Fundamentals of Health Law

Seventh Edition

BY

ANITA BETH ADAMS
BARRY D. ALEXANDER
BERNADETTE M. BROCCOLO
ANTHONY H. CHOE
ANTHEA R. DANIELS
REBECCA E. DITTRICH
SANDRA M. DIVARCO
ANJALI N.C. DOWNS
GEOFF A. DRUCKER
CATHERINE A. HURLEY
RAYMOND J. LINDHOLM
CAROL COLBORN LOEPERE
THOMAS WM. MAYO
JOHN J. MILES
YETUNDE ONI
KRISTEN ROSATI
ROSS E. SALLADE
MICHAEL F. SCHAFF
SUSAN O. SCHEUTZOW
DANIEL J. SCHWARTZ
NANCY A. SHELIGA
KERRIN B. SLATTERY
CRAIG H. SMITH
MELISSA A. SOLIZ

American Health Lawyers Association

Copyright 2018, 2014, 2011, 2008, 2004, 2000, 1995 by

AMERICAN HEALTH LAWYERS ASSOCIATION
1620 Eye Street, NW, 6th Floor
Washington, DC 20006-4010
Web site: www.healthlawyers.org
E-Mail: info@healthlawyers.org

All rights reserved.
No part of this publication may be reproduced, stored in a retrieval system, or transmitted, in any form, or by any means, electronic, mechanical, photocopying, recording, or otherwise, without the express, written permission of the publisher.

Printed in the United States of America
ISBN: 978-1-5221-5332-0 (Nonmember, print)
978-1-5221-5331-3 (Member, print)
978-1-5221-5334-4 (Nonmember, eBook)
978-1-5221-5333-7 (Member, eBook)

"This publication is designed to provide accurate and authoritative information with respect to the subject matter covered. It is provided with the understanding that the publisher is not engaged in rendering legal or other professional services. If legal advice or other expert assistance is required, the services of a competent professional person should be sought."
— from a declaration of the American Bar Association

AHLA Diversity+Inclusion Statement
In principle and in practice, the American Health Lawyers Association values and seeks to advance and promote diverse and inclusive participation within the Association regardless of gender, race, ethnicity, religion, age, sexual orientation, gender identity and expression, national origin, or disability. Guided by these values, the Association strongly encourages and embraces participation of diverse individuals as it leads health law to excellence through education, information, and dialogue.

RECENT TITLES FROM AMERICAN HEALTH LAWYERS ASSOCIATION

False Claims Act & the Health Care Industry: Counseling & Litigation, Seventh Edition

The Law of Digital Health, First Edition

Telehealth Law Handbook: A Practical Guide to Virtual Care, First Edition

Best Practices Handbook for Advising Clients on Fraud and Abuse Issues, First Edition

AHLA's Guide to Health Care Legal Forms, Agreements, and Policies, Second Edition with 2017 Cumulative Supplement

Federal Health Care Laws and Regulations, 2017-2018 Edition

The Fundamentals of Behavioral Health Care Law, First Edition

Enterprise Risk Management Handbook for Health Care Entities, Third Edition

Peer Review Guidebook, Fifth Edition

The Medical Staff Guidebook: Minimizing Risks and Maximizing Collaboration, Fourth Edition

Representing Hospitals and Health Systems Handbook, First Edition

Representing Physicians Handbook, Fourth Edition

Health Care Provider and Supplier Audits Practice Guide, First Edition

Health Plans Contracting Handbook: A Guide for Payers and Providers, Seventh Edition

Health Plan Disputes and Litigation Practice Guide, First Edition

Health Care Finance: A Primer, Third Edition

Data Breach Notification Laws: A Fifty State Survey, Second Edition

Health Care Compliance Legal Issues Manual, Fourth Edition

For more AHLA titles published with LexisNexis,
visit https://store.lexisnexis.com/ahla.

For more information on AHLA's ePrograms, webinar recordings and PDFs,
visit www.healthlawyers.org/store.

Preface

Since the publication of the first edition of *Fundamentals of Health Law* in 1995, dramatic changes have occurred in terms of the entities that provide health care services, how these services are paid for, and the ways in which they are delivered.

A health lawyer's practice today encompasses a wide variety of legal issues, and includes a correspondingly diverse group of clients. Health lawyers may represent hospitals, physicians, and other traditional health care providers, as well as pharmaceutical and device entities, technology vendors, data repositories, and payers—not to mention an ever-evolving range of hybrid entities. Across the breadth of this spectrum, a fundamental core curriculum of health law issues exists, with which anyone practicing health law must be familiar.

This seventh edition of the *Fundamentals of Health Law* addresses these issues: not only the fundamental legal issues a health lawyer may face, but also the structural and operational issues affecting health care providers and payers. In addition, it provides a basic understanding of how health care is administered.

Our goal for this book is to provide lawyers new to the health law arena with an essential resource to aid them in developing their practices. We thank the experienced practitioner authors for participating in this project and for lending their expertise to this important endeavor.

About the Authors

Anita Beth Adams (Chapter 12, Health Care Transactions and Contracting) is a member of the Health Care Group at Baker, Donelson, Bearman, Caldwell & Berkowitz, PC, with a primary focus on advising clients on practice acquisitions, mergers and joint ventures. Clients have included physician practice management companies, individual physicians, physician groups, and ambulatory surgery centers. Ms. Adams builds her health care experience on a broad background of business law, which includes assisting clients with tax issues, transaction structuring, strategic planning and entity formation, joint ventures, mergers and acquisitions, corporate reorganizations, sale and lease agreements, and master service agreements. Prior to joining Baker Donelson, Ms. Adams practiced at Willkie, Farr & Gallagher, LLP, in New York City, and at Neese & Adams in Corinth, Mississippi.

Barry D. Alexander (Chapter 3, Medicare) is a Shareholder of Polsinelli PC, where he provides strategic legal advice to a wide range of health care providers, specialty pharmaceutical and medical device companies, and private equity investors on the complex legal and regulatory environment surrounding the health care industry including reimbursement, billing, and compliance matters arising under the Medicare and Medicaid programs and the implications to business operations in a dynamically changing health care market. He defends health care providers and suppliers under government investigations and audits including those charged with violations of the Federal Civil False Claims Act and he represents organizations in reimbursement-related commercial payer disputes. Barry is a frequent lecturer on Medicare reimbursement matters, an author of numerous publications, and a past Board Member of the American Health Lawyers Association.

Bernadette M. Broccolo (Chapter 6, Tax-Exempt Issues) is a partner in the Chicago office of McDermott Will & Emery LLP and has been counseling health industry organizations for more than 38 years on complex health industry innovation strategies, most recently including provider networks and big data strategies for transitioning to value-based care, development and deployment of digital health solutions, formation of electronic health information networks and exchanges to support improvements, health care quality and accountability, and collaborations for streamlining and accelerating innovations in digital health, translational research, and precision medicine. Her specialties include the full scope of legal and regulatory compliance in the areas of federal taxation of exempt organizations and not-for-profit corporate governance, privacy, human subject protection, and technology contracting. Bernadette is a frequent speaker and author on topics in her areas of practice. She is co-author of *Tax-Exempt Status of Health Care Organizations*, which is part of BNA's Health Law & Business Series. She has served in numerous leadership positions for organizations serving the health industry and the legal profession, including the Board of Directors of the American Health Lawyers Association (AHLA) and she is an AHLA Fellow. She has been selected by her peers to be included in *The Best Lawyers in America* for her expertise in health care law and was named *Best Lawyers'* Chicago Health Care Lawyer of the Year for 2010. Bernadette is listed as a leading individual in health care in *Chambers USA: America's Leading Lawyers for Business*, US Healthcare Expert Guide (EuroMoney Legal Media Group), *Illinois Super Lawyer*, and *Leading Lawyers Network*.

About the Authors

Anthony H. Choe (Chapter 3, Medicare) is a Counsel with Polsinelli PC. He advises provider-sponsored health plans, health care providers, telehealth companies, private equity sponsors, and other industry stakeholders on health care regulatory, compliance, and transactional matters. He routinely advises clients on matters involving Medicare Advantage, Prescription Drug Program, Medicaid managed care, TRICARE, and commercial payer reimbursement issues and disputes. Tony speaks regularly at national conferences and currently serves on the planning committee for the AHLA Fundamentals of Health Law program.

Anthea R. Daniels (Chapter 12, Health Care Transactions and Contracting) is Vice President and General Counsel at Akron Children's Hospital. Anthea is the past president of the American Health Lawyers Association (AHLA). She also chaired AHLA's Fundamentals of Law Program, the Women's Leadership Council, and the AHLA Mentoring Program and is an AHLA Fellow. Anthea is past chairman and president of the Northeast Ohio Chapter of The Healthcare Financial Management Association where she received its Founders, Merit, and Muncie Gold Awards. Anthea is recognized as a "Leading Lawyer for Healthcare" by Chambers USA and has been named an Ohio "Super Lawyer." She has been named a 2013 and 2017 Client Choice Award winner.

Rebecca E. Dittrich (Chapter 11, Post-Acute Providers and Suppliers) is an associate in Reed Smith's Life Sciences Health Industry Group, practicing in the area of health care regulatory law. Her work focuses on fraud and abuse issues, regulatory compliance, health care licensing, and Medicare reimbursement. She has assisted a variety of health care providers, suppliers, and manufacturers in regulatory, compliance, and transactional matters, including DMEPOS suppliers, pharmacies, post-acute care providers, and medical device and pharmaceutical manufacturers. Rebecca received her J.D. from Georgetown University Law Center and her M.P.H from Johns Hopkins Bloomberg School of Public Health.

Sandra M. DiVarco (Chapter 9, Regulation of Hospitals) is a partner in the law firm of McDermott Will & Emery LLP and is based in the firm's Chicago office. Sandy focuses her practice on the representation of hospitals and health systems. She has counseled health care facility and system clients regarding all aspects of health law transactions and health system restructurings. In addition to maintaining an active transactional practice, Sandy has a deep knowledge of regulatory, licensing, and accreditation issues of particular concern to health care providers in today's heightened enforcement climate. Sandy regularly advises clients on the legal aspects of clinical regulatory issues and policy/procedure and operational matters. A significant component of her practice involves assisting health care provider clients across the United States with regulatory, licensure, and accreditation issues, including state-level and Centers for Medicare and Medicaid Services (CMS) survey responses, formulation of successful plans of correction, Joint Commission complaint responses, and Emergency Medical Treatment and Active Labor Act (EMTALA)/regulatory investigations. Drawing on her experience as a registered nurse, and holding a current license in the state of Illinois, Sandy brings a pragmatic perspective and first-hand knowledge of health care operations to these complex and mission-critical matters. Sandy has worked extensively with Catholic organizations within health care and other business areas on transactions, restructurings, and internal inquiries. Prior to practicing law, Sandy worked in an intensive care unit as a registered nurse and as a risk manager at a large academic medical center in Chicago. While in law school, she was a member of the *Loyola Law*

Journal and served as a student articles editor. Sandy is a member of the Firm's Gender Diversity Committee. Sandy is recognized by *The Best Lawyers in America* 2013 to 2018, Health Care Law and *Chambers USA* 2013 to 2017.

Anjali N.C. Downs (Chapter 5, Fundamentals of Health Law Fraud and Abuse) is a partner of Epstein Becker Green's Health Care and Life Sciences Practice in the firm's Washington, D.C., office. She practices in the firm's Health Care Fraud Practice Group, which focuses on federal and state fraud issues, including anti-kickback, self-referral, false claims, secondary payer issues, and false billings. Ms. Downs represents a variety of health care and life science organizations including health systems, pharmaceutical and medical device manufacturers, pharmacies, clinical laboratories, academic medical centers, physician group practices, dialysis providers, and medical transportation providers. Ms. Downs' experiences include conducting internal health regulatory investigations; assisting clients in preparing self-disclosures and advisory opinion requests; representing and defending health care entities undergoing government investigations, inquiries and audits; assisting clients in developing, implementing, and evaluating corporate compliance programs; and advising clients on physician contracting arrangements in a variety of health care joint ventures. In 2017, Ms. Downs was selected to the Washington DC *Rising Stars* list in the area of Health Care.

Geoff A. Drucker (Chapter 15, Dispute Resolution in Health Care) oversees the Dispute Resolution Service of the American Health Lawyers Association. He is also an adjunct professor at the George Washington University School of Law, teaching Mediation and Alternative Dispute Resolution. Geoff is the President of the Board of Directors of the Northern Virginia Mediation Service. His first book, *Resolving 21st Century Disputes: Best Practices for a Fast-Paced World* (Prospecta Press) was published in 2012. Geoff received a B.A. with distinction from Stanford University in 1982, a J.D. from the UCLA School of Law in 1985, and an M.S. in Conflict Analysis and Resolution from George Mason University in 1997.

Catherine A. Hurley (Katie) (Chapter 11, Post-Acute Providers and Suppliers) is counsel in Reed Smith's Life Sciences Health Industry Group, specializing in health care regulatory matters. Katie's practice covers a wide range of complex regulatory matters ranging from government health care fraud investigations to conducting regulatory due diligence and obtaining regulatory approvals in connection with health care transactions. She has particular experience with health care anti-fraud laws, such as the federal Anti-Kickback statute and related prohibitions under federal and state law and the physician self-referral or Stark Law.

Raymond J. Lindholm (Chapter 3, Medicare) is an Associate of Polsinelli PC. He provides guidance on matters ranging from government investigations in fraud and abuse, and administrative audits and appeals, to regulatory advisement related to general corporate contracting and operational issues. Raymond has experience assisting health care organizations under government investigation, representing clients in third party payment disputes with commercial and government payers, and negotiating and drafting agreements related to joint ventures. In addition, he has extensive experience assisting clients with licensure and enrollment issues.

About the Authors

Carol Colborn Loepere (Chapter 11, Post-Acute Providers and Suppliers) is a partner and former Chair of Reed Smith's Life Sciences Health Industry Group, practicing in the area of health care regulatory law. She also serves on the firm's Executive Committee. For over 30 years, she has counseled on regulatory and legislative initiatives affecting health care providers and suppliers including Medicare and Medicaid coverage and reimbursement issues, survey and certification, and contractual arrangements. She also advises clients on business transactions for compliance with physician self-referral and anti-kickback laws, and represents clients in False Claims Act and other government proceedings and investigations. Carol specializes in advising clients on the regulatory requirements and business considerations in connection with health care transactions in the health care industry, focusing on due diligence, change of ownership (CHOW) issues, regulatory approvals and related regulatory issues. Carol is recognized as a leading lawyer in health care law by *Chambers USA* (2009–2016), as a leading lawyer by *Legal 500*, and as a Life Sciences Star by *LMG Life Sciences* (2013–2015).

Thomas Wm. Mayo (Chapter 13, Bioethics) is the Altshuler University Distinguished Teaching Professor and Professor of Law in the Dedman School of Law at Southern Methodist University, Adjunct Associate Professor of Internal Medicine at the University of Texas - Southwestern Medical School; and Of Counsel, Haynes and Boone, all in Dallas. He teaches courses in torts, legislation, nonprofit organizations, health care law, and bioethics and law, as well as a literature course for medical students and law students together (titled, unsurprisingly, "Law, Literature & Medicine"). He co-chairs two hospital ethics committees and is co-founder of the Legal Hospice of Texas, the state's first *pro bono* legal clinic for persons with HIV disease and persons with terminal illnesses. He also was the long-time poetry columnist for the *Dallas Morning News*.

John J. (Jeff) Miles (Chapter 7, Antitrust) is an attorney in the Washington, D.C. office of Baker Donelson. Jeff has limited his practice to antitrust law for over 35 years; the vast majority of his practice involves antitrust issues in the health-care sector. Previously, Jeff was the Assistant Attorney General in charge of the Virginia Attorney General's Antitrust Unit and then a Trial Attorney with the Antitrust Division of the U.S. Department of Justice in Washington. He has undergraduate and graduate degrees in economics from Virginia Tech and a law degree, magna cum laude, from the Washington & Lee University School of Law, where he now serves as an adjunct professor of law teaching the antitrust law course. In addition to his law practice and teaching, he writes and updates yearly a multi-volume treatise on health care antitrust law. He is an AHLA Fellow.

Yetunde Oni (Chapter 11, Post-Acute Providers and Suppliers) is an associate in Reed Smith's Life Sciences Health Industry Group, practicing in the area of health care regulatory law. Her practice focuses on regulatory and transactional matters for a variety of health industry clients, including but not limited to drug and device manufacturers, health care providers and suppliers such as post-acute providers, pharmacies, and DMEPOS suppliers. Yetunde's practice also covers a broad range of regulatory matters including FDA compliance issues, fraud and abuse compliance, and health care transaction requirements such as due diligence, change of ownership, and facility or provider licensing. Prior to joining Reed Smith, Yetunde worked in the pharmaceutical industry, with Pfizer Inc., as a research scientist focusing on clinical trials for vaccines. Yetunde has a Master's degree in Biotechnology from University of Pennsylvania, and received her law degree from University of Maryland, Francis King Carey School of Law.

About the Authors

Kristen Rosati (Chapter 14, Data Sharing for Clinical Integration and other "Big Data" Initiatives) is a partner at Coppersmith Brockelman, PLC. She has deep experience in all things "Big Data," including HIPAA compliance and data breaches, health information exchange, data sharing for research and clinical integration initiatives, clinical research compliance, clinical trials contracting, and biobanking and genomic privacy. Kristen Rosati is a Past President of the American Health Lawyers Association and currently serves on the planning committee for the AHLA's Academic Medical Centers and Teaching Hospitals Institute. Kristen has been listed in *Best Lawyers in America* for health care since 2007, was *Best Lawyers'* 2017 and 2014 Phoenix Health Care Law "Lawyer of the Year" and is ranked by Chambers and Superlawyers. She was chosen as one of the Outstanding Business Women in Arizona in 2017 and one of the 50 Most Influential Women in Arizona Business in 2013, and received the Health Care Leadership Award for Legal Advocate of the Year in 2014. Kristen received her B.A., with high honors, and her J.D., cum laude, from the University of Michigan. She clerked for the late Judge Thomas Tang of the U.S. Court of Appeals for the Ninth Circuit and for Judge Earl H. Carroll of the U.S. District Court for the District of Arizona.

Ross E. Sallade (Chapter 3, Medicare) is a Shareholder in Polsinelli, PC. Ross helps clients navigate state and federal health care regulatory challenges. He regularly counsels clients on structuring business transactions and relationships in compliance with federal and state regulations, including change of ownership requirements and Medicare provider-based guidelines. He counsels clients on program enrollment, state licensure, provider and supplier reimbursement, health care operational matters, diligence support in connection with transactions, compliance with fraud and abuse laws including the Federal Anti-Kickback and Federal Physician Self-Referral (Stark) laws, and professional service and management service agreements, including controlled professional corporations.

Michael F. Schaff (Chapter 10, Representing Physicians) is the Chair of the Corporate and Healthcare Departments and shareholder of Wilentz, Goldman & Spitzer PA. In 2016, Mr. Schaff was elected as a Fellow of the American Health Lawyers Association (AHLA). Michael was a member of the AHLA Board of Directors from 2006 thru 2012, serving on its Executive Committee (2010–2012) and its Finance Committee (2011–2012), and is a past Chair of AHLA Physicians Organization Committee and was the editor of its newsletter. Active in the New Jersey State Bar Association (NJSBA), he is currently a Trustee of the NJSBA (2017–), a past chair (1999–2000 & 2016–2017), a director (1996–2013, 2016–) and was on the Emeritus Board (2013–2016) of the Health Law Section. In December 2016, Mr. Schaff received the New Jersey Institute of Continuing Legal Education's 2016 Distinguished Service award. In March 2008, Mr. Schaff received the Middlesex County Bar Association's Transactional Attorney of the Year Award. Michael was the recipient of an Outstanding Physician Practice Lawyer for 2007 by *Nightingale's Healthcare News*. In May 2006, Michael received the NJSBA Health and Hospital Law Section first Distinguished Service Award. Among his many publications, Michael is Chair of the AHLA Taskforce, author and editor of *Representing Physicians Handbook* 4th Edition (published in 2016) and for the 3rd, 2nd and 1st editions (published in 2012, 2009 and 2006). Michael is the Co-Executive Editor and an author of AHLA's *The ACO Handbook: A Guide to Accountable Care Organizations* 2nd Edition, 2014 and for the 1st Edition (2012). Mr. Schaff is on the Advisory Board of BNA's *Health Law Reports* since 2011. Mr. Schaff has been selected for inclusion in New Jersey *Best Lawyers* list 2003–2017 (2012, 2016 & 2018 Health Lawyer of the Year) and New Jersey *Super Lawyers®* list 2005–2017 (Top 100 attorneys; 2007–

About the Authors

2017), *Chambers USA* 2007–2017 (Band 1, Healthcare 2011–2017). Active in charitable endeavors, Mr. Schaff was awarded the AHLA Pro Bono Champion Award (2012), is an active volunteer in the American Cancer Society (2000–) and was the 2011 recipient of the American Cancer Society's Shining Star Award for Volunteering. Michael was on the Board of Directors for the Susan G. Komen South and Central New Jersey Affiliate (2009–2016) and was the 2016 recipient of the Susan G. Komen Pink Tie Award for volunteering. Michael is also a former Board member for Circle of Life Children's Center (2008–2011).

Susan O. Scheutzow (Chapter 2, Patient Care) is head of the Healthcare Group at Kohrman, Jackson & Krantz PLL. One of Susan's major accomplishments is a book she wrote titled *Ohio Health Care Provider Law*, which is still used by health law attorneys across the state. She is a Fellow of the American Health Lawyers Association, a distinction granted her for her contribution to health care law. She has also served on the Board of Directors of the American Health Lawyers Association and is presently the Editor in Chief of the American Health Lawyers Association's *Journal of Health and Life Sciences Law*. She taught the first health law course offered by Cleveland State University's Cleveland-Marshall College of Law and is currently a member of the faculty at Baldwin-Wallace University teaching a Masters course in health care law and policy and an undergraduate course in health care law and ethics. She has received many awards, including Distinguished Women in Healthcare from the Visiting Nurse Association and has authored numerous law review articles and monographs, including the American Health Lawyers Association publication, *Indemnification in Health Care Contracting*. Susan has practiced law for over 30 years, including serving as in-house general counsel for Southwest General Health Center in Cleveland.

Daniel J. Schwartz (Chapter 8, The Source of Payment: The State and Federal Regulation of Private Health Plans) is a Shareholder in the St. Louis, MO, law firm of Greensfelder, Hemker & Gale, PC. He has practiced primarily in the employee benefits area since 1977, during which he has provided advice on all facets of employee benefits and has represented clients in court in ERISA litigation matters. In 2017, Mr. Schwartz represented a large health care organization in a landmark ERISA case before the U.S. Supreme Court. He is the author of a Bloomberg BNA Tax Management Portfolio entitled *Employee Benefits for Tax-Exempt Organizations*. Mr. Schwartz was named to the IRS Advisory Committee on Tax Exempt and Government Entities (ACT) by the United States Department of Treasury and served as an advisor to the IRS during 2006, 2007 and 2008. In 2000, Mr. Schwartz was elected as a Charter Fellow of the American Academy of Employee Benefits Counsel. Mr. Schwartz received his undergraduate degree from the University of Missouri-Columbia (1974, Phi Beta Kappa) and his law degree from the University of Missouri-Kansas City (1977, Law Review).

Nancy A. Sheliga (Chapter 11, Post-Acute Providers and Suppliers) is a health policy analyst for Reed Smith's Life Sciences Health Industry Group, focusing on health care regulatory law. She works primarily on matters involving licensing and enrollment of health care facilities, Medicare reimbursement, and other state and federal regulatory issues. Nancy has a significant background and experience preparing state licensing and federal Medicare and Medicaid enrollment materials for pharmacies, durable medical equipment suppliers, skilled nursing facilities, and other health care businesses. She also has particular familiarity with compliance matters, having frequently been involved in analyzing the reporting requirements of prior sanctions and disciplinary actions.

About the Authors

Kerrin B. Slattery (Chapter 9, Regulation of Hospitals) is a partner in the law firm of McDermott Will & Emery LLP and is based in the firm's Chicago office. Kerrin maintains a diverse transactional practice focused on the representation of hospitals and health systems, as well as other health industry providers and investors across the country. Kerrin has significant experience in all aspects of health industry transactions, including mergers, acquisitions, affiliations, joint ventures, and system restructurings involving nonprofit hospitals and health systems, academic medical centers, post-acute providers, large medical groups, and other health care providers. She also advises health industry clients on accountable-care strategies and hospital-physician integration initiatives. Kerrin manages large-scale transactions, often involving experienced practitioners throughout the firm with unique health industry knowledge, including in antitrust, employee benefits, environmental, executive compensation, information technology and data privacy, certificate of need, real estate, fraud and abuse, and white collar. In addition, Kerrin regularly advises her health industry clients on corporate and regulatory compliance matters, including licensure, fraud and abuse laws, accreditation, and other state and federal regulations uniquely applicable to health care entities. She also works with numerous Catholic health care organizations and non-Catholic organizations in the unique structuring and operational issues related to the intersection of corporate and Canon laws governing Catholic sponsored entities. Kerrin is recognized by *The Best Lawyers in America* 2012 to 2018 Health Care Law; *Chambers USA* 2008 to 2017; *The Legal 500* US 2015 to 2017, *Leading Lawyer*; and *Ambulatory M&A Advisor*, Top Healthcare Transactional Lawyer of 2014, Leading Lawyer 2016.

Craig H. Smith (Chapter 4, Medicaid Fundamentals) is a partner in the law firm of Hogan Lovells US LLP and is based in the firm's Miami office. Craig is Board Certified in Health Law by the Florida Bar and is the partner-in-charge of the firm's Health Care practice in Florida. Craig previously served as General Counsel for Florida's Agency for Health Care Administration, where he supervised a team of 42 lawyers and oversaw all legal matters for the Florida agency that administers the nation's third largest Medicaid program and licenses over 32,000 health care facilities. At Hogan Lovells, Craig advises health care industry clients on complex transactions as well as compliance and internal investigation matters, and *Chambers USA* ranks him in its top band of health care lawyers in Florida.

Melissa A. Soliz (Chapter 14, Data Sharing for Clinical Integration and other "Big Data" Initiatives) is an Associate at Coppersmith Brockelman PLC in Phoenix, Arizona. The focus of her regulatory health care practice is on federal and state confidentiality laws (with an emphasis on 42 C.F.R. Part 2), data sharing for health information exchange and research, data breach reporting, regulatory compliance and contracting for human subjects research, Arizona licensing and scope of practice requirements, and other state and federal regulatory requirements applicable to health care organizations. She has experience negotiating data sharing agreements and clinical trial agreements, counseling clients on health information privacy and security compliance, conducting internal investigations and responding to OCR requests, and representing clients in civil litigation and administrative proceedings. Melissa received her B.A. degrees in history and political science, summa cum laude, and her J.D., summa cum laude and Order of the Coif/Order of Barristers/Pro Bono Distinction, from Arizona State University, where she was the recipient of the 2005 ASU History Alumni Award for Excellence in Undergraduate Studies, the 2005 Feldt-Barbanell Women's History Award, and the 2011 John S. Armstrong Award (the law school's highest honor). She is also a former Executive Articles Editor of the *Arizona State Law Journal*, Pedrick Scholar and placed second on the 2011 Arizona Bar Exam.

About the Authors

She clerked for Judge Mary Schroeder of the U.S. Court of Appeals for the Ninth Circuit and externed for Judge Susan Bolton (U.S. District Court, District of Arizona) and Judges Patricia Orozco and Donn Kessler (Arizona Court of Appeals).

Table of Contents

Preface iv

About the Authors v

1 Terminology 1
1.1   Glossary 1
1.2   Table of Acronyms and Abbreviations 44

2 Patient Care 53
2.1   Creation of the Provider-Patient Relationship; Duty to Treat and Ending
      Provider-Patient Relationships; Patient Abandonment 53
    2.1.1   Creation of a Provider-Patient Relationship 53
    2.1.2   Requirement that Health Care Facilities and Individual Providers
            Accept Patients 56
          2.1.2.1   Emergency Treatment 56
          2.1.2.2   Non-Emergency Treatment 56
    2.1.3   Conscience Laws 57
2.2   Consent to Medical Treatment 57
    2.2.1   Generally 57
          2.2.1.1   Requirements for Consent Form 59
          2.2.1.2   Disclosure of Special Risk Factors of Providers 59
          2.2.1.3   Exceptions to the Requirement to Obtain Consent 60
          2.2.1.4   Statutes Requiring Special Circumstances 61
          2.2.1.5   Restraint and Seclusion 61
    2.2.2   Constitutional Protection 62
    2.2.3   Incompetent's Right to Make Treatment Decisions 63
    2.2.4   Minors 64
    2.2.5   Consent for Experimentation 65
2.3   End-of-Life Decisionmaking 66
    2.3.1   Competent Person's Right to Refuse Life-Sustaining Medical Treatment 66
    2.3.2   Incompetent Patients 66
    2.3.3   Damages for Rendering Unwanted Care 67
    2.3.4   Advance Directives 67
          2.3.4.1   Living Wills 67
          2.3.4.2   Durable Powers of Attorney for Health Care 68
          2.3.4.3   Do-Not-Resuscitate Protocols 68
    2.3.5   Medical Futility 68
    2.3.6   Physician-Assisted Death 69
2.4   Disclosure and Protection of Patient Medical Information 70
    2.4.1   Patient Confidentiality 70
    2.4.2   Mandatory Disclosure 72

			2.4.2.1	Judicial Disclosure	72
			2.4.2.2	Mandatory Reporting of Medical Conditions and Duty to Warn	73
		2.4.3	HIPAA Privacy Rules		74
			2.4.3.1	Administrative Requirements and Training	74
			2.4.3.2	Use and Disclosure of Protected Health Information	75
			2.4.3.3	Patient Rights under HIPAA	76
			2.4.3.4	Notice of Privacy Practices	76
			2.4.3.5	Breach Notification	77
			2.4.3.6	Business Associate Agreements and Policies	77
			2.4.3.7	Sanctions and Enforcement	78
2.5	Conclusion				78

3	**Medicare**				**79**
3.1	Introduction				79
	3.1.1	The Evolution of Medicare Policy and Law			80
	3.1.2	Chapter Overview			81
3.2	Overview of the Medicare Program				82
	3.2.1	Medicare Basics			82
			3.2.1.1	Part A	82
			3.2.1.2	Part B	82
			3.2.1.3	Part C	83
			3.2.1.4	Part D	84
	3.2.2	Private Contracts			85
	3.2.3	Excluded Services			86
	3.2.4	Beneficiary Cost-Sharing			86
			3.2.4.1	Premiums, Co-Payments, and Deductibles	86
			3.2.4.2	Medicare Supplement Insurance Policies	86
			3.2.4.3	Assistance for Low-Income Beneficiaries	87
	3.2.5	The Secondary Payer Rule			87
	3.2.6	Other Areas Subsidized by Medicare			87
	3.2.7	"Provider" vs. "Supplier"			88
	3.2.8	"Provider-Based"			88
3.3	Program Administration				88
	3.3.1	Organizational Overview			88
	3.3.2	Centers for Medicare & Medicaid Services			88
			3.3.2.1	Administrative History	88
			3.3.2.2	Structural Overview	89
			3.3.2.3	Central and Regional Operations	91
			3.3.2.4	Administrative Guidance	91
			3.3.2.5	Administrator Rulings	91
	3.3.3	Medicare Administrative Contractors, Fiscal Agents			91
	3.3.4	Quality Improvement Organizations			92
	3.3.5	The DHHS Office of Inspector General			92
	3.3.6	The Provider Reimbursement Review Board			93

	3.3.7	Independent Payment Advisory Board	93
3.4	Reimbursement Overview		94
3.5	Eligibility		94
	3.5.1	Medicare Part A	94
	3.5.2	Medicare Part B	94
	3.5.3	Medicare Part C	95
	3.5.4	Medicare Part D	96
3.6	Coverage		96
	3.6.1	Medicare Part A	96
		3.6.1.1	Hospital Services	96
		3.6.1.2	Extended Care or Skilled Nursing Services (SNF)	97
		3.6.1.3	Home Health Services	97
		3.6.1.4	Hospice Services	98
	3.6.2	Medicare Part B	98
		3.6.2.1	Physicians' Services	99
		3.6.2.2	Services by Non-Physician Practitioners	100
		3.6.2.3	Outpatient Providers and Freestanding Supplier Entities	100
	3.6.3	Shared Savings Programs	101
	3.6.4	Medicare Part C	102
		3.6.4.1	Basic Benefits	102
		3.6.4.2	Supplemental Benefits	102
	3.6.5	Medicare Part D	103
	3.6.6	National Coverage Decisions	106
3.7	Certification		106
	3.7.1	Providers	107
	3.7.2	Physicians and Suppliers	108
	3.7.3	MA Organizations	108
	3.7.4	PDP Sponsors	109
3.8	Payment—The Prospective Payment System		109
	3.8.1	Introduction	110
	3.8.2	PPS for Acute Inpatient Hospitals	110
		3.8.2.1	Diagnosis-Related Groups	110
		3.8.2.2	Determining the IPPS Rate	111
		3.8.2.3	Case-Mix Adjustment	113
		3.8.2.4	Special Adjustments and Payments for Certain Costs	113
	3.8.3	Other Hospital PPS	117
		3.8.3.1	Rehabilitation Hospitals	117
		3.8.3.2	Long Term Care Hospitals	117
		3.8.3.3	Psychiatric Hospitals	117
		3.8.3.4	Affordable Care Act Updates	118
	3.8.4	Rural-Area Hospitals	118
	3.8.5	Hospitals Excluded from PPS	118
	3.8.6	Hospital Outpatient Department Services	120
		3.8.6.1	Establishment of the Outpatient Prospective Payment System	120
		3.8.6.2	Payment for Outpatient Drugs and Biologicals	120

Table of Contents

	3.8.6.3	Section 603 of the Bipartisan Budget Act of 2015 and Payment Reductions for Off-Campus Outpatient Departments	122
	3.8.6.4	The Three-Day DRG Payment-Window Rule	124
	3.8.6.5	Unbundling	125
3.8.7	Post-Acute Care Providers		125
	3.8.7.1	Skilled Nursing Facilities	125
	3.8.7.2	Hospice	126
	3.8.7.3	Home Health Agencies	127
3.9	Payment—The Resource-Based Relative Value Scale Fee Schedule		128
3.9.1	Overview		128
3.9.2	RBRVS Fundamentals		129
3.9.3	Coding and Documentation Standards		129
3.9.4	Application of RBRVS to Non-Physician Practitioners and Other Suppliers		130
3.9.5	MACRA		130
	3.9.5.1	Advanced Payment Models or APMs	131
	3.9.5.2.	Merit-Based Payment Incentive System (MIPS)	132
3.9.6	Fee Schedules for Freestanding Supplier Entities		132
3.9.7	Ambulance Services		133
3.10	Payment—Blended Capitation		133
3.10.1	Introduction		133
3.10.2	Determining the MA Payment Rate		134
3.11	Payment—New Competitive "Market-Based" Systems		134
3.11.1	Part B		134
3.11.2	Part C		135
3.11.3	Part D		136
3.12	Assignment and Reassignment		137
3.12.1	Assignment		137
	3.12.1.1	Part A	137
	3.12.1.2	Part B	137
	3.12.1.3	Part C	138
	3.12.1.4	Part D	138
3.12.2	Reassignment		138
3.13	Appeals—Parts A and B		139
3.13.1	Claims Appeals—Parts A and B		140
3.13.2	Cost Report Appeals—Part A Only		141
3.14	Appeals—Part C		142
3.14.1	Enrollee Grievances and Appeals		143
	3.14.1.1	Reconsiderations	143
	3.14.1.2	Independent Review	143
	3.14.1.3	Judicial Review	144
	3.14.1.4	Determinations During an Inpatient Stay	144
	3.14.1.5	Service Terminations	144
3.14.2	MA Organization Contract Appeals		144
	3.14.2.1	Request for Hearing	144
	3.14.2.2	Request for Review by the Administrator of CMS	145

3.15	Appeals—Part D		145
	3.15.1	Part D Sponsor Contract Appeals	146
3.16	Conclusion		146
3.17	Useful Websites and Other Resources		148

4 Medicaid Fundamentals 151

4.1	Introduction			151
4.2	The Evolution of the Medicaid Program			152
	4.2.1	Original Intent of Congress		152
	4.2.2	Medicaid Prior to ACA		152
	4.2.3	Medicaid After the ACA		154
4.3	Administration			156
	4.3.1	Oversight by CMS		156
	4.3.2	Single State Medicaid Agency		156
	4.3.3	Fundamental Elements of a State Medicaid Program		156
	4.3.4	Differences Among State Medicaid Programs		157
4.4	Eligibility			157
	4.4.1	Applying for Medicaid (Changed by ACA)		157
	4.4.2	Eligibility (Changed by the ACA)		158
		4.4.2.1	Mandatory Categorically Needy	158
		4.4.2.2	Optional Categorically Needy	159
		4.4.2.3	Optional Medically Needy	159
			4.4.2.3.1 Financial Criteria for Medically Needy	159
	4.4.3	General Criteria Used to Determine Medicaid Eligibility		160
		4.4.3.1	Meeting Standards for Income and Resources	160
4.5	Covered Benefits			161
	4.5.1	Mandatory Benefits for Categorically Needy		162
	4.5.2	Optional Benefits		163
	4.5.3	Mandatory Benefits for the Medically Needy		164
	4.5.4	Limitations on Covered Services		164
	4.5.5	Cost Sharing		167
		4.5.5.1	Denial of Service for Nonpayment	167
	4.5.6	Specific Rules for Prescribed Drugs		167
		4.5.6.1	Medicaid Drug Rebate Program	168
4.6	Reimbursement and Financing Mechanisms			169
	4.6.1	Fundamental Reimbursement Principles		169
		4.6.1.1	Setting Provider Payment Rates	169
		4.6.1.2	Medicaid Upper Payment Limits	169
		4.6.1.3	Disproportionate Share Hospital (DSH) Payments	171
	4.6.2	Financing the Non-Federal Share of Medicaid Expenditures		171
4.7	Delivery Systems			172
	4.7.1	States Have Options		172
	4.7.2	Traditional Fee-For-Service		172
	4.7.3	Medicaid Managed Care		173
		4.7.3.1	State Plan Amendment (SPA)	173
		4.7.3.2	Section 1915(b) Waiver	173

Table of Contents

			4.7.3.3	Section 1115 Demonstration Projects	173
			4.7.3.4	Home and Community Based Services (HCBS)	174
	4.8	Affordable Care Act of 2010			175
		4.8.1	ACA Expands Medicaid in 2014		175
		4.8.2	Improvements to Medicaid Services		175
		4.8.3	Prescription Drug Coverage		175
		4.8.4	Expansion of Presumptive Eligibility Sites		175
		4.8.5	Increased Physician Reimbursement for Primary Care		176
		4.8.6	Funding and Administrative Support for Quality Initiatives		176
		4.8.7	DSH Payments Reduced		176
		4.8.8	Payment Innovations		176
			4.8.8.1	Extension and Enhancement of CHIP	177
			4.8.8.2	Program Integrity Provisions	177
	4.9	SCOTUS & Medicaid Impact			177
		4.9.1	Medicaid Expansion: Optional Participation for the Newly Eligible		177
		4.9.2	Medicaid Program Changes—Mandatory Participation		178
	Exhibit A	2017 Poverty Guidelines for the 48 Contiguous States and the District of Columbia			181

5 Fundamentals of Health Law Fraud and Abuse 183

5.1	The Federal Health Care Program's Anti-Kickback Statute		184
	5.1.1	Statutory Prohibition	184
	5.1.2	Judicial Interpretation	185
		5.1.2.1 The First 25 Years of Case Law under the Statute: Pre-*Hanlester*	185
		5.1.2.2 The *Hanlester* Decision	186
		5.1.2.3 *United States ex rel. Jamison v. McKesson*	188
	5.1.3	Special Fraud Alerts	188
	5.1.4	Advisory Opinions	189
5.2	Federal Anti-Kickback Safe Harbor Regulations		190
	5.2.1	Investment Interest Safe Harbors	192
		5.2.1.1 Large Investment Interests	192
		5.2.1.2 Small Investment Interests	193
		5.2.1.3 Investments in Entities in MUAs	194
	5.2.2	Space and Equipment Rental, and Personal Services and Management Contracts	194
	5.2.3	Sale of Practice	195
	5.2.4	Referral Services	195
	5.2.5	Warranties	195
	5.2.6	Discounts	196
	5.2.7	Employees	197
	5.2.8	Group Purchasing Organizations	197
	5.2.9	Coinsurance and Deductible Waivers	198
	5.2.10	Beneficiary Incentives Offered by Managed-Care Organizations	198
	5.2.11	Price Reductions Offered to Group Health Plans	199
	5.2.12	Practitioner Recruitment	199

	5.2.13	Obstetrical Malpractice-Insurance Subsidies	200
	5.2.14	Investments in Group Practices	200
	5.2.15	Cooperative Hospital-Services Organizations	201
	5.2.16	ASCs	201
	5.2.17	Referral Agreements for Specialty Services	202
	5.2.18	Ambulance Replenishing/Restocking	202
	5.2.19	Federally Qualified Health Centers	203
	5.2.20	Risk-Sharing Arrangements	203
	5.2.21	Electronic Prescribing	205
	5.2.22	Electronic Health Records and Community-Wide Information System	207
	5.2.23	Accountable Care Organization Waivers	209
	5.2.24	Federally Qualified Health Centers and Medicare Advantage Organizations	209
	5.2.25	Medicare Coverage Gap Discount Program	209
	5.2.26	Local Transportation	209
5.3	Federal "Sunshine Law"		210
5.4	Federal Physician Self-Referral Law		212
	5.4.1	Statutory Prohibition	212
	5.4.2	Regulations	214
	5.4.3	Reporting Requirements	215
	5.4.4	Definition of "Entity"	216
	5.4.5	Advisory Opinions	217
	5.4.6	Self-Referral Disclosure Protocol	218
5.5	Stark Exceptions		218
	5.5.1	Ownership and Compensation Exceptions	218
		5.5.1.1 Physician Services	218
		5.5.1.2 In-Office Ancillary Services	219
		5.5.1.3 Prepaid Plans	220
		5.5.1.4 Academic Medical Centers	221
		5.5.1.5 Implants in ASCs	222
		5.5.1.6 Additional Regulatory Exceptions Applicable to Both Ownership and Compensation Arrangements	222
	5.5.2	Ownership Exceptions	222
		5.5.2.1 Ownership in Publicly Traded Securities and Mutual Funds	222
		5.5.2.2 Hospitals	223
		5.5.2.3 Rural Providers	224
	5.5.3	Compensation Arrangement Exceptions	224
		5.5.3.1 Rental of Office Space and Equipment	224
		5.5.3.2 Bona Fide Employment Relationships	225
		5.5.3.3 Personal-Service Arrangements	225
		5.5.3.4 Unrelated Payments	226
		5.5.3.5 Physician Recruitment and Retention	226
		5.5.3.6 Isolated Financial Transactions	227
		5.5.3.7 Certain Group Practice Arrangements with a Hospital	227
		5.5.3.8 Payments for Items and Services	228

Table of Contents

		5.5.3.9	Fair Market Value Exception	228
		5.5.3.10	Non-Monetary Compensation	228
		5.5.3.11	Medical Staff Incidental Benefits	229
		5.5.3.12	Managed-Care Risk-Sharing Arrangements	229
		5.5.3.13	Compliance Training	229
		5.5.3.14	Indirect Compensation and the "Stand in the Shoes" Analysis	229
		5.5.3.15	Electronic Prescribing and Electronic Health Records	231
		5.5.3.16	Additional Compensation Exceptions	231
		5.5.3.17	Accountable Care Organization Waivers	232
		5.5.3.18	Recruitment of Non-physician Practitioners	232
		5.5.3.19	Timeshare Arrangements	233
	5.5.4	"Special Rules" for Compensation		233
		5.5.4.1	Definition of Fair Market Value	233
		5.5.4.2	Compensation Methodologies	234
		5.5.4.3	Physician's Compensation can be Conditioned on Referrals to a Particular Provider	235
5.6	Federal Criminal Prohibitions Against False Claims and Fraudulent Billing Practices			235
	5.6.1	Social Security Act		235
	5.6.2	Federal Health Care Fraud Offenses		236
		5.6.2.1	General Prohibition	236
		5.6.2.2	Making of False Statements	237
		5.6.2.3	Theft or Embezzlement	237
	5.6.3	Mail and Wire Fraud		237
	5.6.4	Racketeering Violations		238
	5.6.5	Money-Laundering		238
	5.6.6	Other Criminal Statutes		239
5.7	Federal Civil Prohibitions Against False Claims and Fraudulent Billing Practices			239
	5.7.1	The Federal False Claims Act and Qui Tam Actions		239
	5.7.2	Social Security Act		243
	5.7.3	Program Fraud and Civil Remedies Act		243
5.8	Corporate Compliance Programs			244
	5.8.1	The Federal Sentencing Guidelines		244
	5.8.2	Various OIG Guidances to Particular Segments of the Health Care Industry		246
	5.8.3	Corporate Integrity Agreements		247
6	**Tax-Exempt Issues**			**251**
6.1	Introduction			251
	6.1.1	Benefits of Section 501(c)(3) Tax-Exempt Status		252
	6.1.2	Public Charity Status		252
	6.1.3	Recurring Concepts		252
6.2	Exemption Requirements—Generally			252
	6.2.1	The Organizational Test		252
	6.2.2	The Operational Test		253

	6.2.3	The Exempt Purposes Requirement		253
		6.2.3.1	Stand-Alone Exemption—The Community Benefit Standard	253
		6.2.3.2	Stand-Alone Exemption—Charity Care as a Consideration Under the Community Benefit Standard	256
		6.2.3.3	Stand-Alone Exemption—Application of the Community Benefit Standard to Other than Hospitals and Other than Direct Providers of Health Care	259
		6.2.3.4	Stand-Alone Exemption—Lessening the Burdens of Government	262
		6.2.3.5	Annual Information Return Reporting—Compliance with the Community Benefit Standard	264
	6.2.4	"Derivative" or "Integral Part" Theory of Exemption		266
		6.2.4.1	Parent Corporations	268
		6.2.4.2	Joint Operating Companies	268
	6.2.5	Public-Benefit Requirement		269
	6.2.6	Private-Inurement Prohibition		270
	6.2.7	Intermediate Sanctions and the Rebuttable Presumption of Reasonableness		271
		6.2.7.1	The Intermediate Sanctions Excise Taxes	271
		6.2.7.2	Excess-Benefit Transactions and the Rebuttable Presumption	272
		6.2.7.3	Disqualified Persons	272
		6.2.7.4	Relationship to Revocation Sanction	274
	6.2.8	Unrelated Business Activities		275
	6.2.9	Political Activity Prohibition and Lobbying Limitation		276
		6.2.9.1	Political Activity Prohibition	276
		6.2.9.2	Lobbying Limitation	277
6.3	Practical Application of the Fundamental Exemption Requirements			278
	6.3.1	Purchase and Sale of a Business or other Assets		278
	6.3.2	Compensation Arrangements		280
		6.3.2.1	General Principles	280
		6.3.2.2	Incentive Compensation Generally	282
		6.3.2.3	Physician Incentive Compensation	282
		6.3.2.4	Executive Compensation	283
	6.3.3	Physician Recruitment Incentives		285
		6.3.3.1	Background	285
		6.3.3.2	Community Benefit Requirement	286
		6.3.3.3	Income Guarantees	287
	6.3.4	Joint Venture Arrangements Involving Exempt and Non-Exempt Participants		287
		6.3.4.1	Whole Hospital Joint Ventures	288
		6.3.4.2	Ancillary Joint Ventures	289
	6.3.5	Courtesy Discounts		291
	6.3.6	Donation of Electronic Health Record Technology		292
	6.3.7	Use of Taxable Affiliates		292
6.4	Section 509(a) Public Charity Status			293
	6.4.1	Section 509(a)(1) Public Charities		293
	6.4.2	Section 509(a)(2) Public Charities		294
	6.4.3	Section 509(a)(3) Public Charities		294

		6.4.3.1	Organizational Test	295
		6.4.3.2	Operational Test	295
		6.4.3.3	Relationship Test	295
		6.4.3.4	Control Test	297
	6.4.4	Effect of the Pension Protection Act of 2006		298

7 Antitrust Law 299
- 7.1 Introduction 299
  - 7.1.1 Purpose of the Antitrust Laws 300
  - 7.1.2 Relevant-Market Definition 302
  - 7.1.3 Market Share, Market Concentration, and Effect on Competition 304
- 7.2 The Substantive Antitrust Statutes and Their Analyses 305
  - 7.2.1 Section 1 of the Sherman Act 305
    - 7.2.1.1 Agreement 306
    - 7.2.1.2 Unreasonable Restraint on Competition 310
    - 7.2.1.3 Agreements with Potential Section 1 Ramifications 314
      - 7.2.1.3.1 Horizontal Price-Fixing Agreements 315
      - 7.2.1.3.2 Horizontal Agreements to Exchange Pricing Information 318
      - 7.2.1.3.3 Horizontal Market-Allocation Agreements 319
      - 7.2.1.3.4 Horizontal Concerted Refusals to Deal or Group Boycotts 320
      - 7.2.1.3.5 Tying Agreements 321
      - 7.2.1.3.6 Exclusive Dealing Agreements 322
  - 7.2.2 Section 2 of the Sherman Act 324
    - 7.2.2.1 Monopolization 325
    - 7.2.2.2 Attempted Monopolization 328
  - 7.2.3 Section 7 of the Clayton Act 328
    - 7.2.3.1 Definition of the Relevant Product Market 331
    - 7.2.3.2 Definition of the Relevant Geographic Market 332
    - 7.2.3.3 Identification of Competitors in the Relevant Market 333
    - 7.2.3.4 Calculation of Each Competitor's Market Share 333
    - 7.2.3.5 Calculation of the Merging Firms' Post-Merger Market Share, the Level of Market Concentration, and the Increase in Market Concentration Resulting from the Merger 333
    - 7.2.3.6 Examination of Factors that Might Indicate that Post-Merger Market Share or Market Concentration Statistics are Misleading 335
  - 7.2.4 The Federal Trade Commission Act 337
- 7.3 Exemptions, Immunities, and Scope of Coverage 338
  - 7.3.1 Nonprofit Entities 338
  - 7.3.2 Federal Governmental Immunity 338
  - 7.3.3 State-Action Exemption 339
  - 7.3.4 Solicitation of Governmental Action 340
  - 7.3.5 Local Government Antitrust Act 341
  - 7.3.6 Business of Insurance 342
  - 7.3.7 Labor Unions 343

		7.3.8	Health Care Quality Improvement Act	343
7.4	Government Enforcement			344
	7.4.1	The Antitrust Division		345
	7.4.2	The Federal Trade Commission		345
	7.4.3	State Attorneys General		346
7.5	Private Enforcement			347
	7.5.1	Causation		347
	7.5.2	Antitrust Injury		347
	7.5.3	Antitrust Standing		348
	7.5.4	Damages		350
7.6	Conclusion			350
7.7	References			352
8	**The Source of Payment: The State and Federal Regulation of Private Health Care Plans**			**355**
8.1	The Basis of Regulation			355
	8.1.1	The State Regulation of the Business of Insurance		355
	8.1.2	Federal Regulation and the Pre-Emption of State Laws		360
8.2	The State Regulation of Private Health Care Plans			370
	8.2.1	Indemnity Insurers		370
	8.2.2	Preferred Provider Organization		372
	8.2.3	Health Maintenance Organizations		374
		8.2.3.1	Description	374
		8.2.3.2	Scope of State Regulation	380
		8.2.3.3	Typical Areas of Regulation	381
	8.2.4	Point-of-Service Programs		385
	8.2.5	Third-Party Administrators		386
	8.2.6	Provider-Sponsored Networks		387
	8.2.7	Blue Cross and Blue Shield (BC/BS) Plans		392
8.3	The Federal Regulation of Private Health Care Plans			394
	8.3.1	Background		394
	8.3.2	ERISA		395
		8.3.2.1	COBRA	395
		8.3.2.2	Mental Health Parity and Addiction Equality Act	397
		8.3.2.3	Pre-Existing Condition Rule	398
		8.3.2.4	HIPAA's Privacy Rules	399
		8.3.2.5	Qualified Medical Child Support Orders	400
		8.3.2.6	Coverage for Adopted Children	402
		8.3.2.7	Coverage for Pediatric Vaccines	402
		8.3.2.8	Maternity Protection	402
		8.3.2.9	Minimum Cancer Treatment	403
	8.3.3	The Patient Protection and Affordable Care Act		404
		8.3.3.1	No Lifetime or Annual Coverage Limits	406
		8.3.3.2	Prohibition on Rescission	407
		8.3.3.3	The Appeals Process	407

Table of Contents

		8.3.3.4	Coverage of Preventive Health Services	408
		8.3.3.5	Extension of Dependent Coverage	409
		8.3.3.6	Standardization of Coverage Documents	409
		8.3.3.7	Information Regarding Transparency	409
		8.3.3.8	Prohibition of Discrimination in Favor of Highly Compensated Individuals	409
		8.3.3.9	Reporting; Quality of Care	409
		8.3.3.10	Essential Benefits Coverage	410
		8.3.3.11	Prohibition on Excessive Waiting Period	410
		8.3.3.12	Prohibition of Pre-Existing Condition Based on Health Status	410
		8.3.3.13	Prohibition of Discrimination against Individual Participants and Beneficiaries Based on Health Factors	410
		8.3.3.14	Tax Credit for Small Business	411
		8.3.3.15	Employer Requirement to Inform Employees of Coverage Options	413
		8.3.3.16	Shared Responsibility	413
		8.3.3.17	Reporting of Employer Health Insurance Coverage	414
		8.3.3.18	Cafeteria Plan Changes	414
8.4	Conclusion			414
9	**Regulation of Hospitals**			**415**
9.1	Introduction			415
9.2	State and Local Regulations			416
	9.2.1	Licensure		416
	9.2.2	Patient Safety and Patient Rights		417
	9.2.3	Regulations Impacting Medical Staff		418
	9.2.4	Regulation of Individually Identifiable Health Information		418
	9.2.5	Construction of Facilities		419
9.3	Federal Regulation			419
	9.3.1	HIPAA		420
	9.3.2	Treatment of Medical Emergencies		422
	9.3.3	Conditions of Participation and Compliance Programs		424
	9.3.4	Regulation of Medical Staff Disciplinary Procedures and Excluded Provider Verification		425
	9.3.5	Regulation of Hospitals as Employers		426
	9.3.6	Regulation of Unionization of Nurses and Doctors		427
9.4	Accreditation; Survey Activity			428
10	**Representing Physicians**			**433**
10.1	Introduction			433
10.2	Life Cycle of Physician-Practice Association			433
	10.2.1	Overview		434
		10.2.1.1	Who is Your Client?	434
		10.2.1.2	Who Can Employ a Physician?	434
	10.2.2	Employment Contracts		435
		10.2.2.1	Duties and Responsibilities	435
		10.2.2.2	Compensation	435

		10.2.2.3 Benefits and Perquisites	436
		10.2.2.4 Ownership Opportunities	436
		10.2.2.5 Term/Termination	437
		10.2.2.6 Post-Termination Restrictive Covenant	437
		10.2.2.7 Other Issues	438
	10.2.3	Ownership	438
		10.2.3.1 Buy-In	438
		10.2.3.2 Ownership Agreements	439
		10.2.3.3 Employment and Compensation	440
	10.2.4	Retirement/Sale of Ownership Interest	441
		10.2.4.1 Valuation of Ownership Interests	441
		10.2.4.2 Payment Terms and Collateral	442
		10.2.4.3 Funding Buy-Outs with Insurance	443
		10.2.4.4 Post-Termination Restrictive Covenant	443
		10.2.4.5 Breaking Up/Dissolution	444
10.3	Physician/Hospital Arrangements		444
	10.3.1	Employee vs. Independent Contractor	444
	10.3.2	Key Issues/Provisions	445
		10.3.2.1 Term and Termination	445
		10.3.2.2 Duties	446
		10.3.2.3 Compensation	446
		10.3.2.4 Benefits	446
		10.3.2.5 Restrictive Covenant, Hospital Records, and Confidentiality	447
		10.3.2.6 Dispute Resolution	447
10.4	Licensure and Credentialing		447
	10.4.1	State Licensure Law	448
	10.4.2	Reports to the National Practitioner Data Bank	449
	10.4.3	Exclusion from Medicare/Medicaid	451
	10.4.4	Medical Staff Privileges—Credentialing and Other Concerns	454
10.5	Reimbursement Issues		455
	10.5.1	Problems in Reimbursement	456
	10.5.2	Independent Practice Associations	456
	10.5.3	Unionization	457
10.6	Telemedicine		458
10.7	Physician/Patient Relationships		459
10.8	Accountable Care Organizations		460
10.9	Conclusion		460
11	**Post-Acute Providers and Suppliers**		**461**
11.1	Introduction		461
11.2	Home Medical Equipment Suppliers		461
	11.2.1	State Licensure	461
	11.2.2	Medicare	462
		11.2.2.1 Coverage	462

Table of Contents

			11.2.2.1.1 Categories of Coverage	462
			11.2.2.1.2 Statutory Exclusion	463
			11.2.2.1.3 National Coverage Policies	464
			11.2.2.1.4 DME MAC Coverage Policies	464
		11.2.2.2	Requirements of Participation	465
		11.2.2.3	Payment	465
			11.2.2.3.1 Payment Categories	466
			11.2.2.3.2 Payment Updates	468
			11.2.2.3.3 Competitive Bidding	469
			11.2.2.3.4 Inherent Reasonableness	474
		11.2.2.4	Medicare Upgrade Provisions/Advance Beneficiary Notices	475
		11.2.2.5	DMEPOS Furnished in Skilled Nursing Facilities and to Patients of Home Health Agencies	476
	11.2.3	Medicaid		476
	11.2.4	Fraud and Abuse		476
11.3	Home Health Care			478
	11.3.1	State Licensure and Certificate of Need		478
	11.3.2	Medicare		478
		11.3.2.1	Coverage	478
		11.3.2.2	Conditions of Participation	480
		11.3.2.3	36 Month Rule	483
		11.3.2.4	Payment	484
	11.3.3	Medicaid HHAs		487
		11.3.3.1	Coverage	487
		11.3.3.2	Qualifications	488
		11.3.3.3	Payment	488
		11.3.3.4	Fraud and Abuse	488
		11.3.3.5	Audits	490
		11.3.3.6	Hospital Discharge Planning	490
11.4	Hospice Care			490
	11.4.1	Introduction		490
	11.4.2	State Licensure and Certificate of Need		491
	11.4.3	Medicare Conditions of Participation		491
		11.4.4.1	Types of Hospice Care	492
		11.4.4.2	Hospice Services and Personnel	493
		11.4.4.3	Qualifications for Medicare Coverage	494
	11.4.5	Election of Hospice Benefit		494
	11.4.6	Physician Certification		495
	11.4.7	Reimbursement		496
		11.4.7.1	Medicare	496
		11.4.7.2	Medicaid	498
	11.4.8	Fraud and Abuse Issues		499
	11.4.9	Compliance Guidance for Hospices		500
11.5	Long Term Care			501

	11.5.1 State Licensure	501
	11.5.2 State Certificate of Need	501
	11.5.3 Medicare Skilled Nursing Facilities	501
	11.5.3.1 Coverage	501
	11.5.3.2 Requirements of Participation	502
	11.5.3.3 Reimbursement	503
	11.5.3.4 Compliance, Ethics and Accountability Requirements	507
	11.5.4 Medicaid Nursing Facilities	507
	11.5.4.1 Coverage	508
	11.5.4.2 Qualifications	508
	11.5.4.3 Reimbursement	508
	11.5.4.4 Compliance, Ethics and Accountability Requirements	510
	11.5.5 Quality of Care	510
	11.5.5.1 Resident Assessment Instruments (RAIs)	510
	11.5.5.2 Collection and Publication of Quality Information	511
	11.5.5.3 Requirements and Reporting Staffing	511
	11.5.5.4 Nursing Home Value-Based Purchasing Demonstration and SNF Value-Based Payment System	512
	11.5.5 Survey, Certification, and Enforcement for Long Term Care Facilities	512
	11.5.5.1 Survey Policies and Procedures	512
	11.5.5.2 Stronger Enforcement Actions	513
	11.5.5.3 Stronger Federal Oversight of State Inspections	514
	11.5.5.4 Preventing Pressure Ulcers, Dehydration, and Malnutrition, use of Psychotropics	514
	11.5.5.5 Resident Abuse, Neglect and Financial Exploitation	514
	11.5.5.6 Prosecution of Egregious Violations	515
	11.5.5.7 Federal False Claims Actions against Nursing Homes Care	515
	11.5.5.8 Fraud and Abuse, Compliance Program Guidance and the OIG Work Plan	516
11.6	Home and Community-Based Services—Long Term Services and Supports	517
	11.6.1 Introduction	517
	11.6.2 Related Legal Developments	518
	11.6.3 Medicaid Quality Assurance/Quality Improvement and Oversight	520
12	**Health Care Transactions and Contracting**	**521**
12.1	Introduction	521
12.2	Getting Started: Initial Discussions and Preliminary Documents	523
	12.2.1 Business Development Teams and Due Diligence	523
	12.2.2 Non-Disclosure Agreements and Disclosure of PHI	524
	12.2.3 Letters of Intent/Term Sheets	526
12.3	Structure of Health Care Transactions	526
	12.3.1 Acquisitions and Mergers	526
	12.3.1.1 Stock Transactions and Member Substitutions	527
	12.3.1.2 Asset Transactions	528

Table of Contents

		12.3.2	Joint Ventures	528
		12.3.3	Affiliations	530
	12.4	Health Care Corporate Structures		531
		12.4.1	Integrated Delivery Systems	531
			12.4.1.1 Antitrust	532
			12.4.1.2 Fraud and Abuse	532
			12.4.1.3 Stark Law	533
			12.4.1.4 Tax	534
			12.4.1.5 Other Legal Issues	535
		12.4.2	Physician/Hospital Organizations	536
		12.4.3	Independent Practice Associations	539
		12.4.4	Professional Corporations	540
		12.4.5	Management-Services Organizations	541
	12.5	Key Issues in Structuring Transactions		542
		12.5.1	Purpose of the Venture	542
		12.5.2	Operational Issues	542
		12.5.3	Legal Issues	543
	12.6	Unwinding Transactions		543
		12.6.1	Termination Provisions	543
		12.6.2	Rights to Repurchase; Repurchase Obligations	544
		12.6.3	Bankruptcy	544
	12.7	Types of Health Care Contracts		545
		12.7.1	Employment and Independent Contractor Agreements	545
		12.7.2	Physician Recruitment Agreements	548
		12.7.3	Management and Service Agreements	549
		12.7.4	Merger and Acquisition Agreements	551
		12.7.5	Affiliation Agreements	553
	12.8	Termination of Agreements		553
		12.8.1	Indemnification Provisions	554
		12.8.2	Confidentiality and Ownership of Records	555
		12.8.3	Non-Compete and Non-Interference Clauses	556
	12.9	Current Climate of Health Care Transactions and Contracting		557
13	**Bioethics**			**559**
13.1	Human Reproduction			559
	13.1.1	Abortion		559
		13.1.1.1	*Roe v. Wade*	559
		13.1.1.2	Post-*Roe* Developments	560
		13.1.1.3	The Transformation of *Roe*	561
		13.1.1.4	Medical and Emergency Abortion	564
		13.1.1.5	Access to Abortion Facilities	567
		13.1.1.6	Informed-Consent Laws Redux	567
	13.1.2	Access to Contraceptives		569
	13.1.3	Commercial Surrogacy		570

		13.1.3.1 Prohibition and Regulation	571
		13.1.3.2 Custody Disputes	572

13.2 Organ Transplantation 573
    13.2.1 Strategies to Increase the Supply of Organs 574
    13.2.2 Allocation Policies 576
13.3 The New Genetics 577
    13.3.1 Confidentiality..577
    13.3.2 Nondiscrimination..579
        13.3.2.1 Insurance 581
        13.3.2.2 Employment 581
    13.3.3 Genetic Engineering...582
        13.3.3.1 Embryonic and Fetal-Cell Research 582
        13.3.3.2 Cloning..585
13.4 Conclusion..586

14 Data Sharing for Clinical Integration and Other "Big Data" Initiatives 587
14.1 Introduction..587
14.2 Health Insurance Portability and Accountability Act (HIPAA) 588
    14.2.1 Building a Data Repository..588
    14.2.2 Access to a Data Repository for Health Care Operations.........................589
    14.2.3 Access to the Data Repository for Research..594
    14.2.4 Minimum Necessary Standard...598
    14.2.5 Psychotherapy Notes..598
    14.2.6 Individual Right to Withhold Certain PHI from Health Plans..................599
    14.2.7 De-identifying PHI and Access to De-identified Data..............................599
14.3 Federal Confidentiality of Substance Use Disorder (Alcohol and Drug Abuse) Patient Records..602
    14.3.1 Applicability of the Part 2 Regulations' Disclosure Restrictions 602
        14.3.1.1 Substance Use Disorder Identifying Information 602
        14.3.1.2 Part 2 Programs..603
        14.3.1.3 Other Lawful Holders of Part 2 Data...604
    14.3.2 Building a Data Repository..605
    14.3.3 Access to Protected Information in a Data Repository for Health Care Operations..606
    14.3.4 Access to Protected Information in a Data Repository for Research and Data Linkages..606
14.4 State Privacy Laws..607
14.5 Common Rule 608
    14.5.1 Applicability of the Common Rule..609
    14.5.2 Exempt Research 612
        14.5.2.1 Amendments to the Common Rule..613
    14.5.3 Informed Consent and Waiver 614
        14.5.3.1 Amendments to the Common Rule..615
    14.5.4 Application of the Common Rule to Building a Data Repository 618
    14.5.5 Application of the Common Rule to Access to Data in a Data Repository 618

14.6	Antitrust	618
14.7	Nonprofit Tax Exemption	620
	14.7.1 Unrelated Business Income	620
	14.7.2 Private Use of Tax-Exempt Bonds	621

15 Dispute Resolution 623

15.1	Introduction	623
15.2	Arbitration	624
	15.2.1 Potential Advantages	624
	15.2.2 Realizing Time and Cost Savings	626
	15.2.3 Getting Cases Into Arbitration	626
	15.2.4 Employment and Consumer Disputes	627
	15.2.4.1 Agreements with Employees	627
	15.2.4.2 Agreements with Consumers	628
	15.2.4.2.1 Nursing Home Statutes and Regulations	629
	15.2.4.2.2 Limitations on Consumer Choice	629
	15.2.4.2.3 Authority to Agree to Arbitration	630
	15.2.4.2.4 Rules of Procedure	631
	15.2.5 Summary	631
15.3	Mediation	631
	15.3.1 Advantages for Health Law Cases	631
	15.3.2 Mediating Effectively	632
	15.3.2.1 Agreeing to Mediate	632
	15.3.2.2 Selecting a Mediator	633
	15.3.2.3 Preparing for Mediation	634
	15.3.3 Combining Mediation and Arbitration	634
	15.3.4 Summary	635
15.4	Conflict Management	635
15.5	Conclusion	636

Index **637**

1

Terminology[1]

1.1 Glossary

AAPCC: Adjusted average per capita cost. CMS's best estimate of the amount of money it costs to care for Medicare recipients under fee-for-service Medicare in a given area. In computing the AAPCC, CMS uses the U.S. per capita incurred cost and adjusts it by the specified factors to establish an AAPCC for each class of Medicare enrollees.

Abuse: A manner of operation that results in excessive or unreasonable costs to the Medicare or Medicaid programs.

Accelerated Benefits Option: Life insurance provision under which terminally ill persons with life expectancies of less than a year or persons confined to a nursing home can choose to have a certain portion of life insurance proceeds paid out before death to use as they deem appropriate.

Access: The ability to obtain needed medical care. Access is frequently affected by availability of insurance, cost of care, and the geographic location of providers.

Accountable Care Organization (ACO): A network of health care providers that offer the full continuum of health care services for patients. The network receives payment for all care provided to a patient and is held accountable for the quality and cost of care provided. The Affordable Care Act provides financial incentives for these organizations to improve quality and reduce costs by allowing them to share in any savings achieved as a result of these efforts.

Accreditation: Granting of approval or credentials to an agency or facility, based on that agency or facility demonstrating (usually by passing a specific survey or inspection) that standards prescribed by the accrediting body have been met.

Accrete: The term used by CMS for the process of adding new Medicare enrollees to a plan.

Accrual: The amount of money that is set aside to cover expenses. The accrual is the plan's best estimate of what those expenses are and (for medical expenses) is based on a combination of data from the authorization system, the claims system, the lag studies and the plan's history.

---

[1] Thanks to Victoria Ekeanyanwu, Angela Haddon, and Joseph Watkins for updating this chapter for the Seventh Edition. Thanks also to Gillian R. Leene for her work updating this chapter for a previous edition.

ACEs: Accelerated-compensation events. These are medically caused injuries that should not occur. ACEs do not cover all injuries, just classes of adverse outcomes that are usually, although not invariably, avoidable through good medical care.

Actuarial Assumptions: The assumptions that an actuary uses in calculating the expected costs and revenues of the plan. Examples include utilization rates, age, and sex mix of enrollees and cost of medical services.

Actuarial Value: A measure of the average value of benefits in a health insurance plan. It is calculated as a percentage of benefit costs a health insurance plan expects to pay for a standard population, using standard assumptions and taking into account cost-sharing provisions. It represents an average for a population, and does not necessarily represent the actual cost-sharing of an individual.

ADG: Ambulatory diagnostic group. These offer a method of categorizing outpatient episodes.

Administrative Law Judge (ALJ): An employee of the Department of Health and Human Services who presides over civil fraud and abuse administrative hearings brought by the Office of Inspector General. The ALJ's decision is final and binding 30 days after it is served on the parties, unless the decision is appealed to the Departmental Appeals Board (DAB) or the DAB grants an extension of time to file an appeal.

Advance Directives: Written instructions executed by decisionally capable adults that pertain to the future medical treatment preferences or values of the party executing the document. These directives take effect only if the patient is decisionally incapacitated at the time that specific decisions need to be made.

Adverse Selection: The problem of attracting members who are sicker than the general population (specifically, members who are sicker than was anticipated when the budget for medical costs was developed).

Affordable Care Act (ACA): *See* **Patient Protection and Affordable Care Act of 2010**

Aid to Families with Dependent Children (AFDC): The AFDC was created by the Social Security Act to provide grant payments to children deprived of parental support.

Allowed Charge: Discounted fees that insurers will recognize and pay for covered services. Insurers negotiate these discounts with providers in their health plan network, and network providers agree to accept the allowed charge as payment in full. Each insurer has its own schedule of allowed charges.

ALOS: *See* **LOS**.

Alternative Benefits Plan: Rather than follow traditional Medicaid funding plans, states have the option to tailor benefits to meet the needs of specific populations by using an Alternative Benefits Plan.

Ambulatory Surgical Center (ASC): A freestanding, self-contained facility providing outpatient surgical services to patients who do not require inpatient hospitalization.

American Recovery and Reinvestment Act of 2009 (ARRA): Commonly referred to as the "Stimulus," this is the economic stimulus package intended to create jobs and promote investment and consumer spending during the recession. A portion of this money went toward many health care programs such as Medicaid, health information technology, COBRA, health research and construction, community health centers, and more.

Annual Benefit Limit: Insurers place a ceiling on the amount of claims that the insurer will pay for an individual in a given year. After an individual reaches this ceiling during the course of the year, the individual must pay the full cost for all subsequent claims. In 2014, annual benefit limits were prohibited under the Affordable Care Act.

Anti-Kickback Statute: A provision of the Social Security Act that forbids any knowing and willful conduct involving the solicitation, receipt, offer or payment of any kind of remuneration in return for referring an individual for any Medicaid- or Medicare-covered item or service or for recommending or arranging the purchase, lease or order of an item or service that may be wholly or partially paid for through the Medicare or Medicaid programs. Violation of the anti-kickback provision can result in substantial fines for each violation and/or imprisonment for up to five years. The law also mandates exclusion or suspension from government health care programs following a conviction under this statute.

Antisupplementation Provision: A provision of the Social Security Act that makes it a criminal offense to charge a higher amount than the Medicaid rate for a covered service provided to a Medicaid beneficiary. Violation of this provision can subject an individual to a fine and imprisonment.

APG: Ambulatory patient group. A reimbursement methodology developed by 3M Health Information Systems for CMS. APGs are to outpatient procedures what DRGs are to inpatient days. APGs provide for a fixed reimbursement to an institution for outpatient procedures or visits and incorporate data regarding the reason for the visit and patient data. APGs prevent unbundling of ancillary services.

The Administrative Procedures Act (APA): Pub.L. 79–404, 60 Stat. 237, enacted June 11, 1946, is the United States federal statute that governs the way in which administrative agencies of the federal government of the United States may propose and establish regulations.

ASO: Administrative services only; sometimes referred to as an administrative services contract (ASC). A contract between an insurance company and a self-funded plan where the insurance company performs administrative services only and does not assume any risk. Services usually include claims processing but may include other services, such as actuarial analysis, utilization review and so forth. *See also* **ERISA**.

Assignment of Benefits: The payment of medical benefits directly to a provider of care rather than to a member. Generally requires either a contract between the health plan and the provider or a written release from the subscriber to the provider allowing the provider to bill the health plan.

Average Manufacturer Price (AMP): With respect to a covered outpatient drug of a manufacturer, the average price paid to the manufacturer for the drug in the United States by wholesalers for drugs distributed to retail community pharmacies and retail community pharmacies that purchase drugs directly from the manufacturer.

AWP: Any willing provider. This is a form of state law that requires an MCO to accept any provider willing to meet the terms and conditions in the MCO's contract, whether the MCO wants or needs that provider or not.

AWP: Average wholesale price. Commonly used in pharmacy contracting, the AWP is generally determined through reference to a common source of information.

Balance Billing: The practice of a provider billing a patient for all charges not paid for by the insurance plan, even if those charges are above the plan's UCR or are considered medically unnecessary. Managed care plans and service plans generally prohibit providers from balance billing except for allowed copays, coinsurance, and deductibles. Such prohibition against balance billing may even extend to the plan's failure to pay at all (for example, because of bankruptcy).

Basic Health Plan: Beginning in 2014, the Affordable Care Act gave states the option of creating a basic health plan to provide coverage to individuals who have incomes between 133 and 200 percent of poverty instead of having these individuals enroll in the health insurance exchange and include the essential health benefits as defined by the law. Cost-sharing under this plan is limited. In addition, if states choose to offer this plan, the federal government will provide states 95 percent of what it would have paid to subsidize these enrollees in the health insurance exchange.

Beneficiary: A person who has health care insurance through the Medicare or Medicaid program.

Benefit Package: The set of services that are covered by an insurance policy or health plan. Services include physician visits, hospitalizations, and prescription drugs. The benefit package specifies cost-sharing requirements for services, limits on particular services, and annual or lifetime spending limits.

Broker: A person authorized to sell, solicit, or negotiate insurance for compensation.

Blue Cross: Nonprofit (usually) membership corporation providing protection against the cost of hospital care in a limited geographical area.

Blue Shield: Nonprofit (usually) membership corporation providing protection against the cost of hospital care in a limited geographical area.

Capitation: A method of reimbursement where the provider, hospital, or health plan is paid a fixed per patient amount, and is expected to provide all necessary covered services at no additional charge.

Carrier Fraud Control Unit: A fraud control unit housed within a Medicare carrier that receives referrals of potential fraud and abuse cases and conducts case reviews.

Carve-Out: Refers to a set of medical services that are carved out of the basic arrangement. In terms of plan benefits, may refer to a set of benefits that are carved out and contracted for separately; for example, mental health/substance abuse services may be separated from basic medical-surgical services. May also refer to carving out a set of services from a basic capitation rate with a provider (e.g., a capitation rate for cardiac care but carving out cardiac surgery and paying case rates for that).

Case Management: An approach to managing the provision of health care to members with high-cost medical conditions. The goal is to coordinate the care to improve both continuity and quality of care and to lower costs. This generally is a dedicated function in the utilization management department. When focused solely on high-cost inpatient cases, it may be referred to as large case management or catastrophic case management.

Catastrophic Coverage: Insurance coverage option that offers limited benefits and a high deductible, intended to only protect against medical bankruptcy due to unforeseen illness or injury. These plans are generally for young adults in relatively good health.

Case Mix: Refers to the mix of illness and severity of cases for a provider.

Center for Medicare and Medicaid Innovation: A branch of the Centers for Medicare and Medicaid Services created by the Affordable Care Act that is to test innovative payment and delivery system models to improve quality of care and slow the rate of growth in costs in Medicare, Medicaid, and the Children's Health Insurance Program (CHIP).

Centers for Medicare and Medicaid Services (CMS): A federal agency within the United States Department of Health and Human Services (HHS) that administers the following programs: Medicare, Medicaid, the Children's Health Insurance Program (CHIP), and the Health Insurance Marketplace. Formerly known as the Health Care Financing Administration (HCFA).

Certificate of Coverage: Refers to the document that a plan must provide to a member to show evidence that the member has coverage and to give basic information about that coverage. Required under state regulations.

Certification: Granting of approval or credentials to an individual professional, based upon that professional demonstrating (usually through education, experience and specific examination performance) that the standard prescribed by the certifying body has been met.

Children's Health Insurance Program (CHIP): A federal-state program enacted in 1997 that provides health care coverage for uninsured low-income children who are not eligible for Medicaid. States have the option of administering the CHIP through their Medicaid programs, through a separate program, or a combination of both. The Federal government matches state spending for CHIP but Federal CHIP funds are capped.

Churning: The practice of a provider seeing a patient more often than is medically necessary, primarily to increase revenue through an increased number of services. Churning may also apply to any performance-based reimbursement system where there is a heavy emphasis on productivity (in other words, rewarding a provider for seeing a high volume of patients, whether through fee-for-service or through an appraisal system that pays a bonus for productivity).

Civil Investigative Demand: The attorney general has the authority to serve a civil investigative demand on a person who may be in possession of any documents or information relating to a false claims investigation. A demand imposes a broader range of requests than an Office of Inspector General subpoena, including producing documents, providing responses to written interrogatories or giving oral testimony concerning documentary material.

Civil Monetary Penalty Law (CMP): Under this law, the Office of Inspector General (OIG) may bring administrative actions against providers who submit false or fraudulent claims to the United States or its agent for a medical item or service. The OIG need only demonstrate that the person knew or should have known that the claim was false or fraudulent. The penalty for violation of this law can be a substantial fine for each item or service that is submitted in violation of the CMP Law, an assessment of up to three times the amount claimed for each item or service, or a substantial fine for violations regarding patient stabilization and appropriate transfers. In addition, the provider can be terminated from Medicare, Medicaid or other state health care programs.

Claim Fraud: Use of various means (material misrepresentation, exaggeration of an injury, alteration of medical bills and so on) to obtain benefits to which an insured or a physician is not entitled.

Claim Lag: Time incurred between date of a claim and its submission to the insurer for payment; also, the time between claim incurred and payment (check or draft issue or redemption).

Clayton Act: Section 7 of the Clayton Act prohibits mergers and acquisitions where the effect may be substantially to lessen competition, or tend to create a monopoly.

Clinical Laboratory Improvement Amendments of 1988 (CLIA): A federal law subjecting nearly all clinical laboratories operating in the United States—whether they are located in hospitals, physicians' offices or independent—to comprehensive federal quality regulation.

Closed Panel: A managed care plan that contracts with physicians on an exclusive basis for services and does not allow those physicians to see patients for another managed care organization. Examples include staff and group model HMOs. Could apply to a large private medical group that contracts with an HMO.

COA: Certificate of authority. The state-issued operating license for an HMO.

COB: Coordination of benefits. Method of integrating benefits payable under more than one health insurance plan so that the insured's benefits from all sources do not exceed 100% of allowable medical expenses or eliminate appropriate patient incentives to contain costs. For example, an individual may have Blue Cross and Blue Shield through work, and the individual's spouse may have elected an HMO through his or her place of employment. The COB agreement gives the order for what organization has primary responsibility for payment and what organization has secondary responsibility for payment.

COBRA: Consolidated Omnibus Budget Reconciliation Act. Federal statute requiring employers with more than 20 employees to make group health care coverage available for 18 months, at employee expense, to employees who leave the employer for any reason other than gross misconduct. Another portion eases a Medicare recipient's ability to disenroll from an HMO or CMP with a Medicare risk contract. *See also* **Conversion**. The American Recovery and Reinvestment Act (ARRA) provided a temporary subsidy of 65 percent of the premium cost for the purchase of COBRA coverage to people who have lost their job between September 1, 2008 and May 31, 2010.

Coinsurance: A provision in a member's coverage that limits the amount of coverage by the plan to a certain percentage, commonly 80%. Any additional costs are paid by the member out of pocket.

Cold Claim: A claim for medical services received by the plan for which no authorization has been received; that is, it arrives "cold."

Collective Knowledge Doctrine: A doctrine attributing liability to a corporation for the separate actions of several employees who are operating independent of one another. The corporation is considered to have acquired the collective knowledge of its employees and is held responsible for their failure to act lawfully.

Commission: The money paid to a sales representative, broker or other type of sales agent for selling the health plan. May be a flat amount of money or a percentage of the premium.

Commissioner of Insurance: Chief state official responsible for matters related to insurance regulation.

Common Law: Judge-made or court-made law, as opposed to statutes, which are laws enacted by legislative bodies. *Compare* with **Statute**.

Community Rating: The rating methodology required of federally qualified HMOs, HMOs under the laws of many states, and occasionally indemnity plans under certain circumstances. The HMO must obtain the same amount of money per member for all members in the plan. Community rating does allow for variability by allowing the HMO to factor in differences for age, sex, mix (average contract size) and industry factors; not all factors are necessarily allowed under state laws, however. Such techniques are referred to as community rating by class and adjusted community rating. *See also* **Experience Rating**.

Competitive Bidding: Open bidding for federal contracts between independent groups that compete for the contract by providing the best bid. Section 302 of the Medicare Modernization Act of 2003 (MMA) established requirements for a competitive bidding program for certain durable medical equipment, prosthetics, orthotics and supplies (DMEPOS).

CON: Certificate of need. The requirement that a health care organization obtain permission from an oversight agency before making changes. Generally applies only to facilities or facility-based services.

Concurrent Review: Refers to utilization management that takes place during the provision of services. Almost exclusively applied to inpatient hospital stays.

Congressional Budget Office (CBO): The Congressional Budget Office (CBO) is a federal agency within the legislative branch of the United States government that provides budget and economic information to Congress.

Consumer-Directed Health Plan: Plans that seek to increase consumer awareness about health care costs and provide incentives for consumers to consider costs when making decisions about health care. These plans usually have high deductibles along with a consumer-controlled savings account for health care services. The two types of savings accounts are: Health Savings Accounts (HSAs) and Health Reimbursement Arrangements (HRAs).

Consolidated Omnibus Budget Reconciliation Act (COBRA): *See* **COBRA**.

Continuing Care Retirement Community (CCRC): Self-sufficient life-care community in which residents, for a substantial entry fee plus a monthly maintenance fee, enter into a contractual relationship with the community that can last a lifetime.

Contract Year: The 12-month period for which a contract for services is in force. Not necessarily tied to a calendar year.

Contributory Plan: A group health plan in which the employees must contribute a certain amount toward the premium cost, with the employer paying the rest.

Conversion: The conversion of a member covered under a group master contract to coverage under an individual contract. This is offered to subscribers who lose their group coverage (for example, through job loss, death of a working spouse and so forth) and who are ineligible for coverage under another group contract. *See also* **COBRA**.

Coordination of Benefits (COB): *See* **COB**.

Cooperative Hospital Service Organizations (CHSOs): Organizations that are available for hospitals considering certain types of joint ventures with other hospitals.

Copayment: The portion of a claim or medical expense not covered by insurance that a patient must pay for him- or herself.

Corporate Compliance Program: A program designed, implemented, and enforced by a corporation to detect and prevent violations of the fraud and abuse laws.

Corporate Death Sentence: A penalty that may be imposed under the federal Guidelines for Sentencing of Organizations on a corporation that does not take effective measures to prevent wrongdoing among its employees. If a death sentence is imposed on the corporation, the corporation will be fined an amount sufficient to divest it of all net assets.

Corporate Integrity Agreement (CIA): An agreement that a health care company has entered into with the government as part of a global settlement of a government investigation.

Corporate Practice of Medicine Acts or Statutes: State laws that prohibit a physician from working for a corporation; in other words, a physician can only work for himself or herself or another physician. Put another way, a corporation cannot practice medicine. Often created through the effort on the part of certain members of the medical community to prevent physicians from working directly for managed care plans or hospitals.

Cost Sharing: Any form of coverage in which the member pays some portion of the cost of providing services. Usual forms of cost sharing include deductibles, coinsurance and copayments.

Cost Shifting: When a provider cannot cover the cost of providing services under the reimbursement received, the provider raises the prices to other payers to cover that portion of the cost. Some of the costs are shifted to and absorbed by private health insurance.

Credentialing: The most common use of the term refers to obtaining and reviewing the documentation of professional providers. Such documentation includes licensure, certifications, insurance, evidence of malpractice insurance, malpractice history, and so forth. Generally includes both reviewing information provided by the provider and verification that the information is correct and complete.

A less frequent use of the term applies to closed panels and medical groups and refers to obtaining hospital privileges and other privileges to practice medicine.

Current Procedural Terminology (CPT) coding: A set of five-digit codes corresponding to medical services that are frequently used for billing purposes.

Custodial Care: Care provided to an individual that is primarily the basic activities of living. May be medical or nonmedical, but the care is not meant to be curative or as a form of medical treatment, and it is often lifelong. Rarely covered by any form of group health insurance or HMO.

CVO: Credentialing verification organization. This is an independent organization that performs primary verification of a professional provider's credentials. The managed care organization may then rely on that verification rather than requiring the provider to provide credentials independently. This lowers the cost of credentialing.

CWW: Clinic without walls. *See* **GPWW**.

Date of Service: Refers to the date that medical services were rendered. Usually different from the date a claim is submitted.

DAW: Dispense as written. The instruction from a physician to a pharmacist to dispense a brand-name pharmaceutical rather than a generic substitution.

Days Per Thousand: A standard unit of measurement of utilization. Refers to an annualized use of the hospital or other institutional care. It is the number of hospital days that are used in a year for each thousand covered lives.

DCI: Duplicate coverage inquiry. A document used in COB when one plan contacts another to inquire about dual coverage of medical benefits.

Death Spiral: An insurance term that refers to a spiral of high premium rates and adverse selection, generally in a free-choice environment (typically, an insurance company or health plan in an account with multiple other plans or a plan offering coverage to potential members who have alternative choices, such as through an association). One plan, often the indemnity plan competing with managed care plans, ends up having continually higher premium rates such that the only members who stay with the plan are those whose medical costs are so high (and who cannot change because of provider loyalty or benefits restrictions, such as preexisting conditions) that they far exceed any possible premium revenue. Called the death spiral because the losses from underwriting mount faster than the premiums can ever recover, and the account eventually terminates coverage, leaving the carrier in a permanent loss position.

Deductible: The portion of a subscriber's (or member's) health care expenses that must be paid out of pocket before any insurance coverage applies. Common in insurance plans and PPOs, uncommon in HMOs. May apply only to the out-of-network portion of a point-of-service plan. May also apply only to one portion of the plan coverage (for example, there may be a deductible for pharmacy services but not for anything else). Under the Affordable Care Act, deductibles for new plans sold in the small group insurance market are limited to $2,000 for individual policies and $4,000 for family policies.

Defensive Medicine: Physician use of extensive laboratory tests, increased hospital admissions and extended hospital stays for the principal purpose of reducing the likelihood of malpractice suits by patients or providing a good legal defense in the event of such lawsuits.

Deficit Reduction Act of 2005 (DRA): Legislation affecting, among other things, Medicare and Medicaid. The DRA provides states with flexibility to reform their Medicaid programs, Also encourages states to enact their own version of the false claims act.

Delete: The term used by CMS for the process of removing Medicare enrollees from a plan. *See also* **Accrete**.

Departmental Appeals Board (DAB): In a civil action brought by the Office of Inspector General, a party may appeal an ALJ's decision to the DAB. The DAB's decision is final and binding 60 days after the parties are notified of the decision. Any petition for review of the DAB's decision must be filed with the appropriate U.S. Court of Appeals before the 60-day period has expired.

Department of Health and Human Services (DHHS or HHS): Through the Centers for Medicare & Medicaid Services, DHHS administers the Medicare and Medicaid programs, and is the federal agency primarily concerned with health care fraud.

Department of Justice: The agency responsible for the enforcement of health care fraud and abuse at the federal level. Health care fraud may be prosecuted by the antitrust, civil, and/or criminal divisions.

Department of Labor: The agency works to foster, promote, and develop the welfare of the wage earners, job seekers, and retirees of the United States; improve working conditions; advance opportunities for profitable employment; and assure work-related benefits and rights.

Department of Treasury: The agency responsible for maintaining a strong economy and creating economic and job opportunities by promoting the conditions that enable economic growth and stability at home and abroad, strengthening national security by combating threats and protecting the integrity of the financial system, and managing the U.S. Government's finances and resources effectively.

Dependent: A member who is covered by virtue of a family relationship with the member who has the health plan coverage. For example, one person has health insurance or an HMO through work, and that individual's spouse and children, the dependents, also have coverage under that contract.

Designated Health Services (DHS): A specifically defined set of services for billing purposes.

DMO: Dental health maintenance organization. An HMO organized strictly to provide dental benefits.

Diagnosis Coding: A numerical coding system that is used to specify diseases, conditions, injuries, services and items provided to patients.

Diagnosis-Related Group (DRG): *See* **DRG**.

Direct Contracting: A term describing a provider or integrated health care delivery system contracting directly with employers rather than through an insurance company or managed care organization. A superficially attractive option that occasionally works when the employer is large enough. Not to be confused with direct contract model (*see* entry).

Direct Contract Model: A managed care health plan that contracts directly with private practice physicians in the community rather than through an intermediary, such as an IPA or a medical group. A common type of model in open-panel HMOs.

Discharge Planning: That part of utilization management that is concerned with arranging for care or medical needs to facilitate discharge from the hospital. It includes a system of expediting transfer of a patient to a more cost-effective health care facility.

Disease Management: The process of intensively managing a particular disease. This differs from large case management in that it goes well beyond a given case in the hospital or an acute exacerbation of a condition. Disease management encompasses all settings of care and places a heavy emphasis on prevention and maintenance. Similar to case management but more focused on a defined set of diseases.

Disenrollment: The process of termination of coverage. Voluntary termination would include a member quitting because he or she simply wants out. Involuntary termination would include a member leaving the plan because of changing jobs. A rare and serious form of involuntary disenrollment in which the plan terminates a member's coverage against the member's will. This is usually only allowed (under state and federal laws) for gross offenses such as fraud, abuse, nonpayment of premium or copayments or a demonstrated inability to comply with recommended treatment plans.

Disproportionate Share Hospital (DSH) Payments: Payments made by Medicare or a State's Medicaid program to hospitals designated as serving a "disproportionate share" of low-income or uninsured patients. These payments are in addition to the regular payments that hospitals receive for providing inpatient care to Medicare and Medicaid beneficiaries. States have some discretion in determining how much eligible hospitals receive, but the amount of federal matching funds that a state can use to make payments to DSH hospitals is capped at an amount specified in the federal Medicaid statute. The Affordable Care Act reduces the amount of both Medicare and Medicaid DSH funds distributed by the Federal government as more people become insured.

DME: Durable medical equipment. Medical equipment that is not disposable (that is, is used repeatedly) and is only related to care for a medical condition. Examples include wheelchairs, home hospital beds and so forth. An area of increasing expense, particularly in conjunction with case management. DME is covered under Medicare Part B.

Doughnut Hole: The gap in prescription drug coverage under Medicare Part D. The gap begins after beneficiaries enrolled in Part D plans pay 100 percent of their prescription drug costs after their total drug spending exceeds the initial coverage limit until they qualify for catastrophic coverage. The coverage gap will be gradually phased out under the Affordable Care Act, so that by 2020, beneficiaries will be responsible for 25 percent of all prescription drug costs up to the catastrophic level.

Do-Not-Resuscitate (DNR): Also known as no code or allow natural death, is a legal order written either in the hospital or on a legal form to withhold cardiopulmonary resuscitation (CPR) or advanced cardiac life support (ACLS), in respect of the wishes of a patient in case their heart were to stop or they were to stop breathing.

DRG: Diagnosis-related group. A statistical system of classifying any inpatient stay into groups for the purposes of payment. Factors used to determine the DRG payment amount include the diagnosis involved as well as the hospital resources necessary to treat the condition. Also used by a few states for all payers and by many private health plans (usually non-HMO) for contracting purposes. Hospitals are paid a fixed rate for inpatient services corresponding to the DRG group assigned to a given patient.

DRG Creep: The placement of patients in a higher-value DRG than is warranted by the patient's condition to receive increased Medicare reimbursement.

DRG Payment Window: The period of time before a patient's admission to the hospital when the services provided to the patient are eligible for Medicare reimbursement. Between the advent of a prospective payment system in 1983 and 1990, hospitals were eligible for reimbursement for outpatient services performed in the 24 hours prior to admission. In 1990, Congress expanded the DRG payment window to include services provided during the three days prior to admission and expanded services to include not only outpatient services, but services furnished by any entity wholly owned or operated by the hospital.

DSM-IV: Diagnostic and Statistical Manual of Mental Disorders, fourth edition. The manual used to provide a diagnostic coding system for mental and substance abuse disorders.

Dual Choice: Sometimes referred to as Section 1310 or mandating. That portion of the federal HMO regulations that required any employer with 25 or more employees that resided in an HMO's service area, paid minimum wage, and offered health coverage to offer a federally qualified HMO as well. The HMO had to request it. This provision was "sunsetted" in 1995. Another definition, unrelated to the previous one, pertains to point of service.

Dual Eligibles: A term used to describe an individual who is eligible for Medicare and for some level of Medicaid benefits. To promote better coordination of Medicare and Medicaid services for dual eligibles, the Affordable Care Act created a Federal Coordinated Health Care Office within the Centers for Medicare and Medicaid Services.

Dual Option: The offering of both an HMO and a traditional insurance plan by one carrier.

Duplicate Claims: When the same claim is submitted more than once, usually because payment has not been received quickly. Can lead to duplicate payments and incorrect data in the claims file.

DUR: Drug utilization review.

Durable Medical Equipment (DME): *See* **DME**.

EAP: Employee assistance program. A program that a company puts into effect for its employees to provide them with help in dealing with personal problems, such as alcohol or drug abuse, mental health or stress issues and so forth.

Effective Date: The day that health plan coverage goes into effect or is modified.

Eligibility: When an individual is eligible for coverage under a plan. Also used to determine when an individual is no longer eligible for coverage (for example, a dependent child reaches a certain age and is no longer eligible for coverage under his or her parent's health plan).

Emergency Medical Treatment and Labor Act (EMTALA): A federal law enacted in 1986 as part of COBRA that requires hospitals with emergency departments to screen and treat within its capacity any individual with an emergency medical condition who comes to the hospital, regardless of the person's health insurance status or ability to pay.

ELOS: *See* **LOS**.

Employee Retirement Income Security Act of 1974: *See* **ERISA**.

Employer Health Care Tax Credit: An incentive mechanism designed to encourage employers to offer health insurance to their employees. The tax credit enables employers to deduct an amount, usually a percentage of the contribution they make toward their employees' premiums, from the federal taxes they owe. The tax credits are typically refundable so they are available to non-profit organizations that do not pay federal taxes. The Affordable Care Act included a tax credit for small employers that provide health coverage to their employees. The credit is available to employers with 25 or fewer employees and average annual wages of less than $50,000.

Employer Mandate: A provision, such as in the Affordable Care Act, that requires all employers, or at least all employers meeting size or revenue thresholds, to offer health benefits that meet a defined standard, and pay a set portion of the cost of those benefits on behalf of their employees.

Employer Pay-or-Play: An approach that would require employers to offer and pay for health benefits on behalf of their employees, or to pay a specified dollar amount or percentage of payroll into a designated public fund. The fund would provide a source of financing for coverage for those who do not have employment-based coverage.

Encounter: An outpatient or ambulatory visit by a member to a provider. Applies primarily to physician office visits but may encompass other types of encounters as well. In fee-for-service plans, an encounter also generates a claim. In capitated plans, the encounter is still the visit, but no claim is generated. *See also* **Statistical Claim**.

Enrollee: An individual enrolled in a managed health care plan. Usually applies to the subscriber or person who has the coverage in the first place rather than to their dependents, but the term is not always used that precisely.

Entitlement Program: Federal programs, such as Medicare and Medicaid, for which people who meet eligibility criteria have a federal right to benefits. Changes to eligibility criteria and benefits require legislation. The federal government is required to spend the funds necessary to provide benefits for individuals in these programs, unlike the discretionary programs for which spending is set by Congress through the appropriations process. Enrollment in these programs cannot be capped and neither states nor the Federal government may establish waiting lists.

EOB: Explanation of benefits. A statement mailed to a member or covered insured explaining how and why a claim was or was not paid; the Medicare version is called an explanation of Medicare benefits or EOMB. *See also* **ERISA**.

Episode of Care: An episode of care refers to all the treatments and services related to the treatment of a condition. For acute conditions (such as a concussion or a bone fracture), the episode refers to all treatment and services from the onset of the condition to its resolution. For chronic conditions, the episode refers to all services and treatments received over a given period of time, commonly one year. The Affordable Care Act called for for pilot programs to test this method of payment reform in Medicare and Medicaid.

EPO: Exclusive provider organization. An EPO is similar to an HMO in that it often uses primary physicians as gatekeepers, often capitates providers, has a limited provider panel and uses an authorization system. It is referred to as exclusive because the member must remain within the network to receive benefits. The main difference is that EPOs are generally regulated under insurance statutes rather than HMO regulations. Not allowed in many states that maintain that EPOs are really HMOs.

EPSDT: The Early and Periodic Screening, Diagnostic and Treatment mandate of the Medicaid Act. It requires states to provide any service that Medicaid offers and a physician has deemed "medically necessary." Treatment is available to Medicaid-eligible children under the age of 21. EPSDT will also include follow-up diagnostic and treatment services to correct conditions identified during a screening, without regard to whether the state Medicaid plan covers those services for adult beneficiaries.

Equity Model: A term applied to a form of for-profit vertically integrated health care delivery systems in which the physicians are owners.

ERISA: Employee Retirement Income Security Act of 1974. One provision of this act allows self-funded plans to avoid paying premium taxes, complying with state-mandated benefits, or otherwise complying with state laws and regulations regarding insurance, even when insurance companies and managed care plans that stand risk for medical costs must do so. Another provision requires that plans and insurance companies provide an explanation of benefits statement to a member or covered insured in the event of a denial of a claim, explaining why the claim was denied and informing the individual of his or her rights of appeal.

Essential Health Benefits: A benchmark level of benefits created by the Affordable Care Act that is meant to ensure a health plan provides a comprehensive set of services. Essential health benefits must include items and services within at least 10 categories, including ambulatory patient services; emergency services, hospitalization; maternity and newborn care; mental health and substance abuse disorder services; prescription drugs; rehabilitative and habilitative services and devices; laboratory services; preventative and wellness services and chronic disease management; and pediatric services, including oral and vision care. Plans both within and outside of the health insurance exchange will be required to offer at least this level of coverage. Cost-sharing will be limited to the current HSA limits. The Secretary of Health and Human Services is required to define and annually update the benefit package.

Ethics in Patient Referrals Act: The official name for the laws that have become known as the Stark Laws or Stark I and Stark II. *See* **Stark I** and **Stark II**.

Evidence of Insurability: The form that documents whether an individual is eligible for health plan coverage when the individual does not enroll through an open enrollment period. For example, if an employee wants to change health plans in the middle of a contract year, the new health plan may require evidence of insurability (often both a questionnaire and a medical examination) to ensure that it will not be accepting adverse risk.

Experience Rating: The method of setting premium rates based on the actual health care costs of a group or groups. Experience rating was prohibited under the Affordable Care Act beginning in 2014.

Experimental Medical Procedure: Medical practice, procedure, or treatment still in a trial stage—that is, being tested on humans or animals. (*See* **Investigational Medical Procedure** for distinction in meaning.)

Extracontractual Benefits: Health care benefits beyond what the member's actual policy covers. These benefits are provided by a plan to reduce utilization. For example, a plan may not provide coverage for a hospital bed at home, but it is more cost-effective for the plan to provide such a bed than to keep admitting a member to the hospital.

Fair Market Value: The value in arms-length transactions consistent with the general market value, that is the price that is the result of bona fide bargaining between well-informed parties.

False Claims Act (FCA): The criminal FCA makes it illegal to present a claim upon or against the United States that the claimant knows to be false, fictitious, or fraudulent. The civil FCA provides that any person who knowingly presents or causes to be presented to the U.S. government a false or fraudulent claim for payment or approval; knowingly makes, uses or causes to be made or used, a false record or statement to get a false or fraudulent claim paid or approved by the government; or conspires to defraud the government by getting a false or fraudulent claim allowed or paid violates the act. The act also has qui tam provisions. Under the civil provisions of the FCA, a defendant can be assessed a penalty per claim, plus three times the damages incurred by the federal government in its prosecution and investigation of the case. The criminal provisions provide for a fine and up to five years imprisonment upon conviction.

False Statements Statute: A statute that prohibits any false, fictitious, or fraudulent statement to the United States or any government agency. This statute is often used to prosecute health care providers who make false Medicare or Medicaid claims.

Family and Medical Leave Act (FMLA): A federal law that guarantees up to 12 weeks of job protected leave for certain employees when they need to take time off due to serious illness or disability, to have or adopt a child, or to care for another family member.

FAR: Federal acquisition regulations. The regulations applied to the federal government's acquisition of services, including health care services. *See also* **FEHBARS**.

Favored Nations Discount: A contractual agreement between a provider and a payer stating that the provider will automatically provide the payer the best discount it provides anyone else.

Federal Bureau of Investigation (FBI): As the federal government's law enforcement agency, the FBI investigates federal crimes, including health care fraud.

Federal Employee Health Benefits Program (FEHBP): *See* **FEHBP**.

Federal Medical Assistance Percentage (FMAP): The statutory term for the federal Medicaid matching rate—i.e., the share of the costs of Medicaid services or administration that the federal government bears. In the case of covered services, FMAP varies depending upon a state's per capita income. The Affordable Care Act established highly enhanced FMAPs for the cost of services to low-income adults with incomes up to 133% of the Federal Poverty Level (FPL) who are not currently covered. The ACA required the federal government to pay 100 percent of such costs in 2014 through 2016, phasing down to 90 percent in 2020 and beyond.

Federal Qualification: Applies to HMOs and CMPs. It means that the HMO/CMP meets federal standards regarding benefits, financial solvency, rating methods, marketing, member services, health care delivery systems, and other standards. An HMO/CMP must apply for federal qualification and be examined by the OMC, including an on-site review. Federal qualification does place some restrictions on how a plan operates but also allows it to enter the Medicare and FEHBP markets in an expedited way. Federal qualification is voluntary and not required to enter the market.

Federal Trade Commission: The Federal Trade Commission's mission is "working to protect consumers by preventing anticompetitive, deceptive, and unfair business practices, enhancing informed consumer choice and public understanding of the competitive process, and accomplishing this without unduly burdening legitimate business activity."

Federally-Facilitated Exchange/Marketplace: Marketplace for insurance plans that will operate in states that did not choose to build their own marketplace. The Affordable Care Act directs the Secretary of Health and Human Services to establish and operate a federally-facilitated marketplace in any state that is not able or willing to establish a state-based marketplace. In a federally-facilitated marketplace, HHS will perform all marketplace functions. States entering into a partnership marketplace may administer plan management functions, in-person consumer assistance functions, or both, and HHS will perform the remaining marketplace functions.

Federally Qualified Health Centers (FQHC): An entity that has entered into an agreement with CMS to meet Medicare program requirements and is receiving a grant under Sections 329, 330, or 340 of the Public Health Service Act or is receiving funding from such a grant pursuant to a contract with the grant recipient and meets the grant requirements; based on the recommendation of the Public Health Service, is determined by CMS to meet the requirements for receiving such a grant; was treated by CMS as a comprehensively federally funded health center as of January 1, 1990; or is an outpatient health program or facility operated by a tribe or tribal organization under the Indian Self-Determination Act or by an urban Native American organization receiving funds under Title V of the Indian Healthcare Improvement Act.

Federally Qualified Health Maintenance Organization (HMO): An HMO that has met federal standards delineated in the federal HMO Act for legal and organizational status, financial viability, marketing, and health service delivery systems. Federally qualified HMOs are required to provide or arrange for basic necessary services with no limitation as to time, cost, frequency, extent or kind of services actually provided. Federal qualification under the HMO Act is voluntary.

Fee-for-Service: Method of charging whereby a physician or other provider bills for each visit or service rendered.

Fee Schedule: May also be referred to as fee maximums or a fee allowance schedule. A listing of the maximum fees that a health plan will pay for certain services based on CPT billing codes.

FEHBARS: Federal Employee Health Benefit Acquisition Regulations. The regulations applied to OPM's purchase of health care benefits programs for federal employees.

FEHBP: Federal Employees Health Benefits Program. The health insurance program for federal employees and their families. The FEHBP is administered by the U.S. Office of Personnel Management. *See also* **OPM**.

Flexible Benefit Plan: When an employer allows employees to choose a variety of options in benefits up to a certain total amount. The employee then can tailor his or her benefits package among health coverage, life insurance, child care, and so forth to optimize benefits for his or her particular needs.

Forensic Medicine: Specialty area of medicine concerned with the investigation, preparation, preservation, and presentation of medical opinion and other evidence in courts and other legal, correctional, or law enforcement settings.

Formulary: A listing of drugs that a physician may prescribe. The physician is requested or required to use only formulary drugs unless there is a valid medical reason to use a nonformulary drug.

Foundation: A nonprofit form of integrated health care delivery system. The foundation model is usually formed in response to tax laws that affect nonprofit hospitals or in response to state laws prohibiting the corporate practice of medicine. The foundation purchases both the tangible and intangible assets of a physician's practice, and the physician then forms a medical group that contracts with the foundation on an exclusive basis for services to patients seen through the foundation. *See also* **Corporate Practice of Medicine Acts or Statutes**.

Foundation Model: Refers to an integrated health care delivery system in which a nonprofit foundation is responsible for providing the income to a medical group that is exclusive with the foundation. The foundation is usually, but not necessarily, associated with a nonprofit hospital and is often found in states with corporate practice of medicine acts.

FPP: Faculty practice plan. A form of group practice organized around a teaching program. It may be a single group encompassing all the physicians providing services to patients at the teaching hospital and clinics, or it may be multiple groups drawn along specialty lines (for example, psychiatry, cardiology, or surgery).

Fragmented Caims: Billing separately for procedures rather than using a global billing code covering all of these services, when billing separately results in a higher payment rate.

Fraud: Knowing and willful deception or misrepresentation or a reckless disregard of the facts, with the intent to receive an unauthorized benefit.

Fraud Alerts: The OIG has issued Fraud Alerts as a way of informing the health care industry about prohibited practices. The alerts are generally brief documents that describe conduct that the OIG perceives as violating the fraud and abuse laws.

Fraud Enforcement Recovery Act of 2009 (FERA): An Act intended to increase enforcement oversight over the types of financial frauds that contributed to the economic crisis and to recover taxpayers' money lost to these frauds. The Act provides the federal government with more tools to investigate and prosecute these financial frauds.

Freedom of Information Act (FOIA): This law generally provides that any person has the right to request access to federal agency records or information except to the extent the records are protected from disclosure by any of nine exemptions contained in the law or by one of three special law enforcement record exclusions.

FTE: Full-time equivalent. The equivalent of one full-time employee. For example, two part-time employees are 0.5 FTE each, for a total of 1 FTE.

Full Capitation: A loose term used to refer to a physician group or organization receiving capitation for all professional expenses, not just for the services it provides itself; does not include capitation for institutional services. The group is then responsible for subcapitating or otherwise reimbursing other physicians for services to its members. *See* **Global Capitation**.

Full-Time Employee: An employee who works an average of at least 30 hours per week.

Gatekeeper: An informal, although widely used, term that refers to a primary care case management model health plan. In this model, all care from providers other than the primary care physician, except for true emergencies, must be authorized by the primary care physician before rendered. This is a predominant feature of almost all HMOs.

Generic Drug: A drug that is equivalent to a brand-name drug but usually less expensive. Most managed care organizations that provide drug benefits cover generic drugs but may require a member to pay the difference in cost between a generic drug and a brand-name drug or pay a higher copay, unless there is no generic equivalent.

Global Billing Codes: Billing codes used by Medicare to pay for surgical services that cover not only the surgery itself, but also the usual pre- and postoperative services.

Global Capitation: A capitation payment that covers all medical expenses, including professional and institutional expenses. May not necessarily cover optional benefits (e.g., pharmacy). Sometimes called total capitation.

GPWW: Group practice without walls. A group practice in which the members of the group come together legally but continue to practice in private offices scattered throughout the service area. Sometimes called a clinic without walls (CWW).

Gramm-Leach-Bliley Act: Signed into law on November 12, 1999, the act provided for sweeping changes in the regulation of the financial industry allowing, among other things, for affiliations among banks, securities firms and insurance companies that were previously not permitted.

Grandfathered Plan: A health plan that was in place on March 23, 2010, when the Affordable Care Act was enacted, is exempt from complying with some parts of the law, so long as the plan does not make significant changes to its policy, such as eliminating or reducing benefits to treat a specific disease or condition, significantly increasing cost-sharing, or reducing the employer contribution toward the premium, among others. Once a health plan makes such a change to their policy, it becomes subject to all the requirements of the ACA.

Group: The members who are covered by virtue of receiving health plan coverage at a single company.

Group Model HMO: An HMO that contracts with a medical group for the provision of health care services. The relationship between the HMO and the medical group is generally close, although there are wide variations in the relative independence of the group from the HMO. A form of closed-panel health plan.

Group Practice: The American Medical Association defines group practice as three or more physicians who deliver patient care, make joint use of equipment and personnel and divide income by a prearranged formula.

Group Purchasing Organization (GPO): An entity authorized to act as a purchasing agent for a group of individuals or entities who are furnishing services payable by Medicare or a state health care program, and who are neither wholly owned by the GPO nor by subsidiaries of a parent corporation that wholly owns the GPO (either directly or through another wholly owned entity).

Guarantee Issue/Renewal: Requires insurers to offer and renew coverage, without regard to health status, use of services, or pre-existing conditions. This ACA requirement ensures that no one will be denied coverage for any reason.

Health Care and Education Reconciliation Act of 2010 (HCERA): A reconciliation bill that the 111th Congress enacted into law on March 30, 2010, which made several changes to the Patient Protection and Affordable Care Act (ACA) that was enacted 7 days earlier. Among other things, the changes included increasing tax credits to buy insurance, lowering the penalty for not buying insurance, and closing the Medicare Part D "donut hole."

HCFA-1500: A claims form used by professionals to bill for services. Required by Medicare and generally used by private insurance companies and managed care plans.

Health Care Fraud and Abuse Control Program (HCFAC): Efforts to combat fraud were consolidated and strengthened under Public Law 104-191, the Health Insurance Portability and Accountability Act of 1996 (HIPAA). The Act established a comprehensive program to combat fraud committed against all health plans, both public and private. The legislation required the establishment of a national Health Care Fraud and Abuse Control Program (HCFAC), under the joint direction of the Attorney General and the Secretary of the Department of Health and Human Services (HHS) acting through the Department's Inspector General (HHS/OIG).

HCPCS: HCFA Common Procedural Coding System. A set of codes used by Medicare that describes services and procedures. HCPCS includes CPT codes but also has codes for services not included in CPT, such as DME and ambulance. Although HCPCS is nationally defined, there is provision for local use of certain codes.

Health Care Financing Administration: *See* **CMS.**

Healthcare Integrity and Protection Data Bank (HIPDB): A national data collection program for health care fraud and abuse, formed in October 1999 pursuant to the Health Insurance Portability and Accountability Act of 1996 (HIPAA). The HIPDB is intended to complement the National Practitioner Data Bank.

Health Care Quality Improvement Program (HCQIP): In 1992, HCFA established this program, which promotes partnerships between PROs (now QIOs) and hospitals, health plans and physicians. These partnerships profile patterns of medical care, identify areas in which treatment could be improved, assist in the development of quality improvement efforts, and measure improvement.

Healthcare Facilities Accreditation Program (HFAP): is a not-for-profit organization meant to help health care organizations maintain their standards in patient care and comply with regulations and the health care environment.

Health Information Technology for Economic and Clinical Health Act (HITECH): Part of the American Recovery and Reinvestment Act of 2009 (ARRA) that addresses the privacy and security concerns associated with the electronic transmission of health information, much like HIPAA.

Health Insurance Exchange/Marketplace: An arrangement through which insurers offer smaller employers and individuals health insurance plans for purchase. Under the Affordable Care Act, state-based health insurance exchanges were established to set standards for what benefits are to be covered, how much insurers can charge, and the rules insurers must follow in order to participate in the insurance market. Individuals and small employers will then be able to select their coverage within this organized arrangement.

Health Insurance Portability and Accountability Act of 1996 (HIPAA): This statute addresses the availability of private insurance to persons with preexisting medical conditions, among other topics. Its "Administrative Simplification" provisions created duties to protect the privacy and security of personal health information.

Healthcare Fraud and Prevention Partnership (HFPP): is a voluntary public-private partnership between the federal government, state agencies, law enforcement, private health insurance plans, and health care anti-fraud associations.

Health Maintenance Organization (HMO): A system of health care delivery that not only pays for the care, but also arranges for the provision of services. In order for the HMO to pay for the cost of health care, members must receive care from a participating provider who has contracted with the HMO. In most HMOs, members choose a primary care physician from a panel of physicians affiliated with the HMO. The primary care physician serves as a gatekeeper, authorizing all visits to a specialist.

Health Reimbursement Arrangement (HRA): A tax-exempt account that can be used to pay for current or future qualified health expenses. HRAs are established benefit plans funded solely by employer contributions, with no limits on the amount an employer can contribute. HRAs are often paired with a high-deductible health plan, but do not have to be.

Health Savings Account (HSA): A tax-exempt savings account that can be used to pay for current or future qualified medical expenses. Employers may make HSAs available to their employees or individuals can obtain HSAs from most financial institutions. Employers and employees can contribute to the plan. In order to open an HSA, an individual must have health coverage under an HSA-qualified high-deductible health plan.

HEDIS: Health Plan Employer Data Information Set. Developed by the NCQA with considerable input from the employer community and the managed care community, HEDIS is an ever-evolving set of data reporting standards. HEDIS is designed to provide some standardization in performance reporting for financial, utilization, membership, and clinical data so that employers and others can compare performance among plans and across organizational structures. A voluntary system, HEDIS uses primarily process measures but also includes some outcome and structural measures. It covers preventive care, acute care, and chronic care.

High-Deductible Health Plan: Health insurance plans that have higher deductibles (the amount of health care costs that must be paid for by the consumer before the insurance plan begins to pay for services), but lower premiums than traditional plans.

High-Risk Pool: State programs designed to provide health insurance to residents who are considered medically uninsurable and are unable to buy coverage in the individual market.

Hobbs Act: According to the Department of Justice's website, "The Hobbs Act prohibits actual or attempted robbery or extortion affecting interstate or foreign commerce in any way or degree."

Home Health Agency (HHA): An organization that provides certain part-time or intermittent medical, nursing, therapy, and personal care services to individuals in their homes.

Home Health Value-Based Purchasing (HHVBP) Model: CMS implemented this model, on January 1, 2016, to improve the quality and delivery of home health care services to Medicare beneficiaries with specific goals to provide incentives for better quality care with greater efficiency, study new potential quality and efficiency measures for appropriateness in the home health setting; and enhance the current public reporting process.

Hospice: Concept of care provided to terminally ill patients and their families that emphasizes emotional and spiritual needs and coping with pain and death rather than cure.

Hospital Readmissions: When a patient is discharged from a hospital, then later readmitted to a hospital for care within a certain number of days. The number of hospital readmissions is often used to measure quality of care in a hospital and other care settings.

Iatrogenic Injuries: Injuries caused by the medical treatment itself, not the underlying disease.

IBNR: Incurred but not reported. The amount of money that the plan should accrue for medical expenses that it knows nothing about yet. These are medical expenses that the authorization system has not captured and for which claims have not yet hit the door.

IDS: Integrated delivery system; also referred to as an integrated health care delivery system. Other acronyms that mean the same thing include IDN (integrated delivery network), IDFS (integrated delivery and financing system) and IDFN (integrated delivery and financing network). An IDS is a system of health care providers organized to span a broad range of health care services. Although there is no clear definition of an IDS, in its full flower an IDS should be able to access the market on a broad basis, optimize cost and clinical outcomes, accept and manage a full range of financial arrangements to provide a set of defined benefits to a defined population, align financial incentives of the participants (including physicians) and operate under a cohesive management structure. Includes IHO, IPA, PHO, MSO, Equity model, Staff model HMO, and Foundation model.

IHO: Integrated health care organization. An IDS that is predominantly owned by physicians.

Improving Medicare Post-Acute Care Transformation (IMPACT) Act of 2014: Congress passed this Act on September 18, 2014 to change and improve Medicare's post-acute care services and how they are reported. The Act requires LTCHs, SNFs, HHAs, and IRFs to submit standardized patient assessment data with regard to quality measures, resource use, and other measures.

Income-Related Premium: Premiums for Medicare Part B and Part D that apply to higher-income Medicare beneficiaries. The Medicare Modernization Act of 2003 established an income-related Part B premium that took effect in 2007, requiring higher-income Medicare beneficiaries to pay a greater share of average Part B costs. The Affordable Care Act froze the threshold for the income-related Part B premium at 2010 levels through 2019. The ACA also created an income-related Part D premium, effective in 2011, using the same surcharge percentages and income thresholds as for Part B. Similar to the Part B premium provision, the income thresholds for the Part D income-related premium are not indexed to increase annually.

Incurred but Unpaid Claims: Claims that may not have been paid as of some specific date. May include reported and unreported claims. *See also* **Lag Study**.

Indemnification: Obligation, established by contractual agreement or imposed as a matter of tort law, in which one party is required to reimburse another for losses of a particular type.

Independent Payment Advisory Board: Established by the Affordable Care Act, a board of 15 members appointed by the President and confirmed by the Senate for six year terms. The board is tasked with submitting proposals to Congress to reduce Medicare spending by specified amounts if the projected per beneficiary spending exceeds the target growth rate. If the Board fails to submit a proposal, the Secretary of the Department of Health and Human Services is required to develop a detailed proposal to achieve the required level of Medicare savings. The Secretary is required to implement the Board's (or Secretary's) proposals, unless Congress adopts alternative proposals that result in the same amount of savings. The Board is prohibited from submitting proposals that would ration care, increase taxes, change Medicare benefits or eligibility, increase beneficiary premiums and cost-sharing requirements, or reduce low-income subsidies under Part D.

Individual Insurance Market: The market where individuals who do not have group (usually employer-based) coverage purchase private health insurance. This market is also referred to as the non-group market.

Individual Mandate: A requirement that all individuals obtain health insurance. Massachusetts was the first state to impose an individual mandate that all adults have health insurance. The Affordable Care Act established an individual mandate to obtain health insurance, applicable to all Americans with some hardship and income-based exemptions.

Informed Consent: Legal right of all adults, with no upper age limit, to make their own decisions regarding medical, financial, and daily living matters.

Institutional Review Board (IRB): Panel that prospectively reviews and approves biomedical or behavioral protocols involving human subjects that are supported with federal funds. Mandated by the National Research Act of 1973.

Integrated (Carve-Out) Plan: Method of combining two or more benefit plans to prevent duplication of benefits or overinsurance.

Investigational Medical Procedure: Ongoing clinical observation of an approved agent with respect to immediate and long-term effectiveness, complications, consequences and care. (*See* **Experimental Medical Procedure** for distinction in meaning.)

IOM: Institute of Medicine. This organization is part of the National Academy of Sciences in Washington, DC.

IPA: Independent practice association. An organization that has a contract with a managed care plan to deliver services in return for a single capitation rate. The IPA in turn contracts with individual providers to provide the services either on a capitation basis or on a fee-for-service basis. The typical IPA encompasses all specialties, but an IPA can be solely for primary care, or it may be a single specialty. An IPA may also be the "PO" part of a PHO.

Joint Commission: Formerly the Joint Commission on Accreditation of Healthcare Organizations (JCAHO). A nonprofit organization that performs accreditation reviews primarily on hospitals, other institutional facilities, and outpatient facilities. Most managed care plans require any hospital under contract to be accredited by the Joint Commission.

Joint-Operating Agreement/Arrangement (JOA): Transactions between two hospitals or health systems in which both parties are affiliated yet operate independently in certain regards, such as keeping power over the board of directors and assets.

Joint Operating Company (JOC): JOC is formed to serve as the parent to two or more affiliating hospitals. The JOC is created with the expectation that it will qualify as a Section 501(c)(3) organization and will enter into JOAs with the participating hospitals.

Lag Study: A report that tells managers how old the claims are that are being processed and how much is paid out each month (both for that month and for any earlier months, by month) and compares these with the amount of money that was accrued for expenses each month. A powerful tool used to determine whether the plan's reserves are adequate to meet all expenses.

Large Group Health Plan: A group health plan that covers employees of an employer that has 101 or more employees. Until 2016, in some states large groups are defined as 51 or more employees.

Licensure: Permission granted by a state, under requirements and conditions established by statute, to an individual or entity to engage in a particular type of activity (for example, practice medicine, nursing, or social work or operate a hospital, nursing facility, or home health agency).

Life Care at Home (LCAH): Concept of health care finance and delivery program models that resemble a CCRC while allowing an elderly person to live at home instead of at a centralized location.

Lifetime Benefit Maximum: A cap on the amount of money insurers will pay toward the cost of health care services over the lifetime of the insurance policy. Lifetime benefits maximums are prohibited under the Affordable Care Act.

Line of Business: A health plan (e.g., an HMO, EPO, or PPO) that is set up as a line of business within another, larger organization, usually an insurance company. This legally differentiates it from a freestanding company or a company set up as a subsidiary. It may also refer to a unique product type (e.g., Medicaid) within a health plan.

Loading Factor: Amount added to the net premium rate determined for a group insurance plan to cover the possibility that losses will be greater than statistically expected because of older average age, hazardous industry, large percentage of unskilled employees, or adverse experience.

Long Term Care: Continuum of maintenance, custodial and health services to the chronically ill, disabled or retarded. Services may be provided on an inpatient, outpatient or at-home basis.

LOS/ELOS/ALOS: Length of stay/estimated length of stay/average length of stay.

Loss Ratio: *See* **Medical Loss Ratio**.

MAC: Maximum allowable charge (or cost). The maximum, although not the minimum, that a vendor may charge for something. This term is often used in pharmacy contracting; a related term, used in conjunction with professional fees, is fee maximum.

Major Medical Expense Insurance: Form of health insurance that provides benefits for most types of medical expense up to a high maximum benefit. Such contracts may contain internal limits and usually are subject to deductibles and coinsurance.

Managed Care, Managed Care Organization (MCO): A broad term used to describe a system of health care delivery that tries to manage the cost of the health care, the quality of health care, and access to health care. The term encompasses a variety of health care delivery organizations, including HMOs, preferred provider organizations (PPOs), and physician/hospital organizations (PHOs).

Mandated Benefits: Benefits that a health plan is required to provide by law. This is generally used to refer to benefits above and beyond routine insurance type benefits, and it generally applies at the state level (where there is high variability from state to state). Common examples include in-vitro fertilization, defined days of inpatient mental health or substance abuse treatment and other special condition treatments. Self-funded plans are exempt from mandated benefits under ERISA.

Master Group Contract: Also known as a master policy, this is the actual contract between a health plan and a group that purchases coverage. The master group contract provides specific terms of coverage, rights, and responsibilities of both parties.

Material Misrepresentation: A false or misleading statement on an application for an insurance policy that influences the insurer's decision as to the prospective insured's insurability. These statements may create the basis for rescinding the policy.

Maximum Daily Hospital Benefit: Maximum amount payable for hospital room and board per day of hospital confinement.

Maximum Out-of-Pocket Cost: The largest amount of money a member will ever need to pay for covered services during a contract year. The maximum out-of-pocket cost includes deductibles and coinsurance. Once this limit is reached, the health plan pays for all services up to the maximum level of coverage. Applies mostly to non-HMO plans such as indemnity plans, PPOs, and POS plans.

McCarran-Ferguson Act (Public Law 15): Legislation stipulating that federal law would apply to the insurance business only to the extent that it was not regulated by state law.

M+C: *See* **Medicare Advantage Plan**.

MCE: Medical care evaluation. A component of a quality assurance program that looks at the process of medical care.

Medicaid: A federal and state-funded program administered, in part, by CMS and participating states that finance health care for the poor. States receive federal matching funds and are free to design their programs as long as they cover certain federally mandated services and run their programs within federal parameters. Demonstration projects, especially for managed care, may get waivers from certain requirements imposed by the federal government. Medicaid also covers some low-income children and pregnant women without regard to their eligibility for cash assistance programs.

Medicaid Expansion: The Affordable Care Act allowed states to expand their Medicaid programs to cover individuals between the ages of 19 and 65 (parents, and adults without dependent children) with incomes up to 133% of the federal poverty level. The ACA required the federal government to pay for 100% of the cost to expand Medicaid to this new population for three years, phasing down to 90% in 2020 and all subsequent years.

Medicaid Fraud Control Unit (MFCU): Entities located in 49 states and the District of Columbia funded jointly by state and federal money that are charged with investigating and pursuing convictions against health care providers who defraud the Medicaid program. These units are usually affiliated with the state Attorney General's office and directed by an assistant attorney general. An MFCU's authority is concurrent with the OIG at the DHHS.

Medicaid Waivers: Authority granted by the Secretary of Health and Human Services to allow a state to continue receiving federal Medicaid matching funds even though it is no longer in compliance with certain requirements of the Medicaid statute. States can use waivers to implement home and community-based services programs, managed care, and to expand coverage to populations who are not otherwise eligible for Medicaid.

Medical Loss Ratio: The ratio between the cost to deliver medical care and the amount of money that was taken in by a plan. Insurance companies often have a medical loss ratio of 92% or more; tightly managed HMOs may have medical loss ratios of 75% to 85%, although the overhead (or administrative cost ratio) is concomitantly higher. The medical loss ratio is dependent on the amount of money brought in as well as on the cost of delivering care; thus, if the rates are too low, the ratio may be high even though the actual cost of delivering care is not really out of line. The Affordable Care Act requires that health insurance issuers submit data on the MLR and, starting in 2012, requires them to issue rebates to enrollees if this percentage does not meet minimum standards. MLR requires insurance companies to spend at least 80% or 85% of premium dollars on medical care.

Medically Necessary: Term used by insurers to describe medical treatment that is appropriate and rendered in accordance with generally accepted standards of medical practice.

Medical Policy: Refers to the policies of a health plan regarding what will be paid for as medical benefits. Routine medical policy is linked to routine claims processing and may even be automated in the claims system; for example, the plan may only pay 50% of the fee of a second surgeon or may not pay for two surgical procedures done during one episode of anesthesia. This also refers to how a plan approaches payment policies for experimental or investigational care and payment for noncovered services in lieu of more expensive covered services.

Medical Review Criteria: Systematically developed statements that can be used to assess the appropriateness of specific health care decisions, services and outcomes.

Medicare: The federal health insurance program, administered by CMS, that provides coverage for most Americans over age 65, the permanently disabled and people with end-stage renal disease. Medicare is divided into four parts. *See* Chapter 3 **Medicare** for a description of each.

Medicare Access & CHIP Reauthorization Act of 2015 (MACRA): A federal statute enacted among other purposes, to repeal the Medicare sustainable growth rate and strengthen Medicare access by improving physician payments and making other improvements and to reauthorize the Children's Health Insurance Program.

Medicare Administrative Contractor (MAC): MMA permitted CMS to consolidate the Fiscal Intermediary (Part A) and Contractor (Part B) systems into a new system administered by MACs, covering both Part A and Part B claims in one or more geographic jurisdictions.

Medicare Advantage Plan (MA): A Medicare program that offers a full range of coverage options by providing a choice between the traditional fee-for-service program or enrollment in a HMO, preferred-provider organization, point-of-service plan, provider sponsored-organization, or an insurance plan operated in conjunction with a medical savings account. Formerly known as Medicare + Choice Plans (M+C).

Medicare Improvements for Patients and Providers Act (MIPPA): MIPPA allows for grants to low-income seniors and persons with disabilities assistance to pay for Medicare costs.

Medicare and Medicaid Patient and Program Protection Act (MMPPPA): A 1987 federal law that broadened the grounds for excluding health care providers from participation in the Medicare and Medicaid programs. This statute also granted the OIG the authority to exclude from Medicare and state health care program participation individuals or entities who violate the law, even if there has been no criminal conviction.

Medicare Prescription Drug, Improvement, and Modernization Act of 2003 (MMA): Signed into law on December 8, 2003, as the Medicare Prescription Drug, Improvement, and Modernization Act of 2003, the MMA brought about the most sweeping changes to the federal health insurance program for the elderly and disabled since it was created nearly 40 years ago, including adding a prescription drug benefit under Medicare Part D. Providers, physicians, payers, manufacturers, suppliers, employers, and beneficiaries all have been affected profoundly by these changes.

Medicare Secondary Payer Statute: A federal statute providing that when payment sources in addition to Medicare are available, those sources are primary payers and Medicare is secondary.

Medicare SELECT: A 50-state Medicare demonstration program that permits Medicare supplemental insurance companies (Medigap insurers) to offer a preferred provider organization policy to Medicare recipients. Medicare SELECT policies may waive or reduce deductible and coinsurance payments if the plan participant uses a network provider. Plan participants are free to choose a non-network provider, but the Medicare SELECT policies may restrict or eliminate payment of deductibles and coinsurance that the policy would otherwise cover.

Medicare Shared Savings Program (MSSP): Congress created this program to facilitate coordination and cooperation among providers to improve the quality of care for Medicare fee-for-service (FFS) beneficiaries and reduce unnecessary costs.

Medigap: Private insurance designed to supplement Medicare coverage by paying for medical costs that Medicare does not pay, such as deductibles and coinsurance.

Member: An individual covered under a managed care plan. May be either the subscriber or a dependent.

Member Months: The total of all months for which each member was covered. For example, if a plan had 10,000 members in January and 12,000 members in February, the total member months for the year to date as of March 1 would be 22,000.

MET: Multiple employer trust. *See* **MEWA**.

MEWA: Multiple employer welfare association. A group of employers who band together for purposes of purchasing group health insurance, often through a self-funded approach to avoid state mandates and insurance regulation. By virtue of ERISA, such entities are regulated little, if at all. Many MEWAs have enabled small employers to obtain cost-effective health coverage, but some MEWAs have not had the financial resources to withstand the risk of medical costs and have failed, leaving the members without insurance or recourse. In some states, MEWAs and METs are no longer legal.

Midlevel Practitioner: Physician's assistants, clinical nurse practitioners, nurse midwives, and the like. Nonphysicians who deliver medical care, generally under the supervision of a physician but for less cost.

Minimum Essential Coverage: The minimum level of benefits that must be included in a health insurance plan in order for an individual to be considered insured. Under the Affordable Care Act, if an individual does not have minimum essential coverage and does not qualify for an exemption, he/she will be subject to a penalty under the individual mandate.

MIS: Management information system (or service). The common term for the computer hardware and software that provides the support for managing the plan or a department or group that administers and maintains such computer hardware and software.

Mixed Model: A managed care plan that mixes two or more types of delivery systems. This has traditionally been used to describe an HMO that has both closed panel and open panel delivery systems.

MMA: *See* **Medicare Modernization Act**.

Modified Risk: Person who cannot meet the normal health requirements of a standard health insurance policy.

Money Laundering Statute: A federal statute that prohibits any monetary transaction in excess of $10,000 where the money was obtained from certain specified unlawful activities, including theft of federal funds or mail or wire fraud.

Morbidity: Frequency and severity of sicknesses and accidents in a well-defined class or classes of persons.

Morbidity Table: Actuarial statistics showing the expected average frequency and duration of disability, illness, and sometimes accidents.

Mortality: Death rate in a group of people as determined from prior experience.

Mortality Table: Exhibit showing the incidence of death in various age groups.

MSO: Management-service organization. A form of integrated health-delivery system. Sometimes similar to a service bureau, the MSO often actually purchases certain hard assets of a physician's practice and then provides services to that physician at fair market rates. MSOs are usually formed as a means to contract more effectively with managed-care organizations, although their simple creation does not guarantee success. *See also* **Service Bureau**.

Multispecialty Group: Just what it sounds like; a medical group made up of different specialty physicians. May or may not include primary care.

National Coverage Determinations (NCD): Sets forth the extent to which Medicare will cover specific services, procedures, or technologies on a national basis. An NCD is published in the Medicare National Coverage Determinations Manual.

National Labor Relations Act (NLRA): A federal law enacted in 1935 to protect the rights of employees and employers, to encourage collective bargaining, and to curtail certain private sector labor and management practices, which can harm the general welfare of workers, businesses and the U.S. economy.

Navigator: An individual or organization that is trained and able to help consumers, small businesses, and their employees as they look for health coverage options through the health insurance marketplaces, including completing eligibility and enrollment forms. These individuals and organizations are required to be unbiased and their services are free to consumers.

NDC: National drug code. The national classification system for identifying prescription drugs.

Negligence: An unintentional, but legally blameworthy, tort.

Net Revenue: For a hospital, total revenue less deductions for bad debts, charity, and contractual adjustments. Net revenue is the amount of money actually received by the hospital resulting from charges for services provided. Network-based programs: Insurer arrangements with health care providers (such as HMOs, PPOs, and point-of-service programs) under contracts to provide services aimed at managing health care costs.

Network Model HMO: A health plan that contracts with multiple physician groups to deliver health care to members. Generally limited to large single-specialty or multispecialty groups. Distinguished from group model plans that contract with a single medical group, IPAs that contract through an intermediary and direct contract model plans that contract with individual physicians in the community.

Nonpar: Short for nonparticipating. Refers to a provider that does not have a contract with the health plan. Nonprofit insurers: Corporations organized under special state laws to provide medical benefits on a not-for-profit basis (for example, Blue Cross/Blue Shield, dental service corporations).

OBRA: Omnibus Budget Reconciliation Act. What Congress calls the many annual tax and budget reconciliation acts. Most of these acts contain language important to managed care, generally in the Medicare market segment. Occupancy rate: Measure of inpatient health facility use, determined by dividing available bed days by patient days. It measures the average percentage of occupied beds in a hospital, either for the entire institution or for one department or service.

Occupational Rate: Variation in premium based upon occupational class, due to differences among occupations in the incidence of accidents or illness.

Occupational Schedule: Method of insurance listing under which persons are insured for an amount based on their job classifications.

Office for Civil Rights (OCR): The Office for Civil Rights under DHHS. Among other duties, this branch is responsible for developing and disseminating technical-assistance materials designed to help Covered Entities comply with the HIPAA privacy rule. It also is charged with enforcement of that rule.

Office of Audit: The branch of the OIG that performs audits of large health care entities to ensure that they are filing accurate cost reports. The Office of Audit also identifies specific areas of waste or abuse in CMS's administration of these programs.

Office of Evaluations and Inspections: The branch of the OIG that analyzes particular reimbursement or systems issues and produces reports on various topics.

Office of Inspector General (OIG): Every federal agency has an Inspector General who is responsible for ferreting out waste, fraud and abuse in that agency's programs. The DHHS OIG is responsible for enforcing most fraud and abuse civil penalties and programs exclusions. The OIG's office is divided into three sections: (1) the Office of Audit, (2) the Office of Evaluations and Inspections, and (3) the Office of Investigations.

Office of Investigations: The branch of the OIG responsible for investigating health care fraud and abuse cases.

OIG Subpoena: One of the primary ways that investigators and prosecutors obtain information in health care fraud and abuse cases. The OIG subpoena power permits the OIG to compel only documentary information and not testimonial information. The OIG subpoena may request documents for use in criminal, civil or administrative investigations. The OIG may also serve a subpoena on parties who have no immediate connection with the HHS. *See also* **Civil Investigative Demand**.

Onset of Condition: Date an illness or disease first manifested itself—generally when medical treatment and advice were first sought or when symptoms were such that an ordinarily prudent person would seek diagnosis, care, or treatment.

Open Enrollment Period: The period when an employee may change health plans; usually occurs once per year. A general rule is that most managed care plans will have around half their membership up for open enrollment in the fall for an effective date of January 1. A special form of open enrollment is still law in some states. This yearly open enrollment requires an HMO to accept any individual applicant (that is, one not coming in through an employer group) for coverage, regardless of health status. Such special open enrollments usually occur for one month each year. Many Blue Cross and Blue Shield plans have similar open enrollments for indemnity products.

Open Panel HMO: A managed care plan that contracts (either directly or indirectly) with private physicians to deliver care in their own offices. Examples include direct contract HMOs and IPAs.

OPM: Office of Personnel Management. The federal agency that administers FEHBP. This is the agency with which a managed care plan contracts to provide coverage for federal employees.

Original Source: In *qui tam* actions, the term refers to an individual who has direct and independent knowledge of the information on which the allegations are based and has voluntarily provided the information to the government before filing an action.

Outlier: Something that is well outside an expected range. May refer to a provider who is using medical resources at a much higher rate than his or her peers or to a case in a hospital that is far more expensive than anticipated.

Out-of-Pocket Expense: Those medical expenses that an insured must pay that are not covered under the insurance contract.

Out-of-Pocket Maximum: A yearly cap on the amount of money individuals are required to pay out-of-pocket for health care costs, excluding the premium. The Affordable Care Act required new plans offered beginning in 2014 to include an out-of-pocket maximum.

Overhead Expense Insurance: Form of health insurance for business owners designed to help offset continuing business expenses during an insured's total disability.

Pacific Business Group on Health (PBGH): This is a nonprofit organization of large health care purchasers in California and Arizona created in 1989 to improve the quality of health care and address rising costs. One of its projects is the California Collaborative Healthcare Reporting Initiative, which represents the collective interests of health plans, purchasers and provider groups.

Package Pricing: Also referred to as bundled pricing. An MCO pays an organization a single fee for all inpatient, outpatient and professional expenses associated with a procedure, including preadmission and postdischarge care. Common procedures that use this form of pricing include cardiac bypass surgery and transplants.

Par Provider: Shorthand term for participating provider (that is, one who has signed an agreement with a plan to provide services). May apply to professional or institutional providers.

PAS Norms: The common term for Professional Activity Study results of the Commission on Professional and Hospital Activities. Broken out by region; the western region has the lowest average LOS, so that it tends to be used most often to set an estimated LOS. Available as LOS: Length of Stay by Diagnosis, published by CPHA Publications, Ann Arbor, Michigan.

Patient-Centered Medical Home: A system of comprehensive coordinated primary care for children, youth and adults. Patient centeredness refers to an ongoing, active partnership with a personal primary care physician who leads a team of professionals dedicated to providing proactive, preventive and chronic care management through all stages of life.

Patient Protection and Affordable Care Act of 2010 (ACA): The major health reform bill that President Barack Obama enacted into law on March 23, 2010 to expand health insurance coverage and to reduce costs so that all Americans have access to quality, affordable health care. Also referred to as the Affordable Care Act (ACA) or Obamacare.

Patient Self-Determination Act: Congressional act mandating that all Medicare- and Medicaid-certified provider organizations notify patients of their rights to make decisions concerning medical treatment and the right to formulate advance directives.

Pay and Pursue: Refers to a plan paying for a benefit first, then pursuing another source of payment (for example, from another plan). Also referred to as "pay and chase." *See also* **Pursue and Pay**.

Pay for Performance: A health care payment system in which providers receive incentives for meeting or exceeding quality and cost benchmarks. Some systems also penalize providers who do not meet established benchmarks. The goal of pay for performance programs is to improve the quality of care over time.

Payment Bundling: A form of provider payment where providers or hospitals receive a single payment for all of the care provided for an episode of illness, rather than per service rendered. Total care provided for an episode of illness may include both acute and post-acute care. The Affordable Care Act established pilot programs in Medicare and Medicaid to pay a bundled payment for episodes of care involving hospitalizations.

PCCM: Primary care case manager. This acronym is used in Medicaid managed care programs and refers to the state designating PCPs as case managers to function as gatekeepers, but reimbursing those PCPs using traditional Medicaid fee-for-service as well as paying them a nominal management fee, such as $2 to $5 PMPM.

Peer Review Organization (PRO): *See* **QIO**.

Pending Claim: Claim that has been reported but on which final action has not been taken.

Per Cause Deductible: Flat amount that an insured must pay toward the eligible medical expenses resulting from each illness before the insurance company will make any benefit payments.

Percentage Participation: *See* **Coinsurance**.

***Per Diem* Reimbursement:** Reimbursement of an institution, usually a hospital, based on a set rate per day rather than on charges. *Per diem* reimbursement can be varied by service (e.g., medical-surgical, obstetrics, mental health, and intensive care) or can be uniform regardless of intensity of services.

PHO: Physician/hospital organization. These are legal (or perhaps informal) organizations that bond hospitals and their attending medical staff. Frequently developed for the purpose of contracting with managed care plans. A PHO may be open to any member of the staff who applies, or it may be closed to staff members who fail to qualify (or who are part of an already overrepresented specialty).

Physician Payment Sunshine Act (Sunshine Act): Also known as section 6002 of the Affordable Care Act, requires medical product manufacturers to disclose to CMS any payments or other transfers of value made to physicians or teaching hospitals.

PMG: Primary medical group. A group practice made up of primary care physicians, although some may have obstetrician/gynecologists as well.

PMPM: Per member per month. Specifically applies to a revenue or cost for each enrolled member each month.

PMPY: Per member per year. The same as PMPM, but based on a year.

Policyholder (also Policy Owner): The owner of a health insurance policy. In group insurance, the legal entity (employer, union, trustee, creditor) to whom an insurer issues a contract.

Policyholder (Self) Administration: Situation whereby a group policyholder maintains all records and assumes responsibility regarding insureds covered under its insurance plan, including preparing the premium statement for each payment date and submitting it with a check to the insurer. The insurance company, in most instances, has the contractual prerogative to audit the policyholder's record.

Portability: Characteristic of an insurance policy that allows an insured to accumulate and transfer insurance benefits from one employer to another or from an employer to a nongroup or personal policy.

POS: Point-of-service. A plan in which members do not have to choose how to receive services until they need them. The most common use of the term applies to a plan that enrolls each member in both an HMO (or HMO-like) system and an indemnity plan. Occasionally referred to as an HMO swing-out plan, an out-of-plan benefits rider to an HMO or a primary care PPO. These plans provide a difference in benefits (for example, 100% coverage rather than 70%) depending on whether the member chooses to use the plan (including its providers and in compliance with the authorization system) or to go outside the plan for services. Dual choice refers to an HMO-like plan with an indemnity plan, and triple choice refers to the addition of a PPO to the dual choice. An archaic but still valid definition applies to a simple PPO where members receive coverage at a greater level if they use preferred providers (albeit without a gatekeeper system) than if they choose not to do so.

PPM: Physician practice management company. An organization that manages physicians' practices and in most cases either owns the practices outright or has rights to purchase them in the future. PPMs concentrate only on physicians, not on hospitals, although some PPMs have also branched into joint ventures with hospitals and insurers. Many PPMs are publicly traded.

Practice Guidelines: Systematically developed statements to assist practitioner and patient decisions about appropriate health care for specific clinical circumstances.

Precertification: Also known as preadmission certification, preadmission review, and precert. The process of obtaining certification or authorization from the health plan for routine hospital admissions (inpatient or outpatient). Often involves appropriateness review against criteria and assignment of length of stay. Failure to obtain precertification often results in a financial penalty to either the provider or the subscriber.

Preemption: Federal law preempts any State law that is inconsistent with Federal law.

Preexisting Condition: A medical condition for which a member has received treatment during a specified period of time before becoming covered under a health plan.

Preexisting Conditions Limitation: Restriction on payments for those charges directly resulting from an accident or illness for which the insured received care or treatment within a specified period of time (for example, three months) prior to the date of insurance. Pre-existing condition exclusions are prohibited by the Affordable Care Act.

Preferred Provider Organization (PPO): Entities that supply networks of health care providers to employer health benefit plans and health insurance carriers. Providers contracting with PPOs typically agree to abide by procedures designed by the PPO to control the utilization and cost of health services and to accept the PPO's reimbursement structure and payment levels. PPOs provide incentives for enrollees to use network providers. Individuals may choose a nonparticipating provider and still receive coverage, although they will pay a higher coinsurance or deductible amount.

Premium: The amount paid, often on a monthly basis, for health insurance. The cost of the premium may be shared between employers or government purchasers and individuals.

Premium Subsidies: A fixed amount of money or a designated percentage of the premium cost that is provided to help people purchase health coverage. Premium subsidies are usually provided on a sliding scale based on an individual's or family's income. The Affordable Care Act provides premium subsidies through refundable pre-tax credits to individuals with incomes between 133% and 400% of the federal poverty level who purchase policies through the health insurance exchanges beginning in 2014.

Premium Tax Credits: A refundable tax credit that helps eligible individuals and families with low or moderate income afford health insurance purchased through a Health Insurance Marketplace. To get this credit, you must meet certain requirements and file a tax return.

Preventive Care: Health care that emphasizes the early detection and treatment of diseases. The focus on prevention is intended to keep people healthier for longer, thus reducing health care costs over the long term. The Affordable Care Act required new qualified health plans and Medicare to provide coverage without cost-sharing for certain preventive services. The law also included incentives for states to offer the same coverage in their Medicaid programs.

Primary Care: First contact and continuing health care, including basic or initial diagnosis and treatment, health supervision, management of chronic conditions, preventive health services, and appropriate referral.

Primary Care Physician (PCP): A physician (M.D. - Medical Doctor or D.O. - Doctor of Osteopathic Medicine) who directly provides or coordinates a range of health care services for a patient.

Private Inurement: Situation in which a nonprofit business operates in such a way as to provide more than incidental financial gain to a private individual; for example, if a nonprofit hospital pays too much money for a physician's practice or fails to charge fair market rates for services provided to a physician. The IRS frowns heavily on this.

Professional Standards Review Organization (PSRO): Organization responsible for determining whether care and services provided were medically necessary and meet professional standards regarding eligibility for reimbursement under the Medicare and Medicaid programs.

Prognosis: Forecast or prediction of the probable course of a disease or injury.

Program for All-Inclusive Care for the Elderly (PACE): Federal Medicare and Medicaid program through which qualifying individuals receive comprehensive community care, rather than being placed in a nursing home.

Prospective Payment System (PPS): A reimbursement system in which Medicare payment is made based on a predetermined, fixed amount. The payment amount for a particular service is derived based on the classification system of that service (e.g., DRGs for inpatient hospital services).

Prospective Rating: Method of renewal rating that adjusts the rates for the coming policy year in accordance with such factors as known credible past experience, insurance industry and insurance company trends, general business trends (for example, inflation, deflation), current manual rates, and so forth.

Prospective Review: Reviewing the need for medical care before the care is rendered. *See also* **Precertification**.

Provider: Any organization, institution, or individual that provides covered health care services to Medicare beneficiaries (e.g., hospital, skilled nursing facility, home health agency, outpatient physical therapy, comprehensive outpatient rehabilitation facility, end-stage renal disease facility, hospice, physician, non-physician provider, laboratory, supplier, etc.).

Provider Discounts: Element of network-based managed care programs whereby financial arrangements are negotiated with providers to reduce fees for medical services rendered.

Provider Self-Disclosure Protocol: A component of the OIG's activities that provides health care providers with the opportunity to self-disclose any potential fraudulent acts. Self-disclosure may reduce the possibility that the OIG will subject the corporation to a complete audit and investigation, or bring an exclusion action against the provider. In addition, the corporation might be liable for a lower amount of fines and penalties due to its cooperation with the government.

Provider Payment Rates: The total payment a provider, hospital, or community health center receives when they provide medical services to a patient. Providers are compensated for patient care using a set of defined rates based on illness category and the type of service administered.

PSA: Professional services agreement. A contract between a physician or medical group and an IDS or MCO for the provision of medical services.

PSN: Provider-sponsored network; occasionally the acronym stands for provider-service network. Also referred to as a PSO (provider-sponsored organization). A network developed by providers, whether as a vertically integrated IDS with both physicians and hospitals or as a physician-only network. Formed for the purpose of direct contracting with employers and government agencies. A PSN may even end up being an HMO, but its origins are with sponsoring providers rather than nonproviders.

PSO: Provider-sponsored organization. *See* **PSN**.

PTMPY: Per thousand members per year. A common way of reporting utilization. The most common example is hospital utilization, expressed as days per thousand members per year.

Public Plan Option: A proposal to create a new insurance plan administered and funded by federal or state government.

Purchasing Pool: Health insurance providers pool the health care risks of a group of people in order to make the individual costs predictable and manageable. For health coverage arrangements to perform well, the risk pooling should balance low and high risk individuals such that expected costs for the pool are reasonably predictable for the insurer and relatively stable over time.

Pursue and Pay: Refers to a plan not paying for a benefit until alternate sources of payment (for example, another plan) have been pursued. Also referred to as "chase and pay." *See also* **Pay and Pursue**.

QA or QM: Quality assurance (older term) or quality management (newer term).

Qualified Health Plan: Refers to insurance plans that have been certified as meeting a minimum benchmark of benefits (i.e. the essential health benefits) under the Affordable Care Act. This will allow consumers to verify that the plan they have purchased will meet at least the minimum requirements of the individual mandate.

Quality Improvement Organization (QIO): Formerly known as peer-review organizations (PRO), quality improvement organizations are independent, private organizations, generally operating at the state level, that review medical necessity, as well as quality and cost of care for Medicare and Medicaid programs. QIOs conduct reviews primarily in connection with inpatient hospital care. Established under TEFRA.

Qui Tam **Action:** Abbreviation of the Latin phrase "*qui tam pro domino rege quam pro si ipso in hac parte sequitur*," which means, "He who brings the action for the King as well as for himself." *Qui tam* provisions of a statute allow a private person to bring a civil action on behalf of both the United States and herself, and to share in part of the monetary recovery. The individual bringing the *qui tam* action can receive between 15% and 25% of whatever is recovered from the lawsuit, with the remainder going to the government.

Qui Tam **Relator:** The private person who may bring a lawsuit on behalf of the U.S. government as well as herself, based on her knowledge of wrongdoing. A relator is often a current or former employee or an employee of a competitor or subcontractor of the organization accused of wrongdoing.

Racketeer Influenced and Corrupt Organization Act (RICO): A federal statute that prohibits the receipt of any income from a pattern of racketeering activity. To prove a RICO case, the government must show that the activity has an effect on interstate commerce, an association of the defendant with the enterprise and participation in its activities, and the commission of a predicate act (for example, mail or wire fraud) at least twice within 10 years.

Rate: The amount of money that a group or individual must pay to the health plan for coverage. Usually a monthly fee.

Rating: Determining the cost of a given unit of insurance for a given year.

Reasonable and Customary Charges (R&C): Amounts charged by health care providers that are consistent with charges from similar providers for identical or similar services in a given locale.

Reinsurance: Insurance purchased by a health plan to protect it against extremely high-cost cases. *See also* **Stop-Loss Insurance**. The Affordable Care Act provided for a temporary federal reinsurance program for employers that insure early retirees over age 55 who are not eligible for Medicare.

Relative Value Study (RVS): Guide (not a fee schedule) that attempts to show in a general way by a unit or point designation the relationship among the time, competency, experience, severity, and other factors required to perform services under usual conditions. Such a study becomes a schedule when dollar conversion factors are applied.

Renewal Rating: Insurer's review of the premium rates and claim experience for a group plan from which the necessity of rate changes is determined.

Renewal Underwriting: Review of the financial experience of a group case and the establishment of the renewal premium rates and terms under which the insurance may be continued.

Rescission: Voiding of an insurance contract from its date of issue by the insurer because of material misrepresentation on the application for insurance. The act of rescission must take place within the contestable period or Time Limit on Certain Defenses. The policy is treated as never having been issued and the sum of all premiums paid plus interest, less any claims paid, is refunded. Under the Affordable Care Act, insurers will only be able to rescind policies in cases of fraud.

Reserves: The amount of money that a health plan puts aside to cover health care costs. May apply to anticipated costs, such as IBNRs, or to money that the plan does not expect to have to use to pay for current medical claims but keeps as a cushion against future adverse health care costs.

Resource-Based Relative Value Scale (RBRVS): A fee schedule that uses a complex formula to determine the payment due a physician for patient services. Factors that are considered in determining the payment due include the resources used, practice expenses, malpractice expenses, geographic location, and whether the services were provided on an outpatient or inpatient basis. Medicare began phasing in this PPS in 1992. The practical effect has been to diminish reimbursement for procedures such as cardiac surgery and raise reimbursement for primary care office visits.

Responsible Corporate Officer Doctrine: A doctrine holding that an officer, even without criminal intent or actual knowledge of an offense, can be convicted for the criminal acts of lower-level company employees merely because of his or her responsible share in overseeing the company's business activities and failure to correct or prevent the criminal violations.

Retrospective Rating: Method of experience rating that adjusts the final premium of a risk in accordance with the experience of that risk during the term of the policy for which the premium is paid.

Retrospective Reimbursement: Method of payment to providers by a third party after costs or charges have actually been incurred by insureds.

Retrospective Review: Reviewing health care costs after the care has been rendered. There are several forms of retrospective review. One form looks at individual claims for medical necessity, billing errors, or fraud. Another form looks at patterns of costs rather than individual cases.

Risk Management: Management activities aimed at lowering an organization's legal and financial exposures, especially to lawsuits.

Risk Pools: Method operating in some states through which persons who can afford private health insurance but who are uninsurable for medical reasons can obtain access to health insurance.

Safe Harbor: Regulatory or statutory provisions that shield certain designated payment arrangements from criminal prosecution or program exclusion. Safe harbor provisions are contained in the Stark Laws and the Anti-Kickback Statute.

Safety Net: Health care providers who deliver health care services to patients regardless of their ability to pay. These providers may consist of public hospital systems, community health centers, local health departments, and other providers who serve a disproportionate share of uninsured and low-income patients.

Sarbanes-Oxley Act of 2003 (SOA): Imposes substantial obligations on publicly owned corporations to disclose and certify financial conditions.

Section 125 Plan: A section 125 plan allows employees to receive specified benefits, including health benefits, on a pre-tax basis. Section 125 plans enable employees to pay for health insurance premiums on a pre-tax basis, whether the insurance is provided by the employer or purchased directly in the individual market.

Schedule H: Accident and Health Exhibit of an insurer's Annual Statement. Its purpose is to show the profitability of various categories of health insurance business.

SCHIP: *Also CHIP.* The State Children's Health Insurance Program, under Title XXI of the Social Scurity Act, is jointly funded by the Federal and State governments and administered by the States. It provides health insurance for children in need.

SCP: Specialty care physician. A physician who is not a PCP.

Second Opinion: An opinion obtained from another physician regarding the necessity for a treatment that has been recommended by another physician. May be required by some health plans for certain high-costs cases, such as cardiac surgery.

Self-Insured or Self-Funded Plan: A health plan where the risk for medical cost is assumed by the company rather than an insurance company or managed care plan. Under ERISA, self-funded plans are exempt from state laws and regulations, such as premium taxes and mandatory benefits. Self-funded plans often contract with insurance companies or third-party administrators to administer the benefits.

Service Area: The geographic area in which an HMO provides access to primary care. The service area is usually specifically designated by the regulators (state or federal), and the HMO is prohibited from marketing outside the service area. May be defined by county or by ZIP code. It is possible for an HMO to have more than one service area and for the service areas to be either contiguous (that is, they actually border each other) or noncontiguous (that is, there is a geographic gap between the service areas).

Service Bureau: A weak form of integrated delivery system in which a hospital (or other organization) provides services to a physician's practice in return for a fair market price. May also try to negotiate with managed care plans, but generally is not considered an effective negotiating mechanism.

Service Plan: A health insurance plan that has direct contracts with providers but is not necessarily a managed care plan. The archetypal service plans are Blue Cross and Blue Shield plans. The contract applies to direct billing of the plan by providers (rather than billing of the member), a provision for direct payment of the provider (rather than reimbursement of the member), a requirement that the provider accept the plan's determination of UCR and not balance bill the member in excess of that amount, and a range of other terms. May or may not address issues of utilization and quality.

Shadow Pricing: The practice of setting premium rates at a level just below the competition's rates whether or not those rates can be justified. In other words, the premium rates could actually be lower, but to maximize profit the rates are raised to a level that will remain attractive but result in greater revenue. This practice is generally considered unethical and, in the case of community rating, possibly illegal.

Sherman Act: According to the FTC's website, "The Sherman Act outlaws 'every contract, combination, or conspiracy in restraint of trade,' and any 'monopolization, attempted monopolization, or conspiracy or combination to monopolize.'"

Skilled Nursing Facility (SNF): Institution providing that step in progressive care during which a patient receives that degree of medical care required from, or under the supervision of, registered nursing personnel or a physician.

SMG: Specialty medical group. A medical group made up predominantly of specialty physicians. May be a single-specialty group or a multispecialty group.

Social Security Act: Federal law under which the federal government operates the Old Age, Survivors, Disability, and Health Insurance Program (OASDHI). Includes Medicare and Medicaid.

Special Enrollment Period: Is a time outside the yearly Open Enrollment Period when one can sign up for health insurance.

Socialized Medicine: A health care system in which the government operates and administers health care facilities and employs health care professionals.

Specialty Network Manager: A term used to describe a single specialist (or perhaps a specialist organization) that accepts capitation to manage a single specialty. Specialty services are supplied by many different specialty physicians, but the network manager has the responsibility for managing access and cost and is at economic risk. A relatively uncommon model as this book is being written.

Spending Down: Gradual depletion of one's assets until indigent, thus qualifying for Medicaid benefits. Usually associated with nursing home or long term care.

Staff Model HMO: An HMO that employs providers directly, and those providers see members in the HMO's own facilities. A form of closed panel HMO. A different use of this term is sometimes applied to vertically integrated health care delivery systems that employ physicians but in which the system is not licensed as an HMO.

Stark I: Colloquial name for the physician self-referral prohibitions introduced to Congress in 1988 by California representative Fortney "Pete" Stark. The initial Stark Law became effective January 1, 1992, and provides that a physician or an immediate family member who has a financial relationship with an entity may not refer a Medicare patient to that entity for clinical laboratory services, unless an applicable exception exists. In addition, the law prevents an entity with which a physician has a financial relationship from billing Medicare or a beneficiary for clinical laboratory services furnished pursuant to a prohibited referral.

Stark II: The 1993 amendments to Stark I that extend the physician self-referral restrictions to Medicaid services and beneficiaries and expand the referral and billing prohibitions to 10 additional designated health services reimbursable by Medicare or Medicaid. The 10 services are (1) physical therapy, (2) occupational therapy, (3) radiology services, including magnetic resonance imaging, computerized axial tomography scans and ultrasound services, (4) radiation therapy services and supplies, (5) DME and supplies, (6) parenteral and enteral nutrients, equipment and supplies, (7) prosthetics, orthotics, and prosthetic devices, (8) home health services and supplies, (9) outpatient prescription drugs, and (10) inpatient and outpatient hospital services. Stark II became effective on January 1, 1995. The statute contains many exceptions, which can be grouped into categories applicable to all financial relationships, to ownership and investment interests, and to compensation arrangements.

Statistical Claim: Another term for an encounter whereby data are entered by an MCO's claims department but no FFS payment is made. Occurs in a capitated environment.

Statute: A law enacted by an elected legislature. *Compare* with **Common Law**.

Step-Rate Premium: Rating structure in which the premiums increase periodically at predetermined times, such as policy years or attained ages.

Stockholder Derivative Lawsuits: An action brought by a stockholder on behalf of a corporation because the corporation was caused to suffer damage but refuses to redress the act causing the damage.

Stop-Loss Insurance: A form of reinsurance that provides protection for medical expenses above a certain limit, generally on a year-by-year basis. This may apply to an entire health plan or to any single component. For example, the health plan may have stop-loss reinsurance for cases that exceed $100,000. After a case hits $100,000, the plan receives 80% of expenses in excess of $100,000 back from the reinsurance company for the rest of the year. Another example would be the plan providing a stop-loss to participating physicians for referral expenses greater than $2,500. When a case exceeds that amount in a single year, the plan no longer deducts those costs from the physician's referral pool for the remainder of the year.

Subacute Care Facility: A health facility that is a step down from an acute care hospital. May be a nursing home or a facility that provides medical care but not surgical or emergency care.

Subrogation: The contractual right of a health plan to recover payments made to a member for health care costs after that member has received such payment for damages in a legal action.

Subscriber: The individual or member who has health plan coverage by virtue of being eligible on his or her own behalf rather than as a dependent.

Supplemental Medical Insurance: Another term for Medicare Part B coverage.

Supplier: Any company, person, or agency that provides a medical item or service, e.g., a wheelchair or walker.

Surplus: Amount by which the value of an insurer's assets exceeds its liabilities.

Tax Credit: A tax credit is an amount that a person or family can subtract from the amount of income tax that they owe. If a tax credit is refundable, the taxpayer can receive a payment from the government to the extent that the amount of the credit is greater than the amount of tax they would otherwise owe.

Tax Deduction: A deduction is an amount that a person/family can subtract from their adjusted gross income when calculating the amount of tax that they owe.

Tax Relief and Health Care Act: The Tax Relief and Health Care Act, "amends the Internal Revenue Code to grant jurisdiction to the U.S. Tax Court to review taxpayer petitions for equitable relief from joint and several tax liability (i.e., innocent spouse relief)."

TEFRA: Tax Equity and Fiscal Responsibility Act. One key provision of this act prohibits employers and health plans from requiring full-time employees between the ages of 65 and 69 to use Medicare rather than the group health plan. Another key provision codifies Medicare risk contracts for HMOs and CMPs.

Termination Date: The day that health plan coverage is no longer in effect.

Third-Party Administration (or Administrator) (TPA): Method by which an outside person or firm, not a party to a contract, maintains all records regarding the persons covered under the insurance plan. Entity also may pay claims using the draft book system.

Third-Party Payer: Any organization, public or private, that pays or insures health or medical expenses on behalf of beneficiaries or recipients, such as Blue Cross and Blue Shield, commercial insurance companies, Medicare, and Medicaid. A person generally pays a premium for coverage in all such private and in some public programs. The organization then pays bills on the insured's behalf. These payments, called third-party payments, are distinguished by the separation between the individual receiving the service (the first party), the individual or institution providing it (the second party), and the organization paying for it (the third party).

Time-Loss Management: The application of managed care techniques to workers' compensation treatments for injuries or illnesses to reduce the amount of time lost on the job by the affected employee.

Tort: A civil wrong, leading to the imposition of liability, based on the violation of an obligation other than a breach of contract. *See* **Negligence**.

Total Capitation: The term used when an organization receives capitation for all medical services, including institutional and professional. The more common term is global capitation.

TPA: Third-party administrator. A firm that performs administrative functions (e.g., claims processing, membership and the like) for a self-funded plan or a start-up managed care plan. *See also* **ASO**.

TPL: Third-party liability. *See* **COB**.

Triage: In health plans, this refers to the process of sorting out requests for services by members into those who need to be seen right away, those who can wait a little while, and those whose problems can be handled with advice over the phone.

TRICARE: The federal program administered by the Department of Defense that provides health care coverage to families of military personnel, military retirees, certain spouses and dependents of such personnel and certain others. Formerly CHAMPUS.

Twenty-Four-Hour Care: An ill-defined term that essentially means that health care is provided 24 hours per day regardless of the financing mechanism. Applies primarily to the convergence of group health, workers' compensation, and industrial health all under managed care.

Two Midnight Rule: A rule that established Medicare payment policy regarding the benchmark criteria that should be used when determining whether inpatient admission is reasonable and payable under Medicare Part A. Generally, inpatient admissions are payable under Part A if the admitting practitioner expects the patient to require a hospital stay that crosses at least two midnights and the medical record supports that reasonable expectation. There has been ongoing industry criticism and legal challenge regarding this rule.

UB-04/UB-92: The common claim form used by hospitals to bill for services. Some managed care plans demand greater detail than is available on the UB-04 or UB-92, requiring hospitals to send additional itemized bills.

UCR: Usual, customary, or reasonable. A method of profiling prevailing fees in an area and reimbursing providers on the basis of that profile. One common technology is to average all fees and choose the 80th or 90th percentile, although a plan may use other technologies to determine what is reasonable. Sometimes this term is used synonymously with a fee allowance schedule when that schedule is set relatively high.

Unbundling: The practice of a provider billing for multiple components of service that were previously included in a single fee. For example, if dressings and instruments were included in a fee for a minor procedure, the fee for the procedure remains the same, but there are now additional charges for the dressings and instruments.

Uncompensated Care: Health care rendered by providers to persons unable to pay and not covered by private or governmental health insurance plans.

Underinsured: People who have health insurance but who face out-of-pocket health care costs or limits on benefits that may affect their ability to access or pay for health care services.

Underwriting: In one definition, this refers to bearing the risk for something (e.g., a policy is underwritten by an insurance company). In another definition, this refers to the analysis of a group that is done to determine rates and benefits or to determine whether the group should be offered coverage at all. A related definition refers to health screening each individual applicant for insurance and refusing to provide coverage for preexisting conditions.

Underwriting Profit: Insurer's profit from its insurance operations as distinguished from its investment earnings.

Uniform Policy Provisions Law (UPPL): Statutory policy provisions of health insurance policies that specify some of the rights and obligations of the insured and the insurer. These provisions, with some modifications, are part of the insurance laws of all 50 states and the District of Columbia.

Universal Coverage: A system that provides health coverage to all residents.

Upcoding: Using improper billing codes to charge Medicare or Medicaid for an item or service to receive higher payments than would ordinarily be due for the treatment of a patient.

URO: Utilization review organization. A freestanding organization that does nothing but utilization review, usually on a remote basis using the telephone and paper correspondence. It may be independent or part of another company, such as an insurance company that sells utilization review services on a stand-alone basis.

Utilization: Patterns of usage for a single medical service or type of service (e.g., hospital care, prescription drugs, physician visits). Measurement of utilization of all medical services in combination usually is done in terms of dollar expenditures. Use is expressed in rates per unit of population at risk for a given period, such as number of annual admissions to a hospital per 1,000 persons over age 65.

Utilization Review: Program designed to reduce unnecessary hospital admissions and to control the length of stay for inpatients through the use of preliminary evaluations, concurrent inpatient evaluations, or discharge preplanning.

Value-Based Purchasing: A payment reform under which hospitals and other providers are provided bonuses based upon their performance against quality measures. The Affordable Care Act established a value-based purchasing program in Medicare for hospitals and required the development of similar programs for skilled nursing facilities, home health agencies, and ambulatory surgical centers, and the testing of pilot programs for other providers, including psychiatric hospitals, long-term care hospitals, rehabilitation hospitals, and hospice programs.

Variable Deductible: Deductible amount applied to a particular sickness or injury that is the greater of either the minimum deductible stated in the policy or an amount equal to all benefit payments received from any other medical expense coverage for the same eligible expenses.

Volume Discount: Premium rate reduction application to new group case coverages that is based on total case premium (for specific coverages) or total premium and premium per certificate (employee).

Volume Loading: Premium rate increase applicable to new group case coverages that is based on the total case premium (for specified coverages) or total premium and premium per certificate (employee).

Wellness Programs: Employer programs provided to employees to lessen health risks and thus avoid more serious health problems.

Whistleblower: An employee who reports the illegal or wrongful actions of his or her coworkers.

Wire Fraud Statute: A federal statute that prohibits the use of wire, radio, or television communication in interstate or foreign commerce for the purpose of executing a scheme to defraud.

Workers' Compensation: A form of social insurance provided through property-casualty insurers. Workers' compensation provides medical benefits and replacement of lost wages that result from injuries or illnesses that arise from the workplace; in turn, the employee cannot normally sue the employer unless true negligence exists. Workers' compensation has undergone dramatic increases in cost as group health has shifted into managed care, resulting in workers' compensation carriers adopting managed care approaches. Workers' compensation is often heavily regulated under state laws that are significantly different from those used for group health insurance and is often the subject of intense negotiation between management and organized labor.

Wraparound Plan: Commonly used to refer to insurance or health plan coverage for copays and deductibles that are not covered under a member's base plan. This is often used for Medicare.

Yates Memo: A memorandum entitled *Individual Accountability for Corporate Wrongdoing* that Deputy Attorney General Sally Quillian Yates issued on September 9, 2015, which announced that the DOJ will seek accountability from the individuals involved in corporate misconduct.

Zero Down: The practice of a medical group or provider system distributing all the capital surplus in a health plan or group to the members of the group rather than retaining any capital or reinvesting it in the group or plan.

1.2 Table of Acronyms and Abbreviations

Key: a.k.a. – also known as | f.k.a. – formerly known as | n.k.a. – now known as

Relevant Acts and Laws

ARRA	American Recovery and Reinvestment Act of 2009
ACA	Affordable Care Act of 2010
ADA	Americans with Disabilities Act of 1990
BBA	Balanced Budget Act of 1997
BBRA	Balanced Budget Refinement Act of 1999
BIPA	Benefit Improvement and Protection Act of 2000
CLIA	Clinical Laboratory Improvement Amendments of 1988
COBRA	Consolidated Omnibus Budget Reconciliation Act of 1985
DEFRA	Deficit Reduction Act of 1984
DRA	Deficit Reduction Act of 2005
EMTALA	Emergency Medical Treatment and Labor Act of 1986
FAR	Federal Acquisition Regulations
FCA	False Claims Act
FMLA	Family and Medical Leave Act
HCERA	Health Care and Education Reconciliation Act of 2010
HCQIA	Health Care Quality Improvement Act of 1986
HIPAA	Health Insurance Portability and Accountability Act of 1996
HITECH	Health Information Technology for Economic and Clinical Health Act
IMPACT	Improving Medicare Post-Acute Care Transformation Act of 2014
MACRA	Medicare Access and CHIP Reauthorization Act of 2015
MMA	Medicare Modernization Act of 2003 (a.k.a. Medicare Prescription Drug, Improvement, and Modernization Act)
MIPPA	Medicare Improvements for Patients and Providers Act of 2008
OBRA	Omnibus Budget Reconciliation Act ('86, '87, '89, '90, '93, '99 and '00)
OSHA	Occupational Safety and Health Act (or Administration)
PAMA	Protecting Access to Medicare Act of 2014
RICO	Racketeer Influenced and Corrupt Organizations Act
SOA	Sarbanes-Oxley Act of 2003
SSA	Social Security Act
Stark I & II	Physician Self-Referral Laws—part of OBRA '89 and '93, respectively
RICO	Racketeer Influenced and Corrupt Organizations Act
TEFRA	Tax Equity and Fiscal Responsibility Act of 1982

Relevant Agencies, Commissions, Departments, and Programs

AHCPR	Agency for Health Care Policy and Research
CHIP	Children's Health Insurance Program
CMI/CMMI	Center for Medicare and Medicaid Innovation
CMS	Centers for Medicare and Medicaid Services (f.k.a. Health Care Financing Administration (HCFA))
DAB	Departmental Appeals Board
DOL	Department of Labor
DOJ	U.S. Department of Justice
FDA	Food and Drug Administration
FEHBP	Federal Employee Health Benefits Program
FMAP	Federal Medical Assistance Program
FTC	Federal Trade Commission
GAO	Government Accountability Office (f.k.a. Government Accounting Office)
HHS/DHHS	U.S. Department of Health and Human Services
HOQR	Hospital Outpatient Quality Reporting Program
HRSA	Health Resources and Services Administration
IPAB	Independent Payment Advisory Board
MedPAC	Medicare Payment Advisory Commission
MGCRB	Medicare Geographic Classification Review Board
NIH	National Institutes of Health
OCR	Office of Civil Rights (DHHS)
OGE	Office of Governmental Ethics
OIG	Office of Inspector General
OMB	Office of Management and Budget
PRO	Peer Review Organization
PPRC	Physician Payment Review Commission
PRRB	Provider Reimbursement Review Board
PSRO	Professional Standards Review Organization
QIC	Qualified Independent Contractor
SCHIP	State Children's Health Insurance Program
SEC	Securities and Exchange Commission
SHPDA	State Health Planning and Development Agency

Commonly Used Terms and Descriptors

AAPCC	Adjusted Average Per Capita Cost
ACO	Accountable Care Organization
ACR	Adjusted Community Rate (or Rating)
ADC	Average Daily Census
ADG	Ambulatory Diagnostic Group
ADL	Activities of Daily Living
ADS	Alternative Daily Systems
AHP	Accountable Health Partnership

ALOS	Average Length of Stay
AOB	Assignment of Benefits
APC	Ambulatory Payment Class
APM	Advanced Alternative Payment Model
APG	Ambulatory Patient Group
APR	Average Payment Rate
ASC	Ambulatory Surgery Center
ASO	Administrative Services Only Contract
ASP	Average Sales Price
AVG	Ambulatory Visit Group
AWP	Average Wholesale price; *also* Any Willing Provider
BC/BS	Blue Cross/Blue Shield Plans
CAH	Critical Access Hospital
CAP	Capitation
CCN	Community Care Network
CCP	Coordinated Care Program; *also* Corporate Compliance Plan
CCRC	Continuing Care Retirement Community Program
CDLT	Clinical Diagnostic Laboratory Test
CIA	Corporate Integrity Agreement
CF	Conversion Factor
CFC	Conditions for Coverage
CHC	Community Health Center
CHMIS	Community Health Management Information System
CHOW	Change of Ownership
CIA	Corporate Integrity Agreement
CJR	Comprehensive Care for Joint Replacement
CLASS	Community Living Assistance Services and Supports
CMI	Case Mix Index
COA	Certificate of Authority
COB	Coordination of Benefits
COC	Certificate of Coverage
COI	Certificate of Insurance
CON	Certificate of Need
CoP	Conditions of Participation
Copay	Copayment
CORF	Comprehensive Outpatient Rehabilitation Facility
CPI	Consumer Price Index
CPI-MCS	Consumer Price Index-Medical Care Services
CPR	Customary, Prevailing and Reasonable
CPT	Current Procedural Terminology
CQI	Continuous Quality Improvement
CSR	Continued Stay Review
CVO	Credential/Central Verification Organization

CWW	Clinic Without Walls
DCI	Duplicate Coverage Inquiry
DME	Durable Medical Equipment
DMEPOS	Durable Medical Equipment Prosthetics Orthotics & Supplies
DMS	Demand Management Services
DOS	Date of Service
DRG	Diagnosis Related Group
DSA	Disproportionate Share Adjustment
DSH	Disproportionate Share Hospital
DSM	Disease State Management
DUM	Drug Utilization Management
DUR	Drug Utilization Review
DX	Diagnosis
E&M	Evaluation and Management
EACH	Essential Access Community Hospital
EBIS	Employee Benefits Information System
EDI	Electronic Data Interchange
EHR	Electronic Health Record
EMS	Emergency Medical Services
EOB	Explanation of Benefits
EOC	Episode of Care
EOMB	Explanation of Medicare Benefits
EQRO	External Quality Review Organization
ERA	Electronic Remittance Advice
FAS-106	Financial Accounting Standards—Rule 106
Fee Max	Fee Maximum
FFS	Fee for Service
FI	Fiscal Intermediary (n.k.a. MAC)
FPL	Federal Poverty Level
FQHC	Federally Qualified Health Center
FQHMO	Federally Qualified HMO
FTE	Full-time Equivalent
GAF	Geographic Adjustment Factor
GDP	Gross Domestic Product
GHP	Group Health Plan
GPCI	Geographic Practice Cost Index
GPWW	Group Practice Without Walls
HCAHPS	Hospital Consumer Assessment of Healthcare Providers and Systems
HCPCS	HCFA Common Procedure Coding System
HEDIS	Health Plan Employer Data and Information Set
HHA	Home Health Agency
HHPPS	Home Health Prospective Payment System
HHRG	Home Health Resource Group

HHVBP	Home Health Value-Based Purchasing
HMO	Health Maintenance Organization
HOPPS	Hospital Outpatient Prospective Payment System
HPSA	Health Professional Shortage Area
HRA	Health Risk Appraisal
HRA	Health Reimbursement Arrangement
HSA	Health Services Agreement; *also* Health Savings Account
HSR	Hospital Specific Rate
IBNR	Incurred But Not Reported
ICD-10	International Classification of Diseases, Tenth Revision
ICF	Intermediate Care Facility
ICU	Intensive Care Unit
IDS	Integrated Delivery System
IDTF	Independent Diagnostic Testing Facility
IIHI	Individually Identifiable Health Information
IME	Indirect Medical Education
IOM	Internet-Only Manual (CMS publication); *also* Institute of Medicine
IPF	Independent Psychiatric Facility
IPL	Independent Physiological Laboratory
IPPS	Inpatient Prospective Payment System
IQR	Inpatient Quality Reporting
IRB	Institutional Review Board
IRC	Internal Revenue Code
IRF	Inpatient Rehabilitation Facility
IRS	Internal Revenue Service
LCAH	Life Care at Home Program
LCC	Lower of Cost or Charges
LCD	Local Coverage Decision (a.k.a. Local Medical Review Policy)
LLP	Limited Liability Company
LMRP	Local Medical Review Policy
LMRP	Local Medical Review Policy (a.k.a. "Local Coverage Decision")
LOB	Line of Business
LOS	Length of Stay
LTC	Long Term Care
LTCH	Long Term Care Hospital
MA	Medicare Advantage (f.k.a. "Medicare + Choice"); *also* Medical Assistant
MAC	Medicare Administrative Contractor; *also* Maximum Available Coverage
MAP	Maximum Allowable Payment
MAPD	Medicare Advantage Prescription Drug Plan
MaxLOS	Maximum Length of Stay
M+C	Medicare + Choice (n.k.a. MA)
MCE	Medical Care Evaluation
MCM	Medical Case Management

MCO	Managed Care Organization
MCP	Managed Care Plan
MDC	Major Diagnostic Category
MDS-PAC	Minimum Data Set - Post-Acute Care
MEDCAC	Medicare Evidence Development & Coverage Advisory Committee
MED PAR	Medicare Provider Analysis and Review
MEI	Medical Economic Index
MERP	Medical Expense Reimbursement Plan
MET	Multiple-Employer Trust
MFS	Medicare Fee Schedule
MHSS	Military Health Services System
MIG	Medicare-Insured Group
MIP	Medicare Integrity Program; *also* Managed Indemnity Plan
MIPS	Merit-based Incentive Payment System
MLR	Medical Loss Ratio
MM	Member Months
MOB	Maintenance of Benefits Plan
MOR	Monthly Operating Report
MPP	Minimum Premium Plan
MSA	Metropolitan Statistical Area, also Medical Savings Account
MSN	Medicare Summary Notice
MSO	Management-Service Organization
MSP	Medicare Secondary Payer
MSPB	Medicare Spending Per Beneficiary
MTS	Medicare Transaction System
NCA	National Coverage Analysis
NCD	National Coverage Decision/Determination
NDC	National Drug Code
NLR	Net Loss Ratio
NonPARs	Nonparticipating Physicians/Providers
NPDB	National Practitioner Data Bank
NPI	National Provider Identifier
NPP	Notice of Privacy Practices
NPR	Notice of Program Reimbursement
NPRM	Notice of Proposed Rule Making
NTIS	National Technical Information Service
OASIS	Outcome and Assessment Information Set
OMSB	Outcomes Management Standards Board
OOA	Out-of-Area Services
OON	Out-of-Network Services
OOP	Out-of-Pocket Payments
OPM	Office of Personnel Management
OPPS	Outpatient Prospective Payment System

P&T	Pharmacy and Therapeutics Committee
PARs	Participating Physicians/Providers
PAS	Preadmission Screening Program; *also* Professional Activities Survey
PAT	Preadmission Testing
PBM	Pharmacy Benefit Manager
PC	Professional Component
PCCM	Primary Care Case Manager
PCLR	Paid Claims Loss Ration
PCMH	Patient-Centered Medical Home
PCN	Primary Care Network
PCP	Primary Care Physician/Practitioner
PCPM	Per Contract Per Month
PDP	Prescription Drug Plan
PHO	Physician-Hospital Organization
PHP	Prepaid Health Plan
PIN	Provider Identification Number
PIP	Periodic Interim Payment
PIP-DCG	Principal Inpatient Diagnostic Cost Group
PLI	Professional Liability Insurance
PHI	Personal Health Information
PMPM	Per Member Per Month
POP	Premium-Only Plan
POS	Point of Service
PPI-H	Producer Price Index-Hospital
PPO	Preferred Provider Organization
PPP	Private Practice Partnership
PPS	Prospective Payment System
PQRS	Physician Quality Reporting System
PRO	Peer Review Organization (n.k.a QIO)
ProPAC	Prospective Payment Assessment Commission
PSA	Professional Services Agreement
PSAO	Pharmacy Services Administration Organization
PSC	Program Safeguard Contractor
PSN	Provider-Sponsored Network
PSO	Provider Sponsored Organization
PSRO	Professional Standards Review Organization
PSV	Primary Source Verification
PTMPY	Per Thousand Members Per Year
QA	Quality Assurance
QIO	Quality Improvement Organization (f.k.a. PRO)
QIP	Quality Improvement Program
QM	Quality Management
QMB	Qualified Medicare Beneficiary

QPP	Quality Payment Program
QRC	Quality Review Committee
R&C	Reasonable and Customary Charge
RBRVS	Resource Based Relative Value Scale
RFI	Request for Information
RFP	Request for Proposal
RHC	Rural Health Clinic
RHHI	Regional Home Health Intermediary
RIC	Rehabilitation Impairment Category
RRC	Rural Referral Center
RUG	Resource Utilization Group
RVS	Relative Value of Services
RVU	Relative Value Unit
SAP	Service Assessment Program
SGR	Sustainable Growth Rate
SLMB	Specified Low-Income Medicare Beneficiary
SMI	Supplemental Medical Insurance
SNF	Skilled Nursing Facility
SNPs	Special Needs Plans
SPR	Standard Paper Remit
SUR	Statistical Utilization Review
TOP	Transitional Outpatient Payment
TOS	Type of Service
TPA	Third Party Administrator
TQM	Total Quality Management
UB-04	Uniform Billing of 2004 (institutional claim form)
UCDS	Uniform Clinical Data Set
UCR	Usual, Customary, and Reasonable Fees
UHDDS	Uniform Hospital Discharge Data Set
UM	Utilization Management
UPIN	Unique Provider Identification Number
VBM	Physician Value-Based Modifier
UR	Utilization Review
URO	Utilization Review Organization
VPB	Value-Based Purchasing, Value-Based Payment
VPS	Volume Performance Standards
WDC	Weighted Daily Census
WEDI	Workgroup for Electronic Data Interchange
ZEBRA	Zero-Balanced Reimbursement Account

2

Patient Care

Susan O. Scheutzow
Kohrman Jackson & Krantz, LLP

2.1 Creation of the Provider-Patient Relationship; Duty to Treat and Ending Provider-Patient Relationships; Patient Abandonment

2.1.1 Creation of a Provider-Patient Relationship

The existence of a provider/patient relationship is fundamental to the existence of many patient rights, provider liability, and ethical responsibility. A physician-patient relationship usually is required prior to a patient being able to sue for malpractice; it also is necessary in order for a patient to be able to seek continual treatment from a physician (e.g., a physician cannot be responsible for abandonment unless a physician-patient relationship exists.) Many patient rights, including the right to confidentiality, flow from the existence of a provider/patient relationship. Additionally, physicians are often prohibited from taking certain actions, such as prescribing medication for individuals, unless a physician-patient relationship exists. Whether a physician-patient relationship exists is generally a state law issue.

Generally, the provider/patient relationship arises under the theory of implied contract.[1] A person seeks treatment from a physician or other health care provider, and the provider accepts the person as a patient by initially rendering treatment. A physician (or other individual health care provider) generally is under no legal obligation to accept any particular patient into her practice. Many physicians, however, do enter into written contracts obligating them to accept certain persons as patients. Examples of such agreements include agreements with third-party payers (which, at times, require physicians to treat all patients covered by such health plans) or provisions in a hospital's medical-staff bylaws (to which physicians agree) such as those which require the physicians to treat all patients of the hospital's emergency department when the physician is "on-call."

Clearly if a physician treats the patient and bills for the service, a physician-patient relationship has been established. However, a physician-patient relationship may exist even if the physician never treats the patient or offers minimal services and doesn't bill if the physician has undertaken some affirmative action on behalf of the patient.

---

[1] *Childs v. Weis*, 440 S.W. 2d 104 (Ct. Cv. App. TX 1969).

Several courts have found that there is a physician patient relationship established between a physician and patient if the physician is "on-call" through an emergency department and if the physician fails to give advice or treat the patient (either by refusing to treat the patient or not being responsive to a page) and the patient is harmed, the physician may be liable.[2] Whether a physician-patient relationship exists, is a factual determination dependent in large part on whether the physician was obligated under the medical staff bylaws to treat the patient. For example, at least one court has held that a physician who was on call and failed to notify the hospital that he had another physician covering for him remained responsible for patients in the emergency department and would be liable for any damage occurring to patients by his failure to respond.[3] Decisions in these cases are very fact specific, such as a case when a physician was contacted and refused to come in, but it was held that a physician-patient relationship was not formed because the physician hadn't signed up for call but was just contacted by the hospital[4].

Whether or not advice given to other physicians in "hallway consults" establishes a physician-patient relationship is highly fact specific. If the advice given is solely to consult with another physician as how to generally treat certain conditions, a physician-patient relationship is not established. However, if the consulting physician suggests a course of treatment understanding significant details about the specific patient, a physician-patient relationship may be established even if the physician never has a face-to-face meeting with the patient and doesn't bill for the service. One issue in these cases is whether the physician providing the curbside consult actually expected his advice to be followed or was only assisting the physician making the inquiry in coming to his own decision regarding the patient's treatment.

Courts have reached divergent decisions as to whether a physician-patient relationship is established between a physician who supervises residents who render care and patients treated by a resident if the supervising physician never has direct contact with the patient and never is contacted for advice. An Ohio court has ruled that a supervising physician could be liable if the physician assumed an active duty to oversee the performance of the residents and familiarize himself with the condition of the patients.[5] Contrast this to a Texas case in which a physician who was actually present when a resident malpracticed was held not liable because the physician did not provide direct care to the patient.[6]

In an interesting case, the Georgia Court of Appeals would not grant a motion for summary judgment for a physician who had referred a patient to a specialist for care and the specialist allegedly malpracticed, stating that the physician's act of evaluating and sending the patient on for specialty care might be enough to establish a physician-patient relationship for that care.[7]

---

[2] *See, e.g., Milliard v. Cirrado*, Miss. Ct. App. ED Dec 14, 1999, Case No. 75420; *Hiser v. Randolph*, 126 Ariz 608, 617 P. 2d 774 (Ct. App. AZ 1980); *Mead v. Legacy Health System*, No. A130969 (Or. Ct. App. Oct. 28, 2009).

[3] *Brown v. Bailey*, No. ED 86387 (Mo Ct. App. Nov. 14, 2006). Of interest in this case is that the court found that a physician-patient relationship wasn't established; however, the physician had a duty to the patient which was sufficient for a negligence action.

[4] *Seeber v. Ebeling*, No. 94,666 (Kan. Ct. App. Sept. 1, 2006).

[5] *Lownsbury v. VanBuren*, 94 Ohio St. 3d 231 (2002).

[6] *Reynosa v. Huff*, 21 S.W.3d 510 (Tex. App. 4, 2000).

[7] *Harris v. Griffin*, No. A 05A0576, 2005 Ga. App. LEXIS 153 (Ga. Ct. App. Feb. 21, 2005).

Another area currently being developed in the law is whether or not a physician-patient relationship exists when a physician undertakes an examination of a person not for the benefit of the person being examined, but for the benefit of a third party such as an employer or an insurance company. The majority rule appears to be that no physician-patient relationship exists in these situations,[8] but some courts have found that a limited physician-patient relationship exists as to the examination and a physician may be found liable for failing to notify the person being examined if information (such as test results) is obtained which would be necessary for preserving the health of the person being examined.[9] In these cases the physician had a duty to notify the patient of the test results.

Once a physician has rendered care and the physician-patient relationship is established, the provider is under a duty to provide services for the patient until treatment is no longer necessary or either the patient terminates the relationship or the provider ends the relationship in a manner that does not constitute abandonment of the patient. Proper termination of the physician-patient relationship requires the physician both to give notice to the patient that the relationship will end and to give the patient sufficient time to secure substitute care.[10] Some states have statutes or medical board requirements addressing how termination of the physician-patient relationship is to be effected. Although the physician-patient relationship is based in contract (either expressed or implied), patient abandonment is generally characterized as a tort; because the duty to provide continuing care exists until it is properly terminated, if the provider fails to provide the care, then a breach of a duty has occurred.

With the advent of physicians providing services through electronic communications ("telemedicine") many states are establishing what actions must be taken to establish a physician-patient relationship prior to prescribing drugs for the patient.[11] These laws and regulations often require the physician to personally perform and document an appropriate history and physical prior to prescribing. It remains to be seen whether these laws, which define a physician-patient relationship as involving an actual examination (whether via telemedicine or otherwise), will act as a shield for physicians in malpractice actions attempting to impose liability upon physicians who have never seen the patient.

---

[8] *See, e.g., Payne v. Sherrer*, 458 S.E. 2d 916 (Ga. Ct. App. 1995); *Ervin v. American Guardian Life Assurance Co.*, 545 A. 2d 354 (Pa. Super. Ct. 1988).

[9] *See, e.g., Daly v. United States*, 946 F. 2d 1467 (9th Cir. 1991); *Green v. Walker*, 910 F. 2d 291 (5th Cir. 1990); *Reed v. Bojarski*, 166 N.J. 89 (2001).

[10] *See, e.g., Ricks v. Budge*, 91 Utah 307, 64 P. 2d 208 (1937); *Hammonds v. Aetna Cas. & Sur. Co.*, 237 Supp. 96 (N.D. Ohio 1965).

Sample Form Letter to Terminate Physician-Patient Relationship

Dear :

This letter is to inform you that I will cease providing you medical care. Since your condition requires continued medical attention, I suggest that you secure another physician to provide medical care immediately. If you desire, I will continue to provide care to you for a period of thirty (30) days following the date of this letter, but as of _____, I will no longer be available to provide you care.

Upon your request, I will make available your medical records to the physician that you select.

Very truly yours,

---

[11] *See, e.g.*, S.C. Code § 40-47-113.

2.1.2 Requirement that Health Care Facilities and Individual Providers Accept Patients

No general law requires health care providers to provide services to all persons in all circumstances. A number of laws govern treatment in emergency situations and health care providers generally may not discriminate against protected classes in the rendering of treatment.

Although absent a physician-patient relationship, a physician has no obligation to provide medical care to non-patients, many states have passed "Good Samaritan" laws that provide immunity from civil liability to any person who does choose to provide emergency care or treatment outside of the normal provider/patient context.[12]

2.1.2.1 Emergency Treatment

Almost all hospitals that offer emergency care must offer such care to all patients, regardless of a patient's ability to pay. Although this obligation exists in some jurisdictions by common law,[13] this obligation became clear with the passage of the Emergency Medical Treatment and Labor Act (EMTALA),[14] which prohibits hospitals in most circumstances from failing to provide care to stabilize patients in emergencies or active labor. (*See* Section 9.3.2 of this publication for more-detailed analysis of EMTALA.) Hospitals have the duty to provide physicians to render necessary treatment in such emergencies, and hospitals satisfy this requirement by imposing on-call responsibilities upon medical staff members.

In addition to EMTALA, the accreditation standards of The Joint Commission (JC) and the Healthcare Facilities Accreditation Program (HFAP) require hospitals with emergency facilities to provide services to patients requiring such care. Hospitals that are exempt from federal income tax pursuant to Section 501(c)(3) of the Internal Revenue Code also may be required to provide emergency care to all patients who seek such care, or risk their tax-exempt status (*see* Section 6.2.5 of this publication for more-detailed analysis of the public-benefit requirement for attaining and maintaining federal tax-exempt status).

2.1.2.2 Non-Emergency Treatment

In non-emergency situations, hospitals and health care facilities have much more latitude in selecting patients. Nevertheless, a number of restrictions to this generalization apply. Health care providers often contractually agree to accept certain patients by entering into agreements with third-party payers which require the provider to accept all patients covered by such health plans based on the providers' available space or services.

Similarly, any health care facility that participates in the federal Medicare or Medicaid program agrees to accept all Medicare or Medicaid patients to the facility's capacity. Health care facilities that have received funding for construction and modernization under the Federal Hospital Survey and Construction Act (also known as the Hill-Burton Act)[15] have an obligation to provide a "reasonable volume" of services to persons who are unable to pay for such services. Also affecting a facility's

---

[12] *See, e.g.*, OHIO REV. CODE § 2305.231.
[13] *Wilmington Gen. Hospital v. Manlove*, 54 Del. 15, 174 A 2d 135 (1961).
[14] 42 U.S.C. §§ 1395cc, 1395dd.
[15] 42 U.S.C. §§ 291 *et seq.*

ability to refuse patients are many state property-tax exemption statutes that require health care facilities to provide charity care prior to qualifying for a state-tax exemption. Public hospitals also may have significant restrictions on their ability to refuse care.

Regardless of whether a health care provider may otherwise refuse treatment to a particular patient, most health care providers are covered by a variety of federal non-discrimination statutes including Title VI of the Civil Rights Act of 1964, Section 504 of the Rehabilitation Act of 1973, Title III of the Older Americans Amendments of 1975, and the Americans With Disabilities Act of 1990, which prohibits health care facilities from discriminating on the basis of a protected classification such as race, color, national origin, age, or handicap.

2.1.3 Conscience Laws

Most states have some type of conscience law which provides that a provider does not need to provide care which violates the provider's conscience, such as providing abortion or sterilization services. Case law developing in this area focuses on the responsibility of the provider to provide information to a patient to allow the patient the opportunity to receive care from another provider.[16]

2.2 Consent to Medical Treatment

2.2.1 Generally

The right of every individual to be free of undesired personal contact from another is a fundamental tenet of American law, and the United States courts have jealously guarded this right. In the words of the Supreme Court:

> No right is held more sacred, or is more carefully guarded by the common law, than the right of every individual to the possession and control of his own person, free from all restraint or interference of others, unless by clear and unquestionable authority of law.[17]

From this concept of individual autonomy and self-determination flows the doctrine of informed consent. The doctrine of informed consent has two components: first, that the right of a person to determine what may be done to her body includes the right to consent to medical care; and second, that true consent cannot be given unless the patient is given all relevant information and has an opportunity to evaluate the available risks involved.[18] Therefore, if a physician or other health care professional renders medical treatment without a patient's consent, it is actionable as a tort.

Historically, an action based on a lack of informed consent was brought as an action for the intentional tort of battery; unless effective consent was given, rendering medical treatment constituted an unconsented touching or a battery. The requirement of informed consent became so accepted that it is now considered the standard of care and the failure to obtain informed consent now also constitutes negligence or malpractice. In some instances, failure to give complete information may also give rise to

---

[16] *See, e.g., Brownfield v. Daniel Freeman Marina Hosp.*, 208 Cal App 3d 405 (1989) regarding hospital's failure to provide a patient with information regarding the "morning after" contraceptive medication.
[17] *Union Pac. R.R. Co. v. Botsford*, 141 U.S. 250, 251, 11 S. Ct. 1000, 1001, 351 L. Ed. 734, 735 (1891).
[18] *See, e.g., Canterbury v. Spence*, 464 F.2d 772 (D.C. 1972).

an action for misrepresentation or fraud. The characterization of a lack of informed consent as the intentional tort battery or as negligence may have implications for statutes of limitations, insurance coverage, and the ability of a plaintiff to recover punitive damages; as punitive damages are generally not permitted for negligence claims, and insurance policies generally refuse coverage for intentional acts.

The legal standard for proper informed consent is the disclosure of the following to the patient who has the capacity to understand and make a reasoned decision, or to the patient's substitute decision maker:

1. the patient's condition;
2. the nature of the proposed treatment;
3. the benefits reasonably expected from a proposed treatment, together with the material risks and dangers of the proposed treatment; and
4. treatment alternatives, as well as the risks and benefits of such alternatives, including foregoing treatment.[19]

The requirement to provide information to the patient is greater the more serious the risk (regardless of the degree of likelihood of the risk) and greater the more prevalent the risk (regardless of its severity). The current development in the law regarding informed consent has focused on whether the standard for information to be given to the patient is what a "reasonable physician" should provide or what a "reasonable patient" would want to have. Under a "reasonable physician" standard, the patient must be given information that would customarily be given by physicians in the same specialty, in the same circumstances; under the "reasonable patient" standard, the physician must give information that would be relevant to reasonable patients in the same circumstances.[20] A small number of states have adopted a "subjective patient standard," requiring the physician to give information that the specific patient needed to know given that patient's circumstances.[21] The subjective patient standard requires physicians to have knowledge of their patients and may subject the physician to hindsight analysis of the patient's circumstances.[22] In order for a patient to prevail on a suit for lack of informed consent under a negligence theory, a patient must show not only that had he or she received inadequate information but also that he or she would have made a different decision regarding the care because without such a finding, the patient would have no damages.

Generally, consent may be oral or written, although some state statutes provide for statutory presumptions that appropriate informed consent was obtained if state-dictated written-consent forms are completed. The responsibility to obtain informed consent historically has rested with the physician. However, at least one court has stated that if the hospital is responsible for the physician's malpractice on a vicarious liability theory, the hospital may also be held liable for the physician's failure to obtain informed consent.[23]

---

[19] *See, e.g., Nickell v Gonzalez*, 17 Ohio St. 3d 136, 477 N.E.2d 1145 (1985); *Dries v. Grecor*, 424 N.Y.S. 2d 561, 72 A.2d 231 (1980); D. Louisell & H. Williams, *Medical Malpractice* § 2201 (1974); *Holt v. Nelson*, 11 Wash. App. 230, 523 P. 2d 211 (1974).

[20] *See, e.g., Ketchup v. Howard*, 247 Ga. App 54 (2000), which contains a survey of other states' laws regarding informed consent.

[21] *See, e.g., Scott v. Bradford*, 606 P. 2d 554 (Okla. 1979).

[22] For a state by state analysis of the various standards used, *see* King & Moulton, *Rethinking Informed Consent: The Case for Shared Medical Decision Making*, AM. J. OF L. & MED, 32 (2006): 429–501.

[23] *Mueller v. Auker* No, CV-04-399-S-BLW (D. Idaho, April 14, 2006).

While hospitals or other health care facilities historically have had no independent duty to secure consent,[24] it is important for hospitals to have policies requiring informed consent, as the JC and HFAP accreditation guidelines for hospitals require hospitals to have consent policies; further, state-licensing statutes may also require hospital consent procedures. The federal government has also established guidelines for informed consent and documentation regarding informed consent in certain circumstances.[25]

2.2.1.1 Requirements for Consent Form

Informed consent is a process and does not turn on whether or not a form has been signed. The decision to accept or reject all medical treatment is to be based on informed consent. Generally when a patient signs an admission consent form the patient consents to testing for diagnosis and general hospital care, but specific medical treatment requires additional explanation and consent. Notwithstanding the legal requirement that the patient give informed consent for *all* medical treatment, CMS, the JC and HFAP require *written* consent forms for specific procedures such as surgeries and other invasive procedures.[26] Many states provide a statutory presumption that informed consent was given if a consent form is signed that complies with statutory requirements.[27] Generally, these forms do not actually need to provide all the risks and benefits expected because such information is often specific to a particular patient. The form is an acknowledgment by the patient that the patient received relevant information and has the opportunity to ask questions.

Written consent forms are not practical for all medical care[28] but providers should obtain signed consent forms when required by law or an accrediting organization and should also consider consent forms for high risk activities. Regardless of whether a signed consent form is obtained, physicians and other providers should always take care to document in their records that they provided the patient with the relevant information and that the patient consented.

2.2.1.2 Disclosure of Special Risk Factors of Providers

Generally, informed consent involves informing the patient of the risks and benefits associated with various treatment alternatives. Patients have begun to allege that if a health care provider does not disclose information regarding the specific provider's experience and skills, the patient has not provided appropriate consent. In *Johnson v. Kakemoor*,[29] the Wisconsin Supreme Court held that, in order to make an informed decision, a patient may need to have all relevant information presented, and that information regarding a surgeon's experience and skill may be considered relevant for a patient

---

[24] *See, e.g., Bedel v. University OB/GYN Assocs.*, 76 Ohio App. 3d 742, 603 N.E.2d 342 (1991); *Gibson v. Methodist Hosp.*, 822 S.W. 2d 95 (Tex. App. 1991).

[25] 42 C.F.R. § 482.13(b)(2) relative to consent; 42 C.F.R. § 482.24(c)(2)(v) relative to documentation in the medical record; and 42 C.F.R. § 482.51(b)(2) relative to surgical services. *See* the revised Interpretive Guidelines of the federal law published by the Centers for Medicare and Medicaid effective on April 13, 2007. These regulations apply to obtaining informed consent for patients being treated at hospitals certified for participation in the federal Medicare and Medicaid programs.

[26] 42 C.F.R. § 482.51(b)(2).

[27] *See e.g.* OHIO REV. CODE § 2317.54.

[28] There are countless medical interventions given to hospitalized patients and signing a consent form for each intervention is not practiced.

[29] *Johnson v. Kakemoor*, 199 Wis 2d 615, 545 N.W. 2d 495 (Wis. 1996); *Housel v. James*, No. 25031-8-111 (Wash Ct. App., Nov. 15, 2007) (holding that the plaintiff didn't show that the defendants lack of experience was relevant).

to know in order to give informed consent. When the patient specifically asks the physician about his or her experience or credentials and the physician does not provide all of the relevant information, or was not truthful in providing the information, it is easier for the patient to successfully argue that the physician's alleged experience or credentials provided the basis for the patient's consent.[30]

In the twenty years since *Kakemoor*, many courts and some state legislatures have grappled with this issue with contradictory results. For instance, in *Duttry v. Patterson*,[31] the Pennsylvania Court held that even when a patient asked a physician about his experience and the physician lied, the physician's actions did not void the patient's consent to the procedure. The court reasoned that consent is given to a particular procedure and not to a particular provider and the proper action in such a circumstance would be for misrepresentation. The Pennsylvania legislature, however, enacted law which overruled *Duttry* by providing that a physician may be held liable on an informed consent theory if the "... physician knowingly misrepresents to the patient his or her professional credentials, training or experience."[32]

Requirements as to the nuances of informed consent vary from state to state and specific state law must always be analyzed when dealing with issues of informed consent.

2.2.1.3 Exceptions to the Requirement to Obtain Consent

A patient must be fully informed and give express consent to medical procedures except in three circumstances in which actual informed consent is not necessary but, rather, is implied from the circumstances: (1) when additional procedures are necessary to accomplish the initial treatment for which there was consent; (2) in emergency situations when a presumption can be made that the patient would give consent to protect her life; and (3) when giving the patient full and complete information would be harmful to the patient.[33] Some states also permit a patient to waive informed consent.[34]

Although the law consistently has recognized these exceptions to the requirement that a patient gives informed consent, such exceptions may not be used to violate a patient's wishes. For instance, in an emergency situation (when it is not possible to obtain informed consent), the patient's consent is implied when the treatment considered by the physician is necessary to preserve the life or health of the patient; however, if the patient has initially refused to consent to treatment and the patient's condition becomes critical, the physician may not claim that the doctrine of implied consent in an emergency has created the right to render the treatment that was previously refused.

Similarly, while an exception to the requirement for informed consent exists when the risk of disclosure poses a threat to the patient because the patient might become ill or so distraught that treatment is severely hindered or becomes unfeasible,[35] the physician's privilege to withhold information

---

[30] *See Johnson, id.; Willis v. Bender*, 596 F. 3d 1244 (10th Dist., 2010). *But see Howard v. Univ. of Medicine and Dentistry of N.J.*, 172 N.J. 537, 800 A. 2d 73 (2002).
[31] 565 Pa. 130, 771A. 2d 1255 (2001).
[32] 40 Pa. State A§1303.504(d)(2). *See also Healey.*
[33] *See, e.g., Leach v. Shapiro*, 13 Ohio App. 3d 393, 469 N.E.2d 1047 (1984).
[34] *See Stover v. Assoc. of Cardiovascular Surgeons*, 634 A. 2d 47 (Pa. Sup. 1993); New York Public Health Law Section 2805-d(4)(b).
[35] *See Canterbury v. Spence*, 464 F.2d 772 (D.C. 1972).

is severely limited. Information may be withheld only when it is absolutely required for therapeutic reasons that information be withheld, and not simply when the physician fears that the patient will make a treatment decision with which the physician does not agree.

While the exceptions to the need for informed consent generally are derived from common law, some states, such as New York, have statutes which govern when informed consent is not necessary.[36]

2.2.1.4   Statutes Requiring Special Circumstances

Most states provide that special consent must be obtained for specific procedures, e.g., prior to a person undergoing a test to detect the human immunodeficiency virus (HIV), prior to abortion services, and prior to patients receiving a variety of mental health procedures such as electroshock therapy. State law should always be consulted for special-consent statutes.

2.2.1.5   Restraint and Seclusion

The issue of whether hospitalized patients may be restrained and/or subject to seclusion gained national attention with the death of 11-year-old Andrew McClain in 1998 from asphyxiation while being restrained at a psychiatric hospital in Connecticut. A Connecticut newspaper investigated the use of restraints and concluded that 142 patient deaths occurred between 1988 and 1998 due to improper restrains or seclusion. Restraints and seclusion are almost always imposed without the patient's consent. In January 2007, Centers for Medicare and Medicaid final rule on the use of restraints became effective. Restraints are defined as any manual method (including mechanical duress) which reduces the ability of a patient to move his or her arms or legs, body or head or any medication used to manage patient's behavior or restrict freedom of movement if such is not the standard treatment or dosage for the patient's condition, and seclusion which is defined as the involuntary confinement of a person in a room or area where the person is physically prevented from leaving.[37]

The rule which applies to all Medicare participating hospitals provides that a physician or other licensed practitioner must order the least restrictive safety measure which is most likely to be effective. Restraints are not to be used as a routine means of preventing patient falls. Once the use of restraints or seclusion are ordered by a physician or other licensed independent practitioner responsible for the patient's care, the order must be reviewed and rewritten every four hours for adults and more frequently for children, in addition to other requirements. Simultaneous use of restraint and seclusion may only be used with continual monitoring of the patient. In addition to Medicare guidelines, some states have passed laws regarding restraints and seclusion.[38] Seclusion may only be used for the management of violent or self-destructive behavior. The law imposes a high standard on hospitals and other health care providers utilizing restraints and seclusion to control patient's behavior and should be carefully reviewed. Each health care facility should have a restraint and seclusion policy which carefully follows federal and any applicable state law.

---

[36] New York Public Health Law Section 2805-d(4).
[37] *See* 42 C.F.R. § 482.13.
[38] *See* Texas Statutes and Codes Chapter 322.

2.2.2 Constitutional Protection

In addition to the common-law right to give informed consent prior to receiving medical treatment, the courts have recognized the patient's constitutional right to refuse medical treatment. While tort law addresses the liability of physicians and others for treating a patient without the patient's informed consent; unless the right to determine whether to receive medical treatment is recognized as a constitutional right, the state may place restrictions upon an individual's right to determine her own appropriate medical treatment. The constitutional protection of a person's choice of medical treatment has been found to flow from the United States Constitution and through many state constitutions. Some states have characterized it as a protected liberty interest; others a protected right to privacy and in certain circumstances it may be characterized as a valid exercise of one's constitutionally protected religious freedom. Because persons generally refuse medical treatment in the end-of-life context, constitutional issues usually have been addressed in this context, and have become known as the "right to die" cases.

The U.S. Supreme Court addressed the issue in *Cruzan v. Director, Missouri Dept. of Health*[39] and found the right to refuse medical treatment is the constitutionally protected liberty interest under federal law, arising from the Fourteenth Amendment. This right grants a person the right to refuse medical treatment even if that treatment will maintain the person's life. Although the Court acknowledged that many state courts have held that the right to refuse treatment is part of a generalized constitutional right of privacy, the Court reasoned that the right to refuse treatment is more properly analyzed in terms of a Fourteenth Amendment liberty interest. This liberty interest must then be weighed against the state's interests to determine if the deprivation of the liberty interest is constitutionally permissible.

The characterization of the right to refuse treatment as a liberty interest, rather than a fundamental privacy right may have legal significance; because traditionally, a privacy interest may only be overridden by a *compelling* state interest, whereas a liberty interest may be subject to state regulation as long as it is *rationally related* to a legitimate state interest.[40] Therefore, even though the U.S. Supreme Court has characterized the right to refuse treatment as a liberty interest, which allows states to impose restrictions on the right, additional patient rights may be given in the states which characterize the right as a privacy right under their state constitutions. The constitutionally protected right to free exercise of religion also has been raised as a basis for refusal of specific medical treatment.[41]

While *Cruzan* recognized a constitutionally protected right to refuse medical treatment, it does permit a state to abridge that right and require a patient to accept medical treatment if the state has a competing interest. Generally, four possible state interests have been recognized that could counteract the individual's constitutional rights:

- protection of third parties;
- prevention of suicide;

---

[39] *Cruzan v. Director, Missouri Dept. of Health*, 497 U.S. 261, 110 S. Ct. 2841, 111 L. Ed. 2d 224 (1990).
[40] *See Griswold v. Connecticut*, 381 U.S. 479, 85 S. Ct. 1678, 14 L. Ed. 2d 510 (1965); *Eisenstadt v. Baird*, 405 U.S. 438, 92 S. Ct. 1029, 31 L. Ed. 2d 349 (1972); Bopp & Coleson, *Webster and the Future of Substantive Due Process*, 28 Duq. L. Rev. 271, 280 (1990).
[41] *In re Milton*, 29 Ohio St. 3d, 505 N.E.2d 255 (1987).

- preservation of ethical standards of the medical profession; and
- preservation of human life.[42]

In *Cruzan*, the Court permitted the state of Missouri to exercise its interest by requiring that it be shown by clear and convincing evidence that Nancy Cruzan would have refused life-sustaining treatment. Courts have held that the state interests generally weaken and the individual's rights grow as the "degree of bodily invasion [of the procedure] increases and the prognosis dims."[43] Most of the case law has developed in the end-of-life context, as discussed in Section 2.3.

2.2.3 Incompetent's Right to Make Treatment Decisions

Incompetency may result from a person's youth, mental incompetence, illness, injury, or external influence (e.g., drugs or alcohol). Whatever the reason, if a patient is unable to make his or her own treatment decisions and these decisions must be made, someone must make them for the patient.

There is no clear definition of incompetency in the law for purposes of medical decision making. The key in determining mental competency for purposes of medical decisionmaking is whether the patient has the capacity to make informed decisions with respect to medical care.[44]

Historically, principles of decision making for incompetents have been extremely inconsistent. Physicians and other health care professionals often would make decisions based on the medical merits of each case, and might not place much weight on the wishes of the patient's family or the patient's own earlier-expressed intentions. Some early courts took the position that mentally ill patients had no right to make their own treatment decisions, and courts regularly made decisions on behalf of such patients. Alternatively, treatment decisions often were made by health care professionals in consultation with the family.

For years, many courts, professionals, and scholars wrestled with the issue of medical decision-making for incompetents. Public awareness of the issue increased dramatically in the mid 1970s with the case of Karen Ann Quinlan. *In re Quinlan*[45] and its progeny established that, if the personal right to choose medical treatment is to have any meaning, then a person must maintain the right during periods of incompetency, and third parties must be able to exercise it on behalf of the incompetent patient.

The court, in *Superintendent of Belchertown v. Saikewicz*, summed up the rights of incompetents to make medical decisions when it stated: "[W]e recognize a general right in all persons to refuse medical treatment in appropriate circumstances. The recognition of that right must extend to the case of an incompetent, as well as a competent, patient because the value of human dignity extends to both."[46]

---

[42] *Cruzan, supra*.
[43] *In re Quinlan*, 70 N.J. 10, 40, 355 A.2d 647 (1976), *cert. denied*, sub nom. *Garger v. New Jersey*, 429 U.S. 922, 97 S. Ct. 319, 50 L.Ed. 289 (1976); *see also Leach v. Akron Gen. Med. Ctr.*, 68 Ohio Misc. 1, 22 Ohio 3d 49, 426 N.E.2d 809 (Ohio Probate 1980).
[44] *See, e.g., Bartling v. Superior Ct.*, 163 Cal. App. 3d 186, 209 Cal. Rptr. 220 (1984); *In re Quakenbusch*, 156 N.J. Super. 282, 383 A.2d 785 (1978).
[45] *In re Quinlan, supra*.
[46] *Superintendent of Belchertown v. Saikewicz*, 373 Mass. 728, 745, 370 N.E.2d 417, 427 (1977).

It is now widely accepted that incompetents have the right to make medical-treatment decisions and that right may be exercised by a surrogate decision maker. Some dispute continues as to what decisions may be made, who can act in the place of the incompetent in making those decisions, and what standard of decision making should be used.

If the patient lacks the capacity to consent, then consent should be obtained from a third party. Unless the patient has a legal guardian appointed, consent is obtained from the person designated by the patient, or if no such designation exists, by the patient's "next of kin." Some states have statutes authorizing consent from family members and designating a hierarchy of "kinship;" other states have not established statutory designations and health care providers have relied on common interpretations of next of kin.

2.2.4 Minors

When a patient is a minor, consent to medical treatment must be obtained from the parent or legal guardian. Exceptions to parental consent include when the child requires immediate medical care and a parent or guardian is not available,[47] when a child is emancipated and is no longer under the control of her parents[48] and where specific statutes provide when minors may give consent. In addition, some states have adopted a common-law "mature minor" doctrine, which has been invoked in situations where the child is sufficiently mature to make her own health care decisions.[49]

Some states have specifically recognized a "mature-minor doctrine," which allows minors who are mature enough to understand the risks and benefits of the treatment to give their own consent. Some states have adopted broad mature minor statutes that allow a mature minor to consent to all medical care.[50] Most states, even if they do not statutorily recognize a mature minor's right to consent for all treatment, have laws authorizing minors to consent to certain treatment, such as for treatment of sexually transmitted diseases, alcoholism, drug abuse, and mental illness. State statutes must always be consulted.[51] State courts may also make case-by-case decisions regarding a minor's right to make his or her own treatment decisions such as in *In re E.G.* in which the Illinois Supreme Court allowed a 17-year-old to refuse medical treatment on religious grounds.[52]

When a parent makes a medical decision on behalf of a child, the parent is required to make the decision based upon what is in the best interest of the child. State child-neglect laws may include a parent's failure to provide necessary medical care in its definition of "neglect." Generally, a parent's religious-based objections to treatment generally do not justify a refusal of treatment of minors because the religion is the parent's and the child does not have the capacity for determining his or her own religion.[53] When a health care provider believes a parent is making a decision that is not in the best interest of the child, the provider should generally contact the local children's services agency.

---

[47] *See, e.g.*, Miss. Code Ann. § 41-41-3; N.Y. Pub. Health Law § 2504.4.
[48] Not all states have statutes which allow a child to become emancipated.
[49] *Younts v. St. Francis Hosp. & Sch. of Nursing*, 205 Kan. 292, 469 P.2d 330 (1970).
[50] Ark. Stat. Ann. 20-9-602(7); Or. Stat. Ann. 109.640.
[51] *See, e.g.*, Ariz. Rev. Stat. §§ 44-132.01, 44-133.01.
[52] 549 N.E.2d 322 (Ill. 1989).
[53] *See, e.g. Penn. v. Nexon*, 761 A. 2d 1151. (Sup. Ct. Penn., 2000), upholding parents' conviction of involuntary manslaughter and endangering the welfare of a child based on parents' refusal to seek medical treatment and instead treating their child with prayer.

Particularly problematic for health care providers is what to do when parents disagree about treatment; in such cases, judicial intervention or the intervention of local child protection agencies may also be necessary.

The U.S. Supreme Court also recognized a minor's right to make the decision to have an abortion without parental consent if the minor is mature enough to make her own decision or if it is in the minor's best interest to have an abortion without her parents' consent.[54] This follows the state law decisions recognizing the rights of a mature minor to make her own decisions and requiring parents to make decisions for children not able to give their own consent based on the child's best interests. The Court also held that a state can impose restrictions on the minor's right, such as requiring her parents to be notified prior to the abortion.

2.2.5 Consent for Experimentation

Federal regulations require approval by an Institutional Review Board (IRB) for all federally funded research involving human subjects, and research that involves drugs or devices (including clinical trials), regardless of its funding. The IRB is required to review the research proposal to ensure that the subjects are not exposed to any unnecessary risk, and to guarantee that prospective subjects have been given a sufficient opportunity to obtain information and give consent. An IRB must also ensure that individuals are not coerced into participating in the study. Since regulations governing IRBs can be onerous, many institutions and physicians do not have the resources to convene and run an IRB, and because multi-site research may result in many different IRBs reviewing the same study, some hospitals and study sponsors have begun to utilize the services of commercial IRBs, often called "Central IRBs." In June of 2016, the National Institute of Health (NIH) finalized a policy which favors using a Central IRB for multi-site research.[55]

Federally funded research involving human subjects is governed by regulations promulgated by the Department of Health and Human Services (DHHS) Office of Human Research Protections (OHRP). Research involving drugs or devices is subject to Food and Drug Administration (FDA) regulations, which provide for audits by the FDA to guarantee compliance with the regulations.[56] Although some differences exist between DHHS and FDA regulations, they are substantially similar in requiring patients to be informed that the study involves research, the risks of the study, its anticipated benefits, a disclosure of alternatives, the extent to which confidentiality will be maintained, information regarding how the patient could withdraw from the study, and costs of the study.

On January 19, 2017,[57] DHHS and fifteen other federal agencies issued a Final Rule significantly revising the federal regulations on human subject research. Most provisions of the new rule become effective January 19, 2018. The Final Rule clarifies what is not considered research and consequently not required to have IRB approval, and adds exemptions, and makes significant changes to consent requirements and other changes. See Chapter 14 for more analysis of the Common Rule.

---

[54] *Planned Parenthood of Cent. Mo. v. Danforth*, 428 U.S. 52, 96 S. Ct. 2831, 49 L. Ed. 2d 788 (1976).
[55] National Institutes of Health, Final NIH Policy on the Use of a Single Institutional Review Board for Multi-Site Research, Notice Number: NOT-OD-16-094 (June 21, 2016).
[56] 56 Fed. Reg. 28025 (1991).
[57] 82 Fed. Reg. 7149 (Jan. 19, 2017).

2.3 End-of-Life Decisionmaking

2.3.1 Competent Person's Right to Refuse Life-Sustaining Medical Treatment

Based upon the common-law right of informed consent and constitutional protection, an adult patient who has the capacity to understand the risks and benefits of medical treatment (competent patient) should be able to make determinations of what medical treatment to accept or reject, even if refusal of such treatment is life-threatening. If the state has an interest (e.g., the protection of third parties), then it may assert such a position in the courts. Courts have been reluctant to find that the state has a strong interest in maintaining the life of a patient, particularly when that patient has a serious illness. In *Bouvia v. Superior Court of California*,[58] a hospital sought permission to feed a competent 26-year-old woman with cerebral palsy who refused to eat in an attempt to cause her own death. The California state court found that she had a constitutionally protected privacy interest in refusing treatment, and prohibited her being fed against her wishes.

2.3.2 Incompetent Patients

Incompetent patients do not lose their right to make medical decision and forego life-sustaining treatment; however, their rights must be exercised through a surrogate decision maker. If a decision to refuse or withdraw life-sustaining treatment is to be made for an incompetent patient, then one of three standards is used: the subjective standard; the substituted-judgment standard; or the best-interest standard.

The subjective standard is evidence of the patient's subjective wishes regarding treatment. A good example of the subjective wishes of the patient would be an advance directive.[59] The substituted-judgment standard is when a proxy makes decisions based upon what she believes the patient would want. The best-interest standard permits the decisions to be made in the best interest of the patient. Different states require or permit different standards to be used, depending upon the circumstances. For instance, the best-interest standard most often is appropriate when a patient has never been competent, such as mentally handicapped patient, and there is no indication of what the patient would want in such a circumstance.[60]

The constitutional interests involved in end-of-life decisions often have arisen in the context of determining the standard that the state can require before the decision to withdraw or withhold life-sustaining treatment from an incompetent patient must be honored. In *Cruzan*,[61] Missouri law provided that care could not be withdrawn from an incompetent patient without clear and convincing evidence of the patient's wishes, which must have been articulated prior to the patient becoming incompetent (i.e., the subjective standard). The U.S. Supreme Court recognized that the state had interests in preserving life, and permitted the state to prevent life-sustaining treatment from being withdrawn from an incompetent patient unless such a standard was met.

---

[58] *Bouvia v. Superior Court of California*, 225 Cal. Rptr. 297 (Ct. App. 1986).
[59] *See* Section 2.3.4.
[60] *See, e.g., Belchertown v. Saikewicz; In re Conroy*, 486 A.2d 1209 (N.J. 1985).
[61] *Cruzan, supra.*

2.3.3 Damages for Rendering Unwanted Care

Despite the well-settled law that a competent person is able to refuse treatment which may cause the patient's death, and despite well settled law that a patient needs to consent to treatment, courts are very inconsistent about permitting patients to recover damages when a health care provider preserves the life or health of the patient against his or her wishes. Often, the courts' reasoning in refusing such compensation is that saving one's life or health is not damage and, consequently, is not compensable. This position of the courts is seen with particular frequency in cases when a patient is not terminally ill and yet refuses medical treatment that could restore the patient to health. A health care provider faced with a patient who is refusing treatment that might restore her to a full life may wish to weigh the potential liability that could flow from wrongfully not rendering treatment versus the liability from wrongfully treating a patient. Given the court's reluctance to grant significant (or any) damages when a person's life has been maintained, and given the significant damages that could flow from wrongful death, a provider faced with a difficult decision may wish to seek judicial intervention prior to withdrawing or withholding treatment from a competent patient who is not terminally ill.

2.3.4 Advance Directives

With the increase in the health care provider's technological ability to maintain patients' lives, and the growing public awareness of the possibility of having life supports and other highly invasive health care services at the end of life, many people began to write down their wishes about the medical care they want or do not want should they become incompetent to express their wishes. Most states have now legislatively authorized competent adults to execute advance directives regarding health care that can later be used if the person becomes incompetent to make those decisions.

Two types of advance directives generally are used: the living will and the durable power of attorney for health care. Most states have statutes that are very specific about the legal formalities of advance directives (e.g., requiring witnesses or notarization). While the structure and validity of advance directives is a matter of state law, the Patient Self-Determination Act of 1990[62] requires that, at the time of admission to a federal Medicare or Medicaid participating hospital or a nursing facility, or upon enrollment in a participating home health agency, the health care provider must give the patient information about her rights under state law to execute advance directives. Additionally, each health maintenance organization (HMO) must give patients the same information upon a subscriber's enrollment into the HMO. For patients without advance directives, the law continues to be problematic as to who may exercise a patient's wishes and what standard of evidence is necessary, as was evident with the much publicized case of Terri Schiavo in which Ms. Schiavo's husband and parents disagreed as to the withdrawal of treatment and she had no advance directive.

2.3.4.1 Living Wills

Living wills are documents that specify what a person wants to transpire regarding health care should the patient become incompetent and unable to express her own wishes. Living wills generally

---

[62] 42 U.S.C. § 1395cc.

are limited to the issue of whether the patient wants life-sustaining treatment withdrawn or withheld, when a patient is terminally ill or in a persistent vegetative state.

2.3.4.2 Durable Powers of Attorney for Health Care

Durable powers of attorney for health care are documents designating a surrogate decision maker who is empowered to make a wide range of treatment decisions for the patient in the event that the patient is not competent. Durable powers of attorney for health care have greater applicability than living wills because they can be used in circumstances that do not involve life-sustaining or end-of-life treatment. Many states require that, in order for the surrogate decision maker to make decisions regarding the withdrawal or refusal of life-sustaining treatment, the patient must be in a terminal condition or persistent vegetative state, and that the durable power of attorney must specifically grant the surrogate decisionmaker the authority to refuse such treatments. State laws vary as to how end-of-life decisions may be made for incompetent patients without advance directives.

2.3.4.3 Do-Not-Resuscitate Protocols

If a patient is an inpatient in a hospital or nursing home, generally all life sustaining treatment will be rendered in the case of a patient arrest unless a physician has written an order not to resuscitate the patient. Those are known as "Do-Not-Resuscitate" (DNR) orders. Patients who had living wills or durable powers of attorney which indicated that the patient did not want life sustaining treatment have been resuscitated in hospitals in emergency situations because the advance directives were not available. In response to this perceived problem, some states have passed legislation permitting physicians to write DNR orders which individuals wear as armbands or carry as wallet cards. These actual physicians' orders to not resuscitate the patient are to be honored when a patient reaches the hospital or nursing home. The laws also address the immunity from liability for health care providers that follow such orders.

2.3.5 Medical Futility

While it is now well established that patients and their surrogates may refuse life sustaining medical treatment, a growing area of discussion is whether a physician may refuse to provide medical treatment when the patient or her surrogates want treatment but the physician has determined that care is futile and will be of no benefit or only short term benefit. Some state statutes refer to "medically ineffective health care" as care which in reasonable medical judgment will not cure a patient's illness. Courts, when faced with the issue of whether a patient's or surrogate's wishes to continue treatment prevail over the physician's request to discontinue care the physician feels is futile, have been mixed.[63]

In 1999, Texas enacted legislation which allows a physician, if supported by the hospital Ethics Committee after a due process proceeding, to withdraw treatment considered futile by the physician.[64] Under the legislation, the patient's family or representative has 10 days after the due process

---

[63] *See, e.g., Gilgunn v. Mass. Gen. Hosp.* No. 92-4820, Mass Super Ct (1995); *In re Helga Wanglie*, PX-91-238 Minn Dist Ct. Probate Division (1991); *In re Baby K*, 16 F.3d 590 (1990).
[64] Tex. Advance Directives Act, 166 TEX. HEALTH & SAFETY CODE, see § 166.046.

procedure has resulted in a decision to withdraw the care in which to find a facility which will accept and treat the patient. If no facility can be found, the futile treatment may be withdrawn. The Texas law has been invoked many times, often amidst controversy. This area of the law can be expected to develop significantly over the next few years as providers, legislators, and courts grapple with how to handle cases where patients and families want care continued which providers consider to be futile.

While no states other than Texas have enacted a detailed medical futility process, many states have passed immunity laws for physicians who make medical decisions based on the physician's medical judgment that treatment won't be curative,[65] or that provide that in end of life situations health care providers are not obligated to provide care not likely to provide life.[66]

2.3.6 Physician-Assisted Death

Health care providers and the public alike are divided in their views as to whether a competent patient's right to choose to forego or withdraw life-sustaining medical treatment should include the right to have a physician assist in ending a person's life. Suicide—the taking of one's own life—is not a crime, although state laws vary as to whether assisting someone in a suicide is punishable. The issue of physician-assisted death first became a prominent legal and ethical issue with the activities of Dr. Jack Kevorkian in the 1990s.

Initiatives to legalize physician-assisted death were first considered in the state of Washington in 1991 and by California in 1992, where neither initiative passed. Since that time, four states have passed laws permitting physician-assisted suicide and one state, Montana, by judicial decision, permits assisted death. In 1994, voters in Oregon passed an initiative to allow physicians, after screening adult patients for competency and other criteria, to either provide a patient with a prescription for a lethal overdose of medication or to start an IV which the patient could control to cause the patient's death.[67] In 2008, Washington became the second state to pass an initiative to legalize physician-assisted death.[68] In 2013 and 2015, the Vermont General Assembly and the California General Assembly, respectively, passed legislation permitting physician-assisted death.[69] In 2016, Colorado by voter initiation became the sixth state to legalize physician-assisted suicide.

The Supreme Court of Montana ruled late in 2009 that physicians could not be prosecuted for assisting their patients to end their own lives, thereby making physician-assisted death also legal in Montana.[70]

A majority of other states have specific laws making it a crime for a physician to assist a patient's death, while a few states have no law, but leave the issue to prosecutorial discretion to charge physicians under the states' general criminal laws (such as laws preventing murder and assault).

Physician-assisted death initiatives have been placed on many state ballots, and it is expected over time that more states' voters will pass initiatives or state legislatures will pass statutes that authorize

---

[65] *See* DEL. CODE ANN. Title 16 § 2501(m).
[66] N.J. STAT. ANN § 26:2H-67.
[67] OR. REV. STAT §§ 127.800 to 127.897.
[68] *See* the Washington Death with Dignity Act, WA. REV. CODE, Chapter 70.245b.
[69] 18 V.S.A. 113 § 5281–5292.
[70] *See Baxter v. Montana*, 2009 Mt. 449.

patients to receive lethal drug prescriptions from their physicians, provide immunity to physicians who engage in such actions in accordance with their patient's wishes, or both. All of the physician-assisted death laws only apply to physicians assisting in the death of competent patients. So although durable powers of attorney and living wills provide that a person may direct that medical care be withheld or withdrawn if the person becomes incompetent, there is currently no legally recognized manner, even in those states permitting physician-assisted death, by which a patient may in advance request that a physician affirmatively assist with the patient's death if the patient becomes incompetent.

In 1997 the U.S. Supreme Court addressed whether an individual has a constitutionally protected right to have a physician assist in his or her suicide. In the companion cases of *Washington v. Glucksberg*[71] and *Vacco v. Quill*,[72] the Court determined that there was no constitutionally-protected interest and state law prohibiting physician-assisted death does not violate a person's constitutional right to due process or equal protection. The Court determined that, unlike the decision to withdraw or refuse life-sustaining treatment, the ability to commit suicide is not a constitutionally protected interest, and therefore a state may prohibit individuals from assisting a person to commit suicide. The Court also rejected the argument that a prohibition on physician-assisted death was a denial of equal protection. The proponents of physician-assisted death had argued that, because competent patients who had medical conditions that allowed them to die without life-sustaining treatment had a constitutionally protected right to refuse such treatment (and could therefore cause their own death by refusing or withdrawing such medical treatment), those ill patients who could not effect their own death by the withdrawal of treatment were denied equal protection by the law refusing them affirmative intervention to end their lives.

The Supreme Court decisions in *Vacco* and *Quill* left to the individual states the decision of whether physician-assisted death is permitted or prohibited in that state. In November 6, 2001, U.S. Attorney General John Ashcroft attempted to block Oregon's assisted-suicide law by authorizing federal agents to sanction physicians who prescribe medications to assist their terminally ill patients' death for violating the Controlled Substance Act of 1970. The U.S. Supreme Court, however, ruled that the Justice Department lacks the authority to directly counteract a state law in such a manner.[73]

The states are clearly split on the issue of physician-assisted suicide with only five states clearly permitting it, a number of states legislatively prohibiting it, and the majority of states not directly addressing the issue. In any state without specific authorization of physician-assisted suicide, however, physicians may face charges for assisting someone in ending their lives, depending upon state criminal laws.[74]

2.4 Disclosure and Protection of Patient Medical Information

2.4.1 Patient Confidentiality

Health care providers are subject to a wide spectrum of laws and regulations governing the maintenance and disclosure of information. With the passage of the Health Insurance Portability and Accountability Act of 1996 (HIPAA) a comprehensive nation-wide policy came into effect regarding

---

[71] *Washington v. Glucksberg*, 117 S. Ct. 2258 (1997).
[72] *Vacco v. Quill*, 117 S. Ct. 2293 (1997).
[73] *Gonzales v. Oregon*, 543 U.S. 1145 (2005).
[74] See *People v. Kevorkian*, 205 Mich. App. 180, 517 N.W.2d 293 (1994).

patient privacy.[75] HIPAA has been enacted via a series of rules promulgated by DHHS, including the Privacy, Security, and Enforcement Rules in 2003[76] (as updated from time to time) and the Breach Notification Rule in 2013.[77] Each of these rules will be discussed later in this section. Because of the federal supremacy clause, HIPAA applies unless a state law is more stringent. Consequently, practitioners should always be aware of applicable state laws and whether such laws are more or less stringent than federal requirements.

Additionally, as a matter of policy or requirements imposed by licensing boards or accrediting agencies, health care providers keep information about their patients confidential unless release of such information is mandated by state or federal law. It is important to know that HIPAA itself does not create a private cause of action. A patient who believes his confidentiality has been breached may file a complaint against the provider with the Office of Civil Rights of the Department of Health and Human Services (OCR) and the provider may be sanctioned, but HIPAA does not provide other recourse to the patient. Patients seeking damages for violations of their privacy must find a state legal theory on which to base their complaint, such as negligence or other torts or contract. However, many states take HIPAA obligations to set the standard of care for negligence and other tort claims.[78]

In addition to their obligations under federal law, physicians and many other health care professionals are obligated by their licensing statutes to keep patient information confidential. Therefore, if a health care professional releases confidential information, the professional may be subject to professional disciplinary action, and the patient may have a cause of action for such release based either on the state statute or in tort law. Some states' licensure statutes covering hospitals and other health care facilities also require such facilities to keep patient information confidential, and accreditation criteria of the JC and the AOA require information to remain confidential.

In addition to a general right to confidentiality, certain types of information have been subject to heightened protection. For instance, most states place significant restrictions on the release of HIV and acquired immunity deficiency syndrome (AIDS) information;[79] federal law prohibits the release of information regarding anyone receiving drug abuse or alcohol treatment, unless compliance with federal confidentiality protections is at issue;[80] and many state laws protect the release of mental-health information.[81]

Unless a specific state or federal statute governed the release of information, patients who felt their information was released improperly had to base an action either on the breach of an implied contract or an assertion of negligence. In a few instances, invasion-of-privacy or defamation actions could have been supported. In defending these cases, health care providers often were permitted to

---

[75] Health Insurance Portability and Accountability Act of 1996, Pub. L. No. 104-191.
[76] *See* 45 C.F.R. Part 160 and Part 164, Subpart E.
[77] 45 C.F.R. §§ 164.400 *et seq.*
[78] *Byrne v. Avery Ctr. for Obstetrics & Gynecology, P.C.*, 102 A.3d 32, 36 (Conn. 2014); *Walgreen Co. v. Hinchy*, 21 N.E. 99, 105 (Ind. Ct. App. 2014) on reh'g, 25 N.E.3d 748 (Ind. Ct. App. 2015); *Acosta v. Byrum*, 638 S.E.2d 246, 249 (N.C. App. 2006).
[79] *See, e.g.*, OHIO REV. CODE § 2739.02.
[80] Comprehensive Alcohol Abuse and Alcoholism Prevention, Treatment, and Rehabilitation Act of 1970, 42 U.S.C. § 290dd-2; Drug Abuse Office and Treatment Act of 1972, 42 U.S.C. § 290ee-3.
[81] *See, e.g.*, OHIO REV. CODE § 3793.12(c).

show that they had acted reasonably in the disclosure of the information, and that the disclosure of the information was to further the valid needs of the health care provider.

A few states have recognized the tort of breach of confidence, which significantly broadens patient protection for release of information. These cases have made it clear that release of patient information, even if done for a valid purpose for the health care provider, will not be permitted without patient consent. However, some states have held that if the information was released validly under HIPAA, the health care provider had met its obligations of confidentiality.[82]

In *Biddle v. Warren General Hospital*,[83] an Ohio hospital was releasing patient information to its attorneys so that its attorneys could review the patient information and determine if payment should be sought from certain third-party payers. The Ohio Supreme Court held that, absent specific authorization by the patient, the hospital could not turn the records over to its attorneys; no Ohio statutory authority permitted an attorney to obtain confidential patient information. It should be noted that the attorney/client privilege prevents attorneys from testifying about confidential client matters, but does not address an attorney's right to access confidential information given to clients.[84]

In light of this and other cases recognizing the right of patients' to confidentiality, health care providers should ensure that the Notice of Privacy Practices that they provide to their patients and any other authorizations (discussed later) are broad and make it clear that health care providers may give information to attorneys, consultants, and others determined by the health care provider to need such information for the efficient operation of the health care provider.

2.4.2 Mandatory Disclosure

Health care providers are required to release patient information (and therefore will not be liable to the patient for such release) when such a release is mandated by law.

2.4.2.1 *Judicial Disclosure*

Public policy generally requires full disclosure of relevant information in litigation. Therefore, absent common law or statutes giving special protection to information, no person or entity may refuse to testify or produce documents as part of judicial process, and all relevant evidence is admissible in court and discoverable in preparation for trial.

In derogation of the rule of full disclosure of relevant information in litigation, most states have adopted a privilege for communications between health care professionals and their patients. Three major public-policy reasons often are cited for the physician-patient privilege:

- encouraging honest communication between patients and health care workers;

---

[82] *OhioHealth Corp. v. Ryan*, No. 10AP-937, 2012-OH-60 (10th Dist. App., January 10, 2012).
[83] *Biddle v. Warren General Hospital*, 86 Ohio St. 3d 395 (1999).
[84] While *Biddle* is a cautionary tale, it was decided before the HIPAA Privacy Rule was in effect. When an Ohio Appeals Court took up a similar issue in *OhioHealth Corp. v. Ryan*, No. 10AP-937, 2012-OH-60 (10th Dist. App. Jan. 10, 2012), the court made clear that while it would have decided *Biddle* the same as it did in 1999, this was because the hospital in *Biddle* gave its attorneys the *entire* medical record, which was far more than necessary for the attorney to recommend seeking payment.

- protecting patient privacy; and
- protecting the ethics of the medical profession.

Because no physician-patient privilege exists under common law, each state statute has identified those health care professionals covered under the privilege.[85] Some states have physician-patient privilege statutes which are broader than HIPAA in preventing disclosure of information in response to the judicial process.[86] Since HIPAA sets a minimum standard of protection and does not preempt more stringent state law, state statutes must always be considered.

Rule 501 of the Federal Rules of Evidence provides that, for civil federal cases based upon state claims, privileges are determined by state law; further, for all other federal cases, the privileges are based upon federal common law. Generally, no common-law recognition of a communication privilege exists between health care professionals and patients; as a result, no privilege exists for communications made to health care professionals in cases based upon federal claims.[87] The Supreme Court, in *Jaffee v. Redmond*,[88] recognized a common-law privilege between psychotherapists and their patients; to date, however, the Court has not broadened the privilege to cover other professionals.

2.4.2.2 Mandatory Reporting of Medical Conditions and Duty to Warn

Health care providers are subject to a broad range of reporting requirements that take precedence over confidentiality requirements. Mandatory reporting requirements cover a wide spectrum of reportable events, including births, deaths, infectious diseases, child and elderly abuse, cancer, abortions, and others.

A health care provider may also be required to release confidential information when such information is necessary for the protection of a third party. This "duty-to-warn" or "duty to protect" doctrine generally arises in the context of a physician's duty to warn a third party of a communicable illness of the physician's patient, or the duty to warn a third party of the violent propensities of the physician's patient. The best-known case establishing the duty to warn is *Tarasoff v. Regents of Univ. of California*, in which the court determined that, when a psychiatrist determines that a patient poses a direct threat against a third party, the psychiatrist must take steps to warn or protect the third party. In this case, a voluntary outpatient told his psychiatrist that he intended to murder a readily identifiable woman. The psychiatrist did not warn the woman of the danger and, after the patient did in fact kill the woman, her parents successfully sued the psychiatrist for failing to warn her that she was in danger.[89]

State laws regarding a health care provider's duty to warn a person of potential danger from a patient who the provider is treating are undergoing sweeping changes in light of the mass shootings at places such as Aurora, Colorado and Newtown, Connecticut by persons who had been treated

---

[85] Ohio, for instance, recognizes a privilege for patient communications to their physicians, dentists, podiatrists (OHIO REV. CODE ANN. § 2317.02(B)(1)); psychologists (OHIO REV. CODE ANN. § 4732.19); and counselors and social workers (OHIO REV. CODE ANN. § 2317.02(G)).
[86] *See Turk v. Oiler*, 732 F. Supp.2d 758 (2010).
[87] *See United States v. Bek*, 493 F.3d 790 (7th Cir. July 6, 2007) and *Whalen v. Roe*, 429 U.S. 589, 602 n. 28 (1977) ("The physician-patient evidentiary privilege is unknown to the common law.")
[88] *Jaffee v. Redmond*, 518 U.S.1 (1996).
[89] *Tarrasoff v. Rights of Univ. of Calif.*, 17 Cal. 3d 425, 131 Cal. Rptr. 14, 551 P.2d 334 (1976).

for mental illness. At this time, only four (4) states have no significant duty to warn laws, while a majority of states' laws require certain professionals to either warn potential victims or the police of a patient's violent propensities and the remainder of the states provide immunity to providers who voluntarily choose to make such reports.

2.4.3 HIPAA Privacy Rules

HIPAA established standards and requirements for health care providers, health plans, and health care clearinghouses (Covered Entities) to protect confidential patient information. The regulations implementing HIPAA's privacy standards are complex, covering a wide range of topics.[90]

HIPAA's privacy standards impacting Covered Entities and individuals can be organized into four major areas:

- administrative and training requirements;
- the requirement for policies, procedures, and forms regarding how patient information is used and disclosed;
- certain requirements regarding patient access to their own information;
- the requirement to notify patients if their information has been breached; and
- the requirement for agreements and policies regarding how Business Associates keep information confidential.

HIPAA privacy regulations generally do not preempt state laws that are more stringent than the HIPAA privacy standards regarding patient confidentiality or reporting. HIPAA's goal to create uniform confidentiality standards across the states may, in large part, remain unrealized if states maintain or develop confidentiality laws that are more stringent than HIPAA. To date, only a few states have enacted such more stringent requirements than those in the HIPAA regulations.[91]

2.4.3.1 Administrative Requirements and Training

Three basic administrative requirements are posed by the HIPAA privacy regulations: covered individuals and entities must designate a privacy officer; they must train their workforce on HIPAA requirements, emphasizing privacy policies and procedures;[92] and they must put in place administrative safeguards. All new employees must be trained within a reasonable time of their hiring. Compliance with this requirement is to be repeated when material changes are made to the covered individual or entity's privacy policies. It is also highly recommended that ongoing training and reminders be given in response to persistent threats, including threats from malware and e-mail scams. Administrative safeguards include implementing policies and procedures to prevent, detect,

---

[90] Final rules implementing HIPAA privacy standards were originally published on December 28, 2000 (65 Fed. Reg. 82462 (2000)) and were modified on August 14, 2002 (67 Fed. Reg. 53181 (2002)) and again in 2009 (Pub. L. No. 111-005). Compliance was required for most Covered Entities and individuals as of April 14, 2003; and the Health Information Technology for Economic and Clinical Health (HITECH) enacted as part of the American Recovery and Reinvestment Act, Public Law 111-005.
[91] *See, e.g.*, Texas Medical Records Privacy Act, TEXAS HEALTH AND SAFETY CODE, § 181, and New Jersey S562.
[92] 45 C.F.R. § 164.530(b)(1).

contain, and correct security violations, conducting the security awareness training discussed above, and putting into place reasonable processes and procedures to (i) perform periodic security updates; (ii) guard against, detect, and report malicious software; (iii) monitor log-in attempts and report discrepancies; and (iv) manage passwords, including creating, changing, and safeguarding passwords.[93] To this end, the privacy officer is charged with maintaining compliance with federal and state law regarding HIPAA and privacy issues.

2.4.3.2 Use and Disclosure of Protected Health Information

The basic tenet of HIPAA's privacy-related concerns is that protected health information (PHI) may not be used or disclosed unless the disclosure is authorized by the patient or specifically permitted by HIPAA. (Information that cannot identify the patient in any way is not covered by HIPAA restrictions; it is important to note, however, that very specific rules exist as to what constitutes "de-identified" information, and such information frequently has limited uses.)

HIPAA permits PHI to be used without patient consent for treatment, payment, or health care operations. The basic standard of HIPAA, however, is that the use of PHI must be limited to the minimum amount necessary to accomplish the purpose of the disclosure. An exception to this "minimum necessary" standard is where the disclosure is made for treatment purposes. Therefore, if a Covered Entity is disclosing PHI to another provider involved in the patient's treatment, or is making an internal disclosure for treatment purposes, then HIPAA permits full disclosure in the interest of the patient's safety and care. If the Covered Entity is using the information internally for payment or operation's purposes, or is disclosing information to others for any reason other than treatment purposes, then care must be taken to release only the information that is necessary. This means that, even within an institutional health care provider, access to patient information should be limited to those having a need to know the information. Consistent with the training requirement of the Privacy Rules, a provider's workforce therefore needs to be trained to limit the sharing of information between staff.

Release of information for any purpose other than treatment, payment, and health care operations may be made only with the patient's specific authorization unless otherwise permitted by HIPAA. The disclosures permitted under HIPAA are generally related to disclosures required by law (such as mandatory reporting to state agencies), to law enforcement in special circumstances and for certain litigation purposes. Providers may not condition the provision of services on the execution of such an authorization.[94]

---

[93] 45 C.F.R. § 164.308(a)(5).
[94] The privacy regulations are quite specific about the contents of authorizations. Authorizations are required to contain the following:
1. description of the information to be used or disclosed;
2. identification of the persons or class of persons authorized to make the disclosure of the PHI;
3. identification of the persons or class of persons to whom the Covered Entity is authorized to make the disclosure;
4. description of each purpose of the disclosure;
5. an expiration date or expiration criteria;
6. signature and date, or statement of authorization for someone signing on behalf of the patient;
7. statement that the patient may revoke the authorization in writing, and directions as to how that may occur (with a reference to the Covered Entity's notice of privacy practices);

To comply with the privacy regulations, health care providers should review carefully and develop policies regarding release of information to family, friends, clergy, and government personnel (upon request), pursuant to mandatory reporting laws and pursuant to subpoenas. The privacy regulations have tried to be neutral with respect to minors' rights to privacy, and providers should carefully review state law regarding minors in light of the privacy regulations. The regulations also address how covered individuals and entities may use patient identity and information for marketing and fundraising purposes and inclusion in a hospital directory.

2.4.3.3 Patient Rights under HIPAA

Patients are provided with very specific rights under HIPAA relative to their own information. Patients are permitted to request restrictions on how their information is to be used (although Covered Entities may not need to agree to such restrictions), the right to inspect and copy their patient information, the right to request amendments to their patient information, the right to receive an accounting of how their information has been disclosed (except for treatment, payment and health care operations) and the right to receive the Covered Entities Notice of Privacy Practice.

2.4.3.4 Notice of Privacy Practices

The privacy regulations contain specific requirements for Covered Entities to notify patients of the privacy practices of the Covered Entity. This notice is to be presented when the patient initially obtains services from the provider. If these practices change, patients must be notified of such changes. Additionally, providers with a direct-treatment relationship with the patient must make a good-faith effort to obtain the patient's written acknowledgement of receipt of the provider's notice of privacy practices.

Final modifications of the regulations require the patient's acknowledgement be in writing, but give no other direction concerning its form. Providers may adopt whatever form best suits their practices. DHHS has model notices on its website in several forms and in several languages.

The notice requirement may be particularly problematic, because the first encounter with a patient may be by telephone, in an emergency, or another manner in which presentation of the notice may not be feasible. DHHS has provided the following potentially helpful guidance:

- if the first treatment encounter is by telephone, then the provider may satisfy the notice provision by mailing notice to the patient no later than the day of that service, and may include an acknowledgement form to be returned by the patient;
- an initial contact to schedule an appointment does not trigger the notice or acknowledgement requirements;
- if a provider renders services electronically, then DHHS expects it to give notice and obtain an acknowledgement in that form;

---

8. statement that treatment, payment, and other benefits may not be conditioned on the execution of the authorization (or, if an exception under the privacy regulations is met, a statement of the repercussions of any refusal to execute the authorization); and
9. statement that the PHI may be redisclosed by the recipient.

- if a provider revises its notice form, then a new patient acknowledgement is not required unless the patient requests a copy of the revised notice; and
- notice and acknowledgement forms may be included in other mailings to patients, so long as a notice and an authorization are not combined.

2.4.3.5 Breach Notification

The HIPAA Breach Notification Rule requires covered entities and business associates to notify individuals when unsecured protected health information has been breached.[95] Generally, a breach is defined as an impermissible use or disclosure of protected health information that compromises the security or privacy of such information. Notification is only required if the breach involved unsecured protected health information, that is, protected health information that has not been rendered unusable, unreadable, or indecipherable to unauthorized persons through the use of a technology or methodology specified by the Secretary of DHHS. After a breach of unsecured protected health information, covered entities must provide notification of the breach to affected individuals, the Secretary, and, in certain circumstances, to the media. Business associates must also notify covered entities if a breach occurs at or by the business associate.

2.4.3.6 Business Associate Agreements and Policies

HIPAA regulations address the situation of PHI being released from a covered individual or entity to another entity or individual, and provide that the information should not lose its protected nature. The government has extended the protections given the information when maintained by Covered Entities and individuals by requiring that such Covered Entities and individuals enter into contracts with their Business Associates, requiring their Business Associates to keep information confidential and subject the information to the same protections required by the initial Covered Entity. To accomplish this, providers and other Covered Entities must enter into contracts with their Business Associates requiring their Business Associates to maintain the information in a manner similar to the Covered Entity or individual, although changes to the law, effective September 23, 2013, have made business associates subject to civil and criminal penalties directly from the federal government.

While Covered Entities and individuals are free to develop their own Business Associate Agreements, DHHS has provided sample agreements in the Privacy Regulations for the use of Covered Entities and individuals may use. Covered Entities and providers need to enter into agreements with their Business Associates covering the release of PHI. These agreements must be in writing, even if the underlying agreement with the Business Associate is an oral agreement. Failure to have written business associate agreements and update those agreements as a result of changes in law can come at a high cost. A recent settlement with Care New England Health System (CNE) and OCR for $400,000 and a comprehensive corrective action plan was directly related to CNE's failure to update its written business associate agreement with a third party when the law changed in 2013.[96]

---

[95] The Federal Trade Commission enforces similar breach notification provisions for vendors of personal health records and their third party service providers.
[96] *See* DHHS announcement *at* https://www.hhs.gov/hipaa/for-professionals/compliance-enforcement/agreements/wih#sthash.STPNPQmE.dpuf.

2.4.3.7 Sanctions and Enforcement

Enforcement authority for HIPAA's privacy regulations has been placed with the DHHS' Office of Civil Rights (OCR). Criminal penalties and civil monetary penalties alike exist for violations. For unintentional violations, a $100 penalty per occurrence may be assessed, to a maximum of $25,000 per year for the same type of violation. No penalties will be assessed if failure to comply is due to reasonable cause, rather than willful neglect, provided that the person or entity takes action to correct the failure during the first 30 days following either actual knowledge or imputed knowledge of the noncompliance. The OCR is also granted the right to conduct compliance reviews of providers.[97] There is no private right of action for a HIPAA violation,[98] although there may be a private right of action under state law and HIPAA regulations may be cited as the standard of care.

Criminal penalties, including imprisonment, have been established for obtaining information under false pretenses, as well as obtaining information with the intent to sell, transfer, or use the information. The Secretary of DHHS also is authorized to perform compliance audits. One of the biggest current concerns of observers and practitioners is that HIPAA requirements will set the standard for maintaining health information, and that private malpractice suits may be brought for HIPAA violations.

2.5 Conclusion

Patient-care issues continue to be timely and significant, with hospital ethics committees, courts, and politicians addressing related concerns. In large part, these issues are governed by state law; the practicing attorney must take care to know the law of the applicable state.

---

[97] *See* enforcement guidelines, 70 Fed. Reg. 20227–29 (Apr. 18, 2005).
[98] *See, e.g., Rigaud v. Garofalo*, No. Civ A. 04-1866, 2005 U.S. Dist. LEXIS 8735 (E.D. Pa. May 2, 2005).

3

Medicare

Barry D. Alexander
Anthony H. Choe
Raymond J. Lindholm
Ross E. Sallade
Polsinelli, PC

3.1   Introduction

Health care in America has been and continues to be big business. Health care spending consumed approximately 17.2% of the total U.S. gross domestic product (GDP) in 2012.[1] By the year 2022 health care spending is projected to comprise 19.9% of GDP, with 50% of total health care spending coming from government sponsored programs.[2] The Centers for Medicare and Medicaid Services (CMS) is one of the largest purchasers of health care services in the world, having spent a combined $1.12 trillion on health care services in 2012.[3] CMS administers or oversees administration of the Medicare, Medicaid, and State Children's Health Insurance Programs providing health care for one in four Americans. Medicare enrollment has increased from 19 million in 1966 to more than 52 million beneficiaries for fiscal year 2013.[4]

In fiscal year 2013, CMS outlayed approximately $773.4 billion, of which total Medicare benefits alone were approximately $498.6 billion.[5] Total outlays spent by Medicare represent approximately 22% of total federal outlays—only the Social Security Administration outlayed more at $867.4 billion.[6] CMS now predicts that Medicare, which now comprises 3.6% of total GDP, will increase to 9.8% by 2087.[7]

---

[1] Centers for Medicare & Medicaid Services, *National Health Care Expenditures 2012 Highlights*.
[2] *Id.*
[3] Centers for Medicare & Medicaid Services, *National Health Expenditures by Type of Service and Source of Funds: Calendar Years 1960 to 2012*, at www.cms.hhs.gov/NationalHealthExpendData/downloads/highlights.pdf.
[4] Centers for Medicare & Medicaid Services, *Financial Report, Fiscal Year 2013*, at http://www.cms.gov/Research-Statistics-Data-and-Systems/Statistics-Trends-and-Reports/CFOReport/Downloads/2013_CMS_Financial_Report.pdf.
[5] *Id.*
[6] *Id.*
[7] *2013 Annual report of the Boards of Trustees of the Federal Hospital Insurance and Federal Supplementary Medical Insurance Trust Funds*, at https://www.cms.hhs.gov/ReportsTrustFunds/downloads/tr2010.pdf; *see also* http://www.cms.gov/Research-Statistics-Data-and-Systems/Statistics-Trends-and-Reports/ReportsTrustFunds/index.html?redirect=/reportstrustfunds/.

3.1.1 The Evolution of Medicare Policy and Law

Well into the late 19th century, U.S. health care was delivered in a two-tiered arrangement. The first tier catered to the well-to-do, who could afford to pay for health care services. These individuals were treated at home by trained physicians and nursed to health by relatives. The second tier was reserved for the destitute—primarily the young, the aged, and the disabled. The destitute received medical care through a patchwork system of local charities and poorly-trained volunteers. The delivery of health care services, long the domain of local physicians and charities, remained largely outside of the government purview.

The period between 1870 and 1930 witnessed an evolution in public-health practices and medical technology that greatly improved health outcomes. Soon, hospitals were being transformed into places of recovery as well as centers for medical education. As a result, the locus of health care delivery also began to move away from the home and into the hospital. Accompanying these developments were periodic discussions on a national scale over the establishment of a government health-insurance program.

The 1930s witnessed the advent of the federal role in social-welfare issues. Sparked by the Great Depression and the need to "alleviate the unpredictable and uneven incidence of medical costs," President Franklin Roosevelt's administration gave serious consideration to launching a national health-insurance initiative.[8] Fierce opposition by the American Medical Association (AMA), however, coupled with the failure to achieve a consensus on financing the plan, ultimately caused the initiative to be dropped from the proposed social-security legislation.[9]

The role of the federal government in social-welfare issues became institutionalized with the passage of the Social Security Act in 1935.[10] Congress used Social Security to broaden and reformulate traditional public-relief coverage into distinct categories for specific population groups. Categorical eligibility quickly became a politically useful paradigm for federal policymakers to define and "solve" social-welfare problems.

At the same time, the U.S. began experimenting with the concept of voluntary health insurance. A group of Dallas schoolteachers contracted to pay Baylor Hospital a 50-cent monthly premium for a guarantee of up to 21 days of hospital care. The Baylor arrangement, which subsequently expanded to include other hospitals and employers, was later known as the "Blue Cross" plan.[11]

Federal policy during World War II prohibited salary increases but not fringe benefits to employees. This dynamic accelerated the expansion of the Blue Cross plans nationwide. As the popularity of the Blue Cross plans grew, state medical societies began offering similar physician coverage under the "Blue Shield" plan.

By the war's end, the U.S. employer-based model for health insurance had become fully institutionalized. Congress responded to the increased demand for health care services with many

---

[8] U.S. Dep't of Health & Human Servs., *Overview of the Medicare and Medicaid Programs*, HEALTH CARE FIN. REV. (Medicare & Medicaid Statistical Supp. 1998) (hereinafter *1998 Overview*).
[9] Paul Starr, *The Social Transformation of American Medicine* (1982).
[10] 42 U.S.C. §§ 301–1397jj.
[11] *See generally*, Blue Cross Blue Shield, The Health of America, https://www.bcbs.com/the-health-of-america/articles/health-insurance-invention-innovation-history-blue-cross-and-blue (last visited Dec. 20, 2017).

federal subsidies. With the adoption of the Hospital Survey and Construction Act (commonly known as Hill-Burton) in 1946, Congress made construction and modernization grants and loans available to public and nonprofit hospitals, in return for a "reasonable volume" of uncompensated medical care.[12]

The Hill-Burton subsidy greatly accelerated hospital construction and expansion in rural towns and inner cities, areas that typically were bereft of adequate health care facilities. Local governments quickly embraced hospital construction and expansion as key to their continued economic development.[13] Hospitals funded by Hill-Burton soon became symbols of local civic pride, as well as important sources of employment and medical care for the community. Federal policy thus spawned the dramatic rise in employer-funded health care plans and fueled the establishment of local community hospitals.

This further propelled the public's demand for medical services, and the cost of health care began to soar. By the end of the 1950s, health care inflation had begun to "price out" certain consumers (particularly those living on the margins or with fixed incomes) of medical care. As a result, "the widely perceived inadequacy of 'welfare medical care' under public assistance" emerged as a heated political issue on the national scene.[14] Congress responded in 1960 with the Kerr-Mills Amendments to the Social Security Act, which extended grant money to the states for the establishment of a means-tested medical-assistance program for the aged.[15]

With government subsidies of all types proliferating during this period, Congress looked to exert increasing control over programs funded by the federal government. At the same time, pressure mounted on Capitol Hill to create a national health care program for the elderly—one that was free from the stigma of welfare and the vagaries of state control. These factors, coupled with the federal largesse produced by the "New Frontier" and "Great Society" programs of the early 1960s, sparked a complex series of political maneuvers that culminated in the adoption of the Medicare and Medicaid programs in 1965.[16]

3.1.2 Chapter Overview

This Chapter provides an in-depth examination of the Medicare program. The initial sections of the Chapter offer an overview of the program's current organizational structure (Parts A, B, C, and D), followed by a review of features specific to the operation of the Medicare program (including eligibility and cost-sharing, coverage issues, and program administration). The Chapter next presents a detailed discussion of Medicare reimbursement principles and payment methodologies. Lastly, the Chapter ends with a description of the program's grievance and appeals processes, and closes with some prognostications about the future of the Medicare program. Additional resources are located in the Appendix to this Chapter, including useful websites; frequently referenced acts, laws, and programs; and relevant agencies, departments, commissions, advisory committees, and participants. The Medicare program also

---

[12] 42 U.S.C. §§ 291–291o-1. The term "Hill-Burton" refers to the sponsors of the act: Senators Lister Hill (D-AL) and Harold Burton (R-OH).
[13] Grants and loans have been made to over 6,900 facilities since Hill-Burton was implemented in 1946. *See* U.S. Dep't of Health & Human Servs., Health Resources & Servs. Admin., *The Hill-Burton Free Care Program*, at www.hrsa.gov/osp/dfcr/about/aboutdiv.htm.
[14] *1998 Overview* at 2.
[15] Social Security Amendments of 1960 (Kerr-Mills), Pub. L. No. 86-778, 74 Stat. 924 (1960).
[16] 42 U.S.C. §§ 1395–1395hhh and 1396–1396v.

has countless acronyms, abbreviations, and designations that dominate the industry's communications landscape. A listing of some of the common terminology may be found under the Glossary in Chapter 1.

3.2 Overview of the Medicare Program

Established under Title XVIII of the Social Security Act, Medicare is a social health-insurance program that provides health care coverage for Americans who are age 65 years or older. Originally established as "a health insurance program for aged persons to complement the retirement, survivors and disability insurance benefits under Title II of the Social Security Act,"[17] Medicare now insures the long-term disabled, those who require renal dialysis, and certain other persons who may buy into the program regardless of age.[18]

3.2.1 Medicare Basics

The "original" Medicare program consisted of just two parts, Part A (hospital insurance) and Part B (supplementary insurance). Congress has significantly expanded Medicare coverage options for beneficiaries, first in 1997 with the establishment of the Medicare Advantage (MA) program (Part C), and again in 2003 with the creation of the Medicare prescription-drugbenefit program (Part D). As a result, four separate components or "Parts" currently comprise the Medicare program Part A, Part B, Part C, and Part D.[19] The term "Part" refers to divisions within Title XVIII of the Social Security Act.

3.2.1.1 Part A

Borrowing from the Blue Cross model, Medicare Part A covers inpatient hospital and critical access hospital (CAH) care, skilled nursing facility (SNF) care, home health care agency (HHA) services, and hospice care. Medicare Part A is financed through the federal Hospital Insurance (HI) Trust Fund, established at the inception of the program and funded by payroll taxes from workers and employers. The HI Trust Fund balance is dependent on the fund's total income exceeding total outlays; thus, its financial health is sensitive to economic, demographic, and health care cost trends. As a result, the HI Trust Fund has hovered near insolvency at several times.[20]

3.2.1.2 Part B

Borrowing from the Blue Shield model, Medicare Part B covers physician and other professional services, hospital outpatient department services, ambulatory surgical centers (ASCs), laboratory services, some HHA services, physical and occupational therapy, diagnostic services, ambulance services, and durable medical equipment, prosthetics, orthotics, and supplies (DMEPOS). Medicare

---

[17] Health Care Fin. Admin. *Brief Summaries of Medicare and Medicaid, Title XVIII and XIX of the Social Security Act* (Nov. 1, 2006).

[18] Disability and renal dialysis were added as Medicare eligible groups in 1972. Medicare was expanded again in 1973 to include certain non-covered persons who may buy into the program under specific circumstances. U.S. Dep't of Health & Human Servs., *Overview of the Medicare and Medicaid Programs*, 22 HEALTH CARE FIN. REV. 1 (2000).

[19] Title XVII of the Social Security Act also includes a Part E (Miscellaneous Provisions), which governs additional Medicare benefit programs (e.g., Section 1899 Shared Savings Program, Section 1876 Cost Plans). Part E is not addressed separately in this chapter, although certain Part E programs will be discussed.

[20] House Comm. on Ways and Means, 108th cong., Second Session, *2004 Green Book* (Comm. Print 2004) *at* waysandmeans.house.gov/.

Part B, also known as Supplementary Medical Insurance (SMI), is a voluntary program.[21] Medicare Part A beneficiaries may elect to have Part B coverage for a monthly premium that is deducted from their Social Security checks. The major sources of revenue for the SMI Trust Fund Part B account are (i) contributions of the federal government that the law authorizes to be appropriated and transferred from the general fund of the Treasury; and (ii) premiums paid by eligible persons who voluntarily enroll. A source of revenue, which began in 2011 as a result of the Affordable Care Act (ACA), is the annual fees assessed on manufacturers and importers of brand-name prescription drugs. Because the majority of Part B coverage is financed by general revenue, bankruptcy of the SMI Trust Fund has not presented a significant concern. The Medicare Access and CHIP Reauthorization Act of 2015 (MACRA) is positioned to have significant impact on Part B payments to physicians and several other clinicians billing under the Medicare Physician Fee Schedule, with a significant shift away from fee schedule payments and toward value-based payments.

3.2.1.3 Part C

Part C or the Medicare Advantage (MA) program, enacted under the Balanced Budget Act (BBA) of 1997 and first implemented in January 1999, is an alternative to the original Medicare program under Parts A and B. This program, also voluntary, gives eligible Medicare beneficiaries the choice to access their Medicare benefits through private health plans (MA Plans) offered by public and private organizations (MA organizations) contracted with CMS.[22]

MA organizations are authorized to offer MA Plans in a variety of forms: (1) coordinated care plans (CCPs), which include health maintenance organizations (HMOs), with or without point-of-service (POS) options, local and regional preferred provider organizations (PPOs), provider-sponsored organizations (PSOs) and special needs plans (SNPs); (2) medical savings account (MSA) plans; (3) private fee-for-service (PFFS) plans; (4) Part B only plans; (5) employer group waiver plans; and (6) religious fraternal benefit (RFB) plans. In general, MA plans serve specific geographic areas comprised of individual counties and groups of counties except for regional PPOs, which operate in one or several of the 26 regions established by CMS, where a region consists of one or more states.

MA Plans must cover all Part A and Part B benefits that exist under original Medicare (Basic Benefits), and may also elect to offer other medically necessary benefits (not otherwise covered under Parts A/B/D) as Supplemental Benefits. MA plans were intended to serve smaller geographic areas and can also opt to

---

[21] SMI is distinct from the Medicare Supplement Insurance program and is discussed in Section 3.2.4.2. below.
[22] The Balanced Budget Act of 1997, Pub. L. No. 105-33, 111 Stat. 251 (1997) (hereinafter BBA). The BBA added §§ 1851–1859 to the Social Security Act establishing the M+C (now MA) program. The BBA was amended in 1999 by the Medicare, Medicaid & SCHIP Balanced Budget Refinement Act of 1999, Pub. L. No. 106-113, 113 Stat. 536, 1501A-321 (1999) (hereinafter BBRA). The BBRA provided approximately $27 billion in relief to providers over 10 years from the cuts exacted by the BBA. Amended again the following year by the Medicare, Medicaid and SCHIP Benefits Improvement and Protection Act of 2000, Pub. L. No. 106-554, 114 Stat. 2763 (2000) (hereinafter BIPA), BIPA provided approximately $35 million in relief to providers over five years from the financial blows dealt by the BBA. The BBRA and BIPA also added further refinements to the MA program. The Medicare Prescription Drug, Improvement and Modernization Act of 2003, Pub. L. No. 108-173, 117 Stat. 2066 (2003) (hereinafter MMA). The MMA's Title II affected a number of substantive changes to Medicare Part C, including changing the name to "Medicare Advantage" and added additional MA plan options. Economic improvements also were made to Medicare Part C, including a significant rate increase for managed-care plans, as well as the creation of a $10 billion plan entry-and-retention stabilization fund. The MA program was also amended in 2008 by the Medicare Improvements for Patients and Providers Act (MIPPA) and in 2010 by the Affordable Care Act (ACA).

offer other value-added items and services (VAIS) that are not plan benefits and do not incur a cost for the plan (e.g., discounts on gym memberships).[23]

Basic Benefits are financed through payments by CMS to MA organizations drawn from HI or SMI Trust Funds, in proportions calculated by CMS based on the relative actuarial value of total benefits paid for benefits under Parts A and B.[24] Finally, Supplemental Benefits are financed either through premiums paid by MA Plan enrollees or, for mandatory Supplemental Benefits, through bid rebates.[25]

As of the end of calendar year 2017, approximately 18.9 million Medicare beneficiaries were enrolled in Medicare Part C or approximately 31% of the Medicare population.[26] As discussed in greater detail below, the Affordable Care Act of 2010 made substantial changes to Medicare's payment methodology for MA Plans in an effort to curtail perceived "overpayments" to plans (payments in amounts above the costs Medicare Parts A and B would incur under the traditional FFS program) while providing bonuses to plans with high quality ratings. These changes were projected to reduce Medicare spending by $132 billion over 10 years according to the Congressional Budget Office (CBO).[27]

3.2.1.4 Part D

Medicare Part D, or the prescription drug benefit program enacted under the Medicare Prescription Drug, Improvement and Modernization Act of 2003 and first implemented on January 1, 2006, covers certain classes of outpatient prescription drugs which are not otherwise covered under Part A or B.[28] Part D covered drugs include *Medicaid*-covered prescription drugs, biologicals, and vaccines.

The Part D benefit is implemented through private insurers that contract with CMS as either standalone prescription drug plans (PDPs) or as MA prescription drug plans (MA-PDs) that offer integrated prescription drug and health care coverage.[29]

Part D benefits are financed through the Medicare Prescription Drug Account of the SMI Trust Fund and through applicable beneficiary premiums.[30] Under the Part D program, CMS makes capitated payments to plans sponsors to administer the beneficiaries' benefits under the Part D plan's CMS-approved benefit and rate structure. While there are minimum standards that all Part D plans

---

[23] *See* Section 80 to Chapter 4 of the Medicare Managed Care Manual.
[24] 42 U.S.C. § 1395w-24. Section 140.1 to Chapter 8 of the Medicare Managed Care Manual.
[25] 42 C.F.R. § 422.102(c); Section 10.3 to Chapter 4 of the Medicare Managed Care Manual.
[26] CMS Monthly Contract Summary Report – November 2017, *available at* https://www.cms.gov/Research-Statistics-Data-and-Systems/Statistics-Trends-and-Reports/MCRAdvPartDEnrolData/Monthly-Contract-and-Enrollment-Summary-Report.html; and the CMS Medicare Enrollment Dashboard (updated February 2017).
[27] Comparison of Projected Enrollment in Medicare Advantage Plans and Subsidies for Extra Benefits Not Covered by Medicare Under Current Law and Under Reconciliation Legislation Combined with H.R. 3590 as Passed by the Senate, CBO, Mar. 19, 2010.
[28] MMA, Title I (42 U.S.C. § 1395w-101 *et seq.*); *see also* 70 Fed. Reg. at 4194 (Jan. 28, 2005). Although Medicare Part D is commonly thought of as the Medicare prescription drug coverage benefit, there are a number of drugs that continue to be covered under Part B including, among others respiratory drugs (e.g., nebulizer drugs), certain injectable drugs furnished in a physicians' office, infusion drugs including many cancer drugs, oral anti-cancer drugs, oral anti-nausea drugs, ESRD drugs and blood clotting factors such as anti-hemophilic factor.
[29] 42 U.S.C. § 1395w-101(a)(1); *see also* 42 C.F.R. § 423.100.
[30] *Id.*

must meet, each plan has a certain amount of flexibility in structuring its plans in terms of prescription drugs covered, co-pays and deductibles charged and development of its distribution network.[31]

To be covered under Part D, a drug must be: (i) available only by prescription; (ii) approved by the Food and Drug Administration (FDA); (iii) used and sold in the United States; and (iv) prescribed for a medically accepted indication.[32] Insulin, certain vaccines, biological products, and medical supplies may also be covered. Part D generally does not cover drugs that may be excluded under Medicaid or certain drugs that may be eligible for Medicare Part A or Part B coverage.[33]

The definition of "Part D drug" specifically excludes those drugs or classes of drugs, or medical uses of such drugs, that may be excluded from coverage or otherwise restricted under Medicaid, with the exception of smoking cessation agents.[34] These drugs include, for example:

- drugs for anorexia, weight loss, or weight gain;
- drugs used to promote fertility;
- drugs used for cosmetic purposes or hair growth;
- drugs used for the symptomatic relief of cough and colds;
- prescription vitamins and mineral products, except prenatal vitamins and fluoride preparations;
- nonprescription drugs;
- outpatient drugs for which the manufacturer *seeks* to require that associated tests or monitoring services be purchased exclusively from the manufacturer as a condition of sale; and,
- agents used for the treatment of sexual or erectile dysfunction except under certain conditions.[35]

3.2.2 Private Contracts

Medicare also permits the use of "private contracts" between physicians, certain practitioners, and Medicare beneficiaries under which the parties may agree that no claims for reimbursement will be submitted to Medicare. In particular, a "private contract" is a contract between a Medicare beneficiary and a physician or other practitioner who has opted out of Medicare for two years for all covered items and services the physician/practitioner furnishes to Medicare beneficiaries. In a private contract, the Medicare beneficiary agrees to give up Medicare payment for services furnished by the physician/practitioner and to pay the physician/practitioner without regard to any limits that would otherwise apply to what the physician/practitioner could charge.[36]

Physicians and practitioners entering into such contracts must file an affidavit with DHHS affirming that, for two years from the date of the affidavit, they will not submit any claims to Medicare for items or services provided to *any* Medicare beneficiary, nor will they receive payment from Medicare, either directly or indirectly, for items or services provided to any beneficiary. The beneficiary must acknowledge

---

[31] *See* 42 U.S.C. § 1395w-102, 42 C.F.R. § 423.104.
[32] *See* 42 U.S.C. §§ 1395w-102(e); 1396r-8(k)(2).
[33] *See* 42 U.S.C. § 1395w-102(e)(2); *see also* 42 C.F.R. § 423.100.
[34] 42 C.F.R. § 423.100 (definition of "Part D drug").
[35] 42 U.S.C. § 1396r-8(d)(2); Section 20.1 to Chapter 6 of the Medicare Prescription Drug Benefit Manual.
[36] Medicare Benefit Policy (CMS Pub. 100-02), 15, § 40.7.

in writing her unlimited personal liability for the cost of medical care rendered under the contract. A private contract also may not be executed if the beneficiary is experiencing "an emergency or urgent health care situation."[37]

3.2.3 Excluded Services

Medicare does not pay for custodial nursing-home services; immunizations; routine physicals; hearing aids; low vision aids and services, such as for eye glasses; eye examinations; orthopedic shoes and general foot care; dental services; cosmetic surgery and related services; personal comfort services; and any other services which are not deemed to be reasonable and necessary.[38] Also, note that there are many exceptions to the above list for specific circumstances, screenings and tests.

3.2.4 Beneficiary Cost-Sharing

3.2.4.1 Premiums, Co-Payments, and Deductibles

The Medicare program routinely imposes beneficiary cost-sharing mechanisms (e.g., premiums, copayments, and deductibles). For example, Medicare Part A services are delivered in benefit periods, each known as a "spell of illness." A spell of illness begins the day the beneficiary is admitted to the hospital, and ends when the beneficiary has not received hospital or SNF services for 60 consecutive days.[39] Medicare charges Part A beneficiaries an out-of-pocket deductible for each spell of illness.[40] Unlike Part A, Medicare Part B beneficiaries are charged a single deductible per year.[41] Part B beneficiaries also incur copayments for certain medical services.[42] Similarly, MA organizations may require enrollees to contribute to the cost of covered services in the form of deductibles, copayments, or percentage of costs under certain conditions.[43] The prescription drug benefit under Medicare Part D also provides for coinsurance, premiums, and deductibles.[44]

3.2.4.2 Medicare Supplement Insurance Policies

Beneficiaries have the option of purchasing Medicare supplement plan coverage from private commercial insurers. Known as "Medigap," these policies typically offer a range of standardized coverage options for Medicare-excluded services and help defray the cost of coinsurance and deductibles for Medicare beneficiaries.[45] Medigap policies are available only to beneficiaries who are covered under Parts and B of the program. Medigap policies are not Medicare Advantage plans and beneficiaries may not have both types of coverage at the same time.

---

[37] 42 U.S.C. § 1395a; 42 C.F.R. §§ 405.400–.455.
[38] 42 C.F.R. § 411.15. Effective January 1, 2005, the MMA authorizes an initial preventative physical examination for Medicare beneficiaries within six months of enrollment in Part B. MMA, § 611. Also, commencing on January 1, 2011, Medicare now pays for an annual "Wellness Visit." ACA § 4103; 42 U.S.C. § 1395x(hhh); 42 C.F.R. § 411.15.
[39] 42 U.S.C. § 1395x(a).
[40] Id. § 1395e(a)(1). Note that no coverage is provided for stays in excess of 150 days in a benefit period.
[41] Id. § 1395l(b).
[42] Id. § 1395l(a)(1).
[43] Id. § 1395d ww-21(d), 42 C.F.R § 422.100(c).
[44] See id. § 1395w-102, 42 C.F.R. § 423.104.
[45] 42 U.S.C. § 1395ss; 42 C.F.R. §§ 403.200–.258.

3.2.4.3 Assistance for Low-Income Beneficiaries

Financial-assistance programs are available through a combination of Medicare and Medicaid coverage for low-income Medicare beneficiaries who cannot pay their Medicare premiums, coinsurance, and deductibles. These include the Qualified Medicare Beneficiary (QMB) program, the Specified Low-Income Medicare Beneficiary (SLMB) program, and the Qualifying Individual (QI) program. Known as "dual eligibles" in Medicare parlance, beneficiaries who qualify for financial assistance must have total annual incomes that match or fall below 135% of the federal poverty level (FPL).[46]

3.2.5 The Secondary Payer Rule

Medicare does not pay for services for which Medicare is not the "primary" payer. As a result, Medicare payment for any items or services that may be covered under other insurance plans or policies (e.g., workers' compensation, liability insurance, or employer health-benefit plans) or by another entity (e.g., a third party's self-insurance) is prohibited with certain exceptions.[47] Under such circumstances, Medicare's liability for payment is "secondary" to that of the other payer(s).[48] Medicare can "conditionally" pay the medical expenses of a beneficiary for whom Medicare may be the secondary payer, but has authority to recover those expenses from the beneficiary's settlement with a third party or from the entity that finances that settlement.[49] Entities that pay an award or settlement to a Medicare beneficiary or assume responsibility for a beneficiary's medical expenses must self-report the arrangement to the contractor responsible for Medicare coordination of benefits, pursuant to the so-called "Section 111" reporting rules.[50] In 2013, CMS merged the Coordination of Benefits Contractor (COBC) and the Medicare Secondary Payer Recovery Contractor (MSPRC) into the Benefits Coordination & Recovery Center (BCRC).[51] This entity will centralize and consolidate activities related to the collection, management, and reporting of other insurance coverage of Medicare beneficiaries, and the recovery of conditional payments or mistaken primary payments under the Medicare Secondary Payer (MSP) program. The Section 111 reporting obligations, coupled with contractor consolidation and federal budgetary pressures, reflect enhanced attention on the MSP Rule and enforcement of the government's authority to recoup conditional payments.

3.2.6 Other Areas Subsidized by Medicare

Medicare subsidizes the costs associated with operating approved medical residency and allied health-education training programs for teaching hospitals.[52] Hospitals that serve a high proportion of low-income patients receive additional funding from Medicare through a disproportionate-share formula adjustment. Similarly, certain rural hospitals may receive payment from Medicare at an enhanced rate.

---

[46] 42 U.S.C. § 1396d(p). *See also* 42 U.S.C. § 1395w-114 regarding subsidies for low-income beneficiaries under the Part D drug benefit and transitional drug-card program.
[47] 42 U.S.C. § 1395y(b)(2)(A).
[48] *Id.* § 1395y(b)(2); 42 C.F.R. §§ 411.32–.33.
[49] *Id.*; 42 C.F.R. §§ 411.24, 411.37.
[50] 42 U.S.C. § 1395y(b)(8). The administrative guidance for the reporting program is found under the "Coordination of Benefits & Recovery" section *at* https://www.cms.gov/Medicare/Medicare.html.
[51] *See* https://www.cms.gov/Medicare/Coordination-of-Benefits-and-Recovery/Coordination-of-Benefits-and-Recovery-Overview/Overview.html.
[52] *See generally* 42 C.F.R. § 412 subpt. G.

3.2.7 "Provider" vs. "Supplier"

The terms "provider" and "supplier" have special meanings within the Medicare program. Medicare defines "providers" as hospitals, SNFs, HHAs, hospices, CAHs and comprehensive outpatient rehabilitation facilities (CORFs).[53] Medicare defines a "supplier" as "any company, person, or agency that provides a medical item or service."[54] Such entities or persons include physicians, DME companies, ASCs, physical and occupational therapists, speech pathologists, clinical laboratories, renal-dialysis facilities, nurse midwives, physician assistants, chiropractors and audiologists.[55]

3.2.8 "Provider-Based"

The term "provider-based" refers to facilities or organizations that are operated under the name, ownership, financial, and/or administrative control of a provider, typically a hospital.[56] Such facilities/organizations may be located on or off-campus from the main provider. Historically, provider-based entities received enhanced reimbursement from Medicare under the hospital outpatient prospective payment system, and it became increasingly common for hospitals to connect physician clinics to hospital outpatient departments and seek reimbursement under the Hospital Outpatient Prospective Payment System (OPPS). Congress reacted with passage of the Bipartisan Budget Act of 2015, putting an end to higher OPPS reimbursement for new outpatient departments located off of a hospital's campus. This significant reimbursement change for hospitals operating off-campus provider-based outpatient departments is discussed later in this chapter.

3.3 Program Administration

3.3.1 Organizational Overview

Congress creates Medicare law by amendment to the Social Security Act and through the federal appropriations process. The Department of the Treasury manages the two Medicare trust funds through the Medicare Board of Trustees. Eligibility for the Medicare program is determined by the Social Security Administration (SSA). DHHS oversees the Medicare program and issues relevant regulations.

3.3.2 Centers for Medicare & Medicaid Services

3.3.2.1 Administrative History

The Social Security Administration administered the Medicare and Medicaid programs until 1977, when the newly created Health Care Financing Administration (HCFA) took over the daily operation of the programs after a reorganization of the U.S. Department of Health, Education and

---

[53] 42 U.S.C. § 1395x(u). *See also* 42 C.F.R. § 422.2 for the meaning of "provider" within the MA program.
[54] Ctrs. for Medicare & Medicaid Servs., *Medicare—Glossary*, at www.cms.hhs.gov/glossary/; 42 U.S.C. § 1395x(a).
[55] 42 U.S.C. § 1395k(a); Ctrs. for Medicare & Medicaid Servs., *Medicare Benefits Manual* (Pub. 100-02), Ch. 15, §§ 30, 60, 80, 110, 160–240, 260.
[56] 42 C.F.R. § 413.65.

Welfare (now DHHS). An operating division of DHHS, the name "HCFA" was formally changed to CMS on June 14, 2001.[57]

3.3.2.2 Structural Overview

Currently, CMS is organized around three primary service areas: "original" Medicare (Parts A and B); voluntary/optional coverage choices (Parts C and D); and state-administered programs, e.g., Medicaid and the State Children's Health Insurance Program (SCHIP)). Following the enactment of the Affordable Care Act, the Obama Administration re-organized CMS into six primary centers of operation:

- *The Center for Medicare.*[58] This center is the largest center in the Medicare program. This center is responsible for the formulation, coordination, integration, implementation, and evaluation of national Medicare program policies and operations encompassing Parts A through D of the program. This center is responsible for identifying and proposing modifications to Medicare programs and policies. This center serves as CMS's lead for management, oversight, budget and performance issues relating to Medicare Advantage and prescription drug plans, Medicare fee-for-service providers and contractors. This center is also responsible for communication and dissemination of policies, guidance and materials to same to understand their perspectives and to drive best practices in the health care industry.[59]

- *The Center for Medicaid, CHIP and Survey & Certification.*[60] This center oversees the operation of federal programs administered by the states, including Medicaid and the State Children's Health Insurance Program (SCHIP or CHIP). This Center also oversees the planning, coordination and implementation of the survey, certification and enforcement programs for all Medicare and Medicaid providers and suppliers, and for laboratories under the Clinical Laboratory Improvement Amendments (CLIA). This Center also coordinates with the Center for Program Integrity on the identification of program vulnerabilities and implementation of strategies to eliminate fraud, waste, and abuse.

- *The Center for Program Integrity (CPI).*[61] The CPI is responsible for all national and State-wide Medicare and Medicaid programs and CHIP integrity fraud and abuse issues. This center coordinates provider/contractor audits and policy reviews, identifies program vulnerabilities, recommends modifications to programs to reduce program fraud, waste and abuse. This center (1) collaborates with the Office of Legislation on the development and advancement of new legislative initiatives and improvements to deter, reduce, and

---

[57] DHHS published a final regulation that revised all references to the "Health Care Financing Administration" and "HCFA" in Chapters I, IV and V of title 42, and subtitle A, and Chapters II and III of title 45 of the Code of Federal Regulations to the "Centers for Medicare & Medicaid Services" and "CMS," respectively. The technical regulation became effective upon publication. 66 Fed. Reg. 39451 (2001). *See also* Ctrs. for Medicare & Medicaid Servs. Prog. Mem. A-01-113 (2001). According to DHHS, the effective date of the name change was the date of the announcement by DHHS Secretary Tommy Thompson (June 14, 2001). However, the effective date of the corresponding technical revisions to the Code of Federal Regulations was July 31, 2001.

[58] *See* http://www.cms.gov/About-CMS/Agency-Information/CMSLeadership/Office_CM.html.

[59] For a description of the Medicare Centers, the organization chart and current leadership, *see* http://www.cms.gov/CMSLeadership/50_OrganizationalChartASP.asp#TopOfPage.

[60] *See* http://www.cms.gov/About-CMS/Agency-Information/CMSLeadership/Office_CMCSC.html.

[61] *See* http://www.cms.gov/About-CMS/Agency-Information/CMSLeadership/Office_CPI.html.

eliminate fraud, waste and abuse and (2) oversees all CMS interactions and collaboration with key stakeholders relating to program integrity (i.e., U.S. Department of Justice, DHHS Office of Inspector General, state law enforcement agencies, other federal entities, CMS components).

- *The Center Clinical Standards and Quality (CCSQ).*[62] CCSQ is CMS's focal point for all quality, clinical, medical science issues, survey and certification, and policies for all CMS programs. This center is tasked with creating a cohesive approach to improving quality throughout all of CMS by developing and implementing quality standards and programs, best practices and techniques in quality improvement, performance measurement systems, develop and implement participation requirements, and operating the Quality Improvement Organization, among other tasks.

- *The Center for Medicare and Medicaid Innovation (CMMI).*[63] Established in 2010 under the ACA, the CMMI is the center within CMS that is responsible for designing and testing innovative payment and service delivery models to reduce program expenditures, while at the same time improving the coordination, quality and efficiency of the health care services offered to beneficiaries.[64] CMMI is, according to CMS, intended to "explore new approaches to the way we pay for and deliver care to patients so that we have better results both in terms of the quality of care and the affordability of coverage.[65] CMMI, for example, administers the Medicare Advantage Value-Based Insurance Design model and the Part D Enhanced Medication Therapy Management model, as part of its Health Plan Innovation Initiatives.[66]

- *The Center for Strategic Planning (CSP).*[67] CSP handles the planning, formulation and coordination of long-term strategic plans, and future program policy and proposals for CMS. This center also: (1) collaborates with the Office of Legislation on the development and advancement of new legislative initiatives and improvements; (2) conducts environmental scanning, identifying, evaluating and reporting emerging trends in health care delivery and financing and their interactions with CMS programs and implications for future policy development and planning; and (3) oversees strategic, cross-cutting initiatives in coordination with other CMS components and external stakeholders.

CMS also administers the insurance reform provisions of the Health Insurance Portability and Accountability Act (HIPAA) in conjunction with the U.S. Departments of Labor and Treasury.[68]

---

[62] *See* http://www.cms.gov/About-CMS/Agency-Information/CMSLeadership/Office_CCSQ.html.
[63] *See* https://www.cms.gov/About-CMS/Agency-Information/CMSLeadership/Office_CMMI.html.
[64] ACA § 3021. The Patient Protection and Affordable Care Act (ACA) was enacted on March 23, 2010 (H.R. 3590, Pub. L. No. 111-148). The ACA, together with the Health Care and Educational Reconciliation Act of 2010 (HCERA), enacted on March 30, 2010 (H.R. 4872, Pub. L. No. 111-152), constitute two separate legislative enactments that are commonly referred to as the "health care reform" initiative under President Barrack Obama. These two Acts significantly impact the Medicare program, and Medicare reimbursement, but without directly changing Medicare reimbursement systems.
[65] CMS Center for Innovations blog site introducing the CMMI, http://innovations.cms.gov/blog/introducing.shtml.
[66] *See* https://innovation.cms.gov/initiatives/HPI/index.html.
[67] *See* http://www.cms.gov/About-CMS/Agency-Information/CMSLeadership/Office_CMMI.html.
[68] Note that the DHHS Office for Civil Rights is responsible for implementing and enforcing the privacy provisions of HIPAA. 65 Fed. Reg. 82381 (2000).

3.3.2.3 Central and Regional Operations

Headquartered in Washington, D.C., with its principal operational functions based in Baltimore, Maryland, CMS functions with a relatively small staff of approximately 4,600. The central office for CMS directs national program policy and oversees the work of the agency's 10 regional offices.[69] Located around the country, the regional offices are responsible for ensuring that participating providers, physicians, and suppliers meet applicable federal requirements. The regional offices were recently reorganized into a Consortia structure based on CMS's four key lines of business: 1. Medicare Health Plans Operations; 2. Financial Management and Fee For Service Operations; 3. Medicaid and Children's Health Operations; and, 4. Quality Improvement and Survey and Certification Operations.

3.3.2.4 Administrative Guidance

In addition to publishing implementing regulations in the *Federal Register*, CMS publishes interpretative guidance though various administrative manuals. With the exception of the Provider Reimbursement Manual, the agency has transitioned to exclusive use of Internet-only manuals (IOMs).[70] Unlike the paper-based manuals (which are segregated by provider type), the new CMS manual system is organized by functional area (e.g., program integrity, eligibility, entitlement, claims processing). As a result, the IOMs also follow a new publication-numbering system.[71]

3.3.2.5 Administrator Rulings

These rulings are decisions of the Administrator of CMS, and serve as precedent final opinions and orders, as well as agency statement of policy and interpretation. According to CMS, these rulings provide clarification and interpretation of complex or ambiguous provisions of the law or regulations in the areas of Medicare and Medicaid utilization, review by quality improvement organizations (QIOs, formerly called "peer review organizations"), private health insurance, and related matters. Rulings of the Administrator of CMS are binding on all CMS components, MACs, the Provider Reimbursement Review Board (PRRB), and the administrative law judges (ALJs) that hear Medicare Part B appeals including enrollment appeals.[72] However, Administrator rulings are not binding on non-CMS components, but are generally given deference.

3.3.3 Medicare Administrative Contractors, Fiscal Agents

CMS contracts with private organizations (usually large commercial-insurance carriers) to process and pay Medicare claims, and to provide local administrative support for a specific geographic area. In Medicare parlance, the entity that processes Part A claims used to be known as the "fiscal intermediary" or "intermediary."[73] Similarly, the processor of Medicare Part B claims was known as

---

[69] *See* Ctrs. for Medicare & Medicaid Servs., *CMS Regional Offices*, at www.cms.hhs.gov/regionaloffices.
[70] *See* http://www.cms.gov/Regulations-and-Guidance/Guidance/Manuals/index.html.
[71] "Crosswalks" from the paper-based manuals to the new IOMs are located in the individual IOMs at www.cms.hhs.gov/manuals/.
[72] Copies of the rulings are posted to the CMS website at www.cms.hhs.gov.rulings. In addition, a searchable database of Departmental Appeals Board rulings can be found at http://www.hhs.gov/dab/search.html. Finally, a list of PRRB decisions can be accessed at http://www.cms.gov/Regulations-and-Guidance/Review-Boards/PRRBReview/List-of-PRRB-Decisions.html.
[73] 42 U.S.C. § 1395h.

the "carrier."[74] Finally, the processor of Medicare Part B durable medical equipment prosthetics and orthotics claims were carried out by the "durable medical equipment regional carriers" (or DMERCs).

The MMA eliminated the distinction between fiscal intermediaries, carriers, and DMERCs, and established a category of contractor known as the "Medicare Administrative Contractors" (or MACs).[75] The MACs act as multi-state regional contractors that are responsible for administration of both Medicare Part A and Part B according to what was originally planned to be 15 distinct regions.[76] In addition, MACs also issue guidance regarding Medicare payment policy in the form of newsletters (many of which are available through the Internet) and published manuals. CMS is currently in the process of consolidating the 15 MAC regions down to 10, and estimates it will take several years before the consolidation is completed.[77] In addition, there are four regions for the administration of the DMEPOS program, each handled by a separate DME MAC (DMAC). The transition to the MACs began in 2006, with certain administrative functions previously carried out by fiscal intermediaries, carriers, and DMERCS transitioning to the MACs. As of the end of 2013, all jurisdictions have completely transferred from the old fiscal intermediaries, carriers and DMERCs to the MACs and DMACs. The MACs also issue guidance regarding Medicare payment policy in the form of local coverage decisions, newsletters (many of which are available through the Internet) and published manuals.

3.3.4 Quality Improvement Organizations

CMS contracts with one quality improvement organization (QIO) in each state, including the District of Columbia, Puerto Rico, and the U.S. Virgin Islands, which are composed of health care professionals who audit the utilization, quality, appropriateness and necessity of the medical care that is provided to program beneficiaries by physicians, providers, suppliers, Medicare Advantage organizations, and Part D sponsors. QIOs also serve to educate health care professionals about quality of care issues, and are tasked with protecting Medicare Beneficiaries by addressing individual complaints related to provider-based notice appeals, violations of the Emergency Medical Treatment and Labor Act (EMTALA), and other beneficiary complaints. Denial of service coverage by a QIO will generally result in a loss of Medicare reimbursement to the provider or supplier. The QIO can also refer a provider for investigation fraud in the case of excessive claims-denial rates.[78]

3.3.5 The DHHS Office of Inspector General

The DHHS Office of Inspector General (OIG) is responsible for auditing and evaluating the Medicare program. To that end, the OIG conducts financial, performance, and management-evaluation audits and inspections to identify, document, and provide recommendations for the efficient and effective operation of the program. As the enforcement arm of DHHS, the OIG also conducts criminal and civil investigations into Medicare fraud and abuse, working in cooperation with the

---

[74] *Id.* §§ 1395u, 1325m(a)(12); a directory of intermediaries and carriers may be accessed through the CMS website on the Internet at www.cms.hhs.gov/contactinggeneralinformation.
[75] MMA, § 911. The transition to MACs commenced in 2006.
[76] *See* http://www.cms.gov/Medicare/Medicare-Contracting/Medicare-Administrative-Contractors/MACJurisdictions.html.
[77] *See* http://www.cms.gov/Medicare/Medicare-Contracting/Medicare-Administrative-Contractors/A-B_MAC_Jurisdictions.html.
[78] 42 U.S.C. § 1320c.

U.S. Department of Justice, the Federal Bureau of Investigation, and state and local law enforcement agencies.[79] Administrative sanctions, including fixed period and permanent exclusion from the Medicare program, may be imposed by the OIG against providers and suppliers that violate Medicare law.[80] Periodic policy statements, advisory opinions, enforcement actions, and model compliance guidelines also are issued by the OIG in connection with various Medicare fraud and abuse laws. Such materials may be accessed through OIG's website on the Internet.[81]

3.3.6 The Provider Reimbursement Review Board

The PRRB, established by Congress in 1972, offers hospitals and other institutional providers an independent forum outside the fiscal intermediary (now known as MACs) for resolving Medicare payment disputes involving more than $10,000.[82] The PRRB has both rulemaking and subpoena power. PRRB members are appointed by the Secretary of DHHS for a three-year term.[83] The composition of the five-member PRRB includes at least one certified public accountant and two provider representatives. PRRB decisions are subject to review by the Administrator of CMS, as well as the federal courts.[84]

3.3.7 Independent Payment Advisory Board

The Independent Payment Advisory Board (IPAB) was established by the Affordable Care Act ostensibly to ensure that growth in Medicare spending stays within certain prescribed limits. The IPAB is tasked with drafting proposals "containing recommendations to reduce the projected per-capita growth rate" for Medicare spending in the future, provided that such projected growth rate exceeds certain targets.[85] The IPAB must annually submit these proposals, or alternatively, advisory reports, to Congress and the President (starting in 2014 for implementation in 2015) and, annually thereafter, the IPAB must submit a draft proposal to the Medicare Payment Advisory Commission (MedPAC) and the Secretary "by not later than September 1 of the determination year." Generally, the Secretary is required to implement by regulation the proposal recommendations, and may do so under an interim final rule. In what has become a recent theme in many pieces of Medicare legislation, the Affordable Care Act provides that there "shall be no administrative or judicial review under section 1869, section 1878, or otherwise, of the implementation by the Secretary under this subsection of the recommendations contained in a proposal."[86] The IPAB is to be composed of 15 members appointed by the President for six-year terms. The IPAB is prohibited from developing proposals related to Medicare benefits, eligibility or financing.

---

[79] 48 Fed. Reg. 21662 (1983); Ctrs. for Medicare & Medicaid Servs., *Medicare Carriers Manual* (Pub. 14) § 14002.
[80] 51 Fed. Reg. 34764 (1986).
[81] *See* DHHS Office of Inspector General at www.oig.hhs.gov.
[82] 42 C.F.R. §§ 405.1835, 405.1389; Institutional providers include SNFs, HHAs, CORFs, rural primary-care hospitals, hospices, and outpatient physical therapy, speech pathology, and ESRD facilities.
[83] 42 U.S.C. § 1395oo. No member may serve more than two consecutive three-year terms of office. 42 C.F.R. § 1845.
[84] The CMS Administrator has the authority to affirm, modify, reverse or vacate and remand decisions of the PRRB within 60 days of notification to the provider of that decision. *See* S.S.A. § 1878; 42 C.F.R. § 405.1875.
[85] ACA, § 3403.
[86] 42 U.S.C. § 1395kkk(e)(5).

3.4 Reimbursement Overview

Because they encompass more than just payment for medical care, items, and services, Medicare reimbursement principles are relatively complex. The key to understanding how Medicare reimburses providers and suppliers involves a thorough understanding of the basic components that comprise the Medicare reimbursement system.

REIMBURSEMENT— THE FIVE COMPONENTS	
ELIGIBILITY	Is the individual eligible for Medicare benefits?
COVERAGE	Is the item or service covered by Medicare?
CERTIFICATION	Is the provider of the item or service permitted to participate in the Medicare Program?
PAYMENT	How does Medicare pay for the item or service?
ASSIGNMENT/ REASSIGNMENT	Who is entitled to receive Medicare payment?

Each of these elements is described in Sections 3.5 through 3.16 of this Chapter.

3.5 Eligibility

The first step in analyzing the potential reimbursement issues associated with a proposed Medicare item or service is to ascertain whether the individual is eligible for Medicare benefits and, if so, when the effective date of Medicare coverage began.

3.5.1 Medicare Part A

The Medicare program provides Part A coverage to persons who qualify for Social Security retirement or survivor benefits and are age 65 years or older. Under a special transitional provision, some individuals who have reached age 65 but have not met other eligibility requirements are "grandfathered" into the program. Additionally, employees of federal, state, and local governments who are age 65 years and older may be eligible for Part A coverage if their employment was "Medicare qualified" (e.g., the individual was not a temporary employee, prison inmate, or election worker). Permanent residents who have resided in the U.S. for five years and who have attained the age of eligibility, but otherwise are not entitled to Medicare benefits, may voluntarily enroll in Medicare Part A if they pay a monthly premium. Younger individuals who have received disability benefits for at least 25 consecutive months under the Social Security or the Railroad Retirement programs, may apply for Medicare Part A coverage, as well as those with end-stage renal disease (ESRD) or Amyotrophic lateral sclerosis (ALS), commonly known as Lou Gehrig's Disease.[87]

3.5.2 Medicare Part B

Part A beneficiaries are automatically eligible for supplementary medical insurance under Medicare Part B unless they specifically decline the coverage.[88] It is possible, however, for a person

---

[87] 42 U.S.C. § 1395c; 42 C.F.R. § 406.5(a), (b).
[88] 42 C.F.R. § 407.17.

3.5.3 Medicare Part C

To enroll in an MA Plan, an individual must be eligible for Part A and enrolled in Part B,[91] and the electing beneficiary must reside within the MA Plan's geographic service area.[92] Also, because enrollment does not occur automatically, an MA-eligible beneficiary must elect affirmatively to enroll with an MA Plan. Enrollment can be accomplished directly with the MA Plan, through a licensed sales agent or broker, or through CMS's online enrollment tool located at www.Medicare.gov.[93] Further, a beneficiary who has been medically determined to have ESRD may not elect coverage under an MA Plan.[94]

MA organizations may not refuse enrollment to any MA beneficiary eligible for the applicable MA plan who elects MA during the program's coverage election periods with limited exceptions.[95] Moreover, MA-eligible beneficiaries may disenroll from an MA Plan or elect another plan during such periods.[96] Special coverage rules apply as to the effective dates of coverage for beneficiaries who elect MA plans.[97]

MA beneficiaries are subject to specific enrollment lock-in restrictions, meaning that beneficiaries generally must remain in a plan until the next annual enrollment period.[98] Special enrollment and disenrollment periods exist for newly eligible Medicare beneficiaries, enrollees in terminated MA Plans (e.g., plans that cease to operate or offer an MA Plan), dual eligible enrollees, enrollees who have changed their residences, and, in certain instances, where the MA Plan has committed contract violations.[99]

MA organizations may terminate an enrollee's plan election for certain causes, including late premium payments, disruptive behavior by the enrollee, or termination of the enrollee's service area by the plan.[100] In such instances, the enrollee's coverage will revert back to FFS Medicare.[101] However, special enrollment and disenrollment rules apply to enrollees who are terminated due to a reduction in the plan's service area or the termination of the plan from the MA program.[102]

---

[89] 42 U.S.C. § 1395o; 42 C.F.R. § 407.10(a).
[90] 42 U.S.C. § 1395o; 42 C.F.R. § 407.10(a).
[91] 42 U.S.C. § 1395w-21(a)(3); 42 C.F.R. § 422.50(a).
[92] Eligible beneficiaries may obtain information on the availability of MA plans in their area by calling 1-800-MEDICARE or by consulting the Medicare consumers' information website on the Internet at https://www.medicare.gov/find-a-plan/questions/home.aspx (Medicare Plan Finder).
[93] 42 U.S.C. § 1395w-21(c)(2)(A); 42 C.F.R. § 422.50(a)(5).
[94] An exception to this rule is made for beneficiaries who develop ESRD while enrolled in an MA plan or who elect an MA special needs plan that enrolls ESRD individuals. 42 U.S.C. § 1395w-21(a)(3)(B); 42 C.F.R. § 422.50(a)(2).
[95] 42 C.F.R. § 422.60(a)(1)–(2).
[96] 42 C.F.R. § 422.62(a).
[97] *Id.* § 422.68(a)–(f).
[98] *Id.* § 422.62(a).
[99] 42 U.S.C. § 1395w-21(e)(4), (5); 42 C.F.R. § 422.62(b); For a more detailed summary of the special enrollment periods (SEP) under Medicare Part C; *see* CY 2018 MA Enrollment and Disenrollment Guidance.
[100] 42 C.F.R. § 422.74(b).
[101] 42 C.F.R. § 422.74(e).
[102] *Id.* § 422.74(b)(3) and (d)(7).

3.5.4 Medicare Part D[103]

To be eligible to enroll in Part D, a beneficiary must be: (i) entitled to Part A coverage or enrolled in Medicare Part B, (ii) a U.S. citizen or lawfully present in the U.S., and (iii) live in the service area of the Part D plan.[104] Medicare beneficiaries who are eligible for Part D are permitted to select among the various plans offered by the PDPs and MA-PD Plans in their service area.[105]

Initial enrollment for Part D coverage is the same as the annual, coordinated election period. Additional special enrollment periods are available when the beneficiary suffers an involuntary loss of creditable coverage, errors occurred in enrollment, under certain exceptional circumstances, for certain "dual eligible" beneficiaries who are also entitled to Medicaid coverage, and if a discontinuance of MA-PD coverage occurs during the first year of eligibility.[106] PDP enrollment, disenrollment, termination and change of enrollment processes are established by the Secretary of DHHS using rules similar to, and coordinated with those established for MA Plans regarding residency requirements, exercise of choice, coverage and election periods, guaranteed issue and renewal, consumer protections, marketing material, and application forms.[107]

3.6 Coverage

The next step in analyzing the potential reimbursement issues associated with a proposed Medicare service or supply is to determine whether the Medicare program *covers* the item or service.

3.6.1 Medicare Part A

Medicare Part A provides coverage for hospitalization, rehabilitation, and long term care. Part A beneficiaries also may receive hospice care, SNF services, and care that is provided by an HHA.[108]

3.6.1.1 Hospital Services

Inpatient hospital coverage includes the cost of a semi-private room, meals, regular nursing services, operating and recovery room, intensive care, inpatient prescription drugs, laboratory tests, radiology services, psychiatric hospitalization, and inpatient rehabilitation and long term care hospitalization when medically necessary, as well as all other medically necessary services and supplies provided in the hospital. A provider also may contract with outside suppliers to furnish services "under arrangements."[109] Arrangements in this context are limited to those under which the receipt of payment by the provider for the services discharges the liability of the beneficiary, or any other

---

[103] Note that the regulations governing eligibility and enrollment for Part D plans is found at 42 C.F.R. Part 423, Subpart B and in Chapter 3 of the *Part D Prescription drug Benefit Manual*.
[104] 42 U.S.C. § 1395w-101(a)(3)(A); 42 C.F.R. § 423.30; "lawful presence" is defined by 8 C.F.R. § 1.3.
[105] 42 C.F.R. §§ 423.30 and 423.32.
[106] *Id*. § 1395w-101(b)(3); 42 C.F.R. § 423.30.
[107] 42 U.S.C. § 1395w-101(b)(1)(B); 42 C.F.R. § 423.30–.46.
[108] Certain medical supplies also may be covered under Medicare Part A. 42 U.S.C. § 1395x(m).
[109] Ctrs. for Medicare & Medicaid Servs., *Medicare General Information and Eligibility Manual* (Pub. 100-01) Ch. 5 § 10.3.

person, to pay for the services. The provider also must exercise professional responsibility over the arranged-for services as a condition of coverage by Medicare.[110]

3.6.1.2 Extended Care or Skilled Nursing Services (SNF)

SNFs provide inpatient medical, skilled nursing, or rehabilitative services and supplies to patients in a non-acute care hospital setting.[111] Part A coverage is available for each day of extended care or SNF services up to a maximum of 100 days per spell of illness, and is subject to a coinsurance charge.[112] Medicare covers SNF services if a beneficiary has been an inpatient of a hospital for at least three consecutive calendar days and is transferred to a participating SNF within 30 days after discharge from the hospital.[113] Such services also must be certified (and subsequently recertified) as "medically necessary" by a physician, a clinical nurse, or a nurse practitioner.[114]

3.6.1.3 Home Health Services

HHAs provide certain "part-time" or "intermittent" medical, nursing, and therapy services to individuals in their places of residence.[115] Medicare covers home health care services that are furnished in the beneficiary's home (defined as any place in which a beneficiary resides that is not a hospital, SNF, or nursing facility), or in an outpatient setting (which may include a hospital, SNF, or rehabilitation center under certain circumstances).[116] In order to qualify for home health care, a Medicare beneficiary must be:

1. confined to the home;
2. under the care of a physician;
3. receiving services under a plan of care established and periodically reviewed by a physician; and
4. in need of skilled nursing care on an intermittent basis, requires physical therapy or speech-language pathology, or have a continuing need for occupational therapy.

HHA-covered services do not include drugs, biologicals, housekeeping, or transportation services. HHAs also cannot provide home health visits for patients receiving venipuncture (the drawing of blood) as the only skilled nursing service.[117]

---

[110] 42 U.S.C. §§ 1395x(w)(1), 1395cc(a)(1)(H), 1395u(b)(6), 1395yy(e). Ctrs. for Medicare & Medicaid Servs., *Medicare Intermediary Manual* (Pub. 13) § 3007.
[111] *Id.* § 1395i-3(a), (d).
[112] *Id.* § 1395e(a)(3).
[113] 42 C.F.R. §§ 409.30–.36.
[114] *Id.* § 424.20. As a general rule, Medicare will not cover items or services that are not deemed to be "reasonable and necessary" for the diagnosis or treatment of an illness or injury (*see* 42 U.S.C. § 1395y(a)(i)); however, to avoid potential overutilization in the delivery of certain services and equipment, Medicare may require a physician's certification to explain why the service or equipment is necessary.
[115] 42 C.F.R. §§ 409.44–.45. The courts have interpreted "intermittent" to mean six or fewer days of the week, and "part-time" to mean less than eight hours per day. *Duggan v. Bowen*, 692 F. Supp. 1487 (D.D.C. 1988). However, Medicare generally will not pay for home health care that exceeds 28 hours per week without special documentation and/or medical justification. Ctrs. for Medicare & Medicaid Servs., *Medicare Benefit Policy Manual*, (Pub. 100-2), Ch. 7, § 40.1.
[116] 42 C.F.R. § 409.47.
[117] 42 U.S.C. §§ 1395x(m), 1395f(a)(2)(C); 42 C.F.R. §§ 409.47, .42, .49.

HHA services are covered under Medicare Part A and Part B. The first 100 visits for home health care following a beneficiary's three-day hospital or SNF stay are covered under Part A. If the first HHA visit is more than 14 days after discharge from the hospital or SNF, Part B covers the first 100 visits.[118] Under the BBA, Medicare payment for post-institutional HHA services furnished on or after January 1, 1998, for Medicare beneficiaries enrolled in both Part A and Part B during a home health stay (other than the first 100 visits) are covered under Part B.[119] Such services, however, will continue to be covered under Part A for beneficiaries who are enrolled only in Part A and qualify for the home health benefit.[120]

3.6.1.4 Hospice Services

Hospice care is a service provided to terminally ill persons with a life expectancy of six months or less and who elect to forgo the standard Medicare treatment benefits to receive only hospice care.[121] Such care includes pain relief with drugs, supportive medical and social services, physical therapy, nursing services, and symptom management. A beneficiary may receive covered hospice-consultation services from a physician who is also the medical director or employee of a hospice program if the beneficiary has not elected hospice coverage and has not been seen by the physician on a previous occasion.[122]

Beneficiaries must elect to receive hospice care in "periods." Under current Medicare law, there are two 90-day hospice-benefit periods, followed by an unlimited number of 60-day periods. At the beginning of the second 90-day period and for each subsequent 60-day period, the appropriate medical professional must recertify that the beneficiary is terminally ill. Prior to such recertification a hospice physician or nurse practitioner must have a face-to-face encounter with the patient to determine continued eligibility to receive hospice services.[123] By electing to receive hospice care, beneficiaries waive their rights (with exceptions) to receive Medicare benefits other than hospice.

3.6.2 Medicare Part B

Medicare Part B provides coverage for "medical and other health services."[124] Part B services generally fall within one of three primary categories.

- physicians' professional services, including services and supplies that are furnished "incident to" physicians' services;

---

[118] Part A only pays for post-institutional services; Program Memorandum No. A-97-16, Dec. 1, 1997; Program Memorandum No. A-98-49, Dec 1, 1998.
[119] "A post-institutional service" follows a beneficiary's stay in a hospital or SNF for three or more days.
[120] 42 U.S.C. § 1395d.
[121] Federal regulations at 42 C.F.R. § 418.3 further clarify that an individual is considered terminally ill if he or she has a medical prognosis of a life expectancy of six months or less if "the illness runs its normal course."
[122] MMA, § 512; 42 U.S.C. § 1395d(a)(5); 42 U.S.C. § 1395x(dd)(1); 42 C.F.R. §§ 418.20–.30; 67 Fed. Reg. 70363 (proposed Nov. 22, 2002); Centers for Medicare & Medicaid Servs. Prog. Mem. AB-03-008 (2003). BIPA clarified that the certification of terminal illness of an individual who elects hospice "shall be based on the physician's or medical director's clinical judgment regarding the normal course of the individual's illness." This clarification is effective for certifications made on or after December 21, 2000. BIPA, § 322.
[123] ACA, § 3132.
[124] 42 U.S.C. § 1395j-k.

- services provided by outpatient providers and freestanding supplier entities, including suppliers of diagnostic tests; and
- services rendered by non-physician practitioners working under physician supervision or in collaboration with a physician, as required by state law, including services and supplies that are furnished "incident to" certain non-physician practitioners' services.

"Incident to" professional services are services provided incident to the professional services of a physician or certain non-physician practitioners (e.g., physician assistants and nurse practitioners).[125] "Incident to" services are services that are generally not furnished directly to the patient by the physician or non-physician practitioner, but are considered an *essential element* of the physician's or non-physician practitioner's overall professional service. Incident to services may include the services of auxiliary personnel (for example, nurses or technicians) working *under the direct supervision* of the physician, or non-physician practitioner. "Direct supervision" means that the physician or non-physician practitioner is physically present in the office suite and immediately available to provide assistance and direction throughout the time the auxiliary personnel perform services).[126] Non-physician practitioners, who in some circumstances may bill Medicare directly for their services, may also provide services incident to the physician's professional services.[127] In order to qualify for Medicare payment, incident to services must be furnished in a non-hospital setting, such as a physician's office.[128] Note that "incident to" professional services are distinct from hospital outpatient "incident to" services. Medicare Part B separately covers outpatient therapeutic services that are furnished incident to the services of a physician or non-physician practitioner.[129]

Detailed rules for coverage and exclusion also apply to each of the following categories and their related subsets. Such requirements typically involve the level of physician supervision, the location of the services (e.g., inpatient vs. outpatient), and the qualifications of the non-physician practitioners who provide the services.[130]

3.6.2.1 Physicians' Services

Physicians' services that may be covered under Medicare Part B include services rendered to Medicare beneficiaries by medical doctors (MDs) and doctors of osteopathic medicine (DOs). Such services include diagnosis, therapy, surgery, and preventive wellness services, as well as the oversight of the patient's plan of care.[131] Other physicians' services that occur in hospitals and like providers (e.g., anesthesiology, pathology, radiology, and laboratory services) similarly are covered. Part B coverage extends to services and supplies that are incident to those commonly furnished in a physician's office

---

[125] 42 C.F.R. §§ 410.26, 414.34. Ctrs. for Medicare & Medicaid Servs., *Medicare Benefit Policy Manual* (Pub. 100-2), Ch. 15, § 60. *Also see* 66 Fed. Reg. 55246 (2001) and 67 Fed. Reg. 79966 (2002) for further clarification.
[126] *Id.*
[127] 42 C.F.R. §§ 410.26, 414.34. Ctrs. for Medicare & Medicaid Servs., *Medicare Benefit Policy Manual* (Pub. 100-2), Ch. 15, § 60.2.
[128] 42 C.F.R. §§ 410.20–.27; Ctrs. for Medicare & Medicaid Servs., *Medicare Benefit Policy Manual* (Pub. 100-2), Ch. 15, § 60. *Also see Medicare General Information Eligibility and Entitlement Manual* (CMS Pub. 100-1), Ch. 5, § 70.
[129] 42 C.F.R. § 410.267; Ctrs. for Medicare & Medicaid Servs.,*Medicare Benefit Policy Manual* (Pub. 100-2), Ch. 6, § 20.5.2.
[130] *See generally* 42 C.F.R. pt. 410.
[131] 42 U.S.C. § 1395x(q)–(r); Ctrs. for Medicare & Medicaid Servs., *Medicare Benefit Policy Manual* (Pub. 100-2), Ch. 15 § 30.

(e.g., drugs and biologicals that cannot be self-administered), and which are included in the physicians' invoice for professional services.[132] Services provided to Medicare beneficiaries by limited-license practitioners (e.g., dentists, oral and maxillofacial surgeons, optometrists, podiatrists, and chiropractors) also are covered by Part B under the physicians' services coverage definition; however, some of these services are extremely limited.[133]

3.6.2.2 Services by Non-Physician Practitioners

Covered services by non-physician practitioners include services that are rendered by physician assistants, nurse practitioners, and clinical nurse specialists working under physician supervision, as well as services provided by certified registered nurse anesthetists (CRNAs) and anesthesiologist assistants.[134] Outpatient physical therapy services, occupational therapy services, and speech pathology services are similarly covered under Medicare Part B if they are certified as medically necessary by the physician.[135] Part B coverage also extends to the services of qualified clinical psychologists, licensed clinical social workers, certified nurse midwives, and audiologists.[136]

3.6.2.3 Outpatient Providers and Freestanding Supplier Entities

Services rendered by outpatient providers and freestanding supplier entities covered under Medicare Part B include clinical laboratory services, as well as outpatient therapeutic- and diagnostic-testing services conducted by providers such as hospitals and critical access hospitals (CAHs), independent diagnostic testing facilities (IDTFs) and suppliers of portable diagnostic X-ray services.[137] Additionally, Part B coverage encompasses rehabilitation and related services when they are furnished in a CORF, rehabilitation agency, certified rehabilitation clinic, or a public-health agency.[138] Institutional and home dialysis equipment, supplies, and support services provided by renal dialysis providers and facilities also are covered under Part B.[139]

Medicare Part B covers primary health care and related services that are furnished by Federally Qualified Health Centers (FQHCs) or rural health clinics (RHCs).[140] Coverage also is extended to radiation-therapy services that are conducted in a freestanding radiation therapy center under physician supervision.[141] Similarly, surgical procedures performed in an ASC are covered, as are certain services provided in a hospital outpatient department setting.[142]

---

[132] Ctrs. for Medicare & Medicaid Servs., *Medicare Benefit Policy Manual* (Pub. 100-2), Ch. 15 §§ 50 and 60.
[133] 42 U.S.C. § 1395x(r). *Also see Medicare Benefit Policy Manual* (Pub. 100-2), Ch. 15, § 30 and *Medicare General Information Liability and Entitlement Manual* (Pub. 100-01), Ch. 5, § 70. Medicare, for example, does not cover most routine dental services from filings to cleanings. However, in certain inpatient situations, Medicare may cover limited dental services if the beneficiary has an emergency or if the beneficiary has a disease like oral cancer which involves the jaw or a facial tumor removal that requires certain types of jaw reconstruction.
[134] 42 C.F.R. §§ 410.69, .74–.76.
[135] 42 U.S.C. § 1395cc(e); 42 C.F.R. §§ 400.202, 485.701–.729.
[136] 42 C.F.R. §§ 410.32, .71, .73, .77; *Medicare Benefit Policy Manual* (Pub. 100-2), Ch. 15, § 80.3.
[137] 42 C.F.R. §§ 410.27–28, 32–.33, 486.100–110, pt. 493.
[138] *Id.* §§ 410.100–.105, .170.
[139] *Id.* § 410.50–.52.
[140] *Id.* §§ 405.2400–.2415; 410.45, pt. 491.
[141] *Id.* §§ 410.10(f), .35.
[142] *Id.* pt. 416.

Medical equipment, supplies, and prosthetic and orthotic devices that are furnished by DMEPOS suppliers are covered if such services and supplies have been prescribed by a physician and are certified as medically necessary.[143] Ambulance services also are covered under Medicare Part B if certain conditions apply.[144] Lastly, Part B also covers partial hospitalization services that are furnished by participating community mental health centers (CMHCs), hospitals and CAHs, provided such services are delivered pursuant to a physician plan of treatment and are certified by the physician as medically necessary.[145]

3.6.3 Shared Savings Programs

Section 3022 of the ACA created a "shared savings program" under which the Medicare program would share cost savings for high quality care delivered by "accountable care organizations" (ACOs) to Medicare beneficiaries.[146] An ACO is a group of providers or suppliers or a network of groups that are jointly responsible for the cost and quality of health care provided to Medicare beneficiaries.

An ACO must apply and be approved for participation in the shared savings program. Upon approval, the ACO must sign a participation agreement with CMS for a term of at least three years with an effective date of January 1 (except during 2012, when start dates of April 1 or July 1 were permitted). The application must declare the ACO's selection of one of two risk models, either "Track 1" (also called the "one-sided model) or "Track 2" (also called the "two-sided model").[147] Under Track 1, savings but not losses are shared with CMS for all three years of the initial term of the agreement, while under Track 2, both savings and losses are shared with CMS.[148]

Under the program, ACO participating providers and suppliers will continue to be paid by Medicare in the same manner as they otherwise would be under the original Medicare fee-for-service program for Parts A and B. However, ACOs can receive an additional payment from CMS in the form of a shared savings distribution if the ACO meets certain requirements and realizes savings that exceed a "minimum savings rate" (MSR). The savings are calculated by analyzing the ACO's expenditures in comparison to an expenditure benchmark.[149]

If the ACO's expenditures are below the benchmark (i.e., there is a savings), the amount of savings must meet or exceed the MSR before an ACO can share in the savings. For Track 2 ACOs, the MSR is fixed at 2 percent. For Track 1 ACOs, CMS uses a sliding scale MSR between 2.0 percent and 3.9 percent, based on the number of beneficiaries assigned to the ACO with a higher MSR for ACOs with fewer beneficiaries. If there is a savings and if the savings exceed the applicable MSR, Track 2 ACOs can receive a greater share of the savings than Track 1 ACOs. Depending on the quality performance score the ACO receives, once the savings exceed the applicable MSR, Track 2 ACOs can earn up to 60 percent of total savings while Track 1 ACOs can earn up to 50 percent of total savings.[150]

---

[143] *Id.* § 414.200–.232.
[144] *Id.* §§ 410.40–.41.
[145] *Id.* §§ 410.43, 110.
[146] Pub. L. No 111-148 and Pub. L. No 111-152, enacted March 23 and March 30, 2010.
[147] 42 C.F.R. §§ 425.200–222.
[148] 42 C.F.R. §§ 425.600–606.
[149] 42 U.S.C. § 1395jjj(d).
[150] 42 C.F.R. §§ 425.604, 425.606.

Each ACO will determine, based on its unique agreements with its participants, providers, and suppliers, how any shared savings payments may be distributed among them. However, ACOs are required to use part of the shared savings payment to further CMS's triple aim of better health, better health care, and reduced costs.[151]

3.6.4 Medicare Part C

MA organizations offer two coverage categories to beneficiaries within the plan's service area: basic and supplemental benefits. Each year, MA organizations are required to submit their proposed plan benefits and premiums for the following year to CMS for approval.[152] Each MA organization must compute a separate ACR for each MA coordinated-care or private FFS plan offered to Medicare beneficiaries. The ACR is subject to certain adjustment factors that take into account the utilization characteristics of plan enrollees.[153] If the ACR calculation (after adjustment) produces an excess amount, then the MA organization may use all or part of this amount to reduce beneficiaries' liability for premiums or cost-sharing amounts, or use the remainder to fund additional services not covered by Medicare.[154] MA SNPs and certain RFB plans are required to offer Part D coverage, while MSA plans are prohibited from offering prescription drug coverage other than that required under Parts A and B. PFFS plans may offer Part D coverage, and MA CCPs are required to provide at least one plan with prescription-drug coverage. They may also offer plans with no drug coverage for beneficiaries who choose not to enroll in Medicare Part D.[155] The rules for Part D coverage by MA Plans are similar to those for stand-alone PDPs.[156]

3.6.4.1 *Basic Benefits*

"Basic benefits" comprise Medicare Part A and Part B benefits plus other "additional" benefits.[157] Additional benefits may include certain reductions in the Part B premium and other beneficiary cost-sharing reductions subject to an annual cap on out-of-pocket costs. Benefits that are not covered by FFS Medicare but offered by an MA Plan as an additional benefit must be extended to all enrollees within a plan's service area or segment on a uniform premium and cost-sharing basis. The establishment of additional benefits is subject to approval by CMS.

3.6.4.2 *Supplemental Benefits*

Supplemental benefits (aka Medicare supplement or "Medigap" plans) are "extra" benefits (i.e., services not covered by Medicare) that either must or may be purchased by the enrollee depending on the type of benefit coverage. Common examples of supplemental benefits include dental benefits, vision care benefits (Medicare Part B does not, contrary to popular assumption, include vision benefits) and exercise facility memberships. MA allows for two supplemental-coverage

---

[151] 42 C.F.R. § 425.204(d).
[152] 42 C.F.R. § 422.254.
[153] 42 C.F.R. § 422.264.
[154] 42 C.F.R. § 422.266.
[155] 42 C.F.R. § 422.4.
[156] MMA, § 222.
[157] Hospice services are excluded from basic benefits under MA. 42 U.S.C. § 1395w-22(a)(1); 42 C.F.R. §§ 422.2, .100, .101.

categories—"mandatory" and "optional" benefits. MA enrollees may choose to decline the optional benefits, but cannot decline the mandatory coverage (even if they add to the overall cost of the premium). Supplemental benefits may be offered only by coordinated-care and PFFS plans, and are subject to approval by CMS.[158] As a practical matter, MA Plans in a given market offer different plans with varying levels of benefits and premiums and beneficiaries choose the plan and benefit package that meets their needs.

For an enrollee who is an inpatient when MA coverage begins, payment responsibility belongs to the original Medicare program or previous MA organization until the date of discharge, even if this date extends beyond the effective date of an enrollee's MA election. For an enrollee who is an inpatient when MA coverage *ends*, the MA organization remains responsible for payment until the date of discharge (even though no payment was received from CMS for the period after coverage had ended).[159]

3.6.5 Medicare Part D[160]

PDP and MA-PD plans may offer "standard coverage" or an actuarial equivalent (known as "alternative coverage") benefit package approved by CMS.[161] PDP and MA-PD plans may also offer supplemental coverage to beneficiaries, including lower out-of-pocket costs and coverage of Medicare-excluded drugs.[162] Drugs otherwise excluded from Part D coverage may be included as supplemental benefits so long as the drugs otherwise meet the definition of a Part D drug.[163] PDP and MA-PD plans that cover excluded drugs are not, however, allowed to pass those costs on to Medicare and are required to repay CMS if they are found to have billed Medicare in such cases.[164]

Part D also provides drug coverage for dual-eligible beneficiaries, effectively preempting Medicaid prescription drug coverage for dual eligible beneficiaries.[165] Dual eligible beneficiaries are automatically enrolled in a PDP if they have not elected to enroll.[166] Dual eligible beneficiaries also qualify for premium and cost-sharing subsidies based on income.[167]

The Affordable Care Act made a number of changes to the Part D cost-sharing obligations incurred by beneficiaries. First and foremost, the Affordable Care Act eliminates the cost-sharing obligation for full-benefit dual eligible beneficiaries who receive services under a Medicare home

---

[158] 42 U.S.C. § 1395w-22(a)(3); 42 C.F.R. §§ 422.2, .100, .102. Special rules on supplemental benefits apply to MSA plans. 42 C.F.R. §§ 422.103–.104(a). A Point-of-Service option may be offered by coordinated-care plans and network MSAs for a supplemental premium. *Id.* § 422.105.
[159] 42 U.S.C. § 1395w-23(g); 42 C.F.R. § 422.318.
[160] The regulations governing Part D benefits are found at 42 C.F.R. Part 423, Subpart C. Additional information can be found in Ch. 5 of the *Medicare Prescription drug Benefit Manual* and in CMS's annual *Announcement of Calendar Year Medicare Advantage Capitation Rates and Medicare Advantage and Part D Payment Policies and Final Call Letter.*
[161] *See id.* § 1395w-102(a)(1).
[162] *Id.* § 1395w-102(a)(2).
[163] *Id.* § 1395w-102(a)(2)(A)(ii).
[164] *See, e.g.,* OIG-OAS Report A-06-06-00022, *Report on Medicare Drug Discount Card Program Sponsor McKesson Health Solutions,* (Sept. 25, 2006) *available at* https://oig.hhs.gov/oas/reports/region6/60600022.pdf .
[165] 42 U.S.C. § 1395w-114(a)(3)(B)(v).
[166] 42 C.F.R. § 423.34(d).
[167] *Id.* § 1395w-114; 42 C.F.R. §§ 423.286(e), 423.780, and 423.782.

and community-based waiver program.[168] In addition, premium and cost-sharing subsidies are available to low-income beneficiaries with incomes at or below 150% of the FPL.[169] The Affordable Care Act also permits PDPs to waive premiums for beneficiaries who are eligible for the low-income subsidy, effective calendar year 2011, if the premium is *de minimis*.[170]

The standard benefit is updated annually by CMS, based on the rate of per capita Part D spending growth.[171] For 2018, after a $405 deductible, Medicare covers 75% of a beneficiary's "incurred" drug costs, up to $3,750 (known as the Initial Coverage Limit).[172] Thereafter, beneficiaries pay 100% of their incurred drug costs (this gap in coverage is commonly known as the "donut hole") until they reach the "catastrophic coverage limit" of $5,000 in out-of-pocket expenses (i.e., $8,418 in total drug spending or TrOOP).[173] After the catastrophic coverage limit is reached, Medicare reinsures at 80% of the incurred drug costs and the Plan pays for 15%. The beneficiary is responsible for the *greater of* 5% of actual cost *or* nominal copayments of $3.35 for generic and preferred multi-source drugs and $8.35 for all other drugs.[174]

The Affordable Care Act incrementally began to close the donut hole beginning in 2011 thru a combination of reductions in cost sharing obligations on generic and brand-name drugs and discounts on brand-name drugs. In particular, starting in 2011, beneficiary cost-sharing obligations began to be reduced for generic drugs by 7% each year continuing through 2019, and by 12% in 2020 for a total reduction of 75%.[175] Accordingly, by 2020, coinsurance for generic drugs in the coverage gap or donut hole will be 25%, the same co-insurance amount applicable to generic drugs during the Initial Coverage Limit. Second, in 2011, beneficiaries who reach the donut hole will be eligible to receive a 50% discount on brand-name drugs at the point of sale (the Coverage Gap Discount Program). Finally, starting 2013, coverage for brand-name drugs purchased in the donut hole with co-insurance is gradually being reduced to a 75% of the negotiated brand name drug price goal by 2020. When combined with the Coverage Gap Discount Program, Part D enrollees will have co-insurance obligations for brand-name drugs furnished in the donut hole equal to 25% of the negotiated price—the same co-insurance amount applicable to brand name drugs during the Initial Coverage Limit.[176] These three key provisions in the Affordable Care Act effectively eliminate the donut hole coverage gap when fully implemented by 2020.[177]

---

[168] *See* Pub. L. No. 111-148, Sec. 3309 (2010); 42 U.S.C. § 1395w-114(a)(1)(D)(i).
[169] 42 U.S.C. § 1395w-114(a)(1)(D)(ii).
[170] *See* Public L. No. 111-148, Sec. 3303 (2010); 42 U.S.C. § 1395w-114(a)(5).
[171] 42 U.S.C. § 1395w-102(b)(6); 42 C.F.R. § 423.104(d)(5)(iv).
[172] *See* 42 U.S.C. § 1395w-102(b) and 42 C.F.R. § 423.104(d); *see also* CMS Medicare Advantage and Part D Payment Policies and Final Call Letter, 68 (Apr. 3, 2017), *available at* https://www.cms.gov/Medicare/Health-Plans/MedicareAdvtgSpecRateStats/Downloads/Announcement2018.pdf.
[173] *Id.*
[174] 42 C.F.R. § 423.104(d)(5); 2017 Call Letter, *supra* note 191.
[175] *See* Pub. L. No. 111-152, Sec. 1101 (2010); 42 U.S.C. § 1395w-152.
[176] *See* ACA, Pub. L. No. 111-148, Section 330; 42 U.S.C, § 1395w-114a.
[177] The Affordable Care Act requires that the 50% brand-name drug discount be paid for by pharmaceutical manufacturers who must enter into an agreement with CMS in order for their brand name drug to be eligible for coverage under Part D and offered by a plan. Participating manufacturers must make quarterly payments to Part D plan sponsors based upon CMS-supplied date from the agency's third-party administrator based upon prescription drug event data. *See* ACA, Pub. L. No. 111-148, Section 3301 (2010); *see also* 42 C.F.R. Part 423, Subpart W.

Covered Part D drugs include the following: federal legend drugs for a medically-accepted indication that are approved by the Food and Drug Administration (FDA); insulin and diabetic supplies;[178] prescription-based smoking cessation products; biologicals, self-administered injectable and infusion drugs, as well as those items that are administered in a home setting (so long as they are not covered under Medicare Part A or Part B); and compounded prescriptions—as long as at least one of the ingredients is covered under the Part D formulary.[179] Part D also covers a number of drugs or infusion therapy that are covered under Part B in some circumstances but do not meet Part B coverage or medical necessity requirements including IDPN and other infusion therapies.[180] Additionally, the Affordable Care Act mandates Part D sponsors to offer PDPs that include all covered Part D drugs in certain categories and classes identified in the law. Until CMS establishes more specific criteria, the following categories and classes must be included in the formulary: anticonvulsants, antidepressants, antineoplastics, antipsychotics, antiretrovirals, and immunosuppressants for the treatment of transplant rejection.[181] Excluded drugs include non-prescription medications, drugs and supplies covered by Part A or Part B and drugs excluded by Medicaid.[182] Examples of drugs currently excluded by Medicaid include non-prescription drugs, drugs used for weight loss, weight gain or anorexia, and prescription vitamins or minerals (except for prenatal vitamins and fluorides).[183]

PDP and MA-PD plans are not required to pay for all covered Part D drugs.[184] Rather, each PDP and MA-PD plan is permitted to establish its own formulary, or list of covered drugs for which they will make payment, as long as the formulary and benefit structure are not found by CMS to discourage enrollment by certain Medicare beneficiaries.[185] PDP and MA-PD plans can also change the drugs on their formulary during the course of the year with 60 days' notice to affected parties, including direct written notice to enrollees.[186]

---

[178] These supplies covered by Part D include syringes, gauze, insulin pens, and alcohol swabs. Part D does not cover diabetic testing supplies (glucose monitors and test strips) which will continue to be covered under Part B.

[179] 42 C.F.R. § 423.120(d); *see also* 70 Fed. Reg. 4231–32 (Jan. 28, 2005); Part D will only pay for those portions of the compounded drug that meet the definition of a Part D drug; if any of the ingredients in the compound are covered under Part B, the drug is considered a Part B compound.

[180] *See* Medicare Prescription Drug Benefit Manual, Pub. 100-18, ch. 5 § 50.

[181] *See* 42 U.S.C. § 1395w-104(b)(3)(G)(iv). On January 10, 2014 (79 Fed. Reg. 1918) CMS issued a proposed rule with comment period that would have made substantial changes to the Medicare Advantage Program. Among others, CMS proposed to require formulary inclusion of all drugs within the antineoplastic, anticonvulsant, and antiretroviral drug classes (subject to proposed exceptions), but would no longer require all drugs from the antidepressant and immunosuppressant drug classes to be on all Part D formularies. Although antipsychotics would not meet the criteria, they would remain protected at least through 2015 while CMS evaluated additional considerations and the need for any other formulary exceptions. Based upon strong, negative public reaction, CMS Administrator Marilyn Tavenner told Congress on March 10, 2014 that CMS would not move forward with four provisions of the proposed rule governing Medicare's prescription drug program and that, in particular, CMS decided not to finalize the Medicare Part D proposals relating to the "protected classes" definition on three drug classes, standards for preferred pharmacy networks, the number of Part D plans sponsors may offer and clarifications to the noninterference provision. Accordingly, the status of these drug classes remains subject to future rulemaking.

[182] 42 U.S.C. § 1395w-102(e)(2); 42 C.F.R. § 423.100; *see also* 70 Fed. Reg. 4228–31 (Jan. 28, 2005).

[183] 42 U.S.C. § 1396r-8(d); *see also* 70 Fed. Reg. 4228 (Jan. 28, 2005).

[184] 42 U.S.C. § 1395w-104(b)(3) and 42 C.F.R. § 423.120(b).

[185] *Id.*

[186] 42 C.F.R. § 423.120(b)(5).

3.6.6 National Coverage Decisions

Medicare law lists broad categories of items and services that may be covered by the Medicare program. The Secretary of DHHS has the authority to make coverage determinations regarding specific items and services. A national coverage determination (NCD) simply is a policy statement granting, limiting, or excluding Medicare coverage for a specific item or service. Often, an NCD is written in terms of a particular patient population that may receive (or not receive) Medicare reimbursement for a particular item or service. Specifically, the law provides that an NCD is a determination made by the Secretary of DHHS with respect to whether a particular item or service is covered nationally by Medicare, but that it does *not* include a determination about which code, if any, is assigned to a particular item or service, nor does it make a determination with respect to the amount of payment.[187] An NCD itself is a formal instruction to the MACs regarding how to process claims. These instructions have a specific date dictating when claims will be processed according to the new criteria. NCDs may be issued by CMS as a manual instruction or other document (e.g., a program memorandum or ruling) or notice in the *Federal Register*. After issuance, an NCD is binding on all MACs, QIOs, and MA organizations, as well as ALJs during the claims-appeal process.[188]

In the absence of a specific NCD, coverage determinations are made by local MACs within the boundaries established by Medicare law. Usually these determinations are made on a claim-by-claim basis. MACs also publish local coverage determinations (LCDs) that are contractor-specific policies that offer coverage and coding guidance for providers, physicians, and suppliers in a specific geographic area. An LCD may not conflict with an NCD, but the LCD may supplement an NCD.[189] NCDs and LCDs are posted to a CMS internet site that is updated weekly.[190] MA organizations must also comply with the LCDs of the MAC whose jurisdiction covers the service area of the MA Plan.[191]

The Benefits Improvement and Protection Act (BIPA), as amended by the MMA, made significant changes with respect to the timing and circumstances under which coverage determinations may be challenged and appealed.[192]

3.7 Certification

Another crucial step in analyzing the potential reimbursement consequences associated with a proposed Medicare item or service is determining the conditions applicable to coverage. This begins with an evaluation as to whether the individual or entity that provided the service was properly certified to do so by the Medicare program.

---

[187] BIPA, § 522.
[188] 42 U.S.C. § 1395y(a); 42 U.S.C. § 1395ff(f)(1); 42 C.F.R. §§ 405.732, .860; 64 Fed. Reg. 22619 (1999).
[189] BIPA, § 522(a)(2)(B). Note that LCDs were called local medical review policies (LMRPs) until December 7, 2003. *See* CMS Trans. No. 63 (2004) regarding the conversion of LMRPs by CMS to NCDs.
[190] Ctrs. for Medicare & Medicaid Servs., *Medicare Coverage Database at* www.cms.hhs.gov/med/overview.asp.
[191] 42 C.F.R. 422.101(b). An MA plan whose service area encompasses multiple MAC jurisdictions may, with CMS approval, apply the coverage policy most beneficial to enrollees across its entire service area.
[192] BIPA, § 522; MMA, § 731; 42 C.F.R. pt. 426. For background information regarding Medicare policy on coverage determinations prior to the implementation of BIPA, *see* 67 Fed. Reg. 54534 (proposed Aug. 22, 2002). For additional information regarding the revised coverage determination process, *see* Notice, 68 Fed. Reg. 55634 (Sept. 26, 2003); for a list of currently enacted NCD's see: http://www.cms.gov/medicare-coverage-database/indexes/ncd-alphabetical-index.aspx?bc=BAAAAAAAAAAA.

3.7.1 Providers

The Secretary of DHHS uses conditions of participation (CoPs) to establish a provider's eligibility for participating in the Medicare program.[193] CoPs are detailed standards that providers must meet and adhere to in order to receive payment from Medicare. Compliance with the CoPs is determined by the state department of health or similar agency that surveys, inspects, and certifies providers for program participation under an agreement with DHHS. Certain providers may be given "deemed" status for program participation without such a state-assessment survey if they have received full accreditation from the Joint Commission (JC), DNV Healthcare (DNV), Community Health Accreditation Program (CHAP), the American Osteopathic Association (AOA), or similar private accrediting entity that surveys and inspects health care facilities and that has been recognized by Medicare as having authority to accredit providers.[194] In addition, an accreditation program known as National Integrated Accreditation for Healthcare Organizations (NIAHO) is the first hospital accreditation program in the United States that integrates ISO 9001 Quality Management System with the CoPs.[195]

Providers also enter into a written agreement with the Secretary of DHHS, known as the "provider agreement," wherein they agree to comply with all of the Medicare program's requirements.[196] The provider agreement, a 'non-negotiable' agreement, is automatically renewed each year, and may be terminated by the Secretary of DHHS for substantial noncompliance.[197] The Secretary of DHHS also may exclude providers from participation in the Medicare program for certain offenses, such as patient abuse and neglect, submission of false claims, program fraud, and financial misconduct.[198] Provider agreements are automatically assigned in connection with a change of ownership (regardless of whether the transaction is structured as a stock or asset sale) with carry forward liability to the successor in interest unless the acquirer takes specific steps to reject assignment of the provider agreement and, potentially, face a significant gap in Medicare reimbursement while awaiting re-certification as a new provider.

DHHS issues each individual Part A provider a Medicare identification number known as the "CMS Certification Number" (CCN).[199] Program rules require that the CCN appear on every claim for payment that is submitted to the Medicare program. Any correspondence from the provider to the Medicare program also must contain this number.[200]

---

[193] 42 C.F.R. pts. 482–498. HHAs also are required by Medicare to obtain a surety bond. 42 U.S.C. § 1395b-5; 42 C.F.R. §§ 441.16, 489.60–.74. *See also* BBRA, § 304 (clarifies the HHA surety-bond requirements).

[194] 42 U.S.C. § 1395bb; 42 C.F.R. §§ 488.5–.6.

[195] 73 Fed. Reg. 56588 (Sep. 29, 2008); ISO 9001 Quality Management System specifies requirements for a quality management system where an organization (i) needs to demonstrate its ability to consistently provide product that meets customer and applicable regulatory requirements and (ii) aims to enhance customer satisfaction through the effective application of the system.

[196] The basic terms of the provider agreement are contained in 42 U.S.C. § 1395cc; 42 C.F.R. §§ 489.10, .12, .53.

[197] Ctrs. for Medicare & Medicaid Servs., *Program Integrity Manual* (Pub. 100-08) Ch. 10, § 9.

[198] 42 U.S.C. § 1395y(e).

[199] Previously, these numbers were referred to as a "provider identification number" or PIN. They were also referred to as the OSCAR number, and may also be called the Medicare Identification Number, or MIN. Part B and DMEPOS providers are issued Provider Transaction Access Numbers, or PTANs. *See* CMS Pub. 100-08 IOM, Program Integrity Manual, Ch. 15 § 15.1.

[200] Ctrs. for Medicare & Medicaid Servs., *Regional Office Manual* (Pub. 23) § 6170. Note, this manual is now only available to CMS staff.

Under the Affordable Care Act, requirements were added to require the Secretary to establish procedures to screen and monitor potential providers and suppliers of the Medicare, Medicaid and SCHIP programs for fraud, waste and abuse activities.[201] Such screening includes licensure checks, criminal background checks, fingerprinting, site visits, data base checks and other procedures. The procedures applied to all newly enrolling providers and suppliers beginning March 23, 2011 and to existing enrolled providers and suppliers on March 23, 2012.[202]

3.7.2 Physicians and Suppliers

As noted above, suppliers include physicians, DMEPOS suppliers, ASCs and IDTFs. As of May 2008, each physician, supplier, and other providers were required to obtain and use a national provider identifier (NPI).[203] The NPI replaces UPINs and other so called "legacy" numbers as a physician, supplier or provider's identifier for billing and other purposes and is intended to serve as a national identification number across all public (Medicare and Medicaid) and private (e.g., commercial insurers) payers. Certain types of suppliers, including DMEPOS, IDTFs and ASCs, are also subject to on-site inspection or a survey by the applicable MAC.[204] All suppliers are required to execute a written certification statement of program compliance. Suppliers also receive a Provider Transaction Access Number (PTAN) for the purpose of communication with MACs regarding claims status, beneficiary eligibility, check status or other supplier related transactions.[205]

3.7.3 MA Organizations

CMS is responsible for determining whether an entity qualifies as an MA organization, and whether MA Plans (*i.e*, a policy or contract for health benefits coverage) offered by MA organizations meet CMS requirements. As a condition of participation in the Medicare program, MA organizations are required to assume full financial risk on a prospective basis for the provision of health care services. MA organizations may obtain insurance coverage to provide for this risk, or they may make other arrangements as provided by Medicare law. Such arrangements may include the assumption of downstream risk by other health care professionals or institutions in the organization's provider network.[206]

In order to qualify as an MA organization, enroll beneficiaries in any MA Plans, and be paid on behalf of Medicare beneficiaries enrolled in those plans, a prospective MA organization must complete the application process and enter into a contract with CMS.[207] An entity seeking to apply and contract as an MA organization is required to provide documentation of appropriate state licensure and certification, including evidence that the entity is authorized by the state to accept prepaid capitation

---

[201] ACA § 6401(a).
[202] *See* 75 Fed. Reg. 58204 (Sep. 23, 2010).
[203] The original deadline for obtaining an NPI was May 23, 2007. CMS expanded that deadline by 12 months to May 23, 2008.
[204] 42 U.S.C. §§ 1395m(a), 1395x(cc)(2), 1395x(p); 42 C.F.R. §§ 424.57, 400.202. Note also that the Secretary of DHHS has established conditions for coverage with respect to determining the eligibility of certain suppliers to participate in the Medicare program.
[205] *See generally* Ctrs. for Medicare & Medicaid Servs., *Program Integrity Manual* (Pub. 100-08) Ch. 10.
[206] 42 U.S.C. § 1395w-25(b).
[207] 42 C.F.R. §§ 422.503(a).

for providing, arranging, or paying for comprehensive health care services.[208] Contracting entities also must meet certain minimum enrollment requirements, and have administrative and management arrangements satisfactory to CMS.[209] Each contract is for a period of at least 12 months and is automatically renewed annually, contingent on the parties' agreement on the annual bid submission, unless either party has not submitted a notice of their intention not to renew.[210]

3.7.4 PDP Sponsors

Prospective PDP sponsors must submit applications and bid information to CMS at the same time, and in a manner similar to the MA program.[211] Prospective PDPs may choose to participate in Part D as a full-risk, limited-risk, or non-risk bearing fallback plan.[212] PDPs that assume the highest level of risk will receive priority by the Secretary of DHHS for participation in Part D.

The service area for a PDP consists of an entire PDP "region."[213] The SSA requires that eligible beneficiaries have a choice of at least two qualifying plans (one of which must be a PDP) in the area where they reside.[214] This requirement is not satisfied if only one PDP sponsor, or one MA-PD plan, offers all of the qualifying plans for the area. Under such circumstances, the DHHS Secretary is permitted to approve limited-risk contracts to ensure beneficiary access to Part D coverage. In the event such access is still not available, CMS is authorized to solicit bids for a "fallback plan" which does not bear insurance risk.[215]

Every PDP sponsor must enter into a contract with CMS.[216] Such entities must be licensed under state law as risk-bearing organizations eligible to offer health insurance or health benefits in the states where their prescription-drug benefit plans are offered.[217] Similar to MA organizations, PDP sponsors must adhere to certain administrative and management standards, in addition to requirements regarding enrollment, marketing, contracting periods, beneficiary protections, and others applicable to participation in Medicare Part D.[218]

3.8 Payment—The Prospective Payment System

A central element in analyzing the potential reimbursement issues associated with a proposed Medicare item or service is determining the methodology Medicare uses to pay for the item or service.

---

[208] 42 C.F.R. § 422.503(b)(2).
[209] 42 C.F.R. §§ 422.503(b)(3) and (4), 422.514.
[210] *Id.* § 422.505; *see also* §§ 422.506–.512 for contract non-renewal and termination.
[211] 42 U.S.C. § 1395w-111(b).
[212] 42 U.S.C. § 1395w-111(b)(2)(E)(ii).
[213] The MMA directed the Secretary of DHHS to establish and revise PDP regions in a manner that is consistent with the requirements for establishing and revising MA regions; 42 U.S.C. § 1395w-111(a).
[214] *Id.* § 1395w-103; 70 Fed. Reg. 44194.
[215] 42 U.S.C. § 1395w-103(b); Note, however, that certain coverage, marketing, and participation restrictions would apply to such plans.
[216] 42 U.S.C. § 1395w-112(b)(1).
[217] *Id.* § 1395w-112(a)(1). The MMA allows PDP sponsors to meet solvency standards for entities not licensed by the state in a manner similar to the process for provider-sponsored organizations under Part C.
[218] 42 U.S.C. § 1395w-112(b)–(e).

3.8.1 Introduction

PPS was established by the Social Security Act Amendments of 1983, which mandated that Medicare create and implement a prospective payment system (PPS) for the reimbursement of acute inpatient hospitals.[219] Prior to this time, hospitals were paid by Medicare on a retrospective reasonable cost basis. Spiraling health care costs prompted a rethinking of the Medicare payment system by Congress, which resulted in a complete reformulation of the program's methodology for reimbursing hospitals.

3.8.2 PPS for Acute Inpatient Hospitals

The PPS rate for acute inpatient hospitals (IPPS) represents the nationwide average cost of treating a Medicare beneficiary according to the beneficiaries' medical condition. IPPS hospitals are paid a predetermined flat rate per discharge for inpatient care that is based on the patient's principal diagnosis.[220] The full IPPS amount is paid for each stay during which there is at least one Medicare-payable "day of care." The IPPS rate may either exceed or fall short of the hospital's full costs for treating the patient. Any costs incurred by the hospital in excess of the IPPS amount will be absorbed by the hospital.

IPPS includes certain costs and excludes others from the payment rate.[221]

Costs Included in the IPPS Rate	Costs Excluded from the IPPS Rate
Inpatient Operating	Outpatient Services
Routine Ancillary	Direct Medical Education
Intensive Care	Organ Acquisition
Malpractice Insurance	Non-Physician Nurse Anesthetists
Preadmission Services	Services Covered by Parts B, C, and D
Capital-Related	Medicare Excluded Services

Beginning in FY 2005, the MMA tied annual payment updates for IPPS hospitals to the submission of quality indicators established by the Secretary of DHHS. Initially, the list was comprised of 10 such indicators, and was gradually expanded to eventually include 46 measures by FY 2011.[222] Hospitals that do not submit the required quality data on a timely basis receive a 2% reduction in their factor payment update for the fiscal year in question.[223]

3.8.2.1 Diagnosis-Related Groups

The IPPS uses diagnosis-related groups (DRGs) to calculate the payment rate.[224] Developed by Yale University as a patient-care management system in 1969, the DRG method groups diseases

---

[219] Social Security Act Amendments of 1983, Pub. L. No. 98-21, 97 Stat. 65 (1983); 42 U.S.C. § 1395ww(d).
[220] 42 C.F.R. pt. 412.
[221] 42 C.F.R. § 412.2(c)–(e). Note that a PPS for inpatient hospital-related capital costs (i.e., depreciation, interest, rent, and other property-related expenses) was phased in under a 10-year transition period that ended September 30, 2001. 42 U.S.C. § 1395ww(g); 42 C.F.R. pts. 412, 413.
[222] 75 Fed Reg 50,041, 50,183–84 (Aug. 16, 2010).
[223] 42 U.S.C. § 1395ww(B)(viii)(I).
[224] 42 C.F.R. § 412.2(a).

by diagnosis, and assigns them into case types that consider, among other factors, the amount of resources needed to treat the condition. The DRGs are then organized under major diagnostic categories (MDCs) that relate both to single-organ and multiple body systems. Each DRG has a relative value (or case-mix weight) that reflects the cost of treating Medicare patients in that particular group in comparison to the treatment cost of the average Medicare case.

DRG selection is determined by the specific principal diagnosis, as well as the age of the patient. The specific principal diagnosis denotes the cause for admission, as determined after treatment and discharge (note this is not necessarily the preliminary diagnosis, but rather the actual reason for the admission).

Cases are then further subdivided based on the presence of surgery (surgical DRGs) or the absence of surgery (medical DRGs).

Surgical and medical DRGs may be further differentiated by the presence or absence of complications or co-morbidities. Complications are conditions that arise during an inpatient stay that increases the patient's overall length of stay by at least one day in approximately 75% of cases; co-morbidities are any preexisting conditions that increase the patient's length of stay by one day in 75% of cases.

In 2007, CMS overhauled the DRG system with the development of "severity-adjusted DRGs." Specifically, in October 2007, CMS began to replace DRGs with "Medicare-severity DRGs" or "MS-DRGs" through a three year phase-in period that blended payment under the old DRG system and the MS-DRG system. While there are similarities between the two systems in the existence or absence of complications or co-morbidities, the MS-DRG system adds a third category—"major complications and/or co-morbidities." Cases are classified into MS-DRGs for payment based on: the principal diagnosis, up to eight additional diagnoses, and up to six procedures performed during the stay. In a small number of MS-DRGs, classification is also based on the age, sex and discharge status of the patient. The diagnosis and discharge information is reported by the hospital using codes from the ICD-9-CM (the International Classification of Diseases, 9th Edition, Clinical Modification). Hospitals were scheduled to transition to the ICD-10-CM beginning in October 1, 2014; however, on April 1, 2014, the President signed into law the Protecting Access to Medicare Act of 2014 which delays ICD-10-CM implementation until October 1, 2015.[225]

3.8.2.2 Determining the IPPS Rate

Determining payment can be challenging, due to the myriad of special payments and adjustments that may figure into the calculation of a final payment amount. Also, the IPPS rate and related payment adjustments seldom remain static. The IPPS rate adjustments routinely figure into the budgetary deliberations of Congress, and are the subject of an annual rulemaking by DHHS.[226]

---

[225] Pub. L. No. 113-93 § 212; *See* http://beta.congress.gov//bill/113th-congress/house-bill/4302/text.
[226] The Social Security Amendments of 1983 authorized the Secretary of DHHS to determine the rate of increase to the PPS rate, taking into account the recommendation of the Prospective Payment Assessment Commission (ProPAC). The 1983 amendments established ProPAC to advise the Secretary of DHHS on DRG classification, weight adjustments, and increases to the payment rate. Congress used the BBA to combine the functions of ProPAC and the Physician Payment Review Commission (PPRC) into a single commission called the Medicare Payment Advisory Commission (MedPAC).

Similar to an income-tax return, providers prepare a "cost report" that is used to reconcile the estimated IPPS rate adjustments for the cost-reporting year on a claims-made basis.[227] The provider files the cost report with the MAC for auditing and review. A Notice of Program Reimbursement (NPR), which details the Medicare program's final determination and settlement of the provider's total allowable costs and IPPS payments, is issued to the provider by the MAC.

The following examples describe the basic mechanics involved in determining the total payment amount for acute inpatient hospital services.

1. *Determining the Basic Payment Rate.* A payment event occurs when an acute inpatient hospital submits a claim for payment to the MAC for inpatient care that was delivered to a Medicare beneficiary.

2. *The MS-DRG Assignment.* Based on the information provided on a claim, the case is assigned to a DRG. Providers may appeal their MS-DRG assignment within 60 days from the date the claim was filed.[228]

3. *The MS-DRG Weight.* An appropriate weighting factor (which represents the average resources required to care for that specific MS-DRG relative to the average resources used to treat all MS-DRGs) is assigned by the Secretary of DHHS to each MS-DRG (the MS-DRG weight). Changes to the MS-DRG weights resulting from changes in resource patterns, technology, and various other factors are published in an annual rulemaking by the Secretary of DHHS.[229]

4. *The Payment Amount.* The MS-DRG weight is then multiplied by a dollar amount that is based on the average Medicare allowable operating cost per discharge (known as the "standardized amount") for that year.[230] The MMA permanently equalized the standardized amount for all areas. Hospitals in rural and small urban areas are paid the same standardized amount as that utilized by Medicare to pay hospitals in large urban areas.[231]

The standardized amount is divided into a labor and non-labor share. The non-labor component is adjusted by a cost-of-living factor. The labor component is adjusted by the wage index applicable to the area where the hospital is located.

The wage index accounts for variations in area-hospital labor costs (which is established by the Secretary of DHHS based on an annual survey of wage and wage-related costs for short-term acute-care hospitals).[232] The Secretary of DHHS also is required to make an annual determination with respect to the wage index.[233]

BBA, § 4022. MedPAC is charged with advising Congress on payment issues relating to Medicare payment issues. 42 U.S.C. § 1395ww(e). To help fund the costs of reform initiatives in the ACA, market basket updates for inpatient services will be reduced on an annual basis from 2010 to 2019.

[227] CMS requires cost reports from *all hospitals* and their components, as well as from freestanding SNFs, HHAs, and outpatient physical-therapy providers.

[228] 42 C.F.R. § 412.60(d).

[229] Data for DRG relative weights may be obtained from the CMS website on the Internet at www.cms.hhs.gov/AcuteInpatientPPS/FFD/list.asp.

[230] 42 U.S.C. § 1395ww(d).

[231] MMA, § 401.

[232] This data is derived from each hospital's annual Medicare cost report, and reflects the earnings and paid hours of employment by occupational category.

[233] 42 U.S.C. § 1395ww(d)(5)(A); 42 C.F.R. § 412.64.

A hospital may request that it be reclassified or redesignated to a different geographic area for purposes of using the other area's wage index.[234] Reclassification is accomplished by appealing to the Medicare Geographic Classification Review Board (MGCRB).[235] The MMA established a one-time process for hospitals to appeal their wage-index classifications and select another area within the same (or a contiguous) state if they do not otherwise qualify for wage reclassification.[236]

Under MMA the Secretary of DHHS also established a payment adjustment recognizing the out-migration of hospital employees who reside in one county and work in a different area with a higher wage index. Hospitals eligible for this "commuting wage adjustment" must be located in a qualifying county. A "qualifying county" is a county that meets all of the following criteria: (i) hospital employees in the county commute to work in an MSA (or MSAs) with a wage index (or wage indices) higher than the wage index of the MSA or rural statewide area in which the county is located; (ii) at least 10% of the county's hospital employees commute to an MSA (or MSAs) with a higher wage index (or wage indices); and, (iii) the three-year average hourly wage of the hospital(s) in the county equals or exceeds the three-year average hourly wage of all hospitals in the MSA or rural statewide area in which the county is located.[237]

Calculation of the Payment Amount

Step 1	(Labor component) x (MS-DRG weight) x (wage index) = A
Step 2	(Non-labor component) x (MS-DRG weight) = B
Step 3	A + B = Standardized Amount

3.8.2.3 Case-Mix Adjustment

The Secretary of DHHS also may adjust the average standardized amount to "eliminate the effect" of coding and discharge classification changes "that do not reflect real changes in case mix" for discharges occurring on or after October 1, 2001.[238] This is done in the aggregate for all hospitals as part of the annual updating process.

3.8.2.4 Special Adjustments and Payments for Certain Costs

CMS may adjust the IPPS rate or make special payment for certain costs.[239] These include the following categories.

Treatment of Low-Income Patients

A percentage add-on payment is applied to the DRG-adjusted base payment rate for hospitals that serve a "disproportionate share" (DSH) of low-income and indigent patients. In Medicare parlance,

---

[234] BIPA extends the effective duration of a hospital's wage-index reclassification by the MGCRB to three fiscal years. BIPA, § 304(a).
[235] The guidelines concerning the criteria and conditions for hospital reclassification are located at 42 C.F.R. §§ 412.230–.236.
[236] The statutory deadline for hospitals to file an appeal was February 15, 2004. Reclassification is effective for three years starting April 1, 2004. MMA, § 508; 69 Fed. Reg. 661 (2004).
[237] MMA, § 505; 42 C.F.R. 412.64(i).
[238] BIPA, § 301(e). The term "case mix" refers to the types of cases that are treated by the hospital.
[239] 42 C.F.R. § 412.90.

these hospitals are referred to as "DSH hospitals." The DSH adjustment provides for a percentage increase in Medicare payment for hospitals that qualify under either of two statutory formulas designed to identify hospitals that serve a disproportionate share of low-income and indigent patients. For qualifying hospitals, the amount of this adjustment may vary based on the outcome of the statutory calculation. [240]

The ACA dictated that, beginning in fiscal year 2014 (October 1, 2013), and for each subsequent fiscal year, DSH payments will be adjusted to 25% of what the DSH hospital would have otherwise received plus an additional payment based upon one of three factors described in the statute. This adjustment in payment is designed to better conform with the amount that Medicare believes DSH hospitals actually lose from providing services to low-income and indigent patients.[241] These adjustments also reflect a view that, with new health care coverage for millions previously uninsured individuals, the DSH "subsidy" can be decreased over time. However, based upon numerous administration-imposed delays to certain aspects of the Affordable Care Act as well as the impact on many of the nation's hospitals, on March 31, 2014, the U.S. Senate passed the Protecting Access to Medicare Act of 2014 (PAMA), which reauthorized and extended dozens of Medicare payment enhancements including extensions to DSH provisions. Under this Act, implementation of the Medicaid DSH changes is further delayed to 2017, but the revised methodology and allocations are extended through 2024, an additional two years. After 2024, a new provision would revert the calculation of DSH allotments back to the previous methodology, without regard to the provisions governing reductions.[242]

Indirect Medical Education

Approved teaching hospitals may receive a percentage add-on payment for each case paid through IPPS. The indirect medical education (IME) adjustment provides additional IPPS payments to hospitals for the indirect costs attributable to approved medical-education programs for physicians. The IME adjustment varies depending on the ratio of residents-to-beds under IPPS for operating costs, and according to the ratio of residents-to-average daily census under the IPPS for capital costs.[243]

Outlier Cases

Special payment adjustments are made for cases involving extraordinarily high costs compared to most discharges classified in the same DRG.[244] The threshold criteria for determining outlier payment are published in the annual rulemaking by the Secretary of DHHS.[245]

---

[240] 42 U.S.C. § 1395ww(d)(5)(F); 42 C.F.R. §§ 412.2(f)(6), .106, .320. *See also* MMA, §§ 402, 951.
[241] ACA, § 3133; . 42 U.S.C. § 1395ww(r).
[242] Pub. L. No. 113-93 § 221.
[243] 42 U.S.C. § 1395ww(d)(5)(B); 42 C.F.R. §§ 412.105, .322. Note that Medicare Part B provides for a graduate medical education (GME) payment adjustment for a hospital's activities based on a prospectively determined amount per resident. 42 U.S.C. § 1395ww(h)(4); 42 C.F.R. § 413.76.
[244] 42 U.S.C. § 1395ww(d)(5); 42 C.F.R. §§ 412.80–.89. Payment for day outliers was phased out of the Medicare program in 1998.
[245] CMS published a final rule revising its outlier payment policies effective for discharges occurring on or after August 8, 2003, with deferred implementation of various changes until October 1, 2003. 68 Fed. Reg. 34494 (2003).

New Technologies and Medical Services

Hospitals are eligible for an add-on payment for a new medical service or technology, if:

- the medical service or technology is new;
- the medical service or technology is costly such that the MS-DRG rate otherwise applicable to discharges involving the medical service or technology is determined to be inadequate; and
- the service or technology demonstrates a substantial clinical improvement over existing services or technologies.

The amount of the add-on payment depends on the cost incurred by the hospital for the new medical service or technology.[246]

Post-Acute Transfers

IPPS distinguishes between patient "transfers" and "discharges." Medicare considers a patient to be "discharged" when the patient is formally discharged from the hospital, expires while in the hospital, or is transferred to an excluded hospital or distinct-part unit. Activities that *do not* qualify as a "discharge" include the transfer of a patient to another IPPS hospital, or a patient's leave of absence from the hospital. "Discharging" hospitals are paid the full DRG amount.[247]

A patient is considered "transferred" by Medicare when the patient is moved:

1. to another IPPS hospital;
2. from an IPPS hospital;
3. from a hospital excluded from IPPS because of a statewide cost-control program or demonstration project; or
4. to a hospital that has not yet begun its first IPPS cost-reporting period.

The "transferring" hospital is paid a per diem rate for each day of the stay, not to exceed the full DRG payment that would have been made had the patient been discharged without being transferred. The per diem rate is determined by the full DRG divided by the average length of stay for that DRG, multiplied by the length of stay at the transferring hospital. Certain exceptions to the payment-rate standard for transferring hospitals apply to specific DRGs and cost outliers.[248]

DHHS had designated 273 MS-DRGs that commonly require post-hospital care for payment either as "transfers" or "qualified discharges."[249] Medicare updates the DRGs subject to the post-acute care transfer policy every fiscal year in connection with the IPPS rulemaking.[250]

In certain instances, a "special payment methodology" applies whereby Medicare pays qualified discharges at a "fifty/fifty" blend of the transfer/discharge rate for the first day and at the transfer rate

---

[246] 42 U.S.C. § 1395ww(d)(5)(K) and (L); *see also* 42 C.F.R. §§ 412.87–.88.
[247] 42 C.F.R. § 412.4(e).
[248] *Id.* § 412.4(b), (f).
[249] 72 Fed. Reg. 47188 (Aug. 22, 2007); 73 Fed. Reg. 48956 (Aug. 19, 2008).
[250] DHHS has designated 274 MS-DRGs subject to the Post-Acute Care Payment Transfer Rule for FY2014. *See* 78 Fed. Reg. 50495, Table 5; *see also* CMS Internet-Only Manual 100-04, CPIM, Ch. 3 § 40.2.4.

for all subsequent days.[251] Specifically, under the special payment methodology, a hospital is paid 50% of the total IPPS payment plus the average per diem for the first day of the stay, and 50% of the per diem amount for each subsequent day of the stay, up to the full MS-DRG payment amount.[252]

ESRD Discharges

Hospitals receive a payment adjustment for ESRD discharges if these discharges equal 10% or more of the hospital's total Medicare discharges. The ESRD payment adjustment is based on the estimated weekly cost of dialysis and the ALOS of ESRD beneficiaries for the hospital.[253]

Low-Volume Hospitals

A graduated payment adjustment of up to 25% is available to "low-volume" hospitals. Medicare defines a low-volume hospital as a short-term general hospital that is located more than 25 road miles from a similar hospital, and that has less than 200 discharges (including both Medicare and non-Medicare patients) during a fiscal year.[254]

Excluded (Pass-Through) Costs

Certain inpatient hospital costs are excluded from PPS, and thus, continue to be reimbursed by Medicare on a reasonable cost basis. These include, among others, hospital bad debt related to "covered services" that are derived from beneficiary deductible and coinsurance amounts; heart, liver, lung, and kidney acquisition costs incurred by an approved transplant facility; and costs associated with blood-clotting factor.[255]

Value Based Purchasing

Starting in 2013, the Secretary of DHHS, as mandated by the ACA, began to implement a hospital value-based purchasing program (VBP) under which payments can be increased based on a provider's performance score.[256]

Hospital Acquired Conditions

Beginning in fiscal year 2015, hospitals will be ranked based on their number of hospital-acquired conditions and hospitals in the top quarter (i.e., with the most HACs) will have overall inpatient payments further reduced by 1%, in addition to current payment penalties for HACs.[257]

---

[251] 42 U.S.C. § 1395ww(d)(5); 42 C.F.R. § 412.4(f)(5), (6); 65 Fed. Reg. 40953 (1998); 68 Fed. Reg. 45345 (2003); 72 Fed. Reg. 47188 and 47410 (Aug. 22, 2007).
[252] 42 C.F.R. § 412.4(f)(2); 73 Fed. Reg. 48593 (Aug. 19, 2008).
[253] 42 C.F.R. § 412.104(a), (b)(1).
[254] 42 C.F.R. § 412.101. Note, while the statute defines low-volume hospital as hospital with 800 or fewer discharges per year (*see* 42 U.S.C. § 1395ww(d)(12)(C)(i)), the law provides that the term "discharge" refers to total discharges, and not merely to Medicare discharges and the Secretary has interpreted the law to require "an empirically justifiable adjustment formula based on the relationship between costs and discharges for these low-volume hospitals." *See* 69 FR 48,916, 49,099 (2004). Upon performing this calculation, CMS determined the discharge number should be established at 200 or fewer per year.
[255] *See* 42 C.F.R. §§ 412.2(e)(5), .2(f)(8), .2(e)(2), 413.85, 415.160, 412.2(e)(4), .113(c), .113(d), .113(f)(4), .115(a).
[256] ACA, § 3001; 42 U.S.C. § 1395ww(o)(1); *see also* 78 Fed. Reg. 50678, and http://www.cms.gov/Medicare/Quality-Initiatives-Patient-Assessment-Instruments/hospital-value-based-purchasing/index.html.
[257] ACA, § 3008; 42 U.S.C. § 1395ww(p); *see also* http://www.cms.gov/Medicare/Medicare-Fee-for-Service-Payment/HospitalAcqCond/Hospital-Acquired_Conditions.html.

Hospital Readmissions

Beginning in fiscal year 2013, IPPS for hospitals with readmission rates higher than their Medicare-calculated expected readmission rates began to be reduced by the greater of (a) a floor adjustment factor equal to 0.99% for FY 2013, 0.98% for FY 2014 and 0.97% for FY 2015 and subsequent years, or (b) the excess readmissions ratio for the applicable federal fiscal year.[258]

Community-based Care Transition Program

Beginning January 1, 2011 and continuing for a five-year period, funding has been made available to facilities that furnish improved care transition services to high-risk Medicare beneficiaries (for example, post-discharge planning, medication administration counseling, follow-up services, etc.).[259]

3.8.3 Other Hospital PPS

3.8.3.1 Rehabilitation Hospitals

Inpatient rehabilitation facilities (IRFs) and distinct-part units are paid under an IRF PPS. IRF PPS applies to all inpatient rehabilitation facilities except Department of Veterans Affairs (VA) hospitals, hospitals subject to state cost controls (e.g., Maryland hospitals), and hospitals in demonstration projects. The IRF PPS utilizes information from a patient-assessment instrument to classify patients into distinct groups based on clinical characteristics and expected resource needs. Separate payments are calculated for each group, including the application of case- and facility-level adjustments.[260]

3.8.3.2 Long Term Care Hospitals

Long term care hospitals (LTCHs) are paid under a separate LTCH PPS.[261] LTCH PPS applies to hospitals with an average length of stay greater than 25 days. The LTCH PPS uses information from LTCH patient records to classify patients into distinct long term care DRGs based on clinical characteristics and expected resource needs. Separate payments are calculated for each DRG.

3.8.3.3 Psychiatric Hospitals

Inpatient psychiatric facilities (IPF PPS) are paid under a per diem-based payment system. The per diem payment amount reflects the average daily costs of inpatient psychiatric care, including capital-related costs. After adjustment for budget neutrality, the per diem amount is modified by factors for patient and facility characteristics to account for variation in patient resource use. Adjustments also are made to account for area wage levels, rural IPFs, and teaching IPFs.[262]

---

[258] ACA, §§ 3025, 10309; 42 U.S.C. § 1395ww(p); *see also* http://www.cms.gov/Medicare/Medicare-Fee-for-Service-Payment/AcuteInpatientPPS/Readmissions-Reduction-Program.html.
[259] ACA, § 3026; *see also* http://innovation.cms.gov/initiatives/CCTP/.
[260] 42 U.S.C. § 1395ww(j); 42 C.F.R. §§ 412.600 *et seq.*; BBA, § 4421; BIPA, § 305; 66 Fed. Reg. 41316 (2001).
[261] 42 U.S.C. 1395ww(d); 42 C.F.R. §§ 412.500 *et seq.*; BBRA, § 123; BIPA, § 307; 67 Fed. Reg. 55954 (2002). Section 114(d) of the Medicare, Medicaid and SCHIP Extension Act (MMSEA), enacted December 29, 2007, established a three-year moratorium on the establishment of new LTCHs, an increase in the number of certified beds at LTCHs, or the establishment of a satellite facility by an existing LTCH. This moratorium was extended until December 28, 2012 by section 3106(a) of the ACA.
[262] 42 U.S.C. § 1395ww(d)(1)(B); 42 C.F.R. §§ 412.400 *et seq.*

3.8.3.4 Affordable Care Act Updates

Under the Affordable Care Act, market basket updates for IRFs, LTCHs and IPFs were reduced on a sliding scale between the years 2010 and 2019. In addition, beginning in fiscal year 2014, IRFs, LTCHs and IPFs are now required to report data on quality measures, similar to what is already occurring in the hospital and SNF settings. Providers that fail to submit quality data on such measures are now subject to a 2% reduction in market basket updates.[263]

3.8.4 Rural-Area Hospitals

Special payment provisions apply to hospitals identified as isolated or essential hospitals primarily located in rural areas. Such entities include critical access hospitals, sole community hospitals, rural referral centers and Medicare-dependent hospitals.[264] Each is briefly described below.

- *Critical Access Hospitals (CAHs)*—CAHs must have no more than 15 inpatient beds, offer 24-hour emergency care, and be located more than a 35-mile drive from any other hospital. CAHs are reimbursed based on what they spend for each patient, rather than on the average expected cost for specific diagnoses that most hospitals are paid.[265]

- *Sole Community Hospitals (SCHs)*—SCHs are the sole source of care in their area and are eligible for reimbursement as a SCH if they are located at least 35 miles from other similar hospitals or are located in a rural area and meet certain conditions regarding accessibility. SCHs receive the higher of a hospital-specific rate based on their costs in a base year or the IPPS Federal rate based on the standardized amount.[266]

- *Rural Referral Centers (RRCs)*—The RRC program was established to support high-volume rural hospitals that treat a large number of complicated cases. To be eligible to be a RRC, a hospital must be either located in a rural area and have more than 275 beds in use, or meet certain criteria concerning case volume and patient travel.[267]

- *Medicare-Dependent Hospitals (MDHs)*—MDHs have fewer than 100 beds, do not serve as SCHs, and at least 60% of the facility's inpatient days or discharges are for Medicare beneficiaries. An MDH receives the higher of the Federal rate or the Federal rate plus 75% of the amount by which the Federal rate is exceeded by the highest of its FY 1982, FY 1987, or FY 2002 hospital specific rate.[268] Under the Affordable Care Act, the MDH program was extended for another year through October 1, 2012.[269]

3.8.5 Hospitals Excluded from PPS

Certain hospitals are excluded from PPS primarily because the government has been unable to devise a workable PPS methodology for these hospitals. Hospitals *originally* excluded from

---

[263] ACA §§ 3004, 10322; 42 U.S.C. § 1395ww(m)(5).
[264] *See generally* 42 U.S.C. § 1395ww(d); 42 C.F.R. §§ 412.90(a), .92 (SCHs); 42 U.S.C. §§ 1395i; 42 C.F.R. § 412.96 (RRCs); 42 C.F.R. § 412.108 (MDHs).
[265] *See generally* at 42 U.S.C. § 1395ww(d) and specifically at 42 C.F.R. § 413.70.
[266] *See generally* at 42 U.S.C. § 1395ww(d) and specifically at 42 C.F.R. §§ 412.90(a) and 412.92.
[267] *See generally* at 42 U.S.C. § 1395ww(d) and specifically at 42 C.F.R. § 412.96.
[268] *See generally* at 42 U.S.C. § 1395ww(d) and specifically at 42 C.F.R. §§ 412.90(j) and 412.108.
[269] ACA, § 3124.

PPS included IRFs, LTCHs, IPFs, hospitals located in any U.S. territory (except Puerto Rico), children's hospitals, cancer hospitals, VA hospitals, and CAHs.[270] Medicare traditionally reimburses PPS- exempt hospitals for "reasonable costs" subject to the limits imposed by the Tax Equity and Fiscal Responsibility Act (TEFRA), thereby the "TEFRA limit."

The term "reasonable cost" is defined by Medicare law as follows:

> the cost actually incurred, excluding therefrom any part of incurred cost found to be unnecessary in the efficient delivery of needed health services, and shall be determined in accordance with regulations establishing the method or methods to be used and the items to be included in determining such costs....[271]

Reasonable costs encompass "all necessary and proper expenses incurred in furnishing services" including the provider's direct and indirect costs.[272] Reasonable-cost principles contemplate that a provider will be reimbursed the actual costs of providing quality care, regardless of how widely the actual costs may vary from provider to provider and from time to time for the same provider.[273]

Cost-based providers are reimbursed subject to allowable costs. Under the allowable-cost principle, "the costs for individuals covered by the Medicare Program are not borne by others not so covered, and the costs for individuals not so covered are not borne by the Medicare Program."[274] Allowable costs are determined using the claims that are submitted by the provider, the provider's annual cost reports, or a combination of the two. If the provider's operating costs include amounts unrelated to patient care, specifically not reimbursable, or flowing from the provision of luxury items or services, then such amounts will not be deemed "allowable" for payment by Medicare.[275]

In Medicare parlance, PPS-excluded hospitals are frequently referred to as "TEFRA hospitals." These hospitals receive a *per diem* interim payment for the cost of inpatient care that is subject to a final cost-report settlement. Medicare uses the hospital's net cost amount (e.g., exclusive of capital-related and medical-education costs) to determine whether such costs exceed the program's targeted cost threshold (known as the "TEFRA target amount"). Medicare imposes a "penalty payment" on hospitals that exceed the TEFRA target amount, as only a portion of the excess cost will be reimbursed to the hospital. Similarly, hospitals will receive an "incentive payment" from Medicare if their final reimbursable costs fall below the TEFRA limit.[276]

---

[270] *See* discussion regarding transition to IRF PPS, LTCH PPS, and IPF PPS at section 3.8.1.3. *See also* 42 C.F.R. § 413.80 regarding CAHs.
[271] 42 U.S.C. § 1395x(v)(1)(A).
[272] Ctrs. for Medicare & Medicaid Servs., *Medicaid Management Care Manual* (Pub. 100-16), Chap. 17A, § 50.
[273] 42 C.F.R. § 413.9(c)(3). *See also GranCare, Inc. v. Shalala*, 93 F. Supp. 2d. 24 (D.D.C. 2000) regarding the court's interpretation of the "prudent buyer" principle when costs are considered "substantially out of line" with institutions in the same geographic area that are similar in size, scope of services, utilization, and the like.
[274] Ctrs. for Medicare & Medicaid Servs., *Medicaid Management Care Manual* (Pub. 100-16), Ch. 17A, § 50.
[275] 42 C.F.R. § 413.9(c)(3).
[276] Tax Equity and Fiscal Responsibility Act of 1982, Pub. L. No. 97-248, 96 Stat. 324 (1982). TEFRA hospitals are paid a target rate for their operating costs. The "cost with TEFRA limit" reimbursement scenario is set forth in 42 U.S.C. § 1395x(v), which defines "reasonable cost," and at 42 C.F.R. §§ 412.22, 413.40.

3.8.6 Hospital Outpatient Department Services

3.8.6.1 Establishment of the Outpatient Prospective Payment System

A PPS for hospital outpatient department services—the hospital Outpatient Prospective Payment System (OPPS)—became effective August 1, 2000.[277] Under the OPPS, only a hospital may bill Medicare for services furnished by the outpatient department pursuant to an "encounter" in the outpatient department. An "encounter" is defined by Medicare as a "direct personal contact between a patient and physician, or other person" who is authorized under state law or the hospital's bylaws.[278] As discussed further below, payment for hospital outpatient department services changed dramatically under Section 603 of the Bipartisan Budget Act of 2015 and CMS's issuance of implementing regulations in its 2017 OPPS final rule.

The OPPS uses "ambulatory payment classification" (APC) groups to calculate the hospital outpatient rate.[279] Developed by 3M Health Information Systems, the APC system groups outpatient procedures into individual ambulatory payment classes. Each APC contains an aggregation of clinically related and resource-similar services.

The beneficiary coinsurance is calculated for each APC based on 20% of the national median charge for services in the APC. The coinsurance amount for an APC will not change until such time as the amount becomes 20% of the total APC payment. Regardless, no coinsurance amount can be greater than the hospital inpatient deductible in a given year.[280]

The OPPS rate is based on the median cost of the procedures contained within each APC subject to an outlier payment adjustment for high-cost cases established by the Balanced Budget Refinement Act (BBRA).[281] Further, both the total APC payment and the coinsurance amount are adjusted for geographic wage variations. Hospitals may also be paid for more than one APC per patient encounter, depending on the type of service provided.

3.8.6.2 Payment for Outpatient Drugs and Biologicals

The Medicare Modernization Act of 2003 (MMA) established a new payment methodology for "specified covered outpatient drugs" furnished as part of a covered hospital's outpatient department service.[282] "Specified covered outpatient drugs" are drugs that were paid on a pass-through basis prior to December 31, 2002, and for which a separate APC was established.[283] They also address radiopharmaceuticals. Reimbursement for these types of drugs and biologicals furnished in the hospital outpatient department setting migrated to the average sales price (ASP) methodology under

---

[277] 42 U.S.C. § 1395(l); 42 C.F.R. pt. 419. *See also* BBA, § 4523; BBRA, §§ 201–204, 402; and BIPA, §§ 401–406. Although an effective date of January 1, 1999 was established under the BBA, the implementation of the OPPS was delayed by CMS for various reasons until August 1, 2000. Additionally, the effective implementation of OPPS for provider-based facilities was delayed until October 7, 2000.
[278] 42 C.F.R. § 410.2.
[279] *Id.* §§ 419.30–.32.
[280] BBA, § 4523; BBRA, § 204; 65 Fed. Reg. 18434 (2000). *See* BIPA, § 111 for subsequent modifications to the beneficiary copayment amount; 42 C.F.R. §§ 419.42–.44.
[281] BBRA, § 201; 65 Fed. Reg. 18434 (2000). *See also* 67 Fed. Reg. 9556 (2002).
[282] Pub. L. No 108-173.
[283] 42 U.S.C. § 1395l(t).

the MMA.[284] Now, covered Part B drugs and biologicals (including IVIG, orphan drugs, separately payable drugs and biologicals, blood clotting factors, intrathecal drugs and echocardiography contrast agents) are generally paid at the lesser of 106% of ASP or the actual charge, just as in the physician office setting.[285] In some instances, however, the payment amount differs depending upon the type of drug or biological being provided. These include the following:

- Medicare pays the lesser of the actual charge or 106% of the ASP for multiple-source drugs.[286]
- Single source drugs are paid by Medicare at the lesser of the actual charge, 106% of the ASP or 106% of the wholesale acquisition cost (WAC), subject to copays and deductibles.[287]
- The ASP methodology does not apply to infusion drugs furnished through a DME item, certain drugs provided in connection with particular renal dialysis services and blood and blood products.[288]
- The payment allowance limits for radiopharmaceuticals used in the physician office setting or freestanding IDTFs are not subject to the ASP. MACs determine the payment limits for radiopharmaceuticals based on the methodology in place as of November 2003 in the case of radiopharmaceuticals furnished in other than the hospital outpatient department. Some MACs have developed fee-schedules for radiopharmaceuticals while other MACs continue to pay based upon actual "invoice pricing."[289]
- Radiopharmaceuticals in the *hospital outpatient setting* are reimbursed depending upon whether the radiopharmaceutical is a diagnostic supply or a therapeutic agent. For 2014, payment for most radiopharmaceuticals in the hospital outpatient used for diagnostic purposes, including stress agents and Cysview, are not separately reimbursed—namely, the cost of the radiopharmaceutical agent is considered to be 'bundled' or 'packaged' as part of their associated medical procedures or services (and hence reflected by the APC).[290]
- However, policy-packaged drugs (which include the following: anesthesia drugs; drugs, biologicals, and radiopharmaceuticals that function as supplies when used in a diagnostic test or procedure (including contrast agents; diagnostic radiopharmaceuticals, and stress agents); and drugs and biologicals that function as supplies when used in a surgical procedure) are eligible for a pass-through payment amount that would be equal to ASP + 6 percent for CY 2017 because, if not for their pass-through status, payment for these products would be packaged into the associated procedure.[291]
- Vaccines, namely pneumococcal pneumonia, flu, and hepatitis vaccines are paid at reasonable cost when furnished in a hospital outpatient.[292]

---

[284] 70 Fed. Reg. 68516 (Nov. 10, 2005).
[285] 70 Fed. Reg. 68640, 68648, 68661, 68671–72.
[286] 42 C.F.R. § 414.904.
[287] *Id.*
[288] *Id.*; Ctrs. for Medicare & Medicaid Servs., *Medicare Claims Processing Manual* (Pub. 100-04), Ch. 17, § 20.1.3.
[289] Medicare Claims Processing Manual, Chapter 17, Sections 20.1.3. Importantly, where "invoice pricing" is deployed at the local level, some MACs have required copies of actual manufacturer invoices while other MACs have required a certification of the "invoice price."
[290] *See* 42 C.F.R. § 419.2(b)(15) and 78 FR 74826, 75010 (December 10, 2013).
[291] 81 Fed. Reg. 79562, 79663.
[292] *Id.*; Ctrs. for Medicare & Medicaid Servs., *Medicare Claims Processing Manual* (Pub. 100-04), Ch. 17, § 20.5.9.

In the 2018 OPPS final rule released in November of 2017, CMS cut Part B reimbursement for certain 340B drugs from ASP + 6% to ASP – 22.5%.[293] The reduction applies to separately payable, non-pass through drugs with status indicator "K" that meet the definition of "covered outpatient drug" as defined in Section 1927(k) of the Social Security Act.[294] Additionally, the final rule implements a requirement to use certain modifiers on all OPPS claims for 340B-acquired drugs. The reduction is limited to disproportionate share and rural referral center hospitals; sole community and children's hospitals are exempt. The modifiers, however, must be used by all hospitals subject to OPPS. Non-exempt hospitals must report modifier "JG," and exempt hospitals must report modifier "TB."[295] This proposal is implemented in a budget neutral manner and increases the non-drug OPPS conversion factor for all hospitals (including those not participating in 340B) by 3.2%.[296] All changes are set to take effect on January 1, 2018. As of the time of this writing, industry groups have filed suit to enjoin the implementation and challenge the statutory authority of the final rule.[297] Further, on November 14, 2017, Representatives McKinley (R-W.Va.) and Mike Thompson (D-Calif.) introduced a bipartisan bill with the aim of preventing the implementation of the OPPS 340B payment reduction.[298]

3.8.6.3 Section 603 of the Bipartisan Budget Act of 2015 and Payment Reductions for Off-Campus Outpatient Departments

Section 603 of the Bipartisan Budget Act of 2015 (Section 603) requires that Medicare payment for *off-campus* hospital provider-based outpatient department (PBD) services be "site-neutral."[299] The payment changes necessary to implement Section 603 took effect on January 1, 2017. As a result, and as of that date, off-campus PBDs that were not otherwise excepted from Section 603 were no longer be paid at OPPS rates, but, as discussed below, were paid at a lower rate under the Medicare Physician Fee Schedule (MPFS), thereby effectively neutralizing the payment differential hospitals enjoyed when providing services from off-campus PBDs instead of a freestanding supplier type.

Section 603 reflects the culmination of policymakers' concerns that by providing higher reimbursement under the OPPS, hospitals were improperly incentivized to acquire physician practices or other facilities and convert them into PBDs, resulting in higher costs to Medicare and beneficiaries.

Several types of off-campus PBDs were excepted from Section 603, including the following:

- off-campus PBDs that furnished and billed for outpatient department services under the OPPS prior to November 2, 2015. With regards to these excepted PBDs it should be noted that the exception continues even if such off-campus PBDs expand the services they provide, but not if the PBD relocates, unless that relocation is necessary because extraordinary

---

[293] *See* Hospital Outpatient Prospective Payment and Ambulatory Surgical Center Payment Systems and Quality Reporting Programs, 82 Fed. Reg. 52356 (November 13, 2017).
[294] 82 Fed. Reg. 52509.
[295] *Id.*
[296] 82 Fed. Reg. 52509–10.
[297] *Am. Hosp. Ass'n v. Hargan*, No. 1:17-cv-02447, 2017 U.S. Dist. LEXIS 213027 (D.D.C., Dec. 29, 2017).
[298] H.R. 4392, 115th Cong. (1st Sess. 2017).
[299] Pub. L. No. 114-74, enacted November 2, 2015, amending Section 1833(t) of the Social Security Act.

circumstances outside of the hospital's control, such as natural disasters, significant seismic building code requirements, or significant public health and public safety issues;[300]

- off-campus PBDs that meet the definition of a "dedicated emergency department" under EMTALA regulations at 42 C.F.R. § 489.24(b), even if the dedicated emergency departments provide both emergency and nonemergency services;[301] and

- PBDs located on the campus of a hospital or a remote location of a hospital. In this instance, the term "campus" includes that area that is within 250 yards of a hospital or remote location of a hospital and is measured from any point at the hospital or remote location to any point on the PBD.[302]

As indicated above, for those off-campus PBDs that are subject to Section 603, the items and services they deliver are reimbursed under the MPFS.[303] In determining to use the MPFS, CMS reasoned that most off-campus PBDs were initially freestanding physician practices and that most items and services furnished therefrom are commonly furnished in the physician office setting.[304] Despite these reimbursement changes, hospitals billing for items and services rendered from non-excepted off-campus PBDs continue to submit claims for the items and services they provide on institutional claim forms (i.e., CMS UB-04, and not CMS-1500) and continue to include such items and services on their cost reports.[305] However, now, when billing for such items and services, hospitals are required to include payment modifier "PN" in order to identify that the items and services were furnished from a nonexcepted off-campus PBD.[306]

Payment rates for items and services provided by nonexcepted off-campus PBDs were established as follows:

- For calendar year 2017, CMS compared off-campus PBD payment data from 2016 to MPFS rates and used a rate that was approximately 50% of the OPPS rate.[307]

- For calendar year 2018, CMS will use the same methodology as in 2017, although with different scaling at approximately 40% of the applicable OPPS rate rather than 50% of that rate.[308]

- For calendar years 2019 and beyond, CMS intends to pay hospitals for nonexcepted items and services at a MPFS rate that would more directly equalize payment rates between nonexcepted off-campus PBDs and physician offices (for example, a MPFS-based rate equal to the difference between the nonfacility and facility rates for the item or service in question).[309] CMS acknowledges that this more direct MPFS-based payment based approach will require hospitals to bill for nonexcepted items and services on professional or facility claim form rather than an institutional one, and that it will require substantial

---

[300] 42 C.F.R. § 419.48(a)(2); 81 Fed. Reg. 79562, 79704–07 (Nov. 14, 2016).
[301] 42 U.S.C. § 1395l(t)(21)(A); 42 C.F.R. § 419.48(a)(1); 81 Fed. Reg. 79702.
[302] 42 U.S.C. § 1395l(t)(21)(B)(i)(II); 81 Fed. Reg. 79703.
[303] 81 Fed. Reg. 79712–13, 18–19.
[304] 81 Fed. Reg. 79712–13.
[305] 81 Fed. Reg. 79717–18.
[306] 81 Fed. Reg. 79710.
[307] 81 Fed. Reg. 79720–31.
[308] 81 Fed. Reg. 79727–28; 82 Fed. Reg. 52976, 53027–28 (Nov. 15, 2017).
[309] 81 Fed. Reg. 79728.

system changes.[310] Accordingly, in the alternative, CMS is still considering whether to continue with a methodology similar to what it used for 2017 and 2018 (i.e., a scaling of OPPS rates), but is concerned that doing so will continue to result in payments that are higher than would be made for the same service in a physician office, and as a result may incentivize hospitals to acquire certain types of physician practices and convert them to PBDs.[311]

Services not packaged under the OPPS are not subject to CMS's new payment policy. For example, if a hospital furnishes an outpatient laboratory test that is eligible for separate payment under the Clinical Laboratory Fee Schedule (CLFS), the hospital will continue to bill under the CLFS regardless of whether the off-campus PBD is nonexcepted.[312] Part B drugs and other items and services currently paid at the MPFS rate under the OPPS (e.g., therapy and preventive services) are also not subject to this new payment policy.[313]

Beneficiary cost-sharing for nonexcepted items and services will generally be equal to their cost-sharing where the items and services are provided at a freestanding facility (i.e., 20% of the new rate, which is intended to be similar to the MPFS nonfacility rate).[314]

3.8.6.4 The Three-Day DRG Payment-Window Rule

Diagnostic and certain non-diagnostic services performed on an outpatient basis during the three days immediately preceding a patient's date of admission to a PPS hospital, and one day immediately preceding a patient's date of admission to a non-PPS hospital, are not billable to the Medicare program as separate services. This required bundling of services is known as the "Three-Day DRG Payment-Window Rule" (Payment-Window Rule).[315] Due to a statutory change in 2010 that was implemented as part of the 2012 Physician Fee Schedule, all clinically related non-diagnostic services (i.e. therapeutic services) are included in the Payment-Window Rule.[316] It is irrelevant for purposes of the application of the Payment-Window Rule whether the diagnosis for the inpatient admission and outpatient diagnosis of the patient are the same. Rather, the focus of the inquiry is whether the non-diagnostic services are clinically related to a patient's inpatient admission.[317] If a hospital attests that the non-diagnostic services are not clinically related, then the services can be separately billed to Part B.[318]

Further, despite the fact that this rule commonly is known as the "72-hour DRG payment window," a literal reading of the applicable provisions indicates that three days will mean more than 72 hours in most cases. The statute and regulations refer to diagnostic and therapeutic services furnished by a hospital or by an entity wholly-owned by a hospital (e.g., laboratory and radiology services) furnished

---

[310] *Id.*
[311] *Id.*
[312] 81 Fed. Reg. 79725.
[313] *Id.*
[314] 81 Fed. Reg. 79718–19.
[315] This Rule is also sometimes called the "72-hour DRG Payment Window."
[316] Section 102 of the Preservation of Access to Care for Medicare Beneficiaries and Pension Relief Act of 2010 (Pub. L. 111-192); Social Security Act §1886(a)(4).
[317] Ctrs. for Medicare & Medicaid Servs., *Medicare Claims Processing Manual* (Pub. 100-04), Ch. 3, § 40.3B.
[318] *Id.*

during the three days "immediately preceding the date of the patient's admission."[319] The Medicare Hospital Manual, however, refers to services furnished "on the first, second and third calendar days preceding the date of a beneficiary's admission."[320] Thus, the window can be as long as 95 hours and 59 minutes—three days, plus the date of admission.

3.8.6.5 Unbundling

"Unbundling" is the improper practice of billing Medicare for separate procedures that routinely should be reported as a single claim. This practice results in an overall higher cost to the Medicare program for such services. In 1986, Congress extended the 1983 prohibition against the unbundling of hospital inpatient services to include hospital outpatient services.[321]

3.8.7 Post-Acute Care Providers

Medicare also covers certain post-hospital services (e.g., SNF and hospice) for patients who are discharged to a post-acute care setting after a hospital stay, as well as for medical services that are provided to beneficiaries in their homes. Medicare reimburses such providers for post-acute care services using a PPS or fee-based payment methodology. Payment also may be tied to the satisfactory submission of certain additional requirements, such as a physician's certification of medical necessity, patient-assessment data, and/or a written plan of care.

3.8.7.1 Skilled Nursing Facilities

Medicare classifies SNFs as hospital-based, freestanding, or "swing-bed" for payment purposes. In order to be considered "hospital-based," the SNF must be an integral and subordinate part of the hospital, and be subject to the same bylaws and governance as the hospital. Swing-bed SNFs may be converted to either short-term (acute care) or long-term (extended care) use, subject to need. Swing-bed SNFs also must meet specific eligibility requirements, and are subject to special payment rules.

As a condition of participation, Medicare requires all SNFs to have in effect a transfer agreement with a hospital. Medicare also excludes services furnished by SNFs from the three-day DRG payment-window rule.[322]

For cost-reporting periods occurring after July 1, 1998, a PPS *per diem* rate was phased in over a transition period that ended in 2001.[323] The initial PPS *per diem* rate was based on 1995 aggregate cost-report data and is adjusted for case-mix variation using a resident classification system called Resource Utilization Groups (RUGs). The RUGs are based on resident-assessment data (e.g., health conditions, clinical characteristics, and patient service needs), and are weighted by the intensity of

---

[319] 42 U.S.C. § 1395ww(a)(4); 42 C.F.R. §§ 412.2(c)(5), 413.40(c)(2).
[320] Ctrs. for Medicare & Medicaid Servs., *Medicare Claims Processing Manual* (Pub. 100-04), Ch. 3, § 40.3B.
[321] 42 U.S.C. §§ 1395y(a)(14), 1395cc(a)(1)(H); 42 C.F.R. §§ 410.42, 1003.102–.103; 65 Fed. Reg. 18434 (Apr. 7, 2000).
[322] *See* section 3.8.6.1.4 for a discussion of the three-day DRG payment-window rule. 42 U.S.C. §§ 1395tt, 1395x(*l*); 42 C.F.R. §§ 409.20, .32–.33, 412.2(c), .4, 413.114, .40(c); Ctrs. for Medicare & Medicaid Servs., *Medicare Claims Processing Manual* (Pub. 100-04), Ch. 3, § 40.3B.
[323] 42 C.F.R. §§ 413.335, .337; Ctrs. for Medicare & Medicaid Servs., *Medicare Program Integrity Manual* (Pub. 100-08), Ch. 6, § 6.1; *see also* BIPA, §§ 311–315 for subsequent modifications to the SNF payment methodology. Ctrs. for Medicare & Medicaid Servs. Prog. Mem. A-01-08 (Jan. 16, 2001) *at* www.cms.hhs.gov/transmittals/downloads/a0108.pdf.

care and services required. Initially, 44 RUGs were established. Recently that has been expanded to encompass 53 RUGs.[324] The PPS rate is further adjusted for geographic wage variations using the hospital wage index.[325]

The Affordable Care Act required the Secretary of DHHS to develop a plan to implement value based purchasing for SNFs by October 1, 2011.[326] However, as of 2014, CMS was still in the process of complying with this requirement.[327] Therefore, Congress included value-based purchasing program (SNF VBP Program) requirements in PAMA.[328] First, the law requires that the Secretary specify re-admission measures by October 1, 2015 and 2016, respectively, and provide quarterly feedback reports to the SNFs beginning October 1, 2016 based upon these measures.[329] Next, the SNF VBP Program must be implemented for SNF payments beginning October 1, 2018. The law also requires the Secretary to develop and publish scoring and payment formulas, including performance standards for achievement and improvement, at least 60 days prior to the October 1, 2018 deadline. Once implemented, SNF payments will be based on a combination of their adjusted federal per diem rate times the value-based incentive payment percentage, which is based on the SNF's performance score.[330]

3.8.7.2 Hospice

CMS establishes payment rates for specific categories of covered hospice care (e.g., routine home care, continuous home care, inpatient respite day care, general inpatient care) that are subject to a cost cap and an inflation update.[331] Under the Affordable Care Act, the Secretary of DHHS is required to promulgate regulations no earlier than October 1, 2013 implementing revisions to the methodology for the routine homecare payment rate, based upon analytical data gathered beginning in FY2011.[332] CMS has yet to implement revisions to these payment rates due to a lack of data in rebasing six of the nine components of cost that comprise the routine care hospice rate.[333] Medicare beneficiaries must elect to receive hospice care and be certified by a physician as terminally ill at the beginning of the initial hospice-benefit period.[334]

Payment is made for each day during which the beneficiary is eligible and under the care of the hospice, regardless of the amount of services furnished on any given day. Additionally, payment is made for only one of the categories of hospice care for any particular day.[335] The hospice cap, which runs from November 1 of each year until October 31 of the following year, is calculated by the MAC

---

[324] *See* http://www.cms.gov/Medicare/Medicare-Fee-for-Service-Payment/SNFPPS/RUGRefinement.html. Note that under the ACA, the implementation of the RUG-IV system was delayed by one year until October 11, 2011. *See* ACA § 10325.
[325] The hospital wage index is being used by CMS for the SNF geographic-wage adjustment because the agency lacks reliable SNF-specific data to establish a wage index for SNFs. 66 Fed. Reg. 39562 (2001).
[326] ACA § 3006.
[327] *See* http://www.cms.gov/Medicare/Medicare-Fee-for-Service-Payment/SNFPPS/Downloads/SNF-VBP-RTC.pdf.
[328] PAMA § 215; Pub. L. No. 113-93 § 215; 42 U.S.C. 1395yy(h).
[329] PAMA § 215(a).
[330] PAMA § 215(b).
[331] 42 C.F.R. §§ 418.302(b), .308, .309. Medicare also excludes hospice services from the three-day DRG payment-window rule. *Id.* §§ 412.2(c), 413.40(c).
[332] ACA § 3132; 42 U.S.C. 1395f(i)(6)(D)(i).
[333] 78 Fed. Reg. 48234, 48241, 48272.
[334] 42 U.S.C. § 1395d(a)(4), (d)(1); 42 C.F.R. §§ 418.200–.204.
[335] 42 C.F.R. § 418.302(e)(2). *See also* BIPA, § 321(a)–(b) for subsequent modifications to the hospice payment methodology.

at the end of the hospice-cap period. Payments made to a hospice during the cap period that exceed the cap amount are considered overpayments, and must be refunded back to the Medicare program by the hospice.[336] In addition, the total payment to a hospice for inpatient care is subject to a cap as well, not to exceed 20% of the total days that the patient had elected for hospice care.[337]

Similar to other PPS providers, hospice providers, beginning in March 2014, are now required to report quality measures or have their annual market basket updates reduced by 2%.[338] As was done in the context of other PPS payment systems, and to help fund the costs of reform initiatives, market basket updates for hospice services will be reduced on a sliding scale between fiscal years 2013 through 2019.[339]

3.8.7.3 Home Health Agencies

HHAs are classified by Medicare as hospital-based or freestanding for payment purposes. Effective October 1, 1997, HHAs are paid based on the physical location where the HHA services are provided, as opposed to where the HHA that provides the services is located.[340]

Prior to October 1, 1997, HHAs were reimbursed by Medicare on a per-visit cost basis subject to applicable limits. Between October 1, 1997, and September 30, 2000, HHAs were reimbursed under an interim payment system (IPS) that paid HHAs according to the "*lesser*" of (1) the agency's specific costs, (2) the Medicare per-visit limit, or (3) the agency's specific per-beneficiary limit, which is calculated using a statutory formula prescribed under the BBA.[341]

For cost-reporting periods occurring on or after October 1, 2000, HHAs are paid under a PPS. The PPS rate, which is based on data collected from a two-year (1995–1997) demonstration project, is adjusted for case-mix variation using a Home Health Resource Group (HHRG) classification system. The HHRG system classifies HHA patients into 80 case-mix groups that are adjusted for geographic wage variations.

Under PPS, HHAs are paid for each 60-day episode of care. Sixty percent of the estimated base payment for the full 60 days is paid to the HHA when the initial claim is filed with the MAC. The remaining 40% is received by the HHA at the close of the first 60-day episode of care. For subsequent episodes, the HHA receives a 50% initial payment and a 50% residual payment. Additional adjustments may be made for payment outliers, significant changes in a beneficiary's condition, low beneficiary utilization during an episode of care, or when a beneficiary changes HHAs in the middle of an episode of care.[342] Certain items (e.g., DME, oxygen, and related supplies) also are excluded from the PPS rate.[343]

---

[336] 42 C.F.R. §§ 418.308–.309.
[337] 42 C.F.R. § 418.302(f)(1).
[338] ACA §§ 3004, 10322; *see also* http://www.cms.gov/Medicare/Quality-Initiatives-Patient-Assessment-Instruments/Hospice-Quality-Reporting/Downloads/HQRP-General-Information-Fact-Sheet.pdf.
[339] ACA § 3401.
[340] 42 U.S.C. § 1395bbb(g).
[341] *Id.* § 1395x(v)(1)(L); *see also* BBRA, §§ 301–303 for subsequent modifications to the interim payment system and PPS methodologies.
[342] 65 Fed. Reg. 41128 (2000).
[343] BBRA, § 305; 65 Fed. Reg. 41128 (2000).

Beginning in 2014, the CMS issued rules to begin implementing rebasing adjustments to the national, standardized 60-day episode payment rates; the national per-visit rates; and the NRS conversion factor. As a result of these adjustments, payments to HHAs are estimated to decrease by approximately 1.05 percent, or $200 million in CY 2014. These adjustments are intended to better reflect the number, mix and level of intensity of home health services in an episode of care, and the average cost of providing care.[344] This rebasing is being phased in over a four year period, as mandated by the ACA, and will not to exceed adjustments of 3.5% per year.

As with hospitals and SNFs, the Secretary is required to develop a plan to implement value based purchasing for home health agencies.[345] As with the SNF value based purchasing program, CMS is still in the process of designing and implementing its vision for a VBP, beginning with a report to Congress in 2012.[346] The Affordable Care Act also reduces market based updates for HHAs by 1% for calendar years 2011 through 2013.[347] Beginning in 2015, market based updates will be further reduced by a productivity adjustment.

3.9 Payment—The Resource-Based Relative Value Scale Fee Schedule

3.9.1 Overview

Historically, physicians and other Part B suppliers were paid by Medicare on a "reasonable charge" basis. Medicare defines "reasonable charge" as the "lesser" of (i) the submitted charge; (ii) the "customary charge," which is the median of the supplier's historical charges for that service; or (iii) the prevailing charge, which is derived from what the other suppliers charge for the service in the same area.[348] Since the early 1980s, Medicare has moved progressively away from paying physicians and suppliers using the reasonable-charge methodology.

Congress established a new payment program for physicians in 1989. The methodology, which was phased in between 1992 and 1996, pays physicians according to the lesser of the actual charge, or the amount determined from a resource-based relative value scale (RBRVS) fee schedule. Developed by the Harvard School of Public Health under the direction of William Hsiao, the RBRVS fee schedule is based on the relative value of a physician's work (i.e., intensity of effort, skill, and medical judgment) as adjusted for geographic, practice, and malpractice-expense variations.[349] Effective with implementation of the Medicare Access and CHIP Reauthorization Act of 2015 (MACRA) on January 1, 2017, physicians and other clinicians billing under the Medicare Physician Fee Schedule (MPFS) will see a significant shift away from fee schedule payments and toward value-based payments. MACRA is discussed in more detail below.

---

[344] ACA § 3131; 42 U.S.C. 1395fff(b)(3)(A)(iii); 78 Fed. Reg. 72256; *see also* http://www.cms.gov/Center/Provider-Type/Home-Health-Agency-HHA-Center.html.
[345] ACA § 3006.
[346] *See* http://www.cms.gov/Medicare/Medicare-Fee-for-Service-Payment/HomeHealthPPS/downloads/stage-2-NPRM.PDF.
[347] ACA §§ 3401, 10322.
[348] 42 U.S.C. § 1395u(b)(3).
[349] *Id.* § 1395w-4(a); 42 C.F.R. pt. 414. Radiology and anesthesiology services are subject to separate RBRVS fee schedules. 42 C.F.R. §§ 414.22(a)(2), .46.

3.9.2 RBRVS Fundamentals

Each medical procedure is assigned a relative value unit (RVU) for the physician work, practice, and malpractice components that is based on the individual procedure's ranking, relative to the other procedures on the scale.[350] The RVU is then multiplied by a national dollar "conversion factor" to determine the amount of Medicare payment.[351] Individual Geographic Practice Cost Indexes (GPCIs) are used by Medicare to adjust this number to account for geographical differences in practice costs.[352]

For services furnished on or after January 1, 1999, separate facility and non-facility practice-expense RVUs have been established. The lower facility-expense RVU applies to services that are delivered in a hospital, SNF, or ASC. The higher non-facility expense RVU applies to services that are furnished in a physician's office, a patient's home, or a facility that is not an ASC, SNF or hospital.[353]

Medicare participating physicians (PARs) with UPINs are paid based on the full RBRVS payment amount. Non-participating physicians (Non-PARs) are paid based on 95% of the allowable RBRVS amount, and are subject to a maximum limit on what they can charge beneficiaries over the fee-schedule amount. Non-PARs can be subject to sanctions, including civil monetary penalties and program exclusion, for repeatedly billing Medicare beneficiaries in excess of the "limiting charge."[354]

Annual updates to the conversion factor are derived from a market-basket index of medical service costs called the Medicare Economic Index (MEI). To control the overall growth of physician expenditures to the Medicare program, RBRVS historically used a target rate (the Sustainable Growth Rate (SGR)) linked to the growth of the U.S. Gross Domestic Product and certain other factors.[355] Such factors included the estimated weighted percentage increase in fees for all physician services, the estimated changes in the average number of Part B beneficiaries, and the estimated change in expenditures for all physician services due to statutory and regulatory changes. Annual updates to the conversion factor were tied to the SGR. With implementation of MACRA, the SGR is replaced with a new system that links fee-for-service payments to care delivery, quality and value-based variables. Beginning in the second half of 2015 and through 2019, MPFS payment rates have a .5% annual update.[356] Payment rates will then freeze until 2026, at which point payment rates will be updated by .25% (for those participating in MACRA's Merit-Based Incentive Payment System) or .75% (for those participating in MACRA's Alternative Payment Models).[357]

3.9.3 Coding and Documentation Standards

The RVUs have been compiled into HCPCS' common five-character coding arrangement.[358] Eighty percent of all HCPCS codes are compiled under the Practitioner's Current Procedural

---

[350] 42 U.S.C. § 1395w-4(c); 42 C.F.R. §§ 414.20–.28. The MMA effected changes in practice-expense RVUs for drug administration costs. MMA, § 303.
[351] 42 C.F.R. § 414.30.
[352] 42 U.S.C. § 1395w-4(e); 42 C.F.R. § 414.26.
[353] 42 C.F.R. § 414.22.
[354] *Id.* § 414.20.
[355] 42 U.S.C. § 1395w-4(f). The MMA modified the formula for calculating the sustainable growth rate to include a ten-year rolling-average factor. This change applies to SGR computations starting in 2003. MMA, § 601.
[356] 42 U.S.C. § 1395w-4(d)(17), (18).
[357] 42 U.S.C. § 1395w-4(19), (20).
[358] *See* cms.hhs.gov/medhcpcsgeninfo/01_overview.asp for detailed information relating to the HCPCS coding.

Terminology (CPT) for medical services that is updated annually by the AMA. The other 20% include physician and non-physician services not included in the CPT, as well as codes based on local reporting practices. CPT codes are five-digit numerical codes; the other codes are alphanumeric.

In conjunction with the AMA, CMS has developed explicit evaluation and management (E&M) guidelines to assist physicians in properly coding and documenting office visits, hospital visits, medical consultations, and other case-management services in the patient's chart. Components used in proper E&M code selection include the type of medical history taken, the category of medical examination performed, and the complexity level of medical decision making by the physician. Failure to provide adequate documentation in the patient's medical record (i.e., appropriate support for the coding decision) can result in reduced reimbursement and/or allegations that the physician submitted "false claims" to the Medicare program.[359]

Teaching physicians who bill Medicare when services are provided in part by a medical resident are required to adhere to additional documentation standards. For example, the teaching physician must be physically present during *key* portions of the procedure. In cases involving surgery or procedures that are dangerous or complex, the teaching physician must be present during all *critical* portions of the procedure, and must be immediately available to furnish services throughout the entire procedure.[360] Documentation of the physician's presence also must be included in the patient's chart.

3.9.4 Application of RBRVS to Non-Physician Practitioners and Other Suppliers

Medicare uses the RBRVS fee schedule to reimburse limited-license practitioner services, incident to services, radiology services, outpatient physical and occupational therapy services, and certain diagnostic tests exclusive of clinical laboratory tests.[361] Physician assistants, nurse practitioners, clinical nurse specialists, nurse midwives, and CRNAs also are subject to cost limits that are based on a percentage of the RBRVS fee-schedule amount.[362]

3.9.5 MACRA

The Medicare Access and CHIP Reauthorization Act of 2015 (MACRA) and its implementing regulations represent a significant shift in the way that Medicare pays for the services of most physicians and certain other practitioners paid under the MPFS. MACRA establishes a Quality Payment Program (QPP) that, fundamentally, requires a rapid transition from fee-for-service to quality and value-based payments under Part B for the professional services of most physicians and certain other "eligible clinicians."[363] Physicians and certain other "eligible clinicians" are required to participate in the QPP through either (1) Advanced Payment Models (APMs) or (2) the Merit

---

[359] The False Claims Act creates criminal liability for anyone who presents a false, fraudulent, or fictitious claim for payment to the federal government. A violation of the act constitutes a felony offense punishable by imprisonment of up to five years, fines up to $25,000, and exclusion from participation in government health care programs. 18 U.S.C. § 287. *See also* 31 U.S.C. § 3729 (civil False Claims Act).

[360] 42 C.F.R. § 415.172.

[361] *Id.* §§ 410.10, .32, .59.

[362] Revisions to Payment Policies and Adjustments to the Relative Value Units Under the Physician Fee Schedule for Calendar Year 1999, 63 Fed. Reg. 58814 (1998).

[363] *See* 42 C.F.R. § 414.1300 et seq.; 81 Fed. Reg. 77008 (Nov. 4, 2016).

Based Incentive Payment System (MIPS). Presently, MIPS eligible clinicians are physicians, physician assistants, nurse practitioners, clinical nurse specialists, certified registered nurse anesthetists, and groups that include such clinicians,[364] but this definition may be expanded in future rulemaking. Three defined classes of clinicians are excluded from MIPS eligible clinicians: (1) new Medicare-enrolled eligible clinicians, for the first year, (2) low-volume clinicians with less than or equal to $30,000 in Part B-allowed charges or 100 Medicare patients (these clinicians are still subject to some MIPS participation requirements, but are not subject to payment adjustments), and (3) clinicians who participate in qualifying APMs.[365] The following provides a high-level summary of APMs and MIPS.[366]

3.9.5.1 Advanced Payment Models or APMs

MACRA is designed to incentivize clinicians to form and participate in APMs. Through APMs, clinicians and groups participate in initiatives directed at changing how care is delivered, such as the Medicare Shared Savings Program, the Comprehensive Primary Care Plus (CPC+), and certain other Medicare payment initiatives. Those clinicians and groups who participate in APMs are subject to the APM's quality, cost, data reporting, performance, and potential payment incentives under the particular APM program. Participants in an APM are excepted from the MIPS payment adjustments if the APM is an "Advanced APM"[367] (i.e., APMs that require the use of certified electronic health record technology, include quality measure results as a factor for determining payment for professional services, and require the APM entity to bear more than nominal financial risk[368] in its arrangement with CMS).[369]

Advanced APM participants receive a 5% positive lump-sum payment based on the aggregate of professional services furnished during the immediately preceding payment year.[370] Such lump sum payments are in addition to any payments (or losses) under the APM itself. Clinicians participating in Advanced APMs also receive 0.75% annual fee schedule updates beginning in 2026.[371]

---

[364] 42 C.F.R. § 414.1305.
[365] 42 C.F.R. § 414.1310.
[366] Note that CY 2017 represents a transition year for the QPP. During this transition year, clinicians are able to "pick their pace" of participation in the QPP through certain reduced MIPS obligations or participation in an Advanced APM. The transition year requirements are described throughout the MACRA final rule preamble at 81 Fed. Reg. 77008 (Nov. 4, 2016) and the MACRA implementing regulations.
[367] 42 C.F.R. § 414.1310.
[368] The MACRA implementing regulations establish both general and medical home model-specific financial risk standards. Under the general financial risk standard, CMS must be able to use withholds or reduce payments to the APM or its eligible clinicians, or impose repayment obligations on the APM as a vehicle to satisfy the AMP'S financial responsibility to CMS for an applicable performance period. 42 C.F.R. § 414.1415(c)(1). For medical home model APMs, the repayment mechanism described under the general standard above applies, with an additional option that the APM may lose the right to all or part of otherwise guaranteed payments. 42 C.F.R. § 414.1415(c)(2). Beginning in the 2018 performance year, medical home model APMs will be limited to entities that are owned and operated by organizations with 50 or fewer eligible clinicians. Where the APM (including its parent organization and subsidiaries of that parent) has more than 50 eligible clinicians, it will be subject to the general (rather than medical home-specific) standards. *Id.*
[369] 42 C.F.R. § 414.1415.
[370] 42 C.F.R. § 414.1450.
[371] 42 U.S.C. § 1395w-4(20).

3.9.5.2 Merit-Based Payment Incentive System (MIPS)

The Merit Based Payment Incentive System (MIPS) program is a QPP participation vehicle that consolidates and streamlines components of three existing CMS programs set to end on Dec. 31, 2018. Under MIPS, clinicians or groups will be measured and assessed upward or downward payment adjustments based on their achievement in four performance categories:

1. Quality (replacing the Physician Quality Reporting System);[372]
2. Cost (measuring cost of care and replacing the Value Based Payment Modifier);[373]
3. Improvement activities (such as operating a patient centered medical home, promoting care coordination etc.);[374] and
4. Advancing care information (ACI) (replacing the Electronic Health Record Incentive Program (also known as meaningful use)).[375]

MIPS eligible clinicians will be required to report information regarding, and be measured on, these four MIPS performance categories beginning in 2017.[376] Performance in a defined performance year determines whether a clinician or group receives positive or negative MIPS payment adjustments during a payment year two years forward (so 2017 reporting and performance determines payment adjustments for 2019).[377]

MIPS payment adjustments represent an increase or decrease in payment under Part B based on reported achievements in the categories described above. During performance year 2017/payment year 2019, the adjustment percent is +/-4%; during performance year 2018/payment year 2020, the adjustment percent is +/-5%; during performance year 2019/payment year 2021, the adjustment percent is +/-7%, and during performance year 2020/payment year 2022 and beyond, the adjustment percent is +/-9%.[378] In addition, MACRA provides $500 million for payments for "exceptional performance" under MIPS through payment year 2024.[379]

3.9.6 Fee Schedules for Freestanding Supplier Entities

Medicare uses a combination of national fee schedules and cost-charge limitations to pay freestanding supplier entities such as clinical laboratories, DME and prosthetic and orthotic providers, screening mammography suppliers, CORFs, rehabilitation agencies and clinics, ESRD facilities, FQHCs, and RHCs.[380]

---

[372] 42 C.F.R. § 414.1330–40.
[373] 42 C.F.R. § 414.1350.
[374] 42 C.F.R. § 414.1355–65.
[375] 42 C.F.R. § 414.1375.
[376] 42 C.F.R. § 414.1320(a).
[377] *Id*.
[378] 42 C.F.R. § 414.1405(c).
[379] 42 C.F.R. § 414.1405(d).
[380] 42 U.S.C. §§ 1395m, 1395k; Ctrs. for Medicare & Medicaid Servs., *Medicare Claims Processing Manual* (Pub. 100-04), Ch. 15, §§ 10.2, 20, 20.1; Ch. 18, §§ 20.2, 20.3, 20.4.

3.9.7 Ambulance Services

Payment is available according to a national fee schedule under Medicare Part B only if payment is not made under Medicare Part A, directly or indirectly, for the service.[381] There are seven levels of ambulance services, five of which apply to ground ambulances and two of which apply to air ambulances (one for fixed wing and one for helicopters). Each level of service has a slightly different payment schedule amount which is generally determined by adding a base rate to a payment rate per mile which is adjusted by a geographic adjustment factor, multiplied by the number of miles the beneficiary is transported.

For ambulance services where the pickup point is in a rural area, there is an add-on to the mileage rate for both ground (for first 50 miles) and air transport. Further, for a period commencing July 1, 2004, and continuing through April 1, 2015, rural transports will be paid the higher of (a) the current rate payable under the national fee schedule process or (b) a blended rate that is a mix of the national fee schedule and a new, regional fee schedule. Section 414 of MMA requires the Secretary to increase the base rate for certain rural area transports.[382]

The national fee schedule is not applicable to critical access hospitals (CAH) or entities owned or operated by CAHs, which continue to be paid on a reasonable cost basis if there is no other ambulance supplier or provider within a 35-mile drive.

3.10 Payment—Blended Capitation

3.10.1 Introduction

Medicare employs a distinct payment methodology for MA organizations that ties the program's payment to the number of beneficiaries enrolled in the MA Plan. CMS makes advance monthly payments to MA organizations using a per-member per-month (PMPM) methodology known as "capitation."[383]

MA organizations receive an advance monthly payment equal to 1/12th of the annual MA capitation rate for the county or geographic area (i.e., payment area) they serve.[384] Monthly payments to MA organizations reflect existing enrollees, including enrollment that is effective both before and in the month for which payment is being made. CMS can retroactively adjust (reconcile) payments to

---

[381] 42 C.F.R. § 410.40(a)(2).

[382] For example, between July 1, 2004 and 2009, MMA § 414 provided additional funding for transports that originate in a "qualified rural area," long trip mileage and rural transports attributable to low-density areas, and trips in excess of 50 miles in both urban and rural areas. Sections 3105 and 10311 of the Affordable Care Act extended increases in the ambulance fee schedule amounts for covered ground ambulance transports originating in rural areas by 3% and for covered ground ambulance transports originating in urban areas by 2% retroactive to January 1, 2010 through December 31, 2010. The ACA also extended § 414 of the MMA. The Medicare and Medicaid Extenders Act of 2010 (H.R. 4994, signed into law Dec. 15, 2010), further extended these provisions through December 31, 2011 or January 1, 2012 dependent upon the specific provision. Next, Pub. L. No. 113-67, the "Pathway for SGR Reform Act of 2013" extended these rates through March 31, 2014; and PAMA § 104 (H.R. 4302, signed into law Apr. 1, 2014) extended the rates through April 1, 2015.

[383] 42 C.F.R. § 422.304(a).

[384] 42 C.F.R. § 422.304; *see also* 42 C.F.R. § 422.306. Special rules apply to enrollees in MSAs and RFBS plans, as well as to enrollees with ESRD. *Id.* § 422.304(c)(1)–(3).

MA organizations to reflect any differences between the actual number of MA enrollees in a plan and the number on which CMS based the MA organization's advance monthly payment.[385]

3.10.2 Determining the MA Payment Rate

MA Plans (other than medical savings accounts) are required to use a competitive-bidding system for Part A and Part B benefits. The MMA allows for competitive bidding that compares geographically-based benchmarks and bids to calculate beneficiary premiums and plan-payment amounts. Each MA organization must annually submit a monthly aggregate bid for each of its MA Plans.[386] The Secretary of DHHS will determine benchmark amounts for Part A and Part B benefits in geographic areas based on the MA capitation rates. The benchmark amounts, risk adjustment factors, and related information will be announced by the Secretary of DHHS by the first Monday in April of each year.[387]

3.11 Payment—New Competitive "Market-Based" Systems

3.11.1 Part B

The Medicare Prescription Drug, Improvement and Modernization Act of 2003 (MMA) established guidelines for a Competitive Bidding Program for Part B DME, enteral nutrition and off-the-shelf orthotics.[388] This program is ultimately intended to replace the traditional Medicare fee schedule payment system with competitively bid payment amounts for selected items in designated metropolitan statistical areas (MSAs). Pursuant to program guidelines, suppliers submit competitive bids to furnish certain items in the competitive bid areas, which are ultimately awarded by CMS. CMS must re-compete the bids at least once every three years.

Following an initial 2007 Round 1 bid leading to a number of widespread complaints and Congressional scrutiny with respect to CMS's implementation of the Round 1 bids, the agency was directed to conduct a re-bid of the Round 1 Competitive Bidding Program pursuant to the Medicare Improvements for Patients and Providers Act of 2008 (MIPPA).[389] CMS conducted a subsequent "Round 1 Rebid" in 2009 which included (1) Oxygen Supplies and Equipment; (2) Standard Power Wheelchairs, Scooters, and Related Accessories; (3) Complex Rehabilitative Power Wheelchairs and Related Accessories; (4) Mail-Order Replacement Diabetic Supplies; (5) Enteral Nutrients, Equipment and Supplies; (6) Continuous Positive Airway Pressure devices (CPAPs), Respiratory Assist Devices (RADs), and related supplies and accessories; (7) Hospital Beds and Related Accessories; (8) Walkers and Related Accessories and (9) Support Surfaces (Group 2 mattresses and overlays).[390] CMS launched the program on January 1, 2011 in nine different MSAs (Charlotte,

---

[385] *Id.* § 422.308(f).
[386] 42 C.F.R. §§ 422.254–.256.
[387] MMA, § 222(f); 42 C.F.R. §§ 422.264(c) and (e), .312(a).
[388] Section 302 of the Medicare Prescription Drug, Improvement and Modernization Act of 2003, Pub. L. No. 108-173, 117 Stat. 2066 (2003).
[389] The Medicare Improvements for Patients and Providers Act of 2008 (MIPPA), 110 Pub. L. No. 275, 122 Stat. 2494 (2008).
[390] *See* "Competitive Bidding Update—One Year Implementation Update," *available at* http://www.cms.gov/Medicare/Medicare-Fee-for-Service-Payment/DMEPOSCompetitiveBid/index.html. The re-bid for Support Services occurred in the Miami MSA only.

Cincinnati, Cleveland, Dallas-Fort Worth, Kansas City, Miami/Ft. Lauderdale, Orlando, Pittsburgh, and Riverside/San Bernardino, California).[391] CMS estimates that the competitive bidding program saved the fee-for-service program over $200 million in its first year of operation.[392]

MIPPA also required Round 2 of program competition, which occurred in 2011 in 91 additional MSAs and became effective in July 2013.[393] At the same time, CMS commenced a national mail-order competition for diabetic testing supplies, which covers all fifty states, the District of Columbia, Puerto Rico, the U.S. Virgin Islands, Guam, and America Samoa.[394] CMS continues recompetes for Round 1, Round 2, and the national mail-order competition. The ACA required CMS to use either competitive bidding or payment rate adjustments using competitively bid rates in all areas of the country by 2016.[395] Pursuant to 2014 rulemaking, CMS began reimbursement adjustments on January 1, 2016 that applied competitive bid pricing for all areas of the country, with this pricing fully phased in on July 1, 2016.[396] However, Congress—through the 21st Century Cures Act passed in December 2016—retroactively delayed the second round of rate adjustment from July 1, 2016, to January 1, 2017, in order to provide suppliers temporary relief from CMS's substantial reduction in reimbursement payments.[397]

3.11.2 Part C

On January 1, 2006, MA Plans (other than medical savings accounts) were also moved to a competitive-bidding system for Part A and Part B benefits. *See* Section 3.10.2 above.

The most significant change to the MA program since the MMA is, undoubtedly, the Affordable Care Act. Prior to the Affordable Care Act, MA Plans were paid monthly per-capita benefits (except for hospice services) to beneficiaries who enrolled in their MA Plan. Under Section 1853 of the Act, CMS was required to calculate benchmark amounts for MA Plans. MA Plans annually submitted bids that represented the plans estimated monthly revenue requirement for providing covered benefits for the average beneficiary in the upcoming plan year. Under prior guidelines, if the MA Plan's bid equaled the CMS-determined benchmark, CMS would pay the MA organization the benchmark amount and no beneficiary premium would be charged to enrollees. If the MA Plan bid *exceeded* the benchmark, CMS would pay the MA organization the benchmark amount and the MA organization would charge the beneficiary a monthly premium based upon the difference between the bid and the benchmark amount. Likewise, if the MA Plan bid was *less than* the benchmark, CMS would pay the MA organization 75% of the difference between the bid amount and the benchmark—the MA "rebate"—which could be used by the MA organization to (1) lower Medicare cost sharing obligations, (2) provide supplemental benefits (e.g., vision care), or (3) reduce or eliminate monthly premiums.

---

[391] *Id.*
[392] *Id.*
[393] Section 302 of the Medicare Prescription Drug, Improvement and Modernization Act of 2003, Pub. L. No. 108-173, 117 Stat. 2066 (2003); Section 6410 of the ACA (expanding the Round 2 MSAs from 70 to 91).
[394] *See* CMS DMEPOS Competitive Bidding Program, "About the Program," *available at* http://www.dmecompetitivebid.com/palmetto/cbicrd2.nsf/DocsCat/Home.
[395] *See* Section 6410 of the ACA.
[396] 79 Fed. Reg. 66120, 66224–241 (Nov. 6, 2014).
[397] 21st Century Cures Act, Pub. L. No. 114-255 (2016); *see* H.R. 5210 and S. 2736.

The Affordable Care Act made a number of fundamental changes to this process. First and foremost, the Act provided that benchmarks are frozen at 2010 levels. Second, the Act established a new MA benchmark rate methodology that is pegged to a fixed percentage of the Medicare FFS costs for the MA Plan's payment area. To determine the applicable percentage, each MA payment area (i.e., county) was ranked based on its Medicare FFS costs and was grouped into four categories ranging from 95% (for areas that are ranked as high FFS cost areas) to 115% (for areas ranked as low FFS cost areas). This methodology was phased in using a three-tiered approach, beginning in contract year (CY) 2011, with the full methodology in effect for CY 2017 and subsequent years.[398]

For all MA Plans, payments for CY 2011 were frozen at the CY 2010 levels. Thereafter, the methodology was phased in over a three-year period for most MA Plan payment areas. For MA Plans in payment areas where the difference between the current CY 2010 payment rate and the CY 2010 projected benchmark rate (calculated under the new methodology) was $30 or more, the phase-in occurred over a four-year period. In those payment areas where the difference was $50 or more, it occurred over a six-year period. All MA Plans were paid under the new methodology beginning in CY 2017.

Of note, while the Affordable Care Act imposed substantial payment reductions as a result of these changes to the benchmark payment approach, the law also established bonus payments available to MA Plans that achieved a four stars or higher rating under the MA Plan five-star quality rating system used by CMS. In 2012, plans achieving four stars or higher will be eligible for a 1.5% increase, in 2013 a 3% increase, and in 2014 and beyond a 5% increase.[399] Accordingly, the ultimate impact on MA organizations depends upon their geographic location and the ability to meet four stars or higher on the five-star quality rating system currently used by CMS.

3.11.3   Part D

The MMA also incorporates competitive-bidding and benchmark rates into the Part D payment methodology.[400] As a result, beneficiary premiums vary based on the bids of the selected PDP or MA-PD plan.

PDP and MA-PD plans receive subsidies from CMS through four payment mechanisms: (1) a direct premium subsidy; (2) reinsurance subsidies; (3) payment adjustments; and (4) additional payments for low-income subsidy individuals.[401] Beneficiaries pay a monthly premium in addition to their cost sharing obligations (i.e., deductibles and copayments), unless they qualify for low-income subsidies or premium waivers.[402]

The direct subsidy payments CMS makes to the Part D plans equal the approved standardized bid of the individual PDP or MD-PD plan, adjusted for health status less the monthly beneficiary premiums.[403] The health status adjustment amount is based on the formula used by CMS to account for the overall health of a given PDP or MA-PD plan's enrollees.[404]

---

[398] Pub. L. No. 111-152, Section 1102(b) and (c); 42 U.S.C. § 1395w-23.
[399] Pub. L. No. 111-152, § 1102(c); 42 U.S.C. § 1395w-23.
[400] 42 U.S.C. § 1395w-111(b).
[401] 42 U.S.C. § 1395w-115 and 42 C.F.R. § 423.315; 70 Fed. Reg. 4306 (Jan. 28, 2005).
[402] *See* 42 U.S.C. § 1395w-102(b), 42 U.S.C. § 1395w-114, 42 C.F.R. § 423.286, and 42 C.F.R. § 423.771.
[403] 42 C.F.R. § 423.329(a).
[404] 42 C.F.R. § 423.329(b).

CMS also provides the PDP and MA-PD plans with reinsurance and risk-sharing subsidies.[405] Reinsurance is provided to a PDP or MA-PD plan once a beneficiary reaches the out-of-pocket threshold in the amount of 80% of the beneficiary's drug cost for the balance of the year.[406]

The MMA also established risk corridors for PDP and MA-PD plans (i.e., specified percentages above and below a target amount).[407] PDP and MA-PD plans with adjusted allowable costs following below a given risk corridor target receive increased payments.[408] Conversely, if a PDP or MA-PD plan falls below the target, then it is required to refund a percentage of the savings to the government.[409] CMS establishes the adjusted allowable risk corridor costs for each fiscal year; however, the risk percentage may not be less than 5%.[410] CMS may also provide additional reimbursement to a PDP or MA-PD plan if it experiences unexpected expenses not included in its competitive bid.[411]

3.12 Assignment and Reassignment

The final step in analyzing the potential reimbursement issues associated with a proposed service or supply is determining who is entitled to receive payment from Medicare.

3.12.1 Assignment

The term "assignment" is defined by Medicare as an agreement between a physician or supplier and the beneficiary. Under the terms of the assignment, the beneficiary transfers to the physician or supplier her right to benefits based on covered services specified on the assigned claim; in turn, the physician or supplier agrees to accept the approved charge determined by the MAC as the *full charge* for the items or services.[412]

3.12.1.1 Part A

Medicare Part A prohibits direct payment to beneficiaries for "covered services." Part A providers must accept direct assignment of payment from Medicare, and are prohibited from charging program beneficiaries fees in excess of the Medicare payment amount.[413]

3.12.1.2 Part B

Unlike Part A, beneficiaries under Part B may receive direct payment from Medicare, or they may assign this benefit to their treating physician or supplier.[414] Physicians and suppliers who accept assignment from beneficiaries may not charge them more than the Medicare deductible and coinsurance

---

[405] *See id.* § 423.329(c).
[406] *Id.*
[407] 42 C.F.R. § 423.336. Note, the target amount is defined as total payments that are paid to the plan, risk-adjusted, and reduced by total administrative expenses assumed in the plan's approved bid.
[408] *Id.*
[409] *Id.* Note that the subsidy and risk-corridor provisions do not apply to fallback plans.
[410] 42 C.F.R. § 423.336(a)(2).
[411] 42 C.F.R. § 423.315.
[412] 42 U.S.C. § 1395(b)(3)(B)(ii); Ctrs. for Medicare & Medicaid Servs., *Medicare Claims Processing Manual* (Pub. 100-04), Ch. 1, § 30.3.2.
[413] 42 C.F.R. §§ 424.70–.90.
[414] *Id.* §§ 424.53, .55.

amounts. A physician or supplier also may refuse to accept assignment from a Medicare beneficiary on an occasion of service basis. In any case, however, Medicare beneficiaries may not be charged over 115% of the nonparticipant fee-schedule amount by such physicians and suppliers.[415]

3.12.1.3 Part C

Except under certain circumstances (e.g., payments made to health care providers by CMS because the MA organization failed to do so), only the MA organization is entitled to receive payment for health care services that are provided to MA enrollees.[416]

3.12.1.4 Part D

In general, only Part D sponsors are entitled to receive payments for Part D covered services and items that are provided to Part D plan enrollees.[417]

3.12.2 Reassignment

Subject to certain exceptions, Medicare prohibits payment for assigned benefits to anyone other than the physician or supplier who provided the items or services.[418] The MMA liberalized the reassignment rules by eliminating the site of service requirement. Effective as of December 8, 2003, physicians and suppliers may reassign payment for Medicare-covered services, regardless of where the service is furnished, as long as the physician or supplier is an employee of, or has an independent contract with, the entity that will be billing for the physician's services.[419]

An otherwise-correct Medicare payment made to an ineligible recipient under a reassignment will not constitute an overpayment. Nevertheless, the physician's or supplier's right to accept assignment may be subject to revocation for an improper assignment.[420] A violation of the reassignment prohibition also can result in exclusion from the Medicare program.[421] Exceptions include the following:

- *Payment to an Employer.* Payment to an employer of a physician or supplier pursuant to an employment agreement. The agreement must provide the employer with the right to charge and collect payment for the services of the physician or supplier. The employer also must provide CMS with acceptable evidence (e.g., a W-2) of the employer/employee relationship.

- *Payment to an Inpatient Facility.* Payment to an "inpatient" facility (for services furnished in that facility) pursuant to a written agreement that is entered into between the facility and the physician or supplier. The agreement must provide the facility with the right to bill and receive payment for the services of the physician or supplier.

- *Payment to an Organized Health Care Delivery System.* Payment to a "health care delivery system" (for services furnished within the system) if the system and the physician or supplier

---

[415] 42 U.S.C. § 1395w-4(g)(2)(C).
[416] 42 C.F.R. § 422.322(c).
[417] *See* 42 C.F.R. §§ 423.301 & 423.315.
[418] 42 U.S.C. § 1395g.
[419] MMA, § 952.
[420] Ctrs. for Medicare & Medicaid Servs., *Medicare Claims Processing Manual* (Pub. 100-04), Ch. 1, § 30.2.
[421] 42 C.F.R. § 424.82(c).

enter into a contractual arrangement that allows the system to bill and receive payment for services provided by the physician or supplier. Three organization types may provide and administer health care through an organized delivery system—medical group clinics, university-affiliated medical faculty practice plans, and managed care organizations that provide services through a network of contracting providers.

- *Payment to an Agent.* Payment in the name of the party eligible to receive payment to an agent who furnished billing or collection services if the agent receives payment under an agreement with the physician, the agent's compensation is not related to the dollar amounts billed or dependent upon the actual collection of payment, and the agent acts under payment disposition instructions which the physician may modify or revoke at any time.

- *Payment under Reciprocal Billing Arrangements.* Payment under reciprocal billing arrangements where the patient's regular physician submits a claim for covered visit services that the regular physician arranges to be provided by a substitute physician on an occasional reciprocal basis. The term "covered visit services" includes not only those services ordinarily characterized as a covered physician visit, but also other covered items and services furnished by the substitute physician or by others as incident to the physician's services. Reciprocal billing arrangements are limited to 60 continuous days.

- *Payment under* Locum Tenens *Arrangements.* Payment to a *locum tenens* or substitute physician. A *locum tenens* physician substitutes for a physician who is absent from his or her professional practice due to illness, pregnancy, vacation, or continuing medical education. The *locum tenens* physician must be paid on a *per diem* or similar fee-for-time basis by the "regular" physician, and may not provide services to Medicare patients for longer than 60 continuous days.

- *Payment for Diagnostic Tests Subject to the Anti-Markup Rule.* Payment to a physician or medical group for diagnostic laboratory tests (other than clinical) which the physician or group obtains or 'purchases' from an independent physician, medical group, or other supplier are subject to payment limitations. In particular, where the rule applies, the physician's payment is limited to the lowest of the performing supplier's "net charge," the billing physician or other supplier's actual charge, or the Medicare fee schedule amount.

- *Payment to a Bank.* Absent a court order, Medicare payments that are due to a physician may be sent to a bank or similar financial institution for deposit in the physician's account. The physician must have sole control over the account, and the bank may not be providing any direct or indirect financing to the physician.

- *Payment to Others.* Payment also may be made pursuant to a court order; or may be made to a government agency or entity, a medical school, or a university under specific circumstances.[422]

3.13 Appeals—Parts A and B

Payment disputes between Part A providers or Part B suppliers and the Medicare program may be administratively appealed. Under Part A, there are two types of appeals processes available, depending on whether a provider is appealing reimbursement for claim(s) or reimbursement under a cost report.

---

[422] 42 U.S.C. § 1395u(b)(6); 42 C.F.R. §§ 424.73, .80; Ctrs. for Medicare & Medicaid Servs., *Medicare Claims Processing Manual* (Pub. 100-04), Ch. 1, § 30.2.

3.13.1 Claims Appeals—Parts A and B

Rules governing the Part A and B claims appeals processes appear at 42 C.F.R. §§ 405.900 *et seq.* A summary of the appeals process is as follows:

- *Step 1 – Request for Redetermination.* Once an initial determination has been made by the Medicare Administrative Contractor (MAC), a Provider has 120 days to file a request that the Medicare Administrative Contractor revise its determination—i.e., render a redetermination. However, if CMS has made an overpayment determination it will begin recouping the money it has determined the Provider owes beginning 41 days following the initial overpayment demand.[423] Therefore, if the Provider wishes to stay these recoupment efforts, it must file its appeal within this 41 day time frame.[424] After filing a request, the MAC then has 60 days in which to make such a redetermination.

- *Step 2 – Request for Reconsideration.* If the redetermination continues to be adverse to the provider, the provider has 180 days to request that a "qualified independent contractor" (QIC) modify the Medicare Administrative Contractor's determination. This is called a request for reconsideration. Here again, however, if the appeal has to do with an overpayment determination, CMS will begin recouping the determined overpayment beginning on the 60th day from the initial determination (minus the tolled period from Redetermination Appeal).[425] Therefore, if the Provider wishes to continue to stay CMS's recoupment efforts, it must file its request for reconsideration within 30 days from the date of the redetermination decision. As of 2014, there are three QICs: Maximus, Inc., C2C Solutions, Inc., and Q2 Administrators, LLC. The QICs are independent from the Medicare Administrative Contractors; however, they review the appeal based upon the requirements found in the Local and National Coverage Determinations, the Medicare Manuals, as well as the Medicare statutes and regulations. Appeals to the QIC are "record" appeals and are not live hearings. Importantly, § 933 of the MMA requires that all evidence be presented at this point and bars submission of additional evidence at the next or higher levels of appeal, absent just cause. The QIC must render its reconsideration within 60 days. If the QIC cannot complete its review within this timeframe, the appellant has the right to escalate the case to the next level of appeal. Also, note that any overpayment amounts upheld by the QIC will begin to be recouped following the issuance of the reconsideration decision, and the provider will not be able to stay recoupment at any further levels of appeal.

- *Step 3 – Request for Administrative Law Judge Hearing.* If the QIC's reconsideration decision is adverse to the provider, and the amount in controversy is at $150, (the amount is adjusted annually based on a formula prescribed by statute) claims can be aggregated to meet this threshold), the provider may request review by an administrative law judge (ALJ) within 60 days of the QIC's action.[426] These requests are filed with the Office of Medicare Hearings

---

[423] 42 C.F.R. § 405.379(d).
[424] Note that, while technically CMS will not begin recoupment until the 41st day following the initial determination, the MACs actually require that the Request for Redetermination be submitted within 30 days from the initial determination in order to allow for processing time.
[425] 42 C.F.R. § 405.379(e).
[426] The minimum amount in controversy is subject to an annual inflation factor.

and Appeals (OMHA). The ALJ must render his or her ruling within 90 days of the completion of the record. If the ALJ cannot render a decision within this time frame, the appellant may request that the case be escalated to the Medicare Appeals Council. ALJs must give "substantial deference" to LCDs, LMRPs, and CMS guidance, but are not bound by the guidance as the MACs and QICs are. If the ALJ fails to follow this guidance, it must provide reasons why. Note that this third level of appeal has experienced a significant backlog in its caseload, and, as a result, in November of 2013, OMHA released a statement on its website that any requests for ALJ hearing filed after April 1, 2013 would be deferred from assignment to an ALJ for up to 28 months. As of this writing the average processing times for appeals decided in FY2015 was 547 days.[427]

- *Step 4—Medicare Appeals Council.* If the provider continues to be dissatisfied with the ALJ action, the provider may request review by the Department Appeals Board (DAB) Medicare Appeals Council within 60 days of the ALJ's ruling. The Medicare Appeals Council has 90 days to render its ruling.[428] The appellant has the same escalation rights should the Medicare Appeals Council fail to make a timely ruling.

- *Step 5—Federal District Court.* If the provider continues to be dissatisfied with the ruling of the Medicare Appeals Council, and if the amount in controversy is at least $1,050, the provider may request initiate an action in federal district court within 60 days of the decision by the Appeals Council.[429] Appeals for judicial review must be for "final" determinations after all administrative appeals have been exhausted.

Finally, certain types of appeals may be eligible for an expedited review process. These are typically claims involving Home Health Agencies, Skilled Nursing Facilities, Comprehensive Outpatient Rehabilitation Facilities, and Hospices, where the providers anticipate that the beneficiary's Medicare coverage for their services will end.[430]

3.13.2 Cost Report Appeals—Part A Only

After the Medicare Administrative Contractor performs an audit of the provider's cost report, it issues an NPR, which is the Medicare Administrative Contractor's determination of allowable costs, including any underpayment owed to the provider or any overpayment owed by the provider to the Medicare program. A provider has 180 days to appeal the Medicare Administrative Contractor's

---

[427] *See* https://www.hhs.gov/sites/default/files/omha/files/medicare-appeals-backlog.pdf.
[428] The DAB was chartered in 1973 as the Departmental Grant Appeals Board; until the 1980s, DAB jurisdiction was limited to disputes arising under the large public assistance grants, such as Medicaid and Aid to Families with Dependent Children, as well as discretionary grant programs. In 1988, the Secretary delegated to the DAB responsibility for adjudicating civil money penalties and exclusions imposed under a wide range of fraud and abuse authorities. In 1993, the Secretary delegated to the DAB responsibility for hearing appeals in enforcement cases brought by CMS and, in 1995, the Secretary delegated to the DAB the Medicare Appeals Council function of hearing appeals in Medicare coverage and payment cases and entitlement cases. The MAC provides the final administrative review of claims for entitlement to Medicare and individual claims for Medicare coverage and payment filed by beneficiaries or health care providers/suppliers inclusive of claims appeals and enrollment matters (including denials and revocations).
[429] Effective January 1, 2009, this amount was increased to $1060. *Id.*
[430] More information on expedited appeals can be found at: http://www.cms.gov/Medicare/Medicare-General-Information/BNI/Downloads/EDgeneralinfo.pdf.

determination subsequent to the issuance of the NPR. The total dollar amount in controversy generally determines where the provider must file an appeal.[431]

- *Medicare Administrative Contractor.* A reimbursement dispute involving more than $1,000 but less than $10,000 must be appealed to the Medicare Administrative Contractor where the dispute is heard by a hearing officer or a panel that is designated by the Medicare Administrative Contractor. Medicare Administrative Contractor decisions are subject to a reevaluation or "reopening" within 12 months (or four years if the provider can show good cause).[432] Medicare Administrative Contractor hearing decisions may be reviewed by the Administrator of CMS at his or her discretion or at the request of the affected provider.[433] However, such decisions are not subject to judicial review.

- *Provider Reimbursement Review Board Appeals.* A reimbursement dispute involving more than $10,000 must be appealed to the Provider Reimbursement Review Board (PRRB).[434] Decisions by the PRRB may be reviewed by the Administrator of CMS and are subject to judicial review.[435] Individual providers may aggregate their appeals for submission to the PRRB if the aggregate dollar amount in controversy exceeds $50,000 and the appeal involves a question of fact or judicial interpretation common to all providers in the appeal.[436] Medicare also requires providers under common ownership to aggregate their appeals to the PRRB under such circumstances.

- *Right to an Appeal Before the PRRB.* A provider who is dissatisfied with any "final determination" of the MAC or the Secretary of HHS may appeal to the PRRB. "Final determinations" include an original or revised NPR, an amended cost report provided to the Medicare Administrative Contractor before an NPR is issued, refusal to reopen a cost report, rate of payment notices, denial of requests for exception, exemption, and adjustment, including routine cost limit exceptions and TEFRA adjustments, ESRD exception requests for fiscal years ending after August 1983, denial of provider status or classification requests (e.g., sole community hospitals, rural referral centers, etc.) and late NPR determinations.

- *Judicial Review.* Providers may appeal the final administrative decision (whether by the PRRB or from the CMS Administrator's review) to federal court by initiating an action within 60 days from the date of receipt of an adverse decision.[437] Providers also may bypass the hearing process and obtain an expedited judicial review of any action of a Medicare Administrative Contractor that involves the validity of a governing law, regulation or CMS ruling.[438]

3.14 Appeals—Part C

CMS has established procedures for processing MA Plan enrollee appeals regarding coverage denials, payment for services, and other grievances. An MA organization must provide appeal procedures, either directly or by delegation to another entity, for each MA Plan that it offers.

---

[431] 42 C.F.R. §§ 405.1809–.1839.
[432] 42 C.F.R. § 405.750.
[433] 42 C.F.R. § 405.1875.
[434] 42 C.F.R. § 405.1835.
[435] 42 C.F.R. §§ 405.1873–.1877, 405.1878(f).
[436] 42 C.F.R. §§ 405.1837–.1839.
[437] 42 C.F.R. §§ 405.1875, 405.1877.
[438] *Id.* § 405.1842.

3.14.1 Enrollee Grievances and Appeals

Each MA Plan must establish procedures for standard and expedited MA organization determinations, standard and expedited resolution of grievances, and standard and expedited resolution of appeals.[439] The procedures described in this subsection refer to the appeals process. Disputes that do not meet the definition of an initial determination (e.g., items or services to be included in an optional supplemental plan, or complaints about waiting times or inadequate facilities) are categorized as grievances and are not subject to the appeals process.[440]

MA Plans are required to provide timely enrollee-coverage determinations regarding plan benefits. Such determinations must be made by an MA organization "as expeditiously as the enrollee's health condition requires," but no later than 14 calendar days after the date the organization receives the service request and 60 days for a payment request.[441] Either the enrollees or their physician may request a 72-hour "expedited" determination in situations involving serious risk to the enrollee's life, health, or physical functioning.[442]

3.14.1.1 Reconsiderations

An enrollee may request a reconsideration of an adverse organization determination from an MA organization. This request must be made within 60 calendar days from the date of the initial determination notice. The MA organization is required to complete the reconsideration "as expeditiously as the enrollee's health condition requires" or within 30 calendar days for a service request and 60 calendar days for a payment request, depending on the circumstances.[443] The enrollee or the enrollee's physician (acting on the enrollee's behalf) may request a 72-hour determination, provided the same serious-jeopardy standard is met.[444]

3.14.1.2 Independent Review

Adverse reconsiderations affirmed by the MA organization are referred to an independent review entity for resolution.[445] The independent-review process is subject to the same time frames that govern reconsiderations by MA organizations. If the enrollee, or any party other than the MA organization, is dissatisfied with the decision of the independent entity, and the amount in controversy is in excess of the annual threshold amount, then the case may be heard by an ALJ with the Office of Medicare Hearings and Appeals (OHMA).[446] Opportunities for review of the ALJ's decision by the Medicare Appeals Council (MAC) or by a U.S. district court also are available.[447]

---

[439] Ctrs. for Medicare & Medicaid Servs. *Medicare Managed Care Manual* (Pub. 100-16), Ch. 13 § 10.3.
[440] *Id.* § 20.2. Regulations governing grievances can be found at 42 C.F.R. §§ 422.561–.564 and more detail is located in Chapter 13 of the *Medicare Managed Care Manual*.
[441] 42 C.F.R. § 422.568.
[442] 42 U.S.C. § 1395w-22(g); 42 C.F.R. §§ 422.570.
[443] 42 C.F.R. § 422.590.
[444] 42 C.F.R. § 422.590(d).
[445] 42 C.F.R. § 422.592.
[446] 42 C.F.R. § 422.600. For CY 2017, the AIC for ALJ review is $160.
[447] 42 C.F.R. §§ 422.592–.612.

3.14.1.3 Judicial Review

Any party, including the MA organization, may request judicial review of an ALJ's decision if (i) the DAB denied the party's request for a review and (ii) and the amount in controversy is in excess of the annual threshold amount.[448]

3.14.1.4 Determinations During an Inpatient Stay

Special provisions apply when an MA organization determines that an authorized hospital stay is no longer necessary. MA organizations are required to provide enrollees with a formal end-of-coverage-determination notice that specifies the reasons why continued hospitalization is not considered medically necessary by the MA organization. Information regarding the appeal rights of the enrollee and the enrollee's financial liability for continuing the hospital stay also must be included in the notice. An immediate QIO review may be requested by the enrollee, and the enrollee may remain hospitalized throughout the course of the QIO review period without incurring additional financial liability for the continued hospital stay.[449]

3.14.1.5 Service Terminations

An enrollee of an MA organization has a right to a "fast-track" appeal of an MA organization's decision to terminate provider services.[450] An enrollee must make a request for a fast-track appeal by an independent review entity (IRE) by noon of the first day after the day of delivery of the termination notice.[451] If the IRE upholds the MA organization's decision, in whole or in part, then an enrollee may request that the IRE reconsider its original decision.[452]

3.14.2 MA Organization Contract Appeals

Contract-determination disputes between MA organizations and the Medicare program may be administratively appealed.[453] Once CMS has made a contract determination, the agency will send a written notice to the contracting applicant or MA organization stating the reasons for the determination and the right to request a reconsideration of the contract determination by CMS.[454]

3.14.2.1 Request for Hearing

A contracting applicant or MA organization may request a hearing of an adverse contract determination (e.g., termination) or intermediate sanctions by filing a written request with CMS within 15 days of receipt from the date of the contract determination or intermediate sanction.[455] The

---

[448] *Id.* For CY 2017, the threshold amount for judicial review is $1,560.
[449] *Id.* §§ 422.620–.622.
[450] 42 C.F.R. § 422.626(a).
[451] 42 C.F.R. § 422.626(a)(1).
[452] 42 C.F.R. § 422.626(g).
[453] 42 C.F.R. § 422.641, .660. *See also* Ctrs. for Medicare & Medicaid Servs., *Medicare Managed Care Manual* (Pub. 100-16), Ch. 14, § 10 *et seq.*
[454] 42 C.F.R. § 422.644.
[455] 42 C.F.R. § 422.662. A party has a right to a hearing if the applicant has been found to be unqualified to enter into a contract with CMS; if the MA organization contract is terminated or not renewed or if the organization is assessed intermediate sanctions under 42 C.F.R. § 422.660(a).

hearing officer, who is designated by CMS, and need not be an ALJ, must set the hearing date for no later than 30 days from the date the request for hearing was received by CMS.[456] Parties to the hearing may appoint a representative for the hearing, request permission for pre-hearing discovery, and examine/cross-examine witnesses.[457] A decision of a hearing officer may be reopened and revised by another hearing officer designated by CMS within one year of the notice of the hearing decision if the hearing officer who issued the initial decision is unavailable.[458]

3.14.2.2 Request for Review by the Administrator of CMS

An MA organization that has received a hearing decision upholding a contract determination may request review by the Administrator of CMS within 15 days of receiving the hearing decision. A decision by the Administrator of CMS is final and binding. Such decisions may be reopened and revised by the Administrator of CMS, however, upon the administrator's own motion within one year of the date of the notice of determination.[459]

3.15   Appeals—Part D[460]

PDP enrollees, their appointed representatives, prescribing physicians, or other prescribers may, on behalf of enrollees, request coverage determinations, request exceptions to obtain coverage for a non-preferred drug on a plan's tiered formulary or for a drug excluded from a plan's formulary, or appeal the coverage determinations of the Part D plan.[461] Participating pharmacies are required to provide beneficiaries with a notice containing information about the beneficiaries' rights in this regard.[462]

The process begins when the plan issues a coverage determination.[463] Plans are required to notify beneficiaries of initial coverage determinations as expeditiously as the beneficiary's health condition requires, but no later than 72 hours after receipt of request.[464] Each PDP must provide a meaningful process for resolving grievances.[465] PDPs are also required to use a single, uniform exception and appeals process for prescription drug coverage.[466]

Beneficiaries may obtain a covered drug at a more favorable cost sharing level or a covered drug not on a plan formulary through the "exceptions process."[467] More specifically, a beneficiary can

---

[456] 42 C.F.R. § 422.666, .670.
[457] Id. §§ 422.672–.690.
[458] Id. § 422.696(b).
[459] Id. § 422.692–.694. Note that a contract applicant is not entitled to determination review by the Administrator of CMS.
[460] The regulations governing standard and expedited redeterminations and appeals for Part D plans are found at 42 C.F.R. §§ 423.580 – 423.638, and Subpart U. Chapter 18 of the *Part D Prescription drug Benefit Manual* also covers appeals.
[461] 42 U.S.C. §§ 1395w-104; 42 C.F.R. § 423.562(b).
[462] 42 C.F.R. § 423.128(a)(7).
[463] Coverage determinations can include, for example: (1) a PDP decision not to provide or cover a drug; (2) a PDP's failure to provide a timely coverage determination where a delay would harm the beneficiary's health; (3) a PDP decision concerning exceptions requests; or (4) a decision on the required cost sharing amount for a drug. 42 C.F.R. § 423.566(b).
[464] 42 C.F.R. § 423.568(b).
[465] See 42 U.S.C. § 1395w-104(f); 42 C.F.R. § 423.564.
[466] 42 U.S.C. § 1395w-104(b)(3)(H); this process must be available for enrollees' immediate access through a toll-free telephone number and a website.
[467] See 42 U.S.C. § 1395w-104(g)(2); 42 C.F.R. § 423.578.

request an exception under the following circumstances (i) when the beneficiary is using a drug that has been removed from a plan formulary, (ii) a non-formulary drug is prescribed and is medically necessary, (iii) the cost-sharing status of a drug a beneficiary is using changes, or (iv) a drug covered under a more expensive cost sharing tier is medically inappropriate.[468] The plan must act within 72 hours for standard coverage determinations or 24 hours for expedited requests if the standard timeframe for making a decision may seriously jeopardize the life or health of the beneficiary or the beneficiary ability to regain maximum function.[469] If a request is denied, a beneficiary may follow the appeals process.[470]

Part D statutes and regulations describe a five-level appeals process.[471] The beneficiary or, subject to certain conditions, the treating physician or other prescriber acting on behalf of the beneficiary, may initially request a redetermination of an unfavorable coverage determination within 60 days.[472] The redetermination is performed by the Part D plan and its decision must be communicated within seven days of receipt of a standard redetermination request, or within 72 hours for an expedited request.[473] If a beneficiary is dissatisfied with the redetermination, the beneficiary has 60 days to request reconsideration by an Independent Review Entity (IRE), which is due within 7 days (or 72 hours, if expedited).[474] If dissatisfied with the reconsideration and the amount in controversy exceeds a threshold amount established annually (e.g., $160 for 2017), the beneficiary has 60 days to appeal to an administrative law judge, whose decision is due within 90 days (10 days, if expedited). If beneficiaries wish to further appeal, they have 60 days to file before the Medicare Appeals Council, whose decision is due within 90 days (10 days, if expedited). Finally, a beneficiary may elevate an appeal to federal district court, provided the amount in controversy amount is met ($1,560 for 2017).[475]

3.15.1 Part D Sponsor Contract Appeals

Contract-determination disputes between Part D sponsors and the Medicare program may be administratively appealed.[476] Once CMS has made a contract determination, the agency will send a written notice to the contracting applicant or Part D sponsor stating the reasons for the determination and the right to request a reopening of the contract determination by CMS.[477]

3.16 Conclusion

The continued popularity of the Medicare program stands as a testament to America's long-term commitment to safeguarding the nation's elderly and disabled. The establishment of the program, however, not only increased access to medical care for these population groups but also escalated

---

[468] *Id.*
[469] *See* 42 C.F.R. § 423.566(a) *referencing* 42 C.F.R. §§ 423.568, 423.570.
[470] 42 C.F.R. § 423.580.
[471] 42 U.S.C. § 1395w-104(h); 42 C.F.R. §§ 423.580–.638.
[472] 42 C.F.R. § 423.580.
[473] 42 C.F.R. § 423.590(a).
[474] 42 C.F.R. § 423.600.
[475] 42 C.F.R. §§ 423.1970–1976; Note that certain appeal requirements may have to be met at the ALJ, MAC, and judicial review levels, such as those pertaining to the remaining amount in controversy.
[476] 42 C.F.R. § 423.650.
[477] 42 C.F.R. § 423.642.

overall demand for health care services. As the Medicare program mushroomed in size, scope, and complexity, so have the nature, size, and number of its participating providers, physicians, and suppliers—so much so that today Medicare provides a substantial financial underpinning for the entire American health care industry.

As demonstrated by the discussions in this Chapter, many efforts have been made by federal policymakers to reduce program expenditures and to shore up the HI Trust Fund. Beginning with TEFRA target rates in 1982 and PPS for inpatient hospital care in 1983 and additional providers in subsequent years, through RBRVS for physicians in 1989 and the introduction of "market-based" payment systems in the new millennium, Medicare payment policy has attempted to shift more of the program's financial burdens and risks to providers, physicians, and suppliers. The effect of the government's actions *vis-à-vis* changes to Medicare reimbursement policy ripple throughout the health care industry. Other government health care programs—including Medicaid, the VA, FEHBP (the health benefits program for federal employees), TRICARE (the health benefits program for the Department of Defense), as well as commercial insurance carriers—tie many of their own payment methodologies and rates to the Medicare reimbursement system.

The Medicare program has evolved from a government payment system for health care services to a force for dictating American health care policy. Medicare covers a share of costs furnished to hospitals treating a disproportionate share of indigent patients and, also, is a major source of funding for graduate medical education in the United States.

Challenges await federal policymakers in meeting the growing demand for expanded Medicare benefits including stemming the relentless rise in health care expenditures, attempting to inject meaningful quality requirements into Medicare payment provisions and establishing payment systems based upon improved patient outcomes and decreased costs. Policy makers also must prepare for an unprecedented increase in program beneficiaries as American "baby boomers" live longer with Medicare and Generations X and Y rapidly move toward retirement age. Although the BBA stemmed the immediate hemorrhage of the HI Trust Fund, it only delayed the inevitable. Indeed, current projections indicate that the HI Trust Fund will be totally depleted by 2029. As a result, larger premiums, increased means-testing, greater cost-sharing, and a rise in the eligibility age all loom on the horizon as the future of Medicare is debated by Congress.

The Affordable Care Act has also shifted a number of priorities within CMS. The establishment of CMMI was expressly intended by Congress to encourage CMS to develop new payment methodologies including bundled payment methodologies and payments that take into consideration quality of care and savings to the Medicare Program. And, at the same time, the CMS is increasingly focused on eliminating fraud, waste and abuse in what is the largest health care benefit provider in the world. ACOs and other initiatives lay on the horizon as the program and its leadership work to maintain and shape the future of Medicare and shape the future of the payment systems to the complex fabric of providers that make up the Medicare system.

Where Medicare goes from here remains unknown. While some have proposed making Medicare into an entirely private benefit, the Affordable Care Act largely left the structure of the 4-part Medicare Program intact. The exchange-based system espoused by the Affordable Care Act for many Americans was not imposed on Medicare beneficiaries, and yet, while early CBO predictions indicated a drop in enrollment in Medicare Advantage, by 2017, nearly 33% of all Medicare beneficiaries had voluntarily elected to enroll in a Medicare Advantage plan. Is this the future of Medicare as today's generation of Americans, having grown up in a managed care environment, elect to stay with this type of health care coverage as they move into Medicare enrollment? One thing is for certain, the Medicare Program remains dynamic, complex, political and certain to change in the future. Stay tuned.

3.17 Useful Websites and Other Resources

Sources of Medicare Law

- Part A, General Provisions; Part B Peer Review of Utilization and Quality of Health Care Services; and Administrative Simplification: Social Security Act (SSA §§ 1101–1179; 42 U.S.C. §§ 1301–1320d-8)
- Health Insurance for the Aged and Disabled; Part A: Hospital Insurance Benefits; Part B—Supplemental Medical Insurance Benefits for the Aged and Disabled; Provisions Relating to the Administration of Part B, Payment for Physicians Services; Part C—Medicare Advantage Program; Part D—Voluntary Prescription Drug Program; Part E—Miscellaneous Provisions. SSA §§ 1801–1896; 42 U.S.C. § 1395)

Sources of Medicare Regulations

- 42 C.F.R. Parts 400–424; 482–494: Regulations, generally
- 42 C.F.R. Parts 409–410: Coverage, generally
- 42 C.F.R. Parts 482–493: Certification
- 42 C.F.R. Parts 412–414; 416–418; 424: Payment, generally
- 42 C.F.R. § 406: Part A Eligibility
- 42 C.F.R. § 407: Part B Eligibility
- 42 C.F.R. § 411: Exclusions from Medicare Payment *including* Stark law provisions
- 42 C.F.R. § 412: Inpatient Hospital PPS
- 42 C.F.R. § 413: End Stage Renal Disease
- 42 C.F.R. § 416: Ambulatory Surgery Services
- 42 C.F.R. § 420: Program Integrity
- 42 C.F.R. § 422: Medicare Advantage Program
- 42 C.F.R. § 423: Voluntary Medicare Prescription Drug Benefit
- 42 C.F.R. § 424: Conditions for Medicare Payment
- 42 C.F.R. §§ 1000–1008: OIG Regulations including AKBS Safe Harbor Provisions

MEDICARE MANUALS

In addition to publishing implementing regulations in the Federal Register, CMS publishes additional interpretative guidelines though various administrative manuals. Medicare manuals are a repository of operating instructions, policies, and procedures to administer CMS programs. The manuals are based on interpretations of statutes and regulations and were drafted for CMS agencies, contractors, and State survey agencies. The manuals are useful for many as source of technical and professional information about the Medicare and Medicaid programs.

CMS has transitioned to Internet-only manuals (IOMs). Unlike the paper-based manuals, the Internet-only CMS manual system is organized by functional area (i.e., program integrity, eligibility, entitlement, claims processing, etc.).

The IOM manuals include the following:

- Medicare General Information, Eligibility, and Entitlement Manual: CMS Pub 100-01
- Medicare Benefit Policy Manual: CMS Pub 100-02
- Medicare National Coverage Determinations Manual: CMS Pub 100-03
- Medicare Claims Processing Manual: CMS Pub 100-04
- Medicare Secondary Payer Manual: CMS Pub 100-05
- Financial Management Manual: CMS Pub. 100-06
- State Operations Manual: CMS Pub. 100-07
- Program Integrity Manual: CMS Pub 100-08
- Medicare Contractor Beneficiary and Provider Communications Manual: CMS Pub 100-09
- Quality Improvement Organization Manual: CMS Pub 100-10
- End-Stage Renal Disease Network Organizations Manual: CMS Pub 100-14
- Medicare State Buy-In Manual: CMS Pub 100-15
- Medicare Managed Care Manual: CMS Pub 100-16
- Business Partners Systems Security Manual: CMS Pub 100-17
- Medicare Prescription Drug Benefit Manual: CMS Pub 100-18
- Demonstrations: CMS Pub. 100-19
- One Time Notification Manual: CMS Pub. 100-20

The older paper based manuals include the following:

- Coverage Issues Manual: CMS Pub 6
- State Operations Manual: CMS Pub 7
- Outpatient Physical Therapy, Comprehensive Outpatient Rehabilitation Facility and Community Mental Health Center Manual: CMS Pub 9
- Hospital Manual: CMS Pub 10
- Home Health Agency Manual: CMS Pub 11
- Skilled Nursing Facility Manual: CMS Pub 12
- Medicare Intermediary Manual: CMS Pub 13
- Medicare Carriers Manual: CMS Pub 14
- Provider Reimbursement Manual: CMS Pub 15
- Peer Review Organization Manual: CMS Pub 19
- Hospice Manual: CMS Pub 21
- Regional Office Manual: CMS Pub 23
- State Buy In Manual: CMS Pub 24
- Carrier QA Handbook: CMS Pub 25
- Rural Health Clinic Manual: CMS Pub 27
- Renal Dialysis Facility Manual: CMS Pub 29
- Christian Science Sanatorium Hospital Manual Supplement: CMS Pub 32

- State Medicaid Manual: CMS Pub 45
- HMO/CMP Manual: CMS Pub 75
- Federally Qualified HMO Manual: CMS Pub 77
- End Stage Renal Disease Manual: CMS Pub 81

NATIONAL COVERAGE DECISIONS (NCDs)

NCDs set forth whether Medicare will cover specific services, procedures or technologies on a national basis based on a reasonableness standard. NCDs do not make determinations on codes assigned to a service or the amount of payment to be made for the service. An NCD is binding on all Medicare contractors, including, but not limited to, MACs, Medicare carriers, fiscal intermediaries, QIOs and MA organizations. The Medicare contractor must make the coverage decision if an NCD does not specifically exclude an indication or circumstance, or if the item or service is not mentioned in an NCD or Medicare manual. NCDs are located on the CMS Medicare Coverage Homepage website at http://www.cms.gov/mcd/overview.asp?from2=overview.asp&.

IMPORTANT WEBSITES & LINKS

- Social Security Administration (SSA) — www.ssa.gov
- U.S. Dept. of Health and Human Services (HHS) — www.hhs.gov
- Centers for Medicare and Medicaid Services (CMS) — www.cms.hhs.gov
- Consumer Medicare Information — www.medicare.gov
- HHS Office of Inspector General (OIG) — www.oig.hhs.gov
- U.S. Dept. of Justice (DOJ) — www.usdoj.gov
- The Federal Register — www.gpo.gov/fdsys
- Federal Register Advance Desk — www.archives.gov/federal-register/public-inspection/index.html
- CMS Medlearn Matters: https://www.cms.gov/Outreach-and-Education/Medicare-Learning-Network-MLN/MLNMattersArticles/index.html
- Congressional Budget Office (CBO) — www.cbo.gov
- General Accounting Office (GAO) — www.gao.gov
- Office of Management and Budget (OMB) — www.whitehouse.gov/omb
- House Budget Committee — www.house.gov/budget
- House Committee on Ways and Means — https://waysandmeans.house.gov/
- House Committee on Energy and Commerce — https://energycommerce.house.gov/
- Senate Committee on Finance — www.finance.senate.gov

4

Medicaid Fundamentals

Craig H. Smith[1]
Hogan Lovells US LLP

4.1 Introduction

The political battles over the Patient Protection and Affordable Care Act of 2010 (ACA), and the United States Supreme Court's ruling in *National Federation of Independent Business v. Sebelius*,[2] largely upholding the ACA, have raised the public's awareness about Medicaid. While many Americans are very familiar with Medicare, many still are relatively unfamiliar with how Medicaid works and whom it serves.

The United States Supreme Court has described the federal Medicaid statute as "among the most intricate ever drafted by Congress," with a "Byzantine construction" that is "almost unintelligible to the uninitiated."[3] Other federal courts have described the Medicaid statute as a "virtually impenetrable thicket of legalese and gobbledygook,"[4] and "an aggravated assault on the English language, resistant to attempts to understand it."[5] One federal court stated that it "would be hard-pressed to find a more difficult statute to interpret than 42 U.S.C. § 1396a."[6]

This Chapter will attempt, at the very least, to make the Medicaid program's very complicated statutory and regulatory scheme somewhat intelligible. The topics we will cover are (i) the evolution of the Medicaid program since its inception, (ii) how the Medicaid program is administered, (iii) what groups of persons are eligible for Medicaid, (iv) the types of items and services covered by Medicaid, (v) the delivery systems used by states, (vi) the reimbursement and financing systems used by states, and (vii) recent reforms and other developments in the Medicaid program, as well as the ramifications of the Supreme Court's decision in *National Federation*.[7]

---

[1] Mr. Smith thanks Hemi Tewarson, Esq., for sharing her excellent written materials and Jennifer L. Evans, Partner with Polsinelli Shughart PC, for her valuable contributions to this chapter.
[2] 132 S.Ct. 2566 (2012).
[3] *Schweiker v. Gray Panthers*, 453 U.S. 34, 43 (1981).
[4] *Lamore v. Ives*, 977 F.2d 713, 716 (5th Cir. 1992).
[5] *Friedman v. Berger*, 409 F.Supp. 1225, 1226 (S.D. N.Y. 1976).
[6] *Sherman v. Griepentrog*, 775 F.Supp. 1383, 1390 (D. Nev. 1991).
[7] *National Federation of Independent Business v. Sebelius*, 132 S.Ct. 2566 (2012).

4.2 The Evolution of the Medicaid Program

4.2.1 Original Intent of Congress

Congress created the Medicaid program in 1965 (which legislation was initially effective January 1, 1966).[8] The Medicaid program was created as a federal-state partnership in which the federal government provided matching grants to states to finance care for children from low-income families, single parents with dependent children, aged, blind and/or disabled, and individuals receiving federal income maintenance payments and assistance. It was "established in response to the widely perceived inadequacy of welfare medical care under public assistance."[9]

The Medicaid program created an entitlement to a base level of health care coverage for qualifying individuals. Procedural due process protections extended to individuals who met eligibility criteria and received benefits. The federal government matched state funding for the program so long as states complied with minimum federal requirements.

4.2.2 Medicaid Prior to ACA

The Medicaid program is no longer simply a welfare benefit program; rather, it is a complex health care payer system that covers millions of people across a wide variety of eligibility categories. Some notable facts are:

1. *Medicaid is one of the largest federal health insurers.* Expenditures in 2011 for this joint federal-state health care financing program for an estimated 54.7 million individuals totaled approximately $432.4 billion split between the Federal government ($275.1 billion, 64%) and the states ($157.3 billion, 36%).[10] Total expenditures in FY 2011 represented 2.8% of the gross domestic product.[11] Medicaid enrollment is expected to increase by about 18 million people in 2021.[12] In 2011, more than one in five people in the United States were enrolled in Medicaid for some portion of the year.[13]

2. *Medicaid is the third largest social program in the federal budget and one of the largest components of state budgets.* Following expiration of temporary increases in the Federal matching rate provided by the American Recovery and Reinvestment Act of 2009, Pub. L. 111-226, the states' share of Medicaid expenditures have grown significantly to approximately 37% of the total cost of the program.[14] According to the National Association of State

---

[8] *See* Social Security Act (SSA) Amendments of 1965, Pub. L. No. 89-97, § 121, 79 Stat. 343-353 (July 30, 1965) (adding new sections 1901–1905 and amending sections 1109 and 1115 of the SSA).
[9] Centers for Medicare and Medicaid Services, Office of the Actuary, *Brief Summaries of Medicare & Medicaid, Title XVIII and Title XIX of the Social Security Act as of November 1, 2007* at 2.
[10] Klees, B. and Wolfe, C, Office of the Actuary, Centers for Medicare and Medicaid Services, Department of Health and Human Services, *Brief Summaries of Medicare & Medicaid as of November 1, 2013* at 13.
[11] Office of the Actuary, Centers for Medicare & Medicaid Services, U.S. Dept. of Health & Human Services, *2012 Actuarial Report on the Financial Outlook for Medicaid* at i.
[12] *Id.*
[13] *Id.*
[14] Office of the Actuary, Centers for Medicare & Medicaid Services, U.S. Dept. of Health & Human Services, *2016 Actuarial Report on the Financial Outlook for Medicaid.*

Budget Officers (NASBO), in state fiscal year 2016, Medicaid represented an estimated 29 percent of all state government spending.[15]

3. *Medicaid covers some services that typically are not covered by Medicare or private insurers.* For example, unlike the Medicare program, Medicaid covers long term care services for lower and middle income populations. Medicaid payments for long term care benefits accounted for 21% of total Medicaid benefits expenses in 2015 or $112.8 billion. Notably, the trend of higher average per-person expenditures in Medicaid among the aged ($14,323 per person) and disabled ($19,478 per person) population than the population of adults ($4,986 per person) and children (approximately $3,389 per child) covered under Medicaid continued.[16]

4. *The national recession had a significant impact on the growth of enrollment and spending on Medicaid.* Growth in enrollment of Medicaid averaged 5.4 percent in SFY 2009, significantly higher than projected growth of 3.6. States expected growth to continue increasing an average of 6.6 percent above SFY 2009 levels. Medicaid spending grew an average of 7.9 percent in SFY 2009, the highest rate of growth in six years.[17] The American Recovery and Reinvestment Act (ARRA) provided additional federal funds to state Medicaid Programs based upon the state's unemployment rate. Overall ARRA provided an additional $87 billion to states for Medicaid from October 1, 2008 through December 30, 2010. Extension of a portion of ARRA federal match enhancements until June 30, 2011 provided states an additional $16.1 billion in federal Medicaid support. Pub. L. No. 111-5 § 5001.

5. *The structure of the Medicaid program has changed since its inception in a number of ways that have added to its complexity and variation across the nation.* Examples of trends include:

   a. *Movement to Medicaid managed care.* When Medicaid was enacted, states operated their programs by contracting directly with providers. But now Medicaid managed care programs, under which managed care organizations assume the risk of operating a state Medicaid program, are widespread. In 2015, Medicaid expenditures for managed care programs were $243 billion or 46% of total benefit expenditures.[18] In 2014, fully 73.5% of all Medicaid beneficiaries received all or a portion of their Medicaid benefits through a Medicaid managed care program.[19]

   b. *Expansion of populations and services.* Over the years, Medicaid eligibility and service categories have been expanded by Congress, creating a complicated scheme of coverage. In addition to *statutory* changes, a large number of states have chosen to expand their coverage of individuals and services through Section 1115 demonstration projects. Some states have also chosen to reform the way in which they cover populations or services under Medicaid.[20]

---

[15] *FY 2014–2016 State Expenditure Report*, National Association of State Budget Officers, December 2016.
[16] Centers for Medicaid & Medicare Services, Reports 64 (December 2008).
[17] Kaiser Commission on Medicaid and the Uninsured, *The Crunch Continues: Medicaid Spending, Coverage and Policy in the Midst of a Recession* (Sept. 2009).
[18] *2016 Actuarial Report* at 6.
[19] Centers for Medicare & Medicaid Services, 2014 *Medicaid Managed Care Enrollment Report*.
[20] *See CMS's Medicaid-At-a-Glance* (2005).

c. *The ability of states to establish "benchmark" benefit packages that are different than the standard Medicaid benefit package.* Section 6044 of the Deficit Reduction Act of 2005 (DRA) (Pub. L. 109-171, enacted on February 8, 2006) amended the federal Medicaid law by adding a section that allows states to amend their Medicaid state plans to provide for special benefit packages. States such as Kentucky, West Virginia and Idaho have implemented "complete redesigns of their Medicaid benefit packages...."[21] On December 3, 2008, Centers for Medicare and Medicaid Services (CMS) published a final rule to implement those provisions of the DRA.[22] On November, 30, 2009, CMS published a rule that postponed the effective date of December 3, 2008 rule until July 1, 2010.[23] Implementation went into effect on July 1, 2010.[24] This approach of distinguishing benefit packages was further changed by the ACA as discussed herein.

4.2.3 Medicaid After the ACA[25]

The enactment of the ACA introduced significant changes to the Medicaid program both at the federal and state level. The following are a few of these changes:

1. *The ACA created significant expansion of Medicaid.* Significant expansion of the Medicaid program became effective in 2014 for states that choose to expand as a result of enactment of the Patient Protection and Affordable Care Act of 2010, Pub. L. No. 111-148 as amended by the Health Care and Education Reconciliation Act, Pub. L. No. 111-152 (HCERA) (together the ACA). The original expansion included in the ACA was diminished by granting states the option to expand in *NFIB v. Sebelius.*[26]

2. *Expansion of those eligible for Medicaid coverage.* The ACA brought eligibility expansion in 2014, extending benefits to all individuals and children with an income below 138% of the poverty level (133% + 5% income disregard). *See* ACA; 42 U.S.C. § 1396a. Section 2001 requires states to expand Medicaid eligibility to all non-elderly individuals with income up to 138% of the Federal Poverty Level by 2014. Initial projections of Medicaid growth as a result of the ACA, Medicaid (and CHIP) predicted enrollment would increase from 63.4 million in 2013 to 85.2 million in 2014.[27]

3. *Expansion estimates in light of NFIB v. Sebelius.* The 2016 Actuarial Report on the Financial Outlook for Medicaid published by the Office of the Actuary, CMS estimated that 11.2 million newly eligible adult enrollees were covered under the ACA's expanded Medicaid eligibility in 2016 and projected that the total would increase to 13.2 million enrollees by 2025. These estimates were based on the assumption that 50% of the potentially newly eligible enrollees resided in States that expanded eligibility in 2016, and that 55% reside in States that would expand eligibility by 2017 and after.

---

[21] *State Fiscal Conditions and Medicaid*, Kaiser Commission on Medicaid Facts at 2 (November 2007).
[22] 73 Fed. Reg. 73694 (Dec. 3, 2008).
[23] 74 Fed. Reg. 28569 (Nov. 30, 2009).
[24] 75 Fed. Reg. 23068–01.
[25] *See* SCOTUS & Medicaid Expansion, *infra*, 14.9.
[26] 132 S.Ct. 2566 (2012).
[27] CMS: Office of the Actuary, *National Health Expenditure Projections 2009–2019*, Table 3 (Sept. 2010).

4. *Expansion of service.* ACA added mental health services, prescription drug coverage, and family planning services to benchmark benefit packages.[28]

5. *Expansion of the Prescription Drug Rebates.* ACA increases the flat rebate for outpatient prescription drugs from 15.1% to 23.1%, along with an increase of the pediatric drug rebate to 17.1%.[29]

6. *Requiring states to utilize information technology systems.* States must allow potential enrollees the option of enrolling for Medicaid on an Internet website.[30] Additionally, states are required to provide information on the state's Medicaid and CHIP plan on these websites.[31] The goal of this utilization is to allow a streamlined, efficient enrollment process.

7. *Allowing states the option of establishing home and community-based attendant services.* Under this plan, states will receive a 6% increase in federal matching funds if they elect to provide coverage for these services.[32] States may provide these services to qualified individuals whose income is the greater of 150% of the federal poverty level or the cost of institutional services for someone requiring those services (i.e., nursing home services).[33]

8. *Prohibiting funding to services related to provider-preventable conditions.* Under ACA, states are forbidden from reimbursing services that (1) were not in the best interests of the recipients and (2) were preventable as determined by the current medical literature (e.g., wrong surgery or invasive procedure).[34]

9. *A reduction in disproportionate share (DSH) payments.* Because ACA predicts that the number of uninsured will decrease, CMS initially planned to phase out DSH payments beginning in 2014.[35] The statute requires annual reductions as follows: $500 million for FY 2014; $600 million for FY 2015; $600 million for FY 2016; $1.8 billion for FY 2017; $5 billion for FY 2018; $5.6 billion for FY 2019; and $4 billion for FY 2020. On September 18, 2013, CMS published a Final Rule with a methodology to implement the annual reductions for FY 2014 and FY 2015.[36] Based on the methodology CMS adopted, CMS acknowledged that hospitals located in states that have implemented optional Medicaid expansion for the new adult coverage group likely will see greater reductions in hospital Medicaid DSH payments than they would have if all states were to elect to cover the optional coverage group.[37]

---

[28] ACA §§ 2001(c), 2203(c). *See also* 75 Fed. Reg. 23068 (April 30, 2010).
[29] ACA § 2501.
[30] SSA § 1943(b)(1); 77 Fed. Reg. 14143 (Mar. 23, 2012).
[31] *Id.*
[32] ACA § 2401.
[33] ACA § 1915(k).
[34] ACA §§ 1902 and 2702; 42 C.F.R. § 447.26.
[35] ACA § 2551.
[36] 78 Fed. Reg. 57293 (Sept. 18, 2013).
[37] *Id.* at 57294.

4.3 Administration

4.3.1 Oversight by CMS

The Secretary of Health and Human Services (HHS) has assigned oversight of the Medicaid program to CMS (formerly known as the Health Care Financing Administration). This oversight consists of approval of state Plans, state Plan Amendments, waivers of federal Medicaid requirements, and enforcement of federal Medicaid law through promulgation of regulations and other guidance (such as the state Medicaid Manual and Letters to state Medicaid Directors). When a state seeks to make a significant change to its Medicaid program—such as a change in covered populations, reimbursement methodologies for providers, or covered benefits—the state generally must seek approval from CMS.

4.3.2 Single State Medicaid Agency

Each state operating a Medicaid program must designate a "single state agency" to administer or supervise the program.[38] The single state agency, in overseeing this program, may delegate certain functions to other state agencies or private entities, including (a) authority to make eligibility determinations (the state Plan must clarify which agency is making eligibility determinations); and (b) survey and certification of providers.[39]

4.3.3 Fundamental Elements of a State Medicaid Program

In order to qualify for the federal share of payments for Medicaid programs, states must have in place a comprehensive state Medicaid Plan that has been approved by the Secretary of HHS. state Plans must describe administration of the program, eligibility categories, coverage of services, reimbursement methodologies and other beneficiary protections.[40] States with approved state Plans will receive federal financial participation, meaning that the federal government will match state expenditures for covered services provided to Medicaid recipients.[41]

State Medicaid expenditures fall into two categories:

1. *Service-related expenditures.* These are the payments made by states for covered services received by Medicaid recipients. For service expenditures, the federal government pays the applicable Federal Medical Assistance Percentage (FMAP) assigned to the state for the cost of care and the state pays the remainder. FMAP may vary from 50% to 83%. CMS assigns each state a FMAP annually, based on the state's per capita income.[42] In 2010, the ACA expanded Medicaid eligibility and increased FMAP percentages for the newly eligible to 100% for the first three years, starting 2014 and decreasing to 90% in 2020 and thereafter.[43]

2. *Administrative expenditures.* These are costs incurred by states for administering their Medicaid program. For administrative expenditures, the federal government generally pays

---

[38] SSA § 1902(a)(5); 42 C.F.R. § 431.10.
[39] SSA § 1902(a)(5), (33); 42 C.F.R. § 431.10(d), Pt. 488.
[40] *See* SSA § 1902 (setting forth requirements for state Plans).
[41] *See* SSA § 1903(a).
[42] SSA §§ 1101(a)(8), 1903(a)(1), 1905(b).
[43] HCERA § 1201(1)(B); 42 U.S.C. § 1396d(y)(1)(A)–(E).

the state at 50% of the cost (although there are a few statutory exceptions that provide a higher match rate, such as a 90% match rate for family planning services and developing a Medicaid fraud control unit).[44]

4.3.4 Differences Among State Medicaid Programs

Although Medicaid is a voluntary program for states and territories, all of the states, the District of Columbia and territories participate. Within broad federal guidelines, each state determines the design of its program (e.g., eligibility categories, covered benefits, and payment levels). There are many significant differences, therefore, among the various state Medicaid programs, principally because federal law gives states discretion in the following program areas:

1. *Coverage for certain populations*—covering "mandatory" versus "optional" categories.[45]
2. *Coverage of certain services*—covering "mandatory" or "optional" categories and/or imposing permissible amount, duration and scope limits on covered services.[46]
3. *Cost sharing*: Imposing enrollment fees, premiums or other cost sharing upon Medicaid recipients in certain, limited circumstances.[47]
4. *Provider rates*—Setting of payment rates for various providers, consistent with federal parameters.[48]
5. *Financing arrangements*—Financing the non-federal share of expenditures.[49]
6. *Use of managed care*—Implementing a managed care program for Medicaid recipients.[50]
7. *Use of "waiver" programs*—Modifying coverage of populations or services under "waivers" of federal Medicaid requirements.[51]

Even when federal statutes or regulations mandate change in the Medicaid program by a date certain, it is common for the various state Medicaid programs to come into compliance at different times. It is imperative to check the particular Medicaid Program where clients are located to give accurate advice.[52] "A state that requires additional time to comply with the requirements of this Section may apply to the Secretary for an extension."

4.4 Eligibility

4.4.1 Applying for Medicaid (Changed by ACA)[53]

All individuals must be given the opportunity to apply for Medicaid. Subject to certain exceptions, states must respond to applications within 45 days (or 90 days in the case of disability

---

[44] SSA § 1903(a)(2)–(7).
[45] *See, e.g.*, SSA §§ 1902(a)(10), 1905(a); 42 C.F.R. Part 435, Subparts A–I.
[46] *See, e.g.*, SSA § 1905(a); 42 C.F.R. Parts 440 and 441.
[47] *See, e.g.*, SSA §§ 1916, 1916A; 42 C.F.R. Part 447, Subpart A.
[48] *See, e.g.*, SSA § 1902(a)(30)(A); 42 C.F.R. § 447.20 *et seq.*
[49] *See, e.g.*, SSA § 1903(w); 42 C.F.R. Part 433, subpart B.
[50] *See, e.g.*, SSA §§ 1115, 1915(b), 1932; 42 C.F.R. Pt 438.
[51] *See, e.g.*, SSA §§ 1115, 1915(c)–(e).
[52] *See, e.g.*, 42 C.F.R. § 447.520(c).
[53] *See* SCOTUS & Medicaid Expansion, *infra*, 14.9.

determinations).[54] If an individual meets the eligibility categories summarized below, the state generally must make the individual eligible three months prior to the date of application (to the extent the individual met eligibility requirements at that time).[55] If a state denies an application or does not act upon the application with reasonable promptness, the state must afford applicants the requisite due process protections as required under federal Medicaid law.[56] States must develop procedures that enable individuals to apply for, renew, and enroll in coverage through an Internet website.[57] The website must also detail information regarding coverage under Medicaid and CHIP.[58] ACA also requires states to develop a single, streamlined application for all eligibility and enrollment systems for insurance affordability programs.[59]

Once individuals are eligible for Medicaid, states must re-determine their eligibility at least once every 12 months as well as promptly after receiving information about a change in circumstances of the individual.[60]

4.4.2 Eligibility (Changed by the ACA)

Individuals who may be covered under a state Medicaid Plan are classified into three broad categories: mandatory Categorically Needy, optional Categorically Needy, and optional Medically Needy. States are required to identify these covered populations in their state Medicaid Plans.

4.4.2.1 Mandatory Categorically Needy

State Medicaid Plans *must* extend coverage to individuals who qualify as mandatory Categorically Needy.[61] These are individuals who fall into a particular classification and meet general eligibility criteria. General categories of eligible individuals include:

a. *Low-income children and pregnant and postpartum women.* ACA changes mandatory children from 100% to 133% of the federal poverty level (138% after 5% income disregard). For infants (children under the age of 6), the final rule provides coverage up to 185% of the federal poverty level. Effective Oct. 1, 2013, States have the option to provide full Medicaid coverage to all pregnant women, regardless of any income limit.[62]

b. *Aged, blind and disabled individuals who are receiving Social Security Income* (SSI) or may be linked to or otherwise qualify for SSI under less restrictive standards.[63]

c. *Children for whom adoption assistance or foster care maintenance payments are made.*[64]

---

[54] SSA § 1902(a)(8); 42 C.F.R. § 435.911.
[55] SSA § 1902(a)(34); 42 C.F.R. § 435.915.
[56] SSA § 1902(a)(3); 42 C.F.R. § 435.912, 42 C.F.R. Part 431, Subparts D–E.
[57] SSA § 1943(b)(a)(A); 77 Fed. Reg. 14143 (Mar. 23, 2012), 51160.
[58] *Id.*
[59] SSA §§ 1943(b)(3); ACA § 1413.
[60] SSA § 1902(a)(8); 42 C.F.R. § 435.916.
[61] SSA § 1902(a)(10)(A)(i); 42 C.F.R. § 435.100 *et seq.*
[62] 42 C.F.R. § 435.116.
[63] 42 C.F.R. §§ 435.120, 121.
[64] 42 C.F.R. § 435.145.

d. *Former foster care children enrolled in Medicaid and in foster care upon turning 18 until age 26.*[65]

e. *Individuals receiving mandatory state supplements, and individuals with certain special historic coverage or circumstances.*[66]

4.4.2.2 Optional Categorically Needy

States have the option of extending coverage to individuals who qualify under optional Categorically Needy groups.[67] These individuals generally share similar characteristics with mandatory Categorically Needy populations, with certain differences such as relatively higher income or resources. Individuals must meet particular classifications and general eligibility criteria. Starting in 2014, states have the option through a plan amendment to cover individuals under the age of 64 with incomes above 138% of the poverty level.[68]

4.4.2.3 Optional Medically Needy

States have the option of extending coverage to individuals who qualify as "Medically Needy."[69] These individuals would qualify under Categorically Needy category but for the fact that their income and/or resources exceed levels applicable to Categorically Needy groups.

4.4.2.3.1 Financial Criteria for Medically Needy

i. *"Medically needy income level" (MNIL)*: Subject to certain exceptions and limitations, states must set a single income and resource standard for all Medically Needy.[70]

ii. *Income/Resource Eligible*: Individuals will qualify for Medically Needy if they have income and resources that are below the MNIL AND fall under one of the covered populations.[71]

iii. *Spend down*: Individuals will qualify for Medically Needy if they have income which exceeds the MNIL, but have "incurred medical expenses" that reduce their income level to at or below the MNIL AND they fall under one of the covered populations.[72] There are a number of requirements governing how to calculate "spend down," including limitations on applicable time periods and what costs may qualify.[73]

If states decide to cover a Medically Needy population, states generally must cover certain individuals who meet financial criteria, such as children under age 18 and pregnant women who would qualify as Categorically Needy except for family income and resources.[74]

---

[65] SSA § 1902(a)(10)(A)(i)(IX).
[66] *See* 42 C.F.R. §§ 435.122 to 435.172.
[67] SSA § 1902(a)(10)(A)(ii); 42 C.F.R. § 435, Subpart C.
[68] SSA § 1902(a)(10)(A)(ii)(XX); ACA § 2001(e)(1)(A)(iii).
[69] SSA §§ 1902(a)(10)(C), 1905(a); 42 C.F.R. Part 435, Subparts D and I.
[70] SSA §§ 1902(a)(10)(C)(i), 1902(a)(17); 42 C.F.R. §§ 435.301, 435.811, 435.840, 435.1007.
[71] 42 C.F.R. §§ 435.301, 435.811.
[72] 42 C.F.R. §§ 435.301, 435.811.
[73] *See, e.g.*, 42 C.F.R. § 435.831.
[74] *See, e.g.*, 42 C.F.R. §§ 435.301(b), 435.340.

If states decide to cover Medically Needy populations, they have the option of covering individuals who meet financial criteria but would not fall under a mandatory Medically Needy category such as aged, blind or disabled individuals receiving SSI.[75]

4.4.3 General Criteria Used to Determine Medicaid Eligibility

4.4.3.1 Meeting Standards for Income and Resources

The federal minimum eligibility level for Medicaid is calculated by a percentage of the federal poverty level guidelines (FPL). States are required at a minimum to cover children in families ages 0–1 at up to 138% of the FPL; children ages 1–5 at up to 138% of the FPL; and children ages 6–19 at up to 138% of the FPL.[76] However, states have the discretion to increase the income eligibility limits for these groups and the majority of them have. For example, for a family of four, participating states must cover the family's children ages 0–1 if the family's annual income is equal to or less than $28,196; but on average, states nationwide cover children 0–1 for a family of four with annual income equal to or less than $40,883. Likewise, many states cover pregnant women above the federally required income level. On average, states cover pregnant women in a family of four with one income earner whose annual income is less than or equal to $42,018 annually.

> *Income:* Cash income includes employment earnings, pension benefits, and tax refunds. In-kind income includes food or shelter, or something the individual uses to obtain either food or shelter.[77]
>
> *Resources*: Resources include cash or other property that can be liquidated or converted into cash-in-hand such as stocks and bonds.[78]

Subject to certain exceptions, states are required to exempt certain categories of income and resources when determining eligibility. States also possess flexibility in applying income and resource standards to certain children and pregnant women.[79]

Effective January 1, 2014, States were required to harmonize the approach for determining income for purposes of Medicaid Eligibility. States must convert their current net income eligibility thresholds to equivalent modified adjusted gross income (MAGI) thresholds. The MAGI-based methodology is required for both Medicaid and CHIP.[80] MAGI-based income eligibility standards are required to be not less than the effective income levels in place prior to the ACA. States may use a standardized MAGI conversion methodology or propose an alternative method. States have a variety of submission requirements with a completed application for a conversion plan by May 31, 2013. State Plan Amendments were expected by June, 2013 to allow for adequate implementation time in advance of open enrollment on October 1, 2013.[81]

---

[75] *See* 42 C.F.R. §§ 435.301(b), 435.308 *et seq.*
[76] 42 C.F.R. § 435.118.
[77] 20 C.F.R. § 416.1100 *et seq.*
[78] 20 C.F.R. § 416.1201 *et seq.*
[79] *See, e.g.*, SSA §§ 1902(a)(17)(B), 1902(r)(2); 20 C.F.R. § 416.1100 *et seq.*; 20 C.F.R. § 416.1201 *et seq.*
[80] SSA §§ 1902(e)(14)(A), 2102(b)(1)(B)(v).
[81] *See* CMS Letter to State Health Official/Medicaid Director, SHO # 12-003 (Dec. 28, 2012); and 77 Fed. Reg. 17144, 17150–59 (March 23, 2012).

State residency: States may impose residency requirements for Medicaid eligibility subject to certain limits (e.g., states may not impose a minimum time period for residency or require a permanent address).[82]

U.S. citizenship or legal status:[83]

a. U.S. citizens and U.S. nationals must qualify for full Medicaid benefits if they meet other eligibility requirements.[84] Effective financial quarters beginning July 1, 2006, under federal law, individuals must provide proof of citizenship or nationality in order to obtain or retain eligibility for Medicaid. (Previously individuals could self-attest to their citizenship or nationality status.)[85]

b. "Qualified" immigrants must meet a number of requirements solely related to their immigration status in order to qualify for full Medicaid benefits (assuming they meet other Medicaid eligibility requirements). Such requirements include providing acceptable documentation that they are in satisfactory immigration status and in some cases, completion of a waiting period of 5 years after becoming a "qualified" immigrant. Qualified immigrants include but are not limited to lawful permanent residents, refugees, asylees, Cuban/Haitian entrants and certain battered spouses and children with pending or approved visas.[86] Beneficiaries must submit satisfactory documents with respect to their immigration status to continue receiving benefits.

c. Immigrants, both documented and undocumented, who do not qualify for full Medicaid benefits due to their immigration status must receive coverage of emergency medical services. This coverage must be extended only if the individuals meet all other eligibility criteria. This coverage excludes organ transplants.[87]

4.5 Covered Benefits

"Medical assistance" is defined as payments made for a statutorily defined benefit package provided to Medicaid recipients. States must define the scope of "medical assistance" in their state Plans.[88] States, however, also have the option of seeking "waivers" of these requirements in certain circumstances.[89]

---

[82] *See* SSA § 1902(b)(2); 42 C.F.R. § 435.403.
[83] *See* 42 C.F.R. § 435.406.
[84] *See* SSA § 1902(b)(3).
[85] *See* Deficit Reduction Act of 2005 (DRA), Pub. L. No. 109-171, § 6036, 120 Stat. 80-81 (2006) (codified at SSA § 1903(i)(22)). Note that the Tax Relief and Health Care Act of 2006, Pub. L. No. 109-432, § 405 (Dec. 20, 2006) contained certain technical amendments to provisions of the DRA including (i) clarification of the state option for alternative premium and cost sharing (amending sections 6041–6043 of the DRA), (ii) clarification of the treatment of certain annuities (amending section 6012 of the DRA) and (iii) clarification with respect to application of citizenship documentation requirements (amending section 6036 of the DRA). 42 C.F.R. § 435.407.
[86] *See* 8 U.S.C. § 1601 *et seq.*, SSA § 1137(d)(2); 42 C.F.R. §§ 436.406, 436.408.
[87] 8 U.S.C. § 1601 *et seq.*; SSA § 1903(v); 42 C.F.R. §§ 436.128, 440.255.
[88] SSA §§ 1902(a)(10)(A), 1905(a).
[89] *See, e.g.*, SSA § 1115.

4.5.1 Mandatory Benefits for Categorically Needy

States are required to cover the following categories of services for their entire Categorically Needy population (both mandatory and optional categories):[90]

1. Inpatient and outpatient hospital services;
2. Rural health clinic and federally qualified health center services;
3. Laboratory and x-ray services;
4. Nursing facility services for individuals 21 or older (with the exception of institutions for mental disease for individuals between the ages of 22 and 64);[91]
5. Early periodic screening, diagnosis and treatment (EPSDT) services for individuals under 21.
    a. EPSDT covers four types of screening services—medical, vision, hearing and dental, which includes immunizations, laboratory tests and health education.[92]
    b. EPSDT also covers a broad range of services in addition to screening services defined as "any necessary health care, diagnostic services, and treatment needed to correct or ameliorate defects and physical and mental health conditions" discovered by the screenings. This coverage must include any service that a state *may* cover as medical assistance even if the state has not exercised that option under its state Plan.[93]
    c. States must provide transportation and appointment scheduling to children and families as part of EPSDT.[94]
6. Pregnancy-related services and services for other conditions that might complicate pregnancy;
7. Family planning services and supplies (with exception of hysterectomies in certain circumstances);[95]
8. Physician services, including medical and surgical services furnished by a dentist;
9. Services furnished by a nurse-midwife as authorized under state law;
10. Services furnished by a certified pediatric nurse practitioner or certified family nurse practitioner as authorized under state law; and
11. Home health care services for anyone who is entitled to receive nursing facility services (which must include nursing services, home health aide services and durable medical equipment and supplies).[96]
12. Freestanding birth center services and other ambulatory services that are offered by a freestanding birth center and that are otherwise included in the plan.[97]

---

[90] SSA §§ 1902(a)(10)(A), 1905(a)(1)–(5), (7), (17), (21), (28); 42 C.F.R. § 440.210.
[91] 42 C.F.R. § 435.1008.
[92] SSA § 1905(r).
[93] SSA § 1905(r).
[94] 42 C.F.R. § 441.62; State Medicaid Manual § 5150.
[95] 42 C.F.R. § 441.255.
[96] 42 C.F.R. § 440.70.
[97] SSA § 1905(a)(28) [added by ACA].

4.5.2 Optional Benefits

States may choose to cover the following categories of services and if they so choose, must provide coverage of these services for the entire Categorically Needy population (both mandatory and optional categories) covered under the state Plan.[98]

1. Prescription drugs;
2. Home health care for individuals not eligible for nursing services;
3. Private duty nursing services;
4. Clinic services provided by or under the direction of a physician;
5. Dental services;
6. Physical therapy, occupational therapy and speech therapy for individuals with speech, hearing and language disorders;
7. Dentures, prosthetic devices and eye glasses prescribed by a physician or optometrist;
8. Institutions for mental disease services for individuals age 65 and older;
9. Intermediate care facility services for the mentally retarded (with the exception of institutions for mental disease for individuals between the ages of 22 and 64);[99]
10. Inpatient psychiatric hospital services for individuals under 21;
11. Hospice care;
12. Case management services;
13. Respiratory care services for ventilator-dependent individuals;
14. Home and community care for functionally disabled elderly individuals;
15. Community-supported living arrangement services;
16. Personal care services;
17. Primary care case management;
18. Services provided under a program for all-inclusive care for the elderly (PACE);
19. Alcohol and drug treatment;
20. Tuberculosis-related services and drugs;
21. Targeted case management; and
22. Other diagnostic, screening, preventive and rehabilitative services recommended by a physician or other practitioner within the scope of their license, for the maximum reduction of physical or mental disability and restoration of an individual to the best possible functional level;
    a. Medical care or other types of remedial care recognized under state law furnished by licensed practitioners within the scope of their practice (such as podiatrists, optometrists

---

[98] SSA §§ 1902(a)(10)(A), 1905(a)(6)–(16), (18)–(20), (22)–(27); 42 C.F.R. § 440.225.
[99] 42 C.F.R. § 435.1009.

or chiropractors) or approved by the Secretary of HHS. This includes transportation and other travel related expenses necessary to secure treatment.[100]

4.5.3 Mandatory Benefits for the Medically Needy

If states decide to cover Medically Needy populations, they must cover the following categories of services.[101]

1. Prenatal care and delivery services for pregnant women;
2. Ambulatory services as defined under the state Plan for children under 18 and institutionalized individuals;
3. Home health services for individuals otherwise entitled to skilled nursing facility services; and
4. Institutions for mental disease services (excluding individuals from ages 22 through 64) or intermediate care facility for the mentally retarded services. If the state provides coverage of either of these services, it must provide *all* of the mandatory services for the Categorically Needy listed above (with the exception of nurse practitioner services) **OR** any *seven* of the mandatory or optional services for the Categorically Needy listed above.

4.5.4 Limitations on Covered Services

State Plans must specify not only which services are covered for Categorically Needy and Medically Needy, but also the amount, duration and scope of coverage for these services.[102] For example, in their state Plans, states must identify if a service is covered with or without limitation (e.g., whether there is a limit on the number of prescriptions covered). States, however, also have the option of seeking "waivers" of these requirements in certain circumstances.[103]

There are certain fundamental Medicaid principles that states must abide by when considering placing limits on services.

a. *Statewideness*. States must ensure that covered services are available to all recipients on a statewide basis.[104]
b. *Comparability*.
  i. State must provide the same package of benefits to all covered Categorically Needy groups.[105]
  ii. States must provide the same package of benefits within covered Medically Needy groups.[106]

---

[100] 42 C.F.R. § 440.170(a).
[101] SSA §§ 1902(a)(10)(C)(ii)–(iv), 1905(a)(1)–(27); 42 C.F.R. § 440.220.
[102] *See, e.g.*, SSA § 1902(a)(10)(B).
[103] *See, e.g.*, SSA § 1115.
[104] SSA § 1902(a)(1).
[105] SSA § 1902(a)(10)(B)–(C); 42 C.F.R. § 440.240.
[106] SSA § 1902(a)(10)(B)–(C); 42 C.F.R. § 440.240.

iii. States must ensure that the amount, duration and scope of services provided to Medically Needy does not exceed the package of services provided to Categorically Needy.[107]

iv. But for certain services, states may choose to provide coverage for only certain populations. For example, coverage of skilled nursing facility services may be limited to individuals age 21 years and older.[108]

c. *Reasonableness.* Coverage of services for Medicaid recipients must be sufficient in amount, duration and scope to achieve its purpose.[109]

d. *Non-Discriminatory.* States may not "arbitrarily" deny or reduce the amount of mandatory services based on a diagnosis, type of illness or condition.[110]

e. *Freedom of Choice.* States must allow Medicaid recipients to receive services from any qualified provider who is willing to provide the service to recipients.[111]

States do have the authority to place certain limits on coverage of services to the extent the implementation of these controls is consistent with the Medicaid amount, duration and scope principles summarized above.

a. *Utilization controls.* States may impose appropriate utilization controls on both mandatory and optional services for Medicaid recipients. For example, states may implement a prior authorization (PA) program through which recipients would need to seek PA prior to delivery of the service as a condition of coverage (with the exception of emergency services and certain EPSDT services).[112]

b. *Medical necessity.* States limit coverage of mandatory and optional services to when such services are medically necessary for the individual.[113]

But notwithstanding other Medicaid requirements, the Deficit Reduction Act of 2005 (DRA) provided states with the option of submitting a state Plan Amendment through which states may limit Medicaid coverage for certain recipients to "benchmark" or "benchmark equivalent" coverage.[114]

Benchmark coverage is defined as:

i. Insurance equivalent to the Federal Employee Health Benefits Program—the standard Blue Cross/Blue Shield preferred provider option service benefit plan;

ii. Health benefits plan that is offered to state employees;

iii. Coverage offered by a health maintenance organization (HMO) that has the largest insured commercial non-Medicaid enrollment in the state; or

---

[107] SSA § 1902(a)(10)(B)–(C); 42 C.F.R. § 440.240.
[108] 42 C.F.R. § 440.250.
[109] SSA § 1902(a)(10)(B); 42 C.F.R. § 440.230.
[110] SSA § 1902(a)(10)(B); 42 C.F.R. § 440.230.
[111] SSA § 1902(a)(23).
[112] 42 C.F.R. § 440.230.
[113] 42 C.F.R. § 440.230.
[114] *See* DRA, Pub. L. No. 109-171, § 6044, 120 Stat. 88–92 (2006) (codified at SSA § 1937).

iv. Coverage which the Secretary of HHS has determined to provide appropriate coverage for the proposed population.[115]

Benchmark equivalent coverage is defined as:

i. Basic services (changed by ACA)—inpatient and outpatient hospital services, physician surgical and medical services, lab and x-ray services, coverage of prescription drugs, mental health services, well-baby and well-child care and other appropriate preventative services (such as immunizations) as designated by HHS; and

ii. This coverage has an aggregate actuarial value that is equivalent to one of the benchmark benefit packages. If states opt to provide coverage of additional services, any coverage of vision services and hearing services must be equivalent to at least 75% of the actuarial value of benchmark coverage.

States must also ensure that, regardless of the benefit package, individuals have coverage of rural health clinic and Federally Qualified Health Center services.

Minimum Standards—Beginning 2014, any benchmark benefit package must provide at least the following essential health benefits as described in § 1302 of ACA:

i. Ambulatory patient services;
ii. Emergency services;
iii. Hospitalization;
iv. Maternity and newborn care;
v. Mental health and substance use disorder services, including behavioral health treatment;
vi. Prescription drugs;
vii. Rehabilitative and habilitative services and devices;
viii. Laboratory services;
ix. Preventive and wellness services and chronic disease management; and
x. Pediatric services, including oral and vision care.[116]

Certain populations are exempt from the imposition of benchmark or benchmark-equivalent coverage including: pregnant women in mandatory Categorically Needy categories; certain blind and disabled individuals; Medicare eligibles; terminally ill hospice patients; individuals who qualify for long term care services; and children receiving foster care or adoption assistance.

Children who are covered by the benchmark or benchmark-equivalent package must be provided with EPSDT services.

Benchmark and Benchmark-equivalent plans are also known as Alternative Benefit Plans following rules promulgated as a result of the ACA.[117] Alternative Benefit Plans are required to cover

---

[115] 42 C.F.R. § 440.330.
[116] 42 C.F.R. § 440.335.
[117] *See* 78 Fed. Reg. 42160, 42162 (July 15, 2013).

Essential Health Benefits (EHBs).[118] EHBs include items and services in at least 10 statutory benefit categories and equal in scope to a typical employer plan.

4.5.5 Cost Sharing

States have the authority to impose cost sharing (enrollment fees, premiums, deductibles, coinsurance, and copayments on certain mandatory and optional services) upon certain Medicaid recipients. However, states are prohibited from imposing cost-sharing mechanisms on a variety of groups including children under 18 with certain income levels, pregnant women (except for non-pregnancy related services), institutionalized individuals, Indians and on recipients of family planning, emergency and hospice services.[119]

Generally Medicaid providers may only deny services to an eligible individual on account of the individual's inability to pay the cost sharing amount imposed by the state Plan in accordance with the rules at 42 C.F.R. §§ 447.15, 447.52(e).

4.5.5.1 Denial of Service for Nonpayment

States may permit a provider, including a pharmacy or hospital to require an individual to pay cost sharing as a condition for receiving the item or service if

a. The individual has family income above 100% FPL,
b. The individual is not part of an exempt group, and
c. Cost-sharing rules for non-emergent services have been met.[120]

Cost sharing is prohibited for:

a. Emergency services;
b. Family planning services and supplies;
c. Preventive services provided to children under the age of 18;
d. Pregnancy-related services; and
e. Provider-preventable services.[121]

4.5.6 Specific Rules for Prescribed Drugs

Prescribed drugs are those simple or compound substances or mixtures of substances prescribed for the cure, mitigation, or prevention of disease or health maintenance that are (a) approved for safety and effectiveness by the FDA under §§ 505 or 507 of the Food, Drug, and Cosmetic Act, (b) prescribed by a physician or licensed practitioner, (c) dispensed by a licensed pharmacist and (d) dispensed on a written prescription.[122]

---

[118] ACA § 1302. *See also* 45 C.F.R. Parts 147, 155, 156.
[119] *See* SSA § 1916; 42 C.F.R. § 447.56(a).
[120] 42 C.F.R. § 447.52(e).
[121] 42 C.F.R. § 447.56(a)(2).
[122] *See* SSA § 1927(k)(2), 42 C.F.R. § 440.120.

States may place the following certain restrictions on coverage of prescribed drugs:[123]

a. Prior authorization before payment of a drug can be made;
b. Preferred drug lists (PDLs) that include those drugs for which prior authorization is not required;
c. Waiting period for new drugs when the prescribed use is not for a medically accepted indication or the state has excluded the drug from its formulary;
d. Excluding coverage of certain classes of drugs, such as nonprescription drugs, barbiturates, benzodiazepines, "lifestyle" drugs, and agents used for cosmetic purposes or hair growth; and
e. Limiting the number of prescriptions or refills as necessary to discourage waste or address fraud and abuse.

Effective January 1, 2006, for those individuals dually eligible for Medicare and Medicaid, Medicare became the primary payer for Medicare Part D prescription drugs. States may only provide coverage of outpatient prescription drugs to the extent the drug is not coverable under Part D (such as the benzodiazepines and barbiturates). Medicaid programs may not cover part or all of the cost of drugs that Medicare Part D plans *may* cover, even if a particular Part D plan has chosen not to cover a drug.[124]

4.5.6.1 Medicaid Drug Rebate Program

Covered outpatient drugs purchased through a state Medicaid program must be subject to significant price rebates.

Drug manufacturers are required to enter into national rebate agreements with the Secretary of HHS as a condition of receiving Medicaid payments for outpatient drugs. Manufacturers must agree to pay a rebate on each unit of its drug reimbursed under Medicaid as an outpatient prescription.[125] Once an agreement is made, manufacturers then must report product and pricing information every quarter, or else face a civil penalty of up to $10,000 per drug per day.[126]

The rebate amount is a percentage of the average manufacturer's price (AMP) depending on whether the products are innovator or non-innovator, single source or multiple source drugs.[127]

States have the option of negotiating supplemental rebates, equal to or greater than the drug rebates in the national rebate agreement, with manufacturers if the state enters into an agreement with a drug manufacturer that has been approved by CMS.[128]

States may use multi-state pooling arrangements that provide states with bulk purchasing power to negotiate even deeper discounts for outpatient drugs purchased by state Medicaid programs.[129]

---

[123] *See* SSA § 1927(d)(1).
[124] SSA § 1935(d).
[125] SSA § 1927(a).
[126] 77 Fed. Reg. 5318.
[127] SSA § 1927(c).
[128] CMS Letter to state Medicaid Directors #02-014 (Sept. 18, 2002).
[129] CMS Letter to state Medicaid Directors #04-006 (Sept. 9, 2004).

States have the option to cover investigational drugs under Medicaid and other drugs not subject to rebates once the FDA approves the drug for human trials. Reimbursements under this are covered by rules promulgated by the FDA.[130]

4.6 Reimbursement and Financing Mechanisms

4.6.1 Fundamental Reimbursement Principles

4.6.1.1 Setting Provider Payment Rates

Traditional Medicaid programs generally make payments directly to providers who have entered into an agreement with the state and meet the conditions of participation. State Plans must address methodologies by which payments are made to providers for covered services as consistent with the following fundamental Medicaid principles:[131]

a. Set payment rates that are consistent with the efficiency, economy and quality of care;

b. Adequately define the policy and method used in setting payment rates for each type of service;

c. Assure appropriate audit of records if payment is based on the cost of services; and

d. Set payment rates at a level that is sufficient to enlist enough providers so that services under the plan are reasonably available.

4.6.1.2 Medicaid Upper Payment Limits

CMS has interpreted setting payment rates that are consistent with the efficiency, economy and quality of care as requiring that Medicaid payments to certain types of providers must be subject to a limit, as defined by federal regulations.

a. Medicaid may not pay more than the upper limits described in Part 447 of Title 42 of the Code of Federal Regulations. States who pay more than upper limits will not receive FFP for those payments.

b. Generally, for inpatient providers (hospitals, nursing facilities and intermediate care facilities for the mentally retarded) and outpatient providers (hospitals and clinics), "aggregate Medicaid payments to a group of facilities" may not exceed "a reasonable estimate of the amount that would be paid for services furnished by the group of facilities under Medicare payment principles...."[132]

c. For other inpatient and outpatient providers, states may pay the "customary charges of the provider but must not pay more than the prevailing charges in the locality for comparable services under comparable circumstances."[133]

---

[130] 77 Fed. Reg. 5318, 5343.
[131] SSA § 1902(a)(30); 42 C.F.R. Part 447.
[132] 42 C.F.R. §§ 447.272, 447.321.
[133] 42 C.F.R. § 447.325.

d. Drugs are subject to various upper payment limits.[134] These limits are designed to assist the Federal government in purchasing drugs in a prudent manner by taking advantage of current market savings. They have been the subject of much controversy, litigation and legislative revision. On July 15, 2009, the Medicare Improvements for Patients and Providers Act of 2008 (MIPPA), P.L. 110-275 was enacted prohibiting CMS from taking any action, prior to October 1, 2009, to impose Federal Upper Limits for multiple source drugs established under 42 C.F.R. § 447.514(b) and from publishing Average Manufacturer Prices. Enactment of ACA made significant changes to the definition of Average Manufacturer Price and Federal Upper Limits. On February 2, 2012, CMS published proposed rules establishing new criteria on determining the average manufacturer price (AMP) of prescription drugs, setting a new formula for calculating the federal upper limit (FUL), and increasing the rebate percentages for covered drugs under Medicaid.[135] The ACA made significant changes to the Medicaid prescription drug program, including revising the definition of AMP, creating a new formula to calculate FUL, increasing the rebate percentages for covered outpatient drugs dispensed to Medicaid patients and including the resulting rebate offset, and broadening the prescription drug rebates to include covered outpatient drugs dispensed to enrollees of Medicaid MCOs.[136]

e. For non-risk Medicaid managed care contracts, Medicaid payments to the non-risk contractor may not exceed what Medicaid would have paid on a fee-for-service basis plus the net savings of administrative costs achieved by the Medicaid agency by contracting with the plan.[137]

f. For at risk Medicaid managed care contracts, states may only pay capitation rates that are determined to be actuarially sound.[138]

g. When there is no specific upper payment limit, payments to providers must be "consistent with efficiency, economy and quality of care."[139]

h. For Rural Health Centers and Federally Qualified Health Centers, states do not possess the discretion to set payment rates subject to the general principles outlined above. Instead, the Medicare, Medicaid and SCHIP Benefits Improvement and Protection Act of 2000 (BIPA) mandated that states implement a prospective payment system in which payments are made based on the costs of the facilities.[140]

i. On May 29, 2007, CMS published a final rule with comment period that limits reimbursement for health care providers that are operated by state or local governments to an amount that does not exceed a provider's cost. CMS requires that providers demonstrate the retention of the full amount of payment provided to them under a state Plan (or waiver or demonstration).[141]

---

[134] *See* 42 C.F.R. §§ 447.512–447.516.
[135] *See* 77 Fed. Reg. 5317, 5351 (Feb. 2, 2012).
[136] CMS, *Medicaid Prescription Drugs under the Affordable Care Act*, *available at* https://www.medicaid.gov/affordable-care-act/benefits/index.html.
[137] 42 C.F.R. § 447.362.
[138] 42 C.F.R. § 438.6(c)(2)(i).
[139] SSA § 1902(a)(30)(A).
[140] BIPA, Pub. L. No. 106-554, § 702, Appendix F, 114 Stat. 2763A-572-574 (codified at SSA § 1902(bb)).
[141] 72 Fed. Reg. 29748 (May 29, 2007) (The final rule went into effect on July 30, 2007).

4.6.1.3 Disproportionate Share Hospital (DSH) Payments

States must provide payments to hospitals which serve a "disproportionate share of low-income patients with special needs."[142] States receive allotments of DSH funds, from which they make payments to eligible hospitals. DSH payments to hospitals must be limited by hospital-specific DSH caps, which are defined as costs incurred by the hospital for providing services minus Medicaid reimbursement and payments made by the uninsured (those without health insurance during the year), by third parties (i.e., Indian Tribes and prisoners), or those with health insurance but met their annual or lifetime insurance limit. Significant cuts to DSH payments will be phased in between 2014 and 2020 as a result of the ACA.[143]

4.6.2 Financing the Non-Federal Share of Medicaid Expenditures

States have a number of sources from which to generate their share of Medicaid expenditures, which in turn generates "federal match" in accordance with the state's established federal medical assistance percentage (FMAP). Permissible sources include:

i. *State general revenues.* States must utilize state funds for at least 40% of the non-federal share of their Medicaid expenditures.[144]

ii. *Intergovernmental transfers (IGT) and certified public expenditures (CPEs).* Public agencies may transfer monies to the state Medicaid agency for or certify expenses that constitute the cost of the non-federal share of Medicaid expenditures. These public funds may not include federal funds.[145] CMS has determined that many states have used inappropriate financing arrangements, and from August 2003 through August 2006, 29 states ended such programs.[146] CMS has published a proposed rule that would clarify which state and local units of government have the authority to transfer monies or certify expenses. The proposed rule also would impose documentation requirements for CPEs.[147]

iii. *Provider donations.* Using this mechanism, the total amount of expenditures used to compute federal match may include revenues received by the state from provider-related donations.[148] In order to qualify as a provider donation:

    a. Provider donations must be bona fide, meaning that the voluntary donations have no direct or indirect relationship to Medicaid payments to that provider, to providers rendering the same types of services or to any related entity. Donations are presumed to be

---

[142] SSA §§ 1902(a)(13)(A)(iv), 1923.
[143] 42 U.S.C. § 1396r-4(7).
[144] SSA § 1902(a)(2).
[145] SSA § 1903(w)(6)(A); 42 C.F.R. § 433.51.
[146] *See Medicaid Financing: Federal Oversight Initiative is Consistent with Medicaid Payment Principles but Needs Greater Transparency,* GAO-07-214 at 5 (March 2007); *see also Medicaid Financing: Long-Standing Concerns about Inappropriate State Arrangements Support Need for Improved Federal Oversight,* GAO-08-255T (Nov. 1, 2007).
[147] *See Medicaid Program: Cost Limit for Providers Operated by Units of Government and Provisions to Ensure the Integrity of Federal-State Financial Partnership,* 72 Fed. Reg. 2236 (Jan. 18, 2007).
[148] SSA § 1903(w)(1); 42 C.F.R § 433.57 provided certain conditions are met.

bona fide if they do not exceed $5,000 per year for individual providers or $50,000 for health care organizations.[149]

    b.   Provider donations will not be bona fide if a hold harmless practice is in use.

iv. *Provider and health care related taxes.* Using this mechanism, the total amount of expenditures used to compute federal match is reduced by revenues received by the state from provider or health care related taxes that are not broad based and have a hold harmless provision;[150]

Provider and health care related taxes must be broad based, covering a permissible class of items and services and applying to all providers of the items and services within that class;[151]

Provider and health care-related taxes must be uniformly imposed throughout a jurisdiction;[152] and

Provider and health care-related taxes must not violate the hold harmless provision (which means facilities which would have paid more in taxes than they receive in Medicaid rate increases are not subject to taxes).[153]

v. By regulation, CMS established a safe harbor that allowed states to return taxes to providers if they are less than 6 percent of the provider's revenues. The Tax Relief and Health Care Act of 2006, Pub. L. No. 109-432, § 403 (Dec. 20, 2006), codified this six percent limit for 2007. Effective January 1, 2008 through September 30, 2011, this percentage will be reduced to 5.5 percent; after which time it will revert to 6 percent.

In light of recent economic challenges, many states will need to be creative in their efforts to finance their Medicaid programs.[154]

4.7 Delivery Systems

4.7.1 States Have Options

States have a number of options in operating a state Medicaid program. As discussed in Sections III and IV, states have certain choices with respect to covering populations and services. In addition to this flexibility, states also have the ability to choose different delivery systems– fee-for-service or Medicaid managed care.

4.7.2 Traditional Fee-For-Service

Under this model, the single state Medicaid agency will be responsible for setting eligibility categories, service categories and payment methodologies under the state Plan (and as approved by CMS). The Medicaid agency will generally make direct payments to providers in accordance with

---

[149] SSA § 1903(w)(2)(B); 42 C.F.R. §§ 433.52, 433.54.
[150] SSA § 1903(w)(1).
[151] 42 C.F.R. §§ 433.68(c)–(e).
[152] 42 C.F.R. § 433.68(d).
[153] 42 C.F.R. § 433.68(f).
[154] *See* Medicaid: Strategies to Help States Address Increased Expenditures during Economic Downturns, GAO-07-97 (Oct. 18, 2006).

the rates established as part of the state Plan. In setting the parameters for the program, the state must abide by fundamental Medicaid requirements—such as operating on a statewide basis and allowing recipients to receive care from any willing provider.[155]

4.7.3 Medicaid Managed Care

State Medicaid programs may also be operated as a managed care program in which enrollees are assigned to and enrolled in a managed care plan. But because this structure is a departure from traditional fee-for-service, states must choose one of the following three options in order to implement a Medicaid managed care program. On June 1, 2015, CMS issued a proposed Final Rule addressing Medicaid managed care.[156] This rule is the first major update to Medicaid and CHIP managed care regulations in more than a decade. On May 6, 2016, CMS finalized that rule.[157]

4.7.3.1 State Plan Amendment (SPA)

The Balanced Budget Act of 1997 provided states with the ability to implement a mandatory Medicaid managed care program through a SPA that must be approved by CMS. Under this option, state may not require certain populations to enroll in a managed care plan—children under 19 with special needs, individuals dually eligible for Medicare and Medicaid, Qualified Medicare Beneficiaries and certain Native Americans. States must also provide recipients with the choice of at least two managed care plans (with the exception of in rural areas).[158]

4.7.3.2 Section 1915(b) Waiver

States may also obtain CMS approval for "freedom of choice" waivers. Section 1915(b) waivers provide states with the ability to waive statewideness, freedom of choice and comparability of services requirements. This provides states with the authority to mandate enrollment of Medicaid recipients into a managed care plan, provide varying benefit packages to different segments of the population and operate the program in only certain parts of the state.[159]

4.7.3.3 Section 1115 Demonstration Projects

Under 1115 authority, states may receive CMS approval of the same waivers as under a 1915(b) waiver to implement a Medicaid managed care program. Section 1115, however, provides CMS with the authority to waive additional federal Medicaid requirements (subject to certain exceptions) and authorize expenditures as a Medicaid expense if a state can establish that the demonstration is "likely to assist in promoting the objectives of the Medicaid statute." CMS, by policy, also requires that the demonstration is "budget neutral" (which means that the cost of the demonstration will not exceed the

---

[155] *See* SSA §§ 1902(a)(1) and 1902(a)(23).
[156] 80 Fed. Reg. 31097.
[157] 1 Fed. Reg. 27498.
[158] SSA § 1932(a).
[159] SSA § 1915(b).

costs that would otherwise be incurred under state Plan). In addition to implementing managed care, this option provides states with the ability to expand or reform coverage of populations or services.[160] More than 30 Medicaid Programs have received approval of a Section 1115 demonstration project.

4.7.3.4 Home and Community Based Services (HCBS)

Over approximately the past 20 years, many states have worked towards developing home and community-based options as an alternative to institutional care. The U.S. Supreme Court's decision in *Olmstead v. L.C.*, 527 U.S. 581 (1999) applied the Americans with Disabilities Act to the right of certain individuals with disabilities to receive health care in a community-based setting. Under HCBS waiver authority, states may provide coverage of home-based services to individuals in need of institutionalization which are not otherwise covered under the state Plan. In providing states with flexibility to provide this coverage, HHS may waive comparability requirements, statewideness requirements and financial eligibility requirements (with the exception of HCBS waivers for children under 5).[161] Three populations may be covered under an HCBS waiver:

a. Individuals who would be eligible for Medicaid if they were institutionalized in a hospital, nursing facility or ICF/MR and would require such institutionalization if they did not receive HCBS waiver services.[162]

b. Individuals who are 65 years or older and would require care provided in a skilled nursing facility or intermediate care facility as covered by Medicaid if they did not receive HCBS waiver services.[163]

c. Children under 5 who have AIDS or who are drug dependent at birth and who would require care in a hospital or nursing facility if they did not receive HCBS waiver services.[164]

Services covered under a HCBS waiver can include, for example, case management, homemaker, home health aide, personal care, adult day, habilitation, respite care and day treatment services. Services may also include prevocational and habilitative services.[165]

States also have the ability under 1905(i) to provide through a state plan amendment for the provision of medical assistance for HCBS. On January 16, 2014, CMS published a Final Rule concerning HCBS requirements.[166] CMS states that the Final Rule "offers states new flexibilities in providing necessary and appropriate services to elderly and disabled populations."[167] The Final Rule also includes important changes concerning 1915(c) HCBS waivers.

---

[160] SSA § 1115.
[161] SSA § 1915(c)–(e).
[162] SSA § 1915(c).
[163] SSA § 1915(d).
[164] SSA § 1915(e).
[165] *See* 42 C.F.R. §§ 440.180–181.
[166] 79 Fed. Reg. 2948.
[167] *Id.*

4.8 Affordable Care Act of 2010

4.8.1 ACA Expands Medicaid in 2014

Significant expansion of the Medicaid program will be effective in 2014[168] as a result of enactment of the ACA, Pub. L. No. 111-148.

1. Section 2001 of the ACA requires states to expand Medicaid eligibility to all non-elderly individuals with income up to 133% of the Federal Poverty Level by 2014[169] and expands FFP to 100% for newly eligible from 2014–2016, and continues phased down enhanced FFP to 90% in 2020 and beyond.
2. New eligibility category for childless adults who are not otherwise eligible for Medicaid in 2014.[170] States may begin offering such coverage in 2010 with an approved SPA.
3. States must maintain existing income eligibility levels until state exchanges become fully operational.
4. States must maintain existing income eligibility levels for CHIP and Medicaid until 2019.
5. As a result of the ACA, Medicaid (and CHIP) enrollment is projected to grow from 63.4 million in 2013 to 85.2 million in 2014.[171]

4.8.2 Improvements to Medicaid Services

Freestanding Birth Centers. Payments to facilities serving as freestanding birth centers as covered by a state Plan and providers providing professional services in such settings.[172]

Expanded Children's Hospice Benefit. Provides children electing to receive hospice care in the last six months of life are eligible to receive curative treatment simultaneously with hospice care.[173]

Expanded Eligibility for Family Planning. States may provide family planning services on a presumptively eligible basis as an optional categorically needed group.[174]

4.8.3 Prescription Drug Coverage

Rebates. Minimum rebate for single source and innovator multiple source drugs increased to 23.1%.

4.8.4 Expansion of Presumptive Eligibility Sites

Effective 2014, any Medicaid enrolled hospital may become a presumptive eligibility site for Medicaid for all Medicaid eligible populations.[175] On January 24, 2014, CMS issued an Informational

---

[168] *See* SCOTUS & Medicaid Expansion, *infra*, 4.9.
[169] *Id.*
[170] 42 U.S.C. § 1396a(10)(A)(i)(VIII).
[171] CMS, Office of the Actuary, *National Health Expenditure Projections 2009–2019*, Table 3 (Sept. 2010).
[172] ACA § 2301, SSA § 1905.
[173] ACA § 2302; SSA § 1905(o)(1) (Medicaid); SSA 2120(a)(23) (CHIP).
[174] ACA § 2303.
[175] ACA § 2202.

Bulletin entitled "Implementation of Hospital Presumptive Eligibility" in which CMS announced the release of a number of resources designed to assist states with the implementation of hospital presumptive eligibility.[176] In addition to citing numerous resources available, the Informational Bulletin requests that states take into account the following policy considerations as they implement hospital presumptive eligibility: (1) the presumptive eligibility period varies depending on whether an individual submits a full application; (2) a full Medicaid application is not a condition of eligibility for presumptive eligibility; and (3) states may not require verification of information provided as a condition of presumptive eligibility.

4.8.5 Increased Physician Reimbursement for Primary Care

Pediatricians, Family Medicine and general Internal Medicine physicians will see increased reimbursement equal to 100% of Medicare Part B physician fee schedule rates for 2013 and 2014. FFP for resulting rate increases will be 100%.[177]

4.8.6 Funding and Administrative Support for Quality Initiatives

1. Granted funding and increased scope to Medicaid and CHIP Payment and Access Commission (MACPAC).[178]

2. Created CMS Innovation Center to test, evaluate, and expand different payment structures and methodologies to foster patient-centered care, improve quality and slow costs growth in Medicare, Medicaid and CHIP.[179]

4.8.7 DSH Payments Reduced

Significant cuts to DSH payments will be phased in between 2014 and 2020.[180]

4.8.8 Payment Innovations

1. Prohibit payments to states for services related to health care acquired conditions. Regulations to be effective July 1, 2011.[181]

2. Demonstration project for up to five states whereby defined safety net hospital system converts from FFS reimbursement to a capitated, global payment structure.[182]

3. Demonstration project for Pediatric Accountable Care Organizations to earn incentive payments based on shared savings. Providers must agree to participate for at least three years.[183]

---

[176] *See* www.medicaid.gov/Federal-Policy-Guidance/Downloads/CIB-01-24-2014.pdf.
[177] HCERA § 1202.
[178] 42 U.S.C. § 1396(f).
[179] ACA § 3201.
[180] 42 U.S.C. § 1396r-4(7).
[181] ACA § 2701. 42 U.S.C. § 1396b-1.
[182] ACA § 2705.
[183] ACA § 2706.

4.8.8.1 Extension and Enhancement of CHIP

CHIP reauthorized through Sept 30, 2015 and increases CHIP FFP 23% (capped at 100%) from 2016 through 2019. Children of state employees eligible for CHIP.[184]

4.8.8.2 Program Integrity Provisions

Subtitle E and F of ACA adds additional program integrity requirements to Medicaid.

4.9 SCOTUS & Medicaid Impact

The U.S. Supreme Court (SCOTUS) rendered a decision in *National Federation of Independent Businesses, et al. v. Sebelius, Secretary of Health and Human Services et al.* (hereinafter *NFIB*) on June 28, 2012, which contained many important ramifications for the ACA and its mandated changes to the Medicaid program.[185]

The Court upheld the ACA's individual mandate as a constitutional exercise of Congress' taxing power.

The Court held that Medicaid Expansion under the ACA is unconstitutional as written, and Congress is not free "to penalize States that choose not to participate in that new [Medicaid Expansion] program by taking away their existing Medicaid funding…the Secretary cannot apply [the ACA] to withdraw existing Medicaid funds for failure to comply with the requirements set out in the expansion."[186]

Chief Justice Roberts' opinion in *NFIB* declared that Medicaid Expansion should be optional for states operating under the existing Medicaid program. Justice Roberts took care to clearly identify each of the elements that combined to create this new health care program, described as Medicaid Expansion, ultimately supporting his conclusion that this new program should be optional for states operating the existing Medicaid programs. The opinion identifies those elements of Medicaid change in the ACA that are considered Medicaid Expansion, and therefore optional for states. From that, some people infer that those elements that are not considered a new program or Medicaid Expansion, and are therefore mandatory for states continuing to participate in Medicaid.

4.9.1 Medicaid Expansion: Optional Participation for the Newly Eligible

Of the various ACA requirements addressed in *NFIB*, requirements for newly eligible Medicaid beneficiaries were given special attention as having "transformed" the Medicaid program in three ways (below). The newly eligible category was described as going significantly beyond historically accepted amendments to Medicaid to essentially create a new health care program.

(i) Adding a new eligibility category—the newly eligible;
(ii) Creating new funding for the newly eligible; and

---

[184] ACA § 2101.
[185] *Nat'l Fed'n of Indep. Bus. v. Sebelius*, 132 S. Ct. 2566 (2012).
[186] *NFIB*, at 2607.

(iii) Creating a new benefit category of at least minimum essential coverage for the newly eligible.[187]

The new health care program for the newly eligible enlisted the states to participate in it or risk losing the opportunity to participate in Medicaid altogether. The Court held that states must be given a genuine choice to accept the federal government's offer to participate in an expansion of Medicaid to the newly eligible. Consequently, the Court struck down the Secretary's ability to withdraw traditional Medicaid funds for failure to comply with the newly eligible requirements.

4.9.2 Medicaid Program Changes—Mandatory Participation

In light of the holding in *NFIB*, a number of states have indicated an interest in identifying other Medicaid program requirements as optional and not subject to compliance with federal rules as a condition for receiving federal Medicaid funds.

However, the Secretary retains the ability to withhold federal funds from Medicaid programs for failure to comply with Medicaid requirements. The Secretary also maintains the option to enforce Medicaid program requirements by withholding federal funds to noncompliant states except for requirements for the newly eligible.

The holding in *NFIB* is limited only to broad new categories of beneficiaries unrelated to mandatory categories under the existing program. Justice Roberts' holding appears to forbid Congress from coercing the states into participating in a new health care program does not apply either to elements of the Medicaid program previously required or to the expansion of those categories.[188]

Medicaid requirements that are not related to the newly eligible, and are not otherwise transformative, will require mandatory adoption for ongoing programs. Several of these mandatory Medicaid provisions are as follows:

i. *Eligibility for Children in Low Income Families*

   The ACA increased the number of eligible children for Medicaid by granting eligibility to children ages 6–18 in households with income up to 133 percent of the FPL in 2014.[189] This modification is likely to survive any challenges by states using the *NFIB* analysis. CMS published a rule implementing these requirements which will become effective on January 1, 2014.[190] The *NFIB* test requires:

   1. the addition of a new eligibility category;
   2. creation of new funding for that eligibility category; and
   3. creating a new benefit category.

ii. *Extension of Time for States to Return Federal Financial Participation (FFP) Collected from an Overpayment*

---

[187] ACA § 2001(a)(3).
[188] *NFIB* at 2606.
[189] ACA § 2001(a)(5)(B).
[190] 77 Fed. Reg. 17144, 17149 (Mar.23, 2012); codified at 42 C.F.R. § 435.118.

The ACA increased the time from sixty days to one year that state Medicaid programs have to collect provider overpayments before they are required to return the federal share of an identified overpayment.[191] CMS published a final rule implementing this requirement, which became effective June 28, 2012.[192] The rule does not contain any exceptions or distinctions for states based on their participation in Medicaid Expansion.

iii. *Increase Medicaid Primary Care Rates*

The ACA makes changes to the Medicaid program that temporarily increase primary care reimbursement rates of which the federal government grants 100% FFP for such increases in 2013 and 2014.[193] These changes to the existing Medicaid program do not enlist the states to create a new program and are unchanged by *NFIB*. A final rule was published to implement these regulations at 76 Fed. Reg. 66670, 66696–70 (Nov. 6, 2012); codified at 42 C.F.R. § 477, Subpart G.

iv. *Expansion of Recovery Audit Contractor (RAC) Program to Medicaid*

The ACA requires states to establish a RAC program to enable the auditing of claims for Medicaid providers' services.[194] Medicaid RACs must identify overpayments, recoup overpayments, and identify underpayments.[195] There is no indication that this ACA provision is applicable to only those states that participate in Medicaid Expansion. CMS published the final rule which became effective on January 1, 2012.[196]

v. *Diminished DSH Funding*

The *NFIB* decision could have a significant practical effect on hospitals located in states that do not implement Medicaid Expansion. Those hospitals will continue to treat large numbers of uninsured beneficiaries whose Medicaid coverage was expected to offset the reduction in DSH funding. This impact is likely to be greatest for safety net hospitals. In October 2012, the National Association of Public Hospitals and Health Systems published a report concluding that safety net hospitals expect to lose approximately $14.1 billion in federal subsidies as a result of reduced Medicaid DSH payments.[197]

vi. *Medicaid Coverage for Former Foster Care Children*

The ACA extended the Medicaid eligibility to age 24 for individuals who had spent more than six months in foster care.[198] This ACA section extends eligibility of foster care children but does not create a new eligibility category. Further, there are no new federal fund or benefit categories attached to these children, so the program does not appear to meet the elements of an optional Medicaid Expansion program.

---

[191] ACA § 6506.
[192] 77 Fed. Reg. 31499, 31152 (May 29, 2012); codified at 42 C.F.R. § 433.320.
[193] Social Security Act § 1902(a)(13).
[194] ACA § 6411(a).
[195] *Id.* § 6411(a)(1).
[196] 76 Fed. Reg. 57808, 57829 (Sept. 16, 2011); codified at 42 C.F.R. 455.502.
[197] Nat'l Ass'n of Public Hosps. & Health Sys., *Need for a Sustainable Solution: Restoring the Balance in Safety Net Financing* (Oct. 2012), *available at* http://essentialhospitals.org/wp-content/uploads/2015/04/NAPH_uncompensated_care_analysis_FINAL.pdf.
[198] ACA § 2004.

vii. *Payment Adjustments for Provider-Preventable Conditions*

The Secretary of HHS has been directed to prohibit payments to states for any amounts expended for providing medical assistance for health care-acquired conditions.[199] CMS published a final rule effective on July 1, 2011 with compliance not anticipated until July 1, 2012.[200] There is no indication that this ACA provision is applicable to only those states that participate in Medicaid Expansion.

viii. *Maintenance of Effort*

Requirements for maintenance of effort (MOE) in Medicaid do not appear to invoke a significant change that would fit within the *NFIB* test to render the requirements optional. Rather, the provisions specify that existing coverage for adults under the Medicaid program generally must remain in place until the Secretary determines that an Exchange established by the ACA is fully operational, and existing coverage for children must generally remain in place through October 2019.[201] There is no new eligibility category, no new funding, and no new category of benefits. Instead, MOE standards require states to continue their previous participation levels in Medicaid. MOE requirements have been used repeatedly by Congress in the past and CMS has affirmatively declined to issue significant regulatory guidance on implementation of the ACA Medicaid MOE provisions and instead refers to the guidelines previously issued to implement the MOE requirements as required by the ARRA. Medicaid MOE requirements may not apply to a state that certifies that it has, or projects, a budget deficit.[202] All of these factors support the conclusion that the Medicaid MOE provisions in the ACA do not create a separate program of Medicaid Expansion and are not optional for the states.

ix. *Newly Eligible Option—Logistics*

The holding in *NFIB* has clarified that the Medicaid Expansion provisions in the ACA are optional for states' participation in the Medicaid program. However, the options, logistics, decision-making, and eligibility requirements are unclear and various organizations including the National Governor's Association, the National Association of Medicaid Directors, the American Hospital Association, and the Republican Governor's Association have submitted written questions to the President and the Secretary of HHS. In response, CMS has communicated regularly with the provider community regarding these issues. Here is what we know:

1. The majority of Medicaid provisions included in the ACA survived the *NFIB* decision. The only optional provision for states is expanding Medicaid to adults under the age of 65 with incomes up to 133% of the FPL who were not previously eligible for Medicaid.[203]

2. Resources available to states to develop affordable insurance exchanges are not contingent on expanding Medicaid to the newly eligible.[204]

---

[199] ACA § 2702.
[200] 76 Fed. Reg. 32816, 32816–19 (June 6, 2011); codified at 42 C.F.R. § 447.26.
[201] ACA § 2001(b).
[202] *Id.*
[203] Letter from Kathleen Sebelius, Sec'y of HHS to Governors (July 10, 2012).
[204] *Id.*

3. States may choose to expand or discontinue Medicaid to the newly eligible at any time.[205]
4. HHS is moving forward with a final rule to increase FMAP to all states for certain primary care professional services.[206]
5. States may receive additional funding provided in the ACA for Medicaid information technology costs and insurance exchange implementation costs even if they have not decided to expand Medicaid eligibility or run their own exchange. If a state accepts such funding and ultimately decides not to start its own exchange, implementation costs will not need to be refunded.[207]

A variety of waivers have been granted to states to expand Medicaid using HHS/CMS statutory waiver authority including programs in Iowa (effective January 1, 2014), Michigan (effective April 1, 2014), Arkansas (effective January 1, 2014). Pending waiver applications have been submitted for Indiana and Pennsylvania. Wisconsin has not adopted Medicaid expansion, but did amend its existing 1115 waiver to expand coverage to adults up to 100% FPL.

Exhibit A[208]

2018 POVERTY GUIDELINES FOR THE 48 CONTIGUOUS STATES AND THE DISTRICT OF COLUMBIA

Persons in family/household	Poverty guideline
For families/households with more than 8 persons, add $4,180 for each additional person.	
1	$12,140
2	$16,460
3	$20,780
4	$25,100
5	$29,420
6	$33,740
7	$38,060
8	$42,380

---

[205] Statement of Cindy Mann, Dir., Ctr. For Medicaid & CHIP Servs., Panel at the Nat'l Conference of State Legislature 2012 Legislative Summit Health Sessions: *The Health Care Law: What's Next* (NCSL Health Reform Implementation Task Force Meeting) (Aug. 6, 2012).
[206] Cindy Mann, CMS Deputy Adm'r & Dir. of the Ctr. for Medicaid & CHIP Servs., *Affordable Care Act Implementation Update for Clinicians, Hospitals, and other Health Care Providers: Medicaid Expansion*, Sept. 13, 2012.
[207] Letter from Marilyn Tavenner, Acting Adm'r, CMS, HHS, to the Hon. Robert McDonnell, Chairman, Republican Governors Ass'n, July 13, 2012, *available at* www.modernhealthcare.com/assets/pdf/CH80617713.PDF.
[208] Source: https://aspe.hhs.gov/poverty-guidelines.

2018 POVERTY GUIDELINES FOR ALASKA

Persons in family/household	Poverty guideline
For families/households with more than 8 persons, add $5,230 for each additional person.	
1	$15,180
2	$20,580
3	$25,980
4	$31,380
5	$36,780
6	$42,180
7	$47,580
8	$52,980

2018 POVERTY GUIDELINES FOR HAWAII

Persons in family/household	Poverty guideline
For families/households with more than 8 persons, add $4,810 for each additional person.	
1	$13,960
2	$18,930
3	$23,900
4	$28,870
5	$33,840
6	$38,810
7	$43,780
8	$48,750

5

Fundamentals of Health Law Fraud and Abuse

Anjali N.C. Downs*
Epstein Becker Green PC

Developing ways to identify and ferret out health care fraud continues to be a significant focus for both federal and state governments. By way of example, the National Health Care Fraud and Abuse Control Program (HCFAC)[1] was responsible in FY 2016 for returning $2.5 billion in fraudulent and misspent funds. Moreover, more than $31.0 billion has been returned to the Medicare Trust Fund since its creation in 1997.[2] In fact, the return on investment for the HCFAC program over the last three years is $5.00 returned for every $1.00 expended.[3] As another example, since its inception in 2007, the Medicare Fraud Strike Force[4] (Strike Force) has resulted in the charging of over 3,018 defendants, with 2,041 defendants pleading guilty and 275 convicted in jury trials.[5]

In addition to federal and state governments, private organizations and individuals also play a big role in combating fraud. In FY 2016, *qui tam* relators received over $5.26 million. Also, in 2012, the Healthcare Fraud and Prevention Partnership (HFPP) was formed between the federal government, state officials, law enforcement, private health insurance plans and associations, and health care anti-fraud associations. "The purpose of the partnership is to exchange data and information between the partners to help improve capabilities to fight fraud, waste and abuse in the health care industry."[6]

As health care fraud enforcers are targeting a wide array of business arrangements and payment practices as potentially constituting fraud, this Chapter addresses the fundamental legal underpinnings of the broad spectrum of health care fraud and abuse laws. In particular, this Chapter provides a brief overview of the federal laws and regulations, particularly the Anti-Kickback Statute, the physician

---

* The author gratefully acknowledges the valuable contributions made by Daniel Kim, an Associate in the Health Care and Life Sciences practice of Epstein Becker Green PC, to the updating of this chapter.

[1] The HCFAC was established by the Health Insurance Portability and Accountability Act of 1996 (HIPAA). The HCFAC is under the joint direction of the Attorney General for the Department of Justice (DOJ) and the Secretary of the Department of Health and Human Services (HHS), acting through the Inspector General, and is designed to coordinate Federal, state and local law enforcement activities with respect to health care fraud and abuse. *See* Health Insurance Portability and Accountability Act of 1996, Pub. L. No. 104-191, 110 Stat. 1936 (1996).

[2] The Department of Health and Human Services and The Department of Justice Health Care Fraud and Abuse Control Program Annual Report for Fiscal Year 2016, January 2017, *available at* https://oig.hhs.gov/publications/docs/hcfac/FY2016-hcfac.pdf.

[3] *Id.*

[4] The Strike Force is comprised of interagency teams made up of investigators and prosecutors "that focus on the worst offenders in regions with the highest known concentration of fraudulent activities." *See Id.*

[5] *Id.*

[6] *See* HFPP website at https://hfpp.cms.gov/.

self-referral law (known as the Stark Law for its chief legislative architect), and the prohibitions against false claims and fraudulent billing practices. This Chapter also examines the importance of establishing a corporate compliance program.

5.1 The Federal Health Care Program's Anti-Kickback Statute

5.1.1 Statutory Prohibition

The federal health care program's Anti-Kickback Statute makes it a felony to knowingly and willfully solicit or receive remuneration "in return for referring an individual to a person for the furnishing or arranging for the furnishing of any item or service" or "in return for purchasing, leasing, ordering, or arranging for or recommending purchasing, leasing, or ordering any good, facility, service, or item for which payment may be made in whole or in part under a Federal health care program."[7] The Anti-Kickback Statute also prohibits a person from knowingly and willfully offering or paying remuneration to any person to induce that person to refer or purchase, lease, order, or arrange for or recommend the purchasing, leasing, or ordering of items or services for which payment may be made by a federal health care program. Although the Anti-Kickback Statute originally applied to Medicare and Medicaid only, over the years it has been broadened to apply to any "Federal health care program," defined as "any plan or program that provides health benefits, whether directly, through insurance, or otherwise, which is funded directly, in whole or in part, by the United States Government" other than the Federal Employee Health Benefit Program.[8]

Each offense under the Anti-Kickback Statute is punishable by a fine of up to $25,000 and imprisonment for up to five years. Violators of the Anti-Kickback Statute also are subject to exclusion from participation in the federal health care programs, as well as imposition of civil monetary penalties for each violation of (i) up to $50,000, and (ii) three times the amount of the remuneration in question. In addition, as part of the Patient Protection and Affordable Care Act of 2010 along with the Health Care Education Affordability Reconciliation Act of 2010 (referred to collectively as the Affordable Care Act or ACA), Congress established conclusively that a violation of the Anti-Kickback Statute is a false claim for purposes of the federal False Claims Act.[9]

In recognition of the breadth of the prohibition contained in the Anti-Kickback Statute, Congress has enacted several exceptions over the years for certain financial arrangements. Specifically, there are exceptions for:

---

[7] 42 U.S.C. § 1320a-7b(b).

[8] 42 U.S.C. § 1320a-7(g). Examples of federal health care programs include, but are not limited to: Medicare (Title XVIII of the Social Security Act); Medicaid (Title XIX of the Social Security Act); Department of Defense health care programs (*i.e.*, CHAMPUS and TRICARE, Chapter 55 of Title 10, United States Code); programs funded by Maternal and Child Health Block Grants (Title V of the Social Security Act); programs funded by Social Services Block Grants (Title XX of the Social Security Act); a medical care program of the Indian Health Service or of a tribal organization; and a health benefit plan under § 5(e) of the Peace Corps Act.

[9] *See* Patient Protection and Affordable Care Act of 2010, Pub. L. No. 111-148, 124 Stat. 119 § 6402(f)(1) (2010) (codified at 42 U.S.C. § 1320a–7b(g)). Health Care and Education Reconciliation Act of 2010, Pub L. No. 111-152, 124 Stat. 1029 (2010) [hereinafter ACA].

1. discounts that are properly disclosed and reflected in the costs claimed or charges made by the provider;
2. payments by an employer to an employee for bona fide employment in the provision of covered items and services;
3. amounts paid by providers to a group purchasing organization (GPO) where a written agreement is made between the providers and the GPO specifying the fee and the GPO discloses the amount of the administrative fee to providers purchasing from the GPO;
4. waivers of coinsurance amounts in connection with certain Federally Qualified Healthcare Centers (FQHC);
5. activities protected by the safe harbor regulations (which will be described in the following section);
6. certain risk-sharing arrangements;
7. certain arrangements involving FQHCs;
8. waivers of certain cost sharing amounts under Medicare Part D; and
9. certain discounts made under the Medicare coverage gap discount program.[10]

5.1.2 Judicial Interpretation

5.1.2.1 The First 25 Years of Case Law under the Statute: Pre-Hanlester

United States v. Greber[11] is the landmark case on the scope of the Anti-Kickback Statute. In this case, the Third Circuit Court of Appeals adopted the "one-purpose" test. Dr. Greber, an osteopathic physician who was board-certified in cardiology, was president of Cardio-Med, Inc., an organization that provided diagnostic services for cardiac patients. When Cardio-Med performed a test at the request of a referring physician, Cardio-Med also forwarded a portion of the Medicare reimbursement it received to the referring physician. This fee was purportedly for "interpretations" by the referring physician. Evidence was introduced, however, that physicians received these interpretation fees even though Dr. Greber evaluated the tests. In addition, the amount paid to the physicians was more than Medicare allowed for such services. Hence, Dr. Greber was convicted of, among other transgressions, tendering kickbacks in violation of the Anti-Kickback Statute. In upholding his conviction, the Third Circuit Court of Appeals held that "if one purpose of the payment was to induce future referrals, the [Anti-Kickback Statute] has been violated."

After the *Greber* case, the issue confronting the health care industry was whether the broad "one-purpose" test was applicable merely to the egregious facts presented, or whether the test would be generally applicable to *all* kickback cases. For several years, no other kickback cases considered this issue until 1989, when two separate circuit courts considered the *Greber* "one-purpose" test.

---

[10] *See* 42 U.S.C. § 1320a-7b(b)(3); *see also* 42 U.S.C. § 1395w-104(e).
[11] *United States v. Greber*, 760 F.2d 68 (3rd Cir.1985), *cert. denied*, 474 U.S. 988 (1985).

In *United States v. Kats*,[12] a physician owned a 25% interest in Community Clinic, which collected blood and urine specimens and forwarded the specimens to Tech-Lab. Tech-Lab billed Community Clinic, which in turn billed the California Medicaid and Medicare programs. According to the court's description of the facts, 50% of the laboratory payments were "kicked back" to Community Clinic. The Ninth Circuit Court of Appeals followed the *Greber* holding, and upheld a jury instruction allowing conviction unless the payment was "wholly and not incidentally attributable to the delivery of goods and services." The Ninth Circuit stated that it is not a defense to claim that other purposes are behind the payment as long as one of the material purposes is to induce referrals.

United States v. Bay State Ambulance and Hospital Rental, Inc.[13] concerned the award of a hospital ambulance contract. Allegedly, the ambulance company made illegal payments to a hospital official who sat on the bid committee. Such payments consisted of a management-consulting contract, loans, and other consideration including automobiles and cash. The court cited with approval *Greber*'s holding that any amount of inducement is illegal under the Anti-Kickback Statute, but stopped short of explicitly adopting the Third Circuit's broad "one-purpose" test. The district court had instructed the jury that, in order to obtain a conviction under the Anti-Kickback Statute, the *primary* purpose (as opposed to an incidental or minor purpose) of the payments must be improper, and thus the less-favorable *Greber* standard was not directly challenged on appeal. The court in *Bay State Ambulance* also noted that the government was not required to prove that payments received were not reasonable for the work performed, because "the gravamen of Medicare fraud is inducement. Giving a person an opportunity to earn money may well be an inducement to that person to channel potential Medicare payments towards a particular recipient."

5.1.2.2 The Hanlester Decision

On April 6, 1995, the U.S. Court of Appeals for the Ninth Circuit issued a decision in *Hanlester Network v. Shalala*,[14] the first case in which the OIG asserted its civil-sanction authority under the Anti-Kickback Statute. Significantly, the Ninth Circuit determined that the appellants should not be excluded under the statute.

This case involved a network of three clinical laboratories that had been established as physician joint ventures by the Hanlester Network of Santa Ana, California. The joint ventures established by the Hanlester Network were organized as limited partnerships with more than 100 physicians participating as investors. The investment arrangement basically consisted of physicians as limited partners who owned between three and seven shares at $500 per share. Although no express requirement was made that physician investors refer to the laboratory, physician investors were required to sell back their shares if they retired, lost their medical license, or relocated outside the laboratory's service area. In addition, each joint-venture laboratory was operated under a management agreement with SmithKline Beecham Clinical Laboratories (SBCL). The management agreement provided the payment to SBCL of either $15,000 per month or 76% of the revenues generated by the joint-venture laboratory, whichever was greater.

---

[12] *United States v. Kats*, 871 F.2d 105 (9th Cir. 1989).
[13] *United States v. Bay State Ambulance and Hospital Rental, Inc.*, 874 F.2d 20 (1st Cir. 1989).
[14] *Hanlester Network v. Shalala*, 51 F.3d 1390 (9th Cir. 1995), *reh'g en banc denied*, No. 93-55351 (9th Cir. Nov. 15, 1995).

In 1989, the OIG issued notices of proposed program exclusion to five individuals and five entities involved in the joint ventures.[15] The individuals and entities subject to the exclusion action requested an administrative hearing to challenge their proposed program exclusion. Initially, the Administrative Law Judge (ALJ) held that the Anti-Kickback Statute was not violated unless the government demonstrated that there was an actual agreement or *quid pro quo*, whereby the referral of patients to the entity was a condition imposed on physician investors for maintaining their investment interest in the entity. Then, upon initial appeal, the Departmental Appeals Board (DAB) held that the term "inducement" contained in the Anti-Kickback Statute meant something more than "encourage," but something less than "require"—that is, "an intent to exercise influence over the reason or judgment of another in an effort to cause the referral of program-related business." The DAB subsequently remanded the case to the ALJ, who concluded that permissive exclusions were necessary for some but not all of the appellants. The defendants then appealed the DAB's decision to the U.S. District Court for the Central District of California, which affirmed the DAB's decision,[16] and then to the Ninth Circuit Court of Appeals.[17]

Although the Ninth Circuit agreed with the DAB's definition of the term "inducement," it reversed the exclusions against the appellants, apparently based on the particular facts of the case. The Ninth Circuit found that "the fact that a large number of referrals resulted in the potential for a high return on investment, or that the practical effect of low referral rates was failure for the labs, is insufficient to prove that appellants offered or paid remuneration to induce referrals" in violation of the Anti-Kickback Statute. The court noted that limited partners were paid dividends based on their ownership share, not the volume of their referrals, and that payments were made to limited partners regardless of whether they referred business to the joint venture.

The Ninth Circuit did find, however, that the Hanlester Network's Marketing Director, Patricia Hitchcock, had made representations to prospective investors that were indeed in violation of the Anti-Kickback Statute. Thus, Ms. Hitchcock apparently "crossed the line" into illegality by linking a physician-investor's personal referral pattern to his or her participation in the joint venture.

As a result of Ms. Hitchcock's conduct, the Court of Appeals further held that the Hanlester Network and joint-venture laboratories' organizational entities could be held vicariously liable under the Anti-Kickback Statute for Ms. Hitchcock's actions, regardless of the fact that Ms. Hitchcock acted in a manner contrary to the organizations' stated policies. Nevertheless, the Court of Appeals found that no remedial purpose would be served by excluding organizational entities of either the Hanlester Network' or the joint-venture laboratories' from the Medicare or Medicaid programs, because their vicarious liability arose entirely from the conduct of Ms. Hitchcock, who was no longer associated with the organizations.

The court additionally held that vicarious liability cannot extend to the individual partners in the organizational entities, and that they did not act with the requisite intent in order to constitute an independent violation of the statute. Citing U.S. Supreme Court precedent,[18] the Ninth Circuit

---

[15] Simultaneously, the OIG announced the settlement of charges against SBCL for $1.5 million.
[16] *Hanlester v. Sullivan*, CCH Medicare and Medicaid Guide ¶41,076, CV-92-4552 (C.D. Cal. Feb. 10, 1993).
[17] *Hanlester Network v. Shalala, supra.*
[18] See *Ratzlaf v. United States*, 114 S. Ct. 655, 657, 126 L. Ed. 2d 615 (1994).

concluded that a party may violate the Anti-Kickback Statute's *mens rea* requirement (i.e., knowingly and willfully) *only* if he or she *knows* that the Anti-Kickback Statute prohibits offering or paying remuneration to induce referrals *and* engages in the prohibited conduct with the *specific intent* to disobey the law. Although Ms. Hitchcock's conduct was sufficiently egregious to infer the requisite intent to violate the Anti-Kickback Statute, the Ninth Circuit found that the other partners displayed no such conduct.

Significantly, the positions held by the Ninth Circuit in the *Hanlester* case were not universally adopted by other courts.[19] Then, in 2010 as part of the ACA, the Anti-Kickback Statute was amended to provide that "a person need not have actual knowledge of this section or specific intent to commit a violation of this section."[20]

5.1.2.3   United States ex rel. Jamison v. McKesson

On September 28, 2012, a Mississippi district court ruled for defendants finding that the government had failed to prove the requisite scienter necessary to violate the Anti-Kickback Statute. The relator, Jamison, claimed that the defendants defrauded the government by forming improper joint ventures, failing to satisfy DME supplier standards, and submitting fraudulent Medicaid cost reports. Under the joint ventures, medical supply companies created DME suppliers within nursing homes that allowed the nursing homes to seek reimbursement under their own DME supplier numbers. Jamison alleged that the monies derived from these joint ventures were kickbacks, and therefore, all claims submitted by the DME suppliers violated the False Claims Act. The government sought $895 million in damages and penalties.

Asserting an "express false certification" theory of liability, the government claimed that because the defendants had violated the Anti-Kickback Statute, all of the claims submitted also violated the False Claims Act. However, the court ultimately held that there was no violation of the FCA because there was no underlying violation of the Anti-Kickback Statute. In its decision, the court took the position that the government had the burden of establishing fair market value and had failed to prove that the defendants offered its services below fair market value, below actual costs, or at a discount, and therefore failed to prove the inducement required for a violation under the Anti-Kickback Statute. In addition, the court held that the government must provide the Anti-Kickback Statute's knowing and willful standard to meet the scienter requirement.

5.1.3   Special Fraud Alerts

Whereas the safe harbors describe conduct that is explicitly permissible, the OIG also has published various issuances over the past several years that describe conduct that the OIG views as

---

[19] *See, e.g., United States v. Starks*, 157 F.3d 833 (11th Cir. 1998); *United States v. Jain*, 93 F.3d 436 (8th Cir. 1996), *cert. denied*, 520 U.S. 1273 (1997); *United States v. Neufeld*, 908 F. Supp. 491, 497 (S.D. Ohio 1995); *Med. Dev. Network, Inc. v. Prof. Respiratory Care/Home Medical Equip. Servs., Inc.*, 673 S.2d 565 (Fla. Dist. App. 1996); *United States v. Mittal*, 2002 U.S. App. LEXIS 11220 (2d Cir. 2002); *see also United States v. Starks*, 157 F.3d 833 (11th Cir. 1998); *United States v. Anderson*, 85 F. Supp.2d 1047, 1065–68 (D. Kan. 1999), *rev'd sub nom.*; *United States v. McClatchey*, 217 F.3d 823 (10th Cir. 2000); *United States v. Shaw*, 106 F. Supp.2d 103 (D. Mass. 2000); *United States v. Borrasi*, 639 F.3d 774 (7th Cir. 2011).

[20] *See* ACA, § 6402(f)(2) (2010) (codified at 42 U.S.C. § 1320a–7b(h)).

impermissible. Specifically, the OIG issues fraud alerts as a vehicle for identifying fraudulent and abusive practices within the health care industry.

Although the majority of the OIG's fraud alerts are disseminated internally within the government, the OIG has issued several "Special Fraud Alerts" that are distributed directly to members of the health care provider community. To date, the OIG has issued Special Fraud Alerts that address the following:

- joint venture arrangements;
- routine waiver of copayments or deductibles under Medicare Part B;
- hospital incentives to physicians;
- prescription drug marketing schemes;
- arrangements for the provision of clinical lab services;
- home health fraud;
- fraud and abuse in the provision of medical supplies to nursing facilities;
- fraud and abuse in nursing home arrangements with hospices;
- fraud and abuse in the provision of services in nursing facilities;
- rental of space in physician offices by persons or entities to which physicians refer;
- telemarketing by durable medical equipment suppliers;
- physician-owned distributors; and
- laboratory payments to referring physicians.[21]

5.1.4 Advisory Opinions

In 1996, as part of HIPAA, Congress authorized DHHS to issue, upon request, advisory opinions on the applicability of the Anti-Kickback Statute, the safe harbor regulations, and other OIG health care fraud and abuse provisions to either a proposed or an existing financial arrangement.[22]

In order to obtain an advisory opinion, the requesting party must submit to the OIG detailed information on the circumstances of the transaction, including all background information, copies of all existing or proposed operative documents, and detailed statements of all collateral or oral understandings. In disclosing this information to the government, the OIG has confirmed that documents submitted in connection with an advisory-opinion request are subject to the Freedom of Information Act (FOIA).

---

[21] Copies of these Special Fraud Alerts can be found on the OIG's Internet site at https://oig.hhs.gov/compliance/alerts/index.asp. In addition to the Special Fraud Alerts that are listed and address arrangements that may violate the Anti-Kickback Statute, the OIG also has published other types of Special Bulletins and Special Alerts related to other issues (e.g., in 1999, the OIG issued a "Special Bulletin" related to gainsharing arrangements, in 2003 issued a Special Advisory Bulletin entitled "Contractual Joint Ventures", and in 2005 issued a Special Advisory Bulletin entitled "Patient Assistance Programs for Medicare Part D Enrollees").

[22] 42 U.S.C. § 1320a-7d; see also 42 C.F.R. pt. 1008; 62 Fed. Reg. 7350 (1997); 63 Fed. Reg. 38311 (1998). Copies of all advisory opinions can be found on the OIG's Internet site at https://oig.hhs.gov/compliance/advisory-opinions/index.asp.

In addition to the time and costs associated with the requesting party or its representatives preparing the request for an advisory opinion, the requesting party is responsible for reimbursing the OIG for costs in processing the advisory-opinion request.

In July 2008, HHS issued a Final Rule amending its policies relating to the collection and payment by individuals requesting an Advisory Opinion.[23] Under the July 2008 Rule, parties no longer are required to deposit $250 to the U.S. Treasury upon requesting an OIG Advisory Opinion. According to the OIG, this policy change eliminates the resource demands that arise when a party rescinds its request for an advisory opinion and seeks to recoup its initial deposit. The April 2008 rule also sets forth that parties can no longer pay the U.S. Treasury by way of check or money order but instead must pay for these charges directly through wire or electronic funds transfer.

The OIG is required to issue an advisory opinion within 60 days of receipt of an "accepted" request. The 60-day period does not begin until the OIG deems the request to be complete, but it may be tolled at various times.

5.2 Federal Anti-Kickback Safe Harbor Regulations

Congress established a statutory exception for certain payment practices that the Secretary of the Department of Health and Human Services (DHHS) specifies as being "safe harbored" and therefore not subject to the Anti-Kickback Statute. An arrangement that meets the criteria of a safe harbor is fully protected from criminal and civil liabilities under the Anti-Kickback Statute; it is important to note, however, that failure to fall squarely within the terms of a safe harbor does not necessarily mean that the arrangement is illegal or that it will be investigated or prosecuted. Indeed, the OIG has stated that

> [c]ommenters should not infer that because a safe harbor provision does not specifically refer to a particular arrangement or activity, it is unlawful. Nor should [one] interpret that lack of a safe harbor to mean that the [] activit[y] will be subjected to heightened scrutiny. Moreover, safe harbors do not create affirmative obligations on individuals or entities since *compliance with the [ ] safe harbors is purely voluntary*. The failure to comply with a safe harbor means only that the practice or arrangement does not have absolute assurance of protection from anti-kickback liability.[24]

Thus, conduct outside the safe harbors must be analyzed based on its particular facts and circumstances to determine whether a violation exists under the Anti-Kickback Statute.

In 1991, the OIG promulgated the first set of final "safe harbor" regulations, which set forth permissible payment practices in the following 11 areas:

1. investment interests;
2. space rental;
3. equipment rental;

---

[23] 73 Fed. Reg. 40982 (July 17, 2008); 42 C.F.R. § 1008.31(b); 42 C.F.R. § 1008.36(b); 42 C.F.R. § 1008.43(d).
[24] 61 Fed. Reg. 2122, 2124 (1996) (emphasis added).

4. personal services and management contracts;
5. sale of a practice;
6. referral services;
7. warranties;
8. discounts;
9. employees;
10. GPOs; and
11. waiver of beneficiary coinsurance and deductible amounts for Part A inpatient hospital services and certain federally qualified and federally funded health centers and health care facilities.[25]

Although these 11 safe harbors were published as a "final" list, the OIG published "clarifications" to several of these safe harbors in 1999.[26]

With respect to the applicability of the Anti-Kickback Statute to certain managed-care activities, the OIG has confirmed that the Anti-Kickback Statute does, in fact, apply by adopting several managed-care safe harbors. In particular, in 1996, the OIG not only modified the safe harbor for waivers of inpatient and deductible amounts so as to include Medicare "SELECT PPOs," but also adopted safe harbors for incentives offered to beneficiaries in order to encourage the use of the preferred provider network and provider discounts offered to managed-care plans.[27] Then, in 1999, the OIG issued as an interim final rule two safe harbors related to the shared-risk exception that was added to the Anti-Kickback Statute as part of HIPAA.[28]

Also in 1999, the OIG finalized additional safe harbors for several different categories of ambulatory surgery centers (ASCs), for group practices, for referral arrangements for specialty services, and for cooperative hospital service organizations. The OIG also adopted several safe harbors related to financial relationships entered into by and with health care entities located in medically underserved areas (MUAs). Specifically, safe harbors were established for investment interests held in health care entities located in MUAs, for remuneration paid as part of a recruitment package in order to attract professionals to an MUA, and for obstetrical malpractice-insurance subsidies paid to a practitioner who is primarily engaged in an obstetrical practice in a designated Health Professional Shortage Area (HPSA).[29]

In 2001, the OIG established a safe harbor for ambulance arrangements with hospitals and other receiving facilities that replenish drugs and medical supplies used by the ambulance provider when transporting patients to the hospitals or receiving facilities.[30]

---

[25] 42 C.F.R. § 1001.952(a)–(k); *see also* 56 Fed. Reg. 35952 (1991).
[26] *See* 64 Fed. Reg. 63518 (1999); *see also* 59 Fed. Reg. 37202 (1994).
[27] 42 C.F.R. § 1001.952 (k)–(m); *see* 61 Fed. Reg. 2122, (Jan. 25, 1996); *see also* 57 Fed. Reg. 51723 (1992).
[28] 42 C.F.R. § 1001.952(t)–(u); *see* 64 Fed. Reg. 63504 (1999).
[29] 42 C.F.R. § 1001.952(n)–(s); *see* 64 Fed. Reg. 63518 (1999); *see also* 58 Fed. Reg. 49008 (1993).
[30] 42 C.F.R. § 1001.952(v); *see* 66 Fed. Reg. 62979 (2001); *see also* 65 Fed. Reg. 32060 (2000).

In August 2006, the OIG issued regulations creating two safe harbors for non-monetary remunerations involving certain electronic prescribing and electronic health records arrangements,[31] and in October 2007, the OIG published a safe harbor in order to enable FQHCs to more easily provide medical care to underserved populations.[32]

In October 2014, the OIG published a proposed rule[33] to add new safe harbors (Proposed Rule). The Proposed Rule sets forth a number of provisions that codify into the regulations certain exceptions and modifications to the laws that Congress has adopted over the last decade. The Proposed Rule addressed the following:

- Part D cost sharing waivers by pharmacies;
- Cost-sharing waivers for emergency ambulance services;
- FQHCs and Medicare Advantage organizations;
- Medicare coverage gap discount programs; and
- Free or discounted local transportation services.

On December 7, 2016, the OIG issued a Final Rule finalizing all of the safe harbors that were proposed, with certain modifications (2016 Safe Harbor Final Rule).[34] In the 2016 Safe Harbor Final Rule, OIG stated, "Congress intended the safe harbors to evolve with changes in the health care system, and we believe this final rule balances additional flexibility for industry stakeholders to provide efficient, well-coordinated, patient-centered care with protections against fraud and abuse."[35] The OIG acknowledged that the 2016 Safe Harbor Final Rule takes into account the changes in payment and delivery of health care items and services, advances the needs of providers and patients in rural areas, and recognizes the transition from volume to value-based and patient-centered care.

5.2.1 Investment Interest Safe Harbors

The final safe harbor regulations published in 1991 contained two separate sets of criteria for investment interests: (1) investment interests in large, publicly held companies; and (2) investment interests held in smaller health care companies. In 1999, the OIG adopted a third set of criteria related to investment interests held in health care entities that are located in MUAs.[36]

5.2.1.1 Large Investment Interests

Under this safe harbor, a large publicly traded company must have at least $50 million in undepreciated net tangible assets related to the furnishing of health care items or services. Moreover, equity securities must be registered with the Securities and Exchange Commission, and the invest-

---

[31] 42 C.F.R. § 1001.952(x)–(y); see 71 Fed. Reg. 45110 (2006).
[32] 42 C.F.R. § 1001.952(w); see 72 Fed. Reg. 56632 (2007).
[33] Medicare and State Health Care Programs: Fraud and Abuse; Revisions to Safe Harbors Under the Anti-Kickback Statute and Civil Monetary Penalty Rules Regarding Beneficiary Inducements and Gainsharing, 79 Fed. Reg. 59717 (proposed Oct. 3, 2014).
[34] Medicare and State Health Care Programs; Fraud and Abuse; Revisions to the Safe Harbors Under the Anti-Kickback Statute and Civil Monetary Penalty Rules Regarding Beneficiary Inducements, 81 Fed. Reg. 88368 (Dec. 7, 2016).
[35] Id. at 88370.
[36] 42 C.F.R. § 1001.952(a).

ment interest must be obtained "on terms equally available to the public" through trading on a registered national-securities exchange. As a result of the clarifications adopted by the OIG in 1999, language was added to this safe harbor to "clarify" that the investment interest (1) may not be subject to restrictions or limits on transferability that are not applicable to an investment held by members of the public and (2) must be obtained for the same price available to the general public.

Additional requirements under this safe harbor include that neither the entity nor any investor (nor other individual acting on behalf of the entity or any investor in the entity) may make loans or loan guarantees to investors who may be in a position to refer business to the entity. Further, dividends to investors must be in proportion to the amount of the investment, and the entity may not market or furnish its services differently to passive investors than it does to non-investors.

5.2.1.2 Small Investment Interests

With respect to the small entity safe harbor, each of the following eight standards must be satisfied.

1. *"60/40" Investor Rule.* No more than 40% of the value of the investment interests of each class of investments may be held in the previous fiscal year or previous 12-month period by investors who are in a position to make or influence referrals to, furnish items or services to, or otherwise generate business for, the entity. In 1999, the OIG added language to this requirement explaining that equivalent classes of equity investments may be combined.

2. *Terms of Investment.* The terms on which an investment interest is offered to a passive investor who is in a position to make or influence referrals to, furnish items or services to, or otherwise generate business for the entity must be no different than the terms offered to other passive investors.

3. *Investment Not Related to Referrals.* The terms on which an investment interest is offered to an investor who is in a position to make or influence referrals to, furnish items or services to, or otherwise generate business for the entity must not be related to the previous or expected volume of referrals, items, or services furnished, or the amount of business otherwise generated, by that investor to the entity.

4. *No Requirement to Generate Referrals.* No requirement may be made that a passive investor make referrals to, be in a position to make or influence referrals to, furnish items or services to, or otherwise generate business for the entity as a condition for remaining as an investor.

5. *Marketing Efforts.* Neither the entity nor any investor may market or furnish the entity's items or services (or those of another entity as part of cross-referral agreement) to passive investors differently than to non-investors.

6. *"60/40" Revenue Rule.* No more than 40% of the gross revenue of the entity in the previous fiscal year or previous 12-month period may come from referrals or business otherwise generated from investors.

7. *Prohibition on Loans.* Neither the entity nor any investor (nor other individual or entity acting on behalf of the entity or any investor in the entity) may loan funds to or guarantee a loan for an investor who is in a position to make or influence referrals to, furnish items or

services to, or otherwise generate business for the entity if the investor uses any part of such loan to obtain the investment interest.

8. *Investment Return.* The amount of payment to an investor in return for the investment interest must be directly proportional to the amount of the capital investment of that investor.

5.2.1.3 Investments in Entities in MUAs

In contrast to the OIG's proposal in 1993 to adopt a safe harbor for investments held in entities that are located in "rural" areas, in 1999 the OIG expanded the scope of this safe harbor so as to apply to MUAs, which can be located in either a rural or urban area. Although many of the requirements for this safe harbor are similar to the small investment safe harbor, this safe harbor eliminates the 60/40 Revenue Rule, and modifies the 60/40 Investor Rule to a 50/50 Investor Rule (i.e., no more than 50% of the value of the investment interest of each class of investments may be held by investors who are in a position to make or influence referrals to, furnish items or services to, or otherwise generate business for the entity). In addition, the OIG has included a requirement that at least 75% of the business in the previous fiscal year or previous 12-month period be derived from services furnished to persons in an MUA or who are members of a medically underserved population (MUP).

5.2.2 Space and Equipment Rental, and Personal Services and Management Contracts

The OIG created three separate safe harbors for certain contracts related to space rental, equipment rental, and personal services and management contracts. Nevertheless, all three of these safe harbors share common requirements.[37] For example, all three safe harbors require that a written agreement be executed for a term of at least one year that specifies the aggregate payment amount, as well as the premises, equipment, or services covered. If the agreement does not contemplate full-time services, then the agreement must also specify the schedule of intervals, their precise length, and the exact charge for such intervals.

As part of the "clarifications" adopted by the OIG in 1999 and in order to "preclude schemes involving the use of multiple overlapping contracts to circumvent the one-year requirement," the OIG has added a requirement to all three safe harbors that the agreement cover *all* space, equipment, or services for the term of the agreement.

These three safe harbors also require that the payments must be based upon fair market value, and not vary on the volume or value of any Medicare-covered or state health care program-covered referrals or business generated between the parties. For purposes of space rental, fair market value means the value of the rental property for general commercial purposes. For purposes of equipment rental, fair market value means the value of the equipment when obtained from a manufacturer or professional distributor. The assessment of "fair market value" for space and equipment leases, however, may not include additional value for location or convenience to sources of Medicare and/or state health care program business. An additional requirement for personal services and management contracts is that the services performed under the agreement must not involve the counseling or promotion of a business arrangement or other activity that violates any State or federal law.

---

[37] 42 C.F.R. § 1001.952(b)–(d).

5.2.3 Sale of Practice

Although the "sale of practice" safe harbor originally only covered sales between practitioners, the OIG expanded this safe harbor in 1999 to include the sale of a practice by a practitioner in an underserved area to a hospital.[38]

With respect to the sale of a physician's practice to another practitioner, the sale must be completed within one year, and the selling practitioner cannot remain in a position to generate business for the purchasing practitioner beyond the one-year period. Thus, the safe harbor would not protect any situation in which the physician who sells the practice is retained on its staff for any significant period of time following the purchase.

With respect to payments made to a practitioner by a hospital or other entity to purchase the practitioner's practice, the safe harbor requires that: (1) the sale be completed within three years; (2) after the sale is completed, the practitioner not be in a position to make referrals to or generate business for the purchasing entity; (3) the practice be located in a HPSA for the practitioner's specialty; and (4) the purchasing entity must, in good faith, engage in recruitment activities to find a new practitioner to take over the acquired practice.

5.2.4 Referral Services

The final sale-harbor regulations include a safe harbor for payments to "referral services."[39] Under this safe harbor, a referral service may not exclude any person or entity that meets participation qualifications. Although the safe harbor does not require inclusion of *all* physicians in a particular geographic area, the safe harbor requires that, if the referral service qualifies physicians based upon certain criteria, then such criteria must be applied equally to all participants. In addition, the referral service must disclose to persons seeking referrals how individual participants are chosen, whether a fee is paid, the relationship between the participant and the service, and any restrictions that would exclude a participant.

5.2.5 Warranties

The safe harbors protect payments or exchanges of value under certain manufacturer or supplier warranties.[40] In order to qualify for safe harbor protection, the buyer and the manufacturer or supplier alike must comply with specified reporting standards. The buyer must report any price reduction or free item obtained as part of the warranty in its cost report or claim for payment. The supplier or manufacturer, in turn, must report such price reductions or free items on the buyer's invoice (or, if the amount is unknown, the existence of the warranty and the full documentation when known), and inform the buyer of its reporting obligations. The buyer also must furnish the invoice information to the Medicare or relevant state health care program on request. Additionally, the warranty can only be for the item itself, and cannot include payment to an individual or entity other than a beneficiary for any medical, surgical, or hospital expenses incurred by a beneficiary. Finally, the safe harbor not

---

[38] 42 C.F.R. § 1001.952(e).
[39] 42 C.F.R. § 1001.952(f).
[40] 42 C.F.R. § 1001.952(g).

only defines the term "warranty" under the Magnuson-Moss Warranty-Federal Trade Commission Improvement Act's definition of "written warranty" at 15 U.S.C. § 2301(6) governing the sale and warranty of consumer products, but it also includes one manufacturer's or supplier's agreement to replace another manufacturer's or supplier's defective item (which is covered by a "written warranty" under that act) on terms equal to the original written warranty.

5.2.6 Discounts

The Anti-Kickback Statute includes several statutory exceptions, including an exception for "a discount or other reduction in price obtained by a provider of services or other entity under a Federal health care program if the reduction in price is properly disclosed and appropriately reflected in the costs claimed or charges made by the provider or entity...."[41] Despite the existence of a statutory exception, the OIG has adopted safe harbors related to the statutory exceptions as it has taken the position that its role is "to define innocuous arrangements that should not be prosecuted, including the statutory exceptions."[42]

In contrast to the statute, which only requires that the discount be "properly disclosed and appropriately reflected" in the entity's Medicare and Medicaid costs or charges, the safe harbor sets forth a restrictive definition of the term "discount," excluding such typical discount arrangements as discounts not applicable to Medicare or Medicaid, and those discounts given directly to beneficiaries (e.g., coinsurance waivers).[43] In addition, although the safe harbor originally excluded from the definition of "discount" the provision of discounted or free items or services in exchange for the purchase of different items or services, the OIG "clarified" this exclusion so as to allow this type of discount arrangement if the goods and services are reimbursed by the same federal health care program using the same methodology.

The protection provided under the discount safe harbor is categorized based upon the type of party involved in the transaction (buyers, sellers, and offerors) with the safe harbor placing different requirements on the respective parties. Specifically, the safe harbor provides protection to buyers that are Medicare+Choice plans and/or Medicaid risk contractors without imposing any reporting requirements; by contrast, cost-reporting entities not only must report the discount on the cost report, but also must earn the discount within a single fiscal year and claim the benefit of the discount in that or the following fiscal year. All other purchasers, such as Part B suppliers, can only take advantage of discounts made at the time of the original sale, or the terms of the rebate must be fixed and disclosed in writing to the buyer at the time of the initial sale of the good or service.

With respect to sellers, the safe harbor provides protection for discounts given to cost-reporting entities as long as the seller reports the discount on the purchaser's invoice and reasonably notifies the buyer of its obligations to report such discount. For cost-reporting entities, the safe harbor also provides that, if the value of the discount is unknown at the time of the sale, the seller can disclose the existence of the discount program on the invoice and furnish the additional documentation later.

---

[41] 42 U.S.C. § 1320a-7b(3)(A).
[42] 56 Fed. Reg. 35952, 35957 (1991).
[43] 42 C.F.R. § 1001.952(h).

For all other entities, the seller's obligations depend on whether the seller submits a claim or request for payment on behalf of the buyer, or whether the buyer instead submits such claims on its own behalf.

In addition to buyers and sellers, the safe harbor includes protection for offerors, who are individuals or entities who are not sellers but who promote the purchase of an item or service by a buyer at a reduced price. Similar to sellers, the ability of an offeror to qualify for safe harbor protection depends on the offeror satisfying certain requirements that are based upon the type of purchaser.

5.2.7 Employees

The Anti-Kickback Statute includes a statutory exception for "any amount paid by an employer to an employee (who has a bona fide employment relationship with such employer) for employment in the provision of covered items or services."[44] Despite the significant legislative history that surrounded the enactment of this exception, in which Congress explained its intention to include a broad meaning for the term "employee," this position was rejected by the OIG as the OIG defined the term "employee" pursuant to the "usual common law rules."[45] Therefore, independent-contractor arrangements fall outside the employee safe harbor protection, unless they otherwise qualify for the safe harbor governing personal services and management contracts described earlier.

5.2.8 Group Purchasing Organizations

The Anti-Kickback Statute includes a statutory exception for amounts paid by a vendor to a GPO as long as two conditions are satisfied:

1. the person has a written contract with each such individual or entity, which specifies the amount to be paid the person, which amount may be a fixed amount or a fixed percentage of the value of the purchases made by each such individual or entity under the contract; and
2. in the case of an entity that is a provider of services (as defined in § 1861(u)), the person discloses (in such form and manner as the Secretary requires) to the entity and, upon request, to the Secretary the amount received from each such vendor with respect to purchases made by or on behalf of the entity.[46]

Within the safe harbors, the OIG narrowed the scope of the protection offered to GPOs by excluding GPOs that are part of the same corporate family as the entities for whom the GPOs are purchasing.[47] On the other hand, although the statute requires that the agreement specify the amount the vendor pays the GPO, irrespective of the amount, the safe harbor permits the agreement to state that vendors will pay the GPO a fee of 3% or less of the purchase price of the vendor's goods. If the fee is more than 3%, the agreement must specify the amount (or, if unknown, the maximum amount) of the GPO payment by each vendor.

---

[44] 42 U.S.C. § 1320a-7b(b)(3)(B).
[45] 42 C.F.R. § 1001.952(i).
[46] 42 U.S.C. § 1320a-7b(b)(3)(C).
[47] 42 C.F.R. § 1001.952(j). *See* 81 Fed. Reg. 88368 (2016).

5.2.9 Coinsurance and Deductible Waivers

Under the 2016 Safe Harbor Final Rule, the OIG expanded the safe harbor for waivers of coinsurance and deductible amounts to protect waivers under all federal health care programs, where applicable.[48] Under the expanded safe harbor, remuneration does not include any reduction or waiver of a beneficiary's obligation to pay copayment, coinsurance, or deductible amounts as long as all the standards are met within one of the following health care providers, if the cost-sharing amounts are owed:

(1) to a hospital for inpatient hospital services for which a federal health care program pays under the prospective payment system;

(2) by an individual who qualifies for subsidized services under a provision of the Public Health Services Act or under Titles V or XIX of the Act;

(3) to a federally qualified health care center or other health care facility under any Public Health Services Act grant program or under Title V of the Act;

(4) to a pharmacy for cost-sharing imposed under a federal health care program; or

(5) to an ambulance provider or supplier for emergency ambulance services for which a federal health care program pays under a fee-for-service payment system.

5.2.10 Beneficiary Incentives Offered by Managed-Care Organizations

The safe harbor for beneficiary incentives offered by health plans (e.g., differentials in coinsurance and deductible amounts) applies only to Medicare and Medicaid contracting health plans.[49] The term "health plan" has been defined in the safe harbor to apply to a managed care entity that:

1. has a formal contract with the Medicare or Medicaid programs;
2. charges a premium regulated by a state insurance statute or existing state statute governing health maintenance organizations (HMOs) or preferred provider organizations (PPOs);
3. is an Employee Retirement Income Security Act (ERISA) or self-funded/self-insured employer or union plan that contracts directly with health care providers or insurance companies; and
4. acts as an intermediary between contract health care providers and employers, union welfare funds, and/or insurance companies such as PPOs.

Nevertheless, no safe harbor protection exists for commercial managed-care plans that furnish coverage to Medicare eligibles on a fee-for-service basis.

Plans that qualify under the definition of a "health plan" and that have a formal Medicare or Medicaid contract also must meet other requirements, such as not discriminating in offering incentives to all potential enrollees. Consequently, these health plans must offer the same incentives to all Medicare or state health care program enrollees, unless otherwise approved by the federal or state

---

[48] *Id.* § 1001.952(k).
[49] *Id.* § 1001.952(*l*).

program. Moreover, health plans paid on a reasonable cost or similar basis cannot claim the cost of the incentive as a bad debt, or otherwise make additional claims to the federal or state health care program to pay for the incentive.

5.2.11 Price Reductions Offered to Group Health Plans

The managed-care safe harbors also protect price reductions that providers offer to health plans under certain circumstances.[50] Unlike the beneficiary incentive safe harbor, which applies only to Medicare and Medicaid contracting health plans, the price reduction safe harbor enables non-contracting health plans to qualify for safe harbor protection, albeit based on different safe harbor criteria.

First, for all health plans, a contract must be created between the provider and the health plan, and such contract must be for the sole purpose of furnishing covered items and services to health plan enrollees. Thus, contracts for utilization-review or enrollment-screening services would not qualify for safe harbor protection unless they otherwise meet the employment or personal services contracts safe harbor previously issued.

Second, the health plan must meet certain standards, depending on whether the health plan's relationship with the Medicare and Medicaid programs falls under one of the following categories:

1. risk-based health plans with formal program contracts;
2. cost-based health plans with formal program contracts cost contractors;
3. non-contracting health plans that do not pay providers on an at-risk capitated basis; and
4. health plans making capitated payments to providers.

5.2.12 Practitioner Recruitment

In 1999, the OIG added a safe harbor for physician recruitment activities paid to a physician in order to induce the physician who has been practicing her specialty for less than one year to locate her primary practice to a HPSA for such physician's specialty as long as the following nine requirements are satisfied.[51]

1. *Written Agreement.* The arrangement must be set out in writing, specifying the recruitment benefits being provided and the respective parties' obligations.
2. *75% Revenue from New Patients.* If a practitioner is leaving an established practice, at least 75% of the revenues of the new practice must be generated from new patients.
3. *Three-Year Limitation.* The period of the agreement cannot exceed three years, and the terms of the agreement cannot be renegotiated during such three-year period.
4. *No Requirement to Refer.* There may not be any requirement that the physician make referrals to or otherwise generate business for the entity, although the entity may require physician to maintain staff privileges.

---

[50] *Id.* § 1001.952(m).
[51] *Id.* § 1001.952(n).

5. *No Restrictions on Staff Privileges.* The practitioner may not be restricted with respect to where the practitioner may maintain staff privileges.

6. *Amount of Benefits.* The amount of benefits provided to the physician may not vary in any manner based on the volume or volume of any expected referrals to or business generated for the entity.

7. *Agreement to Treat.* The practitioner must agree to treat patients receiving Medicare benefits or assistance from a Federal health care program in a nondiscriminatory manner.

8. *75% of Revenues Generated from Underserved Area.* At least 75% of the revenues of the new practice must be generated from patients who reside in a HPSA or a MUA or who are part of a MUP.

9. *Benefits Only Paid to Practitioner.* Except for the practitioner who is being recruited, no payment or exchange of anything of value given to a person or entity in a position to make or influence referrals may be made.

5.2.13 Obstetrical Malpractice-Insurance Subsidies

This safe harbor protects malpractice subsidies for obstetrical care paid by a hospital or other entity where such payment is for a practitioner (including a certified nurse-midwife) who engages in obstetrical practice as a routine part of her medical practice in a primary care HPSA.[52] Included among the criteria for this safe harbor is a requirement that at least 75% of the practitioner's obstetrical patients, who are treated under the coverage policy, reside in a HPSA or MUA or be part of a MUP. In addition, for practitioners who are not full-time obstetricians or certified nurse-midwives, the safe harbor only protects payments related to obstetrical malpractice insurance.

5.2.14 Investments in Group Practices

The OIG has adopted a safe harbor that protects returns on investments made to a solo or group practitioner investing in her own practice, as long as certain requirements are satisfied. In light of the fact that much of the day-to-day management of most physician groups is given to one physician or a practice manager, the OIG deleted its proposal to require that the group practice be composed of "active investors," and instead merely requires that the group practice be comprised of licensed professionals who practice as part of the group.

Among the other requirements are that the physician's equity interest be held in the group practice itself and not a subdivision of the group, that the group satisfy the Stark Law's requirements for being a "group practice," and that revenues from ancillary services be derived from "in-office ancillary services" that meet the applicable definition under the Stark Law. Moreover, the OIG has required that the group practice be organized "as a unified business with centralized decision-making, pooling of expenses and revenues, and a compensation/profit distribution system that is not based on satellite offices operating substantially as if they were separate enterprises or profit centers."[53]

---

[52] *Id.* § 1001.952(o).
[53] *Id.* § 1001.952(p).

5.2.15 Cooperative Hospital-Services Organizations

This safe harbor protects most cooperative hospital-service organizations (CHSOs) that qualify under § 501(c)(3) of the Internal Revenue Code (IRC), which operate by distributing earnings to members in accordance with the volume of services used by the member hospital.[54] The safe harbor requires that if the patron-hospital makes a payment to the CHSO, the payment must be for *bona fide* operating expenses of the CHSO. On the other hand, if the CHSO makes a payment to the patron-hospital, the payment must be for the purpose of paying a distribution of net earnings required to be made under IRC § 501(e)(2).

5.2.16 ASCs

In 1993, the OIG proposed adding a safe harbor protecting payments to surgeon-investors in ASCs who refer patients directly to the ASC and perform the surgery themselves on those patients. In contrast to other investment interest safe harbors that limit investment by individuals in a position to refer, the proposed ASC safe harbor would have only protected entities whose investment interests were held entirely by such individuals. After the OIG received a great volume of comments on this proposed safe harbor, however, the OIG significantly revised it in 1999.

In the final regulations, the OIG created four different categories of ASC safe harbors: surgeon-owned ASCs; single-specialty ASCs; multi-specialty ASCs (e.g., a mix of surgeons and specialists); and hospital/physician-owned ASCs. In addition to the surgeons, physicians, and/or a hospital that can have an ownership interest in the entity, certain other "non-tainted" investors can own an investment interest as long as they: (1) do not provide items or services to the ASC or its investors; (2) are not employed by the ASC or any investor; and (3) are not in a position to refer patients directly or indirectly to, or generate business for, the ASC or any of its investors.[55]

Applicable to all four categories of ASCs are requirements that the ASC be Medicare certified, that the ASC's operating and recovery room space be dedicated exclusively to the ASC (i.e., if the ASC is located in a hospital, the ASC space must be dedicated exclusively to the ASC and not used by the hospital for the treatment of the hospital's inpatients or outpatients), and that all patients who are referred to the ASC by an investor must receive information about the investor's investment interest. In addition, all four categories include a requirement that all ancillary services be directly and integrally related to primary procedures performed at the ASC, and that none may be separately billed to Medicare or other federal health care programs.

With respect to the first three categories of ASC safe harbors (i.e., surgeon-owned ASCs, single-specialty ASCs, and multi-specialty ASCs), each requires that physician investors satisfy the "One-Third Practice Income Test," which requires that each physician investor derive at least one-third of her medical practice income for the previous 12-month period from her own performance of procedures that require an ASC or hospital surgical setting. Moreover, a physician investor in the third category of ASC (i.e., a multi-specialty ASC) must satisfy another standard whereby at least

---
[54] *Id.* § 1001.952(q).
[55] *Id.* § 1001.952(r).

one-third of the physician's procedures that require an ASC or hospital surgical setting be performed at the ASC in which she is investing (known as the "One-Third/One-Third Test").

With respect to the fourth category (i.e., a hospital/physician ASC), the OIG has included a requirement that the hospital not be in a position to make or influence referrals directly or indirectly to the ASC or to any of its physician investors—a development which, from a practical perspective, may preclude many hospital/physician ASC joint ventures from qualifying for safe harbor protection.

5.2.17 Referral Agreements for Specialty Services

This safe harbor excludes from the purview of the Anti-Kickback Statute any "exchange of value" among individuals or entities where one party "agrees to refer a patient to other party for the provision of a specialty services" in return for an agreement that the other party will "refer that patient back at a mutually agreed upon time or circumstance" as long as certain requirements are met.[56] In particular, the safe harbor requires that the timing and circumstances for the referral back to the originating physician or entity be "clinically appropriate," that the service for which the referral is made not be within the expertise of the referring individual or entity, and that the parties neither receive any payment from each other for the referral nor share or split a global fee in connection with the referred patient. Finally, unless the parties to the agreement belong to the same group practice, the only permitted "exchange of value" is the remuneration the respective parties receive from the third-party payer or the patient for the services furnished to the patient.

5.2.18 Ambulance Replenishing/Restocking

In 2001, the OIG adopted a final regulation establishing safe harbor protection for ambulance "restocking" or "replenishing" arrangements.[57] As described in the preamble to the safe harbor, ambulance "restocking" is the practice of hospitals, or other receiving facilities, restocking ambulance providers with drugs or supplies used during the transport of a patient to the hospital or receiving facility. Operationally, this is done to ensure that, when the ambulance departs the hospital, it is, as the OIG points out, ready for the next emergency call, fully stocked with current medications, sanitary linens, and a full complement of appropriate medications and supplies, and helps to ensure that supplies, such as intravenous tubing and catheters, are compatible with equipment used in local emergency rooms so as to expedite the transfer or critically ill or injured patients to emergency room systems.[58]

The final regulations address three categories of restocking: general restocking (either for free or for a charge); fair-market-value restocking; and government-mandated restocking. Common to all three categories of safe harbors are the following four conditions:

---

[56] *Id.* § 1001.952(s).
[57] *Id.* § 1001.952(v); *see* 66 Fed. Reg. 62979 (2001); *see also* 65 Fed. Reg. 32060 (2000).
[58] 66 Fed. Reg. 62979 (2001). In the preamble, the OIG also explains that, although "restocking" is the term commonly used, the OIG uses the word "replenishing" to make clear that "the safe harbor only applies to the gifting or transfer of drugs and supplies that replace comparable drugs and supplies administered," and that the safe harbor is not applicable to "general stocking of the inventories of ambulance providers." *Id.*

1. under no circumstances may both the ambulance provider and the receiving facility bill for the same replenished drug or supply, and all billing or claims submission for the replenished drugs must comply with all federal health care program payment and coverage rules;
2. one of the parties will maintain records of the replenished drugs and medical supplies;
3. no ties to referrals, and
4. all parties will ensure compliance with all other federal, state, and local laws regulating ambulance services.

5.2.19 Federally Qualified Health Centers

In 2003, Congress amended the Anti-Kickback Statute and include a statutory requirement that the OIG develop a safe harbor for certain agreements involving FQHCs. On October 4, 2007, the OIG published a final rule establishing a safe harbor for FQHCs for certain goods, items, services, donations, and loans provided by individuals and entities to certain health centers funded under Section 330 of the Public Health Service Act, which is a health center program designed to assist individuals living in medically underserved areas and populations with limited access to health care resources.[59]

The safe harbor excludes remuneration between a health center and an individual or entity providing goods, items, services, donations, loans, or a combination of these to the health center pursuant to a contract, lease, grant, loan, or other agreement, provided that the agreement contributes to the health center's ability to maintain or increase its services to the medically underserved. The remuneration must be "medical or clinical in nature or relate directly to patient services" such as billing services, administrative support services, technology support and the like.

5.2.20 Risk-Sharing Arrangements

In 1999, the OIG issued two safe harbors for shared-risk arrangements.[60] The first safe harbor protects price reductions that are offered to "eligible managed care organizations" (EMCOs), which are defined to include HMOs and competitive medical plans (CMPs) with a risk- or cost-based contract; Medicare+Choice organizations that receive capitation payments; certain Medicaid managed care organizations (MCOs), Programs for the All Inclusive Care For the Elderly, and federally qualified HMOs.

This safe harbor is divided into two categories of requirements. The first category sets out standards for arrangements between EMCOs and any individual or entity that contracts directly with the EMCO (referred to as a "first tier" contractor). Among this safe harbor's requirements is the requirement that the EMCO and the first-tier contractor have an agreement that is set out in writing, is for a term of at least one year, specifies the items and services covered under the agreement, and specifies that the first-tier contractor cannot claim payment in any form from a federal health care program for items or services covered under the agreement, except for (1) HMOs and CMPs that have cost-based

---

[59] 42 C.F.R. § 1001.952(w); *see* 72 Fed. Reg. 56632 (2007).
[60] 42 C.F.R. § 1001.952(t)–(u); *see also* 64 Fed. Reg. 63504 (1999).

contracts, (2) federally qualified HMOs without a CMS contract, and (3) federally qualified health centers that claim supplemental payments from a federal health care program.

In addition, the safe harbor requires that, when the parties establish the financial terms of the agreement, neither party gives nor receives remuneration in return for, or to induce the provision or acceptance of, fee-for-service business reimbursed by a federal health care program.

The second category addresses financial arrangements between first-tier contractors and downstream contractors, or between successive tiers of downstream contractors. Although many of the requirements of this section of the safe harbor are similar to the first category, the major difference is that, under this safe harbor, the underlying agreement between the first-tier contractor and the EMCO may *not* involve an HMO or CMP with a cost-based contract, a federally qualified HMO without a CMS contract, or a federally qualified health center receiving supplemental payments.

While the first safe harbor covers most Medicare and HMO plans, the scope of the second safe harbor is very narrow. To qualify under this safe harbor, the risk-sharing arrangement must be part of a "qualified managed care plan" (QMCP), which is defined as a managed-care entity that satisfies the requirements of the definition of a "health plan" located in the managed-care safe harbor related to beneficiary incentives. Moreover, a QMCP must adopt processes and procedures to assure that the health care services are managed (e.g., utilization-review procedures, grievance-procedure requirements). The safe harbor also requires either that no more than 10% of the QMCP's beneficiary population be Medicare beneficiaries (excluding those individuals where Medicare is secondary) or that no more than 50% are Medicare beneficiaries, but only if the premium payments are made on a periodic basis and do not take into account various factors.

Similar to the safe harbor for price reductions offered to EMCOs, this safe harbor provides protection to two categories of entities: first-tier contractors and downstream providers. Both must satisfy the requirement that the applicable party (i.e., the first-tier contractor or the downstream contractor) have substantial financial risk for the cost or utilization of services that it is obligated to provide. The regulations then create four payment methodologies that qualify as placing a contractor at "substantial financial risk": periodic fixed payments per patient, percentages of premiums, diagnosis-related groups (DRGs), and bonus and withhold arrangements.

With respect to the last category of payment methodologies—bonus and withhold arrangements—the OIG has further required that the target payment for individuals and non-institutional providers must be at least 20% greater than the minimum payment, whereas the target payment for an institutional provider (e.g., a hospital or nursing home) must be at least 10% greater. The safe harbor further requires that the amount at risk must be in direct proportion to the ratio of the contractor's actual utilization to its target utilization. Alternatively, for contractors that are physicians, the OIG adopts the definition of "substantial financial risk" based upon CMS's requirements under the physician incentive plan regulations.[61]

---

[61] *See* 42 C.F.R. § 417.479.

5.2.21 Electronic Prescribing

In August 2006, HHS promulgated a final rule establishing an e-prescribing safe harbor,[62] and between 2005 and 2008 HHS promulgated two additional rules, which taken together establish a comprehensive and uniform set of standards for e-prescribing under Medicare Part D.[63]

The final e-prescribing safe harbor incorporates most of the language from the 2005 proposed safe harbor, but the OIG modified a few provisions in order to expand the overall scope of safe harbor protection. Whereas the proposed safe harbor would have protected arrangements relating to the transmission of electronic "drug" information, the final safe harbor protects arrangements relating to the transmission of "any" prescription information, such as information related to drugs, laboratory tests, and durable medical equipment orders.[64] In addition, the OIG has abandoned provisions from the proposed safe harbor that (1) would have imposed a cap on the amount of technology or services that an entity can donate, and (2) would have required a recipient to certify the technical or functional superiority of donated technology over technology already in the recipient's possession. The OIG also dismissed a proposal to create a separate e-prescribing safe harbor for multipurpose technology.[65]

As proposed in 2005, the final safe harbor applies if eight conditions are met. Among these conditions, the items and services may be provided: (a) in the case of a hospital, by the hospital to physicians who are members of its medical staff; (b) in the case of a group practice, by the group practice to prescribing health care professionals who are members of the group practice (including not only physicians, but other health care professionals who are authorized to prescribe by state licensing laws); and (c) in the case of a PDP sponsor or MA organization, by the sponsor or MA organization to pharmacists participating in the network of such sponsor or organization and to prescribing health care professionals.[66]

Safe harbor protection applies to e-prescribing hardware, software, and information technology and training services that are necessary and used solely to receive and transmit electronic prescription information. Examples of protected products and services include electronic clinical support tools, tools that provide access to formulary information, and operating software required for hardware usage.[67]

The e-prescribing safe harbor does not protect the donation of unnecessary technology or technology that is functionally equivalent to products and services already possessed by a recipient. If the OIG discovers that a donor had actual knowledge or acted in reckless disregard or deliberate ignorance of the fact that a recipient already possessed functionally equivalent technology, then neither party can receive safe harbor protection. The final safe harbor has abandoned language from the proposed safe harbor that would have required donors to certify that donated products and services are technically or functionally superior to those already possessed by the recipient. Instead, the OIG

---

[62] 71 Fed. Reg. 45110 (Aug. 8, 2006).
[63] 73 Fed. Reg. 18918 (Apr. 7, 2008); 70 Fed. Reg. 67568 (Nov. 7, 2005).
[64] 71 Fed. Reg. 45114 (Aug. 8, 2006).
[65] *Id.*
[66] *Id.* at 45,117; 42 C.F.R. § 1001.952(x)(1).
[67] 71 Fed. Reg. 45116–117 (Aug. 8, 2006); 42 C.F.R. § 1001.952(x).

recommends that donors make "reasonable inquiries" (which should not usually require the use of technical experts) about a recipient's existing e-prescribing capabilities before donating.[68]

Only technology used solely for e-prescribing purposes can receive safe harbor protection. For technology to serve an e-prescribing purpose, it must provide information or perform functions necessary to formulate, transmit, or receive a medically appropriate prescription for a patient. Technology that directly relates to e-prescribing, such as electronic clinical support software that identifies alternative drug therapies, drug-drug interactions, or payer formulary information, satisfies this requirement. Technology that bundles e-prescribing functions with unrelated functions, such as patient billing or scheduling, will not satisfy this requirement.[69]

Donated e-prescribing technology will not receive safe harbor protection unless it meets HHS standards for e-prescribing systems.[70] These standards, established to ensure that e-prescribing technology is interoperable, consist of rules relating to all aspects of e-prescribing, such as the electronic transmittal of information between providers and pharmacists, eligibility and benefits queries, formulary and benefit information, medication history, and network compatibility. Before being incorporated into law, HHS tested many of these rules through pilot programs conducted at various provider and pharmacy settings throughout the country.[71]

The OIG also conditioned safe harbor protection on compliance with specific rules relating to the selection of donors and recipients. Recipients may not make the donation of e-prescribing technology a prerequisite for doing business with a donor, and neither the donor nor the recipient may directly or indirectly base selection on the volume or value of referrals or other business generated between the parties. The safe harbor permits selection based on the total number of prescriptions written by a recipient, but does not permit selection based on the value of prescriptions written by the recipient, or the volume or value of prescriptions written by a recipient that are reimbursable to any Federal health care program.[72]

Also, parties seeking safe harbor protection must satisfy the following additional requirements: (1) where possible, recipients must have the ability to use donated e-prescribing technology on all patients without regard to payer status;[73] (2) arrangements between donors and recipients must be written and signed by the parties;[74] (3) the donor must not take any action to restrict the compatibility of donated e-prescribing technology with other e-prescribing or electronic health record systems;[75] and (4) such arrangements must identify with specificity the items or services being provided (but do not have to specify the value of the donated technology).[76] The final e-prescribing safe harbor abandoned language from the proposed safe harbor that would have limited the aggregate value

---

[68] *Id.* at 45,115, 45,123.
[69] *Id.* at 45,115.
[70] 42 C.F.R. § 1001.952(x)(2).
[71] 71 Fed. Reg. 45115 (Aug. 8, 2006); Center for Medicare & Medicaid Services, *available at* http://www.cms.hhs.gov/eprescribing/.
[72] 71 Fed. Reg. 45118 (Aug. 8, 2006).
[73] 42 C.F.R. § 1001.952(x)(4).
[74] 42 C.F.R. § 1001.952(x)(7).
[75] 42 C.F.R. § 1001.952(x)(3).
[76] 71 Fed. Reg. 45119 (Aug. 8, 2006); 42 C.F.R. § 1001.952(x)(7).

of e-prescribing technology that a donor could provide to a qualifying recipient. As a result, in the final regulations, there is no cap on the value of services that a donor can provide or a recipient can receive.[77]

5.2.22 Electronic Health Records and Community-Wide Information System

The EHR safe harbor protects technology necessary and used predominantly to create, maintain, and transmit or receive EHRs, such as EHR computer software and related wireless internet services, clinical support tools, electronic messaging services, and helpdesk services.[78] However, the safe harbor does not protect hardware, hardware operating software, software primarily used for non-EHR purposes, or the provision of staff services to perform EHR related tasks such as the conversion of paper medical records into EHRs.[79] The safe harbor also does not protect the donation of unnecessary technology or technology that is functionally equivalent to products and services already possessed by a recipient.[80] If the OIG discovers that a donor had actual knowledge or acted in reckless disregard or deliberate ignorance of the fact that a recipient already possessed functionally equivalent technology, then neither party can receive safe harbor protection. Although donors do not have to certify that donated products and services are technically or functionally superior to those already possessed by the recipient, the OIG recommends that donors make "reasonable inquiries" (which should not usually require the use of technical experts) about a recipient's existing EHR capabilities before donating.[81] The OIG interprets the donation of software upgrades that enhance usability or technology that enhances the interoperability of donor and recipient systems as necessary and functionally superior.[82] In contrast to the safe harbor for e-prescribing, which only covers technology used solely for e-prescribing, the EHR safe harbor covers multi-purpose technology as long as the technology is used predominately for EHR purposes and its other uses relate to patient care. For example, EHR technologies that have secondary functions associated with patient administration, scheduling, and billing can qualify for safe harbor protection.[83]

On December 27, 2013, the OIG issued final regulations to amend the safe harbor concerning electronic health records items and services (EHR Final Rule).[84] Under the EHR Final Rule, the OIG included an update to the provision under which electronic health records software is deemed interoperable, removal of the electronic prescribing capability requirement and extension of the sunset provision from December 31, 2013 to December 31, 2021 (which corresponds to the last year for EHR Medicaid incentive payments). In addition, the EHR Final Rule specifically excluded laboratory companies from the list of eligible "Protected Donors." Finally, to promote the free exchange of information, the EHR Final Rule includes limited clarifications to require that no action be taken to limit or restrict the use, compatibility, or interoperability of items or services with other electronic prescribing or EHR systems.

---

[77] 71 Fed. Reg. 45118, 45119 (Aug. 8, 2006).
[78] 42 C.F.R. § 1001.952(y).
[79] 71 Fed. Reg. 45125 (Aug. 8, 2006).
[80] *Id.* at 45115, 45123.
[81] *Id.* at 45123.
[82] *Id.*
[83] *Id.* at 45124; 42 C.F.R. § 1001.952(x); 42 C.F.R. § 1001.952(y).
[84] 78 Fed. Reg. 79202 (Dec. 27, 2013); 42 C.F.R. § 1001.952(y)(2).

In order to qualify for safe harbor protection, arrangements for the donation and receipt of EHR technology must also comply with interoperability requirements, which the OIG describes as the ability of systems to communicate and exchange data accurately, effectively, securely, and consistently with different information technology systems without altering the meaning of the data.[85] The OIG's decision to create only one safe harbor, instead of separate pre- and post-interoperability safe harbors, reflects progress in the development of interoperability criteria for EHR systems that occurred between the publication of the proposed and final rules. Software is deemed to be interoperable if, "on the date it is provided to the recipient, it has been certified by a certifying body authorized by the National Coordinator for Health Information Technology to an edition of the electronic health record certification criteria identified in the then-applicable version of 45 C.F.R. part 170."[86]

The EHR safe harbor only applies to donors and recipients of EHR technology that meet the following eligibility criteria: entities that provide covered services and submit claims or payment requests to a Federal Health Care Program are eligible donors, and entities that engage in the delivery of health care items and services are eligible recipients. Among eligible donors, the OIG has included health plans, but not laboratory companies, pharmaceutical, medical device, and durable medical equipment manufacturers, or research entities.[87] The EHR safe harbor does not impose a cap on the value of items or services that can be donated or received, but it does require that each recipient contribute at least 15% of the value of the donation.[88]

The OIG also conditions safe harbor protection on compliance with specific rules relating to the selection of donors and recipients. Recipients may not make the donation of EHR technology a prerequisite for doing business with a donor, and donors may not select recipients or determine the value of a donation based on the volume or value of referrals or other business generated between the parties. The OIG identifies as examples of permissible criteria for selecting a recipient selections made in a "reasonable" and "verifiable" manner based on: (1) the total number of prescriptions written by a recipient; (2) the size of a recipient's medical practice; (3) the total number of hours a recipient practices medicine; (4) the recipient's overall use of automated technology for medical care; (5) whether the recipient is a member of the donor's medical staff; and (6) the level of uncompensated care provided by the recipient.[89]

Parties seeking safe harbor protection must satisfy the following additional requirements: (1) where possible, recipients must have the ability to use donated EHR technology on all patients without regard to payer status;[90] (2) arrangements between donors and recipients must be written and signed by the parties;[91] and (3) such arrangements must identify with specificity the items or services being provided, the donor's costs of those items and services, and the recipients contribution.[92] As discussed above, the EHR Final Rule extended the EHR safe harbor to December 31, 2021. After that

---

[85] 42 C.F.R. § 1001.952(y)(2).
[86] 78 Fed. Reg. 79202, 79204 (Dec. 27, 2013); 42 C.F.R. § 1001.952(y)(2).
[87] 42 C.F.R. § 1001.952(y)(1).
[88] 42 C.F.R. § 1001.952(y)(11).
[89] 42 C.F.R. § 1001.952(y)(5).
[90] 42 C.F.R. § 1001.952(y)(8).
[91] 42 C.F.R. § 1001.952(y)(6).
[92] Id.

time, all arrangements involving the donation and receipt of EHR related items and services will be subject to a case-by-case analysis under the Anti-Kickback Statute.[93]

5.2.23 Accountable Care Organization Waivers

On November 2, 2011, the OIG, in conjunction with CMS, issued an interim final rule with comment period establishing waivers of the Anti-Kickback Statute and certain other laws to particular arrangements involving ACOs under the Medicare shared savings program.[94] While not technically a safe harbor, the interim final rule establishes five waivers of application of the Stark law, the Anti-Kickback Statute, and the Civil Monetary Penalty provisions related to gainsharing and beneficiary inducements if certain conditions are met. According to the interim final rule, an arrangement need only fit in one waiver to be protected.

5.2.24 Federally Qualified Health Centers and Medicare Advantage Organizations

In the 2016 Safe Harbor Final Rule, the OIG finalized a safe harbor to protect any remuneration between a federal qualified health center (or an entity controlled by a FQHC) and a Medicare Advantage organization pursuant to a written agreement.[95]

5.2.25 Medicare Coverage Gap Discount Program

The 2016 Safe Harbor Final Rule added a safe harbor to protect a discount in the price of a drug when the discount is furnished to a beneficiary under the Medicare Coverage Gap Discount Program if the discounted drug meets the definition of "applicable drug," the beneficiary receiving the discount meets the definition of "applicable beneficiary"(both as set forth in section 1860D-14(g) of the Act), and the manufacturer of the drug participates in, and is in compliance with the requirements of, the Medicare Coverage Gap Discount Program.[96]

5.2.26 Local Transportation

In the 2016 Safe Harbor Final Rule, the OIG finalized a safe harbor to protect free or discounted services (collectively, transportation services) provided to federal health care program beneficiaries who are *established patients* to obtain medically necessary items or services.[97] The OIG defines established patient as, "a person who has selected and initiated contact to schedule an appointment with a provider or supplier to schedule an appointment, or who previously has attended an appointment with the provider or supplier." To prevent impermissible arrangements, the OIG has imposed a number of requirements on the transportation services.

First, in addition to being available only to established patients, the transportation services, whether free or discounted, must not be determined in a manner related to past or anticipated volume

---

[93] 78 Fed. Reg. 79202 (Dec. 27, 2013); 42 C.F.R. § 1001.952(y)(13).
[94] 76 Fed. Reg. 67992 (Nov. 2, 2011). Significantly, the interim final rule merely appears in the *Federal Register* and has not been codified anywhere in the Code of Federal Regulations.
[95] 42 C.F.R. § 1001.952(z). *See* 81 Fed. Reg. 88368 (2016).
[96] 42 C.F.R. § 1001.952(aa). *See* 81 Fed. Reg. 88368 (2016).
[97] 42 C.F.R. § 1001.952(bb). *See* 81 Fed. Reg. 88368 (2016).

or value of federal health care program business. The transportation services must be set out in a policy that is applied uniformly and consistently.

Second, the OIG has limited the transportation services to only be offered by an "Eligible Entity" which is defined as "any individual or entity, except for individuals or entities (or family members or others acting on their behalf) that primarily supply health care items."

Third, the transportation safe harbor restricts the form of transportation to not include air, luxury (e.g., limousine), and ambulance-level transportation.

Fourth, the Eligible Entity may not (1) publicly advertise or market to patients or to potential referral sources the availability of transportation services; (2) pay drivers or others involved in arranging the transportation on a per-beneficiary transported basis; and (3) market health care items and services during the course of the transportation.

Fifth, the OIG limited the availability of the safe harbor to only apply to local transportation (within 25 miles or 50 miles if the patient resides in a rural area).

Finally, the OIG requires the Eligible Entity to bear the cost of the transportation services and not shift the burden of the costs onto any federal health care program, other payers, or individuals.

5.3 Federal "Sunshine Law"

Section 6002 of the ACA includes provisions from the Physician Payment Sunshine Act (Sunshine Act).[98] Although the Sunshine Act does not prohibit any specific financial relationships, it requires "applicable manufacturers" including all drug, device, biological or medical supply manufacturers to submit electronic "Transparency Reports" disclosing certain payments or transfers of value to "covered recipients." On February 1, 2013, CMS issued final regulations (Final Regulations).[99] Applicable manufacturers and GPOs were required to begin data collection on August 1, 2013, and the first report was due to CMS by March 31, 2014. CMS releases data annually on its website. Between 2013 and 2016, approximately $24.94 billion worth of payments or transfer of value were made between manufacturers and covered recipients.[100]

CMS limited the definition of "applicable manufacturer" to an entity that "operates" in the United States, which means having a physical location or otherwise conducting activities within the United States, and is "engaged in the production, preparation, propagation, compounding, or conversion of a covered drug, device, biological, or medical supply...." An applicable GPO is defined as an entity that, "operates in the United States and purchases, arranges for or negotiates the purchase of a covered drug, device biological or medical supply for a group of individuals or entities, but not solely for use by the entity itself. The Final Regulations made clear that entities based outside the United States with operations inside the United States are subject to the reporting requirements. Also, the Final

---

[98] *See* ACA, § 6002 (201) (codified at 42 U.S.C. § 1320a-7h).
[99] 78 Fed. Reg. 9458 (Feb. 1, 2013).
[100] CMS, The Facts About Open Payments Data (June 30, 2017), *available at* https://openpaymentsdata.cms.gov/summary.

Regulations clarified that entities that manufacture a covered product are applicable manufacturers, even if they do not hold the FDA approval, licensure, or clearance for the covered products.

With regard to reporting of physician ownership and investments, the ownership or investment interest provisions apply to all "physicians" and not just "covered recipients." CMS has interpreted this to mean that ownership and investment interest must be reported for all physicians regardless of whether a physician is an employee of the applicable manufacturer or GPO. Additionally, the requirement to report payments and other transfers of interests apply to such physicians.

CMS specifically declined to expand the scope of applicable GPOs to covered devices or covered medical supplies that, by law, require premarket approval from, or premarket notification to, the FDA. The Final Regulations clarify that entities that engage in rare and circumstantial resale of products are not likely to fall within the scope of an applicable GPO. In an attempt to limit the broad definition of "ownership or investment interest" the Final Regulations only require applicable manufacturers to report those ownership or investment interests that they know to be owned by a physician or an immediate family member[101] of a physician.

Finally, the Final Regulations specify that:

- information related to ownership and investment interest and payment or transfer of interest must be reported separately because of the difference in the reporting requirements;
- reports can be aggregated across all family members who hold interests that are subject to the same ownership and investment terms. If an applicable manufacturer or GPO seeks to aggregate interest across family members, the value of the interest must be aggregated as well;
- in addition to reporting the ownership or investment interests, the Final Regulations require applicable manufacturers or GPOs to report all payments or other transfers of interest made to physicians, or to third parties on behalf of physicians, holding ownership or investment interests. Applicable manufacturers with physician owners should include such transfers in the same report used to capture payments and other transfers to covered recipients. An applicable manufacturer will need to indicate on the report that the recipient was a physician owner or investor.

Penalties for failing to report include, a civil money penalty of not less than $1,000, but not more than $10,000, for each payment or other transfer of value or ownership or investment interest not reported. The total amount of civil money penalties will not exceed $150,000. Knowingly failing to submit payment information will result in a civil money penalty of not less than $10,000, but not more than $100,000, for each payment. The penalty will not exceed $1,000,000. Combined, penalties may not exceed $1,150,000.

---

[101] CMS finalized the proposed definition of "immediate family member" to include the following: spouse; natural or adoptive parent; child or sibling; stepparent, stepchild, stepbrother, or stepsister; father, mother, daughter, son, brother, or sister-in-law; grandparent or grandchild; or spouse of a grandparent or grandchild.

5.4 Federal Physician Self-Referral Law

5.4.1 Statutory Prohibition

The Stark Law prohibits a physician from ordering "designated health services" (DHS) for Medicare patients from entities with which the physician (or an immediate family member) has a "financial relationship."[102] The term "financial relationship" is defined in the Stark Law to include both compensation arrangements and interests in investment and/or ownership. In addition, the term "referral" is defined more broadly than merely recommending a vendor of DHS to a patient. Instead, the term "referral" means, for Medicare Part B services, "the request by a physician for the item or service" and, for all other services, "the request or establishment of a plan of care by a physician which includes the provision of the designated health service."[103]

Although the Stark Law originally only applied to the provision of clinical laboratory services, effective January 1, 1995, the Stark Law was expanded to apply to a host of "designated health services." DHS includes clinical laboratory services as well as the following:

- physical-therapy services;
- occupational-therapy services;
- radiology, including magnetic resonance imaging, computerized axial tomography scans, and ultrasound services;
- radiation-therapy services and supplies;
- durable medical equipment and supplies;
- parenteral and enteral nutrients, equipment, and supplies;
- prosthetics, orthotics, and prosthetic devices;
- home health services and supplies;
- outpatient prescription drugs; and
- inpatient and outpatient hospital services.[104]

However, excluded from the definition of the term "DHS" are services that are reimbursed by Medicare as part of a composite, except for the services listed above that are themselves payable through a composite rate (e.g., home health, outpatient hospital services).

In 2003, Congress modified the Stark Law by adopting an 18-month moratorium on the ability of physicians to own an interest in a specialty hospital.[105] Although the moratorium officially lapsed

---

[102] 42 U.S.C. § 1395nn. The federal physician self-referral statute, as noted, often is referred to as the "Stark Law" after Congressman Fortney "Pete" Stark (D-CA), the Congressman who introduced and strongly supported the enactment of the statute.
[103] 42 U.S.C. § 1395nn (h)(5).
[104] CMS has defined certain designated health services (i.e., clinical laboratory services, physical therapy, radiology, and certain other imaging services, and radiation therapy services) by publishing specific lists of the Current Procedural Terminology and HCFA Common Procedure Coding System codes that physicians and providers most commonly associate with a given service.
[105] Medicare Prescription Drug, Improvement and Modernization Act of 2003, Pub. L. No. 108-173 § 507.

in June 2005, over the last several years, Congress has continued to monitor and debate the issue of whether this exception to the Stark Law should be modified. With the passage of the ACA, Congress again placed significant limitations on physicians' ownership interests in hospitals located both in urban and rural areas.[106]

Violations of the Stark Law are subject to various penalties, including one or more of the following:

- denial of payment for the DHS provided;
- refund of monies received by physicians and facilities for amounts collected;
- payment of civil penalties of up to $15,000 for each service that a person "knows or should know" was provided in violation of the Stark Law, and three times the amount of improper payment the entity received from the Medicare program;
- exclusion from the Medicare program and/or state health care programs including Medicaid; and
- payment of civil penalties for attempting to circumvent the Stark Law of up to $100,000 for each circumvention scheme.

In the Phase II Regulations, CMS adopted an exception to when the government will impose penalties if an arrangement involves "temporary noncompliance." Specifically, CMS provides that a violation has not occurred if: (1) an arrangement met an exception for at least 180 consecutive calendar days preceding the date when the agreement was no longer in compliance; (2) the financial relationship fell out of compliance for reasons beyond the control of the entity; and (3) the arrangement does not violate the Anti-Kickback Statute.[107]

Then, in the 2009 IPPS Final Rule, CMS adopted a provision that allows an entity under certain circumstances to submit a claim for a DHS if the compensation arrangement between the entity and a referring physician fully complied with an applicable exception except with regard to the signature requirement. More specifically, if the failure to comply with the signature requirement was "inadvertent" and the parties obtain the required signature(s) within 90 consecutive calendar days immediately following the date on which the compensation arrangement became noncompliant, the arrangement qualifies for the exception, without regard to whether any referrals occur or compensation is paid within the 90-day period. If the failure to comply was "not inadvertent," the parties must obtain the required signature(s) within 30 consecutive calendar days following the date on which the compensation arrangement became noncompliant to enjoy the protection of the exception.[108] An entity may use the provision for alternative method for compliance with signatures only once every three years with respect to the same referring physician. CMS specifically declines to extend relief to failures to satisfy other prescribed procedural or "form" criteria of an exception such as the amount of compensation or the description of the services.

---

[106] *See* ACA, § 6001(a)(3) (2010) (codified at 42 U.S.C. § 1395nn).
[107] 42 C.F.R. § 411.353(f).
[108] 42 C.F.R. § 353(g); *See also* 73 Fed. Reg. at 48705–09.

In addition to applying to the Medicare program, certain aspects of the Stark Law apply to state Medicaid programs. Specifically, the Social Security Act denies federal financial-participation payment under a Medicaid program to a state for services that would have been prohibited by Medicare under the Stark Law, if Medicare covered the services to the same extent as under the state's Medicaid plan.[109] Under the "Stark II Proposed Regulations" (as will be discussed), CMS has articulated its proposed position that individuals and entities are not precluded from referring Medicaid patients, or from billing for DHS that otherwise would be prohibited under the Medicare Stark Law prohibition. Instead, CMS has taken the position that, in these circumstances, state Medicaid programs may pay for these services even though the states will not be eligible to receive federal financial participation for these services.[110]

5.4.2 Regulations

On August 14, 1995, CMS published final regulations implementing the Stark Law's prohibition against the ordering of clinical laboratory services from an entity with which a physician has a financial relationship (the Stark I Regulations).[111] Then, on January 9, 1998, CMS published as a proposed rule for public comment the "Stark II" regulations (the Stark II Proposed Regulations).[112]

On January 4, 2001, almost three years to the day after the Stark II Proposed Regulations were issued, CMS published in the *Federal Register* "Phase I" of the Final Stark II regulations (Phase I Regulations),[113] which implemented only certain portions of the Stark Law:

1. the Stark Law's prohibition;
2. exceptions to the law that apply to both ownership and compensation arrangements;
3. the definitions of key terms included in the Stark statute; and
4. certain regulatory exceptions.

On March 26, 2004, CMS published Phase II of the Final Stark II regulations (Phase II Regulations) as an interim final rule with comment period.[114] The comment period ended on June 24, 2004, and the Phase II Regulations became effective July 26, 2004. On September 5, 2007, CMS issued Phase III of the Final Stark regulations (Phase III Final Regulations).[115]

While traditionally CMS issued stand-alone Stark regulations, CMS has begun including extensive changes to the Stark regulations in other regulatory issuances such as the Medicare Physician Fee Schedule (MPFS), the Hospital Inpatient Prospective Payment Systems (IPPS), or the Outpatient Prospective Payment System (OPPS). For example, final Stark regulations can be found in the FY

---

[109] 42 U.S.C. § 1396b(s).
[110] 63 Fed. Reg. 1659, 1672 (1998).
[111] *See* 60 Fed. Reg. 41914 (1995) (codified at 42 C.F.R. pt. 411).
[112] *See* 63 Fed. Reg. 1659 (1998).
[113] 66 Fed. Reg. 856 (2001) (codified at 42 C.F.R. Part 411 & 424).
[114] 69 Fed. Reg. 16054 (2004).
[115] *See* 72 Fed. Reg. 51012 (2007).

2008 IPPS Final Rule,[116] the CY 2008 MPFS Final Rule,[117] FY 2009 IPPS Final Rule,[118] the CY 2009 MPFS Final Rule,[119] the CY 2010 MPFS Final Rule,[120] the CY 2011 MPFS Final Rule,[121] the CY 2012 OPPS Final Rule,[122] the CY 2015 OPPS Final Rule,[123] the CY 2016 MPFS Final Rule,[124] and the CY 2017 MPFS Final Rule.[125]

5.4.3 Reporting Requirements

The Stark Law includes certain reporting requirements whereby any entity that provides items or services for which payment may be made under Medicare must submit certain information about the entity's financial relationship with physicians to CMS under time periods prescribed by the entity's Medicare carrier.[126] In the Phase II Regulations, CMS waived all reporting requirements for DHS entities providing fewer than 20 Part A and B services during a calendar year. Moreover, CMS decided not to require regular submission of information of other providers, but instead only requires information to be submitted upon request by CMS.[127]

As part of the Deficit Reduction Act of 2005, Congress required DHHS to develop a strategic and implementing plan to address certain issues relating to physician-owned specialty hospitals.[128] In preparing its report, CMS sent a voluntary survey, the Disclosure of Financial Relationships Report (DFRR), to 130 specialty hospitals and 220 competitor hospitals which sought information regarding, among other things, the hospitals' ownership and investment relationships and their compensation arrangements with physicians. Then, in August 2008, CMS issued its Final Report to Congress and that it would require all hospitals to provide information on a periodic basis concerning the investment interests and compensation arrangements with physicians.[129] As a result, in 2007, CMS began its initiative to implement a survey to investigate the investment/ownership and compensation arrangements between physicians and hospitals to determine whether they are in compliance with the Stark Law and implementing regulations. Under the Paperwork Reduction Act, CMS was required to obtain clearance from the Office of Management and Budget (OMB) prior to sending out the survey. Although the DFRR was under review by OMB for several months, on April 10, 2008, OMB reported that CMS had withdrawn its request for clearance of the DFRR survey.[130] Although CMS

---

[116] 72 Fed. Reg. 47130 (Aug. 22, 2007). *See also* the Proposed FY 2008 IPPS rule at 72 Fed. Reg. 24680 (May 3, 2007).
[117] 72 Fed. Reg. 66222 (Nov. 27, 2007). *See also* the Proposed CY 2008 MPFS rule at 72 Fed. Reg. 38122 (July 12, 2007).
[118] 73 Fed. Reg. 48434 (Aug. 19, 2008). *See also* the Proposed FY 2009 IPPS rule at 73 Fed. Reg. 23528 (Apr. 30, 2008).
[119] 73 Fed. Reg. 69726 (Nov. 19, 2008). *See also* the Proposed CY 2009 MPFS rule at 73 Fed. Reg. 38502 (July 7, 2008).
[120] 74 Fed. Reg. 61738 (Nov. 25, 2009). *See also* the Proposed CY 2010 MPFS rule at 74 Fed. Reg. 33520 (July 13, 2009).
[121] 75 Fed. Reg. 73170 (Nov. 29, 2010). *See also* the Proposed CY 2011 MPFS rule at 75 Fed. Reg. 40140 (July 13, 2010).
[122] 76 Fed. Reg. 74517 (Nov. 30, 2011). *See also* the Proposed CY 2012 OPPS rule at 76 Fed. Reg. 42170 (July 18, 2011).
[123] 79 Fed. Reg. 66987 (Nov. 10, 2014). *See also* the Proposed CY 2015 OPPS rule at 79 Fed. Reg. 40916 (Jul. 14, 2014).
[124] 80 Fed. Reg. 70886 (Nov. 16, 2015). *See also* the Proposed CY 2016 MPFS rule at 80 Fed. Reg. 41686 (Jul. 15, 2015).
[125] 81 Fed. Reg. 80170 (Nov. 15, 2016). *See also* the Proposed CY 2017 MPFS rule at 81 Fed. Reg. 46162 (Jul. 15, 2016).
[126] 42 U.S.C. § 1395nn(f); 42 C.F.R. § 411.361.
[127] 42 C.F.R. § 411.361.
[128] Deficit Reduction Act of 2005, Pub. L. No. 109-171, § 5006.
[129] A copy of the CMS Final Report to Congress can be found at http://www.cms.hhs.gov/PhysicianSelfReferral/06a_DRA_Reports.asp#TopOfPage.
[130] *See* http://www.reginfo.gov/public/do/PRAViewICR?ref_nbr=200710-0938-003.

had not reintroduced this tool, as part of the ACA, Congress adopted another provision requiring the Secretary to collect information regarding physician ownership in hospitals.[131]

5.4.4 Definition of "Entity"

Although in the Phase I Stark II Final Regulations, CMS adopted the definition of the term "entity" as "the person or entity to which CMS makes payment for the DHS,"[132] in 2007, as part of the CY 2008 MPFS Proposed Rule, CMS proposed to revise the definition of the term "entity" to include not only the person or entity that bills for the DHS but also any person or entity that "performs" the DHS as well as any person or entity that "presented a claim or caused a claim to be presented" to Medicare for the DHS.[133]

Although CMS did not finalize its proposal in the CY 2008 MPFS Final Rule, CMS did adopt a modified definition in the FY 2009 IPPS Final Rule so as to include any person or entity that "has performed services that are billed as DHS."[134] By changing the definition of "entity" to include persons and entities that "perform" DHS, CMS specifically stated in the preamble to the regulations that it intended to include within the scope of the Stark Law those physician groups and other organizations that provide inpatient and/or outpatient services to a hospital "under arrangements."[135] Consequently, any physician who maintains a financial relationship with the "under arrangement" organization/DHS entity can only make DHS referrals to the organization if that financial relationship meets a Stark Law exception. While it may be possible to structure a physician's *compensation* arrangement with such an "under arrangement" organization to satisfy a compensation arrangement exception, only under very limited circumstances will a physician be able to maintain an *ownership* or investment interest in an "under arrangement" organization after October 1, 2009.[136]

In the FY 2009 IPPS Final Rule, CMS specifically addresses two sets of services that, in many instances, are provided to hospitals by physician organizations under arrangements: lithotripsy services and cardiac catheterization services. With respect to lithotripsy and as a result of the District of Columbia District Court decision in 2002 finding that lithotripsy is not a DHS, CMS stated in the FY 2009 IPPS Final Rule that lithotripsy services will not be subject to these principles.[137] With respect to cardiac catheterization services, CMS states that the final rule does not prohibit physicians from furnishing services, in part because "[w]here a group practice or other physician organization provides the service and bills for it, the service is not DHS and the physician self-referral statute will not apply."[138] Yet, this statement ignores the practical reality of cardiac catheterization practices as Medicare billing rules provide that cardiac catheterization services generally must be billed by

---

[131] *See* ACA, § 6001(a)(3) (2010) (codified at 42 U.S.C. § 1395nn(i)).
[132] 42 C.F.R. § 411.351; *see* 66 Fed. Reg. at 943.
[133] 72 Fed. Reg. at 38224.
[134] 42 C.F.R. § 411.351; *see* 73 Fed. Reg. at 48721. However, in the FY 2009 IPPS Final Rule, CMS did not adopt the concept of including within the definition of "entity" those who present or cause a claim to be submitted to Medicare.
[135] 73 Fed. Reg. at 48721.
[136] Specifically, the only remaining ownership exception available would be the rural provider exception (*see* Section 3–4(b)(3) for a description of the rural provider exception).
[137] 73 Fed. Reg. at 48730; *see also Lithotripsy Society v. Thompson*, 215 F. Supp. 2d 23 (D.C. 2002).
[138] 73 Fed. Reg. at 48729–30.

a hospital.[139] As a result of this position, a group of physicians and physician-owned entities that provide cardiac catheterization services (Cath Labs) across Colorado brought a lawsuit to overturn CMS's position.[140] To stop the definitional change prior to its October 1, 2009 effective date, plaintiffs sought a declaration that the expanded definition "'is contrary to clear congressional intent, based on an impermissible construction of the Stark Law, arbitrary and capricious, and exceeds the agency's authority,' in contravention of the Administrative Procedure Act [(APA)]...."[141] The district judge's interpretation of the definitional change recognized that "absent an applicable exception, the Stark Law will prohibit the individual physician Plaintiffs from making referrals to their own Cath Labs." However, the court never reached a decision on the merits. The court ultimately dismissed the case for lack of subject matter jurisdiction, reasoning in its Memorandum Opinion that even though the Cath Labs were not entitled to HHS administrative review because they do not bill or receive payments from Medicare, their contracting hospitals could bring such a challenge. However, in 2013, the Council for Urological Interests challenged CMS's revision of the term "entity" as violating the APA.[142] The Court held that CMS's interpretation and changes did not violate congressional intent or the APA.

5.4.5 Advisory Opinions

Prior to the passage of the BBA, neither the OIG nor CMS was specifically authorized to issue advisory opinions under the Stark Law. The Stark Law now requires the issuance of written advisory opinions concerning whether a referral relating to DHS is prohibited under the Stark Law.[143]

On January 9, 1998, CMS promulgated a "Final Rule with Comment Period" that not only sets forth the framework for how a private party can obtain an advisory opinion from CMS, but also incorporates certain limitations that have been placed on the OIG with respect to the substance of advisory opinions under the Anti-Kickback Statute and other fraud and abuse provisions. Specifically, CMS has incorporated the limitations placed on the OIG by stating that, in advisory opinions regarding the Stark Law, it will not assess fair market value for any goods, services, or property, nor will it determine whether an individual is a *bona fide* employee within the meaning of the IRC.[144] Moreover, CMS has verified that each advisory opinion issued will only be binding on the DHHS Secretary and the party or parties who requested the opinion.

In contrast to the numerous advisory opinions that have been issued by OIG under the Anti-Kickback Statute and other fraud and abuse provisions, since 1998, there have been only 15 advisory opinions interpreting the Stark Law.

---

[139] *See* Medicare Provider Reimbursement Manual, Part I, Ch. 21, § 2118.1.
[140] *Colorado Heart Institute v. Johnson*, 609 F. Supp. 2d 30 (D.D.C. 2009).
[141] *Id.* at 34.
[142] *Council for Urological Interests v. Sebelius*, 946 F. Supp. 2d 91 (D.D.C. 2013).
[143] 42 U.S.C. § 1395nn(g)(6).
[144] 63 Fed. Reg. 1646 (1998) (to be codified at 42 C.F.R. §§ 411.370 *et seq.*).

5.4.6 Self-Referral Disclosure Protocol

In 2009, the OIG issued an Open Letter to the health care community that stated the OIG would no longer accept self-disclosures of matters that only involve liability under the Stark Law without any potential liability under other similar laws (e.g., the Anti-Kickback Statute).[145]

As part of the ACA, Congress required CMS to develop a self-disclosure protocol related to Stark Law violations (referred to as the self-referral disclosure protocol or SRDP), which CMS posted on its website on September 23, 2010.[146] In addition to establishing a process by which entities can self-disclose Stark Law violations, this provision authorizes the Secretary to negotiate settlements for an amount less than the amount set forth under the Stark Law. Under the SRDP, HHS can negotiate a settlement down based upon a variety of factors such as the timeliness of the disclosure, the level of cooperation, and the nature of the violation. On May 6, 2016, CMS published a revised SRDP form to "streamline and simplify" the self-disclosure process, which was approved by the Office of Management and Budget on June 1, 2017. As of December 31, 2016, CMS has settled 233 disclosures and an additional 92 disclosures initially submitted to CMS were either withdrawn or settled by CMS's law enforcement partners.[147]

5.5 Stark Exceptions

The Stark Law contains several exceptions, with some applying to both ownership and compensation arrangements, some applying only to ownership arrangements, and the remainder applying only to compensation arrangements.

5.5.1 Ownership and Compensation Exceptions

Exempt from both the ownership and compensation arrangement proscriptions are the following exceptions.

5.5.1.1 Physician Services

An exception is provided for physician services provided personally by, or under the personal supervision of another physician in the same group practice as, the referring physician.[148] CMS adopted a qualifier in that, except for "physician services" defined at § 410.20(a), all other "incident to" services are excluded from the definition of "physician services."[149]

---

[145] http://oig.hhs.gov/fraud/docs/openletters/OpenLetter3-24-09.pdf.
[146] *See* ACA § 6409 (2010) (codified at 42 U.S.C. § 1395nn).
[147] http://www.cms.gov/Medicare/Fraud-and-Abuse/PhysicianSelfReferral/Self-Referral-Disclosure-Protocol-Settlements.html.
[148] 42 U.S.C. § 1395nn(b)(1).
[149] 42 C.F.R. § 411.355(a)(2).

5.5.1.2 In-Office Ancillary Services

This exception relates to DHS furnished by a physician in her office, except for durable medical equipment (excluding infusion pumps) and parenteral and enteral nutrients, equipment, and supplies.[150]

In order to qualify for the in-office ancillary-services exception, the referring physician (or another physician who is a member of the same group practice) must personally furnish the services. If other individuals (e.g., technicians) perform the services, then they must be directly supervised by the referring physician or another physician in the group practice.

To be exempt, in-office ancillary services also must be furnished either:

1. in a "centralized" building used by the group practice for the provision of some or all of the group's clinical laboratory services, or for the centralized provision of the group's DHS (other than clinical laboratory services); *or*

2. in the "same building" in which

    a. the referring physician or group practice has an office that is normally open to their patients at least 35 hours per week, and the referring physician or group members regularly practices medicine and furnishes physician services to patients in that office at least 30 hours per week,

    b. the referring physician or group practice has an office that is normally open to patients at least eight hours per week, and the referring physician regularly practices medicine and furnishes physician services to patients in that office at least six hours per week, or

    c. the referring physician or group has an office that is normally open eight hours per week, and the referring physician or group member regularly practices medicine and furnishes physician services to patients at least six hours per week in that office (including "some" services that are unrelated to DHS) and referring physician must be present and order the DHS in connection with a patient visit during the time the office is open, or the referring physician or a group practice member is present while the DHS is furnished during the time the office is open.[151]

As part of the ACA, Congress adopted a requirement as part of the in-office ancillary services exception that for MRI, CT, PET and any other designated health services identified by the Secretary, the provider must inform the individual in writing at the time of the referral that the individual may obtain the services from another health care provider and provide the patient with a written list of suppliers who furnish services in the area in which such patient resides.[152] As part of the CY 2011 MPFS Final Rule, CMS adopted regulations setting forth the substance of what is to be included in these disclosures (i.e., that the physician must identify five suppliers in a 25-mile radius).[153]

---

[150] 42 U.S.C. § 1395nn(b)(2).
[151] 42 C.F.R. § 411.355(b)(2).
[152] *See* ACA, § 6003 (2010) (codified at 42 U.S.C. § 1395nn).
[153] 75 Fed. Reg. at 73443–47 (Nov. 29, 2010).

Another significant issue under the in-office ancillary services exception is that the Stark Law's definition of the term "group practice."[154] First, a group practice must consist of two or more physicians who are legally organized as a single legal entity primarily for the purpose of being a physician group practice. Second, each physician who is a member of the group must provide substantially the full range of services that the physician routinely provides (including medical care, consultation, diagnosis, or treatment) through the joint use of shared office space, facilities, equipment, and personnel. Third, "substantially all" of the services of the physician group members must be provided through the group, billed in the name of the group, and treated as receipts of the group. Fourth, overhead expenses of and income from the practice must be distributed in accordance with methods previously determined by members of the group. Fifth, no physician group member may receive compensation directly or indirectly based on the volume or value of referrals by the physician, except for certain productivity bonuses. Sixth, group members collectively must personally conduct no less than 75% of the physician-patient encounters of the group practice. In addition, CMS has adopted an additional requirement that the group practice be a "unified business" that has (1) centralized decisionmaking by a body representative of the group practice that maintains effective control over the group's assets and liabilities (including, but not limited to, budgets, compensation, and salaries) and (2) consolidated billing, accounting, and financial reporting.[155]

CMS, in Phase III, revised the definition of "physician in the group practice" to "clarify" that an independent contractor must furnish patient care services pursuant to a contract made directly with the group practice in order for the physician to qualify as a "physician in the group practice." Previously, physicians with contractual arrangements could qualify as "physicians in the group" but not necessarily as "members" of the group, but the Stark regulations did not precisely dictate how the contractual arrangement should be structured, leaving open the possibility for contracting though another entity. However, in Phase III, CMS made an explicit requirement that independent contractors have a direct contractual arrangement with the group. CMS specifically said, in the preamble, that the definition of "physician in the group practice" does not extend to contractors between the group practice and another entity, such as a staffing company.[156] The significance of being a "physician in the group" is that such physicians are included for purposes of determining whether the group qualifies for Stark Law protection under several of the criteria applicable to group practices.

5.5.1.3 Prepaid Plans

The Stark Law includes an exemption for services furnished to enrollees of certain health plans. Such health plans include health plans with Medicare risk or cost contracts, carrier-dealing prepayment organizations, organizations that receive payments on a prepaid basis under certain demonstration projects, federally qualified HMOs, and Medicaid managed-care plans.[157]

---

[154] 42 U.S.C. § 1395nn(h)(4).
[155] 42 C.F.R. § 411.352(f).
[156] 72 Fed. Reg. at 51018.
[157] 42 U.S.C. § 1395nn(b)(3).

5.5.1.4 Academic Medical Centers

CMS adopted an exception for services referred within academic medical centers (AMCs).[158] These requirements focus on the definition of an AMC, the conditions for how the components of an AMC operate, and the requirements on the physicians within the AMC who are making the referrals in question. For purposes of this exception, an "academic medical center" is defined as (1) an accredited medical school or accredited academic hospital; (2) one or more affiliated faculty practice plans; or (3) one or more affiliated hospitals in which a *majority* of the hospital medical staff consists of physicians who are faculty members, and where a *majority* of all hospital admissions are made by physicians who are faculty members. In addition, AMCs need to meet the following additional requirements:

- all monetary transfers between "components" (defined as an affiliated medical school, faculty practice plan, hospital, teaching facility, institution of higher education or departmental professional corporation) of the AMC must directly or indirectly support the missions of teaching, indigent care, research, or community services;
- one or more written agreements, approved by the governing body of each component, must control the relationship between the components of the AMC;
- all money paid to a referring physician for research must be used solely to support bona fide research;
- the physician's compensation arrangement does not violate the Anti-Kickback Statute; and
- the exception also places limitations on its applicability to only certain referring physicians.[159]

In 2008, the Western District of Kentucky reviewed the applicability of the AMC exception.[160] *United States ex rel. Villafane v. Solinger* involved alleged Stark Law violations being bootstrapped into an FCA *qui tam* action. After the government declined intervention, the defendants moved for summary judgment on the basis that the Stark law was not violated because the arrangements fit within the AMC exception. Due to the lack of a "jurisprudential consensus about the meaning or applicability of the AMC's many elements," the judge instead, "looked to the history and evolution of the exception for its primary guidance."[161]

The two main issues in *Villafane* were whether the defendant physicians provided substantial academic or clinical services to the AMC and whether the total compensation received by the physician defendant's from the AMC was at fair market value. The regulations for the AMC exception do provide a "safe harbor" for meeting the substantial academic or clinical services requirement, however the defendants' could not meet the "safe harbor" requirements. This was not dispositive because "a physician who fails to meet this safe harbor 'is not precluded from qualifying' under this requirement."[162] The court concluded that while the defendants did not fall within the safe harbor and failed to use a time keeping system that was of high quality or accuracy, they met the "substantial" requirement

---

[158] 42 C.F.R. § 411.355(e).
[159] *Id.* § 411.355(e)(1).
[160] *United States ex rel. Villafane v. Solinger*, 543 F. Supp. 2d 678, 687 (W.D. Ky. 2008).
[161] *Id.*
[162] *Id.* at 688.

because "Defendants' annual work assignments and performance reviews, as well as curricula vitae indicate they were tasked with and completed substantial academic and clinical services."[163] The judge further determined that the defendants complied with the regulations regarding calculating fair market value by "presenting a 'comparison... [to] aggregate compensation paid to physicians practicing in similar academic settings located in similar environments... demonstrating that their compensation is comparable to similarly situated academics.'"[164]

5.5.1.5 Implants in ASCs

CMS adopted an exception for all prosthetic devices—including introcular lenses used as part of cataract surgery—that are implanted in a Medicare-certified ASC but which may not otherwise be included in the bundled ASC payment rate.[165] CMS created this exception, in part, in order to prevent procedures currently performed in ASCs to be shifted to what CMS considers more-costly hospital-outpatient settings. This exception, however, is limited to only a narrow field of devices, and applies only in certain settings.

5.5.1.6 Additional Regulatory Exceptions Applicable to Both Ownership and Compensation Arrangements

CMS also created a number of additional exceptions for both ownership and compensation arrangements concerning the provision of the following items: eyeglasses or contact lenses that are prescribed after cataract surgery; EPO and other dialysis drugs provided by or in end-stage renal disease facilities; preventive screening tests, immunizations, and vaccines; and intra-family rural referrals.[166]

5.5.2 Ownership Exceptions

Exempt from only the proscription on ownership arrangements are the following exceptions.

5.5.2.1 Ownership in Publicly Traded Securities and Mutual Funds

The Stark Law includes a specific exemption for ownership of publicly traded securities and mutual funds,[167] which applies to ownership of investment securities (including shares or bonds, debentures, notes, or other debt instruments) purchased on terms generally available to the public. The securities must be listed on the New York Stock Exchange, the American Stock Exchange, or any regional exchange in which quotations are published on a daily basis; foreign securities listed on a recognized foreign, national, or regional exchange in which quotations are published on a daily basis are exempted as well. Alternatively, exempt securities could be traded under an automated "inter-dealer" quotation system operated by the National Association of Securities Dealers or listed for trading on an electronic stock market or over-the-counter quotation in which quotations are pub-

---

[163] *Id.* at 689–90.
[164] *Id.* at 692.
[165] 42 C.F.R. § 411.355(f).
[166] 42 C.F.R. § 411.355(g)–(j).
[167] 42 U.S.C. § 1395nn(c); 42 C.F.R. § 411.356(a); 80 Fed. Reg. 70886, 71234 (Nov. 16, 2015).

lished on a daily basis and trades are standardized and publicly transparent. In order to qualify for the exemption, the corporation must have total stockholder equity exceeding $75 million at the end of the corporation's most recent fiscal year, or on average during the previous three fiscal years.

5.5.2.2 Hospitals

Also exempt from the ownership proscription are DHS provided by hospitals located in Puerto Rico, as well as DHS furnished by hospitals outside of Puerto Rico where the referring physician has an ownership interest in the hospital itself (and not in a subdivision of the hospital), and where the referring physician is authorized to perform services at the hospital.[168]

As described above, in 2010 and as part of the ACA, Congress has now placed significant limitations on physicians' ownership interest in hospitals located both in urban and rural areas. Specifically, the Stark Law provides that a hospital cannot be owned by physicians unless the ownership interest was obtained by the physicians prior to enactment of the ACA and that the hospital had a provider agreement in place as of December 31, 2010.[169] In the CY 2016 MPFS Final Rule, CMS provided definitions of when a direct and indirect ownership or investment interest in a hospital exists.[170]

With limited exceptions, physician owned hospitals are precluded from expanding the number of licensed beds, operating or procedure rooms beyond the number that existed as of the date the hospital is licensed following enactment of the law. The ACA establishes that a facility can seek a waiver from the expansion limitation in two separate sets of circumstances: (1) a hospital, that among other things, is in a county that has percentage increase in population over the last five years that is 150% of the population growth in the state; or (2) a hospital that constitutes a "High Medicaid Facility," which is not the sole hospital in a county and, for the three most recent years, has a larger percentage of Medicaid inpatient admissions than any other hospital in the county. Regulations setting forth the process by which a hospital can apply for one of these exceptions were issued on November 30, 2011.[171]

As part of the ACA modifications, Congress imposed additional requirements in order to ensure that the physicians' ownership interests are "bona fide." For example, the terms upon which a physician is offered an ownership interest in the hospital can be no different than the terms upon which a non-physician would be offered the same interest.[172] Congress also provided that, not only is the hospital prohibited from loaning money to a physician, but the hospital cannot guarantee a loan that a physician might obtain from a third party.[173]

Congress also enacted a number of disclosure requirements that the hospital and physician owners must make to patients concerning the existence of the ownership interest. The Affordable Care Act requires the hospital to disclose to patients if the hospital does not have a physician onsite 24/7. Congress adopted the specialty hospital moratorium in 2003 when a number of incidents occurred

---

[168] 42 U.S.C. § 1395nn(d)(1) and (d)(3); 42 C.F.R. § 411.356(c)(2) and (c)(3).
[169] See ACA, § 6001(a)(3) (2010) (codified at 42 U.S.C. § 1395nn).
[170] 80 Fed. Reg. 70886 (Nov. 16, 2015); 42 C.F.R. § 411.362(a).
[171] 76 Fed. Reg. 74122, 74517 (Nov. 30, 2011); 42 C.F.R. § 411.362(c)(2) and (c)(3).
[172] 42 C.F.R. § 411.362(b)(3)(ii); See also 80 Fed. Reg. 70886, 71335 (Nov. 16, 2015).
[173] See 42 C.F.R. § 411.362(b)(4).

at specialty hospitals allegedly because there was not adequate physician coverage. Although CMS adopted regulations a few years ago that require certain of these items to be disclosed by hospitals to patients,[174] Congress apparently saw a need to codify these requirements into the Social Security Act.

The ACA also includes a provision requiring the Secretary to collect information regarding physician ownership in hospitals. Although the Stark Law already included a provision providing the Secretary with the authority to request information regarding physician ownership and compensation arrangements that health care entities may have with physicians, as discussed above, CMS has not been able to finalize a process by which it intends to collect this information.

5.5.2.3 Rural Providers

Currently, the Stark Law exempts DHS furnished by physician-owned entities located in a rural area.[175] The exception applies only if substantially all of the DHS furnished by the entity are furnished to individuals residing in the rural area. Significantly, as part of the ACA, the modifications to the exception for ownership in a hospital also apply to ownership interests in hospitals in rural areas.

5.5.3 Compensation Arrangement Exceptions

The Stark Law contains the following exceptions applicable only to the proscription on compensation arrangements. As explained below, many of the compensation arrangement exceptions require that the arrangement be set out in writing.[176] In 2015, CMS issued the CY 2016 MPFS Final Rule clarifying the writing requirement under these exceptions. CMS acknowledged that while a single written document memorializing the key facts is the easiest way to establish compliance with the applicable exception, there is no requirement that the arrangement be documented in a single formal contract.[177] CMS stated, "[d]epending on the facts and circumstances of the arrangement and the available documentation, a collection of documents, including contemporaneous documents evidencing the course of conduct between the parties, may satisfy the writing requirement of the... exceptions that require that an arrangement be set out in writing."[178]

5.5.3.1 Rental of Office Space and Equipment

The exemption for office space protects arrangements for the use of premises in which the lease is set out in writing, signed by the parties, specifies the premises (which must be used exclusively by the lessee when used by the lessee), and is for a term of at least one year.[179] The space rented or leased must not exceed that which is "reasonable and necessary" for legitimate business purposes. The lessee may make payments for the use of common areas if the payments do not exceed the lessee's pro rata share of expenses for such common space based on the ratio of space used exclusively by the lessee to the total amount of space (other than common areas) occupied by all persons using the

---

[174] 42 C.F.R. § 489.20(u) – (v).
[175] 42 U.S.C. § 1395nn(d)(2); 42 C.F.R. § 411.356(c)(1).
[176] *See* 42 C.F.R. § 411.357 (a), (b), (e), (h), (l), (p), (r), (t), (v), and (w).
[177] 80 Fed. Reg. 70886 (Nov. 16, 2015).
[178] *Id.* at 71315.
[179] 42 U.S.C. § 1395nn(e)(1); 42 C.F.R. § 411.357(a).

common areas. The rental charges over the term of the lease must be set in advance, consistent with fair market value, and not determined in a manner that takes into account the volume or value of any referrals or other business generated between the parties. In addition, the lease must be commercially reasonable even if no referrals were made between the parties.

The exception for equipment rental is similar to the criteria for space rental in that the lease must be set out in writing, signed by the parties, and must specify the equipment covered by the lease. The equipment must be used exclusively by the lessee when used by that lessee. The lease term must be at least one year, and the equipment rented or leased must not exceed that which is "reasonable and necessary" for legitimate business purposes. The rental charges over the term of the lease must be set in advance, consistent with fair market value, and not determined in a manner that takes into account the volume or value of any referrals or other business generated between the parties. In addition, the lease must be commercially reasonable even if no referrals were made between the parties.[180]

Finally, although CMS has adopted certain "special" rules on compensation arrangements that allow for the payment of per-use, per-click and percentage based fees, CMS, in 2008, adopted modifications to these rules such that beginning October 1, 2009, percentage and per-click compensation methodologies are no longer permitted for rental of office space and equipment.[181]

5.5.3.2 Bona Fide Employment Relationships

This exception protects arrangements between employers and physicians (or the immediate family members of either party who have a *bona fide* employment relationship with the employer) for the provision of services. The exception applies if the employment is for identifiable services in which the amount of payment is consistent with fair market value and is not determined in a manner that takes into account (directly or indirectly) the volume or value of any referrals by the referring physician.[182]

The last requirement—that payment made to employees not be determined based on the volume or value of referrals—does not prohibit payments in the form of productivity bonuses based on services performed personally by the employee (or immediate family member of the employee).

5.5.3.3 Personal-Service Arrangements

The exemption for personal-service arrangements protects compensation arrangements between a physician and an entity where the physician is an independent contractor and not an employee of the entity.[183] In order to qualify for the exemption, a written agreement must:

1. specify the services covered by the arrangement;
2. cover all of the services to be provided by the physician to the entity;

---

[180] 42 U.S.C. § 1395nn(e)(1); 42 C.F.R. § 411.357(b).
[181] 73 Fed. Reg. 48434 (Aug. 19, 2008). *See also* 81 Fed. Reg. 80170, 80524–34 (restating that per-unit of service rental charges are prohibited to the extent that such charges reflect services provided to patients referred by the lessor to the lessee).
[182] 42 U.S.C. § 1395nn(e)(2); 42 C.F.R. § 411.357(c).
[183] 42 U.S.C. § 1395nn(e)(3); 42 C.F.R. § 411.357(d).

3. have a term for one year or longer;
4. provide that the aggregate services contracted for must not exceed those that are reasonable and necessary for the legitimate business purposes of the arrangement;
5. require that compensation paid over the term of the agreement is set in advance, not exceed fair market value, and not be determined in a manner that takes into account the volume or value of any referrals or other business generated between the parties; and
6. establish that the services to be performed under the arrangement not involve the counseling or promotion of a business arrangement or other activity that violates any state or federal law.

Although this exception requires that compensation paid to a physician may not be determined in a manner that takes into account the volume or value of any "referrals" or other business generated between the parties, the Stark Law includes a further "exception within an exception" for physician-compensation arrangements specifically related to physician incentive payments that satisfy certain requirements.

5.5.3.4 Unrelated Payments

The statute exempts payments provided by a hospital to a physician if such payments do not relate to the provision of DHS.[184]

5.5.3.5 Physician Recruitment and Retention

The physician recruitment exemption protects payments made by a hospital, FQHC, or RHC (rural health clinic) to a physician to induce the physician to relocate to the geographic area served by the hospital and to become a medical staff member.[185] In order to qualify for this exemption, the physician cannot be required to refer patients to the hospital, and the amount of the payment cannot be determined in a manner that takes into account, directly or indirectly, the volume or value of any referrals by the referring physician. In the Phase II Regulations, CMS provided that a hospital can make payments to an existing group in order to assist the group in recruiting the physician as long as the remuneration is passed directly through to and remain with the recruited physician, except for actual recruitment expenses. In the case of an income guarantee, the costs allocated by the physician or group practice to the recruited physician may not exceed the actual additional incremental costs attributable to the recruited physician.[186] In the Phase III Regulations, CMS revised the exception to prohibit physicians and physician practices from imposing any practice restrictions that "unreasonably restrict" the recruited physician's ability to practice medicine in the geographic area while no longer categorically prohibiting physician practices from imposing non-compete provisions.[187]

As part of the exception, the recruited physician must relocate her medical practice to the geographic area served by the hospital (the area composed of the lowest number of contiguous ZIP codes from which the hospital draws at least 75% of its inpatients) as evidenced by (1) the physician

---

[184] 42 U.S.C. § 1395nn(e)(4); 42 C.F.R. § 411.357(g).
[185] 42 U.S.C. § 1395nn(e)(5).
[186] 42 C.F.R. § 411.357(e). This issue was further addressed in the Phase III Regulations. *See* 72 Fed. Reg. at 51050.
[187] *See* 72 Fed. Reg. at 51054 (2007).

moving her medical practice at least 25 miles or (2) the physician deriving 75% of her revenues from professional services furnished to patients not previously seen by the physician during the prior three years.[188] Until 2015, CMS had not provided guidance as to the geographic area into which an FQHC or RHC could recruit a physician. Recognizing that FQHCs and RHCs often serve patients dispersed in a wider geographic area, in the CY 2016 MPFS Final Rule, CMS defined the geographic area served by the FQHC or RHC as the lowest number of contiguous or noncontiguous zip codes from which the FQHC or RHC draws at least 90 percent of its patients, as determined on an encounter basis.[189]

In addition, in the Phase II Regulations, CMS added an exception for retention payments made *directly* to a physician if the payment is to retain the physician's medical practice in the geographic area served by the hospital that is either a HPSA or is an area with a demonstrated need for the physician (as determined through a Stark advisory opinion). This exception also requires that the physician have a *bona fide* firm and written recruitment offer from an unrelated hospital that specifies the remuneration being offered and that requires the physician to move her practice at least 25 miles *and* to a location outside of the geographic area served by the hospital.[190] Moreover, the retention payment is limited to the *lower of* the amount obtained by subtracting (i) the physician's current income from physician and related services from (ii) the income the physician would receive from comparable services in the *bona fide* recruitment offer or the reasonable costs the hospital would expend in recruiting a new physician.[191] Likewise, there are certain restrictions on payment where the physician provides certification of future employment.[192]

5.5.3.6 Isolated Financial Transactions

This exemption protects isolated transactions, such as a one-time sale of property or practice, where the amount of the payment is consistent with the fair market value and does not take into account, directly or indirectly, the volume or value of any referrals between the parties.[193] In addition, the remuneration provided must be commercially reasonable even if no referrals were made. The transaction also must meet other requirements imposed by regulation to protect against program or patient abuse.

5.5.3.7 Certain Group Practice Arrangements with a Hospital

The Stark Law contains an exception for DHS furnished "under arrangements" to a hospital by a group practice.[194] The exception is essentially a "grandfather" of certain relationships that existed prior to December 19, 1989, and that have continued in effect without interruption thereafter. This exception requires that a written agreement establishes that substantially all of the DHS furnished to

---

[188] 42 C.F.R. § 411.357(e).
[189] 80 Fed. Reg. 70886 (Nov. 16, 2015); 42 C.F.R. § 411.357(e)(6)(ii).
[190] In lieu of a *bona fide* written offer of employment, the physician may certify that he or she has a *bona fide* opportunity for future employment.
[191] 42 C.F.R. § 411.357(t).
[192] *Id. See also* 80 Fed. Reg. 70886 (Nov. 16, 2015).
[193] 42 U.S.C. § 1395nn(e)(6); 42 C.F.R. § 411.357(f).
[194] 42 U.S.C. § 1395nn(e)(7); 42 C.F.R. § 411.357(h).

patients of the hospital are furnished by the group under the arrangement; further, compensation paid over the term of the agreement will be consistent with fair market value, is fixed in advance, and is not determined in a manner that takes into account the volume or value of any referrals or other business generated between the parties.

5.5.3.8 Payments for Items and Services

This exception protects both payments made by a physician to a laboratory in exchange for the provision of clinical laboratory services, as well as payments made by a physician to an entity as compensation for items or services (other than clinical laboratory services), if the items or services are furnished at a price that is consistent with fair market value.[195] However, in the Phase III Regulations, CMS states that the expansion of the fair market value exception (discussed below) to apply not only to items purchased by a physician from DHS provider may make this exception unavailable.[196]

5.5.3.9 Fair Market Value Exception

CMS created an exception for certain fair market value arrangements that largely mirror the existing compensation arrangement exceptions. The most significant issue raised by the fair market value exception might be the requirement that such arrangements meet a safe harbor under the Anti-Kickback Statute, be approved by the OIG under a favorable advisory opinion, or not violate the Anti-Kickback Statute.[197] In the Phase III Regulations, CMS expanded this exception to apply both to arrangements involving payments *to* physicians as well as payments *from* physicians to DHS entities.

5.5.3.10 Non-Monetary Compensation

In the Stark II Proposed Regulations, CMS set out an exception titled "De Minimis Compensation" which permitted noncash items or services to be provided to a physician or her family member that did not exceed $50 per gift and an aggregate of $300 per year. In the proposed version, this exception would apply only if the entity providing the compensation makes it available to all "similarly situated" individuals, regardless of whether they referred patients to the entity. In the final regulations, CMS changed the name of this exception to "Non-Monetary Compensation Up To $300" to eliminate any "unintentional implication" that the $300 limit is inconsequential in producing referrals. In addition, in the final regulations, CMS eliminated the $50-per-gift limit.[198]

This exception provides that this amount is to be adjusted each year based upon any increases in the Consumer Price Index-Urban All Item (CPI-U) for the 12-month period ending the preceding September 30th.[199] Therefore, for the calendar year beginning January 1, 2017, the compensation limit under this exception was increased to $398 per year.[200]

---

[195] 42 U.S.C. § 1395nn(e)(8); 42 C.F.R. § 411.357(i).
[196] *See* 72 Fed. Reg. at 51056–57.
[197] 42 C.F.R. § 411.357(*l*).
[198] *Id.* § 411.357(k).
[199] 42 C.F.R. § 411.357(k).
[200] *See* https://www.cms.gov/Medicare/Fraud-and-Abuse/PhysicianSelfReferral/CPI-U_Updates.html.

5.5.3.11 Medical Staff Incidental Benefits

CMS created an exception that permits hospitals to furnish to their medical staffs certain incidental benefits of low value, such as parking, meals, or free computer/Internet access.[201]

5.5.3.12 Managed-Care Risk-Sharing Arrangements

In response to the unintended effect of the Stark Law on commercial health plans, CMS created a compensation exception for remuneration pursuant to a "risk-sharing arrangement" (including, but not limited to, withholds, bonuses, and risk pools) between a MCO and a physician for the provision of items or services to enrollees of the health plan.[202]

5.5.3.13 Compliance Training

Because CMS views compliance training programs as "beneficial," CMS adopted in the Stark II Final Regulations an exception for compliance training provided to physicians who practice in the DHS entity's community.[203]

5.5.3.14 Indirect Compensation and the "Stand in the Shoes" Analysis

CMS created an exception for indirect compensation arrangements that satisfy the following requirements:

1. the compensation received by the physician from the person or entity with which the referring physician has the direct financial relationship is at "fair market value" for services and items actually provided, "not taking into account" the volume or value of referrals for the entity furnishing DHS;
2. the compensation arrangement between the physician and the entity with which the physician has the direct financial relationship is set out in writing, is signed by the parties, and specifies the services covered (except for *bona fide* employment arrangements, which need not be in writing but must be for identifiable services and commercially reasonable even if no referrals are made to the employer); and
3. the arrangement does not violate the Anti-Kickback Statute or any laws or regulations governing billing or claims submission.[204]

Prior to the Phase III Regulations, financial arrangements between an intermediary physician group or other entity and a DHS entity were analyzed to determine, first, whether the arrangement constituted an "indirect compensation arrangement" under the Stark regulations definition and, second, if yes, whether the arrangement met the exception for indirect compensation arrangements. The analysis generally turned on whether the physicians at the other end of the "chain" of arrangements were paid based in any manner on the volume or value of referrals to the DHS. However, the Phase

---

[201] *Id.* § 411.357(m).
[202] *Id.* § 411.357(n).
[203] *Id.* § 411.357(o).
[204] *Id.* § 411.357(p).

III Regulations adopted the first "stand in the shoes" concept that was designed to treat compensation arrangements between DHS entities and group practices as if the arrangements are also with the referring physicians.[205] As adopted in the Phase III Regulations, a physician is to "stand in the shoes" of his/her "physician organization" and is deemed to have the same compensation arrangement—with the same parties and on the same terms—as the physician organization.[206] The effect of this interpretation of the Stark Law and the application of the stand in the shoes was twofold. First, it rendered some arrangements that would have constituted indirect compensation arrangements to now be direct compensation arrangements that must meet a direct compensation exception. Second, arrangements that did not implicate Stark at all under the prior regulations may now be implicated. Some distinctions between the indirect exception and other potentially relevant direct exceptions is that "indirect" compensation is not subject to the requirement that it be set forth in writing and signed by both parties, or be set in advance for one year, giving parties substantial latitude in establishing and amending their arrangements to meet immediate business needs, so long as those modifications are not based on the volume or value of referrals.

As a result of numerous comments from the health care community, CMS explained in the FY 2009 IPPS Proposed Rule that it was revisiting the "stand in the shoes" policy and that it was looking to achieve the goal of "simplifying the analysis of many financial arrangements" while reducing program abuse. To this end, in the FY 2009 IPPS Proposed Rule, CMS proposed two alternatives to addressing these concerns: (1) a "multi-faceted approach" to analyzing stand in the shoes arrangements; or (2) the development of a new exception for "mission support" payments, leaving the current stand in the shoes rules intact.[207]

However, when CMS issued the FY 2009 IPPS Final Rule, it revised the "physician stand in the shoes" provisions to apply only if "the only intervening entity between the physician and the entity furnishing DHS is his or her physician organization and the physician has an ownership or investment interest in the physician organization."[208] Moreover, CMS adopted a provision in the regulations that physicians with only a "titular ownership interests (that is, physicians without the ability or right to receive the financial benefits of ownership or investment)" are not required to undergo the "stand in the shoes" analysis.[209]

In the 2015 Final Rule, CMS explained that it did not intend the FY 2009 IPPS Final Rule to be interpreted to mean that when "applying the exceptions in § 411.355 and § 411.357 for the purposes of determining whether compensation takes into account the volume or value of referrals or other business generated between the "parties" the only "parties" to consider are the physicians with ownership or investment interest in their physician organization."[210] To address this, CMS revised § 411.354(c)(3)(i) to clarify that its intent was and remains that only physicians who stand in the

---

[205] 42 C.F.R. § 354(c)(3); *see also* 72 Fed. Reg. at 51028.
[206] A "physician organization" means a physician (including a professional corporation of which the physician is sole owner), a physician practice, or a group practice that complies with the regulatory requirements for group practices. A "physician practice" as used in this definition is not defined. 42 C.F.R. § 411.351.
[207] 73 Fed. Reg. at 23686.
[208] 42 C.F.R. § 411.354(c)(3); *see also* 73 Fed. Reg. at 48693–99.
[209] *Id.*
[210] 80 Fed. Reg. 70886, 71322 (Nov. 16, 2015).

shoes of their physician organizations are considered parties to an arrangement for the purposes of the signature requirement of the exception.

In responding to comments, CMS specifically stated that nothing in revised § 411.354(c)(3)(i) impacts the analysis regarding whether an indirect compensation arrangement exists. In addition, CMS stated, "compensation between a DHS entity and a physician organization may not be determined in a manner that takes into account the volume or value of *referrals and other business generated* by any physician in the physician organization, including physicians who do not stand in the shoes of the physician organization. The *compensation from the physician organization to its employed or contracted physicians* is relevant to whether an indirect compensation arrangement exists between the DHS entity and a physician."[211]

5.5.3.15 Electronic Prescribing and Electronic Health Records

As required by MMA, CMS in 2006 created two exceptions for compensation arrangements involving certain electronic prescribing and electronic health records arrangements.[212]

The first of these exceptions applies to the provision of items or services that are necessary and used solely to receive and transmit electronic prescription information. This exception requires compliance with criteria similar to those listed under the Anti-Kickback safe harbor that protects the same arrangements.

Meanwhile, the second exception establishes the conditions under which entities furnishing DHS may donate to physicians interoperable electronic health records software, information technology and training services. In order to qualify for protection under this exception, the relevant items or services must be necessary and used predominantly to create, maintain, transmit or receive the electronic health records of the donor's or physician's patients. Additionally, this exception requires compliance with criteria similar to those listed in the electronic prescribing exception, as well as requiring cost sharing and selection of physician recipients of donated technology. On December 27, 2013, CMS issued a final rule to amend this exception.[213] The proposed revisions to the exception include an update to the provision under which electronic health records software is deemed interoperable, removal of the electronic prescribing capability requirement and extension of the sunset provisions from December 31, 2013 to December 31, 2021.

5.5.3.16 Additional Compensation Exceptions

In the Phase II Regulations, CMS created a number of exceptions for:

- referral service arrangements and obstetrical medical-malpractice insurance that satisfy the requirements under the applicable safe harbors of the Anti-Kickback Statute;[214]

---

[211] *Id.* at 71324 (emphasis in original).
[212] 42 C.F.R. § 411.357(v) and (w).
[213] 78 Fed. Reg. 78751 (Dec. 27, 2013).
[214] 42 C.F.R. § 411.357(q) and (r).

- professional-courtesy discounts offered to all physicians on the entity's *bona fide* medical staff, or in the local community or service area, without regard to volume or value of referrals;[215]

- technology provided as part of a community-wide information system;[216] and

- charitable donations made by physicians.[217]

5.5.3.17 Accountable Care Organization Waivers

On October 29, 2015, the OIG, in conjunction with CMS, issued a final rule establishing waivers of the Stark Law and certain other laws to particular arrangements involving ACOs under the Medicare shared savings program.[218] While not technically a safe harbor, the final rule establishes five waivers of application of the Stark law, the federal anti-kickback statute, and the Civil Monetary Penalty provisions related to beneficiary inducements if certain conditions are met. According to the final rule, an arrangement need only fit in one waiver to be protected.

5.5.3.18 Recruitment of Non-physician Practitioners

On November 16, 2015, in the CY 2016 Physician Fee Schedule, CMS issued a compensation exception to protect remuneration provided by a hospital, FQHC, or RHC to employ, contract with, or otherwise engage a non-physician practitioner (NPP) under a compensation arrangement to furnish primary care services or mental health services.[219] CMS defined an NPP as a physician assistant (PA), nurse practitioner (NP), certified nurse specialist (CNS), certified nurse midwife, clinical social worker, or a clinical psychologist. Of note, if the NPP is an independent contractor then the compensation arrangement must be made directly between the physician and the NPP.

Under the exception, the arrangement must be set out in writing and signed by the parties, including the NPP. The arrangement may not: (1) be conditioned on the physician's or NPP's referrals to the hospital, FQHC, or RHC; (2) exceed 50 percent of the actual compensation, signing bonus, and benefits during a period not to exceed the first two consecutive years of the compensation arrangement between the physician and the NPP; (3) be determined in a manner that takes into account the volume or value of any actual or anticipated referrals by the physician or NPP (or any physician or NPP in the physician's practice) or other business generated between the parties; and (4) exceed fair market value.

The exception also imposes certain geographic limitations. Specifically, the NPP may not, within one year of the commencement of the compensation arrangement with the physician have (1) practiced in the geographic area serviced by the hospital, FQHC, or RHC or (2) been employed or otherwise engaged to provide patient care services by the physician. Finally, with certain exceptions, this

---

[215] *Id.* § 411.357(s).
[216] *Id.* § 411.357(u).
[217] *Id.* § 411.357(j).
[218] 80 Fed. Reg. 66729 (Oct. 29, 2015) (not codified at C.F.R.).
[219] 80 Fed. Reg. 70886, 71301 (Nov. 16, 2015); 42 C.F.R. 411.357(x). Under the exception, substantially all of the services that the NPP furnishes to patients of the physician practice must be primary care services or mental health care services.

exception may only be used by a hospital, FQHC, or RHC once every three years with respect to the same referring physician.

5.5.3.19 Timeshare Arrangements

In the CY 2016 MPFS Final Rule, CMS issued a new exception for timeshare arrangements recognizing the need for such arrangements to ensure adequate access to needed health care services. This exception protects only those timeshare arrangements between a physician and a hospital or physician organization, of which the physician is not an owner, employee, or contractor, under which the physician uses the licensed premises, equipment, personnel, items, supplies, and/or services predominately for the evaluation and management (E/M) of patients.[220]

The equipment covered under the arrangement must be (1) located in the same building where the E/M services are furnished; (2) not used to furnish DHS other than those incidental to the E/M services furnished at the time of the patient's E/M visit; and (3) not be advanced imagining equipment, radiation therapy equipment, or clinical or pathology laboratory equipment.

The compensation must be set in advance, consistent with FMV, and not determined in a manner that takes into account the volume or value of referrals or other business generated between the parties or using a formula based on percentage of revenue raised, earned, billed, or collected or per-unit of service fees that are not time based to the extent that they reflect services provided to patients.

5.5.4 "Special Rules" for Compensation

5.5.4.1 Definition of Fair Market Value

The concept of "fair market value" is relevant to many of the Stark Law exceptions. In the Stark II Final Regulations, CMS provided additional definitional guidance for what constitutes "fair market value."[221] Fair market value means the value of a good or service in arm's-length transactions that are consistent with "general market value." In other words, fair market value for an item or service is the price that an asset would bring as the result of *bona fide* bargaining between, or the compensation in a service agreement negotiated by, well-informed buyers and sellers who are not in a position to generate business for one another. The general benchmark for fair market value is the price at which *bona fide* sales have been consummated for assets of like type, quality, and quantity in the particular market at the time of the transaction, or the compensation included in *bona fide* service agreements with comparable terms at the time of the agreement.

In this regard, CMS states that, when fair market value is included in an exception that also includes the "volume or value" standard, the parties may be precluded from relying on comparables that involve entities and physicians in a position to refer and generate business. CMS also states that the burden of establishing "fairness" rests with the parties.

---

[220] 80 Fed. Reg. 70886, 71325 (Nov. 16, 2015); 42 C.F.R. § 411.357(y).
[221] 42 C.F.R. § 411.351.

With regard to the use of independent valuation consultants to determine fair market value, CMS states that no requirement is made to use such outside sources if other "appropriate" valuation methods are available. Nonetheless, CMS states that, although internally generated surveys can be used to determine fair market value in certain circumstances, such surveys do not have "strong evidentiary value" due to their susceptibility to manipulation and absence of independent verification.

For space leases and equipment rentals, fair market value means the value for commercial purposes, not taking into account its "intended use" or its proximity to referral sources. CMS makes clear that this "intended use" limitation still allows for development upgrades and maintenance that customize premises for health care usages to be factored into fair market value, and allows rental payments that reflect the fair market value of the area in which the property is located (i.e., medical property in a medical community). "Intended use" is taken into account only where the lessee pays inflated amounts to enhance her medical practice—that is, pays additional amounts in excess of those paid by other medical practitioners in the same building.

In the Phase II Regulations, CMS provided guidance in connection with hourly payments for a physician's personal services by using one of two possible methodologies (i.e., an hourly payment that is less than or equal to the average hourly rate for emergency room physician services in the relevant physician market; or an hourly rate based upon the 50th-percentile national compensation level for physicians with the same specialty by benchmarking against various publicly available surveys). CMS, however, eliminated this "safe harbor" for calculating fair market value in the Phase III Regulations. While noting that parties are left to choose their own methodologies, CMS stated that "[r]eference to multiple, objective, independently published surveys remains a prudent practice for evaluating fair market value."[222]

5.5.4.2 Compensation Methodologies

In the Phase III Regulations, CMS confirmed that percentage compensation arrangements are deemed to be "set in advance" if the specific formula for calculating the compensation is set in advance and the compensation does not take into account the volume or value of referrals or other business generated Additionally, CMS stated that entities may continue to use unit-based (per-click) and percentage-based compensation arrangements.[223]

However, in the CY 2008 MPFS Proposed Rule, CMS proposed to modify the special rules on compensation in such a way that a percentage based formula could only be used for paying for personally performed physician services. In addition, CMS proposed to exclude per-click based payments to a physician lessor for services rendered by an entity lessee to patients who are referred to the entity by the physician lessor. CMS commented that these situations are inherently susceptible to abuse because the physician has an incentive to profit from referring a higher volume of patients to the lessee.[224]

---

[222] *See* 72 Fed. Reg. at 51015 (2007).
[223] 42 C.F.R. § 411.354(d); *see* 72 Fed. Reg. at 51030–31.
[224] 72 Fed. Reg. at 38184.

While these proposals were not addressed in the CY 2008 MPFS Final Rule, CMS adopted a number of changes to the ability of entities to use percentage and per click arrangements when the FY 2009 IPPS Final Rule was issued. Specifically, instead of modifying the "special rules on compensation" and the definition of "set in advance," CMS revised several exceptions (i.e., the office space and equipment lease exceptions, as well as the fair market value and indirect compensation arrangements exceptions) to address the use of percentage-based compensation formulae and per-click arrangement. Effective October 1, 2009, these exceptions prohibit compensation arrangements that use a formula based on either: a percentage of the revenue raised, earned, billed, collected, or otherwise attributable to the services performed or business generated in the office space or by the use of the equipment; or per-unit of services rental charges, to the extent that such charges reflect services provided to patients referred between the parties.[225]

5.5.4.3 Physician's Compensation can be Conditioned on Referrals to a Particular Provider

CMS expressly permits compensation paid to a physician pursuant to an employment agreement or a managed-care contract to be conditioned on the physician's referring patients to a particular provider, practitioner, or supplier.[226] Specifically, these types of "mandated referral" requirements are permissible as long as:

1. the arrangement is in writing;
2. the compensation is set in advance and is consistent with fair market value;
3. the arrangement complies with an ownership or compensation exception; and
4. the referral requirement does not apply if a patient expresses a different choice of provider, the patient's insurance decides which provider is used, or if the referral is not in the best medical interest of the patient (as determined by the physician).

5.6 Federal Criminal Prohibitions Against False Claims and Fraudulent Billing Practices

5.6.1 Social Security Act

Section 1128B of the Social Security Act sets forth criminal penalties that are to be imposed upon individuals and entities that engage in certain activities that result in the submission of false or fraudulent claims to a federal health care program. Specifically, the Social Security Act sets forth that it is a felony to commit any of the following:[227]

- knowingly and willfully make or cause to be made any false statement of a material fact in any application for any benefit or payment, or for use in determining rights to such payment, under a federal health care program;

---

[225] 42 C.F.R. §§ 357(a)(5), 357(b)(4), 357(l)(3); and 357(p)(1); *see also* 73 Fed. Reg. at 48709–21.
[226] *Id.* § 411.354(d).
[227] *See* 42 U.S.C. § 1320a-7b.

- conceal information from or fail to disclose information to the government—specifically, information of an event affecting the initial or continued right to a benefit or payment under a federal health care program;

- apply to receive federal benefit or payment for the use and benefit of another and knowingly and willfully converting such payment to another use, or present (or cause to be presented) a claim for physician services knowing that the person who furnished the services is not a licensed physician, or counsel or assist an individual to dispose of assets (including by any transfer in trust) in order for an individual to become eligible for medical assistance; or

- knowingly and willfully make, cause to make, induce, or seek to induce, any false statement or representation of a material fact as to the conditions or operation of any institution, facility, or entity:

  - in order to qualify for certification or recertification as any entity for which certification is required, including a hospital, critical access hospital, skilled nursing facility, intermediate care facility for the mentally retarded, home health agency, health maintenance organization or competitive medical plan; or

  - in response to required disclosure of information under § 1124A of the Social Security Act.

Each violation of any of these provisions by a person in connection with the furnishing by that person of items or services for which payment is made under a federal health care program is a felony punishable by a fine of up to $25,000 and/or up to five years imprisonment. With respect to violations by all other persons, such violations are misdemeanors, and are punishable by a fine of up to $10,000 and/or up to one year of imprisonment.

5.6.2 Federal Health Care Fraud Offenses

As part of HIPAA, the U.S. Criminal Code was amended to include several new health care fraud offenses.

5.6.2.1 General Prohibition

HIPAA enacted a general prohibition that makes it a crime to knowingly and willfully execute, or attempt to execute, a scheme or artifice: (1) to defraud any health care benefit program; or (2) to obtain, by means of false or fraudulent pretenses, representations, or promises, any of the money or property owned by, or under the custody or control of, any health care benefit program.[228]

The term "health care benefit program" is defined as "any public or *private* plan or contract, affecting commerce, under which any medical benefit, item or service is provided to any individual, and includes any individual or entity who is providing a medical benefit, item or service for which payment may be made under the plan or contract."[229] However, the majority of cases concerning fraud offenses under HIPAA center on parties who defrauded public payers, or public payers in conjunction

---

[228] 18 U.S.C. § 1347.
[229] 18 U.S.C. § 24(b) (emphasis added). *See U.S. v. McGovern*, 329 F.3d 247 (1st Cir. 2003); *U.S. v. Whited*, 311 F.3d 259 (3d Cir. 2002).

with private payers. For example, in *United States v. Edwards*, the United States District Court for the Northern District of Texas ordered a former medical clinic executive to serve a 30-month prison term and pay over $370,000 in restitution for filing fraudulently coded claims and diagnosis codes to Medicare, Medicaid, and private insurance companies in order to receive higher payments than those authorized by the payers, in violation of 18 U.S.C. § 1347.[230] In this case, it was alleged that the executive directed employees under her supervision to submit claims that were "upcoded" with higher level physician encounters, additional diagnoses and laboratory tests, and/or additional symptoms that were not approved by the clinician. In *United States v. Davis*, a psychologist was found to have violated 18 U.S.C. § 1347 when he used college students to do the "lion's share of his work while still billing Medicaid as if he had performed the tests himself."[231]

Violation of this statute can result in a fine and/or imprisonment for not more than 10 years; if the violation results in serious "bodily injury," then such person shall be fined and/or imprisoned for not more than 20 years. Finally, if the violation results in death, such person shall be fined and/or imprisoned for any term of years or lifetime imprisonment.

5.6.2.2 Making of False Statements

A person can be subject to a fine and/or imprisonment of up to five years when such person, in any matter involving a health care program, knowingly and willfully (1) falsifies, conceals, or covers up by any trick, scheme, or device a material fact or (2) makes any materially false, fictitious, or fraudulent statements or representations, or makes or uses any materially false writing or document knowing the same to contain any materially false, fictitious, or fraudulent statement or entry.[232]

5.6.2.3 Theft or Embezzlement

HIPAA also added a theft or embezzlement provision specifically applicable to health care. Violation of this provision can result in a fine and/or imprisonment for not more than 10 years. If the value of the property is less than $100, however, violation can result in a fine and/or imprisonment of not more than one year.[233]

5.6.3 Mail and Wire Fraud

The U.S. Criminal Code prohibits the use of the national mail system for the purpose of executing any scheme or artifice to defraud, or for obtaining money or property by means of false or fraudulent representations.[234] Violation of these provisions is a felony punishable by a fine and/or up to twenty years imprisonment for each violation. Health care providers may be prosecuted under the mail-fraud statute for submitting claims for services never rendered, filing claims for services billed at inflated rates, waiving co-payments, and billing for services that were not medically necessary.

---

[230] *See, e.g., United States v. Edwards*, No. 5:07-cr-00076 (N.D. Tex. Mar. 14, 2008).
[231] *United States v. Davis*, 471 F.3d 783, 785 (7th Cir. 2006).
[232] 18 U.S.C. § 1035.
[233] 18 U.S.C. § 669.
[234] 18 U.S.C. § 1341.

5.6.4 Racketeering Violations

The Racketeer Influenced and Corrupt Organizations Act (RICO), enacted as part of the Organized Crime Control Act of 1970, has been applied by the federal government and private parties alike in contexts far beyond organized crime. The federal criminal RICO statute prohibits a person from receiving any income, directly or indirectly, from a pattern of "racketeering activity," which is defined as committing a predicate act (e.g., mail or wire fraud) at least twice within 10 years.[235] As Medicare fraud has been recognized as a predicate act supporting a racketeering claim, health care providers and suppliers must be cognizant that they potentially could be prosecuted under RICO for different forms of alleged health care fraud.[236]

Significantly, RICO provides for a private right of action for persons injured in their business or property.[237] Successful private litigants can be awarded treble (i.e., triple) damages in addition to the cost of the suit, including attorney's fees. It is important to note that the defendant need not be convicted of any predicate act; the plaintiff is required only to show that the defendant engaged in conduct that would amount to a predicate offense.

5.6.5 Money-Laundering

The U.S. Criminal Code prohibits a person from knowingly engaging or attempting to engage in a "monetary transaction in criminally derived property" greater than $10,000 and derived from "specified unlawful activity," including mail and wire fraud. The prohibition also covers theft or bribery in programs involving federal funds, and "any act or activity constituting an offense involving a Federal health care offense."[238]

Although the statute provides criminal and civil penalties, it is most frequently used for its civil-forfeiture and broad civil penalty provisions. Civil penalties (the greater of $21,563 or the value of the transaction) may be imposed against *anyone* who conducts a violative transaction, regardless of whether that person benefits from it. Consequently, this provision could be used to penalize attorneys who assist clients in secreting or moving funds.

Forfeiture can be applied to any property involved in a transaction in violation of the statute, as well as any property traceable to such property. Thus, if both "dirty" and "clean" funds are used to purchase property, the *entire* property can be subject to forfeiture. Additionally, forfeiture can occur without first obtaining a conviction. Indeed, it can occur without notice to the affected individual, based upon the government's *ex parte* application, supported by affidavit, to a district judge.

---

[235] 18 U.S.C. §§ 1961 *et seq.*
[236] *See North Shore Med. Ctr., Ltd. v. Evanston Hosp. Corp.*, No. 92 C 533, 1996 U.S. Dist. LEXIS 10804 (N.D. Ill. July 30, 1996).
[237] 18 U.S.C. § 1964(c).
[238] 18 U.S.C. §§ 1956–1957.

5.6.6   Other Criminal Statutes

The federal government also has in its arsenal of criminal penalties the following: conspiracy to defraud the government;[239] the submission of fictitious or fraudulent claims;[240] and conspiracy to defraud.[241]

5.7   Federal Civil Prohibitions Against False Claims and Fraudulent Billing Practices

5.7.1   The Federal False Claims Act and Qui Tam Actions

The federal False Claims Act (FCA) prohibits a person from "knowingly" submitting claims or making a false record or statement in order to secure payment of a false or fraudulent claim by the federal government.[242] A person found to have violated this statute is liable for a civil penalty for each such claim of not less than $10,781 and not more than $21,563, plus three times the amount of damages sustained by the federal government.[243]

The statute specifically provides that the terms "knowing" and "knowingly" mean that a person "(1) has actual knowledge of the information; (2) acts in deliberate ignorance of the truth or falsity of the information; or (3) acts in reckless disregard of the truth or falsity of the information."[244] Therefore, no proof of specific intent to defraud is required. Under the False Claims Act, civil actions must be brought within six years after the date of the violation, or within three years after the date when material facts are known or should have been known by the government; in any event, no claims may be made more than 10 years after the date on which the violation was committed.[245]

In 2009, Congress enacted the Fraud Enforcement and Recovery Act of 2009 (FERA).[246] Although the primary purpose of FERA was to address fraudulent activity associated with the financial industry,[247] FERA expanded the application of the False Claims Act (FCA) which also significantly impacts the health care industry. For example, FERA amended the liability provisions of the FCA by broadening the scope of FCA violations as well as the types of claims that can constitute a FCA violation, which were specifically intended to override and reverse the Supreme Court's decision in *Allison Engine Co. v. U.S. ex rel. Sanders*[248] and the decision of the United States Court of Appeals

---

[239] 18 U.S.C. § 286.
[240] 18 U.S.C. § 287.
[241] 18 U.S.C. § 371.
[242] 31 U.S.C. §§ 3729 *et seq.*
[243] 81 Fed. Reg. 42491 (June 30, 2016).
[244] 31 U.S.C. § 3729(b).
[245] *Id.* § 3731(b).
[246] Pub. L. No. 111-21, § 4, 123 Stat. 1617, 1621–25 (2009) (codified as amended at 31 U.S.C. §§ 3729–3733).
[247] *See* S. Rep. No. 111-10, at 3–4 (2009) ("This bipartisan legislation will reinvigorate our Nation's capacity to investigate and prosecute the kinds of financial frauds that have so severely undermined our financial markets and hurt so many hard working people in these difficult economic times. . . . The [FCA] must be corrected and clarified in order to protect from fraud the Federal assistance and relief funds expended in response to our current economic crisis.").
[248] 553 U.S. 662 (2008) (holding that liability may only be imposed under section 3729(a)(2) of the FCA when the Government can prove that ("a defendant intended that the government itself pay the claim.")).

for the D.C. Circuit in *United States ex rel. Totten v. Bombardier Corp.*[249] FERA also expanded the reverse false claims provision of the FCA by covering acts in which a person "has possession, custody, or control of property or money used, or to be used, by the Government and *knowingly delivers or causes to be delivered, less than all of that money or property*" as well as "*knowingly conceals or knowingly and improperly avoids or decreases an obligation to pay or transmit money or property to the government.*"[250] Congress also added a definition of the term "obligation" as being "an established duty, whether or not fixed arising from an express or implied contractual, grantor-grantee, licensor-licensee, relationship, from a fee-based or similar relationship, from statute or regulation, or from the retention of any overpayment."[251] In addition to the changes to the False Claims Act by FERA, the Affordable Care Act had a significant impact on the scope and reach of the FCA. Significantly, the ACA amended the Social Security Act and now requires that an overpayment be reported or returned by the later of 60 days after the date the overpayment was identified or the date any corresponding cost report is due to avoid penalties.[252] The ACA defines an "overpayment" as "any fund that a person receives or retains under title XVII or XIX to which the person, after applicable reconciliation, is not entitled...."[253] In CMS's proposed rule regarding overpayments, CMS provided examples of what constitutes an overpayment.[254] CMS also proposed that overpayments must be reported and returned if a person (including a company) identifies overpayments within 10 years of the date it was received.

As described above, through the passage of the ACA Congress established conclusively that Anti-Kickback claims are now claims under the False Claims Act, which does include a private right of action by *qui tam* relators.[255] Prior to the ACA, the government and *qui tam* relators attempted to "bootstrap" Anti-Kickback claims to the False Claims Act to obtain civil penalties. This rested on the theory that, when a provider submitted a claim to a federal health care program, the claim included an implicit certification that the provider was in compliance with the Medicare Act, which required compliance with other laws, including the Anti-Kickback Statute.[256] However, with the modification to the Social Security Act as part of the ACA, there is no longer a question that a violation of the Anti-Kickback Statute is, indeed, actionable under the False Claims Act.

In addition, the Affordable Care Act amended several other false claims provisions contained with the False Claims Act, as well as other statutes. These amendments include limiting the public disclosure bar[257] and subjecting payments made through the state-based Exchanges to the False Claims Act.

---

[249] 380 F.3d 488 (D.C. Cir. 2004), *cert denied*, 544 U.S. 1032 (2005) (holding that FCA liability under 3729(a)(1) requires the presentment of a false or fraudulent claim for payment directly to the government).
[250] 31 U.S.C. § 3729(a)(1)(D) and (G) (emphasis added).
[251] *Id.* § 3729(b)(3).
[252] *See* 42 U.S.C. § 1320a-7k(d) *as amended by* ACA, § 10104(j)(2) (201).
[253] ACA, § 6402 (2010).
[254] 77 Fed. Reg. 9179 (Feb. 16, 2012).
[255] *See* ACA, § 6402(f)(1) (2010) (codified at 42 U.S.C. § 1320a–7b(g)).
[256] *See e.g., United States ex rel. Roy v. Anthony*, No. C-1-93-0559 (S.D. Ohio 1994); *United States ex rel. Pogue v. American Healthcorp., Inc.*, 1995 U.S. Dist. LEXIS 16710 (M.D. Tenn. Sept 1995); *United States ex rel. Pogue v. American Healthcorp., Inc.*, 914 F. Supp. 1507 (1996); *United States ex rel. Pogue v. Diabetes Treatment Centers of America, Inc.*, 238 F. Supp. 2d 258 (D.D.C. 2002).
[257] *See e.g., United States ex rel. Roy v. Anthony*, No. C-1-93-0559 (S.D. Ohio 1994); *United States ex rel. Pogue v. American Healthcorp., Inc.*, 1995 U.S. Dist. LEXIS 16710 (M.D. Tenn. Sept 1995); *United States ex rel. Pogue v.*

In addition to actions initiated by the federal government, the FCA authorizes *qui tam* actions to be brought on behalf of the federal government by a private party having direct knowledge of the fraud. These private parties, who are often referred to as *qui tam* relators, may share in the monetary recovery paid as part of the eventual settlement or disposition of the action in cases whereby the *qui tam* relator's recovery depends on whether the government has intervened in the action. The private party commences such an action in federal court by filing the complaint and relevant documentation "under seal" and serving these documents on the DOJ only. Initially, the defendant is not served. By statute, the DOJ then has at least 60 days to evaluate whether to pursue the action. If good cause can be shown, the government may obtain an extension of time beyond the 60-day period. This may result in a *qui tam* complaint pending for an extended period of time before the defendant is even aware of the action. During this time period, the government will conduct its own investigation of the fraud alleged in the complaint. If, based upon its investigation, the government decides to proceed with the action, then the government has the primary responsibility for prosecuting the action, and the *qui tam* relator has the right to remain as a party to the action. If the government decides not to proceed with the action, the *qui tam* relator may elect to proceed on her own with the action against the defendant; the government, however, may be permitted at a later time to intervene in the case.[258]

More recently, courts have examined the concept of materiality as it relates to the False Claims Act. On June 16, 2016, in *Universal Health Servs. v. United States ex rel. Escobar*, the U.S. Supreme Court held for plaintiffs, finding that the defendant had defrauded the government Medicaid program under the implied false certification theory of liability.[259] This decision upholds the implied certification theory of False Claims Act liability and strengthens the False Claims Act materiality requirement. A teen Medicaid beneficiary had been receiving counseling services at Arbour Counseling Services, a satellite mental health facility owned and operated by defendant, Universal Health Services.[260] After being prescribed medication for a diagnosis of bipolar disorder, the beneficiary had an adverse and fatal reaction.[261] Soon thereafter, investigation of Arbour found that very few of Arbour's employees were licensed, including the clinicians who diagnosed the decedent and prescribed the teen's medication.[262] Yet Arbour submitted reimbursement claims, certifying that services were being provided by or supervised by licensed clinicians.[263]

The Court found that Universal Health (through Arbour) knowingly misled the government Medicaid program when it submitted claims for specific counseling services that were supposed to be rendered by licensed clinicians, and made further misrepresentations when it submitted Medicaid reimbursement claims using National Provider Identification numbers that did not correspond with licensed clinicians.[264] The Court held that the omission of material fact when submitting claims can be the basis for liability if at least two conditions are satisfied: (1) the claim is not merely a request

---

American Healthcorp., Inc., 914 F. Supp. 1507 (1996); *United States ex rel. Pogue v. Diabetes Treatment Centers of America, Inc.*, 238 F. Supp. 2d 258 (D.D.C. 2002).
[258] 31 U.S.C. § 3730(c).
[259] See *Universal Health Servs. v. United States ex rel. Escobar*, 136 S. Ct. 1989, 1998 (2016).
[260] See *id.* at 1997.
[261] See *id.*
[262] See *id.*
[263] See *id.*
[264] See *id.* at 2000.

for payment, but makes specific representations about the goods and services provided; and (2) the defendant fails to disclose noncompliance with material statutory, regulatory, or contractual requirements, making those representations misleading half-truths.[265]

The Court, however, acknowledged that not every undisclosed violation of an express condition of payment automatically triggered FCA liability, but that it turned on whether the undisclosed information was material to the government's decision to reimburse the claim.[266] However, the Court also noted that demonstrating materiality was not as definitive as the government argued it to be.[267] For example, materiality is not shown by the mere demonstration of violating particular statutory, regulatory, or contractual requirement as a condition of payment; nor is it the notion of government nonpayment if it knew of the defendant's noncompliance.[268] Conversely, proof of materiality can include the defendant's knowledge of the government's consistent refusal to pay claims based on noncompliance with the particular statutory, regulatory, or contractual requirement; or the government's payment of a particular claim despite it knowing that certain requirements were violated.[269]

The U.S. Court of Appeals for the Fifth Circuit further addressed materiality in *United States ex rel. Harman v. Trinity Indus.*[270] In *Trinity*, the Fifth Circuit held that evidence showing noncompliance with statutory, regulatory, or contractual obligations for payment was not sufficient to satisfy the materiality requirement when alleging FCA liability. Here, the court found in favor of the defendant, Trinity Industries, when it ruled that the relator, Joshua Harman, failed to both demonstrate materiality as well as rebut the strong presumption against materiality. Here, the relator alleged that Trinity Industries, a manufacturer of highway guardrails, defrauded the Government when it accepted Government payment for sales of the guardrails that had not gone under proper testing protocols.[271] According to Harman, Trinity failed to submit drawings of the modifications it had made to the guardrails prior to its crash test.[272] The Federal Highway Administration (FHWA) was made aware of the omitted report, yet confirmed with various state transportation departments that the modified guardrails were the same guardrails tested and still eligible for reimbursement.[273]

Consistent with *Escobar*, the court assessed whether a misstatement is material by giving weight to the Government's response in light of statutory, regulatory, or violation of contractual obligations for payment. Here, even though FHWA knew of Trinity's omission of modified drawings with its testing report, the agency continued to utilize the guardrails on its highway systems and reimburse Trinity for them.[274] The court found that the Government's persistent and continuous reimbursement weighed heavily in favor of the defendant, showing that the Government did not find Trinity Industries' omission of drawings as material.[275]

---

[265] *See id.* at 2001.
[266] *See id.*
[267] *See id.* at 2003.
[268] *See id.*
[269] *See id.* at 2003–2004.
[270] *United States ex rel. Harman v. Trinity Indus.*, 2017 U.S. App. LEXIS 18902, at *15 (5th Cir. 2017).
[271] *See id.* at *10.
[272] *See id.* at *9.
[273] *See id.*
[274] *See id.* at *48–49.
[275] *See id.* at *54–55.

5.7.2 Social Security Act

In addition to its criminal provisions described earlier, the Social Security Act provides for the imposition of civil money penalties against any person who knowingly presents, or causes to be presented, a claim that is improperly filed. Specifically, the statute provides penalties for filing:[276]

- a claim for a medical item or service that the person knows or should know was not provided as claimed, including engaging in a practice of presenting a claim using a Current Procedural Terminology (CPT) code that the person knows or should know will result in greater payment than using the CPT code the person knows or should have known was applicable to the item or service actually provided;
- a claim for Medicare item or service that the person knows or should know is false or fraudulent;
- a claim for a physician's service by a person who knows or should know that the individual who provided that service was not a licensed physician, was licensed as a physician but such license was obtained through misrepresentation of a material fact, or misrepresented that the physician was certified in a medical specialty;
- a claim for a medical or other item or service furnished during a period in which the person was excluded; or
- a pattern of claims for medical or other items or services that a person knows or should know are not medically necessary.

The statute also provides civil money penalties for other activities that include, but are not limited to, knowingly giving a person information that she knows or has reason to know is false or misleading with respect to coverage of inpatient hospital services under the Medicare program, as well as a physician executing a certification that a patient meets the requirements for home health services when, in fact, the physician knows the requirements are not met.

Violation of these provisions generally results in penalties of not more than $10,000 for each item or service claimed, plus an assessment of up to three times the amount claimed for each such item or service. With respect to giving false or misleading information regarding inpatient hospital services, the penalty is $15,000 for each individual with respect to whom such information was given.

5.7.3 Program Fraud and Civil Remedies Act

The Program Fraud Civil Remedies Act of 1986 provides that any person who makes, presents or submits a claim that the person "knows or has reason to know" is false, fictitious, or fraudulent is subject to CMPs of up to $5,000 per false claim or statement and up to twice the amount claimed in lieu of damages.[277] This statute goes beyond the FCA and the CMPs of the SSA to provide for penalties and assessments against those who make false statements.[278]

---

[276] 42 U.S.C. § 1320a-7a; *see also* 42 C.F.R. § 1003.102.
[277] 31 U.S.C. § 3801 *et seq.*
[278] *Id.* § 3802(a)(2).

Under this statute, the OIG has authority to investigate allegations of liability, and then is required to report its findings and conclusions to the "reviewing official" at DHHS. If adequate evidence exists that a violation has occurred, written notice is sent to the Attorney General who is responsible for either approving or disapproving the referral of these allegations to the "presiding officer." If a reviewing officer refers allegations of liability to a presiding officer, the reviewing officer then provides notice to the person alleged to have violated this statute. Persons so notified may request a hearing regarding these allegations.[279] The statute provides that such hearing must be commenced within six years after the date on which the false claim or statement is made.[280]

5.8 Corporate Compliance Programs

The general principle that a health care company should foster an environment of compliance is not novel. Nevertheless, given the increased focus on fraudulent activities by health care providers, the recommendation that organizations adopt a "corporate compliance program" has been widely endorsed, as a number of benefits follow from implementing an effective program. In the ACA, Congress granted DHHS the authority to require providers and suppliers to establish a compliance program as a condition of enrollment in the Medicare, Medicaid, and CHIP programs.[281]

A well-established corporate compliance program can protect a health care company in the midst of a legal crisis by shielding the company from suffering harsher penalties or stricter sentences. Equally as important, a corporate compliance program can reduce the likelihood of potential violations by clarifying to employees what behavior is acceptable and what is intolerable. Also, an effective corporate compliance program can help management detect violations early enough to enable the company to proactively correct a potential problem. Finally, a compliance program can assist a company to gain credibility with the government as a law-abiding organization in the event of an investigation.

5.8.1 The Federal Sentencing Guidelines

"Corporate compliance programs" were originated in 1991 as part of the Federal Sentencing Guidelines as a means to determine whether a corporation's criminal penalties should be reduced. Specifically, the Federal Sentencing Guidelines provide that an organization's culpability will be lessened "if the offense occurred even though the organization had in place at the time of the offense an effective compliance and ethics program."[282]

In order to have an effective compliance and ethics program, the Sentencing Guidelines state that an organization shall "(1) exercise due diligence to prevent and detect criminal conduct; and (2) otherwise promote an organizational culture that encourages ethical conduct and a commitment to compliance with the law." Furthermore, the Sentencing Guidelines provide the following requirements to prove that an organization has adopted a program that promotes "an organizational culture that encourages ethical conduct and a commitment to compliance with the law."

---

[279] *Id.* § 3803.
[280] *Id.* § 3808(a).
[281] *See* ACA, § 6401(a)(7)(A) (2010).
[282] United States Sentencing Commission, *Guidelines Manual* § 8C2.5(f).

1. The organization shall establish standards and procedures to prevent and detect criminal conduct.

2. (A) The organization's governing authority shall be knowledgeable about the content and operation of the compliance and ethics program and shall exercise reasonable oversight with respect to the implementation and effectiveness of the compliance and ethics program.

   (B) High-level personnel of the organization shall ensure that the organization has an effective compliance and ethics program, as described in this guideline. Specific individual(s) within high level personnel shall be assigned overall responsibility for the compliance and ethics program.

   (C) Specific individual(s) within the organization shall be delegated day-to-day operational responsibility for the compliance and ethics program. Individual(s) with operational responsibility shall report periodically to high-level personnel and, as appropriate, to the governing authority, or an appropriate subgroup of the governing authority, on the effectiveness of the compliance and ethics program. To carry out such operational responsibility, such individual(s) shall be given adequate resources, appropriate authority, and direct access to the governing authority or an appropriate subgroup of the governing authority.

3. The organization shall use reasonable efforts not to include within the substantial authority personnel of the organization any individual whom the organization knew, or should have known through the exercise of due diligence, has engaged in illegal activities or other conduct inconsistent with an effective compliance and ethics program.

4. (A) The organization shall take reasonable steps to communicate periodically and in a practical manner its standards and procedures, and other aspects of the compliance and ethics program, to the individuals referred to in subdivision (B) by conducting effective training programs and otherwise disseminating information appropriate to such individuals' respective roles and responsibilities.

   (B) The individuals referred to in subdivision (A) are the members of the governing authority, high-level personnel, substantial authority personnel, the organization's employees, and, as appropriate, the organization's agents.

5. The organization shall take reasonable steps—

   (A) to ensure that the organization's compliance and ethics program is followed, including monitoring and auditing to detect criminal conduct;

   (B) to evaluate periodically the effectiveness of the organization's compliance and ethics program; and

   (C) to have and publicize a system, which may include mechanisms that allow for anonymity or confidentiality, whereby the organization's employees and agents may report or seek guidance regarding potential or actual criminal conduct without fear of retaliation.

6. The organization's compliance and ethics program shall be promoted and enforced consistently throughout the organization through

(A) appropriate incentives to perform in accordance with the compliance and ethics program; and

(B) appropriate disciplinary measures for engaging in criminal conduct and for failing to take reasonable steps to prevent or detect criminal conduct.

7. After criminal conduct has been detected, the organization shall take reasonable steps to respond appropriately to the criminal conduct and to prevent further similar criminal conduct, including making any necessary modifications to the organization's compliance and ethics program.

The Federal Sentencing Guidelines also state that failure to prevent or detect the offense does not mean that the compliance program was *per se* ineffective.[283]

In November 2015, the Department of Justice Fraud Section retained a compliance counsel expert to "provide expert guidance to Fraud Section prosecutors as they consider the enumerated factors in the [Federal Sentencing Guidelines] concerning the prosecution of business entities, including the existence and effectiveness of any compliance program that a company had in place at the time of the conduct giving rise to the prospect of criminal charges, and whether the corporation has taken meaningful remedial action, such as the implementation of new compliance measures to detect and prevent future wrongdoing."[284]

5.8.2 Various OIG Guidances to Particular Segments of the Health Care Industry

While the Sentencing Guidelines provide an overall structure for an organization's assessment of compliance program effectiveness, the OIG has promulgated more-specific "industry compliance guidances" that provide specific criteria for "effectively" meeting the requirements of the Sentencing Guidelines, as well as examples of what the OIG expects an "effective" compliance program to include. To date, the OIG has issued guidance for:

1. clinical laboratories;[285]
2. home health agencies;[286]
3. hospitals;[287]
4. durable medical equipment, prosthetics, and orthotics suppliers;[288]
5. Medicare+Choice (now referred to as Medicare Advantage (MA)) organizations;[289]

---

[283] *United States Sentencing Commission Guidelines Manual* § 8B2.1(b). The Sentencing Guidelines include an application note regarding § 8B.2.1(b)(7). The note clarifies that subsection (b)(7) has two aspects. First, the organization must appropriately respond to the conduct by taking "reasonable" steps to remedy the harm—including compensating any victims, self-reporting and cooperating with authorities. Second, the organization must take action to avert the potential for such criminal conduct to reoccur by employing the steps set forth in subsections (b)(5) and (c), which may include the "use of an outside professional advisor to ensure adequate assessment and implementation of any modifications."

[284] New Compliance Counsel Expert Retained by the DOJ Fraud Section, *available at* https://www.justice.gov/criminal-fraud/file/790236/download (last accessed Dec. 28, 2016).

[285] 63 Fed. Reg. 45076 (1998).

[286] 63 Fed. Reg. 42410 (1998).

[287] 63 Fed. Reg. 8987 (1998); *see also* 70 Fed. Reg. 4858 (2005) (Supplemental Guidance).

[288] 64 Fed. Reg. 36368 (1999).

[289] 64 Fed. Reg. 61893 (1999).

6. third-party medical-billing companies;[290]
7. skilled nursing facilities;[291]
8. hospices;[292]
9. ambulance providers;[293]
10. individual physicians and small group practices;[294]
11. pharmaceutical manufacturers;[295] and
12. recipients of National Institutes of Health research grants.[296]

Each of the OIG's compliance program guidances is structured around the seven elements delineated in the Federal Sentencing Guidelines. Although adoption of a compliance plan solely based upon a compliance program guidance generally is not mandatory, providers interested in voluntarily implementing a compliance program should incorporate these basic elements into their own individually tailored programs. Adoption of a voluntary compliance program is becoming a requirement in a few settings such as Medicare Advantage Plans as well as by state Medicaid programs (e.g., New York).

Although the first document that the OIG published on corporate compliance programs (which was related to the clinical laboratory industry) referred to the document as being a "model" corporate compliance program, the OIG recognized that no one document can—or should—serve as a "model" for an entire segment of the health care industry. Therefore, the OIG now refers to these documents as "guidance," and has stated that the document itself is not a compliance program, but rather is a statement of the OIG's notions on the basic procedural and structural elements to be included in an organization's compliance program.

To this end, within each such guidance, the OIG sets forth its general views on the value and fundamental principles of corporate compliance programs, then provides specific elements that it believes should be considered by an organization when developing and implementing a compliance program.

5.8.3 Corporate Integrity Agreements

Even though a provider may deny that it has committed any wrongdoing in connection with a health care fraud investigation, the provider may agree to enter into a settlement agreement with the government in order to avoid lengthy and uncertain litigation arising out of such investigations by the federal government. As part of the settlement agreement, the OIG often will agree not to seek to exclude the health care provider from participation in the federal health care programs so long as

---

[290] 63 Fed. Reg. 70138 (1998).
[291] 65 Fed. Reg. 14289 (2000); *see also* 73 Fed Reg. 56832 (2008) (Supplemental Guidance).
[292] 64 Fed. Reg. 54031 (1999).
[293] 68 Fed. Reg. 14245 (2003).
[294] 65 Fed. Reg. 36818 (2000).
[295] 68 Fed. Reg. 23731 (2003).
[296] 70 Fed. Reg. 71312 (2005) (Draft OIG Program Guidance).

the provider agrees to a number of obligations concerning the establishment and maintenance of a compliance program.

Originally, these compliance obligations were included as a section of a global settlement agreement among the health care provider, DOJ, and the OIG. Currently, however, the settlement-negotiation process is bifurcated, whereby the health care provider enters into two separate agreements: (1) a settlement agreement with DOJ; and (2) a CIA with the OIG. Although such agreements with the OIG are generally referred to as CIAs, some organizations have entered into similar agreements with the OIG referred to by a different name.

CIAs outline certain obligations that the health care provider agrees to undergo in order to establish an effective compliance program. CIAs typically address the seven core elements of an effective compliance program, which track the Sentencing Guidelines. For example, the more comprehensive CIAs require that the organization:

- hire a compliance officer/appoint a compliance committee;
- implement Board of Director compliance obligations;
- develop written standards and policies;
- implement a comprehensive employee training program;
- review claims submitted to federal health care programs;
- establish a confidential disclosure program; and
- restrict employment of ineligible persons.[297]

CIAs also include a number of notification and reporting requirements, such as notification to the OIG of any ongoing investigations or legal proceedings conducted or brought by a governmental entity. When an entity subject to a CIA discovers that an overpayment may have occurred, it may be required to make certain notifications to payers and complete specific forms for submission to Medicare Carriers and/or Intermediaries. CIAs also require that if the entity determines that it has engaged in an event that would constitute a "Reportable Event," then it must disclose the event to the OIG within certain timeframes (i.e., within 30 days).

Providers also are required to submit to the OIG an initial "Implementation Report" and then subsequent "Annual Reports" concerning the status of and findings regarding the entity's compliance activities. All such reports submitted to the OIG must include a certification by the organization's compliance officer that the organization is in compliance with all of the CIA's requirements, and that the information in the report being submitted is "accurate and truthful." Consequently, as this certification is being made by compliance officers "under penalty of perjury," it is extremely important that, from the inception of the CIA, the compliance officers develop procedures to ensure that they are confident that all of the CIA's requirements have been satisfied. Therefore, as CIAs generally require that all "Covered Persons" (which includes not only the health care entity's employees, but also its contractors/agents and [for hospitals] members of the hospital's medical staff) receive training, it

---

[297] Copies of various CIAs are *available online at* https://oig.hhs.gov/compliance/corporate-integrity-agreements/index.asp.

will be necessary that the compliance officers have a process by which they can attest that all such covered persons have, in fact, received training.

CIAs reveal that the OIG believes boards of directors of health care companies should be more involved in the organization's corporate compliance programs. Specifically, a number of CIAs require that a Board of Directors (or the relevant Board committee) meet quarterly to review and oversee the companies' compliance with federal health care programs requirements and laws, FDA laws and requirements, the obligations of the CIA, and the corporate compliance program. In addition, a number of CIAs require the Board of Directors to adopt resolutions specifying that the board or board committee has concluded, after a reasonable inquiry that the company has implemented "effective" compliance programs and that each individual member of the board or board committee must certify that he or she agrees with the board's resolution.[298]

The OIG has also begun requiring more from the Board of Directors in connection with oversight on quality of care issues. For example, a number of CIAs require the Board of Directors to: "(i) review the adequacy of the provider's system of internal controls, quality assurance monitoring, and patient care; (ii) ensure that provider's response to state, federal, internal, and external reports of quality of care is complete, thorough, and resolves the issues identified; and (iii) ensure that [the provider] adopts and implements policies and procedures that are designed to ensure that each individual cared for by a Covered Facility receives the highest practicable physical, mental, and psychosocial level of care attainable."[299]

---

[298] *See* Corporate Integrity Agreement between the OIG and Eli Lilly and Company (Jan. 2009), *available at* http://oig.hhs.gov/fraud/cia/agreements/eli_lilly_and_company_01142009.pdf; Corporate Integrity Agreement between the OIG and Cephalon, Inc. (Sept. 2008), *available at* http://oig.hhs.gov/fraud/cia/agreements/cephalon.pdf.

[299] *See e.g.*, Corporate Integrity Agreement between the OIG and Corona Care Convalescent Corporation (Mar. 2008), *available at* http://oig.hhs.gov/fraud/cia/agreements/corona_care_convalescent_corporation_03212008.pdf.

6

Tax-Exempt Issues

Bernadette M. Broccolo
McDermott, Will & Emery LLP

6.1   Introduction

This Chapter focuses primarily on the requirements for obtaining and maintaining exemption from federal income tax under § 501(c)(3) of the Internal Revenue Code (the Code). The Chapter will review the fundamental rules under § 501(c)(3). It will also explore briefly the application of those fundamental rules to mainstream health industry transactions and relationships, such as physician recruitment arrangements, physician practice acquisitions, physician and executive compensation, joint operating companies, use of taxable affiliates, and participation in joint ventures. The majority of the discussion will be devoted to tax exemption for hospitals and health systems, with only brief references to the exemption considerations applicable to other types of health organizations, such as health maintenance organizations (HMOs).

The tax-exemption considerations addressed in this Chapter must be in the forefront of the legal and strategic considerations addressed in planning and implementing transactions, and for relationships involving exempt health care organizations and either individuals or taxable entities, as well as in the development and implementation of corporate compliance programs.

This Chapter will not address related topics such as: (1) the rules on reporting obligations (e.g., Forms 990 and 990-T) and related public disclosure requirements;[1] (2) the rules governing the use of tax-exempt financing under Code §§ 103 and 145 by a § 501(c)(3) health care organization;[2] (3) the ability of a § 501(c)(3) health care organization to qualify for exemptions from state and local taxes (e.g., real estate and sales taxes); and (4) the interplay between § 501(c)(3) compliance and compliance with the federal and state fraud and abuse laws. These related topics will also need to be considered in many circumstances in which § 501(c)(3) tax-exemption issues arise.

---

[1] Section 6.2.3.5 of this Chapter discusses revisions to Form 990, *Return of Organization Exempt from Income Tax*, the annual information return filed by many § 501(c)(3) organizations, particularly tax-exempt health care organizations.
[2] Worth noting, however, is that Section 501(c)(3) tax-exempt organizations that have outstanding tax-exempt bonds should be aware of the issuance of Revenue Ruling 2017-13, which provides new guidance and establishes a new safe harbor for avoiding prohibited private use of assets financed with tax-exempt bond proceeds. Violation of the private use prohibition can result in catastrophic consequences, such as loss of federal income tax-exemption for interest on such bonds. Revenue Procedure 2017-13 replaces the prior guidance and safe harbor set forth in Revenue Procedure 97-13, is more flexible in some ways and more limiting in other ways than Revenue Procedure 97-13, and will have important private use compliance planning implications.

6.1.1 Benefits of Section 501(c)(3) Tax-Exempt Status

Qualifying for and maintaining tax-exempt status under Code § 501(c)(3) offers several important benefits to health care organizations. First and foremost, a § 501(c)(3) tax-exempt organization is exempt from paying federal income tax on its net income. Second, and also quite significant, is the eligibility to borrow funds by issuing tax-exempt bonds under § 103 of the Code, which can be more cost effective than commercial (and taxable) financing alternatives. Third, § 501(c)(3) organizations are more attractive to donors than other forms of federal tax-exempt organizations because a donor's contributions to § 501(c)(3) organizations qualify for charitable deductions. Fourth, having § 501(c)(3) status can enhance an organization's ability to qualify in some states and localities for exemption from taxes such as property tax and sales tax.

6.1.2 Public Charity Status

Every organization that is exempt under § 501(c)(3) is considered a private foundation unless it is described in § 509(a)(1), (2), (3) or (4) of the Code. Organizations described in §§ 509(a)(1), (2), (3) or (4) are commonly referred to "public charities" or "non-private foundations." Generally an organization is presumed to be a private foundation even if it meets the requirement for public charity status unless it gives timely notice to the Internal Revenue Service (IRS) that it is not a private foundation. An organization usually gives such notice at the same time as it files for tax-exempt status under Code § 501(c)(3) (discussed further below).

Disadvantages of being classified as a private foundation include exposure to restrictions and excise taxes on net investment income, excess business holdings, and "self-dealing" between private foundations and disqualified persons; mandatory distributions of income for charitable purposes; filing with the IRS of additional and more detailed reports of financial matters and activities; and less advantageous charitable deduction rules for donors.

6.1.3 Recurring Concepts

The following are the fundamental concepts and terms that will appear frequently in this Chapter's discussion of the requirements for obtaining and maintaining § 501(c)(3) tax-exempt status: (1) exempt purpose and the "community benefit" standard; (2) unrelated business income tax (UBIT); (3) stand-alone exempt status; (4) integral-part exempt status; (5) private inurement; (6) more-than-incidental private benefit; and (7) public charity status.

6.2 Exemption Requirements—Generally

To qualify for tax-exempt status under § 501(c)(3) of the Code, an organization must be *organized* and *operated* exclusively for religious, charitable, scientific, literary, educational, or other specified purposes.

6.2.1 The Organizational Test

An organization is organized exclusively for one or more exempt purposes only if its articles of organization:

(a) Limit the purposes of such organization to one or more exempt purposes;

(b) Do not expressly empower the organization to engage, other than as an insubstantial part of its activities, in activities which in themselves are not in furtherance of one or more exempt purposes;

(c) Do not expressly empower the organization to:

　(i) Devote more than an insubstantial part of its activities to attempting to influence legislation by propaganda or otherwise;

　(ii) Directly or indirectly participate or intervene in (including the publishing or distributing of statements) any political campaign on behalf of or in opposition to any candidate for public office; or

　(iii) Have objectives and engage in activities that characterize it as an "action" organization; and

(d) Permit distribution of the organization's assets, upon dissolution, only for one or more exempt purposes or to the federal, state or local government for a public purpose, or as may otherwise be determined by a court of competent jurisdiction.[3]

These organizational requirements typically are not difficult to meet, and do not become an ongoing compliance issue following the initial filing of the articles of organizations with the relevant secretary of state. However, careful drafting of the organization's articles, bylaws and other governing documents is essential.

6.2.2　The Operational Test

The operational test is more complex and comprehensive, and presents significant challenges for monitoring an organization's day-to-day activities so as to ensure continued compliance with the requirements of exempt status under Code § 501(c)(3). The Operational Test requires that: (1) the organization engage primarily in activities that further one or more recognized exempt purposes (the exempt purposes requirement);[4] (2) such activities serve a public rather than a private purpose (the public benefit requirement);[5] (3) no part of the net earnings of the organization may inure to the benefit of any private shareholder or individual (the prohibition against private inurement); and (4) the organization may not engage in political activity, and no more than an insubstantial part of its activities may be to influence legislation (the political activity prohibition and lobbying limitation).

6.2.3　The Exempt Purposes Requirement

6.2.3.1　*Stand-Alone Exemption—The Community Benefit Standard*

Although the Code and Treasury Regulations do not identify the provision of health care as an exempt purpose, the IRS has recognized that the provision of health care may further charitable

---

[3] Treas. Reg. § 1.501(c)(3)-1(b)(1), (2), (3), and (4).
[4] Treas. Reg. § 1.501(c)(3)-1(c)(1).
[5] Treas. Reg. § 1.501(c)(3)-1(d)(1)(ii).

purposes in certain circumstances. In 1969, the IRS issued Revenue Ruling 69-545,[6] which recognized that the promotion of health is one of the purposes in the general law of charity that is deemed beneficial to the community as a whole even though the class of beneficiaries eligible to receive a direct benefit from its activities does not include all members of the community, such as indigent members of the community, provided that the class is not so small that its relief does not benefit the community.[7]

This 1969 community benefit standard remains the principal standard applied by the IRS today, in determining whether a health care organization qualifies as "charitable."[8] The standard derives primarily from the fact pattern set out in Situation 1 in Revenue Ruling 69-545. In Situation 1, the IRS concluded that the hospital was operated primarily for the promotion of health, and satisfied the community benefit standard because it: (1) operated an emergency room open to all persons regardless of ability to pay; (2) provided hospital care in non-emergency situations for everyone able to pay the cost thereof, either directly or through third-party reimbursement (e.g., private health insurance or public programs such as Medicare or Medicaid); (3) was governed by a board of directors composed of independent civic leaders;[9] (4) extended medical-staff privileges to all qualified physicians in the area; (5) conducted all transactions with its medical staff on an arm's-length basis; and (6) applied any surplus receipts to improving facilities, equipment, patient care, medical training, education, and research.[10]

An organization is not required to establish the presence of all of the factors in Revenue Ruling 69-545 for the organization to satisfy the community benefit standard. The organization must, however, establish the presence of significant factors demonstrating that the organization promotes the health of a class of persons that is broad enough so that the community as a whole benefits. One highly significant factor is an emergency room that is open to all persons, regardless of their ability to pay. In Revenue Ruling 83-157,[11] however, the IRS ruled that a hospital could be tax-exempt despite its lack of an emergency room, provided either that the appropriate governmental health agency has determined that the hospital's emergency room would unnecessarily duplicate other emergency services in the community or that the hospital is specialized and treats conditions that do not require emergency treatment.

The IRS also has identified having a board of trustees comprised of prominent citizens drawn from the community as a significant factor in determining whether hospitals and other health care organizations qualify for § 501(c)(3) status.[12] In the early to mid-1990s, the IRS took the position

---

[6] 1969-2 C.B. 117.
[7] *Id*.
[8] *See* Lawrence M. Brauer, Mary Jo Salins, and Robert Fontenrose, "Update on Health Care," *IRS Exempt Organizations Continuing Professional Education Technical Instruction Program for Fiscal Year 2002*, at 171.
[9] *See, e.g.*, Private Letter Ruling 201744019 (dated August 7, 2017, released November 3, 2017), in which the IRS revoked the § 501(c)(3) status of a rural hospital organization based on the finding that, through the terms of a lease arrangement with an unrelated for-profit entity, the organization's board had ceded complete control over the hospital's operation to the for-profit entity and maintained only an advisory role. Authority cited in support of this ruling included *Est of Hawaii v. Commissioner*, 71 T.C. 1067 (1979), *aff'd* in unpublished opinion 647 F.2d 170 (9th Cir. 1981); *Harding Hospital, Inc. v. United States*, 505 F.2d 1068 (6th Cir. 1974); and Rev. Rul. 98-15, 1998-1 C.B. 718.
[10] *See also* IRS Exempt Organization Handbook (IRM 7751) §§ 349.1(2), 349.2(2), and 349.4(2).
[11] 1983-2 C.B. 94.
[12] Rev. Rul. 69-545, 1969-2 C.B. 17.

that *no more than 20%* of the governing board of a tax-exempt entity formed to operate a physician practice could be comprised of a combination of disinterested persons, including both officers and physicians. In 1996, however, the IRS liberalized its position in its announcement of the following three criteria for demonstrating appropriate community representation on the board: (a) a majority of the voting members of the organization's board are independent community members; (b) the organization has a conflict-of-interest policy applicable to transactions or arrangements with interested persons;[13] and (c) the board and all committees with board-delegated powers, as part of their systems of controls, conduct periodic reviews of the organization's activities to ensure that it is operating for community benefit, rather than private interests, in areas such as compensation arrangements, practice acquisitions, and joint ventures.[14]

At the same time, the IRS also took the following position regarding physician-controlled boards of entities created as subsidiaries of exempt parent organizations:

"In a multi-entity hospital system, the board of a subsidiary non-profit health care organization is considered to be comprised of independent community members if it is controlled by an exempt organization whose board is comprised of a majority of voting members who are independent community members."[15]

In 2000, the IRS expanded this concept of a "derived community board" by applying it in the context of professional corporations (PCs) seeking tax-exemption in those states with strict corporate practice of medicine prohibitions. More specifically, tax-exempt hospitals located in states with strict corporate practice of medicine prohibitions had difficulty forming tax-exempt hospital affiliated group practices because the states in which such hospitals were located required such group practices to be established as PCs, but the IRS would not grant exemption to PCs because of the organizational structure of such entities. In order to rectify this problem, the IRS released a position in which it would agree to recognize tax-exempt hospital affiliated PCs as described in § 501(c)(3) of the Code if certain conditions were satisfied. With respect to board composition, the IRS stated that while the board members of the PCs may be physicians (as required under state law), the community board of the tax-exempt parent must retain and exercise reserved powers that are sufficient to ensure that the PC's activities always accomplish charitable purposes and avoid inurement and private benefit, including the right to: (1) elect, appoint, remove and change the number of the directors; (2) amend, alter or repeal the articles of incorporation and bylaws; and (3) approve significant actions including (a) the annual operating and capital budgets and material deviations from such budgets, (b) the sale, lease, mortgage or other transfer or encumbrance of real or certain valuable personal property; (c) the merger, acquisition, consolidation, liquidation, or dissolution; (d) the settlements of claims and litigation; and (e) the selection of auditors.[16]

---

[13] For the model conflicts policy the IRS has recommended for use by exempt organizations, *see* Instructions to Form 1023 (Rev. June 2006) at http://www.irs.gov/pub/irs-pdf/i1023.pdf, which replaces the model policy first published by the IRS in Lawrence M. Brauer and Charles F. Kaiser III, "Tax-Exempt Healthcare Organizations Revised Conflict of Interest Policy," *IRS Exempt Organizations Continuing Professional Education Technical Instruction Program for Fiscal Year 2000*, at 45 (1999).

[14] Lawrence M. Brauer and Charles F. Kaiser, "Tax-Exempt Healthcare Organizations Community Board and Conflicts of Interest Policy," *IRS Exempt Organizations Continuing Professional Education Technical Instruction Program for Fiscal Year 1997*, at 18 (1996).

[15] 1997 CPE Textbook, at 21.

[16] Fiscal Year 2000 CPE Textbook at 58.

In February 2008, the IRS released a set of governance guidelines for tax-exempt organizations expanding the IRS's guidelines first released in 2007,[17] which updated and clarified in a significant way the IRS's position that a well-governed charity is more likely to obey the tax laws, safeguard charitable assets, and serve charitable interests than one with poor or lax governance. In particular, the guidelines shed light on the IRS's view on important governance-related issues, including (1) the importance of an "active and engaged" board (and how such diligence can be demonstrated); (2) issues associated with boards that are either "too small" or "too large"; (3) director/committee member independence;[18] (4) the benefits associated with the adoption of formal governance policies; (5) the need for boards to exercise oversight of sophisticated investment vehicles—including both joint ventures with for profit entities, as well as complicated and sophisticated financial products or investments and use of competent financial advisors; and (6) executive compensation as a continuing area of IRS focus—including with respect to such matters as the expertise of compensation committee members, the independence of the compensation committee consultant, and the emphasis on accurate and reliable comparability data.[19]

6.2.3.2 Stand-Alone Exemption—Charity Care as a Consideration Under the Community Benefit Standard

Prior to 1969, a hospital's charitable purpose was based on its provision of relief to the poor. Revenue Ruling 56-185[20] sets forth the pre-1969 requirements for a hospital to qualify as a § 501(c)(3) charitable organization. The requirements included, among others, that the hospital (1) operate to the extent of its financial ability for persons who are unable to pay for hospital services rendered, and not exclusively for persons who are able and expected to pay; and (2) generally accept patients who need

---

[17] See "Governance and Related Topics–501(c)(3) Organizations," released February 4, 2008, *available at* http://www.irs.gov/pub/irs-tege/governance_practices.pdf at 1. The IRS had previously released proposed, suggested governance guidelines for tax-exempt organizations in early 2007. The proposed guidelines addressed the following nine general areas: (1) Adoption of a Mission Statement; (2) Adoption of a Code of Ethics and whistleblower policies; (3) Satisfaction for the Duty of Care/Director Diligence; (4) Satisfaction of the Duty of Loyalty/effective conflicts of interest oversight; (5) Constituent transparency; (6) Oversight of fund-raising activity; (7) Stewardship of financial affairs; (8) Payment of reasonable compensation; and (9) Adoption of a document retention policy. *See* "Good Governance Practices for 501(c)(3) Organizations," 1–4, released February 2007, *available at* http://www.mwe.com/info/news/IRS0207.pdf.

[18] The Form 990 Annual Information Return that Section 501(c)(3) organizations are required to file requires disclosure of the number of an organization's "independent" directors. The Form 990 instructions provide a definition of independence for purposes of this disclosure and emphasize that independence and conflict of interest are distinguishable concepts. The Form 990 also requires disclosure of business, family, and other relationships between and among the organization's board members and between and among its board members and officers and other key employees. While such "intra-board/officer" relationships are not technically encompassed within the Form 990's definition of "independence," they are likely to be considered relevant by the IRS in an overall determination of whether an organization's board is representative of a broad public interest, not dominated by employees or others who are likely to be influenced by certain types of individual interests or relationships, and capable of exercising meaningful, unbiased judgment in the exercise of its fiduciary duty.

[19] "Governance and Related Topics," *supra* at 2–5. For additional insight into how the IRS evaluates and examines the governance practices of tax-exempt organizations, *see* "IRS Governance Check Sheet" and the supplemental "Guide Sheet" released by the IRS on December 9, 2009, which can be found at http://www.irs.gov/pub/irs-tege/governance_check_sheet.pdf. The IRS released an informative set of guidelines to assist its agents in the course of examining the governance of tax-exempt organizations. The guidelines include both a "Governance Check Sheet" to be compiled by the agent and a supplementary "Guide Sheet" for the agent to use when completing the check sheet. The new examination guidelines highlight practices likely to be viewed with suspicion or concern by the IRS, such as whether persons with conflicts of interest participate in executive compensation decisions (Question 13 of the check sheet).

[20] 1956-1 C.B. 202.

hospital services, but could not pay for those services. Although this ruling was replaced in 1969, a hospital's care for patients without charge or at below-cost rates remains a factor that demonstrates to the IRS that a hospital promotes health to benefit the community. Unless a hospital did not operate an emergency room, however, the extent to which a health care organization has adopted and implemented a charity-care policy has not, since 1969, been considered as a relevant criteria in determining a hospital's § 501(c)(3) tax-exempt status. The IRS and the courts have instead recognized not-for-profit hospitals as § 501(c)(3) organizations because they further the charitable purpose of promoting the health of the community and they do not operate as proprietary entities.[21]

Despite the absence of charity care as a criterion in Revenue Ruling 69-545, the IRS directed its examination agents in early 2001 to ask a series of questions relating to free and discounted care practices when reviewing the tax-exempt status of a hospital, including the amount of charity care that the hospital actually provides.[22] Among the questions were issues such as: (1) whether the hospital has a specific, written plan or policy to provide free or low-cost health care services to the poor or indigent; (2) under what circumstances might the hospital deviate (or has the hospital deviated) from its stated policies to provide free or low-cost health care services to the poor or indigent; (3) what directives or instructions does the hospital provide to ambulance services about bringing poor or indigent patients to its emergency room; and (4) what documents or agreements must the poor or indigent patients sign before receiving care from the hospital? Worth noting is that Revenue Ruling 69-545 is legally binding on the IRS, while the Field Service Advice Memorandum is not. Nonetheless, the Field Service Memorandum is indicative of the IRS administrative and enforcement mindset at the time it was issued.

The relevance of charity care to a hospital's tax-exempt status was addressed in various contexts since 2001, such as congressional hearings and proposals on tax exemption policy and enforcement, congressional and IRS surveys or "soft contact" audits eliciting information on charity care practices from hundreds of hospitals nation-wide, class action litigation initiated in both federal and state courts, and state attorney general inquiries into hospital charity care practices. The discussion and debate that occurred in these contexts culminated in an overhaul of the Form 990 annual information return filed by tax-exempt organizations,[23] and the adoption of Code § 501(r). While Revenue Ruling 69-545 itself has not been revisited, the Form 990 changes and adoption of § 501(r) demonstrate that charity care and other financial assistance practices will be considered administratively by the IRS in its assessment of the community benefit achieved by exempt health care organizations.

Over 40 years after Revenue Rule 69-545, Congress added requirements that overlay the community benefit standard through the Patient Protection and Affordable Care Act (ACA), the federal health reform legislation enacted on March 23, 2010.[24] Section 501(r) imposes several additional requirements on exempt "hospitals" described in § 501(c)(3) of the Code.[25] Now, *in addition to* complying with the general requirements set forth above, tax-exempt hospitals must: (1) conduct

---

[21] "Update on Health Care," at 172–73.
[22] Field Service Advice No. 200110030 (Feb. 5, 2001).
[23] Please refer to Section 6.2.3.3 for a discussion regarding the revisions to Form 990.
[24] Pub. L. No. 111-148, 124 Stat. 119 (2010), § 9007. The Treasury Department requested comments regarding these new requirements by July 22, 2010. Notice 2010-39, 2010-24 I.R.B. 756.
[25] Patient Protection and Affordable Care Act, Pub. L. 111-148, § 9007(a), 124 Stat. 1035.

a community health needs assessment[26] at least once every three years, adopt an implementation strategy for meeting the needs the assessment identifies, and make the assessment widely available to the public; (2) adopt, publicize and make widely available its financial assistance policy;[27] (3) restrict charges for emergency or medically necessary care provided to patients eligible under the financial assistance policy to no more than the lowest amounts generally charged to insured patients and refrain from using gross charges; and (4) take "reasonable efforts"[28] to determine if a patient qualifies for financial assistance before initiating "extraordinary" collection actions (e.g., referral to collection agencies).[29] These requirements apply for tax years beginning after the ACA's enactment date.[30] The ACA also added § 4959 to the Code, which provides for the imposition of excise taxes for failure to meet the community health needs assessment requirement. Failure to comply with these requirements of § 501(r) may also result in loss of exemption under § 501(c)(3) at either the entity level or at the hospital-specific level.

On December 31, 2014, the IRS issued final regulations implementing Section 501(r).[31] The final regulations are effective for tax years beginning after December 29, 2015. While the final regulations adopt the same framework as, and mirror most of the requirements set forth in, the proposed regulations issued in 2012[32] and 2013,[33] they are intended to simplify the compliance process for charitable hospitals.[34]

In the Spring of 2015, the IRS and Treasury Department also issued Revenue Procedure 2015-21 to describe the process for correcting and disclosing certain Section 501(r) compliance failures which will assist charitable hospital organizations in avoiding significant penalties for violating § 501(r)'s requirements. Notably, the benefits of these correction and disclosure procedures do not apply to errors first identified by the IRS, unless the hospital's Form 990 for the applicable tax period was not yet due (which could be significant given the length of available extensions) and the hospital has already begun correcting its failure.

The ACA requires the IRS to review every tax-exempt hospital's compliance with Section 501(r) once every three years. The IRS selected approximately four hundred tax-exempt hospitals for the

---

[26] The community health needs assessment must incorporate input from a broad cross-section of the community the hospital serves, including those with knowledge and expertise in public health.

[27] The financial assistance policy must incorporate eligibility criteria for financial assistance and address the extent to which such assistance includes free or discounted care, the basis for calculating patient charges, how to apply for financial assistance, and how the policy will be publicly publicized. It must also commit the hospital to provide non-discriminatory emergency medical care, regardless of whether the individual is eligible for assistance under the policy.

[28] The definition of "reasonable efforts" is not included in the statute and will be developed by implementing regulations.

[29] These new requirements are set forth in new Internal Revenue Code § 501(r) and apply for tax years beginning after the Act's enactment date. For example, if a tax-exempt hospital's fiscal year ends on April 30, then these requirements would apply beginning as of May 1, 2010.

[30] For example, if a tax-exempt hospital's fiscal year ends on April 30, then these requirements would apply beginning as of May 1, 2010.

[31] "Additional Requirements for Charitable Hospitals; Community Health Needs Assessments for Charitable Hospitals; Requirement of a Section 4959 Excise Tax Return and Time for Filing the Return," 79 Fed. Reg. 78953.

[32] 77 Fed. Reg. 38148.

[33] 78 Fed. Reg. 20523. Comments on the proposed regulations were due to the IRS by July 5, 2013.

[34] For reporting prior to promulgation of the final regulations, hospitals should be allowed to rely on reasonable interpretations of the actual statute for compliance and should not be subjected to an adverse determination based on the final regulations that had not yet been issued or on proposed regulations which were not binding.

initial round of Section 501(r) audits in 2017. The IRS also officially announced the first hospital revocation under the new Section 501(r) regime on August 4, 2017.[35] The IRS revocation letter references the hospital's failure to have its community health needs assessment approved by the hospital board within the applicable three-year period in which a CHNA was due, to prepare and approve a CHNA implementation strategy, and to make its CHNA "widely available" to the public. According to the IRS revocation letter, hospital representatives informed the IRS during the course of the audit of their intent not to comply with Section 501(r) due to a lack of sufficient resources and the fact that the hospital enjoyed tax-exempt status both as a 501(c)(3) charitable organization and a Section 115 governmental entity. This dual exempt status presents unusual facts and circumstances that may limit the value of this revocation case as guidance regarding the IRS's Section 501(r) enforcement posture.

6.2.3.3 Stand-Alone Exemption—Application of the Community Benefit Standard to Other than Hospitals and Other than Direct Providers of Health Care

While Revenue Ruling 69-545 involved a hospital, the community benefit standard generally applies to any health care organization that seeks tax-exempt status under § 501(c)(3) of the Code. Other types of health care organizations to which the IRS has applied the community benefit standard include HMOs,[36] physician practice organizations,[37] hospices,[38] home health agencies,[39] and fitness centers.[40]

Further, the fact that an organization does not provide health care services will not necessarily preclude it from qualifying as a § 501(c)(3) organization under the "community benefit standard."[41]

---

[35] Priv. Ltr. Rul. 201731014 (8/4/2017).

[36] See Sound Health Ass'n v. Commissioner, 71 T.C. 158 (1978), acq. 1981-2 C.B. 2. Compare, Geisinger Health Plan v. Commissioner, 985 F.2d 1210 (3d Cir. 1993); IHC Health Plans v. Commissioner, Op. No. 01-9013 (10th Cir. 2003); 82 T.C.M. (CCH) 593 (2001); Internal Revenue Manual [7.8.1] 27.8. HMOs may also qualify for tax-exemption as social welfare organizations under Code § 501(c)(4). Code § 501(m), however, precludes tax-exempt status under either § 501(c)(3) or § 501(c)(4) if the organization provides commercial-type insurance as a substantial part of its activities. See also "Update on Health Care," at 155–58; Lawrence M. Brauer and Roderick Darling, "Update on Health Care," IRS Exempt Organizations Continuing Professional Education Technical Instruction Program for Fiscal Year 2001, at 59–65 (2000); Internal Revenue Manual [7.8.7] Chapter 27.

[37] See, e.g., University of Maryland Physicians, P.A., v. Commissioner, 41 T.C.M. (CCH) 732 (1981); University of Massachusetts Med. Sch. Group Practice v. Commissioner, 74 T.C. 1299 (1980); B.H.W. Anesthesia Found. v. Commissioner, 72 T.C. 681 (1979); Physicians Network P.C., IRS Determination Letter (Oct. 23, 1996): Marietta Health Care Physicians, Inc., IRS Determination Letter (Oct. 3, 1995); C.H. Wilkinson Physician Network, IRS Determination Letter (June 19, 1996). See also Charles F. Kaiser and John F. Reilly, "Integrated Delivery Systems," IRS Exempt Organizations Continuing Professional Education Technical Instruction Program for Fiscal Year 1994 at 212 (1993).

[38] See Rev. Rul. 79-19, 1979-1 C.B.193.

[39] See Rev. Rul. 72-209, 1972-1 C.B. 148 (freestanding home health agency); Rev. Rul. 68-375, 1968-2 C.B. 246 (hospital-based home health agency).

[40] See, e.g., Tech. Adv. Mem. 9803001 (June 30, 1997). See also "Update on Health Care," at 163–67; Virginia Richardson, Roderick Darling and Marvin Friedlander, "Health Clubs," IRS Exempt Organizations Continuing Professional Education Technical Instruction Program for Fiscal Year 2000 at 1 (1999).

[41] The "community benefit standard" for exemption is set forth generally in Rev. Rul. 69-545, 1969-2 C.B. 117. In this ruling, the IRS determined the following factors may demonstrate that a health care organization benefits the community rather than serving private interests and, therefore, qualifies for exemption under § 501(c)(3) of the Code: (a) operating a full-time emergency room which provides treatment regardless of patients' ability to pay; (b) providing non-emergency services to all individuals who are able to pay for those services, including Medicare and Medicaid beneficiaries; (c) having an open medical staff whose members deal with the organization only on an arms'-length basis; (d) having a board of directors composed of independent civic leaders drawn from the community (rather than physicians, administrators, or others with a private interest in the organization) (described in more detail below); and (e) using any operational surplus

Stated otherwise, the direct provision of medical, hospital, or nursing care to individuals is *not* the exclusive means by which an organization can establish that it promotes health for the benefit of the community within the meaning of § 501(c)(3). The IRS has ruled that the following organizations promoted health for the benefit of the community within the meaning of § 501(c)(3) of the Code despite the fact that they provided no direct health care services: professional standards review organizations (PSROs);[42] health planning agencies;[43] an organization that constructed a hospital and leased it to a public entity to operate the hospital;[44] an organization operating a free computerized donor authorized retrieval system to facilitate the transplantation of body organs;[45] and a regional health data system formed to conduct studies and propose improvements regarding quality, utilization and effectiveness of health care and health care agencies and to educate those involved in furnishing, administering and financing health care.[46]

In contrast, in the mid-1990s, the IRS characterized physician-hospital organizations (referred to as "PHOs") as an "independent practice association" with a hospital participant formed for the purpose of arranging with managed care payers (e.g., insurance companies or employers), on behalf of the participants in the PHO, to provide physician or hospital care.[47] The IRS characterized a PHO as a "joint marketing arrangement." The IRS stated that a PHO will not qualify for *stand-alone* § 501(c)(3) status because: (a) it does not engage in the practice of medicine or operate a hospital; and (b) despite the hospital's participation, the PHOs primary beneficiaries are its member-physicians rather than the community as a whole (citing Rev. Rul. 86-98, 1986-2 C.B. 74) and its activities are substantially devoted to serving those physicians' interests (and thus cannot satisfy the private inurement or private benefit prohibitions of § 501(c)(3)).[48]

---

to further the organization's exempt purposes by improving the quality of patient care and advancing the organization's medical training, education and research programs.

[42] Rev. Rul. 81-276, 1981-2 C.B. 128 (The PSRO was formed pursuant to the mandate of the Social Security Act Amendments of 1972 and designated to review medical necessity of services billed under the Medicare program. DHHS fully funded the PSRO. The IRS ruled that the organization promoted the health of the community by reducing overutilization and relieving the burdens of government.)

[43] Rev. Rul. 76-455, 1976-2 C.B. 150.

[44] Rev. Rul. 80-309, 1980-2 C.B. 183.

[45] Rev. Rul. 75-197, 1975-1 C.B. 156 ("[b]y facilitating the donation of organs which will be used to save lives, the organization is serving the health needs of the community and, therefore, is promoting health within the meaning of the general law of charity").

[46] Revenue Ruling 76-455 (Specifically, the organization furnished aid for the development of uniform health data record-keeping and reporting procedures, and conducted related studies and educational programs. The data gathered was useful for reviewing patient management patterns, planning for regional and community health needs, and conducting epidemiological research. The members of the organization were other not-for-profit health information organizations, but the health data system maintained by the organization was open to everyone on a free, non-discriminatory basis. The IRS ruled that organization in this ruling was exempt as an organization that was organized and operated primarily for scientific and educational purposes under § 501(c)(3). Nonetheless, the facts and circumstances would be persuasive in making the case for exemption under the community benefit theory for exemption as a charitable organization under § 501(c)(3)).

[47] Charles F. Kaiser, Phyllis D. Haney and T. J. Sullivan, "Integrated Delivery and Joint Venture Dissolution Update," *IRS Exempt Organization Continuing Professional Education Technical Instruction Program for Fiscal Year 1995*, 153 (1994) (hereinafter "1995 CPE Text").

[48] This position is restated by the IRS in its 1996 CPE Text at 401. The 1995 CPE Text also states that a PHO will not qualify for *integral part exempt* status because negotiating managed care contracts for the member-physicians is a substantial activity of the PHO and such activity is not an essential service to the hospital participant in the PHO. In a tax exemption determination letter issued to a PHO affiliate of the University of Kansas Medical Center, however, the IRS granted 501(c)(3) status to a PHO with faculty practice plan characteristics. *See* Charles F. Kaiser and T. J. Sullivan,

Like PHOs, accountable care organizations (ACOs) typically do not provide health care services, but instead serve to bring together tax-exempt organizations and private persons in a common health care related endeavor. In contrast to PHOs, however, ACOs are intended to create and maintain a structure for bringing providers together to define common clinical standards, modify practice patterns, create a high degree of integration and cooperation among health care providers in the delivery of health care, and establish accountability of providers for quality and cost of health care—all for the purpose of improving the efficiency and effectiveness of care, patient experience, and population health.

As further discussed in Section 6.2.3.4 below, in IRS Notice 2011-20, the IRS recognized ACOs that participate in the Medicare Shared Savings Program (MSSP) that meet the eligibility requirements established by the Centers for Medicare & Medicaid Services (CMS) as eligible for exemption under § 501(c)(3) of the Code under the "lessening the burdens of government" theory, but the IRS did not address their eligibility under the "promotion of health" theory.[49] The IRS also acknowledged that ACOs may conduct non-MSSP activities by engaging in shared savings arrangements with health insurance payers other than Medicare (non-MSSP activities), but did not offer guidance on whether such non-MSSP activities are eligible for § 501(c)(3) exemption under either the § 501(c)(3) "lessening the burdens of government" or the "promotion of health" exemption theories. The Notice explained that the IRS did not have sufficient information to address whether non-MSSP ACO activities further exempt purposes and comply with the private inurement and private benefit doctrines, and requested comments on what guidance is needed for tax-exempt organizations that participate in shared savings arrangements with payers other than Medicare, such as commercial health insurers, managed care plans, and self-insured programs.[50] In its request for comments, the IRS acknowledged that promotion of health has long been recognized as a charitable purpose under § 501(c)(3); however, it also cautioned that comments should take into account two principles under existing law: (a) although the promotion of health has been recognized as a charitable purpose, not every activity

---

"Integrated Delivery Systems and Health Care Update," *IRS Exempt Organization Continuing Professional Education Technical Instruction Program for Fiscal Year 1996 (1995)* at 402; Peregrine, Michael W. and Broccolo, Bernadette M. *PHO Tax Planning Update*, THE EXEMPT ORGANIZATION TAX REVIEW, Vol. 11, No. 5 (1995). The faculty practice plan characteristics of this case make it relatively unique and limit its overall applicability.

[49] 2011-1 C.B. at 655; In support of this conclusion, Notice 2011-20 cites Rev. Rul. 81-276, which dealt with a PSRO established by federal statute to review whether the quality of health care services provided to the government's Medicare and Medicaid programs satisfied professionally recognized standards of care. Rev. Rul. 81-276 concluded that PSROs further the tax-exempt purpose of lessening the burdens of government. Interestingly, Notice 2011-20 does not address the "lessening the burdens of government" as an exempt purpose for ACOs that involve Medicaid patients, even though this was part of the basis for concluding that PSROs lessen the burdens of government in Rev. Rul. 81-276 (*i.e.*, PSROs reviewed health care provided to Medicaid patients as well as Medicare patients). *See also* Section 6.2.3.4 below for a further discussion of the lessening the burdens of government exemption theory. In addition, the IRS also suggests that if an ACO participates in non-MSSP activities involving Medicaid patients, the ACO may also be furthering the exempt purpose of "relieving the poor and distressed or the underprivileged." 2011-1 C.B. at 655.

[50] *See* IRS Tax Correspondence, ABA Members Request Additional Guidance on Accountable Care Organizations (Section 501 – Tax-Exempt Organizations), 4-5, July 23, 2013 (Doc 2013-17809) for a detailed discussion of the qualification of non-MSSP ACOs for tax-exempt status under § 501(c)(3). The defining feature of non-MSSP activities is that payers other than Medicare (*e.g.*, Medicaid, commercial health insurers, managed care plans, and self-insured programs) will be the source of incentive payments made to reduce cost and improve quality and patient satisfaction. Experience to date and emerging patterns of practice indicate that many ACO policies and procedures developed and used in the MSSP context will be adopted and used in the non-MSSP context. Other payers will have the very same interests as the MSSP in (i) establishing cost and quality performance standards, (ii) assessing ACO performance against such standards, (iii) assigning beneficiaries to the ACO, and (iv) determining when an ACO is eligible for shared savings incentives and the amount of such incentives.

that promotes health supports tax exemption under § 501(c)(3)[51] and (b) if a tax-exempt organization is a partner (or member, in the case of an LLC) of an ACO treated as a partnership for federal tax purposes, the ACO's activities will be attributed to the tax-exempt organization for purposes of determining both whether the organization operates exclusively for exempt purposes and whether it is engaged in an unrelated trade or business.[52]

Nonetheless, in April of 2016, the IRS released a denial of an application for § 501(c)(3) tax-exempt status for a non-MSSP ACO under both the lessening of the burdens of government and the promotion of health standards for exemption.[53] The IRS concluded that the non-MSSP activities did not qualify as charitable and that the ACO's structure and activities generated impermissible private benefit to its physician participants.[54] The denial letter does not discuss how the IRS applied existing law and standards under § 501(c)(3) to the facts and circumstances presented in the application as a basis for these conclusions or address whether under any circumstances activities undertaken primarily to achieve better coordination and management of health care costs promotes the health of the community. This adverse ruling casts doubt as to whether and on what basis the IRS will recognize other than MSSP activities of an ACO as eligible for treatment as § 501(c)(3) charitable activities under long-standing, well-established exemption laws and standards.[55]

6.2.3.4 Stand-Alone Exemption–Lessening the Burdens of Government

"Lessening the burdens of government" is an alternative to "promotion of health" as a basis for exemption under § 501(c)(3). While its applicability in the health care context is limited, it is a theory worth considering in the current, changing health care context.

Qualification for exemption as an organization described in § 501(c)(3) under a lessening the burdens of government rationale requires satisfaction of a two-part test. First, the organization seeking exemption must demonstrate an objective manifestation by a state or Federal government that the activities engaged in by the organization seeking exemption are a burden of government.[56] Second, the organization must demonstrate that its activities actually lessen such burden.[57]

1. PSROs.

The IRS has determined that a PSRO may qualify under § 501(c)(3) of the Code under the lessening the burdens of government theory.[58] In the ruling, the organization's membership was open

---

[51] *See* IHC Health Plans, 325 F.3d at 1197; Fed'n Pharmacy Serv., 72 T.C. at 691-92; Rev. Rul. 98-15.
[52] *See, e.g.*, Rev. Rul. 2004-51; Rev. Rul. 98-15.
[53] Private Letter Ruling 201615022 (dated January 15, 2016, released April 8, 2016).
[54] *See* Section 6.2.5 below for a discussion of the § 501(c)(3) public benefit requirement.
[55] Promptly following issuance of this adverse ruling, the American Hospital Association petitioned the IRS to issue guidance "affirming that hospitals may participate in ACOs without generating a tax cost or incurring the catastrophic loss of their tax-exempt status . . . to remove what appears to be a serious obstacle for nonprofit hospitals striving to coordinate care for their communities and make other improvements in delivering population health." American Heart Association Letter dated May 16, 2016, *available at* http://www.aha.org/advocacy-issues/letter/2016/160516-let-hatton-koskinen-mazur.pdf.
[56] Rev. Rul. 85-1, 1985-1 C.B. 178.
[57] *Id.*
[58] Rev. Rul. 81-276, 1981-2 C.B. 128. The PSRO in this ruling was formed pursuant to the mandate of the Social Security Act Amendments of 1972 and designated to review medical necessity of services billed under the Medicare program.

without charge to all licensed physicians engaged in the practice of medicine and the composition of the organization's board of directors was not tied to membership or association in any medical society. Revenues for the organization were derived exclusively from contracts with the federal government. Based on the legislative history of the applicable federal statute, the IRS found that Congress' objectives in establishing PSROs were (i) to reduce overutilization of the health services provided under Medicare and Medicaid and (ii) to enable the medical profession to assume the federal government's responsibility for reviewing the appropriateness and quality of services provided under Medicare and Medicaid. Accordingly, the IRS determined that reviewing the appropriateness and quality of services provided under Medicare and Medicaid was a burden of government and that the organization's activities actually lessened such burden.

2. Accountable Care Organizations.

In Notice 2011-20,[59] the IRS recognized MSSP activities of ACOs as charitable under the lessening the burdens of government theory of § 501(c)(3) of the Code. Specifically, the IRS addresses the effect of participation in the MSSP through an ACO on the tax-exemption of hospitals and other health care organizations described in § 501(c)(3). A principal goal of both MSSP and non-MSSP ACOs is to create and maintain a structure for defining common clinical standards, modifying practice patterns, creating a high degree of integration and cooperation among health care providers, and establishing accountability for quality and cost of health care. Notice 2011-20 provides that, to the extent an ACO participates in the MSSP and meets the MSSP eligibility requirements established by the Centers for Medicare & Medicaid Services (CMS), the ACO generally will be regarded as furthering the exempt purpose of lessening the burdens of government, and states its rationale as follows:

> Congress established the MSSP to be conducted through ACOs in order to promote quality improvements and cost savings, thereby lessening the government's burden associated with providing Medicare benefits.[60]

Since the date of issuance of Notice 2011-20, many MSSP ACOs have successfully obtained tax-exempt status under § 501(c)(3) of the Code under the lessening the burdens of government rationale.[61]

3. Health Information Technology.

The IRS also began granting exemption to organizations designed to facilitate the adoption of electronic health information under a § 501(c)(3) lessening the burdens of government rationale.

In addition to holding that the PSRO lessened the burdens of government, the IRS ruled that the organization promoted the health of the community by reducing over-utilization and relieving the burdens of government. As discussed above, the IRS also determined that the PSRO's activities promoted health for the benefit of the community within the meaning of § 501(c)(3) of the Code as well.

[59] 2011-1 C.B. 652. The IRS later issued a fact sheet in Q&A format that confirmed and supplemented Notice 2011-20.
[60] 2011-1 C.B. at 655. In support of this conclusion, Notice 2011-20 cites Rev. Rul. 81-276, which dealt with a PSRO established by federal statute to review whether the quality of health care services provided to the government's Medicare and Medicaid programs satisfied professionally recognized standards of care. Rev. Rul. 81-276 concluded that PSROs further the tax-exempt purpose of lessening the burdens of government. Interestingly, Notice 2011-20 does not address the "lessening the burdens of government" as an exempt purpose for ACOs that involve Medicaid patients, even though this was part of the basis for concluding that PSROs lessen the burdens of government in Rev. Rul. 81-276 (*i.e.*, PSROs reviewed health care provided to Medicaid patients as well as Medicare patients).
[61] *See, e.g.*, North Country ACO, IRS Determination Letter (Sep. 9, 2013).

In reaching its conclusion that these types of organizations lessened the burdens of government, the IRS relied on statements in the legislative history of the Health Information Technology for Economic and Clinical Health Act (HITECH) in which Congress expressly deemed such activities to lessen the burdens of government within the meaning of § 501(c)(3) of the Code.[62]

6.2.3.5 Annual Information Return Reporting—Compliance with the Community Benefit Standard

The redesigned Form 990 introduced by the IRS in December of 2007 elicits significantly more information that will enable the IRS to monitor and enforce a § 501(c)(3) organization's compliance with the community benefit standard and explicitly incorporates charity care as a consideration. As such, it has significant implications for reporting the information upon which the IRS will administratively determine compliance with the "community benefit" standard.[63]

The majority of the community benefit-related questions are contained in "Schedule H – Hospitals."[64] Schedule H requires disclosure of a tax-exempt hospital's charity care and other community benefits and community building activities, in addition to bad debt expenses, Medicare shortfall, debt collection practices, management companies and joint ventures.[65] In addition to providing all these required statistics, hospitals must provide supplemental narrative information describing how the hospital assesses the needs of its community, informs patients of eligibility requirements for charity care, and uses community building activities to promote the health of the residents of its service area.[66]

In addition to enacting Code § 501(r), the ACA amends Code § 6033(b) to require that a tax-exempt hospital include in its Form 990 a description of how the organization is addressing the needs identified in each community health needs assessment, a description of any such needs that are not being addressed, and an explanation of why such needs are not being addressed.[67] Each organization must also include in the Form 990 its financial statements (or the consolidated financial statements, if applicable).[68]

The redesigned Form 990 contains an 11-page core form (Core Form) that must be completed by all filing organizations and includes eight additional sections,[69] including the "Governance, Management and Disclosure" section of the Core Form.[70] It is generally intended to improve tax compliance by providing insight into an organization's governance structure, policies, and practices[71]

---

[62] H.R. 1, S.1, American Recovery & Reinvestment Act of 2009, Health Information Technology for Economic and Clinical Health Act, §§ 13001 *et seq.* (Feb. 17, 2009).
[63] For a detailed discussion of the redesign of Form 990 and the implementation of § 501(r), *see* Michael N. Fine and Christopher M. Jedrey, '*Show Me the Money'–Maintaining Hospital Tax-Exempt Status*, JOURNAL OF TAXATION OF EXEMPT ORGANIZATIONS, at 1–2 (Sept./Oct. 2010).
[64] Schedule H of Form 990 can be found at http://www.irs.gov/pub/irs-pdf/f990sh.pdf.
[65] *Id.* Schedule H has been revised for 2010 and later tax years to reflect the changes made by the enactment of § 501(r).
[66] *Id.*
[67] Internal Revenue Code § 6033(b)(15)(A).
[68] Internal Revenue Code § 6033(b)(4).
[69] A copy of the redesigned Form 990 can be found at http://www.irs.gov/pub/irs-pdf/f990.pdf.
[70] Part VI of the Core Form. Some of the questions in Part VI were previously asked on the Form 990 in several different sections, but they are now consolidated into this one part of the Core Form. A copy of the Form 990 prior to its redesign in 2007 can be found at http://www.unclefed.com/IRS-Forms/2006/f990.pdf.
[71] *See* "IRS Governance Check Sheet" and "Guide Sheet for Completing the Check Sheet" for insight into the IRS's examination of governance practices of tax-exempt organizations.

and it underscores the importance that the IRS attributes to effective corporate governance by tax-exempt organizations.

In particular, this section on governance requires the organization to disclose the number of "independent" voting directors. The corresponding instructions introduce a revised standard for determining director independence. This standard focuses principally on whether the board member (or family member) was involved in a transaction or relationship with the organization. In general, according to the instructions, a board member will be regarded as "independent" only if three specific circumstances are satisfied at all times during the organization's tax year: (a) the board member was not compensated as an *officer* or other employee of the organization or of a *related organization*,[72] except as provided in the religious exception discussed below; (b) the board member did not receive total *compensation* or other payments exceeding $10,000 during the organization's tax year from the organization or from related organizations as an *independent contractor*, other than reimbursement of expenses under an *accountable plan* or *reasonable compensation* for services provided in the capacity as a member of the governing body;[73] and (c) neither the board member, nor any of his or her *family members*, was involved in a reportable transaction with the organization (whether directly or indirectly through affiliation with another organization) for the organization's tax year, or in a transaction with a related organization of a type and amount that would be reportable if required to be filed by the related organization. The instructions also note that a board member will not be considered to lack independence merely because of the following circumstances: (a) the board member is a donor to the organization, regardless of the amount of the contribution; (b) the board member has taken a *bona fide* vow of poverty and either (i) receives *compensation* as an agent of a *religious order* or a § 501(d) religious or apostolic organization, but only under circumstances in which the member does not receive taxable income;[74] (ii) belongs to a religious order that receives sponsorship or payments from the organization which do not constitute taxable income to the member (the "religious exception" referred to above); or (iii) the member receives financial benefits from the organization solely in the capacity of being a member of the charitable or other class served by the organization in the exercise of its exempt function, such as being a member of a § 501(c)(6) organization, so long as the financial benefits comply with the organizations terms of membership. Finally, the Final Instructions provide a series of helpful examples applying this three part independence test.

The new governance section of the Form 990 also requests information concerning business relationships and business transactions between and among directors, trustees, officers, and key employees. The corresponding instructions define "business relationships" between two persons to include any of the following: (a) one person is employed by the other in a sole proprietorship or by an organization with which the other is associated as a trustee, director, officer, key employee or greater than 35% owner; (b) one person is transacting business with the other (other than in the ordinary course of either party's business on the same terms as are generally offered to the public), directly or indirectly, in one or more contracts of sale, lease, license, loan, performance of services, or other

---

[72] *See* Form 990, Schedule R instructions.
[73] For example, a person who receives reasonable expense reimbursements and reasonable compensation as a director of the organization does not cease to be independent merely because he or she also receives payments of $7,500 from the organization for other arrangements.
[74] *See, e.g.*, Rev. Ruls.77-290, 1977-2 CB 26, 80-332, 1980-2 CB 34.

transaction involving transfers of cash or property valued in excess of $10,000 in the aggregate during the organization's tax year (indirect transactions are transactions with an organization with which the one person is associated as a trustee, director, officer, key employee, or greater-than 35% owner); *and* (c) the two persons are each a director, trustee, officer, or greater than 10% owner in the same business or investment entity.[75] In contrast, reportable "business transactions" between the organization and its interested persons (including its current and former officers, directors, trustees, key employees, family members thereof, and certain entities owned or controlled, in part, by those officers, directors, trustees, and key employees) include, for example, excess benefit transactions, loans between the filing organization and interested persons, and grants or other assistance to interested persons. Transactions between the organization and such person's family members or affiliated entities generally are included.[76] The business relationships and business transactions reportable in the new governance section of the Form 990 are similar in that both require the disclosure of certain contracts of sale, lease, license, and performance of services. However, each involves different reporting thresholds and exceptions set forth in their respective instructions.[77]

6.2.4 "Derivative" or "Integral Part" Theory of Exemption

As discussed in Section 6.2.3, a health care organization may qualify for "stand-alone" tax-exempt status if it can demonstrate that its activities are primarily charitable in nature under the community benefit standard. An organization involved in health care whose activities are *not* inherently charitable may nonetheless qualify for tax-exempt status under the § 501(c)(3) "derivative" or "integral part" theory of exemption if they meet *both* of the following requirements: (a) the activities of the organization are ones that could or otherwise would have been performed by another exempt organization (the essential services requirement);[78] and (b) a sufficient structural or financial relationship exists between the organization seeking exemption and such other exempt organization (the relationship requirement).[79] Although the community benefit requirement does not apply to integral-part exempt

---

[75] *See* Form 990 Instructions, at 19–20, http://www.irs.gov/pub/irs-pdf/i990.pdf. Ownership is measured by stock ownership (either voting power or value) of a corporation, profits or capital interest in a partnership or limited liability company, membership interest in a nonprofit organization, or beneficial interest in a trust. Ownership also includes indirect ownership (*e.g.*, ownership in an entity that has ownership in the entity in question). *Id.* at 20.

[76] *Id.* at 74.

[77] *See* IRS Form 990 Instructions for Schedule L, *available at* http://www.irs.gov/pub/irs-pdf/i990sl.pdf. For example, an organization that completes Schedule L, Part IV generally is not required to report transactions with an interested person for a dollar amount that did not exceed the greater of $10,000 or 1% of the organization's total revenue for the exempt organization's tax year, whereas the similar threshold for Part VI, line 2 is simply $10,000. *See* IRS Form 990 Filing Tips: Schedule L.

[78] *See, e.g., Squire v. Students Book Corp.*, 191 F.2d 1018 (9th Cir. 1951); Rev. Rul. 58-194, 1958-1 C.B. 240; Rev. Rul. 67-217, 1967-1 C.B. 181; Rev. Rul. 67-291, 1967-2 C.B. 184; Rev. Rul. 69-538, 1969-2 C.B. 116; Rev. Rul. 76-336, 1976-2 C.B. 143; Gen. Couns. Mem. 39830 (Aug. 24, 1990). *See also* Gen. Couns. Mem. 39830 (Aug. 30, 1990), which states that the services must be "essential" for fulfilling the exempt purposes of the benefited organization.

[79] *See, e.g.*, Treas. Reg. § 1.502-1(b); *Council for Bibliographic & Information Techs. v. Commissioner*, 63 TCM 3186 (1992); *Estate of Thayer v. Commissioner*, 24 T.C. 384 (1955); Rev. Rul. 78-41, 1978-1 C.B. 148; Rev. Rul. 71-529, 1971-2 C.B. 234; Rev. Rul. 69-572, 1969-2 C.B. 119; Rev. Rul. 75-282, 1975-2 C.B. 201; Rev. Rul. 74-614, 1974-2 C.B. 164; Rev. Rul. 58-194, 1958-1 C.B. 240. *Compare with* Rev. Rul. 69-633, 1969-2 C.B. 121; Rev. Rul. 69-528, 1969-2 C.B. 127; Rev. Rul. 72-369, 1972-2 C.B. 245; Gen. Couns. Mem. 39003 (Nov. 29, 1982). A corollary to the derivative theory of exemption is that the provision of services by one exempt organization to one or more other exempt organizations that do not satisfy this relationship requirement is not necessarily an exempt activity unless the nature of the services themselves would support a stand-alone exemption. *See, e.g.*, Tech. Adv. Mem. 98 22 004 (Nov. 10, 1997).

organizations, the other components of the § 501(c)(3) operational test discussed in Section 6.2 do apply. Common examples of health care organizations that have relied on the derivative/integral part theory are parent corporations of diversified hospital systems, malpractice-insurance trusts created to pool risk among various related health care providers,[80] and joint-operating companies formed to implement a "virtual merger" between two previously unrelated health care systems.

The predominant focus of the IRS in making derivative-exemption determinations has been on the relationship requirement. In the health care context, the IRS has displayed a preference for a formal structural relationship, such as a parent/subsidiary relationship. As will be reflected in the following discussion of joint-operating companies, the IRS has also recognized a financial relationship as sufficient under certain facts and circumstances.

The essential services requirement was the focus, however, in the integral-part debate involved in the controversial *Geisinger Health Plan* line of cases. On remand from the Third Circuit, the Tax Court held that Geisinger Health Plan did not qualify for tax-exempt status as an integral part of the Geisinger Health System. The court based its decision on the finding that the plan did not provide services directly, either to its affiliates or to the class of beneficiaries of the charitable purposes of its affiliates, and that the subscribers to the plan included individuals who were not patients of the hospitals in the Geisinger system.[81]

The Tenth Circuit took a somewhat different approach to the essential services requirement in its decision issued in connection with the HMO affiliates of Intermountain Health Care, Inc. (IHC), focusing instead on the nexus between the IHC plans and IHC Health Services, a tax-exempt subsidiary of IHC.[82] Under the Tenth Circuit's interpretation of the integral-part doctrine, the performance of a particular activity that is not inherently charitable may nonetheless further a charitable purpose; the analysis depends on why and how the activity is being conducted. The Tenth Circuit stated that one of the factors to be considered in applying the integral-part doctrine is "whether an essential nexus exists between the organization seeking tax exemption and a tax-exempt affiliate."[83] The Tenth Circuit noted that the electric power subsidiary described in Treasury Regulations § 1.502-1(b) furnished power solely to the tax-exempt affiliate. That fact, together with the facts that the product provided is essential and that the tax-exempt affiliate exercises control over the subsidiary, "support[s] a strong inference that the subsidiary operates for the same purpose as the parent."[84] The Tenth Circuit concluded that it need not decide whether the IHC plans provided an essential service because the required nexus between the activities of the IHC plans and IHC Health Services is lacking. The Tenth Circuit found that, because a substantial portion of IHC plans' subscribers received services from independent

---

[80] Rev. Rul. 78-41, 1978-1 C.B. 148.
[81] *Geisinger Health Plan v. Commissioner*, 100 T.C. 394 (1993), *aff'd on other grounds*, 30 F.3d 494 (3d Cir. 1994). For examples of the bases upon which the IRS and the courts have found the activities of supporting organizations to be sufficient to satisfy the essential services requirement, *see* Gen. Couns. Mem. 39830 (Aug. 24, 1990); Rev. Rul. 78-41, 1978-1 C.B. 148; Gen. Couns. Mem. 39864 (Sept. 28, 1984); Gen. Couns. Mem. 39508 (May 27, 1986); Rev. Rul. 58-194, 1958-C.B. 240; Rev. Rul. 67-217, 1967-1 C.B. 181; Rev. Rul. 67-291, 1967-2 C.B. 184; Rev. Rul. 68-26, 1968-1 C.B. 272; Rev. Rul. 75-282, 1975-2 C.B. 201; University of Maryland Physicians, P.A.; University of Massachusetts Med. Sch. Group Practice; B.H.W. Anesthesia Found.
[82] *IHC Health Plans v. Commissioner*, 82 T.C.M. (CCH) 593 (2001).
[83] *Id.*
[84] *Id.*

physicians, the IHC plans do not function solely to further IHC Health Services' performance of its exempt activities.[85]

6.2.4.1 Parent Corporations

In the mid-1980s, the IRS's Chief Counsel raised, but did not resolve, the issue of whether parent corporations in restructured hospital systems, which do not have an inherently charitable purpose of their own, should be able to derive § 501(c)(3) status from their exempt subsidiaries.[86] Specifically, the Chief Counsel questioned whether, under the relationship requirement, a parent may derive its exempt status from its subsidiaries, rather than vice versa. Nonetheless, the IRS thereafter has issued favorable derivative exemption rulings to parent corporations in hospital systems.[87] In October 1993, for example, the IRS issued derivative exempt status to a "Superparent" or "Grandparent" in a hospital network, even though a layer of other derivatively exempt parent corporations existed between the Superparent and the exempt hospitals from which it derived its status.[88]

6.2.4.2 Joint Operating Companies

In some cases, two or more previously unrelated health systems interested in affiliating with one another have chosen to do so using what has become known as a "joint-operating agreement/ arrangement" (JOA) rather than a formal structural affiliation under a common-parent corporation. Although the specific design components of JOAs may vary from case to case, the advantages most often associated with the JOA concept include: (a) achievement of a significant amount of integration among the hospitals, while preserving both separate identities and current hospital asset ownership (often a prerequisite for religious-sponsored and governmental health care entities); (b) increased attractiveness for managed-care contracting purposes (i.e., allows managed-care firms to negotiate with a single entity, the JOC); (c) enhanced opportunities for efficiencies and cost savings; and (d) no disruption to the existing debt structure of the participating hospitals.

In many JOAs, the parties create a new entity, known as a "joint operating company" (JOC), to assume the direct responsibility for the management and operation of all the health care facilities in the affiliating health systems. In late 1996, the IRS published an essay that articulated its position concerning whether a JOC can qualify for § 501(c)(3) status under the integral-part theory.[89] The discussion in the essay differentiates between a JOC and a parent company that functions as a centralized authority with absolute financial and structural control over the directors and assets of the organizations coming together through the affiliation. It also describes the types of facts and circumstances

---

[85] The Tax Court had relied on the heavy use of independent physicians as the basis for determining that the IHC plans did not provide an essential service to IHC Health Services. *See IHC Care v. Commissioner*, 82 T.C.M. (CCH) 617 (2001); *IHC Group v. Commissioner*, 82 T.C.M (CCH) 606 (2001); *IHC Health Plans*.

[86] Gen. Couns. Mem. 39598 (Jan. 23, 1987) and Gen. Couns. Mem. 39508 (May 27, 1986).

[87] *See* Judith E. Kindell and T.J. Sullivan, "Health Care Update," *IRS Exempt Organizations Continuing Professional Education Technical Instruction Program for Fiscal Year 1995*, 137, 145.

[88] *See* Bernadette M. Broccolo & Michael W. Peregrine, *IRS Issues "Double Derivative" Exemption to Super Parent in Regional Health Network—A Glimmer of Hope for the Future of Integral Part Status?* THE EXEMPT ORGANIZATION TAX REVIEW, Vol. 8, No. 4 at 731 (Oct. 1993).

[89] *See* Roderick Darling and Marvin Friedlander, "Virtual Mergers, Hospital Joint Operating Agreement Affiliations," *IRS Exempt Organizations Continuing Professional Education Technical Instruction Program for Fiscal Year 1997*, 131.

that will be sufficient to demonstrate a relationship that supports integral-part exemption other than one in which a common-parent entity exercises absolute financial and structural control.

The facts and circumstances articulated by the IRS focus on the delegation to the JOC of management and financial authority, the binding nature of the JOA, the dispute-resolution mechanism, and the reservation of powers by the participating systems.[90] Elements of specific JOC management authority cited by the IRS include: (a) authority to establish budgets; (b) authority by the JOA governing body to monitor and audit each participating entity's compliance with its directives; (c) authority to direct services; (d) authority to enter agreements that bind participating entities, particularly agreements with managed-care providers; (d) authority to hire and fire personnel; (e) authority to grant hospital-staff privileges; (f) authority to set or approve fees and prices; (g) authority to buy assets for and sell assets of participating entities; and (h) authority to reallocate income among the participating entities to balance income and expenses in order to ensure financial integration and achieve mutual objectives.

Other relevant factors articulated by the IRS include: (a) whether significant penalties or other hindrances are posed by potentially terminating the agreement; (b) whether mechanisms, such as direct negotiations and binding arbitration, are in place to resolve disputes among the parties; and (c) the degree to which the JOA is permanent. If the authority ceded to the JOC is merely the power to veto actions taken by participating hospitals, then the facts and circumstances necessary to establish the equivalent of a parent/subsidiary relationship would not be present. Similarly, if actions of the JOC governing body are subject to veto by the participating hospitals, then this also would negate a finding that the hospitals function as subordinates of the JOC. Retaining some authority in the governing bodies of the participating systems does not necessarily determine whether the equivalent of a parent/subsidiary relationship has been established. Examples of such authority include authority over ethical or moral issues based on religious principles.[91]

6.2.5 Public-Benefit Requirement

A § 501(c)(3) organization must also be operated for the benefit of public, rather than private, interests. Thus, the organization must establish that it is not organized or operated for the benefit of private interests, such as designated individuals, the creator or the creator's family, shareholders of the organization, or persons controlled (directly or indirectly) by such private interests.[92] It must be capable of demonstrating that any benefits that flow from its corporate activities to private interests are incidental, both qualitatively and quantitatively, to the public benefits derived from the activity.[93]

---

[90] As a word of caution, these facts and circumstances in many cases may not be suitable for the traditional parent in a restructured hospital system, as they would require the parent to have significant direct involvement in the day-to-day affairs of the hospitals coming together under the JOA arrangement.

[91] Private letter rulings issued in the JOA context include Priv. Ltr. Rul. 200245057 (Aug. 13, 2002); Priv. Ltr. Rul. 200238051 (June 28, 2002); Priv. Ltr. Rul. 200108045-47 (Nov. 29, 2000); Priv. Ltr. Rul. 200044040 (Aug. 3, 2000); Priv. Ltr. Rul. 200036049 (June 13, 2000); Priv. Ltr. Rul. 9814039 (Jan. 5, 1998), Priv. Ltr. Rul. 9738038-9738054 (June 26, 1997); Priv. Ltr. Rul. 9722042; Priv. Ltr. Rul. 9721031 (Feb. 26, 1997); Priv. Ltr. Rul. 9714011 (Dec. 24, 1996); 9716021 (Jan. 17, 1997) and 9716026; Priv. Ltr. Rul. 9609012 (Nov. 22, 1995); Priv. Ltr. Rul. 9623011 (Feb. 29, 1996); and Priv. Ltr. Rul. 9651047 (Sept. 24, 1996).

[92] Treas. Reg. § 1.501(c)(3)-1(d)(1)(ii).

[93] *See, e.g.*, Rev. Rul. 73-313, 1973-2 C.B. 174; Gen. Couns. Mem. 39598 (Dec. 8, 1986); Gen. Couns. Mem. 39498 (Apr. 24, 1986); Gen. Couns. Mem. 37789 (Dec. 18, 1978); Gen. Couns. Mem. 35268 (Mar. 14, 1973). Like private

The substantiality of the private benefit is measured in the context of the overall public benefit conferred by the activity.[94] Unlike the private-inurement prohibition, the "private benefit" prohibition is not limited to "insiders." This is commonly referred to as the private-benefit prohibition or the public-benefit requirement. Organizations that violate the public-benefit requirement jeopardize their tax-exempt status.

6.2.6 Private-Inurement Prohibition

§ 501(c)(3) of the Code and the corresponding Treasury Regulations[95] provide that no part of the net earnings of a § 501(c)(3) organization may inure to the benefit of private shareholders or individuals with an "inside" relationship to the charity. This is commonly referred to as the private-inurement prohibition. Private shareholders or individuals, typically referred to as "insiders," are "persons having a personal and private interest in the activities of the organization,"[96] and generally include officers, directors, major donors, and senior management because of their interest in and potential ability to influence the affairs of the tax-exempt organization. In the case of a health care provider, therefore, the IRS may take the position that certain physicians employed by, or on the medical staff of, the organization are "insiders."[97]

An organization may pay or receive "fair market value" or "reasonable compensation" for a good or service without violating the inurement prohibition.[98] If, however, a transaction results in the payment by a hospital of more than fair market value or reasonable compensation for an item or service it purchases, or the receipt of less than fair market value or reasonable compensation for an item or service it sells, then the transaction may result in private inurement.[99] The Code and its regulations do not define private inurement. As a result, whether private inurement occurs depends upon the facts and circumstances surrounding a transaction or arrangement. Organizations that violate the private inurement prohibition jeopardize their tax-exempt status.

---

letter rulings, General Counsel Memoranda are not binding precedent. Nevertheless, they provide insights into the IRS's current policy and enforcement positions.

[94] Gen. Couns. Mem. 39598 (Dec. 8, 1986); Gen. Couns. Mem. 39498 (Apr. 24, 1986); Gen. Couns. Mem. 37789 (Dec. 18, 1978).

[95] Treas. Reg. § 1.501(c)(3)-1(c).

[96] Treas. Reg. § 1.501(a)-1(c); *American Campaign Academy v. Commissioner*, 92 T.C. 1053 (1989). *See also* Mertens, *The Law of Federal Income Taxation* 99 (1986); *Passaic United Hebrew Burial Ass'n v. United States*, 216 F. Supp. 500 (N.J. 1963), citing the *Mertens* text, *Founding Church of Scientology v. United States*, 412 F.2d 1197 (Ct. Cl. 1969).

[97] *See, e.g., Lowry Hosp. Ass'n v. Commissioner*, 66 T.C. 80 (1976); *Harding Hosp., Inc. v. United States*, 505 F.2d 1068 (6th Cir. 1974); Gen. Couns. Mem. 39498 (Apr. 24, 1986); Gen. Couns. Mem. 39862 (Nov. 22, 1991); Gen. Couns. Mem. 39670 (June 17, 1987); Gen. Couns. Mem. 39598 (Dec. 8, 1986). Compare with Rev. Rul. 69-383, 1969-2 C.B. 113; Rev. Rul. 73-313, 1973-2 C.B. 174.

[98] *See, e.g., Alive Fellowship of Harmonious Living v. Commissioner*, ¶41,011 (M) T.C.M. (1984); *World Family Corp. v. Commissioner*, 81 T.C. 958 (1983); *John Marshall Law Sch. v. United States*, 81-2 U.S.T.C ¶9514 (Ct. Cl. 1981); *B.H.W. Anesthesia Found., Inc. v. Commissioner*, 72 T.C. 681 (1979); Rev. Rul. 76-441, 1976-2 C.B. 147; Gen. Couns. Mem. 39498 (Apr. 24, 1986); Rev. Rul. 69-383, 1969-2 C.B. 113; Gen. Couns. Mem. 38283 (Feb. 15, 1980).

[99] *See, e.g., Birmingham Bus. College v. Commissioner*, 276 F.2d 476 (5th Cir. 1960) and *Mabee Petroleum v. United States*, 203 F.2d 872 (5th Cir. 1953), in which the courts found the compensation arrangements to be excessive, and *Anclote Psychiatric Ctr., Inc. v. Commissioner*, T.C. Memo 1998-273, *aff'd*, 190 F.3d 541, in which the court found the organization had sold assets to a for-profit company owned by former board members for less than fair market value.

6.2.7 Intermediate Sanctions and the Rebuttable Presumption of Reasonableness

6.2.7.1 The Intermediate Sanctions Excise Taxes

Code § 4958 contains a series of penalty excise taxes generally referred to as "intermediate sanctions." Under those rules, "disqualified persons" (that is, persons in a position to exercise substantial influence over the affairs of the organization) who receive excess benefits, and the organizational managers who approve such benefits, are subject to the imposition of penalty excise taxes.[100] No penalty excise tax applies to the organization itself. The tax on disqualified persons is a two-tier tax. The initial tax is 25% of the amount of the excess benefit.[101] An additional tax of 200% of the excess benefit is imposed if the excess-benefit transaction is not corrected within the taxable period.[102] The organization manager tax is 10% of the amount of the excess benefit,[103] up to a maximum of $20,000 per transaction.[104]

Congress intended that these excise taxes generally be imposed in lieu of a loss of tax-exempt status for organizations that violate the private-inurement prohibition. In certain circumstances, however, these penalties may be imposed in addition to loss of tax-exempt status. The applicable Treasury regulations provide guidance on the specific factors that the IRS will consider in determining whether a § 501(c)(3) organization jeopardizes its tax-exempt status by engaging in one or more excess benefit transactions.[105] In other words, these regulations address the circumstances under which the IRS would consider revoking an organization's tax-exempt status for engaging in an excess benefit transaction in addition to imposing § 4958 intermediate sanctions. The factors include: (1) the size and scope of the organization's regular exempt activities; (2) the relationship between the size and scope of the excess benefit transaction(s) and the organization's regular exempt activities; (3) whether the organization has a history of engaging in "repeated" excess benefit transactions; (4) whether the organization has adopted compliance measures intended to prevent the occurrence of future intermediate sanctions violations; and (5) whether the excess benefit transaction has been corrected (or the organization has made a good faith effort to seek correction).[106] These regulations should be consulted in analyzing any transaction or arrangement with potential intermediate-sanctions risks.

---

[100] The IRS has published two detailed articles on the intermediate-sanctions excise tax in its Continuing Professional Education Texts. *See* Lawrence M. Brauer and Leonard J. Henzke, "Intermediate Sanctions (IRC 4958) Update," *IRS Exempt Organizations Continuing Professional Education Technical Instruction Program for Fiscal Year 2003* (2002), and Lawrence M. Brauer, Toussaint T. Tyson, Leonard J. Henzke, and Debra J. Kawecki, "An Introduction to I.R.C. 4958 (Intermediate Sanctions)," *IRS Exempt Organizations Continuing Professional Education Technical Instruction Program for Fiscal Year 2002*, 260 (2001). Although "An Introduction to I.R.C. 4958 (Intermediate Sanctions)" was written prior to the publication of the final regulations, much of the discussion remains relevant, and the article contains several helpful checklists. *See also* Internal Revenue Manual [7.8.1] Chapter 28.
[101] I.R.C. § 4958(a)(1).
[102] *Id.* § 4958(b).
[103] *Id.* § 4958(a)(2).
[104] *Id.* § 4958(d)(2).
[105] "Standards for Recognition of Tax-Exempt Status if Private Benefit Exists," 73 Fed. Reg. 16519–25 (Mar. 28, 2008).
[106] *Id.*

6.2.7.2 Excess-Benefit Transactions and the Rebuttable Presumption

For intermediate-sanctions purposes, a benefit is an "excess benefit" if it has a value in excess of the fair market value of the goods and services for which it is given.[107] A benefit will not be an excess benefit if it is reasonable. The legislative history underlying Code § 4958 contains guidelines for raising a "rebuttable presumption" of the reasonableness and fair market value of payments made to disqualified persons.[108] The final Treasury Regulations implement these guidelines by providing that payments under a compensation arrangement are presumed to be reasonable, and the transfer of property is presumed to be at fair market value, if the following three conditions are met: (1) the specific compensation arrangement, or specified terms of a property transfer, is approved in advance by an authorized body (i.e., the board of directors or trustees or appropriately qualified committee thereof) that is composed entirely of individuals that do not have a conflict of interest with respect to the transaction; (2) the board or committee obtained and relied upon appropriate data as to comparability; and (3) the board or committee adequately documented the basis for its determination.[109]

Although the intermediate-sanctions rules only apply to transactions and arrangements involving disqualified persons, the process required to qualify for the rebuttable-presumption protection against intermediate sanctions is a prudent one to follow for any compensation arrangement or purchase and sale transaction involving an exempt organization and an individual or nonexempt organization.

6.2.7.3 Disqualified Persons

The final Treasury Regulations provide important guidance concerning the definition of a "disqualified person." The Treasury Regulations specify certain persons deemed to be persons in a position to have substantial influence, and certain others as persons deemed not to be in a position to have substantial influence.[110] A person is deemed to be in a position to have substantial influence over the affairs of a tax-exempt organization, and thus to be a disqualified person, if he or she: (1) serves on the organization's governing body and is entitled to vote; (2) is the president, chief executive officer, or chief operating officer of the organization;[111] or (3) is the treasurer or chief financial officer of the organization.[112] A person is deemed *not* to have substantial influence, and thus not to be a disqualified person, if (1) the person is an organization described in § 501(c)(3) or (2) the person is an employee receiving total direct and indirect economic benefits in an amount less than the amount of compensation necessary to be highly compensated as

---

[107] *Id.* § 4958(c)(1); Treas. Reg. § 53.4958-1(b); Treas. Reg. § 53.4958-4(a)(1). *See also Caracci v. Commissioner*, 188 T.C. 379 (2002) (property transfer); Tech. Adv. Mem. 200244028 (June 21, 2002) (executive compensation); Tech. Adv. Mem. 200243057 (July 2, 2002) (compensation and benefits).
[108] H. Rep. No. 506, 104th Cong., 2d Sess. 56, 57 (1996).
[109] Treas. Reg. § 53.4958-6(c). See "Intermediate Sanctions (IRC 4958) Update," at E-33-E-38; "An Introduction to I.R.C. 4958 (Intermediate Sanctions)," at 270, 327–33; Rebuttable Presumption Checklists in Appendices 4 and 5.
[110] *See* Treas. Reg. § 53.4958-3(c) and (d); "Intermediate Sanctions (IRC 4958) Update," at E-8-E-9; "An Introduction to I.R.C. 4958 (Intermediate Sanctions)," at 261–63.
[111] An individual is considered to serve in such capacity, regardless of title, if he or she has or shares ultimate responsibility for implementing decisions of the governing body or supervising the management, administration, or operation of the organization. Treas. Reg. § 53.4958-3(c)(2).
[112] An individual is considered to be the treasurer or chief financial officer, regardless of title, if he or she has or shares ultimate responsibility for managing the finances of the organization. Treas. Reg. § 53.4958-3(c)(3).

defined in § 414(q)(1)(B)(i) (currently $115,000), who is not a substantial contributor within the meaning of § 507(d)(2) or otherwise within the definition of disqualified person.[113]

In all other cases, the determination of whether a person is a disqualified person is left to a facts-and-circumstances inquiry. The Treasury Regulations set forth certain facts and circumstances "tending to show" that a person has substantial influence. These include whether the person: (1) is a founder of the organization; (2) is a substantial contributor (within the meaning of Code § 507(d)(2)); (3) is one whose compensation is based primarily on revenues derived from activities of the organization that he or she controls;[114] (4) has or shares authority to control or determine a substantial portion of the organization's capital expenditures, operating budget, or compensation; (5) manages a discrete segment or activity of the organization that represents a substantial portion of the activities, assets, income, or expenses of the organization; (6) owns a controlling interest in an entity that is a disqualified person; or (7) is a non-stock corporation controlled, directly or indirectly, by one or more disqualified persons. The regulations make clear that this list is not exclusive.[115] Therefore, a person who has managerial control over a portion of an organization or over a subsidiary of an organization may nevertheless be in a position to exercise substantial influence over the affairs of the organization.

The Treasury Regulations set forth other facts and circumstances "tending to show" that a person is not a disqualified person. These include:

1. the person has taken a *bona fide* vow of poverty as an employee, agent, or on behalf of a religious organization;
2. the person is an independent contractor (e.g., an attorney, accountant or investment manager, or advisor) whose sole relationship to the organization is providing professional advice (without having decision-making authority) with respect to transactions from which the contractor will not economically benefit either directly or indirectly (aside from customary fees for the professional advice rendered);
3. the direct supervisor of the individual is not a disqualified person;
4. the person does not participate in management decisions affecting the organization as a whole or a discrete segment or activity of the organization that represents a substantial portion of the activities, assets, income, or expenses of the organization, compared to the organization as a whole; and
5. any preferential treatment a person receives based on the size of that person's donation also is offered to all other donors making a comparable contribution as part of a solicitation intended to attract a substantial number of contributions.[116]

The Treasury Regulations include 13 examples analyzing the facts and circumstances of whether a person is a disqualified person, including (among others) a for-profit hospital management company

---
[113] Treas. Reg. § 53.4958-3(d).
[114] Note that this factor does not take into account whether the activities the person controls represent a substantial portion of the overall activities of the exempt organization.
[115] *See* Treas. Reg. § 53.4958-3(e)(2).
[116] *See id.* § 53.4958-3(e)(3).

managing a whole-hospital joint venture, a hospital-employed radiologist, and the head of a hospital's cardiology department.[117]

The legislative history specifically rejects the IRS view that all physicians are insiders.[118] The Treasury Regulations include two examples involving physicians. In the first, a radiologist is deemed not to have substantial influence where the physician is employed by a large acute-care hospital, has no managerial authority over any substantial part of the hospital's operations, does not serve as a supervisor over hospital employees other than giving instructions to staff with respect to the physician's own radiology work, is compensated primarily in the form of a fixed salary, is eligible to receive an incentive award based on revenues of the radiology department, is not related to any other disqualified person at the hospital, and does not serve on the hospital board or as an officer.[119]

A second example, however, involves a cardiologist who is the head of the same hospital's cardiology department and who is deemed to be a disqualified person. Although neither a board member nor an officer, the physician has managerial authority for the cardiology department, which is a major source of patients and represents a substantial portion of the hospital's income, as compared to the hospital as a whole. The physician has authority to allocate the department's budget, including authority to distribute incentive bonuses among cardiologists according to criteria he can set.[120]

The legislative history underlying Code § 4958 states that a person could be in a position to exercise substantial influence over a tax-exempt organization even if the person was not an employee of and was not compensated directly by the tax-exempt organization, but was formally an employee of a subsidiary—taxable or tax-exempt—controlled by the parent exempt organization.[121] The Treasury Regulations make clear that, in the case of multiple organizations affiliated by common control, the determination of whether a person has substantial influence must be made separately for each applicable tax-exempt organization.[122] The Treasury Regulations also provide, however, that an economic benefit may be provided directly or indirectly, including through the use of one or more entities controlled or affiliated with an applicable tax-exempt organization. Thus, where a tax-exempt parent causes a taxable subsidiary to pay excessive compensation to, or engage in a transaction at other than fair market value with, a disqualified person of the parent, these arrangements may well fall within the definition of excess-benefit transactions.[123]

6.2.7.4 Relationship to Revocation Sanction

Intermediate sanction excise tax may be imposed instead of revocation of tax exemption or, in extreme cases, intermediate sanctions may be imposed along with revocation of exemption. The first

---

[117] *Id.* § 53.4958-3(g). Example 5 in the disqualified-person section of the regulations demonstrates that a person who had no prior relationship with the organization prior to the transaction at issue can become a disqualified person as a result of the transaction. The effect of this position, however, is somewhat limited by the special provisions relating to initial contracts set forth in Treas. Reg. § 53.4958-4(a)(3).

[118] H. Rep. No. 506 at 58, n.12.

[119] Treas. Reg. § 53.4958-3(g), Example 10.

[120] *Id.* Example 11.

[121] H.R. Rep. No. 104-506 at 58 n.10 (Mar. 28, 1996).

[122] Treas. Reg. § 53.4958-3(f).

[123] *Id.* § 53.4958-4(a)(2).

Tax Court case to interpret the intermediate sanctions provisions,[124] concluded that disqualified persons were liable for excess benefit taxes but that the tax exemption of the organization should not be revoked. The case involved several § 501(c)(3) corporations owning home health agencies that were controlled by the same family. The exempt organizations transferred all their assets and liabilities to for-profit corporations owned by the family after obtaining a valuation indicating that the exempt organizations' liabilities exceeded their assets. The Tax Court found that the transferred assets far exceeded the consideration paid and indicated that first-level excise taxes were due. The Court of Appeals, however, reversed the Tax Court decision and rendered judgment for the taxpayers, finding that as a matter of law no excess benefits were received.

6.2.8 Unrelated Business Activities

A § 501(c)(3) organization is subject to tax on income generated by its unrelated business activities. An activity is an unrelated trade or business if the conduct of the activity does not have a substantial causal relationship (other than the production of income) to the accomplishment of the organization's exempt purposes. In general, the IRS takes into account the nature of the activity; that is, whether the activity is inherently exempt or commercial in nature. If the activity is not inherently exempt, the organization must demonstrate a substantial causal relationship to the accomplishment of an exempt purpose.

An organization is considered "operated exclusively" for one or more § 501(c)(3) exempt purposes "only if it engages primarily in activities which accomplish one or more of" the exempt purposes specified in its articles of incorporation. If "more than an insubstantial part" of an organization's activities is not "in furtherance of an exempt purpose," such organization will not be regarded as operated exclusively for exempt purposes, and its exempt status may be jeopardized. The phrase "more than an insubstantial part of [an organization's] activities" is not further defined in the regulations under § 501(c)(3). Therefore, the IRS and the courts have made such determinations on a case-by-case basis.

There is no "bright line" for determining what constitutes an insubstantial portion. The IRS is likely to take into account the following five factors in determining whether a § 501(c)(3) organization's unrelated business activities are substantial:

1. the time, attention, and importance given by the officers and directors of the organization to exempt activities as compared with unrelated business activities;
2. the organization's expenditures for exempt activities as compared with expenditures for unrelated business activities;
3. the organization's income from exempt activities as compared with income from unrelated business activities;
4. the organization's reasonable expectation of earning a profit; and
5. staff time spent on exempt activities, as compared with staff time spent on unrelated business activities.

---

[124] *Caracci v. Commissioner*, 118 T.C. 379 (2002), *rev'd*, 456 F.3d 444 (5th Cir. 2006).

An exempt organization will be subject to unrelated business income tax (UBIT) on its share of the income of a partnership or limited-liability company (LLC) taxed as a partnership to the extent that the income was generated from partnership activities that are unrelated to the exempt partner's § 501(c)(3) purposes.[125]

The IRS has found various hospital businesses to be related to the hospital's exempt function: (a) the operation of a gift shop, which is patronized by patients, visitors making purchases for patients, and employees;[126] (b) the operation of a cafeteria and coffee shop for employees and the medical staff;[127] (c) the operation of a parking lot for patients and visitors;[128] (d) the sale of pharmaceuticals by a hospital pharmacy to its "patients";[129] (e) the income received by a teaching and research hospital for the performance of pathological diagnostic tests on samples submitted by physicians associated with the hospital;[130] (f) the sale of durable medical equipment (in certain limited cases);[131] (g) the rental of pagers to staff physicians;[132] and (h) the leasing of space in a medical office building and the furnishing of services to physicians (if the lease enhances the use of diagnostic facilities, helps patient admissions, increases the availability of physicians for duty, and enhances their participation in medical education and research programs).[133]

6.2.9 Political Activity Prohibition and Lobbying Limitation

6.2.9.1 *Political Activity Prohibition*

The Code absolutely prohibits tax-exempt health care organizations from engaging in any political campaign activity. § 501(c)(3) of the Code defines prohibited political activity as participation or intervention in any political campaign on behalf of or in opposition to any candidate for public office.

---

[125] I.R.C. § 512(c).
[126] Rev. Rul. 69-267, 1969-1 C.B. 160.
[127] *Id.* 1969-1 C.B. 160.
[128] *Id.*
[129] "Patients" may be one of six categories of individuals: (1) a person admitted as an inpatient; (2) a person receiving general or emergency diagnostic, therapeutic, or preventive health services from outpatient facilities of a hospital; (3) a person referred to a hospital's outpatient facilities for specific diagnosis or treatment; (4) a person refilling a prescription received during treatment as a patient; (5) a person receiving medical services as a part of a hospital-administered home care program; and (6) a person receiving medical care and services in a hospital-affiliated extended care facility. Rev. Rul. 68-376, 1968-2 C.B. 246; Priv. Ltr. Rul. 8206093, 8131063. Nevertheless, the sale of pharmaceutical supplies by an exempt hospital to *private patients of physicians* who have offices in a medical building owned by the hospital is an unrelated business, with income therefrom constituting UBI. Rev. Rul. 68-375, 1968-2 C.B. 245. Likewise, sales of pharmaceuticals by a hospital to the general public are UBI. To treat such income as exempt from taxation would permit hospital-owned pharmacies to unfairly compete with commercial pharmacies. *Carle Found. v. United States*, 611 F.2d 1192 (7th Cir. 1979), *cert. denied*, 449 U.S. 824 (1980).
[130] *St. Luke's Hosp. of Kansas City v. United States*, 494 F. Supp. 85 (W.D. Mo. 1980); Rev. Rul. 85-109, 1985-2 C.B. 165. Thus, unless such laboratory tests are provided to hospital patients or patients of physicians on the medical staff of a teaching hospital, such services constitute UBI. An exception to this general rule is stated in Rev. Rul. 85-110, 1985-2 C.B. 166, where the service acknowledged a "unique circumstances" exception exists if alternative facilities for providing the service are not available within a reasonable distance, or if the facility is unable or inadequate to conduct such tests, or if the analysis is needed on an emergency basis. In such cases, the income generated from performing the tests is not UBI. *See also* Priv. Ltr. Rul. 9023041 (Mar. 9, 1990).
[131] *See* Rev. Rul. 78-435, 1978-2 C.B. 181, in which the IRS noted that the sale of hearing aids by a hospital whose primary activity is the operation of a clinic that provides various rehabilitation services to handicapped individuals (including testing and evaluating their hearing and recommending necessary hearing aids) was not an unrelated trade or business. By selling hearing aids to such patients, maximum assistance to the patients was assured.
[132] Tech. Adv. Mem. 8452011.
[133] *See* Rev. Rul. 69-463, 1969-2 C.B. 131; Rev. Rul. 69-464, 1969-2 C.B. 132; LTR 8452099.

Any violation of this prohibition will result in the loss of the organization's tax-exempt status, as well as the incurrence of substantial excise-tax penalties.[134]

A candidate is defined as any individual who offers oneself, or is proposed by others, as a contestant for an elective public office, regardless of whether such office is national, state, or local. Neither the Code nor the regulations define the term "public office;" however, the IRS has identified the following as characteristics of a public office: (1) created by statute; (2) continuing; (3) not occasional or contractual; (4) has a fixed term of office; and (5) requires an oath of office.[135]

Prohibited activity includes the publication or distribution of written or printed statements on behalf of or in opposition to a candidate. A written or oral endorsement of a candidate and the rating of candidates (even on a non-partisan basis) are prohibited. A § 501(c)(3) organization also may not provide or solicit financial or other forms of support to or for candidates or political organizations.[136]

Revenue Ruling 2007-41[137] provides formal IRS guidance concerning common situations that my involve political activity, including: (a) individual activities of the leaders of the exempt organization); (b) appearances at exempt organization events by candidates in a candidate or a non-candidate capacity; (c) issue advocacy; and (d) voter education, voter registration, and get-out-the-vote drives.[138] The guidance provides a useful basis for the development of policies and procedures designed to maintain compliance with the § 501(c)(3) political activity prohibition.

6.2.9.2 Lobbying Limitation

In contrast to the Code's absolute prohibition against engaging in political activities, a tax-exempt health care organization may engage in activities with the purpose of influencing legislation, so long as those activities do not become a substantial part of the organization's activities. Unfortunately, no clear guidelines have been established as to when lobbying activities will constitute a substantial part of an organization's activities. § 501(h) of the Code permits some tax-exempt organizations to elect to avail themselves of a special set of rules that provides specific guidelines concerning the permissible amount of expenditures for legislative activities. This election, however, is not available to organizations controlled by a religious order.

Legislative activities include: (i) advocating the adoption or rejection of legislation; (ii) engaging in direct lobbying by communicating with legislators, their staff, and, under certain circumstances, executive-branch officials who participate in the formulation of legislation for the purpose of proposing, supporting, or opposing legislation; and (iii) engaging in "grass-roots" lobbying by

---

[134] I.R.C. § 4962. *But see* Gen. Couns. Mem. 39414 (Sept. 25, 1985), which suggests that in some cases the IRS has excused *de minimis* political activity.
[135] Judith E. Kindell and John Francis Reilly, "Election Year Issues," *IRS Exempt Organizations Continuing Professional Instruction Program for Fiscal Year 2002*, at 335 (2001).
[136] Treas. Reg. § 1.501(c)(3)-1(c)(3)(iii).
[137] 2007-25 I.R.B. (June 18, 2007).
[138] In June 2007, the IRS released an update on the political activity prohibition enforcement activities the IRS undertook during the federal 2006 campaigns as part of its Political Activities Compliance Initiative (PACI) project, which was previously discussed in the IRS' February 2006 fact sheet entitled, "Election Year Activities and the Prohibition on Political Campaign Intervention for Section 501(c)(3) Organizations (FS-2006-17, (February 2007). *See* http://www.irs.gov/pub/irs-tege/2006paci_report_5-30-07.pdf.

urging the public to contact members of a legislative body for the purpose of proposing, supporting, or opposing legislation.[139]

Public education and advocacy are distinct from lobbying. The term "educational" includes the instruction of the public on subjects useful to the individual and beneficial to the community. An activity may be educational even though it advocates a particular position or viewpoint, so long as it presents a sufficiently full and fair exposition of the pertinent facts as to permit an individual or the public to form an independent opinion or conclusion. Therefore, engaging in and making available the results of nonpartisan analysis is study or research, not lobbying. The organization is not engaging in educational activities, however, if it merely presents unsupported opinion.

6.3 Practical Application of the Fundamental Exemption Requirements

IRS policymaking and enforcement initiatives that affect exempt health care organizations have focused on the application of the private-inurement prohibition and the public-benefit requirement in various contexts such as the purchase or sale of a business or other assets, compensation arrangements, physician recruitment arrangements, joint ventures, courtesy discounts, and the use of taxable affiliates.

6.3.1 Purchase and Sale of a Business or other Assets

An exempt organization may purchase or sell a business or other asset (and pay value for that business's intangible assets such as goodwill) from or to a for-profit entity so long as the organization pays or receives no more or less than fair market value for the business or asset.[140] The transaction must be conducted at arm's length, and the amounts paid by the tax-exempt organization must be no greater than the fair market value of the assets, including intangible assets.[141]

The IRS defines fair market value as the price at which a willing purchaser and a willing seller agree, neither operating under any compulsion to buy or sell, and both having reasonable knowledge of the relevant facts.[142] In general, fair market value is determined within the framework of the business enterprise's worth to the most likely hypothetical purchaser, which is assumed to be a commercial health care corporation, even if the purchaser is tax-exempt. The IRS has recognized that fair market value is a question of fact, depending upon the circumstances of each case.

Where an organization purchases assets from an independent third party, a presumption exists that a purchase price arrived at through arm's-length negotiations represents fair market value. Where the purchaser has a close relationship to the seller at the time of sale, however, the nature of the relationship brings into question whether the elements of arm's-length negotiations are present. The IRS has stated that, in situations where the close relationship between purchaser and seller precludes arm's-length negotiations, the fair market value of the assets acquired must be established

---

[139] Treas. Reg. § 1.501(c)(3)-1(c)(3)(ii).
[140] Rev. Rul. 76-91, 1976-1 C.B. 149, in which the IRS approves the use of the capitalization of excess earnings method set forth in Rev. Rul. 68-609, 1968-2 C.B. 327, to value the intangible assets being purchased but does not indicate that this is the only acceptable method of valuing intangible assets.
[141] *Id.*
[142] Rev. Rul. 59-60, 1959-1 C.B. 237.

through a valuation performed by a qualified, independent third party.[143] The IRS will not only look to see if a valuation was performed, but also will scrutinize the valuation methodology and underlying assumptions.[144]

The IRS has not released any binding guidance with respect to the valuation of businesses to be acquired or disposed of by a tax-exempt organization. However, it has released a limited amount of non-binding guidance on valuation of medical practices to be purchased by an exempt organization.[145] While this guidance addresses valuation issues only in the context of medical practice acquisitions, the guidance can be applied generally to purchase and sale transactions in which exempt organizations are involved.

The valuation guidance states that a valuation appraisal should include all recognized approaches for estimating value, including the market approach, cost approach, and income approach. Although the IRS requires an analysis of all three methodologies, it has indicated that the income approaches are the most relevant in the context of valuing a physician practice.[146] The IRS will apply two "income" approaches: (i) the "excess earnings method;"[147] and (ii) the "discounted future cash flow" method.[148] The cost and market approaches generally are used as benchmarks to determine whether the valuation reached under the income approach is reasonable. The IRS also has reiterated that a "weighting" approach is inappropriate, and that "no useful purpose is served by taking an average of several factors... and basing the valuation on the result."[149]

The IRS will scrutinize closely the various assumptions used in an income-approach valuation of a medical practice.[150] For example, the IRS requires the use of after-tax cash flows and will scrutinize revenue and expense projections. The projected future physician-compensation expenses used in the income-approach valuation should be based on the actual compensation that will be paid to the selling physician under a post-acquisition employment arrangement. The valuation may incorporate

---

[143] Rev. Rul. 76-91, 1976-1 C.B. 149.
[144] The Tax Court also has indicated that it will carefully scrutinize valuation methodology and underlying assumptions. In *Caracci*, the Tax Court declined to adopt either parties' approach to the valuation completely, finding certain assumptions by both valuation experts not to be credible, and parts of each methodology flawed.
[145] Much of this guidance can be found in the continuing materials that the IRS prepares for its internal continuing education programs. *See* Charles F. Kaiser, Phyllis D. Haney, and T. J. Sullivan, "Integrated Delivery Systems and Joint Venture Dissolutions Update," *IRS Exempt Organizations Continuing Professional Education Technical Instruction Program for Fiscal Year 1995*, 153 (1994); Charles F. Kaiser and Amy Henchy, "Valuation of Medical Practices," *IRS Exempt Organizations Continuing Professional Education Technical Program for Fiscal Year 1996*, 404 (1995). While the CPE Text represents non-precedential guidance, which means it may not be relied upon by taxpayers or the IRS, the CPE Text does serve as a good indication of what the IRS believes to be the correct statement of law and how the IRS would rule under a particular set of facts.
[146] "Valuation of Medical Practices."
[147] The excess-earnings method is described in Rev. Rul. 68-609, 1968-2 C.B. 327, and was approved for valuation of intangibles in Rev. Rul. 76-91, 1976-1 C.B. 149.
[148] Raymond C. Miller, "Basic Business Appraisals," (1984); 1994 CPE Text, at 236. "Valuation of Medical Practices," at 417-38.
[149] "Valuation," *1978 IRS Exempt Organizations Continuing Professional Education Technical Instruction Program*, Chapter J (1978); *see also* Rev. Rul. 59-60, 1959-1 C.B. 237. The IRS will also take into account whether the primary purpose of a medical practice acquisition is (a) a "bail-out" of a financially distressed medical practice, which is otherwise important to the success of the exempt-organization purchaser; or (b) an attempt to find a purchaser for a practice for which no conceivable market exists. "Integrated Delivery Systems and Joint Venture," at 236.
[150] "Valuation of Medical Practices," at 409.

certain assumptions about future benefits, such as synergy, growth, or expansion; these assumptions, however, should hold true for the entity as a stand-alone business or by virtue of *any* purchaser's ability to achieve such benefits. The valuation should not include assumptions about such matters if they are unique to the particular purchaser. For example, if a hospital-purchaser is exempt from state sales tax, then the projections should not include a reduction in sales-tax expense for the seller.[151]

Although the IRS has expressed a preference for the discounted cash-flow income-valuation approach in medical practice acquisitions, it also began to recognize the validity of the market approach in late 1995. To support the validity of the market approach in a particular case, however, the IRS will insist upon detailed documentation of comparability, including information concerning actual sales of "comparable" physician practices in the same community, but the actual purchase prices must be evaluated, adjusted, and applied to the operating data of the selling practice. Moreover, factors affecting comparability should be discussed (e.g., markets served; competitive position; profitability; growth prospects; risk perceptions; capital structure; physician compensation, age, health, reputation, and productivity; average revenue per physician; cost structure; and average revenue per visit or covered-life-to-revenue mix).[152]

The valuation report should include the following: an executive summary; a review of the nature of the business and history of the enterprise; the economic outlook in general, and that of the specific industry in particular; the book value of the stock and hard assets; the financial condition of the business; the earning capacity of the business; the dividend-paying capacity of the business; the estimated value of the intangible assets; a description of the subject assets; and (where applicable) a discussion of comparable enterprises and their market value.[153]

In the IRS's view, continuing a long-term relationship with the selling physicians helps to protect the exempt purchaser's investment in the anticipated future income stream to be generated by the physicians; the investment is represented by the exempt purchaser's payment for the practice.[154] The IRS has expressed no definitive position on the use of non-competition covenants in this context; however, it has expressed what may be viewed as a preference for using them in connection with practice-acquisition agreements and corresponding service relationships.[155]

6.3.2 Compensation Arrangements

6.3.2.1 General Principles

A tax-exempt organization may pay reasonable compensation to its executives and its employed and non-employed physicians for the services they render without jeopardizing its tax-exempt status. The determination of whether total compensation is reasonable depends on the facts and circumstances of each case, and requires an examination of the total compensation paid, including base salary, bonuses, deferred and incentive compensation, benefits (including fringe benefits), and all

---

[151] *Id.*; *see also* "Integrated Delivery Systems and Joint Venture," at 167–68.
[152] "Valuation of Medical Practices," at 409.
[153] Rev. Rul. 59-60, 1959-1 C.B. 237.
[154] "Integrated Delivery Systems and Joint Venture," at 222.
[155] *Id.*

other items of value (such as beneficial loans and leases) provided to the person delivering services to the organization.[156]

The compensation principles from Code § 162 provide useful guidance for evaluating the reasonableness of compensation for purposes of Code § 501(c)(3)'s private-inurement prohibition and public-benefit requirement. For purposes of Code § 162, "reasonable compensation is the amount that would ordinarily be paid for like services by like organizations in like circumstances."[157] In determining the reasonableness of compensation under Code § 162, the IRS will consider whether the compensation is comparable to what other organizations pay their employees based on the following comparability factors:

- what similar organizations pay persons of comparable experience and qualifications performing comparable services;
- the duties to be performed;
- the time devoted to the duties;
- the employee's background, experience, and knowledge of the business;
- the size of the business;
- the employee's contribution to profit-making;
- the time the employee devotes to the business;
- the character and amount of the employee's responsibility;
- the time of the year when compensation is determined;
- the working conditions;
- the prevalent economic conditions; and
- whether the negotiations for such salaries were conducted at arm's length.[158]

An exempt organization may rely on various third-party sources for data and other information needed to demonstrate comparability.[159] The legislative history underlying Code § 4958 states that an individual need not accept reduced compensation merely because he or she is serving a tax-exempt organization.[160] Many sources of objective comparability data exist for physician compensation for a broad spectrum of specialties.[161]

---

[156] Jean Wright and Jay Rotz, "Reasonable Compensation," *IRS Exempt Organization Continuing Professional Education Technical Instruction Program for Fiscal Year 1992*, 191 (1991); "Compensation," *IRS Exempt Organization Continuing Professional Education Technical Instruction Program for Fiscal Year 1990*, 171 (1989).

[157] Treas. Reg. § 1.162-7(b)(3). The proposed intermediate-sanction regulations under Code § 4958 uses this same definition. Prop. Treas. Reg. § 1.53.4958-4(b)(2).

[158] Internal Revenue Manual 4233, § 232.2 (last revised Mar. 11, 1985).

[159] "Reasonable Compensation," lists 10 such sources.

[160] JCX-7-96, Bureau of National Affairs, DAILY TAX REPORT L-1 (Mar. 22, 1996). The 1992 CPE Text lists five sources for comparability data drawn from for-profit businesses.

[161] For example, the Medical Group Management Association annually publishes a physician compensation survey in its *Physician Advisory Newsletter*. The Graduate Medical Education National Advisory Committee and the American Medical Association publish similar surveys. Other sources of information may include state or local medical societies, national trade associations, the "Big Five" accounting firms, health care consulting firms, benefits and compensation firms (*e.g.*, William Mercer, Hay Associates), and physician-recruiting firms (*e.g.*, Jackson and Coker).

6.3.2.2 Incentive Compensation Generally

The mere establishment of incentive compensation will not *per se* jeopardize an organization's tax-exempt status where the plan advances the exempt purpose of a hospital by improving the quality and efficiency of patient care, and is not a mere device to distribute profits.

Incentive compensation is, however, of special concern to the IRS. Its Hospital Audit Guidelines instruct IRS auditors to scrutinize closely incentive-compensation arrangements for potential inurement.[162] When reviewing incentive-compensation arrangements, the IRS seeks to determine whether the total compensation is reasonable, and whether the method by which incentive compensation is determined is acceptable. In particular, the IRS requires that incentive-compensation arrangements (a) are not either a device to distribute profits or tantamount to giving private individuals an "equity" interest in the exempt organization and (b) do not create a significant conflict between serving the personal interests of the individual involved and serving the tax-exempt purpose of the organization.

Accordingly, the IRS has approved incentive-compensation arrangements, but only with the presence of certain safeguards: (a) an arm's-length relationship; (b) contingent payments that serve a real and discernible business purpose; (c) the amount of compensation is not dependent principally on incoming revenues, but rather on accomplishment of the objectives of the compensation arrangement; (d) to the extent that compensation is related to revenues, the compensation is based on a percentage of gross or adjusted gross revenues (and not on net income); (e) actual results do not indicate abuse or unwarranted benefits; (f) presence of a ceiling or reasonable maximum amount of compensation; and (g) total compensation, including the incentive amount, is reasonable.[163]

If a compensation package satisfies these tests, then the mere fact that the compensation involves the payment of incentive compensation will not *per se* result in private inurement, impermissible private benefit, or an excess benefit for purposes of the intermediate-sanctions excise taxes.

6.3.2.3 Physician Incentive Compensation

In 1999, the IRS discussed the application of these safeguards in the context of physician incentive compensation, and identified the following additional factors to be considered: (a) whether the arrangement was established by an independent board of directors or independent compensation committee; (b) whether the arrangement has the potential for reducing the charitable services or benefits the organization would otherwise provide; (c) whether the arrangement takes into account data that measures quality of care and patient satisfaction; and (d) whether the arrangement rewards the physician based on services the physician actually performs.[164]

It is also important to note that the intermediate-sanction provisions of Code § 4958 includes in the definition of "excess benefit transactions" revenue-sharing arrangements that are defined by

---

[162] Examination Guidelines for Hospitals, Announcement 92-83, 1992-22 I.R.B. 59, § 333.3(6).
[163] Gen. Couns. Mem. 38,905 (Oct. 6, 1982), *citing* Gen. Couns. Mem. 32453 (Nov. 30, 1962).
[164] Lawrence M. Brauer and Charles F. Kaiser III, "Physician Incentive Compensation," *IRS Exempt Organization Continuing Professional Education Technical Instruction Program for Fiscal Year 2000*, 30–33. *See also* IRS Information Letter 2002-0021 (Jan. 9, 2002).

Treasury regulations as resulting in prohibited private inurement.[165] The final Treasury Regulations simply reserve that topic; currently, no such arrangements have been defined.[166]

6.3.2.4 Executive Compensation

In determining whether executive compensation is reasonable, it is necessary to examine the total compensation paid to the executive, including base salary, bonuses, fringe benefits, and other items of value provided to the executive. As discussed in the preceding section, bonuses and other incentive compensation vehicles are permitted if appropriate safeguards are present. An additional area of concern related to executive compensation is fringe benefits. In 2001, the IRS included an extensive discussion of the tax implications of fringe benefits in its Continuing Professional Education Text for Fiscal Year 2002.[167] The discussion focused on a number of issues related to fringe benefits, including how they are analyzed and valued for purposes of determining whether (1) total compensation is reasonable, (2) the benefits are provided in exchange for services, and (3) the benefits are properly reported and taxed.[168] In 2002, the IRS issued two Technical Advice Memoranda involving possible imposition of intermediate-sanctions excise taxes in the context of executive compensation.[169]

In 2004, the IRS conducted a "soft contact audit" initiative in which it sought detailed information from 2,000 exempt organizations concerning their executive compensation practices, including the amount of cash and non-cash compensation paid, the exempt organization's internal compensation review processes (including the use of outside consultants), and the nature and extent of the data supporting the reported compensation levels. The IRS also required identification and discussion of any business or financial ties between the exempt organization's disqualified persons and its independent contractors. In its 2007 summary of the results of the project, the IRS reported that, in general, there were widespread significant reporting errors or omissions for compensation paid or benefits (such as cars or cell phones) to officers or high-ranking employees, and that 31% of the organizations reviewed filed amended returns or schedules.[170]

This soft contact audit initiative culminated in significant revisions to the Form 990 annual information return relating to compensation paid to officers, directors, trustees, key employees and their five highest paid employees, and independent contractors.[171] Among the most notable changes are the following:

1. An organization must disclose compensation and benefits provided to the top 20 current "key employees" (i.e., executives who do not fit within the fairly narrow definition of "officer"). A key employee is defined as an individual who receives $150,000 or more in compensation from the exempt organization and has certain types of responsibilities within the organization

---

[165] I.R.C. § 4958(c)(2).
[166] Treas. Reg. § 53.4958-5. The proposed intermediate sanctions regulations on this topic were abandoned.
[167] "An Introduction to I.R.C. 4958 (Intermediate Sanctions)," at 291–323.
[168] *Id.*
[169] Tech. Adv. Mem. 200244028 and Tech. Adv. Mem. 200243057.
[170] *See* "Report on Exempt Organizations Executive Compensation Compliance Project," at 5, *available at* http://www.irs.gov/pub/irs-tege/exec._comp._final.pdf.
[171] Beginning with the 2008 Form 990, these changes are reflected in Part VII of the Core Form 990 and in Schedule J to the Core Form.

even if they do not bear an officer title. For example, physicians who chair a hospital's medical department would be treated as key employees for this purpose.

2. An organization must also report compensation paid to the five "highest compensated" employees who have certain officer-type responsibilities and who receive over $100,000 but less than $150,000 in reportable compensation.

3. An organization must report compensation paid to "former" officers, directors, trustees, key employees and five highest paid employees, reporting organizations who received compensation during a five-year lookback period.

4. If an organization disclosed any of the following on the Core Form, it must provide additional information on Schedule J to the Core Form: (a) compensation to a "former" officer, director, trustee, key employee, or five highest compensated employee; (b) more than $150,000 in compensation paid to any individual (including compensation from related organizations); or (c) participation in an arrangement in which an unrelated organization paid compensation to at least one of its officers, directors, trustees, key employees, or five highest compensated employees for services performed to the filing organization. Schedule J requires organizations to provide more detailed compensation information than included on the Core Form, such as incentive compensation, deferred compensation, nontaxable benefits, and compensation reported in a prior Form 990. It also requires additional information regarding other compensation practices, including, among others: (a) payment of "sensitive" compensation items including spousal travel, discretionary spending accounts, and tax-gross ups; (b) payment for first-class travel for any person whose compensation is being reported, including first-class upgrades on air travel (if paid for with organization funds); and (c) providing personal services for any person whose compensation is being reported (e.g., payment for legal services).

5. The organization must disclose on the Core Form whether it reviews and approves executive compensation in a manner that qualifies for the IRS safe harbor under § 4958. The IRS contemplates that a "yes" answer would be based, in part, on the use of an independent compensation consultant (or the use of data from an independent consultant).[172]

These Form 990 reporting changes and "soft audits" signal the IRS's continuing focus on executive compensation programs and practices, and they reinforce the importance of approving executive compensation in a manner consistent with the rebuttable presumption of reasonableness, and that the market data being used by the board or board-appointed committee be "appropriate comparability data."[173] Tax-exempt organizations should pay close attention to their board-level process of reviewing and approving executive and physician compensation. A strong process led

---

[172] For this purpose, the IRS provides a fairly broad definition of independence: the consultant is independent if he or she does not have a family or business relationship with the Chief Executive Officer or Executive Director, and if a majority of the consultant's appraisals during the same year are for other organizations, even if the consultant's firm also provides tax and audit services to the organization. This will enable many organizations that use their consultant for multiple engagements to take the position that the consultant is nevertheless independent.

[173] See "Report on Exempt Organizations Executive Compensation Compliance Project," at 1, available at http://www.irs.gov/pub/irs-tege/exec._comp._final.pdf. The IRS has also addressed the importance of tax-exempt organizations implementing policies regarding executive compensation to maintain tax-exempt status. See "Governance and Related Topics – 501(c)(3) Organizations," at 3.

by the board or board-appointed committee, and one in which the data comparison is appropriate for the organization, will be the strongest defense against intermediate sanctions and also against a threat to exempt status.

6.3.3 Physician Recruitment Incentives

6.3.3.1 *Background*

The IRS has recognized that hospitals may need to offer incentives to attract qualified physicians in a particular specialty in order to provide quality health care to the community. The IRS historically has been concerned, however, that physician-recruitment arrangements may result in excessive private benefit to the recruited physician.[174] In the course of the past few years, the IRS has increased its scrutiny of physician recruiting activities.

The most common approach to physician recruitment is for an exempt hospital to provide financial assistance needed to bring a new physician into the community either in his or her own private practice or in the practice of an existing group practice. In such case, the hospital would not retain the physician either as an employee or as an independent contractor to provide services on the hospital's behalf.

In 1997, the IRS published Revenue Ruling 97-21,[175] providing physician-recruitment guidance to tax-exempt hospitals. The ruling applies to employed physicians, independent contractor physicians, and voluntary members of a hospital's medical staff who are establishing a private practice in the hospital's service area. The ruling states that, although the compensation of physicians providing services "to or on behalf of the hospital" is reviewed under a reasonable-compensation analysis, the compensation of physicians *not* providing services to or on behalf of the hospital should be scrutinized under a four-part analysis, including the following factors: (a) furtherance of charitable purposes; (b) potential for private inurement; (c) potential for excessive private benefit; and (d) potential for substantial illegal activities.[176]

The situations set forth in the ruling involved the use of a variety of recruiting incentives without a loss of exemption. The incentives include a one-time cash bonus, below-market rent for a limited number of years, a home-mortgage guarantee, start-up financial assistance, malpractice insurance

---

[174] Rev. Rul. 97-21, 1997-1 C.B. 121. The private-inurement prohibition technically does not apply to recruitment arrangements because a physician being newly recruited does not have an existing relationship that would trigger insider status. It is important in this regard, however, to distinguish between offering incentives to recruit new physicians and offering incentives to retain existing physicians. The inurement prohibition does apply to the latter. The IRS's definition of "Permissible Recruits" in the *Hermann Hospital Closing Agreement*, for example, is a "physician who either (i) is a recent graduate of a residency or fellowship program whether or not in the hospital's community or (ii) has not previously practiced in hospital's community or been affiliated with another hospital serving all or part of the hospital's community." This provision of the *Hermann Hospital Closing Agreement*, however, should be considered relative to subsequent guidance, such as Rev. Rul. 97-21 and the unpublished Priv. Ltr. Rul. dated July 31, 1998, which suggest that cross-town recruitment may be permissible in certain cases.
[175] Rev. Rul. 97-21.
[176] An example of potential illegality would be a violation of the Medicare antifraud and abuse laws. A discussion of the effect of illegal activities is outside the scope of this Chapter, but one can be found in Gen. Couns. Mem. 39862 (Nov. 22, 1991).

and reimbursement of malpractice "tail" coverage, paid moving expenses, private-practice income guarantees for a limited number of years, and use of medical staff. These incentives were not all provided in each case.

Prior to the issuance of Revenue Ruling 97-21, the IRS's positions concerning recruitment were reflected in non-precedential guidance such as private letter rulings, general counsel memoranda, audit guidelines, and closing agreements.[177] Together with Revenue Ruling 97-21, such non-precedential guidance remains a useful source of insight into structuring recruitment arrangements.

6.3.3.2   Community Benefit Requirement

From these formal and informal sources of IRS guidance on physician recruitment emerges the clear message that the IRS will require a hospital to demonstrate and document that achieving a *bona fide* community benefit is the principal purpose of all physician recruitment arrangements (rather than increasing the hospital's market share or improving its competitive position).

The closing agreement in the case of Hermann Hospital provides the following examples of evidence of a demonstrable community need for physician: (a) a deficiency in the population-to-physician ratio for the relevant specialty (relative to the ideal ratio set forth in Graduate Medical Education National Advisory Committee reports); (b) documented demand for a particular medical service, coupled with a documented lack of availability of the service of long waiting periods for it; (c) designation of the relevant community as a "Health Professional Shortage Area;"[178] (d) demonstrated reluctance of physicians to relocate to the hospital's location in a rural or economically disadvantaged inner-city area; (e) a reasonably expected reduction in the number of physicians in a given specialty due to anticipated retirement of existing physician; or (f) documented lack of physicians serving indigent or Medicaid patients, and a commitment by the recruited physician to serve a substantial number of such patients.

In an unpublished IRS Private Letter Ruling, the IRS also provided useful guidance to tax-exempt hospitals on permissible recruitment incentives that can be extended to new physicians entering private practice. It also provides detail concerning the facts and circumstances that supported the community-benefit rationale for the recruitment arrangement in that case.[179] A specific strategic focus of the hospital in recent years had been the development of a series of community health centers providing specialized non-tertiary inpatient and outpatient services. Designed to provide access to the hospital's services to a larger number of community residents, the centers were located in growing areas of the hospital's service area where a need existed for additional primary care and specialist physicians. The centers were being developed in conjunction with a primary care physician group loosely affiliated (i.e., not owned or controlled by) with the hospital. The hospital's most recent community-needs assessment determined that, in order to address a shortage of primary-care physicians

---

[177] *See, e.g.*, Gen. Couns. Mem. 39498 (Apr. 24, 1986); Gen. Couns. Mem. 39598 (Dec. 8, 1986); *Examination Guidelines for Hospitals* § 333.3(5), Announcement 92-83, 1992-22 I.R.B. 59; the *Hermann Hospital Closing Agreement* (Sept. 20, 1994), Bureau of National Affairs, "Highlights and Documents," 648 (Oct. 17, 1994). *See also* unpublished Priv. Ltr. Rul. dated July 31, 1998, in Bureau of National Affairs, Health Law Reporter 960 (June 10, 1999). (It has not been formally released by the IRS, and thus has no specific identifying number.)

[178] Health Professional Shortage Area is defined under 42 C.F.R. §§ 5.1–5.4.

[179] Unpublished Priv. Ltr. Rul. dated July 31, 1998.

and certain physician specialists, additional physicians must be recruited to join the physician's group and to provide care in the communities served by the centers.

6.3.3.3 Income Guarantees

Guaranteeing the private-practice income of a newly recruited physician for a period of time is one of the most common forms of recruitment assistance provided by exempt hospitals. In such arrangements, the hospital agrees to fund the shortfall if the professional revenue generated by the physician during the guarantee period is not sufficient to support a specified level of monthly compensation and expenses. At the end of the guarantee period, the total amount of funds advanced and not repaid is converted to a loan. The following are the factors that the IRS likely would consider in evaluating an income guarantee: (a) whether the physician is relocating to the service area; (b) the reluctance of the physician or other physicians to relocate to the service area; (c) whether the period of any benefit provided is longer than two years; (d) whether sufficient evidence is present of *bona fide* community need; (e) whether the level of income guaranteed is reasonable; (f) whether a reasonable and explicit ceiling is established on the amount of any potential subsidy to be provided under the guarantee arrangement; (g) whether an unconditional obligation has been established to repay amounts advanced; and (h) if the physician's repayment obligation is forgiven in whole or in part, whether the forgiveness arrangement is demonstrably related to community benefit.[180] It is also essential that the terms and conditions of any forgiveness arrangement are structured so as to achieve the community benefit the recruitment arrangement was intended to achieve.[181]

The following are the factors that the IRS would likely consider in evaluating the loan aspects of an income guarantee: (a) whether a reasonable rate of interest (generally 1 to 2% above the prime rate) is charged; (b) whether the loan is secured by adequate assets; (c) whether the loan is approved by the board of directors, whose approval reflects consideration of the payment history of any prior loan; and (d) whether any variance between the terms of the loan and commercially available loan terms is treated and reported as compensation.[182]

6.3.4 Joint Venture Arrangements Involving Exempt and Non-Exempt Participants

Prior to 1980, the IRS generally took the view that participation as a general partner[183] in a joint venture with a for-profit entity was *per se* inconsistent with continued tax-exempt status for a § 501(c)(3) organization.[184] The IRS's *per se* rule was based on the view that (1) the joint venture is a vehicle for sharing profits with other investors, (2) as a general partner the exempt organization has

---

[180] These factors emanate from Rev. Rul. 97-21, and the Examination Guidelines for Hospitals.
[181] For example, any forgiveness of a loan is conditioned upon continued presence in private practice in the community, and is pro-ratable for no less than four years (which time period is specified at the time the loan is made); such forgiveness is supported, at the time provision for forgiveness is made, by evidence of a demonstrable need for the physician and the amount of the incentive. *Hermann Hospital Closing Agreement*.
[182] *Examination Guidelines for Hospitals*, at § 333.3(10); *Hermann Hospital Closing Agreement*.
[183] Participation by an exempt organization as a limited partner has not been raised by the IRS as a threat to exemption. The only issue in that case is whether the exempt organization's share of partnership income is subject to unrelated business income tax. Rev. Rul. 79-22, 1979-2 C.B. 236.
[184] *Compare* GCM 36293 (May 30, 1975) (stating the *per se* position) with GCM 37852 (Feb. 15, 1979) (retreating somewhat from the *per se* rule).

a fiduciary duty under state partnership law to further the private financial interests of its partners, and (3) as a general partner the exempt organization is exposed to unlimited liability for the debts of the partnership, which benefits its partners.

The IRS's *per se* prohibition was rejected by the Tax Court in *Plumstead Theatre Society v. Commissioner*,[185] in which a § 501(c)(3) organization acted as the sole general partner in a limited partnership with a for-profit corporation and individuals. The purpose of the partnership was to raise funds to produce a play. The Tax Court approved Plumstead's role as general partner and found that: (1) the formation of the partnership was the result of arm's length negotiations; (2) the exempt organization was not obligated to use its own funds to return any capital contributed by the limited partners; (3) the partnership had no interest in the exempt organization; (4) the limited partners had no control over the way the exempt organization managed its affairs; and (5) none of the limited partners was an officer or director of the exempt organization.

Since the Tax Court's decision in *Plumstead*, it has been the administrative position of the IRS that, under appropriate circumstances, an exempt organization may participate in a joint venture with a taxable entity without jeopardizing its tax-exempt status. The IRS's post-*Plumstead* position is generally regarded as imposing two basic requirements on an exempt organization serving as the general partner of a joint venture with for-profit participants.[186] The first requirement is that the partnership further the exempt organization's charitable purposes. The second requirement is that the partnership agreement permit the exempt organization as general partner to operate exclusively in furtherance of its exempt purposes, without regard to any state-law duty to maximize profits for other partners.

This two-part test has been interpreted and applied in many GCMs and PLRs that have added various refinements. First, the exempt general partner should receive distributions of partnership income at least in proportion to its capital contribution and its losses should not exceed its share of partnership capital.[187] Second, transactions between the partnership and its for-profit partners must be at arm's length and reflect fair market value, including reasonable compensation for services provided to the partnership.[188] Third, in determining whether the charitable purpose requirement is met, there should be evidence of community benefit such as creation of a new health care provider, expansion of community health care resources, improvement of treatment modalities, reduction of health care costs, or improvement of patient convenience and access to physicians.[189] Finally, there should be protections against conflicts of interest if insiders of the exempt organization general partner invest in the joint venture.[190]

6.3.4.1 Whole Hospital Joint Ventures

In March 1998, the IRS issued its first precedential guidance in this area with the release of Rev. Rul. 98-15.[191] This ruling focused on the type of joint venture referred to as a "whole hospital

---

[185] 74 T.C. 1324 (1980).
[186] GCM 39005 (June 28, 1983). *See also* GCM 39862 (November 22, 1991); GCM 39732 (November 4, 1987); GCM 39546 (Aug. 14, 1986).
[187] GCM 39732 (Nov. 4, 1987).
[188] *Id.*
[189] GCM 39862 (Nov. 22, 1991).
[190] GCM 39444 (July 18, 1985).
[191] 1998-1 C.B. 718.

joint venture, which involves the transfer by an exempt hospital organization of its entire exempt operations into a joint venture in which the exempt hospital is a co-investor with a proprietary entity. The ruling emphasized the exempt organization's degree of control over the venture as a key factor in determining whether participation in the venture jeopardized the exempt organization's tax-exempt status, and expressed a clear preference that the exempt organization have majority control over the venture.

Since the issuance of Rev. Rul. 98-15, two important "whole hospital" joint venture cases have been fully adjudicated. In *Redlands Surgical Services, Inc. v. Commissioner*,[192] which the Tax Court, while not wholly adopting the views of the IRS in Rev. Rul. 98-15, also placed tremendous emphasis on the language contained in the governing documents, the ability of the tax-exempt partner to control the joint venture entity, and the role of the for-profit partners in the management of the joint venture. The case was appealed to the Ninth Circuit Court of Appeals where it was affirmed. In *St. David's Health Care System, Inc. v. United States*,[193] the District Court for the Western District of Texas rendered summary judgment in favor of the tax-exempt participant and against the government. The case was the first to review a whole hospital joint venture and the first to approve a 50-50 joint venture. The district court's grant of summary judgment was reversed and remanded by the Fifth Circuit, which remanded the case to the district court for trial.[194] On remand, a jury rendered a verdict for St. David's.

The IRS is not bound to follow the result in *St. David's*. Moreover, the IRS is unlikely to agree that a tax-exempt organization whose primary activity is holding an interest in a joint venture retains its exemption unless the fact situation very closely adheres to the facts and circumstances the IRS described in the "good" fact pattern in Rev. Rul. 98-15. While the IRS did not ultimately prevail in result in the *St. David's* case, based on the appellate decision the IRS believes it has the support of the courts for its position.

6.3.4.2 Ancillary Joint Ventures

Revenue Ruling 2004-51 addresses an exempt organization's participation in an *ancillary joint venture*, which is a joint venture between an exempt organization and a for-profit entity in which the joint venture's activities represent an insubstantial portion of the total activities of the exempt participant. Revenue Ruling 2004-51 involves the formation of a limited liability company by a tax-exempt university and a for-profit company for the purpose of offering off-campus, summer training programs for secondary school teachers using interactive video technology. The exempt university did not have majority control over the venture. Nonetheless, the Ruling concludes that the university's participation in the joint venture will not adversely affect the university's continued tax-exempt status because the activities the university is conducting through the joint venture are not a substantial part of the university's activities. The Ruling also concludes that the activities the university is conducting through the joint venture are not an unrelated trade or business and do not create UBI for the university. The key factor supporting this conclusion is the exclusive control the exempt university

---

[192] 113 T.C. 47 (1999), *aff'd per curiam*, 242 F.3d 904 (9th Cir. 2001).
[193] (W.D. Texas), 01-CV-46 (June 7, 2002).
[194] *St. David's Health Care System v. United States*, 2003-2 USTC ¶50,713 (5th Cir. 2003).

exercises over the important, educational aspects of the joint venture's activities that affect whether the joint venture operates in a manner consistent with the exempt organization's exempt purposes. The Ruling does not indicate how the IRS determined that the university's participation in the joint venture was an insubstantial part of its activities, and in fact there is no bright-line test for substantiality. However, the Ruling clearly indicates that majority control by the exempt organization is not essential for a favorable ruling on both issues in the context of an ancillary joint venture.

Other facts and circumstances the IRS cites in support of the favorable ruling focus primarily on: the provisions of the LLC governing documents dealing with the purposes and activities of the LLC and their compliance with the exempt status of the university; the equal voice of the members in making non-curriculum or business decisions with respect to the LLC; the allocation of profits and losses of the venture in proportion to each party's capital contribution; and the arm's-length nature and market comparability of the contractual relationships between the LLC and either of the venturers or third parties.[195]

To be able to take a position that an exempt organization's participation in the joint venture does not create unrelated business income or otherwise jeopardize the organization's exemption, the joint venture arrangement, and the associated joint venture documents, should include the following features:

- The purpose of the joint venture is to provide health care in a charitable manner (consistent with the community benefit standard set forth in § 501(c)(3) of the Code).

- If there is a conflict between charitable objectives and profit maximization when the joint venture board or members are making a particular decision, charitable operation will prevail over profit maximization.

- The joint venture may not engage in activities that would jeopardize the exempt joint venturer's tax-exempt status.

- The joint venture documents should not include a binding arbitration requirement, on the theory that the arbitrator will make decisions that are not necessarily in furtherance of charitable purposes.

- The joint venture documents should not include a non-compete provision that completely precludes the exempt joint venturer from providing a type of service. For example, the joint venture documents may provide that neither party may operate a freestanding ambulatory surgery center in a particular area but should not prohibit the exempt organization from providing outpatient surgery in its facility.

---

[195] In connection with its consideration of the application of § 501(c)(3) to an exempt organization's participation in the MSSP described in § 3022 of the ACA enacted on March 23, 2010, Pub. L. 111-148, 124 Stat. 119, the IRS issued Notice 2011-20, 2011-16 I.R.B. 652, to solicit comments concerning two important exemption issues: (1) whether this prior IRS guidance on participation in a joint venture is sufficient with regard to participation in an MSSP ACO, and (2) whether guidance is needed regarding the tax-exemption implications of participating in non-MSSP ACO. Notably, the Notice does not address or seek comments concerning whether the nature of the activities of a joint venture organization created to implement some or all of an accountable care strategy will support a position that an exempt health care organization's share of the income generated by such a joint venture will qualify as related to the exempt health care organization's § 501(c)(3) purposes. Nor does it address or seek comments concerning the ability of a new entity created to implement an ACO strategy (in whole or in part) can qualify for stand-alone exemption.

- The joint venture documents should require reformation of documents if the exempt joint venturer determines that the documents' provisions may affect tax-exempt status, be contrary to law, or preclude billing for services.

If the joint venture enters into a management agreement with a for-profit entity:

- The management agreement should not have a term longer than five years.

- The management agreement should require the manager to operate the facility in conformance with the venture's charitable purposes, and failure to comply with this requirement should be included as a basis for termination and/or non-renewal. Further, there should be an effective means of enforcing this obligation short of dissolution of the joint venture.

- If the management fee is based on a percentage of revenues, it is best that the fee be based on gross charges, not collections, so that the manager is not incentivized to limit charitable care improperly or engage in inappropriate collection practices.

- The management fee should be validated as fair market value as to methodology (e.g., if a percentage of revenues, is there a dollar cap?) and amount.

- The exempt organization's approval should be required for certain key matters that could affect whether the joint venture furthers the exempt organization's charitable purposes or furthers the private interests of the non-exempt participants, such as changes in joint venture services and programs; annual capital and operating budgets or significant variations therefrom; the acquisition or disposition of health care facilities; appointment of joint venture executives; renewal or termination of management agreements; amendment of joint venture organizational documents; the addition of partners to the venture; calls for additional capital contributions; conflicts of interest and charity care policies; and merger, dissolution or declaration of bankruptcy by the venture.

6.3.5 Courtesy Discounts

The IRS historically has taken the position that courtesy discounts offered to physicians, nurses, clergy, members of religious orders, or other individuals may represent private inurement or more-than-incidental private benefit to the extent that they are provided without regard to financial need, unless: (1) the individual entitled to the discount is an employee or otherwise provides services to the organization, and the discounts are part of a package that constitutes no more than reasonable compensation; or (2) the organization can show that the practices are qualitatively and quantitatively incidental to advancing its exempt functions or purposes. The informally reported position of the IRS in certain of its Coordinated Examination Program (CEP) audits is consistent with this position.[196]

In addition, the amount of any actual courtesy discounts provided to an individual must be reported as income on either Form W-2 or Form 1099.

---

[196] For example, in the CEP audit of Baylor University Medical Center in Dallas, Texas, the IRS required Baylor to discontinue its practice of providing discounts on hospital services to members of its medical staff. Medicare Compliance Alert, May 11, 1992.

6.3.6 Donation of Electronic Health Record Technology

A possible private inurement situation faced by tax-exempt hospitals involved whether tax-exempt hospitals could donate electronic health record (EHR) technology items and services to health care providers. In response to requests by the exempt hospital community, the IRS issued a directive on May 11, 2007 (the Directive)[197] concerning exempt hospitals that provide physicians who have staff privileges at those hospitals with assistance to acquire and implement EHR items and services. The Directive states that the IRS will not treat the benefits a hospital provides to its medical staff physicians as an impermissible private benefit or inurement if the hospital meets the following requirements:

- the hospital and the participating physicians comply with the requirements of the EHR Regulations on a continuing basis;
- to the extent permitted by law, the hospital may access all of the electronic medical records created by a physician using the donated items or services;
- the hospital ensures that the donated items and services are available to all of its medical staff physicians; and
- the hospital provides the same level of subsidy to all of its medical staff physicians or varies the level of subsidy by applying criteria related to meeting the health care needs of the community.[198]

It is important to keep in mind that the IRS directive is also, in effect, a safe harbor. That is, a failure to fit squarely within the parameters it sets forth does not result in a *per se* tax-exemption violation. Instead, the hospital would need to develop an alternative facts and circumstances analysis to demonstrate its compliance with tax-exemption requirements. For example, it has suggested that a hospital may provide access to various groups of physicians at different times according to criteria related to meeting the health care needs of the community and that the hospital should develop a plan for providing such access.

6.3.7 Use of Taxable Affiliates

Many health care systems include taxable subsidiaries and affiliates, which often are used to conduct activities that might be characterized as unrelated business activities if conducted by the § 501(c)(3) health care organization. The IRS has taken the position that, in certain circumstances, the activities of a taxable affiliate that violate the private-inurement or private-benefit prohibitions may be attributed to its related § 501(c)(3) organization[199] and thereby jeopardize its tax-exempt status.

The IRS has recognized that the taxable corporation is a separate legal entity and that, where a corporation is organized with a *bona fide* intention that it will have some real and substantial business

---

[197] IRS Memorandum, "Hospitals Providing Financial Assistance to Staff Physicians Involving Electronic Health Records" (May 11, 2007).
[198] *Id.*
[199] *See, e.g.*, Gen. Couns. Mem. 39646 (June 30, 1987); Gen. Couns. Mem. 39598 (Jan. 23, 1987); Gen. Couns. Mem. 39326 (Jan. 17, 1985).

function, its existence may not generally be disregarded for tax purposes.[200] The activities of a separately incorporated subsidiary cannot ordinarily be attributed to its parent organization unless the subsidiary is in reality an arm, agent, or integral part of the parent.[201] Nevertheless, where the parent corporation so controls the affairs of the subsidiary that it is merely an instrumentality of the parent, the corporate entity of the subsidiary may be disregarded.[202] In addition, the corporate entity may be disregarded if the corporation or transaction involved was a sham or fraud without any valid business purpose, or there is a true agency or trust relationship between the entities.[203]

Merely showing that one corporation is wholly owned by another is not, in and of itself, sufficient to allow attribution.[204] The IRS has indicated that the activities of a separately organized subsidiary generally will not be attributed to the parent where the day-to-day management of the subsidiary is separate from the parent and a majority of the subsidiary's directors are unrelated to the parent.[205] Other factors that the IRS has considered in determining whether activities of a taxable affiliate may be attributed to a § 501(c)(3) organization are: (1) whether costs related to shared assets, facilities, or services are allocated between the entities according to proportionate use; (2) whether corporate formalities are observed; (3) whether funds are commingled; (4) whether transactions between the taxable affiliate and the § 501(c)(3) organization reflect arm's-length negotiations; (5) whether the entities have common officers or employees; and (6) whether the funding for the taxable affiliate comes in whole or in part, directly or indirectly, from the § 501(c)(3) affiliate.[206]

6.4 Section 509(a) Public Charity Status

6.4.1 Section 509(a)(1) Public Charities

Some organizations qualify for § 509(a)(1) public charity status on the basis of their principal function rather than on the basis of their financial support. Such organizations include a church, a hospital or a medical research organization operated in connection with a hospital, an organization operated for the benefit of certain state and municipal colleges and universities, a governmental unit or a publicly supported organization. Each of these functions is specifically defined under the applicable treasury regulations. For example, "hospital" is broadly defined to include a principal purpose or function of providing hospital or medical care, whether physical or mental, inpatient or outpatient. Thus, the IRS has granted public charity status as a "hospital" to ambulatory surgical centers, psychiatric hospitals, rehabilitation institutions, outpatient clinics, and community mental health

---

[200] *Moline Properties, Inc. v. Commissioner*, 319 U.S. 436, 438 (1943); *Britt v. United States*, 431 F.2d 227, 234 (5th Cir. 1970).
[201] *Id. See also* Gen. Couns. Mem. 39326.
[202] *Krivo Indus. Supply Co. v. National Distillers & Chem. Corp.*, 483 F.2d 1098, 1106 (5th Cir. 1973).
[203] Gen. Couns. Mem. 39598; Tech. Adv. Mem. 200208027 (Oct. 4, 2001). *See Commissioner v. Bollinger*, 485 U.S. 340 (1988) and *National Carbide Corp. v. Commissioner*, 336 U.S. 422 (1949) for a discussion of the six factors identified by the Supreme Court for determining whether an agency relationship exists.
[204] Gen. Couns. Mem. 39598; Priv. Ltr. Rul. 200130048 (Apr. 19, 2001); Priv. Ltr. Rul. 199941051 (July 22, 1999).
[205] Gen. Couns. Mem. 39598; Priv. Ltr. Rul. 200130048. Gen. Couns. Mem. 39598 clarifies that complete overlap between the directors of the § 501(c)(3) organization and the taxable affiliate is not alone, however, a sufficient basis for attribution.
[206] Gen. Couns. Mem. 39646; Gen. Couns. Mem. 39326. *See also* Priv. Ltr. Rul. 200037050 (June 20, 2000); Priv. Ltr. Rul. 199941048 (July 20, 1999); Priv. Ltr. Rul. 9819046 (Feb. 11, 1998): Priv. Ltr. Rul. 9817034 (Jan. 28, 1998.).

and drug treatment centers. Convalescent homes and homes for children or the aged or institutions whose principal purpose or function is to train handicapped individuals to pursue some vocation do not qualify as a "hospital."

Other organizations qualify for § 509(a)(1) public charity status on the basis of their sources of financial support. Specifically, an organization may qualify as such if it meets the "public support test" of Code § 170(b)(1)(A)(vi). This test generally requires that the organization receive more than one-third of its total support from a governmental unit and/or from contributions made directly or indirectly by the general public. Contributions made by one individual, trust or corporation—other than from a governmental unit or another § 509(a)(1) organization described in 170(b)(1)(A)(vi)—are counted as public support only to the extent they do not exceed 2% of an organization's total support. The public support test typically is calculated as a four-year moving average. Alternatively, the public support test can be met on a facts and circumstances basis if the organization normally receives at least 10% public support and it organization demonstrates it can attract new and additional public support on a continuous basis. Relevant factors include the amount by which the organization's support exceeds 10%, the extent to which an organization makes its facilities or services available to the public, the variety of an organization's supporters and the composition of its governing board.

6.4.2 Section 509(a)(2) Public Charities

An organization qualifies as a § 509(a)(2) public charity if it meets a two-part public supported test. First, more than one-third of the organization's total support must be from gifts, grants, contributions, membership fees, and gross receipts from admissions, sale of merchandise, performance of services or furnishing of facilities in an activity that is not an unrelated trade or business. Support is counted as public support only if it is from persons who are not disqualified persons, from organizations described in § 509(a)(1) or from governmental units. In addition, amounts received from persons in excess of both $5,000 and 2% of total contributions in a given year are totally excluded. Second, an organization may not receive more than one-third of its support from the sum of gross investment income and any net unrelated business income (less taxes paid on that income).

6.4.3 Section 509(a)(3) Public Charities

An organization qualifies as a § 509(a)(3) public charity if it is a "supporting organization" for one or more §§ 509(a)(1) or 509(a)(2) public charities. To qualify, the organization must be organized and at all times thereafter operated exclusively for the benefit of, to perform the functions of, or to carry out the purposes of one or more specified §§ 509(a)(1) or (2) organizations (referred to as the "organizational and operational test");[207] the organization must be operated, supervised or controlled by or in connection with one or more §§ 509(a)(1) or (2) organization (referred to as the "relationship test"); and the organization must not be controlled directly or indirectly by disqualified persons (other than foundation managers of §§ 509(a)(1) or (2) organizations).

---

[207] Treas. Reg. § 1.509(a)-4(b).

6.4.3.1 Organizational Test

An organization is organized exclusively to support or benefit one or more specified publicly supported organizations only if its articles (a) limit its purposes to the purposes permitted under § 509(a), (b) do not expressly empower the organization to engage in activities that are not in furtherance of those purposes, (c) state the specified publicly supported organizations on whose behalf the organization is operated,[208] and (d) do not expressly empower the organization to operate to support or benefit any organization other than the specified publicly supported organizations.[209]

6.4.3.2 Operational Test

An organization is operated exclusively to support one or more specified publicly supported organizations only if it engages solely in activities that support or benefit its specified supported organizations. These activities may include making payments to or for the use of or providing services or facilities for individual members of the charitable class benefited by the specified supported organizations.[210] A supporting organization is also operated exclusively to support one or more specified supported organizations when it makes payment indirectly through another unrelated organization to a member of a charitable class benefited by a specified publicly supported organization, but only if the payment constitutes a grant to an individual rather than a grant to an organization.[211] A supporting organization need not pay over its income to its supported organizations; it may satisfy the operational test by carrying on an independent activity or program that supports or benefits its supported organizations. It may also engage in fund-raising activities on behalf of its supported organizations or the charitable class benefited by such organizations.[212]

6.4.3.3 Relationship Test

There are three categories of 509(a)(3) supporting organizations,[213] referred to as "Type I Supporting Organizations," "Type II Supporting Organizations," and "Type III Supporting Organizations." These three categories are based on which of three relationship tests the § 509(a)(3) supporting organization meets. Those three relationships have historically been referred to, respectively, as "operated, supervised or controlled by," supervised or controlled in connection with," and "operated in connection with."[214]

A Type I relationship is defined as comparable to that of a parent and subsidiary, in which the subsidiary is under the direction of and accountable or responsible to, the parent organization. This relationship is established by the fact that the supported organization(s)' governing body, members of

---

[208] The degree of specificity with which the supported organizations must be named depends on which of the three relationship tests the organization meets. Treas. Reg. § 1.509(a)-4(d)(2)(i)(a) and (b).
[209] Treas. Reg. § 1.509(a)-4(c). Note, Treasury Regulations also provide that a supported organization may engage in activities that support organizations other than the named supported organizations so long as such other organizations are organized and operated to support the same supported organizations. Treas. Reg. § 1.509(a)-4(e)(1).
[210] Treas. Reg. § 1.509(a)-4(e)(1).
[211] Id.
[212] Id. § 1.509(a)-4(e)(2).
[213] These three categories were established by the Pension Protection Act of 2006 (the PPA). P.L. 109-280, 120 Stat. 780.
[214] Treas. Reg. § 1.509(a)-4(f)(2).

the governing body, officers acting in their official capacity, or members officers supported organization appoint or elect a majority of the officers, directors or trustees of the supporting organization.[215]

A Type II relationship is established through common supervision or control by the persons supervising or controlling both the supporting organization and the supported organization. To meet this standard, the control or management of the supporting organization must be vested in the same persons that control or manage the publicly supported organization.[216]

To establish a Type III relationship, the supporting organization must meet both the responsiveness test and the integral part test. The responsiveness test requires either that: (a) one or more officers, directors, or trustees of the supporting organization are elected or appointed by the officers, directors, trustees or membership of the supported organizations; (b) one or more of the members of the governing bodies of the publicly supported organizations are also officer, directors, or trustees of, or hold other important offices in, the supporting organization; or (c) the officers, directors, or trustees of the supporting organization maintain a close and continuous working relationship with the officers, directors, or trustees of the supported organizations; *and* that, by reason of one of the foregoing, the officers, directors, or trustees of the publicly supported organizations have a significant voice in the investment policies of, the timing and manner of making of grants by, and the selection of grant recipients by the supporting organization and in otherwise directing the use of the income or assets of the supporting organization.[217] The integral part test requires that the supporting organization maintains a significant involvement in the operations of one or more publicly supported organizations that depend on the supporting organization for the type of support that it provides. The supporting organization must demonstrate either that (a) it engages in activities for or on behalf of the publicly supported organizations that are in furtherance of the functions or purposes of its supported organizations, and, but for the involvement of the supporting organization, that are ones that would normally be engaged in directly by the publicly supported organizations or (b) make payments of substantially all of its income (85% or more) to or for the use of one or more of its supported organizations, in circumstances in which (i) the amount received by one or more of such supported organizations is sufficient to ensure the attentiveness of such publicly supported organizations to the operations of the supporting organization and (ii) a substantial amount of the total support of the supporting organization goes to those supported organizations that meet the attentiveness requirement.[218]

There are also two subcategories of Type III Supporting Organizations—those that are *functionally integrated*, and those that are *not functionally integrated*, with the organizations they support. Internal IRS guidance issued in late 2007 identified the requirements that the IRS will apply to determine whether an organization is "functionally integrated." The final regulations published in 2012 modified the requirements set forth in the 2007 guidance.[219] However, the 2007 IRS guidance states that compliance with the applicable requirements is not a guarantee of recognition of functionally

---

[215] Treas. Reg. § 1.509(a)-4(g)(1)(i).
[216] Treas. Reg. § 1.509(a)-4(h)(1).
[217] Treas. Reg. § 1.509(a)-4(i)(2).
[218] Treas. Reg. § 1.509(a)-4(i)(3).
[219] IRM 7.20.7, Exempt Organizations Determination Letter Program, IRC 509(a)(3) Supporting Organizations Guide Sheet (Oct. 1, 2007). The IRS and Treasury issued final and temporary regulations on December 28, 2012, (77 Fed. Reg.

integrated status by the IRS if the IRS finds an organization to be "potentially abusive," and this aspect of the 2007 guidance still applies today.

The final regulations provide that a Type III supporting organization is functionally integrated if it (1) meets the "but for" test; (2) is the parent of each of its supported organizations; or (3) supports a governmental supported organization.[220] The supporting organization satisfies the "but for" test if it engages in activities substantially all of which directly further the exempt purposes of the supported organization(s), to which it is responsive, by performing the functions of, or carrying out the purposes of, such supported organization(s) and but for the involvement of the supporting organization, would normally be engaged in by the [public charities] themselves." In determining whether "substantially all" of the supporting organization's activities directly further the supporting organization's exempt purposes, the final regulations call for the consideration of all pertinent facts and circumstances. The final regulations also add to the "but for" test a requirement that a functionally integrated Type III supporting organization's activities must directly further the exempt purposes of the supported organizations to which it is responsive.

The Pension Protection Act of 2006 (the PPA) introduced the concept of a not functionally integrated Type III supporting organization. The PPA directed the Treasury to develop regulations that impose a distribution requirement and an "attentiveness" requirement on these types of organizations. The final regulations provide that an organization that otherwise meets the requirements of the responsiveness test as a Type III supporting organization, but that fails to meet the integral part test for a functionally integrated Type III supporting organization, may still qualify under the integral part test if the organization demonstrates its satisfaction with either a distribution requirement or an attentiveness requirement.[221]

6.4.3.4 Control Test

To satisfy the Control Test, the supporting organization must demonstrate that (a) the disqualified persons may not, by aggregating their votes or positions of authority, require the organization to perform or prevent it from performing any act that significantly affects its operations (e.g., the right of any substantial contributor (or spouse of a substantial contributor) to designate annually the recipients from among the publicly supported organizations of the income attributable to his or her contribution to the supporting organization is considered control for these purposes) and (b) one or

---

76382) regarding classification of Type III supporting organizations, which includes information about the requirements for functionally integrated and not functionally integrated organizations.

[220] The final regulations eliminated the expenditure test found in the 2007 guidance, which required the supporting organization to use substantially all of the lesser of (a) its adjusted net income or (b) 5% of the aggregate fair market value of all its assets (other than assets that are used, or held for use, directly in supporting the charitable programs of the public charities) directly for the active conduct of activities that directly further the exempt purposes of the public charities it supports. The final regulations also eliminated the asset test, which required the organization to devote at least 65% of the aggregate value of all its assets directly for the active conduct of activities that directly further the exempt purposes of the public charities it supports.

[221] The final regulations explain what distributions count toward this distribution requirement. The final regulations withdrew a portion of the 2009 regulations and replaced them with temporary regulations, which require non-functionally integrated Type III supporting organizations to meet a distribution requirement equal to the greater of 85 percent of the organization's adjusted net income or 3.5 percent of the fair market value of the organization's non-exempt-use assets.

more disqualified persons do not possess 50% or more of the total voting power of the organization's governing body or the right to exercise veto power over the actions of the organization.[222]

6.4.4 Effect of the Pension Protection Act of 2006

The PPA added several private foundation-like provisions affecting Type III supporting organizations, particularly non-functionally integrated supporting organizations. For example: (a) § 509(a)(3) supporting organizations are not eligible to receive contributions from individual retirement accounts, unlike other public charities; (b) Type III § 509(a)(3) supporting organizations that are not functionally related may not receive private foundation grants unless expenditure responsibility is exercised; (c) Type III § 509(a)(3) supporting organizations that are not functionally related are subject to the private foundation excess business holding rules; (d) the Department of the Treasury is directed to promulgate regulations requiring Type III § 509(a)(3) supporting organizations that are not functionally related to annually distribute prescribed amounts to a supported organization; (e) Type III § 509(a)(3) supporting organizations may not support a foreign charity; (f) payment of compensation by a § 509(a)(3) supporting organization to its substantial contributors or related parties thereof is an automatic excess benefit transaction subject to intermediate sanctions under Code § 4958, regardless of its reasonableness; (g) private non-operating foundations will be able to count donations to the Type III parent and fundraising foundation towards their required minimum annual distributions; and (h) § 509(a)(3) supporting organizations must file a From 990 annual information return regardless of its income level. The PPA also added provisions that will affect Type I and Type II supporting organizations. These and the other provisions of the PPA could have a potentially significant effect the operations and funding of parents and fundraising foundations in a restructured hospital system.

---

[222] Treas. Reg. § 1.509(a)-4(j).

7

Antitrust Law

John J. Miles
Baker Donelson

7.1 Introduction

Federal and state antitrust laws can affect so many activities of participants in the health care sector that a basic understanding of antitrust principles is crucial to the practice of health law today.[1] Antitrust enforcement in the health care sector today is a major area of focus for the Federal Trade Commission (FTC), Antitrust Division of the U.S. Department of Justice, state attorneys general and private parties.[2] The courts have specifically held that the antitrust laws are fully applicable to health care-sector industries.[3] The Obama administration took aggressive antitrust action against both providers and health plans as exemplified by the FTC's 2016 victories in the Pinnacle Health System/Hershey Medical Center and Advocate Health Network/NorthShore University Health System hospital-merger cases[4] and the Antitrust Division's successful challenges in 2017 to the Anthem/Cigna and Aetna/Humana health-plan mergers.[5]

Application of the antitrust laws to health care sector industries dates primarily from two Supreme Court decisions in the mid-1970s holding that there is no "learned professions" exemption from the antitrust laws[6] and that the activities of a local hospital affect interstate commerce such that the federal antitrust laws provide courts with subject-matter jurisdiction over their allegedly anticompetitive conduct.[7] The late 1970s and 1980s saw a number of "staff-privilege" antitrust cases—practitioners

---

[1] For a much more in-depth treatments of numerous antitrust issues arising in the health care sector, *see* American Health Lawyers Association, *Antitrust and Health Care: A Comprehensive Guide* (2016); 1-6 John J. Miles, *Health Care & Antitrust Law* (1992 and 2013 Supp.); ABA Section of Antitrust Law, *Antitrust Health Care Handbook* (2010); Federal Trade Comm'n & U.S. Dep't of Justice, *Improving Health Care: A Dose of Competition* (2004).
[2] *Cf.* Maureen K. Ohlhausen, Acting Chairman, FTC, *The First Wealth is Health: Protecting Competition in Health Care Markets*, Prepared Remarks Before the American Bar Association Section of Antitrust Law Fall Forum (Nov. 16, 2017) ("As antitrust enforcers, there are probably few markets we touch that are more important to both consumers and the economic health of the country than health care markets. . . . [T]hese markets frequently involve some of the most vital products and services that consumers will ever need. . . . [W]hile protecting competition in health care space is neither easy nor straightforward, it remains a critical focus for me personally and for the FTC as a whole.").
[3] *See, e.g., Boulware v. Nev.*, 960 F.2d 793 (9th Cir. 1991).
[4] *FTC v. Penn State Hershey Med. Ctr.*, 838 F.3d 327 (3d Cir. 2016); *FTC v. Advocate Health Network*, 841 F.3d 460 (7th Cir. 2016), *on remand*, 2017 U.S. Dist. LEXIS 37707 (N.D. Ill., Mar. 16, 2017).
[5] *United States v. Anthem, Inc.*, 855 F.3d 345 (D.C. Cir. 2017); *United States v. Aetna*, 240 F. Supp. 3d 1 (D.D.C. 2017).
[6] *Goldfarb v. Va. State Bar*, 421 U.S. 773 (1975).
[7] *Hosp. Bldg. Co. v. Trs. of Rex Hosp.*, 425 U.S. 738 (1976).

challenging their exclusion from clinical privileges at hospitals. The FTC and Antitrust Division began challenging hospital mergers in the 1980s, and the 1980s and 1990s saw an emphasis on challenges to joint provider negotiation of contracts with health plans resulting in horizontal price-fixing agreements by entities such as independent practice associations (IPAs), preferred-provider organizations (PPOs), and physician-hospital organizations (PHOs). The enforcement emphasis now appears to focus on mergers of health care providers, mergers of health plans, as well as a number of activities in the pharmaceutical industry. Those advising health care clients on antitrust matters wonder whether the new administration in Washington will continue aggressive antitrust enforcement in the health care sector and what issues might draw particular government attention.

This Chapter presents an overview of the purpose of the antitrust laws, the antitrust statutes and their application, exemptions from antitrust coverage, and antitrust enforcement, particularly as they affect firms in the health care sector.[8] It is far from exhaustive, and thus the Chapter concludes with a list of references for more in-depth study.

7.1.1 Purpose of the Antitrust Laws

The antitrust laws protect and promote competition as the primary method by which this nation allocates its economic resources.[9] More specifically, the antitrust laws are a "consumer welfare prescription."[10] They are designed to protect consumers, not competitors *per se*.[11] They protect competitors only when the challenged conduct reduces the number of firms in the relevant market to the extent that the market as a whole fails to perform in a competitive manner and consumers suffer as a result through higher prices, lower quality, fewer choices, poorer access, or less innovation. Thus, a plaintiff always must show harm not merely to itself, but to market-wide competition.[12]

The antitrust laws protect consumers by attempting to shield them from "market power," unless that power is achieved by competition on the merits. Seller market power is the ability of a single seller, or a group of sellers acting in concert, to raise price above (or lower quality below) the competitive level without losing so many sales that the price increase (or decrease in quality) is unprofitable and

---

[8] To aid in understanding application of the antitrust laws to several particular issues arising in the health care sector, the Department of Justice and FTC, in 1996, issued their *Statements of Antitrust Enforcement Policy in Health Care*, at http://www.usdoj.gov/atr/public/guidelines/1791.pdf. These statements discuss hospital mergers, hospital joint ventures, providers' communicating non-fee information to payers, providers' communicating fee-related information to payers, competitor exchanges of price and wage information, group-purchasing arrangements, and provider-controlled contracting networks.

[9] *See generally Northern Pac. Ry. v. United States*, 356 U.S. 1, 4 (1958); *City of Lafayette v. Louisiana Power & Light Co.*, 435 U.S. 389 (1978) ("[i]n enacting the Sherman Act . . . , Congress mandated competition as the polestar by which all must be guided in ordering their business affairs").

[10] *Reiter v. Sonotone Corp.*, 442 U.S. 330, 343 (1979); *see also Glen Holly Entm't Inc. v. Tektronix, Inc.*, 343 F.3d 1000 (9th Cir. 2003) ("customers are the intended beneficiaries of competition").

[11] *See generally Brunswick Corp. v. Pueblo Bowl-O-Mat, Inc.*, 429 U.S. 477 (1977); *Metro Net Servs. Corp. v. US W. Communc'ns*, 329 F.3d 986 (9th Cir. 2003).

[12] *E.g., Sterling Merch., Inc. v. Nestle, S.A.*, 656 F.3d 112 (1st Cir. 2011); *Benson v. St. Joseph's Reg'l Health Ctr.*, 575 F.3d 542 (5th Cir. 2009); *Four Corners Nephrology Assocs., P.C. v. Mercy Med. Ctr.*, 582 F.3d 1216 (10th Cir. 2009) ("Plaintiff must show not only that he was harmed by [defendant's] conduct, but that the injury he suffered involved harm to competition. . . . After all, it is the 'protection of competition or prevention of monopoly[ ] which is plainly the concern of the Sherman Act,' not the vindication of general 'notions of fair dealing,' which are the subject of many other laws.") (citation omitted).

thus must be rescinded.[13] A seller, or group of sellers acting jointly, exercises market power by restricting output, which increases price, misallocates resources,[14] and inappropriately transfers income from buyers to sellers. In general, a firm's degree of market power is a function of its market share, the alternatives available to its customers, and the level of any entry barriers into the market.

Buyer market power, of equal concern to the antitrust laws, is the ability of a purchaser, or group of purchasers acting jointly, to depress the price they pay for a product or service below the competitive level by restricting the amount of that product or service they purchase. Called "monopsony power," buyer market power also misallocates resources and inappropriately transfers income from sellers to buyers.[15] In general, a purchaser's monopsony power depends on its market share as a purchaser, the alternative purchasers available to sellers, and whether new purchasers would enter the market in light of the price reduction. Providers frequently allege that health plans exercise monopsony power in their contracting relationships with providers.

Even if the challenged conduct creates market power, it may also achieve offsetting benefits to competition that must be considered in determining its lawfulness. These offsetting benefits are usually referred to generally as "efficiencies"—more technically, "productive efficiencies," which refer to the ratio of a firm's outputs to its inputs: the greater that ratio, the more efficient the firm is.[16] Efficiencies usually result from some type of "economic integration" among firms, i.e., the combination of resources, functions, and operations among them in ways that "the whole is greater than the sum of its parts."[17] Efficiency benefits include any benefits from the integration that benefit consumers, including lower prices resulting from the firms' lower costs, higher quality, greater innovation, higher output, and improved access.

Antitrust analysis, conceptually and at its most basic level, requires identifying, assessing, and balancing the market-power and efficiency effects of the conduct under examination. In general, if the conduct generates no market-power effects, it raises no antitrust concern, regardless of its efficiency effects. If it generates, maintains, or increases market power but not efficiencies, it usually is unlawful. The most difficult situation is that where the conduct generates both effects, and balancing them becomes necessary. In some situations, that can be done quantitatively through econometric analysis, but doing so is extremely complex and expensive (and in many cases, impossible).[18] This

---

[13] *See, e.g., Eastman Kodak Co. v. Image Tech. Servs., Inc.*, 504 U.S. 451 (1992) (explaining that market power is the ability of a seller to restrict output and thus raise price). For excellent discussions of market power and how it is identified, *see* ABA Section of Antitrust Law, *Market Power Handbook: Competition Law and Economic Foundations* (2d ed. 2012); IIB Phillip E. Areeda, Herbert Hovenkamp & John L. Solow, *Antitrust Law* Chs. 4A, 4B, and 5 (4th ed. 2014); William Landes & Richard Posner, *Market Power in Antitrust Cases*, 94 Harv. L. Rev. 937 (1981).

[14] *See generally* Dennis W. Carlton & Jeffrey M. Perloff, *Modern Industrial Organization* Ch. 4 (4th ed. 2005).

[15] Monopsony is analytically the same as monopoly, but on the buyer side rather than the seller side. *See Weyerhaeuser Co. v. Ross-Simons Hardwood Co.*, 549 U.S. 312 (2007). For a full discussion of monopsony power, *see* Roger D. Blair & Jeffrey L. Harrison, *Monopsony: Antitrust Law and Economics* (2d ed. 2010); *see also* Mark V. Pauly, *Managed Care, Market Power, and Monopsony*, 33 Health Servs. Research 1439 (1998).

[16] *See generally* Herbert Hovenkamp, *Federal Antitrust Policy* § 2.3c at 100 (5th ed. 2016) ("A firm that produces a product valued at $100 and requires inputs valued at $80 is more efficient than a firm that produces a product valued at $100 but requires inputs valued at $90.").

[17] *See generally Broadcast Music, Inc. v. Columbia Broad. Sys.*, 441 U.S. 1 (1979).

[18] *See* Herbert Hovenkamp, *Federal Antitrust Policy* § 5.6b at 339–40 (5th ed. 2016) (explaining that courts are ill-equipped to balance effects); Robert Pitofsky, *A Framework for Antitrust Analysis of Joint Ventures*, 74 Geo. L.J. 1605, 1623 (1986) (noting that "except in rare cases, it is almost impossible, at least at the present state of economic learning, to quantify efficiencies").

is often especially true in health care sector antitrust cases because quality improvements are often the primary efficiency, and they are notoriously difficult to measure. Fortunately, very few antitrust cases reach the point where balancing is necessary.

7.1.2 Relevant-Market Definition

It is usually impossible to assess whether particular firms have market power, or to determine the effect of a practice on competition, without first determining the market that the conduct affects, i.e., the "relevant market."[19] In general, a relevant antitrust market consists of a firm, or the smallest group of firms acting together, that could exercise market power by profitably raising price if it or they attempted to do so.[20] In other words, if a firm is able to exercise market power by itself, *e.g.*, significantly and profitably raise price and sustain its price increase, it is the only firm in the relevant market. If the presence of competitors constrains it from exercising market power, then only those firms that prevent the firm from exercising market power are included in the relevant market. Other firms that compete in the relevant market are "market participants," and their shares in the relevant market are counted in calculating market shares and concentration.[21] Thus, the purpose and methodology for defining the relevant market are to identify and include in the relevant market those firms that could prevent or constrain a hypothetical monopolist from profitably raising prices.[22]

Several sources of potential constraints on firms attempting to exercise market power exist, based primarily on the availability of (1) substitute products and (2) more-distant substitute suppliers, to which consumers could turn to escape the seller's hypothetical price increase. Examining these two factors results in defining the "relevant product market" and the "relevant geographic market," each of which must be defined and which together constitute the "relevant market." In essence, the relevant market consists of those firms with the ability to take significant amounts of business away from one another.[23]

If a seller attempts to exercise market power by increasing the price of its product, consumers might substitute other products. If they do in sufficient volume, the seller's price increase will

---

[19] *E.g., Se. Mo. Hosp. v. C.R. Bard, Inc.*, 642 F.3d 608 (8th Cir. 2011); *Little Rock Cardiology Clinic, PA v. Baptist Health*, 591 F.3d 591 (8th Cir. 2009) ("Without a well-defined relevant market, a court cannot determine the effect that an allegedly illegal act has on competition.").

[20] *See generally* U.S. Dep't of Justice & Federal Trade Comm'n, *Horizontal Merger Guidelines* § 4 (2010) (*Merger Guidelines*), at http://www.justice.gov/atr/public/guidelines/hmg-2010.pdf; *FTC v. Whole Foods Mkt., Inc.*, 548 F.3d 1028 (D.C. Cir. 2008).

[21] *See generally Merger Guidelines* § 5.1.

[22] *See generally Ky. Speedway, LLC v. Nat'l Ass'n of Stock Car Auto Racing, Inc.*, 588 F.3d 908 (6th Cir. 2009) ("This test measures whether increasing a product's price—usually by five percent—results in a substantial number of consumers purchasing an alternative product."); *Geneva Pharms. Tech. Corp. v. Barr Labs., Inc.*, 386 F.3d 485 (2d Cir. 2004) ("The goal in defining the relevant market is to identify the market participants and competitive pressures that restrain an individual firm's ability to raise prices or restrict output."); *Doctors' Hosp. v. Se. Med. Alliance*, 123 F.3d 301 (5th Cir. 1997); *Rebel Oil Co. v. Atl. Richfield Co.*, 50 F.3d 1421 (9th Cir. 1995) ("'A market' is any grouping of sales whose sellers, if unified by a monopolist or hypothetical cartel, would have market power in dealing with any group of buyers. . . . If the sales of other producers substantially constrain the price-increasing ability of [these firms], these other producers must be included in the market."); *FTC v. Cardinal Health, Inc.*, 12 F. Supp. 2d 34, 46 (D.D.C. 1998) ("definition of the relevant market rests on a determination of available substitutes"). For an excellent discussion, *see* Jonathan B. Baker, *Market Definition: An Analytical Overview*, 74 Antitrust L.J. 129 (2007).

[23] *Gordon v. Lewistown Hosp.*, 373 F. Supp. 2d 393 (M.D. Pa. 2003), *aff'd*, 423 F.3d 184 (3d Cir. 2005).

be unprofitable, and it will be forced to rescind it.[24] Thus, the relevant product market includes all products that are "reasonably interchangeable" with one another (sometimes referred to as "demand substitutability").[25] The degree of interchangeability between two products or services can be assessed by examining their price "cross-elasticity of demand"—i.e., the percentage change in quantity demanded of Product B for a given percentage change in the price of Product A.[26] A high price cross-elasticity of demand between two products, e.g., a relatively large increase in the quantity demanded of Product B resulting from a relatively small increase in the price of Product A, indicates that Products A and B are in the same relevant product market because it suggests that consumers of A would readily substitute B if the producer of A attempted to exercise market power by increasing its price. In hospital-merger cases, for example, several courts have determined that the price cross-elasticity of demand between inpatient acute-care hospital services and outpatient services is low and thus that they are not in the same relevant product market.[27]

In addition to demand substitutability, some courts also consider supply substitutability in defining relevant product markets. Supply substitutability (or price elasticity of supply) measures the degree to which firms not producing Product A at present would quickly do so if producers of A attempted to increase its price. Elasticity of supply is high (and those firms are included in the relevant market) if they would significantly increase supply of the relevant product quickly as a result of the attempted exercise of market power, thus rendering the price increase unprofitable.[28] Elasticity of supply is also a function of the degree to which firms already producing the relevant product in the market could and would expand their output of the product if its producers raised its price.

In some situations, products that are neither demand substitutes nor supply substitutes can be "clustered" into a single relevant market for antitrust purposes because they are sold or purchased together as a package[29] or are provided under similar competitive conditions.[30] In hospital-merger

---

[24] *See generally Merger Guidelines* § 4.1.1; *FTC v. Whole Foods Mkt.*, 548 F.3d 1028 (D.C. Cir. 2008); *United States v. Oracle Corp.*, 331 F. Supp. 2d 1098 (N.D. Cal. 2004).
[25] *See generally Eastman Kodak Co. v. Image Technical Servs.*, 504 U.S. 451 (1992); *Brown Shoe Co. v. United States*, 370 U.S. 294 (1962); *Little Rock Cardiology Clinic, PA v. Baptist Health*, 591 F.3d 591 (8th Cir. 2009); *Reifert v. S. Cent. Wis. MLS Corp.*, 450 F.3d 312 (7th Cir. 2006); *Nat'l Hockey League Players Ass'n v. Plymouth Whalers Hockey Club*, 419 F.3d 462 (6th Cir. 2005); *Queen City Pizza, Inc. v. Domino's Pizza, Inc.*, 124 F.3d 430 (3d Cir. 1997).
[26] *See generally United States v. E.I. du Pont de Nemours & Co.*, 351 U.S. 377 (1956).
[27] *E.g., United States v. Rockford Mem'l Corp.*, 898 F.2d 1278 (7th Cir. 1990); *Evanston Nw. Healthcare Corp.*, 2007-2 Trade Cas. (CCH) ¶75,814 (FTC 2007).
[28] *See, e.g., United States v. Columbia Steel Co.*, 334 U.S. 495 (1948); *Gulf States Reorg. Group, Inc. v. Nucor Corp.*, 721 F.3d 1281 (11th Cir. 2013); *Geneva Pharms. Tech. Corp. v. Barr Labs., Inc.*, 386 F.3d 485 (2d Cir. 2004); *AD/SAT v. Associated Press*, 181 F.3d 216 (2d Cir. 1999) (explaining that "cross-elasticity of supply . . . depends on the extent to which producers of one product would be willing to shift their resources to producing another product in response to an increase in the price of the other product"); *Blue Cross & Blue Shield v. Marshfield Clinic*, 65 F.3d 1406 (7th Cir. 1995) (holding that "products are in the same market if producers can easily shift production from one to the other").
[29] *See FTC v. Advocate Health Network*, 841 F.3d 460 (7th Cir. 2016) ("products can be 'clustered' together if the "'cluster' is itself an object of consumer demand'"); *United States v. Carilion Health Sys.*, 892 F.2d 1042 (4th Cir. 1989) (per curiam) (unpublished opinion reprinted at 1989-2 Trade Cas. (CCH) ¶68,859); *Cal. v. Sutter Health Sys.*, 130 F. Supp. 2d 1109 (N.D. Cal. 2001); *ProMedica Health Sys.*, 2012-1 Trade Cas. (CCH) ¶77,840 (FTC 2012); *see also Green Country Food Market, Inc. v. Bottling Group, LLC*, 371 F.3d 1275 (10th Cir. 2004) ("A 'cluster market' exists where a seller provides a full line of products or services that create a separate product market consisting of the 'cluster' of products or services.").
[30] *FTC v. ProMedica Health Sys.*, 749 F.3d 559 (6th Cir. 2014) ("If these condition are similar for a range of services, then the antitrust analysis should be similar for each of them . . . [and] we can cluster those services when analyzing a merger's competitive effects.").

cases, for example, most courts have uniformly clustered different types of inpatient acute-care hospital services into a single relevant product market even though the different services are poor substitutes for one another (*e.g.*, hernia and open-heart surgeries), rather than examining each as a separate relevant product market. This is largely because health plans typically do not contract separately for the different types of inpatient services but rather purchase them as a "cluster, or because the competitive conditions under which the clustered services are sold are similar."

Once the relevant product market is defined, the relevant geographic market must be delineated. Broadly stated, the relevant geographic market is the "area of effective competition"[31] or the area in which the seller in question operates, plus those areas (and thus more distant suppliers) to which purchasers practicably would turn for the relevant product if that seller attempted to exercise market power by raising price.[32] As in defining the relevant product market, the goal is to identify those firms (here, more-distant firms) that would constrain the ability of the seller to raise prices profitably because many of its customers would switch their purchases to more distant firms.[33] So, for example, if two cardiology practices in Town A merge, cardiology practices in Town B would be included in the relevant geographic market if health plans and their enrollees would substitute those practices for the merged Town A group to the extent that a post-merger price increase by the Town A group would be unprofitable. But if not enough business would shift, then the merged Town A group would be the only practice in the relevant geographic market.

As in the case of the relevant product market, the relevant geographic market includes only those firms sufficient to prevent the firm in question from profitably raising price. But other firms that sell in that market are "market participants" and have market shares in that market. Thus, if analysis shows that Firm A could profitably raise price, it is the only firm in the relevant geographic market, but that does not mean that it has a 100 percent market share.

7.1.3 Market Share, Market Concentration, and Effect on Competition

Market definition is not an end in itself, but rather one tool for helping assess an action's effect on competition.[34] It identifies competitors or market participants and thus is a necessary step in calculating a firm's market share and the level of market concentration, which permit predictions and inferences about market power and thus effect on competition. Market concentration is a measure of the number and relative sizes of firms competing in the relevant market. All else being equal, the larger a firm's market share, the greater its market power and the greater the potential for an adverse effect on competition. Likewise, the greater the degree of market concentration, *e.g.*, the fewer the number of competitors in the market, the greater the potential for anticompetitive effects because the easier

---

[31] *United States v. Philadelphia Nat'l Bank*, 374 U.S. 321 (1963).

[32] *E.g., Tampa Elec. Co. v. Nashville Coal Co.*, 365 U.S. 320 (1965); *see also E.I. du Pont de Nemours & Co. v. Kolon Indus.*, 637 F.3d 435 (4th Cir. 2011); *Little Rock Cardiology Clinic, PA v. Baptist Health*, 591 F.3d 591 (8th Cir. 2008) ("The end goal in this analysis is to delineate a geographic area where, in the medical setting 'few patients leave . . . and few patients enter.'") (citation omitted); *Gordon v. Lewistown Hosp.*, 423 F.3d 184 (3d Cir. 2005); *FTC v. Tenet Health Care Corp.*, 186 F.3d 1045 (8th Cir. 1999).

[33] For helpful discussions of the appropriate methodology, *see FTC v. Advocate Health Network*, 841 F.3d 460 (7th Cir. 2016); *FTC v. Penn State Hershey Med. Ctr.*, 838 F.3d 327 (3d Cir. 2016); *St. Alphonsus Med. Ctr. v. St. Luke's Health Sys.*, 778 F.3d 775 (9th Cir. 2015); *Evanston Nw. Healthcare Corp.*, 2007-2 Trade Cas. (CCH) ¶75,814 (FTC 2007).

[34] *E.g., Law v. NCAA*, 134 F.3d 1010 (10th Cir. 1998).

and more likely that firms in a market will engage in coordinated conduct—either express collusion or interdependent coordinated interaction,[35] which can lead to higher prices.

In some situations, an adverse effect on competition can be shown directly—*e.g.*, by evidence of higher-than-competitive prices, lower-than-competitive output, or lower-than-competitive quality. In those situations, some courts have held that formal proof of the relevant market and firm market shares are unnecessary or that the relevant market can be defined in very rough fashion.[36] Where, for example, economic evidence shows that a consummated hospital merger has actually resulted in hospital reimbursement higher than would have resulted absent the merger, it may not be necessary for a plaintiff to prove the relevant market.[37] Or another interpretation of that evidence is that the merged firm is the only firm in the relevant market.

7.2 The Substantive Antitrust Statutes and Their Analyses

The basic antitrust statutes are Sections 1 and 2 of the Sherman Act,[38] Section 7 of the Clayton Act,[39] Section 5 of the Federal Trade Commission Act (FTC Act),[40] and the Robinson-Patman Act (which is part of the Clayton Act).[41] Each requires that a plaintiff allege and prove, in addition to its other elements, some connection between the parties or their actions and an effect on interstate commerce.[42] In addition to the federal antitrust laws, almost every state has a set of state antitrust laws, most of which mirror, and are interpreted in conformance with, the federal antitrust laws. The antitrust statutes are few in number but extremely broad and ambiguous in language. As the Supreme Court has explained, the antitrust statutes are akin to constitutional provisions that supply the "skeleton" to which the courts add "meat."[43]

7.2.1 Section 1 of the Sherman Act

Section 1 of the Sherman Act prohibits agreements that unreasonably restrain competition. It is the most important and most frequently invoked antitrust law. The essential elements of a Section 1

---

[35] *E.g., FTC v. H.J. Heinz Co.*, 246 F.3d 708 (D.C. Cir. 2001); *FTC v. Arch Coal Co.*, 329 F. Supp.2d 109 (D.D.C. 2004) (explaining that "in a market with few rivals, firms are able to coordinate behavior, 'either by overt collusion or implicit understanding' to restrict output and achieve anticompetitive profits").

[36] *E.g., Republic Tobacco Co. v. N. Atl. Trading Co.*, 381 F.3d 717 (7th Cir. 2004) (indicating that "it is unnecessary to prove that the defendant wielded market power in a properly defined market" when plaintiff can adduce "direct evidence of anticompetitive effects").

[37] *See Evanston Nw. Healthcare Corp.*, 2007-2 Trade Cas. (CCH) ¶75,814 (FTC 2007) (Rosch, Comm'r, concurring).

[38] 15 U.S.C. §§ 1, 2.

[39] *Id.* § 18. Not discussed here is Section 7A of the Clayton Act, 15 U.S.C. § 18a, the Hart-Scott-Rodino premerger notification provisions. For an overview of them, *see* ABA Section of Antitrust Law, *Antitrust Law Developments* 394–401 (7th ed. 2012).

[40] 15 U.S.C. § 45. Section 5 is not technically an "antitrust law" as that term is defined in Section 1 of the Clayton Act, 15 U.S.C. § 12. As interpreted, however, it applies to conduct that violates Sections 1 and 2 of the Sherman Act.

[41] 15 U.S.C. §§ 12–27; 29 U.S.C. § 52.

[42] For discussions of the interstate-commerce requirement, *see Summit Health, Ltd. v. Pinhas*, 500 U.S. 322 (1991); *McLain v. Real Estate Bd.*, 444 U.S. 232 (1980); *Hosp. Bldg. Co. v. Trustees of Rex Hosp.*, 425 U.S. 738 (1976); *Gulf Coast Hotel-Motel Ass'n v. Miss. Gulf Coast Golf Course*, 658 F.3d 500 (5th Cir. 2011).

[43] *See Appalachian Coals, Inc. v. United States*, 288 U.S. 344 (1933) (comparing the breadth and lack of detail in the antitrust laws to constitutional provisions); *BCB Anesthesia Care, Ltd. v. Passavant Mem'l Area Hosp. Ass'n*, 36 F.3d 664 (7th Cir. 1994) ("The Sherman Act is perhaps the quintessential delegation by the Congress to the courts of the task of fashioning a legal structure to govern conduct.").

violation are (1) an agreement (or other form of concerted action) between two or more entities legally capable of agreeing that (2) unreasonably restrains competition.[44] Importantly, it is the agreement itself that is unlawful, and thus the agreement need not be implemented or successful for a violation to result (although it would need to be both implemented and successful for a plaintiff to suffer injury and thus recover damages).[45]

7.2.1.1 Agreement

Unilateral action, i.e., action by a single firm, *never* violates Section 1, regardless of its effect on competition.[46] Rather, the challenged conduct must result from concerted or joint action. Determining if Section 1's agreement requirement is met often requires answering two questions: (1) whether the alleged co-conspirators are legally capable of agreeing (or "conspiring"); and, if so, (2) whether, as a factual matter, the challenged conduct resulted from concerted action, rather than unilateral action.

As to the first question, the Supreme Court, in *Copperweld Corp. v. Independence Tube Corp.*,[47] held that the individual components of a single, integrated enterprise are incapable of conspiring for antitrust purposes even if, as a technical matter, they are separate legal entities. The *Copperweld* decision, itself, held only that a parent corporation and its wholly-owned subsidiaries are a single entity, and thus legally incapable of entering an agreement among themselves for purposes of the antitrust laws. Numerous decisions hold the same.[48] The rationale of *Copperweld*, however, applies to many other relationships as well. For example, wholly-owned "sister" corporations of the same corporate parent are legally incapable of conspiring among themselves or with their parent,[49] and the unincorporated divisions of the same corporation are incapable of conspiring among themselves or with the corporation.[50] The courts have emphasized that in determining whether two entities are a single entity or separate entities for purposes of the antitrust laws, the analysis should focus on the substance of the relationship between them rather than on form.[51]

---

[44] *E.g., Se. Milk Antitrust Litig.*, 739 F.3d 262 (6th Cir. 2014); *Evergreen Partnering Group, Inc. v. PactIV Corp.*, 720 F.3d 33 (1st Cir. 2013); *Realcomp II, Ltd. v. FTC*, 635 F.3d 815 (6th Cir. 2011); *Gordon v. Lewistown Hosp.*, 423 F.3d 184 (3d Cir. 2005).

[45] *E.g., Summit Health, Ltd. v. Pinhas*, 500 U.S. 322 (1991) (explaining that "the essence of any violation of § 1 is the illegal agreement itself—rather than the overt acts performed in furtherance of it"); *United States v. United States Gypsum Co.*, 438 U.S. 422 (1978); *United States v. Rose*, 449 F.3d 627 (5th Cir. 2006) ("[C]onspiracies under the Sherman Act are not dependent on any overt act other than the act of conspiring."); *Blades v. Monsanto Co.*, 400 F.3d 562 (8th Cir. 2005) ("The mere act of agreeing to raise prices, even if the undertaking is 'wholly nascent or abortive,' violates . . . section 1 of the Sherman Act.").

[46] *E.g., Bell Atl. Corp. v. Twombly*, 550 U.S. 544 (2007) (noting that § 1 does not prohibit all restraints on competition but only those resulting from concerted action); *Fisher v. City of Berkeley*, 475 U.S. 260 (1986); *Abraham v. Intermountain Health Care, Inc.*, 461 F.3d 1249 (10th Cir. 2006); *Am. Chiropractic Ass'n v. Trigon Healthcare, Inc.*, 367 F.3d 212 (4th Cir. 2004); *Capital Imaging Assocs., P. C. v. Mohawk Valley Med. Assocs., Inc.*, 996 F.2d 537 (2d Cir. 1993).

[47] 467 U.S. 752 (1984).

[48] *E.g., Total Benefits Planning Agency, Inc. v. Anthem Blue Cross & Blue Shield*, 552 F.3d 430 (6th Cir. 2008).

[49] *E.g., Gonzalez-Maldonado v. MMM Healthcare, Inc.*, 693 F.3d 244 (1st Cir. 2012); *Advanced Health-Care Servs. v. Radford Cmty. Hosp.*, 910 F.2d 139 (4th Cir. 1990).

[50] *E.g., Gregory v. Ft. Bridger Rendezvous Ass'n*, 448 F.3d 1195 (10th Cir. 2006) ("The general rule, sometimes termed the 'single-entity rule'. . . is that coordinated activity within a corporation does not represent the plurality of actors necessary to establish concerted action."); *Alvord-Polk, Inc. v. F. Schumacher & Co.*, 37 F.3d 996 (3d Cir. 1994).

[51] *See, e.g., Am. Needle, Inc. v. NFL*, 560 U.S. 183 (2010); *Copperweld Corp. v. Independence Tube Corp.*, 467 U.S. 752 (1984); *Deutscher Tennis Bund v. ATP Tour, Inc.*, 610 F.3d 820 (3d Cir. 2010).

The key question in determining whether two entities are single or separate entities for purposes of the antitrust laws is whether they have a single, unified economic interest or, conversely, whether their economic interests do or might diverge.[52] Thus, if two firms completely integrate all their operations in such a way that they have no economic incentives to compete with each other or if there becomes a single center of decision making rather than separate centers, they are deemed to be one entity for antitrust purposes. The same is true if, as in *Copperweld Corp.*, one entity controls the other.

As the structural and operational relationship between the alleged co-conspirators becomes more attenuated, the question of whether they have the capacity to conspire becomes more difficult to answer and may require in-depth discovery and factual analysis. Typically, a business entity is incapable of conspiring with its own employees, officers, or directors,[53] although some circuits apply an exception when the employee has an "independent personal stake," separate from his or her employer, in the success of the conspiracy.[54]

The case law is not in complete accord about the ability of less-than-wholly-owned subsidiaries to conspire with their parents[55] or the ability of separate corporations owned by the same individuals to conspire with each other or their owners.[56] Some courts hold that total, or almost total, ownership is necessary,[57] while other courts require only control by one company of the other as a factual matter.[58]

The activities of joint ventures are usually deemed to result from concerted action among the venturers (and thus are subject to Section 1), rather than from unilateral action undertaken by a single entity,[59] unless the venturers cease competing against one another and completely integrate the lines of

---

[52] *See, e.g., Am. Needle, Inc. v. NFL*, 560 U.S. 183 (2010); *Robertson v. Sea Pines Estate Cos.*, 679 F.3d 278 (4th Cir. 2012); *Jack Russell Terrier Network v. Am. Kennel Club, Inc.*, 407 F.3d 1027 (9th Cir. 2005); *City of Mt. Pleasant v. Associated Elec. Co-Op., Inc.*, 838 F.2d 268 (8th Cir. 1988).
[53] *E.g., Solla v. Aetna Health Plans*, 182 F.3d 901 (2d Cir. 1999) (Table); *Nurse Midwifery Assocs. v. Hibbett*, 918 F.2d 605 (6th Cir. 1990); *Am. Chiropractic Ass'n v. Trigon Healthcare, Inc.*, 258 F. Supp. 2d 461 (W.D. Va 2003). *But cf. Reddy v. Puma*, 2006-2 Trade Cas. (CCH) ¶75,497 (E.D.N.Y. 2006) (noting that, depending on facts, hospital-employed physicians may be capable of conspiring among themselves and with their hospital: "Due to the tangled economic relationships that exist among employers and employees in the medical field, the intra-corporate conspiracy doctrine will not always apply.").
[54] *E.g., N.C. State Bd. of Dental Examiners v. FTC*, 717 F.3d 359 (4th Cir. 2013), *aff'd*, ___ U.S. ___, 135 S.Ct. 1101 (2015); *Stark v. Ear, Nose & Throat Specialists*, 185 Fed. App'x 120 (3d Cir. 2006); *St. Joseph's Hosp. v. Hosp. Corp. of Am.*, 795 F.2d 948 (11th Cir. 1986); *New York Medscan LLC v. New York Univ. Sch. of Med.*, 430 F. Supp. 2d 140 (S.D.N.Y. 2006). Other courts reject the exception. *Am. Council of Certified Podiatric Physicians & Surgeons v. Am. Bd. of Podiatric Surgery, Inc.*, 185 F.3d 606 (6th Cir. 1999).
[55] *Compare Square D Co. v. Schneider S.A.*, 760 F. Supp. 362 (S.D.N.Y. 1991) (parent can conspire with partially owned subsidiary) *with Bell Atl. Bus. Sys. Servs. v. Hitachi Data Sys. Corp.*, 849 F. Supp. 702 (N.D. Cal. 1994) (no conspiracy possible between parent and 80%-owned subsidiary).
[56] *Compare Century Oil Tool Corp. v. Prod. Specialties, Inc.*, 737 F.2d 1316 (5th Cir. 1984) (conspiracy not possible) *with Fishman v. Wirtz*, 807 F.2d 520 (7th Cir. 1986) (conspiracy possible).
[57] *E.g., Aspen Title & Escrow, Inc. v. Jeld-Wen, Inc.*, 677 F. Supp. 1477 (D. Ore. 1987) (holding that *Copperweld* doctrine applies only if parent owns 100% or a de minimis amount less than 100% of the subsidiary).
[58] *E.g., Livinston Downs Racing Ass'n v. Jefferson Downs Corp.*, 257 F. Supp. 2d 819 (M.D. La. 2002) (indicating that a mere majority control suffices for two corporations to constitute a single entity).
[59] *Am. Needle, Inc. v. NFL*, 560 U.S 183 (2010); *NCAA v. Bd. of Regents*, 468 U.S. 85 (1984).

business involved in the venture.[60] This is a very uncertain area of antitrust law at present. For example, it is frequently difficult to determine whether certain types of joint ventures between hospitals and physicians constitute a single entity or separate entities for antitrust purposes.

Capacity-to-conspire issues arise frequently in health care antitrust cases. In staff-privilege antitrust cases, for example, most courts hold that hospital medical staffs are combinations of their members,[61] but that the hospital and its medical staff, when engaging in peer-review credentialing, are a single entity because the medical staff acts as the hospital's agent when conducting peer review.[62] Additionally, partially integrated provider-controlled networks (e.g., an IPA), is a combination of its members, rather than a single entity; thus, Section 1 applies to its activities—as it does to most activities of any organization controlled by competitors.[63] On the other hand, if two parties completely integrate, such as medical practices or hospitals—through, e.g., a merger, asset or stock acquisition, or consolidation—they become a single entity for antitrust purposes and are no longer capable of conspiring amongst themselves for purposes of the antitrust laws.[64]

If the parties are capable of conspiring, the question becomes whether their challenged conduct resulted from unilateral action or concerted action as a factual matter. Technically, a "conspiracy" for antitrust purposes is a conscious commitment by two or more parties to a common scheme designed to achieve an unlawful objective, or a "meeting of the minds" in an unlawful agreement.[65] As a practical matter, however, any agreement or understanding meets the Section 1 concerted-action requirement; no formal agreement is necessary.[66] Indeed, the terms "contract," "conspiracy," "combination," "agreement," and "understanding" are synonymous, meaning generally any type of concerted action.[67] The point worth emphasizing is that, for antitrust purposes, the concept of "agreement" is broad and that juries have significant leeway in finding (even by inferring) an agreement from circumstantial evidence.[68]

---

[60] *Texaco, Inc. v. Dagher*, 547 U.S. 1 (2006); *HealthAm. Pa. v. Susquehanna Health Sys.*, 278 F. Supp. 2d 423 (M.D. Pa. 2003).

[61] *E.g., Oksanen v. Page Mem'l Hosp.*, 945 F.2d 696 (4th Cir. 1991) (en banc); *Wesley v. Howard Univ.*, 3 F. Supp. 2d 1 (D.D.C. 1998).

[62] *E.g., Oksanen v. Page Mem'l Hosp.*, 945 F.2d 696 (4th Cir. 1991) (*en banc*); *Nurse Midwifery Assocs. v. Hibbett*, 918 F.2d 605 (6th Cir. 1990); *Nanavati v. Burdette Tomlin Mem'l Hosp.*, 857 F.2d 96 (3d Cir. 1988); *Rowell v. Valley Health Sys.*, 2010-2 Trade Cas. (CCH) ¶77,214 (N.D. Cal. 2010). A minority of courts hold otherwise. *E.g., Crosby v. Hosp. Auth.*, 93 F.3d 1515 (11th Cir. 1996); *Fox v. Good Samaritan Hosp.*, 2008-1 Trade Cas. (CCH) ¶76,008 (N.D. Cal. 2007).

[63] *N.C. State Bd. of Dental Examiners v FTC*, 717 F.3d 359 (4th Cir. 2013), *aff'd*, ___ U.S. ___, 135 S.Ct. 1101 (2015); *N. Tex. Specialty Physicians v. FTC*, 528 F.3d 346 (5th Cir. 2008) ("When an organization is controlled by a group of competitors, it is considered to be a conspiracy of its members."); *Capital Imaging Assocs., P.C. v. Mohawk Valley Med. Assocs., Inc.*, 996 F.2d 537 (2d Cir. 1993) ("As members of the [IPA], the doctors are not staff physicians employed by the HMO . . . , that is, they are not agents of the HMO. Instead, these health care professionals are independent practitioners with separate economic interests."); *see also Podiatrist Ass'n, Inc. v. La Cruz Azul*, 332 F.3d 6 (1st Cir. 2003); *Perinatal Med. Group, Inc. v. Children's Hosp.*, 2010-1 Trade Cas. (CCH) ¶77,078 (E.D. Cal. 2010).

[64] *E.g., Smith v. N. Mich. Hosps.*, 703 F.2d 942 (6th Cir. 1983); *Georgandellis v. Holzer Clinic, Inc.*, 2009-1 Trade Cas. (CCH) ¶76,651 (S.D. Ohio 2009).

[65] *E.g., Am. Tobacco Co. v. United States*, 328 U.S. 781 (1946); *W. Penn Allegheny Health Sys. v. UPMC*, 627 F.3d 85 (3d Cir. 2010) ("an agreement exists when there is a unity of purpose, a common design and understanding, a meeting of the minds, or a conscious commitment to a common scheme").

[66] *E.g., United States v. Beaver*, 515 F.3d 730 (7th Cir. 2008).

[67] *See generally In re Ins. Brokerage Antitrust Litig.*, 618 F.3d 300 (3d Cir. 2010).

[68] *See, e.g., Flat Panel Antitrust Litig.*, 385 F.3d 350 (3d Cir. 2004).

The conspiracy-in-fact analysis tends to be quite fact-intensive and fact-specific. The requisite concerted action may be proved by either direct or circumstantial evidence.[69] Typically, direct evidence of an agreement (e.g., testimony that the parties agreed or an agreement in a document) is sufficient to prove the requisite concerted action.[70] Where the evidence of conspiracy is circumstantial and thus ambiguous, however, the range of permissible inferences from that evidence is limited.[71] Thus, even at the summary-judgment stage, the plaintiff must present evidence tending to exclude the possibility that the defendants acted independently.[72] A number of courts have held, for example, that if the inference of unilateral action is as justified from the evidence as that of concerted action (i.e., the evidence is in "equipoise"), a jury cannot infer that the challenged action resulted from an agreement and thus the court should grant the defendants summary judgment.[73] Indeed, the Supreme Court has indicated that even at the motion-to-dismiss stage, a plaintiff must plead facts plausibly suggesting that the challenged action resulted from concerted, and not unilateral, action.[74]

The issue can be particularly difficult when there is no direct evidence of an agreement, but the parties have engaged in "conscious parallelism"—i.e., taken identical or almost identical action believing that their competitors would take the same action.[75] The Supreme Court and lower courts have clearly held that the fact-finder cannot infer the necessary agreement from consciously parallel action by itself,[76] although conscious parallelism does constitute circumstantial evidence and is probative of an agreement. When the evidence of concerted action is circumstantial, courts examine a number of factors, none of which is independently determinative, in assessing whether the inference of an agreement is permissible. These include whether:

1. the defendants had a motive to conspire;[77]
2. they had the opportunity to conspire, or met or communicated frequently;[78]

---

[69] *E.g., Theatre Enters., Inc. v. Paramount Film Distrib. Corp.*, 346 U.S. 537 (1954); *N.C. State Bd. of Dental Examiners v. FTC*, 717 F.3d 359 (4th Cir. 2013); *Evergreen Partnerning Group, Inc. v. PactIV Corp.*, 720 F.3d 33 (1st Cir. 2013).
[70] *E.g., Champagne Metals v. Ken-Mac Metals, Inc.*, 458 F.3d 1073 (10th Cir. 2006).
[71] *E.g., Matsushita Elec. Indus. Co. v. Zenith Radio Corp.*, 475 U.S. 574 (1986); *see also Omincare, Inc. v. UnitedHealth Group, Inc.*, 627 F.3d 697 (7th Cir. 2010).
[72] *E.g., Monsanto Co. v. Spray-Rite Serv. Corp.*, 465 U.S. 574 (1984); *see also Nitro Distrib., Inc. v. Alitor Corp.*, 565 F.3d 417 (8th Cir. 2009); *Golden Bridge Tech., Inc. v. Motorola, Inc.*, 547 F.3d 266 (5th Cir. 2008); *Abraham v. Intermountain Health Care, Inc.*, 461 F.3d 1249 (10th Cir. 2006); *Mitchael v. Intracorp, Inc.*, 179 F.3d 847 (10th Cir. 1999).
[73] *E.g., Race Tires Am., Inc. v. Hoosier Racing Tire Corp.*, 614 F.3d 57 (3d Cir. 2010); *Williamson Oil Co. v. Philip Morris USA*, 346 F.3d 1287 (11th Cir. 2003); *Blomkest Fertilizer, Inc. v. Potash Corp.*, 203 F.3d 1028 (8th Cir. 2000) (en banc); *Thompson Everett Co. v. Nat'l Cable Adver., L.P.*, 57 F.3d 1317 (4th Cir. 1995).
[74] *Bell Atl. Corp. v. Twombly*, 550 U.S. 544 (2007); *see also In re Text Messaging Antitrust Litig.*, 630 F.3d 622 (7th Cir. 2010).
[75] *See generally Valspar Corp. v. E.I. Du Pont De Nemours & Co.*, 873 F.3d 185 (3d Cir. 2017); *In re Blood Reagents Antitrust Litig.*, 266 F. Supp. 3d 750 (E.D. Pa. 2017).
[76] *E.g., Bell Atl. Corp. v. Twombly*, 550 U.S. 544 (2007).
[77] *E.g., Mayor and City Council of Baltimore v. Citigroup, Inc.*, 709 F.3d 129 (2d Cir. 2013); *Cason-Merenda v. Detroit Med. Ctr.*, 862 F. Supp. 2d 603 (E.D. Mich. 2012).
[78] *E.g., Todorov v. DCH Healthcare Auth.*, 921 F.2d 1438 (11th Cir. 1991); *Cason-Merenda v. Detroit Med. Ctr.*, 862 F. Supp. 2d 603 (E.D. Mich. 2012).

3. parallel behavior would be expected in the circumstances absent an agreement[79] (i.e., "whether the defendants' actions, if taken individually without agreement, would be contrary to their economic self-interest");[80]

4. they put forth a legitimate explanation and justification for their individual actions;[81]

5. the plaintiff's theory of conspiracy makes any economic sense;[82] and

6. the plaintiff shows that any justifications put forth by the defendants for the action are a pretext.[83]

Typically, one party's mere acceptance of another's recommendation does not constitute a conspiracy or agreement between the two[84]—as when, for example, a hospital board follows the recommendation of its medical staff not to grant staff privileges to a practitioner.[85]

7.2.1.2 Unreasonable Restraint on Competition

If the challenged activity results from an agreement, the question becomes whether the agreement "unreasonably restrains competition." Section 1, notwithstanding its literal language, does not prohibit "[e]very" restraint on competition, but rather only those that "unreasonably" restrain competition.[86] The "reasonableness" of a restraint depends on two factors, one a minus, the other a plus:

---

[79] "Consciously parallel action" occurs when parties act knowing or believing that their competitors will take the same action. Their action is "interdependent"—that is, not successful in achieving their goal unless all take the same action—as in an oligopoly. In an oligopoly—*i.e.*, a market with few competitors—firms hesitate to lower their prices because they know that their competitors will do the same and they will lose any competitive advantage they might gain from the price reduction. As a result, even absent a price-fixing agreement, prices remain above competitive levels through what some courts call "tacit collusion." *Compare generally Interstate Circuit, Inc. v. United States*, 306 U.S. 208 (1939) ("[i]t was enough that, knowing that concerted action was contemplated and invited, the [alleged conspirators] gave their adherence to the scheme and participated in it") *with Theatre Enters., Inc. v. Paramount Film Distrib. Corp.*, 346 U.S. 537 (1954) (consciously parallel action, by itself, is not sufficient to prove conspiracy). For more recent discussions, *see Bell Atl. Corp. v. Twombly*, 550 U.S. 544 (2007) (emphasizing that a conspiracy cannot be inferred from consciously parallel action by itself); *Erie County, Ohio v. Morton Salt, Inc.*, 702 F.3d 860 (6th Cir. 2012); *Burtch v. Milberg Factors, Inc.*, 662 F.3d 212 (3d Cir. 2011); *In re Flat Panel Glass Antitrust Litig.*, 385 F.3d 350 (3d Cir. 2004) (discussing the factors in addition to consciously parallel action that a plaintiff must prove).

[80] *E.g., Mayor and City Council of Baltimore v. Citigroup, Inc.*, 709 F.3d 129 (2d Cir. 2013); *Nat'l Hockey League Players Ass'n v. Plymouth Whalers Hockey Club*, 419 F.3d 462, 475 (6th Cir. 2005) ("A showing that defendants' actions, taken independently, would be contrary to their economic self-interest will ordinarily 'tend to exclude the likelihood of independent conduct'").

[81] *E.g., Mayor and City Council of Baltimore v. Citigroup, Inc.*, 709 F.3d 129 (2d Cir. 2013); *Cooper v. Forsyth County Hosp. Auth.*, 789 F.3d 278 (4th Cir. 1986); *see also City of Tuscaloosa v. Harcros Chems.*, Inc., 158 F.3d 548 (11th Cir. 1998); *Fleischman v. Albany Med. Ctr.*, 728 F. Supp. 2d 130 (N.D.N.Y. 2010); *Merck-Medco Managed Care, Inc. v. Rite-Aid Corp.*, 22 F. Supp. 2d 447 (D. Md. 1998), *aff'd per curiam*, 201 F.3d 436 (4th Cir. 1999) (Table).

[82] *E.g., JTC Petrol. Co. v. Piasa Motor Fuels, Inc.*, 179 F.3d 1073 (7th Cir. 1999).

[83] *E.g., Re/Max Int'l, Inc. v. Realty One, Inc.*, 173 F.3d 995 (6th Cir. 1999); *Boczar v. Manatee Hosp. & Health Sys.*, 993 F.2d 1514 (11th Cir. 1993).

[84] *E.g., Abraham v. Intermountain Health Care, Inc.*, 461 F.3d 1249 (10th Cir. 2006); *Gordon v. Lewistown Hosp.*, 423 F.3d 184 (3d Cir. 2005); *Untracht v. Fikri*, 454 F. Supp. 2d 289 (W.D. Pa. 2006), *aff'd*, 249 Fed. App'x 268 (3d Cir. 2007); *Veesom v. Atchison Hosp. Ass'n*, 2006 U.S. Dist. LEXIS 68576 (D. Kan., Sept. 22, 2006).

[85] *E.g. Mathews v. Lancaster Gen. Hosp.*, 87 F.3d 624 (3d Cir. 1996).

[86] *E.g., Bell Atl. Corp. v. Twombly*, 550 U.S. 544 (2007); *Texaco, Inc. v. Dagher*, 547 U.S. 1 (2006) (noting that the Court has never taken a "literal approach" to Section 1's language); *NYNEX Corp. v. Discon, Inc.*, 525 U.S. 128 (1998) (the Sherman Act's prohibition of "[e]very agreement in 'restraint of trade,'. . . prohibits only agreements that unreasonably restrain trade"); *W. Penn Allegheny Health Sys. v. UPMC*, 627 F.3d 85 (3d Cir. 2010) ("Despite its seemingly absolute language, section 1 has been construed to prohibit only *unreasonable* restraints of trade.")

(1) the degree of the restraint's adverse effect on competition and (2) the degree of any procompetitive effects from the restraint. In assessing the agreement's effect on competition, the first question is the standard or analytical methodology that applies—the *per se* rule, full-blown rule of reason, or a standard between the two referred to as the "quick-look" or "truncated" rule of reason.[87] Perceived important factors other than an agreement's effect on competition (e.g., other social goals, public health goals, and public welfare goals) are irrelevant in antitrust analysis.[88]

Agreements that, by their nature, are so obviously anticompetitive on their face that no analysis of their actual effect on competition is necessary are "*per se* illegal,"[89] meaning that a plaintiff need not prove any actual or likely anticompetitive effect from the agreement, and the court will not consider any proferred justifications for it. Rather, the *per se* rule has the force and effect of a statutory command that the challenged practice is unlawful.[90] It creates a conclusive presumption that the agreement unreasonably restrains competition without further analysis.[91]

The *per se* rule applies to limited types of agreements among competitors that facially appear to be of a type that always (or almost always) tend to restrict competition by decreasing output or increasing prices, rather than being designed to increase economic efficiency or to otherwise generate procompetitive effects.[92] In general, the *per se* rule applies only to naked horizontal price-fixing, market-allocation, and other agreements among competitors not to compete, including bid-rigging agreements,[93] and agreements not to solicit one another's employees (so-called

---

(emphasis in original); *N.C. State Bd. of Dental Examiners*, 2011-2 Trade Cas. (CCH) ¶77,705 (FTC 2011), *petition for review denied*, 717 F.3d 359 (4th Cir. 2013), *aff'd*, ___ U.S. ___, 135 S.Ct. 1101 (2015).

[87] E.g., *N.C. State Bd. of Dental Examiners v. FTC*, 717 F.3d 359 (4th Cir. 2013) (listing the three standards and noting that they are on a continuum), *aff'd*, ___ U.S. ___, 135 S.Ct. 1101 (2015) For the analytical framework applied by the Antitrust Division and Federal Trade Commission in analyzing the lawfulness of agreements among competitors under Section 1 and Section 5 of the Federal Trade Commission Act, *see* Federal Trade Comm'n & U.S. Dep't of Justice, *Antitrust Guidelines for Collaborations Among Competitors* (2000). For an excellent discussion of the relationship between the three standards, *see* Herbert Hovenkamp, *Federal Antitrust Policy* § 5.6b at 335-40 (5th ed. 2016).

[88] E.g., *Nat'l Soc'y of Prof'l Engr's v. United States*, 435 U.S. 679 (1978); *Schering-Plough Corp. v. FTC*, 402 F.3d 1056 (11th Cir. 2005) ("A restraint on competition cannot be justified solely on the basis of social welfare concerns."); *In re NCAA Student-Athlete Name & Licensing Litig.*, 37 F. Supp. 3d 1126 (N.D. Cal.2014).

[89] See, e.g., *Ariz. v. Maricopa County Med. Soc'y*, 457 U.S. 332 (1982); *California v. Safeway, Inc.*, 651 F.3d 1118 (9th Cir. 2011) (en banc); *Total Benefits Planning Agency, Inc. v. Anthem Blue Cross & Blue Shield*, 552 F.3d 430 (6th Cir. 2008) ("The *per se* standard recognizes that there are some methods of restraint that are so inherently and facially anti-competitive that an elaborate and burdensome inquiry into a demonstrable economic impact on competition in a relevant market is not required.").

[90] *FTC v. Superior Court Trial Lawyers Ass'n*, 493 U.S. 411 (1990); *In re Cardizem CD Antitrust Litig.*, 332 F.3d 896 (6th Cir. 2003).

[91] *Arizona v. Maricopa County Med. Soc'y*, 457 U.S. 332 (1982); *Se. Milk Antitrust Litig.*, 739 F.3d 262 (6th Cir. 2014) (explaining that when the per se rule is applied, the requisite anticompetitive effects are "inferred" without plaintiff's having to prove any actual anticompetitive effects); *InterVest, Inc. v. Bloomberg, L.P.*, 340 F.3d 144 (3d Cir. 2003).

[92] E.g., *Texaco, Inc. v. Dagher*, 547 U.S. 1 (2006) ("*Per se* liability is reserved for only those agreements that are 'so plainly anticompetitive that no elaborate study of the industry is needed to establish their illegality.'"); *Nw. Wholesale Stationers, Inc. v. Pac. Stationery & Printing Co.*, 472 U.S. 284 (1985); *Broadcast Music, Inc. v. Columbia Broad. Sys.*, 441 U.S. 1 (1979); *Nitro Distrib., Inc. v. Alitor Corp.*, 565 F.3d 417 (8th Cir. 2009); *Paycom Billing Servs., Inc. v. MasterCard Int'l, Inc.*, 467 F.3d 283 (2d Cir. 2006) ("The *per se* label is applied '[o]nce experience with a particular kind of restraint enables the Court to predict with confidence that the rule of reason will condemn it.'"); *Nat'l Hockey League Players Ass'n, v. Plymouth Whalers Hockey Club*, 419 F.3d 462 (6th Cir. 2005) ("The *per se* rule is appropriate where the challenged practice is 'entirely devoid of redeeming competitive rationales.'").

[93] E.g., *In re Ins. Brokerage Antitrust Litig.*, 618 F.3d 300 (3d Cir. 2010).

"anti-poaching agreements")[94] where the parties have not integrated their operations in ways likely to achieve efficiencies. It never applies to vertical agreements.

At the other end of the continuum from the per se rule, courts apply a more lenient standard—the "rule of reason"—when the effect of the agreement on competition is not clear from its nature and character. Broadly stated, the question under full-blown rule-of-reason analysis is whether, after identifying and weighing an agreement's procompetitive and anticompetitive effects, the agreement, on balance, results in substantial or significant anticompetitive effects. If it does, it is unlawful.[95] Although the analysis is typically quite expensive and time-consuming,[96] the rule of reason is the accepted standard for testing whether an agreement unreasonably restrains competition—a sort of default standard.[97] Application of the *per se* rule is limited to those agreements that always or almost always would restrict competition without providing any offsetting procompetitive benefits.[98]

In recent years, many courts, in applying the rule of reason, have adopted a broad three-step "burden shifting" framework. First, the plaintiff must prove that the agreement has or would have a substantial anticompetitive effect, typically by proof that the defendants have market power. If the plaintiff sustains this burden, the burden of going forward shifts to the defendants to show that the agreement has significant procompetitive effects. "Procompetitive effects" is a broad term, generally encompassing any effect that benefits consumers,[99] although the defendants' justification must relate to the conduct's effect on competition, not to some other factor such as public health or safety.[100] Improvements in quality do constitute efficiencies. If the defendants carry their burden, then the burden shifts back to the plaintiff to show that those benefits could have been achieved in a manner less restrictive of competition or that, on balance, the agreement's anticompetitive effects significantly outweigh its procompetitive effects.[101] The ultimate burden of persuasion always remains on the plaintiff.

---

[94] *See* U.S. Dep't of Justice & Fed. Trade Comm'n, *Antitrust Guidance for Human Resource Professionals* (Oct. 2016), *available at* http://www.justice.gov/atr/file/903511/download (viewing such agreements as per se unlawful and subject to criminal antitrust prosecution).

[95] *E.g.*, *Nat'l Soc'y of Prof'l Eng'rs v. United States*, 435 U.S.679 (1978) (noting that the question under rule of reason analysis is whether the agreement promotes or suppresses competition); *N. Tex. Specialty Physicians v. FTC*, 528 F.3d 346 (5th Cir. 2008) (noting that under rule-of-reason analysis, the fact-finder decides, under all the relevant circumstances, whether the agreement imposes an unreasonable restraint on competition); *Flegel v. Christian Hosp.*, 4 F.3d 682 (8th Cir. 1993); *Bhan v. NME Hosps.*, 929 F.2d 1404 (9th Cir. 1991).

[96] *E.g.*, *United States v. Realty Multi-List, Inc.*, 629 F.3d 1351 (5th Cir. 1980) (noting that rule-of-reason analysis is "copious"); *Cal. v. Safeway, Inc.*, 615 F.3d 1171 (9th Cir. 2010) (explaining that "[f]ull rule of reason analysis is data intensive, and, consequently, expensive for litigants; it also consumes large amounts of the courts' time and resources."), *on rehearing en banc*, 651 F.3d 1118 (9th Cir. 2011).

[97] *E.g.*, *Cal. v. Safeway Stores, Inc.*, 651 F.3d 1118 (9th Cir. 2011).

[98] *E.g.*, *Leegin Creative Leather Prods., Inc. v. PSKS, Inc.*, 551 U.S. 827 (2007).

[99] *See generally California v. Safeway, Inc.*, 615 F.3d 1171 (9th Cir. 2010) ("Procompetitive effects include efficiency gains, the development or improvement of products and other benefits to consumers and society."), *on rehearing en banc*, 651 F.3d 1118 (9th Cir. 2011).

[100] *E.g.*, *Nat'l Soc'y of Prof'l Eng'rs v. United States*, 435 U.S. 679 (1978); *N.C. State Bd. of Dental Examiners*, 2011-2 Trade Cas. (CCH) ¶77,705 (FTC 2011), *petition for review denied*, 717 F.3d 359 (4th Cir. 2013), *aff'd*, ___ U.S. ___, 135 S.Ct. 1101 (2015).

[101] *See, e.g.*, *Agnew v. NCAA*, 683 F.3d 328 (7th Cir. 2012); *In re Ins. Brokerage Antitrust Litig.*, 618 F.3d 300 (3d Cir. 2010); *In re Ciprofloxacin Hydrochloride Antitrust Litig.*, 544 F.3d 1323 (Fed. Cir. 2008); *Nilavar v. Mercy Health Sys.*, 244 Fed. App'x 690 (6th Cir. 2007); *Gordon v. Lewistown Hosp.*, 423 F.3d 184 (3d Cir. 2005); *Schering-Plough Corp. v. FTC*, 402 F.3d 1056 (11th Cir. 2005); *Levine v. Cent. Fla. Med. Affiliates, Inc.*, 72 F.3d 1538 (11th Cir. 1996); *Capital Imaging Assocs., P.C. v. Mohawk Valley Med. Assocs., Inc.*, 996 F.2d 537 (2d Cir. 1993).

As a threshold matter, proving anticompetitive effects usually requires the plaintiff to show that the defendants have significant market power or that their agreement would result in their obtaining market power. Indeed, some courts have held explicitly that no violation of Section 1 can result under rule-of-reason analysis absent proof that the defendants have or would, from the agreement, obtain or maintain market power.[102] Anticompetitive effects include increased prices, reduced output, or lower quality resulting from the exercise of market power.[103]

A plaintiff can prove the requisite anticompetitive effect or market power (i.e., meet its initial burden) by direct or circumstantial evidence.[104] Direct evidence of market power includes proof of supracompetitive prices, sub-competitive output, or sub-competitive quality. Under this approach, some courts hold that the plaintiff need not prove the relevant market, the defendants' market share, or the existence of entry barriers.[105] Under the circumstantial-evidence approach, those factors are precisely what the plaintiff must prove—the relevant market; that the defendants have a substantial share of that market, typically 40% or more; and that entry and expansion barriers would prevent new firms from entering the market and incumbent firms from expanding their output.[106]

The third standard—the "quick-look" or "truncated" version of the rule of reason—stands between the *per se* and full-blown rule-of-reason standards. It applies to agreements among competitors that clearly would, all else being equal, restrict output or increase prices, but which may have significant procompetitive justifications.[107] The court conclusively presumes that the defendants have the necessary market power for a violation and takes a "quick look" at the defendants' purported justifications to determine whether they are plausible.[108] If not and the potential anticompetitive effects of

---

[102] *E.g., In re Sulfuric Acid Antitrust Litig.*, 703 F.3d 1004 (7th Cir. 2012); *Menasha Corp. v. News Am. Mkting. In-Store, Inc.*, 354 F.3d 661 (7th Cir. 2004) ("The first requirement in every suit based on the Rule of Reason is market power...."); *Digital Equip Corp. v. Uniq Digital Tech., Inc.*, 73 F.3d 756 (7th Cir. 1996) (noting that in the Seventh Circuit, substantial market power is an ingredient of every claim under the rule of reason); *see also E. Food Servs., Inc. v. Pontifical Catholic Univ. Servs. Ass'n, Inc.*, 357 F.3d 1 (1st Cir. 2004) (explaining that "absent market power there is ordinarily no detriment and no reason to engage in any weighing").

[103] *E.g., W. Penn Allegheny Health Sys. v. UPMC*, 627 F.3d 85 (3d Cir. 2010).

[104] *E.g., Realcomp II, Ltd. v. FTC*, 635 F.3d 815 (2d Cir. 2011); *Republic Tobacco Co. v. N. Atl. Trading Co.*, 381 F.3d 717 (7th Cir. 2004) (explaining that "there are some circumstances where to establish a violation of the antitrust laws it is unnecessary to prove that defendant wielded market power in a properly defined product and geographic market, and plaintiff may rely instead on direct evidence of anticompetitive effects"); *Levine v. Cent. Fla. Med. Affiliates, Inc.*, 72 F.3d 1538 (11th Cir. 1996); *N.C. State Bd. of Dental Examiners*, 2011-2 Trade Cas. (CCH) ¶77,705 (FTC 2011), *petition for review denied*, 717 F.3d 359 (4th Cir. 2013), *aff'd*, ___ U.S. ___, 135 S.Ct. 1101 (2015); *Peoria Day Surgery Ctr. v. OSF Healthcare Sys.*, 2010-1 Trade Cas. (CCH) ¶76,870 (C.D. Ill. 2009); *Minn. Ass'n of Nurse Anesthetists v. Unity Hosp.*, 5 F. Supp. 2d 694 (D. Minn. 1998), *aff'd*, 208 F.3d 655 (8th Cir. 2000).

[105] *See generally FTC v. Ind. Fed'n of Dentists*, 476 U.S. 477 (1986); *see also Angelico v. Lehigh Valley Hosp.*, 184 F.3d 268 (3d Cir. 1999).

[106] *E.g., Rebel Oil Co. v. Atl. Richfield Co.*, 51 F.2d 1421 (9th Cir. 1995); *United States v. Brown Univ.*, 5 F.3d 658 (3d Cir. 1993); *Gordon v. Lewistown Hosp.*, 272 F. Supp. 2d 393 (M.D. Pa. 2003), *aff'd*, 423 F.3d 184 (3d Cir. 2005).

[107] For development and application of the quick-look rule of reason by the Supreme Court, *see Cal. Dental Ass'n v. FTC*, 526 U.S. 756 (1999); *FTC v. Ind. Fed'n of Dentists*, 476 U.S. 447 (1986); *NCAA v. Bd. of Regents*, 468 U.S. 85 (1984); *Broadcast Music, Inc. v. Columbia Broad. Sys.*, 441 U.S. 1 (1979).

[108] For examples or discussion of quick-look analysis, *see N.C. State Bd. of Dental Examiners v. FTC*, 717 F.3d 359 (4th Cir. 2013), *aff'd*, ___ U.S. ___, 135 S.Ct. 1101 (2015); *N. Tex. Specialty Physicians v. FTC*, 528 F.3d 346 (5th Cir. 2008) (applying quick-look analysis to price fixing by an IPA), *granting petition for review in part and remanding* 2005-2 Trade Cas. (CCH) ¶75,032 (FTC 2005) (FTC decision holding that IPA's joint negotiations and other conduct constituted horizontal price fixing); *FTC v. Polygram Holding, Inc.*, 416 F.3d 29 (D.C. Cir. 2005); *Gordon v. Lewistown Hosp.*, 423 F.3d 184 (3d Cir. 2005) ("The [quick-look rule of reason] applies where *per se* condemnation is inappropriate but where no elaborate industry analysis is required to demonstrate the anticompetitive

the agreement are obvious, the agreement is condemned summarily, as under the *per se* rule, without any examination of relevant markets, market power, or the agreement's actual effect on competition. If the justifications are plausible, however, the court applies a more in-depth analysis, potentially up to and including full-blown rule-of-reason analysis.[109]

The quick-look rule of reason has significant applicability to health care antitrust issues. For example, in examining whether the joint pricing of physician services by partially integrated, provider-controlled physician contracting networks (such as IPAs) constitutes a *per se* unlawful price-fixing agreement, it frequently is necessary to first examine whether the physicians have partially integrated their practices into the network through risk sharing or clinical integration in ways that likely will improve patient care or create other efficiencies. If so, this may provide the plausible competitive justification for applying a more in-depth analysis, rather than the *per se* rule, to the physicians' joint negotiations of prices.[110]

7.2.1.3 Agreements with Potential Section 1 Ramifications

Agreements can be horizontal (i.e., among actual or potential competitors), vertical (i.e., between firms at different levels in the chain of production or distribution), or conglomerate (among firms with no discernable economic relationship).[111] Horizontal agreements are the primary concern of the antitrust laws because, as agreements among competitors, they have the greatest potential to affect competition directly and adversely.[112]

---

character of an inherently suspect restraint. . . . Rather, the competitive harm is presumed and the defendant must set forth some competitive justification for the restraints."); *Cont'l Airlines, Inc., v. United Airlines, Inc.*, 277 F.3d 499 (4th Cir. 2003); *Law v. NCAA*, 134 F.3d 1010 (10th Cir. 1998); *Retina Assocs., P.A. v. S. Baptist Hosp.*, 105 F.3d 1376 (11th Cir. 1997) (*per curiam*).

[109] *See Cal. Dental Ass'n v. FTC*, 526 U.S. 726 (1999) (rejecting application of quick-look analysis to dental association's restraints on advertising because the restraints were not obviously anticompetitive on balance and their effect on competition could not be determined without further analysis); *In re Ins. Brokerage Antitrust Litig.*, 618 F.3d 300 (3d Cir. 2010) (explaining that "[u]nder a quick look analysis . . . , competitive harm is presumed and the defendant must set forth some procompetitive justification for the restraints. . . . If no plausible justification is forthcoming, the restraint will be condemned. . . . 'If the defendant offers sound procompetitive justifications, however, the court must proceed to weigh the overall reasonableness of the restraint. . . .'") (citations and internal quotation marks omitted). In fact, there is no bright-line distinction between the three different standards. Rather, there is a continuum. The quest is simply to determine how much information a court needs before it can determine whether the agreement unreasonably restrains competition. *See* Herbert Hovenkamp, *Federal Antitrust Policy* § 5.6b at 335 (5th ed. 2016).

[110] *See generally* United States Dep't of Justice & Federal Trade Comm'n, *Statements of Antitrust Enforcement Policy in Health Care*, Statements 8 & 9 (1996) (discussing potential rule-of-reason application to "Physician Network Joint Ventures" and "Multiprovider Networks"); *see also* FTC Staff Advisory Opinion to TriState Health Partners (Apr. 13, 2009), at http://www.ftc.gov/os/closings/staff/090413/tristateaoletter.pdf.

[111] *E.g., Se. Milk Antitrust Litig.*, 739 F.3d 262 (6th Cir. 2014).

[112] *E.g., Se. Milk Antitrust Litig.*, 739 F.3d 262 (6th Cir. 2014) ("Horizontal restraints are considered to be more threatening [than vertical restraints], and thus result in *per se* treatment more regularly."). For the analytical framework the federal antitrust enforcement agencies apply in analyzing horizontal restraints, *see* Federal Trade Comm'm & U.S. Dep't of Justice, *Antitrust Guidelines for Collaborations Among Competitors* (2000), at http://www.ftc.gov/os/2000/04/ftcdojguidelines.pdf.

7.2.1.3.1 Horizontal Price-Fixing Agreements

A horizontal price-fixing agreement is any type of agreement among competitors that directly affects the prices they charge (seller price fixing) or pay (buyer price fixing) for their goods or services.[113]

The breadth of conduct constituting price fixing is sweeping, and the Supreme Court has noted that "[n]o antitrust offense is more pernicious than [horizontal] price fixing."[114] It encompasses much more than the classic image of a smoke-filled hotel room meeting where the competitors, all undoubtedly wearing trench coats, hats, and dark glasses, explicitly agree on the prices they will charge. Rather, price-fixing agreements include such activities as the use of a single agent by competitors to negotiate their prices[115] and agreements on profit margins, pricing formulae, ranges of prices, discounts, output, and the like.[116] Buyer price-fixing agreements include, for example, agreements among firms on the salaries or salary increases of their employees.[117]

"Naked" horizontal price-fixing agreements are *per se* unlawful, regardless of whether engaged in by sellers or buyers[118] and are frequently prosecuted criminally by the Antitrust Division. "Ancillary" price-fixing agreements are analyzed under the rule of reason. A price-fixing agreement is "naked" if it is not closely connected to a venture in which competitors partially integrate or combine their operations in ways likely to achieve efficiencies, and thus there is no likelihood of any significant procompetitive effects. A price-fixing agreement is ancillary if it:

1. is related to and implemented in connection with a larger venture that itself is likely to generate procompetitive effects because the parties have significantly integrated their operations;

2. significantly promotes, or is reasonably necessary to, the venture's achievement of those procompetitive effects; and

---

[113] *See generally United States v. Socony-Vacuum Oil Co.*, 310 U.S. 150 (1940) (noting that a horizontal price-fixing agreement is any agreement or understanding among competitors that increases, decreases, pegs, or stabilizes the prices at which they sell their products).

[114] *FTC v. Ticor Title Ins. Co.*, 504 U.S. 621, 629 (1992).

[115] *See New York v. St. Francis Hosp.*, 99 F. Supp. 2d 399 (S.D. N.Y. 2000) (applying the *per se* rule to an agreement among hospitals to negotiate contracts jointly with managed-care plans).

[116] For a list of the types of conduct that courts have held constitute price fixing, *see* 1 John J. Miles, *Health Care & Antitrust Law* § 3:2 at 3-8 through 3-15 (Supp. 2015).

[117] *See* U.S. Dep't of Justice & Fed. Trade Comm'n, *Antitrust Guidance for Human Resources Professionals* (Oct. 2016), *available at* http://www.Justice.gov/atr/file/903511/download ("An agreement among competing employers to limit or fix the terms of employment for potential hires may violate the antitrust laws if the agreement constrains individual firm decision making with regard to wages, salaries, or benefits; terms of employment; or even job opportunities.").

[118] *See Ariz. v. Maricopa County Med. Soc'y*, 457 U.S. 332 (1982); *In re Publ'n Paper Antitrust Litig.*, 690 F.3d 51 (2d Cir. 2012); *Omnicare, Inc. v. UnitedHealth Group, Inc.*, 629 F.3d 697 (7th Cir. 2011) (alleged buyer price-fixing agreement); *Freeman v. San Diego Ass'n of Realtors*, 322 F.3d 1133 (9th Cir. 2003) ("No antitrust violation is more abominated than the agreement to fix prices."); *All Care Nursing Servs., Inc. v. High Tech Staffing Servs., Inc.*, 135 F.3d 740 (11th Cir. 1998) ("That price fixing is equally violative of antitrust laws whether it is done by buyers or sellers is . . . undisputed."); *Cason-Merenda v. Detroit Med. Ctr.*, 862 F. Supp. 2d 603 (E.D. Mich. 2012) (alleged buyer price fixing); *Doe v. Ariz. Hosp. & Healthcare Ass'n*, 2009-1 Trade Cas. (CCH) ¶76,591 (D. Ariz. 2009) (same); *N. Jackson Pharm., Inc. v. Caremark Rx, Inc.*, 385 F. Supp. 2d 740 (N.D. Ill. 2005) (same).

3. no obvious other method exists for achieving those procompetitive effects that would have a significantly less restrictive effect on competition.[119]

The ultimate question is whether the parties' joint activity results in merely a "cartel" that does no more than fix prices, or, on the other hand, in a joint venture or other integrated operation likely to achieve procompetitive benefits, and the agreement on price is reasonably necessary to achieve those benefits.[120] Merely calling the collaboration a joint venture, however, does not make it one for antitrust purposes.

The "naked"/"ancillary" price-fixing distinction is particularly important in determining whether partially integrated, provider-controlled contracting networks (e.g., IPAs, PPOs, accountable care organizations (ACOs), and PHOs) can themselves establish fee-for-service prices for their providers' services in contracting with commercial health plans without running afoul of the *per se* rule against price fixing, or whether they must use some form of "messenger-model" arrangement through which each provider-member of the network independently determines whether to accept health plan contract offers.[121] In 1996, the FTC and Antitrust Division issued their *Statements of Antitrust Enforcement Policy in Health Care,* two of which address provider-controlled contracting networks.[122] They provide that economic integration sufficient to permit the network to establish prices without committing a *per se* violation of Section 1 can result from either (1) the provider members' sharing substantial financial risk by contracting with health plans on a shared-risk basis[123] or (2) "clinically integrating" with one another by ensuring that the network has strong and effective utilization-review, quality-assurance, reporting, monitoring, case management, and credentialing programs likely to improve the quality of services provided and reduce their cost.[124] The FTC has issued five staff-advisory opinions discussing

---

[119] This definition of "ancillary restraint" is a synthesis from numerous sources. The seminal decision is *United States v. Addyston Pipe & Steel Co.,* 85 F. 271 (6th Cir. 1898), *modified and aff'd,* 175 U.S. 211 (1899). Other important decisions discussing when a restraint is ancillary include *In re Sulfuric Acid Antitrust Litig.,* 703 F.3d 1004 (7th Cir. 2012); *Major League Baseball Props., Inc. v. Salvino,* 542 F.3d 290 (2d Cir. 2008) (Sotomayor, J., concurring); *Freeman v. San Diego Ass'n of Realtors,* 322 F.3d 1133 (9th Cir. 2003); *SCFC ILC, Inc. v. Visa U.S.A., Inc.,* 36 F.3d 958 (10th Cir. 1994); *Rothery Storage & Van Co. v. Atlas Van Lines, Inc.,* 792 F.2d 210 (D.C. Cir. 1986); *Nat'l Bancard Corp. v. VISA U.S.A.,* 779 F.2d 592 (11th Cir. 1986); *Polk Bros. v. Forest City Enters.,* 776 F.2d 185 (7th Cir. 1985); *Gen. Leaseways, Inc. v. Nat'l Truck Leasing Ass'n,* 744 F.2d 588 (7th Cir. 1984); *see also* Federal Trade Comm'n & U.S. Dep't of Justice, *Antitrust Guidelines for Collaboration Among Competitors* § 3.2 (2000). For a helpful discussion in the context of an FTC challenge to a physician-controlled contracting network's allegedly negotiating prices in contracts with health plans on behalf of its members, challenged by the FTC, *see N. Tex. Specialty Physicians,* 2005-2 Trade Cas. (CCH) ¶75,032 (FTC 2005), *petition for review granted in part and remanded,* 528 F.3d 346 (5th Cir. 2008).
[120] *Compare Ariz. v. Maricopa County Med. Soc'y,* 457 U.S. 332 (1982) (cartel) *with Broadcast Music, Inc. v. Columbia Broad. Sys.,* 441 U.S. 1 (1979) (joint venture in which the price-fixing agreement was ancillary because it was necessary for the joint venture product to be offered at all).
[121] For a discussion of the antitrust ramifications of provider-controlled networks, *see* John J. Miles, *Joint Venture Analysis and Provider-Controlled Health Care Networks,* 66 Antitrust L.J. 127 (1997). For a discussion of the antitrust issues raised by messenger-model networks, *see* Jeff Miles, *Ticking Antitrust Time Bombs: A Message to Messed-Up Messenger Models,* AHLA Health Lawyers News, Nov. 2002 (Vol. 6, Number 11), at 4. For a discussion of "messenger models" used to avoid price-fixing agreements, *see* ABA Section of Antitrust Law, *Messenger Model Handbook* (2008).
[122] U.S. Dep't of Justice & Federal Trade Comm'n, *Statements of Antitrust Policy in Health Care* (1996) (*Health Care Statements*).
[123] For a helpful discussion of the antitrust ramifications of shared financial risk in the context of provider-controlled contracting networks, *see* Susan A. Creighton, Director, Bureau of Competition, FTC, "Diagnosing Physician-Hospital Organizations," Prepared Remarks Before the AHLA Program on Legal Issues Affecting Academic Medical Centers and Other Teaching Institutions (Jan. 22, 2004), at http://www.ftc.gov/speeches/other/creightonphospeech.shtm.
[124] *"Health Care Statements* 8 & 9 (1996).

the antitrust ramifications of clinically integrated provided-controlled contracting networks.[125] The agencies have brought numerous enforcement actions challenging alleged price-fixing agreements among providers, particularly physicians, for jointly refusing to contract, or threatening to refuse to contract, with health plans absent reimbursement increases.[126]

Even if a network is sufficiently integrated and its joint negotiations are reasonably necessary to achieve the efficiencies from its integration, a second step—rule-of-reason analysis—is necessary because the network's joint negotiations are still unlawful if, by aggregating the market power of the network's members, the network can increase their reimbursement. Whether a provider-controlled contracting network has market power is largely a function of two variables: (1) whether it includes a large percentage of all area providers of the services offered by the network, and (2) whether it is "exclusive" in the sense that participating providers contract with health plans only through that network and refuse to contract directly or through mechanisms other than the network.[127]

The Affordable Care Act, part of the Obama administration's health care reform legislation, directed the Secretary of the Department of Health and Human Services, through its Center for Medicare and Medicaid Services (CMS), to establish a Medicare "shared-savings program" by the creation of accountable care organizations, or ACOs, to manage and coordinate the care of Medicare beneficiaries in the Medicare fee-for-service program.[128] ACOs share in cost savings to Medicare they generate if they meet certain quality performance and cost-saving goals and distribute the money they receive to participating providers.

ACOs are, in effect, clinically integrated provider-controlled contracting networks that likely will contract not only with Medicare but also with commercial health plans by negotiating contracts jointly on behalf of their provider participants. CMS has issued a rule that governs their creation and operation.[129] Because joint negotiations by ACOs with commercial health plans potentially raise significant antitrust issues, the FTC and Antitrust Division issued, in 2011, a *Statement of Antitrust Policy Regarding Accountable Care Organizations Participating in the Medicare Shared Savings*

---

[125] FTC Staff Advisory Opinion to Norman Physician Hospital Organization (Feb. 13, 2013), at https://www.ftc.gov/sites/default/files/documents/advisory-opinions/norman-physician-hospital-organization/130213normanphoadvltr_0.pdf; FTC Staff Advisory Opinion to TriState Health Partners, Inc. (Apr. 13, 2009), at https://www.ftc.gov/sites/default/files/documents/advisory-opinions/tristate-health-partners-inc./090413tristateaoletter.pdf; FTC Staff Advisory Opinion to Greater Rochester Independent Practice Association (Sept. 17, 2007), at https://www.ftc.gov/sites/default/files/documents/advisory-opinions/greater-rochester-independent-practice-association-inc./gripa.pdf; FTC Staff Advisory Opinion to Suburban Health Organization (Mar. 28, 2006), at https://www.ftc.gov/sites/default/files/documents/advisory-opinions/suburban-health-organization/suburbanhealthorganizationstaffadvisoryopinion03282006.pdf; FTC Staff Advisory Opinion to MedSouth, Inc. (Feb. 19, 2002), at https://www.ftc.gov/policy/advisory-opinions/advisory-opinion-miles-02-19-02.

[126] *See, e.g., United States v. Chiropractic Assocs.*, 2013-2 Trade Cas. (CCH) ¶78,501 (D.S.D. 2013) (consent decree); *United States v. Okla. State Chiropractic Independent Physicians Ass'n*, 2013-1 Trade Cas. (CCH) ¶78,394 (N.D. Okla. 2013) (consent decree); *Praxedes E. Alverez*, 155 F.T.C. 874 (2013) (consent order); *Sw. Health Alliance, Inc.*, Dkt. No. C-4327 (FTC Jul. 8, 2011) (consent order); *Minn. Rural Health Coop.*, 150 F.T.C. 795 (2010) (consent order); *United States v. Idaho Orthopaedic Soc'y*, 2010-1 Trade Cas. (CCH) ¶77,142 (D. Idaho 2010) (consent decree); *Boulder Valley Individual Practice Ass'n*, 149 F.T.C. 1147 (2010) (consent order).

[127] *Health Care Statements*, Statements 8.A, 9.B.

[128] Patient Protection and Affordable Care Act, Pub. L. 111-148, § 3022, as amended by the Health Care and Education Reconciliation Act of 2010, Pub. L. 111-152.

[129] Medicare Shared Savings Program: Accountable Care Organizations, 76 Fed. Reg. 67973 (Nov. 2, 2011).

Program.[130] The Statement provides that ACOs meeting CMS's eligibility criteria are deemed sufficiently clinically integrated so that their joint negotiations are tested under the rule of reason rather than summarily condemned under the per se rule. The market-power analysis under the Statement focuses on the ACO's market shares in the services provided by its participating providers in their primary service areas. The Statement also provides a process by which parties may obtain an antitrust review letter from either the FTC or Antitrust Division stating whether the agency believes the ACO will raise antitrust concerns.

7.2.1.3.2 Horizontal Agreements to Exchange Pricing Information

Agreements among competitors to exchange price information can raise three issues under Section 1 of the Sherman Act. First, they may be the first step toward a horizontal price-fixing agreement that is *per se* unlawful.[131] Second, they are probative circumstantial evidence of a *per se* unlawful price-fixing agreement.[132] Third, even short of a resulting price-fixing agreement, they can result in price stabilization or facilitate oligopolistic tacit collusion and thus violate Section 1 regardless of any agreement to fix prices.[133] On the other hand, the exchange or dissemination of pricing information can be procompetitive by facilitating better informed and rational business decisions.[134] As a result, they are analyzed under the rule of reason.[135] The exchange is more likely to have an unlawful effect on prices when:

- the relevant market is highly concentrated;
- the price information exchanged concerns present or future prices, as opposed to historical prices;
- the price information exchanged is firm- or transaction-specific;
- the products or services sold are fungible; and
- demand for the product or services is price-inelastic (i.e., an increase in the product's price results in a less-than-proportional decrease in quantity demanded).

Statement 6 of the agencies' *Statements of Antitrust Enforcement Policy in Health Care* discusses "provider participation in exchanges of price and cost information," specifically providing an "antitrust safety zone" for competitor price and cost exchanges if the program meets certain requirements. The antitrust rules and principles governing agreements among competitors to exchange information about their prices apply equally to agreements among competitors to exchange the prices they pay for their inputs, *e.g.*, an agreement among competing hospitals to exchange information about their wage

---

[130] U.S. Dep't of Justice & Federal Trade Comm'n, *Statement of Antitrust Enforcement Policy Regarding Accountable Care Organizations Participating in the Medicare Shared Savings Program*, 76 Fed. Reg. 67026 (Oct. 28, 2011).
[131] *See, e.g., Morton Salt Co. v. United States*, 235 F.2d 573 (10th Cir. 1956); *Jung v. Am. Ass'n of Med. Colls.*, 300 F. Supp. 119 (D.D.C. 2004).
[132] *E.g., Fleischman v. Albany Med. Ctr.*, 728 F. Supp. 2d 130 (N.D.N.Y. 2010).
[133] *E.g., United States v. Container Corp. of Am.*, 393 U.S. 333 (1969); *Omnicare, Inc. v. UnitedHealth Group, Inc.*, 629 F.3d 697 (7th Cir. 2011) (noting that "[i]nformation exchange can help support an inference of a price-fixing agreement").
[134] *Int'l Healthcare Mgmt. v. Haw. Coalition for Health*, 332 F.3d 600 (9th Cir. 2003).
[135] *United States v. Citizens & S. Nat'l Bank*, 422 U.S. 86 (1975); *Burtch v. Milberg Factors, Inc.*, 662 F.3d 212 (3d Cir. 2011); *Todd v. Exxon Corp.*, 275 F.3d 191 (2d Cir. 2001).

levels for nurses or their participation in third-party surveys of wage levels.[136] The FTC and Antitrust Division have issued several advisory opinions discussing price surveys by health care providers.[137]

7.2.1.3.3 Horizontal Market-Allocation Agreements

A horizontal market-allocation agreement is an agreement among competitors by which they allocate among themselves sales in designated geographical areas, sale of particular goods or services, or sales to particular types of customers, agreeing not to compete along those dimensions. For example, two hospitals might agree that one will provide open-heart surgical services and the other will establish a cancer center of excellence and that they will not compete against each other in providing those services. Market-allocation agreements destroy competition along all competitive dimensions, not just price and so are arguably more destructive of competition than price-fixing agreements.[138] "Naked" market-allocation agreements are *per se* unlawful,[139] but "ancillary" market-allocation agreements (i.e., those that are part of an efficiency-enhancing cooperative effort and reasonably necessary for the venture to function efficiently) are tested under the rule of reason.[140]

In the health care context, market-allocation-agreement problems frequently arise from agreements among competing hospitals about which will provide particular services—efforts to reduce "unnecessary duplication," such as two open-heart programs, neither of which operates at capacity or minimum efficient scale.[141] Two of the federal antitrust enforcement agencies' *Health Care Statements* discuss the issue: Statement 2, dealing with "hospital joint ventures involving high technology or other expensive health care equipment," which includes an antitrust safety zone; and Statement 3, dealing with "hospital joint ventures involving specialized clinical or other expensive health care services," but which includes no safety zone. The Statements indicate that, in many instances, because

---

[136] For examples of health care antitrust cases involving the exchange of price information, *see United States v. Utah Soc'y for Health & Human Res. Admin.*, 1994-2 Trade Cas. (CCH) ¶70,845 (D. Utah 1994) (consent decree); *United States v. Burgstiner*, 1991-1 Trade Cas. (CCH) ¶69,422 (S.D. Ga. 1991) (consent decree). Because wages are the prices paid for inputs, exchanges of wage information among employers competing for employees also can raise serious antitrust issues. *See generally Todd v. Exxon Corp.*, 275 F.3d 191 (2d Cir. 2001); *see also Cason-Merenda v. Detroit Med. Ctr.*, 862 F. Supp. 2d 603 (E.D. Mich. 2012) (nurse wage-fixing and exchanges of wage information); *Fleischman v. Albany Med. Ctr.*, 728 F. Supp. 2d 130 (N.D.N.Y. 2010) (same); *Jung v. Ass'n of Am. Med. Colls.*, 226 F.R.D. 7 (D.D.C. 2005) (rejecting plaintiff's motion to amend complaint alleging numerous graduate medical education programs agreed to fix the stipends paid medical residents), *aff'd*, 184 Fed. App'x 9 (D.C. Cir. 2006).

[137] *See, e.g.*, FTC Staff Advisory Opinion to Medical Group Management Association (Nov. 3, 2003), at https://www.ftc.gov/sites/default/files/documents/advisory-opinions/re-transfer-pharmaceuticals-cost-non-profit-hospital-patients-non-profit-free-clinic/mgma031104.pdf; FTC Staff Advisory Opinion to PriMed, Inc. (Feb. 6, 2003), at http://www.ftc.gov/bc/adops/030206dayton.shtm; Antitrust Division Business Review Letter to Washington State Medical Association (Sept. 23, 2002), at http://www.usdoj.gov/atr/public/busreview/200260.pdf; *see also United States v. Prof'l Consultants Ins. Co.*, 2005-2 Trade Cas. (CCH) ¶75,031 (D.D.C. 2005) (consent decree). (Antitrust Division enforcement action challenging allegedly unlawful information sharing).

[138] *See Blue Cross & Blue Shield v. Marshfield Clinic*, 65 F.3d 1406 (7th Cir. 1995) ("It would be a strange interpretation of antitrust law that forbade competitors to agree on what price to charge, thus eliminating price competition among them, but allowed them to divide markets, thus eliminating all competition among them.").

[139] *E.g., Palmer v. BRG of Ga.*, 498 U.S. 46 (1990) (per curiam); *Anderson News, L.L.C. v. Am. Media, Inc.*, 680 F.3d 162 (2d Cir. 2012); *In re Ins. Brokerage Antitrust Litig.*, 618 F.3d 300 (3d Cir. 2010); *Nitro Distrib., Inc. v. Alitor Corp.*, 565 F.3d 417 (8th Cir. 2009); *Kentuckiana Med. Ctr., LLC v. Clark County*, 2008-1 Trade Cas. (CCH) ¶76,011 (S.D. Ind. 2006).

[140] *E.g., Polk Bros. v. Forest City Enters.*, 776 F.2d 185 (7th Cir. 1985).

[141] *See New York v. St. Francis Hosp.*, 94 F. Supp. 2d 399 (S.D.N.Y. 2000) (applying the *per se* rule to an agreement among hospitals allocating services).

of the efficiencies they can generate, the agencies will assess horizontal market-allocation agreements in these contexts under the rule of reason unless "the joint venture arrangement is . . . one that uses the joint venture label but is likely to merely restrict competition and decrease output"[142]—i.e., is in reality nothing more than a cartel. And the Antitrust Division has challenged several market-allocation agreements between hospitals.[143] The Division also brought a case against a Blue Cross plan where the plan and a number of hospitals agreed that the hospitals would use Blue Cross as their employees' insurer and not compete against Blue Cross in selling health insurance.[144] And in another twist, the Division has brought two enforcement actions challenging agreements between hospitals not to advertise or solicit patients from the other's primary territory.[145]

7.2.1.3.4 Horizontal Concerted Refusals to Deal or Group Boycotts

A concerted refusal to deal or "group boycott" is an agreement between at least two competitors not to deal in some way with another firm, usually a competitor of the boycotting parties.[146] Conduct of this description is ubiquitous throughout the economy and certainly is prevalent in health care—for example, a medical staff including competitors of an applicant for staff privileges recommending against granting the applicant staff privileges, preventing him or her from competing; similarly, a provider-controlled contracting network such as an IPA may deny membership to a provider wishing to join,[147] or a professional association may reject an application for membership by a competitor of the group's members.[148]

Until 1985, many courts stated that group boycotts were *per se* unlawful, although they frequently found ways to circumvent applying the strict *per se* rule.[149] In 1985, however, the Supreme Court, in *Northwest Wholesale Stationers, Inc. v. Pacific Stationery & Printing Co.*,[150] held specifically that, at a minimum, the boycotting parties must have market power or exclusive access to some relationship necessary for effective competition before the *per se* rule applies. Moreover, courts today almost uniformly permit defendants to attempt to justify their group boycotts on procompetitive grounds.[151] As a practical matter, most courts, now apply an almost full rule of reason analysis

---

[142] *Health Care Statements*, Statement 2 n.5.
[143] *See United States v. Charleston Area Med. Ctr.*, 2006-1 Trade Cas. (CCH) ¶75,313 (S.D.W.Va. 2006) (consent decree and competitive impact statement); *United States v. Bluefield Reg'l Med. Ctr., Inc.*, 2005-2 Trade Cas. (CCH) ¶74,916 (S.D. W.Va. 2005) (consent decree).
[144] *United States v. Blue Cross Blue Shield*, 2012-1 Trade Cas. (CCH) ¶77,872 (D. Mont. 2012) (consent decree).
[145] *E.g., United States v. W.A. Foote Mem'l Hosp.*, 2017 U.S. Dist. LEXIS 209031 (E.D. Mich., Dec. 20 2017).
[146] *E.g., NYNEX Corp. v. Discon, Inc.*, 525 U.S. 128 (1998); *Bogan v. Hodgkins*, 166 F.3d 509 (2d Cir. 1999); *Balaklaw v. Lovell*, 14 F.3d 793 (2d Cir. 1994).
[147] *See generally Reifert v. S. Cent. Wis. MLS Corp.*, 450 F.3d 312 (7th Cir. 2006) ("A group boycott traditionally occurs when a particular group or individual is prohibited from joining an organization."); *Doctor's Hosp. v. Se. Med. Alliance*, 123 F.3d 301 (5th Cir. 1997) (hospital expulsion from PPO); *Levine v. Cent. Fla. Med. Affiliates*, 72 F.3d 1538 (11th Cir. 1996) (refusal to permit physician to join a PPO); *Hassan v. Indep. Practice Assocs., P.C.*, 698 F. Supp. 679 (E.D. Mich. 1988).
[148] *E.g., Kreuzer v. Am. Acad. of Periodontology*, 735 F.2d 1479 (D.C. Cir. 1984).
[149] *E.g., FMC v. Aktiebolaget Svenska Amerika Linien*, 390 U.S. 238 (1968) (holding that "[u]nder the Sherman Act, any agreement by a group of competitors to boycott a particular buyer or group of buyers is illegal *per se*").
[150] 472 U.S. 284 (1985).
[151] *E.g., Gregory v. Ft. Bridger Rendezvous Ass'n*, 448 F.3d 1195 (10th Cir. 2006); *Palladin Assocs., Inc. v. Mont. Power Co.*, 328 F.3d 1145 (9th Cir. 2003); *Hassan v. Independent Practice Assocs.*, P.C., 698 F. Supp. 679 (E.D. Mich. 1988).

to group boycotts,[152] and this is particularly true in cases involving the health care sector.[153] Some courts, however, continue to state or suggest that group boycotts are *per se* illegal.[154]

7.2.1.3.5 Tying Agreements

A tying agreement results when a seller and buyer agree that the seller will sell the buyer one product or service (the "tying" product), but only if the buyer purchases a second separate product or service (the "tied" product) as well.[155] The antitrust concern from tying agreements is that competitors in the market for the tied product may be foreclosed from that market, raising the possibility that the seller of the tying product may obtain market power in the tied-product market.

In the health care context, tying arrangements arise most frequently when a hospital enters into an exclusive contract with a single group of hospital-based physicians by which that group is the exclusive provider of specified services at the hospital. Many hospitals have such arrangements with hospital-based physicians, such as anesthesiologists, radiologists, and pathologists. A physician seeking to provide the same services at the hospital but whose application is rejected argues that to obtain hospital services (the "tying" service), the patient must purchase the professional services offered by the exclusive group (the "tied" service), excluding other providers from competing for those patients.[156] Another example is a hospital's conditioning the sale of certain hospital services (such as trauma care) to health plans on the condition that they also contract for the hospital's less sophisticated services as well. This may or may not foreclose the hospital's competitors selling the latter services, depending on whether the health plan is willing to contract with other hospitals, too. The same is true where a multi-hospital system refuses to contract with a health plan for the services of one of its hospitals unless the plan agrees to contract with all its hospitals. As hospitals continue to employ physicians, tying issues may arise if the hospital conditions its sale of hospital services on a health plan's also contracting for its employed physicians' services.

Traditionally, courts have held that tying agreements violate Section 1 of the Sherman Act if a plaintiff proves:

1. the existence of separate tying and tied products;

---

[152] *See, e.g., Buccaneer Energy (USA), Inc. v. Gunnison Energy Corp.*, 846 F.3d 1297 (10th Cir. 2017); *Tunica Web Adver. v. Tunica Casino Operators Ass'n*, 496 F.3d 403 (5th Cir. 2007).

[153] *E.g., Cohlmia v. Ardent Health Servs., LLC*, 448 F. Supp. 2d 1253 (N.D. Okla. 2006) ("Although group boycotts have frequently been cited as examples of a *per se* antitrust violation, not all group boycotts are predominantly anticompetitive. . . . '[C]ourts have generally applied the rule of reason, holding that a hospital must be allowed, in conjunction with its medical staff, to exclude individual doctors on the basis of their lack of professional competence or unprofessional conduct.'") (citation omitted); *Welchlin v. Tenet Healthcare Corp.*, 366 F. Supp. 2d 338 (D.S.C. 2005) ("As a threshold matter, the court notes that '[a] group boycott is not . . . always a *per se* violation.'") (citation omitted); *see also Health Care Statements*, Statement 9.B.2.c (providing that the rule of reason applies to exclusion of providers by provider-controlled contracting networks).

[154] *E.g., Anderson News. L.L.C. v. Am. Media, Inc.*, 680 F.3d 162 (2d Cir. 2012); *Campfield v. State Farm Mut. Auto. Ins. Co.*, 532 F.3d 1111 (10th Cir. 2008); *Med. Ctr. v. Premier Health Ptrs.*, 2012-2 Trade Cas. (CCH) ¶78,040 (S.D. Ohio 2012).

[155] *E.g., Eastman Kodak Co. v. Image Technical Servs., Inc.*, 504 U.S. 451 (1992); *Jefferson Parish Hosp. Dist. No. 2 v. Hyde*, 466 U.S. 2 (1984); *Brantley v. NBC Universal, Inc.*, 675 F.3d 1192 (9th Cir. 2012).

[156] *E.g., Jefferson Parish Hosp. Dist. No. 2 v. Hyde*, 466 U.S. 2 (1984); *Beard v. Parkview Hosp.*, 912 F.2d 138 (6th Cir. 1990).

2. a requirement (or coercion) by the seller forcing the purchaser to buy the tied product, either from it or from a source designated by it, as a condition for purchasing the tying product;

3. the seller has market power in the market for the tying product (including definition of the relevant market for the tying product); and

4. an effect from the tying arrangement on a "not insubstantial" volume of interstate commerce in the tied product.[157]

In most circuits, the plaintiff, when the defendant mandates that the tied product must be purchased from a third party as a condition to its selling the tying product, must also show that the seller of the tying product has a direct economic interest in the sale of the tied product,[158] a condition usually not met when hospitals enter into exclusive contracts with non-employee hospital-based physicians.[159] In addition, more recent decisions also require the plaintiff to prove at least some adverse effect on competition in the market for the tied product or service[160]—i.e., at least some foreclosure of competitors selling the tied product or service from the market.[161] For example, if the seller forces the purchaser to purchase the tied product, but the purchaser would not have purchased the tied product from anyone absent the tying agreement, no competitors are foreclosed from the tied-product market and there is no restraint on competition.[162] The same is true if there are no competitors in the tied-product market. The Supreme Court has recognized that many tying arrangements are competitively benign.[163]

7.2.1.3.6 Exclusive Dealing Agreements

An exclusive-dealing contract results when a buyer and seller agree either that (1) the seller will sell to only one buyer and not to that buyer's competitors (sometimes called an "output contract"); or (2) a buyer will buy only from a single seller and not from its competitors (called a "requirements contract").[164] The antitrust concern is the same as that with tying agreements—competitor foreclosure from the market and thus potential market power of a participant to the contract. To the extent a party

---

[157] *See generally Eastman Kodak Co. v. Image Technical Servs., Inc.*, 504 U.S. 451 (1992); *Suture Express, Inc. v.Owens & Minor Distrib., Inc.*, 851 F.3d 1029 (10th Cir. 2017); *¶Palmyra Park Hosp. v. Phoebe Putney Mem'l Hosp.*, 604 F.3d 1291 (11th Cir. 2010); *Michigan Div. v. Mich. Cemetery Ass'n*, 524 F.3d 726 (6th Cir. 2008); *Gordon v. Lewistown Hosp.*, 423 F.3d 184 (3d Cir. 2005); *Talone v. Am. Ostegpathic Ass'n*, 2017 U.S. Dist. LEXIS 89395 (D.N.J., Jun. 12, 2017); *Warren Gen. Hosp. v. Amgen, Inc.*, 2010-1 Trade Cas. (CCH) ¶77,043 (D.N.J. 2010), *aff'd*, 643 F.3d 77 (3d Cir. 2011).

[158] *E.g., Abraham v. Intermountain Health Care, Inc.*, 461 F.3d 1249 (10th Cir. 2006); *U.S. Philips Corp. v. Int'l Trade Comm'n*, 424 F.3d 1179 (Fed Cir. 2005); *CTUnify, Inc. v. Nortel Networks, Inc.*, 115 Fed. App'x 831 (6th Cir. 2004); *White v. Rockingham Radiologists*, 820 F.2d 98 (4th Cir. 1988).

[159] For an example, *see Healow v. Anesthesia Ptrs.*, 92 F.3d 1192 (9th Cir. 1996) (per curiam unpublished opinion reprinted at 1996-2 Trade Cas. (CCH) ¶71,567).

[160] *E.g., E&L Consulting, Ltd. v. Doman Indus., Ltd.*, 472 F.3d 23 (2d Cir. 2006); *CTUnify, Inc. v. Nortel Networks, Inc.*, 115 Fed. App'x 831 (6th Cir. 2004) ("More importantly, [plaintiff] has not concretely alleged any anticompetitive effect that the defendant's tying agreement has had on the tied market."); *Highland Capital, Inc. v. Franklin Nat'l Bank*, 350 F.3d 558 (6th Cir. 2003).

[161] *See, e.g., In re Cox Enters., Inc. Set-Top Cable Television Box Antitrust Litig.*, 871 F.3d 1093 (10th Cir. 2017); *Blough v. Holland Realty, Inc.*, 574 F.3d 1084 (9th Cir. 2009) (holding that no tying violation results absent foreclosure of competition in the tied-product market); *Reifert v. S. Cent. Wis. MLS Corp.*, 450 F.3d 312 (7th Cir. 2006).

[162] *Jefferson Parish Hosp. Dist. No. 2 v. Hyde*, 466 U.S. 2 (1984); *Brantley v. NBC Universal, Inc.*, 675 F.3d 1192 (9th Cir. 2012).

[163] *Ill. Tool Works, Inc. v. Independent Ink, Inc.*, 547 U.S. 28 (2006) ("Many tying arrangements . . . are fully consistent with a free competitive market.").

[164] *E.g., ZF Meritor, LLC v. Eaton Corp.*, 696 F.3d 254 (3d Cir. 2012); *Allied Orthopedic Appliances, Inc. v. Tyco Health Group, LP*, 592 F.3d 991 (9th Cir. 2010).

agrees to sell to or buy from only one party, competitors of the buyer or seller may be foreclosed from the market. For example, if a health plan agrees with a hospital not to contract with that hospital's competitors, competing hospitals are foreclosed from the plan's members. If the plan's market share of all commercially insured patients in the area is substantial, competing hospitals may be weakened competitively, increasing the contracting hospital's market power.

Because they usually generate procompetitive effects, exclusive contracts are always analyzed under the rule of reason.[165] The plaintiff must (1) define the relevant market affected by the exclusive contract;[166] (2) show that the contract forecloses a significant percentage of that market;[167] and (3) show that the duration of the exclusive relationship is sufficiently long that, given the percentage of foreclosure from the contract, it likely will have a significant anticompetitive effect because the party with the contract will obtain or maintain significant market power.[168] Importantly, the court must consider any offsetting procompetitive benefits from the contract[169] and then subjectively balance the procompetitive and anticompetitive effects to determine which effect predominates.

By far, the most important variable in the analysis is the percentage of the market foreclosed to competitors by the exclusive arrangement. There is no black-letter foreclosure percentage that results in unlawfulness because a host of other variables are relevant in assessing the contract's effect. But most courts indicate that concern should not arise at foreclosure percentages less than 30% or 40%.[170] And there is a trade-off between the foreclosure percentage and the duration of the exclusive arrangement—e.g., the shorter the duration of the contract, the larger the permitted percentage of

---

[165] *Jefferson Parish Hosp. Dist. No. 2 v. Hyde*, 466 U.S. 2 (1984); *Tampa Elec. Co. v. Nashville Coal Co.*, 365 U.S. 320 (1961); *ZF Meritor, LLC v. Eaton Corp.*, 696 F.3d 254 (3d Cir. 2012); *Imaging Ctr., Inc. v. W. Md. Health Sys., Inc.*, 158 Fed. App'x 413 (4th Cir. 2005).

[166] E.g., *Tampa Elec. Co. v. Nashville Coal Co.*, 365 U.S. 320 (1961); *Chuck's Feed & Seed Co. v. Ralston Purina Co.*, 810 F.2d 1289 (4th Cir. 1987).

[167] E.g., *Allied Orthopedic Appliances, Inc. v. Tyco Health Group, LP*, 592 F.3d 991 (9th Cir. 2010); *B&H Med., L.L.C. v. ABP Adm'rs, Inc.*, 526 F.3d 257 (6th Cir. 2008); *Imaging Ctr., Inc. v. W. Md. Health Sys., Inc.*, 158 Fed. App'x 413 (4th Cir. 2005) ("The inquiry into exclusive dealing arrangements focuses on whether the arrangement forecloses competition among producers or suppliers in a substantial share of the affected market."); *Geneva Pharms. Tech. Corp. v. Barr Labs., Inc.*, 386 F.3d 485 (2d Cir. 2004) ("Exclusive dealing is an unreasonable restraint of trade and a § 1 violation only when the agreement freezes out a significant fraction of buyers or sellers from the market."); *Republic Tobacco Co. v. N. Atl. Trading Co.*, 381 F.3d 717 (7th Cir. 2005) ("Exclusive dealing arrangements violate the antitrust laws only when they foreclose competition in a substantial share of the line of commerce at issue.");

[168] E.g., *ZF Meritor, LLC v. Eaton Corp.*, 696 F.3d 254 (3d Cir. 2012) (decided under § 2 of the Sherman Act, but including an extended discussion of exclusive contracts); *Omega Envtl., Inc. v. Gilbraco, Inc.*, 127 F.3d 1157 (9th Cir. 1997); *Balaklaw v. Lovell*, 14 F.3d 793 (2d Cir. 1994); *Rome Ambulatory Surgery Ctr., LLC v. Rome Mem'l Hosp.*, 349 F. Supp. 2d 389 (N.D.N.Y. 2004). For an in-depth discussion of the analysis of exclusive dealing contracts, see *McWane, Inc.*, 2014-1 Trade Cas. (CCH) ¶78,670 (FTC 2014), aff'd, 783 F.3d 814 (11th Cir. 2015).

[169] E.g., *Jefferson Parish Hosp. No. 2 v. Hyde*, 466 U.S. 2 (1984) (O'Connor, J., concurring) (listing several efficiency benefits from exclusive contracts); *Race Tires Am., Inc. v. Hoosier Racing Tire Corp.*, 614 F.3d 57 (3d Cir. 2010); *Barr Labs. v. Abbott Labs.*, 978 F.2d 98 (3d Cir. 1992) (court must consider legitimate business justifications for the exclusive contracts).

[170] E.g., *ZF Meritor, LLC v. Eaton Corp.*, 696 F.3d 254 (3d Cir. 2012); *Sterling Merch., Inc. v. Nestle, S.A.*, 656 F.3d 112 (1st Cir. 2011); *Stop & Shop Supermarket Co. v. Blue Cross & Blue Shield*, 373 F.3d 57 (1st Cir. 2004) (indicating that the exclusive contract must foreclosure some 30% or 40% of the market or more to raise antitrust concern); *Morales-Villalobos v. Garcia-Llorens*, 316 F.3d 51 (1st Cir. 2003); *U.S. Healthcare, Inc. v. Healthsource, Inc.*, 986 F.2d 589 (1st Cir. 1993) (explaining that substantial foreclosure is a threshold element in proving an exclusive contract unlawful); *United States v. Microsoft Corp.*, 87 F. Supp. 2d 30 (D.D.C. 2000) (holding that unlawfulness requires a 40% foreclosure percentage), rev'd in part on other grounds, 253 F.3d 34 (D.C. Cir. 2001) (per curiam); *Colonial Med. Group, Inc. v. Catholic Healthcare W.*, 2010-1 Trade Cas. (CCH) ¶77,039 (N.D. Cal. 2010) (noting that foreclosure percentages of less

foreclosure and vice-versa. But the important ultimate question is whether the contract's foreclosure of the contract beneficiary's competitors will result in its obtaining or maintaining market power.[171]

Exclusive dealing contracts are common in the health care sector. Examples include hospital exclusive contracts with hospital-based physicians, health maintenance organization exclusive contracts with a single provider group in some specialties, exclusive contracts between health plans and hospitals, and group purchasing organization single-source contracts with vendors of hospital supplies.[172] For the contract to constitute an exclusive contract, it need not spell out exclusivity specifically.[173] Exclusivity can be inferred from the parties' dealings. For example, in its United Regional Health Care System enforcement action,[174] the Antitrust Division alleged that a large hospital offered health plans a substantially lower price if they excluded a competing hospital from their provider panels than if they included it, which resulted in a de facto exclusive contract. And in its Blue Cross and Blue Shield of Michigan enforcement action,[175] the Division alleged that Blue Cross's use of most-favored-nations provisions in contracts with hospitals effectively foreclosed competing health plans from markets—another form of de facto exclusive dealing arrangement. Exclusive or semi-exclusive contracts can take numerous forms, including bundled discount arrangements,[176] loyalty and market-share discount arrangements,[177] selective contracting arrangements between health plans and providers, hospital restriction of health-plan ability to steer patients to other providers,[178] most-favored-nations provisions,[179] and seller discounts conditioned on the buyer's refusing to deal with the seller's competitors.[180] The potential competitive concern is always the same, however: potential foreclosure of competitors resulting in market power for the contract beneficiary.

7.2.2 Section 2 of the Sherman Act

Section 2 of the Sherman Act prohibits monopolization, attempted monopolization, and conspiracies to monopolize.[181] In general, the monopolization and attempted monopolization provisions apply to single firms with substantial market power that engage in conduct preventing other firms from encroaching on that power (i.e., "exclusionary" or "predatory" conduct that forecloses competitors from the market based on factors other than the merits of their products). Both violations usually require, prelimi-

---

than 30% or 40% are unlikely to create antitrust concern), *aff'd*, 444 Fed. App'x 937 (9th Cir. 2011); *Natchitoches Parish Serv. Dist. v. Tyco Int'l*, 2009-2 Trade Cas. (CCH) ¶76,815 (D. Mass. 2009) (same).

[171] *E.g., Kolon Indus. v. E.I DuPont De Nemours & Co.*, 748 F.3d 160 (4th Cir. 2014) ("Once a plaintiff has demonstrated substantial foreclosure, it must then demonstrate that the conduct had 'a negative impact on competition a whole.'").

[172] *See, e.g., Stop & Shop Supermarket Co. v. Blue Cross & Blue Shield*, 373 F.3d 57 (1st Cir. 2004); *Woman's Clinic, Inc. v. St. John's Health Sys.*, 252 F. Supp. 2d 857 (W.D. Mo. 2002).

[173] *See generally LePage's, Inc. v. 3M*, 324 F.3d 141 (3d Cir. 2003) (*en banc*).

[174] Compl., *United States v. United Reg'l Health Care Sys.*, No. 7:11-cv-00030 (N.D. Tex. Feb. 11, 2011).

[175] Compl., *United States v. Blue Cross Blue Shield*, No. 10-cv-14155-DPH-MKM (E.D. Mich. Oct. 18, 2010).

[176] *Se. Mo. Hosp. v. C.R. Bard, Inc.*, 642 F.3d 608 (8th Cir. 2011); *Cascade Health Solutions v. PeaceHealth*, 515 F.3d 883 (9th Cir. 2008); *LePage's, Inc. v. 3M*, 324 F.3d 141 (3d Cir. 2003) (en banc).

[177] *E.g., Concord Boat Corp. v. Brunswick Corp.*, 207 F.3d 1039 (8th Cir. 2000).

[178] *United States v. Charlotte-Mecklenburg Hosp. Auth.*, 248 F. Supp. 3d 720 (W.D.N.C. 2017).

[179] *E.g., United States v. Blue Cross Blue Shield*, 809 F. Supp. 2d 665 (E.D. Mich. 2011).

[180] *E.g., United States v. United Reg'l Health Care Sys.*, 2011-2 Trade Cas. (CCH) ¶77,619 (N.D. Tex. 2011) (consent decree).

[181] The conspiracy-to-monopolize violation is not discussed here. The essential elements are (1) a conspiracy or agreement, (2) specific intent to monopolize, and (3) an overt act in furtherance of the agreement. *E.g., Stewart Glass & Mirror, Inc., v. U.S. Auto Glass Discount Ctrs.*, 200 F. 3d 307 (5th Cir. 2000).

narily, definition of the relevant market.[182] Of course, a firm cannot monopolize or attempt to monopolize a market in which it is not a competitor.[183] So, for example, a hospital cannot monopolize or attempt to monopolize a market for physicians' services unless it employs physicians in the relevant market.

7.2.2.1 Monopolization

Monopolization requires proof of two essential elements: (1) monopoly power and (2) the willful acquisition or maintenance of monopoly power by "predatory" or "unreasonably exclusionary" conduct, as opposed to a superior product, business acumen, historical accident, or competition on the merits.[184] Importantly, a "monopoly" or monopoly power, by itself, is not unlawful. To constitute monopolization, that power must have been acquired or maintained by competitively inappropriate—i.e., "predatory"—conduct.[185]

The legal definition of "monopoly power" is "the power to control prices or exclude competition."[186] As a matter of economics, monopoly power is simply a substantial degree of market power,[187] and the terms are often used interchangeably. As in the case of market power, monopoly power can be proved either directly or circumstantially.[188] Direct evidence of monopoly power includes proof of supracompetitive pricing and restricted output.[189] To prove monopoly power by circumstantial evidence—the usual mode of proof—a plaintiff must prove:

1. the relevant market allegedly monopolized;

---

[182] *E.g., IGT v. Alliance Gaming Corp.*, 702 F.3d 1338 (Fed. Cir. 2012); *M&M Med. Supplies & Serv., Inc. v. Pleasant Valley Hosp.*, 981 F.2d 160 (4th Cir. 1992) (*en banc*); *Levine v. Cent. Fla. Med. Affiliates, Inc.*, 72 F.3d 1538 (11th Cir. 1996).
[183] *E.g., Lucas v. Citizens Commc'ns Co.*, 244 Fed. Appx 744 (9th Cir. 2007); *RxUSA Wholesale, Inc. v. Alcon Labs., Inc.*, 661 F. Supp. 2d 218 (E.D.N.Y. 2009), *aff'd without published opinion*, 2010 U.S. App. LEXIS 18200 (2d Cir. Aug. 30, 2010).
[184] *United States v. Grinnell Corp.*, 384 U.S. 563 (1966); *Diaz Aviation Corp. v. Airport Aviation Servs.*, 716 F.3d 256 (1st Cir. 2013); *Allied Orthopedic Appliances, Inc. v. Tyco Health Group, LP*, 592 F.3d 991 (9th Cir. 2010); *HDC Med., Inc. v. Minntech Corp.*, 474 F.3d 543 (8th Cir. 2007).
[185] *E.g., Pac. Bell Tele. Co. v. linkLINE Commc'ns, Inc.*, 555 U.S. 438 (2009); *Verizon Commc'ns, Inc. v. Law Offices of Curtis V. Trinko, LLP*, 540 U.S. 398 (2004) ("The mere possession of monopoly power, and the concomitant charging of monopoly prices, is not . . . unlawful. . . . [T]he possession of monopoly power will not be found unlawful unless it is accompanied by an element of anticompetitive conduct."); *Rambus, Inc. v. FTC*, 522 F.3d 456 (D.C. Cir. 2008); *Christy Sports, LLC v. Deer Valley Resort Co.*, 555 F.3d 1188 (10th Cir. 2009) ("Under both types of § 2 claims, [plaintiff] must . . . plead both power in a relevant market and anticompetitive conduct."); *Gulf States Reorg. Group, Inc. v. Nucor Corp.*, 466 F.3d 961 (11th Cir. 2006) ("The antitrust laws allow legal monopolies to compete vigorously on the merits . . . , even if such competition drives out competitors."); *Total Renal Care, Inc. v. W. Nephrology & Metabolic Bone Disease, P.C.*, 2009 U.S. Dist. LEXIS 80821 (D. Colo. Aug. 21, 2009).
[186] *United States v. E.I. du Pont de Nemours & Co.*, 351 U.S. 377, 391 (1957); *Four Corners Nephrology Assocs., P.C. v. Mercy Med. Ctr.*, 582 F.3d 1216 (10th Cir. 2009). Of course, a seller cannot "control prices" unless it can "exclude competition."
[187] *E.g., Queen City Pizza, Inc. v. Domino's Pizza, Inc.*, 124 F.3d 430 (3d Cir. 1997) ("Monopoly power under § 2 requires 'something greater' than market power under § 1.").
[188] *E.g., Novell, Inc. v. Microsoft Corp.*, 731 F.3d 1064 (10th Cir. 2013); *Diaz Aviation Corp. v. Airport Aviation Servs.*, 716 F.3d 256 (1st Cir. 2013); *Geneva Pharms. Tech. Corp. v. Barr Labs., Inc.*, 386 F.3d 485 (2d Cir. 2004).
[189] *Harrison Aire, Inc. v. Aerostar Int'l, Inc.*, 423 F.3d 374 (3d Cir. 2005) ("Monopoly power can be demonstrated with either evidence of supracompetitive pricing and high barriers to entry . . . , or with structural evidence of a monopolized market. . . . Plaintiffs relying on market share as a proxy for monopoly power must plead and produce evidence of a relevant product market, of the alleged monopolist's dominant share of that market, and high barriers to entry."); *Rebel Oil Co. v. Atl. Richfield Co.*, 51 F.3d 1421 (9th Cir. 1995).

2. that the defendant has a dominant share of the relevant market (usually at least 65%);[190]

3. significant entry barriers prevent new competitors from entering the market; and

4. significant barriers to expansion prevent incumbent competitors from expanding their output.[191]

Section 2 prevents firms with substantial market power from engaging in unnecessarily exclusionary conduct that prevents other competitors or potential competitors from challenging that power—in antitrust jargon, "predatory conduct." In general, conduct is predatory if it has significant exclusionary effects on the defendant's actual or potential competitors, thus facilitating the firm's attainment or maintenance of monopoly power, *and* it promotes none of the values that competition is meant to promote (i.e., lower prices, greater efficiency, higher quality, greater choice, and increased innovation).[192] Conduct is not predatory if the defendant can show that it has a procompetitive "legitimate business justification" or "valid business reason" for engaging in it,[193] although some courts, especially in recent decisions, require a balancing of the procompetitive and anticompetitive effects of the conduct as under Section 1 rule-of-reason analysis.[194]

Distinguishing between anticompetitive predatory conduct and merely aggressive procompetitive conduct is often quite difficult. The latter can exclude competitors but benefit consumers. One example is an efficient firm, even one with monopoly power, charging very low, but not below-cost, prices that harm its less efficient competitors. The focus in determining whether conduct is predatory is its effect on the defendant's competitors, not its customers. For example, a firm with legitimately obtained monopoly power (e.g., because it "built a better mousetrap")[195] can lawfully charge any price the market will bear, including the monopoly price.[196] High prices do not exclude or foreclose competitors from the market; indeed, they invite both new entry into the market and competitors to undercut those prices.

Although difficult to define precisely, predatory conduct is conduct that permits a firm to obtain or maintain its substantial market power but generates no consumer benefits—exclusionary conduct not constituting competition on the merits, undertaken solely to harm competitors[197] It can include predatory pricing (i.e., a firm's pricing below some measure of its cost to destroy competitors and

---

[190] *See generally Cal. v. Safeway, Inc.*, 615 F.3d 1171 (9th Cir. 2010) (noting that a market share between 60 and 70% was sufficient to establish monopoly power), *on rehearing en banc*, 651 F.3d 1118 (9th Cir. 2011); *United States v. Aluminum Co. of Am.*, 148 F.2d 416 (2d Cir. 1945) (stating the classic standard: A 90% market share "is enough to constitute a monopoly; it is doubtful whether sixty or sixty-five per cent would be enough; and certainly thirty-three percent is not").
[191] *Novell, Inc. v. Microsft Corp.*, 731 F.3d 1064 (10th Cir. 2013); *Image Technical Servs., Inc. v. Eastman Kodak Co.*, 125 F.3d 1195 (9th Cir. 1997).
[192] *Cf. Wichita Clinic, P.A. v. Columbia/HCA Healthcare Corp.*, 45 F. Supp. 2d 1164 (D. Kan. 1999) ("Predatory practices are illegal only if they impair opportunities of rivals, are not competition on the merits or go beyond reasonable competition, and appear reasonably capable of contributing significantly to creating or maintaining monopoly power.").
[193] *E.g., Eastman Kodak Co. v. Image Tech. Servs.*, Inc., 504 U.S. 451 (1994); *Gordon v. Lewistown Hosp.*, 423 F.3d 184 (3d Cir. 2005); *United States v. Dentsply Int'l, Inc.*, 399 F.3d 181 (3d Cir. 2005).
[194] *E.g., United States v. Microsoft Corp.*, 253 F.3d 34 (D.C. Cir. 2001) (per curiam).
[195] *See, e.g., Morgan v. Ponder*, 892 F.2d 1355 (8th Cir. 1989).
[196] *E.g., Ocean State Physicians Health Plan v. Blue Cross & Blue Shield*, 883 F.2d 1101 (1st Cir. 1989).
[197] *See generally W. Penn Allegheny Health Sys. v. UPMC*, 637 F.3d 85 (3d Cir. 2010) ("Broadly speaking, a firm engages in anticompetitive conduct when it attempts to 'exclude rivals on some basis other than efficiency,' . . . or when it competes 'on some other basis than the merits.'"); *Race Tires Am., Inc. v. Hoosier Racing Tire Corp.*, 614 F.3d 57 (3d Cir. 2010); *Cascade Health Solutions v. PeaceHealth*, 515 F.3d 883 (9th Cir. 2008) (explaining that predatory conduct is "behavior

then recouping its losses by later charging a supracompetitive price),[198] "bundled" discounts that competitors cannot match (i.e., pricing a package of goods or services below the prices at which they would be sold separately),[199] some refusals by firms with market power to deal with their competitors,[200] a firm's refusal to provide competitors with access to an "essential facility" or relationship necessary for effective competition,[201] assertion of a fraudulently obtained patent,[202] "sham" litigation,[203] and leveraging.[204] These are not the only forms of conduct that can be predatory,[205] but they are the most frequently alleged. Practices that violate Section 1 of the Sherman Act, such as tying and exclusive dealing agreements, can also constitute the predatory conduct element of a Section 2 violation.[206]

Of these, the type of predatory conduct alleged most often is some type of refusal by a firm with market power to deal or provide support to its competitors. The applicable principle is that, except in very limited circumstances, even a firm with monopoly power has no general duty to deal with or aid its competitors.[207] Before finding a refusal to deal predatory, most courts require that there have been previously profitable cooperation between the parties that the defendant terminated the relationship for no procompetitive reason, indicating that it was sacrificing short-term profits solely to damage a competitor rather than for any procompetitive reason.[208]

The mirror image of a seller-side monopolization claim on the buyer side is "monopsonization," where a buyer has substantial market power as a purchaser of a relevant product or service.[209] To prove a violation, a plaintiff seller would have to prove that the defendant buyer has monopsony power and obtained or maintained that power by excluding other buyers from the market, perhaps

---

that tends to impair the opportunities of rivals and either does not further competition on the merits or does so in an unnecessarily restrictive way").

[198] *E.g., Brooke Group, Ltd. v. Brown & Williamson Tobacco Co.*, 509 U.S. 209 (1993); *see also R.J. Reynolds Tobacco Co. v. Cigarettes Cheaper!*, 462 F.3d 690 (7th Cir. 2006); *United States v. AMR Corp.*, 335 F.3d 1109 (10th Cir. 2003).
[199] *Se. Mo. Hosp. v. C.R. Bard Co.*, 616 F.3d 888 (8th Cir. 2010).
[200] *See generally Aspen Skiing Co. v. Aspen Highlands Skiing Corp.*, 472 U.S. 585 (1986); *SmileCare Dental Group v. Delta Dental Plan*, 88 F.3d 780 (9th Cir. 1996).
[201] The classic discussion of the essential-facilities doctrine is *MCI Commc'ns Corp. v. Am. Tel. & Tel. Co.*, 708 F.2d 1081 (7th Cir. 1983). *See also Otter Tail Power Co. v. United States*, 410 U.S. 366 (1973); *McKenzie v. Mercy Hosp.*, 854 F.3d 365 (10th Cir. 1988). Significantly, the Supreme Court never has approved the doctrine. *Verizon Commc'ns, Inc. v. Law Offices of Curtis V. Trinko, LLP*, 540 U.S. 398 (2004).
[202] *E.g., Dippin' Dots, Inc. v. Mosey*, 476 F.3d 1337 (Fed. Cir. 2007).
[203] *See, e.g., Prof'l Real Estate Invs., Inc. v. Columbia Pictures Indus.*, 508 U.S. 49 (1993); *Armstrong Surgical Ctr., Inc. v. Armstrong Mem'l Hosp.*, 195 F.3d 154 (3d Cir. 1999).
[204] *AD/SAT v. Associated Press*, 181 F.3d 216 (2d Cir. 1999) (per curiam); *Am. Airlines, Inc. v. United Airlines, Inc.*, 948 F.2d 536 (9th Cir. 1991); *Berkey Photo, Inc. v. Eastman Kodak Co.*, 603 F.2d 263 (2d Cir. 1979).
[205] For a more complete list, *see* 1 ABA Section of Antitrust Law, *Antitrust Law Developments*, 245–303 (7th ed. 2012).
[206] *E.g., E.I. du Pont de Nemours & Co. v. Kolon Indus.*, 637 F.3d 435 (4th Cir. 2010); *United States v. Microsoft Corp.*, 253 F.3d 34 (D.C. Cir. 2001) (per curiam).
[207] *See generally Pac. Bell Tel. Co. v. linkLINE Commc'ns, Inc.*, 555 U.S. 438 (2009); *Verizon Commc'ns, Inc. v. Law Offices of Curtis V. Trinko, LLP*, 540 U.S. 398 (2004); *Aspen Skiing Co. v. Aspen Highlands Skiing Corp.*, 472 U.S. 585 (1986); *Four Corners Nephrology Assocs., P.C. v. Mercy Med. Ctr.*, 582 F.3d 1216 (10th Cir. 2009).'
[208] *E.g., Novell, Inc. v. Microsoft Corp.*, 731 F.3d 1064, (10th Cir. 2013); *Eatoni Ergomomics, Inc. v. Research in Motion Corp.*, 486 Fed. App'x 186 (2d Cir. 2012) (non-precedential summary order); *Williams v. Citigroup, Inc.*, 433 Fed. App'x. 36 (2d Cir. 2011) (summary order).
[209] *See generally Powderly v. Blue Cross & Blue Shield*, 2008-2 Trade Cas. (CCH) ¶76,321 (W.D.N.C. 2008) (explaining that "it is beyond dispute that a *provider of health insurance* services is also a *buyer* of *health care services* capable of exercising monopoly power over the market for doctor's services") (emphasis in original); *see also Campfield v. State Farm Mut. Auto. Ins. Co.*, 532 F.3d 1111 (10th Cir. 2008).

through a predatory buying scheme.²¹⁰ It is not unlawful, however for a buyer with legitimately obtained monopsony power (e.g., a health plan in contracting with providers) to obtain the lowest price it can in purchasing its inputs.²¹¹

7.2.2.2 Attempted Monopolization

Section 2's attempted-monopolization provision prohibits firms with substantial, but less than monopoly-level, market power from engaging in predatory conduct to achieve an actual monopoly.²¹² A plaintiff must show that the defendant (1) had a "specific intent" to monopolize the relevant market, (2) engaged in predatory conduct to implement that intent, and (3) had a "dangerous probability" of actually acquiring monopoly power if its predatory conduct continued.²¹³

By "specific intent to monopolize," the courts mean a "specific intent to destroy competition or build a monopoly."²¹⁴ Specific intent can be proved from the defendant's documents²¹⁵ or by inference from its predatory conduct.²¹⁶ The plaintiff also must prove that if the predatory conduct were to continue, a dangerous probability exists that the defendant would obtain actual monopoly power. In general, to prove the "dangerous probability of monopolization" element—the requirement on which most attempted monopolization cases focus—the plaintiff must normally show that the defendant has a large market share (typically, 40% or more), that entry barriers would prevent new entry, that firms already in the market lack the capacity to expand their output, and that the defendant's market share is likely to increase to a monopoly level (typically at least 65%).²¹⁷

7.2.3 Section 7 of the Clayton Act

Section 7 of the Clayton Act prohibits all types of mergers and other forms of acquisition that "may" lessen competition substantially.²¹⁸ A first important issue, regardless of whether the transaction presents any competitive concern, is whether the parties must report the transaction to

---

²¹⁰ *See, e.g., Weyerhaeuser Co. v. Ross-Simmons Hardwood Lumber Co.*, 549 U.S. 312 (2007); *see generally Cascades Computer Innovation LLC v. RPX Corp.*, 2013-2 Trade Cas. (CCH) ¶78,604 (N.D.Cal. 2013); *Se. Milk Antitrust Litig.*, 801 F. Supp. 2d 705 (E.D. Tenn. 2011).

²¹¹ *E.g., W. Penn Allegheny Health Sys. v. UPMC*, 627 F.3d 85 (3d Cir. 2010) ("A firm that has substantial power in the buy side of the market (*i.e.*, monopsony power) is generally free to bargain aggressively when negotiating the prices it will pay for goods and services."); *Ocean State Physicians Health Plan v. Blue Cross & Blue Shield*, 883 F.3d 1101 (1st Cir. 1989).

²¹² *See generally Ind. Grocery, Inc. v. Super Valu Stores*, 864 F.2d 1409 (7th Cir. 1988).

²¹³ *Spectrum Sports, Inc. v. McQuillan*, 506 U.S. 447 (1993); *W. Penn Allegheny Health Sys. v. UPMC*, 637 F.3d 85 (3d Cir. 2010); *E. Portland Imaging Ctr., P.C. v. Providence Health Sys.–Ore.*, 280 Fed. App'x 584 (9th Cir. 2008); *Gordon v. Lewistown Hosp.*, 423 F.3d 184 (3d Cir. 2005).

²¹⁴ *Times-Picayune Publ'g Co. v. United States*, 345 U.S. 594, 626 (1953).

²¹⁵ *E.g., Browning-Ferris Indus. v. Kelco Disposal, Inc.*, 845 F.2d 404 (2d Cir. 1988) (document stating that defendant wanted to "squish" plaintiff "like a bug").

²¹⁶ *E.g., E.I. du Pont de Nemours & Co. v. Kolon Indus.*, 637 F.3d 435 (4th Cir. 2011); *Great W. Directories, Inc. v. Sw. Bell Tel. Co.*, 63 F.3d 1278 (5th Cir. 1995) ("Intent can be inferred by anticompetitive practices or proven by direct evidence.").

²¹⁷ *E. Portland Imaging Ctr., P.C. v. Providence Health Sys.–Ore.*, 280 Fed. App'x 584 (9th Cir. 2008); *Full Draw Productions v. Easton Sports, Inc.*, 182 F.3d 745 (10th Cir. 1999); *Rebel Oil Co. v. Atl. Richfield Co.*, 51 F.3d 1421 (9th Cir. 1995).

²¹⁸ 15 U.S.C. § 18.

the Antitrust Division and the FTC under Section 7A of the Clayton Act,[219] the Hart-Scott-Rodino pre-merger notification provisions. It also is important to ensure that the parties will integrate sufficiently through the transaction so they constitute a single entity for antitrust purposes after the transaction.[220] If not, Section 1 of the Sherman Act continues to apply to their actions.[221] So, for example, if two physician practices supposedly "merge" but fail to totally integrate their operations, they may not constitute a single entity (i.e., may not be "*Copperwelded,*") and their joint negotiation of prices with health plans may constitute an unlawful horizontal price-fixing agreement.[222]

Mergers are horizontal (between competitors, meaning participants in the same relevant market); vertical (between buyers and sellers or firms at different levels in the chain of production or distribution); or conglomerate. Only horizontal mergers are discussed here because they raise the most antitrust concern. The analysis of vertical mergers is similar to that of exclusive dealing contracts; the primary concern is whether competitors of the merging firms will be foreclosed from needed inputs or customers to the extent that the merged firm will obtain or maintain market power.[223] In the *St. Alphonsus Medical Center* case, for example, where a hospital acquired a large physician group, a competing health care system claimed that the group would then admit most or all its patients to its hospital employer, foreclosing the plaintiff hospital from a significant percentage of patients, thus increasing the defendant hospital's market power.[224]

In the last several years, the FTC has become very active in investigating and challenging hospital mergers[225] and mergers between hospitals and other providers, including outpatient facilities[226] and

---

[219] 15 U.S.C. § 18a. Implementing regulations are at 16 C.F.R. §§ 801–03.

[220] *See generally Med. Ctr. v. Premier Health*, 827 F.3d 934 (6th Cir. 2016); *HealthAm. Pa., Inc. v. Susquehanna Health Sys.*, 278 F. Supp. 2d 423 (M.D. Pa. 2003) (holding that a hospital joint-operating agreement sufficiently integrated the hospitals so that they constituted a single entity for antitrust purposes). For discussion of this issue, *see* Mark J. Botti, Assistant Chief, Litigation I Section, Antitrust Division, "Virtual Mergers of Hospitals: When Does the *Per Se* Rule Apply?", and John J. Miles, "A Conceptual and Practical Approach to the Antitrust Analysis of Virtual Mergers," Prepared Remarks Before the American Health Lawyers Association Antitrust in the Healthcare Field seminar (Feb. 18, 2000); *see also* John J. Miles, *The Importance of Integration in Healthcare Antitrust Counseling:* Yakima *and* Susquehanna, AHLA HEALTH LAWYERS NEWS, March 2004, at 16.

[221] *E.g., New York v. St. Francis Hosp.*, 34 F. Supp. 2d 399 (S.D.N.Y. 2000) (insufficient hospital integration for single-entity status).

[222] *E.g., Surgical Specialists of Yakima, P.L.L.C.*, 136 F.T.C. 840 (2003) (consent order) (FTC price-fixing enforcement action against allegedly "sham" merger entity negotiating contracts on behalf of competing medical practices).

[223] *See, e.g., Ford Motor Co. v. United States*; *HTI Health Servs., Inc. v. Quorum Health Group, Inc.*, 960 F. Supp. 1104 (S.D. Miss. 1997).

[224] *St. Alphonsus Med. Ctr. v. St. Luke's Health Sys.*, 2014-1 Trade Cas. (CCH) ¶78,667 (D.Idaho 2014). The court did not need to assess this vertical restraint's effect on competition. The acquiring hospital already employed physicians in the same specialty as the acquired group, and the court condemned the transaction based on horizontal analysis.

[225] *See, e.g., FTC v. Phoebe Putney Health Sys.*, 568 U.S. 216 (2013) (FTC challenge to hospital merger in Albany, Georgia); *ProMedica Health Sys. v. FTC*, 749 F.3d 559 (6th Cir. 2014); Compl., *Reading Health Sys.*, Dkt. No. 9353 (FTC Nov. 16, 2012); *FTC v. OSH Healthcare Sys.*, 852 F. Supp. 2d 1069 (N.D. Ill. 2012); *Universal Health, Inc.*, 151 F.T.C. 219 (2011) (consent order) (requiring divestiture of psychiatric hospitals); *Inova Health Sys. Found.*, Dkt. No. 9326 (FTC June 17, 2008) (order dismissing case after parties abandoned transaction); *Evanston Nw. Healthcare Corp.*, 2007-2 Trade Cas. (CCH) ¶75,814 (FTC 2007) (finding that hospital merger violated § 7).

[226] *Carilion Clinic*, Dkt. No. 9338 (FTC Oct. 7, 2009) (consent order) (requiring hospital to divest ambulatory surgery center and imaging center).

physicians.[227] It has also filed high-profile cases challenging laboratory[228] and pharmaceutical mergers as well, and this trend is likely to continue.[229]

In analyzing horizontal mergers, the most important sources of guidance are the recently decided cases themselves and the Department of Justice and FTC 2010 *Horizontal Merger Guidelines*.[230] The agencies' *Merger Guidelines* require close study by any attorney representing health-care clients in planning and implementing a merger. They are not "the law," but courts rely on them heavily in determining the antitrust ramifications of mergers.[231] The *Merger Guidelines* explain in some detail how the agencies analyze horizontal mergers, the factors they consider important in determining whether to challenge particular mergers, and the types and sources of evidence on which they rely.[232]

The *Merger Guidelines* explain that "mergers should not be permitted to create, enhance, or entrench market power or to facilitate its exercise."[233] In general, a plaintiff must show it reasonably likely that the merger will result in anticompetitive effects; Section 7 deals with probabilities, not certainties.[234] The twin potential antitrust concerns from horizontal mergers are that they might (1) permit the merging parties by themselves to exercise market power—so called "unilateral effects"[235] or (2) result in a market sufficiently highly concentrated that several or all firms in the market will interact in a coordinated manner and raise prices, thus exercising market power jointly—so-called "coordinated effects"[236] or "tacit collusion."

The primary concern in recent merger challenges, including those challenging health care sector mergers, has been the potential for unilateral effects.[237] In determining whether adverse unilateral effects are likely, the most important variables are the merging parties' post-merger market share and

---

[227] *See St. Alphonsus Med. Ctr. v. St. Luke's Health Sys.*, 2014-1 Trade Cas. (CCH) ¶78,667 (D. Idaho 2014). *See also* Compl., *Sanford* Health, Dkt. No. 9376 (FTC June 21, 2017) (challenging hospital acquisition of large physician practice); Statement *of Bureau of Competition Director Richard Feinstein on the Abandonment by Providence Health & Services of its Plan to Acquire Spokane Cardiology and Heart Clinics of the Northwest in Spokane Washington* (Apr. 8, 2011).

[228] *E.g.*, Lab. Corp. of Am. Holdings, Dkt. No. C-4341 (FTC Dec. 8, 2011) (consent order); *FTC v. Lab. Corp. of Am.*, 2011 U.S. Dist. LEXIS 20354 (C.D. Cal., Mar. 11, 2011) (denying FTC motion for preliminary injunction).

[229] *FTC v. Lundbeck, Inc.*, 650 F.3d 1236 (8th Cir. 2011) (pharmaceutical merger).

[230] U.S. Dep't of Justice & Federal Trade Comm'n, *Horizontal Merger Guidelines* (2010) (*Merger* Guidelines), at http://www.ftc.gov/os/2010/08/100819hmg.pdf.

[231] *See, e.g., ProMedica Health Sys. v. FTC*, 749 F.3d 559 (6th Cir. 2014) (noting that the *Merger Guidelines* are "useful but not binding"); *Chicago Bridge & Iron Co. v. FTC*, 515 F.3d 447 (5th Cir. 2008) (explaining that "the Merger Guidelines are not binding on the courts and the agency during adjudication but are only highly persuasive authorities as a 'benchmark of legality'").

[232] *See Merger Guidelines* § 1 (explaining that the *Guidelines* "describe the principal analytical techniques and the main types of evidence on which the Agencies usually rely to predict whether a horizontal merger may substantially lessen competition").

[233] *Id.*

[234] *E.g., Brown Shoe v. United States*, 370 U.S. 294 (1962); *United States v. H&R Block, Inc.*, 833 F. Supp. 2d 36 (D.D.C. 2011).

[235] *Merger Guidelines* § 6. *See, e.g., FTC v. Butterworth Health Corp.*, 946 F. Supp. 1285 (W.D. Mich. 1996), *aff'd per curiam without published opinion.*, 121 F.3d 708 (6th Cir. 1997); *FTC v. Staples, Inc.*, 970 F. Supp. 1066 (D.D.C. 1997).

[236] *Merger Guidelines* § 7; *see, e.g., Hosp. Corp. of Am. v. FTC*, 807 F.2d 1381 (7th Cir. 1986); *Chicago Bridge & Iron Co.*, 138 F.T.C. 1024 (2004) ("First, a merger may result in a single firm that so dominates a market that it is able to maintain prices above the level that would prevail if the market were competitive. . . . Second, a merger may result in only a few firms accounting for most of the sales of a product and thereby enable those firms to exercise market power by explicitly or tacitly coordinating their actions."), *petition for review denied*, 515 F.3d 447 (5th Cir. 2008).

[237] *See, e.g, FTC v. Penn State Hershey Med. Ctr.*, 838 F.3d 327 (3d Cir. 2016) (concern was that the merged Pinnacle and Hershey hospitals, themselves, could increase reimbursement from health plans).

particularly the degree of direct competition between them prior to the merger. All else being equal, the larger the post-merger market share of the merging parties or the greater the strength of competition between them (as opposed to the strength of competition between them and other area firms), the more likely that the merger will result in anticompetitive unilateral effects.[238] The most important variables in determining whether the merger will result in coordinated effects are the level of market concentration resulting from the transaction, the degree to which the merger increases that level, and the susceptibility of the market to interdependent competitive decision making.[239]

Traditional antitrust merger analysis usually proceeds through the following steps.

7.2.3.1 Definition of the Relevant Product Market

The Supreme Court and lower federal courts have stated unequivocally that plaintiffs, in challenging mergers, must define the relevant market in which the merger affects competition.[240] Generally, as discussed before, the relevant product market includes the products or services sold by the merging firms and their reasonably interchangeable substitutes.[241] The *Merger Guidelines*, however, specify that, in defining the relevant product market, the agencies will apply the "hypothetical monopolist" methodology. After identifying a product or service sold by both merging parties, the question is whether a hypothetical monopolist of that product, i.e., the only firm selling the product, could profitably increase its price by a small but significant amount because too few customers would divert to substitute products to make the price increase unprofitable. If so, that product constitutes a relevant product market. If not, the next-best substitute product is added to this "candidate market" and the test repeated. Once a hypothetical monopolist of all the added products could profitably increase their price, those products constitute the relevant product market. Importantly, under this methodology for defining the market, the relevant product market usually will not include all reasonably interchangeable substitutes, but only those close substitutes that would permit a monopolist of them to profitably raise their price—i.e., exercise market power.[242] Courts have applied the hypothetical monopolist methodology in delineating relevant product markets (and relevant geographic markets) in every recent merger decision.

In hospital merger cases, courts have universally found a relevant product market consisting of the cluster of inpatient acute-care services offered by the merging hospitals and sold to commercial health plans.[243] Outpatient services are excluded, although they may constitute a separate relevant

---

[238] *See, e.g., ProMedica Health Sys. v. FTC*, 749 F.3d 559 (6th Cir. 2014) (nothing that the extent of direct competition between the merging firms is crucial in evaluating the likelihood of unilateral effects); *United States v. Bazaarvoice, Inc.*, 2014 U.S. Dist. LEXIS 3284 (N.D. Cal. Jan. 8, 2014) ("Economic theory predicts that the merger will result in significant unilateral effects for customers that viewed [the merging parties, individually] as the most attractive suppliers . . . and for whom the third-best supplier has a distinctly inferior product."); *United States v. H&R Block, Inc.*, 833 F. Supp. 2d 36 (D.D.C. 2011); *Evanston Nw. Healthcare Corp.*, 2007-2 Trade Cas. (CCH) F75,814 (FTC 2007).

[239] *E.g., United States v. H&R Block Co.*, 833 F. Supp. 2d 36 (D.D.C. 2011).

[240] *E.g., United States v. Marine Bancorporation*, 418 U.S. 602 (1974); *FTC v. Advocate Health Care Network*, 841 F.3d 460 (7th Cir. 2016).

[241] *See generally City of N.Y. v. Group Health Inc.*, 649 F.3d 151 (2d Cir. 2011); *HTI Health Servs., Inc. v. Quorum Health Group, Inc.*, 960 F. Supp. 1104 (S.D. Miss. 1997).

[242] *Merger Guidelines* § 4.1.1.

[243] *E.g., ProMedica Health Sys. v. FTC*, 749 F.3d 559 (6th Cir. 2014); *FTC v. Tenet Health Care Corp.*, 186 F.3d 1045 (8th Cir. 1999); *FTC v. OSF Healthcare Sys.*, 852 F. Supp. 2d 1069 (N.D. Ill. 2012); *United States v. Mercy Health Servs.*, 902 F. Supp. 968 (N.D. Iowa 1995), *vacated and remanded with instructions to dismiss as moot*, 107 F.3d 632 (8th Cir. 1997).

product market requiring examination. A court may carve out separate relevant product markets where both merging hospitals offer a particular service but competitive conditions for them differ from those for the cluster services—for example, a tertiary service with a broader relevant geographic market than that for the clustered primary and secondary services.[244] As hospitals continue to acquire physician practices, investigations of hospital mergers now almost always examine the effect of the merger on physician-service markets as well as hospital markets.[245] In defining relevant product markets in physician-practice mergers or in analyzing other issues involving physician market power, a frequent question is whether the relevant product market includes physicians in different specialties where both provide certain common services, or whether the product market is limited to services provided by a single medical specialty.[246] The answer is fact-specific, depending primarily on whether health plans could substitute physicians in one specialty for those in the other in their networks.[247]

7.2.3.2 Definition of the Relevant Geographic Market

As noted before, the relevant geographic market is the area of effective competition—the area in which the sellers in question operate and to which their customers would turn in sufficient numbers to make a seller's price increase unprofitable.[248] The courts have emphasized the necessity for including in the relevant geographic market the more-distant sellers to whom customers could turn for services if sellers in closer proximity increased prices.[249] The relevant geographic market for most health care services is relatively local, and could encompass a city (or even only part of a large metropolitan area) or a county.[250] As the services constituting the relevant product market become more complex and sophisticated (e.g., organ transplants), the size of the relevant geographic market usually increases[251] because patients are willing to travel greater distances for them and thus their health plans are willing to contract with more distant providers for their networks.

Again, the agencies, and more and more the courts, apply the hypothetical monopolist methodology in defining relevant geographic markets.[252] Indeed, appropriate application of the test was the primary issue in the two most-recent hospital merger decisions[253] and another merger decision find-

---

[244] *E.g., ProMedica Health Sys. v. FTC*, 749 F.3d 559 (6th Cir. 2014) (finding a product market limited to obstetrical services in addition to a cluster market of inpatient acute-care services).

[245] For example, in the FTC's successful challenge to the merger of two hospitals in Rockford, Illinois, it also alleged that the merger would have anticompetitive effects in physician markets. *FTC v. OSF Healthcare Sys.*, 852 F. Supp. 2d 1069 (N.D. Ill. 2012).

[246] *Cf.* Antitrust Division Business Review Letter to Allied Colon and Rectal Specialists (Jul. 1, 1996) (finding that general surgeons were substitutable for colon-rectal surgeons and thus part of the relevant product market), at https://www.justice.gov/atr/response-allied-colon-and-rectal-specialists-request-business-review-letter.

[247] *See* Antitrust Division Business Review Letter to Childrens' Healthcare, P.A. (Mar. 1, 1996) (opining that general practitioners were not substitutable for pediatricians), at http://www.justice.gov/atr/public/busreview/0555.pdf.

[248] *E.g., Brown Shoe Co. v. United States*, 370 U.S. 294 (1962).

[249] *E.g., FTC v. Freeman Hosp.*, 69 F.3d 260 (8th Cir. 1995); *Cal. v. Sutter Health Sys.*, 130 F. Supp. 2d 1109 (N.D. Cal. 2001).

[250] *ProMedica Health Sys. v. FTC*, 749 F.3d 559 (6th Cir. 2014) (parties agreed that relevant geographic market was limited to one county; court's discussion suggests that market could have been limited to only one portion of the county).

[251] *Merger Guidelines* § 1.2.

[252] *Merger Guidelines* § 4.2.

[253] *FTC v. Advocate Health Network*, 841 F.3d 460 (7th Cir. 2016); *FTC v. Penn State Hershey Med. Ctr.*, 838 F.3d 327 (3d Cir. 2016).

ing a hospital's acquisition of a large physician practice unlawful.[254] The analyst chooses the smallest area (the "candidate market") and asks whether a hypothetical monopolist of the relevant product in that area could profitably increase price a small but significant amount. If so, that area constitutes the relevant geographic market. If not, the next-closest alternative supplier is included, and the test repeated until the included suppliers, together, could profitably increase price. The included firms constitute the firms in the geographic market.

In the case of relevant geographic markets for hospitals, patient-discharge data showing where patients seek hospital services can provide significant insight into the relevant geographic market, but the agencies have warned that patient-discharge analysis is far from sufficient, by itself, to define relevant geographic markets.[255] The views of health plans regarding the substitutability of hospitals in particular areas for their networks, as well as party documents and econometric studies, are quite important.

7.2.3.3 Identification of Competitors in the Relevant Market

The purpose for defining the relevant market is to identify competitors of the merging firms. Once the relevant product and geographic markets are delineated, competitors in those markets can be identified.

7.2.3.4 Calculation of Each Competitor's Market Share

The competitors' or "market participants'" market shares should be calculated using several "universes." In hospital mergers, for example, applicable measures include licensed beds, staffed beds, admissions, inpatient days, and revenue. The *Merger Guidelines* provide that revenue is usually the most appropriate measure.[256] Competitors or market participants include not only firms located "in" the relevant market, but also firms that have sales within that market.[257]

7.2.3.5 Calculation of the Merging Firms' Post-Merger Market Share, the Level of Market Concentration, and the Increase in Market Concentration Resulting from the Merger

The merging firms' post-merger market share provides an indication of whether they, together as a single firm, could exercise market power. No precise combined market share signals unlawfulness; nevertheless, concern generally begins to arise at a post-merger share of about 35%.[258]

If the potential concern from the merger is post-merger coordination of decision making by competitors (i.e., "coordinated effects" in the jargon of the *Merger Guidelines*), the level of market concentration and the degree to which the merger increases that level are the most important variables. "Market concentration," as noted before, refers to the number and relative sizes of competitors in a market—the fewer the number and the more disparate their market shares, the more concentrated the

---

[254] *FTC v. St. Alphonsus Med. Ctr.*, 778 F.3d 775 (9th Cir. 2015).
[255] *See generally* Federal Trade Comm'n & U.S. Dep't of Justice, *Improving Health Care: A Dose of Competition*, Ch. 4 at 5–14 (2004).
[256] *Merger Guidelines* § 5.2.
[257] *Merger Guidelines* § 5.1.
[258] *See generally United States v. Philadelphia Nat'l Bank*, 374 U.S. 321 (1963).

market.[259] Economic theory predicts an inverse relationship between the level of market concentration and market performance.[260] All else being equal, the more the merger increases the level of concentration, the greater the probability and degree of likely anticompetitive coordinated effects because the more likely that firms in the market will establish their prices jointly or interdependently—i.e., the market tends to become an oligopoly.

The *Merger Guidelines* and the courts apply the Herfindahl-Hirschman Index, or HHI, to measure market concentration.[261] To calculate the *post-merger* HHI:

1. add the market shares of the merging firms;
2. square that share and the share of each other participant in the relevant market; and
3. sum the squares.

This results in a figure between almost zero (an infinite number of market participants) and 10,000 (one firm—a monopoly). To calculate the amount by which the merger would increase the HHI, multiply the market shares of the merging firms by each other, and that product by two. Thus, if two urology practices merge, one with a market share of 10% and the other with a share of 5%, the merger will increase the HHI by 100.

If the merging firms' post-merger market share or the level of market concentration and its increase are sufficiently high, the merger is *prima facie*, or rebuttably presumed, unlawful. The burden of going forward then shifts to the merging parties to show that the market share and concentration statistics provide an inaccurate indicator of the merger's likely effect on competition.[262]

According to the *Merger Guidelines*, a post-merger HHI of 1,500 or less indicates an "unconcentrated" market and thus that the merger raises no antitrust issue regardless of the amount by which it would increase concentration. (The HHI for a market with six equal-size firms is about 1,500.) If, after the merger, the HHI is between 1,500 and 2,500, the market is "moderately concentrated," but no antitrust concern arises if the increase in the HHI does not exceed 100. If the increase exceeds 100, however, the merger "potentially raise[s] significant competitive concerns" depending on other factors, and further analysis may be warranted. If the post-merger HHI is above 2,500, the market is deemed "highly concentrated." (The HHI for a market with four equal-size firms is 2,500.) Still, however, if the HHI increase is 100 or less, no problem should arise; if the increase is between 100 and 200, concern can arise depending on other factors and thus more in-depth analysis may be required; and if the increase is more than 200, the merger, according to the *Merger Guidelines*, "will be presumed to create or enhance market power," but this presumption can be rebutted.[263] The case

---

[259] *See, e.g.*, Robert S. Pindyck & Daniel L. Rubinfeld, *Microeconomics* 358 (6th ed. 2005) ("When only a few firms account for most of the sales in a market, we say that the market is highly *concentrated*.") (emphasis in original).
[260] *See generally* F. M. Scherer & David Ross, *Industrial Market Structure and Economic Performance* 4–5, 277–79 (3d ed. 1990).
[261] *Merger Guidelines* § 5.3.
[262] *E.g., United States v. General Dynamics Corp.*, 415 U.S. 486 (1974); *see also ProMedica Health Sys. v. FTC*, 749 F.3d 559 (6th Cir. 2014); *Chicago Bridge & Iron Co. v. FTC*, 515 F.3d 447 (5th Cir. 2008); *United States v. Bazaarvoice, Inc.*, 2014 U.S. Dist. LEXIS 3284 (N.D. Cal., 2014 Jan. 8, 2014); *FTC v. Butterworth Health Corp.*, 946 F. Supp. 1285 (W.D. Mich. 1996), *aff'd per curiam without published opinion*, 121 F.3d 708 (6th Cir. 1997); *FTC v. Cardinal Health, Inc.*, 12 F. Supp. 2d 34 (D.D.C. 1998).
[263] *Merger Guidelines* § 5.3.

law indicates the same: if the government shows that the merger will result in a significant level of market concentration, it is prima facie, or rebuttably presumed, unlawful.[264]

If the potential concern from the merger is possible unilateral effects, i.e., the ability of the merging firms, by themselves, to raise price, the most important variable is the degree of substitutability in the eyes of customers and health plans between them as compared to their substitutability with other competitors in the area.[265] That degree of substitution can be measured or estimated by calculation of the "diversion ratios" between the merging parties. Diversion ratios measure the percentage of one party's customers that would divert to the other, as opposed to other competitors, if the first did not exist or if it attempted to raise its price. The greater those percentages, the greater the likelihood the merger will permit the merged entity to raise prices unilaterally.[266]

An example explains why. Suppose hospitals A and B intend to merge and that they are the first and second choices of a significant percentage of a health plan's members, while hospitals C and D, although competitors, are considered poor substitutes. Prior to the merger, a health plan could force A and B to compete by threatening to exclude one if the plan considered its reimbursement demands too high. But if the hospitals merge and demand higher reimbursement, that competition is lost. The health plan must choose either to accede to the merged hospital's demand for higher reimbursement or attempt to force its members to use inferior substitutes. If the latter, the plan is likely to lose members and thus profits. Thus, the merger increases the merged hospitals' bargaining leverage to an extent greater than that their power prior to the merger. The merged hospital likely will exercise unilateral market power. This has been the primary concern or theory of concern in every recent hospital merger and health plan merger case.

7.2.3.6 Examination of Factors that Might Indicate that Post-Merger Market Share or Market Concentration Statistics are Misleading

Assuming the plaintiff proves a prima facie case, the burden of going forward shifts to the merging parties to rebut the presumption of unlawfulness. A number of factors can indicate that notwithstanding high post-merger market concentration, high post-merger market share, or high substitutability between the merging parties, the merger would not likely lead to unilateral or coordinated effects. In general, these so-called "rebuttal factors" fall into four categories:

1. low entry barriers into the relevant market and thus the likelihood of new entry;[267]
2. if the potential concern is coordinated interaction, market characteristics indicating that competitor tacit or explicit collusion, including interdependent competitive conduct among firms in the market, is not feasible or likely;[268]

---

[264] *E.g., St. Alphonsus Med. Ctr.-Nampa, Inc. v. St. Luke's Health Sys., Inc.*, 778 F.3d 775 (9th Cir. 2015); *ProMedica Health Sys. v. FTC*, 749 F.3d 559 (6th Cir. 2014); *Polypore Int'l, Inc. v. FTC*, 686 F.3d 1208 (11th Cir. 2012); *FTC v. OSF Healthcare Sys.*, 825 F. Supp. 2d 1069 (N.D. Ill. 2012).
[265] *Merger Guidelines* § 6.1. *See also St. Alphonsus Med. Ctr.-Nampa, Inc. v. St. Luke's Health Sys.*, 778 F.3d 775 (9th Cir. 2015) (noting that because the merging parties were "each other's closest substitutes . . . , the district court found that the acquisition limited the ability of insurers to negotiate with the merged entity").
[266] *Merger Guidelines* § 6.1.
[267] *Merger Guidelines* § 9; *see generally United States v. Baker Hughes, Inc.*, 908 F.2d 981 (D.C. Cir. 1990).
[268] *Merger Guidelines* § 7; *see generally FTC v. Elders Grain, Inc.*, 868 F.2d 901 (7th Cir. 1989).

3. the financial weakness of one of the merging firms;[269] and
4. efficiencies generated by the merger.[270]

Thus far, however, none of these factors has carried the day in hospital-merger challenges. Under the *Merger Guidelines*, new entry must be "timely," "likely," and "sufficient" to replace the competition lost by the merger.[271] Entry barriers into hospital markets are typically high, particularly in states with certificate-of-need laws.

The *Merger Guidelines* provide that in some situations, the efficiencies from a merger may offset its likely anticompetitive effects, but the requirements for proving that the efficiencies are "cognizable," and thus help to rebut the prima facie case are strict. They must be "merger specific," "verifiable," and the benefits passed on to consumers.[272] Both the agencies and the courts are skeptical about efficiencies claims, with several wondering if efficiencies count in favor of the transaction at all or whether there is any "efficiencies defense."[273] Indeed, several have noted that in no appellate decision have efficiencies rebutted a prima facie case.[274]

Regarding financial weakness of one of the merging parties, the *Merger Guidelines* provide for a "failing firm" defense, which, if proven, is a dispositive affirmative defense.[275] But the requirements are strict, and the defense has succeeded in only one litigated hospital merger challenge.[276] Proponents of the merger can also argue that although the hospital in question is not "failing" as a technical matter, it is so financially weak and ailing that its current market share grossly overstates its future competitive strength. This "weakened competitor" or "flailing firm" argument, if proved, is merely one factor the court will consider in determining whether the defendants have rebutted the prima facie case. But again, the requirements are strict. In general, the merging parties must prove that within a reasonable period time, the weakened competitor's market share would fall to a level such that the post-merger level of market concentration or the parties' post-merger market share would not raise the rebuttable presumption of unlawfulness.[277] Indeed, the *ProMedica* court stated

---

[269] *E.g., Merger Guidelines* § 11; *see also ProMedica Health Sys. v. FTC*, 759 F.3d 559 (6th Cir. 2014) (rejecting the argument); *Cal. v. Sutter Health Sys.*, 130 F. Supp. 2d 1109 (N.D. Cal. 2001) (explaining that the acquired hospital was a failing firm, thus permitting the merger even were it otherwise unlawful); *FTC v. Univ. Health, Inc.*, 938 F.2d 1206 (11th Cir. 1991) (explaining that although the acquired hospital was not failing, a firm's weakness as a competitor is a factor in favor of the merger).

[270] *Merger Guidelines* § 10. For helpful discussions, *see* Debra A. Valentine, General Counsel, Federal Trade Commission, "Health Care Mergers: Will We Get Efficiencies Claims Right?," prepared remarks before the St. Louis University School of Law (Nov. 14, 1997); Thomas R. McCarthy, et al., "Efficiencies Analysis in Hospital Mergers," text of remarks before the ABA Antitrust Law Section and Health Law Section Seminar, Oct. 15, 1998. *See also FTC v. OSF Healthcare Sys.*, 852 F. Supp. 2d 1069 (N.D. Ill. 2012) (rejecting hospitals' efficiency arguments).

[271] *Merger Guidelines* §§ 9, 9.1–.3.

[272] *Id.* § 10.

[273] *See, e.g., St. Alphonsus Med. Ctr.-Nampa v. St. Luke's Health Sys.*, 778 F.3d 775 (9th Cir. 2015) ("We remain skeptical about the efficiencies defense in general and about its scope in particular.").

[274] *See, e.g., id.* ("none of the reported appellate decision have actually held that a § 7 defendant has rebutted a prima facie case with an efficiencies defense").

[275] *Merger Guidelines* § 11 ("Failure and Exiting Asssets").

[276] *Cal. v. Sutter Health Sys.*, 130 F. Supp. 2d 1009 (N.D. Cal. 2001).

[277] *See ProMedica Health Sys. v. FTC*, 749 F.3d 559 (6th Cir. 2014) ("Courts 'credit such a defense only in rare cases, when the [acquiring firm] makes a substantial showing that the acquired firm's weakness, which cannot be resolved by any competitive means, would cause that firm's market share to reduce to a level that would undermine the government's *prima facie* case.'").

that the argument "is the Hail Mary pass of presumptively doomed mergers—in this case, thrown from ProMedica's own end zone."[278]

In addition to challenging hospital mergers, the agencies have challenged mergers in markets such as physician services,[279] nursing homes,[280] outpatient dialysis facilities,[281] pharmaceuticals,[282] cardiac stents,[283] health plans,[284] medical tests,[285] and others. State attorneys general have challenged physician-practice mergers[286] and joined the FTC in challenges to hospital mergers and hospital acquisitions of physician practices. The Antitrust Division, in business review letters, has threatened to challenge physician-practice mergers but has not yet brought any actions.[287]

7.2.4 The Federal Trade Commission Act

Section 5(a)(1) of the FTC Act prohibits "[u]nfair methods of competition in or affecting commerce."[288] Only the FTC can enforce the Act; there is no private right of action.[289] Section 5 applies only to entities "organized to carry on business for [their] own profit or that of [their] members."[290] Sometimes referred to as the "nonprofits exemption," this provision means, in practical effect, that the FTC lacks authority to investigate and prosecute conduct that would violate Section 5 when the action is implemented by nonprofit hospitals.[291] The Antitrust Division, however, can challenge the same conduct if it violates the Sherman Act. Normally, professional associations are subject to Section 5 because they generate benefits for their members.[292]

Congress granted the FTC broad authority to determine those practices that constitute "unfair methods of competition." In general, the FTC may declare conduct that violates either the "letter" of any of the antitrust laws[293] or their "spirit"[294] to be an unfair method of competition,[295] and in 2015, the

---

[278] *Id.*
[279] *E.g. Keystone Orthopaedic Specialists, LLC*, Dkt. No. C-4562 (FTC Dec. 14, 2015) (consent order).
[280] *See, e.g., United States v. Beverly Enters.*, 1984-1 Trade Cas. (CCH) ¶66,052 (M.D. Ga. 1984) (consent decree).
[281] *E.g., Fresenius AG*, Dkt. No. C-4348 (FTC May 23, 2012) (consent order).
[282] *E.g., FTC v. Lundbeck, Inc.*, 650 F.3d 1236 (8th Cir. 2011).
[283] *Boston Scientific Corp.*, Dkt. No., C-4164 (FTC Jul. 25, 2006) (consent order).
[284] *See, e.g., United States v. Anthem, Inc.*, 855 F.3d 345 (D.C. Cir. 2017); *United States v. Aetna, Inc.*, 240 F. Supp. 3d 1 (D.D.C. 2017); *United States v. Humana, Inc.*, 2013-1 Trade Cas. (CCH) ¶78,228 (D.D.C. 2012) (consent decree); *United States v. UnitedHealth Group, Inc.*, 2008-2 Trade Cas. (CCH) ¶76,318 (D.D.C. 2008) (consent order and competitive impact statement).
[285] *Inverness Med. Instruments*, Dkt. No. C-4244 (FTC Jan. 23, 2009) (consent order).
[286] *E.g., Me. v. Me. Heart Surgical Assocs., P.A.*, 1996-2 Trade Cas. (CCH) ¶71,653 (Me. Sup. Ct. 1996) (consent decree).
[287] *See* Antitrust Division Business Review Letter to Gastroenterology Assocs., Ltd. (Jul. 7, 1997), at https://www.justice.gov/atr/response-gastroenterology-associates-ltd-gi-associates-pcs-and-valley-gastroenterologists.
[288] 15 U.S.C. § 45(a)(1).
[289] *E.g., Am. Airlines, Inc. v. Christensen*, 967 F.2d 410 (10th Cir. 1992).
[290] 15 U.S.C. § 44.
[291] Importantly, however, the "exemption" does not apply merely because the entity is established as a nonprofit entity. For discussions of the relevant analysis, *see Cal. Dental Ass'n v. FTC*, 526 U.S. 756 (1999); *Daniel Chapter One v. FTC*, 405 Fed. App'x 505 (D.C. Cir. 2011) (memo); *Am. Med. Ass'n v. FTC*, 638 F.2d 443 (2d Cir. 1980), *aff'd by an equally divided court*, 455 U.S. 676 (1982).
[292] *See Cal. Dental Ass'n v. FTC*, 526 U.S. 756 (1999).
[293] *E.g., FTC v. Motion Picture Adver. Serv. Co.*, 344 U.S. 392 (1953).
[294] *E.g., FTC v. Sperry & Hutchinson Co.*, 405 U.S. 233 (1972).
[295] For a helpful discussion of the scope of Section 5, *see Rambus, Inc.*, Dkt. No. 9302 (FTC Jul. 31, 2006) (Leibowitz, Comm'r, concurring), *rev'd on other grounds*, 522 F.3d 456 (D.C. Cir. 2008).

FTC issued a statement providing some guidance regarding the circumstances under which it believes conduct would constitute an unfair method of competition.[296] The FTC has no authority to enforce the Sherman Act, but nevertheless can challenge conduct that violates the Sherman Act (plus other conduct) under Section 5.[297] In determining whether a practice is an unfair method of competition, the FTC can consider values beyond those embedded in the letter or spirit of the antitrust laws.[298] Still, the antitrust laws and their goals serve as the guiding light in determining whether conduct is an unfair method of competition,[299] and the FTC must show that conduct challenged under Section 5 has an anticompetitive effect.[300]

7.3 Exemptions, Immunities, and Scope of Coverage

A number of situations arise in which the antitrust laws are simply inapplicable to certain conduct or to certain parties or, although the antitrust laws apply regarding liability, plaintiffs cannot recover damages for violations. Antitrust exemptions—always disfavored and narrowly construed[301]—can be either express, such as when encompassed explicitly in a federal statute, or created by the courts through judicial decision making. The exemptions most germane to health care industries are discussed below.

7.3.1 Nonprofit Entities

As a general rule, the antitrust laws apply to nonprofit entities as well as to for-profit entities.[302] A number of courts, however, have held that the antitrust laws do not apply to "noncommercial" activities because they do not constitute "trade or commerce."[303] In some situations, however, it can be difficult to distinguish between commercial and noncommercial activities.

7.3.2 Federal Governmental Immunity

The antitrust laws do not apply to the conduct of the federal government, its agencies, or its individual agents.[304] For example, an antitrust suit against the Department of Health and Human Services, alleging monopsonization of the purchase of health care provider services would be futile.

---

[296] Fed. Trade Comm'n, *Statement of Enforcement Principles Regarding "Unfair Methods of Competition" Under Section 5 of the FTC Act* (Aug. 13, 2015), *available at* https://www.ftc.gov/system/files/documents/public_statements/735201/150813section5enforcement.pdf.

[297] *E.g., FTC v. Superior Court Trial Lawyers Ass'n*, 493 U.S. 411 (1990); *Polygram Holding Co. v. FTC*, 416 F.3d 29 (D.C. Cir. 2005).

[298] *E.g., FTC v. Sperry & Hutchinson Co.*, 405 U.S. 233 (1972).

[299] *FTC v. Ind. Fed'n of Dentists*, 476 U.S. 477 (1986); *see also E.I. Du Pont de Nemours & Co. v. FTC*, 729 F.2d 128 (2d Cir. 1984); *Boise Cascade Corp. v. FTC*, 637 F.2d 573 (9th Cir. 1980).

[300] *See Rambus, Inc. v. FTC*, 522 F.3d 456 (D.C. Cir. 2008).

[301] *E.g., Jefferson County Pharm. Ass'n v. Abbott Labs.*, 460 U.S. 150 (1983).

[302] *Bd. of Regents v. NCAA*, 468 U.S. 85 (1984); *Am. Soc'y of Mech. Eng'rs v. Hydrolevel Corp.*, 456 U.S. 556 (1982).

[303] *Bassett v. NCAA*, 528 F.3d 426 (6th Cir. 2008); *Big Bear Lodging Ass'n v. Snow Summit, Inc.*, 182 F.3d 1096 (9th Cir. 1999) ("A nonprofit organization that engages in commercial activity . . . is subject to federal antitrust laws."); *Smith v. NCAA*, 139 F.3d 180 (3d Cir. 1998); *Hamilton Chapter, Alpha Delta Phi, Inc. v. Hamilton Coll.*, 128 F.3d 59 (2d Cir. 1997); *United States v. Brown Univ.*, 5 F.3d 658 (3d Cir. 1993).

[304] *E.g., United States Postal Serv. v. Flamingo Indus. (USA) Ltd.*, 540 U.S. 736 (2004); *McCarthy v. Middle Tenn. Elec. Corp.*, 466 F.3d 399 (6th Cir. 2006); *Home Health Licensing Specialists, Inc. v. Leavitt*, 2008-2 Trade Cas. (CCH) ¶76,448 (N.D. Tex. 2008); *Med. Ass'n v. Schweiker*, 554 F. Supp. 955 (M.D. Ala.), *aff'd per curiam sub nom. Med. Ass'n v. Heckler*, 714 F.2d 107 (11th Cir. 1983).

7.3.3 State-Action Exemption

The state-action exemption is relevant when a conflict arguably exists between a state regulatory scheme or statute contemplating anticompetitive activity and the federal antitrust laws.[305] The standard for determining the exemption's applicability depends in large part on the status of the party undertaking the challenged action.[306] Anticompetitive conduct undertaken by a sovereign branch of the state—the legislature, the supreme court, and, presumably, the executive—is automatically exempt.[307] At the other end of the spectrum, for the actions of private parties to enjoy state-action exemption protection, their action must, in the words of the Supreme Court, meet a two-pronged standard: "First, the challenged restraint [imposed by the private party] must be one clearly articulated and affirmatively expressed as state policy; second, the policy must be 'actively supervised' by the state itself."[308] In the middle, subordinate state agencies and local governmental entities need only meet the first (i.e., the "clearly-articulated") requirement; the state need not actively supervise their activities for the exemption to apply.[309] Recently, however, the Supreme Court held that the actions of state professional regulatory boards controlled by practitioners who compete with the parties they regulate and are elected by those parties are treated as action by a private party for state-action exemption purposes and thus that active state supervision of their activities is necessary for the exemption to apply.[310]

To be "clearly articulated" by the state, the state need not require or even explicitly authorize the challenged conduct. But there must be evidence that the state intended to replace competition with regulation, that the conduct was generally authorized by the state, and that its anticompetitive effects were foreseeable and reasonably contemplated by the state.[311] The "active-supervision" element requires that the state have ultimate control over the challenged conduct of private entities and actually exercise the power to review and disapprove conduct not in accordance with state policy.[312] There must be actual supervision by the state, not merely the potential for supervision.[313]

An anticompetitive state statute or regulatory scheme is preempted by the Supremacy Clause of the U.S. Constitution if it mandates conduct by private parties that constitutes a per se violation of the antitrust laws in all situations.[314] For example, the antitrust laws would preempt a state statute

---

[305] *Parker v. Brown*, 317 U.S. 341 (1943).
[306] *See generally Edinboro Coll. Park Apartments v. Edinboro Univ. Found.*, 850 F.3d 567 (3d Cir. 2017); *S. C. State Bd. of Dentistry v. FTC*, 455 F.3d 436 (4th Cir. 2006).
[307] *Hoover v. Ronwin*, 466 U.S. 558 (1984); *see also Neo Gen Screening, Inc. v. New Eng. Newborn Screening Program*, 187 F.3d 24 (1st Cir. 1999).
[308] *Cal. Retail Liquor Dealers Ass'n v. Midcal Aluminum, Inc.*, 445 U.S. 97, 105 (1980); *see also Kay Elec. Coop. v. City of Newkirk*, 647 F.3d 1039 (10th Cir. 2011); *Shames v. Cal. Travel & Tourism Comm'n*, 607 F.3d 611 (9th Cir. 2010); *Brentwood Acad. v. Tenn. Secondary Sch. Athletic Ass'n*, 442 F.3d 410 (6th Cir. 2006).
[309] *Town of Hallie v. City of Eau Claire*, 471 U.S. 34 (1985); *see also City of Columbia v. Omni Outdoor Adver., Inc.*, 499 U.S. 365 (1991); *Stratienko v. Chattanooga-Hamilton Hosp. Auth.*, 402 Fed. App'x 990 (6th Cir. 2010); *Lafaro v. N.Y. Cardiothoracic Group, PLLC*, 570 F.3d 471 (2d Cir. 2009); *Surgical Ctr. v. Hospital Serv. Dist.*, 171 F.3d 231 (5th Cir. 1999) (*en banc*).
[310] *N.C. State Bd. of Dental Examiners v. FTC*, ___ U.S. ___, 135 S.Ct. 1101 (2015).
[311] *FTC v. Phoebe Putney Health Sys.*, 568 U.S. 216 (2013); *S. Motor Carriers Rate Conf. v. United States*, 471 U.S. 48 (1985); *see also City of Columbia v. Omni Outdoor Adver., Inc.*, 499 U.S. 365 (1991); *Danner Constr. Co. v. Hillsborough County*, 608 F.3d 809 (11th Cir. 2010); *Jackson Hosp. Co. v. W. Tenn. Healthcare, Inc.*, 414 F.3d 608 (6th Cir. 2005).
[312] *Patrick v. Burget*, 486 U.S. 94 (1988).
[313] *FTC v. Ticor Title Ins. Co.*, 504 U.S. 621 (1992); *Ky. Household Goods Carrier Ass'n v. FTC*, 199 Fed. App'x 410 (6th Cir. 2006).
[314] *E.g., 324 Liquor Corp. v. Duffy*, 479 U.S. 335 (1987); *Rice v. Norman Williams Co.*, 458 U.S. 260 (1986); *Yakima Valley Mem'l Hosp. v. Wash. Dep't of Health*, 654 F.3d 919 (9th Cir. 2011); *Flying J, Inc. v. Van Hollen*, 621 F.3d 658 (7th Cir. 2010).

that mandated that competing physicians to come together and agree on the prices they charge. But even then, the defendants can escape liability if their conduct meets the requirements for state-action exemption protection.[315]

In health care, the state-action exemption arises in a number of contexts, including staff-privilege antitrust cases where a governmental hospital rejects or terminates a staff physician's privileges.[316] State-action exemption questions can also arise in the context of hospital mergers where the acquiring entity is a local governmental body.[317] Another important state-action exemption question, as yet unanswered, is whether state certificate-of-public-advantage laws, designed to sustain state-action-exemption protection for collaborative hospital activities and mergers, will do so.[318] The exemption also arises frequently in antitrust cases resulting from state certificate-of-need activities.[319]

7.3.4 Solicitation of Governmental Action

The so-called "Noerr-Pennington" antitrust-immunity doctrine protects private parties when they individually or collectively solicit the government to take anticompetitive action.[320] This exemption is probably the broadest and most important of all the antitrust exemption doctrines. It applies to non-antitrust federal and state claims, as well as to state and federal antitrust claims because of its First Amendment underpinnings based on the constitutional right to petition the government.[321] The type, branch, or level of government at which the petitioning is aimed is immaterial,[322] as is the petitioners' anticompetitive intent in soliciting the action[323] and whether they "conspired" with government officials to induce them to take the anticompetitive action.[324]

---

[315] *E.g., Danner Constr. Co. v. Hillsborough County*, 608 F.3d 809 (11th Cir. 2010); *Freedom Holdings, Inc. v. Cuomo*, 624 F.3d 38 (2d Cir. 2010).

[316] *Martin v. Mem'l Hosp.*, 86 F.3d 1391 (5th Cir. 1996), *subsequent decision*, 130 F.3d 1143 (5th Cir. 1997).

[317] *See FTC v. Phoebe Putney Health Sys.*, 568 U.S. 216 (2013) (rejecting application of state-action exemption to hospital merger).

[318] *See generally* Sarah S. Vance, *Immunity for State-Sanctioned Provider Collaboration After Ticor*, 62 Antitrust L.J. 409 (1994).

[319] *E.g., Armstrong Surgical Ctr. v. Armstrong County Mem'l Hosp.*, 185 F.3d 154 (3d Cir. 1999). In general, the state-action exemption applies where there is a conflict between the federal antitrust laws and a state regulatory scheme replacing competition with regulation. Situations also arise presenting a conflict between the federal antitrust laws and a federal regulatory scheme. Where there is a clear repugnancy between the two, the antitrust laws are "impliedly repealed" to the extent necessary for the federal regulatory scheme to achieve its goals. *See Credit Suisse Secs. (USA) LLC v. Billing*, 551 U.S. 264 (2007); *Nat'l Gerimedical Hosp. & Gerontology Ctr. v. Blue Cross*, 452 U.S. 378 (1981).

[320] The doctrine takes its name from two of the Supreme Court decisions establishing the exemption. *UMW v. Pennington*, 381 U.S. 657 (1965); *E. R.R. Presidents Conf. v. Noerr Motor Freight*, 365 U.S. 127 (1961).

[321] *See, e.g., BE&K Constr. Co. v. NLRB*, 536 U.S. 526 (2002); *Coll v. First Am. Ins. Co.*, 642 F.3d 876 (10th Cir. 2011); *Sosa v. DIRECTV, Inc.*, 437 F.3d 923 (9th Cir. 2006) (applying doctrine to federal RICO and state unfair business statutes). *See also Andrx Pharms., Inc. v. Elan Corp.*, 421 F.3d 1227 (11th Cir. 2005); *Knology, Inc. v. Insight Commc'ns, L.P.*, 393 F.3d 656 (6th Cir. 2004) (explaining that the doctrine "allows businesses to combine and lobby to influence the legislative, executive, or judicial branches of government or administrative agencies without antitrust . . . liability, because the First Amendment's right to petition protects such activities").

[322] *E.g., Cal. Motor Transp. v. Trucking Unlimited*, 404 U.S. 508 (1972); *Freeman v. Lasky, Haas & Cohler*, 410 F.3d 1180 (9th Cir. 2005).

[323] *E.g., VIBO Corp. v. Conway*, 669 F.3d 675 (6th Cir. 2012); *Marian v. Fisher*, 338 F.3d 189 (3d Cir. 2003) ("That immunity is so potent that it protects petitioning notwithstanding an improper purpose or motive."); *Sandy River Nursing Care v. Aetna Cas.*, 985 F.2d 1138 (1st Cir. 1993) (the exemption applies even if defendants' motives were "entirely anticompetitive").

[324] *E.g., City of Columbia v. Omni Outdoor Adver., Inc.*, 499 U.S. 365 (1991); *Tal v. Hogan*, 453 F.3d 1244 (10th Cir. 2006); *Boulware v. Nev.*, 960 F.2d 793 (9th Cir 1992).

In determining whether the exemption applies to particular petitioning conduct, the key question is whether the challenged restraint on competition results directly from the action of the private parties (if so, the exemption does not apply unless their activity is "incidental" to their legitimate solicitation of governmental action)[325] or from the governmental action they solicit (in which case the exemption does apply).[326] The exemption does not apply to coercive action by the petitioners against the government to force it to adopt their views[327]—such as an agreement among physicians not to participate in the state's Medicaid program unless the state increases the level of Medicaid reimbursement.[328]

The doctrine does not protect "sham" petitioning.[329] In general, the sham exception to the Noerr-Pennington doctrine applies where "persons use the governmental *process*—as opposed to the *outcome* of that process—as an anticompetitive weapon."[330] For example, litigation (the filing of which is normally exempt under the doctrine) constitutes sham petitioning if it is objectively baseless in the sense that no reasonable person would expect it to succeed and the defendant's subjective intent is to interfere directly with the business relationships of a competitor, rather than to obtain the relief sought from the court.[331]

The exemption has been applied in a number of health care contexts, such as a hospital's lobbying a municipality not to zone property so a competitor could build a medical facility[332] and a hospital's opposing its competitor's certificate-of-need applications.[333] In each of these cases, the courts applied the exemption even though the applicants alleged that the firms provided false and misleading information to the governmental bodies.

7.3.5 Local Government Antitrust Act

Even if the state-action exemption does not provide a local governmental entity with protection from antitrust liability, the Local Government Antitrust Act provides it with absolute protection from damages in antitrust cases.[334] The term "local government" includes "special function governmental unit[s]," which include governmental hospital districts and authorities.[335]

---

[325] *See E. R.R. Presidents Conf. v. Noerr Motor Freight*, 365 U.S. 127 (1961).
[326] *E.g., Allied Tube & Conduit Corp. v. Indian Head, Inc.*, 486 U.S. 492 (1988); *see also Armstrong Surgical Ctr., Inc. v. Armstrong County Mem'l Hosp.*, 185 F.3d 154 (3d Cir. 1999).
[327] *Superior Court Trial Lawyers Ass'n v. FTC*, 493 U.S. 411 (1990).
[328] *E.g., Mich. State Med. Soc'y*, 101 F.T.C. 191 (1983).
[329] *See generally Freeman v. Lasky, Haas & Cohler*, 410 F.3d 1180 (9th Cir. 2005); *Kottle v. Nw. Kidney Ctrs.*, 146 F.3d 1056 (9th Cir. 1998).
[330] *City of Columbia v. Omni Outdoor Adver., Inc.*, 499 U.S. 365, 380 (1991) (emphasis in original); *See also VIBO Corp. v. Conway*, 669 F.3d 675 (6th Cir. 2012).
[331] *Prof'l Real Estate Invs., Inc. v. Columbia Pictures Indus.*, 508 U.S. 49 (1993); *Kaiser Found. Health Plan, Inc. v. Abbott Labs, Inc.*, 552 F.3d 1033 (9th Cir. 2009); *Andrx Pharms., Inc. v. Elan Corp.*, 421 F.3d 1227 (11th Cir. 2005); *Total Renal Care, Inc. v. W. Nephrology & Metabolic Bone Disease, P.C.*, 2009 U.S. Dist. LEXIS 80821 (D. Colo. Aug. 21, 2009). The FTC has held that deliberate misrepresentations to government agencies in certain circumstances negate the exemption. *Union Oil Co.*, 138 F.T.C. 1 (2004). Case law on this issue is not completely clear. *See generally Mercatus Group, LLC v. Lake Forest Hosp.*, 641 F.3d 834 (7th Cir. 2011).
[332] *Mercatus Group, LLC v. Lake Forest Hosp.*, 641 F.3d 834 (7th Cir. 2011).
[333] *Armstrong Surgical Ctr. Inc. v. Armstrong County Mem'l Hosp.*, 185 F.3d 154 (3d Cir. 1999); *Kottle v. Nw. Kidney Ctrs.*, 146 F.3d 1056 (9th Cir. 1998).
[334] 15 U.S.C. §§ 34–36; *see generally Emlich v. OhioHealth*, 2016 U.S. Dist. LEXIS 177373 (E.D. Ohio, Dec. 22, 2016).
[335] *E.g., Bloom v. Hennepin County*, 783 F. Supp. 418 (D. Minn. 1992).

The immunity from damages also applies to officials of local governments acting in their official capacities and to other persons, including private parties, engaged in official action directed by the local government. In general, individuals enjoy the immunity from damages if their actions are authorized and supervised by the local governmental entity.[336] Their motives and those of the government are immaterial.[337] A plaintiff, however, still may obtain injunctive and declaratory relief if it proves a violation.[338]

7.3.6 Business of Insurance

The McCarran-Ferguson Act[339] provides the "business of insurance" with a limited exemption from the antitrust laws. For the Act's protection to apply, a defendant must prove that:

1. the challenged conduct constitutes the "business of insurance";
2. the state regulates the business of insurance; and
3. the challenged conduct does not constitute "boycott, coercion, or intimidation."

In determining whether particular conduct constitutes the "business of insurance," courts examine three factors: whether the conduct (1) transfers or spreads policyholder risk, (2) is an integral part of the relationship between the insurer and its insureds, and (3) is limited to those within the insurance industry.[340] Based on these standards, provider agreements between health insurers and their participating providers do not constitute the business of insurance,[341] although contracts between insurers and their insureds do.[342]

The state must regulate the business of insurance for the Act's protection to apply. The courts have interpreted this requirement leniently, however, and it rarely raises an issue. Even the most general type of state-insurance regulation suffices,[343] and even it need not be effective.[344]

Finally, the challenged conduct must not constitute "boycott," "intimidation," or "coercion." Boycott, for purposes of the McCarran Act, refers to secondary boycotts—refusals to deal seeking an objective collateral to the main transaction[345] or "a refusal to deal in a collateral transaction as a means to coerce terms in a primary transaction."[346]

---

[336] *See generally Wee Care Child Ctr., Inc. v. Lumpkin*, 680 F.3d 841 (6th Cir. 2012); *Sandcrest Outpatient Servs., P.A. v. Cumberland County Hosp. Sys.*, 853 F.2d 1139 (4th Cir. 1988).
[337] *GF Gaming Corp. v. City of Blackhawk*, 405 F.3d 876 (10th Cir. 2005); *Cohn v. Bond*, 953 F.2d 154 (4th Cir. 1991).
[338] *Lancaster Cmty. Hosp. v. Antelope Valley Hosp. Dist.*, 940 F.2d 397 (9th Cir. 1991); *Swarz Ambulance Serv. v. Genesee County*, 666 F. Supp. 2d 721 (E.D. Mich. 2009) (declaratory judgment).
[339] 15 U.S.C. §§ 1011–15.
[340] *E.g., Union Labor Life Ins. Co. v. Pireno*, 458 U.S. 119 (1982); *Katz v. Fid. Nat'l Title Ins. Co.*, 685 F.3d 588 (6th Cir. 2012); *In re Ins. Brokerage Antitrust Litig.*, 618 F.3d 300 (3d Cir. 2010); *Arroyo-Melecio v. Puerto Rican Am. Ins. Co.*, 398 F.3d 56 (1st Cir. 2005).
[341] *Group Life & Health Ins. Co. v. Royal Drug Co.*, 440 U.S. 205 (1979); *Arroyo-Melecio v. Puerto Rican Am. Ins. Co.*, 398 F.3d 56 (1st Cir. 2005).
[342] *E.g., Health Care Equalization Comm'n v. Iowa Med. Soc'y*, 851 F.2d 1020 (8th Cir. 1988).
[343] *E.g., Klamath-Lake Pharm. Ass'n v. Klamath Med. Servs. Bureau*, 701 F.2d 1276 (9th Cir. 1983).
[344] *FTC v. Nat'l Cas. Co.*, 357 U.S. 560 (1958) (noting that there need not even be state enforcement).
[345] *Hartford Fire Ins. Co. v. Cal.*, 509 U.S. 764 (1993); *Arroyo-Melecio v. Puerto Rican Am. Ins. Co.*, 398 F.3d 56 (1st Cir. 2005); *Gilchrist v. State Farm Mut. Auto. Ins. Co.*, 390 F.3d 1327 (11th Cir. 2004); *Slagle v. ITT Hartford*, 102 F.3d 494 (11th Cir. 1996).
[346] *Uniforce Temporary Personnel, Inc. v. Nat'l Council on Compensation Ins., Inc.*, 87 F.3d 1296 (11th Cir. 1996).

7.3.7 Labor Unions

There is a *statutory* antitrust exemption for the conduct of labor unions flowing from Sections 6[347] and 20[348] of the Clayton Act and Sections 1,[349] 4,[350] 5,[351] and 13[352] of the Norris-LaGuardia Act. In addition, a *"nonstatutory"* labor exemption,[353] created by the courts, exists for agreements—primarily collective-bargaining agreements—between unions and employers that meet certain requirements.[354] The labor exemption, however is limited.

The major union-related antitrust issue to arise so far in health care has focused on the desire of some competing physicians to increase their bargaining strength with health plans by "unionizing." A union, they believed, would permit them to bargain collectively with health plans and thus increase their reimbursement. For a group to constitute a *bona fide* union, however, an employee-employer relationship must exist between them and the party with which they bargain. The exemption does not usually apply to collective bargaining between independent contractors and those who purchase their services.[355] Thus, the unionized physician-employees of a staff-model HMO or hospital enjoy the labor exemption when they bargain collectively with the HMO or hospital, but independent contractor physicians bargaining collectively with health plans do not.[356] Indeed, the Antitrust Division has challenged the collective-bargaining activities of one physicians' union several times.[357]

Physicians and other providers have sought, without success thus far, federal and state legislation permitting them to bargain collectively with health plans.

7.3.8 Health Care Quality Improvement Act

The Health Care Quality Improvement Act[358] provides those engaging in the credentialing (or any "professional review action" by a "professional review body") of physicians with immunity from damages if the peer-review process meets certain requirements. The Act provides immunity only from

---

[347] 15 U.S.C. § 17.
[348] *Id.* § 52.
[349] 29 U.S.C. § 101.
[350] *Id.* § 104.
[351] *Id.* § 105.
[352] *Id.* § 113.
[353] *See generally Brown v. Pro-Football, Inc.*, 518 U.S. 231 (1996) (discussing the nonstatutory labor exemption); *Cal. v. Safeway, Inc.*, 651 F.3d 1118 (9th Cir. 2011) (same).
[354] *See generally Cal. v. Safeway, Inc.*, 651 F.3d 1118 (9th Cir. 2011) (en banc); *Clarett v. NFL*, 369 F.3d 124 (2d Cir. 2004); *Burlington N. Santa Fe Ry. v. Int'l Bhd. of Teamsters*, 203 F.3d 703 (9th Cir. 2000) (*en banc*); *Detroit Auto Dealers Ass'n v. FTC*, 955 F.2d 457 (6th Cir. 1992) (explaining that the nonstatutory exemption applies to agreements between unions and employers where the restraint affects primarily only the parties to a collective-bargaining agreement, the agreement concerns subjects of mandatory collective bargaining, and the agreement results from *bona fide* arm's-length bargaining).
[355] *See generally Columbia River Packers Ass'n v. Hinton*, 315 U.S. 143 (1942).
[356] For a helpful discussion of the physician-unionization issue, *see* Edward B. Hirschfeld, *Physicians, Unions, and Antitrust*, J. Health L. 43 (Winter 1999).
[357] *United States v. Fed'n of Physicians and Dentists*, 2008-1 Trade Cas. (CCH) ¶76,062 (S.D. Ohio 2008) (consent decree); *United States v. Fed'n of Physicians and Dentists*, 2005-2 Trade Cas. (CCH) ¶75,006 (S.D. Ohio 2005) (consent decree); *United States v. Fed'n of Physicians and Dentists, Inc.*, 2002-2 Trade Cas. (CCH) ¶73,868 (D. Del. 2002) (consent decree).
[358] 42 U.S.C. §§ 11101–52.

damages, not from liability or injunctive relief.[359] It also provides that the defendants may recover their attorneys' fees if the plaintiff's suit challenging their professional-review action is frivolous.[360] The Act applies most frequently, but not exclusively, in staff-privilege antitrust cases when a hospital denies a physician's application for staff privileges or terminates or otherwise adversely affects those privileges.

For the immunity from damages to attach, the professional review action must have been taken:

1. in the reasonable belief that it would improve quality health care;
2. after reasonable efforts to discover all the facts;
3. after adequate notice and hearing to the affected physician or after other fair procedures; and
4. with the reasonable belief that the action taken was warranted.[361]

The Act provides a presumption that the defendants' action met these requirements, which the plaintiff-physician may rebut by a preponderance of the evidence.[362] Thus, at the summary-judgment stage, the plaintiff, rather than the defendants, has the burden to adduce sufficient evidence to show that the defendant is not entitled to summary judgment on the question of immunity.[363] An objective, rather than subjective, standard applies in determining whether the Act's requirements are met, so the reviewers' biases or motives are not relevant.[364] There is no private right of action for violation of the Act based on failure of the professional review action to meet the Act's requirements.[365]

7.4 Government Enforcement

The antitrust laws are enforced by the Antitrust Division of the U.S. Department of Justice, the Federal Trade Commission, and state attorneys general. As discussed in Section 7.5, private parties injured by antitrust violations may sue for damages and injunctive relief.

---

[359] *E.g., Islami v. Covenant Med. Ctr.*, 822 F. Supp. 1361 (N.D. Iowa 1992).

[360] 42 U.S.C. § 11113; *see generally Cohlmia v. St. John Med. Ctr.*, 749 F.3d 1175 (10th Cir. 2014) (affirming a $733,000 fee award to defendant under the Health Care Quality Improvement Act); *Addis v. Holy Cross Health Sys. Corp.*, 88 F.3d 482 (6th Cir. 1996); *Stratienko v. Chattanooga-Hamilton Hosp. Auth*, 2009 U.S. Dist. LEXIS 44272 (E.D. Tenn., May 27, 2009); *Gordon v. Lewistown Hosp.*, 2006-2 Trade Cas. (CCH) ¶75,454 (M.D. Pa. 2006).

[361] 42 U.S.C. § 11112(a). *See, e.g., Cohlmia v. St. John's Med. Ctr.*, 693 F.3d 1269 (10th Cir. 2012).

[362] 42 U.S.C. § 11112(a); *see generally Cohlmia v. St. John's Med. Ctr.*, 693 F.3d 1269 (10th Cir. 2012); *Moore v. Williamsburg Reg'l Hosp.*, 560 F.3d 166 (4th Cir. 2009); *Wahi v. Charleston Area Med. Ctr.*, 562 F.3d 599 (4th Cir. 2009); *Lee v. Trinity Lutheran Hosp.*, 408 F.3d 1064 (8th Cir. 2005); *Singh v. Blue Cross/Blue Shield*, 308 F.3d 25 (1st Cir. 2002); *Brader v. Allegheny Gen. Hosp.*, 167 F.3d 832 (3d Cir. 1999); *Mathews v. Lancaster Gen. Hosp.*, 87 F.3d 624 (3d Cir. 1996); *Bryan v. James E. Holmes Reg'l Med. Ctr.*, 33 F.3d 1318 (11th Cir. 1994).

[363] *See, e.g., Johnson v. Christus Spohn*, 334 Fed. App'x 673 (5th Cir. 2009); *Gordon v. Lewistown Hosp.*, 423 F.3d 184 (3d Cir. 2005) (noting that "this presumption of immunity creates an unusual standard for reviewing summary judgment orders, as the plaintiff bears the burden of proving that the professional review process was not reasonable and thus did not meet the standard for immunity.").

[364] *E.g., Poliner v. Tex. Health Sys.*, 537 F.3d 368 (5th Cir. 2008) (noting that the reviewers' good or bad faith in conducting the review is irrelevant).

[365] *E.g., Tabrizi v. Faxton-St. Luke's Healthcare*, 2011 U.S. Dist. LEXIS 149278 (N.D.N.Y., Dec. 29, 2011); *Rowell v. Valleycare Health Sys.*, 2010-2 Trade Cas. (CCH) ¶77,214 (N.D. Cal. 2010); *MacArthur v. San Juan County*, 416 F. Supp. 2d 1098 (D. Utah 2005); *Jadali v. Alamance Reg'l Med. Ctr.*, 225 F.R.D. 181 (M.D.N.C. 2004), *aff'd*, 167 Fed. App'x 961 (4th Cir. 2006).

7.4.1 The Antitrust Division

The Antitrust Division primarily enforces Sections 1 and 2 of the Sherman Act, and Section 7 of the Clayton Act. The Sherman Act is both a civil and criminal statute, and the Antitrust Division has authority to investigate and prosecute both civil and criminal violations.[366] Almost all criminal prosecutions result from alleged violations of Section 1 of the Sherman Act. The Antitrust Division normally limits its criminal prosecutions to hard-core *per se* violations—naked horizontal price-fixing, market-allocation, and bid-rigging agreements. Criminal prosecutions in the health care sector are rare, but not unheard of.[367] In its civil-enforcement actions, the Antitrust Division can obtain only injunctive relief, including disgorgement[368]—not damages or civil penalties, although it can recover damages for injury to the United States resulting from antitrust violations.[369] The overwhelming majority of all Antitrust Division enforcement actions are quickly settled by consent decrees, usually filed simultaneously with the complaint.

The Antitrust Division has a "Business Review Procedure" by which parties that intend to undertake specific activity can write the Division, explain their proposed conduct, and ask the Division whether, if they proceed, the Division will file suit.[370] Attorneys representing health care clients have used the process frequently,[371] especially for the review of joint contracting activities by provider-controlled contracting organizations, such as IPAs.[372]

The Division, in recent years, has focused its health care antitrust enforcement efforts on antitrust issues involving health plans rather than providers. For example, it has challenged several exclusionary arrangements by health plans,[373] as well as health-plan mergers,[374] while the FTC, discussed next, has focused on provider conduct.

7.4.2 The Federal Trade Commission

The FTC, an independent regulatory administrative agency led by five commissioners appointed by the President, enforces primarily Section 5 of the FTC Act and Section 7 of the Clayton Act. It lacks authority to enforce the Sherman Act, but it can reach the same conduct under Section 5 of the

---

[366] Violation is a felony punishable by, in the case of a corporation, a fine not exceeding $100 million per violation; and in the case of individuals, a fine not exceeding $1 million and imprisonment not exceeding 10 years per violation.

[367] *See United States v. A. Lanoy Alston, D.M.D., P.C.*, 974 F.2d 1206 (9th Cir. 1992) (horizontal price fixing); *United States v. Country Lake Optometric Soc'y*, Cr. No. W9CR114 (W.D. Tex. Jul. 9, 1996) (same).

[368] *United States v. KeySpan Corp.*, 763 F. Supp. 2d 633 (S.D.N.Y. 2011).

[369] *See* Section 4a of the Clayton Act, 15 U.S.C. § 15a.

[370] *See* 28 C.F.R. § 50.6.

[371] *See* 3 John J. Miles, *Health Care & Antitrust Law* App. C (Supp. 2014) (including full text of all health care business review letters).

[372] *See, e.g.*, Antitrust Business Review Letter to Michigan Hospital Group, Inc. (Apr. 3, 2002) (hospital contracting network), *at* https://www.justice.gov/atr/response-michigan-hospital-group-incs-request-business-review-letter; Antitrust Division Business Review Letter to Rio Grande Eye Associates, P.A. (Aug. 29, 2001) (physician contracting network), at https://www.justice.gov/atr/response-rio-grande-eye-associates-pas-request-business-review-letter.

[373] *E.g., United States v. Charlotte-Mecklenburg Hosp. Auth.*, 248 F. Supp. 3d 720 (W.D.N.C. 2017); *United States v. United Reg'l Health Care Sys.*, 2011-2 Trade Cas. (CCH) ¶619 (N.D. Tex 2011) (consent decree).

[374] *E.g., United States v. Anthem, Inc.*, 855 F.3d 345 (D.C. Cir. 2017).

FTC Act. It cannot prosecute criminally; it sometimes does seek restitution or profit disgorgement[375] in addition to injunctive relief to stop the challenged conduct and prevent its recurrence. Most of its enforcement actions are settled by consent orders. The FTC's rules provide for two types of advisory opinions—formal commission advisory opinions and staff advisory opinions.[376] It has issued a large number of staff advisory opinions dealing with health care antitrust issues.[377]

7.4.3 State Attorneys General

All states (except one) have their own state antitrust statutes,[378] most of which are patterned closely after the federal antitrust laws and are interpreted consistently with federal antitrust precedent.[379] But there can be significant differences, so review of state antitrust laws and precedent is important. In addition to enforcing their own antitrust laws, states can enforce the federal antitrust laws in some circumstances. Under Section 4C of the Clayton Act,[380] for example, states can file so-called *parens patriae* suits to recover damages on behalf of their citizens injured by violations of the federal antitrust laws.[381] States may file suit for damages as private parties under Section 4(a) of the Clayton Act[382] when the state suffers damages from an antitrust violation—e.g., as purchasers of goods or services from parties engaged in price fixing.[383] Several states have become quite active in investigating and prosecuting antitrust problems in the health care sector,[384] and states often conduct joint investigations and become co-plaintiffs with the federal enforcement agencies in bringing enforcement actions.[385]

---

[375] *See FTC v. Mylan Labs.*, 1999-2 Trade Cas. (CCH) ¶72,573 (D.D.C. 1999) (refusing to dismiss, for failure to state a claim, FTC's prayer that defendant disgorge $120 million in overcharges); *FTC v. Coll. of Physicians-Surgeons*, No. 97-2466 (D.P.R. Oct. 2, 1997) (consent decree) ($300,000 in restitution).

[376] *See* 16 C.F.R. §§ 1.1—1.4. For excellent discussions of the FTC advisory opinion process, *see* Judith A. Moreland, Staff Attorney, Bureau of Competition, FTC, "Overview of the Advisory Opinion Process at the Federal Trade Commission," text of remarks before the National Health Lawyers Association Antitrust in the Health Care Field Seminar (Feb. 13, 1997); FTC, "Guidelines from Staff of the Bureau of Competition's Health Care Division on Requesting and Obtaining an Advisory Opinion", at https://www.ftc.gov/system/files/attachments/competition-advisory-opinions/advisoryopinion-guidance-bctextjune2011_update_links_oct_2015.pdf.

[377] *E.g.*, These are collected in 4 John J. Miles, *Health Care & Antitrust Law* App.D (Supp. 2017). For a relatively complete listing of the FTC's health care-sector antitrust initiatives, *see* Markus H. Meier, Assistant Director, Bradley S. Albert, Deputy Assistant Director & Saralisa C. Brau, Deputy Assistant Director, Bureau of Competition, FTC, "Overview of FTC Actions in Health Care Services and Products" (Apr. 2017) at https://www.ftc.gov/system/files/attachments/competition-policy-guidance/overview_health_care_april_2017.pdf.

[378] State antitrust statutes are collected at 6 Trade Reg. Rep. (CCH) ¶¶30,201 through 35,602.

[379] *Cf. Kissing Camels Surgery Ctr., LLC v. Centura Health Corp.*, 2014 U.S. Dist. LEXIS 18335 (D. Colo., Feb. 13, 2014) ("The parties agree that federal antitrust principles control both the federal and state antitrust claims.").

[380] 15 U.S.C. § 15c.

[381] For an example, *see Pa. v. Mid-Atl. Toyota Distribs.*, 704 F.2d 125 (4th Cir. 1983).

[382] 15 U.S.C. § 15(a). *See generally In re Optical Disk Antitrust Litig.*, 2014-1 Trade Cas. (CCH) ¶78,734 (N.D. Cal. 2014) (parens patriae suit brought by State of Florida).

[383] *See, e.g., FTC v. Mylan Labs.*, 62 F. Supp. 2d 25 (D.D.C. 1999).

[384] *See, e.g., Pa. v. Geisinger Health Sys.*, No. 1:13-cv-02647-YK (M.D. Pa. Oct. 25, 2013) (proposed final order) (hospital merger); *Wis. v. Kenosha Hosp. & Med. Ctr.*, 1997-1 Trade Cas. (CCH) ¶71,669 (E.D. Wis. 1996) (consent decree permitting hospital merger to go forward under certain constraints).

[385] *E.g.*, Compl., *FTC v. St. Luke's Health Sys.*, No 13-cv-116-BLW (D. Idaho Mar. 26, 2013) (challenge to hospital's acquisition of a physician practice filed jointly by the FTC and State of Idaho); *FTC v. Lundbeck, Inc.*, 650 F.3d 1236 (8th Cir. 2011) (FTC and Minnesota attorney general unsuccessful joint action to rescind pharmaceutical merger).

7.5 Private Enforcement

Section 4(a) of the Clayton Act authorizes parties injured by antitrust violations to recover treble damages plus attorneys' fees.[386] A plaintiff can sue for injunctive relief as well as damages and is entitled to its attorneys' fees if successful.[387] The statute of limitations for recovery of damages in antitrust cases is four years,[388] although it does not apply to suits for injunctions. In general, to recover damages, a plaintiff must prove that:

1. it is a "person";
2. it was "injured";
3. the injury was to its "business or property";
4. the injury was "caused" by the antitrust violation;
5. the injury caused by the antitrust violation constituted "antitrust injury";
6. the plaintiff has "antitrust standing";
7. the plaintiff suffered damages as a result of the antitrust injury; and
8. the amount of its damages.

Several of these requirements are discussed here.

7.5.1 Causation

To prove causation, the plaintiff must prove that its injury resulted from the antitrust violation rather than from some other cause.[389] There must be some link between the violation and the plaintiff's injury. Although the antitrust violation need not be the sole cause of the plaintiff's injury, it must be a "material," "substantial," or "but for" cause of the injury in order for the plaintiff to recover.[390]

7.5.2 Antitrust Injury

In addition to causation, the plaintiff must show that its injury resulted from the anticompetitive effects of the violation. This "antitrust injury"—the type of injury the antitrust laws were meant to prevent—must flow from the effect that makes the conduct unlawful.[391] For a plaintiff to recover dam-

---

[386] 15 U.S.C. § 15(a); *see, e.g., Gulfstream III Assocs., Inc. v. Gulfstream Aerospace Corp.*, 995 F.2d 414 (3d Cir. 1993).
[387] 15 U.S.C. § 26.
[388] 15 U.S.C. § 15(b); *see generally Zenith Radio Corp. v. Hazeltine Research, Inc.*, 401 U.S. 321 (1971); *Z Techs. Corp. v. Lubrizol Corp.*, 753 F.3d 594 (6th Cir. 2014) (also discussing the "continuing conspiracy" exception to the statute of limitations); *Champagne Metals v. Ken-Mac Metals, Inc.*, 458 F.3d 1073 (10th Cir. 2006); *Midwestern Mach. Co. v. Nw. Airlines, Inc.*, 392 F.3d 265 (8th Cir. 2004); *Varner v. Peterson Farms*, 371 F.3d 1011 (8th Cir. 2004).
[389] *Simon v. Value Behavioral Health, Inc.*, 208 F.3d 1073 (9th Cir. 2000).
[390] *E.g., J.B.D.L. Corp. v. Wyeth-Ayerst Labs., Inc.*, 485 F.3d 880 (6th Cir. 2007); *Gulf States Reorg. Group, Inc. v. Nucor Corp.*, 466 F.3d 961 (11th Cir. 2006); *SAS, Inc. v. Puerto Rico Tel. Co.*, 48 F.3d 39 (1st Cir. 1995).
[391] *Brunswick Corp. v. Pueblo Bowl-O-Mat, Inc.*, 429 U.S. 477 (1977); *see also Eastman Kodak Co. v. Goodyear Tire & Rubber Co.*, 114 F.3d 1547 (Fed. Cir. 1997) (explaining that the purpose for the antitrust-injury requirement is to "ensure that the harm for which plaintiff seeks compensation corresponds to the rationale for finding a violation").

ages, its injury must have resulted from the competition-reducing effects of the violation.[392] Conduct that injures the plaintiff, but not competition, does not constitute antitrust injury[393]—e.g., where the challenged conduct injures the plaintiff but increases competition. A plaintiff must prove antitrust injury in actions to both recover damages[394] and obtain injunctive relief.[395] And the plaintiff must prove antitrust injury even if the challenged conduct is *per se* unlawful under Section 1 of the Sherman Act, when the adverse effect on competition is presumed.[396] It is entirely possible for defendants to engage in conduct that violates the antitrust law and injures the plaintiff, but the plaintiff not suffer antitrust injury because its injury results from some cause other than the competition-reducing effect of the violation.

7.5.3 Antitrust Standing

Congress did not intend that every party suffering some peripheral damage from an antitrust violation recover their damages.[397] Thus, the antitrust standing requirement requires determining whether the plaintiff is an appropriate party to enforce the antitrust laws. It is a narrower concept than Article III constitutional standing, which requires merely that the plaintiff suffer some injury caused by the violation and have a redressable claim.[398]

It is entirely possible for a plaintiff who is injured by the competition-reducing effect of an antitrust violation not to have antitrust standing to recover damages.[399] The Supreme Court has explained that courts should examine and balance six factors in determining whether a plaintiff has antitrust standing and thus is a proper party to recover:

1. the causal connection between the violation and any harm to the plaintiff;

2. whether the defendant intended to cause the harm to the plaintiff resulting from the violation;

3. the nature of the plaintiff's injury, particularly whether the plaintiff was a customer or competitor in the relevant market affected by the violation;

---

[392] *E.g., Se. Mo. Hosp. v. C.R. Bard, Inc.*, 616 F.3d 888 (8th Cir. 2010); *Paycom Billing Servs., Inc. v. MasterCard Int'l, Inc.*, 467 F.3d 283 (2d Cir. 2006); *Cape & Sons v. PCC Constr. Co.*, 453 F.3d 396 (7th Cir. 2006) (agreeing with and affirming district-court holding that antitrust injury must involve a loss resulting from acts that reduce output or raise prices); *Johnson v. Univ. Health Servs.*, 161 F.3d 1334 (11th Cir. 1998); *McKenzie-Willamette Hosp. v. PeaceHealth*, 2004-2 Trade Cas. (CCH) ¶74,600 (D. Ore. 2004) (explaining that plaintiff must show that defendant's conduct injured it "and that the harm flowed from conduct that was antithetical to market-wide competition").

[393] *E.g., Hodges v. WSM, Inc.*, 26 F.3d 36 (6th Cir. 1994); *Williams v. Univ. Med. Ctr.*, 688 F. Supp. 2d 1134 (D. Nev. 2010); *Veesom v. Atchison Hosp. Ass'n*, 2006 U.S. Dist. LEXIS 68576 (D. Kan., Sept. 22, 2006) ("To show an antitrust injury, plaintiff would need to show that defendants' conduct 'affected the prices, quantity or quality of goods or services, not just his own welfare.'") (citation omitted); *Davies v. Genesis Med. Ctr.*, 994 F. Supp. 1078 (S.D. Iowa 1998).

[394] *E.g., Brunswick Corp. v. Pueblo Bowl-O-Mat, Inc.*, 429 U.S. 477 (1977).

[395] *E.g., Cargill Corp. v. Montfort of Colo., Inc.*, 479 U.S. 104 (1986); *Daniel v. Am. Bd. of Emergency Med.*, 428 F.3d 408 (2d Cir. 2005).

[396] *E.g., Atl. Richfield Co. v. USA Petrol. Co.*, 495 U.S. 328 (1990).

[397] *Associated Gen. Contractors v. Cal. State Council of Carpenters*, 459 U.S. 519 (1983).

[398] *See generally Summers v. Earth Inst.*, 555 U.S. 488 (2009); *see also Sunbeam Tele. Corp. v. Nielsen Media Research, Inc.*, 711 F.3d 1264 (11th Cir. 2013).

[399] *E.g., Fisher v. Aurora Health Care*, 558 Fed. App'x 653 (7th Cir. 2014) (holding that a physician whose privileges were terminated would not have antitrust standing even had he alleged a violation because patients and health plans would be the more directly injured parties if the termination restrained competition among physicians).

4. the directness or indirectness of the injury, including whether there are other parties whose injury was more direct than the plaintiff's and who would likely sue;

5. whether the plaintiff's damages are highly speculative; and

6. the risk of duplicative recoveries and complex damage-apportionment problems if the plaintiff is granted antitrust standing.[400]

Several courts synthesize these factors into a two-pronged test by examining whether the plaintiff (1) suffered antitrust injury and (2) is an "efficient enforcer" of the antitrust laws.[401] Antitrust injury is always a necessary, but not sufficient, condition for antitrust standing.[402]

A number of courts have held or suggested that, to have antitrust standing, a plaintiff must be either a customer or competitor in the relevant market adversely affected by the alleged violation.[403] The Supreme Court, however, has indicated that plaintiffs whose injuries are "inextricably intertwined" to the injury to competition in that market also have antitrust standing, even if they are not a participant in that market.[404]

Finally, so-called "indirect purchasers" cannot recover the overcharge they pay when they purchase from a "direct purchaser" who purchased from, e.g., alleged price-fixers or a monopolist. For example, assume that manufacturers of medical supplies conspire to fix the prices of their goods and overcharge the wholesalers to whom they sell. The wholesalers resell the supplies to hospitals, passing-on some of the overcharge they paid as a result of the price-fixing conspiracy. Under the indirect-purchaser doctrine, only the wholesalers (the "direct purchasers") are deemed injured and have antitrust standing to sue. The hospitals (the "indirect purchasers") have no remedy under the federal antitrust laws, even though they suffered some damage from the portion of

---

[400] *Associated Gen. Contractors v. Cal. State Council of Carpenters*, 459 U.S. 519 (1983); *see also Gatt Commc'ns, Inc. v. PMC Assocs., LLC*, 711 F.3d 68 (2d Cir. 2013); *Palmyra Park Hosp., Inc. v. Phoebe Putney Mem'l Hosp.*, 604 F.3d 1291 (11th Cir. 2010); *Stark v. Ear, Nose & Throat Specialists*, 185 Fed. App'x 120 (3d Cir. 2006); *Daniel v. Am. Bd. of Emergency Med.*, 428 F.3d 408 (2d Cir. 2005); *Am. Med. Ass'n v. UnitedHealthcare Corp.*, 588 F. Supp. 2d 432 (S.D.N.Y. 2008).

[401] E.g., *Bocobo v. Radiology Consultants*, 477 Fed. App'x 890 (3d Cir. 2012); *Palmyra Park Hosp., Inc. v. Phoebe Putney Mem'l Hosp.*, 604 F.3d 1291 (11th Cir. 2010) ("We employ a two-prong test for antitrust standing . . . : first, the plaintiff must have alleged an antitrust injury, and second the plaintiff must be an efficient enforcer of the antitrust laws."); *Tal v. Hogan*, 453 F.3d 1244 (10th Cir. 2006); *Ertag v. Naples Cmty. Hosp.*, 121 F.3d 721 (11th Cir. 1997) (per curiam unpublished opinion reprinted at 1997-2 Trade Cas. (CCH) ¶71,966); *Todorov v. DCH Healthcare Auth.*, 921 F.2d 1438 (11th Cir. 1991); *Pierson v. Orlando Reg'l Health-Care Sys.*, 619 F. Supp. 2d 1260 (M.D. Fla. 2009).

[402] *Palmyra Park Hosp., Inc. v. Phoebe Putney Mem'l Hosp.*, 604 F.3d 1291 (11th Cir. 2010); *McCollough v. Zimmer, Inc.*, 382 Fed. App'x 225 (3d Cir. 2010); *Elliot Indus. Ltd. P'ship v. BP Am. Prod. Co.*, 407 F.2d 1091 (10th Cir. 2005); *Giampollo v. Somerset Hosp. Ctr. for Health*, 189 F.3d 464 (3d Cir. 1999) (unpublished opinion reprinted at 1999-2 Trade Cas. (CCH) ¶72,574) ("First we must determine whether a claimant suffered antitrust injury . . . Second, we must determine whether a claimant was the most efficient enforcer of the antitrust laws.").

[403] E.g., *SigmaPharm, Inc. v. Mut. Pharm. Co.*, 454 Fed. App'x 64 (3d Cir. 2011); *W. Penn Allegheny Health Sys. v. UPMC*, 627 F.3d 85 (3d Cir. 2010) ("As a general matter, the class of plaintiffs capable of satisfying the antitrust injury requirement is limited to consumers and competitors in the restrained market."); *McCollough v. Zimmer, Inc.*, 382 Fed. App'x 225 (3d Cir. 2010); *Norris v. The Hearst Trust*, 500 F.3d 454 (5th Cir. 2007).

[404] *Blue Shield v. McCready*, 457 U.S. 465 (1982); *McCollough v. Zimmer, Inc.*, 382 Fed. App'x 225 (3d Cir. 2010); *Novell, Inc. v. Microsoft Corp.*, 505 F.3d 302 (4th Cir. 2007).

the overcharge passed-on to them.[405] The primary reason is the difficulty in tracing the overcharge through levels of distribution and determining the amount of the overcharge that was passed-on. Many state antitrust laws, however, permit indirect purchasers to recover the damages they incur from the passed-on overcharge.

Just as indirect purchasers cannot recover damages under the federal antitrust laws, an antitrust violator cannot defend a damage claim by direct purchasers by arguing that they passed on any overcharges to their customers, the indirect purchasers.[406] Rather, the direct purchaser can recover the full amount of the overcharge even if some or all were passed on to the indirect purchaser.

7.5.4 Damages

Once a plaintiff proves with reasonable certainty that the antitrust violation caused its damages,[407] the standard to prove the amount of damages is relaxed. That amount need not be proved with exactness, but rather can be reasonably estimated based on relevant data using several types of damage-measurement methodologies.[408] Nevertheless, proof of the amount of damages cannot be based on conjecture, guesswork, or speculation[409] and the plaintiff can recover only for damages caused by the antitrust violation, not for damages resulting from other causes.

7.6 Conclusion

Antitrust laws apply fully to the health care sector.[410] The types of antitrust issues arising are almost endless, including hospital mergers,[411] physician-practice mergers,[412] exclusive contracts between hospitals and physicians as to particular services rendered at the hospital,[413] hospital decisions not to grant or to terminate the staff privileges of practitioners based on peer review,[414] hospital staff-privilege moratoriums,[415] squeezing physicians out after a hospital merger,[416] price-fixing

---

[405] *See generally Illinois Brick Co. v. Illinois*, 431 U.S. 720 (1977); *See also Kan. v. UtiliCorp United, Inc.*, 497 U.S. 199 (1990); *Lakeland Reg'l Med. Ctr. v. Astellas US, LLC*, 763 F.3d 1280 (11th Cir. 2014); *Simon v. Keyspan Corp.*, 694 F.3d 196 (2d Cir. 2012); *Warren Gen. Hosp. v. Amgen, Inc.*, 643 F.3d 77 (3d Cir. 2011); *Del. Valley Surgical Supply, Inc. v. Johnson & Johnson*, 523 F.3d 1116 (9th Cir. 2008).
[406] *Hanover Shoe, Inc. v. United Shoe Mach. Corp.*, 392 U.S. 481 (1968).
[407] *See generally Amerinet, Inc. v. Xerox Corp.*, 972 F.2d 1483 (8th Cir. 1992).
[408] *See generally* ABA Section of Antitrust Law, *Proving Antitrust Damages* (2d ed. 2010).
[409] *Zenith Radio Corp. v. Hazeltine Research, Inc.*, 395 U.S. 100 (1969); *Bigelow v. RKO Pictures, Inc.*, 327 U.S. 251 (1946); *see also Texaco, Inc. v. Hasbrouck*, 496 U.S. 543 (1990).
[410] *See Boulware v. Nev.*, 960 F.2d 793 (9th Cir. 1991).
[411] *United States v. Long Island Jewish Med. Ctr.*, 983 F. Supp. 121 (E.D.N.Y. 1997).
[412] Antitrust Division Business Review Letter to Gastroenterology Associates, Ltd. (Jul. 7, 1997), *at* https://www.justice.gov/atr/response-gastroenterology-associates-ltd-gi-associates-pcs-and-valley-gastroenterologists.
[413] *E.g., Jefferson Parish Hosp. Dist. No. 2 v. Hyde*, 466 U.S. 2 (1984); *Lafaro v. N.Y. Cardiothoracic Group, PLLC*, 570 F.3d 471 (2d Cir. 2009); *Colonial Med. Group, Inc. v. Catholic Healthcare W.*, 2010-1 Trade Cas. (CCH) ¶77,039 (N.D. Cal. 2010), *aff'd*, 444 Fed. App'x 937 (9th Cir. 2011); *Perinatal Med. Group, Inc. v. Childeren's Hosp.*, 2010-1 Trade Cas. (CCH) ¶77,078 (E.D. Cal. 2010).
[414] *E.g., Moore v. Williamsburg Reg'l Hosp.*, 560 F.3d 166 (4th Cir. 2009); *Four Corners Nephrology Assocs., P.C. v. Mercy Med. Ctr.*, 582 F.3d 1216 (10th Cir. 2009); *Benson v. St. Joseph's Reg'l Health Ctr.*, 575 F.3d 542 (5th Cir. 2009); *Vesom v. Atchison Hosp. Ass'n*, 279 Fed. App'x 624 (10th Cir. 2008).
[415] *Allen v. Washington Hosp.*, 34 F. Supp. 2d 958 (W.D. Pa. 1999).
[416] *Samuel v. Herrick Mem'l Hosp.*, 201 F.3d 830 (6th Cir. 2000).

by provider networks,[417] exclusion of providers from membership in provider networks,[418] different types of joint ventures,[419] hospital acquisitions of physician practices,[420] hospital acquisitions of individual physicians,[421] health plan mergers,[422] physician unionization,[423] certificate-of-need disputes,[424] payer refusals to contract with certain types of providers,[425] discriminatory prices granted by suppliers to nonprofit entities,[426] hospital tying arrangements with payers,[427] pharmaceutical price-fixing and price discrimination,[428] health-insurer use of most-favored-nations clauses,[429] provider standard-setting programs,[430] tobacco medical-cost suits,[431] hospital attempts to force managed-care plans not to contract with other hospitals,[432] exclusive contracts between payers and single groups of physicians,[433] provider fee-review programs,[434] provider association advertising restraints,[435] pharmaceutical distributor mergers,[436] pharmaceutical manufacturer mergers,[437] pharmaceutical manufacturers "reverse payments" delaying entry of generic drugs,[438] "sham" patent-infringement litigation,[439] pharmacy boycotts of networks,[440] expulsion of physicians from their medical group,[441] hospital group purchasing of nursing services,[442] hospital price fixing of employed nurses' wages,[443] hospital price-fixing of prices paid for traveling nurses,[444] group purchasing organization exclusive vendor

---

[417] *N. Tex. Specialty Physicians*, 140 F.T.C. 715 (2005), *petition for review granted in and part and remanded*, 528 F.3d 346 (5th Cir. 2008); *Roaring Fork Valley Physicians I.P.A., Inc.*, 149 F.T.C. 1221 (2010) (consent order); *Boulder Valley Individual Practice Ass'n*, 149 F.T.C. 1147 (2010) (consent order); *J. Allen Ramey, M.D., Inc. v. Pac. Found. for Med. Care*, 999 F. Supp. 1355 (S.D. Cal. 1998).

[418] *Solla v. Aetna Health Plans*, 14 F. Supp. 2d 252 (E.D.N.Y. 1998), *aff'd*, 182 F.3d 901 (2d Cir. 1999) (Table).

[419] *See New York v. St. Francis Hosp.*, 94 F. Supp. 4d 399 (S.D.N.Y. 2000).

[420] *HTI Health Servs., Inc. v. Quorum Health Group, Inc.*, 960 F. Supp. 1104 (S.D. Miss. 1997).

[421] *Wichita Clinic, P.A. v. Columbia/HCA Healthcare Corp.*, 45 F. Supp. 2d 1164 (D. Kan. 1999).

[422] *E.g., United States v. UnitedHealth Group, Inc.*, 2008-2 Trade Cas. (CCH) ¶76,318 (D.D.C. 2008) (consent decree).

[423] *United States v. Fed'n of Physicians and Dentists*, 2002-2 Trade Cas. (CCH) ¶73,868 (D. Del. 2002) (consent decree).

[424] *Kottle v. Nw. Kidney Ctrs.*, 146 F.3d 1056 (9th Cir. 1998).

[425] *Cont'l Orthopedic Appliances, Inc. v. Health Ins. Plan*, 40 F. Supp. 2d 109 (E.D.N.Y. 1999).

[426] FTC Staff Advisory Opinion to Community CarePartners, Inc. (Jul. 2, 2010), at https://www.ftc.gov/sites/default/files/documents/advisory-opinions/community-carepartners-inc./100702carepartnersopinion.pdf.

[427] *E.g., Palmyra Park Hosp. v. Phoebe Putney Mem'l Hosp.*, 604 F.3d 1291 (11th Cir. 2010).

[428] *In re Brand Name Prescription Drugs Antitrust Litig.*, 186 F.3d 781 (7th Cir. 1999).

[429] Compl., *United States v. Blue Cross Blue Shield*, No. 2:10-cv-14155-DPH-MKM (E.D. Mich Oct. 18, 2010); *United States v. Med. Mut.*, 1999-1 Trade Cas. (CCH) ¶72,465 (N.D. Ohio 1999) (consent decree).

[430] *DM Research, Inc. v. College of Am. Pathologists*, 170 F.3d 53 (1st Cir. 1999).

[431] *Steamfitters Local Union No. 420 v. Philip Morris, Inc.*, 171 F.3d 912 (3d Cir. 1999).

[432] *Surgical Ctr. v. Hospital Dist.*, 171 F.3d 231 (5th Cir. 1999) (en banc).

[433] *Albani v. S. Ariz. Anesthesia Servs., P.C.*, 1997-2 Trade Cas. (CCH) ¶71,927 (D. Ariz. 1997).

[434] *Mitchael v. Intracorp, Inc.*, 179 F.3d 847 (10th Cir. 1999).

[435] *Cal. Dental Ass'n v. FTC*, 526 U.S. 756 (1999).

[436] *FTC v. Cardinal Health, Inc.*, 12 F. Supp. 2d 34 (D.D.C. 1998).

[437] *E.g., Watson Pharms.*, Dkt. No. C-4373 (FTC Dec. 13, 2012) (consent order); *Novartis, AG*, Dkt. No. C-4364 (FTC Sept. 4, 2012) (consent order); *Johnson & Johnson*, Dkt. No. C-4363 (FTC Aug. 7, 2012) (consent order).

[438] *E.g., FTC v. Actavis, Inc.*, 570 U.S. 136 (2013).

[439] *E.g., Bristol-Myers Squibb Co.*, 135 F.T.C. 444 (2003) (consent order).

[440] *Merck-Medco Managed Care, Inc. v. Rite Aid Corp.*, 22 F. Supp. 2d 447 (D. Md. 1998), *aff'd per curiam without published op.*, 201 F.3d 436 (4th Cir. 1999) (Table) (opinion reprinted at 1999 U.S. App. LEXIS 21487).

[441] *Marshall v. Planz*, 13 F. Supp. 2d 1231 (M.D. Ala. 1998).

[442] *All Care Nursing Servs., Inc. v. High Tech Staffing Servs., Inc.*, 135 F.3d 740 (11th Cir. 1998).

[443] *Fleischman v. Albany Med. Ctr.*, 728 F. Supp. 2d 130 (N.D.N.Y. 2010).

[444] *Doe v. Ariz. Hosp. & Healthcare Ass'n*, 2009-2 Trade Cas. (CCH) ¶76,591 (D. Ariz. 2009); *United States v. Ariz. Hosp. & Health Ass'n*, 2007-2 Trade Cas. (CCH) ¶75,869 (D. Ariz. 2007) (consent decree and competitive impact statement).

contracts,[445] provider price fixing to increase reimbursement from payers,[446] tying the purchase of third-party administration services and participation in a network,[447] use of bundled discounts in contracts between hospitals and payers[448] and between group purchasing organizations and vendors,[449] physician efforts to destroy allied-practitioner competitors,[450] boycotts of practitioners by specialty boards,[451] competition from the state in providing medical air-transport services,[452] hospital efforts to stifle competition from members of the medical staff establishing physician-owned specialty hospitals and outpatient facilities,[453] pharmaceutical-purchaser price-fixing agreements facilitated by pharmacy benefit management companies,[454] and challenges to anticompetitive state health care regulatory board decisions.[455]

As even this incomplete list shows, antitrust is an integral part of health law today.

7.7 References

A number of websites and publications provide particular assistance in researching issues relating to health care antitrust law and antitrust economics. The following is a partial list of helpful resources.

- American Health Lawyers Association Antitrust Practice Group: https://www.healthlawyers.org/Members/PracticeGroups/Antitrust/Pages/Default.aspx

- American Health Lawyers Association, *Antitrust and Health Care: A Comprehensive Guide* (2d ed. 2016)

- 1–6 John J. Miles, *Health Care & Antitrust Law* (1992 and Supp. 2017) (Thomson/West Group)

- ABA Section of Antitrust Law, *Antitrust Law Developments* (8th ed. 2017)

- ABA Section of Antitrust Law, *Antitrust Health Care Handbook* (4th ed. 2010)

- ABA Section of Antitrust Law, *Health Care Mergers and Acquisitions Handbook* (2003)

---

[445] *E.g., Se. Mo. Hosp. v. C.R. Bard, Inc.*, 616 F.3d 888 (8th Cir. 2010); *Allied Orthopedic Appliances, Inc. v. Tyco Health Group, LP*, 592 F.3d 991 (9th Cir. 2010).
[446] *United States v. Idaho Orthopaedic Soc'y*, 2010-2 Trade Cas. (CCH) ¶77,142 (D. Idaho 2010) (consent decree).
[447] *Brokerage Concepts, Inc. v. U.S. Healthcare, Inc.*, 140 F.3d 494 (3d Cir. 1998).
[448] *Cascade Health Solutions v. PeaceHealth*, 515 F.3d 883 (9th Cir. 2008).
[449] *E.g., Warren Gen. Hosp. v. Amgen, Inc.*, 2010-1 Trade Cas. (CCH) ¶77,043 (D.N.J. 2010) (not-for-publication opinion), *aff'd*, 643 F.3d 77 (3d Cir. 2011).
[450] *Minn. Ass'n of Nurse Anesthetists v. Unity Hosp.*, 208 F.3d 655 (8th Cir. 2000).
[451] *Ezekwo v. Am. Bd. of Internal Med.*, 18 F. Supp. 2d 271 (S.D.N.Y. 1998).
[452] *Evac, LLC v. Pataki*, 89 F. Supp. 2d 250 (N.D.N.Y. 2000).
[453] *Little Rock Cardiology Clinic, PA v. Baptist Health*, 591 F.3d 591 (8th Cir. 2009); *Kissing Camels Surgery Ctr., LLC v. Centura Health Corp.*, 2014 U.S. Dist. LEXIS 18335 (D. Colo., Feb. 13, 2014); *Med. Ctr. v. Premier Health Ptrs.*, 2012-2 Trade Cas. (CCH) ¶78,040 (S.D. Ohio 2012); *Peoria Day Surgery Ctr. v. OSF Healthcare Sys.*, 2010-1 Trade Cas. (CCH) ¶76,870 (C.D. Ill. 2009); *Tex. v. Mem'l Hermann Healthcare Sys.*, 2009-1 Trade Cas. (CCH) ¶76,479 (Tex. Dist. Ct., Jan. 26, 2009) (consent decree); *Heartland Surgical Specialty Hosp., LLC v. Midwest Div.*, 527 F. Supp. 2d 1257 (D. Kan. 2007); *Surgical Care Ctr. v. Hospital Serv. Dist. No. 1*, 2001-1 Trade Cas. (CCH) ¶73,215 (E.D. La. 2001), *aff'd*, 309 F.3d 936 (5th Cir. 2002).
[454] *Bellvue Drug Co. v. Advance PCS*, 2004-1 Trade Cas. (CCH) ¶74,329 (E.D. Pa. 2004).
[455] *N.C. State Bd. Of Dental Examiners v. FTC*, ___ U.S. ___, 135 S.Ct. 1101 (2015); *S.C. State Board of Dentistry*, Dkt. No. 9311 (FTC Sept. 6, 2007) (consent order).

- ABA Section of Antitrust Law, *State Enforcement Handbook* (2d ed. 2008) (chapter on state antitrust enforcement in health care)
- 1–15 Phillip Areeda & Herbert Hovenkamp, *Antitrust Law* (various dates)
- Phillip E. Areeda & Herbert Hovenkamp, *Fundamentals of Antitrust Law* (2003 and Supps.)
- Herbert Hovenkamp, *Federal Antitrust Policy* (5th ed. 2016)
- Federal Trade Commission & U.S. Department of Justice, *Improving Health Care: A Dose of Competition* (Jul. 2004)
- Roger D. Blair & David L. Kaserman, *Antitrust Economics* (2d ed. 2009)
- Paul J. Feldstein, *Health Care Economics* (6th ed. 2005)
- Federal Trade Commission: http://www.ftc.gov
- National Association of Attorneys General/Antitrust: http://www.naag.org/antitrust.php
- U.S. Department of Justice, Antitrust Division: https://www.justice.gov/atr

8

The Source of Payment: The State and Federal Regulation of Private Health Care Plans

Daniel J. Schwartz
Greensfelder, Hemker, & Gale PC

This Chapter will discuss the nature and extent of state and federal regulation of employer sponsored private health care plans,[1] in light of the historic rights granted to the states to regulate insurance and the sweeping changes made by the federal government through the Patient Protection and Affordable Care Act.[2]

8.1 The Basis of Regulation

8.1.1 The State Regulation of the Business of Insurance

The McCarran-Ferguson Act of 1945 endows states with the primary authority to regulate the "business of insurance."[3] State regulation of the insurance industry, however, did not commence with the passage of the McCarran-Ferguson Act. To the contrary, as early as 1851, states began enacting laws to regulate what was then becoming a burgeoning insurance industry.[4] Not everyone was enamored with the state regulation of insurance. Not surprisingly, the insurance industry was particularly concerned with the burdens of complying with multiple state regulatory schemes and, as a result, often chose to ignore the laws of other states. The first United States Supreme Court case to consider the right of the states to regulate insurance arose in this context.[5]

In *Paul v. Virginia*, the court was asked to overturn Samuel Paul's conviction in the state of Virginia for the unauthorized business of insurance. Mr. Paul was an insurance agent for New York-licensed

---
[1] Generally, for purposes of this Chapter, an employer sponsored health care plan is a non-governmental entity or organization that provides indemnity against certain medical expense, or otherwise provides for or arranges for the provision of, and pays for, certain covered health care services. A detailed description of those organizations that operate health plans, as well as those organizations that are an integral part of many health plans, is discussed in Section 8.2. For a discussion of governmental sponsored health programs (*e.g.*, Medicare), see Chapter 3. Keep in mind, however, that sometimes a governmental program (*e.g.*, the Medicaid+Choice Program or the Federal Employees Health Benefits Program), will contract with a private health plan to obtain coverage for the beneficiaries of the governmental plan.
[2] P.L. 111-148.
[3] 15 U.S.C. §§ 1011–1015.
[4] *See* Susan Randall, *Insurance Regulation in the United States: Regulatory Federalism and the National Association of Insurance Commissioners*, 26 FLA. ST. U. L. REV. 625, 630 (1999) (hereafter Randall).
[5] *See Paul v. Virginia*, 75 U.S. (8 Wall.) 168 (1869). *See also* Randall, at 630–36.

insurers. Although he applied for an agent's license in Virginia, he refused to deposit the necessary bond and was denied a license. He nonetheless acted as an insurance agent in Virginia, and was ultimately convicted of acting as an agent without a license.[6]

On appeal, Mr. Paul argued that the power to regulate insurance resided in the federal government under the Commerce Clause of the United States Constitution. The court held that the issuance of an insurance policy was "not the transaction of commerce," thus leaving the regulation of insurance to the states.[7] The court reaffirmed its *Paul* decision in 1913,[8] and the *Paul* case remained good law until 1944, when the court reversed itself in *United States v. South-Eastern Underwriters Association*.[9] In reversing its earlier decision, the court held that insurance contracts do affect interstate commerce and, therefore, are subject to federal regulation under the Commerce Clause.[10]

In the nearly 100 years that passed between the enactment of the first state insurance law and the Supreme Court's ruling that insurance contracts are subject to federal regulation, many states had developed comprehensive regulatory schemes.[11] Therefore, it is not surprising that, in response to the *South-Eastern Underwriters Association* case, an organization comprised of state insurance regulators[12] proposed a bill that would squarely place the primary authority to regulate insurance back with the states. This bill, which would become known as the McCarran-Ferguson Act, became law in 1945.[13]

Specifically, the McCarran-Ferguson Act exempts the business of insurance from federal antitrust regulation to the extent that it is regulated by the states.[14] More importantly for purposes of this Chapter, the McCarran-Ferguson Act provides that states have the express authority to regulate the business of insurance, and that no federal law or regulation shall preempt that authority unless the federal law specifically relates to the business of insurance.[15]

Though the McCarran-Ferguson Act provides for state regulation of the business of insurance, it does not itself define what constitutes the "business of insurance." Interestingly, many states do not fill this void by including such a definition in their state regulatory schemes. Other states provide statutory definitions that lack clarity or provide multiple conflicting definitions that vary depending upon the activity that is the subject of the particular statutory provision.[16] Those states that do provide a statutory definition, however, generally define the business of insurance as involving a contract

---

[6] *Paul*, at 169.
[7] *Id.*
[8] *See New York Life Ins. Co. v. Deer Lodge County*, 231 U.S. 495 (1913).
[9] *United States v. South-Eastern Underwriters Ass'n*, 322 U.S. 533 (1944). *See also Randall, supra*, at 633.
[10] *United States v. South-Eastern Underwriters Ass'n*, at 510.
[11] *Randall*, at 632.
[12] *Randall*, at 633. This organization would become known as the National Association of Insurance Commissioners (NAIC). The nature and role of NAIC is discussed in Section 8.2.1.
[13] *Randall*, at 633. For general discussion of the McCarran-Ferguson Act, *see* Charles D. Weiller, *The McCarran-Ferguson Act's Antitrust Exemption for Insurance: History and Policy*, 1978 Duke L.J. 587 (1978).
[14] 15 U.S.C. § 1012.
[15] *Id.*
[16] Stephen K. Phillips & Daniel K. Settlelmayer, *Provider Risk Sharing and Provider Sponsored Organizations* 5 (Health Lawyers 1998).

under which one party undertakes, on behalf of another party, to indemnify against certain expenses, or directly pay certain costs, upon the occurrence of certain contingencies.[17]

Though not all states statutorily define the business of insurance, state-court decisions have produced a fairly consistent common-law definition which includes as its essential components the existence of an insurable interest, the shifting of the risk of loss of that insurable interest, for the payment of a fee, from an insured to an insurer who is able to assume that risk by pooling together the payments received from all individuals, thereby spreading the risk among a defined population.[18]

Of course, some level of risk is present in almost every arrangement whereby one person pays another person for something of value. For instance, in the case of a restaurant that operates an "all you can eat" buffet for a set price, the restaurant owner has assumed the risk that the set price charged for the buffet per person, when added together with all the revenues received from all other diners, will not only cover the owner's cost but will, in fact, produce a profit. More specifically, the owner assumes that some people will eat a lot, and some people will eat a little, but by spreading the cost of the food and service among all diners on an equal basis (regardless of the amount they actually consume), the restaurant can bear the risk of those large-capacity eaters.

One certainly could argue that, analyzed in those terms, the "all you can eat" buffet represents an insurance arrangement, because it meets all five of these common-law elements. Under that example, however, the strict application of the five elements produces an absurd result. For this reason, in applying the five essential elements cited, state courts have recognized a distinction between "business risk" and "insurance risk."[19] Specifically, state courts distinguish between situations in which the key objective is the provision of a service (e.g., an all-you-can-eat buffet) and situations in which the key objective is the provision of indemnity (i.e., financial reimbursement for the cost of a particular loss).[20]

The case of *Transportation Guaranty Co., Ltd. v. Jellins* illustrates this distinction.[21] The *Jellins* case involved a plaintiff truck-maintenance corporation that agreed, in exchange for a set monthly fee, to maintain specified trucks owned by the defendant in "mechanical repair [and] to garage and fuel said" trucks.[22] The defendant breached these contracts, and the plaintiff sued for damages. In response, the defendant alleged that the maintenance contracts were void and unenforceable because the plaintiff was engaged in the unlicensed business of insurance. In finding in favor of the plaintiff, the Supreme Court of California ruled that this arrangement did not constitute an insurance

---

[17] *See, e.g.,* Colo. Rev. Stat. § 10-1-102(7); Fla. Stat. Ann. § 624.02; N.C. Gen. Stat. § 58-1-10. *See generally* Nat'l Ass'n of Ins. Comm'rs, *The Regulation of Risk Bearing Entities*, app. at A-IV-4(V) (1997) (hereafter NAIC White Paper); Allison Overbay & Mark Hall, *Insurance Regulation of Providers That Bear Risk*, 22 Am. J.L. & Med. 361 (1996).
[18] *See, e.g., Guaranteed Warranty Corp., Inc. v. State ex rel. Humphrey*, 533 P.2d 87, 90 (Ariz. Ct. App. 1975); *McMullan v. Enter. Fin. Grp., Inc.*, 247 P.3d 1173, 1179 (Okla. 2011).
[19] *See generally* Ericka L. Rutenberg, *Managed Care and the Business of Insurance: When is a Provider Group Considered to be at Risk?*, 1 DePaul J. Health Care L. 267, 272–80 (1996).
[20] *Id. See also* Douglas J. Witten, *Regulation of "Downstream" and Direct Risk Contracting by Health Care Providers: The Quest for Consumer Protection and a Level Playing Field*, 23 Am. J.L. & Med. 449, 458–62 (1997).
[21] *Transp. Guar. Co. v. Jellins*, 174 P.2d 625 (Cal. 1946). Other cases make this distinction as well. *See, e.g., Griffin Sys., Inc. v. Ohio Dep't of Ins.*, 575 N.E.2d 803 (Ohio 1991); *Prof'l Lens Plan v. Dep't of Ins.*, 387 So.2d 548 (Fla. 1980); *Cal. Physicians' Serv. v. Garrison*, 172 P.2d 4 (Cal. 1946); *Nat'l Auto Serv. Corp. v. State*, 55 S.W.2d 209 (Tex. Civ. App. 1932).
[22] 174 P.2d at 626.

contract, because the plaintiff corporation merely agreed to provide its service and labor but never agreed to indemnify the purchaser of the arrangement against a risk of loss.[23] In so holding, the court explained that "every business arrangement entails some assumption of risk, some gambling."[24] Therefore, a party's assumption of risk is not determinative. Rather, one must look at the arrangement, as a whole, to determine whether the principle objective is service or indemnity.

Historically, courts have made similar distinctions in cases involving health care-related arrangements.[25] *Jordan v. Group Health Association* is the seminal case in this area.[26] The *Jordan* case explored the nature of the arrangement between a nonprofit corporation, Group Health Association (GHA), and its members. Specifically, GHA members would pay fixed monthly membership dues to GHA, depending on whether the individual purchased a family or individual membership. In exchange for the payment of these monthly dues, GHA arranged for its members to receive medical and surgical services, subject to certain limitations, from specified providers.[27]

In order to provide these services, GHA paid a fixed annual fee to its physician providers (payable in monthly installments) for providing covered services. This fixed payment did not vary with the volume of services that the physicians rendered. Although GHA accepted the membership dues, and used these dues to enter into prepaid arrangements with physician providers, the GHA bylaws made it clear that GHA's only obligation was to enter into these provider contracts. GHA expressly disclaimed any guaranty that these providers would perform their obligations, and further disclaimed any liability for any such failure to perform or for the negligent performance of those obligations.[28]

Given those facts, the court ruled that GHA was really a "consumer cooperative" and not an insurer.[29] As a consumer cooperative, its main purpose was to arrange for its members to receive a service at a reasonable price through the pooling of purchasing power and other economies of scale. GHA's primary purpose was not to provide financial protection against loss caused by a specified occurrence.[30] Acknowledging that GHA's arrangement may include some element of risk-distribution or assumption, the court stated that a focus only on the element of risk, rather than looking at the contract as a whole, would result in insurance statutes "engulf[ing] practically all contracts."[31]

Interestingly, with the advent of managed care, the distinction between the provision of health care (the "service") and the financing of health care (the "indemnity") has become blurred. As the line between service and indemnity has become less clear, state regulators have become less willing to apply this "service vs. indemnity" analysis to determine whether an arrangement constitutes the business of insurance. As a result, some states have enacted regulatory schemes or espoused policy

---

[23] *Id.* at 631.
[24] *Id.* at 629.
[25] *See, e.g., Mich. Podiatric Med. Ass'n v. Nat'l Foot Care Program, Inc.*, 438 N.W.2d 350 (Mich. 1989); *Professional Lens Plan v. Dep't of Ins.*, 387 So.2d 548 (Fla. Dist. Ct. App. 1980); *New Mexico Life Ins. Guar. Ass'n v. Moore*, 596 P.2d 260 (N.M. 1979); *Cal. Physicians' Serv. v. Garrison*, 172 P.2d 4 (Cal. 1946); *State v. Cmty. Health Serv., Inc.*, 30 A.2d 44 (N.J. 1943); *State ex rel. Fishback v. Universal Serv. Agency*, 87 Wash. 413 (1915).
[26] *Jordan v. Group Health Ass'n*, 107 F.2d 239 (D.C. Cir. 1939).
[27] *Id.* at 242.
[28] *Id.* at 241–44.
[29] *Id.* at 247.
[30] *Id.*
[31] *Id.* at 248.

positions that would provide for some level of regulation over an activity that, under the analysis of these court cases, probably involves the provision of a service.

The United States Supreme Court has had myriad opportunities to define the business of insurance. These opportunities have arisen in connection with the application of the McCarran-Ferguson Act and ERISA. The Supreme Court first explored the definition of the "business of insurance" in the context of the McCarran-Ferguson Act in the case of *Group Life and Health Insurance Co. v. Royal Drug Co.*[32] The *Royal Drug* case involved an antitrust challenge by a group of pharmacies to a participating pharmacy agreement entered into between Blue Shield of Texas and certain pharmacies. The Supreme Court did not consider the merits of the antitrust challenge. Rather, the sole issue before the court was whether Blue Shield's participating pharmacy program—in particular, its contractual arrangement with participating pharmacists—constituted the "business of insurance" so as to render those contracts exempt from federal antitrust laws under the McCarran-Ferguson Act.[33]

The specific practice under review in *Royal Drug* was an arrangement under which Blue Shield insureds were entitled to get their prescriptions filled at participating pharmacies for $2.00. Insureds also could get their prescriptions filled at non-participating pharmacies. If the insured exercised that option, however, the insured would only receive reimbursement equal to 75% of the difference of the amount paid for the drugs and $2.00. In order to offer this benefit, Blue Shield entered into agreements with participating pharmacies. Under these agreements, the participating pharmacy would agree to accept, as payment in full for services rendered, the $2.00 received from the insured plus an additional reimbursement from Blue Shield equal to the pharmacy's cost of acquiring the drugs.[34]

In the *Royal Drug* case, the Supreme Court found that the participating-pharmacy agreements between Blue Shield and its participating pharmacists did not constitute the business of insurance. After acknowledging that the McCarran-Ferguson Act did not define the business of insurance, the court looked to the legislative history of the McCarran-Ferguson Act in order to determine what Congress meant by the "business of insurance." In this regard, the court found that "Congress understood the business of insurance to be the underwriting and spreading of risk."[35] Having made that determination, the court then shifted its focus to whether the arrangement between Blue Shield and its participating pharmacists involved the transfer and spreading of risk. Relying heavily on the *Jordan* case discussed earlier, the court found that the arrangement between Blue Shield and its participating pharmacists involved only an agreement that Blue Shield purchase goods at a set price.[36] Therefore, the arrangement between Blue Shield and its participating pharmacies did not constitute the business of insurance, because it did not involve a true underwriting of risk.

Subsequently, in *Union Labor Life Insurance Co. v. Pireno*,[37] the United States Supreme Court considered whether an insurer's use of a peer-review committee to decide the reasonableness and necessity of services provided by chiropractors involved the business of insurance so as to exempt the insurers

---

[32] *Group Life and Health Ins. Co. v. Royal Drug Co.*, 440 U.S. 205 (1979).
[33] *Id.* at 209.
[34] *Id.* at 205.
[35] *Id.* at 220–21 (citing legislative history contained in House reports).
[36] *Id.* at 229.
[37] 458 U.S. 119 (1982).

from an antitrust challenge by chiropractors with respect to this practice.[38] In holding that the use of a peer-review committee did not involve the business of insurance, the court articulated the following three elements as relevant to the determination of whether the activity involved the business of insurance:

1. whether the practice involved the transfer or spreading of risk of policyholders;
2. whether the practice was an integral part of the policy relationship between the insurer and the insured; and
3. whether the practice is limited to entities within the insurance industry.[39]

Later United States Supreme Court cases have consistently reaffirmed these criteria, which frequently are referred to as the "McCarran-Ferguson factors."[40]

The McCarran-Ferguson Act continues to serve as the foundation of a state's authority to regulate insurance. In accordance with the requirements of the McCarran-Ferguson Act, however, subsequent federal laws (e.g., ERISA,[41] the Consolidated Omnibus Reconciliation Act of 1985 (COBRA), the Health Insurance Portability and Accountability Act of 1996 (HIPAA),[42] and the Patient Protection and Affordable Care Act (ACA)) have placed limits on this state power through express regulation of certain aspects of the business of insurance.

8.1.2 Federal Regulation and the Pre-Emption of State Laws

Although motivated (through the development and passage of ERISA) to prevent mismanagement of employee-benefit funds, Congress did not want to thwart the continued growth of employer-sponsored programs. The preemption provision of ERISA was a way to balance these interests. On the one hand, ERISA preemption provided for uniform federal regulation of benefit programs that ensured ERISA protections to all plan beneficiaries across the country. At the same time, however, the preemption provision released employers from the burdens of complying with "conflicting or inconsistent state and local regulation of employee benefit plans,"[43] thereby reducing the cost of plan administration.

Intuitively, courts and lawyers have struggled with the ERISA preemption statute since its inception. Indeed, the statute has been notorious for producing divergent results in virtually identical fact patterns. In *Rush Prudential HMO, Inc. v. Moran*, U.S. Supreme Court Justice David Souter observed that "[t]he unhelpful drafting of these antiphonal clauses . . . occupies a substantial share of this Court's time . . ."[44]

The ERISA preemption provision is not absolute. The limitations imposed on federal preemption are best understood by analyzing the three separate clauses that together comprise ERISA's preemption provision:

---

[38] *Id.* at 122.
[39] *Id.* at 126.
[40] *See, e.g., Pilot Life Ins. Co. v. Dedeaux*, 481 U.S. 41 (1987); *Metropolitan Life Ins. Co. v. Massachusetts*, 471 U.S. 724 (1985). *See also UNUM Life Ins. Co. of Am. v. Ward*, 526 U.S. 358 (1999).
[41] 29 U.S.C. §§ 1001–1461.
[42] Health Insurance Portability and Accountability Act of 1996, Pub. L. No. 104-191, 110 Stat. 1936 (1996).
[43] *See* 120 CONG. REC., 29,933 (1974) (Statement of Senator Williams). *See also Shaw v. Delta Airlines, Inc.*, 463 U.S. 85, 105 (1983).
[44] *Rush Prudential HMO, Inc. v. Moran*, 536 U.S. 355, 364–65 (2002).

1. the "preemption clause;"[45]
2. the "saving clause;"[46] and
3. the "deemer clause."[47]

Under the preemption clause, ERISA supersedes any and all state laws that "relate to" an employee-benefit plan subject to ERISA.[48] The saving clause "saves" from the preemption clause certain state laws regulating the business of insurance. Specifically, ERISA does not preempt state laws that regulate insurance, even if those laws otherwise "relate to" an ERISA plan.[49] Finally, the deemer clause creates an exception to the savings clause by providing that no employee-benefit plan, or trust established under such a plan, may be deemed to be "an insurance company or other insurer . . . for purposes of any state law purporting to regulate insurance companies [or] insurance contracts."[50] Synthesizing these three components of ERISA's preemption provision has produced two clear concepts.

First, states can continue to regulate the business of insurance, even if the state laws that regulate the business of insurance sometimes impact ERISA plans. For instance, states may enact laws applicable to health-insurance companies, even though health-insurance companies sometimes contract to provide group health coverage to beneficiaries of a plan subject to ERISA. As a result, when an employer purchases insurance to provide benefits for plan beneficiaries under the terms of the insurer's policy, that insurer is subject to state insurance regulation.

Second, states may not impose insurance regulation on self-insured ERISA benefit plans even if those plans are otherwise engaged in the "business of insurance" by state definition. In other words, if an employer bears all or most of the risk for medical claims, then states may not regulate the benefit-plan activities of the employer by calling it "insurance."

Unfortunately, however, as will be discussed more fully, the application of these two "clear" concepts in the context of specific arrangements is often anything but clear. First, it is not always clear when a state law constitutes the regulation of insurance, thus "saving" the law from preemption even if the law in question relates to an ERISA benefit plan. A state's mere inclusion of a law within its insurance code does not automatically make that law an insurance regulation. Second, determining when ERISA preempts a state law that does not constitute the regulation of insurance because that state law "relates to" an ERISA plan is similarly challenging. As stated, if a state law does not constitute the regulation of insurance, but also does not "relate to" an ERISA plan, then ERISA preemption does not occur. Finally, analyzing the interplay between the saving clause and the deemer clause against the backdrop of contemporary health care financing and reimbursement arrangements poses special questions. Specifically, the line between when an ERISA plan is self-funded and when it is insured may be hard to determine. For this reason, analyzing certain state laws for purposes of determining whether they are preempted by ERISA can seem more like an art than a science.

---

[45] 29 U.S.C. § 1144(a).
[46] 29 U.S.C. § 1144(b)(2)(A).
[47] 29 U.S.C. § 1144(b)(2)(B).
[48] 29 U.S.C. § 1144(a).
[49] 29 U.S.C. § 1144(b)(2)(A).
[50] 29 U.S.C. § 1144(b)(2)(B).

Nevertheless, a growing body of case law, particularly United States Supreme Court decisions, does provide useful guidance. While many questions remain unanswered, these cases form the basis of the current ERISA-preemption analytical framework.

Under early case law, it seemed as though almost every state law that did not directly relate to the regulation of the business of insurance was within the reach of ERISA's preemption provision. This is because early cases, including early Supreme Court decisions, interpreted the "relate to" phrase literally. For instance, in its 1983 decision in *Shaw v. Delta Airlines, Inc.*, the United States Supreme Court stated that a "state law 'relates to' an employee benefit plan, in the normal sense of the phrase, if it has a connection with or reference to such plan."[51] Later Supreme Court decisions continued to apply this expansive reading of the "relate to" language.[52] In 1995, however, the Supreme Court, in *New York State Conference of Blue Cross & Blue Shield Plans v. Travelers Insurance Co.*,[53] retreated from this broad, literal interpretation that liberally found the necessary connection between a state law and an ERISA plan, and moved towards a more narrow interpretation that attempts to define parameters for what laws "relate to" a benefit plan through analysis of ERISA's objectives.

In the *Travelers* decision, the court was asked to consider whether ERISA preempted a New York law requiring hospitals to collect surcharges from certain HMOs, as well as from patients whose commercial-insurance coverage was purchased by an employee-health care plan.[54] Several commercial insurers and their trade association filed actions against New York state officials, claiming that ERISA preempted the New York surcharge law on the basis that the surcharge law relates to an employee-benefit plan. The court ruled that ERISA did not preempt this New York state law.[55] In so holding, the court observed that "if 'relate to' were taken to extend to the furthest stretch of its indeterminacy, then for all practical purposes preemption would never run its course, for really, universally, relations stop nowhere."[56] In making this observation, the court acknowledged that its prior attempts to construe the phrase "relate to" do not give much help drawing an appropriate line.[57]

The court then stated that, in order to draw that line and determine whether a law has a connection with an ERISA plan, it must look to the objectives of the ERISA statute "as a guide to the scope of the state law that Congress" intended to preempt.[58] The court noted that the objective of ERISA was to eliminate the threat of conflicting and inconsistent state and local regulation—in other words, to avoid a multiplicity of regulation in order to permit a nationally uniform administration of employee-benefit

---

[51] *Shaw v. Delta Airlines, Inc.*, 463 U.S. 85, 96–97 (1983).
[52] *See, e.g., FMC Corp. v. Holliday*, 498 U.S. 52 (1990); *Ingersoll-Rand Co. v. McClendon*, 498 U.S. 133 (1990); *Pilot Life Ins. Co. v. Dedeaux*, 481 U.S. 41 (1987).
[53] *New York State Conference of Blue Cross & Blue Shield Plans v. Travelers Ins. Co.*, 514 U.S. 645 (1995).
[54] *Id.*
[55] *Id.* at 661.
[56] *Id.* at 655 (quoting H. James, Roderick Hudson (New York ed., World's Classics 1980)).
[57] *Id.*
[58] *Id.* at 656. Citing *Shaw v. Delta Airlines, Inc.*, 463 U.S. 85, 96–97 (1983), the court noted that a law relates to an ERISA plan if it either has a connection with or makes reference to such a plan. *Id.* at 656. The court went on to explain that the law in question clearly did not make a "reference" to an ERISA plan because the surcharges are imposed on patients and HMOs, regardless of whether the coverage is ultimately secured by an ERISA plan. *Id.* The real question for the court, therefore, was whether the surcharge law otherwise had a "connection" with an ERISA plan. *Id.*

plans.⁵⁹ Therefore, the intent of the preemption language was to preempt those state laws that would affect the ability of plan administrators to implement nationally uniform benefit levels.

In the case under review, the New York statute did not in any way impact or preclude a uniform administrative practice or the provision of a uniform interstate benefit package. Rather, it merely impacted the cost of providing those benefits in one state (New York) versus another. The court concluded by saying that cost uniformity was not an objective of ERISA. Accordingly, a state statute that affects the *cost* of providing a benefit, but not the *administration* of the benefit, does not bear the requisite "connection with" an ERISA plan so as to trigger the preemption.⁶⁰

The court's holding, however, was not without limitation. Specifically, the court acknowledged that, in some cases, a state law might produce such acute economic effects so as to force an ERISA plan to adopt certain substantive provisions, or otherwise effectively restrict its choice of insurers, and that such a state law might be preempted under ERISA. In the present case, however, the court found that the New York surcharges did not fall within that category.⁶¹

Though reaching different results in terms of whether the state law in question was preempted, later Supreme Court decisions have continued to apply the *Travelers* "ERISA objectives" analysis when determining whether ERISA preempted the specific state laws under review.⁶² Specifically, when the Supreme Court determines that a state law operates to "frustrate [the] objectives" of ERISA, it continues to find that ERISA preempts the state law in question.⁶³ On the other hand, when a state law merely imposes an increased cost upon an ERISA plan but does not dictate the choices available to the plan, the court has found that ERISA does not preempt the state law.⁶⁴

As noted, whether a state law involves the regulation of insurance is one aspect of ERISA preemption analysis. ERISA does not preempt state laws that regulate insurance, even when such laws relate to an ERISA benefit plan. The only exception to this broad saving clause is that states may not impose insurance regulation on ERISA self-funded benefit programs.

The Supreme Court has provided guidance with respect to what constitutes the business of insurance. As stated in Section 8.1.1, the court initially interpreted what constitutes the "business of insurance" in the context of the McCarran-Ferguson Act antitrust exemption. Under that exemption,

---

⁵⁹ *Id.* at 657.
⁶⁰ *Id.* at 662.
⁶¹ *Id.* at 668.
⁶² *See, e.g., Rush Prudential HMO, Inc. v. Moran*, 536 U.S (2002); *Boggs v. Boggs*, 520 U.S. 833 (1997); *Cal. Div. of Labor Standards Enforcement v. Dillingham Constr. Co.*, 519 U.S. 316 (1997); *DeBuono v. NYSA-ILA Med. & Clinical Servs. Fund*, 520 U.S. 806 (1997). The *Travelers* decision and its progeny are consistent with general federal "field" and "conflict" preemption analysis. Specifically, the case law dealing with issues of federal preemption indicates that federal preemption includes three categories: (1) express preemption, where Congress specifies preemption in the text of an act; (2) "field" preemption, where federal regulation of a particular field is so pervasive that one may reasonably infer that Congress intended to dominate the field and preclude state laws; and (3) "conflict" preemption, where there is a direct conflict in state and federal law such that a private party could not possibly comply with both laws. *See, e.g., Cal. Div. of Labor Standards Enforcement v. Dillingham Constr. Co.*, 519 U.S. 316 (1997); *Dalton v. Little Rock Family Planning Servs.*, 516 U.S. 474 (1996); *Lorincie v. Southeastern Penn. Transp. Auth.*, 34 F. Supp.2d 929 (E.D.Pa.1998). For a discussion of the court's movement towards traditional field and conflict preemption in the context of ERISA, see the concurring opinion of Justice Scalia in *Dillingham*. 519 U.S. at 334.
⁶³ *Boggs v. Boggs*, 520 U.S. 833 (1997).
⁶⁴ *Dillingham*, 519 U.S. 316; *De Buono v. NYSA-ILA Med. & Clinical Servs. Fund*, 520 U.S. 806 (1997).

if a particular practice constituted the business of insurance, then it was immune from federal antitrust scrutiny to the extent regulated by state law. In this context, the court developed the three-part McCarran-Ferguson factors referenced earlier.

In *Metropolitan Life Insurance Co. v. Massachusetts*, the Supreme Court first applied this three-part test to determine whether a state law involved the regulation of insurance so as to save that law from ERISA preemption.[65] In applying the three McCarran-Ferguson factors developed under the McCarran-Ferguson Act, the court explained that the "business of insurance" must be defined consistently for purposes of ERISA and the McCarran-Ferguson Act.

Thus, in *Metropolitan Life*, a Massachusetts statute that required specified minimum mental-health care benefits for persons covered under an insurance policy was saved from preemption. In so holding, the court explained that determining whether a law is saved from ERISA preemption as the regulation of insurance requires the application of a two-part analysis. First, from a "common-sense standpoint," does the statute in question constitute insurance regulation? Second, applying the three McCarran-Ferguson factors, does the statute regulate the business of insurance?

Having determined that the mandated benefit law satisfied the common-sense test, the court, applying the three McCarran-Ferguson factors, found that the mandated benefit law in question constituted the regulation of insurance, because the law met all three McCarran-Ferguson factors. Specifically, the law mandating coverage for certain mental-health benefits did the following:

1. spread policyholder risk by spreading the risk of mental health care;
2. regulated an integral part of the relationship between the insurer and the policyholder by limiting the type of insurance that an insurer may sell to the policyholder; and
3. applied only to entities within the insurance industry.[66]

Having found that the mandated benefit law met all three of the McCarran-Ferguson factors, the court held that the law was saved from preemption.

After *Metropolitan Life*, lower courts were uncertain as to the specific importance of the three McCarran-Ferguson factors, which created a split among the circuits. Specifically, the lower courts did not agree whether, under Supreme Court precedent, a practice had to meet all three McCarran-Ferguson factors in order to be saved from preemption. Some courts held that a law had to regulate a practice that met all three McCarran-Ferguson factors for the saving clause to apply.[67] Other courts held that each of the three factors were "relevant," but that none was dispositive in determining whether a law constituted insurance regulation. Under this view, a state statute may be saved from preemption as the regulation of insurance even if it does not satisfy all three McCarran-Ferguson factors.[68]

---

[65] *Metropolitan Life Ins. Co. v. Massachusetts*, 471 U.S. 724 (1985).
[66] *Id.* at 743.
[67] *See, e.g., Texas Pharmacy Ass'n v. Prudential Ins. Co. of Am.*, 105 F.3d 1035 (5th Cir. 1997).
[68] *See, e.g., Community Health Partners, Inc. v. Kentucky*, 230 F.3d 1357 (6th Cir. 2000).

In 1999, the Supreme Court addressed this question in the case of *UNUM Life Insurance Co. of America v. Ward*.[69] The *UNUM* case involved an ERISA preemption challenge to California's notice-prejudice rule. Under this law, California insurers could not deny benefits to a plan beneficiary solely on the basis of a late claim submission unless the insurer could establish prejudice. In this case, the court clearly held that, although the three McCarran-Ferguson factors are all "relevant" factors to consider, none is individually dispositive. In so holding, the court explained that "*Metropolitan Life* asked first whether the law therein questioned fit a common-sense understanding of insurance regulation . . . and then looked to the McCarran-Ferguson factors as checking points or guideposts, not separate essential elements that must each be satisfied."[70] Accordingly, a law relating to a practice that does not satisfy all three McCarran-Ferguson factors may still regulate the business of insurance and, therefore, be saved from ERISA preemption. In specific reference to the California notice-prejudice rule, the court found that it constituted the regulation of insurance, even though it did not clearly satisfy the second McCarran-Ferguson factor. Taken as a whole, using the McCarran-Ferguson factors as guideposts, the notice-prejudice rule constituted insurance regulation.[71]

In *Kentucky Association of Health Plans, Inc. v. Miller*, the Supreme Court revamped its approach regarding the savings-clause analysis. In *Miller*, the court addressed the issue of whether ERISA preempted two broad Kentucky "any willing provider" statutes.[72] The two statutes (one directed to providers in general, and one directed to chiropractic care) prohibited a health insurer from discriminating against any provider who was willing to meet the terms and conditions for participation established by the insurer.

The court adopted the Sixth Circuit's assumption that the Kentucky laws related to employee benefits plans, and instead devoted its analysis to the question of whether the laws regulated insurance. In departing from the McCarran-Ferguson Act analysis that had pervaded most previous circuit court opinions, Justice Antonin Scalia in a unanimous opinion reasoned that ERISA's savings clause is not concerned (as is the McCarran-Ferguson Act) with how to characterize conduct undertaken by private actions, but rather with how to characterize state laws in regard to what they "regulate."[73] Kentucky's laws "regulate" insurance by imposing conditions on the right to engage in the business of insurance. To come within ERISA's savings clause, those conditions must also substantially affect the risk-pooling arrangement between insurer and insured.

The court concluded:

Today we make a clean break from the McCarran-Ferguson factors and hold that for a state law to be deemed a "law . . . which regulates insurance" under Section 1144(b)(2)(A), it must satisfy two requirements. First, the state law must be specifically directed towards entities engaged in insurance . . . second . . . the state law must substantially affect the risk pooling arrangement between the insurer and the insured.[74]

---

[69] *UNUM Life Ins. Co. of Am. v. Ward*, 526 U.S. 358 (1999).
[70] *Id.* at 374.
[71] *Id.* at 375–77.
[72] *Kentucky Ass'n of Health Plans, Inc. v. Miller*, 538 U.S. 329 (2003).
[73] *Id.* at 337–39.
[74] *Id.* at 341–42.

As discussed, ERISA saved from preemption those state laws that regulate the business of insurance. Congress, however, created an exception to this broad "saving clause" that prohibits states from regulating self-funded ERISA plans by calling them "insurance." In short, as courts have observed, just as states cannot regulate an employee-benefit plan by labeling it insurance, neither can an insurance program avoid state regulation by calling itself an employee-benefit plan.[75]

Although the exact application of the deemer clause remains elusive, understanding the distinction between a self-funded program and an insured program creates a beginning framework for understanding the interplay between the saving clause and the deemer clause.

Case law points to the following common elements of an ERISA self-funded program that distinguish a self-funded program from an insured program:

1. An ERISA-qualified employer promises to provide to employees a benefit defined in the plan.

2. The employer retains ultimate liability for the "losses" covered under the plan. This employer specifically retains this liability even if the employer transfers some financial risk to another party. In short, the employer remains responsible to perform if such other party fails to honor its obligations.

3. No direct contract is made between the employee and any person other than the employer relative to the securing of covered benefits. In other words, there is no privity of contract between the employee and any third party who may have agreed, on behalf of an employer, to assume certain risk of loss.

4. The benefit program is not marketed to the general public.[76]

For example, the Fourth Circuit has held that ERISA preempted a Maryland state law seeking to regulate stop-loss coverage purchased by an ERISA employer as health insurance, because the ERISA employer maintained a self-funded plan that the state could not deem to be an insurer. The court found that the employer's plan was self-funded, even though the employer purchased stop-loss coverage to protect against some of the losses covered under the plan. Specifically, the employer remained responsible for coverage if the stop-loss carrier failed to perform, and no relationship existed between the stop-loss carrier and the employees. The stop-loss carrier's only obligation was to provide the employer with stop-loss coverage when the employer's claims experience reached the attachment point of the policy.[77] Likewise, a Kansas District Court has found that a purported employee-benefit plan was really insurance, because it was provided by a third party, there was a direct relationship between that party and the employees, and the employer was not even made aware when the employee elected to purchase the plan.[78]

Again, it is clear that states may regulate the business of insurance, even when such regulation impacts an ERISA plan. Mandated benefit laws applicable to health-insurance companies, such as the

---

[75] *See Bell v. Employee Sec. Ben. Ass'n*, 437 F. Supp. 382 (D. Kan. 1977).

[76] *See, e.g., id.*; *Bill Gray Enterprises, Inc. Employee Health & Welfare Plan v. Gourley*, 248 F.3d 206 (3d Cir. 2001); *American Med. Sec., Inc. v. Bartlett*, 111 F.3d 358 (4th Cir. 1997).

[77] *American Med. Sec., Inc. v. Bartlett*, 111 F.3d 358 (4th Cir. 1997).

[78] *Bell*, 437 F. Supp. at 392.

law in question in *Metropolitan Life*, provide a clear example of this point. In other cases, however, the practical application of the *Travelers* "relates to" test or the analysis of McCarran-Ferguson factors is not so clear.

In two Supreme Court cases, the court analyzed ERISA's interrelationship with state laws affecting the operation of HMOs. In both cases (perhaps constituting a trend), the court allowed state laws to stand in the face of an ERISA challenge. In *Rush Prudential HMO, Inc. v. Moran*,[79] the United States Supreme Court, continuing its *Traveler's* analysis, held that ERISA did not preempt an Illinois law establishing an independent medical review process. Under the law, an HMO is obligated to provide services in the event that a reviewing physician determines that the services are medically necessary. The plaintiff, Deborah Moran, sought treatment for numbness and pain in her right shoulder. Defendant Rush Prudential HMO (Rush), which provided the coverage, denied Moran's request to have surgery by an unaffiliated specialist on the ground that the procedure was not medically necessary, despite her physician's recommendation that she would be "best served" by the procedure.[80] Ms. Moran pursued her right to an independent medical review under the Illinois law. However, Rush refused Ms. Moran's demand, and Ms. Moran sued in state court. The court ordered the review, which found the treatment necessary, but Rush again denied the claim. While the suit was pending, Ms. Moran had the surgery and amended her complaint to seek reimbursement, at which time the case was removed to federal court. The district court treated Ms. Moran's claim as a suit under ERISA, and denied it on the ground that ERISA preempted the Illinois statute. The Seventh Circuit reversed, concluding that the state act was not preempted as a state law that relates to an employee-benefit plan because the state act also regulates insurance under ERISA's savings clause.[81] In a five-to-four decision, with Justice Souter delivering the opinion, the court agreed with the Seventh Circuit's findings.

The analysis turned on the view that the Illinois law fell within the "savings clause" of ERISA because it "regulates insurance." In deciding whether a law regulates insurance, the court considered a commonsense view of the matter looking in part at whether the law was specifically directed toward the insurance industry. Because HMO organizations are simultaneously providers of health care and entities that assume risk, the HMO was considered to be undertaking the traditional functions of an insurance company. Moreover, because states typically have regulated HMO activity through state insurance departments, commonsense dictated that the law was regulating insurance. The court reviewed the McCarran-Ferguson factors to confirm its common-sense view of the savings clause. The court recognized that, although a state law does not have to satisfy all three factors to survive preemption, the Illinois law clearly satisfied two—the factor that a provision regulate an integral part of the relationship between the insurer and the insured, and the factor that the law be aimed at a practice limited to entities within the insurance industry.[82]

The court dismissed the argument that "conflict preemption" nullified the savings clause approach. That doctrine provides that, where a conflict exists, the congressional policy of exclusive

---

[79] *Rush Prudential HMO, Inc. v. Moran*, 536 U.S. 355 (2002).
[80] *Id.* at 360.
[81] *Id.* at 361–64.
[82] *Id.* at 366–75.

federal remedies overrides the state's regulation of insurance. The court held that the doctrine did not apply, because the state statute did not enlarge the claim process beyond the benefits that were available under ERISA, and it did not interfere with the congressional policy to provide a uniform federal system of rights and obligations under ERISA.[83]

Although not a preemption case, in *Pegram v. Herdrich*,[84] the court further addressed the interrelationship between HMOs and ERISA. In *Pegram*, the court held that physicians were not ERISA fiduciaries when making mixed eligibility/treatment decisions. In this case, the medical plan and its related management company functioned as an HMO organized for profit, named Carle, with the physicians who provided prepaid medical services to the participants serving as its owners. A Carle physician, defendant Lori Pegram, examined a covered participant, plaintiff Cynthia Herdrich, who was experiencing pain in the midline area of her groin. Six days later, Dr. Pegram discovered an inflamed mass in Ms. Herdrich's abdomen. Dr. Pegram did not order an ultrasound, but decided that Herdrich would have to wait eight more days for a diagnosis. In the interim, Herdrich's appendix ruptured, causing peritonitis. Herdrich sued the HMO in state court for fraud (among other violations), with Carle responding that ERISA preempted the claim. The district court granted Carle's summary judgment on one count, but granted Herdrich's leave to amend the other. Her amended count alleged that the provision of medical services was a breach of an ERISA fiduciary duty because the structured arrangement with the physicians rewarded limited medical treatment. The district court granted Carle's motion to dismiss, on the ground that Carle was not acting as an ERISA fiduciary. On appeal, however, the Seventh Circuit reversed the dismissal.[85]

The Supreme Court, in an opinion written by Justice Souter, held that mixed treatment and eligibility decisions by HMO physicians are not fiduciary decisions under ERISA. Here, Herdrich's claim of medical malpractice was inextricably linked with her claim of a breach of an ERISA fiduciary duty, as Herdrich's physician was also responsible for administering her ERISA plan's benefits. In its unanimous opinion, the court held that the answer to the question of whether Carle was a fiduciary when acting through its physician owners did not depend on the ownership status of the physicians, but rather on the background of the facts and laws about HMO organizations, medical benefit plans, and fiduciary obligations. The court concluded that the traditional guideposts of determining ERISA fiduciary status should be used. Ms. Herdrich's claim that Carle became a fiduciary acting through its physicians when it created the arrangement, and that it then then breached that duty by making decisions affecting medical treatment while influenced by a self-serving reimbursement plan, was not persuasive. The court recognized that the claim encompassed decisions related to eligibility and treatment, and that Congress did not intend for an HMO be treated as a fiduciary to the extent that it makes such mixed decisions acting through its physicians.[86] Finally, the court declared that, while ERISA might provide a convenient avenue for relief, there would be no value to a participant by federalizing state law-based malpractice claims.[87]

---

[83] *Id.* at 379–80.
[84] *Pegram v. Herdrich*, 530 U.S. 211 (2000).
[85] *Id.* at 215–218.
[86] *Id.* at 222–31.
[87] *Id.* at 235–37.

Rush and *Pegram* both suggest that the states may have a far broader reach in regulating managed care entities than originally thought. In fact, states establishing statutory causes of action against these entities may now find that their statutes survive preemption.[88]

In addition to favorable judicial treatment towards state statutes regulating managed care entities, courts have seemed willing to sustain another type of law that has an impact on ERISA plans: any-willing-provider (AWP) laws. AWP laws come in various shapes and sizes. Generally speaking, however, they have one common element: These laws require that any "insurer" that maintains a panel of preferred providers allow any provider willing to accept the insurer's contract terms to participate in the preferred panel. Supporters of these laws contend that they increase patient access to providers of choice and prevent HMOs and insurers from arbitrarily excluding competent providers. Opponents contend that AWP laws increase costs by denying the HMO or insurer the ability to deliver a high volume of patients to selected providers in exchange for reduced rates.

Although it was generally accepted that AWP laws "relate to" ERISA plans, the issue was whether the statute was "saved" from preemption as the regulation of insurance. Prior to the Supreme Court's decision in *Miller*, the circuits were split on this issue, with the Fourth and Sixth Circuits holding that the state statute was saved from preemption and the Eighth and Fifth Circuits holding that it was not.[89]

In *Kentucky Association of Health Plans, Inc. v. Miller*,[90] the United States Supreme Court resolved the division among the circuits, and held that Kentucky's AWP statutes were not preempted by ERISA. In so holding, Justice Scalia discarded the McCarran-Ferguson factors that had been used as guideposts in previous cases in favor of a two-pronged test. The court held that, for a state law to be deemed a "law . . . which regulates insurance," it must:

- be specifically directed towards entities engaged in insurance; and
- substantially affect the risk-pooling arrangement between the insurer and the insured.[91]

The court found that the Kentucky statute was specifically directed toward the insurance industry. The court held that the statutes, by their terms, imposed prohibitions on "health insurers" and "health benefit plans that include chiropractic benefits."[92] The fact that other non-insurance entities

---

[88] *See* § 3428 of the California Civil Code, requiring health care service plans and managed-care entities to operate under a duty of ordinary care, and § 88.002 of the Texas Civil Practices and Remedies Code, requiring the same. However, in *Aetna Health, Inc. v. Davila*, 542 U.S. 200 (2004), the Supreme Court held that a plaintiff's cause of action under the Texas statute alleging that an HMO breached the ordinary standard of care in denying coverage for a physician-recommended treatment is preempted by ERISA. The *Davila* court noted that whereas in *Pegram* a medical malpractice claim was inextricably linked with an ERISA claim, the cause of action in *Davila* against an HMO was solely about coverage under an ERISA plan. Accordingly, a cause of action purely to remedy the denial of benefits under an ERISA plan is properly brought under ERISA, not a state statute like California's or Texas's.
[89] *See Kentucky Ass'n of Health Plans, Inc. v. Commissioner of Kentucky Dept. of Insurance*, 227 F.3d 352 (6th Cir. 2000), *cert. granted*, 122 S.Ct. 2657 (2002); *Stewart Circle Hosp. Corp. v. Aetna Health Management*, 995 F.2d 500 (4th Cir. 1993); *Prudential Ins. Co. of Am. v. Nat'l Park Med. Ctr.*, 154 F.3d 812 (8th Cir. 1998); *Tex. Pharmacy Ass'n v. Prudential Ins. Co. of Am.*, 105 F.3d 1035 (5th Cir. 1997), *cert. denied*, 118 S.Ct. 75 (1997); *Cigna Health Plan v. Louisiana*, 82 F.3d 642 (5th Cir. 1996), *cert. denied*, 117 S.Ct. 387 (1996).
[90] *Miller*, 538 U.S. 329.
[91] *Id.* at 342.
[92] *Id.* at 335.

(e.g., providers) may have been affected by the law was not persuasive to the court, because regulations directed toward certain entities will almost always disable other entities from certain activity.

Secondly, the court found that the Kentucky law had a substantial effect on the risk-pooling arrangement between the insurer and the insured. The court reasoned that, by expanding the number of providers from whom an insured may receive health services, state AWP laws alter the scope of permissible bargains between insurers and insureds in a manner similar to the mandated benefit laws.

Miller fits squarely within the trend established by *Rush* and *Pegram*. In all three cases, state laws regulating an important aspect of an HMO's operation were held to survive challenges. Moreover, ERISA (which was designed to establish national uniformity with respect to the operation of health care plans) seems to have "taken a back seat" to the concept of the state regulation of insurance. At a minimum, it is clear that ERISA's statutory structure enacted in the 1970s is ill-equipped to regulate the delivery systems which have evolved.

8.2 The State Regulation of Private Health Care Plans

In order to adequately understand the scope of state regulation of private health plans, it is important to first identify the key players that form the basis of the health care-financing system. In some cases, these players are themselves health plans. In other cases, these players represent an integral part of a health plan's operations or the health plan's delivery of benefits to its insureds. The nature and extent of state regulation of health plans varies as the core functions of these players shift from pure indemnity on the one hand to comprehensive delivery systems (which integrate the financing and health care-delivery functions) on the other.

These key players include the following entities or organizations: indemnity insurers, preferred provider organizations (PPOs), health maintenance organizations (HMOs), point-of-service programs (POS), third party administrators (TPAs), provider-sponsored networks (PSNs), and Blue Cross and Blue Shield plans. A description of these entities and the regulatory schemes under which they operate follows.

8.2.1 Indemnity Insurers

An indemnity health insurer is a company that provides an insured with "indemnity" against a specified medical expense in exchange for the payment of a premium. Coverage is typically catastrophic in nature. This means that the insured has coverage for expenses arising from illness or accident, but not for preventive care. This form of health coverage is primarily a financing system as opposed to a health care delivery system. In other words, when the insured (the patient) incurs a specified loss (a health care related expense), the insurer reimburses, or indemnifies, the patient for that loss up to a specified limit. Under a pure indemnity contract, absent an assignment of benefits, the insurer makes payment directly to the insured (and not the health care provider) upon the submission of a claim. Indemnity policies typically include deductibles (costs that the insured must incur and bear before becoming eligible for coverage). They also include coinsurance, which requires the insured to pay a certain portion of covered expenses.[93]

---

[93] *See generally* Paul J. Routh & Ronald A. Kladder, *Welfare Benefits Guide 1999*, at 183–85 (West 1999).

As health care expenses began to spiral in the 1980s, many "indemnity insurers" began to incorporate "managed care" concepts into their policies. For example, many insurers added a "medical necessity" requirement into their coverage documents.[94] Specifically, the insurer would not pay for certain services listed in the benefits schedule unless the delivery of that service was medically necessary. The definition of medical necessity is discussed in Section 8.2.3.1 below.

Similarly, insurers began to impose second-opinion and pre-certification requirements upon their insureds. Under second-opinion programs, the insured is required to obtain a second opinion from a qualified practitioner supporting the need for certain procedures. Some second-opinion requirements apply to all surgical procedures, and others apply only to certain surgical procedures (e.g., hysterectomies) that insurers believe are subject to abuse. Under pre-certification requirements, the insured is required to obtain a certification from the insurer that a proposed hospitalization is "medically necessary" prior to admission. Typically, the insurer "pre-certifies" a specified number of inpatient days based on established criteria. If the patient stay is going to extend beyond the days initially certified, then the insured is required to obtain certification for those additional days.

States regulate indemnity insurers through their departments of insurance. Due to the financing focus of the health coverage provided by an indemnity insurer, state laws regulating health insurers traditionally focused on financial regulation by prescribing capital and financial reserve requirements, as well as requiring insurers to submit to annual financial examinations. In fact, most of the National Association for Insurance Commissioners (NAIC) core model laws required for accreditation relate to financial matters.[95]

States also generally provide certain consumer protections and filing requirements. From a consumer-protection standpoint, states prohibit insurers from engaging in unfair claims practices, and they require certain disclosures. They may also include mandated benefits that require the insurer to provide coverage for certain services, and may prohibit the insurer from discriminating against certain classes of providers in providing such coverage.

From a filing-requirement standpoint, states generally require insurers to file, and obtain insurance department approval of, insurance contracts and marketing materials. Some states also regulate rate-setting endeavors, requiring insurers to submit rates for approval before use. Finally, states subject insurers to periodic market-conduct reviews by the department of insurance, which are designed to ensure that insurers have complied with all applicable laws.

As indemnity insurers have begun to impose certain managed-care requirements upon insureds, states have begun enacting laws that impose requirements on those administrative functions performed by the insurer that play a role in determining (through coverage decisions) whether, where, and under what circumstances a medical service is provided. For instance, many states have enacted laws regulating the insured's performance of the utilization-review function through which the insurer makes its medical necessity determinations. These statutes often address who may make such

---

[94] *Id.* at 271–72, 294–95.
[95] *See generally* Nat'l Ass'n of Ins. Comm'rs, *Nat'l Ass'n of Ins. Comm'rs Model Laws Regulations and Guidelines* (1997). In addition to its model laws, the NAIC, through its Health Organizations Risk-Based Capital Working Group, has been working on the development of a risk-based capital formula for health organizations. The purpose of this formula is to measure the risk profile of particular organizations based on the level of risk assumed, and to then establish capital standards consistent with this risk profile.

decisions (e.g., only a qualified physician licensed in that state), how quickly they must be made, and the types of appeal processes that the insurer must maintain relative to coverage denials.[96]

8.2.2 Preferred Provider Organization

As the name implies, a PPO is an organization that creates a panel of "preferred" providers from which beneficiaries may obtain care as part of their health-benefits program. Beneficiaries generally are rewarded for obtaining services from these preferred providers in two ways. First, they receive increased coverage when they obtain services from a preferred provider. This increased coverage is usually in the form of lower deductibles or decrease of other out-of-pocket expenses. For instance, the insurer may reduce a $500 deductible to $200 if the insured obtains services from a preferred provider. A second way that beneficiaries are encouraged to obtain services from a provider who is part of the PPO network is through the reduction of paperwork. Specifically, due to their contractual arrangement with the health plan, the preferred provider will submit claims directly to the health plan for payment. As a result, the beneficiary has no responsibility for submitting claims.

A PPO may be part of an insured health-benefits program. In other words, a traditional indemnity insurer often will offer its insureds a preferred-provider option. Under this option, insureds may obtain care from preferred providers in order to obtain higher levels of coverage, but the insureds remain free to obtain covered services from a provider of their choosing.

TPAs also can operate a PPO. Such an administrator develops, through contractual arrangements, a network of preferred providers. The TPA then "rents" that network to insurance companies or self-funded benefit plans. In those situations, the TPA is not, generally speaking, financially at risk.[97] The providers look to the applicable payer (e.g., the insurance company or the self-funded plan) for payment.

Contracts between PPOs and their participating providers generally reflect the following reimbursement methodologies.[98]

1. *Discounted fee-for-service reimbursement methodologies*, under which the provider receives, as compensation for the services the provider renders, a percentage of the provider's usual, reasonable, and customary charge for these services or a discounted fee based on the payer's fee schedule.

2. *Case rate payments*, under which the provider receives a set case rate as compensation for a defined course of treatment. An example of this is a surgical case rate under which a surgeon receives a fixed case rate for performing the surgery, and for providing specified pre-operative and post-operative care.

---

[96] *See, e.g.,* Mo. Rev. Stat. §§ 376.1350 to .1399, which imposes requirements on the utilization review activities of all "health carriers" including insurers and HMOs.

[97] Though uncommon due to the nature of a PPO, some PPOs do accept some form of financial risk even when providing services on an administrative basis. The American Managed Care Review Association conducted a survey in October 1994, which found that of the respondents only 4% of PPOs were at risk. This survey also found that, of the respondents, 16% of PPOs placed hospitals at some financial risk and 7% of PPOs placed physicians at some financial risk. *See* AMCRA Foundation, 1994–95 Managed Health Care Overview 20 (1995).

[98] *See* Rutenburg, *supra*, at 287.

3. *Per-diem rates,* under which a hospital or other facility receives a set payment for all services provided during a single day, regardless of the actual intensity of service provided.
4. *Payments based on diagnosis-related groups* (DRGs), under which hospitals receive a set payment that covers all services provided by the hospital to patients admitted with a particular diagnosis, regardless of their length of stay or intensity of care.

Given their nature, PPOs generally do not compensate preferred providers on a "risk" basis. In other words, PPOs do not transfer to providers any financial risk for the cost of health services. This is true for two reasons. First, as stated, PPOs themselves often are not at financial risk. Second, because beneficiaries are given a choice of obtaining care from preferred providers or from their selected provider, it is difficult to predict how many enrollees will receive care from participating providers; further, of those who seek services from participating providers, it is difficult to predict the specific participating provider from whom they will obtain services. Being able to create a defined population is critical in establishing risk arrangements. Specifically, from an actuarial perspective, it is difficult to accurately predict the cost of care provided by preferred providers without knowing, without any degree of certainty, the number of plan beneficiaries who will obtain treatment from the preferred providers. (Risk arrangements are more fully described in Section 8.2.3.1.)

PPOs operated by an insurance company as part of an insurance product are regulated by the insurance statutes of the state(s) in which they operate. Those that operate as an independent administrative function (i.e., that create a network and rent the network to others), however, may not be subject to state regulation. Only about one-half of the states have adopted some form of PPO statute or regulation. Of those states, about six have adopted the NAIC model act.[99]

Of those states that have adopted some form of PPO regulation, the most frequent areas of regulation include:

- mandatory provider-contract provisions;
- prohibitions against certain restrictions in provider participation;
- patient access-to-care requirements; and
- restrictions on provider incentives; and requirements relative to the PPO's utilization-review program.[100]

In some cases, these laws include broad "any willing provider" provisions that require the PPO to include, in its provider panel, any provider willing to accept the contract terms (including the financial terms) offered by the PPO to participating providers. Many state laws, similar to the NAIC's model act, specifically exempt self-funded ERISA benefit plans from the requirements of the law.[101] Although the state still would require a PPO providing services on behalf of a self-funded ERISA

---

[99] *See* Nat'l Ass'n of Ins. Comm'rs., *Model Regulation Service* (Oct. 1997).
[100] *Id. See generally* Group Health Ass'n of Am. & Am. Managed Care and Review Ass'n, *Guide to State PPO Laws and Regulations* (1995).
[101] Interestingly, merely making reference to an "ERISA plan" in a statute by expressly excluding ERISA plans from the application of the law may in and of itself result in preemption. *See Prudential Ins. Co. of Am. v. Nat'l Park Med. Ctr.*, 154 F.3d 812 (8th Cir. 1998); *CIGNA Healthplan of La., Inc v. State of Louisiana*, 82 F.3d 642 (5th Cir. 1996). *See also District of Columbia v. Greater Wash. Bd. of Trade*, 506 U.S. 125 (1992).

health-benefit program to obtain state certification or registration, the PPO would not be subject to the requirements of the law (e.g., access-to-care provisions, any-willing-provider requirements) when serving as a third-party administrator of an ERISA health-benefit program.

8.2.3 Health Maintenance Organizations

8.2.3.1 Description

As of January 2016, over 92 million Americans received their health care through HMOs—a significant market penetration since HMOs first came on the scene in force in the 1970s.[102] HMOs have evolved over time and are continuing to undergo dramatic change in response to market dynamics, technological developments, and liability exposure. Historically, HMOs organized as nonprofit corporations that operated as "pre-paid" plans. This meant that HMOs would contract with select providers on a pre-paid (risk) basis to provide care to the HMO's enrollees. In other words, the HMO would pay the provider a fixed periodic payment to provide all medical services to enrollees, without regard to the actual volume or value of services rendered. The arrangement between GHA, its members, and its participating providers as described in the *Jordan* case (*see* Section 8.1.1) is a good example of an early HMO in terms of the role of an HMO and the financial relationship between an HMO, its enrollees, and participating providers.

Today, HMOs are more complex and, in many respects, look and act a lot like insurance companies. Specifically, HMOs are organized on both a nonprofit and for-profit basis, and often reimburse their providers on a fee-for-service basis in addition to, or in lieu of, a prepaid-reimbursement risk-based methodology.

Some key distinctions between HMOs and indemnity plans remain, however. First, unlike traditional indemnity insurers, HMOs are responsible for providing, or arranging for the provision of, certain basic health care services for their enrollees. The "M" in HMO stands for "maintenance;" these basic health care services focus on preventive care—not just coverage for services connected with illness and injury. Therefore, HMOs must provide or arrange, and pay, for a broad array of preventive-health services.

Second, as stated, HMOs are required to "provide or arrange" for these basic health services. In order to do this, HMOs must create a comprehensive health care-delivery network covering the full spectrum of covered health services (e.g., physician services, hospital services, ancillary services) through contractual arrangements with providers. In turn, enrollees must obtain care from the HMO's participating providers except in cases of emergency. In other words, except in the case of emergency services, HMO enrollees are not covered for the services provided by non-participating providers. An exception to this rule exists for those enrollees participating in an HMO that offers a "point of service" option. (A discussion of this option can be found in Section 8.2.4 below.)

Third, HMOs generally require their enrollees to select a primary care physician (PCP) responsible for maintaining the enrollee's health and coordinating the overall health care provided to the

---

[102] Henry J. Kaiser Family Foundation, *Total HMO Enrollment*.

enrollee. This means that the PCP is responsible for making referrals, as appropriate, to other providers and ensuring that the enrollee receives all appropriate medical services. HMO coverage documents typically provide that enrollees do not have coverage for health services unless provided or arranged for by their selected PCP. For this reason, the PCP is sometimes referred to as the "gatekeeper." Generally, PCPs include general practitioners, family practitioners, internists, and pediatricians, although gynecologists may also serve as a PCP in some plans. Under certain "open access" options, enrollees often are not required to select a PCP.

Fourth, HMOs provide coverage only for "medically necessary" services. There is not one set definition of medical necessity. Generally speaking, however, a medical treatment or procedure is "medically necessary" if, given the nature of the patient's condition and/or illness, the proposed treatment or procedure is: (i) likely to produce therapeutic benefits; (ii) provided in the lowest-cost setting and level, and for the shortest length, likely to produce the best outcome that can reasonably be expected; and (iii) not provided in a manner based on provider or patient convenience. For instance, if a provider can effectively and safely provide a patient with treatment for a specific condition on an outpatient basis, then inpatient services for the treatment of that condition are not medically necessary. HMOs take a proactive role in encouraging the provision of medically necessary services through a variety of administrative functions including provider credentialing, medical management, and provider contracting.

From a credentialing standpoint, an HMO may monitor the performance of its participating providers, and may continue to contract with only those providers who meet both quality and medical-management criteria. This is sometimes known as "economic credentialing."

From a medical-management standpoint, HMOs may employ a variety of techniques. Originally, medical management (which was then often called utilization review) focused primarily on pre-certification, concurrent review, and discharge planning. Today, medical management is much broader and includes techniques (e.g., case management or disease management) under which the HMO closely monitors the care provided to patients with complex medical conditions or specific diseases in order to ensure that the enrollee receives cost-effective quality care. Under these programs, the HMO may establish practice guidelines for particular conditions. These guidelines provide recommended treatment protocols for those conditions. HMOs may also assume an active role in the overall coordination of the enrollee's care. For instance, the HMO will try to ensure that the enrollee receives the appropriate tests and treatment at the appropriate time, that the enrollee does not receive duplicative tests or treatment, and that the enrollee has the appropriate social support in order to enable the enrollee to adhere to the treatment plan.

Today's medical management also may include data-driven processes and systems. Under such systems, the HMO collects data regarding the items and services provided to its enrollees, and uses this data to conduct outcome studies or create provider profiles. These profiles may include data regarding a physician's utilization of health care resources against established norms, or data comparing the outcomes achieved by the patients of specific providers to the outcomes of other plan providers or providers nationally. The HMO may then use this data to develop "best practices" (e.g., treatment protocols), educate providers, or educate their "consumers" regarding which providers render the most cost-effective care consistent with quality outcomes.

From a contracting perspective, HMOs will contractually require participating providers to participate in, and cooperate with, the HMOs' medical-management and other programs. These contracts often contain provisions designed to align the economic incentive of the provider with the economic incentive of the HMO by placing the provider at whole, or partial, financial risk for services provided. (A more detailed discussion of various risk arrangements is described later in the Chapter.)

Finally, unlike indemnity carriers (which impose deductible and coinsurance requirements), HMOs usually require enrollees to pay only nominal copayments for each service the patient receives. These are usually stated as a specific dollar amount, but may sometimes be stated as a percentage of the cost of the service.

As a result of these characteristics, HMOs promote a high degree of integration between the financing element of health care delivery and the actual delivery of care. This high level of integration has given rise to liability exposure, which is not common elsewhere in the insurance industry. For instance, HMOs are often sued on a vicarious-liability basis for the negligent performance of their participating providers.[103] Such suits typically allege an ostensible agency relationship between the HMO and the provider.[104] In addition, HMOs also are sued on a direct-liability basis for their own corporate negligence. Such actions include allegations that the HMO: (i) negligently performed its credentialing functions;[105] (ii) negligently performed medical management;[106] (iii) created inappropriate financial incentives;[107] or (iv) negligently provided care (when the HMO is seen to have evolved into a health care provider).[108]

HMOs create a delivery system of participating providers through five different models, each of which will be described in turn: the Staff Model HMO; the Group Model HMO; the Network Model HMO; the Independent Practice Association (IPA) Model HMO; and the Direct Contract Model HMO.[109] Keep in mind, however, that most HMOs do not operate in accordance with these rigid classifications. Instead, HMOs often create their networks of participating providers through a combination of two or more of these models.

1. **Staff Model HMOs.** A Staff Model HMO is one that actually employs a variety of providers (including physicians), and provides care through clinics it owns and operates. Some Staff Model HMOs employ only physicians, physician-support personnel, and allied health professionals; other Staff Model HMOs have actually owned and operated hospitals. The providers under these models are salaried employees of the HMO, and do not practice outside the HMO's clinics. Though Staff Model HMOs were once prevalent out of necessity,

---

[103] *See, e.g., Petrovich v. Share Health Plan of Ill., Inc.*, 719 N.E.2d 756 (Ill. 1999).
[104] *Id.*
[105] *See, e.g., Harrell v. Total Health Care*, No. W.D. 39809, slip op., 1989 Mo. App. LEXIS 577 (Mo. Ct. App. Apr. 25, 1989), *rev'd on other grounds*, 781 S.W.2d 58 (Mo. 1989).
[106] *See, e.g., Ardary v. Aetna Health Plans of Cal., Inc.*, 98 F.3d 496 (9th Cir. 1996).
[107] *See, e.g., Pegram v. Herdrich*, 530 U.S. 211 (2000).
[108] *See, e.g., In re U.S. Healthcare, Inc.*, 193 F.3d 151 (3d Cir. 1999).
[109] The IRS has recognized four of these models (the Staff Model, Group Model, IPA Model, and Network Model). *See* Gen. Couns. Mem., 39,829 (Aug. 30, 1990). In addition, four of these models (the Staff Model, Group Model, IPA Model, and Direct Contract Model) are recognized in the Federal Health Maintenance Organization Act of 1973 and its accompanying regulations. 42 U.S.C. §§ 300 *et seq.* and 42 C.F.R. § 417. For a general discussion of these models, *see Rutenberg, supra*, at 284–86.

HMOs have moved away from this model as other forms of providing, or arranging for, care on a cost-effective basis (e.g., risk-contracting with independent providers on a group and individual basis), have become possible.

2. **Group Model HMOs.** Although very similar to a Staff Model HMO, the key distinction is that a Group Model HMO does not directly employ its own providers. Instead, the HMO contracts with a single independent medical group (which, in turn, employs its own providers) to provide care to the HMO's enrollees. These groups are typically closely affiliated with the HMO, and generally have exclusive contracts with the HMO that prevent the group from providing care to patients other than the HMO's enrollees.

3. **Network Model HMO.** In a Network Model HMO, the HMO contracts with not just one medical group, but rather with several different medical groups in order to provide care to its enrollees. These groups are usually, but not always, less closely affiliated with the HMO than the group that contracts with the Group Model HMO.

4. **IPA Model HMO.** Under an IPA Model HMO, the HMO contracts with one or more IPAs comprised of independent physicians. Specifically, the HMO holds a contract with the IPA, which in turn contracts with independent participating providers who agree to provide services to the HMO's enrollees.

5. **Direct Contract Model HMO.** In a Direct Contract Model HMO, the HMO directly contracts with individual physicians and other providers.

Because enrollees of HMOs are required to obtain care from participating providers—and, in most instances, enrollees are required to select a primary care physician—it is easy to create defined populations comprised of either the entire HMO enrollment base or particular subsets of the HMO enrollment base (i.e., all enrollees who have selected particular primary care physicians). As a result, it is possible for HMOs to contract with providers in a manner that transfers some degree of financial risk to the provider for services rendered. Moreover, as indicated, HMOs traditionally operated prepaid plans that involved fixed payments to providers.

Risk arrangements vary and, often, HMOs and their providers combine several forms of risk sharing into a single agreement. Nevertheless, risk arrangements entered into between HMOs and their participating providers can be separated into the five risk models, which are described as follows.

1. Withhold Arrangements
    - A withhold arrangement is any arrangement under which the HMO retains a portion of the provider's compensation for services rendered. For instance, the HMO may retain 20% of the compensation otherwise payable to the physician.
    - Withhold arrangements can be used in connection with both fee-for-service arrangements and prepaid arrangements such as capitation. (Capitation arrangements are described later in the Chapter.)
    - The HMO will return to the provider the aggregate amount of the withhold after a specified period of time, depending on the provider's performance against established goals. These goals may be either financial (e.g., actual health care expenditures are lower than projections) or clinical (e.g., the provider's adherence to preventive health guidelines,

documentation guidelines) in nature. Sometimes, an HMO will include both financial and quality goals in its contract.

2. Bonus Arrangements
   - A bonus arrangement is an arrangement under which an HMO pays a provider an additional "bonus" tied to performance. Similar to the withhold model described, payment of the bonus is tied to the provider's achievement of the specified goals.
   - As with a withhold arrangement, bonus arrangements can be tied to financial performance, clinical performance, or both. A bonus arrangement can work in conjunction with both fee-for-service and prepaid arrangements. In practice, little distinction usually is made between a withhold arrangement and a bonus arrangement. In order to create a bonus arrangement in lieu of a withhold, the HMO may opt merely to reduce the amount of its reimbursement to providers.
   - It is not unusual for agreements to include both a withhold component and a bonus component. These separate components may be tied to separate factors, or may be tied to achievement of the same factors.

3. Capitation Arrangements
   - A capitation arrangement is any prepayment mechanism under which the HMO pays a provider a specified dollar amount for each "assigned member" for each month in return for providing a specified scope of services. This is known as a "per member per month" (PM/PM) payment. This PM/PM payment does not vary based on the volume or value of services rendered by the provider or the amount of payment that the HMO receives in premium. The agreement will define those enrollees that are considered "assigned" under the agreement. Usually, "assigned members" will be all enrollees who have selected particular physicians as their primary care physicians. In other situations, the assigned members may be all members enrolled in a particular product offered by the HMO.
   - The capitation payment may cover only services provided by the at-risk provider. For instance, HMOs frequently pay their primary care physicians on a capitated basis for the services they provide to their assigned enrollees. Other times, a capitation payment may also cover services provided by other providers. For example, a physician may sometimes accept risk for certain services, such as referral services or inpatient care, provided by others.
   - In addition to traditional capitation, some HMOs will pay specialty providers on a "contact" capitation basis. Under contact capitation, an HMO may pay its specialists a set payment for each "contact" that specialist has with the enrollee. Generally, each visit with the specialist does not constitute a contact. Rather, the contact is defined as all of the services provided by that specialist to the enrollee for the condition for which the enrollee was referred to that specialist.
   - A plan may have capitation rates that are adjusted based on the age or gender of the enrollee, may have different capitation rates for different benefit plans or programs, or may have one or more "blended" rates.

- A capitation arrangement can include a withhold or bonus feature (or both).
- Capitation arrangements can also be used in conjunction with pool/fund arrangements. (See the discussion of pool/fund arrangements later in this Chapter.)

4. Percent-of-Premium Arrangements
   - A percent-of-premium arrangement is any prepaid arrangement under which an HMO pays a provider a specified portion (x percent) of the premium revenue received by the HMO for providing a specified scope of services on a monthly basis with respect to all "assigned" members. The scope of service may be broad (covering all plan benefits), or may be more narrow (covering only a subset of plan benefits).
   - Similar to a capitation arrangement, the percent-of-premium arrangement will not vary based on the volume or value of services that the provider renders or the assigned members receive. The payment will vary, however, depending upon the rate charged to the contract holder.
   - Again similar to capitation arrangements, the percent of premium received by a particular provider may be designed to cover only the services provided by that provider, or they may be designed to cover the services of other providers, thereby placing the provider at risk for referral services.
   - Percent-of-premium arrangements do not typically have a "withhold" in the classic sense, though they often are operated in conjunction with, or administered through, pool/fund arrangements. (*See* following discussion of pool/fund arrangements.)

5. Pool/Fund Arrangements
   - Pool/Fund arrangements are often used as a mechanism to administer withhold/bonus arrangements or prepaid arrangements, such as capitation and percent-of-premium arrangements.
   - A pool or fund arrangement is any arrangement under which an HMO sets up a financial budget relative to the cost of providing specified covered services. Generally, the HMO establishes the budget by crediting the "pool" with a specified PM/PM payment. The HMO retains control over the pool. This PM/PM payment may be a capitation payment, or may be a specified percent of premium. The HMO then "debits" from the pool amounts it has paid on behalf of assigned members for covered health care services.
   - If, after a specified period of time (usually one year), the amount of the total debits for claims paid by the HMO is less than the amount of the credits, then the pool is in a "surplus" position. The provider typically receives all or some defined portion of the "surplus." The provider, may, however, also be liable for all, or a portion, of the deficits.
   - The plan may have one overall pool or may have a series of separate pools (e.g., a professional-services fund, institutional fund, and pharmacy fund) covering different types of service.

Under some of these arrangements, the HMO may delegate some of its administrative functions (e.g., claims payment or medical management) to the provider. In many cases, however, the HMO continues to perform these functions.

Of course, as stated, today it is not uncommon for HMOs to compensate providers on a non-risk basis. Such compensation mechanisms include the discounted fee-for-service, case rates, *per diem* arrangements, and DRG-based reimbursement.

Sometimes, however, HMOs will incorporate a risk component into even these reimbursement models. For instance, an HMO might take a typical case-rate arrangement, under which the physician provides a specific course of treatment in exchange for a fixed case-rate fee and add a risk component by including, within the case rate, reimbursement for the services provided by others. An illustration of this is an agreement between an HMO and an orthopedic surgeon under which the surgeon receives a fixed case-rate payment for the orthopedist's own services in connection with total hip-replacement surgery, as well as for the related inpatient services and physical therapy. Such an arrangement places the orthopedist at risk for not only the cost of the professional orthopedic services, but also for the cost of the related hospital and physical-therapy services. If a particular patient requires more hospitalization or therapy than anticipated, then the surgeon is nonetheless responsible for that cost.

8.2.3.2 Scope of State Regulation

Initially, HMOs were not regulated as part of the business of insurance. Given their pre-paid nature, they were often viewed as providing a predominantly service-related function, rather than a predominantly indemnity-related function. As HMOs began to evolve over time and to perform functions that looked indemnity-like (e.g., compensating providers on a fee-for-service basis), however, states began enacting distinct regulatory schemes with laws and regulations tailored to an HMO's unique integration of the financing and delivery of health care. As a result, in addition to the detailed financial regulation to which HMOs are subject, HMOs also are subject to regulation relating to the delivery of care.[110] Likewise, although states generally regulate HMOs through their departments of insurance, many states also regulate HMOs through a department of health or similar regulatory body that the state considers better able to provide regulatory oversight of an HMO's health care-delivery function.

Of course, ERISA may sometimes preempt state "insurance" laws (regardless of whether the law is included within the state's insurance code or HMO act) if the law in question does not constitute insurance regulation based on the application of the McCarran-Ferguson factors. In fact, in 1973 Congress enacted the Health Maintenance Organization Act, which served to establish certain basic requirements for federally qualified HMOs and had the effect of pre-empting onerous conflicting state law. In addition to ERISA preemption, under the Balance Budget Act of 1997 (the BBA), Congress provided for federal preemption of certain state-insurance laws when applied to

---

[110] Although HMOs are subject to financial regulation, HMOs are often subject to less-stringent financial regulation than traditional indemnity insurers for several reasons. HMOs maintain a closed panel of providers, many of whom are compensated on a risk basis, and all of whom are subject to statutory hold-harmless provisions under which the providers are prohibited from seeking payment from the HMO's enrollees in the event of HMO nonpayment for any reason including insolvency.

organizations that contract with the Centers for Medicare & Medicaid Services (CMS) to provide benefits to Medicare+Choice beneficiaries (M+C).

Specifically, the BBA provides that the federal laws governing M+C organizations preempt state laws relating to the inclusion or treatment of providers.[111] As a result, at least with respect to their enrollment, M+C organizations are not subject to state "any willing provider" laws that would otherwise apply to a state-licensed HMO. Due to federal M+C preemption, M+C organizations also may be exempt from other state laws governing the relationship between the M+C organization and its providers (e.g., laws restricting or prohibiting financial-incentive arrangements). Similarly, the scope of coverage and duration of benefits under the M+C program preempts conflicting state law.[112] Finally, the BBA's implementing regulations provide that M+C standards and contract requirements supersede any conflicting state laws and regulations.[113]

Financial regulation of HMOs generally covers net-worth and reserve requirements, as well as solvency protections. Similar to insurers, HMOs are generally required to submit, on an annual basis, audited financial statements. HMOs are also subject to market conduct surveys.

8.2.3.3 Typical Areas of Regulation

As stated, however, given the unique attributes of HMOs, states also have regulatory schemes (which are often complex) designed to address the pre-paid nature of HMOs, as well as the role they play in the delivery of health care. A sampling of these types of regulations is provided. This is an evolving list. States enacted sweeping managed-care reforms as a response to quality-of-care concerns expressed by physicians and patients. For this reason, the scope of HMO regulation has been increasing, and may continue to increase in the future.

(a) Member Hold-Harmless Provisions. Under these laws, HMOs are required to include in their provider contracts language under which the provider agrees not to seek payment from the HMO enrollee (or anyone acting on the enrollee's behalf) for covered services under *any* circumstances—including the event of the HMO's non-payment, insolvency, or breach of the provider's agreement.

(b) Continuity of Care. These laws require HMOs to include language in their provider contracts that requires providers to continue to provide care after the termination of their provider agreement with the health plan in certain circumstances. At a minimum, these laws tend to require the provision of continued care to enrollees who are hospital inpatients on the date of contract termination. Some continuation-of-care laws, however, require continuation of care for a specified period of time to all enrollees under active treatment (not just inpatients), as well as enrollees with certain chronic conditions.[114]

(c) Insolvency Protection. These laws require HMOs to include special hold-harmless and continuity-of-care requirements in their provider contracts that apply in the event that the provider

---

[111] 42 U.S.C. § 1856(b).
[112] 42 U.S.C. § 1856.
[113] 42 C.F.R. § 422.402.
[114] *See* National Conference of State Legislatures, *Health Policy Tracking Service Issue Brief, Finance: Continuity of Care* (Oct. 1, 1999).

terminates the contract due to the HMO's insolvency. Typically, the provider is required to continue to provide care to all enrollees (regardless of health status) for the duration of time for which premiums were paid to the HMO. The provider is required to hold the enrollee harmless for the cost of any care provided during this continuation period.

(d) Quality Assurance. Under these provisions, HMOs are required to operate quality-assurance programs that stress health outcomes and provide review by physicians and other health care professionals of the processes followed in the provision of care that meet certain requirements. HMOs often are required to submit summaries of the activities that they conduct through their quality-assurance program to the state regulatory body that provides oversight of quality-of-care functions. In some states, HMOs are deemed to meet the requirements of these laws if they maintain accreditation in good standing with a nationally recognized accreditation body, such as the National Committee for Quality Assurance.

(e) Mandated Benefits/Coverage Requirements. HMOs are required to provide coverage for specific services. At a minimum, this includes coverage for "basic health care" services. With some limitations, basic health care services generally include the full scope of medical and hospital services necessary for the diagnosis and treatment of illness or injury, as well as preventive care such as physicals and related testing (e.g., mammography) designed to maintain good health.[115] In most states, basic health care services do not include services such as pharmaceuticals, durable medical equipment (DME), or dental care, although states allow HMOs to offer these benefits on a "supplemental" basis.

In addition to basic health care services, common-coverage mandates include coverage for specific hospital lengths of stay following childbirth, coverage for reconstructive breast surgery following a mastectomy, and coverage for one "well-woman" exam by a gynecologist per year without the necessity of a referral from a primary care provider.[116] Finally, states generally prohibit HMOs from imposing deductibles relative to basic health care services, and strictly regulate the nature and extent of any enrollee copayment that HMOs may impose.

(f) Women's Health. In addition to mandates regarding one well-woman exam per year with a gynecologist, some states require that women be allowed to designate an obstetrician/gynecologist (OB/GYN) as their primary care physicians.[117]

(g) Emergency Services/Prudent-Layperson Standard. In most states, HMOs must provide coverage for emergency services without authorization in the event that a "prudent layperson" possessing average knowledge of medicine would have believed that her symptoms or conditions required emergency treatment, regardless of whether the actual diagnosis confirmed the existence of an emergency.[118]

---

[115] Note, however, that many states have adopted limited health services legislation under which "HMO-like" organizations that provide or arrange for, and pay for, a single, specialty service (such as vision or dental services) may obtain limited licensure to provide those benefits without offering a broader scope of basic health care services.

[116] *See* National Conference of State Legislatures, *Health Policy Tracking Service Issue Brief, Finance: Mandated Benefits* (Sept. 28, 1999).

[117] *Id.*

[118] *See* National Conference of State Legislatures, *Health Policy Tracking Service Issue Brief, Finance: Emergency Care* (Nov. 12, 1999).

(h) Network Adequacy. These laws require HMOs to ensure that they meet specific network-adequacy standards. These requirements are designed to ensure that an HMO's provider network is adequate to appropriately care for the needs of the HMO's members. For instance, state law may require HMOs to maintain certain enrollee-to-provider ratios, as well as meet certain standards for geographic coverage (e.g., drive time to certain providers) and wait times for appointments.

(i) Access to Specialists. These laws require HMOs to issue a "standing" referral to a specialist for an entire course of treatment, and allow enrollees with chronic conditions to designate specific specialists as the enrollee's primary care physician. Some states allow enrollee access to non-contracted specialists when the HMO's network does not contain a specialist "qualified" to provide treatment for the enrollee's condition.[119]

(j) Anti-Gag Clause Rules. A large number of states have enacted laws that prohibit HMOs from including clauses in their contracts with participating providers that prohibit providers from communicating with their patients regarding the provider's treatment recommendations. These laws often specifically provide that providers must be free to communicate all treatment alternatives to their patients, regardless of whether those treatments are covered under the patient's plan. They further provide that the HMO cannot take action against a provider for serving as a patient advocate.

(k) Regulation of Certain Financial Incentives. Increasingly, states are enacting provisions that prohibit HMOs from paying incentives to providers to reduce or limit medically necessary services to any specific enrollee.[120] Unfortunately, states often have failed to provide meaningful guidance (e.g., through promulgation of regulations) regarding the types of arrangements that would be prohibited under these laws. When states do provide guidance, they sometimes adopt very restrictive views regarding, and impose significant restrictions on, the level of risk that is permissible.[121]

(l) Enrollee Grievances and Appeals. These laws require HMOs to maintain specific enrollee-grievance and appeal processes, including expedited appeal processes in the case of urgently needed care. In more than one-half of the states, these provisions allow (after the enrollee's exhaustion of the HMO's internal appeal mechanisms) for an appeal to an independent external-review body.[122] States often require HMOs to maintain detailed logs of enrollee's grievances, documenting the nature of the grievance and the resolution thereof.

---

[119] *See* National Conference of State Legislatures, *Health Policy Tracking Service Issue Brief, Finance: Direct Access* (Oct. 1, 1999).

[120] About one-half of all states have adopted statutes or regulations prohibiting financial incentives that seek to limit medically necessary care. *See* D. Pimley, *States Tell Health Plans that Incentives May Not Limit Medically Necessary Care*, 7 HEALTH L. REP. (BNA) No. 40, at 1581 (Oct. 8, 1998).

[121] *See, e.g.*, Consent Order between Commission of the Texas State Department of Insurance and Methodist Health Plan, Inc. (Aug. 19, 1998). Though not applicable to private health plans unless they contract with CMS as a Medicare+Choice organization, CMS has promulgated regulations imposing restrictions regarding the type and level of risk, which physicians and physician groups may assume. *See* 42 C.F.R. § 417.

[122] As of July 2008, 44 states and D.C. had adopted managed-care reform legislation that includes a provision for external reviews. *See* American Association of Health Plans, *State External Review Laws and Regulations* (July 20, 1999) (Available from AAHP). *See also* National Conference of State Legislatures, *Health Policy Tracking Service Issue Brief, Finance: Consumer Grievance Procedures: Internal and Independent Appeals* (Oct. 1, 1999).

At least one court has held that mandating external reviews is preempted by ERISA. This court reasoned that such a law did not constitute insurance regulation, because it did not meet the third McCarran-Ferguson factor.[123]

(m) Provider Selection and Deselection. These laws require HMOs to provide certain providers with a minimum amount of notice prior to termination of the provider's HMO-participation contract without cause. In addition, they often give providers certain appeal rights, and prohibit HMOs from taking action against providers for advocating on behalf of their patients. Finally, most states require HMOs to maintain written credentialing criteria; some states require HMOs to disseminate a copy of the HMO's credentialing criteria to providers upon request.

(n) Indemnification Provisions. Nearly half the states have enacted laws prohibiting HMOs from including clauses in their provider contracts requiring the provider to indemnify the HMO for the losses arising out of the HMO's coverage determinations.[124]

(o) Utilization-Management Laws. HMOs are required to maintain written medical-management policies that meet certain requirements in connection with the operation of these utilization or medical-management programs. For instance, HMO laws often require HMOs to make and communicate utilization-management decisions within specific timeframes, depending on whether the recommended treatment is emergent, urgent, or routine. HMO laws also may require that any person who makes medical-management decisions meet certain qualifications (e.g., licensure as a physician under the laws of that state). Finally, HMOs may be prohibited from retroactively denying coverage for a treatment that the HMO preauthorized through its utilization-review process. In other words, if a provider or an enrollee obtains preauthorization from an HMO before providing or obtaining a service, then that HMO cannot later deny coverage for the authorized service. Exceptions apply in cases of fraud or a loss of health-plan coverage.[125]

Though not yet typical, a handful of states have enacted laws that specifically allow enrollees to sue HMOs for medical malpractice, or that remove barriers which would have prohibited enrollees from suing.[126] One court to consider an ERISA-preemption challenge to this type of legislation held that this provision was not preempted because it did not "relate to" an ERISA plan under the ERISA objectives analysis annunciated in the *Travelers'* decision.[127] Specifically, quality control of benefits is a field traditionally regulated by the states. Shifting from the traditional state regulation of the quality of health care received to the federal government was not an objective of ERISA.

---

[123] *See Corporate Health Ins. Co. v. Tex. Dept. of Ins.*, 215 F.3d 526 (5th Cir. 2000).

[124] National Conference of State Legislatures, *Health Policy Tracking Service Issue Brief, Finance* (Oct. 1, 1999).

[125] Though not directly related to insurance regulation, it is important to note a trend in the case law for courts to find that utilization management constitutes the practice of medicine. *See, e.g., Murphy v. Bd. of Med. Examiners*, 949 P.2d 530 (Ariz. App. 1997); *Morris v. D. C. Bd. of Med.*, 701 A.2d 364 (D.C. Ct. App. 1997). *But see* Ohio Op. Att'y. Gen. 99-044 (1999), wherein Ohio's attorney general opined that, under existing Ohio statutory law, utilization-review activities do not constitute the practice of medicine. Applying state practice-of-medicine requirements on health plans could have significant impact on plan operations.

[126] *See, e.g.,* S.B. 386, 75th Leg. Tex. § 1 (1997). *See generally* National Conference of State Legislatures, *Health Policy Tracking Service* (Oct. 1, 1999).

[127] *Corporate Health Ins. Co. v. Tex. Dept. of Ins.*, 215 F.3d 526 (5th Cir. 2000).

8.2.4 Point-of-Service Programs

In general, a POS program refers to a plan that combines features of both HMOs and PPOs: participants are subject to a limited provider network, but they may also obtain benefits from non-network providers so long as they first obtain a referral from an in-network PCP. The PCP acts as the enrollee's "point-of-service," hence the name. Enrollees are given financial incentives to stay in-network, such as lower deductibles and coinsurance, or no cost-sharing at all. With out-of-network providers, participants are typically subject to indemnity-type benefits with higher cost-sharing requirements, in some cases including the payment of an additional premium. The covered services under a POS program can be just as broad as those covered in-network, or they may be more limited.

Despite this general framework, the specific meaning of a "point-of-service" program under state law can vary widely. Most commonly, POS programs are adjuncts to an HMO product.[128] In these states, HMOs may (or sometimes *must*) offer a POS option, which is in essence an indemnity option, under their HMO license (with certain restrictions, such as limits on the amount of expenses that may be made under the POS program), typically through a supplemental-benefits rider. Some of these states allow the HMO itself to provide the benefits, while others allow (or in some cases, *require*) the HMO to contract with a licensed insurance company to provide the POS benefits.

In other states, however, POS programs may extend to other managed care plans or health plans besides HMOs, and some state laws specifically *prohibit* POS programs from requiring participants to obtain referrals or prior authorization from the HMO or another provider before visiting out-of-network providers (effectively eliminating the "point-of-service" from the POS programs).[129] Given the wide variation in the definition and requirements of a POS plan under state law, practitioners should be careful to understand the specific context in which the term is being used.

POS programs are sometimes confused with "open access" programs. These programs, however, are fundamentally different. Again, under a POS program, an enrollee *may* obtain certain services from non-participating providers. Under an open-access program, on the other hand, the enrollee typically does not have the option of obtaining services from non-participating providers; rather, the enrollee has "open access" to all of the HMO's participating providers without referral. In other words, the enrollee may obtain covered services from any participating provider without first obtaining a referral from a PCP or the HMO.

---

[128] *See, e.g.*, Ark. Code Ann. § 23-86-404; 215 Ill. Comp. Stat. Ann. 125/4.5-1; Ind. Code Ann. §§ 27-13-1-26, 27-13-13-8, 27-13-4-1; Me. Rev. Stat. tit. 24-A, §§ 4202-A, 4207-A; Md. Code Ann., Health-Gen. § 19-710.2; Mo. Rev. Stat. Ann. § 354.551; Mont. Code Ann. § 33-31-306; Tex. Ins. Code Ann. §§ 843.107, 843.108, 1273.001(4); Utah Code Ann. § 31A-8-408; Va. Code Ann. § 38.2-3407.12.

[129] *See, e.g.*, Alaska Stat. Ann. § 21.86.078 (an HMO's POS option must cover out-of-network services "without obtaining a referral or prior authorization from the [HMO]"); Fla. Stat. Ann. § 641.31 (an HMO's POS rider "may not require a referral from the [HMO] for the point-of-service benefits"); Iowa Code Ann. § 514C.13 (a POS program must be offered under any managed care plan); Minn. Stat. Ann. § 62Q.51(health plans (not just HMOs) must offer a POS option that reimburses non-network providers, "without regard to whether the enrollee was referred to the provider by another provider"); N.J. Stat. Ann. § 26:2S-10(a) (managed care plans must offer a POS option, but out-of-network providers must be covered "without having to obtain a referral or prior authorization from the carrier"); Or. Rev. Stat. Ann. § 743B.220 (a POS must be offered under *any* arrangement in which participants must designate a PCP, not just HMOs). In North Carolina, PPO plans are required to allow participants to visit non-participating providers, except that it is not called a "point-of-service" plan (that name is already taken by HMOs), and participants are *not* required to obtain approval prior to going out-of-network. N.C. Gen. Stat. Ann. §§ 58-50-56(i), 58-67-35(a)(6)(d); 11 N.C. Admin. Code 12.1803 (preferred provider plan requirements).

8.2.5 Third-Party Administrators

A TPA is any independent third party that provides certain administrative services incident to the operation of a health-benefits program by another party. TPAs contract to provide services on behalf of licensed insurers, as well as self-funded benefit programs. Services available on a third-party basis include claims-adjudication services, provider-network development and access (*see* discussion of PPOs in Section 8.2.2), and utilization and medical-management services. These medical-management services may include traditional utilization review, case or disease-management services, or both.

Given the nature of TPAs, their services typically are not provided on a risk basis. In other words, the TPA provides administrative services—but it is in no way *financially* responsible for the cost of care. In certain circumstances, however, the TPA may be eligible for incentive payments for meeting certain performance standards. In addition, a TPA providing utilization-management services may receive a portion of the "savings" achieved through the TPA's utilization-review activities.

More than half the states have laws or regulations governing the activities of TPAs that perform the claims-adjudication function, many of which have adopted the NAIC model legislation or similar legislation.[130] Similarly, a majority of states have enacted statutes or regulations governing utilization review agents, with a smaller number that have adopted the NAIC model act or similar legislation.[131]

In the utilization-review context, these laws often regulate: how quickly the TPA must make and communicate utilization-review decisions; who is qualified to make specific utilization-review decisions (particularly adverse-coverage determinations); and the enrollee-appeal processes that must be in place. Furthermore, in some cases, these laws may specifically prohibit a utilization-review agent from accepting compensation on the basis of the savings achieved.[132] In many cases, these laws specifically provide an exemption for activities provided by, or on behalf of, self-funded ERISA plans.[133] In fact, the NAIC's "Third Party Administrator Statute" specifically provides for such an exception.[134] Most courts that have reviewed the issue of preemption in the context of TPAs have found that these statutes are preempted by ERISA as they relate to services provided on behalf of ERISA self-funded benefits programs.[135] Some courts, however, have reached contrary decisions.[136]

States do not require licensed entities (e.g., HMOs or insurers) to obtain separate licensure under these laws to the extent that they are providing services on behalf of their own enrollees. If, however, they provide services on behalf of another party (e.g., a self-funded benefit program), then they must obtain separate licensure. Likewise, if an HMO delegates any of these functions, such as when an HMO delegates medical management to a provider group as part of a risk agreement, then state laws often require the delegate to obtain and maintain licensure or registration under these TPA laws.

---

[130] *See* National Assoc. of Ins. Comm'rs, *Model Regulation Service* (July 1999).
[131] *Id.*
[132] *See, e.g.*, Mo. Rev. Stat. § 376.1361.9.
[133] *See, e.g.*, Mo. Rev. Stat. § 376.500.6(d).
[134] *See* Nat'l Ass'n of Ins. Comm'rs, *Model Regulation Service* (July 1999).
[135] *See, e.g., Self-Insurance Inst. of Am. v. Gallagher*, 11 Employee Benefits Cas. (BNA) 2162 (N.D. Fla. 1989), *aff'd*, 909 F.2d 1491 (11th Cir. 1990). When a law expressly excludes an ERISA plan from its scope, however, that law may make a "reference to" an ERISA plan which subjects the law to ERISA preemption.
[136] *See Benefax Corp. v. Wright*, 757 F. Supp. 800 (W.D. Ky. 1990).

8.2.6 Provider-Sponsored Networks

Generally speaking, a PSN is an organization comprised of health care providers who have formed together to create a provider network capable of contracting with health plans to provide specific services. Sometimes these networks will be broad (covering the full spectrum of the health care-delivery system); in other cases, they may narrowly cover a particular specialty.

PSNs will enter into a contract with a health plan to provide, or arrange for the provision of, services to the beneficiaries of the plan. Sometimes that health plan is the payer itself (e.g., an insurance company or an HMO); at other times, that health plan is a TPA that is merely contracting with a PSN to obtain access to its network of providers on behalf of a payer. The PSN will provide or arrange for the contracted services through its contracts with participating providers.

The nature of the reimbursement arrangement between the PSN and its participating providers usually depends on the nature of the reimbursement agreed to between the health plan and the PSN. For instance, if the health plan and the PSN have entered into a discounted-fee arrangement, then the "downstream" payment to the PSN-participating provider will be on a discounted fee-for-service basis. If, on the other hand, the health plan and the PSN have entered into some type of risk arrangement, then the downstream reimbursement arrangement between the PSN and the participating provider may range from a discounted fee-for-service arrangement to any or all of the types of risk arrangements discussed in Section 8.2.3.1.[137]

PSNs come in a variety of forms. These include, for instance, physician/hospital organizations (PHOs) and IPAs. PHOs and IPAs are generally comprised of independent competing providers who have formed together to create a network for managed-care contracting. PHOs and IPAs are substantially similar. As the name implies, PHOs include a hospital participant that usually plays some role in the governance structure of the organization. IPAs, on the other hand, typically include physicians or other providers, but do not include (at least at the governance level) a hospital partner. Many IPAs, however, subcontract with hospitals in order to arrange for hospital services for which they have assumed financial risk.

Fully integrated medical groups, in which physicians share in the profits and losses of the practice, can also operate as a PSN. Medical-group model PSNs sometimes will contract only to provide or arrange for services that are within the scope of practice of the medical group. Medical-group PSNs also may contract to arrange, and be at financial risk, for the services provided by others. In those situations, that medical-group PSN often will subcontract with other providers to access those services. In addition, medical groups will sometimes operate a "wrap-around" IPA. Specifically, the medical group will contract on behalf of its own employed physicians, as well as certain individual physicians who have agreed to participate in that medical group's contracting network.

In addition to contracting to provide or arrange for specific services, PSNs often agree to perform certain administrative services. This is particularly common in the context of risk agreements.

---

[137] Although outside the scope of this Chapter, antitrust laws impact the nature of the compensation arrangements entered into between the PSN and the health plan, as well as the downstream arrangements between the PSN and its participating providers in those situations in which the PSN is comprised of independent competing providers.

These administrative services may include claims-payment or medical-management services. In the claims-payment context, HMOs may pay a PSN a specified capitation or percent of premium for specified services, and then require the PSN to pay all claims related to such services. Given concerns over PSN solvency, however, HMOs are becoming less willing to delegate claims payment. Instead, they often will administer capitation or percent-of-premium arrangements through pool/fund arrangements under which the HMO retains the claims-adjudication function.

The scope of state regulation of PSNs as relates to their health-plan contracting activities depends on the nature and extent of the services that the PSN provides (i.e., medical care only or also certain administrative functions), the nature of the compensation arrangement between the health plan and the PSN, and whether the health plan is a licensed entity or an ERISA self-funded benefits program.

State regulation of PSNs has received the most attention in the context of PSN risk-contracting activities. From a purely regulatory perspective, state insurance regulators seek to achieve three primary objectives: protect consumers, regulate risk-bearing entities that perform similar functions similarly (i.e., regulation by function), and adapt to the evolving health insurance market. Through the enactment of laws or the issuance of insurance bulletins, states have adopted different positions on the issue of the regulation of risk-bearing PSNs. These positions vary depending on how the applicable state generally defines the business of insurance and, when the PSN is contracting with a self-insured ERISA plan, how the state interprets the interplay between ERISA's saving clause and deemer clause.

(a) State Approaches to Regulation. The majority of states take the position that, when a PSN contracts on a "full risk" basis directly with an unregulated entity (an entity not regulated by the department of insurance, e.g., an ERISA self-funded benefit plan), that PSN is engaged in the unlicensed business of insurance unless it obtains a license as a HMO or insurer.[138] A PSN accepts "full risk" when it is paid on a pre-paid and capitated basis for all covered medical services.[139] Similarly, most states permit PSNs to accept "downstream" risk, even on a full-risk basis, from a licensed entity such as an HMO or indemnity insurer.

In other words, if the PSN has entered into a full-risk agreement with an HMO, then the PSN is not engaged in the unlicensed business of insurance. When that same PSN, however, enters into the same arrangement with a self-funded ERISA plan, it is engaged in the unauthorized business of insurance.

Interestingly, though this position addresses the consumer-protection objective of insurance regulation described earlier, it does not necessarily achieve the objective of treating like risk-bearing entities performing like services in the same manner. Nor is it necessarily consistent with a "business of insurance" analysis. Specifically, if a PSN that contracts with an ERISA self-funded plan is engaged in the unauthorized business of insurance, then it is not clear why that same entity is *not* engaged in the unauthorized business of insurance when it contracts with a *licensed* entity. Neither the definition of the business of insurance based on the McCarran-Ferguson factors nor the common-law definition of insurance seem to support that distinction.

---

[138] *See* Group Health Ass'n of Am., *Fifty States' Survey of Regulator's Attitudes Toward PHO Licensure* (1995) (the GHAA Survey).
[139] *See* GHAA Survey.

From a regulatory perspective, the distinction between these situations is clear. When a PSN contracts with a licensed entity such as an HMO, the licensed entity (which is ultimately responsible for the cost of care if the PSN fails to perform) is subject to comprehensive state regulatory oversight, including solvency regulation. In addition, the state can impose regulations on the licensed entity that set forth certain PSN contracting requirements designed to provide consumer protections. For instance, the state may enact laws or regulations prohibiting or restricting certain risk arrangements, or requiring the regulated entity to only contract with PSNs that meet certain requirements. Regardless of the merits of this position from a public-policy perspective, it is not entirely clear that this position is consonant with principles of ERISA preemption. ERISA preemption in this context is discussed further in later sections of this Chapter.

Interestingly, although a majority of the states clearly take the position that an unlicensed PSN may not accept full risk from an unregulated entity, a few states have taken the position that PSNs are *not* subject to state regulation when: (i) the full-risk arrangement involves the transfer of risk from an ERISA qualified self-funded plan to a provider; and (ii) the employer ultimately remains at risk for health care costs should the PSN fail to perform.[140] These states reason that, when the employer retains ultimate responsibility for the financial risk if the PSN fails to perform, and when no direct contractual arrangement exists between the beneficiaries and the PSN, the PSN is not engaged in the business of insurance. Only when the PSN has a direct contractual relationship with the beneficiary and assumes ultimate risk is the PSN engaged in the business of insurance. At least one group of employers publicly has taken the position that ERISA preempts such regulation.[141]

Less consistency exists among the states on the issue of whether a PSN can accept some type of partial risk from a self-funded benefit plan without being deemed to be engaged in the unauthorized business of insurance.[142] Some states have adopted a very strict view, taking the position that any acceptance of risk by a PSN from an unregulated entity constitutes the unauthorized business of insurance unless the PSN is appropriately licensed.[143] For instance, in response to a question regarding whether some "degree" of risk assumption may be assumed by a provider (for instance if a provider accepted a capitation payment only for services that provider could personally render) without being engaged in the unauthorized business of insurance, the deputy director of the Ohio Department of Insurance responded that there is no degree of risk assumption that would be considered *de minimis*: "It's like being a little bit pregnant."[144]

Although this position may address regulatory concerns about PSN solvency (and therefore achieve consumer-protection objectives), it appears inconsistent with case-law precedent, including the Supreme Court's *Royal Drug* opinion, which recognizes a service vs. indemnity distinction in what constitutes the business of insurance. Other states have taken a more pragmatic view, indicating

---

[140] *See* Illinois Department of Insurance, Insurance Bulletin, *Provider-Based Market Systems—When to Regulate* (Apr. 1996).
[141] *See Witten, supra*, at 481–84.
[142] *See* GHAA Survey, *supra*.
[143] *See* Memo from David J. Randall, Deputy Director, Ohio Department of Insurance, to John E. Callender, Senior Vice President, Ohio Hospital Association (July 28, 1994).
[144] *Id.*

that whether a partial-risk arrangement involves assumption of insurance risk by the provider would depend on the nature and extent of the risk arrangement.[145]

Just as some states diverge from the majority view that risk-bearing PSNs that contract with ERISA self-funded plans must obtain appropriate state licensure to assume that risk, some states diverge from the majority view that risk-bearing PSNs may freely contract with regulated entities (e.g., insurers and HMOs). For instance, at least two states require even those entities that accept downstream risk from a licensed carrier to obtain some degree of licensure.[146]

In addition, several states, though allowing risk-bearing PSNs to engage in downstream contracting with HMOs without licensure, impose special requirements upon HMOs with respect to their downstream risk arrangements. For instance, some states require HMOs to include mandatory provisions in their contracts with risk-based providers. Other states regulate the type of entity that may accept risk, as well as the type of risk that the PSN may assume.[147]

Finally, although most states have taken the position that PSNs may not accept direct risk from an unlicensed entity, a few states have developed special regulatory schemes under which PSNs may obtain a license to contract directly with employers. If a state does not permit PSNs to engage in direct risk-contracting with unlicensed entities and has not adopted a special regulatory scheme, then PSNs operating in that state must be licensed as an HMO or insurer. States that have adopted special regulatory schemes include Iowa, Minnesota, and Texas.[148]

As will be discussed more fully, NAIC does not favor the creation of special insurance laws applicable to PSNs. Instead, NAIC supports the creation of a uniform licensing scheme that applies to all risk-bearing entities equally, regardless of the "form" of the risk bearer. Of course, even NAIC would recognize an exception for downstream risk arrangements from regulated entities. Though NAIC has not yet produced any model legislation in this area to date, at least one state (Ohio) has adopted a managed- care uniform-licensure act that clearly requires all risk-bearing "health insuring corporations" to obtain licensure.[149] Under this uniform act, all risk-bearing entities would need to obtain a certificate of authority under the application of the same rules, regardless of whether the health-insuring corporation was a PSN or an HMO. The uniform act does not, however, require licensure for entities only accepting downstream risk.

(b) Legal Analysis. No clear judicial pronouncement has been made to date in this area relative to the issue of ERISA preemption. Nor is there general agreement among commentators regarding whether ERISA preempts state attempts to regulate risk-contracting by PSNs with ERISA self-funded

---

[145] *See* GHAA Survey, *supra*.

[146] *See* GHAA Survey, *supra*. Most notable is California's Knox-Keene Act, under which physicians can accept risk for services which they personally provide but cannot accept any risk for other services, such as hospital services. *See also* Rutenberg, *supra*, at 300–04.

[147] For instance, statutes in both Florida and Pennsylvania have contracting requirements that impact the arrangement between the licensed HMO and the PSN. In addition, under Texas law, only an approved nonprofit health corporation may accept full risk from a licensed carrier. *See* Kathrin E. Kudner, *Risk Regulation—Fifty State Survey*, paper presented at the National Health Lawyers Association Managed Care Institute (Dec. 11–13, 1996). *See generally Rutenberg, supra*.

[148] *Id.*

[149] OHIO REV. CODE ANN. § 1751.

employers.[150] One could certainly argue that, because a self-funded insurer cannot be "deemed" to be engaged in the business of insurance, ERISA preempts any state attempt to regulate risk-bearing PSNs that contract with ERISA plans when the ERISA plan retains the ultimate responsibility for payment if the PSN fails to perform. Specifically, the risk-bearing arrangement with the PSN does not convert the employer's self-funded plan into an insured plan because of the following elements: (1) the employer remains ultimately at risk for the specified loss; (2) no direct contractual arrangement exists between the PSN and the plan beneficiaries; and (3) neither the employer nor the PSN markets the plan to the general public. Under similar facts, courts have held that ERISA's deemer clause results in the preemption of certain insurance laws applicable to entities to whom the employer has shifted some degree of risk.[151]

Moreover, to the extent that a PSN accepts only partial risk from a self-funded ERISA employer in the form of a capitation payment for services personally provided by the PSN's providers, it could be argued that such a PSN is not engaged in the business of insurance on the basis of the "service objective" versus "indemnity objective" distinction made by many courts in defining whether an organization is engaged in the business of insurance.[152] Therefore, ERISA would preempt state attempts to regulate such arrangements to the extent that they relate to an ERISA benefit plan.[153]

On the other hand, as was discussed in Section 8.1.2, the exact interplay between the deemer clause and saving clause remains elusive. Moreover, the practical application of the McCarran-Ferguson factors against the backdrop of specific practices is not always clear. It is certainly possible to argue that, focusing solely on the activities of the PSN, full-risk arrangements meet more than one (if not all) of the McCarran-Ferguson factors. If risk-contracting by a PSN constitutes the business of insurance, then regulation of risk-bearing PSNs is saved from preemption. With compelling arguments on both sides, it is very difficult to reconcile ERISA's saving clause and deemer clause in the context of risk-bearing PSNs.

(c) NAIC View. Although the correct application of ERISA preemption in this context may not be entirely clear, NAIC released in 1995 a memorandum from its Health Plan Accountability Working Group of the Regulatory Framework Task Force (HPAWG), in which NAIC took the position that PSNs can accept either full or partial downstream risk from entities licensed by an insurance department.[154] When a PSN, however, assumes full or partial financial risk for the delivery of health care services from an unlicensed entity, including an ERISA employer, that PSN is engaged in the unauthorized business of insurance.[155] In reaching this conclusion, NAIC pointed to what has, in essence, become the accepted common-law definition of insurance. In applying the common law definition, however, the NAIC made no reference to the business vs. indemnity distinction often made by the courts.

---

[150] Some commentators argue that ERISA would clearly preempt this type of regulation, while others are equally as adamant that ERISA would not preempt such regulation.
[151] *Id.*
[152] *See Group Life and Health Ins. Co. v. Royal Drug Co.*, 440 U.S. 205 (1979).
[153] *See* discussion regarding the "relate to" test as established by the Travelers' case and its progeny in Section 8.1.2.
[154] *See* Memorandum from Kenney Shipley, Chair, NAIC Health Plan Accountability Working Group, to the Insurance Commissioners, Directors and Superintendents (Aug. 10, 1995) (NAIC Memorandum).
[155] *Id.*

This memorandum was issued as part of NAIC's Consolidated Licensure of Entities Assuming Risk (CLEAR) initiative. Pursuant to the CLEAR initiative the HPAWG was charged with considering the development of a single model health care-licensing act for all "health carriers" (the CLEAR Model Act). The purpose of this CLEAR Model Act is to foster the creation of a uniform-licensing scheme that would apply to all risk-bearing entities equally, regardless of the "form" of the risk-bearer. According to NAIC, this would promote a "more competitive market place by ensuring that entities that perform the same or similar functions are subject to a level regulatory playing field." In 1997, in anticipation that the states would adopt the CLEAR Model Act, NAIC issued its white paper on the regulation of risk-bearing entities in order to provide guidance to the states regarding the analysis of this issue. NAIC has yet to release its CLEAR Model Act.[156]

(d) PSOs that Contract as M+C Organizations. Although the issue of ERISA preemption with respect to state regulation of PSNs is not clear, Congress has created a limited exception from state licensure requirements under certain circumstances for provider-sponsored organizations or (PSOs) contracting with CMS under the M+C program. Specifically, under the BBA, PSOs may contract to become M+C organizations. Although such organizations are required to be licensed to accept risk under applicable state law, the BBA provided a special exception for PSOs; a PSO seeking to become an M+C organization can apply to the Secretary of the Department of Health and Human Services (DHHS) for a waiver of the state licensing requirements.[157] In order to obtain such a waiver, the PSO must have applied no later than November 1, 2002. The DHHS Secretary may grant a waiver if it determines that any of the following criteria are met:

1. The state failed to complete action on a PSO's licensing action within 90 days;
2. The state denied the PSO licensure based on discriminatory treatment; or
3. The state denied the PSO's licensing application on the basis of the organization's failure to meet the state's solvency requirements (assuming that they are different from the M+C solvency requirements).

Waivers are issued for non-renewable 36-month periods.[158] As a result of the BBA, a PSN that otherwise meets the qualifications of a PSO may contract with the M+C program on a risk basis, even if not licensed under state law, if it obtains a waiver.

8.2.7 Blue Cross and Blue Shield (BC/BS) Plans

What we think of today as BC/BS Plans actually have their roots as separate organizations. Blue Cross was originally formed as a prepaid hospital plan. Blue Cross traces its origins to 1929, when Justin Ford Kimball, then working for Baylor University, designed a plan to provide schoolteachers with coverage for a specified number of hospital days at a set price.[159] This concept began to flourish, and other Blue Cross plans emerged. Eventually, these independent prepaid hospital plans formed

---

[156] The NAIC did issue its White Paper, however, to provide guidance to the states regarding the analysis of this issue in anticipation that the states would adopt the CLEAR Model Act.
[157] *See* Balanced Budget Act of 1997, Pub. L. No. 105-33, 111 Stat. 312, § 1855(a) (1997).
[158] *Id.*
[159] *See generally,* Blue Cross and Blue Shield Association, *The Blue Cross Blue Shield System, available at* https://www.bcbs.com/about-us/blue-cross-blue-shield-system.

a national organization that became known as the Blue Cross Association. Plans that met certain guidelines were allowed to use the Blue Cross symbol.

At around the same time, prepaid medical plans began to surface. These early plans were usually designed by employers (typically in the lumber and mining industries) who provided medical services for their employees by entering into prepaid arrangements with physicians who agreed to provide the employees with specified medical service for a fixed fee. From these roots, the first modern-day Blue Shield plan emerged when California Physicians' Service, touted as the nation's first medical-service prepayment plan, was incorporated in 1939. This plan enrolled low-income subscribers who paid a fixed monthly fee in exchange for coverage of physician office visits.[160] A group of independent Blue Shield plans formed what eventually became known as the National Association of Blue Shield Plans in 1948. Like the system adopted by Blue Cross plans, those prepaid medical plans that met certain conditions were allowed to use the Blue Shield symbol.

Though Blue Cross plans and Blue Shield plans have separate origins, they have a common core: Both were developed as nonprofit local organizations, and both were largely formed in order to provide an alternative to government- and commercial- based indemnity health insurance, particularly for the less-affluent members of society. Even with this common core, the Blue Cross Association and the National Association of Blue Shield Plans remained independent for many years. It was not until 1982 that the two organizations formally merged, forming the Blue Cross and Blue Shield Association. Today, the Blue Cross and Blue Shield Association licenses its trademarks and names to independent plans that meet and maintain specified standards. One of the most notable of these standards, that plans maintain nonprofit status, was dropped in 1994.[161]

Like early HMO regulation, state laws regulating BC/BS plans reflected their unique character as local, nonprofit prepaid plans that directly furnish or provide reimbursement for certain medical services to "members." Though the laws governing these plans are highly state-specific, most have special legislative schemes that limit licensure to nonprofit corporations, and provide for exemption from certain taxes (e.g., state premium tax) in recognition of their nonprofit, service-oriented, status. Like insurers and HMOs, however, BC/BS plans are subject to financial regulation in the form of capital and reserve requirements, and are also subject to financial filings and examinations.

As indicated, the traditional regulation of BC/BS plans involves a regulatory scheme tailored to the business of a local, nonprofit prepaid plan. Nevertheless, given the changes in the health care market over the last fifteen years and in order to remain competitive, most BC/BS plans today operate a variety of products and programs, many of which involve activities beyond those authorized under

---

[160] *See* Robert Cunningham, III & Robert Cunningham, Jr., *The Blues: A History of the Blue Cross and Blue Shield System* 45–46 (Northern Univ. Press 1997).

[161] Rosemary A. Stevens, Foreword to Cunningham & Cunningham. The topic of nonprofit conversion is outside the scope of this Chapter. It is important to note, however, that as the market began to change, many BC/BS plans began to "convert" from nonprofit to for-profit organizations. Although the term "convert" has no precise definition, a conversion from nonprofit to for-profit status is generally considered to have occurred when the nonprofit, through one or more transactions, transfers all, or a substantial portion, of its assets to a for-profit entity. A variety of factors are cited as encouraging this trend. The most commonly cited factor is the need to raise capital in order to build the infrastructure necessary to maintain a competitive managed-care product. Given the exemption from state premium tax generally enjoyed by BC/BS plans, states often challenge these conversions under cy pres doctrine, and on the basis that these conversions were not carried out in accordance with applicable statutory authority.

these traditional licensure statutes. These products include indemnity products, PPO programs, and HMO products, as well as administrative-services arrangements whereby the BC/BS plan serves as a TPA for a licensed insurer or self-funded ERISA employer. When offering these products, BC/BS plans operate under the licensure scheme applicable to the product being offered. For this reason, most BC/BS plans hold multiple licenses (e.g., an HMO license, an insurance license, and a license as a health-services corporation) either directly or through one or more affiliates.

8.3 The Federal Regulation of Private Health Care Plans

8.3.1 Background

Congress enacted ERISA in 1974[162] in response to growing concerns that employer sponsors of welfare and pension programs were not managing plan assets appropriately, thereby threatening the availability of those assets for plan beneficiaries when needed.[163] At the same time, however, Congress wanted to preserve the voluntary growth of employer-sponsored benefit plans.[164] In order to provide the beneficiaries of these employer-sponsored programs with the desired protection, while simultaneously continuing to motivate employers to voluntarily offer benefit programs, ERISA created a federal statutory scheme with a broad federal preemption provision, applicable to all employers (except certain governmental employers and church plans) offering welfare and pension plans.

This statutory scheme established standards of conduct, including reporting and disclosure mandates,[165] and imposed fiduciary responsibilities on plan administrators.[166] It also created participation and vesting requirements,[167] as well as funding standards.[168] Finally, it created criminal sanctions for certain violations, and established a comprehensive civil-enforcement scheme.[169]

At the outset, ERISA did not require that plan sponsors offer specific benefits, nor did it dictate the substance of any benefit plan.[170] It simply provided a structure regarding how such plans operate, providing guidance on such matters as claims procedures and fiduciary responsibility. However, Congress steadily and with greater boldness increased its imprint on the substantive operation of private health care plans. The march toward federal regulation reached its high water mark with the 2010 enactment of the Patient Protection and Affordable Care Act (ACA). As explained below, while the ACA represents a radical escalation of the federal regulation of private health care, in the broader view it can be seen as a continuation of a process begun with the enactment of ERISA.

---

[162] 29 U.S.C. §§ 1001–1461.
[163] 29 U.S.C. § 1001(a). *See also Shaw v. Delta Airlines, Inc.*, 463 U.S. 85 (1983). *See generally* Margaret G. Farrell, *ERISA Preemption and Regulation of Managed Healthcare: The Case for Managed Federalism*, 23 AM. J.L. & MED. 251 (1997); Brummond, *Federal Preemption of State Insurance Regulation Under ERISA*, 62 IOWA L. REV. 57 (1976).
[164] Farrell, *supra*, at 251.
[165] 29 U.S.C. §§ 1002–1031.
[166] 29 U.S.C. §§ 1101–1114.
[167] 29 U.S.C. §§ 1051–1061.
[168] 29 U.S.C. §§ 1081–1086.
[169] 29 U.S.C. §§ 1131–1145.
[170] *Shaw v. Delta Airlines, Inc.*, 463 U.S. 85, 91 (1983).

8.3.2 ERISA

8.3.2.1 COBRA

Signed into law by President Reagan on April 7, 1986, COBRA amended ERISA, the Internal Revenue Code, and the Public Health Service Act (PHSA). This act requires that, under certain conditions, a group health plan must provide former participants and their dependents the opportunity to elect and pay for extended health-insurance coverage after an event that would cause a loss of coverage.[171] COBRA applies to group health plans provided by public and private employers other than: (1) churches; (2) governmental entities of the United States; (3) state and local government agencies not receiving funds from the Public Health Service Act; and (4) employers whose total number of employees is fewer than 20 on a "typical business day" in the prior calendar year.[172]

Under COBRA, a qualified beneficiary who would otherwise lose his or her coverage must be allowed to elect continuation coverage for a certain period of time upon the occurrence of a qualifying event.[173] A qualified beneficiary is any individual covered by a group health plan on the day before a qualifying event and includes the employee's spouse and dependent children.[174]

The type of qualifying event determines the requisite length of the extended-coverage period. If the qualifying event is the covered employee's termination or reduction in hours, then the required extended coverage period is eighteen months from the event.[175] In most other instances, the extended coverage period is 36 months.[176] COBRA coverage may be terminated before the otherwise applicable coverage period if:

- the employer terminates any group health coverage to any employee;
- coverage ceases because of a failure to make a timely health-insurance premium payment;
- the qualified beneficiary obtains group health insurance (as long as the new health plan does not exclude or limit coverage on the basis of any preexisting condition of the beneficiary); or
- a beneficiary becomes eligible for Medicare; or legal separation between the spouse and employee terminates the coverage.[177]

Plan-provided continuation coverage must be identical to the plan's coverage for similarly situated beneficiaries who have not experienced a qualifying event.[178] The employee or beneficiary may be required to pay a premium not exceeding 102% of the otherwise-applicable plan premium.[179]

---

[171] 29 U.S.C. § 1161(a); John K. DiMugno & Paul E.B. Glad, *Group Health, Disability and Life Insurance*, CAL. LAW INS. HANDBOOK § 36.05. COBRA provisions are contained in the Internal Revenue Code and ERISA. For simplicity, citations to ERISA will be used.
[172] 29 U.S.C. § 1161(b).
[173] 29 U.S.C. § 1161(a).
[174] 29 U.S.C. § 1162. In certain circumstances, a retired employee, retired employee's spouse, and dependent children may also be included as qualified beneficiaries.
[175] 29 U.S.C. § 1162(2)(A).
[176] 29 U.S.C. § 1162(2)(A)(ii)–(iv).
[177] 29 U.S.C. § 1162(2)(C)(D).
[178] 29 U.S.C. § 1162(1).
[179] 29 U.S.C. § 1162(3)(A). The beneficiary may choose to pay the premiums in monthly installments. 29 U.S.C. § 1162(3)(B).

At the end of the 18- or 36-month period, the employer must offer conversion to an individual policy if the group plan includes a conversion privilege.[180]

Qualifying events for an employee include:

- voluntary termination;
- involuntary termination (except for gross misconduct);
- reduction in hours rendering the employee ineligible under the insurance plan;
- a covered employee's entitlement to benefits under Title XVIII of the Social Security Act; or
- a proceeding in a case under Title XVI of that act beginning on or after July 1, 1986, with respect to the employer from whose employment the covered employee retired at any time.[181]

The principal qualifying events that allow a qualified *beneficiary* who is a spouse or dependent to elect continuation coverage are: (1) a covered employee's death; (2) a covered employee's termination (other than for gross misconduct), or reduction in hours; (3) divorce or legal separation from a covered employee; (4) a covered employee's becoming entitled to Social Security benefits; or (5) a dependent child's ceasing to be a dependent under the plan.[182] Upon the occurrence of a qualifying event, the plan must give the qualifying beneficiary at least 60 days in which to elect continuation coverage.[183]

COBRA requires that qualified beneficiaries be provided with two notices.[184] The first notice must be sent to employees and their spouses when COBRA coverage first becomes effective, or when new employees and their spouses first become eligible to participate in the plan.[185] The second notice must be sent upon the occurrence of a qualifying event.[186] In the event of death, termination of employment, or entitlement to benefits under the Social Security Act, the employer must notify the plan administrator within 30 days of the date of such event.[187] In case of a divorce or legal separation from a covered employee, or the reaching of independent status of a covered employee's child, the employee or qualified beneficiary must notify the plan administrator within 60 days.[188] At that time, the plan administrator must, within 14 days, inform each qualified beneficiary of his or her right to elect continuation coverage.[189] The plan administrator must provide notification, regardless of whether the employee is aware of her rights to continuation coverage under COBRA.

COBRA governs employer-sponsored medical expense plans, HMO options, dental plans, vision-care plans, prescription-drug plans, and often includes employee assistance plans.[190] In the

---

[180] 29 U.S.C. § 1162(5); Employee Benefit Research Institute, *Fundamentals of Employee Benefit Programs* 218 (1997).
[181] 29 U.S.C. § 1163.
[182] *Id.*
[183] 29 U.S.C. § 1165.
[184] 29 U.S.C. § 1166.
[185] 29 U.S.C. § 1166(a)(1).
[186] 29 U.S.C. § 1166.
[187] 29 U.S.C. § 1166(a)(2).
[188] 29 U.S.C. § 1166(a)(3).
[189] 29 U.S.C. § 1166(c).
[190] 29 U.S.C. § 1161.

event of the failure of a state, political subdivision, or agency to comply with the COBRA requirements, an individual may enforce her COBRA rights through ERISA.[191]

8.3.2.2 Mental Health Parity and Addiction Equality Act

Although equality between mental-health coverage and other types of medical coverage had long been the subject of much discussion, the concept of parity in insurance plans did not become nationally significant until the 1990's.[192] On September 26, 1996, President Clinton signed into law the Mental Health Parity Act of 1996.[193] The Mental Health Parity and Addiction Equality Act of 2008 (MHPAEA), signed by President Bush, supplements the prior version by extending the Act to substance use disorders.

Specifically, the MHPAEA requires group health plans or health insurance issuers to make certain that the financial requirements and treatment limitations applicable to mental health or substance use disorder benefits are no more restrictive than the requirements or limitations on medical or surgical benefits.[194] Although the MHPAEA originally only applied to plans sponsored by employers with more than 50 employees and insurers offering coverage for such plans,[195] the ACA extended its application to small plans, individual health insurance, coverage under Medicaid-managed programs, CHIP, and Medicaid alternative benefit plans. The mandate only exempts plans in which the cost of compliance would exceed 1 percent[196] and "grandfathered" small group plans in existence prior to March 23, 2010.[197]

The MHPAEA does not obligate any plan to alter its coverage to include mental health benefits.[198] But the ACA includes mental health and substance abuse treatments as an essential health benefit that must be covered.[199]

The MHPAEA applies regardless of whether plans administer their mental health benefits along with or separately from their medical and surgical benefits. For this reason, a plan cannot avoid mental health parity by offering separate coverage for both benefits.[200] If a group health plan offers two or more benefit package options under the plan, however, the requirements of the MHPAEA apply separately to each option.[201]

On November 13, 2013, final MHPAEA regulations were published and apply to group health plans and health insurance issuers for plan years beginning on or after July 1, 2014.[202]

---

[191] 29 U.S.C. § 1132.
[192] Christopher Aaron Jones, Special Project: Current Issues in Mental Health Care: Legislative "Subterfuge"?: Failing to Insure Persons with Mental Illness Under the Mental Health Parity Act and the Americans With Disabilities Act, 50 VAND. L. REV. 753, 754 (1997).
[193] Id. at 757.
[194] 29 U.S.C. § 1185a.
[195] 29 U.S.C. § 1185a(c).
[196] Id. As to the exemption for plans where the application of the act results in an increase in the cost under the plan of at least 1%, the MHPAEA does not discuss what costs must be considered, or how the exemption is to be administered.
[197] 29 C.F.R. § 2590.715–1251.
[198] 29 U.S.C. § 1185a(b)(1).
[199] 45 C.F.R. § 156.110.
[200] Id.
[201] 29 U.S.C. § 1185a(d). For instance, if a plan offers employees a choice between indemnity insurance and an HMO, then mental-health benefits within each option need match only the medical and surgical benefits of that same option. Id.
[202] 78 Fed. Reg. 68240 (Nov. 13, 2013.

Many states have adopted their own parity laws requiring more favorable treatment of mental health benefits under health insurance coverage offered by issuers. Such state laws are not preempted by the MHPAEA provisions. This is due to the fact that, although group health plans must comply with the federal parity requirements, *issuers* are subject to state law.

8.3.2.3 Pre-Existing Condition Rule

Signed into law on August 21, 1996, one purpose of HIPAA was to increase the portability of health coverage by limiting group health plans' use of preexisting-condition exclusions.[203] A "preexisting condition exclusion" is defined as a limitation or exclusion of benefits relating to a condition based on the fact that the condition was present before the date of enrollment for such coverage whether any medical advice, diagnosis, care, or treatment was recommended or received before such date.[204]

For plan years beginning on or after January 1, 2014, health plans and health insurance issuers cannot impose any preexisting condition exclusions.[205]

A "preexisting condition exclusion" is defined as a limitation or exclusion placed on the benefits a plan will provide for costs with respect to a participant or beneficiary's physical or mental condition that existed before the date of enrollment in the plan by the participant or beneficiary, regardless of whether the participant or beneficiary received any medical advice, diagnosis, care, or treatment before the enrollment date. Group health plans may apply preexisting condition clauses if the HIPAA requirements are met, the exclusions apply uniformly to all similarly situated individuals, and they are not directed at individual participants and beneficiaries.

Under HIPAA, a group health plan may only impose a preexisting-condition exclusion if:

- the exclusion concerns a physical or mental condition, regardless of its cause, for which medical advice, diagnosis, care, or treatment has been suggested and received within the six-month period ending on the enrollment date;
- the exclusion applies for no longer than 12 months after the enrollment date (or 18 months, in the case of a late enrollee);
- and the period of any exclusion is reduced by the aggregate periods of creditable coverage applicable to the participant or beneficiary as of the date of enrollment.[206]

If, for example, a patient has had diagnosed scoliosis for years, but has not sought treatment in the six months prior to enrolling in a group health plan, then the plan cannot exclude coverage for scoliosis treatment. Furthermore, even in situations where the preexisting-condition exclusion is applied, payment cannot be denied for conditions unrelated to the preexisting condition. Continuing with the previous example, even in the event that the patient diagnosed with scoliosis had received treatment in the six months preceding enrollment (and therefore scoliosis was an

---

[203] 29 U.S.C. § 1181.
[204] 29 U.S.C. § 1181(b).
[205] 45 C.F.R. § 147.108.
[206] 29 U.S.C. § 1181(a), (c).

excludable preexisting condition), a myocardial infarction she experiences on the first day of her new plan's coverage may not be excluded, because it is unrelated to the scoliosis.

As stated, plans must reduce any preexisting-condition exclusion period by the length of prior continuous coverage.[207] This is known as "creditable coverage."[208] If no break in coverage occurs, an insurer may not refuse to provide coverage to a person with a preexisting condition. Waiting periods required by plans prior to commencing coverage do not qualify as breaks in coverage. If there is a break in coverage of 63 days or more, however, then a health plan may exclude a preexisting condition.[209] Employers or plan sponsors must provide certification of prior coverage when (1) an individual loses coverage or becomes covered under COBRA, (2) COBRA coverage ends, or (3) an individual requests such certification (provided the request is made no more than 24 months after coverage ceases).[210] The effect of the creditable-coverage requirement is that individuals with existing medical conditions may now change jobs without fear that they will lose their insurance coverage.

Group plans also cannot exclude from coverage newborns or adopted children under the age of 18, as long as the child is enrolled within 30 days after birth, adoption, or placement for adoption.[211] This exception does not apply to an individual after the end of the first 63-day period, during all of which the individual was not covered under any creditable coverage.[212] In addition, HIPAA prohibits the imposition of a preexisting-condition exclusion based on pregnancy.[213] This prohibition applies regardless of the period of creditable coverage.[214]

8.3.2.4 HIPAA's Privacy Rules

HIPAA required, in the event that Congress failed to enact a privacy law within 36 months of its effective date, that DHHS promulgate regulations to serve as minimum privacy standards.[215] As Congress did not enact a privacy law, DHHS carried out its assignment with the publication of proposed privacy standards on November 3, 1999,[216] and final privacy standards on December 28, 2001.[217]

The final regulations set forth an extensive and highly complex set of rules that will be difficult for health care plans to follow. In essence, these rules provide that individually identifiable health data shall be held in confidence unless a specific exemption applies. Incident to the basic premise, handlers of individually identifiable health data are subject to strict behavioral guidelines governing the confidential treatment of data. Also, individuals have certain rights to access their medical records.

---

[207] 29 U.S.C. § 1181(c); Auxillium West, The Health Insurance Portability and Accountability Act (HIPAA) of 1996, available online at www.auxillium.com/hipaa.shtml.
[208] 29 U.S.C. § 1181(c); Anne Maltz, *Insurance Law: Understanding the ABCs*, 673 P.L.I. Litig. 359, 376 (2002).
[209] 29 U.S.C. § 1181(c).
[210] 29 U.S.C. § 1181(e).
[211] 29 U.S.C. § 1181(d)(1)–(2).
[212] 29 U.S.C. § 1181(d)(4).
[213] 29 U.S.C. § 1181(d)(3).
[214] 29 U.S.C. § 1181(d)(4).
[215] Health Insurance Portability and Accountability Act, Pub. L. No. 104-191, 821 1996.
[216] 64 Fed. Reg. 59917.
[217] 45 C.F.R. 160, as amended by 65 Fed. Reg. 82461 (2000); 45 C.F.R. 164; 65 Fed. Reg. 82461 (2000).

As general principle, group health plans, along with other Covered Entities under HIPAA (e.g., health care clearinghouses and health care providers) may not use or disclose protected health information without first receiving the consent of the identified individual.[218] The regulations provide for several exceptions to the rule, which in large part are designed to accommodate the public-policy goals of law enforcement, public safety, emergency needs, and patient care.[219] Data sharing initiatives are discussed in Chapter 14.

8.3.2.5 Qualified Medical Child Support Orders

In order to help children of divorced parents receive health care coverage, medical child support was established under Part D, Title IV of the Social Security Act.[220] This provision requires state agencies administering child support to include medical coverage as part of a child-support order whenever health care coverage is reasonably available to the noncustodial parent.[221] When such support is granted, the notice given to the applicable health plan must conform to the Qualified Medical Child Support Order (QMCSO) requirements of ERISA.[222] If a state court's notice conforms to QMCSO, then the group health plan is required to provide health benefits to the participant's child (assuming benefits are generally available to children).[223] In addition, the QMCSO is excepted from the ERISA supersedure clause, and the state may bring a civil action to enforce compliance.[224]

A QMCSO recognizes the right of a group health-plan participant's child to receive benefits for which the participant is eligible.[225] To qualify as a QMCSO, an order must meet the following requirements:

1. it must be a judgment, decree, or order made by a court of competent jurisdiction or issued through an administrative process, which (i) provides for health benefit coverage for a child, pursuant to a state domestic-relations law, and relates to benefits under such plans or (ii) is pursuant to a law that relates to the medical child support in section 1908 of the Social Security Act;[226]

2. it must clearly specify the name and last known mailing address of the participant and each alternate recipient;[227]

3. it must describe the type of coverage (or how such coverage will be determined) for each alternate recipient;[228]

---

[218] 45 C.F.R. § 164.500.
[219] 45 C.F.R. §§ 506 *et seq.*
[220] 42 U.S.C. § 652(f).
[221] *Id.*
[222] 29 U.S.C. § 1169.
[223] 29 U.S.C. § 1144(a); 29 U.S.C. § 1144(8) (exception granted to QMCSOs).
[224] 29 U.S.C. § 1132(a)(7).
[225] 29 U.S.C. § 1169(a)(2)(A) and (C).
[226] 29 U.S.C. § 1169(a)(2)(B).
[227] 29 U.S.C. § 1169(a)(3)(A) (under some circumstances, the name and mailing address of an official of a state may be substituted for that of each alternate recipient). An alternate recipient is a child of a participant who is recognized as having a right to enrollment in a group health plan under a QMCSO. *Id.*
[228] 29 U.S.C. § 1169(a)(3)(B).

4. it must define the period to which the order applies;[229] and
5. it must not require the plan to provide any options or benefits that the plan does not normally provide, unless otherwise required by law.[230]

When a group health plan's administrator receives a child support order, she is to notify the participant and the alternate recipients that such notice has been received.[231] The plan administrator shall then follow the plan's established procedures for determining whether the order is a QMCSO.[232] After the administrator has made a determination, she must notify the participant and each alternate recipient of her determination.[233] When determining whether the alternate recipient is eligible for coverage under the group health plan, the administrator must not consider whether the child is eligible for state medical assistance (e.g., Medicaid).[234]

The Child Support Performance and Incentive Act of 1998 (CSPIA) provided for the promulgation of a National Medical Support Notice to be issued by states enabling them to enforce the health coverage provisions of child support orders.[235] Under the direction of CSPIA, the Secretary of DHHS and the Secretary of Labor jointly issued regulations providing for National Medical Support Notice.[236] Once such notice has been received by a group health plan and has been determined to be a QMCSO, the plan administrator must, within 40 business days, notify the state agency that issued the QMCSO as to whether the child is covered by the plan and, if so, the effective date of such coverage.[237] During this same timeframe, the plan administrator must notify the custodial parent of coverage availability, in addition to any additional steps that must be taken for coverage to be effectuated.[238]

Once coverage begins, any payment of benefits or medical reimbursements under the plan must be distributed to the alternate recipient, the custodial parent, or legal guardian of such alternate recipient.[239] This payment provision is intended to ensure that the party paying for the medical expenses receives the benefit of the group plan coverage, thus alleviating the problem of a custodial parent

---

[229] 29 U.S.C. § 1169(a)(3)(C).
[230] 29 U.S.C. § 1169(a)(4). The order may require the plan to provide benefits or options it would not otherwise provide to the extent required to meet the guidelines relating to medical child support in § 1908 of the Social Security Act. *See id. See also* 42 U.S.C. § 1369g-1.
[231] 29 U.S.C. § 1169(a)(5)(A).
[232] 29 U.S.C. § 1169(a)(5)(A)(ii) and (B). The group health plans' procedures for determining whether a medical child-support order qualifies as a QMCSO must meet the following requirements: (i) it must be in writing; (ii) it must provide for the notification of each person the order grants benefits; and (iii) it must permit an alternate recipient to designate a representative. 29 U.S.C. § 1169(a)(5)(B)(i)–(iii).
[233] 29 U.S.C. § 1169(a)(5)(A)(ii).
[234] 29 U.S.C. § 1169(b)(2).
[235] 29 U.S.C. § 1169(a)(5)(C), as added by the Child Support Performance and Incentive Act of 1998, Pub. L. No. 105-200 § 401(b).
[236] 29 U.S.C. § 1169(a)(5)(C)(i), as added by the Child Support Performance and Incentive Act of 1998, Pub. L. No. 105-200 § 401(b)(5). *See also* 29 C.F.R. 2590.609-2.
[237] 29 U.S.C. § 1169(a)(5)(C)(ii).
[238] *Id.* There may be additional forms that the custodial parent will have to fill out for the child to receive coverage under the group health plan. A QMCSO, however, does not require the group health plan to offer benefits or eligibility under the plan that are generally not provided under the plan. *See* 29 U.S.C. § 1169(a)(5)(C)(iii).
[239] 29 U.S.C. § 1169(a)(8). Payment to a state official whose name has been substituted for that of the alternate participant's will satisfy the required payment. *See* 29 U.S.C. § 1169(a)(9). Such payment for benefits must be made in accordance with any assignment of rights made on behalf of the participant, or beneficiary of such participant, in accordance

having to request reimbursement from their former spouse, or of a legal guardian having to request reimbursement from the child's natural parents.

8.3.2.6 Coverage for Adopted Children

If a group health plan provides coverage for the dependent children of its participants or beneficiaries, then it must also provide benefits for children placed for adoption with such participants or beneficiaries.[240] These benefits must be granted on the same terms as any natural child of the participant or beneficiary.[241] In addition, the benefits granted on behalf of an adopted child must not be restricted on the basis of a preexisting condition.[242]

8.3.2.7 Coverage for Pediatric Vaccines

Section 609(e) of ERISA bars group health plans from reducing their coverage for the cost of pediatric vaccines below the coverage provided as of May 1, 1993.[243] The COBRA continuation-coverage excise-tax penalty applies in the event that a group health plan fails to follow the pediatric-vaccine coverage requirement.[244] Of course, most group health plans today are required to cover immunizations and vaccines for children from birth to age 18 without cost-sharing, as part of the ACA's coverage of preventive health services.

8.3.2.8 Maternity Protection

On September 26, 1996, Congress enacted the Newborns' and Mothers' Health Protection Act of 1996 (NMHPA).[245] The NMHPA amended ERISA and the Public Health Service Act. This act imposes certain requirements on health plans with respect to coverage of newborns and mothers.[246] The NMHPA mandates that all health plans be designed to include payment for in-hospital coverage for at least 48 hours following a normal vaginal delivery, and 96 hours following a delivery by caesarian section.[247] Discharge from the hospital is permitted sooner *only* when the decision is made by an attending provider, in consultation with the mother.[248] This law generally applies to persons enrolled in group health plans and to persons who have individual health care coverage alike.[249]

---

with a state plan for medical assistance under title XIX of the Social Security Act. 29 U.S.C. § 1169(b)(1). In this manner, the state may acquire the right of payment with respect to such participant. 29 U.S.C. § 1169(b)(3).

[240] 29 U.S.C. § 1169(c)(1). To qualify, the child must be younger than 18 on the date of adoption or placement for adoption. 29 U.S.C. § 1169(c)(3). A "placement for adoption" occurs when the person with whom the child is being placed assumes and retains the legal obligation for total or partial support of the child in anticipation of adoption. *See id.*
[241] *See id.*
[242] 29 U.S.C. § 1169(c)(2).
[243] 29 U.S.C. § 1169(e).
[244] INTERNAL REVENUE CODE § 4980B(f).
[245] Utah Law Review Society, *Insurance Law Amendments*, 2000 UTAH L. REV. 964, 968 (2000) (ULRS).
[246] Michael J. Canan & William D. Mitchell, *Other Laws Concerning Health Benefits, Employee Fringe and Welfare Benefit Plans* § 10.4 (West).
[247] 29 U.S.C. § 1185; Ann H. Nevers, *ERISA Right to Sue: An Rx for Health Care that Places Forum Over Substantive Consumer Rights*, 31 NEW MEXICO L. REV. 493, 495 (2001). These regulations specify that a hospital stay begins at the time of delivery if the delivery occurred in a hospital, or at the time of admission if the mother or newborn was admitted after a delivery occurring outside the hospital.
[248] 29 U.S.C. § 1185(a)(2).
[249] 29 U.S.C. § 1185(a)(1).

The NMHPA allows plans to impose copayments and deductibles for hospital stays in connection with childbirth.[250] Despite this, a group health plan may not provide incentives to mothers to stay less than the required minimum time, nor may they deny or restrict plan coverage or benefits of any portion of the required minimum hospital stay as an inducement to circumvent the act's requirements.[251] Furthermore, the act does not require a mother to give birth in a hospital, or to stay in the hospital for a fixed period of time following the birth of her child.[252] The act, however, does not limit an insurance company from intervening after the 48-hour minimum stay.

The NMHPA provisions are effective with respect to plan years beginning on or after January 1, 1998. In addition, although the NMHPA requirements always apply to self-insured group health plans, the law does not apply to plans provided through health insurance coverage if: (1) a state law requires at least a 48-hour hospital stay after normal delivery, and at least a 96-hour stay after caesarian section; (2) a state law requires maternity and pediatric care coverage in accordance with guidelines established by the American College of Obstetricians and Gynecologists, the American Academy of Pediatrics, or other established professional medical associations; or (3) a state law requires that the hospital length of stay for maternity care is left to the decision of the attending provider, in consultation with the mother.[253]

DHHS, the DOL, and the Department of the Treasury are responsible for implementation and enforcement of the NMHPA. On October 27, 1998, these departments developed a Joint Interim Rule. This rule applies to plans and issuers in the group and individual markets for plan years or health-insurance coverage beginning on or after January 1, 1999. The interim rule provides guidance on how the NMHPA will be implemented and enforced, and explains the jurisdiction of each department.

8.3.2.9 Minimum Cancer Treatment

As Congressional awareness of the problems women face in the context of managed care began to rise by the end of the 105th Congress, Democrats and Republicans together focused on passing legislation addressing women's health concerns.[254] The Women's Health and Cancer Rights Act of 1998 (WHCRA), signed into law on October 21, 1998, is one such piece of legislation.[255] This act amended ERISA and the Public Health Service Act, and is administered by the DOL and DHHS.[256]

The WHCRA applies to women covered by insured and self-insured plans, as well as HMOs provided by private and governmental employees.[257] The WHCRA mandates that these health plans

---

[250] 29 U.S.C. § 1185(c)(3).
[251] 29 U.S.C. § 1185(b).
[252] 29 U.S.C. § 1185(c).
[253] 29 U.S.C. § 1185(f).
[254] Tiffany F. Theodos, *The Patients' Bill of Rights: Women's Rights Under Managed Care and ERISA Preemption*, 26 AM. J.L. AND MED. 89, 102 (2000).
[255] 29 U.S.C. § 1185b; Dennis K. Schaeffer, *Insuring the Protection of ERISA Plan Participants: ERISA Preemption and the Federal Government's Duty to Regulate Self-Insured Health Plans*, 47 BUFFALO L. REV. 1085, 1130 (1999). The WHCRA passed as part of the omnibus appropriations bill. *Id.* at 102–03.
[256] U.S. Department of Labor, Employee Benefits Security Administration, *Your Rights After a Mastectomy* (Aug. 2017), *available at* https://www.dol.gov/sites/default/files/ebsa/about-ebsa/our-activities/resource-center/publications/your-rights-after-a-mastectomy.pdf.
[257] 29 U.S.C. § 1185b(a); Mary Anne Bobinski and Phyllis Griffin Epps, *Women, Poverty, Access to Health Care, and the Perils of Symbolic Reform*, 5 J. GENDER RACE & JUST. 233, 255 (2002).

notify women about the coverage it requires upon enrollment for insurance, and thereafter on a yearly basis.[258] It requires health plans already providing coverage for mastectomies to provide reimbursement for breast reconstructive surgery and surgery to achieve breast symmetry, prostheses, and treatment for physical complications, as needed, following mastectomy.[259] Coverage for reconstructive surgery may not be denied or reduced on the grounds that it is cosmetic in nature, or that it otherwise does not meet the coverage definition of "medically necessary."[260]

Because the WHCRA applies to all types of group health plans and individual health plans, this regulation benefits most women. At the same time, however, the act only mandates coverage of reconstructive services where mastectomy benefits are already provided; it does not require health plans or issuers to pay for mastectomies.

At the time this law was enacted, several states already had in effect regulations requiring health plans covering mastectomies to provide coverage for breast reconstructive surgery following a mastectomy.[261] This act does not preempt any such state laws.[262] Thus, the WHCRA covers those plans not currently covered by state law, and sets a minimum standard securing this service for all women in all states.[263]

8.3.3 The Patient Protection and Affordable Care Act

The federal regulation of health care began in earnest in 1965 with the enactment of the Social Security Act of 1965, which created two revolutionary programs: Medicare and Medicaid. Nine years later, federal effort to regulate health care took another forward leap with the enactment of ERISA. Although ERISA's primary focus was designed to secure the promise of qualified plans, owing largely to the failed promise of certain multi-employer pension plans, welfare plans were also regulated. Further federal regulation of health care plans occurred through the enactment of COBRA continuation coverage in 1986 and the enactment of HIPAA in 1996.

Serious efforts at overhauling the health care system at the federal level were undertaken by President Clinton. On March 26, 1997, President Clinton appointed the Advisory Commission on Consumer Protection and Quality in the Health Care Industry to "advise the President on changes occurring in the health care system and recommend measures as may be necessary to promote and ensure health care quality and value, and protect consumers and workers in the health care system." As part of its work, the President asked the Commission to draft a "Consumer Bill of Rights and Responsibilities," and in November 1997, the Commission produced its recommended Consumer Bill of Rights consistent with its charge. However, as a result of, among other things, crushing lobbying pressures, the legislative effort stalled and comprehensive health care reform under the Clinton administration never materialized.

---

[258] 29 U.S.C. § 1185b(a); American Cancer Society, Women's Health and Cancer Rights Act, (ACS Cancer Rights Act). These health-insurance carriers were also required to notify individuals of coverage directly after the enactment of the WHCRA.
[259] 29 U.S.C. § 1185b(a).
[260] 29 U.S.C. § 1185b(c).
[261] ACS Cancer Rights Act, *supra*.
[262] 29 U.S.C. § 1185b(e).
[263] *Id.*

Further efforts at overhaul occurred in 2003. On December 8, 2003, President George W. Bush ensured that there would be sweeping changes to the Medicare system by enacting the Medicare Prescription Drug, Improvement, and Modernization Act (Medicare Modernization Act or MMA) into federal law. The MMA allowed for the establishment of Medicare Advantage Plans, which offered great advantages over Medicare+Choice plans for insurers. These plans, among other things, allowed enrollees to sign on to the plan for an entire year, restricted care to a network of providers, allowed the use of formularies to restrict prescription drug choices, created the possibility for prescription drug coverage to be deferred to the patient or a prescription plan, restricted care other than emergency care to a particular region, and allowed for the adjustment of federal reimbursement according to the health risk of particular enrollees. While the MMA was great for insurers, it also offered advantages to Medicare recipients, particularly for the elderly and disabled. Among its most important changes was the introduction of an entitlement benefit for prescription drugs, which would be funded through tax breaks and subsidies.

The next large scale health reform did not occur until the House of Representatives passed the ACA on March 21, 2010[264] and, on March 23, 2010, President Obama signed the ACA into federal law. [265]

Congress immediately exercised its reconciliation powers and enacted the Health Care and Education Reconciliation Act (H.R. 4872) in order to make its desired changes to the ACA. The House of Representatives passed the Act on March 21, 2010, and then the Senate also passed the act on March 25, 2010. President Obama signed the Health Care and Education Reconciliation Act into law on March 30, 2010, one week after the ACA.[266] The goal of the Health Care and Education Reconciliation Act is to "ensure that all Americans have access to quality, affordable health insurance . . . ."[267]

Paired together with the ACA, the Health Care and Education Reconciliation Act makes great strides toward a complete health care overhaul. The Act contains provisions that aim to, among other things, reduce premiums for seniors and fill the Medicare prescription drug "donut hole," extend reforms to grandfathered plans, enhance premium tax credits to make coverage more affordable, strengthen provisions attacking waste and fraud in Medicare and Medicaid, increase funding for community health centers, make improvements to Medicaid, improve shared responsibility between individuals and employers, and make fees more reasonable.[268]

Since the ACA was enacted into law, the act has faced several challenges to its Constitutionality.[269] The challenges centered on the ACA's "individual mandate," which requires individuals to purchase

---

[264] Reconciliation Act of 2010: Vote on H.R. 4872 Before the House of Representatives, 111th Cong., Mar. 21, 2010, *available at* http://clerk.house.gov/evs/2010/roll167.xml.
[265] Sheryl Stolberg and Robert Pear, *Obama Signs Health Care Overhaul Bill, With a Flourish*, NY TIMES, Mar. 23, 2010, *available at* http://www.nytimes.com/2010/03/24/health/policy/24health.html.
[266] William Branigin, *Obama Signs Higher-Education Measure Into Law*, WASHINGTON POST, March 30, 2010, *available at* http://voices.washingtonpost.com/44/2010/03/obama-signs-higher-education-m.html?hpid=topnews.
[267] Staff of H. Comms. on Ways and Means, Energy and Commerce, and Education and Labor, 111th Cong., Report on Affordable Health Care for America (Comm. Print Mar. 18, 2010), *available at* http://docs.house.gov/energycommerce/SUMMARY.pdf.
[268] *Id.*
[269] *State of Florida v. United States Department of Health and Human Services* (C.A. No.: 3:10-cv-91-RV/EMT) (N.D. FLA); *Commonwealth of Virginia v. Kathleen Sebelius* (C.A. No.: 3:10-cv-00188-HEH) (E.D. VA); *Liberty*

health insurance or pay a penalty for failing to maintain coverage. The argument against the Constitutionality of the ACA is that requiring an individual to purchase insurance is beyond the scope of the Commerce Clause.

The United States Supreme Court upheld the Constitutionality of the ACA on June 28, 2012.[270] In a 5-to-4 vote, the court ruled that the individual mandate was permissible pursuant to Congress' power to tax and spend, rather than pursuant to the Commerce Clause. Although the ACA labeled the consequence for not purchasing health insurance as a "penalty," Chief Justice Roberts stated that labels are not the deciding factor, and that the determinative factor was instead the substance and application of the exaction. The court also ruled that individual states could not be forced to participate in Medicaid expansion.

In an attempt to derail the regulatory machinery supporting the ACA, President Trump, on January 20, 2017, issued Executive Order 13765 which directs relevant federal agencies to "exercise all authority and discretion available to them to waive, defer, grant exemptions from, or delay the implementation of any provision or requirement of the [ACA] that would impose a fiscal burden on any State or a cost, fee, tax, penalty or regulatory burden on individuals, families, healthcare providers, health insurers, patients, recipients of healthcare services, purchasers of health insurance, or makers of medical devices, products or medications."

Further, as described in Section 8.3.3.16, effective for months after December 31, 2018, the so-called individual mandate is repealed.

8.3.3.1 No Lifetime or Annual Coverage Limits

Prior to the March 23, 2010 enactment of the ACA, group health plans were permitted to set lifetime and annual dollar limits on the benefits received by the covered individuals. In fact, over half of individuals who received employer-provided benefits in 2009 had policies containing lifetime limits of $1 million or $2 million.[271] On the other hand, annual dollar limits were much less common, and were utilized by only 8% of large employer plans, 14% of small employer plans, and 19% of individual market plans.[272]

Effective September 23, 2010, group health plans are no longer allowed to set lifetime dollar limits on essential benefits, such as hospitalization, doctor's office visits, and prescriptions.[273] The use of annual limits will also be restricted, and eventually eliminated altogether, contingent on an exception for pre-2014 annual limits.[274] Group health plans may enforce a restricted annual limit for all plans issued before January 1, 2014, on the value of benefits received by a covered group or

---

University, Inc. v. Timothy Geithner (C.A. No.: 6:10-cv-00015-nkm-mfu) W.D. VA); *Thomas More Law Center v. Barack Hussein Obama* (C.A. No.: 2:10-cv-11156-GCS-RSW) (E.D. MI); *Mead v. Holder* (C.A. No.: 1:10-cv-00950-GK) (D.C.).
[270] *National Federation of Independent Business v. Sebelius* (132 S.Ct. 2566).
[271] The Impact of Lifetime Limits, Prepared for the National Hemophilia Foundation on behalf of the Raise the Caps Coalition (PriceWaterhouseCoopers), Mar. 2009.
[272] Fact Sheet: The Affordable Care Act's New Patient's Bill of Rights, healthreform.gov, June 22, 2010, *available at* http://www.nh.gov/insurance/consumers/documents/fed_ref_pbor.pdf.
[273] 42 U.S.C. §300gg-11(a)(1).
[274] 42 U.S.C. § 300gg-11(a)(2).

individual for "essential health benefits," which are defined by the Secretary of Health and Human Services.[275] The Secretary's responsibility is to make sure that insurance premiums are not significantly raised due to the provision of necessary services.[276] Importantly, group health plans will still be free to impose a lifetime or annual dollar limit on spending for health care benefits that are not considered "essential."[277]

8.3.3.2 Prohibition on Rescission

Prior to the passage of the ACA, group health plans were free to rescind an enrollee's coverage for a multitude of reasons and group health plans and insurers often took advantage of this right.

Upon the passage of the ACA, the guaranteed renewability provisions of the PHSA were expanded to prohibit group health plans and health insurance issuers from rescinding coverage except in cases of fraud or misrepresentation of a material fact.[278] If an insurer plans to rescind coverage, prior notice must be provided to afford covered parties an opportunity to appeal.[279]

8.3.3.3 The Appeals Process

The ACA imposes several requirements for "internal" claims or appeals, including:

- The definition of "adverse benefit determination" includes a rescission of coverage, even if that rescission does not have an adverse effect on benefits (for example, coverage is rescinded but the participant had not actually incurred any claims that could be affected by that rescission).[280]

- In situations in which a participant requires urgent care, a plan administrator must notify the participant of its coverage decision as soon as possible, but in any event within 72 hours of receiving the initial claim for urgent care benefits.[281]

- A participant must be allowed to continue coverage while his or her appeal is pending, except in cases where there is an appeal of a rescission of coverage.[282]

- Notifications of benefit determinations must be provided in a culturally and linguistically appropriate manner.[283]

Adherence to the internal requirements—both the existing requirements under ERISA *and* the ACA mandates—will be *strictly* required under joint regulations issued by the IRS, DOL and HHS. A plan's failure to closely follow these rules will mean that participants will automatically be deemed to have exhausted the internal process and can proceed to an external review of their claims or even

---

[275] *Id.*, reference 42 U.S.C. § 18022(b)(1) for a definition of "essential health benefits."
[276] *Id.*
[277] 42 U.S.C. § 300gg-11(b).
[278] 42 U.S.C § 300gg-12.
[279] *Id.*
[280] 45 C.F.R. § 147.136(a)(2)(i).
[281] 29 C.F.R. § 2560.503-1(f)(2)(i).
[282] 45 C.F.R. § 147.136(b)(2)(iii).
[283] 45 C.F.R. § 147.136(e)(1).

proceed directly to litigation.[284] Even minor or "de minimis" violations of these requirements by the plan may result in a deemed exhaustion if certain criteria are not met.[285]

The ACA requires that participants may take advantage of an "external" review process. For many insured plans, state law may already require an external review process, and procedures are already in place for complying with these requirements. For self-funded plans, however, this requirement alone may make maintaining grandfathered status a particularly important issue. More specifically, the external appeals requirements provide that:

- If a plan (such as a fully insured plan or a church plan) is subject to state law and that state has a process for external appeals that satisfies minimum standards set forth in the Regulations (based on the National Association of Insurance Commissioners Uniform Model), the plan must comply with that state process.[286]

- If a plan (such as a self-funded plan) is *not* subject to state law (or if a plan is subject to a state process that does not satisfy the minimum federal standards), the plan must comply with federal requirements.[287] In general, the federal requirements follow the National Association of Insurance Commissioners Uniform Model.[288]

In general, the appeals rules took effect for plan years beginning on or after September 23, 2010.[289] For calendar year plans, this means compliance generally began January 1, 2011.

However, there was a limited "safe harbor" for some plans effective through December 31, 2017. During this transition period, a non-grandfathered, self-funded plan was considered to satisfy the minimum federal standards if the plan complied with a State process that satisfied NAIC-similar standards. Once the transition period has ended, non-grandfathered self-funded plans in a state that has not implemented NAIC-parallel standards must comply with the federal external review processes.

8.3.3.4 Coverage of Preventive Health Services

The ACA requires all group health plans and health insurance issuers to provide coverage for preventive services, effective for plan years beginning on or after September 23, 2010.[290] These services must be provided without any cost sharing and at a minimum must include certain services supported by the U.S. Preventive Task Force and the Health Resources and Services Administration.[291] Value-based insurance designs may be utilized by plans and issuers upon the Secretary of Health and Human Service's development of guidelines for such coverage.[292]

---

[284] 45 C.F.R. § 147.136(b)(2)(ii)(F)(1).
[285] 45 C.F.R. § 147.136(b)(2)(ii)(F)(2).
[286] 29 C.F.R. § 2590.715-2719(c)(1).
[287] 29 C.F.R. § 2590.715-2719(d).
[288] The National Association of Insurance Commissioners Uniform Model may be found at https://www.dol.gov/sites/default/files/ebsa/laws-and-regulations/laws/affordable-care-act/for-employers-and-advisers/externalreview-modelact.pdf.
[289] 29 C.F.R. § 2590.715-2719(g).
[290] 42 U.S.C. § 300gg-13(a).
[291] *Id.*
[292] 42 U.S.C. § 300gg-13(c).

8.3.3.5 Extension of Dependent Coverage

The ACA requires all group health plans covering dependent children to provide health coverage until the dependent attains age 26.[293] With respect to dependents who have not attained age 26, a plan may not define the term "dependent" for purposes of eligibility for coverage other than in terms of a relationship between the participant and child.[294] The result of this change is that a plan may no longer require an adult child to be a full-time student or live with parents to remain eligible for group health coverage.[295] Grandfathered plans are not exempt from extending dependent health coverage to children until they have reached age 26.

8.3.3.6 Standardization of Coverage Documents

In an effort to provide a more meaningful explanation of health care benefits, the Secretary of Health and Human Services was required to develop standards for group health plans and insurers regarding benefit summaries and coverage explanations.[296] Final regulations on this topic were issued on June 16, 2015, to be effective on August 17, 2015.[297] The Summary of Benefits and Coverage (SBC) is limited to four pages, must be culturally and linguistically appropriate, and must use terminology that is understandable by the average participant.[298] A fine of up to $1,000 may be imposed for each willful failure to meet the aforementioned criteria.[299]

8.3.3.7 Information Regarding Transparency

A group health plan or health insurer seeking to become a provider under the exchanges created by the ACA must provide claims and enrollment information to the relevant state insurance commission, Secretary of Health and Human Services and the exchange authorities.[300]

8.3.3.8 Prohibition of Discrimination in Favor of Highly Compensated Individuals

Self-insured health care plans have been and are currently prohibited from discriminating in favor of highly compensated employees, both as to benefits and eligibility under § 105(h) of the Internal Revenue Code. Under the ACA, insured plans must now comply with the same non-discrimination requirements.[301] Insured grandfathered plans were exempt from this requirement until 2014.

8.3.3.9 Reporting; Quality of Care

On or before March 23, 2012, the Secretary of Health and Human Services was required to develop quality reporting requirement standards in connection with coverage and reimbursement

---

[293] 42 U.S.C. § 300gg-14(a).
[294] 45 C.F.R. § 147.120(b).
[295] *Id.*
[296] 42 U.S.C. § 300gg-15(a).
[297] 45 C.F.R. § 2950.
[298] 42 U.S.C. § 300gg-15(b).
[299] 42 U.S.C. § 300gg-15(f).
[300] 42 U.S.C. § 300gg-15a.
[301] 42 U.S.C. § 300gg-16(a).

arrangements for group health plans and insurers.[302] Group health plans and insurers are now required to annually report to the federal government and to enrollees as to whether the coverage:

- improves health outcomes;
- includes activities to prevent hospital readmissions
- includes activities to improve patient safety;[303] and
- implements wellness and health promotion activities.

8.3.3.10 Essential Benefits Coverage

Starting in 2014, qualified health benefit plans offered by private insurers are made available through a state-operated market place know as an Exchange. In order to be offered through the Exchange, the qualified health benefit plan must offer coverage which provides for "minimum essential benefits," limits on cost-sharing, and provides either bronze, silver, gold, or platinum levels of coverage.[304] The "minimum essential benefits" must include: (1) ambulatory patient services; (2) emergency services; (3) hospitalization; (4) maternity and newborn care; (5) mental health and substance abuse services, including behavioral health treatment; (6) prescription drugs; (7) rehabilitation and habilitative devices; (8) laboratory services; (9) preventive and wellness services and chronic disease management; and (10) pediatric services, including oral and vision care.[305]

8.3.3.11 Prohibition on Excessive Waiting Period

For plan years beginning on or after January 1, 2014, group health plans may not require an individual to experience a waiting period of greater than 90 days.[306] A waiting period is the time that a potential participant or beneficiary must wait to become covered by a health care plan.[307]

8.3.3.12 Prohibition of Pre-Existing Condition Based on Health Status

Effective for plan years beginning on or after January 1, 2014, group health plans and insurers may not impose a pre-existing condition exclusion.[308]

8.3.3.13 Prohibition of Discrimination against Individual Participants and Beneficiaries Based on Health Factors

For plan years beginning on or after January 1, 2014, group health plans and health insurance issuers are prohibited from imposing conditions for eligibility on an individual or dependent of an individual based on the following health factors: health status, medical condition (physical or mental), claims experience, receipt of health care, medical history, genetic information, evidence of insurability,

---

[302] 42 U.S.C. § 300gg-17(a)(1).
[303] 42 U.S.C. § 300gg-17(a)(1)(A) – (D); 42 U.S.C. § 300gg-17(a)(2)(A).
[304] 42 U.S.C. § 18022(a)(1) – (3).
[305] 42 U.S.C. § 18022(b)(1).
[306] 42 U.S.C. § 300gg-7.
[307] 42 U.S.C. § 300gg-3(b)(4).
[308] 42 U.S.C. § 300gg-3(a).

disability, or any other factor deemed appropriate by the Secretary of Health and Human Services.[309] Group health plans and health insurers are not permitted to use these factors in order to require any individual to pay a larger premium or contribution than that paid by a similarly situated individual or dependent of that individual enrolled in the same plan.[310] Similarly, group health plans and health insurance issuers are not allowed to request or require that an individual undergo genetic testing for underwriting purposes, or as a condition for eligibility for participation in the plan.[311] "Wellness programs," or programs offered by employers that are designed to promote health or prevent disease, will not violate the nondiscrimination rule as long as all similarly situated individuals are given the option to participate, and conditions for securing a premium discount, rebate, or other reward are not based on satisfying a standard related to the above-listed health status factors.[312]

Even if securing a premium discount, rebate, or other reward for participation in a wellness program is in fact conditioned on an individual satisfying a standard related to a health status factor, such a program may still be permissible if the following conditions are met: (1) the reward for the program, along with rewards for other programs that consider particular health status factors, does not exceed 30% of the cost of employee-only coverage under the plan; (2) the program is reasonably designed to promote health or prevent disease; (3) individuals eligible for the program are afforded the opportunity to qualify for the reward under the program at least once each year; (4) all similarly situated individuals have access to the full reward under the program, including by completing a reasonable alternative standard; and (5) the reasonable alternative standard is disclosed in all plan materials that describe the terms of the program.[313]

If conditions for obtaining premium discounts, rebates, or other rewards under the program are not based on satisfying a standard that is related to a health status factor and participation in the plan offering the program is offered to all similarly situated individuals then the wellness program will comply with the nondiscrimination requirements. Examples of such permissible wellness programs include the following: a program that reimburses all or part of the cost for memberships in a fitness center; a diagnostic testing program that provides a reward for participation and does not base the reward on outcomes; a program that encourages preventive care related to a health condition through the waiver of the copayment or deductible requirement under the group health plan for the costs of certain items or services related to a health condition; a program that reimburses individuals for the costs of smoking cessation programs without regard to whether the individual quits smoking; and a program that provides a reward to individuals for attending a periodic health education seminar.[314]

8.3.3.14 Tax Credit for Small Business

If an eligible small employer makes nonelective contributions that pay for at least 50% of the cost of health insurance premiums for the coverage of its participating employees, then that employer

---
[309] 42 U.S.C. § 300gg-4(a).
[310] 42 U.S.C. § 300gg-4(b)(1).
[311] 42 U.S.C. § 300gg-4(c)(1).
[312] 42 U.S.C. § 300gg-4(j)(1).
[313] 42 U.S.C. § 300gg-4(j)(3).
[314] 42 U.S.C. § 300gg-4(j)(2).

may claim a tax credit in tax years beginning after 2009.[315] The amount of such a tax credit in tax years beginning in 2010 through 2013 is equal to 35% of the lesser of either the sum of nonelective employer contributions or the sum of nonelective contributions which the employer would have made if each employee had enrolled in a qualified health plan.[316] This limitation serves to prevent an employer from claiming the tax credit on the portion of employer paid premiums that exceeds the average premium charges in the State's small group market.[317]

An eligible small employer may also claim a health insurance credit for any tax year beginning after 2013, with the credit period being the two-consecutive-tax year period beginning with the first tax year in which the employer offers a qualified health plan to its employees through an Exchange.[318] The amount of such a tax credit for a tax year beginning after 2013 is equal to 50% of the lesser of either the sum of nonelective employer contributions or the sum of nonelective contributions that would have been made during that taxable year if each employee had enrolled in a qualified health plan.[319] The credit is phased out over time with some protection for small employers with 10 or fewer employees and overage wages of not more than $25,000 as adjusted.[320]

In order to receive the tax credit, employers must make nonelective contributions through an "arrangement."[321] For tax years beginning in 2010 through 2013, the arrangement must consist of the employer making nonelective contributions on behalf of each enrolled employee that equal a uniform percentage that is greater than 50% of the premium cost of the qualified health plan.[322] In order for an employer contribution to be considered "nonelective," it simply must be something other than a contribution pursuant to a salary reduction agreement.[323] In the instance of a tax year beginning after 2013, the arrangement must offer the insurance through an Exchange as discussed above, while the use of an Exchange is optional for tax years earlier than 2013.[324]

Only an "eligible" employer may take advantage of the tax credit. To be considered an eligible small employer the employer must have no more than 25 full-time employees for that taxable year, its employees' average annual wages must not exceed twice the applicable dollar amount for that tax year, and it must have a qualified health care arrangement in effect.[325]

There are special rules for an eligible small employer that also has tax-exempt status. For tax years beginning in 2010 through 2013, the credit percentage for an eligible small employer with tax-exempt status is 25%.[326] For tax years beginning after 2013, the credit percentage increases to 35%.[327]

---

[315] 26 U.S.C. § 45R.
[316] 26 U.S.C. § 45R(b).
[317] U.S. Congress, The Staff of the Joint Committee on Taxation, Technical Explanation of the Revenue Provisions of the Reconciliation Act of 2010, as Amended, in Combination with the Patient Protection and Affordable Care Act (JCX-18-10), text from Committee Reports, *available at* http://www.jct.gov/publications.html?func=startdown&id=3673.
[318] 26 U.S.C. § 45R(e)(2).
[319] 26 U.S.C. § 45R(b).
[320] 26 U.S.C. § 45R(c).
[321] 26 U.S.C. § 45R(d)(4).
[322] *Id.*
[323] 26 U.S.C. § 45R(e)(3).
[324] 26 U.S.C. § 45R(g)(3).
[325] 26 U.S.C. § 45R(d)(1).
[326] 26 U.S.C. § 45R(g)(2).
[327] *Id.*

In order for a small employer to qualify under these special rules, that employer must be "eligible," as described above, and it also must be an Internal Revenue Code § 501(c) organization that is exempt from the tax code under Internal Revenue Code § 501(a).[328] If the amount of the tax credit is greater than the amount of payroll taxes paid by the employer during a particular taxable year, then the credit amount is capped by the amount paid in payroll taxes.[329]

8.3.3.15 Employer Requirement to Inform Employees of Coverage Options

As of March 1, 2013, employers must provide to each employee at the time of hiring a written notice:

- informing the employee of the existence of an exchange, a description of the services provided by the exchange and the manner in which to contact the exchange;
- if the employer plan's share of total allowed costs of benefits is less than 60%, that the employee may be entitled to certain tax and cost-sharing benefits, if benefits are purchased through an exchange; and
- if the employee purchases a benefit through an exchange and the employer does not offer a free choice voucher, the employee may lose the employer contribution to any health benefit plan and that all or a portion of the contribution may be excludable from income.[330]

8.3.3.16 Shared Responsibility

Generally, employers who employ an average of at least 50 full-time employees per calendar year will be required to provide an offer of coverage under a health plan with minimum essential coverage to 95% of their full-time employees or pay a penalty tax if at least one of their full-time employees enrolls through the exchange and is certified for a premium tax credit.[331] The penalty tax equals 1/12 of $2,000 (indexed for inflation—$2,260 for 2017) for any month in which coverage is not offered to at least 95% of full-time employees, multiplied by the number of full-time employees employed by the employer.[332] Even if an employer offers a health plan with minimum essential coverage, the employer will be penalized with respect to each employee who purchases insurance through the exchange and is certified for a premium tax credit, if the coverage offered by the employer is not affordable or does not provide minimum value. The monthly penalty tax is equal to 1/12 multiplied by $3,000 (indexed for inflation—$3,390 for 2017) multiplied by the number of affected full-time employees.[333]

Under the ACA, individuals who were not covered by a health plan that provided at least minimum essential coverage were required to pay a "shared responsibility payment" (also referred to as a penalty) with their federal tax return. Unless an exception applied, the tax was imposed for any month that an individual did not have minimum essential coverage. Under the Tax Cuts and Jobs Act

---

[328] 26 U.S.C. § 45R(f)(2).
[329] 26 U.S.C. § 45R(f)(1); "Payroll taxes" are calculated pursuant to 26 U.S.C. § 45R(f)(3)(A).
[330] 29 U.S.C. § 218(b).
[331] 26 U.S.C. § 4980H(a).
[332] 26 U.S.C. § 4980H(c)(1).
[333] 26 U.S.C. § 4980H(b).

passed by Congress on December 20, 2017, for months beginning after Dec. 31, 2018, the amount of the individual shared responsibility payment is reduced to zero.[334]

8.3.3.17 Reporting of Employer Health Insurance Coverage

Employers who on average employ at least 50 full-time employees and certain other employers who offer minimum essential coverage are required to file a report with the Secretary of Treasury.[335] The report will essentially describe the scope and extent of coverage afforded to full time employees.[336] In addition, the report must also be provided to each full-time employee who is covered under the plan.[337]

8.3.3.18 Cafeteria Plan Changes

Effective for tax years beginning after December 31, 2012, a health flexible spending account is limited to a maximum of $2,500 (indexed for inflation) per year.[338] Further, effective December 31, 2013, employees will not be able to utilize an employer's cafeteria plan to pay for health care benefits purchased through an exchange. Certain small employers electing to offer benefits through an exchange are exempted from this rule.[339]

8.4 Conclusion

After nearly a century of state regulation of private health care plans, the enactment of ERISA and the ACA has brought about a sweeping era of federal regulation of private health care plans. Practitioners representing employers, health plans, or providers must accordingly become familiar with the unique federal regulatory scheme impacting health plans.

---

[334] 26 U.S.C. § 5000a(c), as amended by Sec. 11081 of the Tax Cuts and Jobs Act).
[335] 26 U.S.C. § 6056(a).
[336] 26 U.S.C. § 6056(b).
[337] 26 U.S.C. § 6056(c)(1).
[338] 26 U.S.C. § 125(i)(1).
[339] IRS Notice 2013-54.

9

Regulation of Hospitals

Sandra M. DiVarco
Kerrin B. Slattery
McDermott Will & Emery LLP

9.1 Introduction

The operation of hospitals has never been more complex than it is today. The concept of a "hospital" includes many different types of institutions, though each has the common feature of providing diagnostic and therapeutic services to inpatients. The United States has approximately 5,500 general acute care hospitals.[1] Almost 2,000 hospitals are organized as charitable, nonprofit, tax-exempt corporations. Approximately 1,000 hospitals are owned and operated as for-profit enterprises (e.g., with public company ownership). Some hospitals are single, freestanding, and unaffiliated organizations, while others are part of regional systems or nationwide chains. Less than 1,000 hospitals are owned by state or local municipalities (e.g., hospital districts or authorities), or are city or county-owned hospitals. Still others are owned and operated by the federal government (e.g., Department of Veterans' Affairs (VA) hospitals).

Hospitals serve diverse communities, from rural areas to densely populated metropolitan regions, and collectively form the backbone of the health care delivery system in the United States. Hospitals are also a vital part of the economic system, and are often one of the largest employers in the communities they serve. As a result, state and local governments have an interest in regulating the operation of hospitals in order to protect the public. Further, because of the significant cost involved in providing care in hospitals, almost all hospitals participate in governmental funding programs. As a result, hospitals are also subject to regulation by the federal government, which focuses on the protection of federal health care program beneficiaries' health and welfare in addition to the fiscal integrity of federal health care programs.

In addition, passage of the Patient Protection and Affordable Care Act of 2010 (ACA) has resulted in sweeping nationwide health care reforms and an emphasis on quality and data reporting, requiring hospitals around the country to develop and enhance processes to comply with new requirements in order to obtain reimbursement for care. While the ultimate legacy of the changes—including those related to the ACA and any successor legislation—remains to be seen, the need to control cost, quality and increase access still remains. Health care reform is driving continued consolidation of hospitals

---

[1] American Hospital Ass'n, *Fast Facts on US Hospitals*, *available at* www.aha.org.

and health care systems, which events trigger the need to comply with various state and federal requirements pertaining to change of ownership and control.

Given the variety of hospitals, this Chapter will primarily focus on regulation of general, acute care hospitals, and will not address all the particular requirements for specialty or single-service hospitals (e.g., children's hospitals, heart hospitals, psychiatric hospitals or long-term acute care hospitals) or VA/federal facilities. Further, the discussion will apply to for-profit, non-profit and governmental hospitals alike, rather than any unique issues arising from particular types of ownership.

This Chapter highlights in summary fashion the breadth and nature of the regulation of hospitals by federal and state governments, as well as by accrediting organizations. In order to get a full picture of the regulatory landscape within which hospitals operate, the authors suggest that all readers explore the Chapters in this book that address in greater detail the complex regulations with which general acute care hospitals must comply.

9.2 State and Local Regulations

9.2.1 Licensure

All states regulate the operation of hospitals to one degree or another, based on the premise that the public good demands careful oversight of health care provided to state residents. State regulation generally takes the form of licensure laws and regulations. Obtaining a license to operate a hospital typically requires the filing of a detailed application by the proposed operator with the appropriate state authority (most often a department of public health (DPH)). The application usually requires a description of the intended operations at the hospital and detailed information regarding ownership of the facility. Not all general acute care hospitals provide all medical services to their patients, but generally there are minimum requirements for hospital operation which vary by state (e.g., emergency department, laboratory, etc.). Many hospitals specialize in particular services, and even more hospitals limit their scope of services for financial or other practical reasons. In many states, specialty hospitals are licensed separately from acute care hospitals, and the delivery of inpatient mental health care and skilled nursing care may be separately licensed within an already-licensed facility.

Many states regulate the types of hospital services provided in their jurisdiction. Some states take these steps as part of Certificate of Need (CON) laws (as further discussed in Section 9.2.5), and others do so merely to maintain an inventory of available health resources. All states regulate the standards used for building construction, including the construction of hospitals, which standards are largely directed at enhancing patient safety (i.e., earthquake protection requirements in California) and fire safety. Increasingly, DPHs also require or recommend the reporting of errors in hospitals, and may levy fines for certain types of errors.

In addition, numerous other licenses and permits are required to operate a hospital in compliance with state and local regulations. Examples of permits required by state and local regulation that impact hospitals range from licensure of pharmacy and laboratory, to building permits (e.g., boiler, elevator), to heliport, radioactive materials, food service, and gift shop licenses.

9.2.2 Patient Safety and Patient Rights

A number of state regulations governing hospitals focus on patient rights and patient safety issues. Such regulations include mandatory dissemination of patient rights information and specific rights and restrictions related to patient restraint and seclusion, the ability to make a complaint or grievance regarding care and imposition of mandatory staffing ratios. State agencies target these areas in an attempt to inform individuals of their rights as patients and to protect them from harm in the course of receiving hospital care. Although the scope of this Chapter does not permit a detailed exploration of all such regulations, the following discussion is illustrative of the type of such regulations.

The use of restraint or seclusion of patients in health care facilities has long been a focus of patient safety regulations. A patient might need to be restrained while in a hospital bed for protective reasons; for example, if the patient has a psychiatric condition, then the patient might need to be physically restrained or chemically restrained through the use of medication to prevent them from harming themselves or others (e.g., staff or other patients). However, the use of restraints can carry significant risk of patient injury. Over the years, patients have been killed or injured due to the type of restraint used, the manner in which a restraint was imposed, the duration of the use of the restraint, and/or the failure to appropriately monitor the patient while the restraint was in use. Because of this potential for patient harm, use of restraints has become a highly regulated activity, and the use of restraints is presumed to be an intervention of "last resort" in most settings.

A second realm of patient rights is the requirement for hospitals to have in place a patient grievance process to investigate and respond to patient complaints about their care in the hospital. Hospitals can be penalized for failing to establish, maintain, and monitor such a program.

Finally, the statutory imposition of nurse-to-patient staffing ratios is yet another example of state-level regulation intended to protect the health and safety of patients within the hospital. In states with such staffing regulations, hospitals are charged with staffing patient care units in compliance with law rather than based solely upon perceived or actual patient acuity. Mandatory staffing ratios are viewed by some as the most efficient way to address the potential association between nurse workload and patient mortality and morbidity. However, studies on the efficacy of such programs in improving morbidity and mortality vary widely, and the American Hospital Association and other groups have opposed laws mandating specific nurse-to-patient staffing ratios due to the impact on hospital scheduling and staffing flexibility in the face of continual nursing shortages. Bolstered by the support of nurse associations and nurse unions, mandatory staffing legislation remains under consideration in a number of states.

When states enact or amend regulations or standards, hospitals must review and adapt policies and procedures to fit the new regulatory environment. Moreover, hospital administrators must hold educational sessions with hospital employees and hospital medical staff to ensure that the new standards are understood and adhered to on a continuous and consistent basis within the hospital. In addition to training staff, hospitals must implement ongoing internal auditing mechanisms to ensure continued compliance. Thus, for example, even in the case of a hospital that has never experienced a patient injury from the use of a restraint, the hospital would still need to have policies and procedures in place, continuously educate its staff and remain aware of and comply with the state's restraint regulations. Failure to do so could be used as evidence of malpractice in a lawsuit alleging the provision of substandard care by the hospital, in addition to the potential loss of licensure, or the imposition of fines or penalties for failure to comply with state law.

9.2.3 Regulations Impacting Medical Staff

Beyond issues pertaining to patient safety, state regulations also govern how hospitals relate to physicians and other health professionals who practice within the hospital. The reasons for these regulations are multifaceted. On one level, by regulating who can practice within a hospital, a state can foster the careers of particular medical practitioners, or impede the ability of other medical practitioners to practice their chosen profession. Thus, in many states, only persons licensed as particular types of medical practitioners are allowed to be members of a medical staff, while other individuals who provide health care services may be prohibited from joining a medical staff. For example, a chiropractic physician may be licensed by the state to provide services while being prohibited under state law from being a full member of the hospital medical staff.

Regulation of a hospital's relationships with its medical staff also relates to the idea that many medical staff practitioners need a hospital in which to practice their professions. Accordingly, it is in the interest of the public, as well as those practitioners, to enforce rules pertaining to how a hospital relates to practitioners that use the hospital, or how a hospital may limit particular practitioners in the practice of their profession. The theory underlying these regulations and related case law is that the power of the state must be used to protect the individual medical practitioner against the perceived market power of a local hospital, which may be an essential part of the practitioner's professional activities. In this way, regulations often relate to whether a hospital provides practitioners with all available opportunities to argue their case for medical staff membership and/or clinical privileges; the question of whether "due process" was followed by a hospital is a major part of many of these regulations.

9.2.4 Regulation of Individually Identifiable Health Information

In addition to federal laws regarding the privacy, security and breach of individually identifiable health information (as described in Section 9.3.1), applicable state laws may regulate the confidentiality of medical records, the privacy of particularly sensitive categories of health information (e.g., HIV status, mental health information, substance abuse treatment information), and the privacy, security and breach of personal information more broadly (e.g., Social Security numbers and financial information). Public concern continues to rise about persons playing no role in an individual's medical care obtaining access to sensitive information in the individual's medical or payment records, such as diagnosis or treatment information, and payment card information. Particular concerns include that employers will use medical information in an adverse action against the employee, that members of the general public would discriminate against individuals if people knew of their medical conditions, or that bad actors will use such information for financial gain. Cyberattacks targeting health and personal information, including ransomware attacks, have emerged as an acute problem for health care organizations, including hospitals. In order to avoid those problems—or the mere perception of such problems—regulators have proposed a myriad of standards for the processing and handling of medical records. Hospitals are required to adhere to these regulations, in addition to ensuring that members of a hospital medical staff and employees comply.

For privacy reasons, many states have recognized specific statutory protections for certain patient conditions. Hospitals therefore are required to process patient records and deal with patients in ways that minimize the possibility of misusing health information and medical records. Examples of this type of specific regulation of medical records and patterns of practice are the laws pertaining to the confidentiality of "highly confidential" information, such as that related to psychiatric treatment, substance abuse treatment or treatment of sexually transmitted diseases. Thus, although a hospital licensing statute in a particular state is normally the primary source of regulations of hospitals in that state, practitioners are well served to determine whether particular statutes governing records or treatment of particular illnesses or conditions also impose requirements on the operations of hospitals. Limitations on data sharing are explored further in Chapter 14.

9.2.5 Construction of Facilities

Many states regulate development of hospital facilities and services through CON laws and regulations. Such regulatory frameworks, originally outgrowths of federal health planning initiatives that have long since expired, still continue in effect in thirty-five (35) states.[2]

CON laws generally prohibit construction of new hospitals, addition of new hospital beds, establishment of major hospital services, acquisition of expensive medical equipment, or sale or transfer of ownership or control of a hospital without obtaining the prior approval of the state agency. Such laws also usually prohibit the cessation of services or the closure of a hospital without prior approval. CON laws and regulations are intended to protect the public from an oversupply of hospital services or unanticipated withdrawal of services that would unnecessarily escalate the cost of hospital care, as well as the entry of unqualified or financially unstable operators owning essential health care facilities within the state. CON regulations are extraordinarily complex and prescriptive. The process of administrative review and appeal often subjects these highly competitive projects to lengthy administrative and (on appeal) judicial proceedings. Any hospital in a state where CON laws still exist must be intimately familiar with the intricacies of the system in their state before undertaking significant projects and those in the ordinary course of operations.

9.3 Federal Regulation

Federal regulation of general acute care hospitals was relatively limited until the federal Medicare program was established in 1966.[3] The program was established in order to promote the provision of nondiscriminatory, cost-effective, and cost-efficient services to Medicare and Medicaid beneficiaries. The Centers for Medicare & Medicaid Services (CMS), the agency responsible for Medicare and Medicaid regulation, oversight, survey and certification, has developed an incredibly complex series of regulations affecting almost every aspect of hospital operations.

---

[2] Nat'l Conf. of State Legislators, *CON Programs*, available at www.ncsl.org.
[3] 42 U.S.C. § 1395.

In order to be eligible to bill the federal government for care provided to a Medicare or Medicaid program beneficiary, a hospital must first qualify as a provider in the program. As a program provider, a hospital must comply with the statutory Medicare Conditions of Participation for Hospitals (CoPs),[4] along with subsidiary and ancillary regulations of the Medicare and Medicaid programs. Although such participation in Medicare and Medicaid is voluntary, most hospitals realistically cannot exist without being providers under these programs, due to the number of patients who are beneficiaries of those programs.

Federal oversight of a hospital's compliance with the CoPs is exercised by state DPH surveyors or CMS Regional Office (CMS RO) survey teams, either on a periodic basis or resulting from complaints made by patients or others. Surveyors will survey a hospital by reviewing medical records, conducting staff interviews and facility tours, etc., which will ultimately result in a report of surveyor findings (Statement of Deficiencies). Hospitals have certain regulatory timeframes in which to respond to the Statement of Deficiencies, depending in large part upon the severity of the findings, and must file a corrective action plan with the state and/or CMS (Plan of Correction). The Plan of Correction must address in detail the steps taken to come into compliance with the CoPs in order to avoid the ultimate penalty of termination of the hospital's provider agreement with CMS. In cases where surveyors identify an immediate threat to patient health and safety, also known as "immediate jeopardy" in CMS parlance, this termination can occur as soon as 23 days after the survey. In other cases, a longer 90-day termination track is imposed. Failure to timely submit an acceptable Plan of Correction, or failure to carry through on corrective actions set forth therein, could ultimately result in termination of the hospital's provider agreement that permits it to participate in Medicare.[5] As one could easily imagine, termination of a hospital's provider agreement would have significant financial impact in that the hospital would no longer be eligible to receive payment for Medicare patients. In addition, termination of a hospital's provider agreement can trigger even more negative consequences, such as termination of Medicaid participation, termination of managed care payer contracts where enrollment as a Medicare provider is a condition to the contract, or violation of bond or financing covenants that require ongoing participation in the programs.

The ACA contemplates the establishment and ongoing maintenance of quality-related initiatives and metrics in almost every aspect of health care, and requires health plans and insurers, insurance exchanges, hospitals and other health care facilities, as well as physicians, to compile, report, and receive payment adjustments related to quality metrics. The parameters of these new processes continue to evolve, and with additional health reform on the horizon it is expected that significant additional regulation will continue to result from the ACA or any replacement legislation that may be implemented.

9.3.1 HIPAA

The Health Insurance Portability and Accountability Act of 1996 (HIPAA)[6] was enacted by Congress on August 21, 1996, and it established, for the first time, federal privacy and security protections for

---

[4] 42 C.F.R. Part 482.
[5] Additional remedies short of termination are also provided for, and state law may also provide for the imposition of fines or other penalties where certain deficiencies are identified on survey.
[6] Health Insurance Portability and Accountability Act of 1996, Pub.L. 104-191 (1996).

certain individually identifiable health information. In 2009, Congress further amended and expanded HIPAA by passing the Health Information Technology for Economic and Clinical Health Act (HITECH)[7] as part of the American Recovery and Reinvestment Act. In 2013, the Department of Health and Human Services (HHS) announced the Omnibus Final Rule implementing the HITECH Act, expanding patient rights, expanding the reach of HIPAA regulations and strengthening enforcement mechanisms.[8] The final rule extended HIPAA Privacy and Security Rule requirements to individuals or entities that receive protected health information, such as contractors and subcontractors (Business Associates). The 2013 Final Rule furthered individual patient rights regarding the use of their health information, set limits on how information is used and disclosed for marketing and fundraising purposes and prohibited the sale of an individuals' health information without their permission and clarified when breaches of unsecured health information must be reported to HHS.[9]

HIPAA applies to Covered Entities and their Business Associates. The term "Covered Entities" means health plans, health care clearinghouses or health care providers, including hospitals, that transmit health information in connection with certain electronic transactions, such as claims and payment.[10] HIPAA is enforced by the Office of Civil Rights within the HHS. As described in more detail below, HHS issued a series of implementing regulations under HIPAA governing, among other things, the privacy and security of individually identifiable health information, the adoption of uniform code set standards for certain electronic transactions and the adoption of notification rules in the event of a breach of unsecured, individually identifiable health information.

The HIPAA privacy regulations define the circumstances and parameters under which Covered Entities and their Business Associates may use or disclose individually identifiable health information held or transmitted by Covered Entities or their Business Associates, in any form or media, whether electronic, paper or oral (otherwise known as "protected health information").[11] As a general rule, Covered Entities and their Business Associates may not use or disclose an individual's protected health information, except as (1) otherwise permitted by law (e.g., for treatment, payment and health care operations; for certain public interest and benefit activities); (2) otherwise required by law (e.g., to HHS in connection with a compliance investigation); or (3) as authorized by the individual who is the subject of the information.[12] The HIPAA privacy regulations also establish certain rights an individual has with respect to his or her protected health information, such as the right to access or amend the protected health information under certain circumstances.[13]

The HIPAA security regulations govern the security of electronic protected health information that is created, received, maintained or transmitted by a Covered Entity and its Business Associates. Specifically, Covered Entities and their Business Associates are required to implement appropriate

---

[7] Health Information Technology for Economic and Clinical Health Act, Title XIII of Division A and Title IV of Division B of the American Recovery and Reinvestment Act of 2009, Pub. L. No. 111-5, 123 Stat. 226 (Feb. 17, 2009) (codified at 42 U.S.C. §§ 300jj *et seq.*, §§ 17901 *et seq.*).

[8] HHS press release, dated Jan. 17, 2013 *available at* http://wayback.archive-it.org/3926/20170118235404/https://www.hhs.gov/about/news/2013/01/17/new-rule-protects-patient-privacy-secures-health-information.html.

[9] *Id.*

[10] 45 C.F.R. § 160.103.

[11] 45 C.F.R. §§ 160 and 164; 45 C.F.R. § 160.103.

[12] 45 C.F.R. § 164.502(a).

[13] 45 C.F.R. § 164.524; 45 C.F.R. § 164.526.

administrative, physical and technical safeguards to ensure the confidentiality, integrity and security of electronic protected health information.[14] These measures include, for example, implementing physical security measures (e.g., locked facilities) as well as software-security measures (e.g., user authentication) and data-transmission protections (e.g., encryption).[15]

Under the HIPAA regulations, known as the Transaction and Code Set Standards,[16] Covered Entities are required to use uniform electronic transmission standards for certain administrative transactions transmitted over electronic data interchanges (EDI), such as health plan enrollment or disenrollment, patient eligibility determinations, health care claims and payment transactions. As of January 1, 2012, most Covered Entities were required to implement standards, known as HIPAA Version 5010, to conduct electronic transactions.[17]

Under the HIPAA breach notification regulations, Covered Entities and their Business Associates must provide notification following a breach of unsecured protected health information.[18] Covered Entities are required to notify every individual affected by a breach of unsecured protected health information without unreasonable delay and in no case later than 60 days after discovery of the breach. For larger-scale breaches involving more than 500 residents of a state or jurisdiction, a Covered Entity must also notify prominent media outlets in the applicable state or jurisdiction. In addition, HHS must be notified without unreasonable delay and in no case later than 60 days after the discovery of the breach if the breach involves 500 or more individuals, or within 60 days of the end of the calendar year if breach involves fewer than 500 individuals.

Depending on the culpability level of the covered Entity or Business Associate, the civil monetary penalties may range from $100 per violation for unknowing violations up to $1.5 million per violation of an identical requirement per year for uncorrected and willfully negligent violations.[19]

9.3.2 Treatment of Medical Emergencies

In 1986, Congress passed the Emergency Medical Treatment and Labor Act (EMTALA).[20] At its most basic, EMTALA requires Medicare-participating hospitals to medically screen all persons who present to the hospital for emergency care without delay, and to stabilize those with emergent conditions, regardless of the individual's ability to pay. EMTALA provides that, if an individual comes to the emergency department of a hospital and the individual requests (or a request is made on that individual's behalf) examination or treatment of a medical condition, then the hospital must provide an appropriate medical screening examination within the capabilities of the hospital. If the hospital determines that the individual has an emergency medical condition, then the hospital is further obligated to provide either necessary stabilizing treatment or an appropriate transfer.

---

[14] 68 Fed. Reg. 8334 (Feb. 20, 2003); 45 C.F.R. § 164.306(a).
[15] 45 C.F.R. § 164.310(a); 45 C.F.R. § 164.312.
[16] 74 Fed. Reg. 3296 (Jan. 16, 2009).
[17] Id.
[18] 45 C.F.R. §§ 164.402 – 164.410. Unsecured protected health information is protected health information that is not rendered unusable, unreadable or indecipherable to unauthorized individuals through the use of technology or methodology specified by HHS.
[19] 45 C.F.R. § 160.402; 45 C.F.R. § 160.404.
[20] 42 U.S.C. § 1395dd; 42 C.F.R. § 489.24.

CMS has defined "hospital with an emergency department" to include only those departments operated as "dedicated emergency departments."[21] A dedicated emergency department refers to a specially equipped and staffed area of the hospital that is used a significant portion of the time for the initial evaluation and treatment of outpatients for emergency medical conditions. It can be located on the main hospital campus or off the main hospital campus. Examples of dedicated emergency departments include an emergency department, a labor and delivery department, an outpatient psychiatric department that provides drop-in evaluations, and off-campus urgent-care sites. Other off-campus departments of hospitals, however, are not obligated to comply with EMTALA obligations unless the location meets the definition of a dedicated emergency department.

Although EMTALA was enacted in response to concerns that indigent patients were being denied emergency care because of their inability to pay, violation of the statute does not require proof that a hospital refused treatment for economic reasons. EMTALA's purpose is to ensure that all patients receive medical care as soon as possible. Therefore, all hospital actions in the emergency room, even routine questions pertaining to financial information in the patient registration process, must be undertaken in a manner that is in full compliance with EMTALA and its implementing regulations.

EMTALA obligations are satisfied with respect to an individual who presented at a hospital for emergency services, was determined to have an emergency medical condition, and whose condition is stabilized as documented by relevant clinical data in the individual's medical record, even if the individual's medical condition later declines. Moreover, a hospital has no responsibility under EMTALA to an inpatient who is admitted for elective (nonemergency) diagnosis or treatment, even if such individual has an abrupt deterioration of her medical condition after admission. Rather, the general Medicare CoPs exist to protect inpatients.

In addition to a hospital's obligation to screen and stabilize individuals, EMTALA governs the emergent transfer of patients from one hospital to another. When a hospital emergently transfers a patient to another institution for care, it is required to document notification of the other institution prior to the transfer, obtain the signature of the transferring physician on a form attesting to the condition of the patient and the need for the transfer, among other details. Even in the event that a patient does not complain about a transfer or the receiving institution does not complain about a transfer, if the paperwork surrounding the patient's transfer is not accurately completed, and such deficiency is discovered upon a subsequent survey of the institution, that incomplete paperwork can be the basis for an allegation of a violation of the statute.

Other requirements under EMTALA include adoption and enforcement of written policies and procedures to ensure compliance with the statute, reporting obligations, posting of EMTALA-explanatory signage, record-keeping, and maintaining a central log and a list of on-call physicians.

With regard to maintaining a list of on-call physicians, on-call lists need to include, by name, the physician on call for a particular specialty. Every hospital is expected to provide, in medical staff bylaws or through policies and procedures, how quickly a physician is expected to respond to a page for emergency services and how quickly he or she must come to the emergency department if it is

---

[21] 42 C.F.R. § 489.24(b).

determined that the doctor's presence is necessary for the patient's screening or stabilizing treatment. Each hospital has the discretion to maintain the on-call list in a manner to best meet community needs. Physicians, including specialists and subspecialists, are not required to be on-call at all times; hospitals, therefore, must have policies and procedures to be followed when a particular specialty is not available or when the on-call physician is unable to come to the hospital. Hospitals may also participate in "community call plans" to share the responsibility for physician coverage that may otherwise be difficult to maintain.

9.3.3 Conditions of Participation and Compliance Programs

All health care facilities that participate in the federal Medicare program are required to comply with the regulations adopted by CMS to implement the program, including, for hospitals, the CoPs. As noted previously, hospitals that are determined to be operating outside of compliance with the CoPs, which may be determined through a state DPH or CMS survey, risk termination of their provider agreement with CMS.

During the 1980s, CMS became concerned that many hospitals and physicians were not complying fully with the CoPs. As a result, the government started to implement a program for health care that was similar to one which had been implemented in the defense industry: individual hospitals were required to have a compliance policy, a senior level committee responsible for compliance issues, and an individual who would be designated as the compliance officer. The intent of this initiative was to establish within a hospital a hierarchy of individuals whose primary purpose was to ensure that the organization fully complied with the CoPs and other federal laws.

This effort was augmented by the adoption of the Federal Sentencing Guidelines in 1991 and their updates in 2015.[22] The Federal Sentencing Guidelines require a federal court to impose severe economic sanctions on an entity convicted of a criminal violation. The purpose of removing judicial discretion was to provide just punishment, adequate deterrence, and incentives for organizations to maintain internal mechanisms for preventing, detecting, and reporting criminal conduct. The Federal Sentencing Guidelines require the sentence to be based on the seriousness of the offense and the culpability of the defendant organization, as measured by significant factors such as whether high level personnel participated in or condoned the criminal behavior. A mitigating circumstance, however, is the presence within the defendant organization of an effective program designed to detect violations of law. In addition, if the defendant self-reported the violation and cooperated in the investigation, then its "culpability score" is once again reduced. Reductions in a culpability score significantly reduce the amount of fines that can be assessed against the defendant organization.

Almost all hospitals have adopted compliance programs in accordance with guidelines for hospital compliance programs published by the Office of the Inspector General (OIG) of HHS (Compliance Program Guidance for Hospitals).[23] Following the Compliance Program Guidance for Hospitals is not mandatory; despite this, however, most hospitals attempt to follow it as closely as possible. The presumption is that a fully functioning compliance program will minimize the possibility that the

---

[22] *Available at* http://www.ussc.gov/guidelines/2015-guidelines-manual.
[23] 63 Fed. Reg. 8987 (Feb. 23, 1998), as revised 70 Fed. Reg. 4858 (Jan. 31, 2005).

organization will violate federal law, and that, if such a violation were to occur, a fully functioning compliance program will mitigate the imposition of penalties. Moreover, private enforcement of health care fraud received a significant enhancement through the 1986 amendments to the Civil False Claims Act,[24] which empowers private individuals to sue on behalf of the government through *qui tam* or "whistleblower" suits and receive a percentage of any recovery of monies by the federal government.

Implementation of an effective compliance program has become one of the more important regulatory realities for the hospital industry. All hospital executives must pay as much attention to compliance regulations as they dedicate to hospital licensing standards and complying with standards promulgated by accrediting bodies such as The Joint Commission. There is a risk that, if a hospital violates federal law, the OIG or a private whistleblower likely will cause the violation to be reported and/or discovered; further, if a conviction results, then subsequent penalties are likely to be imposed, which will be much more severe and restricting than they would have been if an effective compliance program had been in place.[25]

9.3.4 Regulation of Medical Staff Disciplinary Procedures and Excluded Provider Verification

The Health Care Quality Improvement Act of 1986 (HCQIA)[26] was passed by Congress with the intent to offer health care institutions, including hospitals, a limited form of immunity if the institution performed credentialing actions regarding its medical staff in accordance with minimum due process procedures as set forth in statute and its implementing regulations. As a result of HCQIA, hospitals include in their medical staff bylaws a process to permit medical staff members the appropriate period of time required by HCQIA (i.e., 30 days) within which to respond to notices of adverse actions, to provide for the use of attorneys at disciplinary hearings, and to adopt other minimum standards for evidentiary decisions.

Another component of HCQIA was the establishment of a national repository for practitioner information, the National Practitioner Data Bank (NPDB).[27] The NPDB was designed to afford hospitals and other entities associated with medical practitioners a means to find out information about the issues of patient care or professional competence such practitioners might have experienced at other institutions. The obvious intent was to make it difficult for poor quality practitioners to move from one institution to another without anyone knowing about their practice history. Because of the perceived negative impact on a health care practitioner as a result of a report filed in the NPDB, the ability to discipline a medical staff practitioner has moved from a somewhat collegial activity to one where the medical practitioner believes his or her career may

---

[24] 31 U.S.C. § 3729, as amended.
[25] *See, e.g.*, S. Yates, Deputy Attorney General, *Individual Accountability for Corporate Wrongdoing*, U.S. Department of Justice, Sept. 9, 2015 (the "Yates Memo"). The Yates Memo set forth guidance to be used by U.S. Department of Justice civil and criminal attorneys "in any investigation of corporate misconduct" in order to "hold to account the individuals responsible for illegal corporate conduct," thereby providing a framework for imposition of individual liability in instances of corporate misconduct and increasing the scrutiny applied to cooperation credit.
[26] Health Care Quality Improvement Act of 1986, 42 U.S.C. §§ 11101 *et seq.*
[27] 45 C.F.R. § 60.1.

be at stake—an escalation often resulting in heightened degree of activity among lawyers for the individual and the institution alike.

Hospitals are required to file a report with the NPDB in certain instances, for example, if there has been a "professional review action" (as defined by HCQIA) that is based on matters related to the professional competence or conduct of a medical practitioner which has adversely affected clinical privileges for a period longer than 30 days. In addition, if the practitioner voluntarily surrenders or agrees to a restriction of his or her clinical privileges while under investigation or in order to avoid an adverse professional review action, then the hospital also must report that action to the NPDB. Malpractice judgments and settlements are also reportable to the NPDB.

Hospitals are also charged with reviewing the listing of individuals who have been sanctioned by the Medicare programs so that the hospital does not do business with any individual who has previously been removed as a Medicare provider. Federal law authorizes the imposition of civil monetary penalties against health care providers and entities that employ or enter into contracts with excluded individuals or entities to provide items or services to federal health care program beneficiaries.[28] The basis of this restriction is the theory that an individual or entity found to have violated Medicare rules would be more likely to commit that action in the future. CMS has established a website listing the names of all such sanctioned individuals.[29] Hospitals are expected to check the listing each time they enter into a contract with an individual, begin an employment relationship, or grant medical staff privileges and regularly thereafter. If a hospital allows a sanctioned individual to join or remain on its medical staff, to perform as its employee, or to serve as one of its contractors, the hospital can be subject to civil monetary penalties. Because of the seriousness of these penalties, hospitals have made it a part of their policies and procedures to verify the status of all individuals or entities as qualified providers under the Medicare program, and many have contracted with third party vendors to conduct regular screening of all employees and contractors (e.g., monthly or quarterly screenings) to avoid potential liability.

9.3.5   Regulation of Hospitals as Employers

In many communities, the largest employer is the local hospital and its related health care operations. As employers, hospitals are regulated much the same as any other business with employees. However, the specific laws and regulations that govern health care add an additional layer of complexity to hospital operations.

State law impacts how physicians and other licensed health care professionals are employed. In many states, the corporate practice of medicine (or, in some cases, other professions) doctrine limits the ability of corporations to directly employ licensed professionals. Exceptions are commonly provided for by law, for example, statutes explicitly permitting hospitals to employ physicians or other professionals as part of the hospital's purpose of providing health care, so long as the health care professionals are permitted to use independent medical judgment in providing care.

---

[28] Publication of the OIG Special Advisory Bulletin on the Effect of Exclusion from Participation in Federal Health Care Programs, 64 Fed. Reg. 52791 (Sept. 30, 1999).
[29] This website can be accessed by visiting http://www.npdb-hipdb.hrsa.gov/.

Moreover, and as described in greater detail below, hospitals may have a partially or completely unionized workforce, which brings special challenges.

9.3.6 Regulation of Unionization of Nurses and Doctors

Physicians are increasingly becoming employed by hospitals and hospital-affiliated medical groups, and those who are employed in this manner are eligible under the National Labor Relations Act (NLRA) to engage in collective-bargaining activities.[30] Currently, most physicians who are represented by unions are interns, residents, or doctors employed by state or federal governments. However, with the increasing pressures on physician incomes, many physicians employed by private hospitals, medical schools, universities, ambulatory-care centers and other providers may be more receptive in the future to organizing efforts by various collective-bargaining organizations. The American Medical Association has established a policy in support of establishing a collective-bargaining unit, as have a number of state medical societies.

However, due to federal antitrust laws, self-employed physicians are not eligible to engage in collective bargaining with entities such as commercial health plans. Self-employed physicians are considered to be competitors of each other, and are not considered to be "employees" as defined under the NLRA. In addition, even among employed physicians, many individual physicians will not be eligible to join unions because they would be categorized as "supervisors" under the National Labor Relations Board (NLRB) rules. A supervisor is a person who can make hiring and other personnel decisions concerning other employees and who is entitled to use independent judgment in making those decisions.[31] Other persons also will be deemed to be managerial employees (and thus also ineligible to join a union) if they participate in the formulation of the policies of the employing entity and if their status within the entity establishes an element of conflict of interest between employees of the entity and the employing entity.

If physicians were to organize on a general basis, then presumably they would seek to acquire some enhanced degree of control over their employment situations. Many physicians have indicated, however, that they would not seek to develop a union for the purpose of having the right to strike (and, therefore, refuse to deliver patient care services).

Nurses and other categories of health care workers have been members of unions for quite some time. Their organizing efforts have not been without difficulty, however. In 2001, the U.S. Supreme Court held that registered nurses (RNs) are supervisors under Section 2(11) of the NLRA because their duties were conducted in the interests of the employer and used independent judgment in their job duties, even though the judgment involved the use of technical or professional judgment.[32] In 2006, the NLRB decided three cases in which it redefined its test for determining supervisory status (creating new definitions for the terms "assign," "responsibly direct" and "independent judgment"), making it easier for an employer to demonstrate supervisory status of RNs.[33] Nevertheless,

---

[30] 29 U.S.C. § 151.
[31] 29 U.S.C. § 152.
[32] *N.L.R.B. v. Kentucky River Cmty. Care, Inc.*, 532 U.S. 706, 713 (2001).
[33] *Oakwood Healthcare, Inc.*, 348 NLRB No. 37 (Sept. 29, 2006); *Golden Crest Healthcare Center*, 348 NLRB No. 39 (Sept. 29, 2006); and *Croft Metals, Inc.*, 348 NLRB No. 38 (Sept. 29, 2006).

the issue is not entirely resolved, legislation to limit a finding of supervisory status has been proposed but not enacted, and the contest of this issue will continue.

Another issue that could affect organizing efforts among physicians and other health care professionals is the growing trend within the industry of outsourcing workers and "right-sizing" through the engaging of part-time or temporary workers. Anyone employed by an entity and then "leased" by that entity to another company is not a direct employee of the second company. Thus, persons with whom workers have day-to-day contact may not in fact be their fellow workers, which would make it difficult to establish organizing efforts. However, in 2015 the NLRB expanded the scope of the "joint employment" doctrine by holding that either direct or indirect control of certain aspects of a leased employee or contractor could render the leasing entity subject to bargaining and other obligations under the NLRA.[34] (That decision has been appealed and legislation has been introduced to overturn the holding.) Additionally, the NLRB held in 2016 that direct and leased employees working together and sharing a community of interest may form a common bargaining unit without the consent of both employers.[35]

Private health care institutions are subject to the NLRA, but most public health care facilities are excluded from such coverage. The NLRA imposes upon health care providers the obligation to bargain with their employees and with union organizers in good faith. In order to avoid a proliferation of bargaining units in hospitals, the NLRB has developed criteria pertaining to appropriate bargaining units in a hospital. There are eight such groups, made up of separate units for nurses, physicians, professionals other than nurses and physicians, technical employees, skilled maintenance employees, business office clerical employees, guards, and all nonprofessional employees (other than technical employees, skilled maintenance employees, and guards). These eight units are the only permitted bargaining units within a hospital. These units may, however, be combined in certain circumstances, including circumstances in which fewer than five employees are represented within a particular unit. These rules apply to hospitals whose average length of stay is less than 30 days, including general acute care facilities.

In addition to the NLRA, the federal Labor Management Relations Act[36] limits certain union efforts in connection with strikes and picketing. In particular, unions are required under this law to give a minimum of 10 days' written notice of an intention to strike or picket, because health care organizations need an adequate amount of time to make alternative arrangements for patients who might be adversely affected by a work stoppage.

9.4 Accreditation; Survey Activity

The Medicare program requires, as a basic premise, that all participating hospitals be organized and operated in a manner beneficial to their patients. This premise is sound, as CMS has a vested interest in paying only for an appropriate level of quality care for federal health care program beneficiaries. Hospitals demonstrate their compliance with the CoPs through the survey and certification process, either through state agency jurisdiction (where a state DPH surveys and maintains oversight

---

[34] *Browning-Ferris Industries of Calif., Inc.*, 362 NLRB No. 186 (2015).
[35] *Miller & Anderson, Inc.*, 364 NLRB No. 39 (2016).
[36] Labor Management Relations Act, 29 U.S.C. § 141 (2011).

of a facility on behalf of CMS) or through accreditation by an accrediting body with the ability to confer "deemed status"—in other words, that compliance with accreditation requirements is a proxy for satisfying the CoPs.

Virtually all hospitals seek accreditation by an accrediting body CMS has recognized as having sufficient standards, policies, and personnel to perform an inspection of the hospitals and facilities and confer deemed status upon the hospital. The three accrediting bodies currently authorized by CMS to confer "deemed status" upon hospitals are The Joint Commission, the Healthcare Facilities Accreditation Program (HFAP, first formed to accredit osteopathic hospitals) and Det Norske Veritas (DNV). Compliance with the accreditation standards of The Joint Commission, in its *Comprehensive Accreditation Manual for Hospitals, The Official Handbook* (CAMH), or as set forth in the manuals of HFAP or DNV, as verified by survey, is the path to "deemed status." In addition, compliance with the standards of The Joint Commission, HFAP or DNV has become an accepted measure of quality within the industry and is typically included as one of the requirements of financing instruments used by hospitals to obtain necessary capital financing. Of entities that have deeming authority, The Joint Commission has been in existence the longest and continues to accredit a majority of the market and, as such, is the focus of our discussion in this area.

The CAMH (and the manuals of HFAP and DNV) consists of thousands of individual standards and elements that describe virtually every aspect of hospital operations, from governance to the environment of care. Given the broad scope of accreditation, each hospital seeking to obtain or maintain accreditation typically assigns individuals to be responsible for maintaining compliance with the standards within their respective areas of responsibility. Most hospitals, by necessity, look upon compliance with the standards as an integral part of ongoing operations. Joint Commission accreditation expires no later than three years from the date of the last survey of the hospital, which is commonly referred to as the triennial survey.

The Joint Commission surveys hospitals on an unannounced basis to ensure that the hospital integrates standards compliance into daily operations, not only when a survey is expected. Hospitals are accredited in accordance with their CMS certification number (CCN, formerly known as the provider number). Specifically, related hospitals with separate CCNs will be surveyed and accredited separately; similarly, two or more hospitals that share a CCN that may have been accredited separately in the past are now surveyed and accredited as a single organization. Related entities and service providers may be surveyed as part of a hospital if there are Joint Commission standards applicable to such entity and there is organizational and functional integration between the related entity and the hospital.[37] Physician practices are also included where the practice is reported on the hospital's cost report as a provider-based practice.[38] The Joint Commission communicates with accredited facilities primarily through a proprietary web-based site available to each accredited facility.

Triennial surveys by The Joint Commission are conducted in person, on-site at the hospital over the course of a week or more. Additional surveys may be triggered by complaints made to The Joint Commission by patients or health care providers. The Joint Commission utilizes a "tracer" methodology

---

[37] *See* 2017 Comprehensive Accreditation Manual for Hospitals (CAMH) at ACC-7.
[38] *See* CAMH at ACC-10.

that follows care delivered to patients from admission to discharge as a means of reviewing all aspects of hospital operations and ensuring quality and compliance with standards at every step. Each survey also includes interaction with hospital leadership, a review of provider credentialing and privileging, reviews of the environment of care and Life Safety Code compliance, and additional interactions with hospital staff as the surveyors' request. The results of the survey are compiled and scored by The Joint Commission, and shared with the hospital via the extranet site. If recommendations for improvement (RFIs) with standards compliance are made, hospitals must demonstrate and provide evidence of standards compliance (ESCs) for each RFI. The ESCs must specify in detail how the hospital came into compliance with the elements of the standard and measured its success with compliance.

The Joint Commission has developed a new Survey Analysis for Evaluating Risk (SAFER) matrix for accredited hospitals, and plans to replace the current scoring methodology for identified deficiencies. This change will do away with the categorization of deficiencies and identification of direct and indirect impact elements of performance (EPs) and instead utilize a matrix to evaluate the likelihood that the deficiency will cause harm to patients, staff, or visitors based on the surveyor's review.[39] The use of a matrix is designed to provide organizations with additional information related to risk of deficiencies to help prioritize and focus corrective actions. Implementation of the SAFER matrix will also change the submission time frame for submitting ESCs to a consistent time period, as a single time frame of 60 days for corrective action will apply to all cited deficiencies (rather than 45 days in some cases, and 60 days in others).

Upon acceptance of the ESCs by The Joint Commission, the hospital will receive a decision of "Accredited", indicating that the hospital is fully accredited by The Joint Commission, allowing it to have deemed status with CMS. If the RFIs are not acceptable, there is a range of levels of accreditation below the "Accredited" level which provide the opportunity to come into compliance with additional action.[40] These levels may also be imposed where an accredited hospital is found to have ongoing or significant standards compliance issues via a for-cause survey (sometimes referred to as a "complaint" survey).[41] Mechanisms of review and appeal are provided through and until there is a determination of Denial of Accreditation.

Ongoing periodic performance review is an integral part of the triennial Joint Commission accreditation process, inasmuch as it focuses on assisting accredited facilities in remaining compliant with accreditation standards on a day-to-day basis. Further day-to-day monitoring of standards compliance is inherent in other Joint Commission guidelines, such as the reporting of sentinel events[42] and the performance of related root cause analyses.[43]

In addition to visits from The Joint Commission, accredited hospitals also can anticipate unannounced visits by CMS RO or state DPH surveyors (acting on behalf of CMS) to track compliance

---

[39] *See* CAMH at ACC-48-52.
[40] *See* CAMH at ACC-52-53.
[41] *See* CAMH at ACC-71 (*See also* ACC-24-25 for the Joint Commission's process for responding to a complaint).
[42] Defined by The Joint Commission as "[a] patient safety event (not primarily related to the natural course of the patient's illness or underlying condition) that reaches a patient and results in death, permanent harm, or severe temporary harm." *See* CAMH at GL-37.
[43] Which analyses are focused on identification of the factors that underlie variation in performance, including the occurrence or possible occurrence of a sentinel event and related causal or contributory factors. *See* CAMH at SE-6.

with the CoPs and to investigate complaints that a hospital may have violated the CoPs. If the CMS RO or state DPH identifies noncompliance with CoPs, an accredited hospital's deemed status is removed pending resolution, placing the hospital under the jurisdiction of the state agency on behalf of CMS rather than The Joint Commission. As with the RFI process, hospitals must clearly set forth and provide evidence of steps taken to come into compliance and to facilitate ongoing compliance in the post-survey period (as described in Section 9.3).

Once the Plan of Correction is accepted, accredited hospitals may be resurveyed on all CoPs and required to prepare additional Plans of Correction to address any additional deficiencies identified by the surveyors. Upon successful completion of the survey cycle, the hospital is returned by CMS to deemed status as conferred by The Joint Commission. The Joint Commission may elect to make a separate inquiry into resolution of the matter before deemed status is reinstated.

In summary, although this Chapter has only touched the surface of the regulations applicable to hospitals, each practitioner should be aware of the incredibly diverse and in-depth scope of federal and state regulation that may apply to such facilities. A full examination of all such regulations is simply beyond the intent of this Chapter.

10

Representing Physicians

Michael F. Schaff
Wilentz, Goldman & Spitzer PA

10.1 Introduction[1]

As with other clients, it is important for attorneys who represent physicians to recognize characteristics attributable to most physicians. Generally, physicians are intelligent over-achievers who are extremely dedicated to their profession. The vast majority of physicians, however, do not think about or analyze business issues in the same way that business people traditionally do. Physicians have spent significant time in school studying to earn their degrees and, during that time, are usually isolated from the business world. This makes representing physicians different than representing most other individuals who own and operate small businesses. Additionally, the dynamics of a physician group are unique; one physician normally takes the lead in business decisions, and the other physicians are more interested in practicing medicine than running the practice's business. An attorney should take a *proactive* approach in representing physicians: recognizing the role of physicians as health care providers, counsel should be prepared to expend extra time to explain to their physician clients the ramifications of each scenario in order to effectively guide the physicians' practices and the resultant effect on their professional careers.

This chapter is written for attorneys who do not have extensive experience representing physicians. The basic issues and concepts are laid out to give practical insight into the dynamics of physicians and physician groups. Attorneys with extensive experience in representing physicians may be better served by other Health Lawyers publications including the *American Health Lawyers Representing Physicians Handbook, Fourth Edition.*[2] Because the vast majority of physicians are currently employed in the private practice of medicine—and not in academia, research, or hospital employment—this chapter focuses on representing physicians in the private practice of medicine.

10.2 Life Cycle of Physician-Practice Association

Most physicians in the private practice of medicine tend to follow a similar path through their career development. This path generally begins with association or employment with a practice,

---

[1] The author gives a special thanks to Grace D. Mack, Esq., Jason Krisza, Esq., Lisa Gora, Esq. and Patrick Harrity, Esq. who assisted with the update of this chapter.
[2] REPRESENTING PHYSICIANS HANDBOOK (Am. Health Lawyers Ass'n, 4th ed. 2016) [hereinafter REPRESENTING PHYSICIANS HANDBOOK].

followed by ownership, and (hopefully) ends with retirement. Although this process appears to be simple, many issues arise in each phase that can trigger the need for the physician to retain an attorney.

10.2.1 Overview

10.2.1.1 Who is Your Client?

Of key importance to the attorney representing physicians and physician practices is the question of "Who is your client?" The answer to this question will indicate the approach to take in creating and negotiating employment contracts for physicians. Attorneys who have recently commenced their practices are more likely to initially represent employed physicians individually, rather than the group itself. In this regard, this chapter is geared to raising issues necessary for an attorney to advise an individual or employed physician.

10.2.1.2 Who Can Employ a Physician?

Unlike the situation inherent in the employment of unlicensed individuals, states regulate who can employ a physician. In some states, employment is regulated through the "Corporate Practice of Medicine Doctrine." The Corporate Practice of Medicine Doctrine varies from state to state, requiring physicians and their attorneys to review all relevant local laws and regulations governing the specific physician. Often, prohibitions regarding the Corporate Practice of Medicine Doctrine are set forth in the applicable licensure regulations for physicians (*see* Section 10.4.1). Some states strictly enforce the Corporate Practice of Medicine Doctrine, while others practically have abandoned it; the scope of the doctrine varies from state to state.

The Corporate Practice of Medicine Doctrine generally prohibits unlicensed individuals or entities from "practicing medicine." "Practicing medicine" may include the employment of certain health care professionals; the ownership of professional practices; and the provision of medical diagnoses, fee splitting, and/or the treatment or care of patients. These prohibitions can extend to, for example, the prohibition of ownership of diagnostic testing facilities by anyone other than a plenary licensed physician, and even may extend to the broad concept of "excessive influence" over physicians and their clinical judgment.

Historically, the Corporate Practice of Medicine Doctrine arose out of fear that laypersons and general corporations, driven to increase "bottom line" profits, would unduly influence physicians and their medical decisions, with the provision of possibly unnecessary health care (or too little care) as a result. The concern was that a business interest in profit would conflict with a physician's commitments to serve patients and provide the best treatment available. Thus, some jurisdictions prohibit physicians from splitting fees from professional services with unlicensed individuals or entities. Other jurisdictions may simply treat such activity as evidence that a professional is enabling an unlicensed person or entity to practice medicine.

Under the current law of many states, physicians cannot be employed by unlicensed entities, general business corporations, or general business limited liability companies (LLCs). Many states, however, allow a physician to form a professional corporation or LLC, which allows physicians to enjoy the limited liability protection of a corporation or LLC, except for limitation of a liability for their malpractice.

Regarding the restriction on employment of physicians, most states that follow the Corporate Practice of Medicine Doctrine provide exceptions that allow physicians to be employed by health maintenance organizations (HMOs) and other licensed facilities. In addition, licensed entities (e.g., hospitals, fraternal organizations, and other state-licensed entities) may often employ physicians and other health care practitioners in limited roles. Physicians involved in nontraditional practices should be aware of all state laws which may govern their particular entity's structure. In addition, states may differentiate between employment of physicians and employment of other health care practitioners of more limited license. Again, these exceptions, and the question of whether a Corporate Practice of Medicine Doctrine is effective in the state in which the physician will be employed, are state-specific and require individual research.

Although the Corporate Practice of Medicine Doctrine is often honored in its breach, violation of existing state law can result in the exclusion of a physician from the Medicare/Medicaid programs and other insurance programs. Therefore, even if the respective state does not strictly enforce or adhere to its Corporate Practice of Medicine rules or regulations, physicians should be careful to comply with any existing laws.[3]

10.2.2 Employment Contracts

Although employment agreements vary in complexity, certain general topics make up the substance of most physician-employment agreements. Attorneys representing physicians should look for the following items to be incorporated in any physician-employment agreement.[4]

10.2.2.1 Duties and Responsibilities

It is important to understand what duties and responsibilities an employed physician will be required to perform for the employer. The employment agreement should delineate the work schedule (including night and weekend on-call duties); the requirement for staff privileges at certain hospitals or facilities; the location of the physician's employment; and specific responsibilities regarding supervision of nurses, clerical staff, and other physicians. The physician may be required to perform administrative functions. Under all circumstances, a physician's duties should be consistent with and commensurate with the position as a physician.[5]

10.2.2.2 Compensation

Compensation of employed physicians varies widely depending on the area of specialty, years of practice, and geographic region. The employment agreement should specify both the amount and timing of compensation. Many employment agreements contain either a base compensation or a

---

[3] *See* PATIENT CARE AND PROFESSIONAL RESPONSIBILITY: IMPACT OF THE CORPORATE PRACTICE OF MEDICINE DOCTRINE AND RELATED LAWS AND REGULATIONS (NHLA/AAHA 1997), https://www.healthlawyers.org/hlresources/.
[4] Employment contracts are also discussed in Chapter 4 of REPRESENTING PHYSICIANS HANDBOOK.
[5] *See id.* § 4.4.4.

formula compensation based on productivity measures. In addition, many employment agreements provide for bonuses to employed physicians on the occurrence of certain events. It is important to ensure that these events are attainable, so physician clients can perform a proper analysis of the total compensation package offered. Compensation formulas sometimes are very complicated; in practice, some may not work. In this regard, the agreement should include an example regarding the respective formula using expected numbers in order to avoid any confusion as to future interpretation.[6]

10.2.2.3 Benefits and Perquisites

A significant portion of a total compensation package includes the perquisites (more often called "perks") or fringe benefits that are granted to the employed physician. By structuring certain "perks" and fringe benefits separately from compensation, the employed physician may be able to save a significant amount of money in taxes, due to the fact that these benefits are generally not taxable if paid by the employer, but may be taxable income if the employer included them in compensation and the employee purchased these benefits separately. Key benefits include: continuing medical education reimbursement; payments for periodicals and subscriptions; car, or cellular telephone fees; automobile allowance; and health, life, disability, and malpractice insurance. Other benefits can include reimbursement of moving expenses, retirement plans, vacation, and disability/sick/maternity leave.

It is important to understand the distinction between "occurrence" and "claims made" malpractice insurance. Occurrence malpractice insurance covers the physician if she had insurance on the date the malpractice occurred, regardless of whether she has insurance on the date the claim is made. "Claims made" insurance covers the physician only if she has insurance on the date the claim is made. It is important to note that a physician who has claims made insurance will need to purchase a "tail" insurance policy to protect the physician and the practice from malpractice actions that occurred while employed and whose claim is made after the claims made policy lapsed. Tail insurance involves a significant cost, and it is important to spell out whether it is the employer's or employee's obligation to maintain such insurance upon termination.

While advising physicians of the total compensation package, attorneys should ask their clients questions to ascertain which benefits are most important to them. Making a list of types of benefits, and reviewing the agreement to see if those benefits are included, should be of great help. Be proactive; suggest types of benefits that may be of interest to the client, and ask the opposing counsel why a particular benefit has not been included. In many cases, employers may include that benefit without changing the employed physician's salary and/or bonus formula. Attorneys may also request that the employer pay for legal fees associated with review of the proposed agreement (an attempt that works about 20% of the time).[7]

10.2.2.4 Ownership Opportunities

In assessing the merits of an employment offer, physicians generally consider the long-term relationship that will develop while associating with a specific practice. It is in the physician-employee's

---

[6] *See* REPRESENTING PHYSICIANS HANDBOOK, *supra* note 2, § 4.4.5.
[7] *See id.* § 4.4.6.

best interest to work out (in advance) the terms and conditions of any ownership opportunities in the practice. This includes not only the time at which the physician-employee becomes eligible for "partnership," but also the economic ramifications associated with becoming an owner, including any buy-in amounts, compensation, and buy-out obligations (*see* Section 10.2.3). The structure of a buy-in has unique tax consequences, and physicians should consult with their tax advisors regarding tax issues.

Many employers are reluctant to guarantee future ownership opportunities in an initial employment agreement. The physician client's interests can be protected by adding a simple paragraph that lays out the terms of ownership, indicates that these terms are only the current intentions of the parties, and emphasizes that neither party is bound by these provisions. Even if nonbinding, such a provision is important; most physicians tend to honor these written current intentions when "partnership" opportunities arise, due to the fact that a relationship usually develops between the employed physician and the employer over the course of employment.

It is also advantageous to build in a review process where the employer periodically reviews and advises the employed physician on whether the employed physician is on "partnership track."[8]

10.2.2.5 *Term/Termination*

The employment agreement should have defined commencement and expiration dates. Whether a long or short-term agreement is desirable depends upon the client's particular circumstances. Many agreements provide for an "evergreen clause," a provision allowing the contract to continually renew from year to year. This type of clause is generally advantageous from the employed physician's perspective; if an evergreen clause is inserted, however, the compensation section should provide for periodic increases or review of compensation.

In the absence of a specific provision in the agreement, employment is generally "at will" and can be terminated by either party without notice for any reason. In representing the employed physician, it is preferable to limit the employer's ability to terminate to specific causes. The agreement should include a notice provision, as well as the ability to cure any alleged default, breach, or cause in a reasonable period of time. The definition of "cause" is normally hotly negotiated, and its operational definition with respect to the agreement should be carefully reviewed to ensure that the client understands each of the reasons for termination for cause.[9]

10.2.2.6 *Post-Termination Restrictive Covenant*

Employers generally incorporate a post-termination restrictive covenant in their employment agreements. These covenants generally include both noncompetition and nonsolicitation elements. They are designed to prevent the employed physician from competing with the employer in a particular geographic area for a specific period of time, and may also include a prohibition on soliciting patients, referral sources, and employees of the former employer.

---

[8] For further discussion of the specific terms associated with ownership, see *infra* Section 10.2.3; *see also* REPRESENTING PHYSICIANS HANDBOOK, *supra* note 2, § 4.4.17 and ch. 5.

[9] *See infra* Section 10.2.3.3. Term and termination also discussed in REPRESENTING PHYSICIANS HANDBOOK, *supra* note 2, §§ 4.4.7–4.4.8.

To be legally enforceable, restrictive covenants in any form must be reasonable in scope and duration, must not be injurious to the public at large, and should not prohibit the employed physician from pursuing activities not engaged in by the employer. These provisions should be discussed at length and in a detailed manner with a physician client to ensure that, upon termination, the physician will retain the ability to practice medicine without major disruption.

In some instances, the employment agreement includes a pre-termination restrictive covenant prohibiting the employed physician from "moonlighting" or having other employment. This may not be important to a client, but it should be specifically addressed. Attorneys should also note that, in some states, a post-termination restrictive covenant is not enforceable, so applicable state law should also be reviewed.[10]

10.2.2.7 Other Issues

Employment agreements also contain provisions dealing with recordkeeping, legal compliance, dispute resolution, assignability, notice, and many others that are not unique to physician-employment agreements. Although such items are not addressed here due to limitation of space, counsel should take care to account for these and similar measures.

10.2.3 Ownership

Most employed physicians strive to become owners in the medical practices where they work. Becoming an owner, in their eyes, means that they have "arrived." Similar to becoming a partner in a law firm, becoming an owner in a medical practice instills maturity and a sense of stewardship in physicians' careers. Depending on the specific medical practice, ownership has many meanings. Ownership can include the ability to assist with or make decisions, share in the profits or losses of the practice, and grant the physician equity and appreciation in the value of the practice.

10.2.3.1 Buy-In

As a physician becomes an owner of a practice, a significant number of documents may be used to evidence the buy-in. Documents may be labeled differently depending upon whether the practice is a corporation, an LLC, a partnership, or a sole proprietorship. Although the names of these documents will differ and the types of ownership that will be acquired have different names, they essentially have similar characteristics. These documents can include: (1) a purchase agreement for the ownership interest that takes the form of a stock, partnership, or LLC member interest (hereinafter referred to as a Purchase Agreement); (2) an ownership agreement (e.g., a stockholders' agreement and bylaws for a corporation, a partnership agreement in a partnership, and an operating agreement for an LLC); (3) new employment agreements commensurate with being an owner; (4) termination pay agreements; and (5) other documents, depending on the business structure.

Of initial importance is the Purchase Agreement, whereby the physician employee becomes an owner in the practice. That document should specifically set forth the individual's ownership

---

[10] Restrictive covenants also referenced in REPRESENTING PHYSICIANS HANDBOOK, *supra* note 2, § 4.4.15.

percentage, the purchase price, and the payment terms. Purchase Agreements generally provide significant representations and warranties by the seller and the practice, which disclose important information about the practice.

Typical representations and warranties may include disclosure of the assets owned and liabilities owed by the practice; whether the practice is in good standing in the state; that the practice has filed all required tax returns and paid all taxes; that entering into the Purchase Agreement does not and will not violate any agreements under which the practice may be obligated; and that the books, records, and tax returns of the practice reflect its business history.

Of particular importance to an employed physician buying into the practice will be a representation and warranty of the seller and the practice setting forth all transactions where the existing owners of the practice, their family, or friends are involved. For example, it is possible that the other owners of the practice (or their families or friends) own the facility where the practice is located and lease the space to the practice. In these instances, the rental value should be based on fair-market rent, not an inflated rent whereby the existing owners are funneling practice money into their (or their families' or friends') pockets. In addition, a representation and warranty should be included that all billing has been done in accordance with law.[11]

10.2.3.2 Ownership Agreements

Upon buying into a medical practice, the owners usually set forth rights and obligations as owners in an ownership agreement. Ownership agreements generally deal with two major issues: (1) control and management; and (2) transferability of ownership interests. The first major issue will be discussed in this section, and the second is discussed in Section 10.2.4.

Depending on the practice size and dynamics, control and management issues have a varying degree of importance. From a legal point of view, a group practice is managed by its officers, board of directors, or managers (depending on the legal structure of the practice). In reality, the management titles usually have no real importance (they often are based on seniority), and the functions and the responsibilities for each physician owner often are delegated based upon their ability. The legal significance of these positions, however, is important. Should a dispute arise between the owners of the practice, the managing positions assigned to the physician-client could have an impact as to what legal rights and recourse exist. For instance, specific rights inherent to the position of "president" will allow the president to hire or fire employees, absent any provisions or agreements to the contrary.

Typically, a practice will allow each owner to have an equal vote in the management of the practice. Nevertheless, voting may be based instead upon factors such as seniority, ownership percentage, productivity, compensation, or any other factor the practice may deem relevant. It is important to ensure that clients understand the voting rights they obtain upon their buy-in, as well as the voting rights of the other owners.

---

[11] *See* Chapter 5 Fundamentals of Health Law Fraud and Abuse; *See also* Representing Physicians Handbook, *supra* note 2, ch. 5.

In large practices, it is common to have an executive or management committee that is responsible for the day-to-day operations of the practice. In these circumstances, the executive or management committee may have the legal authority to make decisions on certain issues without receiving the input or consent of all of the practice's owners. The practice's documentation should set forth the powers of any executive or management committee. The executive and management committees typically have the ability to negotiate and execute managed-care contracts on behalf of the practice, physician hiring and discipline, check signing, determination of compensation, and other major administrative issues.

If physician-clients are concerned that the practice may make decisions and take certain actions without their consent, then minority-owner protection issues should be addressed. In these circumstances, certain actions should be delineated that require a supermajority (i.e., above 51%, such as 60%, 66%, 75% or greater) or unanimous vote before they are taken. Examples of such actions might include purchasing equipment over an agreed-upon dollar amount, hiring new physicians or terminating employed physicians, obtaining loans on behalf of the practice, entering into related-party transactions, selling all or part of the practice, issuing ownership interests to new or existing owners, amending the practice's organization documents, or making a capital call (asking owners for more money).

Too often, and despite their clear importance, control and management issues are not discussed or set forth in ownership documents. In those instances, a majority vote controls. Once signed, these documents usually are "put in a drawer" and are not looked at again unless a problem develops. At that time, the client will be glad that her rights are spelled out and protected.[12]

10.2.3.3 Employment and Compensation

Employment agreements for physician owners are similar to the employment agreements for associate physicians set forth in Section 10.2.2, but they differ in at least three major areas.[13]

One difference between a physician owner's employment agreement and an associate's employment agreement comes in the area of compensation and fringe benefits. As an owner, the physician client should have a larger risk in the profits and/or losses of the practice, resulting in a base salary that is proportionally lower than total compensation; normally, the remaining amount is paid as funds become available via a bonus mechanism. Nonetheless, spelling out the ways in which compensation is determined and any bonus is calculated remains very important.

A second difference between employee agreements applicable to physician owners and those for physician employees is how each may be terminated by the practice. Generally, employment agreements for physician owners limit termination by the practice only for cause, while practices reserve the right to terminate non-owners without cause. Some physician-owner employment agreements, however, permit termination by the practice without cause by a vote of a supermajority vote of the shareholders (usually 60% or greater). This is an important distinction, because the applicability of

---

[12] *See* REPRESENTING PHYSICIANS HANDBOOK, *supra* note 2, § 5.3.
[13] For further discussion distinguishing physician owner employment agreements from associate employment agreements, see REPRESENTING PHYSICIANS HANDBOOK, *supra* note 2, §§ 5.3–5.4.

a post-termination restrictive covenant may depend on the reason the employment is terminated; if employment is terminated without cause by the practice, then the restrictive covenant may not be germane.

Termination for cause can have either a broad or a narrow definition. The physician-owner will be wearing two "hats" in determining whether the definition should be construed broadly or narrowly. When wearing the "owner" hat, the physician owner may want a broad definition that would give the practice the ability to terminate other physician owners if required. When wearing the "employee" hat, the physician-employee may want a narrow definition that would limit the practice's discretion on termination. Because this inherent conflict does not permit both approaches, it is important to advise physician clients of this duality and the need to use a consistent approach. A new physician-owner should also review the existing physician owners' employment agreements to ensure that they are comparable to the employment agreement being signed. Termination "for cause" provisions include, but are not limited to, the following: termination for loss of license; regulatory violations (including federal, state, hospital, medical society); insubordination (or failure to comply with direction); criminal activities (embezzlement, drug possession, or use); damage to reputation of the entity (or moral turpitude); bankruptcy; inability to maintain malpractice insurance at standard rates; low productivity or hours; and/or the ineffective or incompetent practice of medicine.

A third difference may be in the definition of disability. Practices tend to compensate a physician-owner during disability for a longer period of time than an employed physician, and they allow physician-owners a greater period of time to recover prior to terminating their employment. These different standards for disability between owners and non-owners are prevalent in the medical community. The physician-client should analyze any differences to determine the impact of these changes on disability-insurance policies.[14]

10.2.4 Retirement/Sale of Ownership Interest

The physician's life cycle of association ceases upon the occurrence of certain triggering events. These triggering events generally include death, disability, retirement, or termination of employment (whether with or without cause). Ownership agreements generally prohibit or restrict transferability of ownership interests. Thus, any attempt at voluntary termination will normally be deemed a breach of contract, as well as trigger an automatic offer to the remaining owners to purchase the offered ownership interests. Each triggering event has different ramifications with respect to buy out obligations, as well as any post-termination restrictions.[15]

10.2.4.1 Valuation of Ownership Interests

A medical-practice valuation is comprised of three basic elements: (i) hard (tangible) asset valuation, which incorporates all the physical assets of the practice, including desks, chairs, medical equipment, computers, and other such items; (ii) accounts receivable, including the billings for services rendered that have not been collected by the practice (which are generally worth significantly less

---

[14] *See infra* Section 10.2.4.3.
[15] *See* REPRESENTING PHYSICIANS HANDBOOK, *supra* note 2, § 5.5.

than their face value, because managed care has led to significant discounts from billed amounts); and (iii) "goodwill value," a nebulous term that basically reflects the going concern value of a practice, or the value of continuing the business. Depending upon the triggering event, different valuation approaches may be applicable.

Owners should discuss the value of the ownership interest, and they may wish to annually arrive at and confirm an "agreed value" for their ownership interest. This alleviates any argument as to the value of the interest when an owner leaves, but it may create other problems. The most typical problem arises when many years pass without any change in the established agreed value. To combat this, most ownership agreements provide that if the valuation is stale (e.g., over 12 to 18 months old), then either party can reject the price. In those instances, an alternate valuation approach is generally laid out in the form of a formula value, which could either be a specific formula or an adjustment to the agreed price based on the change in the value of the assets since the date of the last valuation. These valuation approaches should be delineated to avoid any confusion or argument. It might be advantageous from a tax perspective for both the practice and the remaining owners to limit the valuation of the ownership interest to the net "book value" of the practice (the value of the hard assets, as set forth earlier), with the accounts receivable and the goodwill value incorporated in either a severance package or a termination pay or severance agreement. The tax analysis associated with these issues is beyond the scope of this chapter; in this event, consultation with a tax attorney or accountant is recommended.[16]

10.2.4.2 Payment Terms and Collateral

In any buy-out, the practice and remaining physician-owners would experience undue hardship if they were forced to pay a lump sum to the departing owner. Because of this hardship, most buy-out agreements provide for an extended payout with reasonable interest. Typically, these extended payouts are anywhere from 2 to 10 years, depending on the triggering event. If insurance funding has been obtained (*see* Section 10.2.4.3), then the insurance proceeds are paid up front, with the remaining amount (if any) payable over a period of 12 to 24 months, depending on the amount remaining. Any termination or severance payment that is deferred is generally represented by a promissory note, which may be guaranteed by the practice or the remaining owners. In general, promissory notes will include provisions concerning interest rate, payment terms, and default. Normally, a reasonable cure period regarding any default is included so that the outstanding principal does not accelerate upon default. The goal should be to represent this as an obligation and not as a "bank."

To create collateral for the promissory note and the future payment obligations, the typical buy-out includes a pledge of the ownership interest that was purchased, as well as the guarantees of the other owners or the practice, depending on who the purchaser is. In some instances, a security interest is granted on the assets of the company, which will act as additional collateral. In those instances, it should be noted that granting a security interest in the accounts and assets of the practice might have a negative effect on the practice's credit availability with other lenders. In these instances, a subordination agreement will be appropriate.[17]

---

[16] *See id.*
[17] *See id.*

10.2.4.3 Funding Buy-Outs with Insurance

In some cases, it may be appropriate for the practice and the remaining owners to purchase life or disability buy-out insurance on each owner to fund a death or disability buyout. Any purchase of life insurance or disability buy-out insurance should be coordinated with the particular valuation approach chosen. The benefit of purchasing insurance is that the funds will be readily available on the occurrence of a triggering event, and neither the practice nor its remaining owner(s) will be burdened by an unexpected payout. Having insurance proceeds available also will ease the burden on any spouse of a deceased owner, because funds will be immediately available to pay a significant portion of the purchase price, and no negotiations in price will be necessary. Many types of insurance exist; some are quite complicated, so consultation with a reputable insurance agent is recommended.

One major issue regarding insurance is determining who bears the costs of the insurance policy: Determining whether the practice or the individual owners hold the policy, and who pays the premiums associated therewith, can have different tax consequences. Again, this issue should be analyzed with a tax expert to ensure that clients' economic interests are properly protected.

Many physicians become confused about the difference between disability-income insurance and disability buy-out insurance. Simply put, disability-income insurance is used to supplement the loss of base salary on account of disability. Usually, the insurance policy will not begin to pay lost salary for 30 to 90 days. If the physician pays the premiums with after-tax dollars, then the disability payments received by the disabled physician are generally tax-free. If these premiums are deducted by the practice, then generally the payments under the disability policy are taxable income when received by the disabled physician. Conversely, disability buy-out insurance provides a lump sum or periodic payment to fund the buyout of a physician's ownership interest in the practice upon the occurrence of the physician's permanent disability. It is important to review the definitions in the policies (and the ownership agreement) in order to maintain appropriate coverage.[18]

10.2.4.4 Post-Termination Restrictive Covenant

Ownership agreements generally provide for a post-termination restrictive covenant similar to the restrictive covenant that an employed physician signs (*see* Section 10.2.2). The major difference in the buy-out situation is that the practice or the remaining owners are paying the departing owner for the value of her interest in the practice, which may include an amount for goodwill. Whenever a goodwill payment is made, it is reasonable to require the departing owner(s) to restrict their practice so that the remaining owners and the practice actually receive the value paid on account of the goodwill. In these instances, it is typical for the duration of the restrictive covenant to be expanded by a few years, or be parallel to the payout term under the buyout. In many cases, if there is a breach of the restrictive covenant, then the buy-out payments cease, and monies paid under the buyout must be returned. Post-termination restrictive covenants generally have longer durations, and greater restrictive areas, than restrictive covenants for employed physicians. Sometimes the departing physician-

---

[18] Further discussion regarding funding of buy-outs with insurance can be found in REPRESENTING PHYSICIANS HANDBOOK, *supra* note 2, § 5.5.

owner may waive out of a restrictive covenant by paying an agreed-upon amount or giving up a portion of the total buy-out amount. This issue is often hotly negotiated.[19]

10.2.4.5 Breaking Up/Dissolution

Many ownership agreements provide that if the owners are not getting along, the practice will dissolve or "break up." The following three issues are of key importance in any dissolution or break up: (i) the future use of the office location; (ii) the use of the telephone number; and (iii) possession of patient charts. In many cases, the most senior owner retains the right to use the office location and telephone number without having to pay for them, because the senior owner is often the "founder" of the practice, and it could be inequitable for the younger owners to receive the benefit of the established locale and phone number. In many cases, however, the telephone can be answered by a "phone intercept." A typical phone intercept is a service (i.e., voice mail) that either directs callers to a new phone number for the physicians or directly connects the caller to an individual physician's office. For example, the phone-intercept message might be, "If you would like Dr. Jones, please press 1; for Dr. Smith, please press 2; for Dr. Green, please press 3."

Phone intercepts help avoid potential future conflict as to whether a caller was given the appropriate locale or telephone number of the departed physician(s). Typically, patient charts follow the physician who will continue to perform services for the patients.

In many instances, the assets of the practice are divided based upon their value and the ownership percentages of each owner. It is important that the practice is represented by an accountant who is trusted by each of the physicians to coordinate the economics of the dissolution. Each physician also may wish to obtain individual representation by attorneys and/or accountants to ensure that her individual interest is represented.[20]

10.3 Physician/Hospital Arrangements

As the health industry evolves, many physicians are seeking direct employment with hospitals and health systems (Hospitals). When negotiating with hospitals and or health systems, attorneys need to be cognizant of the nuances associated with negotiating contracts with larger entities. Generally speaking, attorneys should recognize the increased chances of the physician being terminated by a hospital and plan accordingly.

10.3.1 Employee vs. Independent Contractor

As with any service arrangement, hospitals may engage physicians through employment arrangements (Internal Revenue Service (IRS) Form W-2) or independent contractor arrangements (IRS Form 1099). If structured as an employment relationship, the employer will withhold taxes and may provide the physician/employee with certain employee benefits, such as paid vacation, health insurance, and a number of other employee benefits. If the relationship is an independent

---

[19] *See id.*
[20] Breaking up/dissolution also referenced *in* REPRESENTING PHYSICIANS HANDBOOK, *supra* note 2, § 5.5 and ch. 8.

contractor relationship, the employer will not typically be required to withhold taxes nor provide employee benefits.

The determination of whether an individual is an independent contractor or an employee is a question of law and the attendant facts. The mere designation of a physician as an "independent contractor" is not dispositive. The IRS offers significant guidance in determining whether an individual is an employee or an independent contractor. While the IRS generally classifies individuals as employees over independent contractors, the determination ultimately turns on the facts related to control, which include:

- The extent to which the services rendered are an integral part of the principal's business;
- The permanency of the relationship;
- The amount of the alleged contractor's investment in facilities and equipment;
- The nature and degree of control by the principal;
- The alleged contractor's opportunities for profit and loss;
- The amount of initiative, judgment, or foresight in open market competition with others that is required for the success of the claimed independent contractor; and
- The degree of independent business organization and operation.[21]

As the determination of whether an individual is an independent contractor or an employee hinges upon facts, attorneys must consider whether a classification is accurate. This consideration is especially important when a hospital incorrectly classifies a physician as an independent contractor as this may have serious economic consequences for the physician. We suggest that the physician's tax advisor be brought into any discussions of this issue.

10.3.2 Key Issues/Provisions

10.3.2.1 Term and Termination

Similar to being employed by a medical practice (see Sections 10.2.2.5 and 10.2.3.3), the term and termination provisions play an important role in contracts between a physician and a hospital, as they govern, among other things, the commencement of the relationship, the length of the relationship, and how the relationship can be ended. Particular attention must be given to the termination provision of any contract.

Many employers include clauses providing for the ability for either party to terminate with cause or without cause. "For cause" termination allows one party to terminate the agreement based on the occurrence or the non-occurrence of a specific event, such as the suspension of the employee's license to practice medicine or the breach of the contract. When representing physicians, it is important to request notice and cure provisions so that an unknowing breach, or an inadvertent breach, will not give the hospital right to terminate the agreement.

---

[21] United States Department of Labor, Fact Sheet 13, *available at* http://www.dol.gov/whd/regs/compliance/whdfs13.htm.

Most employment agreements also provide the parties with the ability to terminate the agreement without cause. "Without cause" termination provides one or both parties the ability to terminate the relationship for any reason or without a reason. An attorney should always ensure that without cause termination provisions should be mutual. This notice provision provides the non-terminating party with a certain time limit so they can, in the case of the physician, find a new job, or in the case of the hospital, find a new physician. Regardless of the stated term of the agreement, a without cause termination provision provides the physician with the only guaranteed term of employment, i.e., the notice period. A notice period between thirty (30) and one hundred twenty (120) days is typical.

10.3.2.2 Duties

Each employment contract should specifically set forth the physician's duties and conditions of employment. The agreement should set forth the (i) types of services the physician is required to perform; (ii) physician's schedule; and (iii) physician's call responsibilities. When representing the physician, it is important to keep these duties as specific as possible and include provisions prohibiting the hospital from changing the terms of the agreement post-execution. Generally, hospitals will add broad language that refers to hospital policies. Ensure your client has access to these policies, is provided advance written notice and copies of any new policies, and will not be subjected to policies unless they apply to all physician employees of the hospital. It is important to include language that allows the physician to terminate the agreement if he or she does not agree with the new policies without being bound by a restrictive covenant.

10.3.2.3 Compensation

Another important component of a physician contract is the consideration or compensation payable to the physician for services. There are numerous compensation models including, but not limited to, fixed salary, productivity/relative value units (RVUs), or compensation based on revenue or collections. Physician compensation payable by a hospital is heavily regulated. In all cases, compensation should be fair market value and not take into account the volume or value of referrals. There is no single way to value the work of a physician, and fair market value is not set at a specific number, but rather is a range that the compensation must fall within. If the arrangement is comprised of some measurable factor such as RVUs, it is important for the physician to have a contractual right to audit such methodology.

10.3.2.4 Benefits

As discussed in Section 10.3.1, most hospitals provide employees with benefits that independent contractors are not provided. Typically, when representing the physician, it is important to ensure that all benefit provisions are not qualified with clauses that allow the hospital to revoke or change certain benefits without amending the contract. These benefits can include paid time off, retirement plans, malpractice insurance, and reimbursement for certain expenses. In some cases, the hospital will merely state that the physician will be awarded benefits in accordance with hospital policies which may be amended from time to time. These provisions should be negotiated to prohibit the hospital from amending such policies without the mutual consent of the physician. In the event that the hospital refuses to include language, it is important to include a clause allowing the physician to terminate the agreement if they do not agree to the amended methodology without being subject to a restrictive covenant.

10.3.2.5 *Restrictive Covenant, Hospital Records, and Confidentiality*

Hospitals consider patient and referral relationships as valuable assets. Upon the termination of a relationship with a physician, the hospital needs to have adequate assurances from the physician that she will not directly compete with the hospital or use the confidential information gained from her employment against the hospital. As such, hospitals will often insert provisions prohibiting the physicians from soliciting patients and employees for a period of time after termination, limiting or eliminating the use of confidential information post-employment, and restricting the physician from practicing within a certain geographic area around the hospital's location for a period of time. When representing physicians, it is important to discuss the impacts of the proposed restrictive covenants.

States vary on the extent to which they will enforce a restrictive covenant (if at all), so it is important that the state laws governing the arrangement are reviewed to determine if, and to what extent, a restrictive covenant will be enforced.[22]

Additionally, hospitals generally include provisions setting forth ownership and access to the medical records following the termination of the agreement. Often, a hospital will want to retain ownership and physical possession of the medical records post-termination. Ensure that the physician can access these records both during and after employment for defending any claim, for example, malpractice actions, payer audits, or disciplinary issues.

10.3.2.6 *Dispute Resolution*

It is often in the best interest of the parties to set forth specific dispute resolution language so it is clear how disagreements will be governed. It is common to have all claims resolved through mediation or arbitration, as these provide parties with cheaper alternatives than filing suit in court.

10.4 Licensure and Credentialing

Although matters surrounding employment and ownership of physician practices are important, a more basic and crucial area to consider when representing physicians is licensure and credentialing. Every physician must be licensed in order to practice medicine in every state in which the physician renders medical care. In addition, most physicians maintain specialty and sometime subspecialty certifications conferred by private accrediting boards, and are required by regulation to do so in order to promote themselves as specialists. Certification in a relevant specialty is also often required in order for the physician to maintain the privilege of admitting privileges at hospitals or other facilities. This section will discuss these and related issues.

---

[22] *See infra* Section 10.2.2.6, Restrictive covenants also referenced in REPRESENTING PHYSICIANS HANDBOOK, *supra* note 2, § 4.4.15.

10.4.1 State Licensure Law

Every state has standards governing the licensure of health care professionals that create a minimum competency level for each health care practitioner in the state. The licensure laws ostensibly ensure quality of care in the medical profession. Health care practitioners can be penalized for practicing in states in which they are not licensed, or for practicing outside the scope of their respective licenses. Medical doctors and doctors of osteopathy generally have "plenary" licenses, which enable them to perform services in virtually any field of medicine in the states in which they are licensed. Because licensure is state-specific, attorneys representing physicians must be careful to check the laws and regulations of the states in which their clients are practicing medicine.

The laws of the several states do have some universal features, however, such as the creation of boards or agencies to oversee medical professionals (e.g., a Board of Medical Examiners, Board of Chiropractic Examiners), a definition of "practicing medicine," educational and professional training pre-requisites and examination requirements for becoming licensed to practice medicine and continuing education requirements to maintain licensure, and delineation of behavior that can result in the imposition of sanctions, such as loss or suspension of a license. States usually have standards governing the admission of physicians who have been trained in foreign countries.[23]

Many states' laws restrict the business structure of physician practices by explicit regulation or under the "corporate practice" doctrine, which generally holds that when a business entity (such as a corporation or limited liability company) that does not hold a professional license employs or otherwise engages a licensed physician or other licensed professional to perform professional services on its behalf, the *entity* is engaged in the unlicensed practice of the profession. In states where the "corporate practice" doctrine is applied, only certain types of entities, such as professional corporations or partnerships owned only by licensed professionals, and hospitals or other types of licensed health care facilities, may employ or otherwise engage professionals to perform professional services.

State-by-state physician licensing requirements sometime conflict with recent developments in technology and the medical economics—such as the advent of telemedicine,[24] the national standard of care now applied to physicians, and the trend toward larger group practices—creating barriers to practicing medicine in an increasingly managed care-oriented and technological world. For instance, telemedicine may be construed as "practicing medicine across state lines." This raises the question of whether physicians can be said to practice medicine in states in which they are not physically present. Many states allow interstate consultations without licensure in the particular state, especially for highly specialized areas of medicine, but individual state laws vary on this point. In addition, large physician groups are becoming more common as physicians realize that they have increased bargaining power in greater numbers. In areas such as the "tri-state area" of New York, New Jersey, and Connecticut, for example, it is not unusual for patients to cross state lines for care; the next logical step is that group practices likewise will cross state lines. Under the current status of licensure, each of the physicians in the group may need to be licensed in each state in which the group practices or

---

[23] For a more in-depth discussion of licensure, *see* SCOTT BECKER, HEALTH CARE LAW: A PRACTICAL GUIDE, Ch. 17 (Matthew Bender, 2d ed. 2001); *see also* REPRESENTING PHYSICIANS HANDBOOK, *supra* note 2, § 2.6.

[24] *See infra* Section 10.6. For a more in-depth discussion of telemedicine, *see* Tara Kepler, *Telemedicine*, Chapter III *in* REPRESENTING PHYSICIANS, THIRD EDITION (Am. Health Laws. Ass'n. 2012).

advertises its services. Attorneys representing physicians in multi-state practices must be familiar with the licensure laws in each state to adequately protect their physician clients.

10.4.2 Reports to the National Practitioner Data Bank

The National Practitioner Data Bank (NPDB) is a centralized system that was established by the Health Care Quality Improvement Act of 1986 (HCQIA).[25] Originally, only certain actions taken against physicians were to be reported to the NPDB, including revocation or suspension of a license by a state medical board (including censure, reprimand, or surrender of a license due to reasons related to professional conduct or competence), medical-malpractice claims paid by malpractice-insurance companies, peer-review actions that result in suspension of at least 30 days, and resignation during a peer-review action that is related to the peer-review action. Failure to report such actions may result in sanctions.[26]

Nonetheless, in addition to the NPDB, the secretary of the Department of Health and Human Services (DHHS) also maintained the Healthcare Integrity and Protection Data Bank (HIPDB) to which federal and state government agencies and health plans were required to report the following final adverse actions to the HIPDB:

- Civil judgments in federal or state court against a health care provider, supplier, or practitioner related to delivery of health care;
- Criminal convictions against a health care provider, supplier, or practitioner related to delivery of health care;
- Actions by agencies responsible for licensure and certification of health care providers, suppliers, or practitioners;
- Exclusion from a federal or state funded health care program; and
- Anything else the secretary of DHHS establishes by regulation relating to final adverse actions taken against health care practitioners, providers, and suppliers.[27]

Recognizing that there was some overlap between the NPDB and the HIPDB, two developments occurred in 2010 that drastically affects the maintenance of the two databases. The first of these took effect on March 1, 2010. As of that date, all licensure actions taken by state licensure authorities that were a result of a formal proceeding against all health care practitioners, not just physicians and dentists, and all health care entities must now be reported to the NPDB. Additionally, peer review organizations and private accreditation entities (if they have due process mechanisms) will report certain "negative actions or findings" to the NPDB even if the health care entity chooses not to act on such recommendation, if taken as the result of a formal proceeding against a health care practitioner, physician, dentist, hospital or other health care entity.[28] Peer review organizations are groups of organizations staffed by local practicing physicians that were established by the Tax Equity and Fiscal

---

[25] *See* 42 U.S.C. §§ 11101–11152; NPDB GUIDEBOOK (2015), https://www.npdb.hrsa.gov/resources/NPDBGuidebook.
[26] 42 U.S.C. §§ 11131–11133.
[27] 42 U.S.C. §§ 1301 *et seq.*
[28] *See* National Practitioner Data Bank for Adverse Information on Physicians and Other Health Care Practitioners: Reporting on Adverse and Negative Actions, 75 Fed. Reg. 4656 (Jan. 28, 2010) (amending 45 C.F.R. Pt. 60).

Responsibility Act of 1982 to evaluate the quality, necessity, cost, and adherence to professional standards of medical care provided to Medicare patients as a prerequisite for payment of the medical services by Medicare. A private accreditation entity is an entity or organization that:

- Evaluates and seeks to improve the quality of health care provided by a health care entity;
- Measures a health care entity's performance based on a set of standards and assigns a level of accreditation;
- Conducts ongoing assessments and periodic reviews of the quality of health care provided by a health care entity; and
- Has due process mechanisms available to health care entities.

A "negative action or finding" includes:

- A final determination of denial or termination of an accreditation status from a Private Accreditation Entity that indicates a risk to patients' safety or quality of health care services;
- A recommendation by a Peer Review Organization to sanction a health care practitioner, physician or dentist; or
- A negative action or finding that under the state's law is publicly available information and rendered by a licensing or certification authority, including, but not limited to, limitations on the scope of practice as well as "liquidations, injunctions, and forfeitures."

Entities that have access to the NPDB have always included licensing boards, hospitals, and HMOs that have, or may have, a relationship with the physician. Additionally, effective March 1, 2010, several government agencies, including those administering federal and state health care programs, federal and state law enforcement officials and agencies and state Medicaid Fraud Control Units now have access to the NPDB.[29] Hospitals may now self-query themselves as well.

The second major development affecting the NPDB occurred due to the passing of the Patient Protection and Affordable Care Act (ACA) on March 23, 2010. Pursuant to Section 6403 of the ACA, the HIPDB was terminated and all of the data in the HIPDB was transferred to the NPDB. Further, the DHHS now maintains a national health care fraud and abuse data collection program for reporting certain adverse actions taken against health care providers, suppliers, and practitioners, These actions are also be reported to the NPDB.[30]

Patients do not have access to the NPDB, but it is presumed that hospitals have checked the NPDB when they have admitted doctors to the medical staff. In limited circumstances, however, an attorney for an injured patient (or a patient representing herself) may obtain information from the NPDB and use this information to show that a hospital was negligent in granting privileges to a physician who was involved in the patient's care.

Once a physician has been reported to the NPDB, the physician can find it very difficult to obtain employment elsewhere. A letter, censure, or reprimand in a peer-review action thus may be preferable

---

[29] *See* National Practitioner Data Bank, 75 Fed. Reg. 4656.
[30] *Id.*

to disciplinary action, because such reprimands are not reported to the NPDB. Physicians often challenge reports to the NPDB, and a formal process exists for disputing reports.[31]

10.4.3 Exclusion from Medicare/Medicaid

Physicians who receive reimbursement for their professional services from Medicare and/or Medicaid must comply with the federal laws and regulations regarding submission of claims and prohibitions against fraud and abuse.[32] Violation of these laws can lead to exclusion from the Medicare and Medicaid programs, as well as other federally funded programs. As a result, no federal health care program payments will be made for any items or services (i) furnished, whether directly or indirectly, by the excluded person or entity, or (ii) directed or prescribed by an excluded physician when the person furnishing the item or service knew or had reason to know of the exclusion.[33]

The Office of the Inspector General (OIG) of DHHS released a Special Advisory Bulletin on September 28, 1999 (1999 Bulletin) stating that health care providers will be held responsible for excluded employees or contractors, and that they must determine whether potential and current employees and independent contractors have been excluded from Medicare and/or Medicaid.[34] The general rule is that no federal funds can be used to pay an excluded individual or entity in any way, regardless of whether the funds pay salary, expenses, perquisites, or other benefits, or whether the excluded individual or entity provides direct patient care. Thus, an employer who employs or contracts with an excluded entity or individual must ensure that all payments derive solely from nonfederal funding, and that all services performed are for nonfederal program patients.

In addition to the ability to exclude individuals and entities from federal-program payment, the OIG's power also extends to imposition of civil monetary penalties (CMPs) against excluded individuals or entities that seek reimbursement, including entities that employ or contract with the excluded individuals or entities for provision of services under federal programs after being excluded.[35] Penalties can run as high as $10,000 for each item or service provided by an excluded entity or individual; further, the responsible party can be held accountable for treble the amount claimed. Thus, physicians and physician groups must be very aware of the employees and independent contractors they hire, and be cautious when merging with other physician group practices.

---

[31] *See* 45 C.F.R. § 60.21 (2013) regarding disputing reports.
[32] *See* Chapter 3 Medicare and Chapter 5 FUNDAMENTALS OF HEALTH LAW FRAUD AND ABUSE. Exclusions also referenced in REPRESENTING PHYSICIANS HANDBOOK, *supra* note 2, § 2.3.
[33] 42 C.F.R. § 1001.1901 (2016).
[34] *See* DHHS OIG Special Advisory Bulletin, *The Effect of Exclusion from Participation in Federal Health Care Programs*, U.S. Dep't. Health & Hum. Serv. (Sept. 28, 1999), http://www.oig.hhs.gov/exclusions/effects_of_exclusion.asp (The OIG was established as a part of DHHS to identify and eliminate fraud and abuse in DHHS programs, which the OIG does by auditing, inspecting, and investigating health care providers. The OIG is responsible for periodically issuing special advisory bulletins, in addition to advisory opinions (which are in response to specific queries) to provide guidance about fraud and abuse issues to the health care industry. These advisories are designed to help prevent fraud and abuse, and to promote ethical use of the federal funding systems).
[35] The OIG Web site contains a List of Excluded Individuals/Entities for health care providers to query in order to avoid potential liability. *See* https://oig.hhs.gov/exclusions/exclusions_list.asp.

The OIG's exclusion power and authority to impose CMPs on providers was greatly expanded by the ACA.[36] Although the specific expanded circumstances in which the OIG may wield this power is beyond the scope of this chapter, it is important to understand how expansive and devastating to the bottom line exclusion can be. Further, states, as the administrators of Medicaid, now have limited exclusion authority as well. Section 6501 of the ACA requires states to terminate providers or individuals from Medicaid upon their termination from Medicare or another state's Medicaid program, with certain exceptions.[37] Also, Section 6502 requires state Medicaid agencies to exclude providers or individuals from participation in Medicaid for a period of time if they own, control or manage an entity that: (i) has failed to repay overpayments; (ii) has been suspended, terminated or excluded from any Medicaid program; or (iii) is affiliated with an entity or individual that has been suspended, terminated or excluded.[38]

In May 2013, the OIG released an updated Special Advisory Bulletin on the Effect of Exclusion from Participation in Federal Health Care Programs (Update).[39] Generally the Update reiterates earlier guidance on the scope and effect of an OIG exclusion, but also, among other things, clarifies and expands on certain concepts of the 1999 Bulletin which were previously unclear, and also makes recommendations to providers in connection with the monitoring of employees and contractors. Five such clarifications and/or expansions are set forth below:

1. Pursuant to the 1999 Bulletin, if a person is "excluded," no federal health care program payment may be made for any items or services furnished by that excluded individual or for any items or services directed or prescribed by the excluded individual or even items or services furnished at the medical direction of that excluded individual.[40] It was previously unclear as to what "program payment" actually meant and what type of payment was prohibited. The Update clarifies this point and provides that the payment prohibition applies to all methods of federal health care program payment, whether from itemized claims, cost reports, fee schedules, capitated payments, a prospective payment system or other bundled payments, or other payment system and applies even if the payment is made to a state agency or a person that is not excluded.[41]

2. An excluded provider may refer a patient to a non-excluded provider as long as the excluded provider does not furnish, order, or prescribe any services for the referred patient, and the non-excluded provider treats the patient and independently bills federal health care programs for the items or services that he or she provides.

3. Any provider participating in federal health care programs that is owned in part five percent (5%) or more by an excluded person is potentially subject to CMPs. For instance, an exclusion does not directly prohibit an excluded person from owning a provider that participates in Medicare or state health care programs; having a control interest in such a provider; or

---

[36] *See* Pub. L. No. 111-148 § 6402; § 6406(c); § 6408(a).
[37] *Id.* at § 6501.
[38] *Id.* at § 6502.
[39] *See* DHHS OIG Updated Special Advisory Bulletin, *The Effect of Exclusion from Participation in Federal Health Care Programs*, U.S. Dep't. Health & Hum. Serv. (May 8, 2013), http://oig.hhs.gov/exclusions/files/sab-05092013.pdf.
[40] DHHS OIG Special Advisory Bulletin, *supra* note 30.
[41] DHHS OIG Updated Special Advisory Bulletin, *supra* note 35, at 12.

being an officer or man-aging employee of such provider; however, the OIG, at its sole discretion, may exclude the provider if certain circumstances regarding the ownership are present[42] and may subject the provider to CMP liability.

4. A provider may reduce or eliminate its CMP liability when relying on a third-party to per-form a check of the List of Excluded Individuals and Entities (LEIE) found on the OIG website,[43] provided that the provider is able to demonstrate that it reasonably relied on the third-party to per-form a check of the LEIE for the individuals furnished by the third-party, e.g., a staffing agency, physician group, or third-party billing or coding company, who agreed by contract to perform the screening of the LEIE and the provider exercised due diligence in ensuring that the third-party was meeting its contractual obligations. The OIG recommends that the provider validate that the third-party agency/contractor is conducting such screening on behalf of the provider by requesting and maintaining screening documen-tation from the third-party agency/contractor. Please note that the OIG does not address that the provider could seek indemnification from the contractor if the contract so allows.

5. Practitioners who have valid licenses or drug enforcement agency (DEA) numbers can still be excluded individuals. Therefore, it is important not to assume that because a prescription contains a valid license number or DEA number that the practitioner is not an excluded individual.

The Update also provides a recommendation by the OIG of how providers should go about determining which individuals and entities to screen. The OIG states that the provider should:

- Check the LEIE prior to employing or contracting with persons and periodically check the LEIE to determine the exclusions status of current employees and contractors. This applies whether the individuals are employees or are independent contractors or subcontractors.

- Review each job category or contractual relationship to determine whether the item or ser-vice being provided is directly or indirectly, in whole or in part, payable by a federal health care program. If the answer is yes, then the best mechanism for limiting CMP liability is to screen all persons that perform under that contract or that are in that job category.

- Use the LEIE as the primary source of information about OIG exclusions since the LEIE is maintained by the OIG; is updated monthly; and provides more details about persons excluded by the OIG than other data banks. For example, the LEIE allows for verification of a provider's identity by using Social Security numbers (which are only accessible in the online searchable database and not in the downloadable excel spreadsheet database),[44] dates

---

[42] *See* Section 1128(b)(8) of the Social Security Act.
[43] *See* https://oig.hhs.gov/exclusions/exclusions_list.asp. (Please note that the LEIE is searchable in two formats: (i) the online searchable database; and (ii) the downloadable excel spreadsheet which can be downloaded to a per-sonal computer.)
[44] 5 U.S.C. § 552a (The Privacy Act) prohibits disclosing Social Security numbers (SSN); therefore, the downloadable Excel list of excluded individuals/entities on the OIG Website does not include SSNs. However, the online searchable database format of the LEIE uses the SSN input by the user as one of the matching criteria. It does not supply SSNs to users. If you are a user of the downloadable Excel spreadsheet database, have a possible match on an individual, and want to verify with a SSN, you should use the online searchable database's SSN feature to verify an identity.

of birth, and National Provider Identifiers (NPI). The LEIE also includes information regarding waivers[45] of exclusion granted by the OIG.

- Search all names of an individual, e.g., maiden name and previous married names, because the LEIE includes only names known to the OIG at the time of the individual's exclusion.[46]

10.4.4 Medical Staff Privileges—Credentialing and Other Concerns

Either by employment contract or by necessity, physicians are generally required to be members of the medical staffs of hospitals or other health care facilities (e.g., ambulatory surgery centers or nursing homes). The medical staff is a group of physicians who are permitted to treat patients in, and admit patients to, a particular hospital or health care facility. Not every physician can become a member of a particular facility's medical staff; the physician must first apply to become a member and undergo a review process. The medical staff, acting as a body in accordance with its own bylaws and regulations, has responsibilities with regard to care provided to patients at the facility, including making recommendations the facility concerning granting, revoking and restricting medical staff memberships and clinical privileges.

The term that comes up most often when discussing medical staffs is "credentialing." Medical staff credentialing is used to refer to the obtaining and reviewing of documentation of professional providers who apply to obtain medical-staff privileges at a health care facility. Such documentation includes, but is not limited to, licensure, certifications, insurance, evidence of malpractice insurance, and malpractice history. This process generally occurs in two phases: First, the members of a credentials committee (or similar group) collect, verify (or re-verify in the case of reappointment), and evaluate the pertinent information about an applicant for appointment or reappointment to the medical staff. Once this information has been collected and verified, this first stage requires the credentials committee to review an applicant's application and ensure that all the criteria for appointment have been satisfied. Medical education must be confirmed, membership and certification by specialty boards must be checked, all licensure requirements must be established, confirmation of professional liability insurance must be obtained, and all other pertinent background information must be scrutinized. Once the credentials committee has confirmed to the best of its ability that all required criteria for appointment have been met, the credentials committee must decide whether the information provided establishes that the applicant possesses the requisite credentials for appointment to the medical staff. When the credentials committee decides that an applicant has the necessary credentials, the credentials committee must determine to which category of the medical staff the applicant should be assigned, and what specific clinical privileges should be granted to the applicant. Second, once the application is complete, a typical progression is for the credentials committee to make a preliminary recommendation regarding the application and submit the recommendation and application to the executive committee of the medical staff for comment. The executive committee should consider all recommendations of the credentials committee and shall either accept the recommendation of the credentials committee, refer the recommendation back to the credentials committee for further

---

[45] *See* Section 1128(c)(3)(B) of the Social Security Act (Act) and 42 C.F.R. § 1001.1801(b) (The OIG has the authority to waive an individual or entity's exclusion from participating as a provider in federal health care programs and such current waivers are found at https://oig.hhs.gov/exclusions/waivers.asp).

[46] *Id.*

consideration, or take action adverse to a favorable recommendation of the credentials committee. Medical staff credentialing is thus a form of licensure, in that it creates parameters that must be met in order for physicians to function within a particular facility.[47]

Medical staff credentialing is a sensitive area that often leads to litigation, as it can prevent physicians from accessing hospitals and other essential health care facilities. Further, it can lead to malpractice suits for hospitals (and for physicians, if physicians are not appropriately credentialed). Thus, courts will review denial of access to medical staffs, but the courts are split on what degree of review is appropriate. One view is that courts should only review the procedural aspect of the medical staff's bylaws to ensure that the procedure was followed.[48] The other view, however, will review both the procedural aspect of the denial of privileges and the substantive aspect (i.e., whether it was fair to deny privileges).[49] The case law in this area varies from state to state; attorneys representing physicians in credentialing actions must be aware of the standard for review in their respective states.

If a denial or revocation of medical-staff privileges does not follow the proper procedures set forth in the medical staff's bylaws, then courts will require the facility to follow its own bylaws, even if the entity is private. It is important to note, however, that courts are deferential to the medical judgment exercised in peer review, and that patient care is considered the realm of the health care facility and the members of the medical staff, rather than that of the courts.

Employment contracts often spell out the medical staff privileges that a physician-employee is expected to maintain, and termination of employment can sometimes be based upon loss of medical staff privileges. Therefore, it is important for physicians and their attorneys to have an understanding of the bylaws at the hospitals and other health care facilities in which the physicians have staff privileges. In that way, in the event credentialing issues arise, attorneys and their clients are properly prepared to challenge any action that could realistically affect the rest of the physicians' careers.

10.5 Reimbursement Issues

The term "reimbursement" is used to denote payment to physicians or other health care providers in exchange for their services, equipment or supplies. Reimbursement comes from a variety of payers: (i) patients may pay privately; (ii) private insurance companies may pay on a traditional fee-for-service basis; (iii) managed care companies may pay capitated rates to physicians each month; or (iv) federal programs such as Medicare and Medicaid may reimburse physicians for their services based on a complex calculation called a resource based relative value scale (RBRVS) fee schedule.[50] The Medicare Access and CHIP Reauthorization Act of 2015 (MACRA) will implement the most extensive collection of changes to Medicare payment methodologies since RBRVS were introduced in 1992. In common jargon, reimbursement is often specifically associated with payments from

---

[47] Credentialing also discussed in REPRESENTING PHYSICIANS HANDBOOK, *supra* note 2, § 10.1.
[48] *See generally Mahmoodian v. United Hosp. Ctr., Inc.*, 404 S.E.2d 750 (W. Va. 1991).
[49] *See generally Nanavati v. Burdette Tomlin Mem. Hosp.*, 107 N.J. 240, 526 A.2d 697 (N.J. 1987).
[50] *See* Chapter 3 Medicare and Chapter 5 FUNDAMENTALS OF HEALTH LAW FRAUD AND ABUSE for further information on federal reimbursement issues.

Medicare and Medicaid. Chapters 3 and 4 of this book discuss Medicare and Medicaid in more detail; this chapter will address basic reimbursement issues facing physicians.[51]

10.5.1 Problems in Reimbursement

Historically, patients either paid privately for physicians' services or they obtained fee-for-service insurance that paid physicians a discounted rate for any services rendered to a member of the insurance plan. The advent of HMOs and managed care contracting has changed the way physicians are paid for their services. Instead of payment per patient visit, certain physicians (e.g., general practitioners) are paid on a capitated basis, which usually means that they receive a flat fee each month based upon the number of patients that he or she treats in a particular health plan (regardless of the actual number of patient visits). Thus, under certain payment arrangements, physicians have been forced to bear the risk in managed care contracting, whereas in traditional fee-for-service insurance, the insurance companies bear the risk of patients' illness, and costs.[52]

The result is that physicians have been forced to find ways to service the large number of patients that managed care organizations (MCOs) send to them, while still earning enough money to remain in the profession. In furtherance of that, physicians have been finding ways to collaborate in order to negotiate with MCOs and reduce the bargaining power held by the MCOs. One method for cooperation is called horizontal integration, in which groups of physicians have formed service organizations. Another method, called vertical integration, also has occurred, in which hospitals and physicians work together in order to improve efficiency and create more complete packages to MCOs. An examination of the variations of such arrangements is too complex to explore in this discussion, so this section will only address two of the most common horizontal-integration relationships.

Many states have laws regarding payment by traditional insurers and MCOs that delineate the amount of time payers may take to reimburse physicians for their services. Each state's laws differ, so attorneys representing physicians must be aware of the laws and regulations in their jurisdictions so that they know how to answer the inevitable question of "When do I get paid?"

10.5.2 Independent Practice Associations

An independent practice association (IPA, also sometimes called an independent provider association or independent physician association) is an entity that is created and owned by physicians and/or physician groups practicing independently. The primary purpose of an IPA is to contract with MCOs. IPAs differ from group practices in that the physicians in the IPA do not combine their practices and do not necessarily contract solely through the IPA. IPAs may negotiate the terms and conditions of MCO contracts, as well as other third-party payer contracts, on behalf of the members of an IPA and process the claims for services performed by members of the IPA.

IPAs can have different structures and levels of commitment by the physicians and physician groups involved. Many IPAs are "messenger model" IPAs, which means that the IPA acts as a mes-

---

[51] Reimbursement also referenced in REPRESENTING PHYSICIANS HANDBOOK, *supra* note 2, ch. 9.
[52] *See* Chapter 8 The Source of Payment: The State and Federal Regulation of Private Health Care Plans for more information on insurance and related issues.

senger system to broker contracts for the members of the IPA; each physician in the IPA then independently decides if the terms of the contract are acceptable. The messenger cannot coordinate the responses of the IPA physicians, communicate their decisions to other physicians in the IPA, or enable the providers to collude in entering into contracts. Such actions will raise serious antitrust concerns.[53]

There are also disadvantages to joining an IPA. Attorneys representing physicians must help their clients to also consider the ramifications of being part of an IPA before joining one. The fact that an IPA itself contracts with a payer for Medicare and/or Medicaid reimbursement can affect a physician's individual status with Medicare and Medicaid. For instance, a physician's individual levels of reimbursement from Medicare and Medicaid can be affected by membership in an IPA. In addition, IPAs are often less efficient than group practices in terms of overhead costs and other administrative issues, which can lead to the failure of the IPA if the physicians involved are unable to see the long-term benefits. Also, if physicians render more services to the patients of an IPA than to their own patients, then they may be considered employees (as opposed to independent contractors) of the IPA by the Internal Revenue Service.[54] IPAs can run into antitrust problems if a large number of physicians from a geographic location participate in the IPA.[55] Attorneys should also be alert to "most favored nation" clauses, which require providers in the IPA to accept as full reimbursement the lowest amount paid by any patient of the provider. Such clauses are now frowned upon by federal agencies because they raise antitrust concerns; these clauses are seen as restraints on natural price competition. Although IPAs may assist physicians in building or maintaining a patient base, these and other issues must be raised so that physician-clients understand the issues associated with joining an IPA.

10.5.3 Unionization

The predominance of managed care in the medical industry has created a renewed interest in physician unions and the potential bargaining power they promise. It is important to understand that only employed physicians (meaning physicians employed by hospitals or other health care entities) can consider unionization; self-employed physicians may not unionize, as it is considered a violation of the antitrust laws. Thus, the same physicians who lack bargaining power and/or protection from MCOs are the ones who cannot unionize or bargain collectively with health care plans. The American Medical Association's policy is to seek changes in the law to expand physicians' ability to negotiate collectively with payers.[56]

Some states are beginning to pass laws that allow physicians to collectively bargain with insurance companies. Movements have begun to alter federal law in order to allow unionization and/or collective bargaining by physicians with MCOs and other health care plans.[57]

---

[53] *See* Statements of Antitrust Enforcement Policy in Health Care (U.S. Dep't. of Just. and the F.T.C. Aug. 1996), https://www.justice.gov/atr/statements-antitrust-enforcement-policy-health-care. Additionally, *see generally* DAVID MARX JR. AND JAMES H. SNEED, ANTITRUST AND HEALTHCARE: MEETING THE CHALLENGE, SECOND EDITION (Am. Health Laws. Ass'n. 1998).
[54] *See generally* BRUCE JOHN SHIH, HEALTHCARE TRANSACTIONS: A GUIDE TO MERGERS, ACQUISITIONS AND INTEGRATION (Am. Health Laws. Ass'n. 1998).
[55] For more information on antitrust issues in health care, see Statements of Antitrust Enforcement Policy in Health Care, *supra* note 45.
[56] *See* American Medical Association (AMA) Policy, H-385.973, H-385.976. The AMA does not advocate withholding patient care in order to gain bargaining leverage. *See id.* at H-405.998.
[57] *See* REPRESENTING PHYSICIANS HANDBOOK, *supra* note 2, § 16.3.

10.6 Telemedicine

Telemedicine is a broad term that has no universal definition. The Institute of Medicine has defined it as the use of electronic information and communications technologies to provide and support health care when distance separates participants. This can include electronic transmission of medical images, video conferencing, and dispatching information to a distant—often otherwise unreachable—location. The Centers for Medicare and Medicaid Services (CMS) defines telemedicine as "multimedia communications equipment that includes, at a minimum, audio and video equipment permitted two-way, real-time interactive communication between the patient and distant site physician or practitioner. Telephones, facsimile machines, and electronic mail systems do not meet the definition of an interactive telecommunications system."[58]

As mentioned earlier, the use of telemedicine may be considered to be practicing medicine across state lines. An attorney representing a physician practicing via telemedicine should review interstate licensure laws and regulations associated with telemedicine and the practice of medicine across state lines. Many states allow interstate consultations, especially for highly specialized areas of medicine, but individual state laws must be consulted.

Malpractice is a concern with respect to the use of telemedicine. Many related interstate issues remain largely unresolved, including whether a physician/patient relationship exists, the standard of care to be applied to telemedicine relationships, and which state's law would apply in the event of a malpractice suit. These issues are compounded by the undefined nature of telemedicine, and that a simple telephone call across state lines could violate licensure regulations. A related sub-issue is whether malpractice insurance would cover physicians practicing medicine in state A to reach a patient in state B (or in another country) via telemedicine. These issues are worthy of consideration for a client who practices telemedicine.

Additionally, questions arise as to whether medical practitioners will be reimbursed for services provided by telemedicine. Insurance companies do not encourage experimental procedures; telemedicine could easily be rejected for that reason, or as being simply too expensive to cover. Generally, Medicare covers certain consultations, office and other outpatient visits, individual psychotherapy, pharmacological management, psychiatric diagnostic interview examinations, and end stage renal disease services delivered via telecommunications systems.[59] Such coverage is subject to strict requirements before payment may be made, including requirements as to the "originating site."[60] Some states have enacted "parity laws" which require reimbursement for telemedicine services on the same terms as reimbursement for traditional medical services.[61]

---

[58] 42 C.F.R. § 410.78(a)(3) (2016).

[59] For a more in-depth discussion of telemedicine, *see* Thomas Wm. Mayo, Esquire et al., *Telemedicine: Survey and Analysis of Federal and State Laws*, (Health Lawyers Expert Series, Am. Health Laws. Ass'n. 2007); *see also* REPRESENTING PHYSICIANS HANDBOOK, *supra* note 2, ch. 3.

[60] *Id.*

[61] *E.g.* CAL. INS. CODE § 10123.85; CAL. HEALTH & SAFETY CODE § 1374.13; COLO. REV. STAT. § 10-16-123, amended by 2015 Colo. HB. 1029; GA. CODE § 33-24-56.4(d); HAW. REV. STAT. §§ 431:10A-116.3(c), 432:1-601.5(c), 432D-23.5(c); KY. REV. STAT. § 304.17A-138; N.M. STAT. § 24-25-5(B); TEX. INS. CODE § 1455.004 *See also* REPRESENTING PHYSICIANS HANDBOOK, *supra*, ch. 3 § 3.5.

The confidentiality of health information involved in the practice of telemedicine is also at issue. Physicians must be familiar with the HIPAA Privacy Regulations, the HIPAA Security Regulations, HITECH, other relevant federal privacy requirements, and the privacy requirements of the states in which the services are being delivered *and* received.

Of particular note, some fraud and abuse issues arise in telemedicine. In an important Advisory Opinion,[62] the OIG found that, based on the facts presented, no prohibited remuneration was taking place because the use of the telemedicine equipment was not intended to induce referrals.[63] Two anti-kickback safe harbors are relevant to telemedicine. The safe harbors apply when a physician receives free electronic prescribing items or services or free electronic health records items or services.[64] Similar exceptions to the Stark law are also applicable to telemedicine.[65]

Generally, the provision of equipment and/or loans for telemedical equipment can create a concern about kickbacks and other fraud and abuse issues that should be addressed specifically. Any leasing or subleasing of equipment for telemedicine should meet the elements for the OIG's equipment rental "safe harbor." In addition, federal and state self-referral prohibitions, along with state laws and regulations regarding fee-splitting, could be sources of concern. For further information on fraud and abuse issues, *see* Chapter 5 Fundamentals of Health Law Fraud and Abuse.

10.7 Physician/Patient Relationships

Generally, a physician/patient relationship[66] is initiated when both parties manifest consent to the relationship; the physician functions as a health care professional, and the patient relies on the advice or diagnosis given.[67] Physicians are not generally obligated to enter into a physician/patient relationship and treat individuals requesting treatment in accordance with the professional standard of care, except situations where there has been an affirmative undertaking by the physician, or an existing contractual obligation to the patient or a health plan or undertaking to provide physician coverage for a hospital's emergency department.[68] Once a physician/patient relationship exists, however, only certain procedures will end the relationship.

Although the law on termination of physician/patient relationships varies from state to state, some basic tenets apply. The physician/patient relationship will continue until (1) the patient has no further need for medical care; (2) the patient affirmatively terminates the relationship; or (3) the physician terminates the relationship after giving the patient reasonable notice and affords the patient an opportunity to obtain alternate care. If, however, the patient is unable to obtain care with another qualified physician, then the treating physician who wishes to terminate the physician/

---

[62] *See* OIG Advisory Opinion 98-18 (Nov. 25, 1998), https://oig.hhs.gov/fraud/docs/advisoryopinions/1998/ao98_18.htm.
[63] The OIG made this conclusion due to the facts that (1) the optometrist with the consultative telemedicine equipment did not intend to advertise the equipment, (2) neither the optometrist nor the ophthalmologist intended to bill Medicare or another insurer for the consultations, and (3) patients were free to choose any ophthalmologist for follow-up care. These elements should be considered in any telemedicine consultative arrangement.
[64] 42 C.F.R. § 1001.952(x) and (y) (2016).
[65] *Id.* § 411.357(v) and (w).
[66] Chapter 2 Patient Care discusses patient issues, so this chapter will only briefly touch on physicians' obligations to patients in terms of terminating patient relationships.
[67] *See* BECKER, *supra* note 19, § 13.03.
[68] *See O'Neill v. Montefiore Hosp.*, 11 A.D.2d 132, 202 N.Y.S.2d 436 (N.Y. App. Div. 1960).

patient relationship may have an obligation to continue care, or the physician may be liable for patient abandonment and open to malpractice liability.[69]

In addition, some state regulations require physicians who participate in a managed care plan to continue to treat certain patients after the physician's agreement to participate in the plan terminates. For example pregnant women and patients who have begun a course of care with the physician would be entitled to continued care by the physician throughout the pregnancy or the course of care, and the physician would be required to accept payment in accordance with the otherwise terminated agreement between the physician and the plan. Physicians are not, otherwise, generally bound to continue relationships with patients who are not under continuing care at the time the contract's termination.

The law in this area may vary from state to state, so it is very important for an attorney representing physicians to consult local laws and regulations. The governing regulations applicable to physicians in a given state may not be under the aegis of one agency; for example, they may be the result of a combination of regulations promulgated by a board of medical examiners, the department of health, and the department of insurance. Thus, a thorough search is necessary in order to advise a physician who plans to terminate patient relationships.

10.8 Accountable Care Organizations

One of the most prominent components of health care reform is the encouragement of the development of Medicare Accountable Care Organizations (ACOs). While certainly not new, ACOs previously existed in relative obscurity until the passage of the ACA. Section 3022 of the ACA required DHHS to develop a Medicare shared savings program through an ACO.[70] More information on ACOs is available in *The ACO Handbook Second Edition* published by American Health Lawyers Association.[71]

10.9 Conclusion

Representing physicians requires an extensive knowledge of many areas. Hopefully, this chapter has laid a framework of some of the physician-representation issues that health care attorneys will encounter. The American Health Lawyers Association's Physician Organizations Practice Group has a Task Force, which the author currently chairs, that has recently published its fourth edition of the *Representing Physicians Handbook* which delves into greater detail on many of the issues discussed in the chapter and discusses other advanced issues with respect to representing physicians.

---

[69] *See, e.g., Groce v. Myers*, 224 N.C. 165, 29 S.E.2d 553 (1944). The case law in this area is well established, dating back to the late 1800s.

[70] Pub. L. No. 111-148 § 3022.

[71] *See* THE ACO HANDBOOK: A GUIDE TO ACCOUNTABLE CARE ORGANIZATIONS SECOND EDITION (Am. Health Laws. Ass'n 2015); *see also* REPRESENTING PHYSICIANS HANDBOOK, *supra* note 2, § 12.1.7.

11

Post-Acute Providers and Suppliers

Carol Colborn Loepere
Catherine A. Hurley
Yetunde D. Oni
Rebecca E. Dittrich
Nancy A. Sheliga
Reed Smith, LLP

11.1 Introduction

When patients leave the acute care setting, they often require ongoing medical care at home or in another institutional setting. Post-acute providers and suppliers cater to these needs. Like acute care and other types of health care providers, home care providers, such as home medical equipment (HME) suppliers, home health agencies (HHAs), and hospices, are subject to extensive regulation at the state and federal levels. Similarly, long-term care facilities must abide by state and federal laws and regulations. These health care entities in particular are under increased scrutiny for compliance with quality-of-care, billing, and medical necessity requirements. This chapter sets forth a summary of the basic regulatory state licensure, certificate of need (CON), and Medicare and Medicaid regulatory requirements for these providers, as well as key legal issues to be considered with respect to fraud and abuse and compliance.

11.2 Home Medical Equipment Suppliers

HME suppliers (sometimes known as durable medical equipment (DME) suppliers) are providers of medical equipment and supplies to patients for use in the home. Examples of home medical equipment include wheelchairs, walkers, oxygen and oxygen equipment, and hospital beds.

11.2.1 State Licensure

A majority of the states require licenses for most types of HME/DME, while the remaining states only require HME/DME suppliers to be licensed to provide certain selected items. For example, Illinois requires suppliers of "home medical equipment and services" to be licensed.[1] Similarly, Florida requires licensure of any person or entity that holds itself out as providing HME.[2] HME is broadly defined by the

---

[1] *See* 225 ILL. COMP. STAT. 51/15.
[2] FLA. STAT. § 400.93(1).

Florida statute to include: (1) "any product as defined by the Food and Drug Administration's Federal Food, Drug, and Cosmetic Act"; (2) any product reimbursed by Medicare Part B; or (3) any product reimbursed by the Florida Medicaid program, with the exception of: prosthetics and orthotics; splints, braces, or aids custom fabricated by a licensed health care practitioner; motorized scooters; personal transfer systems; and medically-necessary specialty beds.[3] The scope of some state licensure statutes is limited, however, to those devices, apparatuses, machines, or similar articles that *must be prescribed* by a physician for use in the home. Other states limit licensure requirements to medical equipment that is life-sustaining or technologically sophisticated. When consulting state law to determine whether HME suppliers must be licensed, it is important to review the scope of the licensure because some types of HME may not be covered by the statute.[4] HME suppliers should also be aware that many states require not only in-state suppliers but also out-of-state suppliers shipping into the state to be licensed.

State licensure may also be a condition of participation in state Medicaid programs, and is a requirement for Medicare participation.[5] Suppliers who provide drugs for use with HME must be licensed under state pharmacy statutes. Medicare DME suppliers are required to obtain oxygen from a state-licensed oxygen supplier (as applicable in the state)[6] and are generally permitted to contract with another licensed individual or entity to perform licensed services, unless state law expressly prohibits such an arrangement.[7]

11.2.2   Medicare

11.2.2.1   *Coverage*

Medicare covers DME under a specific coverage category of the Social Security Act (SSA). In addition, HME suppliers often provide other categories of products (including prosthetics, orthotics, and supplies) which are covered under separate provisions of the SSA. These products collectively are known as DME, prosthetics, orthotics, and supplies (DMEPOS).

11.2.2.1.1   *Categories of Coverage*

The SSA sets forth broad categories of covered DMEPOS.[8] These general categories are defined by federal statute as follows:

(A) *Durable medical equipment* means equipment, furnished by a supplier or a home health agency that—

    (1)   Can withstand repeated use;

---

[3] *Id.* § 400.925(6).

[4] The National Supplier Clearinghouse (NSC) has compiled a DMEPOS State Licensure Directory, available by clicking on "View Your DMEPOS State License Directory," once on the following web page: http://www.palmettogba.com/palmetto/providers.nsf/DocsCat/Providers~National%20Supplier%20Clearinghouse~Resources~Licensure%20Information~7GLS4M6340?open&navmenu=||. This is a useful guide; however, it is advisable to consult the specific state law.

[5] *See* 42 U.S.C. § 1395m(j); 42 C.F.R. § 424.57(c)(1).

[6] *See* 42 C.F.R. §§ 424.57(c)(1) and (27).

[7] *See* 42 C.F.R. § 424.57(c)(1); *see also* Section 11.2.2.2; *see also* FAQs relating to supplier enrollment on the National Supplier Clearinghouse website *at* https://www.palmettogba.com/palmetto/providers.nsf/docsCat/National%20Supplier%20Clearinghouse~Supplier%20Enrollment~FAQs.

[8] *See generally* 42 U.S.C. § 1395m and 42 U.S.C. § 1395x.

(2) Effective with respect to items classified as DME after January 1, 2012, has an expected life of at least 3 years;

(3) Is primarily and customarily used to serve a medical purpose;

(4) Generally is not useful to an individual in the absence of an illness or injury; and

(5) Is appropriate for use in the home.

(B) *Prosthetic and orthotic devices* means—

(1) Devices that replace all or part of an internal body organ, including ostomy bags and supplies directly related to ostomy care, and replacement of such devices and supplies;

(2) One pair of conventional eyeglasses or contact lenses furnished subsequent to each cataract surgery with insertion of an intraocular lens; and

(3) Leg, arm, back, and neck braces, and artificial legs, arms, and eyes, including replacements if required because of a change in the beneficiary's physical condition.[9]

Supplies and drugs prescribed for the effective use of DME, a prosthetic, or an orthotic also are covered. This can include such items as the albuterol sulfate used in nebulizers, the oxygen in an oxygen concentrator, or the batteries in a pacemaker.

Coverage for products is limited to certain indications and circumstances, as set forth in national and local Coverage Determinations. For example, oxygen is covered only for patients with designated blood gas-oxygen levels who meet other specified conditions. A Foley catheter is considered a prosthetic device and is covered only when prescribed for a patient with permanent urinary incontinence because it replaces the function of a permanently inoperative internal body organ. Catheters are not otherwise covered as prosthetic devices.[10]

In addition, the following specific categories of items are commonly supplied by HME suppliers, reimbursed through the regional Medicare administrative contractors, and covered under Medicare through separate statutory benefits:

- home dialysis equipment and supplies;
- immunosuppressive drugs;
- therapeutic shoes for diabetics; and
- surgical dressings.

11.2.2.1.2 Statutory Exclusion

The SSA's basic threshold for when products, procedures, or services will be covered (and thus reimbursed) is that the items and services must be "reasonable and necessary": "[N]o payment may be made under Part A or Part B . . . for any expenses incurred for items or services . . . which . . . are not *reasonable and necessary* for the diagnosis or treatment of illness or injury or to improve the

---

[9] 42 C.F.R. § 414.202.
[10] *See* 42 C.F.R. § 414.202; *see also Medicare Benefit Policy Manual* (CMS Pub. 100-02), Chapter 15 § 120(A).

functioning of a malformed body member."[11] If a patient fails to meet the coverage criteria for an item of DMEPOS, coverage will be denied on the grounds that the item is not "reasonable and necessary."

11.2.2.1.3 National Coverage Policies

To enforce this statutory "reasonable and necessary" limitation, the Centers for Medicare & Medicaid Services (CMS) makes national coverage policies known as National Coverage Determinations (NCDs), which are binding on all Medicare administrative contractors. Congress has statutorily restricted the judicial review of NCDs and has provided that the determinations cannot be challenged on the grounds that CMS failed to abide by the Administrative Procedure Act.[12]

11.2.2.1.4 DME MAC Coverage Policies

Suppliers submit claims to one of four special regional Medicare contractors known as Durable Medical Equipment Medicare Administrative Contractors (DME MACs, formerly known as Durable Medical Equipment Regional Carriers or DMERCs). Each region also has an affiliated Zone Program Integrity Contractor (ZPIC)[13] to perform selected Medicare program integrity functions, including fraud investigations, prepay and post-pay medical review of claims, and data analysis. In addition, Recovery Audit Contractors (RACs) also identify Medicare overpayments and underpayments made to health care providers and suppliers. The geographic areas covered by the four RACs mirror the DME MAC jurisdictions.

Although regional contractors must defer to national policy, in the absence of a national policy on a given issue, the contractors may make a local coverage policy, known as Local Coverage Determinations (LCDs). LCDs are more likely to be based upon issues of overuse and abuse, while NCDs are generally focused on the clinical safety and efficacy of a product. DME MACs can review procedures, devices, and services to develop coverage policies that are effective only in the contractor's geographic area. Generally, however, the regions are expected to have consistent coverage policies.[14] For some items of DMEPOS, certificates of medical necessity or other specific medical necessity documentation are required for coverage. These coverage requirements are set forth in the regional Supplier Manuals.[15]

---

[11] 42 U.S.C. § 1395y(a) and § 1395y(a)(1)(A) (emphasis added).

[12] 5 U.S.C. § 553. *See* 42 U.S.C. § 1395ff(f)(1).

[13] *See Medicare Program Integrity Manual* (CMS Pub. 100-08), Chapter 4. Note that CMS is currently in the process of transitioning Medicare program integrity functions from ZPICs to new contract entities called Unified Program Integrity Contractors (UPIC). UPICs will be responsible for "conducting program integrity activities for both the Medicare and Medicaid programs. CMS plans to award all UPIC contracts by the end of calendar year 2017." *See* U.S. GOV'T ACCOUNTABILITY OFF., GAO-17-710, MEDICARE CMS FRAUD PREVENTION SYSTEM USES CLAIMS ANALYSIS TO ADDRESS FRAUD, 2, n.5 (2017) *available at* http://www.gao.gov/assets/690/686849.pdf.

[14] *See* 42 C.F.R. § 400.202; additionally, *see Medicare Program Integrity Manual* (CMS Pub. 100-08), Chapter 13.

[15] The supplier manuals are available directly from the DME MACs and through various legal publishers. They also are available on the websites for each of the DME MACs:
- Jurisdiction A: https://med.noridianmedicare.com/web/jadme/education/supplier-manual;
- Jurisdiction B: https://cgsmedicare.com/jb/pubs/pdf/jb_supplier_manual_fall2017.pdf;
- Jurisdiction C: https://cgsmedicare.com/jc/pubs/supman/index.html; and
- Jurisdiction D: https://med.noridianmedicare.com/web/jddme/education/supplier-manual.

11.2.2.2 Requirements of Participation

HME/DME suppliers under Medicare must meet the following statutory requirements:

- comply with all applicable [s]tate and [f]ederal licensure and regulatory requirements;
- maintain a physical facility on an appropriate site;
- have proof of appropriate liability insurance; and
- meet such other requirements as the Secretary [of the Department of Health and Human Services (HHS)] may specify.[16]

The primary regulatory requirement for a supplier is compliance with the Medicare supplier standards.[17] These standards both implement the requirements in the SSA and set forth additional criteria for qualification as a Medicare supplier. Such criteria include, for example: (1) responsibility for delivery of covered items to beneficiaries; (2) honoring all warranties both express and implied; (3) the direct or contractual maintenance and repair of items rented to beneficiaries; (4) maintaining a complaint resolution process; and (5) documentation criteria, including providing a copy of the supplier standards to all Medicare beneficiaries. The standards also generally prohibit suppliers from sharing a practice location with any other Medicare supplier or provider (with certain exceptions); impose physical facility requirements on suppliers, including square footage, accessibility, signage, and storage requirements; clarify the prohibition on the direct solicitation of Medicare beneficiaries; allow suppliers to contract with another individual to perform licensed services, unless prohibited under state law; require the use of a primary business telephone; and establish minimum hours of operation, among other requirements.[18] The NSC engages inspectors to conduct site surveys to verify compliance with the supplier standards. If a DMEPOS supplier is found to be out of compliance, the supplier's Medicare Part B supplier number will be revoked, and the supplier will no longer be able to bill Medicare.

The supplier standards require all suppliers to be accredited as meeting quality standards established by CMS.[19] Finally, most Medicare-enrolled DMEPOS suppliers must obtain a surety bond.[20] Specifically, suppliers are required to post a surety bond from an authorized surety unless an exemption applies.[21]

11.2.2.3 Payment

Medicare payment for DMEPOS is based on the statutory category into which the equipment is classified. Payments are updated annually according to statutory formula. Special payment provisions apply to items subject to competitive bidding and in certain special circumstances.

---

[16] 42 U.S.C. § 1395m(j).
[17] *See* 42 C.F.R. § 424.57.
[18] *Id.*
[19] 42 C.F.R. § 424.57(c)(22).
[20] 42 C.F.R. § 424.57(d).
[21] 42 C.F.R. § 424.57(d)(15).

11.2.2.3.1 Payment Categories

DMEPOS payment categories include the following:

1. capped rental;
2. inexpensive or routinely purchased items;
3. customized items;
4. orthotics and prosthetics;
5. oxygen equipment and supplies; and
6. payment for items requiring frequent and substantial servicing.

In addition, the Medicare Part B program also covers certain drugs administered through DME (including inhalation and infusion drugs administered through DME).

Except for those items subject to competitive bidding, payment generally is made at the lesser of the supplier's actual charge or a fee schedule amount (which varies by state), as reduced by applicable deductible and coinsurance requirements. Additional details regarding the complex payment rules associated with the various types of DMEPOS are highlighted below.

Capped Rental & Oxygen Payment

Items classified as capped rental are paid at the lesser of (1) the actual charge for the equipment or (2) a fee-schedule amount determined according to a statutory payment formula. Under the DME payment formula, monthly rental payments are initially made at 10% of the "national limited purchase price" of the equipment. After three months, the rental payment percentage changes to 7.5%.[22] The rental payments continue for the period during which a medical need exists for the equipment, but historically have been limited to 15 continuous months. If the period of medical need extended for a period beyond 15 months, no payment would have been made for the next six months. Until recently, for each succeeding period of six months, however, a maintenance and servicing payment could be made (for parts and labor not covered by the seller's or manufacturer's warranty) during the first month of each such six-month period. Notably, no actual repair or servicing was required to receive payment, but the patient must have had a continuing medical need for the product. Under longstanding rules, capped rental items used for 10 consecutive months were required to be offered for purchase, and power-driven wheelchairs were required to be offered for purchase in addition to rental when the item was first furnished by the supplier.

The Deficit Reduction Act of 2005 (DRA)[23] modified this longstanding DME rental policy. Specifically, the DRA eliminated the 15-month rental option for capped rental DME. Instead, suppliers are required to transfer the title of capped rental DME to the beneficiary after 13 months. The option for beneficiaries to purchase power-driven wheelchairs when initially furnished was retained, although the Health Care and Education Reconciliation Act of 2010[24] (collectively known as the Affordable Care Act or ACA) subsequently eliminated the purchase option for power-driven wheelchairs other

---

[22] 42 U.S.C. §§ 1395m(a)(7) & (8).
[23] Pub. L. No. 109-171, 120 Stat. 2005.
[24] Health Care and Education Reconciliation Act of 2010, Pub. L. No. 111-152, 124 Stat. 1029.

than complex, rehabilitative power wheelchairs. The ACA also modified the rental payment framework for power-driven wheelchairs. Effective for items furnished on or after July 1, 2011, payment is set at 15% (rather than 10%) of the purchase price for the first three months, changing to 6% (rather than 7.5%) of the purchase price for each of the remaining 10 months (with special rules for items furnished pursuant to the competitive bidding program, which is discussed below).

The DRA also eliminated automatic maintenance and servicing payments; such payments now are made only if reasonable and necessary, and only cover parts and labor not otherwise covered by the supplier's or manufacturer's warranty.[25]

Moreover, the DRA limited the rental period for oxygen equipment to 36 months, after which the title transfers to the beneficiary (although rental payments for oxygen contents are still available). Maintenance and servicing payments are made if determined by the Secretary to be reasonable and necessary and not otherwise covered by the supplier's or manufacturer's warranty.[26]

Inexpensive or Routinely Purchased Items

For inexpensive or routinely purchased items of DME ("routinely purchased" in this context means purchased more than 75% of the time), including speech generating devices and accessories furnished on or after October 1, 2015, and before October 1, 2018, CMS has a fee schedule that is based upon historical charges for each product. The state payment levels, however, are subject to payment limitations. The national floor is 85% of the median of all the state fees, and the ceiling is the median of all the state fees. Alaska, Hawaii, and Puerto Rico are excluded from these payment limitations. Payment is made on a rental basis or lump-sum amount at the time of purchase.[27]

Payment for Items Requiring Frequent and Substantial Servicing

Payment for items which must be frequently and substantially serviced in order to avoid risk to a patient's health is made on a monthly rental basis, based on the historic average reasonable charge in the area for the rental of the item or device, subject to annual updates, a national floor set at 85% of the median of all local payment amounts, and a national ceiling set at the median of all local payment amounts.[28]

Customized Items

Customized items (e.g., certain custom wheelchairs) are defined as items that must be uniquely constructed or substantially modified for a specific beneficiary, according to the description and orders of a physician, and thereby are made to be so different from another item used for the same purpose that the two cannot be grouped together for the purpose of pricing. Payment is made on a lump-sum basis, with the amount determined by the carrier's individual consideration and judgment of a reasonable payment amount for each customized item.[29]

---

[25] 42 U.S.C. § 1395m(a)(5).
[26] 42 U.S.C. § 1395m(a)(5).
[27] 42 U.S.C. § 1395m(a)(2); 42 U.S.C. § 1395m(a)(10).
[28] 42 U.S.C. § 1395m(a)(3).
[29] 42 C.F.R. § 414.224; 42 U.S.C. § 1395m(a)(4).

Prosthetic and Orthotic Devices

For prosthetics and orthotics that do not require custom fitting and adjustment, Medicare uses 10 regional fee schedules. As with the fee schedule for inexpensive and routinely purchased DME, the fee schedules for prosthetics and orthotics are subject to payment limitations. The national floor is 90% of the average of all the regional fees, and the ceiling is 120% of the average. Payments are increased annually with an update for inflation, subject to periodic statutory limitations.[30]

On January 12, 2017, CMS issued a proposed rule that laid out stringent qualifications for providers and suppliers that furnish, fabricate, or bill for prosthetics and custom-fabricated orthotics under the Medicare program.[31] Comments were accepted through March 13, 2017. No final rule was issued, however, and the Trump Administration formally withdrew the proposed rule as of October 4, 2017, citing the cost and time burdens it would create for providers and suppliers (especially small businesses) and the complexity of the issues raised in public comments.[32]

Drugs Administered Through DME

Certain drugs administered through DME (including inhalation and infusion drugs administered through DME) are covered under the Medicare Part B program, despite longstanding limitations on Medicare coverage of self-administered drugs prior to the establishment of the Medicare Part D outpatient drug benefit in 2006. Under reimbursement policy implemented pursuant to the Medicare Prescription Drug, Improvement, and Modernization Act of 2003 (MMA), inhalation drugs administered through DME generally are reimbursed using an Average Sales Price (ASP) plus-6-percent formula. The MMA also set Medicare payment for infusion drugs provided in connection with DME at 95% of the April 1, 2003 average wholesale price rate.[33] The 21st Century Cures Act (Cures Act) enacted in December of 2016 revised Medicare payment for drugs infused through DME to the ASP price plus 6 percent payment methodology, effective January 1, 2017. The Cures Act also excludes DME infusion drugs from the DME competitive bidding program. Previously, CMS indicated that it planned to include DME infusion drugs in the competitive bidding process (discussed below) and the HHS Office of Inspector General (OIG) has endorsed this suggestion as a possible way to address payment issues associated with DME infusion drugs.[34]

11.2.2.3.2 Payment Updates

Payment amounts are updated annually by the consumer price index for urban consumers (CPI-U), subject to certain adjustments mandated by Congress. For instance, payment levels were frozen by the Balanced Budget Act of 1997 (BBA) for a period of five years, beginning in 1998. The Balanced

---

[30] 42 U.S.C. § 1395m(h).

[31] 82 Fed. Reg. 3678 (January 12, 2017). Previously, under the Medicare, Medicaid, and SCHIP Benefits Improvement and Protection Act of 2000 (BIPA), Congress directed the Secretary of HHS to use negotiated rulemaking to establish standards for those suppliers billing Medicare for prosthetics and certain custom-fabricated orthotics. While a negotiated rulemaking committee was convened, it was unable to reach a consensus.

[32] 82 Fed. Reg. 46181 (October 4, 2017).

[33] 42 U.S.C. § 1395u(o); 42 U.S.C. § 1395w–3a.

[34] HHS Office of Inspector General Report in Brief "CMS Should Address Medicare's Flawed Payment System for DME Infusion Drugs" September 2016, OEI-12-16-00340.

Budget Refinement Act of 1999 (BBRA) restored a portion of the increases for 2001 and 2002.[35] Subsequently, BIPA further modified payments for DME (other than oxygen and oxygen equipment) by including a full inflation update for DME provided in 2001 and a zero percent update for 2002. The MMA again imposed a freeze on Medicare payment amounts for DME (other than Class III medical devices) for the years 2004 through 2008; thereafter, rates were scheduled to increase by the percentage increase in the CPI-U. The MMA also required the Secretary of HHS to reduce the payment amounts in 2005 for specific items of DME if the HCPCS code for the item or supply was identified by the OIG as being excessive compared to payments under other government programs.[36]

Most recently, the ACA also eliminated the full inflation update to the DME fee schedule. Instead, beginning in 2011, DMEPOS rates increase annually by the rate of increase in the CPI minus a "productivity adjustment"[37] designed to reflect productivity gains in delivering health care services and to encourage more efficient care.

11.2.2.3.3 Competitive Bidding

Certain types of DME and related items are subject to a bidding process under which suppliers must meet certain program standards in order to supply covered items within the competitive acquisition area.[38] Items included in competitive acquisition are: (1) DME (including DME used with infusion and drugs, other than inhalation drugs) and supplies used in conjunction with DME; (2) enteral nutrients, equipment, and supplies; and (3) off-the-shelf orthotics. This requirement builds on earlier CMS demonstration projects in Polk County, Florida and in the San Antonio, Texas area that used competitive bidding to significantly reduce Medicare payment for certain DMEPOS items.

Excluded from competitive acquisition are: inhalation drugs; parenteral nutrients, equipment, and supplies; and Class III devices under the federal Food, Drug & Cosmetic Act. The Secretary of HHS may exempt certain rural areas as well as areas with low population density in urban areas. Competitive acquisition areas may differ for different items and services. The MMA required the program to be phased in, applying to 10 of the largest metropolitan statistical areas (MSAs) in 2007, 80 such areas in 2009, and additional areas thereafter, although this timeframe subsequently was modified. Only successful bidders meeting all program standards may supply the covered items in the acquisition area, and they are reimbursed based on bid amounts.

On April 10, 2007, CMS published its final rule establishing the Medicare DMEPOS competitive bidding program.[39] The rule required suppliers to meet a number of program requirements (including being accredited). To participate, suppliers must bid on all specified codes within the designated product category, and reimbursement will be set at the median of the winning suppliers' bids for the bid items.

---

[35] *See* 42 U.S.C. § 1395m(a).
[36] This provision applied to oxygen and oxygen equipment, standard wheelchairs, nebulizers, lancets and testing strips used for management of diabetes, hospital beds, and air mattresses. For these items, the payment amount was reduced by the percentage difference between the Medicare payment in 2002 and the median Federal Employees Health Benefit Program (FEHBP) price for the same item as identified by the OIG.
[37] The productivity adjustment equals the percentage change in the 10-year moving average of changes in annual economy-wide private nonfarm business multi-factor productivity, as reported by the Bureau of Labor Statistics.
[38] MMA § 302.
[39] 72 Fed. Reg. 17992 (Apr. 10, 2007) (to be codified at 42 C.F.R. pts. 411 and 414).

11.2.2.3.3   *Fundamentals of Health Law*

In 2007, CMS conducted the first round of bidding in the following 10 competitive bidding areas (CBAs): Charlotte-Gastonia-Concord (NC-SC); Cincinnati-Middletown (OH-KY-IN); Cleveland-Elyria-Mentor (OH); Dallas-Fort Worth-Arlington (TX); Kansas City (MO-KS); Miami-Fort Lauderdale-Miami Beach (FL); Orlando-Kissimmee (FL); Pittsburgh (PA); Riverside-San Bernardino-Ontario (CA); and San Juan-Caguas-Guaynabo (PR). CMS selected the following product categories for the first round of bidding: (1) Oxygen Supplies and Equipment; (2) Standard Power Wheelchairs, Scooters, and Related Accessories; (3) Complex Rehabilitative Power Wheelchairs and Related Accessories; (4) Mail-Order Diabetic Supplies; (5) Enteral Nutrients, Equipment, and Supplies; (6) Continuous Positive Airway Pressure Devices, Respiratory Assist Devices, and Related Supplies and Accessories; (7) Hospital Beds and Related Accessories; (8) Negative Pressure Wound Therapy Pumps and Related Supplies and Accessories; (9) Walkers and Related Accessories; and (10) Support Surfaces (Group 2 and 3 mattresses and overlays). The latter product category was bid only in the Miami-Fort Lauderdale-Miami Beach, FL and San Juan-Caguas-Guaynabo, PR CBAs. The contract term for all product categories except mail order diabetes supplies was three years.

CMS offered contracts to 23% of bidding suppliers, with prices averaging 26% below Medicare fee schedule amounts. The program briefly went into effect on July 1, 2008, but significant concerns about the program implementation resulted in Congress taking the rare step of terminating round one contracts through enactment of MIPPA.[40] MIPPA directed CMS to conduct a new round one rebid in nine geographic areas in 2009, and conduct a second phase of bidding in 2011 in an additional 70 of the largest MSAs. MIPPA also added a series of beneficiary safeguards and made certain procedural improvements to the bidding process. The delay in bidding was financed by cutting fee schedule payments for items included in round one by 9.5% nationwide beginning on January 1, 2009, followed by a 2% increase in 2014 (although that increase subsequently was repealed by the ACA).

CMS conducted the round one rebid in 2009 in the same CBAs as the round one bid, expect that it excluded the San Juan-Caguas-Guaynabo (PR) CBA. MIPPA directed that the round one rebid include all product categories selected for the initial round of bidding in 2007, except for negative pressure wound therapy (which was excluded from the round one rebid) and group three complex rehabilitative wheelchairs (which were excluded from both the round one rebid and all subsequent rounds of competition). On July 2, 2010, CMS announced that payment amounts under the round one rebid would average 32% below the Medicare DMEPOS fee schedule amounts. Contract prices went into effect on January 1, 2011 and expired on December 31, 2013 (for all items except mail order diabetic supplies).[41]

CMS is required by law to recompete contracts under the DMEPOS competitive bidding program at least once every three years. Therefore, the agency conducted a "recompete" for six product categories in the round one rebid areas, which took effect on January 1, 2014. The round one recompete included additional items beyond those in the round one rebid and grouped certain similar items and accessories into larger, more consolidated product categories. The round one recompete product

---
[40] MIPPA § 154.
[41] CMS announcements regarding implementation of the program are *available at* http://www.cms.gov/DMEPOSCompetitiveBid/01_overview.asp. In addition, the competitive bidding implementation contractor (CBIC) has posted bid instructions and a variety of other guidance documents *at* http://www.dmecompetitivebid.com/palmetto/cbic.nsf/DocsCat/Home.

categories were: 1) Respiratory Equipment and Related Supplies and Accessories including oxygen, oxygen equipment, and supplies; continuous positive airway pressure (CPAP) devices, respiratory assist devices (RADs), and related supplies and accessories; and standard nebulizers; 2) Standard Mobility Equipment and Related Accessories including walkers, standard power and manual wheelchairs, scooters, and related accessories; 3) General Home Equipment and Related Supplies and Accessories including hospital beds and related accessories, group 1 and 2 support surfaces, transcutaneous electrical nerve stimulation (TENS) devices, commode chairs, patient lifts, and seat lifts; 4) Enteral Nutrients, Equipment and Supplies; 5) Negative Pressure Wound Therapy Pumps and Related Supplies and Accessories; and 6) External Infusion Pumps and Supplies.

Subsequently, CMS again recompeted the supplier contracts awarded under the Round 1 Recompete, which expired on December 31, 2016. The "Round 1 2017" contracts went into effect on January 1, 2017. The Round 1 2017 configuration generally aligned with the Round 1 Recompete categories, except CMS: deleted the external infusion pumps and supplies product category; created a separate TENS category (rather than including such items in the General Home Equipment category); and created a nebulizer product category (rather than including such items in the Respiratory Equipment category). CMS initially intended to add another product category—Non-invasive Pressure Support Ventilators—in eight CBAs but subsequently dropped it. CMS conducted the Round 1 2017 competition in the same nine metropolitan statistical areas that were included in the Round 1 Recompete. Because of changes to zip codes and boundary changes adopted by CMS to ensure that no CBA was included in more than one state, however, the number of CBAs expanded from nine CBAs in the Round 1 Recompete to 13 CBAs in the Round 1 2017 competition,

The Round 1 2017 contracts will apply from January 1, 2017 through December 31, 2018. CMS extended 1,523 contract offers to 198 "winning" Round 1 2017 bidders with 603 locations. 97% of the offers were extended to bidders that previously furnished items in the awarded area or within the product category. CMS did not release data comparing the new payment amounts to then current fee schedule payments, but it did note that since implementation of competitive bidding on January 1, 2011, CMS has saved about $220 million per year in the nine Round 1 metropolitan statistical areas "due to competitive bidding and other CMS fraud, waste, and abuse initiatives." CMS continues to assert that its "data indicate that the program implementation is going smoothly with few inquiries or complaints and no negative beneficiary health outcomes."

MIPPA also authorized competition for national mail order items and services after 2010. The ACA further expanded competitive bidding, requiring the Secretary to include a total of 91 of the largest MSAs in the second round of bidding.

In addition, the ACA requires the Secretary to use competitive bidding payment information to adjust DMEPOS fees in areas outside of competitive bidding areas beginning in 2016.[42] On November 6, 2014, CMS published a final rule[43] to implement this requirement, subjecting DMEPOS suppliers nationwide to steep cuts for many items included in the DMEPOS competitive bidding program. As fully implemented in the second half of 2016, fees for many items were

---

[42] ACA § 6410.
[43] 79 Fed. Reg. 66119 (Nov. 6, 2014).

reduced by 50% – 80% compared to 2015 rates, leading Congress to extend the transition to the fully-adjusted DMEPOS fee schedule. With enactment of the Cures Act in December of 2016, Congress retroactively revised DMEPOS fee schedule amounts for the period of July through December 2016, extending a transition period which set rates using a 50/50 blend of adjusted and unadjusted fee schedule amounts, with full implementation beginning on January 1, 2017.

The November 6, 2014 final rule also established a mechanism to test the use of bundled monthly payment amounts in lieu of capped rental policies for standard power wheelchairs and continuous positive airway pressure devices furnished under the competitive bidding program. Under this policy, the single payment amount for the monthly rental of DME in no more than ten competitive bidding areas will be based on bids for the monthly rental of DME and all item and service associated with the rental equipment, including all related supplies, accessories, maintenance, and servicing. Separate payment for replacement of equipment, repair or maintenance and servicing of equipment, or for replacement of accessories and supplies necessary for the effective use of the equipment would not be allowed.

The Cures Act also requires CMS to consider additional information before adjusting DMEPOS fee schedule amounts based on competitive bidding pricing, effective for items and services furnished on or after January 1, 2019. First, in making any such adjustments, the Secretary must solicit and consider stakeholder input. CMS sought public comments in this regard in the spring of 2017. Second, the Secretary must consider the highest amount bid by a winning supplier in a CBA, along with relative travel distances and costs, volumes of items and services, and number of suppliers in CBAs and non-CBAs.

Round two of the competitive bidding program went into effect on July 1, 2013.[44] It expanded the list of items bid in the round one rebid by combining standard manual wheelchairs, standard power wheelchairs, and scooters to form a new expanded standard mobility device product category, expanded bidding for support surfaces throughout all round two areas, and added negative pressure wound therapy pumps and related supplies and accessories as an additional product category. Group two complex rehabilitative power wheelchairs, which were bid in the round one rebid, were not included in round two. The round two product categories were: 1) Oxygen, Oxygen Equipment, and Supplies; 2) Standard (Power and Manual) Wheelchairs, Scooters, and Related Accessories; 3) Enteral Nutrients, Equipment, and Supplies; 4) Continuous Positive Airway Pressure (CPAP) Devices and Respiratory Assist Devices (RADs) and Related Supplies and Accessories; 5) Hospital Beds and Related Accessories; 6) Walkers and Related Accessories; 7) Support Surfaces (Group 2 Mattresses and Overlays); and 8) Negative Pressure Wound Therapy Pumps and Related Supplies and Accessories.

CMS also conducted a national mail-order competition for diabetic testing supplies at the same time as the round two competition. (Note, however, that Medicare beneficiaries are not limited to using contract suppliers to obtain retail/storefront diabetes supplies.) The national mail-order competition

---

[44] The CBIC, which is administering the DMEPOS competitive bidding program on CMS's behalf, has posted a variety of information about round two *at* http://www.dmecompetitivebid.com/palmetto/cbicrd2.nsf/DocsCat/Home. CMS also has compiled information aimed at beneficiaries and referral sources *at* http://www.cms.gov/Outreach-and-Education/Outreach/Partnerships/DMEPOS_Toolkit.html.

included all parts of the United States, including the District of Columbia, Puerto Rico, the U.S. Virgin Islands, Guam, and American Samoa. It also became effective on July 1, 2013.

CMS subsequently recompeted the supplier contracts awarded in Round 2 of the DMEPOS Competitive Bidding Program and the National Mail-Order diabetic testing supplies competition, with the new contracts beginning on July 1, 2016. For the recompete, CMS made changes to both the composition of the product categories (including adding new products) and the number of competitive bidding areas (CBAs). Specific changes included: combining the Oxygen and CPAP Devices/Respiratory Assist Devices product categories; combining the Walkers and Wheelchairs/Scooters categories; creating a General Home Equipment category which includes the previous Hospital Beds and Support Surfaces categories in addition to new products; and adding a TENS devices product category. CMS conducted the Round 2 Recompete in the same geographic areas that were included in Round 2. Because of changes to the metropolitan statistical areas and boundary changes to ensure that no CBA is included in more than one state, however, there were be 117 CBAs in the Round 2 Recompete (compared to 100 in the prior competition).

CMS also conducted the National Mail-Order Recompete for diabetic testing supplies concurrently with the Round 2 Recompete. The competition included all parts of the United States, including the 50 states, the District of Columbia, Puerto Rico, the U.S. Virgin Islands, Guam, and American Samoa.

CMS offered 12,181 contracts to 637 Round 2 Recompete bidders, along with 9 contracts for the national mail-order program for contracts that took effect on July 1, 2016. CMS did not release data comparing the new single payment amounts to then existing current fee schedule payments, but the agency noted that during the first two years of Round 2 and the national mail-order programs (July 1, 2013-June 30 2015), Medicare saved approximately $3.6 billion as a result of the contract rates. The CMS announcement was followed shortly by release of an HHS Office of Inspector General (OIG) report that flagged problems with the state licensure status of some contract suppliers currently participating in the competitive bidding program.

On November 4, 2016, CMS published a final rule[45] which included competitive bidding program requirements for 2017 and revisions to the methodology for updating Medicare DMEPOS fee schedule amounts based on competitive bidding program pricing. Specifically, the final rule implemented a Medicare Access and CHIP Reauthorization Act of 2015 (MACRA) provision requiring entities bidding in the DMEPOS competitive bidding program to submit proof of an authorized "bid surety bond" for each competitive bidding area (CBA) in which the supplier is bidding. Under the final rule, the surety bond amount will be set at $50,000 for each CBA associated with the bid. If the bidder is offered but declines a contract for any product category in the CBA, and the supplier's bid for the product category was at or below the median composite bid rate used to calculate single payment amounts, the bid bond will be forfeited, and CMS will collect on the bond. In all other cases, the bid bond will be returned to the bidder within 90 days of CMS's public announcement of the contract suppliers for the CBA. The rule establishes penalties for bidders that provide falsified surety bonds or accept a contract offer and then renege on it in order to avoid surety bond forfeiture.

---

[45] 81 Fed. Reg. 77834 (Nov. 4, 2016).

The final rule also: implements a MACRA provision that prevents a contract from being awarded to a bidding entity unless the bidding entity meets applicable state licensure requirements; expands contract suppliers' appeal rights in the event of a breach of contract action by CMS; changes how CMS sets bid limits for individual items based on associated DMEPOS fee schedule amounts prior to adjustment based on CBP information; adopts complex methodological changes to address "price inversions" among similar products features (including specific groups of codes for hospital beds, mattresses and overlays, power wheelchairs, seat lift mechanisms, TENS devices, and walkers).that sometimes occur in the competitive bidding program, whereby the single payment amount (SPA) for an item with fewer features is higher than the SPA for the item with more features; and addresses the potential impact of inverted bidding prices on adjustments to Medicare DMEPOS fee schedule amounts outside of CBAs by using the weighted average of the prices for the similar items in a product category as the revised price for the items that will then be used to adjust the fee schedule amounts.

A Government Accountability Office report issued in the fall of 2016 found that the number of Medicare beneficiaries who received DME items generally fell after Round 2 of the competitive bidding program and the national mail-order program for diabetes testing supplies were implemented July 1, 2013.[46] Despite the study and reports of beneficiaries experiencing access issues by advocacy groups, CMS maintains that its routine monitoring of beneficiary access has not identified access issues. However, discharge planners and state hospital associations have echoed these concerns.

On January 31, 2017, CMS revealed plans for "Round 2019" of the DMEPOS competitive bidding program, which would have consolidated Round 1 2017, Round 2 Recompete, and the National Mail-Order Recompete. CMS stated its intention to conduct bidding in the summer for 11 product categories in 141 competitive bidding areas, with Round 2019 contracts in effect from January 1, 2019 through December 31, 2021. CMS indicated that it intended to implement a number of revisions to the bidding process with the new round, including a new "lead item" bidding methodology and a surety bond requirement. However, on February 7, CMS announced a "temporary delay" in order "to allow the new administration further opportunity to review the program." CMS did not release any details on its timeline for making a determination on whether or how to proceed with the next round of bidding.[47]

11.2.2.3.4 Inherent Reasonableness

As discussed, payment for some DMEPOS remains on the basis of a fee schedule, which is based upon historical reasonable charges for products. GAO, CMS, and the OIG have observed in several reports that fee schedule payments commonly are much higher than both marketplace charges and charges to other governmental health care programs (e.g., the Veterans' Administration). The Medicare statute allows CMS or the DMERCs (now called DME MACs) to impose payment adjustments on items of DMEPOS of up to 15% by providing limited notice and without consulting suppliers. Reductions in excess of 15% can be made by CMS if notice and comment is provided in

---

[46] See U.S. Gov't Accountability Off., GAO-16-570, CMS's Round 2 Durable Medical Equipment and National Mail-order Diabetes Testing Supplies Competitive Bidding Programs 15 (2016), *available at* https://www.gao.gov/products/GAO-16-570.

[47] See CMS DMEPOS Competitive Bidding Home, https://www.cms.gov/Medicare/Medicare-Fee-for-Service-Payment/DMEPOSCompetitiveBid/index.html.

the *Federal Register* and if CMS meets other legislative criteria such as considering the impact of such reductions on suppliers.[48]

The criteria for making these "inherent reasonableness" (IR) adjustments are whether the fee-schedule amounts for the products are not inherently reasonable because they are grossly excessive or grossly deficient. Use of this authority is significant for DMEPOS, because payment changes traditionally have occurred slowly over time. IR authority provides CMS with the ability to make significant changes in payment relatively quickly.

The process for CMS to adjust payments for Medicare Part B services (other than physician services) when existing payment amounts are determined to be either grossly excessive or deficient is further spelled out in the implementing regulations.[49] Notably, CMS decided not to apply IR adjustments unless the difference between the current and proposed payment amounts are at least 15% (although CMS did not preclude adjustments of less than 15% in a given year once it is determined that an overall adjustment of 15% or more is justified). Nevertheless, the IR adjustment process can have a significant impact on Medicare payments for DME and other Part B services.

11.2.2.4 Medicare Upgrade Provisions/Advance Beneficiary Notices

The BBA provided that Medicare beneficiaries purchasing or renting items of DME can choose an upgraded item in place of a standard item, effective upon publication of implementing regulations. Under this provision, suppliers receive payment from the Medicare program as if the item were a standard item, and the Medicare beneficiary pays the difference between the standard item and the upgraded item.

In 2002, CMS implemented a process by which suppliers may bill on an assignment basis for upgraded DME using Advance Beneficiary Notices (ABNs).[50] The ABNs, based on section 1879 of the SSA, inform beneficiaries that they may be responsible for payment for items, given the fact that the supplier expects Medicare payment for these items to be denied. Under the ABN process, the supplier is permitted to bill on an assigned or unassigned basis for the item that would be covered by Medicare. The supplier then bills the beneficiary for the difference between Medicare's allowed amount and the cost of the upgraded feature.

ABNs must be issued when Medicare is expected to deny payment for an item or service because it is not reasonable and necessary under Medicare Program standards or because Medicare considers it custodial care. In addition, DME suppliers are required to issue ABNs before providing a beneficiary with items or services in a number of additional situations, including when 1) the provider violated the prohibition against unsolicited telephone contacts, 2) the supplier has not met supplier number requirements, 3) the supplier is a noncontract supplier providing an item listed in a competitive bidding area, and 4) Medicare requires an advance coverage determination.

---

[48] *See also* 63 Fed. Reg. 687 (January 7, 1998) (codified at 42 C.F.R. pt. 405).
[49] 67 Fed. Reg. 76684 (Dec. 13, 2002) (codified at 42 C.F.R. § 405.502).
[50] 67 Fed. Reg. 21617 (May 1, 2002). Also see 42 C.F.R. § 411.404(b) and (c). Copies of the ABNs, as well as additional details about the ABN requirements, are available on the CMS website at http://www.cms.gov/BNI/01_overview.asp.

11.2.2.5 DMEPOS Furnished in Skilled Nursing Facilities and to Patients of Home Health Agencies

Skilled nursing facilities (SNFs) are paid by Medicare Part A under a prospective payment system (PPS) for services provided to Medicare beneficiaries. The SNF PPS consists of *per diem* rates, which vary based on the intensity of resources required by each resident. With a few exceptions, the PPS rate covers all routine, ancillary, and capital costs of services furnished to patients during a covered Part A stay.[51] This means that for patients in a covered Part A stay, suppliers generally do not receive separate reimbursement for items and services; rather, they must look to the SNF for payment.

Like SNFs, HHAs are paid under a PPS for HHAs,. As part of this payment system, payment for home health items and services is made only to the HHA that establishes the beneficiary's home health plan of care, regardless of whether the item or service was furnished by the agency, by others under arrangement, or under any other contracting or consulting arrangement.[52]

However, DME and oxygen and oxygen supplies (but not medical supplies) are excluded from the consolidated-billing requirement. In other words, DME and oxygen suppliers may bill the Medicare program directly for items and services provided under the home health benefit, rather than be dependent on an HHA for payment.[53]

11.2.3 Medicaid

In general, HME is covered under most state Medicaid benefits. Consult state law for specific determination of HME benefits. In order to receive payment, Medicaid HME suppliers must enroll as state Medicaid providers, after meeting state standards and conditions of participation. Many state Medicaid programs require prior authorization before paying for DMEPOS. Under the Consolidated Appropriations Act of 2016, Medicaid DME reimbursement rates were to be limited to Medicare FFS rates applicable in the state, including applicable competitive bidding rates, beginning January 1, 2019. The Cures Act has accelerated this provision, limiting Medicaid DME rates to Medicare rates effective January 1, 2018.[54]

11.2.4 Fraud and Abuse

While the health care industry as a whole has long been subject to scrutiny by law-enforcement officials, in recent years the HME industry has been one of the main targets of government fraud and abuse efforts. HME has been singled out for certain abusive billing practices, problems with the proper documentation of medical necessity, kickbacks for referrals, and improper marketing. The OIG also has noted that "low barriers to entry and weak oversight and enforcement of enrollment standards make DMEPOS a compelling target for fraudulent suppliers," while excessive Medicare reimbursement levels "makes DMEPOS fraud particularly lucrative, further attracting bad actors to the system."[55]

---

[51] *See* 42 U.S.C. § 1395yy(e).
[52] 42 U.S.C. § 1395fff; 42 U.S.C. § 1395u(b)(6).
[53] Medicare Claims Processing Manual, Chapter 10 – Home Health Agency Billing.
[54] 21st Century Cures Act, Pub. L. No. 114-255, § 5002, 130 Stat. 1033 (2016).
[55] Testimony of Daniel R. Levinson, Inspector General, HHS, House Committee on Energy and Commerce, Subcommittee on Health Hearing on "Medicare's Competitive Bidding Program for Durable Medical Equipment: Implications for Quality, Cost and Access," Sept. 15, 2010.

Such concerns have prompted a number of focused enforcement efforts, such as a two-year HHS pilot project announced on June 28, 2007 designed to prevent Medicare DME fraud in Southern California and Southern Florida. This pilot project required DMEPOS suppliers in the demonstration locales to reenroll in Medicare, expanded the reasons for revoking Medicare billing privileges, and subjected suppliers to an enhanced fraud review, including site visits. Likewise, in September of 2003, CMS and the OIG launched "Operation Wheeler Dealer" to combat improper Medicare payments for power wheelchairs.

Since 2007, HHS also has teamed with the Department of Justice (DOJ) to use "Strike Forces" to target fraudulent Medicare billing, including fraud involving DMEPOS suppliers, in selected geographic areas. According to the OIG, in the first year of Strike Force activity in Miami, Florida, Medicare billing for DMEPOS decreased by $1.7 billion or 63%, compared to the previous year's billing.[56] As of June 2016, Medicare Fraud Strike Forces have charged more than 2,900 individuals and organizations that have billed Medicare for more than $8.9 billion.[57] Likewise, in May of 2009, DOJ and HHS launched an interagency effort called the Health Care Fraud Prevention and Enforcement Action Team (HEAT) to target Medicare fraud patterns and trends using state-of-the-art technology and data analysis techniques.

Because of significant fraud and abuse concerns related to the Medicare DMEPOS benefit, the OIG released a comprehensive set of compliance guidelines for the entire industry in July of 1999. These guidelines, called the "OIG's Compliance Program Guidance for the DMEPOS Industry," address "suspect practices" which could trigger scrutiny by regulators and outline the specific elements that each DMEPOS supplier should consider when developing and implementing an effective compliance program.[58] The guidance is an excellent summary of the rules and requirements applicable to HME suppliers.

The ACA also included a number of program integrity provisions aimed at DMEPOS suppliers. Among other things, the ACA: requires physicians to document a face-to-face encounter with a beneficiary during the six-month period preceding a written order for any DME; allows the Secretary to disenroll for up to one year a Medicare supplier that fails to maintain and provide access to written orders for DME; authorizes the HHS Secretary to hold Medicare claims for up to 90 days for certain new DME suppliers if the Secretary determines that there is a significant fraud risk; and mandates a variety of new screening procedures for Medicare and Medicaid providers. On September 23, 2010, CMS published a proposed rule to implement the ACA provider/supplier screening requirements.[59] Notably, the proposed rule would classify new DMEPOS suppliers and HHAs (unless publicly-traded) as "high risk" entities subject to the most stringent screening requirements, including background checks and fingerprinting. On February 2, 2011, the final rule was implemented. Among

---

[56] *Id.*

[57] U.S. Department of Justice Press Release, *National Health Care Fraud Takedown Results in Charges against 301 Individuals for Approximately $900 Million in False Billing*, JUSTICE NEWS (Jun. 22, 2016), *available at* https://www.justice.gov/opa/pr/national-health-care-fraud-takedown-results-charges-against-301-individuals-approximately-900.

[58] 64 Fed. Reg. 36368 (July 6, 1999). The guidance also is available on the OIG website *at* http://oig.hhs.gov/compliance/compliance-guidance/index.asp.

[59] Medicare, Medicaid, and Children's Health Insurance Programs; Additional Screening Requirements, Application Fees, Temporary Enrollment Moratoria, Payment Suspensions and Compliance Plans for Providers and Suppliers, 75 Fed. Reg. 58204 (proposed Sept. 23, 2010).

many other things, it authorizes CMS and the states to impose temporary moratoria on the enrollment of new providers when deemed necessary to protect against a high risk of fraud and to suspend payments pending an investigation of a credible allegation of fraud.[60] On July 26, 2013, CMS exercised its authority under the ACA for the first time to impose temporary moratoria on new provider enrollment by announcing that it would impose temporary moratoria on the enrollment of new home health agencies and suppliers of DMEPOS in three parts of the country identified as "fraud hot-spots."[61] *See* Section 11.3.3.4 for further discussion of the temporary moratoria.

11.3 Home Health Care

11.3.1 State Licensure and Certificate of Need

HHAs and private duty nursing companies are home care providers that bring nurses and other practitioners to the patient's home. HHAs generally provide skilled nursing, therapy, or social services to patients in their homes, in addition to certain medical supplies and equipment. HHAs may be either freestanding or hospital-based in organization. HHAs are generally subject to state licensure requirements. In some states, licensure is only required if the entity provides skilled nursing and at least one type of therapy service. In others, the provision of skilled nursing services alone (e.g., through a private-duty nursing agency or a home infusion-therapy company) may trigger licensure. Some states (e.g., New York) require a CON to operate an HHA.[62] In other states, only institutional providers are subject to CON. It is important to consult applicable state law and regulations to determine specific requirements.

11.3.2 Medicare

11.3.2.1 Coverage

In order to qualify for Medicare coverage of HHA services, a Medicare beneficiary must be:

- confined to the home;
- under the care of a physician;
- receiving services under a plan of care established and periodically reviewed by a physician; and
- in need of intermittent skilled nursing care, physical therapy, or speech-language pathology, or have a continuing need for occupational therapy.[63]

---

[60] Medicare, Medicaid, and Children's Health Insurance Programs; Additional Screening Requirements, Application Fees, Temporary Enrollment Moratoria, Payment Suspensions and Compliance Plans for Providers and Suppliers, 76 Fed. Reg. 5862 (Feb. 2, 2011).

[61] Notice of Medicare, Medicaid, and Children's Health Insurance Programs: Announcement of Temporary Moratoria on Enrollment of Ambulances Suppliers and Providers and Home Health Agencies in Designated Geographic Areas, 78 Fed. Reg. 46339 (July 31, 2013).

[62] *See, e.g.*, N.Y. Pub. Health § 3606.

[63] *See* 42 U.S.C. §§ 1395f(a)(2)(C), 1395n(a)(2)(A).

As of 2011, a physician or specified non-physician practitioner must also certify through a face-to-face encounter that a beneficiary needs home health services.[64] The face-to-face encounter is only required for the initial certification and must be appropriately documented.[65] This encounter must occur no more than 90 days before or 30 days after the services begin.[66] In addition to the initial certification, the continuous provision of home health services under the plan of care must be periodically recertified by the physician.[67] In 2014, the OIG reviewed the extent of physician compliance with the face-to-face encounter requirement.[68] Based on a sample of 644 face-to-face encounter documents between April 1, 2011 and December 31, 2012, the OIG concluded that documentation did not meet Medicare requirements for 32% of home health claims that required face-to-face encounters, which the OIG estimated resulted in $2 billion in inappropriate payments. The OIG also found inconsistent physician completion of the narrative portion of the face to face documentation. The OIG characterized CMS oversight of the face-to-face requirement as "minimal." In light of these findings, the OIG recommended that CMS: (1) consider requiring a standardized form for the face-to-face documentation; (2) develop a specific strategy to communicate directly with physicians about this requirement, and (3) enhance oversight. CMS concurred with these recommendations and has since invited comments on voluntary home health electronic and paper "progress note" templates intended to assist physicians with documenting a face-to-face examination for purposes of the Medicare home health benefit.[69]

"Intermittent" is defined as skilled nursing care that is either provided or needed on fewer than seven days per week, or less than eight hours per day for periods of 21 days or less (with extensions in exceptional circumstances when the need for care is finite and predictable).[70]

Historically, CMS and the home health and hospice Medicare Administrative Contractors (MACs) that process claims for home health services required the patient literally to be confined to the home in order to qualify as "homebound." As such, if the patient left the home for nonmedical purposes, these absences would have to be for short periods of time or occur only infrequently.

In 2000, Congress expanded the homebound definition to allow patients to attend adult daycare programs or religious services.[71] Further, in 2002, CMS issued changes to require Medicare contractors to be more flexible in determining if a severely disabled individual is qualified as homebound for purposes of the Medicare home-health benefit.[72] CMS policy stated that chronically disabled individuals who otherwise qualified as homebound should not lose home health services because they leave their homes infrequently for short periods of time for special occasions, such as family reunions,

---

[64] *See* ACA § 6407(a).
[65] *See Medicare Benefit Policy Manual*, CMS Pub. 100-02, Chapter 7, § 30.5.1.1(2) (setting forth the encounter documentation requirements).
[66] *See Medicare Benefit Policy Manual*, CMS Pub. 100-02, Chapter 7, § 30.5.1.1.
[67] *See Medicare Benefit Policy Manual*, CMS Pub. 100-02, Chapter 7, § 30.5.2.
[68] OIG, Limited Compliance With Medicare's Home Health Face-to-Face Requirement, OEI-01-12-00390 (Apr. 2014).
[69] See CMS CMS-10564, *available at* https://www.cms.gov/Regulations-and-Guidance/Legislation/PaperworkReductionActof1995/PRA-Listing-Items/CMS-10564.html?DLPage=1&DLEntries=10&DLSort=1&DLSortDir=descending; see also 80 Fed. Reg. 48320 (Aug. 12, 2015).
[70] *See Medicare Benefit Policy Manual*, CMS Pub. 100-02, Chapter 7, § 30.
[71] Consolidated Appropriations Act, 2001, Pub. L. No. 106-554, § 507(a) (amending 42 U.S.C. §§ 1395f(a) and 1395n(a)).
[72] *See* CMS Transmittal 302 (July 26, 2002) (clarifying homebound criteria), *available at* https://www.cms.gov/Regulations-and-Guidance/Guidance/Transmittals/downloads/R302HHA.pdf.

graduations, or funerals.[73] However, effective November 19, 2013, CMS established new criteria for purposes of meeting the homebound criteria. Specifically, CMS revised the Medicare Benefit Policy Manual to state that an individual will be considered "confined to the home" (i.e., homebound) if the following two criteria are met:

Criteria One:

The patient must either:

- Because of illness or injury, need the aid of supportive devices such as crutches, canes, wheelchairs, and walkers; the use of special transportation; or the assistance of another person in order to leave their place of residence;

OR

- Have a condition such that leaving his or her home is medically contraindicated. If the patient meets one of the Criteria-One conditions, then the patient must *also* meet two additional requirements defined in Criteria Two below:

Criteria Two:

- There must exist a normal inability to leave home;

AND

- Leaving home must require a considerable and taxing effort.

If the patient does in fact leave the home, the patient may nevertheless be considered homebound if the absences from the home are infrequent or for periods of relatively short duration, or are attributable to the need to receive health care treatment. This could include, for example, attendance at adult day centers to receive medical care, outpatient kidney dialysis, or outpatient chemotherapy or radiation therapy. The Manual continues to provide some examples of homebound patients to show when a homebound condition exists. It is clear, however, that CMS is taking a much more restrictive view on determining homebound status. If there is a question on whether a patient is confined to home, the HHA is responsible for furnishing the intermediary with information necessary to establish that the patient is homebound, as set forth in the Manual.[74]

11.3.2.2 Conditions of Participation

Medicare-certified HHAs are subject to relatively detailed federal standards.[75] These standards, called "conditions of participation (or CoP)," govern issues such as the qualifications of personnel, furnishing services, developing plans of care, and the like.[76] A hospital or SNF is not considered to be

---

[73] *See Medicare Benefit Policy Manual*, CMS Pub. 100-02, Chapter 7, § 30.1.1 (providing examples of the factors used to determine whether a homebound condition exists) (2012).
[74] *See* Medicare Benefit Policy Manual, CMS Pub. 100-02, Chapter 7, § 30.1.1 (eff. Nov. 19, 2013).
[75] 42 U.S.C. § 1395m.
[76] *See* 42 C.F.R. §§ 484.1 *et seq.*

the patient's home for purposes of HHA coverage;[77] an assisted living facility, however, may be the patient's home for coverage of HHA services.[78]

HHAs are subject to a variety of penalties—including civil monetary penalties (CMPs) of up to $10,000 per day—if they do not comply with these standards.[79] Specifically, if CMS finds that an HHA is non-compliant with one or more conditions of participation, CMS may issue alternative or intermediate sanctions such as directing the: (1) appointment of a temporary manager over the agency;[80] (2) in-service training of staff;[81] and/or (3) plan of correction.[82] Under the first, the assigned temporary manager has the power to hire, fire, reassign staff, and change agency policies, and the agency is required to pay the salary and other expenses of the temporary manager.[83] If the HHA refuses the temporary management, CMS has the authority to terminate the provider agreement.[84] Additionally, CMS may require an HHA to utilize a third party with recognized expertise to provide in-service staff training, and the agency would be responsible for these costs as well.[85] Finally, instead of allowing an HHA to develop its own plan of correction in response to survey findings, CMS may direct the agency to take corrective action to achieve specific outcomes within specific timeframes.[86] Additional sanctions and penalties include CMPs that are based on not only condition-level deficiencies, but also repeat standard-level deficiencies.[87] CMS has also issued guidance on alternative sanctions for HHAs as a new chapter of the State Operations Manual (SOM), entitled "Survey and Enforcement Process for Home Health Agencies."[88]

On January 13, 2017, CMS published a final rule that extensively revises the conditions of participation.[89] The rule gives HHAs greater flexibility to meet quality care standards, focuses provider efforts on patient care through an interdisciplinary approach, and requires enhanced quality assessment and performance improvement efforts. In particular, CMS has added new conditions of participation in the following four areas: (1) patient rights;[90] (2) care planning, coordination of services, and quality care;[91] (3) quality assessment and performance improvement (QAPI);[92] and (4) infection prevention and control.[93] The "patient rights" CoP emphasizes the HHA's responsibility to respect and promote the rights of each home health patient. This includes providing the patient with a written notice of rights during his or her initial evaluation visit, informing the patient of the HHA's policies on transfer and discharge, and routinely investigating complaints. HHAs must also grant patients

---

[77] 42 C.F.R. § 409.42(a).
[78] *See Medicare Benefit Policy Manual*, CMS Pub. 100-02, Chapter 7, § 30.1.2.
[79] *See* 42 U.S.C. § 1395bbb(e)–(f).
[80] *See* 42 C.F.R. § 488.835.
[81] *See* 42 C.F.R. § 488.855.
[82] *See* 42 C.F.R. § 488.850.
[83] *See* 42 C.F.R. § 488.835.
[84] *Id.*
[85] *See* 42 C.F.R. § 488.855.
[86] *See* 42 C.F.R. § 488.850.
[87] *See* 42 C.F.R. § 488.845.
[88] *See* CMS, State Operations Manual (CMS Pub. 100-07), Ch. 10.
[89] *See* 82 Fed. Reg. 4504 (Jan. 13, 2017).
[90] 42 C.F.R. § 484.50.
[91] 42 C.F.R. § 484.60.
[92] 42 C.F.R. § 484.65.
[93] 42 C.F.R. § 484.70.

the freedom to exercise their rights, unless limited by court order.[94] As part of the new "care planning, coordination of services, and quality care" CoP, HHAs must give patients and their care givers written instructions that outline the patient's visit and medication schedules, treatments to be administered, and any other pertinent information regarding the patient's plan of care. Those instructions must include the HHA clinical manager's contact information.[95] The QAPI CoP requires HHAs to "develop, implement, evaluate, and maintain an effective, ongoing HHA-wide, data-driven [quality assessment and performance improvement] program."[96] The HHA must track quality indicators and utilize quality indicator data to design its QAPI program.[97] Finally, to comply with the "infection prevention and control" CoP, CMS requires HHAs to prioritize an infection control program designed to prevent and reduce the spread of infections and communicable diseases, including by educating staff, patients, and caregivers on proper infection control procedures.[98]

The final rule removes many process details from the previous conditions of participation where they do not achieve the goal of ensuring desired outcomes, based on the notion that those details created "unnecessary procedural burdens on providers."[99] Notably, the conditions of participation place quality and performance improvement responsibilities squarely within the responsibility of the provider. HHAs are responsible for identifying their own performance problems through their QAPI programs, addressing them, and continuously striving to improve the quality of care through mandatory annual performance improvement projects.[100] The conditions of participation also are designed to enable surveyors to look at outcomes of care and "assess how effectively the provider was pursuing a continuous quality improvement agenda."[101] HHAs must comply with the new conditions of participation by January 13, 2018, a six-month extension from the final rule's July 13, 2017 original effective date.[102] CMS has delayed enforcement to give HHAs more time to come into compliance, considering the additional resource allocation, staffing, and infrastructure HHAs may require.[103] At the time of publication, CMS has released draft interpretive guidelines, and so additional delays in enforcement are not anticipated.[104]

As an additional condition of participation in Medicare, HHAs must provide notice to Medicare beneficiaries if the HHA believes that items or services may not be covered.[105] These requirements apply, for example, where a beneficiary faces potential liability for care that has been received but may be reduced or terminated, where the HHA has reason to believe a service that is generally covered may be found not to be reasonable or necessary in a given situation, or where the HHA decides for its own reasons no longer to provide some or all of its care. In late 2013, CMS replaced

---

[94] 42 C.F.R. § 484.50, *et seq.*
[95] 42 C.F.R. § 484.60.
[96] 42 C.F.R. § 484.65.
[97] 42 C.F.R. § 484.65(a)-(b).
[98] 42 C.F.R. § 484.70.
[99] 82 Fed. Reg. 4504 (Jan. 13, 2017).
[100] 42 C.F.R. § 484.65(d).
[101] 82 Fed. Reg. 4504, 4569 (Jan. 13, 2017).
[102] 82 Fed. Reg. 31729 (July 10, 2017).
[103] *See id.*
[104] *See* CMS-3819-F Medicare and Medicaid Program: Conditions of Participation for Home Health Agencies Interpretive Guidelines – DRAFT, *available at* http://report.nahc.org/wp-content/uploads/2017/10/3819-F-HomeHealthAgency-CoPs_IGs.pdf.
[105] 42 C.F.R. § 484.10(e).

the previous standardized form used by HHAs to provide advanced notice to Medicare beneficiaries, the Home Health Advance Beneficiary Notice (HHABN), CMS-R-296, with two other standardized forms that are available on CMS's website.[106] Depending on the circumstances, HHAs must provide beneficiary notice through the use of either the standardized Advance Beneficiary Notice (ABN), CMS Form-R-131, or Home Health Change of Care Notice (HHCCN), CMS Form-10280.[107] Prior to the provision of an item or service that is usually paid for by Medicare, but may not be covered because it is, among other things, not considered medically reasonable and necessary under the circumstances, the HHA must provide notice to a beneficiary by providing the standardized ABN, CMS Form-R-131. Additionally, prior to the HHA reducing or discontinuing care listed in a beneficiary's plan of care because, for example, a physician ordered a change in the plan of care, or there is no physicians' order to continue the care, the HHA must provide notice to a beneficiary by providing the standardized HHCCN, CMS Form-10280.

11.3.2.3   36 Month Rule

Under the "36 Month Rule" for HHAs, if the owner of an HHA sells (including asset sales or stock transfers), transfers or relinquishes ownership of the HHA within 36 months after the effective date of the HHA's initial enrollment in Medicare or any "change in ownership" subsequent to the initial enrollment, then the provider agreement and Medicare billing privileges do not convey to the new owner.[108] CMS states that the purpose of this rule is to ensure that HHAs that are sold remain in compliance with Medicare's conditions of participation. CMS also asserts that this change was needed to avoid individuals buying HHAs solely for resale with no intention of operating the business.[109] According to CMS the "36 Month Rule" rule "will help to ensure that individuals establishing an HHA are doing so with the long-term view of furnishing services, rather than establishing a business for the purposes of selling it a short time later."[110] Importantly, the rule does not apply to "indirect" stock ownership changes. Moreover, there are several exceptions to the rule. The rule does not apply if:

- The HHA has submitted 2 consecutive years of full cost reports. (For purposes of this exception, low utilization or no utilization cost reports do not qualify as full cost reports.)
- The HHA's parent company is undergoing an internal corporate restructuring, such as a merger or consolidation.

---

[106] *See* CMS, Beneficiary Notices Initiative (BNI), *available at* http://www.cms.gov/Medicare/Medicare-General-Information/BNI/HHABN.html.

[107] *See* CMS's Change Requests (CRs) 8403 and 8404 and related *Medicare Learning Network* materials for additional guidance on the use of the HHCCN and ABN by HHAs.

[108] 42 C.F.R. § 424.550(b)(1); *see* Medicare Program Integrity Manual (CMS Pub. 100-08), § 15.26.1; *see also* Medicare Program; Home Health Prospective Payment System Rate Update for Calendar Year 2011; Changes in Certification Requirements for Home Health Agencies and Hospices, 75 Fed. Reg. 70372 (Nov. 17, 2010). The previous version of the "36 Month Rule" was limited to an HHA's initial enrollment in Medicare and also limited the circumstances constituting a "change in ownership" to only a merger or asset sale. *See* Medicare Program; Home Health Prospective Payment System, 74 Fed. Reg. 58078, 58118 (Nov. 10, 2009).

[109] *See* Medicare Program; Home Health Prospective Payment System Rate Update for Calendar Year 2011; Changes in Certification Requirements for Home Health Agencies and Hospices, 75 Fed. Reg. 70372 (Nov. 17, 2010) (reiterating that the purpose of the 36 Month Rule is not only to address the broader problem of new owners of HHAs entering Medicare without having undergone state survey compliance, but also the specific issue of "flipping" HHAs without real operations).

[110] Medicare Program; Home Health Prospective Payment System, 74 Fed. Reg. 58078, 58118 (Nov. 10, 2009).

- The HHA is changing its existing business structure—such as from a corporation, a partnership (general or limited), or an LLC to a corporation, a partnership (general or limited) or an LLC—and the owners remain the same.
- An individual owner of the HHA dies.[111]

11.3.2.4 Payment

Historically, HHA services were reimbursed on a reasonable cost basis. The BBA imposed strict per-beneficiary and per-visit caps, known as the interim payment system (IPS), which was an interim system until a prospective system for HHAs was implemented.

The BBA directed the Secretary of HHS to establish a PPS for home health services beginning October 1, 1999, although actual implementation was delayed until 2000. Under the BBA, all services covered and paid on a reasonable-cost basis at the time of enactment (including medical supplies) were to be paid under the PPS. Services reimbursed on the basis of a fee schedule, including DME and orthotics and prosthetics, were not included in the PPS rate. Congress directed the HHS Secretary to determine an appropriate unit of service, along with the number, type, and duration of visits provided within the unit; their costs; and a "general system design that provides for continued access to quality services."[112] No particular type of unit (e.g., per visit or per episode) was specified.

Payment amounts initially were based on the most current audited cost-report data available to the HHS Secretary, and total payment amounts for fiscal year (FY) 2000 were required to equal the amount that would have been made if the PPS system had not been in effect, subject to a 15% reduction in cost limits and per-beneficiary limits effective September 30, 1999. Actual payments were to be adjusted to reflect case mix, area wages, and inflation. Additional outlier payments or adjustments were permitted, but they could not exceed 5% of the total PPS payments estimated to be made in that year.

The BBA also required consolidated billing by the HHA for home health items and services furnished to an individual who (at the time the item or service is furnished) "is under a plan of care of a home health agency," without regard to whether or not the item or service was furnished by the agency, by others under arrangement with the agency, due to any other contracting or consulting arrangement, or otherwise.[113] In other words, if a beneficiary is receiving care under an HHA plan of care, most items and services must be billed by the HHA, rather than the supplier.

Under the prospective payment system (PPS) implemented by CMS in October 2000, HHAs receive a standardized payment for each 60-day episode of home health care that a Medicare beneficiary receives.[114] The payment covers skilled nursing care, home health aide visits, therapy medical social services, and routine and nonroutine medical supplies provided by HHAs.[115] HHAs use a standardized evaluation instrument known as the Outcomes and Assessment Information Set (OASIS) to document the care needs and services for every patient admitted for services and to assess

---

[111] 42 C.F.R. § 424.550(b)(2).
[112] *See* BBA, Pub. L. No. 105-33, 111 Stat. 273, § 4603(a) (amending 42 U.S.C. § 1395ffff).
[113] BBA, Pub. L. No. 105-33, 111 Stat. 273, § 4603(c) (amending 42 U.S.C. § 1395u).
[114] Medicare Program; Prospective Payment System for Home Health Agencies, 65 Fed. Reg. 41128 (July 3, 2000).
[115] *Id.*

the patient's continuing need for home health care. The OASIS is also used to categorize patients for payment purposes under the Medicare prospective payment system for HHAs.

Key elements of the home health PPS are as follows:

- *The unit of service is a 60-day episode of care.* There are no limits to the number of episodes a beneficiary who is eligible for the home health benefit can receive. HHAs receive half of the payment up front, and the balance after the 60-day period (unless there is an applicable adjustment).
- *Case-mix adjusted payment.* Based on the OASIS resident-assessment instrument, patients are classified into one of 153 home health resource groups (HHRGs) by clinical severity, patient functional status, and service intensity. Payment thus is intended to reflect the care needs of the patient.
- *Payment rates are subject* to wage indices to account for geographical variations in labor costs applicable to the furnishing of home health services.
- There are three principal adjustments to the payment rates, including the following:
    - *Low Utilization Payment Adjustment (LUPA).* Payments are adjusted when the patient needs four or fewer visits during the 60-day period. The LUPA essentially converts the PPS to a fee-for-service payment for these types of patients.[116]
    - *Partial Episode Payment Adjustment (PEP).* Payments are adjusted when a patient changes HHAs during the 60-day period, or is discharged and readmitted to the same HHA during the 60-day period. The "old" period begins when the last visit occurs, and the "new" episode begins as for the first visit. Payment is pro-rated based on the number of days the patient is under the care of the agency. The PEP does not apply when a beneficiary transfers to an HHA that has common ownership.
    - *Outlier Payments.* Payments are adjusted for patients where the costs of care exceeds the fixed payment rate under the HHRG greater than the outlier threshold. The outlier payment is the difference between the cost of the episode and the outlier threshold. HHAs are paid at 80% of the costs above the outlier threshold (known as the loss-sharing ratio). Notably, the outlier adjustment does not make up for all of the costs exceeding the HHRG payment. Rather, as the name implies, it is a way for the HHA to make up some, but not all, of its costs. Effective January 1, 2010, outlier payments may compromise no more than 10% of an HHA's total home health PPS payments for the year. Under the ACA, beginning in CY 2011, the 10% outlier cap is permanent.
    - *Consolidated Billing.* HHAs must bill for all home health items and services provided to the patient as set forth in the plan of care except DME, including oxygen and oxygen supplies. Notably, however, most medical supplies still are subject to the consolidated billing requirement.[117]

---

[116] Originally the HHA PPS had a Significant Change in Condition Payment Adjustment for when the patient's condition changed during the 60-day episode. This was eliminated effective January 1, 2008. *See* Medicare Program; Home Health Prospective Payment System Refinement and Rate Update for Calendar Year 2008, 72 Fed Reg. 49,762, 49,850 (Aug. 29, 2007).

[117] Information and links regarding HHA billing are available at https://www.cms.gov/center/hha.asp.

11.3.2.4

CMS has made a number of refinements to the home health PPS over the years, both pursuant to statutory mandates, such as the ACA, and under CMS's general rulemaking authority. Such payment policies have involved capping outlier payments, paying rural HHAs additional reimbursement, rebasing the payment formula, making adjustments for inflation and other factors, and imposing quality reporting requirements on HHAs, among many other things.

In the 2016 final rule, CMS finalized its Home Health VBP model, which shifts from volume-based payments to a framework that promotes the delivery of higher quality care to Medicare beneficiaries.[118] Effective January 1, 2016, CMS implemented the VBP model in the following nine states representing each geographic area in the nation: Massachusetts, Maryland, North Carolina, Florida, Washington, Arizona, Iowa, Nebraska, and Tennessee. All Medicare-certified HHAs delivering services within these states are required to compete for payment adjustments based on quality performance, with a baseline year of 2015 and first performance year of 2016. The maximum quality-based payment adjustment (upward or downward) is 3% in 2018 (down from 5% in the proposed rule), 5% in 2019, 6% in 2020, 7% in 2021, and 8% in 2022. The final rule included a detailed discussion of the initial set of VBP measures (six process measures, 10 outcome measures, and five Home Health Care Consumer Assessment of Healthcare Providers and Systems Survey (HHCAHPS) measures), and the scoring/payment adjustment methodology. While there is aggregate increase or decrease in payments to HHAs competing in the model, CMS projected an estimated $380 million in total savings in CY 2018 through 2022 from the VBP program. Specifically, based on what CMS contends is a "very conservative savings estimate," CMS expects a 6% annual reduction in unnecessary hospitalizations and a 1% drop in skilled nursing facility admissions as a result of greater quality improvements in the home health industry.

In addition, the final rule updated the Home Health Quality Reporting Program (HH QRP) to establish a standardized "cross-setting measure" related to skin integrity as authorized by the Improving Medicare Post-Acute Care Transformation Act of 2014 (the IMPACT Act). The final rule also established a minimum threshold for submission of OASIS assessments for purposes of quality reporting compliance. The initial threshold was set at 70% of all patients with episodes of care occurring during the reporting period starting July 1, 2015, increasing by 10% in each of the subsequent periods (July 1, 2016 and July 1, 2017) to reach 90%.

The 2017 final rule reduced Medicare home health PPS payments by 0.7%, or $130 million overall.[119] CMS adopted a 2.5% home health payment update percentage (derived from a 2.8% market basket update minus a 0.3% multifactor productivity adjustment). This increase was more than offset by other negative adjustments, however, including a -0.97% adjustment for nominal case-mix coding intensity growth (the second year of a three-year phase in period), and a -2.3% rebasing adjustment (the final year of a four-year phase-in). The final rule also recalibrated home health PPS case-mix weights, updated the home health wage index, and modified the methodology used to calculate high-cost outlier payments.

---

[118] 81 Fed. Reg. 76702 (Nov. 3, 2016).
[119] 81 Fed. Reg. 76702 (Nov. 3, 2016).

Additionally, the final rule updated the HH QRP, including the addition of four post-acute care measures under the Improving Medicare Post-Acute Care Transformation Act of 2014, effective beginning with the 2018 payment determination. It removed 28 Home Health Quality Initiative measures that were "topped out" and/or of limited clinical and quality improvement value, along with six topped out process measures. The rule also updated the VBP model, Changes to the VBP model address calculation of benchmarks and achievement thresholds, data submission and reporting timeframes, minimum cohort size, applicable measures, and recalculation and reconsideration processes. Finally, effective January 1, 2017, CMS implemented a statutory provision to require separate payment to HHAs for disposable Negative Pressure Wound Therapy (NPWT) devices furnished under the Medicare home health benefit, 7. This payment equals the amount that would otherwise be made under the Medicare Outpatient Prospective Payment System, as required by statute.

Most recently, CMS published the 2018 final rule[120] that decreases Medicare home health PPS payments by 0.4%, or $80 million. As part of the final rule, CMS continues the third year of a three-year reduction to the national, standardized 60-day episode payment rate, through a -0.97% case mix adjustment. This adjustment is intended to account for case-mix growth not rooted in patient acuity. The final rule also adds a 1.0% market basket. CMS maintains the fixed-dollar loss ratio at 0.55% to pay up to 2.5% of total payments as outlier payments.

In addition, the 2018 rule finalizes changes to the Home Health VBP model. The rule requires 40 HHCAHPS submissions to receive a performance score on any HHCAHP measure; it also indicates CMS's intention to remove the OASIS-based measure on drug education to patients and providers. The final rule also implements changes to the HH QRP. Those changes include: (1) replacing the pressure ulcer quality measure, and adopting measures on the percent of residents with one or more falls with major injury, and the percent of LTC hospital patients with an admission and discharge functional assessment and responsive care plan; (3) implementing exception and extension requirements; and (4) executing reconsideration and appeals procedures. Finally, the rule ends the rural add-on provision. While CMS also intends to implement a new payment model through the HH Groupings Model (HHGM) for CY2019, it has yet to finalize those changes and is unlikely to do so before 2020.

11.3.3 Medicaid HHAs

11.3.3.1 Coverage

The provision of home health services is an optional requirement for state Medicaid programs, but most states provide such benefits.[121] States also may provide payment for private-duty nursing.[122] Most state Medicaid programs follow Medicare coverage rules for HHAs. Some offer programs that cover other types of home care services (e.g., personal care services).[123]

---

[120] 82 Fed. Reg. 51676 (Nov. 7, 2017).
[121] 42 U.S.C. §§ 1396a(10)(A), 1396d(a)(7).
[122] *Id.* § 1396d(a)(8).
[123] *Id.* § 1396d(a)(24).

11.3.3.2 Qualifications

Most states follow the Medicare HHA conditions of participation, as well as state licensure.

11.3.3.3 Payment

Payment is determined by each state Medicaid program, and methodologies differ among the states. Some states apply a flat rate per visit, where actual cost is not a factor. Others use cost reports to set a prospective rate, subject to applicable caps. Still others use a retrospective cost reimbursement system, subject to applicable caps. Consult state law.

11.3.3.4 Fraud and Abuse

HHAs continue to be the subject of DOJ, OIG, and contractor audits and investigations. Key concerns have included submission of false cost reports, providing care to patients not considered "homebound,"[124] billing for services not rendered, kickbacks for referrals, and improper marketing. In light of these concerns, in August 1998, the OIG issued an HHA Compliance Program Guidance identifying specific elements HHAs should consider when developing and implementing an effective compliance program and "risk areas" to be addressed.[125] The guidance is a useful summary of rules and regulations applicable to HHAs. Since then, HHAs have been subject to the federal government's efforts to combat fraudulent Medicare practices.

In December 2012, the OIG issued a report assessing CMS and Medicare contractor oversight of HHAs in light of persistent concerns about Medicare fraud, waste, and abuse involving HHAs.[126] In the report, the OIG concluded that the effectiveness of existing oversight efforts was mixed, and recommended that CMS establish additional contractor performance standards for high-risk providers in fraud-prone areas and to prevent inappropriate payments made to HHAs with suspended or revoked billing privileges.

Pursuant to its authority under ACA,[127] CMS announced the imposition of temporary moratoria on enrollment of new home health providers under Medicare, Medicaid, and the Children's Health Insurance Program (CHIP) in three areas of the country identified as "fraud hot-spots."[128] As of July 30, 2013, the temporary moratoria applied to the enrollment of new HHAs in the Miami, Florida and Chicago, Illinois areas. These areas and services were selected by CMS, in consultation with the OIG and DOJ, because of the high potential fraud risk indicated by factors such as a disproportionate number of providers and suppliers relative to beneficiaries, a rapid increase in enrollment applications from providers and suppliers, and extremely high utilization of services. During the moratoria,

---

[124] *See* Section 11.3.2.1 for discussion of definition of "homebound."

[125] Publication of the OIG Compliance Program Guidelines for Home Health Agencies, 63 Fed. Reg. 42410 (Aug. 7, 1998), *available at* http://oig.hhs.gov/authorities/docs/cpghome.pdf.

[126] *See* OIG, *CMS and Contractor Oversight of Home Health Agencies* (Dec. 2012), *available at* https://oig.hhs.gov/oei/reports/oei-04-11-00220.pdf.

[127] Specifically, CMS imposed temporary moratorium on Medicare enrollment of HHAs under its authority at 42 C.F.R. §§ 242.570(a)(2)(i) and (a)(2)(iv).

[128] *See* Notice of Medicare, Medicaid, and Children's Health Insurance Programs: Announcement of Temporary Moratoria on Enrollment of Ambulances Suppliers and Providers and Home Health Agencies in Designated Geographic Areas, 78 Fed. Reg. 46339 (July 31, 2013).

existing providers and suppliers may continue to provide and bill for services, but new provider and supplier applications for these provider types will not be approved in the selected geographic areas. Beginning January 30, 2014, CMS extended these moratoria, and expanded them to include the enrollment of new HHAs in the Fort Lauderdale, Florida; Detroit, Michigan; Houston, Texas; and Dallas, Texas areas. These moratoria were subsequently extended at 6 month intervals through July 29 2016, when CMS expanded them further to the entire states of Florida, Illinois, Michigan, and Texas,[129] and have been continually extended through 2017.[130]

CMS also announced that it will implement a pre-claim review demonstration for HHAs in five states—Illinois, Florida, Texas, Michigan, and Massachusetts—identified as particularly susceptible to home health services fraud.[131] This pre-claim review demonstration mandates that HHAs seeking Medicare reimbursement for home health services submit currently-mandated documentation to the Medicare Administrative Contractor (MAC) earlier in the claims payment process. Although HHAs need not wait for a determination prior to furnishing services, the documentation is intended to determine if the service level complies with Medicare coverage requirements. CMS intends this review process to aid investigative and enforcement efforts by both CMS and OIG.

Meanwhile, on June 22, 2016 the OIG issued a report[132] detailing its nationwide analysis of common characteristics in home health fraud cases, as well as an Alert[133] on improper arrangements and conduct by and among HHAs and physicians. The report discussed selected characteristics commonly found in OIG-investigated cases of home health fraud. The five distinct characteristics common to these investigations were: (1) high percentage of episodes for which the beneficiary had no recent visits with the supervising physician; (2) high percentage of episodes that were not preceded by a hospital or nursing home stay; (3) high percentage of episodes with a primary diagnosis of diabetes or hypertension; (4) high percentage of beneficiaries with claims from multiple HHAs; and (5) high percentage of beneficiaries with multiple home health readmissions in a short period of time. The Alert warns that OIG will continue aggressively prosecuting HHAs, individuals, and heads of home-visiting physician companies that defraud Medicare" by "making (or accepting) payments for patient referrals, falsely certifying patients as homebound, and billing for medically unnecessary services or for services that were not rendered." The OIG cautions HHAs and physicians to take extra care to ensure that arrangements between them reflect fair market value and are commercially reasonable even in the absence of federal health care program referrals. Additionally, the Alert cautions HHAs on the need to ensure that beneficiaries receiving their services meet the detailed regulatory requirements applicable to providing home health services, including that beneficiaries are confined to their homes and that specific services provided are medically necessary.

---

[129] *See* 81 Fed. Reg. 51120 (Aug. 3, 2016).
[130] 82 Fed. Reg. 35122 (July 28, 2017).
[131] 81 Fed. Reg. 37598 (Jun. 10, 2016).
[132] *See* OIG, Nationwide Analysis of Common Characteristics in OIG Home Health Fraud Cases, OEI-05-16-00031 (Jun. 21, 2016), *available at* https://oig.hhs.gov/oei/reports/oei-05-16-00031.pdf.
[133] *See* OIG, Alert: Improper Arrangements and Conduct Involving Home Health Agencies and Physicians (Jun. 22, 2016), *available at* https://oig.hhs.gov/compliance/alerts/guidance/HHA_%20Alert2016.pdf.

11.3.3.5 Audits

Medicare contractors perform sample audits of the medical necessity of home health services provided to Medicare beneficiaries, and sometimes extrapolate sample results to the entire "universe" of patient claims for the relevant period. HHAs therefore need to perform routine internal audits to make sure documentation supports the care provided, that the plan of care is appropriately updated, and that patients who do not qualify for the Medicare home health benefit are discharged.

11.3.3.6 Hospital Discharge Planning

The Medicare hospital conditions of participation require hospitals to evaluate patients for post-acute hospital services and the availability of those services.[134] The Medicare statute and implementing regulations specifically require hospitals to consider a patient's home health, hospice and post-hospital extended care service needs.[135] In response to concerns about hospitals steering patients to specific HHAs, including those in which they had a financial interest, Congress enacted legislation requiring hospitals to provide Medicare beneficiaries in need of home health services with a list of all Medicare-certified HHAs in the area that have requested to be listed by the hospital. The list must also indicate the HHAs that are enrolled in managed care organizations. Hospitals must inform patients of their freedom of choice of home-health providers, and cannot limit or restrict qualified HHAs that may wish to care for patients following discharge.[136] Hospitals must document in the patient record that the list was presented to the patient or person acting on behalf of the patient.[137] The discharge plan must also identify any HHA to which the patient is referred in which the hospital has a disclosable financial interest.[138] HHAs cannot undertake discharge-planning functions required of the hospital, but can undertake an evaluation of the patient once a referral to the HHA has been made.

11.4 Hospice Care

11.4.1 Introduction

Patients who are terminally ill may elect to receive hospice care, which is available under Medicare, and many health insurance plans, including Medicaid in those states that elect to provide hospice coverage.[139] By electing hospice care, the beneficiary decides to forgo curative medical intervention in favor of palliative care to ease the final stages of the beneficiary's life. Hospice care is provided under an established plan of care by an interdisciplinary group of professionals and volunteers who attend to the physical, social, and spiritual needs of the patient.

---

[134] 42 C.F.R. § 482.43(a) and (b).
[135] *See* 42 U.S.C. § 1395x(ee)(2); 42 C.F.R. § 482.43.
[136] *See* 42 U.S.C. § 1395x(ee)(2); 42 C.F.R. § 482.43(c).
[137] 42 C.F.R. § 482.43(c)(6).
[138] *Id.* § 482.43(c)(8).
[139] *See* 42 U.S.C. § 1395d, f, x(dd), § 1396.

11.4.2 State Licensure and Certificate of Need

Most states license hospices. Many state licensure laws closely track the federal Medicare conditions of participation.[140] Others impose additional or more specific requirements.[141] All hospice employees also must be properly licensed in accordance with applicable federal, state, and local laws. Finally, certain states require hospices to obtain a CON prior to establishing the hospice program.[142] Consult individual state's laws and regulations regarding licensure and CON requirements.

11.4.3 Medicare Conditions of Participation

As with other types of Medicare providers, hospices are subject to specific federal standards.[143] These standards, called "conditions of participation," govern issues such as the qualifications of personnel, furnishing services, developing plans of care, and the like.[144] The conditions of participation for hospices are set forth in the Code of Federal Regulations[145] and the Medicare State Operations Manual (SOM) provides further guidance on how CMS and state survey agencies interpret these regulations.[146] CMS periodically updates the conditions of participation through formal rulemaking.[147]

In general, the conditions of participation address a variety of practices that a hospice is required to adopt in order to be eligible for Medicare certification. For example, the conditions of participation address: hospice benefit periods, documentation requirements to support certification and recertification of terminal illness, hospice admission procedures, hospice discharge procedures (discharges from hospice for cause are allowed under very limited circumstances), patients' rights; patient assessments, the interdisciplinary group, care planning, coordination of services. In addition, the conditions of participation address staffing policies (including, for example, requirements that the physician member of the interdisciplinary group and the medical director are employees of or under contract with the hospice, and that nurse practitioners be permitted to provide services to beneficiaries receiving hospice care if state law permits), and a hospice's responsibility for care provided to hospice patients residing in a nursing facility.[148]

Hospices must also implement "an effective, ongoing, hospice-wide data-driven quality assessment and performance improvement (QAPI) program," but have flexibility "to decide how to implement the QAPI requirement in a manner that reflects its own unique needs and goals."[149]

---

[140] *See, e.g.*, FLA. STAT. ANN. § 400.6085.
[141] *See, e.g.*, WIS. ADMIN. CODE § HHS 131.21 (establishing detailed patient and family bill of rights).
[142] *See, e.g.*, FLA. STAT. ANN. §§ 400.606(5), 408.031–408.045.
[143] 42 U.S.C. § 1395m.
[144] *See generally* 42 C.F.R. §§ 418.1 *et seq.*
[145] *See* 42 C.F.R. 418, Subparts C & D.
[146] *See Medicare State Operations Manual* (CMS Pub. 107), Appendix M (available on the CMS website at http://www.cms.hhs.gov/manuals/downloads/som107_Appendicestoc.pdf.
[147] *See e.g.*, 70 Fed. Reg. 70532 (Nov. 22, 2005); 73 Fed. Reg. 32088 (June 5, 2008).
[148] 73 Fed. Reg. 32088 (June 5, 2008).
[149] 73 Fed. Reg. 32088, 32193 (June 5, 2008).

11.4.4.1 Types of Hospice Care

A hospice provider may furnish care to beneficiaries in a variety of settings, including a freestanding hospice facility, a SNF, a hospital, or in the beneficiary's home. Hospice care falls into four basic categories:

- *Routine home care* is the typical level of care provided to a hospice patient, and is furnished in the patient's home or in a facility that is the patient's residence.
- *Continuous home care* is provided for eight to 24 hours per day for brief periods while a hospice patient is in crisis but can be maintained at home. If a hospice provides this level of care, 51% of the care must be provided by a licensed RN.
- *Inpatient respite care* is provided when the hospice patient's family or caregiver requires a temporary reprieve, which is not related to the patient's physical decline. This level of care can be provided in a facility for up to five days and, after five days, the hospice patient must be converted to another level of care. An RN must be available to provide direct patient care 24 hours a day.
- *General inpatient care* is provided when a hospice patient requires admission to an inpatient facility for pain control, or for acute or chronic symptom management that cannot be accomplished in another setting.[150]

Inpatient hospice care for pain control, symptom management, or respite purposes must be provided in a participating Medicare or Medicaid facility.[151] A hospice facility that provides inpatient hospice care directly must meet certain requirements concerning physical plant, room-like décor, and extended visiting hours.[152] All the hospice inpatient facilities must provide: (1) 24-hour nursing services that are sufficient to meet the patient's needs; (2) a registered nurse on each shift who provides direct patient care; and (3) patient area requirements to meet the comfort and privacy of patients and their families.[153]

A hospice that contracts with a hospital or SNF to provide inpatient care must ensure that:

- the agreement specifies the inpatient services to be furnished;
- the hospice will furnish a copy of the patient's plan of care;
- the inpatient provider's policies are consistent with the hospice;
- the inpatient provider will abide by the hospice's patient-care protocols;
- the medical record will include all inpatient services furnished; and
- the hospice retains responsibility for hospice care training for all personnel involved in providing care pursuant to the agreement.[154]

---

[150] *See* 42 C.F.R. § 418.302. *See also Medicare Benefit Policy Manual* (CMS Pub. 100-02), Chapter 9.
[151] *See id.* § 418.108.
[152] *See id.* § 418.100(c); (e); (f).
[153] *See id.* §§ 418.100(c); 418.64(b); 418.110(f).
[154] *See id.* § 418.112.

As noted, hospice services may be provided in long-term care facilities and assisted-living facilities where that is the patient's home. Hospices that provide services to residents of a long-term care facility must have a written agreement with the facility that sets forth the provision of hospice services at the facility.[155] Among other things, the agreement must address how the parties will communicate, what must be communicated (for example, changes in the patient's condition), and the respective responsibilities of each party to ensure the care and well-being of the patient.[156]

11.4.4.2   Hospice Services and Personnel

The hospice provides and supervises services through an interdisciplinary group comprised of at least the following individuals, who (except for the physician)[157] must be employees of the hospice:

- a doctor of medicine or osteopathy;
- a registered nurse;
- a social worker; and
- a pastoral or other counselor.[158]

This interdisciplinary group is responsible for establishing, periodically reviewing, and updating the hospice patient's plan of care, as well as establishing policies governing the daily provision of hospice care.[159]

The hospice must provide certain "core" covered services, which include physician services, nursing services, medical social services, and counseling services.[160] Except during periods of peak patient load or under extraordinary circumstances, core services must be provided by hospice employees. If the hospice provides any services under arrangements with contracted staff, then "the hospice must maintain professional, financial, and administrative responsibility for the services."[161]

The hospice physician is responsible for the palliation and management of the patient's terminal illness and related conditions, as well as any general medical needs that are not being met by the patient's attending physician.[162] Nursing services must be provided by, or under the supervision of, a registered nurse in accordance with recognized standards of practice.[163] Medical social services must be provided to a hospice patient "by a qualified social worker, under the direction of a physician."[164]

Several types of counseling services must be available to the hospice patient and the patient's family. Bereavement counseling must be provided through an organized program under the supervision of a qualified professional. The hospice must establish a plan of care for bereavement services that

---

[155] 78 Fed. Reg. 38594 (Jun. 27, 2013).
[156] *See* 42 C.F.R. § 418.112(c).
[157] *See* 42 U.S.C. § 1395xdd(2) (providing that the hospice physician may be an independent contractor or employee).
[158] *See* 42 C.F.R. § 418.56(a).
[159] *See id.* § 418.56.
[160] *See id.* § 418.64.
[161] *Id.* § 418.100(e).
[162] *See id.* § 418.64(a).
[163] *See id.* § 418.64(b).
[164] *Id.* § 418.64(c).

adequately reflects the needs of the patient's family.[165] The hospice also must provide dietary counseling by a qualified individual, as needed, for the hospice patient.[166] In addition, the hospice must make spiritual counseling available to the hospice patient and the patient's family.[167]

In addition to these core services, the hospice must make available and provide as appropriate physical therapy, occupational therapy, and speech-language pathology services either through employees or under arrangements.[168] Hospice aides and homemaker services also must be available and be provided under supervision.[169] The hospice is required to use volunteers, as well, who must provide administrative or direct patient care equal to at least "5% of the total patient care hours of all paid hospice employees and contract staff."[170]

11.4.4.3 Qualifications for Medicare Coverage

Generally, to qualify for Medicare coverage of hospice care, the beneficiary must be diagnosed with a terminal illness, which is defined as a life expectancy of six months or less if the illness runs its normal course.[171] The beneficiary's terminal prognosis must be certified by both the hospice's medical director and the patient's attending physician (if any).[172] The beneficiary must consent to receive only palliative care to manage discomfort and relieve the symptoms of the illness, thereby waiving Medicare benefits for curative medical treatments.[173] The hospice care must be furnished under a plan of care established by the attending physician, the hospice's medical director, and the interdisciplinary group.[174] The hospice must maintain complete and accurate documentation for each patient in a clinical record.[175]

11.4.5 Election of Hospice Benefit

An individual who is entitled to Medicare Part A benefits and is certified as terminally ill is eligible to elect the hospice benefit.[176] An eligible individual may elect the hospice benefit for an initial 90-day period, followed by a second 90-day period, and then unlimited subsequent 60-day periods for the beneficiary's lifetime.[177]

If the beneficiary is mentally or physically incapacitated at the beginning of the initial or a subsequent hospice election period, then the individual must be certified as incapacitated to make health care decisions pursuant to applicable state law.[178] Many states require at least one physician

---

[165] *See id.* § 418.64(d).
[166] *See id.* § 418.64(d)(2).
[167] *See id.* § 418.64(d)(3).
[168] *See id.* § 418.7.
[169] *See id.* § 418.76. Aides must be supervised by a registered nurse and homemakers must be supervised by a member of the interdisciplinary group. *Id.*
[170] *Id.* § 418.78.
[171] *See* 42 C.F.R. § 418.3; *see also* Section 11.4.6.
[172] *Id.* § 418.22(c).
[173] *See id.* § 418.24(b), (d).
[174] *See id.* § 418.56.
[175] *See id.* § 418.56.
[176] *See id.* § 418.20.
[177] *See* 42 U.S.C. § 1395d(d); 42 C.F.R. § 418.21.
[178] 42 C.F.R. § 418.24.

(and some require two physicians) to certify that the patient is incapacitated to make health care decisions. A health care guardian or representative then must be appointed, pursuant to state law, to make health care decisions for the incapacitated individual.

A Medicare beneficiary who elects hospice care must file with the designated hospice an election statement that (1) identifies the designated hospice, (2) specifies the effective date of the election, and (3) is signed by the beneficiary or the beneficiary's representative.[179] The election statement also must acknowledge the beneficiary's or representative's informed consent to the palliative (rather than curative) nature of hospice care.[180] In addition, the election statement must include an acknowledgment of the beneficiary's or representative's waiver of other Medicare and Medicaid benefits for the treatment of the terminal illness (except services furnished by the attending physician), and waiver of benefits for services rendered by another hospice, unless those services are provided under arrangements with the designated hospice.[181]

An individual or representative may revoke the hospice election at any time by filing a signed statement revoking the hospice election for the remainder of that period. The individual then will resume the Medicare benefits previously waived through the election of hospice care.[182]

11.4.6 Physician Certification

Both the hospice's medical director (or physician member of the hospice interdisciplinary group) and the individual's attending physician (if any) must provide the initial certification that an individual is terminally ill. For subsequent benefit periods, only the hospice's medical director or physician member of the interdisciplinary group is required to recertify the individual for hospice care.[183] The hospice facility must have a written physician certification or recertification for each benefit period.[184] If the hospice cannot obtain a written certification at the beginning of a benefit period, then the hospice may accept an oral certification, but must obtain the written physician certification within two calendar days and before it submits a claim for payment.[185] The written certifications must be filed in the hospice patient's clinical record.[186]

Physicians must include a brief narrative explanation of the clinical findings that supports a life expectancy of six months or less as part of the certification and recertification forms, or as an addendum to the certification and recertification forms.[187] The hospice physician or nurse practitioner is also required to: (1) have a face-to-face encounter with each hospice patient prior to the 180th-day recertification and each subsequent recertification to determine continued eligibility for hospice care, and (2) attest that such visit took place.[188]

---

[179] *See* 42 C.F.R. § 418.24(a), (b).
[180] *See id.* § 418.24(a)(2).
[181] *See id.* § 418.24(a)(3), (d).
[182] *See id.* § 418.28.
[183] *See id.* § 418.22(c).
[184] *See id.* § 418.22(a)(1).
[185] *See id.* § 418.22(a)(3).
[186] *See id.* § 418.22(d).
[187] 74 Fed. Reg. 39384 (Aug. 6, 2009).
[188] ACA § 3132; 42 C.F.R. § 418.22(a)(4). *See also Medicare Benefit Policy Manual* (CMS Pub. 100-02), Chapter 9, § 20.1.

An issue that arises often in hospice care is the attending physician's uncertainty regarding when a patient has reached the terminal stage of an illness and qualifies for the hospice benefit. In many cases, attending physicians also may be uncertain of what constitutes a terminal illness (e.g., the end stages of Alzheimer's disease, which now is recognized as a terminal illness). The result is that patients often have been referred for hospice care when the patient has far less than six months to live and cannot utilize the full benefits of hospice care.

In response to concerns regarding the chilling effect on physicians and hospices concerning patient eligibility for hospice care, Congress amended the Medicare statute in 2000 to provide that the certification by the physician of the patient's terminal illness must be based on the physician's or medical director's "clinical judgment" regarding the "normal course of the individual's illness."[189] The purpose of this amendment was to make clear that the six-month certification requirement was not a "hard and fast" rule, but rather one based on the physician's clinical judgment. Likewise, in May 2002, CMS Administrator Thomas A. Scully issued a letter to physicians acknowledging the difficulty in making end-of-life care prognoses and, in particular, making accurate or exact prognoses. He noted that making these determinations is not an exact science and that the impact of a hospice's services may initially improve a patient's condition. Thus, Medicare regulations use the terms "expectancy" and "if the terminal illness runs its normal course" to indicate that it is possible for hospice services to be needed for more than a six-month period. He also noted the statutory requirement, coupled with the recognition of the difficulty in making exact predictions, as evidence that physicians certifying Medicare patients for hospice care are expected only to use their best "clinical judgment regarding the normal course of the individual's illness."[190] Such initiatives have resulted in an increase in hospice lengths of stay.[191] In response to the trend toward longer-stay patients, Congress required the Secretary to establish procedures for medical review of patients whose stays exceed 180 days in hospices with high levels of long-stay patients.[192]

11.4.7 Reimbursement

11.4.7.1 Medicare

Medicare reimburses providers under Part A for covered hospice services rendered to eligible beneficiaries. Medicare Part A pays a separate *per diem* rate for routine, continuous, inpatient-respite, and general inpatient hospice services.[193] The Part A payment also covers the general supervisory services furnished by the hospice medical director, as well as services rendered by other hospice-employed physicians.[194] Medicare limits the total payment to the hospice per beneficiary to the cap amount set by the program for the cap period (referred to as the hospice aggregate cap).[195] The Medicare program also sets a cap on the total amount of reimbursement to the hospice for inpatient

---

[189] BIPA § 322 amending § 1814(a) of the Social Security Act, 42 U.S.C. § 1395f(a).
[190] A copy of this letter is available online at http://www.medicareadvocacy.org/old-site/News/Archives/Hospice_CMSconfirmsCoverage.htm.
[191] See MedPAC Report to the Congress: Medicare Payment Policy, at 150 (Mar. 2010).
[192] 42 U.S.C. § 1395f(a)(7)(D)(ii). The Secretary had not yet implemented this requirement as of the date of this publication.
[193] *See* 42 C.F.R. § 418.302.
[194] *See id.* § 418.304(a), (b).
[195] *See id.* § 418.308.

care days for Medicare patients.[196] The cap amount is adjusted each year for inflation or deflation.[197] Payment for the hospice's total number of inpatient care days (general or respite) may not exceed 20% of the total number of days for which Medicare patients received hospice care.[198]

Medicare Part B reimburses for services furnished by the patient's attending physician not employed by the hospice, and for services rendered by other physicians for care that is not related to the patient's terminal illness.[199]

Even though hospice payments are based on *per diem* amounts regardless of actual services rendered, hospices are subject to detailed reporting, coding, and other claims submission requirements to identify the services provided, including the time spent on various patient care-related activities, and changes to the level of care. For example, hospices must include site-of-service codes on their claims. Specifically, hospices must report a HCPCS code along with each revenue code to identify the type of service location where that level of care was provided.[200]

In addition, hospices must report visits in 15-minute intervals by discipline (nursing, hospice aide, medical social work, physical therapy, occupational therapy, or speech language therapy) provided each day at each site of service other than for patients receiving general inpatient care.[201] Physician visits are to be reported daily, at a procedure code level and are subject to the correct coding policy requirements.[202] All visits up to 15 minutes are reported as one 15-minute increment, regardless of the length of the visit. Visits longer than 15 minutes are rounded to the nearest 15-minute increment (up or down). Hospices may report social worker telephone calls for providing or coordinating care or counseling the patient's family as long as they are described in the plan of care and documented in the patient's clinical record. Also, each reportable call should be reported on the claim as a billable visit. Travel time and time in interdisciplinary group meetings do not count as a visit because these are not patient care activities. Where multiple health care providers are providing care at the same time, each interaction counts as a visit as long as the visits (1) are required for the palliation and management of the terminal illness and related conditions as described in the plan of correction and (2) are not listed for the purposes of increasing the number of visits. For example, a nurse teaching another nurse to perform a procedure would not comprise two visits. A nurse and an aide turning a difficult patient would constitute one visit each (although there would likely be other tasks performed as part of those visits).

Hospices must also report a separate service line for each level of care each time the level of care changes. For example, if the level of care starts at routine home care, then becomes continuous home care, followed by another period of routine home care, the claim should report two lines for routine

---

[196] *See id.* § 418.302(f).
[197] *See id.* § 418.309.
[198] *See id.* §§ 418.98(c), 418.302(f)(1).
[199] *See id.* § 418.304(c).
[200] *See* Change Request 5245 (July 28, 2006), *available at* http://www.cms.hhs.gov/transmittals/downloads/R1011CP.pdf; *see also* http://www.cms.hhs.gov/mlnmattersarticles/downloads/MM5345.pdf.
[201] *See* Change Request 6440 (Apr. 24, 2009), as revised, *available at* https://www.cms.gov/transmittals/downloads/R1738CP.pdf.
[202] *See Medicare Claims Processing Manual* (CMS Pub. 100-04), Chapter 12, § 30.

home care and one line for each day of continuous home care. The line item date of service for each of the level of care lines should reflect the first day at that level of care.[203]

Hospices are required to report line-item visit data for hospice staff providing general inpatient care to hospice patients in skilled nursing facilities or in hospitals. This includes visits by hospice nurses, aides, social workers, physical therapists, occupational therapists, and speech-language pathologists, on a line-item basis, with visit and visit length reported as is done for the home levels of care. It also includes certain calls by hospice social workers on a line-item basis, with call and call length reported as is done for the home levels of care.[204]

Hospices that do not submit data on quality measures as specified by the Secretary, will have their annual update reduced by 2 percentage points.[205]

Other types of payment reform have, and continue to be proposed and implemented. For example, in 2015, CMS adopted a proposal to create two different payment rates for routine home care (RHC), which became effective in January 2015.[206] Under this policy, CMS applies a higher base payment rate for the first 60 days of hospice care and a reduced base payment rate for subsequent days.[207] Additionally, CMS adopted a service intensity add-on (SIA) payment for services provided in the last 7 days of a beneficiary's life.[208] In order to qualify for the SIA, the following criteria must be met: (1) the day must be billed as an RHC level of care day; (2) the day must occur within the last 7 days of the life of the beneficiary who has been discharged dead; and (3) direct patient care must be provided by a registered nurse or social worker.[209]

11.4.7.2 Medicaid

Hospice is an optional state benefit.[210] If a state provides a hospice benefit, then the coverage must be equivalent in scope and payment to the Medicare benefit.

When a Medicaid-eligible nursing home resident elects the hospice benefit, the state is required to pay an amount, referred to as the "unified rate," that is equal to 95% of the Medicaid *per diem* rate for nursing-home room and board. The state pays the room and board rate in addition to the Medicaid *per diem* rate paid to cover hospice care, if applicable. Both the room-and-board and hospice *per diem* rates are paid to the hospice which, in turn, pays the nursing facility for the hospice patient's room and board.[211]

---

[203] *See* Change Request 6791 (January 29, 2010), *available at* https://www.cms.gov/transmittals/downloads/R1897CP.pdf.
[204] *See* CMS Transmittal 2747 (Change Request 8358), *Additional Data Reporting Requirements for Hospice Claims* (Jul. 26, 2013).
[205]
[206] 80 Fed. Reg. 47142 (Aug. 6, 2015).
[207] *Id.*
[208] *Id.*; *see also* 42 C.F.R. § 418.302(b)(1)(i).
[209] *Id.*
[210] *See* 42 U.S.C. § 1396d(a)(18), (o).
[211] *See id.* §§ 1396a(a)(13)(B), 1396d(o)(3).

11.4.8 Fraud and Abuse Issues

Like other health care providers, hospice providers continue to be the subject of audits and investigations by DOJ and the OIG as part of their focus on fraudulent and abusive practices within the health care industry. Particular areas of concern for hospice include ineligibility of individuals for hospice care, improper physician certification, lack of informed consent in electing the hospice benefit, falsified medical records and plans of care, improper billing practices, and improper patient solicitation activities, including incentives offered to actual or potential referral sources.

The government is especially wary of hospice arrangements with referral sources (for example, nursing facilities), which may be particularly vulnerable to fraud and abuse. On March 25, 1998, the OIG released a Special Fraud Alert on "Fraud and Abuse in Nursing Home Arrangements with Hospices."[212] In the Special Fraud Alert, the OIG cited instances of hospices offering free goods, goods at prices below fair market value, and inflated payments to nursing homes for room and board and "additional" services as potential kickbacks to influence the referral of patients to hospices. The OIG conducted a 2007 review concluding that Medicare beneficiaries in nursing facilities typically spend more time in hospice care and are associated with higher Medicare hospice care reimbursement than beneficiaries in other settings.[213] A separate 2009 OIG report also found that 82% of hospice claims for beneficiaries in nursing facilities did not meet at least one Medicare coverage requirement.[214] The OIG also has focused attention on hospice billing for physician services. In a 2010 report, the OIG noted that Medicare paid nearly $566,000 in 2009 to physicians for hospice care that the OIG characterized as "questionable" because the physician was paid for the service both under Part A and Part B.[215] The OIG work plan for 2017 discussed numerous hospice-related activities, including a review of vulnerabilities in payment, compliance, oversight, and quality of care; a review of hospice medical records to determine whether services met Medicare conditions of payment; and a review of whether hospice nurses made on-site visits at the appropriate frequency, in accordance with Medicare requirements.[216] Finally, based on an October 2016 review of Medicare hospice election statements and certifications of terminal illness, OIG recommended that CMS develop and disseminate model text for hospice election statements, instruct surveyors to strengthen their review of election statements and certifications of terminal illness, educate hospices about these topics, and provide guidance to hospices clarifying the effects of revocation.

The government has used the federal False Claims Act (FCA)[217] as a basis for suing hospice providers, alleging that fraudulent practices result in the submission of false claims for Medicare and/or Medicaid reimbursement. Likewise, whistleblowers have brought actions against hospice providers under the FCA alleging that hospices have submitted false claims to the Medicare program. Many of these cases have alleged that hospices billed the Medicare program for services provided

---

[212] See 64 Fed. Reg. 54031 (1999). This guidance is also available online at http://oig.hhs.gov/authorities/docs/hospicx.pdf.
[213] OIG Report, "Medicare Hospice Care: A Comparison of Beneficiaries in Nursing Facilities and Beneficiaries in Other Settings" (2007).
[214] OIG Report, "Medicare Hospice Care for Beneficiaries in Nursing Facilities: Compliance With Medicare Coverage Requirements" (2009).
[215] OIG Report, "Questionable Billing for Physician Services for Hospice Beneficiaries" (2010).
[216] OIG Work Plan for Fiscal Year 2017, available at https://oig.hhs.gov/reports-and-publications/archives/workplan/2017/HHS%20OIG%20Work%20Plan%202017.pdf.
[217] 31 U.S.C. § 3729.

to hospice patients who were not terminally ill and hence were ineligible for the Medicare hospice benefit. In two notable cases, AseraCare[218] and Vista Hospice Care,[219] the hospice providers have prevailed, with courts finding that because physician determinations with respect to terminal illness can differ, there is no objective standard of falsity from which to establish a false claim.

Other hospice providers have settled similar cases arising out of FCA enforcement actions for large dollar amounts, including, among others, the following:

- Chemed Corporation and various wholly-owned subsidiaries, including Vitas Hospice Services LLC and Vitas Healthcare Corporation ($75 million, October 2017);[220]
- Odyssey Healthcare, Inc. ($25 million, February 2012);[221]
- Hospice Care of Kansas LLC and Voyager HospiceCare Inc. ($6.1 million, June 2012);[222] and
- Hospice of Arizona L.C. and its affiliates ($12 million, March 2013).[223]

11.4.9 Compliance Guidance for Hospices

On September 30, 1999, the OIG issued its final version of Compliance Program Guidance for Hospices.[224] The OIG's hospice compliance guidelines, like other compliance guidelines, outlines the elements for inclusion in any hospice compliance program, and identifies the "risk areas" to be addressed in policies and procedures. Generally, a hospice compliance program should demonstrate clearly the hospice's commitment to compliance with all applicable federal, state, and private insurance standards, and should emphasize the prevention of fraud and abuse. The OIG's Compliance Program Guidance for Hospices is a useful summary of areas the OIG believes may present compliance risks for hospices. For example, the OIG urges caution in the areas of physician certification, informed consent to elect the hospice benefit, patient solicitation activities, medical records, and billing procedures.

---

[218] *U.S. v. AseraCare*, Nos. 2:12-cv-0245-KOB, 2:12-cv-2264-KOB and 2:09-cv-067-KOB, 2012 U.S. Dist. LEXIS 152591 (N.D. Ala., Oct. 24, 2012); original qui tam suit (*States ex rel. Richardson and Brown v. Golden Gate National Senior Care LLC dba Golden Living et al.*, No. 2:09-cv-00627 (N.D. Ala.)). On March 31, 2016, the district court granted summary judgment to AseraCare based on the government's failure to prove a falsity. The DOJ appealed to the 11th Circuit and that appeal was pending as of the date of this publication.
[219] *U.S. ex rel. Misty Wall v. Vista Hospice Care, Inc. d/b/a Vistacare and VistaCare, Inc.* No. 3:07-cv-00604-M (N.D. Tex. June 20, 2016).
[220] Department of Justice press release is available at https://www.justice.gov/opa/pr/chemed-corp-and-vitas-hospice-services-agree-pay-75-million-resolve-false-claims-act.
[221] Department of Justice press release is available at https://www.justice.gov/opa/pr/hospice-provider-odyssey-healthcare-agrees-pay-25-million-resolve-false-claims-act.
[222] Department of Justice press release is available at http://www.justice.gov/opa/pr/2012/June/12-civ-768.html.
[223] Department of Justice press release is available at http://www.justice.gov/opa/pr/2013/March/13-civ-326.html.
[224] *Available at* http://oig.hhs.gov/fraud/complianceguidance.asp.

11.5 Long Term Care

11.5.1 State Licensure

All states require licensure or its equivalent to operate a nursing home. The majority of states require licensure to operate an assisted living facility or a residential care facility. A licensed facility is subject to certain requirements pertaining to staffing, provision of services, and physical plant, as set forth in the applicable licensure statute and regulations.

11.5.2 State Certificate of Need

Approximately two-thirds of states require a CON or its equivalent to develop or construct a new health care facility (such as a nursing home), incur a capital expenditure by or on behalf of a health care facility above a specified expenditure threshold, add beds/services to an existing health care facility, change the location of a facility, and, in some cases, acquire or change a majority of ownership of an existing health care facility. Consult state law and regulations governing the projects subject to review, any exemptions, any expedited review process, or the standard review process, if applicable. Some states have placed moratoria on new construction; others impose requirements on new health care facilities (e.g., participation in the state Medicaid program). A few states (e.g., New Jersey) subject assisted-living facilities to CON review.[225]

11.5.3 Medicare Skilled Nursing Facilities

Nursing facilities participating in the Medicare program are known as skilled nursing facilities (SNFs). A facility may have one wing or floor that is a Medicare-certified SNF, or the whole facility may be certified by Medicare. Current Medicare payment rules provide fewer advantages to partial certification than had been granted under the previous cost-based reimbursement system. Some states require facilities to certify the whole facility for Medicare participation. The services offered by SNFs generally include: nursing care; room and board; physical, occupational, and speech therapy; social services; and other necessary services, supplies, and equipment.[226]

11.5.3.1 Coverage

Medicare SNF coverage applies for Medicare beneficiaries who have been in a hospital for at least three days and enter a SNF within 30 days of discharge. The benefit only extends for 100 days per spell of illness; Medicare pays 100% for the first 20 days, and beneficiaries are responsible for a daily deductible for the next 80 days.[227] Residents must also require a skilled level of care.[228]

---

[225] *See* N.J. ADMIN. CODE § 8:36-2.1.
[226] *See* 42 U.S.C. § 1395x(h) (describing the various extended care services that may be furnished to SNF residents); *id.* 1395i-3(a)(defining a SNF).
[227] *See id.* §§ 1395d(a)(2), 1395e(a)(3).
[228] *See* 42 C.F.R. § 409.30; *Medicare Benefit Policy Manual* (CMS Pub. 100-02), Chapter 8, § 30.

11.5.3.2 Requirements of Participation

SNFs must meet extensive quality standards set forth in requirements for participation (ROPs), and are subject to strict enforcement remedies for failure to comply with applicable standards. SNFs are required to provide the care and necessary services "to attain or maintain the highest practicable physical, mental, and psychosocial well-being of each resident."[229]

Among the specific quality requirements SNFs must meet are: minimum nurse staffing standards; required training of nurses aides; the obligation to provide, or arrange for, all of the resident's care needs; and residents' rights requirements.[230] On October 4, 2016, CMS issued a final rule comprehensively updating and extensively revising the ROPs for SNFs participating in the Medicare program. Key areas include requirements for improving quality of care and patient safety, nursing facility staffing, care planning, infection control, residents' rights, compliance and ethics programs, and banning pre-dispute arbitration agreements. In response to comments regarding the cost and resources required to achieve compliance with these significant new requirements, CMS is phasing in implementation in three phases. Phase One, which includes many of the health and safety requirements, is effective as of the date of the regulations, November 28, 2016. Phase Two and Phase Three require compliance by one year and three years, respectively, from the effective date of the rule (i.e., November 28, 2017 and November 28, 2019).[231]

Failure to adhere to these standards, as determined by an onsite survey conducted by the state survey agency, can result in a wide range of remedies: appointment of temporary management, denial of Medicare payment for new admissions, directed plans of correction, closure of facilities, termination of Medicare participation, and CMPs up to $20,628 per day or per instance.[232] Penalties can be increased for repeat deficiencies and repeat findings of substandard quality of care (defined as deficiencies in the areas of resident behavior and facility practices, quality of life, or quality of care that are widespread with actual harm or potential for more than minimal harm, or that constitute immediate jeopardy).[233] Remedies are subject to an informal dispute resolution process (by state) and administrative appeal.[234]

SNFs that arrange for the provision of hospice care through an agreement with Medicare-certified hospice providers must have written agreements that delineate responsibilities and requirements of each entity.[235] Among other things, the agreement must address how the parties will communicate,

---

[229] 42 U.S.C. § 1395i-3(b)(2).

[230] *See id.* § 1395i-3(b)–(d).

[231] 81 Fed. Reg. 68688 (Oct. 4, 2016), *available at* https://www.gpo.gov/fdsys/pkg/FR-2016-10-04/pdf/2016-23503.pdf. On November 7, 2016, the United States District Court for the Northern District of Mississippi, Oxford Division issued an order preliminarily enjoining CMS from enforcing section 483.70(n)(1), the ban on pre-dispute arbitration. See *American Health Care Association v. Burwell*, Civil Action No. 3:16-CV-00233 (Nov. 7, 2016). CMS will not enforce 483.70(n)(1) until and unless the injunction is lifted. *See* CMS Survey & Certification Memorandum to State Surveyors, 17-12-NH (Dec. 9, 2016).

[232] By statute, the maximum CMP is $10,000. However, the CMP amounts are increased for inflation. *See* 81 Fed. Reg. 61538, 61549 (Sept. 16, 2016) (interim final rule increasing CMP amounts for inflation, consistent with the requirements of the Bipartisan Budget Act (BBA) of 2015).

[233] 42 C.F.R. §§ 488.404, 488.414.

[234] *Id.* §§ 488.331, 498.5(b).

[235] 42 C.F.R. § 483.75(t). *See also* 78 Fed. Reg. 38594 (Jun. 27, 2013).

what must be communicated (for example, changes in the patient's condition), and the respective responsibilities of each party to ensure the care and well-being of the patient.[236]

11.5.3.3 Reimbursement

Historically, the Medicare program reimbursed SNFs for the "reasonable costs" of providing covered Part A services, subject to certain limits.[237] SNFs were responsible for providing or arranging for the provision of covered Part A services, and billed for their costs of providing these services. In cases where the SNF did not provide ancillary services through its own employees and, instead, opted to outsource these services to an outside ancillary service provider, the SNF would report the ancillary service provider's charge on its Medicare cost report.

Once a patient's eligibility for benefits under Medicare Part A was exhausted, a patient could still be eligible for coverage of certain ancillary services (e.g., therapy services) under Medicare Part B, Medicaid, or other third-party payment programs. Under these circumstances, as well as where certain Part A services were not furnished by the facility,[238] the outside ancillary service provider would bill Medicare Part B, Medicaid, or other third-party payers directly for services furnished to patients. The Medicare program then would pay the outside supplier based on the applicable Part B or other payment methodology.

The BBA required the Secretary of HHS to establish, for cost-reporting periods beginning on or after July 1, 1998, a PPS for Part A SNF services consisting of *per diem* rates that vary based on the intensity of resources required by each resident. With a few exceptions, the PPS rate covers all routine, ancillary and capital costs of services furnished to patients during a covered Part A stay.[239] Residents are placed in a particular resource utilization group (RUG) based upon clinical and other information collected in the minimum data set (MDS) assessment tool. Payment is based on 66 RUGs that are intended to reflect the resources needed to care for the resident. Currently, CMS reimburses under the RUG-IV classification system.

On October 1, 2010, CMS announced the current 66-group Version 4 of the RUGs (RUG-IV)[240]. Under the ACA, this implementation was delayed until October 1, 2011 (FY 2012); however, certain components of RUG-IV (concurrent therapy and look-back revisions) were applied effective October 1, 2010 (FY 2011).[241]

The SSA requires CMS to update federal rates annually.[242] The rate changes are updated by the SNF market basket index, which is intended to reflect pricing changes of an appropriate mix of goods and services included in SNF services.[243] Under the ACA, the SNF market basket update is

---

[236] *See* 42 C.F.R. § 418.112(c).
[237] *See* 42 C.F.R. Part 413.
[238] *See, e.g., Medicare Claims Processing Manual* (CMS Pub. 100-04), Chapter 12, § 10.
[239] *See* 42 U.S.C. § 1395yy(e).
[240] *See* Medicare Program; Prospective Payment System and Consolidated Billing for Skilled Nursing Facilities for FY 2010, 74 Fed. Reg. 40288, 40294 (Aug. 11, 2009).
[241] *See generally* https://www.cms.gov/Medicare/Medicare-Fee-for-Service-Payment/SNFPPS/index.html.
[242] 42 U.S.C. § 1395yy(e)(4)(H). By law the rates must be provided to the *Federal Register* prior to the August 1 that precedes the October 1 start of each new federal FY.
[243] 42 U.S.C. § 1395yy(e)(5)(a).

subject to a full productivity adjustment beginning in October 1, 2011, which is intended to account for increases in provider productivity that could reduce the actual cost of providing services.[244] Rates are also revised to incorporate a "forecast error adjustment" whenever the difference between the forecasted and actual change in the market basket exceeds a 0.5 percentage point threshold for the most recently available fiscal year for which there is final data. Federal rates are then adjusted for geographic differences to reflect changes in local wage rates, using the latest hospital wage index.[245]

SNF payment rates have been subject to various adjustments over the years to achieve certain policy goals or fund other programs (such as the SNF value-based purchasing program discussed below). For example, the Medicare Access and CHIP Reauthorization Act of 2015 (MACRA) established a special rule for FY 2018 that requires the market basket percentage, after application of the productivity adjustment, to be 1.0%. Notably, in the absence of MACRA, the proposed update would equal 2.3%, or 2.7% (the proposed 2014-based SNF market basket percentage change) less 0.4% (the multifactor productivity adjustment). Likewise, the IMPACT Act reduces the annual update by 2 percentage points for SNFs that fail to submit required quality data to CMS under the SNF Quality Reporting Program (QRP), beginning with FY 2018.

The BBA, as amended by BBRA and BIPA, also imposed "consolidated billing" under which the SNF must submit Medicare claims to the Part A Medicare administrative contractor (MAC) all services that its residents receive (except for certain specifically excluded services)[246] in a Part A stay, and for all Part B rehabilitation therapy services (e.g., physical, occupational, and speech-language pathology therapy services) provided in the SNF. In other words, where previously a third party therapy provider may have furnished certain services to a SNF resident and billed the program directly, these services must now *only* be billed to the Medicare program by the SNF. For other Part B services, suppliers may continue to bill directly. The SNF must furnish the services either directly or under an arrangement with an outside provider, and the SNF must bill Medicare. In addition, the BBA requires that Part B services furnished to SNF residents and outpatients (i.e., nonresidents receiving care at the facility) be reimbursed according to the otherwise-applicable fee schedule (or actual charge, if it is less than the applicable fee amount).[247]

Because of the consolidated billing requirements for Medicare Part B outpatient therapy furnished to residents of SNFs, SNFs are directly impacted by limitations imposed on Medicare Part B payment for therapy services. The BBA imposed annual statutory Part B therapy caps on combined physical and speech-language pathology services therapy, and occupational therapy (which have been inflation adjusted over time). Through various legislative actions the therapy caps have been suspended, reinstated and subject to an exceptions process while CMS continues to develop a payment system

---

[244] *See* ACA § 3401.
[245] *See generally* https://www.cms.gov/Medicare/Medicare-Fee-for-Service-Payment/SNFPPS/index.html?redirect=/SNFPPS/.
[246] *See* http://www.cms.gov/Medicare/Medicare-Fee-for-Service-Payment/SNFPPS/ConsolidatedBilling.html. Excluded services for Part A patients in a covered stay include: physician's professional services; certain dialysis-related services; certain ambulance services; Epoetin Alfa (EPO, trade name Epogen) for certain dialysis patients; hospice care; chemotherapy; chemotherapy administration services; radioisotope services; magnetic resonance imaging; cardiac catheterization; hospital outpatient radiation therapy; hospital outpatient angiography; lymphatic and venous procedures; and customized prosthetic devices.
[247] *See* 42 U.S.C. §§ 1395u(b)(6), 1395yy(e)(9).

for outpatient therapy services.[248] The current exception process expires December 31, 2017, but may be extended by Congress. In the meantime, the Supplemental Medical Review Contractor (SMRC) continues to perform medical review of therapy claims over the thresholds on a post-payment basis.[249]

The PPS and consolidated-billing requirements create powerful incentives for SNFs to adopt cost-effective methods of delivering ancillary services. Some SNFs have responded to these challenges by bringing certain activities "in-house." Others have contracted with ancillary suppliers, to control costs or share the risk of increased costs. These arrangements may include discounts, *per diem* rates, "risk corridor" arrangements, or similar approaches. In some cases, discounts may apply only to Part A patients; in others, the arrangement may cover all of the patients at a particular facility. The OIG has warned that providing deep discounts on Medicare Part A items and services in return for the referral of Part B business that the vendor bills at standard rates could be found to constitute an illegal kickback under the federal anti-kickback statute and could subject the vendor to exclusion for billing Medicare "substantially in excess" of other payers.[250]

The ACA has several provisions focused on innovative reimbursement methodologies, which include SNF services. In January 2013, CMS announced certain health facilities selected to participate in its Bundled Payments for Care Improvement Initiative (BPCI). This initiative is comprised of four broadly defined models of care, which link payments for multiple services beneficiaries receive during an episode of care, rather than payments to providers for each of the individual services they furnish to beneficiaries for a single illness or course of treatment.[251]

Two other bundled payment initiatives may impact payment for SNF services, but the future of these initiatives is uncertain as the Trump Administration has proposed significant changes in one and canceling the second. First, in November 2015, CMS issued a final rule establishing a *mandatory* Medicare Comprehensive Care for Joint Replacement (CJR) model in 67 metropolitan statistical areas.[252] Under this model, effective April 1, 2016, hospitals in the selected geographic areas receive a bundled payment for an episode of care for lower extremity joint replacement surgery, covering all services provided during the inpatient admission through 90 days post-discharge. The bundled payment is paid retrospectively through a reconciliation process; hospitals and other providers and suppliers continue to submit claims and receive payment via the usual Medicare fee-for-service payment systems, with the reconciliation occurring later. The program includes waiver of certain

---

[248] The MMA suspended application of the therapy caps and the requirement for focused therapy claims reviews through December 31, 2005. Caps were reinstated January 1, 2006. At that time, CMS adopted an exception process to the therapy caps for patients with documented complex care needs. As a practical matter, most residents of SNFs were exempt from the cap. The exception process was set to expire December 31, 2009; however, various legislative actions extended the exception process. The Protecting Access to Medicare Act of 2014 (PAMA) extended the exceptions process for outpatient therapy caps through March 31, 2015. The following year, in the Medicare Access and CHIP Reauthorization Act of 2015 (MACRA) Congress again extended the therapy cap exception process through December 31, 2017 and modified the requirement for manual medical review for services over the $3,700 therapy threshold.

[249] For more information on Part B therapy caps, *see* http://www.cms.gov/Research-Statistics-Data-and-Systems/Monitoring-Programs/Medical-Review/TherapyCap.html.

[250] *See* OIG Advisory Opinion 99-2 (Mar. 1999).

[251] More information on this initiative is available at http://innovation.cms.gov/initiatives/bundled-payments/.

[252] 80 Fed. Reg. 73274 (Nov. 24, 2015).

fraud and abuse laws to give hospitals flexibility in entering bundling arrangements.[253] These waivers include allowing episode-initiating hospitals to use gainsharing payments with other providers, called "collaborators," and waiving CMPs for beneficiary inducements to permit hospitals to offer certain items or services to Medicare beneficiaries during the episode of care if certain conditions to further patient engagement in the program.

Second, on August 2, 2016, CMS proposed a multi-faceted plan to promote certain hospitals to participate in Medicare episode payment models (EPMs) for acute myocardial infarction (AMI), coronary artery bypass graft (CABG), and surgical hip/femur fracture treatment (SHFFT) procedures furnished in designated areas of the country and to refine the CJR model and integrate these payment programs into the Medicare physician quality/payment framework. This proposal continued the Obama Administration's initiative to move the Medicare system away from fee-for-service (FFS) payments and towards alternative payment models that reward quality of care rather than volume of services.[254] On January 3, 2017, CMS published the final rule,[255] but the Trump Administration subsequently delayed implementation until January 1, 2018 while modifications were considered.[256]

In the meantime, on August 17, 2017, CMS issued a proposed rule[257] to *cancel* the still-pending EPM rule and dramatically scale back mandatory participation in the ongoing CJR program, with an option for participating hospitals in about half of the current CJR locations to shift to voluntary participation. While CMS appears to be moving away from mandatory participation for many hospitals, the agency continues to consider how to incentivize eligible hospitals to elect to continue participating in the CJR model for the remaining years of the model and to further incentivize all participant hospitals to advance care improvements, innovation, and quality for beneficiaries. The role of SNFs and other post-acute providers in these EPMs remains uncertain.

While the SNF PPS has been in place for nearly 20 years, CMS,[258] the OIG,[259] and the Medicare Payment Advisory Commission (MedPAC)[260] have raised concerns about the SNF payment system and called for reforms. In particular, they have asserted that the SNF PPS encourages providers to deliver rehabilitation therapy services to residents based on financial goals and not patient need. As a result, CMS has proposed through an advanced notice of rulemaking a potentially ground-breaking rule to replace the SNF PPS RUG-IV case-mix classification methodology, which forms the basis for SNF payment, with the resident Classification System, Version I (RCS-I), effective as early as FY 2019.[261] The RCS-I case-mix model, which was developed by a CMS contractor, attempts to address prior concerns by removing service-based metrics from the SNF PPS and deriving payment,

---

[253] Notice of Waivers of Certain Fraud and Abuse Laws in Connection with the Comprehensive Care for Joint Replacement Model (November 16, 2015), *available at* https://www.cms.gov/Medicare/Fraud-and-Abuse/PhysicianSelfReferral/Fraud-and-Abuse-Waivers.html.
[254] 81 Fed. Reg. 50794 (Aug. 2, 2016), *available at* https://www.gpo.gov/fdsys/pkg/FR-2016-08-02/pdf/2016-17733.pdf.
[255] 82 Fed. Reg. 180 (Jan. 3, 2017).
[256] *Id.* 22,895 (May 19, 2017).
[257] 82 Fed. Reg. 39310 (Aug. 17, 2017).
[258] *See* "Observations on Therapy Utilization Trends," *available at* https://www.cms.gov/Medicare/Medicare-Fee-for-Service-Payment/SNFPPS/Downloads/Therapy_Trends_Memo_04212014.pdf.
[259] https://oig.hhs.gov/oei/reports/oei-02-13-00610.asp.
[260] *See generally* http://www.medpac.gov/.
[261] 82 Fed. Reg. 20980 (May 4, 2017).

almost exclusively, from objective resident characteristics. Most notably, the proposed RCS-I case-mix model would:

- ***Divorce therapy minutes from payment*** by no longer using minutes of therapy provided to a resident to classify the resident for payment purposes, and impose a 25% limit on group therapy and a 25% limit on concurrent therapy, thereby ensuring that residents receive at least 50% of their therapy minutes on an individual basis;
- ***Establish new case-mix components*** by classifying each resident into four case-mix adjusted components (physical therapy/occupational therapy, speech therapy, nursing and non-therapy ancillaries (NTA)) based, almost exclusively, on objective resident characteristics, and rely on each component to determine the per-diem payment received by a SNF;
- ***Front-load payments*** to incorporate variable per-diem payment adjustments for the physical therapy/occupational therapy and NTA components, which would reduce the payment amount associated with the physical therapy/occupational therapy and NTA components over time consistent with research that suggests a SNF's costs for physical therapy/occupational therapy and NTA decrease during a resident's stay; and
- ***Significantly revise the assessment schedule*** to require only (i) 5-day Scheduled PPS Assessments, (ii) Significant Change in Status Assessments, and (iii) PPS Discharge Assessments.

SNF and patient advocacy groups have raised questions about whether the proposed methodology has been adequately tested and would have unintended consequences that would reduce the adequacy of payment for patient care. As of late 2017, CMS is still considering comments on the proposal.

11.5.3.4 Compliance, Ethics and Accountability Requirements

The ACA implemented various requirements for improved SNF transparency on compliance and ethics. For example, both SNFs and Medicaid nursing facilities were required to have an operational compliance and ethics program within 36 months of enactment, i.e., by March 2013.[262] Additionally, the ACA requires the establishment of a quality assurance and performance improvement program for facilities by December 31, 2011. The final ROPs for long-term care facilities require a compliance and ethics program by November 28, 2019, and a quality assurance and improvement plan by November 28, 2017 with full implementation by November 28, 2019.[263] Further, the ACA expanded the SNF ownership disclosure requirements already found in the SSA, but those have not yet been fully implemented by regulation.[264]

11.5.4 Medicaid Nursing Facilities

Nursing homes participating in a state Medicaid program are known as nursing facilities (NFs). A nursing home may have one wing or floor that is a Medicaid-certified NF, or the whole facility

---

[262] ACA § 6102.
[263] 81 Fed. Reg. 68688 (Oct. 4, 2016), *available at* https://www.gpo.gov/fdsys/pkg/FR-2016-10-04/pdf/2016-23503.pdf.
[264] *See* ACA § 6101.

may be certified. Many states require facilities to certify the whole facility for Medicaid participation. SNFs and NFs are generally required to provide the same level of care. For example, as with SNFs, the services offered by NFs generally include: nursing care; room and board; physical, occupational, and speech therapy; social services; and other necessary services, supplies, and equipment. The amount and degree vary based upon each particular state's Medicaid-program requirements. Increasingly, states are moving to managed Medicaid programs under which private payers oversee the benefits and payments for Medicaid beneficiaries.

11.5.4.1 Coverage

State Medicaid programs are required by federal law to provide coverage for NF services.[265] The amount and scope is based upon the state's Medicaid state plan, subject to federal Medicaid requirements. Consult state law.

11.5.4.2 Qualifications

NFs must meet the same extensive quality standards as Medicare SNFs, and are subject to similar enforcement remedies for failure to comply with applicable standards.[266] NFs are required to provide the care and necessary services "to attain or maintain the highest practicable physical, mental, and psychosocial well-being of each resident."[267] Among the specific quality requirements NFs must meet are: minimum nurse-staffing standards; required training of nurse's aides; the obligation to provide, or arrange for, all of the resident's care needs; and residents' rights requirements.[268] Failure to adhere to these standards, as determined by survey, can result in a wide range of remedies, including: appointment of temporary management; denial of Medicaid payment for new admissions; directed plans of correction; closure of facilities; termination of Medicaid participation; and CMPs up to $20,628 per day or per instance.[269] Significantly, if Medicare terminates a facility from program participation, then the state Medicaid program is also required to terminate the facility from the Medicaid program.[270]

11.5.4.3 Reimbursement

Historically, the federal Medicaid statute and regulations contained specific reimbursement requirements for NFs. As a general matter, facilities were required to be reimbursed at a rate that was "reasonable and adequate to meet the costs that must be incurred by efficiently and economically operated facilities in order to provide care and services in conformity with applicable State and Federal laws, regulations, and quality and safety standards."[271] This standard commonly is referred to as the Boren Amendment. Under a separate provision, a state's institutional reimbursement rates

---

[265] 42 U.S.C. §§ 1396a(a)(10), 1396d(a)(4)(A).
[266] *Id.* § 1396a(28).
[267] *Id.* § 1396r(b)(2).
[268] *See* 42 U.S.C. § 1396r(b)–(d); 42 C.F.R. § 483.1.
[269] ACA § 6012.
[270] 42 C.F.R. § 488.456.
[271] This language previously appeared at 42 U.S.C. § 1396a(a)(13) and was replaced by language from BBA, Pub. L. No. 105-33 § 4711(a)(1).

could not, in the aggregate, result in greater payments than can reasonably be estimated to be made for comparable services under Medicare payment principles.[272] This provision is generally known as the "Medicare upper limit." Further, federal law requires state Medicaid plans to "[a]ssure that payments are consistent with efficiency, economy, and quality of care and are sufficient to enlist enough providers so that care and services are available under the plan at least to the extent that such care and services are available to the general population." This provision is known as the "equal access" clause.[273]

The BBA repealed the Boren Amendment, thus granting states considerable flexibility in establishing Medicaid rates for NFs. The Boren Amendment has been replaced with a "notice and public process" procedure under which states must "publish" and provide "justifications" for rates.[274] State Medicaid plans must still comply with various requirements for establishing payment rates, including the equal access clause.[275]

States employ a variety of rate-setting methodologies to establish NF rates. A rate-setting methodology may be either retrospective or prospective. Under a retrospective methodology, Medicaid makes interim cost-based payments throughout the year, and reconciles the interim payments with the provider's actual reported costs at the end of the year. Under a prospective system, the state establishes a rate in advance of the year by "trending forward" previous years' costs through an inflation factor. Facilities that keep their costs within the prospectively set rate keep the difference; those with costs greater than that rate suffer a loss. In addition to the retrospective/prospective distinction, states' Medicaid rates can be established on either a class or individual basis. In a class-based system, a state groups similar facilities together for rate-setting purposes, and each of the facilities within the class receives the same rate. In an individual-facility rating system, a facility's rate will be set on the basis of its costs.

State rate-setting methods also may take into account the level of services to be provided to the individual through the use of level of care distinctions, diagnosis-related groups, or case-mix indices (similar to the RUGs system used for Medicare SNFs). Under these systems, the state generally pays higher rates for residents with greater care needs. Finally, some states pay supplemental amounts for "administratively necessary" days (i.e., days in which the patient is in the facility awaiting placement in the community) and "reserved bed days" (i.e., days in which a nursing-facility patient is in the hospital).[276] Increasingly state Medicaid programs have adopted managed care programs under which states contract with private managed care organizations (MCOs) to administer and arrange for the delivery of Medicaid health benefits and additional services. Most arrangements involve a set per member per month (capitation) payment for these services. The MCOs, in turn, contract with providers to furnish care and pay on a fee schedule or capitated basis.[277]

---

[272] 42 C.F.R. § 447.272.
[273] 42 U.S.C. § 1396a(a)(30)(A); *see also* 80 Fed. Reg. 67575 (2015) (final rule implementing the equal access clause).
[274] 42 U.S.C. § 1396a(a)(13)(A).
[275] 42 C.F.R. §§ 447.201 *et seq.* and 447.250 *et seq.*
[276] For a general summary of state Medicaid payment methodologies, *see* CCH Medicare & Medicaid Guide Explanations and Annotations ¶ 14,724.
[277] *See generally* https://www.medicaid.gov/medicaid/managed-care/index.html.

11.5.4.4 Compliance, Ethics and Accountability Requirements

The ACA implemented various requirements for improved NF transparency on compliance and ethics. Both SNFs and NFs were required to have an operational compliance and ethics program within 36 months of enactment, i.e., by March 2013.[278] Additionally, the ACA requires the establishment of a quality assurance and performance improvement program for facilities by December 31, 2011. As noted, the final ROPs for long-term care facilities require a compliance and ethics program by November 28, 2019, and a quality assurance and improvement plan by November 28 2017 with full implementation by November 28, 2019.[279] The ACA also expands the nursing facility ownership disclosure requirements already found in the SSA disclosure of ownership information, but those have not yet been fully implemented by regulation. Consult state law for state-specific Medicaid ownership disclosure requirements.[280]

11.5.5 Quality of Care

11.5.5.1 Resident Assessment Instruments (RAIs)

CMS requires long-term care facilities to conduct comprehensive, accurate, standardized, reproducible assessments of each resident's functional capacity and to transmit this information to CMS using a standard form known as the minimum data set (MDS) assessment instrument. The information from the MDS is compiled into an electronic data system. The instrument includes information about the patient and the patient's health status.[281] States must use either the federally established resident assessment instrument, or an alternate instrument designed by state and approved by CMS. The assessment is intended, among other things, to help CMS and state surveyors identify nursing homes for immediate onsite inspections, detect and correct systemic problems early, and ultimately help nursing homes improve quality. Beginning July 1, 2002, a shorter version of the MDS—the Medicare PPS Assessment Form (MPAF)—became available for use to satisfy Medicare assessment requirements. CMS estimates that the MPAF roughly half the time to complete as the original MDS.[282]

The most recent iteration of this assessment tool is the MDS 3.0. The MDS 3.0 was developed to improve the reliability, accuracy, and usefulness of the MDS, after some expressed concern that the MDS 2.0 failed to obtain critical information since it did not include items that relied on direct resident interviews. Some also expressed concern regarding the reliability, validity, and relevance of MDS 2.0.[283] Consequently, MDS 3.0 was developed to improve the reliability, accuracy, and usefulness of the MDS. MDS 3.0 includes resident assessment and other standard protocols used in other settings. The FY 2010 SNF payment rule also required that version 3.0 of the MDS (MDS 3.0) go

---

[278] ACA § 6102.
[279] 81 Fed. Reg. 68688 (Oct. 4, 2016), *available at* https://www.gpo.gov/fdsys/pkg/FR-2016-10-04/pdf/2016-23503.pdf.
[280] ACA § 6101.
[281] Medicare and Medicaid; Resident Assessment in Long Term Care Facilities, 62 Fed. Reg. 67174 (Dec. 23, 1997) (codified at 42 C.F.R. part 483).
[282] Medicare Program; Notice of Modification of Beneficiary Assessment Requirements for Skilled Nursing Facilities, 67 Fed. Reg. 38128 (May 31, 2002).
[283] CMS, MDS 3.0 for Nursing Homes and Swing Bed Providers, https://www.cms.gov/Medicare/Quality-Initiatives-Patient-Assessment-Instruments/NursingHomeQualityInits/NHQIMDS30.html.

into effect October 1, 2010 for FY 2011. Finally, the FY 2014 SNF payment rule added a requirement for reporting the number of distinct therapy days.[284]

11.5.5.2 Collection and Publication of Quality Information

Increasing focus on nursing home quality information has resulted in CMS publication of Quality Measures (QMs) for facilities in all states, the District of Columbia and some U.S. territories. The purpose of the QMs is to make people aware of the performance of individual nursing homes. The information can be used by Medicare beneficiaries and families to make placement decisions and for nursing homes to improve the quality of care.

In January 2004, CMS began reporting an enhanced set of QMs endorsed by the National Quality Forum (a voluntary standard setting, consensus-building organization representing providers, consumers, and researchers), which makes it easier for consumers to compare nursing home quality, deficiency, and staffing information. The 18 enhanced QMs (13 for long-stay and 5 for short-stay residents) build on the original 10 measures and are publicly posted on the Nursing Home Compare website.[285]

In 2005, CMS and several industry groups adopted an initiative called Advancing Excellence in America's Nursing Homes to focus on eight areas for quality improvement: reducing high-risk pressure ulcers; reducing use of physical restraints; pain management for short- and long-term residents; setting specific targets for quality improvement; assessing resident and family satisfaction; increasing staff retention; and making staffing assignments more consistent. Facilities are asked to focus on three of eight areas.

Additional information is collected by surveyors as "Quality Indicators" (QIs). Unlike access to QMs, which are for the use of consumers and the public, access to QIs is restricted. QIs measure 24 indicators relating to chronic populations.[286] There are some QMs that overlap with the QIs.

11.5.5.3 Requirements and Reporting Staffing

Federally-certified nursing facilities must post staffing information in a clearly visible location. Legislation has been introduced in Congress to impose daily nursing home staffing minimums but such efforts have not moved beyond committee in either the House or Senate. The final ROPs include requirements for staff competencies and training in various areas such as nursing, dietary and infection control, but do not establish minimum staffing levels.[287]

The ACA required that within two years of enactment, facilities must electronically submit direct staffing information based on payroll, as well as other verifiable and auditable data, in a uniform

---

[284] *See* Medicare Program; Prospective Payment System and Consolidated Billing for Skilled Nursing Facilities for FY 2014, 78 Fed. Reg. 47936 (Aug. 6, 2013).
[285] *See* https://www.cms.gov/Medicare/Quality-Initiatives-Patient-Assessment-instruments/NursingHomeQualityInits/NHQIQualityMeasures.html.
[286] For more information, *see* Marilyn J. Rantz et al., *Improving Care in Nursing Homes Using Quality Measures/Indicators and Complexity Science*, 25 Journal of Nursing Care Quality 5 (2010).
[287] *See generally* 81 Fed. Reg. 68688.

format.[288] In response to this statutory mandate, CMS developed a system for facilities to submit staffing and census information called the Payroll-Based Journal (PBJ). This system allows staffing and census information to be collected on a regular and more frequent basis than previously collected. It is also auditable to ensure accuracy. All long term care facilities have access to this system at no cost. The first mandatory reporting period began July 1, 2016.[289]

11.5.5.4 Nursing Home Value-Based Purchasing Demonstration and SNF Value-Based Payment System

Since July 1, 2009, CMS has operated a demonstration project in Arizona, New York and Wisconsin aimed at improving the quality and efficiency of care furnished to Medicare beneficiaries.[290] The Nursing Home Value Based Purchasing (NHVBP) demonstration tests the "pay for performance" concept applied to the nursing home setting. CMS is assessing the performance of participating nursing homes based on selected measures of quality of care: staffing, appropriate hospitalizations, MDS outcomes, and survey deficiencies. CMS award the nursing homes certain points based on the nursing home's performance on each of those measures. A nursing home's score will determine whether the home is eligible for a share of the state's savings pool. CMS has not completed the evaluation of participants' performance during the first year of the demonstration.

The ACA directed the Secretary to submit a plan to Congress no later than FY 2012 showing how to move SNFs into a value-based purchasing (VBP) payment system. Subsequently, the Protecting Access to Medicare Act (PAMA) of 2014, enacted into law on April 1, 2014, authorized the SNF VBP program. PAMA requires CMS to adopt a VBP payment adjustment for SNFs beginning October 1, 2018 (i.e., FY 2019). Among other things, CMS is required to develop a methodology for assessing performance scores; adopt performance standards on a quality measure that include achievement and improvement; and rank SNFs based on their performance from low to high. The highest ranked facilities will receive the highest payments, and the lowest ranked 40 percent of facilities will receive payments that are less than what they otherwise would have received without the program. The first performance measure to be implemented is the SNF 30-Day All Cause Readmission Measure (SNFRM). CMS has also adopted the SNF 30-Day Potentially Preventable Readmission (SNFPPR) Measure for future use in the SNF VBP program. The SNFPPR measure assesses the risk-standardized rate of unplanned, Potentially Preventable Readmissions (PPRs) for Medicare FFS SNF patients within 30 days of discharge from a prior hospitalization.

11.5.5 Survey, Certification, and Enforcement for Long Term Care Facilities

11.5.5.1 Survey Policies and Procedures

The survey Protocol and Interpretive Guidelines providing guidance to surveyors on how to interpret and apply regulatory request to long term care facilities to contain in the SOM, Appendices P

---

[288] ACA § 6106.
[289] For information on this program including frequently asked questions, *see* https://www.cms.gov/Medicare/Quality-Initiatives-Patient-Assessment-Instruments/NursingHomeQualityInits/Staffing-Data-Submission-PBJ.html.
[290] For information on this demonstration program, *see* https://innovation.cms.gov/initiatives/Nursing-Home-Value-Based-Purchasing/.

and PP in the SOM.[291] There have been many changes to the SOM over the years. The following highlights significant revisions.

The data-driven survey system and reporting tool includes Quality Indicators (QIs), as discussed above. Standard surveys are to be completed on consecutive workdays, whenever possible, and may be conducted at any time during the day, including weekends. The SOM also includes criteria for ensuring that surveys are unannounced. As discussed above, various enforcement mechanisms, including civil monetary penalties (CMPs) may be issued per instance or per day for violations.

Individual nursing home survey results and violation records are posted on the Internet to increase accountability and flag repeat offenders for families and the public. The Nursing Home Compare website provides detailed information about the past performance of every Medicare and Medicaid certified nursing home in the country. It is one of the most popular tools on www.medicare.gov. The ACA requires certain information to be included on the Nursing Home Compare website, such as staffing data for facilities, links to state websites with information on state surveys, certifications, and inspection reports, information on substantiated complaints, and the number of adjudicated instances of a SNF's criminal violations.[292]

In 2005, CMS launched a demonstration project in five states called the Quality Indicator Survey (QIS) project to use customized software to guide surveyors through the survey. The goal was to improve consistency and accuracy of quality of care and quality of life problems. Unlike the standard survey that uses the QM/QI indicator report (discussed below), surveyors use MDS data and the QIS Data Collection Tool software to identify a larger sample of residents to review prior to their onsite inspection. Surveyors then use onsite observations and data to identify care issues. According to the Final Report issued in 2007, the results of the study were mixed and did not lead to any firm conclusions regarding the effectiveness of the QIS.[293] In 2011, another report brought to light other issues with the QIS.[294] Nonetheless, CMS continues to phase in implementation of the QIS as a replacement for the current (traditional) survey process. See Appendix P to the SOM.

11.5.5.2 Stronger Enforcement Actions

CMS continues to actively enforce the nursing home safety and quality regulations, including the following:

- increasing citations for conditions alleged to present "serious and immediate jeopardy" to residents;
- imposing immediate sanctions and not permitting a "grace period" to allow facilities to correct problems and avoid penalties;

---

[291] The SOM is available at http://www.cms.gov/Regulations-and-Guidance/Guidance/Manuals/Internet-Only-Manuals-IOMs.html.
[292] ACA § 6103; *see* https://www.medicare.gov/nursinghomecompare/search.html.
[293] Evaluation of the Quality Indicator Survey (QIS), Final Report (Dec. 2007), *available at* https://www.cms.gov/medicare/provider-enrollment-and-certification/certificationandcomplianc/nhs.html.
[294] *See* Government Accountability Office (GAO) report to Congress regarding this CMS report, *available at* http://www.gao.gov/products/GAO-11-403R.

- revising the revisit policy so that states must conduct an onsite revisit for any deficiency greater than substantial compliance (more serious than an "A," "B," or "C" deficiency) if there is a "G" or higher deficiency at any time in the survey cycle; and
- directing states to identify special-focus facilities (SFFs) in their states to focus their enforcement efforts on nursing homes with a record of noncompliance with federal rules; these facilities are being terminated from Medicare program participation if they are unable to achieve substantial compliance with program requirements.[295]

11.5.5.3 Stronger Federal Oversight of State Inspections

To target states with weak inspection systems, CMS has:

- provided additional training and other assistance to surveyors in states that are not adequately protecting residents;
- enhanced federal review of the surveys conducted by the states, including implementation of standard evaluation protocols in every state; and
- monitored state surveyors' enforcement of CMS's policy to sanction nursing homes with serious violations, and required that sanctions cannot be lifted until after an onsite visit has verified compliance.

11.5.5.4 Preventing Pressure Ulcers, Dehydration, and Malnutrition, use of Psychotropics

CMS has stepped up its review of nursing homes' ability to prevent pressure ulcers, dehydration, and malnutrition. Nursing homes with patterns of serious violations will be sanctioned. CMS is also working with a variety of entities (including the Administration on Aging, the American Dietetic Association, clinicians, consumers, and nursing homes) to develop a repository of "best-practice" guidelines for residents at risk of weight loss and dehydration. CMS has also focused on efforts to reduce the use of psychotropics.[296]

11.5.5.5 Resident Abuse, Neglect and Financial Exploitation

State inspectors will review each nursing home's system to prevent, identify, and stop physical or verbal abuse, neglect, and misappropriation of resident property. A description of each nursing home's abuse-prevention plan will be shared with residents and families. CMS and the OIG also have directed nursing homes to enquire about criminal convictions when interviewing potential personnel.

---

[295] While originally there were two facilities per state, currently states have greater discretion to select a larger number if warranted based upon the number of facilities in the state and survey history. A SFF that fails to achieve and maintain significant progress in correcting deficiencies on the first and subsequent standard survey will receive an immediate sanction. If after 18 months and 3 surveys after being selected as a SFF a nursing home fails to make significant progress, the facility is terminated from participation in Medicare and Medicaid. Conversely, if a facility has no higher than an "E" on two successive standard surveys without intervening complaint-related deficiencies of an "F" or greater, the facility may be removed from the SFF program. For more information on survey and certification compliance, including the SFF program, see. https://www.cms.gov/medicare/provider-enrollment-and-certification/certificationandcomplianc/nhs.html.

[296] See "National Partnership to Improve Dementia Care in Nursing Homes," *available at* https://www.cms.gov/Medicare/Provider-Enrollment-and-Certification/SurveyCertificationGenInfo/National-Partnership-to-Improve-Dementia-Care-in-Nursing-Homes.html.

Additionally, the ACA requires each individual owner, operator, employee, manager, agent, or contractor of a long-term care facility that receives at least $10,000 in federal funds annually to report to the Secretary of HHS and one or more local law enforcement entities, any "reasonable suspicion" of a crime against anyone who is a resident of, or is receiving care from, the facility. Steep penalties can be imposed on individuals for failure to report within specified timeframes. The law also contains whistleblower protections for facility employees and provides for additional penalties for retaliation. In addition, each facility must post conspicuously in an appropriate location a sign, in a form to be specified by the Secretary, specifying the rights of employees under the law. Such signs shall include a statement that an employee may file a complaint with the Secretary against a facility that violates the law, and information regarding how to file such a complaint. Terms such as "abuse," "elder justice," "exploitation" and "neglect," among others, are specifically defined in the ACA.[297] Finally, the law requires facilities to include as part of initial nurse aide training and competency evaluation programs patient-abuse prevention training.[298]

11.5.5.6 Prosecution of Egregious Violations

CMS is working with the OIG and DOJ to ensure that state-survey agencies and others refer appropriate cases to DOJ for prosecution under federal civil and criminal statutes, particularly cases that result in harm to individual patients. The OIG also will work with CMS to conduct training for, and provide technical assistance to, federal survey and certification staff and CMS contractors on how to make appropriate referrals to the OIG.[299]

11.5.5.7 Federal False Claims Actions against Nursing Homes Care

The government has used the federal False Claims Act (FCA), 31 U.S.C. § 3729 *et seq.*, as a basis for filing actions against providers, alleging that fraudulent practices resulted in the submission of false claims for Medicare and/or Medicaid reimbursement. There have been two main types of cases: 1) medical necessity cases, in which the government asserts that skilled nursing facilities furnished unnecessary rehabilitation therapy services to Medicare patients, resulting in increased RUG levels and so overcharged the government; and 2) quality of care cases and more traditional payment related cases. In the quality of care cases, the government has applied two principal theories:

- *implied certification theory:* provider certified that it met the Medicare/Medicaid requirements for participation but did not, and
- *worthless services theory:* the care was so deficient as to be the equivalent of providing no services at all.

---

[297] ACA § 6703 (adding new § 2011 of the SSA).
[298] ACA § 6121.
[299] Individual nursing home survey results and violation records now are posted on the Internet at http://www.medicare.gov/nursinghomecompare/search.html. This is intended to increase accountability and flag repeat offenders for families and the public.

In the 2016 decision *Universal Health Services, Inc. v. U.S. ex rel. Escobar*,[300] a unanimous U.S. Supreme Court upheld the validity of the implied certification theory of FCA liability. In so doing, the Court discarded a judicially created check some courts had imposed on the theory (i.e., whether the requirement related to a condition of participation vs. a condition of payment), but set forth strict limits on the implied certification theory; announced a rigorous materiality requirement; and strongly reiterated that the FCA is not intended to be used to remedy minor regulatory violations or contractual breaches. Courts will now focus on whether the alleged noncompliance was material to the services provided, and thus could form the basis for a FCA action.

11.5.5.8 Fraud and Abuse, Compliance Program Guidance and the OIG Work Plan

Nursing homes, like others in the health care industry, continue to be subject to investigations and enforcement actions by the HHS OIG, DOJ, and State Medicaid Fraud Control Units (MFCUs). In 2000, the OIG issued its Compliance Program Guidance (CPG) for Nursing Facilities.[301] The guidance outlines the elements to be included in an effective compliance program and the "risk areas" to be addressed. The guidance is also a useful summary of rules and regulations applicable to nursing homes. In 2008, the OIG published supplemental CPG addressing issues that have arisen since the original CPG was published, including quality of care issues, billing issues, and kickback concerns.[302]

The OIG's Work Plan summarizes the major projects the OIG intends to pursue in each of HHS' major operating areas, including CMS.[303] The OIG's priorities for SNFs include:

- assessing Medicare Part B payments for ambulance services subject to Part A SNF consolidated billing requirements;
- determining whether State survey agencies investigate nursing home complaints alleging immediate jeopardy and actual harm within the required timeframes;
- examining potentially avoidable hospitalizations of Medicare- and Medicaid-eligible nursing facility residents;
- evaluating whether portable x-ray suppliers provide diagnostic imaging services at patients' locations (often group living facilities, such as nursing homes) have been improperly paid s for return trips to nursing facilities, i.e., multiple trips to a facility in 1 day, and whether payments were correct and were supported by documentation;
- assessing SNF use of the SNF adverse event screening tool; and
- determining the extent to which Medicare beneficiaries residing in SNFs meet the 3-day qualifying hospital stay requirements.

---

[300] 136 S. Ct. 1989 (2016).
[301] OIG Compliance Program Guidance for Nursing Facilities, 65 Fed. Reg. 14289 (Mar. 16, 2000), *available at* http://oig.hhs.gov/authorities/docs/cpgnf.pdf.
[302] OIG Supplemental Compliance Program Guidance for Nursing Facilities, 73 Fed. Reg. 56832 (Sept. 30, 2008), *available at* http://edocket.access.gpo.gov/2008/pdf/E8-22796.pdf.
[303] *See* OIG Work. https://oig.hhs.gov/reports-and-publications/workplan/index.asp.

11.6 Home and Community-Based Services—Long Term Services and Supports

11.6.1 Introduction

The ACA includes a provision that expresses the Sense of the Senate that Congress should address long-term services and support services for the elderly and disabled so that they are guaranteed the necessary care both in the community and in institutions.[304] A growing trend in caring for elderly and disabled individuals is the provision of home and community-based services (HCBS). In fact, the ACA creates financial incentives for states to shift Medicaid beneficiaries out of nursing homes and into HCBS.[305]

HCBS include a range of health services provided to individuals in their homes and the community, including residents of ALFs, to promote functional independence and individuals at whatever age to be able to live outside institutions in the setting that is as integrated as possible into the community. Some of the most common home and community services are:

- *Adult Day Service (ADS) programs*, designed to meet the needs of adults with cognitive or functional impairments, as well as adults needing social interaction and a place to go when their family caregivers are at work. They provide a variety of health, social, and other support services in a protective setting during part of the day. Adult day centers typically operate programs during normal business hours five days a week; some have evening and weekend hours. These programs do not provide 24-hour care.

- *Case managers/geriatric care managers* are health care professionals (typically nurses or social workers) who specialize in assisting patients with long-term care needs. This includes but is not limited to assisting, coordinating, and managing long-term care services; developing a plan of care; and monitoring long-term care needs over extended periods of time. These are often provided through managed care programs or demonstration projects.

- *Emergency response systems*, which provide an automatic response to a medical or other emergency via electronic monitors.

- *Friendly visitor/companion services*, which are typically staffed by volunteers who regularly pay short visits (under two hours) to someone who is frail or living alone.

- *Home health care/home care* (discussed above).

- *Homemaker/chore services* provide general household activities such as meal preparation, routine household care, and heavy household chores such as washing floors, windows, or shoveling snow.

- *Meals programs*, which include both home-delivered meals (e.g., Meals-on-Wheels) or congregate meals, which are provided in a variety of community settings.

---

[304] ACA § 2406. The ACA also provides $10 million funding to state Aging and Disability Resource Centers for FYs 2010 to 2014. *Id.*, § 2405.
[305] *See* ACA Reconciliation Act, § 10202 (describing financial incentives, including, subject to certain conditions, increases in FMAP matching funds to states seeking to rebalance their total HCBS expenditures).

- *Respite Care*, which gives families temporary relief from the responsibility of caring for family members who are unable to care for themselves. Respite care is provided in a variety of settings including in the home, at an adult day center, or in a nursing home.
- *Senior Centers*, which provide a variety of services including nutrition, recreation, social and educational services, and comprehensive information and referral to help people find the care and services they might need; and
- *Transportation services* to help patients get to and from medical appointments, shopping centers and access a variety of community services and resources.

Payment has traditionally been private pay, community block grants, or some Medicaid funding. The Home and Community Based Services Waiver Provision of the SSA gives the Secretary of the HHS authority to waive certain Medicaid provisions in order to allow long-term care services to be delivered in community settings.[306] This program is the Medicaid alternative to providing comprehensive long-term services in institutional settings. While initially used sporadically, many states now have various § 1915(c) waiver programs reflecting an increasing trend toward seeking Medicaid funding for non-institutional long-term care.

States desiring an alternative to waivers now have another option under the ACA. The ACA directs the Secretary to issue regulations to give states options to provide HCBS through a state plan amendment to individuals with higher levels of need. Additionally, the ACA gives states the option to extend full Medicaid benefits to individuals receiving HCBS under a state plan amendment.[307]

11.6.2 Related Legal Developments

In 1999, the Supreme Court issued what has come to be known as the "integration mandate" in *Olmstead v. L.C.*[308] the Court ruled that states are required to administer services, programs, and activities "in the most integrated setting appropriate to the needs of qualified individuals with disabilities." The Olmstead decision interpreted Title II of the Americans with Disabilities Act (ADA), which gives civil rights and protections to individuals with disabilities and guarantees equal opportunity for individuals with disabilities in public accommodations, employment, transportation, state and local government services, and telecommunications. Patient advocates have used this law to advocate for more funding for community-based services.

The New Freedom Initiative (NFI) was announced by President Bush on February 1, 2001, followed up by the Executive Order 13217 on June 18, 2001. The initiative is a nationwide effort to remove barriers to community living for people of all ages with disabilities and long-term illnesses and to support states' efforts to comply with the *Olmstead* decision. Two recent cases demonstrate the government's commitment to upholding the tenets of *Olmstead*. In *United States v. Virginia*,[309]

---

[306] 42 U.S.C. § 1396n(d). *See generally* https://www.medicaid.gov/medicaid/hcbs/index.html.
[307] ACA § 2402.
[308] 527 U.S. 581 (1999).
[309] No. 3:12-cv-00059-JAG (E.D. Va. Aug. 23, 2012).

DOJ alleged that Virginia's practice of housing disabled individuals in state-run training centers violated the ADA. The settlement agreement Virginia entered into seeks to prevent the unnecessary institutionalization of individuals with developmental disabilities who are living in the community, and ensure that people who are currently in institutions have a meaningful opportunity to receive services that meet their needs in the community. Moreover, in *United States v. North Carolina*,[310] DOJ contended that North Carolina unnecessarily institutionalized thousands of people with mental illness—people who could have been better served in community-based settings. In the settlement agreement, North Carolina agreed to expand its community-based services for the mentally ill over the next eight years.

The DRA includes a provision to allow states to add HCBS to their permanent array of benefits without having to go through a waiver program. The DRA also includes the Money Follows the Person (MFP) "rebalancing" initiative to provide grants to states to encourage the use of HCBS.[311] Currently, 45 states and the District of Columbia have implemented MFP Demonstration Programs, and in July 2010, CMS issued an MFP grant solicitation to encourage states not yet involved to apply for grant funds. As of December 2015, over 63,300 people with chronic conditions and disabilities have transitioned from institutions back into the community through MFP programs.[312]

Under the DRA, these grants are to design programs with four major objectives:

- increase the use of home and community-based, rather than institutional, long-term care services;
- eliminate barriers or mechanisms that prevent Medicaid-eligible individuals from receiving support for appropriate and necessary long-term services in the settings of their choice;
- increase the ability of the state Medicaid program to assure continued provision of home and community based long-term care services to eligible individuals who choose to move from an institutional to a community setting; and
- ensure that procedures are in place to provide quality assurance for individuals receiving Medicaid home and community-based long-term care services and to provide for continuous quality improvement in such services.

Through the ACA, the MFP Rebalancing Demonstration Project has been extended through September 30, 2016. Additionally, the ACA changed the eligibility requirements for individuals participating in the project from six months to 90 consecutive days and excludes short-term rehabilitation stays.[313]

---

[310] No. 5:12-cv-557 (E.D.N.C. Aug. 23, 2012).
[311] For information on the MFP initiatives, *see* https://www.medicaid.gov/medicaid/ltss/money-follows-the-person/index.html.
[312] *See id.*
[313] ACA § 2403.

11.6.3 Medicaid Quality Assurance/Quality Improvement and Oversight

CMS has taken action to implement an HCBS Quality Framework to ensure that states are measuring and working toward seven desired outcomes. These outcomes include participant access, sufficient provider capacity and capabilities, participant rights and satisfaction, and system performance.[314] Consult individual state program websites for more information on implementation of this guidance in oversight programs.

---

[314] Links to information regarding the HCBS quality initiatives are available at https://www.medicaid.gov/medicaid/quality-of-care/improvement-initiatives/hcbs/index.html.

12

Health Care Transactions and Contracting

Anita Beth Adams
Baker, Donelson, Bearman, Caldwell & Berkowitz, PC

Anthea R. Daniels
Vice President, General Counsel, Akron Children's Hospital

12.1 Introduction

Health care mergers, acquisitions, and contracting surged in the wake of the enactment of the Patient Protection and Affordable Care Act (ACA),[1] which contained hundreds of changes that impacted health care providers and reimbursements, leading many providers to choose to either acquire or be acquired in order to weather the ACA storm.[2]

However, the ACA was not the first time the health care industry experienced such a rush for consolidation and integration. Historically, many hospital systems consolidated in the 1980s and 1990s for numerous economic and regulatory reasons, including capitation, managed care, fraud and abuse, financial stability and diversification of types of providers. For example, various health care providers (including hospitals, physician groups, and nursing homes) and ancillary health care providers (including ambulatory surgery centers (ASCs), durable medical equipment (DME) suppliers, and home health care (HHC) and hospice providers) joined together with other health care providers or health care payers (including traditional indemnity-insurance companies, health maintenance organizations (HMOs), and preferred provider organizations (PPOs)) to form integrated delivery systems or enter into joint ventures and affiliations.[3]

---

[1] Patient Protection and Affordable Care Act, Pub. L. No. 111-148, 124 Stat. 119 (2010).
[2] In the first decade of the 21st Century, there were 597 announced hospital mergers and acquisitions. Richard Pizzi, *600 Hospital Mergers in Last Decade*, HEALTHCARE FINANCE NEWS (May 11, 2010), *available at* http://www.healthcarefinance-news.com/news/600-hospital-mergers-last-decade. The second half of the decade saw a 140 percent increase in total capital committed to fund these deals over the first half. *Hospital Pricing Indicators Rose in 2009, Despite Reduced M&A Activity, According to New Irving Levin Five-Year Hospital M&A Report*, BUSINESS WIRE (June 22, 2010, 8:30 AM), *available at* http://www.businesswire.com/news/home/20100622005708/en/Hospital-Pricing-Indicators-Rose-2009-Reduced-MA.
[3] For example, in 1999, HealthSouth Corp., a publicly traded integrated delivery system based in Birmingham, Alabama, had more than 1,900 facilities (primarily outpatient surgery and rehabilitation facilities) in every state and in Puerto Rico, the United Kingdom, and Australia. 29 MODERN HEALTHCARE (Aug. 30, 1999). (This was, of course, prior to the accounting scandal revealed in 2003 that rocked the company and led to a steady decline in its profits and the divesture of certain of its operating divisions for several years following, when its number of integrated delivery systems declined as a result.) In 2008, Hospitals Corporation of America (HCA) was the largest private hospital system in the United States, with 163 hospitals, 105 freestanding surgery centers, and revenues exceeding $28 billion. *See* HCA Fact Sheet, *available at* http://hcahouston.prod.ehc.com/util/documents/CurrentFactSheet1.pdf.

These integrated and/or affiliated entities were formed for various reasons, including: (i) providers, such as a hospital wanting to be able to offer a complete array of health care services to their patients; (ii) providers wanting to improve and enhance their access to capital; (iii) providers wanting to negotiate and obtain financially favorable managed-care contracts and better reimbursement rates; (iv) certain providers wanting to eliminate or decrease their business and administrative responsibilities; and (v) certain providers had no other choice as they were forced to either go out of business or join forces. Many providers and payers in the health care marketplace believed that "bigger" would be "better" and that it was necessary to provide a full array of services in order to capture patients and lucrative insurance contracts.

As a result of all of this integration activity (e.g., acquisitions, mergers, joint ventures, and affiliations), the health care marketplace has undergone and continues to undergo significant consolidation, leaving far fewer choices in hospital providers today in certain heavily consolidated regions. For example, while a major metropolitan city may have had eight independent hospitals 20 years ago, today that same region may have only three hospitals or hospital systems that operate those same eight hospitals, or perhaps a few were merged into other hospitals or closed. Many of these providers are health care powerhouses that offer a wide range of services encompassing a complete continuum of care, from outpatient services to tertiary care, rehab services, nursing home services, and even HMOs. As a result of these transactions, a myriad of contractual arrangements were and continue to be established between the providers (e.g., hospitals and physicians) and other providers and payers. Thus, the concept of Accountable Care Organizations (ACO) for large health care systems may not be as daunting as for a smaller provider who has to enter into numerous contractual arrangements before it could form an ACO.

Despite the consolidation of the past two decades and the fact that, based on the current political climate, the state of the ACA remains somewhat uncertain, health care mergers, acquisitions, and contracting are still strong. In 2016, a PricewaterhouseCoopers report called 2016 the "year of merger mania."[4] While 2017 deal values and volumes declined somewhat, certain portions of the industry—including behavioral health and managed care—experienced growth and the industry witnessed more than 200 deals in the third quarter of 2017 alone.[5] Thus, it seems that integration and consolidation among providers is still active in today's landscape.

This Chapter will explore various types of health care transactions and contractual arrangements, and provide an overview of certain current legal issues and contractual terms that will need to be reviewed when structuring, drafting, and negotiating health care transactions and contracts. Although one may consider the structures for integration to be well established (and they are), the marketplace finds itself full of surprises even today.[6] Thus, understanding the basics is crucial.

---

[4] *See Healthcare Mergers and Acquisitions in 2016: Running List*, HEALTHCARE FINANCE (December 28, 2016), *available at* http://www.healthcarefinancenews.com/slideshow/healthcare-mergers-and-acquisitions-2016-running-list.

[5] *See* Nick Donkar, *PwC Deals, US Health Services Dals Insights Q3 2017*, PwC's DEALS PRACTICE, *available at* https://www.pwc.com/us/en/health-industries/publications/pdf/pwc-health-services-deals-insights-q3-2017.pdf (last visited December 6, 2017).

[6] Recently, two large health systems found themselves in a position to merge even despite certain antitrust concerns. On September 19, 2017 and October 27, 2017, the Tennessee Health Commissioner and the Commissioner of the Virginia Department of Health, respectively, approved the merger of Wellmont Health System and Mountain States Health

12.2 Getting Started: Initial Discussions and Preliminary Documents

One of the first—and perhaps most important—decisions that hospitals, providers, and/or payers must make in determining how to integrate and align their businesses and interests is the structure such integration will take, and often, these initial considerations do not include the legal teams of one or even both sides. Therefore, before the focus of this Chapter turns to the possible structures that can be used to achieve the integrations, a brief discussion on the mechanics leading up to choosing the proper structure is warranted.

12.2.1 Business Development Teams and Due Diligence

In today's landscape, Buyers often have business development teams, and these teams target potential providers for a Buyer to partner with to expand the Buyer's scope of services. Part of this identification includes the initial discussions with a potential Seller, and those discussions cover a whole host of issues to which legal counsel may not be privy. Some of these discussions are solely business related: Are you interested in integration? How do you envision such an integration (stock sale, asset sale, lots of integration, remain relatively autonomous)? And, so on. Some of these discussions, however, trend over into matters that can later be impacted by legal due diligence, most notably the determination of the purchase price (Are there capital leases, creditors or assumed liabilities that require a reduction in the purchase price?).

While sometimes these conversations are initiated by a brokerage firm hired by a provider desiring to be acquired or by a potential seller/target itself, the mechanics follow these same patterns. After the Buyers and Sellers have engaged in these discussions and determined there is a desire to move forward, the Buyer, if it has not already, will perform due diligence to better understand the potential business partner and ascertain if the Buyer can ultimately move forward to a definitive agreement with the Seller. Due diligence is a comprehensive review of the Seller's business, assets, and known and contingent liabilities. Initial due diligence typically culminates in a proposed purchase price and transaction structure, from which the parties can thereafter paper the deal with documents.

Diligence is typically conducted by the Buyer and its attorneys, accountants, billing experts, consultants, and its employees and agents, who review the Seller's corporate books and records, tax records, financial, audit and cost reporting statements, contracts, deeds, title searches, leases, environmental audits, billing records, litigation, risk management reports, physical plant, labor, employee-benefit issues, bond issues, intellectual property, medical staff and physician issues, legal compliance, Health Insurance Portability and Accountability Act of 1996 (HIPAA) compliance,[7]

System, despite opposition from the Federal Trade Commission. Details about this merger, the state approvals, and required regulatory oversight can be found at http://becomingbettertogether.org.

[7] As discussed in more detail in Section 12.2.2 below, as Buyers review diligence, PHI will almost certainly be included. Thus, it is important that the parties consider who is in control of the data room (if a data room exists). Is it the Buyer or the Seller? It is not unusual in an acquisition to find that a sophisticated Buyer is in a better position to set up and maintain an efficient data room, and often this is an extra cost that a potential Seller is willing to allow the Buyer to bear. However, Sellers must be aware that this sensitive information, as well as a great deal of other sensitive information of the potential Seller, is being uploaded into a data room under the control of the Buyer, and, in the event the deal is not consummated, the parties must have an understanding, preferably documented in writing, as to how

privacy, security and IT, in addition to many more areas of operations and their related documents. However, today's Buyers often assemble a "core" in-house business team to initially vet a potential partner's entire enterprise, including a high level review of many, if not most, of these categories. Any results from this in-house due diligence will be useful and should be considered by legal counsel and accountants, and as the deal continues to progress, should be used by these agents as a reference as they are faced with their own due diligence.

A Seller may also conduct due diligence of the Buyer. However, it typically is limited to certain concerns that the Seller may have. For example, if the Seller is taking a note (as opposed to all cash or all stock) in the transaction, the Seller may want to ensure that the Buyer has the appropriate finances to enter into the deal or has the cash to pay at closing of the sale. If the Seller is a nonprofit tax-exempt entity, Seller may want to conduct due diligence to ensure that the Buyer is also a tax-exempt entity and that it is not operating in such a manner as to potentially jeopardize its charitable status and put at risk the Seller's charitable assets.

Finally, it is important that clients and their counsel appreciate the important role of diligence. The purpose of the Buyer's due diligence is to ensure that the Buyer is aware of the Seller's operations, the condition of the assets or business it is acquiring, and any potential liabilities associated with the acquisition. Given the scope of all of the liabilities assumed in a stock transaction, due diligence will often be more thorough and exhaustive; it must cover every aspect of the entity being acquired. Thus, due diligence covers myriad topics. In health care transactions, certain key health care due-diligence areas include Medicare and Medicaid billing and cost-reporting issues; federal and state government investigations; health care accreditation and licensure; HIPAA compliance; contracts with providers and payers; tax-exempt issues; bond financing; FDA compliance; NIH and grant compliance; contractual relationships; and joint ventures with physicians. All of these considerations are in addition to the more typical corporate due-diligence issues referenced above. Due diligence is also an important process because the results will affect the terms of the agreement, potentially increasing or decreasing the purchase price, post-closing conditions and the nature and scope of the representations and warranties the Seller will make to the Buyer in the acquisition agreement (discussed below in Section 12.7.4).

12.2.2 Non-Disclosure Agreements and Disclosure of PHI

As business development teams develop their discussions and proposals with a potential Seller, due diligence, including sensitive financial, accounts receivable, and sometimes patient information, is required. Although confidentiality agreements are not always requested by a potential Seller or Target Company, oftentimes a savvy Seller will request a confidentiality or non-disclosure agree-

---

and when the information (and particularly the PHI) will be returned to the Seller and permanently removed from the data room, as well as how and when any copies downloaded or printed by the potential Buyer will be returned to the Seller or satisfactorily destroyed. For best practices purposes, any writing between the parties that details such return or destruction of sensitive information should require that, when no deal is consummated, an affidavit executed by the CEO/President of the potential Buyer should be promptly delivered to the Seller confirming that all agreed upon steps for return or destruction of information have been taken by the Buyer and to confirm that, with the delivery of the affidavit, any return of information or destruction thereof has been completed. *See infra* Section 12.2.2 for a more detailed discussion of the disclosure of PHI during the due-diligence period.

ment prior to sharing any of this sensitive financial information with a potential Buyer. In the event a brokerage firm is involved in helping a Seller find and choose a potential Buyer, a confidentiality agreement will almost certainly be requested, and in the event legal counsel is consulted concerning the initial stages, a confidentiality agreement should be requested.

A main concern of any potential Seller or Target Company should be the disclosure of protected health information (PHI), and the safeguards that should be in place before any such information is shared. Generally, HIPAA provides that a covered entity may disclose minimally necessary PHI for certain "Health Care Operations" that include the health care transactions discussed in the Chapter.[8] However, certain limitations are also imposed. In particular, in the preamble to the modification to the Standards for Privacy of Individually Identifiable Information in August 2002, HHS clarified:

> [a] covered entity may use or disclose protected health information in connection with a sale or transfer of assets to, or a consolidation or merger with, *an entity that is or will be a covered entity upon completion of the transaction*; and to conduct due diligence in connection with such transaction. The modification also makes it clear it is also a health care operation to transfer records containing protected health information as part of the transaction. For example, if a pharmacy which is a covered entity buys another pharmacy which is also a covered entity, protected health information can be exchanged between the two entities for purposes of conducting due diligence, and the selling entity may transfer any records containing protected health information to the new owner upon completion of the transaction.[9]

Although some question whether this exception for disclosure without patient authorization is valid in the event the transaction is not consummated (and the potential Buyer is not already and therefore does not become a covered entity), such considerations are beyond the scope of this Chapter. Additionally, certain fact specific situations could potentially fall outside this definition of "Health Care Operations," and therefore, careful consideration of any use or disclosure of PHI by a Seller must be carefully evaluated prior to the disclosure based on the relevant facts.

Notwithstanding, confidentiality agreements are useful for incorporating the parties' rights and obligations under HIPAA and state law, but also for the disclosure of sensitive financial, business operations, group practice, and other non-publically known information. The most important term in a confidentiality agreement is that one or both of the parties agree to keep certain information confidential. Thus, best practices would be to enter into a confidentiality agreement before any information is exchanged. This ensures neither party is able to disclose the information that it learns about the other party during the negotiation and due-diligence process. The key provision in a confidentiality agreement is the term that sets forth what information will be maintained as confidential, and for how long. Usually, the parties are required to maintain the confidentiality of the information indefinitely, and there may also be a provision that one party has to notify the other in the event of receiving a subpoena to disclose the confidential information covered by the agreement. Additionally, if this agreement is used as a precursor to negotiations of a merger or acquisition, then customarily a "no-shop" provision will be included in the agreement. A no-shop provision precludes

---

[8] 45 C.F.R. §§ 164.501 & .502.
[9] 67 Fed. Reg. 53182, 53190–53191 (Aug. 14, 2002) (emphasis added).

typically a Seller from entering into any negotiations with any other party regarding the merger or sale under discussion for a certain length of time. This often may be a benefit to the Buyer if the Buyer fears that the Seller may be "shopping" the business or assets to multiple potential Buyers.

There are not many legal issues to review in these types of agreements; usually the necessary terms can be memorialized in a very short document.[10] State confidentiality laws should be reviewed, however, to ensure that the provisions in the confidentiality agreement are enforceable under state law. Traditionally, no payment terms are specified in a confidentiality agreement; as a result, the typical health care legal issues do not apply.

In all circumstances, careful attention should be given to the definition of confidential information, any exceptions for permitted disclosures, and the return or destruction of such information in the event discussions cease without an actual deal resulting.

12.2.3 Letters of Intent/Term Sheets

After a Buyer has completed its due diligence and determined that an integration with the potential Seller is beneficial, a letter of intent setting forth the basic terms of the deal is often, although not always, generated. Generally speaking, the letter of intent contains the basic understanding of the terms of the proposed acquisition to be completed between the Buyer and the Seller (i.e., the purchase price, the targeted closing date, the structure of the transaction (stock, asset, merger, etc.), retention of employees or key employees, selling shareholder employment, tax consequences to the parties, summary of representations and warranties to be included (which may simply be those customary in deals of the same nature), confidentiality terms, and the no-shop/exclusivity period for purposes of negotiating the definitive agreements and completing final due diligence). While many of the provisions of the letter of intent are often explicitly described as "non-binding" on the parties, there are certain terms of the letter of intent that should be binding, such as a no-shop/exclusivity period provision during the negotiation period, the term of the letter of intent, and the confidentiality provisions (which should incorporate or reference any confidentiality agreement executed between the parties).

12.3 Structure of Health Care Transactions

As noted above, before providers and/or payers can enter into any type of arrangement, they must first agree on the basic structure of the transaction. Generally, a health care transaction among these parties can be structured in various ways depending on the goals of the parties involved, which do not always align. This section of the Chapter will address several types of transactional structures and the key determinants that drive each one.

12.3.1 Acquisitions and Mergers

An acquisition is where one entity (the Buyer) acquires another entity (the Seller or the Target Company). There are three basic forms of acquisitions: the stock transaction, the asset transaction,

---

[10] "The Confidentiality Agreement is often in letter form from the Company to Buyer. . . ." *Id.*

and the merger. Sellers generally prefer that a Buyer acquire the stock of the entity to be acquired, while Sellers generally prefer to acquire only those assets deemed necessary and desirable (while leaving behind any unwanted liabilities). However, there are a host of factors and considerations that can impact this crucial decision.

12.3.1.1 Stock Transactions and Member Substitutions

In a stock transaction or LLC unit transaction, the Buyer purchases certain or all of the stock or units of the Seller, and the sale proceeds from the sale of the stock, after liabilities are extinguished,[11] and are distributed to the selling owners of the Seller.

If the Seller is a nonprofit entity rather than a for-profit entity, then under nonprofit state laws, it has members rather than shareholders. A nonprofit "stock" deal is sometimes referred to as a member substitution arrangement.[12] Unlike shareholders, the members do not "own" any part of the health care entity; instead, the members protect the nonprofit entity and its charitable assets on behalf of the community. Thus, if the members sell the "membership" of the health care entity to a Buyer, the members are not entitled to divide the purchase price among themselves, as a for-profit entity would among its shareholders. Instead, any monies received, after all liabilities are extinguished, would typically be donated to another nonprofit tax-exempt entity pursuant to specific provisions on distribution of assets upon sale as set forth in the selling organization's organizational documents or as required by state law and federal tax-exempt laws.

In this type of arrangement, whether it be a stock sale or a member substitution, the Buyer becomes the new member or the shareholder of the Target Company. Thus, the Buyer, XYZ Company, now controls and has become the shareholder or member of ABC Health Care entity. As the sole shareholder or sole member of ABC Health Care entity, XYZ Company typically has the ability to appoint all of ABC's board of trustees or directors, who in turn elects all of the officers of ABC Health Care, who control its day-to-day operations. Often a transaction will be structured as a stock deal or a member substitution because either the Buyer wants to make sure it is buying all of the assets and business of the Seller or the Seller wants to sell the entire business, in order to extinguish all of its liabilities and obligations regarding the business. However, a Buyer may not want to acquire all of the liabilities of the business, and would rather only purchase certain assets and liabilities that it chooses, leaving certain liabilities behind. Obviously, this is one of the initial deal points that is negotiated between the parties and can become a potential deal breaker if there is not a meeting of the minds between the parties. Additionally, it can sometimes be the case that, after more involved due diligence is completed, the potential Buyer realizes that there are too many significant liabilities of the potential Target Company to make a stock deal feasible. This can result in a restructuring of the deal, or a complete abandonment of the transaction if the parties cannot agree.

---

[11] Generally speaking, Buyers desire to buy an entity on a debt-free basis, meaning that on or prior to the closing of the acquisition, all indebtedness of the Target Company will be paid in full, either by the owners or out of the purchase price proceeds. Certain exceptions to this may apply, such as the assumption of a capital lease or other liability, which could in turn reduce the purchase price.

[12] GERALD R. PETERS, HEALTHCARE INTEGRATION: A LEGAL MANUAL FOR CONSTRUCTING INTEGRATED ORGANIZATIONS 68 (1995); *see also* BRUCE JOHN SHIH, HEALTHCARE TRANSACTIONS: A GUIDE TO MERGERS, ACQUISITIONS & INTEGRATION (1998).

This transaction could also be accomplished by a merger wherein ABC Health Care entity is merged into XYZ Company (or vice versa), where either XYZ Company or ABC Health Care is the surviving entity. Unlike a stock deal or member substitution where there are still two entities after the closing of the transaction (the parent corporation and a subsidiary), with a merger or asset acquisition there is typically only one entity remaining after the merger, or the assets become part of the Buyer's entity as described further below.

12.3.1.2 Asset Transactions

In asset transactions, some or all of the assets of the Seller are acquired by the Buyer. Transactions may be structured as asset deals because: (1) the Buyer does not want to purchase all of the Seller's assets; (2) the Seller only wants to sell a portion of its business or a specific line or division of its business; or (3) the Buyer does not want to assume the Seller's liabilities as with a stock deal. Often health care transactions are structured as asset deals because the Buyer does not want to assume the Seller's Medicare and Medicaid billing agreements/provider numbers and wants to avoid the potential successor liability for the prior billing acts of the Seller. Notwithstanding such desires, certain courts have still held that, even in asset transactions, the Buyer may still be responsible for the Seller's prior billing liabilities when the Medicare provider agreements/numbers are purchased but the Seller agrees to retain all liabilities for prior billing acts.[13]

12.3.2 Joint Ventures

Sometimes health care entities strategically decide to collaborate with another provider but may not want to merge or be acquired. In this instance, the parties may establish a joint venture. A joint venture is an arrangement whereby the parties agree to collaborate for a specific purpose. According to the Internal Revenue Service (IRS), "[a] joint venture is created when two or more persons enter into an arrangement to invest in a project and the parties share the control, benefits, and risks of the project."[14] The joint venture may establish collaboration on anything from a single service to a variety of services, or have the entities venturing into a new geographic area or for numerous other reasons. Unrelated hospitals, health systems, physicians, and numerous other types of providers have entered into joint ventures for various projects.

---

[13] *See, e.g., United States v. Vernon Home Health, Inc.*, 21 F.3d 693 (5th Cir. 1994); *Delta Health Grp., Inc. v. U.S. Dep't of Health & Human Servs.*, 459 F.Supp.2d 1207, 1210 (N.D. Fla. 2006) (denying Delta Health Group's claim to recover $250,000 in civil monetary fines assessed against it for violations incurred by a corporation whose provider agreement and number Delta had acquired). In *Vernon*, the court held Vernon Home Health Care was liable for the Medicare overpayments to a corporation whose assets Vernon purchased. *Vernon Home Health, Inc.*, 21 F.3d at 694. Because Vernon had acquired the corporation's Medicare agreement and provider number, it was jointly and severable for the debts created under the agreement, even though the purchase agreement provided that Vernon had purchased assets and assumed no liabilities. *Id.* at 696. The court noted that the government had conceded the case would have been different if Vernon had not assumed the provider number. *Id.* The Eighth Circuit has cited *Vernon* for the proposition that applying for a new provider agreement prevents a new operator from liabilities incurred under the old agreement. *See Deerbrook Pavilion, LLC v. Shalala*, 235 F.3d 1100, 1105 (8th Cir. 2000).

[14] Mary Jo Salins et al., *Whole Hospital Joint Ventures, 1999 CPE Text for Exempt Organizations*, 2, *available at* https://www.irs.gov/pub/irs-tege/eotopica99.pdf (last visited December 6, 2017). "The Tax Court has defined a joint venture as 'a special combination of two or more persons where in some specific venture a profit is jointly sought without any actual partnership or corporate designation.'" *Id.* (quoting *Sierra Club v. Comm'r*, 103 T.C. 307, 322 (1994), rev'd, 86 F.3d 1526 (9th Cir. 1996)).

Unlike an acquisition or a merger, the parties to a joint venture remain independent entities. The joint venture is created by a written contract or by creating a new entity that would be jointly owned by the parties. At times, a joint venture may be the first step toward further integration of the parties. Many health care joint ventures have recently been structured as limited liability companies (LLCs). As with a shareholder, an LLC member does not have liability for the debts of the LLC in excess of the amount paid for the member's units. Additionally, an LLC can be treated for tax purposes as a pass-through entity and thus avoid double-level taxation as with a corporation. The individual members of the LLC are taxed on their distributions.

Physicians and hospitals have established joint ventures to jointly own or operate ancillary services providers (i.e., ASCs), medical office buildings, clinics, medical imaging centers, hospitals, and physician hospital organizations (PHOs), described in Section 12.3.2. However, the Anti-Kickback Statute[15] and the Stark laws[16] make the formation of such joint ventures challenging when trying to structure these arrangements. Certain providers have formed joint ventures and have obtained an Advisory Opinion from the Office of the Inspector General (OIG) of the Department of Health and Human Services (DHHS) to guarantee that the arrangement does not violate the Anti-Kickback Statute is deemed to be the type of arrangement that would be investigated by the federal government as violat(ing) the Anti-Kickback Statute.[17]

Notwithstanding the regulatory challenges, there are many reasons providers continue to enter into joint ventures. One reason is that one party may bring resources and capital to the joint venture, while the other party brings expertise. For example, two hospitals may form a joint venture to construct and operate an ASC where the one hospital will finance a majority of the project and the other hospital has management expertise in operating ASCs. Alternatively, perhaps these parties decide to joint venture the ASC because the community only needs one ASC. In this case, rather than each hospital operating its own ASC, the parties will collaborate and avoid duplicate facilities, services, and costly equipment. Additionally, the parties may pursue a joint venture on a risky project in order to spread the risk among a larger group of participants.

Another joint-venture example is a surgeon owned and operated ASC where all of the investors provide services at the facility. In this scenario, the joint venture's success relies upon obtaining many active referring investors so that the facility will be used. For the last several decades and the move from Medicare cost reimbursement to fee schedule reimbursement (e.g., DRG and RVS), many independent physicians, not employed by hospitals, want to provide ancillary services, whether by joint venture or within their practice, because they are looking for additional revenue sources and it often is a convenience to their patients to offer the service in the office. Alternatively, hospitals want to joint venture with physicians in order to cement the physician's loyalty to the facility, which in turn means the physician may utilize that hospital for its patients and the physician stays in the community.

---

[15] 42 U.S.C. § 1320a-7b(b).

[16] 42 U.S.C. § 1395nn.

[17] In one Advisory Opinion, a hospital and a group of radiologists created a joint venture of a medical imaging center. The OIG stated that, although the arrangement does not fit within a safe harbor, the activity does not violate the Anti-Kickback Statute because radiologists do not refer patients to the facility or the hospital, but rather merely provide radiology services to patients who are referred by other physicians. OIG Advisory Opinion 97-5 (Oct. 6, 1997).

In recent years, the industry has seen an increase in joint ventures for co-management operations. The goal of such a joint venture is to elevate the performance in a particular service line of a hospital, such as cardiology, general surgery, oncology, etc. The structure of the co-management arrangement can take the form of a separate joint venture management entity, owned by the hospital and the physicians. This management company then enters into a management agreement with the hospital to manage the applicable service line. The compensation arrangement in a co-management venture is two-fold: There is a fixed fee, which must be consistent with fair market value based on the time and efforts of the physicians for developing, managing, and overseeing the service line, and there is an incentive fee, which must also be fair market value but is based upon the achievement of certain pre-determined quality metrics. These quality metrics must be objective, verifiable, and tracked. This type of joint venture is attractive to both physicians and hospitals. Physicians have the potential for an increase in compensation, all subject to fair market value, that would not otherwise be available to them. However, the hospital gains great benefits, too: direct physician participation, improved operations and efficiencies, enhanced service lines and, sometimes most importantly, more integrated and aligned goals of physicians and hospitals in delivering quality patient care.[18]

Unlike acquisitions and mergers, joint ventures may be either limited in duration to a specific amount of time (as set forth in a joint-venture agreement) or perpetual. While some joint ventures are perpetual, it is not unusual to have a joint venture effective for a three to five-year period of time, with provisions permitting one party to terminate the joint venture if certain incidences occur (e.g., breach by the other party of the terms in the joint-venture agreement). In this situation, the parties may or may not have created a separate corporate entity that holds the asset. If a separate corporate entity is not established, then the parties agree, via a contractual arrangement, to share the expenses and profits of the lithotripter. Hence, the joint venture is established by a contract rather than via a separate entity owned by the joint-venture participants. Either way, a definitive shareholder, operating, or venture agreement sets forth the relationship of the parties and the obligations of each.

12.3.3 Affiliations

In the world of corporate transactions, affiliation arrangements typically require the least amount of integration of the parties involved. There does not appear to be a uniform definition of what constitutes an affiliation. There is no clearly identifiable type of affiliation arrangement common to all affiliation arrangements. Rather, an affiliation can be created between two or more parties to accomplish anything the parties desire. Often, an affiliation arrangement will be memorialized in an agreement executed by the parties. Unlike a joint venture, the activities may be more informal. Health care entities have entered into affiliations with one another for various reasons, including creating loose networks as to explore further integration. Entities may enter into an affiliation arrangement because they are not organizationally or fiscally prepared to merge, sell, or buy. Thus, a party may enter into an affiliation arrangement in order to explore such possibilities.

---

[18] Although the co-management arrangement discussed here contemplates a separate joint venture entity, the co-management arrangement is also achievable by a direct management contract between a hospital and physician group. Generally, in such a contractual arrangement, an operating committee would develop and oversee the quality metrics required for inventive payments.

Another common type of affiliation agreement is between a hospital or an integrated delivery system (IDS) and an educational institution (i.e., a medical, nursing, or physical therapy school). These educational institutions enter into affiliation agreements with hospitals so that their students can receive training from the hospitals. Typically, these agreements do not involve any compensation provisions. Instead, the key sections of the contract are the insurance, indemnification, and description of the responsibilities of the parties. (Section 12.7.5 discusses the structure of affiliation agreements.)

12.4 Health Care Corporate Structures

12.4.1 Integrated Delivery Systems

IDSs started to be formed in the 1980s and 1990s and continue to evolve in the 21st century, with some continuing to grow especially in light of the ACA and the formation of ACOs. Notwithstanding, some health care systems are shrinking because the health system perhaps expanded into an area that was not profitable, was beyond its core services, or did not fully understand how to operate such entity (e.g., health maintenance organizations, long term care facilities). IDSs are defined as a variety of health care providers that are integrated as part of one corporate structure or system. There is no one specific corporate organizational model for IDSs. Thus, one IDS may have four hospitals, three physician groups, and a DME company all in one corporation; another IDS may have one hospital, one nursing home, a physician group, an HMO, and a management services organization, all in separate corporate entities with a parent holding company. The structure will primarily be dictated by tax, liability, financial, and other business concerns.

IDSs are formed by health care providers for many reasons. Many systems want to create an entity that would be a full-service provider of health care services that a patient may need. For example, an IDS would have physician employees who may refer patients to the IDS's hospital and other providers. Once discharged, the patient would receive at-home services from the IDS's HHC, and might purchase a wheelchair from the IDS's DME company. If the patient needed further sub-acute care, then the patient could be referred to the IDS's step-down facility or assisted-living facility. Hence with the IDS, the patient has "one-stop shopping," and does not need to look for health care services outside of the IDS. In turn, the IDS can coordinate care for a patient among all of its entities, and perhaps provide better care to its patients because of the coordination between all of the providers in the IDS and the sharing of one medical record. In addition, if all of the providers of the IDS have access to the same electronic medical record, then time efficiencies and improved quality of care are expected outcomes.

Another reason for the wave of creating IDSs was to create a structure that would have sufficient leverage and power to negotiate favorable contracts with managed-care payers. An IDS that negotiates on behalf of six hospitals and 2,000 physicians most probably would be able to obtain more favorable rates and contractual terms than an individual hospital. An IDS will also have larger amounts of capital available to withstand decreases in government reimbursement, commercial revenues and/or increased competition. For whatever reason, the health care industry has consolidated, and the individual hospital entity is almost extinct in urban areas as the IDS has become the norm.

Many legal issues need to be analyzed when structuring and operating an IDS. In fact, several books are completely dedicated to addressing this issue.[19] This Chapter will provide a brief overview of the certain legal issues surrounding an IDS.

12.4.1.1 Antitrust

When entities integrate to form an IDS, various antitrust laws need to be reviewed to ensure that a proposed IDS is in compliance with federal and state antitrust laws. Specifically, a proposed IDS needs to be reviewed under Section 2 of the Sherman Act to ensure that the IDS would not be deemed to constitute a monopoly if it has significant market share (and thus makes it prohibitive for others to enter the marketplace). Monopolizations apply to an entity that has significant market power and prevents other participants from competing in that industry.[20]

In addition to monopoly and market-power issues, when health care entities decide to merge or integrate, the entities may need to provide premerger notification. The premerger-notification report is referred to as a Hart-Scott-Rodino premerger notification (Hart-Scott filing), and must be made to the Federal Trade Commission (FTC), as required by Section 7 of the Clayton Act, and to the Department of Justice (DOJ). After the filing is made, an applicable waiting period must expire before the parties are permitted to close their transaction.[21] The necessity of a Hart-Scott filing depends on the size of the Buyer and the Seller. A Hart-Scott filing will be necessary if the value of the assets or voting securities to be acquired meet or exceed certain standards. Typically, very few physician-acquisition transactions or small hospital acquisitions will require a Hart-Scott filing; by contrast, many hospital-acquisition transactions may require a Hart-Scott filing depending on the specific revenues and assets of the parties involved.

12.4.1.2 Fraud and Abuse

Fraud and abuse issues also need to be reviewed when structuring an IDS to ensure that the proposed structure does not create a potential for an anti-kickback violation.[22] When structuring an

---

[19] *See supra*, footnote 13, to this chapter.
[20] A monopoly is defined by having "the power to control prices or exclude competition." *United States v. E.I. DuPont de Nemours & Co.*, 351 U.S. 377, 391 (1957). Chapter 7 provides further discussion on monopolies and the Sherman Act.
[21] 15 U.S.C. § 18a (the waiting period will "end on the thirtieth day" after receipt of the appropriate documentation, or on the fifteenth day "in the case of a cash tender offer," unless the FTC or Attorney General extends the deadline by requesting additional relevant information).
[22] 42 U.S.C. § 1320a-7b(b) provides:
  (1) Whoever knowingly and willfully solicits or receives any remuneration (including any kickback, bribe, or rebate) directly or indirectly, overtly or covertly, in cash or in kind—
     (A) in return for referring an individual to a person for the furnishing or arranging for the furnishing of any item or service for which payment may be made in whole or in part under a Federal health care program, or
     (B) in return for purchasing, leasing, ordering, or arranging for or recommending purchasing, leasing, or ordering any good, facility, service, or item for which payment may be made in whole or in part under a Federal health care program,
  shall be guilty of a felony and upon conviction thereof, shall be fined not more than $25,000 or imprisoned for not more than five years, or both.
  (2) Whoever knowingly and willfully offers or pays any remuneration (including any kickback, bribe, or rebate) directly or indirectly, overtly or covertly, in cash or in kind to any person to induce such person—

IDS, the parties want to be particularly careful if the IDS includes physicians or physician groups. Because the Anti-Kickback Statute generally prohibits any type of payment to a person (including a physician) in exchange for a referral of a government-sponsored patient, which includes Medicare and Medicaid recipients in addition to recipients under other government-sponsored programs, any arrangement with physicians needs to be scrutinized to ensure that any payments to the physicians are not deemed to be a kickback in exchange for a referral of a government beneficiary.[23] The parties should also review the safe harbors to the Anti-Kickback Statute[24] to determine whether the proposed structure for the IDS fits within one of the applicable safe harbors.

Typically when forming an IDS, the safe harbors that may be applicable are the investment interests safe harbors,[25] which includes a safe harbor for publicly traded companies and another for entities owned by either active or passive investors. If the arrangement is a joint venture to create an ASC, then the ASC safe harbor should be reviewed.[26] Also potentially applicable when structuring such a transaction are the safe harbors for employment arrangements, agreements with independent contractors, and leases for real and personal property. Because the safe harbors are narrowly written, not all transactions satisfy all of a particular safe harbor's criteria. Notwithstanding this dilemma, it is important to remember that the mere fact that an arrangement does not fit within a safe harbor does not make the transaction illegal; instead, the transaction is subject to review by the government and may be a violation of the law.

12.4.1.3 Stark Law

The Ethics in Patient Referrals Act of 1989 (Stark Law)[27] also needs to be reviewed to ensure that the IDS does not violate this law. In general, the Stark Law prohibits a physician (and certain family members of such physician) from having a financial relationship, including ownership and compensation arrangements, with an entity that provides designated health services (DHS), as well as from referring Medicare patients to such entity for a DHS[28] unless a Stark exception is satisfied.

(A) to refer an individual to a person for the furnishing or arranging for the furnishing of any item or service for which payment may be made in whole or in part under a Federal health care program, or

(B) to purchase, lease, order, or arrange for or recommend purchasing, leasing, or ordering any good, facility, service, or item for which payment may be made in whole or in part under a Federal health care program, shall be guilty of a felony and upon conviction thereof shall be fined not more than $25,000 or imprisoned for not more than five years, or both.

42 U.S.C. § 1320a-7b(b). Please see Chapter 5 for a complete discussion of the Anti-Kickback Statute.

[23] The Patient Protection and Affordable Care Act (ACA) has clarified the meaning of "knowingly and willingly" within the meaning of the Anti-Kickback Statute by stating that a violator need not have specific knowledge the action violates the Anti-Kickback Statute or specific intent to violate the law. Patient Protection and Affordable Care Act, Pub. L. No. 111-148, § 6402, 124 Stat. 759 (2010). The ACA also makes False Claims Act violations easier to prove, by making the establishment of a violation of the Anti-Kickback rules the establishment of the filing of a false claim. *Id.* The False Claims Act makes anyone who knowingly makes false claims to the government liable for up to three times the amount of the claim plus mandatory penalties. 31 U.S.C. § 3729(a).

[24] 42 C.F.R. § 1001.952; *see also Safe Harbor Regulations*, OFFICE OF INSPECTOR GENERAL, U.S. DEPARTMENT OF HEALTH & HUMAN SERVICES, https://oig.hhs.gov/compliance/safe-harbor-regulations/index.asp (last visited December 6, 2017) (providing access to proposed and final rules as published in the Federal Register).

[25] 42 C.F.R. § 1001.952(a).

[26] 42 C.F.R. § 1001.952(r).

[27] Social Security Act 1877; 42 U.S.C. § 1395nn.

[28] The 11 designated health services set forth in the Stark Law are: clinical lab services; physical therapy services; occupational therapy services; radiology services (including magnetic resonance imaging, computerized axial tomography

Thus, if the IDS has a financial arrangement with a physician and the physician refers patients to the hospital, then the arrangement must satisfy a Stark exception. If the arrangement does *not* satisfy an exception, then the physician would be precluded from referring any Medicare patients to the IDS for a DHS. Because the list of DHS is comprehensive, since one DHS is hospital inpatient and outpatient services, most compensation/investment arrangements with physicians must satisfy a Stark exception. ACA made several changes to the Stark Law, and some of the ACA Stark changes impact integration.[29] For example, ACA froze the ability to create a new physician-owned hospital after 2010.[30] Additionally, those in operation will be severely limited in expanding their facilities unless they can show need in the community.[31]

12.4.1.4 Tax

Various tax laws will need to be reviewed when structuring an IDS. For example, if a tax-exempt hospital is acquiring entities to create an IDS,[32] then the hospital needs to be cautious if creating an IDS with for-profit entities, which would include physicians and physician groups, proprietary health systems, etc. The tax-exempt hospital needs to ensure that it will not be jeopardizing its tax-exempt status by engaging in private inurement or private benefit, and expose the facility to intermediate sanctions, by forming the IDS.[33] Such a situation could arise if the hospital offered a physician a purchase price for the physician's practice that exceeds the practice's fair market value. The excess amount paid to the physician could be deemed a benefit to a private individual, and could expose certain parties to penalties under the intermediate sanctions that are available to the IRS in the event that the physician is deemed to be a disqualified person.[34] Other tax issues to review are unrelated business income tax issues, as well as reviewing each transaction in light of the tax-exempt mission and applicable IRS determination letter to ensure ongoing recognition by the IRS as a tax-exempt entity.

---

scans, and ultrasound services); radiation therapy services and supplies; durable medical equipment and supplies; parenteral and enteral nutrients, equipment and supplies; prosthetics, orthotics, and prosthetic devices and supplies; home health services; outpatient prescription drugs; and inpatient and outpatient hospital services. 42 U.S.C. § 1395nn(h)(6).

[29] Patient Protection and Affordable Care Act, Pub. L. No. 111-148, § 6001, 124 Stat. 684 (2010); *see also* Sean A. Timmons, *Fraud and Abuse Provisions in the Patient Protection and Affordable Care Act*, NORTH CAROLINA BAR ASSOCIATION'S PROGNOSIS NEWSLETTER, May, 2010.

[30] *See* Patient Protection and Affordable Care Act, Pub. L. No. 111-148, § 6001, 124 Stat. 684 (2010); *see also* Timmons, *Fraud and Abuse Provisions in the Patient Protection and Affordable Care Act* (noting that two of the Stark law exceptions, codified at 42 U.S.C. § 1395nn(d)(2) and (3)—the rural provider exception and the hospital owner exception—will not apply to physician owned hospitals created after Dec. 31, 2010).

[31] *See* Timmons, *Fraud and Abuse Provisions in the Patient Protection and Affordable Care Act* (suggesting that the number of physician owned hospitals will significantly decrease after Dec. 31, 2010).

[32] Section 501(c)(3) of the Internal Revenue Code states:

> Corporations... organized and operated exclusively for religious, charitable, scientific, testing for public safety, literacy, or educational purposes... no part of the net earnings of which inures to the benefit of any private shareholder or individual, no substantial part of the activities of which is carrying on propaganda, or otherwise attempting, to influence legislation... and which does not participate in, or intervene in... any political campaign on behalf of (or in opposition to) any candidate for public office.

26 U.S.C. § 501(c)(3).

[33] 26 U.S.C. § 4958.

[34] *Id.*

12.4.1.5 Other Legal Issues

Various other legal issues affect the structuring of an IDS. For example, certain states have corporate practice of medicine statutes that prohibit a corporation from being owed by a non-physician and in turn that entity practicing medicine.[35] Hence, if the IDS wants to employ physicians directly, then the IDS's counsel should review the applicable state(s) statutes to see whether any prohibition is made on such employment, and upon which entity, and whether the state allows certain entities, such as hospitals, or others in rural areas to directly employ physicians. Various states, however, have corporate practice of medicine statutes that prohibit even a *hospital* from employing a physician.[36]

Reimbursement issues also need to be addressed when structuring an IDS. Applicable Medicare and Medicaid regulations should be reviewed prior to any transactions to see if the amount of government reimbursement will be affected, limited, or prohibited by the proposed structure of the IDS. For example, when physician practices are acquired by a hospital and become part of an IDS, depending upon the circumstances, the physician services may be billed as either hospital-based services or freestanding services (which are rendered in a physician's office).[37] If the service is billed as hospital-based to Medicare, then typically two bills are generated to the Medicare program: one for the technical component of the service (i.e., office overhead, non-professional assistance, supplies) and the other for the professional component of the service (the physician's service). If the service is billed as freestanding, then one professional bill is sent to the Medicare carrier, which incorporates an overhead component. In order for the IDS to determine how it should bill, the Medicare regulations and other advisory information should be reviewed, including the Medicare provider based rules and regulations. Additionally, CMS has recently added further limitations on new facilities of a hospital being able to qualify for hospital-based status. Additionally, the "incident to" rules[38] under Medicare will often affect the structuring of physician entities within an IDS, as well as the successor-liability issues with acquiring provider agreements/numbers.

---

[35] The prohibition on corporate medicine is against any person or entity other than a licensed physician/dentist/optometrist holding herself out as a provider of diagnoses, treatment, or care of patients, billing in the name of such non-licensed entity for such diagnoses, treatment or care of patients, and/or ownership or other control of professional medical, dental, or optometric delivery systems by non-licensed persons or entities. *Patient Care and Professional Responsibility: Impact of the Corporate Practice of Medicine Doctrine and Related Laws and Regulations*, NHLA/AAHA (1997), *available at* https://www.healthlawyers.org/hlresources/PI/ConvenerSessions/Documents/PatientCare.PDF; *see also* Mary Michal et al., *Corporate Practice of Medicine Doctrine: 50 State Survey Summary* (September 2006), *available at* https://www.nhpco.org/sites/default/files/public/palliativecare/corporate-practice-of-medicine-50-state-summary.pdf (briefly stating the law in each state as of 2006 along with a short summary of legal guidance).

[36] *See, e.g.*, OHIO REV. CODE ANN. § 1701.03 (prohibiting a corporation formed for the combination of professional services from controlling the professional judgment of doctors and other health care providers); *see also* COLO. REV. STAT. ANN. § 25-3-103.7 (3); *Conrad v. Med. Bd. of California*, 55 Cal. Rptr. 2d 901 (Cal. Ct. App. 1996) (hospitals may not employ physicians but may use them as independent contractors); *Gupta v. E. Idaho Tumor Inst., Inc.*, 140 S.W.3d 747, 752 (Tex. App. 2004) (illegal for a corporation comprised of lay persons to hire physicians to treat patients); Iowa Op. Att'y Gen. 91-7-1 (July 12, 1991) (the legality of employment of physicians is determined on an individual basis and depends on degree of control exercised).

[37] 42 C.F.R. § 413.65; 65 Fed. Reg. 18538 (Apr. 7, 2000).

[38] *See Medicare Carriers Manual* § 2050. Billable incident services are those that are: (1) "an integral, although incidental, part of the physician's professional service," § 2050.1; (2) "commonly rendered without charge or included in the physician's bill," § 2050.1A; (3) "of a type that are commonly furnished in physician's offices or clinics," § 2050.1A; and (4) "furnished by the physician or by auxiliary personnel under the physician's direct supervision," § 2050.1B.

State certificate of need (CON) issues may also need to be reviewed if the IDS operates in a state that has CON laws that affect the transaction.[39] Certain states have CON laws which require a state health department's approval prior to a health care entity providing certain types of activities within the state. For example, a CON may be necessary for the acquisition of health care facilities, construction or renovation of facilities, or the acquisition of specialized health care equipment (e.g., lithotripter or magnetic resonance imagining equipment). CON laws were initially enacted to discourage overbuilding of health care entities (i.e., an ASC on every corner, a hospital on every major street), as well as to ensure that facilities that provide highly technical services, such as organ transplant procedures and open-heart surgery, can provide a sufficient volume of those services in order to obtain proficiency and ensure quality. Thus, the CON laws limit the number of facilities constructed within the state, as well as the types of procedures that can be performed. State law should be reviewed to determine whether a CON law exists, and what impact the CON law would have on the proposed transaction.

In summary, each IDS formation and transaction is unique. Thus, a myriad of legal issues may influence how the IDS is structured in order to comply with all applicable federal and state laws. All of these laws (and others, depending on the specifics) should be reviewed during the structuring phase of the transaction.

12.4.2 Physician/Hospital Organizations

Physician/hospital organizations (PHOs) were created in the early 1990s by hospitals that were interested in establishing a bond with physicians in order to offer an attractive, full-service provider product to managed-care payers, third-party administrators, and employers. A PHO can be structured in various ways, but it is typically structured by creating a new entity that is jointly owned by physicians and a hospital. Customarily, a PHO is established either as a for-profit corporation, a partnership, or a limited liability company.

Historically, the specialty physicians (e.g., cardiologists, surgeons, anesthesiologists, radiologists) were not offered ownership in the PHO; rather, the PHO would contract with such physicians to provide that type of specialty medical services to the PHO's patients. Specialty physicians are typically not offered ownership opportunities in the PHO because, unlike primary care physicians, a specialist usually does not manage care in the same way a primary care physician does. Specialists typically may not have regular appointments with a patient, and thus do not monitor a patient's care in a general fashion. Specialty physicians are not deemed to be "gatekeepers," as primary care physicians are in the managed care environment. For example, a primary care physician sees a patient and determines whether the patient should be sent to a gastroenterologist. The primary care physician has the opportunity to try to keep the patient well so that she will not have to be referred to a specialist; the physician's goal is to eliminate an unnecessary referral to a specialist when it is not medically necessary. This is one of the basic premises concerning the economics of managed care: if primary care physicians properly manage the care of their patients and keep their patients healthy, then patients should need fewer services from specialty physicians and ancillary providers, as well as fewer hospital inpatient and emergency room visits.

---

[39] *See, e.g.*, ALA. CODE § 22-21-260; CAL. HEALTH & SAFETY CODE § 127170; OHIO REV. CODE ANN. § 3702.51.

Once formed, the PHO would then contract directly with managed-care plans, which would now have a "one-stop-shopping" type of arrangement with the PHO: In one contract, the managed care plan simultaneously arranges for the PHO provision of hospital tertiary-care services, primary care services, and specialty-physician services. The managed care organization (MCO) would no longer need to enter into several agreements with individual physicians and specialists; instead, the MCO would have an agreement for the entire scope of services from the PHO. Some PHOs also contract with other types of ancillary providers who would, like the specialists, be contract providers to the PHO and not owners of the PHO. Those providers might include nursing homes, HHC providers, and DME suppliers. And everything old is new again as we see the resurgence of the PHO in the concept of ACOs where patients will receive wellness care and incentives to not utilize services and health care providers will financially benefit if they do not render services and keep the patient healthy. Also, PHOs have fallen out of favor since many large hospital systems in the Country have a physician employed model and can negotiate rates on behalf of all of their physician employees without the need of a PHO.

As with all health care transactions, a wide variety of legal issues influence the formation of a PHO. One of the most fundamental legal issues to review is tax concerns. If the hospital is an entity that is deemed to be tax-exempt under federal law (a § 501(c)(3) organization under the Internal Revenue Code), and if the hospital is going to enter into a joint venture with physicians or any other entity to create the PHO, then the tax-exempt hospital must receive a commercially appropriate percentage of the joint-venture vehicle in exchange for its investment in order not to be subject to tax penalties or loss of tax-exempt status.

For example, if the hospital provides 50 percent of the capital to establish the PHO, it should receive 50 percent of the partnership or the stock of the PHO, depending on its corporate structure. If it does not receive its fair share of the PHO for its investment, then the IRS may view this as the hospital engaging in private inurement or private benefit by offering the physicians a greater investment portion of the PHO in relation to the physicians' investments. A hospital may be tempted to do this because the physicians may not have the necessary capital, the physicians do not want to borrow funds, or the physicians selected are ones who use the hospital's services and refer a lot of patients to the hospital. Such a transaction, if reviewed by the IRS, could jeopardize the tax-exempt status of the hospital because it would be deemed to have wasted its charitable assets on a private individual or for the benefit of private persons. In such instance, the IRS has the ability to revoke the hospital's tax-exempt status or, pursuant to regulations, the IRS could impose financial sanctions on the hospital[40] for entering into excess-benefit transactions with the physicians. (*See* Chapter 6 for more discussion on private inurement, private benefit, and intermediate sanctions.)

In addition to the necessary tax analysis, the structure of a PHO has to be reviewed to ensure compliance with the Stark laws and the Anti-Kickback Statute. A Stark exception may have to be satisfied if the PHO will provide designated health services (DHS), and if the physicians will refer Medicare and Medicaid patients to the PHO for such DHS. Often a PHO does not directly provide any health care services, but rather is an entity that is created for collective managed-care contracting purposes and not as a provider of services. Instead, the PHO contracts with providers who will render the DHS or other services. Thus, the Stark laws might not apply.

---

[40] 26 U.S.C. § 4958.

If the PHO provides DHS and a Stark exception is not satisfied, then the physician would be precluded from referring Medicare patients for DHS to the PHO. Eleven DHS categories have been established, encompassing a vast array of health care services such as clinical laboratory services, radiology services, and hospital inpatient and outpatient services. The Stark Law sets forth various exceptions, including for ownership arrangements, compensation arrangements, and ownership and compensation arrangements. Because a proposed PHO would involve an ownership arrangement between the hospital and the physicians, and because the physicians would have an ownership interest in the PHO, an ownership exception would need to be satisfied.

Under the Anti-Kickback Statute, the PHO arrangement would be reviewed to determine whether referrals are made between the parties. The analysis will change depending on whether the PHO is also a provider. Nevertheless, the PHO's advisors should review the arrangement and comply with the Anti-Kickback Statute, given that most probably the physicians will refer patients to the hospital. Thus, the arrangement should not be deemed to constitute a kickback to the physicians in exchange for their referrals. An example of a gross violation would be if the PHO's distributions (profits) were allocated based on referrals to the hospital, or if a physician received a PHO percentage distribution disproportionate to her capital investment in the PHO. Therefore, the structure of the PHO should be reviewed, in addition to any other contracts with parties who are referral sources and, thus, implicate the fraud and abuse laws.

Additionally, depending on the structure of the PHO, there may be antitrust implications if there is not sufficient integration of the parties and sharing of risk. The Federal Trade Commission and the Department of Justice look at these factors (in addition to others) to ensure appropriate integration of the PHO. The goal of the PHO is to allow the parties to the PHO, who are competitors, the ability to negotiate jointly reimbursement fees with the MCOs for professional services rendered by the PHO's providers.

Certain PHOs have been formed in part to contract directly with an employer so that the PHO may provide services directly to an employer's employees without the involvement of an insurance company. Many large employers have contracted with PHOs in order to obtain better rates by eliminating the MCO, as well as to establish more control over who are the employer's health care providers. In these arrangements, the employer does not have to be limited to the MCO's providers; instead, the employer can select its own providers. Depending on the employer's expertise, the employer may contract with a third-party administrator (TPA) who would pay the providers' claims, administer the health care plan on behalf of the employer, credential the providers, and provide utilization review services for cost and quality-control measures. This arrangement between an employer and providers is often referred to as direct contracting. When direct contracting is a possibility, employers and PHOs should review their state insurance laws to determine whether the PHO would be deemed to be an insurance entity as a result of having taken on the business of insurance. This analysis usually turns on whether the party has assumed "insurance risk" rather than "business risk," as defined in the particular state's laws. Therefore, the state insurance laws and regulations should be reviewed. Other legal issues that could arise include corporate practice of medicine issues (because of the possible employment by the PHO of physicians), as well as billing and collection issues.

12.4.3 Independent Practice Associations

Similar to a PHO, an Independent Practice Association (IPA) is typically a group of unaffiliated physicians who join together to create an organization for managed-care contracting and administrative-efficiency purposes. (It is important to note that an IPA commonly also will refer to an independent physician association or independent professional association.) IPAs come in many sizes, from several doctors to several hundred doctors. For example, an IPA can be organized in several ways, including as a corporation or a partnership or limited liability company, a physician or a physician group can purchase an equity interest in the IPA and an IPA can enter into a contract with payers to provide physician services to the payer's beneficiaries.

The IPA's participating providers (which either can be limited to owner-physicians of the IPA or expanded to include other health care providers who have contracted with the IPA) agree to provide services to the MCO's beneficiaries. As noted in the earlier discussion of PHO structures, MCOs find contracting with IPAs beneficial because a potentially large group of physicians can serve a large number of the MCO's enrollees as a result. Rather than requiring the MCO to contract with 100 individual doctors, it can enter into *one* contract with the IPA. One downside from the MCO's perspective is that the MCO may now be negotiating this contract with a large entity that has greater bargaining power because of its number of providers. Thus, the IPA may be able to negotiate better terms (e.g., higher reimbursement, definition of what constitutes a covered service) in the managed-care agreements than the individual physician who does not have sufficient bargaining power and often has to sign a form agreement.

Aside from managed-care contracting, some IPAs are also formed to offer administrative services to its provider members. For example, the IPA may provide marketing services, billing and collection services, or supplies and equipment to the IPA's members. An IPA will provide these services hoping to achieve some "economies of scale," as the IPA is able to purchase items or services in larger quantities and then distribute them to its members.

Physician-investors contract with the IPA to provide various services. Additionally, the IPA provides billing and collection services for noninvesting physician groups or individual physicians via contracts in which the physician group pays the IPA for billing and collection services.

Many physicians also participate in IPAs because they want to have the benefits of affiliation (e.g., greater bargaining power in managed-care contracts) without total integration. Thus, with an IPA, the physicians typically still own their separate medical practices, and they continue to provide their professional services in their own practices. The IPA merely provides a vehicle in which unaffiliated parties can unite and enter into a joint venture for specific purposes (e.g., managed-care contracting and group purchasing).

The paramount legal issue that needs to be reviewed when structuring an IPA is the antitrust laws because the potential exists for price fixing whenever unaffiliated parties that are deemed to be competitors join together to negotiate prices amongst themselves in order to offer a fee schedule or payment terms to an MCO. In general terms, however, the antitrust laws allow competitors to share and discuss pricing information if an appropriate level of shared risk and integration exists.[41] If this is the case, then the arrangement may be deemed to be pro-competitive rather than anti-competitive, and may not be deemed to be a violation of the antitrust laws. Hence, when structuring an IPA, a thorough review of the antitrust laws and applicable guidelines must be made. Specifically, the joint FTC and DOJ Antitrust Guidelines for Collaboration Among Competitors should be reviewed.[42]

12.4.4 Professional Corporations

A Professional Corporation (P.C.) is usually a corporation recognized by state statute, allowing professionals of the same or different specialties to join together and form a corporation to provide professional services. If physicians want to integrate more fully than in an IPA model and operate as a single physician practice, then the next step would be for the physicians to create a P.C. In such an arrangement, each physician could be a shareholder of the P.C., in addition to providing professional services on behalf of the P.C. as an employee. Some state statutes prohibit nonprofessionals from directly holding shares in a professional corporation.[43]

Very few sophisticated legal issues affect the structuring of a P.C. Unlike an IPA, for the most part a P.C. does not implicate antitrust issues because the physicians have integrated into one organization; thus, it cannot conspire with itself to set fees. However, a P.C. may pose antitrust concerns if it has so many physician shareholders in the community that it could be considered a monopoly. Additionally, P.C.s in states with corporate practice of medicine statutes should ensure that all of its shareholders are permitted under state law to be shareholders. In the last decade, physicians have been organizing and utilizing a limited liability company structure rather than the P.C. structure for ease of documentation and the ability to "pass through" profits and losses.

The distribution of profits and salaries among the physicians should also be analyzed under the Stark Law and the Anti-Kickback Statute. For example, there could be an anti-kickback problem if one physician in the P.C. is paid a salary that takes into account referrals to other persons in the P.C. or to a hospital[44] Additionally, under this hypothetical situation, if the P.C. provides DHS (e.g., clinical lab service), then the Stark exception for in-office ancillary services would probably not be satisfied due to the fact that the P.C. probably does not satisfy the Stark definition of a group practice, as compensation is based on referrals.[45] Thus, this arrangement would also create a Stark problem. Lastly, many states have created their own state statutory versions of the Stark and Anti-Kickback Laws.[46]

---

[41] *See* U.S. Department of Justice and Federal Trade Commission, Statement of Antitrust Enforcement Policy in Health Care 61 (1996), *available at* https://www.justice.gov/sites/default/files/atr/legacy/2007/08/15/1791.pdf (Statement 8 - Physician Network Joint Ventures).

[42] Federal Trade Commission and the U.S. Department of Justice, Antitrust Guidelines for Collaboration Among Competitors (2000), *available at* https://www.ftc.gov/sites/default/files/documents/public_events/joint-venture-hearings-antitrust-guidelines-collaboration-among-competitors/ftcdojguidelines-2.pdf.

[43] *See, e.g.*, Ohio Rev. Code Ann. § 1701.01 *et. seq.*

[44] The federal government may not deem payments among members in a group practice to violate the Anti-Kickback Statute if the organization satisfies the definition of a group practice in section 1877(h)(4) of the Social Security Act and the implementing regulations, which is the Stark Law. 42 C.F.R. § 1001.952(p); 64 Fed. Reg. 63518, 63555 (1999).

[45] In the Stark Law regulations and requirement of a group practice, the definition requires "no physician who is a member of the group directly or indirectly receives compensation based on the volume or value of referrals by the physician." 42 U.S.C. § 1395nn(h)(4)(A)(iv).

[46] *See, e.g.*, Kathryn Leaman, Note, *State Anti-kickback Statutes: Where the Action Is*, 9 J. Health Care Compliance 23 (2007).

Therefore, counsel for such practitioners should review the applicable state statutes with respect to any state limitations regarding payments to physicians and other providers.

12.4.5 Management-Services Organizations

A management-services organization (MSO) is an entity that provides various types of administrative and management services to providers in their practices. The types of services offered by MSOs can include billing and collection; credentialing; marketing; insurance; provision of staff support, supplies, and equipment; office space; utilization review; HIPAA compliance; managed care; and other contracting. Many hospitals and IDSs have established MSOs as part of their system to provide services to their physicians and medical staff. Hospitals and IDSs constantly are in search of ways to create a closer bond with these physicians if they have not directly employed them already. Notwithstanding the ACA, there are still many physicians who are not interested in selling their practices to and becoming employees of the IDS. Some physicians have sold practices to the IDSs, only to have the practices sold back to the physicians after the arrangement failed. Many of these physicians wanted to retain their autonomy, and did not desire or trust an employment relationship with the IDS. In other situations, the integration proved to be financially impossible, and the practices were sold back to the physicians. In light of current economic and compliance trends, however, physicians have sought assistance from MSOs and other administrative providers, desiring to purchase various services from an MSO in order to relieve various administrative burdens and for the providers to concentrate on practicing medicine.

From the IDS's viewpoint, this creates a contractual relationship between the physician and the IDS, and perhaps will foster some loyalty of the physician to the IDS and the services it provides. These MSO services can also be offered to other hospitals, clinics, ASCs, nursing homes, and other providers and facilities. Additionally, some providers may choose to purchase one service, while others purchase a wider range of services. In some instances, this contractual arrangement has been a precursor to further integration between the parties. This contractual arrangement thus affords the parties the opportunity to get to know each other and become acquainted with one another's operations before committing to an employment or independent-contractor relationship. Additionally, some MSOs are now also becoming providers of health care services.

As with all other potential arrangements between a hospital or IDS and a physician, the Stark and Anti-Kickback Laws need to be reviewed. For example, the Anti-Kickback Laws established a safe harbor for personal services and management contracts between parties that have a potential referral relationship. In order for an MSO contractual arrangement to fit within the safe harbor, it would have to satisfy all of the criteria of that specific safe harbor.[47] Again, however, even if the MSO contract does not satisfy all seven parts of the safe harbor, it does not mean that the arrangement is illegal; rather, the contract would be subject to scrutiny and might be deemed a violation.

---

[47] The requirements of the personal services and management contracts safe harbor are as follows: (i) the agreement must be in writing and signed by the parties; (ii) the agreement specifies all of the services provided and covers all of the services provided by the agent; (iii) if the services are sporadic, the agreement has a schedule for such services and the resulting charges; (iv) the term of the agreement is for at least one year; (v) the aggregate service charge is set in advance and based on arm's-length negotiations, and does not take into account any referrals of government sponsored patients; (vi) the services under the agreement do not promote or involve a business activity that violates any state or federal law; and (vii) the aggregate services contracted for do not exceed those that are reasonably necessary to accomplish the commercially reasonable business purposes of the services. 42 C.F.R. § 1001.952(d).

With regard to the formation of the MSO, typically these entities are wholly owned by the IDS, a hospital, or a group of physicians. If the MSO is owned by a combination of these participants, then Stark and anti-kickback issues would need to be analyzed to ensure that the ownership investments are proportional to the specific amount invested by each investor, as discussed earlier in this Chapter. For example, if a physician invests only 10 percent of the capital but gets 50 percent ownership of the MSO, then the arrangement likely will lead to an anti-kickback problem, a Stark violation, and/ or potential tax problems (if a charitable entity is involved). Specifically, an anti-kickback problem might result because the government would most probably question the inequity. Specifically, why did the physician receive a 50 percent ownership interest, rather than a 10 percent ownership interest, because the other owners of the MSO offered this extra 40 percent investment interest to the physician in order to encourage her to refer government-sponsored patients to the IDS's facilities?

Similarly, a Stark violation would follow from physician-investor referral of Medicare patients to the MSO for DHS if a Stark ownership exception is not satisfied.

There would also be a tax problem if the IDS is a tax-exempt entity. In such case, the IRS might deem the physician to be an "insider" of the IDS for tax purposes, and *any* amount of benefit given to the physician (e.g., the excess 40 percent ownership interest) would be deemed to be private inurement, which could either jeopardize the tax-exempt status of the IDS and its facilities or allow the IRS to impose intermediate sanctions, the latter of which could include financial penalties on both the physician and the IDS and its managers.

12.5 Key Issues in Structuring Transactions

12.5.1 Purpose of the Venture

Before the parties (and their lawyers, accountants, and consultants) start structuring the transaction and drafting documents to reflect such structure, the parties should make sure that they have reviewed the purposes for the venture. If the parties do not understand what the goals of the venture are and whether they can be satisfied, then perhaps the parties should not enter into the transaction. Some element of risk is always present with a new venture, and it may be impossible to ascertain the possibility or probability of reaching the goals of the venture. In such an instance, perhaps the parties should discuss, earlier rather than later, what will happen if the goals are not satisfied. These issues are discussed more fully in Section 12.6.

12.5.2 Operational Issues

As important as it is to be aware of the purpose of the transaction that is being contemplated, it is just as important to understand the operational issues of the client. For example, if one party wants to ensure that the billing of Medicare services after the closing of the transaction will be handled in a certain manner, then it is important when structuring the transaction to make sure that the operational billing issues of that party are satisfied, or that the party is fully aware of the potential problems or complications. Another example may be that a client wants to employ the physicians as part of the transaction. Therefore, the deal may have to be structured so as not to violate a state prohibition on the corporate practice of medicine or a Medicare billing limitation. Thus, it is important to devote significant time to discussing the key operational issues or goals that the parties hope to resolve or accomplish by entering into the transaction and flush out any legal concerns or challenges at an early stage.

12.5.3   Legal Issues

As was discussed earlier in this Chapter, a myriad of legal issues affect the types of transactions that are available to the parties, and many of these same issues impact structuring the specifics of the transaction. In many instances, health care providers may want to engage in some form of transaction that will not be possible due to legal constraints. For example, many hospitals and physicians want to create a joint venture to share imaging centers or clinical labs. Many such arrangements are impossible to structure, however, without violating the Stark laws and the Anti-Kickback Statute.

In general, hospitals have wanted to enter joint ventures with physicians to create a stronger relationship between the parties, but it is clear that the Stark, fraud and abuse, and tax-exemption laws sometimes make such a transaction illegal, or otherwise create a risky arrangement that could be challenged by governmental authorities. Instead, the parties may have to choose another structure or forego the entire proposed transaction because of the legal prohibitions.

Because of the varied regulatory issues that affect health care transactions, the parties should be aware of the legal issues when initially contemplating the structure of a transaction, so that the parties do not have to change the structure or unwind the transaction due to a violation of applicable laws and regulations. Sometimes providers will structure a transaction and agree on the specifics of the deal only to find out, at a later date, that the transaction is illegal and impossible to restructure in order to comply with existing federal and state laws and regulations. Therefore, it is best to include the legal team in the initial discussions and negotiations of the structure so that the proposed transaction or arrangement complies with applicable federal and state laws.

12.6   Unwinding Transactions

At a stage when the parties are structuring a deal and entering into a new venture, no one wants to focus on issues that may arise if the transaction is unsuccessful. The parties to a transaction are typically optimistic, and do not want to contemplate what should happen if the transaction does not materialize as the parties intended. However, because of this optimism, this is in fact the best time to contemplate and address these very issues: when the parties are not reactive to bad circumstances (and sometimes fueled by anger) but can think rationally and with a goal of minimizing the cost and disruption to their business in the future. It is simply a fact of life that not all transactions will be successful Therefore, the following issues should be discussed and addressed in the transactional documents.

12.6.1   Termination Provisions

If the venture does not roll out as one or both parties intended, then the parties may want to make sure legal means are available to terminate the arrangement. This is typically not an issue if all of the parties mutually consent to terminate the agreement. In the event that only one party wants to terminate, however, this could be a big problem if no termination provisions are included in the governing documents. Transactions involving the acquisition of an entity (either through a merger, stock transaction, or asset transaction) usually cannot be reversed after the transaction closes, and will only be unwound under extraordinary circumstances. In a non-acquisition arrangement (i.e., an affiliation, joint venture, or service agreement), however, the arrangement can easily be terminated if the governing document allows for termination in various circumstances. (*See* Section 12.8 for further discussion on termination provisions.) Even if the agreement provides for termination, the parties may not want to terminate the arrangement without receipt of the assets that they sold or contributed to the venture. Thus, certain agreements contain a repurchase right for the terminating party under certain circumstances and in accordance with specific terms in the agreement.

While it is not unusual in non-acquisition agreements to find certain termination provisions for breach of material terms or certain other specified occurrences, it is also the case that oftentimes one or both parties may terminate the agreement for convenience. This may be considered desirable from the perspective of one or both parties, but it is important to be mindful of the time and money already invested in the integration. Therefore, when determining appropriate convenience termination provisions, careful consideration to these factors should be considered. It may be appropriate in certain circumstances to limit such terminations after a certain amount of time has passed (for example, no party can terminate for convenience until two years have passed), and it may be appropriate for parties to consider why each party may be pushing for a convenience termination provision (for example, is the other side really committed to the arrangement, or do they intend to affiliate for a time and then retire?).

12.6.2 Rights to Repurchase; Repurchase Obligations

In certain transactions, the parties may want to include a provision in the governing documents that sets forth a repurchase right in the event that certain circumstances occur, or if the parties mutually agree to terminate the relationship. The repurchase right may be a compulsory obligation imposed on the party that sold or contributed the asset at the time of termination. The repurchase clause could also be a discretionary right that is given to a terminating party who contributed or sold assets to the venture. In either case, it is best if the governing agreement sets forth the particulars of a buy-back, specifying whether it is a compulsory obligation or discretionary right, the latter of which can be exercised if elected by the former owner of the assets.

The agreement may also delineate the type of event that must occur in order for the repurchase rights or obligations to be triggered. The agreement would also set forth the terms of the repurchase (e.g., purchase price or valuation methodology, timing of transaction, post-transactional issues). If the agreement does not contain a repurchase provision and only one party wants to terminate the contractual relationship, then (notwithstanding a breach, which might allow one party to terminate the agreement and buy back the assets) the other party would not be legally required to sell the assets back to the original seller.

12.6.3 Bankruptcy

In a typical contractual service arrangement, a party is able to terminate the relationship if the other party files for receivership or bankruptcy. This situation might also trigger a contractual right on one party to buy back the business or assets that were originally sold to the purchaser. For example, a P.C. that purchased the assets of a physician's practice and later files for bankruptcy might afford the physician (via her employment agreement with the P.C.) the opportunity to terminate the agreement and repurchase the assets from the P.C. If the terms of the contractual relationship do not afford the other party the right to terminate in such instances, then the parties may be mired in a relationship with a party who is in receivership or in bankruptcy proceedings.

12.7 Types of Health Care Contracts

Written contracts serve to memorialize the understanding and formal agreement between the parties, setting forth all of the details of the arrangement. The written agreement not only clearly defines the terms of the arrangement, but also addresses how to resolve disputes if they arise in the future. The document should address how to resolve such issues based on the agreed-upon terms in the agreement. Parties should be very cautious when using form agreements or documents from a prior transaction because each agreement and arrangement is unique to the specific facts of each situation. Therefore, if a form is used, it may not include, for example, indemnification provisions or other terms that are crucial to one of the parties. Thus, when using a form document, each party should review each term in the agreement to ensure that it is appropriate for the specific deal at hand.

Parties will often spend hours, days, weeks, and months negotiating the agreement. Often, however, certain points that have been agreed to may not be memorialized in the agreement, perhaps due to oversight. Thus, each party should review the agreement carefully to ensure that all agreed-upon points have been incorporated into the agreement in a clear and unambiguous manner.

12.7.1 Employment and Independent Contractor Agreements

In structuring various types of transactions, the arrangement may include the employment of a professional or some other type of contractual relationship. For example, if an IDS has purchased the assets of a physician's practice, then the IDS will usually employ or enter into an independent-contractor relationship with the physician, unless the physician is retiring or moving to another community. The main theoretical difference between employing a physician and merely contracting with the physician as an independent contractor is the amount of control that can be exercised by the employer over the physician. In an employment relationship, the employer is expected to exert control over its employees; in an independent contractor arrangement, on the other hand, the independent contractor performs the services under his or her own direction with very little supervision.

One key contractual element to be aware of in these types of agreements is the section of the agreement that addresses the status of the parties. It should be clearly stated in the agreement whether the parties have entered into an employment or independent-contractor relationship. This is extremely important for tax reasons, as there are severe penalties that can be imposed in the event the Internal Revenue Service determines the status of workers has been misclassified. For example, if the status of the parties is unclear, or the IDS exercises too much control over the physician, then the IRS may deem the relationship to be an employment arrangement, regardless of whether the parties called it an "independent contractor" relationship. In this case, the perceived "employer" would be penalized by the IRS for not withholding taxes, as well as being held responsible for paying all related employment taxes on behalf of the employee. Even if the agreement sets forth that the parties are independent contractors, in the event that the IDS possesses too much control over the physician, the IRS can still find an employment relationship and penalize the "employing" party. The IRS has released guidance on whether someone should be deemed an employee or an independent contractor, and this guidance should be carefully considered based on the specific facts at hand.[48] Some agreements may incorporate a provision that, in the event of a determination by the IRS that one party is deemed to be an employee, the independent contractor will indemnify the other party for all taxes, interest, and penalties imposed by the IRS on the "employer."

Another key provision is the "non-compete" clause or restrictive covenant. This term customarily prohibits a physician or other type of health care provider from providing services for a specific period of time, and within a defined geographical area, during the agreement's term and after the termination or expiration of the agreement. Typically, the geographical area covered by the non-compete clause will surround the location in which the physician or provider rendered services during the term of the agreement.[49] Although legal in some jurisdictions, these provisions are unenforceable in others or are only enforceable if the person agreed to the non-compete as part of a sale of assets or stock.[50] Those jurisdictions that enforce covenants not to compete consider whether the non-compete provision is (i) reasonably limited in time or geographic scope and (ii) serves the purpose of protecting the former employer from unfair competition without being harmful to the public or unduly burdensome to the former employee. (*See* Section 12.8.3 for a further discussion on non-compete clauses.)[51]

---

[48] The most important issue in this determination is the right to control how the services are performed. In 1987, IRS compiled a list of 20 factors based on its examination of court cases and ruling in order to determine whether a worker is an employee. *See* Rev. Rul. 87-41, 1987-1 C.B. 296. These factors are as follows:
1. To what degree does the recipient direct the worker?
2. Does the employer provide training?
3. Is the worker distinguished from the employer's regular employees?
4. Is the work performed characterized by personal service?
5. Are assistants subject to control by the employer?
6. Does the worker provide continuing services for the employer?
7. Are work hours set by the employer?
8. Does the worker devote full time to one employer?
9. Is the work performed at the employer's place of business?
10. Does the employer designate the order or sequence of work to be performed?
11. Is the worker required to submit regular reports?
12. Is the worker paid per time intervals?
13. Does the employer of the services pay business and traveling expenses?
14. Are tools furnished by the employer?
15. Has the worker made significant investments in his or her business?
16. Is the worker exposed to normal profit and loss risks associated with operating a business?
17. Does the worker provide services to more than one employer?
18. Does the worker provide service to the general public?
19. Under what conditions can the worker be fired?
20. Is the worker subject to a breach of contract charge if he or she prematurely terminates the working relation-ship?

More recently, the IRS identified three categories of evidence that may be relevant in determining whether the requisite control exists and has grouped illustrative factors under these categories: behavioral control, financial control, and rela-tion-ship of the parties. Department of the Treasury, Internal Revenue Service, Independent Contractor or Employee? Training Materials, Training 3320-102 (10-96) TPDS 84238I, at 2–7, *available at* https://www.irs.gov/pub/irs-utl/emporind.pdf. This document is publicly available through the IRS website, irs.gov.

[49] *See, e.g., Prairie Eye Center, Ltd. v. Butler*, 768 N.E. 2d 414 (Ill. App. Ct. 2002).

[50] CAL. BUS. & PROF. CODE §§ 16600 & 16601; *see also Edwards v. Arthur Anderson LLP*, 189 P.3d 285, 292 (Cal. 2008) (non-compete contracts are invalid per se unless needed to protect trade secrets).

[51] Additionally, certain states, such as Tennessee, may require a mandatory buy-back be included for non-competes to be enforceable in certain circumstances. *See* Tenn. Code Ann. § 63-2-204(f)(2).

Compensation terms also are often heavily negotiated. When physicians are employed by hospitals and offered a fixed salary, the physician may lose her entrepreneurial spirit and not be as productive for the employer as when she was self-employed. To cure this, hospitals and IDS have tried to incorporate financial incentives in order to encourage the physicians to treat a certain volume of patients, comply with protocols, and watch overhead expenses.[52] Physicians are often compensated for their services based on their RVU production, gross billables, or net collections as well as satisfying quality metrics and patient satisfaction data. Notwithstanding these attempts, hospitals have terminated relationships with physicians on account of a lack of productivity and financial viability. More and more in today's landscape, hospitals and health systems are continually striving to keep physicians from lagging.[53]

In addition to key provisions of an employment or agency agreement, it is also important to be aware of the key legal issues that affect these agreements. For example, in states prohibiting the corporate practice of medicine, a physician cannot be employed by corporations other than professional corporations or other specified entities. Thus, it is important to check the applicable state statutes and determine which entities are legally permitted to employ physicians and other ancillary health care professionals.

Liability concerns may be another reason for structuring an arrangement as either an employment or agency relationship. In an employment relationship, the employer is liable for the acts of its employees. Thus, the employer will purchase and maintain malpractice and general-liability insurance on behalf of its employees. In an independent-contractor arrangement, independent contractors will purchase their own malpractice insurance. In a health care transaction agreement, however, one party may impose an amount and type of insurance that must be acquired and maintained by an independent contractor. Notwithstanding the foregoing, cases abound in which one party may be held liable for the acts of its independent contractors because of a presumed employment arrangement. This liability, which is imposed on one party, is referred to as "respondent superior."[54] A specific example is when a hospital is held liable for the acts of its independently contracted emergency room physicians.[55]

---

[52] A 2009 survey found that "seventy percent of physicians employers have incentive based compensation." Sullivan, Cotter and Associates, *Physician Compensation Survey Reveals Shrinking Income Gap Between Primary Care and Specialty Physicians* (May 5, 2010, 08:57 AM), *available at* http://www.marketwired.com/press-release/Physician-Compensation-Survey-Reveals-Shrinking-Income-Gap-Between-Primary-Care-Specialty-1160289.htm. Fifty-four percent of organizations used measurements based on quality or patient satisfaction. *Id.*

[53] For additional information on changing models and the continued search for new payment models, *see* Wolk and Apple, Building *a Better Physician Compensation and Performance Model*, NEJP Catalyst (Sept. 13, 2017), which may be found at https://catalyst.nejm.org/building-a-better-physician-compensation-and-performance-model/; *see also Changing How Doctors Get Paid*, Modern Healthcare (Mar. 11, 2017), which may be found at http://www.modernhealthcare.com/article/20170311/MAGAZINE/303119983 and *How 4 organizations are shaking up physician compensation*, The Advisory Board (Mar. 14, 2017), which may be found at https://www.advisory.com/daily-briefing/2017/03/14/physician-compensation.

[54] "Generally, an employer or principal is vicariously liable for the torts of its employees or agents under the doctrine of *respondeat superior*, but not for the negligence of an independent contractor over whom it retained no right to control the mode and manner of doing the contracted-for work." *Clark v. Southview Hosp. & Family Health Ctr.*, 628 N.E.3d 46, 48 (Ohio 1994).

[55] In *Clark*, the court reviewed various factors in making its determination that the hospital is liable for the acts of its independent contractors. *Id.* at 54. Two factors that the court reviewed in making its determination were that the hospital held itself out as a provider of a full range of medical services, and that no evidence was present that the patient was

Other legal issues that need to be reviewed include the Stark laws and the Anti-Kickback Statute. The compensation paid to the physician needs to be reviewed to ensure that a Stark exception is satisfied, given that the physician probably will refer patients to the employer for DHS. If no referrals are made, then Stark will not apply. Similarly, the Anti-Kickback Statute needs to be reviewed to ensure that the compensation paid to the provider is not deemed to be a kickback to encourage the physician to refer patients to the employer.[56] Stark laws and the Anti-Kickback Statute alike feature exceptions and safe harbors for employment and agency relationships.[57]

12.7.2 Physician Recruitment Agreements

One common type of health care arrangement is a physician recruitment agreement. A physician recruitment contract is usually between a physician and an IDS, a hospital, or physician practice group. The recruitment agreement provides for a physician to be recruited, to relocate, or to remain in a certain community after completing a residency in exchange for certain financial benefits, which either are delineated in the recruitment agreement or offered to a practicing physician that may be relocating. These agreements are usually made between the physician in question and a hospital, rather than other forms of health care providers, because community hospitals often need to recruit primary-care physicians or certain specialists in order to provide a full range of health care services to the community, as well as the fact that they have the funds to offer recruitment and relocation incentives.

A hospital may enter into a recruitment agreement with an oncologist, for example, if a demonstrable need exists for an oncologist in the hospital's community. Typically, these agreements will offer the physician certain financial perks for accepting the agreement. For example, if the physician relocates and practices in the community for a specific number of years, she may be offered a signing bonus, relocation expenses, malpractice insurance, or a guaranteed amount of compensation for a specific time period. Often, these agreements contain provisions that obligate the physician to repay some of these financial incentives in the event that the physician leaves the community before the time frame set forth in the agreement. It is important to note, however, that these agreements are neither employment arrangements nor service agreements where the physician provides services to

---

informed or knew that the emergency care was being rendered by an independent contractor who merely used the site to provide services and was not an employee. *Id.* at 53.

[56] For example, in 2010, the Health Alliance, and one of its former members, Christ Hospital, settled an Anti-Kickback suit brought by a whistleblower and joined by the Justice Department, for $108 million. Mary Vanac, *Cincinnati Health Alliance, Christ Hospital Settle Suit for $108M*, MEDCITY NEWS (May 21, 2010, 4:20 PM), https://medcitynews.com/2010/05/cincinnati-health-alliance-christ-hospital-settle-suit-for-108m/. The suit alleged that the hospital violated the Anti-Kickback Statute by remunerating doctors for referring cardiac patients to the hospital in a "pay-to-play" scheme. The suit further alleged that the scheme violated the False Claims Act because any claim filed to Medicare or Medicaid as a result of an illegal kickback constitutes a violation of that act. Because Christ Hospital refused to enter into a Corporate Integrity Agreement in conjunction with the settlement, the U.S. Department of Health and Human Services was considering dropping Christ Hospital from Medicare and Medicaid reimbursement. *See Christ Hospital Could Lose Medicare, Medicaid Reimbursement*, CINCINNATI BUSINESS COURIER (May 28, 2010), *available at* https://www.bizjournals.com/cincinnati/stories/2010/05/24/daily58.html. The Corporate Integrity Agreement would have permitted additional government oversight of the hospital. *Id.*

[57] With respect to the Stark laws, please see the Social Security Act 1877 § 1877(e)(2) and (3). 42 U.S.C. § 1395nn. For fraud and abuse topics please see 42 C.F.R. § 1001.952(d) and (i).

the other contracting party. Instead, these agreements set forth some minimum qualifications that the physician must satisfy in order to be entitled to such recruitment incentives.

Various legal issues need to be reviewed before entering into a recruitment agreement. The Stark laws and their implementing regulations need to be reviewed to ensure that a compensation exception is satisfied, due to the fact that the physician will most likely make referrals of patients to the contracting party (i.e., the hospital or IDS). The fraud and abuse laws also should be reviewed to make sure that there is no requirement to refer patients in exchange for the benefits, and that the physician has been legitimately recruited. There is a practitioner-recruitment safe harbor, but it is limited to practitioners who are recruited to work in a "health professional shortage area."[58] Thus, if the physician is being recruited to work in an area that is not recognized as a health professional shortage area, then this safe harbor does not lend any specific protection.

Additionally, if the recruiting party is federally recognized as a tax-exempt entity, then the remuneration offered to the physician must be reviewed to make sure that it is not deemed to be a private inurement or an arrangement that constitutes an excess benefit, which is subject to IRS intermediate sanctions. In general, the remuneration offered to the physician under all of these federal laws (Stark, fraud and abuse, and tax) require that the compensation be reasonable and independent of any referrals by the physician to the other party. Additionally, the benefits should represent fair market value for the value of relocating the physician to the community (or, alternatively, for the benefit to be gained by the physician relocating to the area). Because there may not be any services provided by the physician in a recruitment agreement, the value of the physician moving to the community and staying for an amount of time agreed upon by the parties should be valued to determine whether the payment is appropriate and not a violation of these laws.

12.7.3 Management and Service Agreements

Due to the integration and consolidation of health care providers, a myriad of management and service agreements have developed. For example, if a hospital purchases a physician's practice but does not employ the physician, then the hospital may enter into a service agreement with the physician to provide professional medical services to the hospital's practice. Alternatively, if the hospital was not able to purchase the physician's practice (perhaps because the physician did not want to sell the practice or because the hospital did not want to own the physician's practice), then the hospital might offer management services to the physician's practice, either directly or through a subsidiary organization. In any of these situations, the hospital and the physician must enter into some form of a services agreement.

---

[58] This safe harbor only applies to practitioners working in their specialties for less than one year or relocating their practices. Additionally, the practitioner must be relocating to a health professional shortage area (HPSA). There are nine standards to the safe harbor: (1) the agreement must be in writing and signed by the parties; (2) 75 percent of the revenues of the new practice must be generated from new patients; (3) benefits can only be offered for a maximum of three years, and the terms of the agreement cannot be renegotiated during the term of the agreement; (4) there can be no requirement to refer, and the recruiting entity can require the physician to maintain privileges at its facility; (5) the entity cannot restrict the practitioner from obtaining privileges elsewhere; (6) the benefits offered to the physician do not vary based on volume or value of referrals; (7) there is an agreement to treat all federal health care beneficiaries in a nondiscriminatory manner; (8) at least 75 percent of revenues of the new practice must be generated from persons residing in a HPSA or medically underserved area, or be part of a medically underserved population; and (9) the payment can only be to a practitioner and not to any other person or entity in position to make or influence referrals to recruiting entity. 42 C.F.R. § 1001.952(n).

Many physicians prefer these arrangements because they allow physicians to dedicate their time to the practice of medicine while a third party provides the administrative services. Some management-service agreements may provide the physician with all nonprofessional administrative services. Thus, the physician has what is commonly referred to as a "turnkey" operation: the physician merely enters the premises and provides her professional services; meanwhile, the management company provides all of the other services as the physician's independent contractor. For example, the management company provides office space and personnel, billing and collection services, medical-records maintenance, compliance with laws including HIPAA, supplies, malpractice insurance, contracting, and all other services.

In other arrangements, the physician might contract with the entity for one or two specific services. Often physicians will contract with a third party to provide billing and collection services because many companies specialize in physician coding and billing. Additionally, many hospitals have contracted with third parties to outsource various services that the hospitals had traditionally provided in-house. Some of these services include billing and collection, food services, laundry, housekeeping, cafeteria, pharmacy, plant operations, equipment maintenance, credentialing of physicians, and the like. Many hospitals also are interested in outsourcing maintenance services. Because of the different types of relationships, there are many different types of service and management arrangements among health care providers and health care-service entities.

The key terms in a service or management contract are contained in the section that delineates all of the services to be provided and what the payment is for such services. Other important provisions include hold-harmless provisions, in which one party agrees to hold the other party harmless for its acts and the acts of its employees. Thus, it is important to have a clear delineation of what services each party provides so that a hold-harmless provision is meaningful. For example, if the third party provides billing and collection services, then the billing company may agree in the contract to hold the physician practice harmless for its billing errors if the activity was that of the third party. Other key provisions include malpractice-insurance requirements and ownership of medical records, especially if a third party is hired to maintain them.

Several legal issues will need to be reviewed when structuring management and service agreements. Depending on the parties to the contract and the services being contracted for, the following laws should be reviewed. Antitrust laws may be implicated if the entities will provide managed-care contracting services. If such services are provided for in the contract, then the contract may be prohibited if not structured properly because the parties may not be appropriately integrated and may be deemed competitors. Therefore, a thorough review of the antitrust laws (and especially the antitrust guidelines for the health care industry) must be undertaken. Stark and fraud and abuse implications will also need to be reviewed (in addition to tax laws, if at least one of the entities is tax-exempt). Additionally, certain Medicare and Medicaid rules and regulations may affect the contractual arrangement depending on the structure of the contract. For example, certain regulations must be satisfied in order for a physician to be able to reassign her right to a third party to bill the Medicare program for her services.[59]

---

[59] This Medicare regulation permits a physician the right to reassign to a third party his or her right to bill and collect from the Medicare program for services rendered by the physician. Some of the permittable assignees include the

12.7.4 Merger and Acquisition Agreements

In acquisition and merger agreements, various terms are essential to the arrangement. In a merger agreement, in which one entity will be subsumed by the other, one essential provision is determining which entity will be the surviving corporation. The merger agreement generally will set forth the surviving corporation, along with which governance documents apply and who will be the officers of the surviving corporation. Even though one corporation is chosen as the surviving corporation, however, that in itself does not mean that all of that corporation's operations will stay intact. For example, the parties may still negotiate and incorporate into the merger agreement the identities of the officers of the newly merged company, especially because mergers usually result in redundancies in officers (e.g., two chief executive officers, two chief financial officers, etc.). All of these issues, in addition to any other major post-merger operational issues, should be addressed specifically in the merger agreement.

In acquisition documents, the parties should clearly set forth in the agreement whether the Buyer is purchasing the stock or assets of the target company. As was discussed in Section 12.3.1, if the target company is a nonprofit entity, then members of the corporation rather than shareholders, are the "owners;" further, if the Buyer is purchasing the entire business of the nonprofit target company, then the transaction is often referred to as a member substitution transaction. Because no stock purchase is involved, the acquisition document will reflect that the Buyer is becoming the sole member of the target company. Thus, the previous members of the target company cease to exist as members and are replaced by the Buyer.

Naturally, the amount of the purchase price and how it will be paid are also important terms in acquisition agreements. Many entities will obtain an independent appraisal of the assets being acquired from a qualified independent appraiser, which serves to establish and reflect the fair market value of the business being purchased.[60] With regard to the payment terms, some agreements may have the Buyer withhold a portion of the purchase price for a period of time after the closing of the transaction. For example, the Buyer may withhold a portion of the purchase price to cover some potential anticipated liabilities of the target company. After a certain amount of time following the closing, the Buyer would remit that amount to the Seller if those liabilities did not materialize and/ or become a debt of the Buyer. If the transaction is an acquisition of assets, then the Buyer wants to be precise concerning what assets and liabilities it is assuming. This is also an important issue for

---

employer of the physician, the hospital, or other facility where the services are provided in which there is a contractual arrangement between the physician and facility that allows the facility to submit such bills, and to an entity that provides coverage of the services under a health benefits plan. 42 U.S.C. § 1395u(b)(6).

[60] The Office of the Inspector General (OIG) has expressed concern with hospitals acquiring physician practices if the amount of the purchase price exceeds the value of the acquired stock or assets. The OIG believes that such excess amount could be paid to the physician in order to encourage the physician to refer patients to the hospital after the closing is complete. According to a December 22, 1992, letter from D. McCarty Thornton, DHHS General Counsel's Office, to T.J. Sullivan, IRS:

> Merely because another buyer may be willing to pay a particular price is not sufficient to render the price paid to be fair market value. The fact that a buyer, in a position to benefit from referrals, is willing to pay a particular price may only be a reflection of the value of the referral shown that is likely to result from the purchase.

D. McCarty Thornton, Letter to Mr. T.J. Sullivan (Dec. 22, 1992), https://oig.hhs.gov/fraud/docs/safeharborregulations/acquisition122292.htm.

the target company because liabilities that are not assumed by the Buyer will remain the responsibility of the Seller. Thus, it is important to clearly delineate which liabilities will remain the legal responsibility of the Seller.

Another key provision may be the acquisition of the Seller's Medicare billing provider agreement and billing number. If the Buyer assumes such number, then it is also assuming the liability for all prior inappropriate or false claims made by the Seller in its billing activities.[61] For these reasons, many deals are structured so as not to assume the Medicare billing agreement and number, instead choosing to either use the Buyer's existing number or have the Buyer apply for a new Medicare number. One problem with trying to obtain a new Medicare billing number is that it can take several months before Medicare issues the number. This may lead to financial constraints on the Buyer, due to the fact that it likely would be rendering services already and would be unable to bill for them until receipt of the Medicare number. Additionally, often a provider is precluded from billing for services which were rendered prior to survey and certification. All of this is dependent upon the type of provider number being requested. Therefore, it is necessary to check the specific terms required for a Medicare provider agreements and numbers.

Other important terms in an acquisition agreement are the representations and warranties. Representations are descriptions by each of the parties about their company, assets, employees, filings, etc. These representations are usually made by both parties; however, the Seller usually gives more exhaustive representations than the Buyer because the majority of the representations address the Seller's knowledge regarding its business, in addition to the condition of its assets and potential liabilities. For example, the Seller will represent to the Buyer that the assets are in good condition, no environmental problems exist regarding the property, no liens have been made on the property or the assets, no unions or threats of unionization exist, and no litigation is pending. Parties will usually give such representations with a caveat that the representations are true except as set forth on a schedule to the agreement, or are given pursuant to a "best effort" or "good-faith" basis. Any such schedule(s) would then delineate, for example, all of the threatened or pending litigation claims against the Seller. In the event that one of the representations is untrue and the Buyer finds this out after the closing of the transaction, then the Buyer would be able to seek damages as permitted in the indemnification provisions, which are discussed further in Section 12.8.1. In fact, the American Bar Association's Business Law Section has declared:

> Bare representations, if false, may support claims in tort and for federal securities act violations [if applicable] and also claims for breach of an implied warranty, breach of an implied promise that a representation is true, or breach of an express warranty if the description is basic to the bargain.[62]

In addition to the myriad of contractual terms that make up an acquisition agreement, several legal terms affect mergers and acquisitions. Antitrust laws must be reviewed in both merger and

---

[61] In *Vernon*, discussed above, the acquiring entity was held liable for the billing activities of the predecessor company because the billing number was one of the assets acquired. *United States v. Vernon Home Health, Inc.*, 21 F.3d 693 (5th Cir. 1994); *see also Deerbrook Pavilion, LLC v. Shalala*, 235 F.3d 1100 (8th Cir. 2000) (finding successor nursing home liable for civil monetary penalties incurred by predecessor under the same Medicare provider agreement).

[62] American Bar Association, Business Law Section, *Model Stock Purchase Agreement* 47 (1995).

acquisition transactions, as was discussed earlier in this Chapter. Some states have premerger notice or approval requirements that mandate that an entity not merge or be acquired without state notice or approval.[63] Additionally, depending on the specifics of the transaction, securities laws, tax issues, fraud and abuse, Stark laws, and Medicare reimbursement laws and regulations may be applicable to the transaction (among other potentially applicable laws). Acquisitions and mergers are very fact-specific situations and, depending on the specific structure, could require the review of various laws at the federal and state level.

12.7.5 Affiliation Agreements

This type of agreement is used to create an affiliation between parties. As stated earlier in this Chapter, many hospitals enter into affiliation agreements with other hospitals or physician groups because they are not prepared to merge, sell, or be acquired. Thus, the parties enter into an affiliation agreement as an intermediate transitional step. Because most of these affiliation agreements have no specific clauses that trigger further integration (e.g., there is no clause which requires a merger or acquisition at a specific future date), these agreements often are ignored. For certain entities, these agreements nevertheless provide an opportunity for parties to affiliate and discuss potential future integration options.

Because most affiliation agreements are unique, no standard terms or forms exist. Nevertheless, all affiliation agreements should set forth the purpose for the affiliation. Additionally, an expiration date should be specified for the affiliation. Perhaps such an expiration (i.e., the affiliation exists only for a two-year period) will encourage the parties to commence merger, acquisition, or next-step negotiations.

Depending on the specifics of the affiliation, various legal issues may be implicated. For example, if the parties are affiliating to negotiate managed-care contracts with managed-care payers, then such affiliation needs to be reviewed under the antitrust laws to ensure that the affiliation arrangement is not deemed to be a conspiracy between competitors, which would make it illegal for such persons to share pricing information and negotiate fees jointly. Other laws may apply to the affiliation arrangement based on the specific terms of the affiliation.

12.8 Termination of Agreements

Parties often exclusively focus on entering into an agreement and/or closing the merger or acquisition. Parties rarely focus on the potential termination of the transaction or what to do if the deal fails, and one party wants to terminate the relationship or unwind the transaction. Termination, exit, repayment, and post-termination provisions are key aspects of all acquisition agreements. It is

---

[63] *See, e.g.*, OH. REV. CODE. ANN. § 109.34(B) (requiring the approval of the Ohio Attorney General if a for-profit entity acquires a nonprofit hospital or HMO). Under Ohio law, the nonprofit must provide the Attorney General with certain information, including the names of the parties and the terms of the transactions. *Id.* Different notification rules apply when both parties to the transaction are tax-exempt nonprofits. OH. REV. CODE. ANN. § 109.34 (G). Certain states may also have Certificate of Need laws, which require state approval before acquisitions can be completed. *See generally Certificate of Need State Laws*, NATIONAL CONFERENCE OF STATE LEGISLATIONS (August 25, 2016), *available at* http://www.ncsl.org/research/health/con-certificate-of-need-state-laws.aspx (providing an overview of which states have Certificate of Need laws).

important for the parties to discuss these issues relating to the termination of the transaction when structuring deals. By requiring the parties to focus some of their time and attention on defining the parties' responsibilities if the transaction is terminated, the parties may be able to avoid disputes and potential litigation in the future. In some situations (i.e., a merger), there are no longer two corporations. Hence, it may be virtually impossible to undo the transaction. With respect to a member substitution, on the other hand, the parties could enter into an agreement to undo what the "member substitution" transaction had accomplished earlier. Thus, the acquiring member could decide to end its membership, and the corporation put in place a new member. In the case of a hospital acquisition of a physician's practice, the hospital could resell the assets or stock back to the physician and/or terminate the professional service arrangement between the two parties.

Some parties commit the fatal flaw of not including a way—or enough ways—in which a party can terminate an agreement. For example, the agreement may only permit termination by a party in the event of bankruptcy, loss of license or accreditation, death, or permanent disability. The physician in the situation, however, may want to have the right to terminate the agreement immediately on account of nonpayment of the physician's salary. Thus, the parties should try to anticipate what types of complications may occur in the future, and draft appropriate termination and post-termination provisions. For example, in an acquisition document, the parties may want to set forth the purchase price in the event of a repurchase of the assets by the Seller.

Various other terms in an agreement become important after the termination or expiration of the agreement. A sound agreement addresses not only issues during the term, but also for certain actions after the agreement has expired or terminated. This section presents a brief discussion of some of those terms.

The following are some terms that only become important after the closing of a transaction, but that must be given great consideration during negotiations.

12.8.1 Indemnification Provisions

Indemnification clauses are traditionally part of a stock or asset transaction. An indemnification provision provides that, if one of the representations and warranties made by a Seller is false, then the Buyer who relied on such representation or warranty can seek indemnification for the resultant damages incurred by the Buyer. This indemnification is sought from the party who made the false statement. For example, in an asset acquisition, a physician may buy assets from another physician. One of the assets could include real property. Typically, in transactions with real property, the Buyer will conduct an investigation of the property regarding title and environmental issues. In addition, the Buyer may also want the Seller to give a real estate representation. This representation may set forth that, to the best of the Seller's knowledge, there are no defects in the title or any claims made by a third party against the property (including liens), and that the property does not contain any environmental hazards or toxic substances. If, after the closing, the Buyer discovers underground leaking storage tanks that must be removed, then the Buyer will seek to recover its costs from the Seller for cleaning the property pursuant to the indemnification provisions in the acquisition agreement. The Buyer will have a right to recover its costs for cleaning the property from the Seller because the Seller breached the real estate representation contained in the acquisition agreement by failing to disclose the presence of leaking underground storage tanks to the Buyer. Notwithstanding the existence of indemnification clauses, disputes may arise concerning which party is actually responsible for the acts or omissions that resulted in the damages.

Indemnification clauses are written in various ways. Typically, however, they contain a survival clause or a time limit. Thus, a party may be able to seek indemnification for a period of three years after the closing date. Hence, in our hypothetical situation, if the physician becomes aware of the tanks four years after the closing date, then the Seller is not contractually obligated to indemnify the Buyer. Additionally, the parties may agree to limit the amount of indemnification that one party can seek to recover from the other party. For example, the amount of indemnification may be capped at the amount of the purchase price of the assets. Some indemnification clauses incorporate minimum thresholds (i.e., floor) that must be reached before one party can bring a claim for indemnification against the other party. This requirement eliminates one party seeking indemnification for an immaterial matter.

In a member substitution or a merger, the Seller either ceases to exist or becomes part of the Buyer; no corporate entity "Seller" remains from which a Buyer may seek indemnification. In certain situations where a charitable Seller was involved, the purchase price may be paid to a foundation that is established by the former members of the entity merged out of existence.[64] In exchange for the purchase price, the former members may guarantee the representations and warranties contained in the acquisition agreement and indemnify the Buyer. For example, in a transaction where a for-profit hospital chain has acquired a nonprofit hospital, the nonprofit hospital converts to a for-profit hospital and becomes part of the for-profit hospital chain. It would be meaningless for the nonprofit hospital to indemnify the for-profit chain due to the fact that, once the closing occurs, the nonprofit hospital is *part* of the for-profit chain. If the for-profit hospital paid the purchase price to a foundation or other third party, however, and such entity also provided the representations to the Buyer, then the foundation or third party may agree to indemnify the Buyer for any breach of the representations and warranties contained in the acquisition agreement.

12.8.2 Confidentiality and Ownership of Records

These provisions usually codify that certain parties are obligated to maintain the confidentiality of all records, which may include business and medical records. Additionally, ownership of the records after the termination or expiration needs to be addressed in the agreement.

Confidentiality provisions are important, especially in professional service contractual arrangements. For example, a clinic may employ a physician for a five-year period to provide professional medical services to the clinic. When the five-year period expires, the physician leaves the clinic. At this time, a dispute may arise between the parties concerning ownership or access to the medical records. Thus, it is important in this type of arrangement (where medical records are created and maintained

---

[64] *See, e.g.*, Andrew Wineke, *Memorial Sale Could Create Heavy-Hitting Health Charity*, THE GAZETTE (June 16, 2010), *available at* http://www.gazette.com/articles/health-100369-mean-few.html (reporting that the Colorado Attorney General stated that the proceeds of the sale of a city-owned hospital would have to be used for charitable purposes in accordance with the state's Hospital Transfer Act). These foundations may also be given a right of first refusal if the for-profit hospital wishes to sell the formerly nonprofit hospital or a substantial part of the hospital. *See, e.g., Found. for Seacoast Health v. HCA Health Services of New Hampshire, Inc.*, 953 A.2d 420 (N.H. 2008) (discussing the foundation's right to first refusal created by acquisition agreement).

during the contract) to incorporate an explicit provision in the agreement that sets forth who owns the medical records after the termination or expiration of the agreement. Additionally, if the clinic maintains the records, then the physician or the physician's counsel may want to ensure that the clinic (and its employees, agents, and the like) maintain the confidentiality of those records and to provide the physician with access to such records to defend herself for audits, etc. It is necessary to review state law to determine whether a statutory requirement exists for certain parties to maintain the confidentiality of the medical records, in addition to the HIPAA federal privacy restrictions.

Problems could arise if a clinic maintains the records without a confidentiality requirement, and if state law does not require such entity to maintain the confidentiality of such records. The clinic might then disclose the medical record information to third parties. Because a privileged relationship exists between the patient and the physician (and not necessarily between the patient and the clinic) in many states, the physician may be subject to liability claims brought by the patient claiming that the physician owed the patient the duty to maintain the confidentiality of the medical records. Notwithstanding these state laws, the federal HIPAA regulations require all types of health care providers to maintain the confidentiality of all patient records.

Notwithstanding the HIPAA regulations, it is advisable to incorporate a contractual clause that requires all parties, at all times, to maintain the confidentiality of the medical records, limit disclosure of such information, and perhaps even incorporate a provision to protect other *business* information of the parties that is disclosed during the relationship. If a clinic was contractually obligated to maintain the confidentiality of the records, and if the clinic disclosed the records to a third party, then the physician would have recourse against the clinic for breach of contract for violating the confidentiality provision. Parties are currently addressing confidentiality by having a provision which requires the parties to comply with HIPAA.

12.8.3 Non-Compete and Non-Interference Clauses

These clauses are very important in professional agreements and acquisition transactions. A non-compete provision or a restrictive covenant usually prohibits a person (for the term of the agreement and for a certain period of time after the termination or expiration of the agreement) from providing similar services as those set forth in the agreement. Usually, these provisions have a geographic and time limitation, as well as a specific limitation with respect to the certain services provided. For example, a hospital who employs a physician may include a non-compete provision in the employment agreement so that, for a period of one year after the termination or expiration of the agreement, the physician cannot provide professional medical services within the same city, county, or within a ten-mile radius of the employer hospital. Further, certain services may be excluded from the covenant because the party had been providing such service prior to entering into the agreement that contains the restrictive covenant. For example, an emergency room physician may have an exclusive arrangement with Hospital A, and has agreed to a covenant not to compete with Hospital A, but with a caveat that allows such physician to provide services to Hospital B in recognition of the fact that the physician rendered services to Hospital B prior to entering into the agreement which contained the restrictive covenant.

Although some states have upheld the legality of non-compete clauses for physicians and other medical professionals,[65] other states find such provisions to be illegal and unenforceable.[66] In a Massachusetts case, the physician employment contract did not contain a non-compete provision, but a specific dollar penalty was imposed if the physician were to practice in a certain area after the expiration of the agreement.[67] The court found this provision to be unenforceable and likening it to a non-compete provision, which would be prohibited in that jurisdiction.[68] The court noted that the state favors the public interest in allowing patients to choose their physicians over the benefit to the medical profession in upholding covenants not to compete.[69]

Non-compete clauses are also common in transactions where an entire business is purchased and the Buyer wants to prohibit the Seller from practicing or operating a similar business in the same marketplace for a specific period of time after the closing of the transaction.

Non-diversion and non-solicitation clauses, on the other hand, basically prohibit a party from contacting the other party's employees, agents, customers, and patients after the expiration or termination of the agreement. As with restrictive covenants, these provisions usually have a specific timeframe as to when the non-diversion and non-solicitation applies. These provisions typically are not as controversial or litigated as a covenant not to compete. These provisions nevertheless are customary and necessary in certain industries. For example, in managed-care contracting, MCOs often include a non-diversion provision so that their providers cannot solicit the MCOs' beneficiaries after the expiration of the agreement. Often, the physician will want to send a notice to his or her patients to alert them that the physician participates in other managed care plans, or provide similar notifications. Perhaps some of these patients would be willing to switch health plans in order to be treated by the same physician. Customarily, however, a non-diversion and non-solicitation clause would prohibit the physician from sending such letters.

These post-termination provisions are only a sampling but represent some of the more important post-termination issues that may be incorporated into an agreement. Depending on the specific situation, facts, parties, and their goals, however, other post-termination provisions are also important, including billing and collection post-closing, arbitration, and final payment issues.

12.9 Current Climate of Health Care Transactions and Contracting

As was discussed in the introduction to this Chapter, for over three decades, health care organizations and providers have been in a merger and acquisition "mania" to partner together. This

---

[65] *See, e.g., Prairie Eye Center, Ltd. v. Butler*, 768 N.E. 2d 414 (Ill. App. Ct. 2002); *Bollengier v. Gulati*, 233 A.D.2d 721 (N.Y. App. Div. 1996).
[66] *See, e.g.*, CAL. BUS. & PROF. CODE § 16600 (stating that "every contract by which anyone is restrained from engaging in a lawful profession, trade, or business of any kind is to that extent void"); COLO. REV. STAT. § 8-2-113(3) ("Any covenant not to compete provision of an employment, partnership, or corporate agreement between physicians which restricts the right of a physician to practice medicine, [as defined under Colorado law], upon termination of such agreement, shall be void; except that all other provisions of such an agreement enforceable at law, including provisions which require the payment of damages in an amount that is reasonably related to the injury suffered by reason of termination of the agreement, shall be enforceable.").
[67] *Falmouth Ob-Gyn Assocs., Inc. v. Abisla*, 629 N.E.2d 291 (Mass. 1994).
[68] *Id.*
[69] *Id.*

integration currently continues as health care providers evolve and face new challenges. Additionally, many transactions have not been successful for various reasons, and so the parties have unwound these transactions, whether through bankruptcy, repurchase arrangements, or sales to third parties, which creates a whole new opportunity for corporate transactional work. Nevertheless, hospitals and other institutional providers continue to seek ways in which to affiliate with physicians or other types of health care providers or suppliers in joint ventures and service arrangements, and to create meaningful alliances. Many health care providers have entered into transactions in order to be a part of a bigger health care system so that they will survive by having enough physicians on staff, capital for improvements and acquisitions, and a full complement of services so that loyal patients do not stray to a competitor for other services. Many physicians merely want to practice medicine and not bother themselves with the ever-growing regulatory nightmare of Medicare, Medicaid, and ACA. What we have seen in the last 30 years is that health care providers have entered into these arrangements, have divested such arrangements and then, years later, once again entered into similar types of arrangements in the constant battle of physician integration. The climate continues to be ripe for integration and affiliation, and it appears that these collaborations will continue in the future, especially in light of the unknown impact of federal health care reform.

13

Bioethics

Thomas Wm. Mayo
Professor, SMU/Dedman School of Law
Adjunct Associate Professor, University of Texas–Southwestern Medical School
Of Counsel, Haynes and Boone, LLP

Bioethics is a growing area of concern for health lawyers, no matter who their clients may be. This Chapter addresses major legal developments in three fields: human reproduction (abortion and surrogacy); organ transplantation; and genetics. Treatment issues in connection with dying patients and human research issues are discussed in Chapter 2.

13.1   Human Reproduction

13.1.1   Abortion

13.1.1.1   *Roe v. Wade*

Few issues in the past 30 years have been more politically controversial or have focused more attention on the unique role of the United States Supreme Court in the federal judicial system. Nevertheless, the law of abortion has been relatively stable, at least in broad outline, since the Court's decision in *Roe v. Wade*[1] in 1973. At issue in *Roe* was the constitutionality of Texas's abortion laws—similar to those of a majority of states at the time—which made it a crime to "procure an abortion" except "by medical advice for the purpose of saving the life of the mother."

One of the bedrock issues fueling the abortion debate concerns the moral status of the fetus: is it a "person" with the attributes and rights associated with that status? Or is the fetus an inchoate being of another sort, more than a clump of cells but not yet possessed of "personhood"? The rhetoric of abortion policy and politics is grounded on this question, but it is a question the Court chose not to answer. Instead, it concluded that, for purposes of the Fourteenth Amendment (which confers its protections upon "persons"), a fetus is not a "person." Once the Court ruled that a fetus has no constitutionally protectable interests, the *Roe* opinion turned to the rights of the pregnant woman, creating an analysis of the state's interests in limiting those rights.

---

[1] *Roe v. Wade*, 410 U.S. 113 (1973).

The *Roe* Court was built primarily upon its 1965 decision in *Griswold v. Connecticut*,[2] which struck down a Connecticut law that made it a crime for any person to use "any drug, medicinal article or instrument for the purpose of preventing conception," as well as to "counsel" or "assist" a person to violate the prohibition of the use of contraception. The Court held that a "zone of privacy" is created by "specific guarantees in the Bill of Rights [that] have penumbras, formed by emanations from those guarantees that help give them life and substance,"[3] and that this zone of privacy is broad enough to protect "an intimate relation of husband and wife and their physician's role in one aspect of that relation."[4]

Although various justices in *Griswold* offered a number of possible sources for this constitutional right of privacy, the Court did not coalesce around one answer until *Roe v. Wade*. Despite the checkered history of the constitutional doctrine of "substantive due process," a majority of the justices nonetheless anchored the Court's privacy doctrine "in the Fourteenth Amendment's concept of personal liberty and restrictions upon state action."[5] Recognizing that the right of privacy is "fundamental" but not absolute, the Court balanced the pregnant woman's interest in deciding whether to continue or to terminate her pregnancy against the state's interests in the promotion of maternal health and the protection of fetal life. In perhaps its most controversial move (in an opinion that had many of them), the Court ruled that the interests of the state, and the weight that should be accorded to those interests, changed in each of the trimesters of the pregnancy:

> A state criminal abortion statute of the current Texas type, that excepts from criminality only a life-saving procedure on behalf of the mother, without regard to pregnancy stage and without recognition of the other interests involved, is violative of the Due Process Clause of the Fourteenth Amendment. (a) For the stage prior to approximately the end of the first trimester, the abortion decision and its effectuation must be left to the medical judgment of the pregnant woman's attending physician. (b) For the stage subsequent to approximately the end of the first trimester, the State, in promoting its interest in the health of the mother, may, if it chooses, regulate the abortion procedure in ways that are reasonably related to maternal health. (c) For the stage subsequent to viability, the State in promoting its interest in the potentiality of human life may, if it chooses, regulate, and even proscribe, abortion except where it is necessary, in appropriate medical judgment, for the preservation of the life or health of the mother.[6]

13.1.1.2 Post-Roe Developments

Using the trimester approach outlined in *Roe*, the Court subsequently ruled on the constitutionality of a number of state abortion regulations. The Court struck down state laws: (i) that required abortions to be performed in a hospital accredited by a private accrediting organization, that required the procedure to be approved by the hospital staff abortion committee, and that required two physicians in

---

[2] *Griswold v. Connecticut*, 381 U.S. 479 (1965).
[3] *Id.* at 484.
[4] *Id.* at 482.
[5] 410 U.S. at 153.
[6] *Id.* at 164–65.

addition to the patient's attending physician concur in the procedure;[7] (ii) that imposed a spousal-consent requirement, a parental-consent requirement, and an obligation on the attending physician to exercise all care and diligence to preserve the life and health of the fetus without regard to the stage of viability;[8] (iii) that required all abortions after the first trimester to be performed in a hospital;[9] (iv) that imposed a variety of detailed informed-consent requirements deemed by the Court to be intended to discourage abortion, rather than to help inform the pregnant woman's choice;[10] and (v) that required a 24-hour waiting period after the woman had given her informed consent to the procedure.[11]

On the other hand, the Court held that *Roe*'s trimester approach permitted states to require: (i) that an abortion be based upon the physician's "best clinical judgment that an abortion was necessary;"[12] (ii) that abortions be performed either in a hospital or a licensed outpatient clinic (if licensing standards are consistent with accepted medical practice);[13] (iii) that tissue removed during clinic abortions be submitted to pathologic testing, and that a second physician be present during post-viability abortions to assist in saving the life of the fetus;[14] and (iv) that either one parent or both parents be notified of a minor's intent to obtain an abortion, as long as a judicial-bypass mechanism was available.[15] The Court also ruled that the privacy doctrine in *Roe* did not require either Congress or the states to provide public funding for abortions.[16] That reasoning also extended to a state's prohibition against the use of public facilities, employees, and resources for abortions (unless necessary to save the life of the mother).[17]

13.1.1.3 The Transformation of Roe

Roe's trimester approach to the right to privacy lasted 19 years. During this time the Court considered and rejected a number of invitations to overrule *Roe*. Many litigants and commentators (and at least some justices) believed that the ruling (1) was constitutionally illegitimate, (2) had plunged the Court into matters that were reserved by the Constitution to the states, (3) invited the Court to make political and policy judgments rather than legal ones, and (4) led to unpredictable results based upon increasingly labored distinctions that threatened to undermine public confidence in the Court. Against this onslaught, *Roe*'s "days were numbered," and its number finally came up in *Planned Parenthood of Southeastern Pennsylvania v. Casey*.[18]

Although the Court in *Casey* invalidated Pennsylvania's spousal-notification requirement, it upheld the state's detailed informed-consent requirements, its mandated 24-hour waiting period, a requirement that minors obtain the consent of at least one parent (subject to a judicial bypass procedure), and

---

[7] *Doe v. Bolton*, 410 U.S. 179 (1973).
[8] *Planned Parenthood v. Danforth*, 428 U.S. 52 (1976).
[9] *City of Akron v. Akron Ctr. for Reproductive Health*, 462 U.S. 416 (1983).
[10] *Id.; see also Thornburgh v. American College of Obstetricians & Gynecologists*, 476 U.S. 747 (1986).
[11] *Akron Ctr. for Reproductive Health*.
[12] *Doe v. Bolton*.
[13] *Simopolous v. Virginia*, 462 U.S. 506 (1983).
[14] *Planned Parenthood Ass'n v. Ashcroft*, 462 U.S. 476 (1983).
[15] *Ohio v. Akron Ctr. for Reproductive Health*, 497 U.S. 502 (1990); *Hodgson v. Minnesota*, 497 U.S. 417 (1990).
[16] *Harris v. McRae*, 448 U.S. 297 (1980); *Poelker v. Doe*, 432 U.S. 519 (1977); *Maher v. Roe*, 432 U.S. 464 (1977); *Beal v. Doe*, 432 U.S. 438 (1977).
[17] *Webster v. Reproductive Health Servs.*, 462 U.S. 416 (1983).
[18] *Planned Parenthood of Southeastern Pennsylvania v. Casey*, 505 U.S. 833 (1992).

extensive reporting requirements on abortion facilities. Most of these provisions would probably not have survived the strict scrutiny required by *Roe*, but a three-justice plurality (consisting of Justices O'Connor, Kennedy, and Souter) abandoned *Roe*'s trimester approach as too rigid and not necessary to carry out the "essential holding" of *Roe*. In an opinion that mentioned neither "fundamental right" nor "strict scrutiny," the three justices wrote:

> *Roe*'s essential holding, the holding we reaffirm, has three parts. First is a recognition of the right of the woman to choose to have an abortion before viability and to obtain it without undue interference from the State. Before viability, the State's interests are not strong enough to support a prohibition of abortion or the imposition of a substantial obstacle to the woman's effective right to elect the procedure. Second is a confirmation of the State's power to restrict abortions after fetal viability, if the law contains exceptions for pregnancies which endanger the woman's life or health. And third is the principle that the State has legitimate interests from the outset of the pregnancy in protecting the health of the woman and the life of the fetus that may become a child.[19]

Since 1992, lower courts have struggled to apply the *Casey* Court's "undue burden" test largely without additional guidance from the Court itself.[20] A considerable measure of guidance came from the Court in 2016 in *Whole Woman's Health v. Hellerstedt*,[21] in which the Supreme Court considered whether a Texas law's admitting-privileges and surgical-center requirements imposed an undue burden on a woman's right to seek an abortion. The admitting-privileges restriction required all physicians performing abortions to have active admitting privileges at a hospital within a 30-mile radius of their abortion clinic. The surgical-center restriction subjected abortion facilities to ambulatory service center health and safety standards. The five-justice majority found both provisions unconstitutional and reversed the U.S. Court of Appeals for the Fifth Circuit's ruling that the requirements were valid.

While recognizing the state's "legitimate interest" in facilitating "maximum safety" for women seeking abortions, the Court reiterated that a statute can still be invalidated if it "has the effect of placing a substantial obstacle in the path of a woman's choice," despite its furtherance of a valid state interest.[22] The Court noted its obligation to consider both the burdens a law imposes as well as the benefits that the law confers. It concluded that neither of the provisions at issue offered any benefit to women's health, yet both imposed significant obstacles to abortion access.

---

[19] *Id.* at 846.
[20] *See, e.g., Fargo Women's Health Org. v. Schafer*, 18 F.3d 526 (8th Cir. 1994) (informed-consent and 24-hour waiting period requirements not unconstitutional, in part because counseling may be done by telephone and therefore two trips to the clinic are not required); *Planned Parenthood, Sioux Falls Clinic v. Miller*, 63 F.3d 1452 (8th Cir. 1995) (a parental notification provision that does not include judicial bypass option except for abused or neglected minors is unconstitutional on its face), *cert. denied sub nom.*, 517 U.S. 1174 (1996); *Barnes v. Mississippi*, 992 F.2d 1335 (5th Cir.) (upholding two-parent consent requirement with constitutionally adequate judicial bypass option), *cert. denied*, 510 U.S. 976 (1993). The Supreme Court has not been totally silent. In addition to the late-term abortion cases discussed in the text, the Court decided *Lambert v. Wicklund*, 520 U.S. 292 (1997), *rev'g*, 93 F.3d 567 (9th Cir. 1996)), which upheld the judicial-bypass provision of a Montana statute that allowed waiver of notice requirement if notification of parent or guardian was not in minor's best interest.
[21] 136 S.Ct. 2292 (2016).
[22] *Id.* at 2309.

The alleged purpose of the admitting-privileges requirement was to provide women with "easy access" to a hospital in the event that complications arose during abortion procedures. However, evidence indicated that prior to the passage of Texas House Bill 2, abortion in Texas was "extremely safe with particularly low rates of serious complications and virtually no deaths occurring on account of the procedure."[23] Therefore, there was no identifiable health-related problem for the provision to alleviate. However, the requirement introduced a sizable obstacle—its enforcement coincided with the closure of almost half of the abortion facilities in Texas, which caused a shortage of doctors, longer waiting times, and increased crowding.[24] In the absence of a health benefit, the admitting-privileges provision imposed an unconstitutional undue burden on women's right to abortion.

The surgical-center requirement, purporting to promote women's health, subjected abortion clinics to exceptionally demanding health and safety standards. For example, it required facilities providing abortions to maintain "specific corridor widths."[25] The Court determined that this requirement was not "'reasonably related to' preserving women's health" due in large part to the fact that abortions performed in abortion facilities are "safer than numerous procedures that take place outside hospitals and to which Texas does not apply its surgical-center requirements."[26] For example, colonoscopies, which are not subject to surgical-center requirements, have a mortality rate ten times higher than an abortion. The Court maintained that many of the standards had "such a tangential relationship to patient safety in the context of abortion as to be nearly arbitrary."[27] The Court's conclusion that this requirement was unnecessary, taken together with evidence that it imposed a substantial obstacle to abortion access by further reducing the number of abortion facilities, led the Court to reject the restriction as unconstitutional.

In *Carhart v. Stenberg*,[28] the Court considered another major abortion issue—whether states may prohibit late-term abortions (called "partial-birth abortions" by opponents of the procedure). Late-term abortion involves the extraction of a fetus, legs first, through the birth canal. Because the procedure is performed up to approximately the 24th week of gestation, the size of the skull usually requires that the skull be cut, its contents drained, and the skull itself reduced in size in order for delivery to be completed.

Carhart affirmed the U.S. Court of Appeals for the Eighth Circuit's decision to strike down a Nebraska statute prohibiting late-term abortion. Justice Breyer deemed the Nebraska statute unconstitutional for two reasons. First, it did not contain an exception for situations in which a late-term abortion might be necessary to save the life of the pregnant woman. Second, as the Eighth Circuit had noted, the statute's definition of the procedure was overbroad, and could include not only the late-term abortion procedure (dilation and extraction) but also the much more commonly performed dilation and evacuation procedure, which is usually performed early in the second trimester. The Supreme Court held that the potential restriction of dilation-and-evacuation procedures unconstitutionally limited a woman's right to choose abortion.

---

[23] *Id.* at 2311.
[24] *Id.* at 2313.
[25] *Id.* at 2315.
[26] *Id.* at 2315.
[27] *Id.* at 2316.
[28] 530 U.S. 914 (2000).

After the Court handed down its decision in *Stenberg*, Congress passed the Partial Birth Abortion Act of 2003,[29] which is nearly identical to the Nebraska statute struck down in *Stenberg*. The Act makes it a crime (punishable by a fine or up to two years' imprisonment or both) for a physician to perform a dilation and extraction procedure, except if it is necessary to save the life of the mother. After three district courts and three courts of appeals—all relying principally upon the Court's opinion in *Carhart*—struck down the federal law, many observers were surprised when the Supreme Court upheld the Act in *Gonzales v. Carhart*.[30] Opponents of the law claimed that it had the same defects as the Nebraska law: the procedure was described in terms that could make it illegal to perform second-trimester dilation-and-extraction procedures, and the law lacked an exception for the protection of a woman's *health*.

The Court held that the Act was neither void for vagueness nor an undue burden on a woman's right to abortion based on its overbreadth or lack of a health exception. The Court distinguished the Act from the Nebraska statute in *Stenberg*, holding that it could not reasonably be read to prohibit the standard dilation-and-evacuation procedure. The Court also upheld the act's failure to provide for an exception to protect the pregnant woman's health, based upon Congress' detailed (and controversial) findings that dilation and extraction is never needed to protect a woman's health. In dissent, Justice Ginsburg called the decision "alarming" and noted that little had changed in the years since it handed down *Stenberg* other than the Court's membership. Ginsburg wrote, "[the majority decision] tolerates, indeed applauds, federal intervention to ban nationwide a procedure found necessary and proper in certain cases by the American College of Obstetricians and Gynecologists," adding that "the Court's defense [of the ban] cannot be understood as anything other than an effort to chip away at a right declared again and again by this Court."

13.1.1.4   Medical and Emergency Abortion

Other methods of abortion remain controversial. Medical (i.e., drug-induced, as opposed to surgical) abortion, though legal in other countries for years, was banned in the United States until 1993.[31] On September 28, 2000, the Food and Drug Administration (FDA) approved mifepristone, the so-called "abortion pill," also known as RU-486 or Mifeprex. Taken in combination with a prostaglandin, this drug causes uterine contractions and bleeding, terminating over 95% of pregnancies of fewer than seven weeks' gestation. The FDA approved the drug solely for the termination of early pregnancy, defined as 49 days or fewer as measured from the beginning of the woman's last menstrual period.[32] It warned that the drug should not be used for women with certain medical conditions (e.g., ectopic pregnancy or bleeding disorders), and that complications, including severe bleeding, may occur that would require surgical intervention.

In 2016, the FDA approved a supplemental application for Mifeprex, which can now be used, together with another medication called misoprostol, to end a pregnancy through 70 days' gestation

---

[29] *See, e.g.*, 18 U.S.C. § 1531.
[30] 127 S. Ct. 1610, 550 U.S. 124 (2007).
[31] The first President Bush banned the importation of mifepristone, but the ban was lifted by President Clinton in his first term.
[32] United States Department of Health and Human Services, HHS News P00-19, *FDA Approves Mifepristone for the Termination of Early Pregnancy* (Sept. 28, 2000).

(70 days or less since the first day of a woman's last menstrual period).[33] After reviewing the supplemental application, the agency determined that Mifeprex is safe and effective when used to terminate a pregnancy in accordance with the revised labeling. The new regimen also cut the drug's dosage by two-thirds, a move that decreases the cost.[34]

On August 24, 2006, the FDA approved the emergency contraceptive drug levonorgestrel, also known as "Plan B" or the "morning-after pill," as an over-the-counter option for women aged 18 and older.[35] In December 2011, the FDA approved the over-the-counter sale of "Plan B One-Step" for all women 17 years of age and older but still required a prescription for young women under the age of 17.[36] In April 2013, the U.S. Department of Justice appealed a ruling by U.S. District Judge Edward Korman that removed all age restrictions for over-the-counter sales of Plan B to women and girls.[37] After a resulting deluge of criticism from abortion and women's rights groups and many other parts of the Democratic coalition, President Obama instructed the U.S. Department of Justice to drop the appeal and begin work on an implementation plan for the removal of age restrictions.[38]

On August 13, 2010, the Food and Drug Administration approved a new form of emergency contraception that can prevent pregnancy as many as five days after sex.[39] The prescription-only product, ulipristal acetate (called ella™), can prevent pregnancy if taken within 120 hours after contraceptive failure or unprotected sex.[40]

The FDA's approval of ella has reopened the heated abortion debate. Ella is a progesterone agonist/antagonist that works by blocking progesterone's activity and therefore delaying ovulation.[41] Critics claim that ella's chemical similarities to RU-486, which also blocks progesterone, make it another "abortion drug."[42] They also worry that ella's classification as an emergency contraceptive, instead of an abortion pill, will make it eligible to receive federal subsidies which are not available for RU-486.[43] Because it is only available by prescription, ella will also likely contribute to the ongoing debates

---

[33] U.S. Food and Drug Admin., *Mifeprex (mifepristone) Information* (Mar. 30, 2016), *available at* https://www.fda.gov/drugs/drugsafety/postmarketdrugsafetyinformationforpatientsandproviders/ucm111323.htm.

[34] Kimberly Leonard, *Changes to Abortion Pill Guidance Will Make It More Available*, U.S. News, Mar. 30, 2016, *available at* https://www.usnews.com/news/articles/2016-03-30/fda-updates-abortion-pill-guidance.

[35] U.S. Food and Drug Admin., *Plan B: Questions and Answers - August 24, 2006; updated December 14, 2006* (Aug. 26, 2013), archived at https://wayback.archive-it.org/7993/20170406045431/https://www.fda.gov/Drugs/DrugSafety/PostmarketDrugSafetyInformationforPatientsandProviders/ucm491173.htm. Levonorgestrel works like a birth-control pill to prevent pregnancy mainly by stopping the release of an egg from the ovary, or possibly by preventing fertilization of the egg, or by preventing a fertilized egg from attaching to the uterus. Plan B does not work if pregnancy has already occurred. *See also* Nat'l Conference of State Legislatures, *Emergency Contraception State Laws* (Aug. 24, 2012), *available at* http://www.ncsl.org/research/health/emergency-contraception-state-laws.aspx.

[36] Nat'l Conference of State Legislatures, *supra*.

[37] Linda Feldman, *Morning-after Pill: How the Politics of Plan B Changed for Obama*, Christian Sci. Monitor, June 11, 2013, *available at* http://www.csmonitor.com/USA/Politics/DC-Decoder/2013/0611/Morning-after-pill-how-the-politics-of-Plan-B-changed-for-Obama.

[38] *Id.*

[39] Press Release, U.S. Food & Drug Admin., *FDA Approves ella™ Tablets for Prescription Emergency Contraception* (August 16, 2010), *available at* https://rushprnews.com/2010/08/16/fda-approves-ellatm-tablets-for-prescription-emergency-contraception. *See also* Gardiner Harris, *F.D.A. Approves 5-Day Emergency Contraceptive*, N.Y. Times, Aug. 13, 2010, *available at* http://www.nytimes.com/2010/08/14/health/policy/14pill.html.

[40] *Id.*

[41] *Id.*

[42] Rob Stein, *FDA Approves ella as 5-Day-After Emergency Contraceptive*, Wash. Post, Aug. 14, 2010, at A01.

[43] *Id.*

about conscience clauses as applied to both doctors who refuse to write prescriptions and pharmacists who refuse to fill them.

Proponents point out that there is no evidence that ella works as anything other than a contraceptive and that it has only been tested within five days of unprotected sex.[44] "According to the product's labeling, women with known or suspected pregnancy and women who are breastfeeding should not use ella. A patient package insert also will be provided to ensure that women are fully informed of the benefits and risks involved in the use of ella."[45] Officials from HRA Pharma of Paris, which makes ella, claim that there are no plans to test it as an abortion drug and that it did not appear to cause any problems for the handful of women who became pregnant after taking the drug.[46]

Ella was approved in Europe in 2009 and is available in at least 22 European countries.[47] It became available in the United States in December 2010.[48]

Following upon the FDA's approvals in this field, all but a small handful of states have statutes related to emergency contraception.[49] State laws vary widely, however. Some increase access while others restrict is. Most states provide Medicaid funding for ella or Plan B or both.

These state laws have prompted the latest debate over reproductive rights.[50] One of the major issues involves pharmacists refusing to dispense birth control or emergency contraception.[51] In some states, legislators are pushing laws that would grant pharmacists the right to refuse to dispense drugs related to contraception or abortion on moral grounds.[52] Other states require pharmacists to fill any legal prescription for birth control.[53] Still others have enacted laws to make the morning-after pill

---

[44] *Id.*

[45] Press Release, U.S. Food & Drug Administration, *supra.*

[46] Stein, *supra.*

[47] *Id.*

[48] *See* Press Release, Watson Pharmaceuticals, Watson Launches ella® (ulipristal acetate) Emergency Contraceptive (Dec. 1, 2010), *available at* http://www.prnewswire.com/news-releases/watson-launches-ella-ulipristal-acetate-emergency-contraceptive-111109109.html.

[49] *See, e.g.*, CAL. INS. CODE § 10604.1; 410 ILL. COMP. STAT. § 70/2.2; ANN. LAWS OF MASS. Ch. 41 § 97B; N.J. STAT. ANN. § 26:2H-12.6c and 26:2H-12.6e; N.Y. PUB. HEALTH LAW § 2805-p; 28 PA. CODE §§ 117.53, .55, .57; TEX. HEALTH & SAFETY CODE ANN. § 171.012. For a full list of these states, *see* State Laws and Policies: Emergency Contraception (as of October 1, 2017), Guttmacher Institute, *available at* https://www.guttmacher.org/state-policy/explore/emergency-contraception.

[50] *See* Nat'l Women's Law Ctr., *Pharmacy Refusals 101*, at 3 (Aug. 4, 2015), *available at* http://www.nwlc.org/resource/pharmacy-refusals-101. (discussing the legislative and administrative responses to pharmacist refusals).

[51] *See, e.g.*, Lora Cicconi, *Pharmacist Refusals and Third-Party Interests: A Proposed Judicial Approach to Pharmacist Conscience Clause*, 54 UCLA L. REV. 709 (2007).

[52] These are the "conscience clause bills" that allow pharmacists to refuse to dispense contraceptives if they have moral or religious objections. Four states already have pharmacist-refusal statutes in place. *See* ARK. CODE ANN. § 20-16-304; GA. COMP. R. & REGS. 480-5-.03; MISS. CODE ANN. § 41-107-5; S.D. COD. LAWS § 36-11-70. Illinois, Colorado, Florida, Maine, Tennessee, and Washington have broad refusal clauses that do not specifically mention pharmacists. *See* 745 ILL. COMP. STAT. ANN. § 70/1-70/14; COLO. REV. STAT.§ 25-6-102(9); FLA. STAT. ANN. § 381.0051, *amended by* LAWS 2012, Ch. 2012-184, eff. Apr. 27, 2012; ME. REV. STAT. ANN. tit. 22 § 1903(4); TENN. CODE ANN. § 68-34-104; WASH. REV. CODE ANN. § 48.43.065. Several other states have statutes protecting government employees who refuse to provide family planning services. *See, e.g.*, COLO. REV. STAT. § 25-6-207; GA. CODE ANN. § 49-7-6; OR. REV. STAT. § 435.225; W. VA. CODE § 16-2B-4; WYO. STAT. ANN. § 42-5-101.

[53] Seven states—California, Illinois, Maine, Massachusetts, Nevada, New Jersey, and Washington—explicitly require pharmacists to ensure legal prescriptions are filled. In Illinois, then-Governor Rod Blagojevich issued emergency rules that required pharmacists to provide the morning after pill. *See* ILL. ADM. CODE tit. 77, § 545.95. Seven state pharmacy boards—Alabama, Delaware, New York, North Carolina, Oregon, Pennsylvania, and Texas—have issued policy statements

more accessible by requiring hospitals to offer it to rape victims or allowing certain pharmacists to sell it without a prescription.[54]

Abortion rights advocates contend that the emergency contraception pill is not an abortion drug because it does not destroy an embryo, but instead it prevents ovulation or fertilization or blocks a fertilized egg from becoming implanted in the uterus. Advocates of the drug say it is crucial for pharmacists to stock the morning-after pill because women have only a small window of time after sex in which to obtain and use it, and the pill would lead to fewer abortions. Opponents argue that the emergency contraception pill has the same effect of an abortion drug destroying life because it can prevent an already fertilized egg from implanting in the uterus.

13.1.1.5 Access to Abortion Facilities

The ongoing controversy over abortion has generated not only public debate but also violence against women who choose to undergo or perform abortions. Congress passed the Freedom of Access to Clinic Entrances (FACE) Act of 1994[55] to protect and promote the public safety and health. The act established federal criminal penalties and civil remedies for violent, threatening, obstructive, and destructive conduct intended to injure, intimidate, or interfere with persons seeking to obtain or provide reproductive health services. In 1994, the National Organization for Women, Inc. (NOW), a nonprofit organization that supports legal availability of abortions and abortion clinics, brought a class action suit against individuals and organizations that oppose legal abortions, alleging that they violated the Racketeer Influenced and Corrupt Organizations Act[56] (RICO) by engaging in a nationwide conspiracy to shut down abortion clinics through racketeering and extortion. After 12 years of litigation, the Supreme Court held that threatening or committing violent acts unrelated to robbery or extortion falls outside the Hobbs Act,[57] therefore the Pro-Life Action Network (PLAN) was not liable for conspiracy.

13.1.1.6 Informed-Consent Laws Redux

Another disputed issue involves attempts to regulate professional communications between health care providers and their patients. Under the first Bush administration, the Department of Health and Human Services (DHHS) took steps to distance taxpayer dollars from abortion services. DHHS implemented regulations prohibiting clinics receiving federal funds under Title X of the Public Health Service Act[58] from engaging in abortion counseling, referral, and activities advocating abortion as a method of family planning. Physicians who supervised Title X funds questioned the constitutionality of these regulations in *Rust v. Sullivan*.[59] The Supreme Court declared the regulations permissible:

> The regulations do not violate the First Amendment free speech rights . . . by impermissibly imposing viewpoint-discriminatory conditions on Government subsidies. There is no question

---

that prohibit pharmacists from obstructing patient access to medication or from refusing to transfer prescriptions to another pharmacy. *See* http://www.nwlc.org/sites/default/files/pdfs/AppendixA-update.pdf.
[54] *See, e.g.,* CAL. BUS. & PROF. CODE § 4052; ANN. LAWS OF MASS. Ch. 111 § 70E(o).
[55] 18 U.S.C. § 248.
[56] 18 U.S.C. §§ 1961–68.
[57] *Nat'l Org. for Women, Inc. v. Scheidler*, 510 U.S. 249 (1994); *see also Scheidler v. Nat'l Org. for Women, Inc.*, 547 U.S. 9 (2006).
[58] Public Health Service Act, § 1008, as amended, 42 U.S.C. §§ 300a, 300a-6.
[59] *Rust v. Sullivan*, 500 U.S. 173 (1991).

but that § 1008's prohibition is constitutional, since the Government may make a value judgment favoring childbirth over abortion and implement that judgment by the allocation of public funds. In so doing, the Government has not discriminated on the basis of viewpoint; it has merely chosen to fund one activity to the exclusion of another.[60]

The dissent argued that the Court was impinging upon free speech by manipulating the doctor/patient dialogue, in an effort "to deter a woman from making a decision that, with her physician, is hers to make."[61] It also asserted that the Court's actions were "nearly as noxious as overruling *Roe* directly, for if a right is found to be unenforceable, even against flagrant attempts by government to circumvent it, then it ceases to be a right at all."[62]

In 2005, South Dakota amended its informed-consent law to add a number of specific required disclosures that must be made by a physician or the physician's agent before an abortion procedure is performed with sole exception where, "the physician determines that obtaining an informed consent is impossible due to a medical emergency . . ."[63] The disclosures, which must be provided in writing at least two hours before the procedure, include:

1. That the abortion will terminate the life of a whole, separate, unique, living human being;
2. That the pregnant woman has an existing relationship with that unborn human being and that the relationship enjoys protection under the United States Constitution and under the laws of South Dakota;
3. That by having an abortion, her existing relationship and her existing constitutional rights with regards to that relationship will be terminated; [and]
4. A description of all known medical risks of the procedure and statistically significant risk factors to which the pregnant woman would be subjected, including:

    (a) Depression and related psychological distress;

    (b) Increased risk of suicide ideation and suicide;

    (c) A statement setting forth an accurate rate of deaths due to abortions, including all deaths in which the abortion procedure was a substantial contributing factor;

    (d) All other known medical risks to the physical health of the woman, including the risk of infection, hemorrhage, danger to subsequent pregnancies, and infertility.[64]

A district court preliminarily enjoined the enforcement of these four disclosure requirements in 2005,[65] and the U.S. Court of Appeals for the Eighth Circuit affirmed concluding that the compelled

---

[60] *Id.* at 174 (citations omitted).

[61] *Id.* at 219 (Blackmun dissenting) (quoting *Thornburgh v. Am. Coll. of Obstetricians & Gynecologists*, 476 U.S. 747, 759 (1986)).

[62] *Id.* at 220 (Blackmun, J., dissenting).

[63] S.D. CODIFIED LAWS § 34-23A-10.1; *see also Planned Parenthood Minnesota, N. Dakota, S. Dakota v. Rounds*, 650 F.Supp.2d 972 (D.S.D. 2009) (upholding constitutionality of emergency exception).

[64] *Id.* at 10.1(1)(b)–(e).

[65] *Planned Parenthood Minnesota v. Rounds*, 375 F. Supp. 2d 881 (S.D.S.D. 2005) *vacated and remanded sub nom. Planned Parenthood Minnesota, N. Dakota, S. Dakota v. Rounds*, 530 F.3d 724 (8th Cir. 2008).

statements were ideological speech, rather than medical facts.[66] However, after a re-hearing was granted, the same court upheld the disclosure requirements maintaining only the emergency exception.[67]

13.1.2 Access to Contraceptives

Under the Patient Protection and Affordable Care Act (ACA),[68] employers are required to provide their female employees with certain preventive health care products and services without any of the costs being passed on to the women utilizing those services. If employers do not meet this requirement, they can be fined for each day that the coverage is not provided. Many forms of birth control are offered under this provision, including four types that might prevent a fertilized egg from attaching to the uterus. In specific cases, religious organizations and nonprofit employers that have religious objections to these types of birth control may be exempted from the mandate to provide them to their employees. Under this exception, contraceptive services are still offered free of charge to the female employees of the exempt organization; however, none of the costs for those services are passed on to either the employer, its insurance plan, or its other employee beneficiaries. In this case, the owners of three closely held for-profit corporations, which at that time did not qualify for the religious exemption, brought suit arguing that the ACA's requirement that their businesses provide insurance coverage that included access to four types of birth control they found objectionable violated their religious rights.

The Supreme Court held for the corporate owners,[69] finding that the contraceptive mandate at issue violated the Religious Freedom Restoration Act (RFRA).[70] RFRA prohibits governments from burdening a person's religious beliefs unless the government can show that the burden being applied furthers a compelling governmental interest and that the least restrictive means are being used to achieve that compelling interest. First, the Court found that corporations are "persons" for the purposes of RFRA because Congress designed RFRA to ensure broad protections of religious liberty, and under these protections, business owners should not have to choose between maintaining the rights guaranteed by RFRA and their desire to access the security of incorporation.[71] Then, the Court found that forcing these "persons" to choose between providing contraceptives they viewed as morally offensive or being fined large monetary penalties by the government burdened their sincerely held religious beliefs.[72] The Court concluded that the means chosen by the government was not the least restrictive because these employers could easily be exempted using the plan already in place, while the government still maintained its interest in ensuring that all female employees had no-cost access to these important preventive health care services.[73]

---

[66] *Planned Parenthood Minnesota v. Rounds*, 467 F.3d 716 (8th Cir. 2006).
[67] *Id.* at 722. On January 6, 2007, the Eighth Circuit vacated the panel's opinion and granted rehearing en banc, and oral argument was held on April 11, 2007. http://www.ca8.uscourts.gov/tmp/053093.html. Then in 2011 the court reversed on all disclosures except suicide, which it reversed in 2012. *See* 530 F.3d 724 (2008) (vacating injunction and remanding the case); 650 F. Supp. 2d 972 (2009) (cross motions for summary judgment); 653 F. Supp. 3d 662 (2011) (upholding biological and protected relationship disclosures); 662 F. 3d 1072 (2011) (enjoining the all known risks and suicide disclosure allowance); 686 F. 3d 889 (2012) (upholding all known risks and suicide disclosures).
[68] 42 U.S.C. § 300gg–13(a)(4).
[69] *Burwell v. Hobby Lobby Stores, Inc.*, 134 S.Ct. 2751 (2014).
[70] 42 U.S.C. §§ 2000bb *et seq.*
[71] *Id.* at 2767–75.
[72] *Id.* at 2775–79.
[73] *Id.* at 2780–85.

13.1.3 Commercial Surrogacy

Surrogacy—the practice by which a woman bears a child for a woman who cannot conceive or cannot carry a fetus to term—has biblical roots.[74] Commercial surrogacy, by contrast, appears to be a modern invention. As the term implies, commercial surrogacy involves the payment of a fee to the surrogate mother. Commercial surrogacy is usually facilitated by a broker who matches infertile couples with a woman who agrees to become pregnant, carry the fetus to term, and turn the newborn over to the couple, who assume the role of "social parent."[75] Commercial surrogacy has increased the supply of potential surrogate mothers, and has moved surrogate parenting outside the traditional circle of family and friends. In so doing, it has brought strangers together in ways strangers have seldom interacted before, which has created legal issues that have not yet been completely resolved.

Prior to the development of reliable *in vitro* fertilization techniques, conception with a surrogate mother occurred through either coitus or artificial insemination; as a result, the surrogate mother was both the genetic parent and the gestational parent of the offspring so conceived. *In vitro* fertilization eventually became an option that permitted couples to contribute their own genetic material to an embryo that was created in a fertility laboratory and subsequently transplanted into the womb of the surrogate. As a result, it has become possible for a second type of surrogacy, a purely "gestational surrogacy," to occur, in which the surrogate mother contributes her womb for nine months, but not her gametes. Although other combinations of genetic, gestational, and social parents can be imagined,[76] traditional and gestational surrogacy are by far the two most common types of surrogacy arrangement.

The ethical and public-policy issues surrounding surrogacy have been intensely debated. Critics argue that the practice constitutes an undesirable "commodification" of life, is indistinguishable from the universally prohibited practice of baby-selling, reduces surrogate mothers to "baby machines"[77] and "fetal containers,"[78] is a form of prostitution or slavery, is unfair to the child and its siblings, and exploits surrogate mothers whose life situations may make them particularly vulnerable to the allure of a fee of $25,000 or more.[79] Defenders of the practice note that reproductive decisions are generally given the highest degree of constitutional protection[80] and argue that the autonomous reproductive decisions of competent adults are entitled to respect, that laws "protecting" women from their bargains

---

[74] *See Genesis* 16:1–6, 30:1–13 (King James).

[75] "With techniques of assisted fertility, three types of mother can be defined: (1) genetic, (2) gestational, and (3) social. A woman may be one, two, or all three types of mother to a child . . . [A social mother is] a woman who rears the baby after birth." MILLER-KEANE & MARIE T. O'TOOLE, MILLER-KEANE ENCYCLOPEDIA AND DICTIONARY OF MEDICINE, NURSING, AND ALLIED HEALTH (7th ed. 2003).

[76] *See* Alexander M. Capron, *Alternative Birth Technologies: Legislative Challenges*, 20 U.C. DAVIS L. REV. 679, 682 (1987) (describing eight surrogacy scenarios, including the "Brave New World" surrogacy arrangement: five different, unrelated persons contribute the male and female gametes, gestation, and social parents of the child).

[77] *See* Iver Peterson, *Baby M Trial Splits Ranks of Feminists*, N.Y. Times (Feb. 24, 1987), *available at* http://www.nytimes.com/1987/02/24/nyregion/baby-m-trial-splits-ranks-of-feminists.html.

[78] Carol Lawson, *Couples' Own Embryos Used in Birth Surrogacy*, N.Y. Times (Aug. 12, 1990), *available at* http://www.nytimes.com/1990/08/12/us/couples-own-embryos-used-in-birth-surrogacy.html?pagewanted=all.

[79] *See* UTAH CODE ANN. § 78B-15-801 (although gestational carrier contracts are legal in the state of Utah, the intended gestational mother may not currently be receiving Medicaid or any other state assistance).

[80] Cf. *Skinner v. Oklahoma*, 316 U.S. 535, 541, 545 (1942) (procreation deemed a fundamental right); *Eisenstadt v. Baird*, 405 U.S. 438, 453–54 (1972) (procreative decisions fall within the right of privacy).

are unnecessarily paternalistic, and that the human desire for offspring that are related to one or more of the intended (social) parents should be accorded respect. [81]

The legal issues created by surrogate parenting generally fall into two categories. First, what should the state's policy be with respect to the practice itself? The options range from outright prohibition to detailed judicial supervision of every aspect of the practice. Second, in the event that the surrogate agreement is violated, when and on what basis should the state provide a remedy? In particular, how should courts rule when the surrogate mother refuses to relinquish her parental rights (which is a rare, but dramatic, occurrence)?

13.1.3.1 Prohibition and Regulation

A surrogacy arrangement is a daunting legal task even in instances when a pregnancy is uneventful—the child is born in good health, and all individuals involved behave exactly as they have agreed (assuming no state-law obstacles to the practice). In most jurisdictions it will involve a relinquishment of parental rights by the surrogate mother (and probably by her spouse, if she is married), as well as an adoption by one or both of the social parents. It may also involve the execution of collateral documents intended to overcome various common-law and statutory presumptions of parentage that were not developed with surrogate parenting in mind.[82] An additional element of uncertainty results when state laws provide (as most states do) that the relinquishment of parental rights, the consent to adoption, and the adoption decree itself do not become final and irrevocable until some time after the birth of the child. The Uniform Status of Children of Assisted Conception Act (USCACA) provides alternative approaches for adopting states, which can either declare surrogacy arrangements to be void or provide for a type of preconception adoption proceeding.[83] So far only two states have adopted the USCACA;[84] Virginia chose the regulatory option, while North Dakota refuses to enforce traditional surrogacy arrangements (in which the surrogate is also genetically related to the resulting child), but allows for gestational surrogacy (in which the intended parents are genetically related to the child).[85]

---

[81] State laws reflect a similar divergence in opinion about commercial surrogacy. *Cf.* Mich. Comp. Laws Ann. § 722.855–59 (deeming surrogate parentage contracts for compensation to be unlawful and against public policy); N.H. Rev. Stat. Ann. § 168-B:1-22 (enforcing strict guidelines with the purpose of protecting all parties to a surrogacy arrangement).

[82] For example, under the Uniform Parentage Act (UPA) of 2000, if a married woman, with the consent of her husband, has been artificially inseminated with semen donated by someone other than her husband, then the husband is deemed to be the natural father of the child so conceived. Unif. Parentage Act (2000) § 705. In a surrogacy arrangement that is subject to this law, therefore, the surrogate's husband typically must execute a statement that he does not consent to the artificial insemination of his wife in order to avoid the creation of a legislative presumption that he, rather than the donor of the sperm, is the natural father of the child.

[83] The pre-birth adoption decree solves one vexing problem that faces hospitals in which a surrogate mother delivers a child. Hospital policies routinely call for newborns to be sent home with their birth mothers. With a surrogacy arrangement, that is not the parents' usual intention, but on what basis should a hospital release the newborn to someone who is not the birth mother, and may not be the genetic mother either? A court order upon which the hospital presumably may rely would clear the matter up considerably.

[84] *See* N.D. CENT. CODE § 14-18-05 (surrogacy contracts are void); VA. CODE ANN. §§ 20-156 to 20-165 (surrogacy contracts are subject to regulation and judicial supervision).

[85] The UPA was revised in 2000 and amended in 2002 to reflect technological changes, such as exact genetic identification for paternity tests. The National Conference of Commissioners on Uniform State Laws addressed modern developments through additional uniform laws: the Uniform Putative and Unknown Fathers Act (UPUFA) (1988) and the USCACA (1988). As already noted in the main text, only two states adopted the USCACA, and the UPUFA was

At least 26 states have enacted laws that specifically address surrogate parenting. Some states regard all surrogacy contracts to be void,[86] while others refuse to enforce commercial surrogacy arrangements,[87] and a third group specifically declare surrogacy arrangements to be lawful and enforceable.[88] States in this last group typically provide for judicial approval of the agreement, as well as continuing jurisdiction to resolve disputes under the agreement as they arise.[89] At least Florida and Texas explicitly require "pure gestational" surrogacy (i.e., surrogacy contracts must provide for the use of an egg other than one from the surrogate's body).[90]

13.1.3.2 Custody Disputes

Although the vast majority of surrogacy arrangements are uneventful, a small number have resulted in dramatic litigation that occasionally has commanded national attention. Three of these cases mark the evolution of custody law as it applies to three distinct surrogate relationships. The most famous of these is *In re Baby M*,[91] in which the surrogate mother (that is, the genetic and gestational mother) renounced her obligations under the surrogacy contract and refused to relinquish custody of the child to the intended parents. The parents sued to enforce their rights under the surrogacy contract, which the New Jersey Supreme Court ruled was void and unenforceable on public-policy grounds. Applying the traditional "best interests of the child" standard, the court concluded that the intended parents should be awarded custody and that the surrogate was entitled to visitation rights on a basis to be determined on remand to the trial court.

The surrogate mother fared less well in *Johnson v. Calvert*.[92] This case involved a gestational surrogacy arrangement, a deteriorating relationship between the surrogate and the intended parents throughout the pregnancy, and competing lawsuits in which the surrogate and the intended parents each sought a declaration of parentage. The California Supreme Court held that California law permitted only one person to be a "mother," and that person should be the intended (and genetic) mother, not the gestational surrogate.[93]

---

not adopted anywhere. The revision to the UPA "attempts to integrate the best of [the three uniform acts]." *See* John J. Sampson, *Uniform Parentage Act (2000) with Prefatory Note and Comments*, 35(1), FAMILY LAW QUARTERLY, 83, 92095 (2001). The conference also withdrew all previous versions of the UPA, as well as the USCACA and UPUFA. *Id.*

[86] *See, e.g.*, KY. REV. STAT. ANN. § 199.590; MICH. COMP. LAWS ANN. § 722.855; N.Y. DOM. REL. LAW § 122.

[87] *See, e.g.*, WASH. REV. CODE ANN. § 26.26.230.

[88] *See, e.g.*, FLA. STAT. ANN. § 742.15; TEX. FAM. CODE ANN. § 160.754; VA. CODE ANN. §§ 20-159, 20-160. All require that the intended mother must be infertile. Additionally, Virginia requires advance judicial approval of the surrogacy agreement, and limits who may act as a surrogate.

[89] One type of dispute that might arise involves the surrogate mother's promise to avoid unhealthy or dangerous practices (smoking, drinking, ingesting controlled substances, skydiving), to seek regular medical care, and to follow all recommendations of her obstetrician. These promises create difficult issues when the intended parents seek enforcement through injunctive decrees or rescission on grounds of a material breach. *See* Thomas Wm. Mayo, *Medical Decision Making During a Surrogate Pregnancy*, 25 HOUS. L. REV. 599 (1988).

[90] FLA. STAT. ANN. §§ 742.13–742.15; TEX. FAM. CODE ANN. § 160.754(c).

[91] *In re Baby M*, 537 A.2d 1227 (N.J. 1988).

[92] *Johnson v. Calvert*, 851 P.2d 776 (Cal.), *cert. denied*, 510 U.S. 874 (1993).

[93] Justice Kennard vigorously challenged this conclusion in his dissenting opinion, in which he identified "three discrete aspects of motherhood: genetic, gestational, and social," *id.* at 791 (Kennard, J., dissenting), not one of which provided a solid basis for a judicial decree of parentage. Justice Kennard concluded that the best interests of the child, not the genetic bond or the intent of the parties, should control. *Id.* at 798. In a commercial surrogacy case, *In re Roberto, d.B.*, 923 A.2d 115 (Md. 2007), the Court of Appeals of Maryland granted certiorari to hear a father, whose sperm was used to fertilize donor's eggs and implanted into a gestational carrier, petition the court to issue a birth certificate that did not list

A third surrogacy case, *In re Buzzanca*, was noteworthy for two reasons: the baby was not genetically related to either intended social parent; and the genetic and surrogate parents (as well as one of the intended social parents) did not want custody.[94] According to a surrogacy contract, the Buzzancas, a married couple, both wished to initiate the process of having a baby. They created an embryo, using genetic material that was not theirs, and implanted the embryo into a surrogate mother. The couple separated before the baby was born, and Mr. Buzzanca tried to disclaim any parental responsibility. Mrs. Buzzanca asked the court to declare that she and Mr. Buzzanca were the legal parents.

The Buzzanca child could have had any of six possible legal parents: either of the genetic parents; the gestational mother or her spouse; or Mr. or Mrs. Buzzanca. However, a trial court declared the baby a legal orphan. The California Court of Appeals reversed, declaring that the legislature had declared a "preference for assigning individual responsibility for the care and maintenance of children, not leaving the task to taxpayers."[95] The court designated the Buzzancas the legal parents, reasoning by analogy to artificial insemination. Section 7613 of the California Family Code states that, when a husband gives permission for his wife to be artificially inseminated by another man, the husband is treated in law as the natural father.[96] The court also stated that, even if Mrs. Buzzanca had promised to shoulder all parental responsibilities, as Mr. Buzzanca argued, this promise was void and unenforceable.

Surrogacy contracts remain difficult legal ground; the court in *Buzzanca* was careful to note that it was not ruling on the enforceability of the surrogacy contract, but rather on "the consequences of those agreements as *acts* which *caused the birth* of the child."[97] The court called on the legislature to clarify parental rights and responsibilities in the legal area of artificial reproduction.[98]

13.2 Organ Transplantation

The framework for organ procurement, allocation, and transplantation is provided by the National Organ Transplant Act (NOTA),[99] which authorizes DHHS to contract with a private entity to establish and operate the Organ Procurement and Transplantation Network (OPTN).[100] The only contractor in the history of the OPTN has been the United Network for Organ Sharing (UNOS), a nonprofit corporation whose bylaws and policies have been the cornerstone of federal organ-transplant policy.[101]

---

the carrier as the mother on the birth certificate. The court held that the best-interest-of-the-child standard did not apply; the carrier was not required to be listed as the mother on birth certificates; and under the Equal Rights Amendment both males and females can challenge their parental status based on their genetic connection.

[94] *In re Buzzanca*, 61 Cal. App. 4th 1410 (Cal. App. 1998).
[95] *Id.* at 1424.
[96] CAL. FAM. CODE § 7613. One court even decided that a similar law should apply to the transgender partner, physiologically female but living as a man, of an artificially inseminated woman, where the couple had obtained a marriage license. *Karin T. v. Michael T.*, 484 N.Y.S.2d 780 (N.Y. Fam. Ct. 1985).
[97] *Buzzanca*, 61 Cal. App. 4th at 1423.
[98] *Id.* at 1428.
[99] 42 U.S.C. §§ 273–274g.
[100] *Id.* § 274(a)–(b).
[101] Hospitals in which transplants are performed must, as a condition of participation in the Medicare and Medicaid programs, be members of UNOS and comply with its policies and rules. *Id.* § 1320b-8(a)(1)(B). UNOS policies may be found at https://unos.org/policy/policy-brochures/ and bylaws are posted at https://www.unos.org/wp-content/uploads/unos/UNOS_Bylaws.pdf.

NOTA prohibits the purchase or sale of organs in interstate commerce,[102] as does the Uniform Anatomical Gift Act (UAGA).[103] Consequently, the United States relies on an entirely voluntary system for organ donation. Federal law currently requires Medicare- and Medicaid-eligible hospitals to inform families of potential organ donors of the option to donate (and their right to decline) and to notify their local organ procurement organization (OPO) of potential organ donors.[104]

13.2.1 Strategies to Increase the Supply of Organs

The number of organs produced by the voluntary-donation system falls woefully short of the demand for transplantable organs. As a result, many attempts have been made to increase the supply, not all of them successful.

The UAGA provides that an anatomical gift takes effect upon or after the death of the donor. The determination of death is a matter of state law; although a majority of states still follow cardio-respiratory standard for determining death,[105] all states have adopted the whole-brain-death standard, as well.[106] Under the "brain death" standard, death occurs when all brain functions—those of the brain stem as well as the cerebral hemispheres—cease.[107] The brain-death standard has been useful for transplant purposes; it allows a determination of death to be made even while an individual's cardiac and respiratory functions are being artificially maintained, thus precluding a determination of death according to cardio-respiratory criteria.

Occasionally, however, waiting for all of the brain-death criteria to be satisfied will result in the loss of transplantable organs. This has led to occasional attempts to get around the brain-death criteria and declare death on some other basis. For example, in *In re T.A.C.P.*,[108] parents of an anencephalic newborn petitioned for a declaration that their child was "dead" for purposes of organ donation. Because an anencephaly denotes the absence of the cerebral hemispheres but the presence of some or all of the brain stem, the Florida Supreme Court ruled that an anencephalic newborn could not be declared dead. The infant, therefore, could not be an organ donor until her brainstem ceased to function or she satisfied the cardio-respiratory criterion for death, even though that meant the organs of most anencephalic infants would not be transplantable.

Similarly, patients in a persistent (or permanent) vegetative state (PVS) have suffered the irreversible loss of higher-brain functions, while some or all of their brain-stem functions are intact.

---

[102] 42 U.S.C. § 274e(a). Federal law, however, does permit "the reasonable payments associated with the removal, transportation, implantation, processing, preservation, quality control, and storage of a human organ or the expenses of travel, housing, and lost wages incurred by the donor of a human organ in connection with donation of the organ." *Id.* § 274e(c)(2).
[103] Uniform Anatomical Gift Act (UAGA) § 10 (1987). All 50 U.S. states adopted the 1968 version of the UAGA, which was silent on the subject of organ sales; 27 states subsequently repealed the 1968 UAGA and enacted the 1987 UAGA (which departs significantly from the Uniform Act's language in some instances). *See* "General Notes," *id.* (2003). Thus, approximately 20 states still do not prohibit the purchase or sale of human organs, although the point is largely moot as long as federal law prohibits the practice. *See* Comment, *Organ Donation, Procurement and Transplantation: The Process, The Problems, The Law*, 65 UMKC L. Rev. 201, 218 (1996).
[104] 42 U.S.C. § 1320b-8(a)(1)(A)(i) and (iii).
[105] Cardio-respiratory criteria usually provide that death occurs upon the irreversible cessation of spontaneous cardiac and respiratory functions. *See, e.g.*, Dan W. Brock, *Death and Dying*, in *Medical Ethics* 363, 364 (Robert M. Veatch ed.,
[106] *See* Alan Meisel & Kathy L. Cerminara, *The Right to Die* § 6.04[A] (3rd ed. 2004).
[107] *See* Bernard Lo, *Resolving Ethical Dilemmas: A Guide for Clinicians* 164 (5th ed. 2013).
[108] *In re T.A.C.P.*, 609 So. 2d 588 (Fla. 1992).

The wait for death according to brain-death criteria may mean the loss of transplantable organs in PVS situations, especially when the PVS results from sudden trauma and cardio-pulmonary functioning has been restored before the organs have suffered from lack of oxygen. This loss could be avoided in many such cases if the states were to adopt a "neocortical" or "higher-brain" criterion for determining death, rather than the "whole-brain" criteria that are now universally recognized. Although the "higher-brain" proposal has been eloquently defended,[109] it has not gained much support.[110]

With the strong encouragement of UNOS and the Joint Commission and the support of the Institute of Medicine,[111] some hospitals are returning to cardio-respiratory criteria to determine death in at least some circumstances. These donors are referred to as "non-heart-beating cadaver donors," and their deaths are declared in the operating room, rather than the intensive care unit, after the removal of artificial life support and two to five minutes[112] of asystole and either pulselessness or fibrillation (ineffectual "quivering" action of the heart muscle fibers).[113] Drugs usually are administered at this point (if not sooner) to dilate the patient's blood vessels and to impede the clotting process, both in an attempt to maintain maximum blood flow to the organs. Several criticisms have been raised against the use of non-heart-beating cadaver donors,[114] and it is not yet clear whether societal intuitions concerning death will embrace or reject this approach to increasing the supply of cadaveric organs, although it appears to be gaining in acceptance.[115]

Finally, In 2007 the Department of Justice determined that paired organ exchanges among couples who do not match within their own family but do match someone else on the waiting list do not violate NOTA's prohibition against organ sales.[116] Congress subsequently amended NOTA to express its agreement with Justice that a paired organ exchange does not constitute "valuable consideration" within the meaning of the law.[117]

---

[109] *See, e.g.*, Robert M. Veatch, *The Impending Collapse of the Whole-Brain Definition of Death*, 23 HASTINGS CTR. REP'T 18–24 (July–Aug. 1993).

[110] The principal objections are (i) the higher-brain criterion confuses "loss of personhood," which arguably occurs with PVS and anencephaly, with "death;" (ii) no reliable tests are available to date to establish that higher-brain-death has occurred; and (3) the symbolism of burying or cremating a person who still has a pulse and is still breathing offends deep-seated intuitions about the nature of death. *See* Bernard Lo, *supra*, at 165.

[111] *See* Robert Steinbrook, *Organ Donation After Cardiac Death*, 357 NEW ENG. J. MED. 209 (2007).

[112] Early protocols called for a two-minute loss of cardio-pulmonary function and, despite a recommendation by the Institute of Medicine to increase the period to five minutes, most organ procurement protocols have retained the two-minute standard. *See* Stuart J. Youngner, Robert M. Arnold & Michael A. DeVita, When is "Dead"?, 29 HASTINGS CTR. REP'T 14 (Nov.–Dec. 1999).

[113] Gina Kolata, *Organ Shortage Leads to Nontraditional Transplants, and Ethical Concerns*, N.Y. TIMES, June 2, 1993, at A15, col. 1.

[114] The concerns include the following: (i) whether donors truly satisfy the cardio-respiratory criteria for the determination of death (in theory or in practice); (ii) the extent to which terminal care of patients may be compromised; (iii) the potentially undignified manner by which a patient/donor will die if he continues to breathe or have a pulse for "too long," and is returned to the intensive-care unit; and (iv) the possibility that death might occur not from the removal of life-support but from the organ-retrieval process itself, thus stepping over the line between "letting die" and "killing." *See* Bernard Lo, *supra*, at 296. These concerns are rigorously analyzed by John A. Robertson in *Policy Issues in a Non-Heart-Beating Donor Protocol*, 3 KENNEDY INSTIT. OF ETHICS J. 241–50 (1993).

[115] *See* Steinbrook, *supra*, at 213.

[116] *See Mem. Op. for the General Counsel, Dep't of Health and Human Services: Legality of Alternative Organ Donation Practices Under 42 U.S.C. § 274e*, (Op. O.L.C. 1, 3 (U.S. Dep't of Justice, Mar. 28, 2007).

[117] Pub. L. No. 110-144, § 2, 121 Stat. 1813 (2007).

Other proposals have been suggested but not implemented in this country. These include repealing the federal ban on organ sales[118] and creating a "presumed consent" rule, the latter having been adopted by a number of European countries. At the present time, however, little support exists for either option.

13.2.2 Allocation Policies

Because of the extreme shortage of organs for transplant, a great deal of attention has focused on the development of allocation rules for organs. UNOS has dominated the issue pursuant to a Congressional mandate to set national policy; until 1999, DHHS largely deferred to UNOS's lead.

Organs are allocated through a two-step process. First, a potential recipient has to be placed on the UNOS list for an organ, a decision that is guided by UNOS policies and, ultimately, left up to the patient's physician. Although the policies are specific as to the criteria to be used in deciding whether to put a patient on the list, their execution seems to have varied in the following ways: considerable variation has appeared among hospitals and regions; transplant centers adopted different approaches to liver and intestinal organs, on the one hand, and thoracic organs on the other; and some centers "gamed" the system by prematurely admitting a patient to the ICU and listing patients on multiple regional lists.[119]

The second step in the process involves matching patients on the UNOS's waiting list to a particular organ. Historically, UNOS' policies provided for a match to be made first locally (within the OPO's service area); if no match is possible locally, then the search moved to regional lists and, absent a match at that level, the national list. This system was designed to avoid (to the extent possible) the detriment that transportation causes to fragile organs; moreover, a potential donor often is encouraged by the knowledge that her organs would be given to someone from her area. Such a largely geography-driven system, however, resulted in two types of disparity. First, significant differences were seen in waiting times for patients on the UNOS list, seemingly a function of widely different local levels of supply and demand. This led to a second feature of the system: when organs were matched locally or regionally, patients on the national list who were far sicker and medically needier often had to continue to wait for an organ that survived the system's preference for local-then-regional matches.[120]

On October 20, 1999, DHHS published a final rule that attempted to address these disparities.[121] The rule directs the OPTN to develop allocation policies that will distribute cadaver organs to the maximum extent feasible on the basis of medical need, without regard to geographic location.[122] Thoracic organs—because of their relative fragility outside the body—continue to be allocated on a geographical basis, and "zero-antigen-mismatch" kidneys are matched anywhere in the country that

---

[118] *See, e.g.*, Lloyd R. Cohen, *Increasing the Supply of Transplant Organs: The Virtues of a Futures Market*, 58 GEO. WASH. L. REV. 1–51 (1989).

[119] *See Developments in the Law: Medical Technology and Law*, 103 HARV. L. REV. 1614 (1990).

[120] These disparities are documented and analyzed by the *Institute of Medicine* in *Organ Procurement and Transplantation: Assessing Current Policies and the Potential Impact of the DHHS Final Rule* (1999), *available at* https://www.nap.edu/read/9628/chapter/1.

[121] *Organ Procurement and Transplantation Network*, 64 Fed. Reg. 56650 (Oct. 20, 1999), codified at 42 C.F.R. Part 121.

[122] This description is vastly oversimplified, but accurate as far as it goes. In addition to the separate policies noted in the text for thoracic organs and "zero-antigen-mismatch" kidneys, UNOS has separate allocation rules for pediatric patients. *See, e.g.*, Organ Procurement and Transplantation Network (OPTN) Policies 3.E, 6.1.D, 6.1.E, 6.1.F, 6.1.G, 6.5.E, 9.1.B, 9.1.C, 9.3.D, 9.6, *available at* https://optn.transplant.hrsa.gov/media/1200/optn_policies.pdf.

such a match can be made, in recognition of the increased prospect of a successful graft. The rule also brings the OPTN squarely within the regulatory orbit of DHHS, which was technically but not factually the case before 1999.

13.3 The New Genetics

As a result of the Human Genome Project, a greater understanding of the genetic basis of many diseases and conditions promises as great a revolution in health care as the germ theory of disease produced 150 years ago. In the areas of genetic testing, counseling, and therapy, new techniques are developed almost daily for detecting an individual's genetic predisposition to particular illnesses. This information, however, creates new and challenging ethical and legal dilemmas. Congress addressed this when it appropriated funds for the Human Genome Project by simultaneously earmarking 3% (later increased to 5%) of the total budget for the study of ethical, legal, and social issues.[123] Areas of major concern include confidentiality of genetic information, nondiscrimination, and the use of embryonic and fetal tissue cells in research.

13.3.1 Confidentiality

All states require that medical information and medical records be kept confidential. In addition to these generic requirements, however, many states have statutes that specifically protect the confidentiality of genetic information or prohibit genetic discrimination by employers and insurers,[124] and bills on this topic were introduced at least as far back as 1990.[125] The rationale for these statutes is that the unauthorized release of genetic information has the potential for creating a unique mixture of injuries—not only to the privacy and autonomy interests of the individual tested, but also the privacy interests of that person's extended family, as well as to his or her economic interests (i.e., employment opportunities, and the cost and availability of insurance) and social and psychological well-being.[126]

In addition to any genetic privacy law that may emerge from Congress in the future, DHHS's final privacy rule[127] enforcing that portion of the Health Insurance Portability and Accountability Act

---

[123] See Archive: Ethical, Legal and Social Issues, Human Genome Project, available at www.ornl.gov/sci/techresources/Human_Genome/elsi/elsi.shtml (describing much of the work in this area).

[124] See, e.g., 410 ILL. COMP. STAT. § 513/15; TEX. INS. CODE ANN. § 546.102; VA. CODE. ANN. § 38.2-508.4. Karen H. Rothenberg analyzes many of these state laws in Genetic Information and Health Insurance: State Legislative Approaches, 23 J. LAW, MED. & ETHICS 312 (1995) (discussing statutes enacted by Alabama, California, Colorado, Florida, Georgia, Maryland, Minnesota, New Hampshire, North Carolina, Ohio, Oregon, Virginia, and Wisconsin). See also Deborah Hellman, What Makes Genetic Discrimination Exceptional?, 29 AM. J. L. & MED. 77 (2003); Sharona Hoffman, Legislation and Genetic Discrimination, 16 J.L. & HEALTH 47 (2001); Genetic Privacy Laws, Nat'l Conference of State Legislatures, available at http://www.ncsl.org/research/health/genetic-privacy-laws.aspx.

[125] See, e.g. H.R. 493 and S. 358, Cong. 110 (2007) (Genetic Information Nondiscrimination Act of 2008); S. 306, Cong. 109 (2005) (Genetic Information and Nondiscrimination Act of 2005); H.R. 3636 IH, Cong. 108 (2003) (Genetic Privacy and Nondiscrimination Act of 2003); H.R. 602, Cong. 107 (2001) (Genetic Nondiscrimination in Health Insurance and Employment Act); H.R. 1057 & S. 573, Cong. 106 (1999) (Medical Information Privacy and Security Act); H.R. 2878, Cong. 106 (1999) (Medical Privacy in the Age of New Technologies Act of 1999); H.R. 5612, Cong. 101 (1990) (Human Genome Privacy Act). These culminated with the passage of the Genetic Information Nondiscrimination Act of 2008 (GINA), Pub. L. No. 110-233, 122 Stat. 881.

[126] See Lawrence O. Gostin, Genetic Privacy, 23 J. L. MED. & ETHICS 320, 324 (1995).

[127] The HIPAA privacy rule has a long and tortuous history, the explication of which is beyond the scope of this Chapter. Much of it is recounted in the preambles to the final rule and its various corrections and amendments. In 2013 HIPAA was substantially revised to include changes to the privacy, security, enforcement, and breach of notification rules. These changes

(HIPAA) is already in place. It places significant restrictions on the communication of health information without at least notification to the patient; for some uses, the patient's affirmative consent is needed. HIPAA also contains hefty penalties for its violation. The rule preempts contrary state laws that are less protective of individually identifiable health information; thus, the state laws discussed earlier, and the state cases that will be discussed, need to be reconsidered in light of this federal standard for privacy protection.

Confidentiality is not an absolute value; as a practical matter, the storage and dissemination of genetic information is relatively easy and has potential benefits. Accordingly, difficult issues arise concerning when and under what circumstances *may* genetic information be disclosed without a person's consent, and whether a *duty to disclose* such information exists at any point. At least two courts have considered whether a treating physician may have a duty to inform close family members that the patient has a disease for which the family members may be at risk due to the heritability of the gene that is linked to the disease. In *Pate v. Threlkel*,[128] the Florida Supreme Court accepted, for purposes of reviewing a dismissal for failure to state a claim, the allegation that the prevailing standard of care required a physician to warn a patient of the genetically transferable nature of her disease, and ruled that such a duty would run to the benefit of third parties, such as the patient's children. The court stopped short of imposing a duty to warn third parties directly, however:

> If there is a duty to warn, to whom must the physician convey the warning? Our holding should not be read to require the physician to warn the patient's children of the disease. In most instances the physician is prohibited from disclosing the patient's medical condition to others except with the patient's permission . . . . Moreover, the patient ordinarily can be expected to pass on the warning. To require the physician to seek out and warn various members of the patient's family would often be difficult or impractical and would place too heavy a burden upon the physician. Thus, we emphasize that in any circumstances in which the physician has a duty to warn of a genetically transferable disease, that duty will be satisfied by warning the patient.[129]

A New Jersey appellate court rejected the Florida Supreme Court's resolution of the issue in *Safer v. Pack*,[130] in which an adult daughter sued the estate of her father's physician on the ground that the physician failed to warn her that her father's diagnosis put her at increased genetic risk of contracting cancer. The court ruled that (i) "the duty to warn of avertable risk from genetic causes, by definition a matter of familial concern, is sufficiently narrow to serve the interests of justice,"[131] and (ii) it would not rule that disclosure of the familial risk to the patient satisfied the physician's duty to warn. The court did not "resolve a conflict between the physician's broader duty to warn and his fidelity to an

---

incorporate increased penalties, prohibit against the use of information for underwriting purposes, and they also incorporate a change in the length which information is protected to fifty years after death. *See Standards for Privacy of Individually Identifiable Health Information*, 65 Fed. Reg. 82462 (Dec. 28, 2000) (original final rule); 65 Fed. Reg. 82944 (Dec. 29, 2000) (technical corrections); 66 Fed. Reg. 12434 (Feb. 26, 2001) (correction of effective and compliance dates); 67 Fed. Reg. 53182 (Aug. 14, 2002) (substantial modifications to final rule); 78 Fed. Reg. 5566 (Jan. 25, 2013) (final rule with modifications to the privacy, security, enforcement, and breach of notification rules of HIPAA).

[128] *See Pate v. Threlkel*, 661 So.2d 278 (Fla. 1995).
[129] *Id.* at 282.
[130] *See Safer v. Pack*, 677 A.2d 1188 (N.J. Super. A.D.), *cert. denied*, 683 A.2d 1163 (N.J. 1996).
[131] *Id.* at 1192.

expressed preference of the patient that nothing be said to family members about the details of the disease,"[132] because the case had not yet been tried and there was not yet a factual record that would require the court to rule on the question.

13.3.2 Nondiscrimination

State legislatures have focused primarily upon genetic discrimination in the insurance and employment contexts, recognizing the reality that businesses have a strong economic incentive to find out about an individual's genetic predisposition for certain expensive medical conditions, and to act on that information. Before addressing state requirements and prohibitions, however, federal legislation must be considered.

In 2008 the Federal government passed the Genetic Information Nondiscrimination Act (GINA), which also focuses on discrimination in the context of insurance and employment. It prohibits discrimination in health insurance coverage and employment based on genetic information.[133] GINA provides a minimum level of protection on a nation-wide basis. Thus, "all entities that are subject to [it] must, at a minimum, comply with all applicable GINA requirements, and may also need to comply with more protective state laws."[134]

The statute defines "genetic information" as

information about an individual's genetic tests, genetic tests of the individual's family members, genetic tests of any fetus of an individual or family member who is a pregnant woman, and genetic tests of any embryo legally held by an individual or family member utilizing assisted reproductive technology, the manifestation of a disease or disorder in family members, any request for, or receipt of, genetic services or participation in clinical research that includes genetic services by an individual or family member."

"Genetic test" is defined as "analysis of human DNA, RNA, chromosomes, proteins, or metabolites that detects genotypes, mutations, or chromosomal changes." This definition does not include "analyses of proteins or metabolites that are directly related to a manifested disease, disorder, or pathological condition that could reasonably be detected by a health care professional with appropriate training and expertise in the field of medicine involved."[135]

Title I of GINA, in conjunction with HIPAA,[136] "generally prohibits health insurers or health plan administrators from requesting or requiring genetic information of an individual or the individual's

---

[132] *Id.* at 1192–93.
[133] *See* GINA, *supra*.
[134] *See* Genetic Information Nondiscrimination Act of 2008: Information for Researchers and Health Care Professionals, DEP'T OF HEALTH AND HUMAN SERVICES 1, 1 (Apr. 6, 2009), *available at* https://www.genome.gov/pages/policyethics/geneticdiscrimination/ginainfodoc.pdf.
[135] *Id.* at 2.
[136] In passing HIPAA, Congress limited the ability of group health plans to exclude subscribers on the basis of a preexisting condition. *See* 42 U.S.C. § 300gg. "Genetic information" is not a "condition" for which an insurer may impose a preexisting-condition exclusion "in the absence of a diagnosis of the condition related to such information." *See id.* This limitation does not extend to rating policies or establishing premiums on the basis of genetic information, and provides no protection to applicants or insureds in individual policies.

family members, or using it for decisions regarding coverage, rates, or preexisting conditions." It is enforced by the Department of Labor, the Department of Treasury, and the Department of Health and Human Services, and "remedies for violations include corrective action and monetary penalties."[137]

Title II of GINA "prohibits most employers from using genetic information for hiring, firing, or promotional decisions, and for any decisions regarding terms of employment" and will be enforced by the Equal Employment Opportunity Commission (EEOC).[138] As with Title I, the remedies for violation under Title II include corrective action and monetary penalties, although Title II also provides a "right to pursue private litigation."[139]

GINA provides a "research exception" to its application. Health plans are permitted to request, but not require, that a plan participant or beneficiary undergo a genetic test for "research purposes" if the following conditions are met:

(a) The request is made in writing and complies with relevant state and federal laws;

(b) The plan or issuer clearly indicates

   i. Compliance is voluntary; and

   ii. Non-compliance will have no effect on enrollment status or premiums

(c) None of the information collected shall be used for underwriting purposes

(d) The plan or issuer notifies the Secretary in writing that activities will be conducted pursuant to the exception.[140]

Additionally, "GINA does not extend to life insurance, disability insurance and long-term care insurance, "does not mandate coverage for any particular test or treatment," and "does not prohibit health insurers or health plan administrators from obtaining and using genetic test results in making health insurance payment determinations."[141] The employment provisions "generally do not apply to employers with fewer than 15 employees."[142]

One of GINA's limitations is that its nondiscrimination rule as applied to insurers does not extend to discrimination based upon an actual diagnosis of disease based upon the appearance of symptoms. This is hardly surprising, in light of GINA's focus upon discrimination based upon genetic information alone. The Patient Protection and Affordable Care Act, however, responded to this criticism in its prohibition of preexisting condition exclusions by providing that "[g]enetic information shall not be treated as a [preexisting] condition in the absence of a diagnosis of the condition related to such information."[143] The effect of this definition was to leave genetic-information-only discrimination in GINA's domain and to extend the federal nondiscrimination principle to symptoms through the Affordable Care Act.

---

[137] *Id.*
[138] *Id.*
[139] *Id.*
[140] *See* Pub. L. No. 110-233, § 101, 122 Stat 881, 833–88.
[141] *See* Genetic Information Nondiscrimination Act of 2008: Information for Researchers and Health Care Professionals, *supra*, at 2–3.
[142] *See id.* at 3.
[143] *See* 42 U.S.C. § 300gg-3(b)(1)(B).

13.3.2.1 Insurance

With respect to insurers, the several states have pursued a number of different strategies. Some have prohibited an insurer from denying coverage because of genetic information.[144] Several states prohibit insurers from limiting coverage, or determining rates or premiums, based on genetic information.[145] Several states also prohibit insurers from canceling or refusing to renew policies on the basis of such information.[146] Florida, Louisiana, Nevada and Tennessee prohibit an insurer from considering whether the applicant made a request for a genetic test.[147] Oregon and Texas have laws that prohibit an insurer from using favorable genetic tests as an inducement for coverage,[148] while Indiana and Illinois allow insurers to consider the results of a genetic test if the results are voluntarily submitted and favorable to the applicant or insured.[149] Several states forbid insurers from seeking information about a person's genetic characteristics for any nontherapeutic purpose.[150] Georgia has declared that genetic information is the unique property of the individual tested.[151]

13.3.2.2 Employment

As is the case with insurers, employers have an economic interest in screening job applicants or employees for genetic conditions that may lead to a higher rate of health-insurance claims, as well as a higher incidence of absenteeism and disability claims.[152] Title I of the federal Americans with Disabilities Act (ADA) provides that "no covered entity shall discriminate against a qualified individual on the basis of *disability* in regard to job application procedures, the hiring, advancement, or discharge of employees, employee compensation, job training, and other terms, conditions, and privileges of employment."[153] A "disability" within the meaning of the ADA includes a condition that is regarded by others to be a disability, regardless of the actual impact of the condition upon a major life activity.

The Equal Employment Opportunity Commission (EEOC) has the responsibility to develop standards and guidelines to implement the ADA. In its first formally published statement on the subject, the EEOC concluded that genetic discrimination fell within the scope of the ADA.[154] The EEOC's

---

[144] *See, e.g.,* CAL. INS. CODE § 10140(b); D.C. CODE § 2-1402.11(a); FLA. STAT. ANN. § 627.4301(2)(a); GA. CODE ANN. § 33-54-4; 410 ILL. COMP. STAT. § 513/20(b); MASS. ANN. LAWS ch. 175 § 108H; N.J. STAT. ANN. § 17B:30-12(e)–(f); N.Y. INS. LAW ANN. § 3221(q)(1)(F); TEX. INS. CODE § 546.052; VA. CODE ANN. § 38.2-508.4(B).

[145] *See, e.g.,* CAL. INS. CODE § 10140(b); FLA. STAT. ANN. § 627.4301(2)(a); MASS. ANN. LAWS. ch. 175 § 108H; N.J. STAT. ANN. § 17B:30-12(e)(1); OHIO REV. CODE ANN. § 3901.491(B); TEX. INS. CODE ANN. § 546.052; VA. CODE ANN. § 38.2-508.4(B).

[146] *See, e.g.,* CAL. INS. CODE § 10140(b); FLA. STAT. ANN. § 627.4301(2)(a); MASS. ANN. LAWS. ch. 175 § 108H; N.J. STAT. ANN. § 17B:30-12(f); TEX. INS. CODE § 546.052; VA. CODE ANN. § 38.2-508.4(B).

[147] *See* FLA. ST. ANN. § 627.4301(2)(b); LA. REV. STAT. ANN. 22:1023(B)(1); NEV. REV. STAT. § 689A.417; TENN. CODE ANN. § 56-7-2703.

[148] *See* OR. REV. STAT. § 746.135(2); TEX. INS. CODE ANN. § 546.051(c).

[149] *See* IND. CODE ANN. § 27-8-26-9; 410 ILL. COMP. STAT. § 513/20(c).

[150] *See* CAL. INS. CODE § 10140(c); GA. CODE ANN. § 33-54-4; IND. CODE ANN. § 27-8-26-5; MO. ANN. STAT. § 375.1303.

[151] *See* GA. CODE ANN. § 33-54-1.

[152] *See* Mark Rothstein, *Genetic Discrimination in Employment and the Americans with Disabilities Act*, 29 HOUS. L. REV. 23, 27 (1992).

[153] 42 U.S.C. § 12112(a) (emphasis added).

[154] Melinda B. Kaufmann, *Genetic Discrimination in the Workplace: An Overview of Existing Protections*, 30 LOY. U. L.J. 393, 414 (1999).

compliance manual now includes a short statement that addresses the "regarded as having a substantially limiting impairment" prong of the ADA's disability test. The statement provides that the ADA "[a]pplies to individuals who are subjected to discrimination on the basis of genetic information relating to illness, disease, or other disorders."[155]

President Clinton issued an Executive Order on February 8, 2000[156] prohibiting discrimination in federal employment based on genetic information. In general, the order protects information about an individual's genetic tests, or the genetic test of an individual's family member, and information about the occurrence of disease, medical condition, or disorder in family members of the individual.

Employment discrimination appears not to have attracted as much state legislative attention as insurance discrimination. In 1981, New Jersey was the first to enact legislation addressing employment discrimination based on genetic testing. This law prohibited "employment discrimination based on an individual's atypical hereditary cellular or blood trait."[157] In 1996, New Jersey revised this law to ban discrimination based on "genetic information," including information "that may derive from an individual or family member."[158]

Iowa, New Hampshire, Texas, and Wisconsin provide virtually identical statutory provisions. They prohibit an employer, labor organization, employment agency, or licensing agency from: (1) directly or indirectly soliciting, requiring, or administering genetic testing as a condition of employment, labor organization membership, or licensure; (2) affecting the terms, conditions, or privileges of employment, labor organization membership, or licensure of any individual based on genetic testing; or (3) terminating the employment, labor organization membership, or licensure of any individual based on genetic testing.[159]

13.3.3 Genetic Engineering

In some ways, the topic of genetic engineering brings this Chapter "full circle:" from decisions about reproduction (terminating a pregnancy, aiding a pregnancy) to scenarios similar to that in the novel *Brave New World* for reproducing human life in the laboratory. Predictably, the political and public-policy thicket of abortion, with which this Chapter began, also marks the developments (or the lack thereof) in this field.

13.3.3.1 Embryonic and Fetal-Cell Research

Genetic therapies that use fetal cells have long been thought to hold promise for curing or ameliorating the symptoms of many diseases; the potential for medical advances based upon embryonic

---

[155] EEOC Compliance Manual (BNA) § 902.8(a) (1995).
[156] Exec. Order No. 13145, 3 C.F.R. § 1 (2000).
[157] *See* Mark A. Rothstein, *The Law of Medical and Genetic Privacy in the Workplace*, in Genetic Secrets: Protecting Privacy and Confidentiality in the Genetic Era 281, 291 (Mark Rothstein, ed., 1997) (citing N.J. Stat. Ann. § 10:5-5(x), which states that "atypical hereditary cellular or blood trait [means] sickle cell trait, hemoglobin C trait, thalassemia trait, Tay Sachs trait, or cystic fibrosis trait.").
[158] *Id*, citing N.J. Stat. Ann. § 10:5-5(oo).
[159] *See* Iowa Code Ann. § 729.6(2); N.H. Rev. Stat. Ann. § 141-H:3(1); Tex. Labor Code §§ 21.402; Wis. Stat. Ann. § 111.372(1).

cells—especially stem cells[160]—is regarded as one of the most significant scientific achievements of the past decade.[161] Most federally sponsored research using embryonic and fetal cells, however, stopped when Congress enacted a ban in 1985 on most fetal research,[162] followed by a ban in 1997 on the use of federal funds "for the creation of a human embryo or embryos for research purposes . . . or research in which a human embryo or embryos are destroyed, discarded or knowingly subjected to risk of injury or death."[163] The National Institutes of Health (NIH) tested the limits of this federal ban by proposing "Draft Guidelines for Research Involving Human Pluripotent Stem Cells."[164] The guidelines were based upon an opinion issued by the general counsel of DHHS that pluripotent stem cells are not "embryos" within the meaning of the federal research ban, and therefore NIH could legally fund stem-cell research.[165] Under the guidelines, federally sponsored researchers could not derive stem cells from embryos, but they were permitted to conduct research on stem cells that were so derived by private (nonfederally funded) researchers.

In August 2001, President Bush announced that federal funds may be awarded for research using human embryonic stem-cell lines that meet certain criteria, such as "where the life and death decision has already been made."[166] According to the president, approximately 60 cell lines met the specifications: their derivation process began before 9:00 pm E.D.T. on August 9, 2001; they were derived from an embryo created for reproductive purposes; and informed consent was obtained from the embryo donor, without financial inducement. Some have criticized the president's decision, accusing him of unnecessarily and arbitrarily restricting scientific progress. Others, however, have praised the decision as an appropriate restriction on potentially unethical and dangerous research. NIH has implemented the president's decision by creating a Human Embryonic Stem Cell Registry, which lists the human embryonic stem cells that meet the eligibility criteria.[167]

In March 2009, President Obama issued an Executive Order (Removing Barriers to Responsible Scientific Research Involving Human Stem Cells) that revoked President Bush's Executive Order of August 9, 2001.[168] The order provides that, "[t]he Secretary of Health and Human Services, through the director of NIH, may support and conduct responsible, scientifically worthy human stem cell research, including human embryonic stem cell research, to the extent permitted by law."[169]

---

[160] Stem cells have the ability to divide for indefinite periods in culture and to give rise to specialized cells. "Pluripotent" stem cells can give rise to many types of cells, and could help to identify the factors involved in the cellular decision-making process that results in cell specification. *Stem Cell Information*, Nat'l Institutes of Health (June 17, 2001), https://stemcells.nih.gov/info/2001report/execSum.htm.
[161] *See* Stephen S. Hall, *The Recycled Generation*, N.Y. TIMES MAG., Jan. 30, 2000.
[162] Pub. L. No. 99-158 § 498, 99 Stat 820, 877–78 (1985), *codified at* 42 U.S.C. § 289g. The law makes an exception for research that will not result in harm to the fetus, but that exception is of no real use to fetal-cell researchers.
[163] Pub. L. No. 105-78 § 513, 111 Stat. 1467, 1517 (1997). The prohibition was re-enacted in Pub. L. No. 105-277 § 511, 112 Stat. 2681, 2681–386 (1998); and Pub. L. No. 106-113 § 510, 113 Stat. 1501, 1501A-275 (1999).
[164] *See* Draft Nat'l Institute of Health Guidelines for Res. Involving Hum. Pluripotent Stem Cells, 64 Fed. Reg. 67576 (Dec. 2, 1999).
[165] *See* Guidelines for Res. Using Hum. Pluripotent Stem Cells, 65 Fed. Reg. 51975 (Aug. 25, 2000). The opinion also stated that stem cells derived from human fetal tissue falls within the definition of human fetal tissue and would continue to be subject to the federal prohibition.
[166] White House Press Release, Fact Sheet, *Embryonic Stem Cell Research*, Aug. 9, 2001.
[167] *See* NIH Human Embryonic Stem Cell Registry, Nat'l Institutes of Health, (July 13, 2011), https://grants.nih.gov/stem_cells/registry/current.htm.
[168] Exec. Order No. 13,505, 74 Fed. Reg. 10667 (Mar. 9, 2009).
[169] *Id.* at § 2.

The intended effect of this order was to allow for federal funding of research on many more stem cell lines than the 21 lines in existence when President Bush issued his order in 2001. The order directed NIH to "review existing NIH guidance and other widely recognized guidelines on human stem cell research" and "issue new NIH guidance on such research that is consistent with this order."[170]

In response to the order, NIH published draft guidelines entitled "Draft Guidelines for Human Stem Cell Research Notice" in April 2009.[171] The Draft Guidelines allowed "funding for research using human embryonic stem cells that were derived from embryos created by *in vitro* fertilization (IVF) for reproductive purposes and were no longer needed for that purpose."[172] The final Guidelines, published on July 7, 2009, set forth eligibility requirements to determine which embryonic stem cell lines could be used in research funded by NIH.[173]

Under these guidelines, applicant institutions proposing research on human embryonic stem cells (hESCs) derived from embryos donated in the U.S. on or after the effective date of the NIH guidelines must use hESCs that are posted on the NIH registry, or establish eligibility for NIH funding by submitting a certificate of compliance with Section II(A) of the NIH guidelines.[174] Section II(A) requires that research involves only ESCs that were derived from human embryos that "were created using *in vitro* fertilization for reproductive purposes and were no longer needed for this purpose" and "were donated by the individuals who sought reproductive treatment . . . and who gave voluntary written consent for the human embryos to be used for research purposes."[175] Section II(A) further requires documentation of the following:

a. All options available in the health care facility where treatment was sought pertaining to the embryos no longer needed for reproductive purposes were explained to the individual(s) who sought reproductive treatment.

b. No payments . . . were offered for the donated embryos.

c. Polices and/or procedures were in place at the health care facility where the embryos were donated that neither consenting nor refusing to donate embryos for research would affect the quality of care provided to potential donor(s).

d. There was a clear separation between the prospective donor(s)'s decision to create human embryos for reproductive purposes and the prospective donor(s)'s decision to donate human embryos for research purposes.[176]

In order to comply with the congressional ban on funding for research in which an embryo is destroyed, section V(A) of the Guidelines provides, "NIH funding of the derivation of stem cells from human embryos is prohibited by the annual appropriations ban on funding of human embryo research . . . , otherwise known as the Dickey Amendment."[177]

---

[170] *Id.* at § 3.
[171] Nat'l Institutes of Health, *Draft Guidelines for Human Stem Cell Research Notice*, 74 Fed. Reg. 18578 (Apr. 23, 2009).
[172] *Id.*
[173] Nat'l Institutes of Health, *Guidelines for Human Stem Cell Research*, 74 Fed. Reg. 32170 (July 7, 2009).
[174] *See id.* at 32174.
[175] *Id.*
[176] *Id.*
[177] *Id.* at 32175.

On August 23, 2010, United States District Court for the District of Columbia issued a preliminary injunction that blocked federal funding of stem cell research pursuant to the Guidelines.[178] The court held that

> [I]f one step or "piece of research" of an ESC research project results in the destruction of an embryo, the entire project is precluded from receiving federal funding by the Dickey-Wicker Amendment. Because ESC research requires the derivation of ESCs, ESC research is research in which an embryo is destroyed.[179]

Therefore, "by allowing federal funding of ESC research, the [NIH] Guidelines are in violation of the Dickey-Wicker Amendment."[180] The court concluded that the language of the Dickey-Wicker Amendment is clear, unambiguous, and intended to "encompass *all* 'research in which' an embryo is destroyed, not just the 'piece of research' in which the embryo was destroyed."[181] On appeal, the U.S. Court of Appeals for the D.C. Circuit held that the Dickey-Wicker Amendment was ambiguous and vacated the preliminary injunction.[182] The court reasoned that "because the Congress wrote with particularity and in the present tense—the statute says 'in which' and 'are' rather than 'for which' and 'were'—it was entirely reasonable for the NIH to understand Dickey-Wicker as permitting funding for research using cell lines derived without federal funding, even as it barred funding for the derivation of additional lines."[183]

13.3.3.2 Cloning

When the news first broke in 1996 that a laboratory in Scotland had successfully cloned a sheep,[184] the worldwide reaction was not primarily concerned with the implications for animal husbandry and herd control. Instead, political and opinion leaders immediately asked, "are human beings next?" and "should they be?" Although the answer to the first question was "probably not,"[185] the answer to the second question was a resounding "no!"

The legal response has been swift and varied. Some states have encouraged stem-cell research without specifically addressing cloning, while others have prohibited cloning even when stem-cell research is otherwise encouraged.[186] At the federal level, then-President Clinton concluded that the federal ban on embryo research might not be fully effective in stopping cloning research, and issued a memorandum to all executive-department and agency heads in 1997 "direct[ing] that no Federal

---

[178] *Sherley v. Sebelius*, 704 F. Supp. 2d 63, 73 (D.D.C. 2010).
[179] *Id.* at 71–72.
[180] *Id.* at 72.
[181] *Id.* at 70–71 (emphasis added).
[182] *Sherley v. Sebelius*, 644 F.3d 388, 399 (D.C. Cir. 2011).
[183] *Id.* at 396. On remand, the district court granted the government's motion for summary judgment, 776 F. Supp. 2d 1, 24–25 (D.D.C. 2011), and the D.C. Circuit affirmed, 689 F.3d 776, 785 (D.C. Cir. 2012), *cert. denied*, 568 U.S. 1087 (2013).
[184] *See* K.H.S. Campbell *et al.*, *Sheep Cloned by Nuclear Transfer from a Cultured Cell Line*, 380 NATURE 64–66 (Mar. 7, 1996).
[185] *See* Lee M. Silver, *Remaking Eden: Cloning and Beyond in a Brave New World* 102–05 (1997) (arguing that safety issues strongly counsel cloning experiments with other mammals first).
[186] *See* Embryonic and Fetal Research Laws, Nat'l Conference of State Legislatures, (Jan. 1, 2016), http://www.ncsl.org/research/health/embryonic-and-fetal-research-laws.aspx.

funds shall be allocated for cloning of human beings."[187] President Clinton also requested the National Bioethics Advisory Commission to review the ethical and legal issues raised by human cloning, and to make recommendations for federal policy. That commission's report, issued in June 1997, concluded that "it is morally unacceptable for anyone in the public or private sector, whether in a research or clinical setting, to attempt to create a child using somatic cell nuclear transfer cloning."[188] The commission also recommended a continuation of the moratorium announced by President Clinton, as well as enactment of federal legislation "to prohibit anyone from attempting, whether in a research or clinical setting, to create a child through somatic cell nuclear transfer cloning."[189] Although bills were introduced in the 106th House of Representatives,[190] Congress *did not* enact legislation adopting the commission's recommendation.

President Bush stated that, although two types of human cloning have been distinguished in public debate, he "believe(s) all human cloning is wrong, and both forms of cloning ought to be banned."[191] He endorsed a proposed bill in 2001 that would ban all human cloning in the United States, including the cloning of embryos for research. The "Human Cloning Prohibition Act of 2003" passed in the House of Representatives,[192] but failed in the Senate.

The first report of the President's Council on Bioethics[193] recommended (by a 9-7 vote, with one member abstaining) in July 2002 that "cloning-to-produce-children" be banned and that Congress should enact a four-year moratorium on "cloning-for-biomedical-research."[194]

13.4 Conclusion

The challenging topic of bioethics is perhaps a fitting way to end a volume that attempts to present the fundamentals of health law. From the earliest stirring of human existence, through the disposition of human tissue and organs after death, bioethics represents the struggle to forge public policy in the face of technological advances and ethical uncertainty. The entire field of health law faces a similar challenge: to eke out a legal response to the constantly moving target of enlightened health policy. At any moment, the picture that emerges is at best a work in progress, as complex as the needs and strivings of our large and diverse population.

---

[187] William J. Clinton, *Memorandum for the Heads of Executive Departments and Agencies Re: Prohibition on Federal Funding for Cloning of Human Beings*, Mar. 4, 1997.
[188] Nat'l Bioethics Advisory Comm'n, *Cloning Human Beings* at iii (1997).
[189] *Id.* at iv.
[190] H.R. 571 and H.R. 2326, 106th Cong (1999).
[191] White House Press Release, *President Bush Calls on Senate to Back Human Cloning Ban: Remarks by the President on Human Cloning Legislation*, Apr. 10, 2002. The president noted a difference between "reproductive cloning" and "research cloning": the former creates embryos for implantation and childbirth, whereas the latter creates embryos for research and stem cell derivation.
[192] H.R. 534, 108th Cong. (2003) (passed in the House Feb. 27, 2003). The same bill passed in the House of Representatives during the 107th Congress as well, but it stalled in the Senate. Numerous bills aimed at prohibiting human cloning have been introduced since 2003, but none have passed.
[193] This group was created after President Bush's statement on stem-cell research in August 2001. *See* Executive Order 13237, 66 Fed. Reg. 59851 (Nov. 28, 2001).
[194] *See* President's Council on Bioethics, Human Cloning & Human Dignity: An Ethical Inquiry (July 2002), archived at https://bioethicsarchive.georgetown.edu/pcbe/reports/cloningreport/fullreport.

14

Data Sharing for Clinical Integration and Other "Big Data" Initiatives

Kristen Rosati and Melissa Soliz[1]
Coppersmith Brockelman PLC

14.1 Introduction

Many hospitals and other provider organizations are now entering into "Big Data"[2] arrangements under which they are sharing substantial amounts of clinical, genomic, and other types of data with other entities. These Big Data arrangements have the potential to improve health services and reduce the cost of health care through support for clinical integration across legal entities, to improve care management through data sharing, to facilitate powerful research and shorten the drug development pipeline by reforming how we conduct clinical trials, and to utilize data for important public health activities such as active drug safety surveillance across multiple data sources.

The utility of Big Data is clear, but the risks are substantial without thoughtful data governance that reflects the legal restrictions around data sharing. This Chapter explores the legal issues in data sharing, including compliance with the Health Insurance Portability and Accountability Act and its implementing regulations (HIPAA), the federal Confidentiality of Substance Use Disorder Patient Records regulations, state health information confidentiality laws, the Common Rule, antitrust laws, and laws related to tax exempt entities.

The first step in the use of Big Data for clinical integration, research, and other data sharing activities is generally building a data repository to house and curate the data. The data repository may itself be a shared data resource, or one of the parties to the data sharing arrangement may be responsible for hosting and curating the data. Because data repositories are essential to most Big Data arrangements, this Chapter explores the legal parameters around building data repositories and then providing access to that data to multiple legal entities.

---

[1] Sam Coppersmith, a founding partner at Coppersmith Brockelman PLC whose practice centers on business and transaction issues, contributed to the nonprofit tax exemption section of this Chapter.
[2] TOM WHITE, HADOOP: THE DEFINITIVE GUIDE 3 (3d ed. 2012). Big Data describes the "collection of data sets so large and complex that it becomes difficult to process using on-hand database management tools or traditional data processing applications."

14.2 Health Insurance Portability and Accountability Act (HIPAA)

14.2.1 Building a Data Repository

The process of creating a data repository is a "health care operation" function under the HIPAA Privacy Rule.[3] A covered entity may, of course, create a data repository with its own protected health information (PHI), because it may use or disclose PHI for its own health care operations.[4]

A covered entity may also create a shared data repository with other covered entities. A covered entity may enlist another entity to host its PHI in a data repository, as long as there is a business associate agreement in place (BAA) between the parties.[5] Thus, one covered entity may disclose its PHI to another, acting as a business associate on its behalf, in order for the business associate to host its PHI in a data repository. There is no limit under HIPAA on the *creation* of a shared data repository (only the use of information within the data repository). That is because HIPAA does not regulate *how* PHI is stored (other than the need to have a BAA with the repository holder and compliance with the HIPAA Security Rule requirements); rather, the HIPAA Privacy Rule regulates *who has access* to PHI and *for what purpose*. That issue is addressed in the next section.

However, building a data repository for research (or repurposing an existing data repository for research) is itself a research activity that should comply with one of the HIPAA rules. In its guidance document on HIPAA's application to research repositories, the U.S. Department of Health and Human Services (HHS) explained that the creation of a research repository is itself a separate research activity that should comply with one of the HIPAA rules.[6]

Organizations generally want to populate their data warehouses with all PHI from their electronic information systems; waiver of HIPAA authorization is the most practical approach to this end

---

[3] *See* 45 C.F.R. § 164.501 (defining health care operations).
[4] *See* 45 C.F.R. § 164.506(c)(1).
[5] *See* 45 C.F.R. § 160.103 (defining business associate); 45 C.F.R. § 164.502(e). A covered entity may be the business associate of another covered entity. *Id.*
[6] *See* NIH, Research Repositories, Databases and the HIPAA Privacy Rule (NIH Pub. No. 04-5489) (Jan. 2004), http://privacyruleandresearch.nih.gov/pdf/research_repositories_final.pdf:

> "Q: How may a covered entity use or disclose PHI for the creation of a research repository or database when it is unknown at the time of collection what specific protocols will make use of the repository or database in the future?
>
> A: There are two separate activities to consider: (1) The use or disclosure of PHI for creating a research database or repository, and (2) The subsequent use or disclosure of PHI in the database for a particular research protocol. A covered entity's use or disclosure of PHI to create a research database or repository, and use or disclosure of PHI from the database or repository for a future research purpose, are each considered a separate research activity under the Privacy Rule. In general, the Privacy Rule requires Authorization for each activity, unless, for example, an IRB or Privacy Board waives or alters the Authorization requirement. (*See* Overview of Privacy Rule's Impact on Repositories and Databases.) Documentation of a waiver or an alteration of Authorization to use or disclose PHI to create a research database requires, among other things, a statement that an IRB or Privacy Board has determined that the researcher [the holder of the repository] has provided adequate written assurances that PHI in the database will not be further used or disclosed except as permitted by the Privacy Rule (*e.g*, for research uses and disclosures with an Authorization or waiver). A covered entity also could use or disclose a limited data set to create a research repository or database under conditions set forth in a data use agreement."

because of the large number of individuals involved. To waive HIPAA authorization, the institutional review board (IRB) would be required to document the following determinations:

- The use or disclosure of the identifiable information involves no more than minimal risk to the privacy of the patients/members (the participants), based on: (a) an adequate plan to protect information identifying the participants from improper use and disclosure; (b) an adequate plan to destroy information identifying the participants at the earliest opportunity consistent with conduct of the research (unless there is a health or research justification for retention or if retention is required by law); and (c) adequate written assurances that the information identifying the participants will not be reused or disclosed to any other person or entity, except as required by law, for authorized oversight of the study, or for other research permitted by the rules;

- The research could not practicably be conducted without the waiver or alteration of authorization; and

- The research could not practicably be conducted without access to and use of information identifying the participants.[7]

A covered entity may rely on another organization's IRB for this purpose.[8]

14.2.2 Access to a Data Repository for Health Care Operations

A covered entity generally may release PHI to another covered entity for: (1) the releasing entity's own health care operations, and (2) the health care operations of the recipient entity, but only for the health care operations activities listed in the first two paragraphs of the Privacy Rule's definition of "health care operations" and fraud and abuse compliance activities, and only for individuals who

---

[7] 45 C.F.R. § 512(i)(2).

[8] The HIPAA Privacy Rule does not require the covered entity to conduct its own IRB review; rather, a covered entity may rely on waiver documentation generated by an outside IRB if that IRB is established under the Common Rule. *See* 45 C.F.R. § 164.512(i)(1)(i) ("Board approval of a waiver of authorization. The covered entity obtains documentation that an alteration to or waiver, in whole or in part, of the individual authorization required by § 164.508 for use or disclosure of protected health information has been approved by either: (A) An Institutional Review Board (IRB), established in accordance with [citations omitted]; or (B) A privacy board that [meets certain requirements]."). *See also* OCR, *Institutional Review Boards and the HIPAA Privacy Rule,* at http://privacyruleandresearch.nih.gov/pdf/IRB_Factsheet.pdf, pg. 2 ("The Privacy Rule does not impose any requirements for the location or sponsorship of an IRB convened for the purposes of acting on a request for approval of a waiver or an alteration of the Authorization requirement. Thus, an IRB approval for a waiver or an alteration of Authorization may be issued by an IRB that is unrelated to the institution conducting or sponsoring the specific research project, unrelated to the covered entity that creates or maintains the PHI to be used or disclosed for research, or different from the IRB with responsibility for monitoring the underlying research project. As a result, a waiver of alteration of the Privacy Rule's Authorization requirements could be obtained from a single IRB in connection with a multisite research activity or where the PHI necessary for the research is to be used or disclosed by more than one covered entity.").

The Common Rule also permits institutions covered by those federal regulations to rely on outside IRBs, if the relying institution has an IRB authorization agreement in place and lists the reviewing IRB on its Federal wide Assurance. *See* 45 C.F.R. § 46.114 ("Cooperative research projects are those projects covered by this policy which involve more than one institution. In the conduct of cooperative research projects, each institution is responsible for safeguarding the rights and welfare of human subjects and for complying with this policy."); 45 C.F.R. § 46.103(b)(2) (requiring designation of the reviewing IRB on the institution's Federal wide Assurance (FWA)).

Under the amendments to the Common Rule, the use of a central IRB will be required for most multi-site studies. 82 Fed. Reg. 7149, 7209 (Jan. 19, 2017). The requirement to use a central IRB will be effective on February 20, 2020. *Id.*

have or had a relationship with the recipient entity[9] (unless the entities participate in an organized health care arrangement (OHCA), which we discuss below).

---

[9] *See* 45 C.F.R. § 164.506(c):
"(c) Implementation specifications: Treatment, payment, or health care operations.
    (1) A covered entity may use or disclose protected health information for its own treatment, payment, or health care operations.
    (2) A covered entity may disclose protected health information for treatment activities of a health care provider.
    (3) A covered entity may disclose protected health information to another covered entity or a health care provider for the payment activities of the entity that receives the information.
    (4) *A covered entity may disclose protected health information to another covered entity for health care operations activities of the entity that receives the information, if each entity either has or had a relationship with the individual who is the subject of the protected health information being requested, the protected health information pertains to such relationship, and the disclosure is:*
        (i) For a purpose listed in paragraph (1) or (2) of the definition of health care operations; or
        (ii) For the purpose of health care fraud and abuse detection or compliance.
    (5) A covered entity that participates in an organized health care arrangement may disclose protected health information about an individual to another covered entity that participates in the organized health care arrangement for any health care operations activities of the organized health care arrangement." (emphasis added).

See also 45 C.F.R. § 164.501 (defining "health care operations"):

"Health care operations" means any of the following activities of the covered entity to the extent that the activities are related to covered functions:
    (1) Conducting quality assessment and improvement activities, including outcomes evaluation and development of clinical guidelines, provided that the obtaining of generalizable knowledge is not the primary purpose of any studies resulting from such activities; population-based activities relating to improving health or reducing health care costs, protocol development, case management and care coordination, contacting of health care providers and patients with information about treatment alternatives; and related functions that do not include treatment;
    (2) Reviewing the competence or qualifications of health care professionals, evaluating practitioner and provider performance, health plan performance, conducting training programs in which students, trainees, or practitioners in areas of health care learn under supervision to practice or improve their skills as health care providers, training of non-health care professionals, accreditation, certification, licensing, or credentialing activities;
    (3) Underwriting, premium rating, and other activities relating to the creation, renewal or replacement of a contract of health insurance or health benefits, and ceding, securing, or placing a contract for reinsurance of risk relating to claims for health care (including stop-loss insurance and excess of loss insurance), provided that the requirements of § 164.514(g) are met, if applicable;
    (4) Conducting or arranging for medical review, legal services, and auditing functions, including fraud and abuse detection and compliance programs;
    (5) Business planning and development, such as conducting cost-management and planning-related analyses related to managing and operating the entity, including formulary development and administration, development or improvement of methods of payment or coverage policies; and
    (6) Business management and general administrative activities of the entity, including, but not limited to:
        (i) Management activities relating to implementation of and compliance with the requirements of this subchapter;
        (ii) Customer service, including the provision of data analyses for policy holders, plan sponsors, or other customers, provided that protected health information is not disclosed to such policy holder, plan sponsor, or customer.
        (iii) Resolution of internal grievances;
        (iv) The sale, transfer, merger or consolidation of all or part of a covered entity with another covered entity, or an entity that following such activity will become a covered entity and due diligence related to such activity; and
        (v) Consistent with the applicable requirements of § 164.514, creating de-identified health information or a limited data set, and fundraising for the benefit of the covered entity.

Many of the typical uses of PHI in a data repository for clinical integration activities are for treatment or for care management and quality improvement, activities that fall under the first two paragraphs of the HIPAA definition of "health care operations."[10] These might include activities such as evaluating quality metrics from a combination of clinical and claims data; determining prescription compliance rates; managing transitions of care and managing the care of patients; and developing predictive models to target care management and care coordination efforts. However, other potential uses of data within clinical integration efforts may fall outside of those limited health care operations, including the use of data for more traditional business purposes, such as business planning, studying new business lines, or risk management.

In addition, covered entities may share PHI for each other's health care operations only if the recipient entity has or had a relationship with the patient and the PHI "pertains to such relationship."[11] As related to provider exchanges with plans, the HHS Office for Civil Rights (OCR) has concluded that "pertains to such relationship" means PHI that "overlaps with the period for which the individual is or was enrolled in the health plan."[12] It is unclear from the guidance provided how narrowly the OCR will apply this restriction, so parties are advised to document why the particular data that will be accessed pertains to the accessing entity's relationship with the individuals in the data set.

However, another rule will allow for greater data sharing between parties for health care operations purposes: the rule governing OHCAs. The Privacy Rule provides that a covered entity that participates in an OHCA may disclose PHI to another participating covered entity "for any health care operations activities of the [OHCA]." Thus, one advantage of an OHCA is that parties may share PHI for *all* health care operations "of the OHCA," not just the limited list of health care operations in the first two paragraphs of the definition of health care operations and fraud and abuse compliance activities, as discussed above. Also, such disclosures do not require that both entities have a relationship with the individual.[13]

---

[10] 45 C.F.R. § 164.501 (defining "health care operations").

[11] *See* 45 C.F.R. § 164.506(c)(4).

[12] *See* FAQ at http://www.hhs.gov/ocr/privacy/hipaa/faq/disclosures/265.html ("Question: May a health care provider disclose protected health information to a health plan for the plan's Health Plan Employer Data and Information Set (HEDIS)? Answer: Yes, the HIPAA Privacy Rule permits a provider to disclose protected health information to a health plan for the quality-related health care operations of the health plan, provided that the health plan has or had a relationship with the individual who is the subject of the information, and the protected health information requested pertains to the relationship. *See* 45 C.F.R. 164.506(c)(4). Thus, a provider may disclose protected health information to a health plan for the plan's Health Plan Employer Data and Information Set (HEDIS) purposes, *so long as the period for which information is needed overlaps with the period for which the individual is or was enrolled in the health plan.*") (emphasis added).
See also 67 Fed. Reg. 14776, 14782–83 (Mar. 27, 2002) ("These proposed modifications to allow disclosures for health care operations of another entity are permitted only to the extent that each entity has, or has had, a relationship with the individual who is the subject of the information being requested. Where the relationship between the individual and the covered entity has ended, a disclosure of protected health information about the individual only would be allowed if related to the past relationship. The Department believes that this limitation is necessary in order to protect the privacy expectations of the individual. An individual should expect that two providers that are providing treatment to the individual, and the health plan that pays for the individual's health care, would have protected health information about the individual for health care operations purposes. However, an individual would not expect a health plan with which the individual has no relationship to be able to obtain identifiable information from his or her health care provider. Therefore, this proposed limitation would minimize the effect on privacy interests, while not interfering with covered entities' ability to continue to provide access to quality and effective health care.").

[13] *See* 67 Fed. Reg. 53182, 53217 (Aug. 14, 2002) ("[A]s clarified by § 164.506(c)(5), covered entities that participate in an OHCA may share[PHI] for the health care operations of the OHCA, without the condition that each covered entity

The rule limits disclosures between covered entities for the health care operations activities *of the OHCA*.[14] The OCR has not adequately clarified what the "health care operations activities of the [OHCA]" means, although some language in the preamble indicates that OHCA participants may share PHI for health care operations of another participant in the OHCA. During the comment period, health plans had commented that they wanted to be able to receive PHI for health care operations they conducted that are not included in the first two paragraphs of the definition.[15] The OCR explained that the OHCA rules adequately addressed those concerns:

> The [OCR] also was not persuaded by the comments that the proposal should be broadened to allow disclosures for other types of health care operations activities, such as resolution of internal grievances, customer service, or medical review of auditing activities. The [OCR] believes that the provisions at § 164.506(c)(5), which permit covered entities that participate in an OHCA to share information for any health care operations activities of the OHCA, adequately provides for such disclosures. *For example, a health plan and the health care providers in its network that participate as part of the same OHCA are permitted to share information for any of the activities listed in the definition of "health care operations." The [OCR] understands the need for entities participating in these joint arrangements to have shared access to information for health care operations purposes and intended the OHCA provisions to provide for such access.*[16]

In another section of the preamble, the OCR stated: "While [PHI] may be freely shared among providers for treatment purposes under other provisions of this rule, some of these joint activities also support the health care operations *of one or more participants in the joint arrangement.* Thus, special rules are needed to ensure that this rule does not interfere with legitimate information sharing among the participants in these arrangements."[17]

Other statements in the preamble discuss the support of *joint* activities, but do not address activities that don't support joint activities:

- The "Privacy Rule allows legally separate covered entities that are integrated clinically or operationally to be considered an OHCA for purposes of the Privacy Rule if protected health information must be shared among the covered entities *for the joint management and operations of the arrangement.*"[18]

- If covered entities engage "jointly in one or more of the listed activities, the participating covered entities will need to share [PHI] to undertake such activities and to improve their joint operations. [For] example, the physician participants in the IPA [independent physician association] may share financial risk through common withhold pools with health plans or similar arrangements. The IPA participants who manage the financial arrangements need [PHI] about all the participants' patients in order to manage the arrangement. . . . If the

---

have a relationship with the individual who is the subject of the information.").
[14] 45 C.F.R. § 164.506(c)(5).
[15] *See* 67 Fed. Reg. at 53216.
[16] 67 Fed. Reg. at 53217 (emphasis added).
[17] 65 Fed. Reg. 82461, 82494 (Dec. 28, 2000) (emphasis added).
[18] *See* 67 Fed. Reg. at 14783.

participants in the IPA engage in joint quality assurance or utilization review activities, they will need to share [PHI] about their patients much as participants in an integrated clinical setting would. Many joint activities that require the sharing of [PHI] benefit the common enterprise, even when the benefits to a particular participant are not evident."[19]

The OCR explained that the purpose of the rule is to support broad sharing of information among OHCA participants for health care operations and that a "key component" of OHCAs is "that the individuals who obtain services from them have an expectation that these arrangements are integrated and that they jointly manage their operations"[20] and would thus not be surprised if their PHI was shared with another participant in the OHCA. As long as both parties' Notice of Privacy Practices discuss the information exchange between them, or other information is widely available to individuals about the information sharing so that they would not be surprised to see information exchanged, the risk should be low that the OCR would conclude that sharing of PHI must be limited to the types of health care operations that support the joint operations of the parties (such as joint utilization review or quality assessment and improvement activities).

A shared data repository could meet the second definition of an OHCA, as an "organized system of health care in which more than one covered entity participates." To meet this definition, the participating covered entities must "hold themselves out to the public as participating in a joint arrangement" and must participate in at least one of the following joint activities: (1) utilization review, in which health care decisions by participating covered entities are reviewed by other participating covered entities (or by a third party on their behalf); (2) quality assessment and improvement activities, in which treatment provided by participating covered entities is assessed by other participating covered entities (or by a third party on their behalf); or (3) payment activities, if the financial risk for delivering health care is shared, in part or in whole, by participating covered entities through the joint arrangement and if PHI created or received by a covered entity is reviewed by other participating covered entities (or by a third party on their behalf) for the purpose of administering the sharing of financial risk.[21] Many clinical integration activities include aspects of joint quality improvement and

---

[19] 65 Fed. Reg. at 82494.
[20] 65 Fed. Reg. at 82494.
[21] *See* 45 C.F.R. § 160.103:
"Organized health care arrangement means:
  (1) A clinically integrated care setting in which individuals typically receive health care from more than one health care provider;
  (2) An organized system of health care in which more than one covered entity participates and in which the participating covered entities:
    (i) Hold themselves out to the public as participating in a joint arrangement; and
    (ii) Participate in joint activities that include at least one of the following:
      (A) Utilization review, in which health care decisions by participating covered entities are reviewed by other participating covered entities or by a third party on their behalf;
      (B) Quality assessment and improvement activities, in which treatment provided by participating covered entities is assessed by other participating covered entities or by a third party on their behalf; or
      (C) Payment activities, if the financial risk for delivering health care is shared, in part or in whole, by participating covered entities through the joint arrangement and if protected health information created or received by a covered entity is reviewed by other participating covered entities or by a third party on their behalf for the purpose of administering the sharing of financial risk.

some share financial risk, so meeting the OHCA requirements in a clinical integration arrangement should not be difficult.

14.2.3 Access to the Data Repository for Research

Under HIPAA, covered entities may internally use or externally disclose protected health information (PHI) only as expressly permitted by the HIPAA Privacy Rule.[22] Use or disclosure of PHI is permitted for research if the requirements of at least *one* of the provisions in the HIPAA Privacy Rule are met, including:[23]

1. The research involves only de-identified data;[24]
2. The research uses or discloses a "Limited Data Set" and the covered entity has a "Data Use Agreement" in place with the recipient of the Limited Data Set;[25]
3. The research subject or the subject's authorized representative has signed a written HIPAA authorization;[26]
4. An IRB has waived the requirement for authorization;[27]
5. The activities are just to prepare for research and required representations are obtained from the researchers;[28]

---

    (3) A group health plan and a health insurance issuer or HMO [health maintenance organization] with respect to such group health plan, but only with respect to protected health information created or received by such health insurance issuer or HMO that relates to individuals who are or who have been participants or beneficiaries in such group health plan;

    (4) A group health plan and one or more other group health plans each of which are maintained by the same plan sponsor; or

    (5) The group health plans described in paragraph (4) of this definition and health insurance issuers or HMOs with respect to such group health plans, but only with respect to protected health information created or received by such health insurance issuers or HMOs that relates to individuals who are or have been participants or beneficiaries in any of such group health plans."

[22] *See* 45 C.F.R. Part 160 and Part 164, Subpart E.

[23] Where multiple rules exist that may permit use or disclosure of PHI, it is not necessary to meet the terms of all of those rules. *See* 45 C.F.R. § 164.502:

"(a) Standard. A covered entity may not use or disclose protected health information, except as permitted or required by this subpart or by subpart C of part 160 of this subchapter.

    (1) Permitted uses and disclosures. A covered entity is permitted to use or disclose protected health information as follows:

        (i)   To the individual;

        (ii) For treatment, payment, or health care operations, as permitted by and in compliance with § 164.506;

        (iii) Incident to a use or disclosure otherwise permitted or required by this subpart, provided that the covered entity has complied with the applicable requirements of § 164.502(b), § 164.514(d), and § 164.530(c) with respect to such otherwise permitted or required use or disclosure;

        (iv) Pursuant to and in compliance with a valid authorization under § 164.508;

        (v) Pursuant to an agreement under, or as otherwise permitted by, § 164.510; and

        (vi) As permitted by and in compliance with this section, § 164.512, or § 164.514(e), (f), or (g)." (emphasis added).

[24] 45 C.F.R. § 164.514(a)–(b).

[25] 45 C.F.R. § 164.514(c).

[26] 45 C.F.R. § 164.508.

[27] 45 C.F.R. § 164.512(i).

[28] 45 C.F.R. § 164.512(i).

Chapter 14 Data Sharing and Other "Big Data" Initiatives 14.2.3

6. The use or disclosure is for patient recruitment purposes;[29]
7. The research involves only the information of decedents and required representations are obtained from the researchers;[30]
8. The disclosure of the PHI is required by law;[31] or
9. The research is "grandfathered" under the HIPAA rules (which rarely applies).[32]

In its guidance document on HIPAA's application to research repositories, HHS explained how use of PHI in a clinical data repository complies with the HIPAA Privacy Rule:

For subsequent use or disclosure of PHI for research purposes from a repository or database maintained by the covered entity, the covered entity may:

- Obtain the individual's Authorization for the research use or disclosure of PHI as specified under section 164.508;
- Obtain documentation of an IRB or Privacy Board's waiver of the Authorization requirement that satisfies section 164.512(i);
- Obtain satisfactory documentation of an IRB or Privacy Board's alteration of the Authorization requirement as well as the altered Authorization from the individual;
- Use or disclose PHI for reviews preparatory to research with representations that satisfy section 164.512(i)(1)(ii) of the Privacy Rule;
- Use or disclose PHI for research on decedents' PHI with representations that satisfy section 164.512(i)(1)(iii) of the Privacy Rule;
- Provide a limited data set and enter into a data use agreement with the recipient as specified under section 164.514(e); or
- Use or disclose PHI based on permission obtained prior to the compliance date of the Privacy Rule—informed consent of the individual to participate in the research, an IRB waiver of such informed consent, or Authorization or other express legal permission to use or disclose the information for the research as specified under section 164.532(c) of the Privacy Rule.[33]

Covered entities may also de-identify PHI according to standards set forth in the Privacy Rule so that its use and disclosure are not protected by the Privacy Rule.[34]

Applying these rules to a data repository, if a researcher wants access to PHI in the data repository, the researcher should submit a protocol to an IRB for approval of the specific study, as well as a

---

[29] 45 C.F.R. § 164.506 (treatment or health care operations).
[30] 45 C.F.R. § 164.512(i).
[31] 45 C.F.R. § 164.512(a).
[32] 45 C.F.R. § 164.512(i).
[33] NIH, RESEARCH REPOSITORIES, DATABASES AND THE HIPAA PRIVACY RULE (NIH Pub. No. 04-5489) (Jan. 2004), https://privacyruleandresearch.nih.gov/pdf/research_repositories_final.pdf.
[34] *Id.*

14.2.3 *Fundamentals of Health Law*

request for waiver of HIPAA authorization.[35] The standards for waiver of authorization are discussed above.

Second, the organization may provide access to Limited Data Sets[36] if it obtains a Data Use Agreement with the recipient that complies with the regulations.[37] This requirement to sign a Data Use Agreement applies to internal personnel, as well as external researchers.[38] There are a variety of informatics tools available (such as the i2b2 open-source software), which can extract Limited Data Sets or de-identified information from the PHI in the data repository, to create "research marts" that are useful and easily accessible to researchers.

Finally, an organization may allow researchers access to the PHI in a data repository for "preparatory to research activities" under HIPAA—activities to prepare for research, such as determining whether there are sufficient numbers of patients in the organization's records for particular studies. To provide access for this purpose, the organization must obtain the following representations in writing from the researcher: (1) the information is sought solely to prepare for research; (2) the information is necessary to prepare for research; and (3) no information identifying individuals will be removed from the premises in the course of the review.[39]

Because of the last requirement that no identifying information be removed from the premises, this rule poses substantial barriers to allowing researchers remote access to the data repository to

---

[35] If a researcher submits approval and waiver of HIPAA authorization of the IRB of a separate organization, the covered entity may rely on that outside IRB. Again, the HIPAA Privacy Rule does not require the covered entity to conduct its own IRB review; rather, a covered entity may rely on waiver documentation generated by an outside IRB if that IRB is established under the Common Rule. *See* 45 C.F.R. § 164.512(i)(1)(i) (A); *see also* OCR, *Institutional Review Boards and the HIPAA Privacy Rule*, at http://privacyruleandresearch.nih.gov/pdf/IRB_Factsheet.pdf, pg. 2.

[36] A Limited Data Set excludes all of the direct "identifiers" listed in the HIPAA regulations, but may include: (1) geographic designations above the street level or PO Box; (2) dates directly related to a patient, such as dates of service, birth date, admission date, discharge date, or date of death; or (3) any other unique identifying number, characteristic, or code that is not expressly listed as an "identifier." 45 C.F.R. § 164.514(c).

[37] *See* 45 C.F.R. § 164.514(e). A Data Use Agreement must:

"(A) Establish the permitted uses and disclosures of such information by the limited data set recipient [the purpose of which must be limited to research, public health activities or health care operations]. The data use agreement may not authorize the limited data set recipient to use or further disclose the information in a manner that would violate the requirements of this subpart, if done by the covered entity;

(B) Establish who is permitted to use or receive the limited data set; and

(C) Provide that the limited data set recipient will:

(1) Not use or further disclose the information other than as permitted by the data use agreement or as otherwise required by law;

(2) Use appropriate safeguards to prevent use or disclosure of the information other than as provided for by the data use agreement;

(3) Report to the covered entity any use or disclosure of the information not provided for by its data use agreement of which it becomes aware;

(4) Ensure that any agents, including a subcontractor, to whom it provides the limited data set agrees to the same restrictions and conditions that apply to the limited data set recipient with respect to such information; and

(5) Not identify the information or contact the individuals."

[38] The Preamble to the HIPAA Privacy Rule is clear that a covered entity that wants to create and use a limited data set for its own research purposes must have its own workforce member enter into an agreement containing the requirements of a data use agreement. 67 Fed. Reg. 53182, 53236 (Aug. 14, 2002). *See also* NIH Publication Number 03-5388, "Protecting Personal Health Information in Research: Understanding the HIPAA Privacy Rule," at p. 16 (last revised July 13, 2004), *available at* http://privacyruleandresearch.nih.gov/pdf/HIPAA_Booklet_4-14-2003.pdf.

[39] 45 C.F.R. § 164.512(i).

identify potential research participants, or to otherwise screen information to prepare for research. In its guidance documents, HHS has explained that this rule permits remote access to a repository, but that the researchers should be prohibited from downloading or printing the information:

Q: May a researcher access PHI through a remote access connection as a review preparatory to research?

A: Under certain, specified conditions and reasonable and appropriate security safeguards, yes. However, covered entities must comply with the relevant standards in both the Privacy Rule and Security Rule. . . before access to PHI through a remote access connection for preparatory research purposes is permitted to occur.

Under the Privacy Rule, covered entities are permitted to use or disclose PHI for reviews preparatory to research if the researcher provides representations that satisfy section 164.512(i)(1)(ii). The required representations must, among other things, provide that no PHI will be removed from the covered entity by the researcher in the course of the review. Remote access connectivity (*i.e.*, out-of-office computer access achieved through secure connections with access permissions and authentication) involves a transmission of electronic PHI, which is not necessarily a removal of PHI under the Privacy Rule. However, although the access to PHI through a remote access connection is not itself a removal of PHI, the printing, copying, saving, or electronically faxing of such PHI would be considered to be a removal of PHI from a covered entity.

The Privacy Rule permits a covered entity to rely on representations from persons requesting PHI if such reliance is reasonable under the circumstances. In the case of a request by a researcher to access PHI remotely, this means that, among other things, the risk of removal, as described above, should be assessed in order to determine whether it is reasonable to rely on the researcher's representation that the PHI will not be removed from the covered entity. The covered entity should determine whether its reliance is reasonable based on the circumstances of the particular case. For example, a covered entity may conclude that it can reasonably rely on representations from researchers who are its employees or contractors because their activity is manageable through the covered entity's employment and related policies establishing sanctions for the misuse of PHI. On the other hand, where the researcher has no connection to the covered entity, the covered entity may conclude that it cannot reasonably rely on the researcher's representations that PHI will not be removed from the covered entity, unless the researcher's activity is managed in some other way.

Covered entities that permit their workforce or other researchers to access PHI via a remote access connection must also comply with (on and after the compliance date) the Security Rule's requirements for appropriate safeguards to protect the organization's electronic PHI. Specifically, the standards for access control (45 C.F.R. § 164.312(a)), integrity (45 C.F.R. § 164.312(c)(1)), and transmission security (45 C.F.R. § 164.312(e)(1)) require covered entities to implement policies and procedures to protect the integrity of, and guard against the unauthorized access to, electronic PHI. The standard for transmission security

(§ 164.312(e)) also includes addressable specifications for integrity controls and encryption. This means that the covered entity must assess its use of open networks, identify the available and appropriate means to protect electronic PHI as it is transmitted, select a solution, and document the decision.[40]

This guidance limits the usefulness of this rule, particularly because it prevents downloading of information onto a remote server. Moreover, because the guidance suggests that a covered entity should not rely on the representations of non-employed researchers that they will observe these limitations, there is some risk of permitting researchers outside the organization to access PHI without IRB approval and waiver, even though the Privacy Rule technically might permit it. So, the better option is to provide access only to Limited Data Set information to outside researchers (and require Data Use Agreements), even if the purpose is to prepare for research.

14.2.4 Minimum Necessary Standard

A covered entity must limit its disclosures of PHI for health care operations and research purposes to the minimum necessary amount of information required for the particular purpose.[41] Thus, access to PHI in a data repository will be subject to the minimum necessary standard. To comply with the minimum necessary standard, personnel may only view information that is relevant to the request. To implement this, covered entities should consider limiting direct access to PHI to those who are maintaining the repository and curating the PHI for various requests, and should provide only de-identified information or a Limited Data Set to others to use for health care operations purposes.

14.2.5 Psychotherapy Notes

The HIPAA Privacy Rule has strict requirements on the use and disclosure of "psychotherapy notes," defined as "notes recorded (in any medium) by a health care provider who is a mental health professional documenting or analyzing the contents of conversation during a private counseling session or a group, joint, or family counseling session and that are separated from the rest of the individual's medical record. Psychotherapy notes do not include medication prescription and monitoring, counseling session start and stop times, the modalities and frequencies of treatment furnished, results of clinical tests, and any summary of the following items: Diagnosis, functional status, the treatment plan, symptoms, prognosis, and progress to date."[42] Use or disclosure of psychotherapy notes would

---

[40] NIH, Health Services Research and the HIPAA Privacy Rule (NIH Pub. No. 05-5308) (May 2005), http://privacyrule-andresearch.nih.gov/pdf/HealthServicesResearchHIPAAPrivacyRule.pdf.

[41] See 45 C.F.R. § 164.502(b); FAQ at http://www.hhs.gov/ocr/privacy/hipaa/faq/minimum_necessary/208.html ("**Question**: Won't the HIPAA Privacy Rule's minimum necessary restrictions impede the delivery of quality health care by preventing or hindering necessary exchanges of patient medical information among health care providers involved in treatment?
Answer: No. Disclosures for treatment purposes (including requests for disclosures) between health care providers are explicitly exempted from the minimum necessary requirements. Uses of protected health information for treatment are not exempt from the minimum necessary standard. However, the Privacy Rule provides the covered entity with substantial discretion with respect to how it implements the minimum necessary standard, and appropriately and reasonably limits access to identifiable health information within the covered entity. The Rule recognizes that the covered entity is in the best position to know and determine who in its workforce needs access to personal health information to perform their jobs. Therefore, the covered entity may develop role-based access policies that allow its health care providers and other employees, as appropriate, access to patient information, including entire medical records, for treatment purposes.").

[42] 45 C.F.R. § 164.501.

not be permitted for business analytics purposes.[43] Because psychotherapy notes, by definition, are not included in the medical record, however, they should not be present in electronic clinical information systems that populate a data repository. If they are present in the data sources that populate the data repository, they must be segregated.

14.2.6 Individual Right to Withhold Certain PHI from Health Plans

Section 13405(a) of the Health Information Technology for Economic and Clinical Health Act (HITECH Act) (*codified at* 42 U.S.C. § 17935(a)) requires a covered entity to grant an individual's request not to disclose PHI to a health plan, where that PHI is solely related to a health care item or service for which the individual has paid in full out-of-pocket. The HIPAA Privacy Rule sets forth those basic statutory requirements and states: "A covered entity must agree to the request of an individual to restrict disclosure of [PHI] about the individual to a health plan if: (A) The disclosure is for the purpose of carrying out payment or health care operations and is not otherwise required by law; and (B) The protected health information pertains solely to a health care item or service for which the individual, or person other than the health plan on behalf of the individual, has paid the covered entity in full."[44] If a health plan will be participating in the clinical integration activity or otherwise has access to a shared data repository, the parties should develop a way to meet this requirement.

14.2.7 De-identifying PHI and Access to De-identified Data

Covered entities may de-identify the PHI in a data repository to create de-identified data sets that are not subject to HIPAA restrictions on use and disclosure. The HIPAA Privacy Rule protects "individually identifiable health information." Individually identifiable health information is "health information, including demographic information collected from an individual" that identifies an individual or where "there is a reasonable basis to believe the information can be used to identify the individual."[45] PHI is a subset of individually identifiable health information that excludes certain health information held by employers and educational institutions."[46]

HIPAA provides two ways in which PHI may be "de-identified" so that it is no longer protected by the Privacy Rule.[47] First, a covered entity may follow the "safe harbor" method of de-identification and remove or code all of the HIPAA "identifiers" in the information. These identifiers include all of the following data about individuals and their family members, household members, or employers:

- Name;
- Street address, city, county, precinct, or zip code (unless only the first three digits of the zip code are used and the area has more than 20,000 residents);

---

[43] 45 C.F.R. § 164.508(a)(2).
[44] *See* 45 C.F.R. § 164.522.
[45] 45 C.F.R. § 160.103 (defining "individually identifiable information" as "information that is a subset of health information, including demographic information collected from an individual, and: (1) Is created or received by a health care provider, health plan, employer, or health care clearinghouse; and (2) Relates to the past, present, or future physical or mental health or condition of an individual; the provision of health care to an individual; or the past, present, or future payment for the provision of health care to an individual; and (i) That identifies the individual; or (ii) With respect to which there is a reasonable basis to believe the information can be used to identify the individual."
[46] 45 C.F.R. § 160.103 (defining "protected health information").
[47] 45 C.F.R. § 164.514(a)–(b).

- All elements of dates (except year) directly related to an individual;
- Age over 89 (unless aggregated into a single category of age 90 and older);
- Telephone numbers;
- Fax numbers;
- Email addresses;
- Social security numbers;
- Medical record numbers;
- Health plan beneficiary numbers;
- Account numbers;
- Certificate/license numbers;
- Vehicle identifiers, serial numbers, and license plate numbers;
- Device identifiers and serial numbers;
- Web Universal Resource Locators (URLs) and Internet Protocol (IP) addresses;
- Biometric identifiers, such as fingerprints;
- Full-face photographs and any comparable images; or
- Any other unique identifying number, characteristic, or code.

If a covered entity has actual knowledge that, even with these identifiers removed the remaining information could be used alone or in combination with other information to identify the individual, then the information must be treated as PHI.[48]

One issue is particularly relevant to data repositories and the use of that data. The Privacy Rule treats as identifiers "all elements of dates (except year) for dates directly related to an individual, including birth date, admission date, discharge date, [and] date of death."[49] An OCR/NIH fact sheet explains that time periods of less than one year are considered to be elements of dates under § 164.514(b)(1) of the Privacy Rule:

Q: May information de-identified under the Privacy Rule's "safe-harbor" method contain a data element that identifies a time period of less than a year (*e.g*, the fourth quarter of a specific year)?

A: No. The Privacy Rule's "safe-harbor" method for de-identifying health information requires removal of, among other elements, all elements of dates directly related to an individual, except for year. Thus, a data element such as the fourth quarter of a specified year must be removed if a covered entity intends to de-identify data using the "safe-harbor" method. However, fewer identifiers may need to be removed under the Privacy Rule's alternative method for deidentification, where a qualified statistician, applying generally accepted statistical and scientific principles and methods for rendering information not individually identifiable, determines that the risk of re-identification is very small. Thus, it may

---

[48] 45 C.F.R. § 164.514(b)(2).
[49] 45 C.F.R. § 164.514(b)(2)(C).

be possible for certain elements of dates to be considered de-identified where this second method allows it. See section 164.514(b)(1) of the Privacy Rule.

As an alternative to de-identified data, the Privacy Rule would permit a covered entity to use or disclose information about dates in the form of a limited data set.[50]

Information may be de-identified under the safe harbor method by coding (rather than removing) the identifiers. Codes may not be derived from any information about the individual, such as the individual's social security number, medical record number or name (such as initials), and may not be capable of being translated to identify the individual.

The second method of de-identification is to have a qualified statistical expert determine that the risk is very small that the information could be used alone, or in combination with other available information, to identify the patient.[51] The statistical expert must be a person with knowledge of and experience with generally accepted statistical and scientific principles and methods for rendering information non-individually identifiable, and must document the methods and results of the analysis that justifies the conclusion of very small risk.[52] For this analysis, whether or not there are "identifiers" in the information is not necessarily relevant. For example, a statistical expert could conclude that there is a very small risk of identification if certain dates of service are present in the information.

The process of de-identifying PHI is treated as a covered entity "health care operation," which may be done without the individual's authorization.[53] If the covered entity uses a third party to de-identify the information, the covered entity must first have a BAA in place with that third party.[54] When a business associate de-identifies PHI on behalf of a covered entity, that process is a "health care operations" function of the covered entity, *whether or not the covered entity participates in the financial benefit of using the de-identified data.* The HIPAA Privacy Rule specifically says that a covered entity may disclose PHI to a business associate for purposes of de-identification "whether or not the de-identified information is to be used by the covered entity."[55] Moreover, the definition of health care operations does not carry any requirement that the covered entity receive financial or

---

[50] *See* "Health Services Research and the HIPAA Privacy Rule," NIH Pub. No. 05-5308, *available at* http://privacyruleandresearch.nih.gov/pdf/HealthServicesResearchHIPAAPrivacyRule.pdf.
[51] 45 C.F.R. § 164.514(b) ("(1) A person with appropriate knowledge of and experience with generally accepted statistical and scientific principles and methods for rendering information not individually identifiable: (i) Applying such principles and methods, determines that the risk is very small that the information could be used, alone or in combination with other reasonably available information, by an anticipated recipient to identify an individual who is a subject of the information; and (ii) Documents the methods and results of the analysis that justify such determination . . . .").
[52] *Id.*
[53] *See* 45 C.F.R. § 164.501, defining health care operations as "any of the following activities of the covered entity to the extent that the activities are related to covered functions: ***
    (6) Business management and general administrative activities of the entity, including, but not limited to:***
        (v) Consistent with the applicable requirements of §164.514, creating de-identified health information or a limited data set, and fundraising for the benefit of the covered entity." *See also* 45 C.F.R. § 164.506 (use or disclosure of PHI for health care operations).
[54] 45 C.F.R. § 164.502(e); 45 C.F.R. § 164.504(e).
[55] 45 C.F.R. § 164.502(d)(1). *See also* "Clinical Research and the HIPAA Privacy Rule" (NIH Feb. 2004), *available at* http://privacyruleandresearch.nih.gov/pdf/clin_research.pdf (concluding that a covered entity may disclose its PHI to a third party researcher, for the researcher to de-identify that information to support the researcher's research (not the covered entity's research)).

other benefit from the activity.[56] After the de-identification process, the business associate may not retain the fully identifiable information for research without following one of the other HIPAA rules for use or disclosure of PHI for research.

14.3 Federal Confidentiality of Substance Use Disorder (Alcohol and Drug Abuse) Patient Records

Title 42, United States Code (U.S.C.) § 290dd-2, protects the confidentiality of records containing the identity, diagnosis, prognosis, or treatment of any patient that are maintained in connection with the performance of any federally assisted program relating to substance abuse education, prevention, training, treatment, rehabilitation, or research. On January 17, 2017, the Substance Abuse and Mental Health Services Agency (SAMHSA) issued amended Confidentiality of Substance Use Disorder Patient Records regulations, which are located at 42 C.F.R. Part 2 (the Part 2 Regulations), and implement the protections in 42 U.S.C. § 290dd-2.[57] SAMHSA further amended the Part 2 Regulations on January 3, 2018.[58] The last substantive update to these regulations was in 1987.[59] The amended regulations went into effect on March 21, 2017 and February 2, 2018, respectively.[60] This paper discusses compliance with the amended Part 2 Regulations for Big Data arrangements and notes where the amended Part 2 Regulations depart significantly from the 1987 regulations.

14.3.1 Applicability of the Part 2 Regulations' Disclosure Restrictions

The Part 2 Regulations' disclosure restrictions have limited application. They apply to information that (1) identifies a patient as having (or having had) a substance use disorder, and (2) was obtained by a "federally assisted program" called a "Part 2 program"[61] (collectively, Part 2 data).[62] The Part 2 Regulations' disclosure restrictions also apply to health plans, as well as other individuals or entities, that receive Part 2 data under certain circumstances—these other individuals and entities are referred to under the amended regulations as "other lawful holders of patient identifying information."[63]

14.3.1.1 Substance Use Disorder Identifying Information

Only information that identifies a patient as having (or having had) a substance use disorder either directly or by reference to other publicly available information, or through verification of identification by another person, is subject to the Part 2 Regulations' disclosure restrictions.[64] These restrictions do not apply to information that does not identify the patient as a substance abuser. For

---

[56] *See* 45 C.F.R. § 164.501 (defining "health care operations").
[57] 82 Fed. Reg. 6052 (Jan. 18, 2017).
[58] 83 Fed. Reg. 239 (Jan. 3, 2018).
[59] 82 Fed. Reg. at 6053.
[60] 82 Fed. Reg. 10863 (Feb. 16, 2017); 83 Fed. Reg. at 239 (SAMHSA has delayed the date for complying with the requirements in 42 C.F.R. § 2.33(c) until February 2, 2018).
[61] 42 C.F.R. § 2.11 (definition of "Part 2 program").
[62] 42 C.F.R. § 2.12(a)(1).
[63] 42 C.F.R. § 2.12(d)(2).
[64] 45 C.F.R. § 2.12(a)(1)(i).

example, demographic information that does not identify the patient as a substance abuser is not considered Part 2 data.[65]

14.3.1.2 Part 2 Programs

Additionally, the Part 2 Regulations' disclosure restrictions only apply if the information is obtained by a "a federally assisted program."[66] A program is "federally assisted" if it: (1) is conducted entirely or in part by any federal agency or department (with some exceptions for Veterans Administration and Armed Forces programs); (2) is conducted under a license, certificate, registration, or other authorization granted by any federal agency or department, including certified Medicare providers, authorized methadone maintenance treatment providers, and programs registered under the Controlled Substances Act to dispense controlled substances for substance use disorder treatment; (3) is tax-exempt or contributions to it are tax deductible; or (4) is the recipient of any federal funds.[67] Thus, any tax-exempt organization or organization that participates in Medicare/Medicaid is "federally assisted."

A "program" is defined as:

(1) An individual or entity (*other than a general medical facility*) who holds itself out as providing, and provides, substance use disorder diagnosis, treatment, or referral for treatment; or

(2) An identified unit within a general medical facility that holds itself out as providing, and provides, substance use disorder diagnosis, treatment, or referral for treatment; or

(3) Medical personnel or other staff in a general medical facility whose *primary function* is the provision of substance use disorder diagnosis, treatment, or referral for treatment, and who are identified as such providers.[68]

The Part 2 Regulations provide this explanation of applicability:

. . . . These regulations cover any information (including information on referral and intake) about patients receiving diagnosis, treatment, or referral for treatment for a substance use disorder created by a part 2 program. Coverage includes, but is not limited to, those treatment or rehabilitation programs, employee assistance programs, programs within general hospitals, school-based programs, and private practitioners who hold themselves out as providing, and provide substance use disorder diagnosis, treatment, or referral for treatment. However, the regulations in this part would not apply, for example, to emergency room personnel who refer a patient to the intensive care unit for an apparent overdose, unless the primary function of such personnel is the provision of substance use disorder diagnosis,

---

[65] SAMHSA, *Frequently Asked Questions: Applying the Substance Abuse Confidentiality Regulations to Health Information Exchange (HIE)* (2010), at Q16, *available at* https://www.samhsa.gov/sites/default/files/faqs-applying-confidentiality-regulations-to-hie.pdf [hereinafter "*HIE FAQs*"].
[66] 42 C.F.R. § 2.11 (definition of "Part 2 program").
[67] 42 C.F.R. § 2.12(b).
[68] 42 C.F.R. § 2.11 (definition of "Program") (emphasis added).

treatment, or referral for treatment, and they are identified as providing such services or the emergency room has promoted itself to the community as a provider of such services.[69]

In sum, the Part 2 Regulations historically have applied to, and will continue to apply to, any program that is federally assisted and holds itself out as providing, and provides, substance use disorder diagnosis, treatment, or referral for treatment, including an identified unit or medical personnel or other staff within a general medical facility. Hospitals, clinics, and other general medical practices are not "programs" unless they have an identified unit that holds itself out as providing substance use disorder diagnosis, treatment, or referral for treatment, or unless they have personnel whose *primary function* is this type of service.

14.3.1.3   Other Lawful Holders of Part 2 Data

Part 2 data is also protected from re-disclosure by individuals or entities who receive Part 2 data under certain circumstances. The Part 2 Regulations refer to such recipients as "other lawful holders of patient identifying information." SAMHSA declined to define this term in the Part 2 Regulations, reasoning that the term defies definition because "such determinations are fact-specific."[70] Instead, SAMHSA describes such "lawful holders" as "an individual or entity who has received such information as the result of a part 2-compliant patient consent (with a prohibition on re-disclosure notice) or as permitted under the part 2 statute, regulations, or guidance and, therefore, is bound by 42 C.F.R. [Code of Federal Regulations] part 2."[71]

For purposes of Big Data arrangements, this means that the following individuals or entities who are not Part 2 programs but who *receive* Part 2 data are subject to the Part 2 Regulations' disclosure restrictions with respect to the Part 2 data:

- Individuals or entities who receive Part 2 data with the required prohibition on re-disclosure notice,[72] regardless of its source;[73]
- Health plans that receive records directly from a Part 2 program or from a Part 2 program through an intermediary organization, such as a health information organization, whether or not those records are accompanied by the re-disclosure notice;[74]

---

[69] 42 C.F.R. § 2.12(e)(1).
[70] 82 Fed. Reg. at 6068.
[71] 82 Fed. Reg. at 6068.
[72] Each disclosure made with the patient's written consent must be accompanied by a prohibition on re-disclosure notice that states: "This information has been disclosed to you from records protected by federal confidentiality rules (42 CFR part 2). The federal rules prohibit you from making any further disclosure of information in this record that identifies a patient as having or having had a substance use disorder either directly, by reference to publicly available information, or through verification of such identification by another person unless further disclosure is expressly permitted by the written consent of the individual whose information is being disclosed or as otherwise permitted by 42 CFR part 2. A general authorization for the release of medical or other information is NOT sufficient for this purpose (*see* §2.31). The federal rules restrict any use of the information to investigate or prosecute with regard to a crime any patient with a substance use disorder, except as provided at §§2.12(c)(5) and 2.65." 42 C.F.R. § 2.32.
[73] 42 C.F.R. § 2.12(d)(2)(i)(C); *see also* 82 Fed. Reg. at 6069.
[74] 42 C.F.R. § 2.12(d)(2)(i)(A).

- Entities having direct administrative control over a Part 2 program and who receive records from the Part 2 program in connection with the provision of diagnosis, treatment, or referral for treatment of patients with substance use disorders;[75]

- Qualified service organizations (QSOs) of Part 2 programs[76] and the "contract agents" of QSOs;[77]

- Contractors of other lawful holders who receive Part 2 data pursuant to a patient's written consent for payment and/or health care operations purposes and their "contract agents";[78]

- Researchers and data repositories that receive Part 2 data without patient consent under the research exception, which is discussed in greater detail below;[79] and

- Others as specified in the Part 2 Regulations or guidance with respect to the Part 2 data, which are not necessarily relevant to Big Data arrangements.[80]

14.3.2 Building a Data Repository

The Part 2 Regulations permit a Part 2 program or lawful holder who received the Part 2 data pursuant to a patient's written consent for payment and/or health care operations to supply Part 2 data to a third party hosting a data repository for purposes of storing and curating the data. In these circumstances, the host of the data is acting as a QSO[81] (a Part 2 business associate or a lawful holder contractorfn (a non-Part 2 business associate),[82] and the contract with the host must integrate the required QSO language.[83] The host can then make the Part 2 data available to the data source for the general purposes of the data repository, consistent with the disclosure rules under the Part 2 Regulations. The de-identified information in the data repository can be shared for research purposes.[84]

---

[75] 42 C.F.R. § 2.12(d)(2)(i)(B).
[76] 42 C.F.R. § 2.11 (definition of "Qualified Service Organization").
[77] *HIE FAQs*, at Q10, *supra*.
[78] 42 C.F.R. § 2.33(b)–(c).
[79] 42 C.F.R. § 2.52.
[80] *See* 82 Fed. Reg. at 6068.
[81] 42 C.F.R. § 2.11 (definition of "Qualified Service Organization").
[82] 42 C.F.R. § 2.33.
[83] 42 C.F.R. § 2.11 (definition of "Qualified Service Organization," requiring that the QSO "(i) Acknowledges that in receiving, storing, processing, or otherwise dealing with any patient records from the part 2 program, it is fully bound by the regulations in this part; and (ii) If necessary, will resist in judicial proceedings any efforts to obtain access to patient identifying information related to substance use disorder diagnosis, treatment, or referral for treatment except as permitted by the regulations in this part."); 42 C.F.R. § 2.33(c) ("Lawful holders who wish to disclose patient identifying information pursuant to paragraph (b) of this section must have in place a written contract or comparable legal instrument with the contractor or voluntary legal representative, which provides that the contractor, subcontractor, or voluntary legal representative is fully bound by the provisions of part 2 upon receipt of the patient identifying information. In making any such disclosures, the lawful holder must furnish such recipients with the notice required under § 2.32; require such recipients to implement appropriate safeguards to prevent unauthorized uses and disclosures; and require such recipients to report any unauthorized uses, disclosures, or breaches of patient identifying information to the lawful holder. The lawful holder may only disclose information to the contractor or subcontractor or voluntary legal representative that is necessary for the contractor or subcontractor or voluntary legal representative to perform its duties under the contract or comparable legal instrument. Contracts may not permit a contractor or subcontractor or voluntary legal representative to re-disclose information to a third party unless that third party is a contract agent of the contractor or subcontractor, helping them provide services described in the contract, and only as long as the agent only further discloses the information back to the contractor or lawful holder from which the information originated" *Id.*
[84] 82 Fed. Reg. at 6096.

14.3.3 Access to Protected Information in a Data Repository for Health Care Operations

Part 2 programs (and other lawful holders of Part 2 data) may disclose Part 2 data to others, without patient consent, only for limited types of health care operations purposes (*i.e.*, audit and evaluation activities).[85] Any use of Part 2 data for other types of health care operations would require consent of the patient.[86] Pending federal legislation introduced this year, if signed into law, will loosen this restriction and permit disclosures for treatment, payment, and health care operations purposes without patient consent.[87]

14.3.4 Access to Protected Information in a Data Repository for Research and Data Linkages

Part 2 data may be released for research, without patient consent, in only limited circumstances. SAMHSA relaxed the disclosure restrictions for research purposes in the amended Part 2 Regulations so that patients suffering from substance use disorders have the same opportunity to benefit from research as patients suffering from physical disorders.[88] The revised research exception now permits Part 2 data to be disclosed by Part 2 programs and other lawful holders of Part 2 data to qualified personnel for the purpose of conducting scientific research if the researcher provides documentation of meeting other existing requirements for protection of human research subjects.[89] This is a significant change from the 1987 regulations, which limited disclosures for research to disclosures with approval by Part 2 program directors and operated without deference to the Common Rule or HIPAA.[90]

Under the amended Part 2 Regulations, a Part 2 program or other lawful holder of Part 2 data may disclose such data for the purpose of conducting scientific research if an individual designated by the disclosing organization as director, managing director, or otherwise vested with the authority to act as chief executive officer or their designee, makes a determination that the recipient satisfies the following requirements:

- If the recipient is a HIPAA-covered entity or business associate, the recipient has obtained and documented authorization from the patient, or a waiver or alteration of authorization consistent with the HIPAA Privacy Rule at 45 C.F.R. §§ 164.508 or 164.512(i), as applicable.[91]

- If the recipient is subject to 45 C.F.R. part 46 (the Common Rule), the recipient either provides documentation that the researcher is in compliance with the requirements of the Common Rule for informed consent or a waiver of consent (45 C.F.R. §§ 46.111 and 46.116) or that the research is exempt (45 C.F.R. §§ 6.101(b)) and any successor regulations.[92]

---

[85] 42 C.F.R. § 2.53.
[86] SAMHSA has proposed additional regulations that would allow individuals and entities who received Part 2 data pursuant to a valid consent to disclose this data without patient consent to contractors and subcontractors for specific types of payment and health care activities. 82 Fed. Reg. 5485, 5487 (Jan. 18, 2017).
[87] 115 H.R. 3545 (July 28, 2017); *see also* 115 S.B. 1850 (Sept. 25, 2017).
[88] *See, e.g.*, 82 Fed. Reg. at 6099.
[89] 42 C.F.R. § 2.52(a).
[90] 52 Fed. Reg. 21796, 21812 (June 9, 1987).
[91] 42 C.F.R. § 2.52(a)(1).
[92] 42 C.F.R. § 2.52(a)(2). SAMHSA issued this revised regulation predicated on the *current* version of the Common Rule. 82 Fed. Reg. at 6100. SAMHSA has indicated that "[s]hould conflicting policies be created in the future," as a result of changes to the Common Rule, it "will take appropriate action (*e.g*, issue an NPRM or technical correction)." *Id.*

- If the recipient is both a HIPAA covered entity or business associate and is subject to the Common Rule, the recipient has met the requirements of both HIPAA and the Common Rule (as reflected in the first two paragraphs above).[93]
- If the recipient is neither a HIPAA covered entity or business associate or subject to the Common Rule, the rule governing research does not apply.[94] We presume that means that patient consent would then be required.

Additionally, any individual or entity conducting scientific research that receives Part 2 data from a Part 2 program or other lawful holder of Part 2 data:

- Is fully bound by the Part 2 Regulations and must resist in judicial proceedings any efforts to obtain access to patient records except as permitted by the Part 2 Regulations;
- Must not re-disclose patient identifying information except back to the individual or entity from whom that patient identifying information was obtained or as permitted under the data linkage provisions at 42 C.F.R. § 2.52(c) (see discussion on data linkages below);
- May include Part 2 data in research reports only in aggregate form in which patient identifying information has been rendered non-identifiable such that the information cannot be re-identified and serve as an unauthorized means to identify a patient, directly or indirectly, as having or having had a substance use disorder;
- Must maintain and destroy patient identifying information in accordance with the security policies and procedures established under 42 C.F.R. § 2.16; and
- Must retain records in compliance with applicable federal, state, and local record retention laws.[95]

Researchers who have met these requirements may also request linkages to data sets from both federal and non-federal data repositories.[96] SAMHSA is permitting data linkages because the process of linking two or more streams of data opens up new research opportunities that will benefit patients suffering from substance use disorders.[97] SAMHSA also clarified that this "provision is not intended to prohibit a researcher from linking a data set in the researcher's possession that contains part 2 data with a data set from a third party source, so long as the part 2 data is not further disclosed in the data linkage process and the researcher adheres to any applicable confidentiality, privacy, and security requirements and safeguards."[98]

However, such data linkages are subject to a number of conditions. Specifically, the researcher must:

---

[93] 42 C.F.R. § 2.52(a)(3).
[94] 42 C.F.R. § 2.52(a)(4).
[95] 42 C.F.R. § 2.52(b).
[96] 42 C.F.R. § 2.52(c); *see also* 82 Fed. Reg. at 6101.
[97] 82 Fed. Reg. at 6101.
[98] 82 Fed. Reg. at 6101.

- Have the request reviewed and approved by an IRB registered with HHS Office for Human Research Protections (OHRP) to ensure patient privacy is considered and the need for identifiable data is justified;
- Upon request, provide evidence of the IRB approval of the research project that contains the data linkage component; and
- Ensure that patient identifying information obtained is not provided to law enforcement agencies or officials.[99]

A data repository, which is fully bound by the Part 2 Regulations upon receipt of Part 2 data, also has the following obligations:

- After providing the researcher with the linked data, destroy or delete the linked data from its records, including sanitizing any associated hard copy or electronic media, to render the patient identifying information non-retrievable in a manner consistent with the policies and procedures established under 42 C.F.R. § 2.16; and
- Ensure that the patient identifying information obtained in accordance with 42 C.F.R. § 2.52(a) is not provided to law enforcement agencies or officials.[100]

14.4 State Privacy Laws

Entities must consider whether their data sharing arrangement will comply with applicable state laws. Counsel should consider state laws that are applicable to the types of information (such as mental health or substance abuse treatment, Human Immunodeficiency Virus (HIV) and communicable disease information, or genetic information) and the types of entities sharing data (such as state hospital licensure regulations or health plan insurance regulation).

14.5 Common Rule

On January 19, 2017, the OHRP and other federal agencies that have adopted the Common Rule[101] published final regulations amending the Common Rule.[102] These regulations were long awaited: an Advance Notice of Proposed Rule Making was published July 26, 2011[103] and the Notice of Proposed Rule Making (NPRM) was published on September 8, 2015.[104] While the final rule makes substantial changes to the Common Rule, the regulations did not adopt the more controversial aspects of the NPRM, such as requiring consent to use de-identified biospecimens.

While the amendments originally were to become effective January 19, 2018 (with the exception of the rule mandating the use of a single IRB for multi-site studies, effective on January 20, 2020), HHS first announced that it was reviewing a proposed rule to delay the implementation of the

---

[99] 42 C.F.R. § 2.52(c)(1).
[100] 42 C.F.R. § 2.5(c)(2).
[101] The "Common Rule" regulations are regulations common across many federal agencies that conduct human subjects research. The Department of Health and Human Services regulations are found at 42 C.F.R. Part 46.
[102] 82 Fed. Reg. 7149 (Jan. 19, 2017).
[103] 76 Fed. Reg. 44512 (July 26, 2011).
[104] 80 Fed. Reg. 53933 (Sept. 8, 2015).

Common Rule revisions.[105] Then on January 22, 2018, the agencies published an interim final rule delaying the effective date until July 19, 2018.[106] The agencies explained that the delay is needed to provide additional time for regulated entities to make preparations to implement the amended Common Rule, and for the agencies to get input on whether further delay is warranted.[107] Because it is unclear when the amended Common Rule will be effective, this Chapter addresses both the current rule and the final amendments where applicable to the discussion.

14.5.1 Applicability of the Common Rule

The Common Rule applies to human subjects research that is conducted or supported by a federal department or agency that has adopted the Common Rule (such as HHS).[108] "Research" is defined in the Common Rule as "a systematic investigation, including research development, testing and evaluation, designed to develop or contribute to generalizable knowledge."[109] Under the amended Comment Rule the definition of "research" has been revised to expressly exclude a number of activities, including:

- Certain scholarly and journalistic activities;[110]
- Public health surveillance;[111]
- Criminal justice and investigations; and[112]
- Homeland security.[113]

The distinction between "research" under the Common Rule and other activities (such as quality improvement, public health surveillance, and innovative health care) is often a thin one, notwithstanding the amended Common Rule's changes to the definition of "research." That is because these activities often employ the same methodology as "research" by looking systematically at large data

---

[105] *See* OIRA, https://www.reginfo.gov/public/do/eoDetails?rrid=127614 (RIN 0937-AA05) (Oct. 7, 2017); *see also* OIRA, https://www.reginfo.gov/public/jsp/EO/eoDashboard.jsp (RIN 0937-AA06) (Jan. 4, 2018).

[106] 83 Fed. Reg. 2885 (Jan. 22, 2018). The interim final rule does not delay the compliance date for use of a single IRB for multi-site studies. *Id.*

[107] 83 Fed. Reg. at 2885.

[108] 45 C.F.R. § 46.101; § 46.103. OHRP has issued "Human Subjects Regulations Decision Charts" at http://www.hhs.gov/ohrp/policy/checklists/decisioncharts.html that are helpful in understanding the analysis of what activities are subject to IRB review.

[109] 45 C.F.R. § 46.102; *see also* 82 Fed. Reg. at 7260 (amended Common Rule § ___.102(l)).

[110] 82 Fed. Reg. at 7260–61 (amended Common Rule § ___.102(l)(1)) (excluding scholarly and journalistic activities (*e.g*, oral history, journalism, biography, literary criticism, legal research, and historical scholarship), including the collection and use of information, that focus directly on the specific individuals about whom the information is collected).

[111] 82 Fed. Reg. at 7260–61 (amended Common Rule § ___.102(l)(2)) (excluding public health surveillance activities, including the collection and testing of information or biospecimens, conducted, supported, requested, ordered, required, or authorized by a public health authority. Such activities are limited to those necessary to allow a public health authority to identify, monitor, assess, or investigate potential public health signals, onsets of disease outbreaks, or conditions of public health importance (including trends, signals, risk factors, patterns in diseases, or increases in injuries from using consumer products). Such activities include those associated with providing timely situational awareness and priority setting during the course of an event or crisis that threatens public health (including natural or man-made disasters).

[112] 82 Fed. Reg. at 7260–61 (amended Common Rule § ___.102(l)(3)) (excluding collection and analysis of information, biospecimens, or records by or for a criminal justice agency for activities authorized by law or court order solely for criminal justice or criminal investigative purposes).

[113] 82 Fed. Reg. at 7260–61 (amended Common Rule § ___.102(l)(4)) (excluding authorized operational activities (as determined by each agency) in support of intelligence, homeland security, defense, or other national security missions).

sets using statistics to analyze the data. Moreover, organizations often desire to disseminate the results of their quality activities to help other organizations improve care, leading to a concern that the activities are designed to contribute to "generalizable knowledge." Because Big Data likely will be used for quality improvement analyses during clinical integration activities, this paper focuses on the distinction between research and quality improvement activities.

The OHRP issued FAQs that are somewhat helpful in determining the distinction between research and quality improvement.[114] In essence, the use of data to evaluate or improve clinical care at a single institution (or within a network) would not be research.[115] On the other hand, a project to collect information about patient outcomes from untested clinical interventions *would* constitute research.[116] While many organizations use the intent to publish as an easy "rule of thumb" to deter-

---

[114] *See* http://answers.hhs.gov/ohrp/categories/1569.

[115] *Id.*, Q. "Do the HHS regulations for the protection of human subjects in research (45 C.F.R. part 46) apply to quality improvement activities conducted by one or more institutions whose purposes are limited to: (a) implementing a practice to improve the quality of patient care, and (b) collecting patient or provider data regarding the implementation of the practice for clinical, practical, or administrative purposes?"

A. "No, such activities do not satisfy the definition of "research" under 45 C.F.R. 46.102(d), which is ". . .a systematic investigation, including research development, testing and evaluation, designed to develop or contribute to generalizable knowledge. . ." Therefore the HHS regulations for the protection of human subjects do not apply to such quality improvement activities, and there is no requirement under these regulations for such activities to undergo review by an IRB, or for these activities to be conducted with provider or patient informed consent.

Examples of implementing a practice and collecting patient or provider data for non-research clinical or administrative purposes include:

- A radiology clinic uses a database to help monitor and forecast radiation dosimetry. This practice has been demonstrated to reduce over-exposure incidents in patients having multiple procedures. Patient data are collected from medical records and entered into the database. The database is later analyzed to determine if over-exposures have decreased as expected.

- A group of affiliated hospitals implements a procedure known to reduce pharmacy prescription error rates, and collects prescription information from medical charts to assess adherence to the procedure and determine whether medication error rates have decreased as expected.

- A clinic increasingly utilized by geriatric patients implements a widely accepted capacity assessment as part of routine standard of care in order to identify patients requiring special services and staff expertise. The clinic expects to audit patient charts in order to see if the assessments are performed with appropriate patients, and will implement additional in-service training of clinic staff regarding the use of the capacity assessment in geriatric patients if it finds that the assessments are not being administered routinely."

Q. "Do quality improvement activities fall under the HHS regulations for the protection of human subjects in research (45 C.F.R. part 46) if their purposes are limited to: (a) delivering healthcare, and (b) measuring and reporting provider performance data for clinical, practical, or administrative uses?"

A. "No, such quality improvement activities do not satisfy the definition of "research" under 45 C.F.R. 46.102(d), which is ". . .a systematic investigation, including research development, testing and evaluation, designed to develop or contribute to generalizable knowledge. . ." Therefore the HHS regulations for the protection of human subjects do not apply to such quality improvement activities, and there is no requirement under these regulations for such activities to undergo review by an IRB, or for these activities to be conducted with provider or patient informed consent.

The clinical, practical, or administrative uses for such performance measurements and reporting could include, for example, helping the public make more informed choices regarding health care providers by communicating data regarding physician-specific surgical recovery data or infection rates. Other practical or administrative uses of such data might be to enable insurance companies or health maintenance organizations to make higher performing sites preferred providers, or to allow other third parties to create incentives rewarding better performance."

[116] Q. "Are there types of quality improvement efforts that are considered to be research that are subject to HHS human subjects regulations?"

mine whether an activity is research, the OHRP has concluded that publication alone does not make a project research.[117]

Whether or not an activity is "research," the Common Rule does not apply if the research does not involve "human subjects." An organization does not conduct "human subjects" research under the HHS regulations as long as both of the following conditions are met: (1) the data was not collected for currently proposed research; and (2) the investigator cannot readily ascertain the identity of the subjects.[118] Thus, access to data is not human subjects research if it was collected for clinical care, payment, or administrative purposes by the organization and if the information in the repository is de-identified or in Limited Data Set format, and thus an investigator most likely will not be able to "readily ascertain the identity of a subject." (The only potential way de-identified information or Limited Data Sets could be identifiable to a particular researcher is if the researcher is a clinician that treats patients with a particularly rare condition. The repository can control for this through limiting the display of "small cell" data, where only a limited number of patients with a particular condition are displayed.) The OHRP FAQs are consistent.[119]

A. "Yes, in certain cases, a quality improvement project may constitute non-exempt human subjects research conducted or supported by HHS or otherwise covered by an applicable FWA. For example, if a project involves introducing an untested clinical intervention for purposes which include not only improving the quality of care but also collecting information about patient outcomes for the purpose of establishing scientific evidence to determine how well the intervention achieves its intended results, that quality improvement project may also constitute nonexempt human subjects research under the HHS regulations."

[117] *Id.*, Q. "If I plan to carry out a quality improvement project and publish the results, does the intent to publish make my quality improvement project fit the regulatory definition of research?"

A. "No, the intent to publish is an insufficient criterion for determining whether a quality improvement activity involves research. The regulatory definition under 45 C.F.R. 46.102(d) is "Research means a systematic investigation, including research development, testing and evaluation, designed to develop or contribute to generalizable knowledge." Planning to publish an account of a quality improvement project does not necessarily mean that the project fits the definition of research; people seek to publish descriptions of nonresearch activities for a variety of reasons, if they believe others may be interested in learning about those activities. Conversely, a quality improvement project may involve research even if there is no intent to publish the results."

[118] 45 C.F.R. § 46.102; *see also* OHRP, "Guidance on Research Involving Coded Private Information or Biological Specimens" (Oct. 16, 2008), *available at* http://www.hhs.gov/ohrp/policy/cdebiol.html.

[119] OHRP, "Quality Improvement Activities FAQs," *available at* https://www.hhs.gov/ohrp/regulations-and-policy/guidance/faq/quality-improvement-activities/index.html.

Q: "Can I analyze data that are not individually identifiable, such as medication databases stripped of individual patient identifiers, for research purposes without having to apply the HHS protection of human subjects regulations?"

A: "Yes, whether or not these activities are research, they do not involve "human subjects." The regulation defines a "human subject" as "a living individual about whom an investigator conducting research obtains (1) data through intervention or interaction with the individual, or (2) identifiable private information.... Private information must be individually identifiable (*i.e.*, the identity of the subject is or may readily be ascertained by the investigator or associated with the information) in order for obtaining the information to constitute research involving human subjects." Thus, if the research project includes the analysis of data for which the investigators cannot readily ascertain the identity of the subjects and the investigators did not obtain the data through an interaction or intervention with living individuals for the purposes of the research, the analyses do not involve human subjects and do not have to comply with the HHS protection of human subjects regulations. (*See* OHRP Guidance on Research Involving Coded Private Information or Biological Specimens, October 2008, *available at* http://www.hhs.gov/ohrp/policy/cdebiol.pdf)."

14.5.2 Exempt Research

The current Common Rule identifies six categories of research exempt from the Common Rule.[120] These categories include:

- Some research conducted in educational settings;[121]
- Some research involving educational tests, surveys, interviews, or observation of public behavior;[122]
- Research involving the use of existing data and specimens that are publicly available;[123]
- Research involving the use of existing data and specimens, where the investigator records information about the research subject in a way that can't identify the subject (including no links);[124]
- Public benefit research;[125] and
- Food quality studies.[126]

---

[120] 45 C.F.R. § 46.101(b). None of these exemptions apply to research involving prisoners. See 45 C.F.R. 46, Subpart C; 82 Fed. Reg. at 7261 (amended Common Rule § ___ .104(b)(2)). All of the exemptions are applicable to pregnant women, human fetuses and neonates involved in research. 45 C.F.R. § 46.201(b); see also 82 Fed. Reg. at 7261 (amended Common Rule § ___ .104(b)(1)).

[121] 45 C.F.R. § 46.101(b)(1) (exempting research conducted in educational settings, involving normal educational practices, such as (i) research on regular and special education instructional strategies, or (ii) research on the effectiveness of or the comparison among instructional techniques, curricula, or classroom management methods).

[122] 45 C.F.R. § 46.101(b)(2) (exempting research involving the use of educational tests (cognitive, diagnostic, aptitude, achievement), survey procedures, interview procedures or observation of public behavior, unless: (i) information obtained is recorded in such a manner that human subjects can be identified, directly or through identifiers linked to the subjects; and (ii) any disclosure of the human subjects' responses outside the research could reasonably place the subjects at risk of criminal or civil liability or be damaging to the subjects' financial standing, employability, or reputation). This exemption does not apply to research involving children, except for research involving observation of public behavior if the investigator does not participate in the observed activities. 45 C.F.R. § 46.101(i), n.1; see also 82 Fed. Reg. at 7261 (amended Common Rule § ___ .104(b)(3).

45 C.F.R. § 46.101(b)(3) (exempting research involving the use of educational tests (cognitive, diagnostic, aptitude, achievement), survey procedures, interview procedures, or observation of public behavior that is not otherwise exempt as described above, if: (i) the human subjects are elected or appointed public officials or candidates for public office; or (ii) federal statute requires without exception that the confidentiality of the personally identifiable information will be maintained throughout the research and thereafter).

[123] 45 C.F.R. § 46.101(b)(4) (exempting research involving the collection or study of existing data, documents, records, pathological specimens, or diagnostic specimens, if these sources are publicly available).

[124] 45 C.F.R. § 46.101(b)(4) (exempting research involving the collection or study of existing data these sources are publicly available or if the information is recorded by the investigator in such a manner that subjects cannot be identified, directly or through identifiers linked to the subjects).

[125] 45 C.F.R. § 46.101(b)(5) (exempting research and demonstration projects which are conducted by or subject to the approval of department or agency heads, and which are designed to study, evaluate, or otherwise examine: (i) public benefit or service programs; (ii) procedures for obtaining benefits or services under those programs; (iii) possible changes in or alternatives to those programs or procedures; or (iv) possible changes in methods or levels of payment for benefits or services under those programs).

[126] 45 C.F.R. § 46.101(b)(6) (exempting research involving taste and food quality evaluation and consumer acceptance studies that examine: (i) if wholesome foods without additives are consumed; or (ii) if a food is consumed that contains a food ingredient at or below the level and for a use found to be safe, or agricultural chemical or environmental contaminant at or below the level found to be safe, by the Food and Drug Administration (FDA) or approved by the Environmental Protection Agency or the Food Safety and Inspection Service of the U.S. Department of Agriculture).

14.5.2.1 Amendments to the Common Rule

The amendments to the Common Rule add new exemption categories, the most significant being exemptions for secondary research regulated by HIPAA and secondary research with identifiable private information or identifiable biospecimens after "broad consent." "Secondary" research is research using data or biospecimens for purposes other than the specific research being conducted, including for clinical purposes or for research repositories intended for future research. The new categories of exempt research most relevant to Big Data arrangements include:[127]

- Exemption for HIPAA-regulated research: Secondary research with identifiable information is exempt from the Common Rule if the research is regulated by HIPAA for the purposes of health care operations, research, or public health activities and purposes, as those terms are defined or described by HIPAA.[128] Thus, as long as the identifiable information stays within organizations that are regulated by HIPAA (covered entities and business associates), the research will be exempt from the Common Rule.

- Exemption for storage and use of data and biospecimens collected with "broad consent" after "limited" IRB Review: Both the storage of identifiable information for potential secondary research, and the actual use for secondary research, is exempt from the Common Rule if certain requirements are met.[129] The storage of such information is exempt if an IRB conducts a limited IRB review and makes the determination that "broad consent" will be obtained and documented, and that there are provisions to protect privacy and confidentiality in the event of a change in the way the information is stored.[130] Secondary research may then be conducted with the stored information if broad consent was obtained and documented, an IRB conducts a limited IRB review and makes the determination that the research is within the scope of the broad consent, and the researchers will not return individual research results to individuals.[131] The requirements of broad consent are discussed in greater detail below.

- Exemption for publicly available information and biospecimens: Secondary research using identifiable information and biospecimens is exempt from the Common Rule if the identifiable information or biospecimens are publicly available.[132]

- De-identified, non-linked information: Secondary research using identifiable information is also exempt from the Common Rule if it is recorded by the investigator in such a manner that the identity of the human subjects cannot readily be ascertained directly or through

---

[127] There is also an exemption for secondary research involving identifiable private information or identifiable biospecimens where: "The research is conducted by, or on behalf of, a Federal department or agency using government-generated or government-collected information obtained for nonresearch activities, if the research generates identifiable private information that is or will be maintained on information technology that is subject to and in compliance with section 208(b) of the E-Government Act of 2002, 44 U.S.C. 3501 note, if all of the identifiable private information collected, used, or generated as part of the activity will be maintained in systems of records subject to the Privacy Act of 1974, 5 U.S.C. 552a, and, if applicable, the information used in the research was collected subject to the Paperwork Reduction Act of 1995, 44 U.S.C. 3501 et seq." 82 Fed. Reg. at 7261–62 (amended Common Rule § ___.104(d)(4)(iv)).
[128] 82 Fed. Reg. at 7261–62 (amended Common Rule § ___.104(d)(4)(iii)).
[129] 82 Fed. Reg. at 7261–63 (amended Common Rule § ___.104(d)(7)–(8)).
[130] 82 Fed. Reg. at 7261–62 (amended Common Rule § ___.104(d)(7)) (criteria for exemption); 82 Fed. Reg. at 7264 (amended Common Rule required § ___.111(a)(8) (IRB determinations)).
[131] 82 Fed. Reg. at 7261–62 (amended Common Rule § ___.104(d)(8)) (criteria for exemption).
[132] 82 Fed. Reg. at 7261–62 (amended Common Rule § ___.104(d)(4)(i)).

identifiers linked to the subjects, the investigator does not contact the subjects, and the investigator will not re-identify subjects.[133]

Additionally, the amended Common Rule now permits an IRB to approve a research proposal in which the investigator will obtain information or biospecimens for "preparatory to research activities" (*e.g*, for purposes of screening, recruiting, or determining the eligibility of prospective subjects) without informed consent if the investigator either obtains the information: (1) through oral or written communication with the prospective subject or his/her legally authorized representative; or (2) by accessing records or stored identifiable biospecimens.[134] OHRP describes this in the preamble to the amended Common Rule as an exception to the informed consent requirement, not a waiver.[135] Although "preparatory to research activities" are not "exempt" under the amended Common Rule, the amended Common Rule is now more closely aligned with HIPAA, which also permits such activities without obtaining patient authorization if certain conditions are met.[136] The amended Common Rule is a change from the current rule, which requires an IRB to determine that informed consent can be *waived* before investigators may use such information for "preparatory to research activities."[137]

Finally, the amended Common Rule also slightly modifies some of the existing exemption categories.[138]

14.5.3 Informed Consent and Waiver

Unless activities are not "research" or are otherwise "exempt" from the Common Rule, a research subject's informed consent is required under both the current and amended Common Rule.[139] The basic requirements for informed consent under the current Common Rule include the following:

- A statement that the study involves research, an explanation of the purposes of the research and the expected duration of the subject's participation, a description of the procedures to be followed, and identification of any procedures which are experimental;

- A description of any reasonably foreseeable risks or discomforts to the subject;

- A description of any benefits to the subject or to others which may reasonably be expected from the research;

- A disclosure of appropriate alternative procedures or courses of treatment, if any, that might be advantageous to the subject;

---

[133] 82 Fed. Reg. at 7261–62 (amended Common Rule § ___.104(d)(4)(ii)).
[134] 82 Fed. Reg. at 7266–67 (amended Common Rule § ___.116(g)).
[135] 82 Fed. Reg. at 7227.
[136] *See* discussion in 14.2.3 Access to the Data Repository for Research, above.
[137] *See* 82 Fed. Reg. at 7227.
[138] The amended Common Rule exempts survey and interview research if "[t]he information obtained is recorded by the investigator in such a manner that the identity of the human subjects can readily be ascertained, directly or through identifiers linked to the subjects, and an IRB conducts a limited IRB review to make the determination required by § ___.111(a)(7)." 82 Fed. Reg. at 7261–62 (amended Common Rule § ___.104(d)(2)(iii)). This exemption does not apply to research involving children. *Id.* at 7261 (amended Common Rule § ___.104(b)(3)). Additionally, there is a new exemption for benign behavioral interventions involving adults. *Id.* at 7261–62 (amended Common Rule § ___.104(d)(3)).
[139] 42 C.F.R. § 46.116; 82 Fed. Reg. at 7265 (amended Common Rule § ___.116).

- A statement describing the extent, if any, to which confidentiality of records identifying the subject will be maintained;
- For research involving more than minimal risk, an explanation as to whether any compensation and an explanation as to whether any medical treatments are available if injury occurs and, if so, what they consist of, or where further information may be obtained;
- An explanation of whom to contact for answers to pertinent questions about the research and research subjects' rights, and whom to contact in the event of a research-related injury to the subject; and
- A statement that participation is voluntary, refusal to participate will involve no penalty or loss of benefits to which the subject is otherwise entitled, and the subject may discontinue participation at any time without penalty or loss of benefits to which the subject is otherwise entitled.[140]

Additionally, the current Common Rule generally requires that the information be given in a language understandable to the subject or representative and not include any exculpatory language through which the subject or representative waives (or appears to waive) any legal rights.[141]

An IRB may waive or alter the informed consent requirement under the current Common Rule if it finds that: (1) the research involves no more than minimal risk to the subjects; (2) the waiver or alteration will not adversely affect the rights and welfare of the subjects; (3) the research could not practically be carried out without the waiver or alteration; and (4) whenever appropriate, the subjects will be provided with additional pertinent information after participation.[142]

14.5.3.1 Amendments to the Common Rule

The amendments to the Common Rule make three substantial changes to consent requirements by: (1) adding to the informed consent requirements; (2) changing when and what elements of informed consent may be waived or altered by an IRB; and (3) introducing the concept of "broad consent," which an entity may use (in place of a full informed consent or IRB waiver of informed consent) if it is seeking consent for the storage or use of identifiable information or biospecimens for secondary research (where the information was collected for non-research purposes or for purposes other than the proposed research).[143]

---

[140] 45 C.F.R. § 46.116(a). Additional elements that might be required, if appropriate, include:
  "(1) A statement that the particular treatment or procedure may involve risks to the subject (or to the embryo or fetus, if the subject is or may become pregnant) which are currently unforeseeable;
  (2) Anticipated circumstances under which the subject's participation may be terminated by the investigator without regard to the subject's consent;
  (3) Any additional costs to the subject that may result from participation in the research;
  (4) The consequences of a subject's decision to withdraw from the research and procedures for orderly termination of participation by the subject;
  (5) A statement that significant new findings developed during the course of the research which may relate to the subject's willingness to continue participation will be provided to the subject; and
  (6) The approximate number of subjects involved in the study." Id. § 46.116(b).

[141] 46 C.F.R. § 46.116(a).

[142] 45 C.F.R. § 46.117(c)–(d); 45 C.F.R. § 46.101(i) and 61 Fed. Reg. 51531 (Oct. 2, 1996) (waiver of informed consent in emergency research).

[143] 82 Fed. Reg. at 7266–67 (amended Common Rule § ___.116(d)).

With respect to full informed consent, the amended Common Rule adds the following requirements:

- The consent must begin with a concise, focused, and plain presentation of the key information that is most likely to assist one in understanding the reasons why one might or might not want to participate in the research.[144]

- It must, as a whole, present information with sufficient detail and be organized in a way that facilitates understanding.[145] A listing of isolated facts is not sufficient.[146]

- If the research involves the collection of identifiable private information or identifiable biospecimens, it must include a statement that either: (i) identifiers might be removed and that, after such removal, the information or biospecimens could be used for future research studies or distributed to another investigator for future research studies without additional informed consent; or (ii) that the subject's information or biospecimens, even if identifiers are removed, will not be used or distributed for future research studies.[147]

- If the research involves biospecimens, a statement that the subject's biospecimens (even if identifiers are removed) may be used for commercial profit and whether the subject will or will not share in this commercial profit.[148]

- If appropriate, a statement regarding whether clinically relevant research results, including individual research results, will be disclosed to subjects, and if so, under what conditions.[149]

- If the research involves biospecimens, a statement regarding whether the research involves whole genome sequencing (*i.e.*, sequencing of a human germline or somatic specimen with the intent to generate the genome or exome sequence of that specimen).[150]

By contrast, the elements of the new "broad consent" concept for the storage and secondary research use of identifiable information or biospecimens incorporate some of the basic and additional elements of full informed consent,[151] and require that the following elements be included:

- A general description of the types of research that may be conducted with the identifiable information.[152] The description must include enough information that a reasonable person would expect the broad consent to permit the future research conducted.[153]

---

[144] 82 Fed. Reg. at 7265 (amended Common Rule § ___.116(a)(5)(i)).
[145] 82 Fed. Reg. at 7265–66 (amended Common Rule § ___.116(a)(5)(ii)).
[146] 82 Fed. Reg. at 7265–66 (amended Common Rule § ___.116(a)(5)(ii)).
[147] 82 Fed. Reg. at 7265–66 (amended Common Rule § ___.116(b)(9)).
[148] 82 Fed. Reg. at 7265–66 (amended Common Rule § ___.116(c)(7)).
[149] 82 Fed. Reg. at 7265–66 (amended Common Rule § ___.116(c)(8)).
[150] 82 Fed. Reg. at 7265–66 (amended Common Rule § ___.116(c)(9)).
[151] 82 Fed. Reg. at 7265–66 (amended Common Rule § ___.116(d)(1) (". . . . [T]he following shall be provided to each subject or the subject's legally authorized representative: The information required in paragraphs (b)(2), (b)(3), (b)(5), and (b)(8) and, when appropriate, (c)(7) and (9) of this section.").
[152] 82 Fed. Reg. at 7265–66 (amended Common Rule § ___.116(d)(2)).
[153] 82 Fed. Reg. at 7265–66 (amended Common Rule § ___.116(d)(2)).

- A description of the identifiable information that might be used in research, whether sharing might occur, and the types of institutions or researchers that might conduct the future research.[154]

- A description of the period of time that the identifiable information may be stored and maintained and/or used for research purposes.[155] The period of time for either could be indefinite.[156]

- Unless the subject or legally authorized representative will be provided details about specific research studies, a statement that they will not be informed of such details, including the purposes of the future research.[157] The statement must also inform the subject or legally authorized representative that they might have chosen not to consent to some of those specific research studies.[158]

- Unless it is known that clinically relevant research results, including individual research results, will be disclosed to the subject in all circumstances, a statement that such results may not be disclosed to the subject.[159]

- An explanation of whom to contact for answers to questions about the subject's rights, storage, and use of the subject's identifiable information or biospecimens, and whom to contact in the event of a research-related harm.[160]

Under the amended Common Rule, researchers are not required to use broad consent. A researcher can take the "traditional" route of obtaining full IRB-approved informed consent as described above or seek a waiver of informed consent to store and use identifiable information for research.[161]

The amended Common Rule also changes requirements for waiver of alteration of informed consent. In addition to the four existing criteria for waiver or alteration, an IRB will be required to find that, if the research involves using identifiable information or identifiable biospecimens, the research could not practicably be carried out without using the information in an identifiable format.[162] This criterion was modeled on the comparable element of waiver under HIPAA.[163] Additionally, if alteration of consent is sought, the amended Common Rule will not allow certain core elements of informed consent to be changed or omitted.[164]

With respect to alteration of the broad consent requirements, the amended Common Rule does not permit any omission or changes to these requirements.[165] The amended Common Rule also will prohibit waiver of informed consent for individuals who previously were asked to sign a "broad con-

---

[154] 82 Fed. Reg. at 7265–66 (amended Common Rule § ___.116(d)(3)).
[155] 82 Fed. Reg. at 7265–66 (amended Common Rule § ___.116(d)(4)).
[156] 82 Fed. Reg. at 7265–66 (amended Common Rule § ___.116(d)(4)).
[157] 82 Fed. Reg. at 7265–66 (amended Common Rule § ___.116(d)(5)).
[158] 82 Fed. Reg. at 7265–66 (amended Common Rule § ___.116(d)(5)).
[159] 82 Fed. Reg. at 7265–67 (amended Common Rule § ___.116(d)(6)).
[160] 82 Fed. Reg. at 7265–67 (amended Common Rule § ___.116(d)(7)).
[161] 82 Fed. Reg. at 7265–66 (amended Common Rule § ___.116(d)).
[162] 82 Fed. Reg. at 7265–67 (amended Common Rule § ___.116(f)(3)(iii)).
[163] 82 Fed. Reg. at 7224.
[164] 82 Fed. Reg. at 7226, 7267 (amended Common Rule § ___.116(f)(2)).
[165] 82 Fed. Reg. at 7265–97 (amended Common Rule § ___.116(f)(2)).

sent" to store or use the information for future research, but declined to sign.[166] Thus, before using or disclosing information pursuant to an IRB waiver of informed consent, organizations should confirm that none of the individuals previously declined to sign a broad consent concerning the information collected.

14.5.4 Application of the Common Rule to Building a Data Repository

Before a data repository is used for federally-funded research, an organization must obtain IRB review and approval for the repository. As noted above, if the data stays within entities subject to HIPAA, under the amendments to the Common Rule, the data repository will not be regulated by the Common Rule.

Because of the large amount of data that will flow to a repository, most organizations request an IRB to waive informed consent for that purpose (along with waiver of HIPAA authorization).

14.5.5 Application of the Common Rule to Access to Data in a Data Repository

If a researcher wants access to identifiable information in the data repository, it is human subjects research that requires approval by an IRB (unless the new HIPAA exemption or other exemption applies under the revised Common Rule applies).[167] If data is curated to remove identifiable information before access by researchers, access is not human subjects research and would not require approval by an IRB.

14.6 Antitrust

Federal antitrust laws are implicated when competing health care providers or health plans directly or indirectly exchange or share competitively sensitive information. Competitively sensitive information might include current or future prices, employee wages, strategic plans such as planned market entry or exit, or prices paid for inputs used to produce services. Although exchanging information is not, in and of itself illegal, such exchanges, particularly when there are only a few competitors in a relevant market, can be used to facilitate price fixing or otherwise suppress competition. Any competitively sensitive information therefore should not be shared between competing providers or competing plans, and data sharing should be structured to comply with the Department of Justice (DOJ) Antitrust Division and Federal Trade Commission (FTC) 1996 Statements of Antitrust Enforcement Policy in Health Care (the Health Care Statements)[168] and the 2014 Statement of Antitrust Policy Regarding Accountable Care Organizations in the Medicare Shared Savings Program.[169]

---

[166] 82 Fed. Reg. at 7267 (amended Common Rule § ___.116(f)(1)–(2)).
[167] An organization may rely on waiver documentation generated by an outside IRB if that IRB is established under the Common Rule. *See* OCR, *Institutional Review Boards and the HIPAA Privacy Rule*, at http://privacyruleandresearch.nih.gov/pdf/IRB_Factsheet.pdf, pg. 2.
[168] DOJ & FTC, STATEMENTS OF ANTITRUST ENFORCEMENT POLICY IN HEALTH CARE (Aug. 1996), *available at* https://www.ftc.gov/sites/default/files/attachments/competition-policy-guidance/statements_of_antitrust_enforcement_policy_in_health_care_august_1996.pdf.
[169] DOJ & FTC, PROPOSED STATEMENT OF ANTITRUST ENFORCEMENT POLICY REGARDING ACCOUNTABLE CARE ORGANIZATIONS PARTICIPATING IN THE MEDICARE SHARED SAVINGS PROGRAM (2011), *available at* https://www.justice.gov/sites/default/files/atr/legacy/2014/09/17/269155.pdf.

The focus of these antitrust concerns is on exchanges of information among *competing* entities. Single entities, such as a single hospital system with employed physicians, are free to exchange information internally without raising antitrust concerns. Moreover, information gathered from non-competing levels in the health care supply chain would not be subject to antitrust laws for sharing. For example, if an academic medical center and a health plan were to share information, they do not compete with one another because they are at separate levels of the health care distribution system. The antitrust laws regulate the exchange of sensitive information among *competitors*.

The federal antitrust enforcement agencies, the DOJ and the FTC recognize that the flow of information in the health care industry may be pro-competitive or competitively neutral. In the 1996 Healthcare Statements, the agencies explained that the collection and exchange of medical information generally will not raise antitrust concerns: "Providers' collective provision of underlying medical data that may improve purchasers' resolution of issues relating to the mode, quality, or efficiency of treatment is unlikely to raise any significant antitrust concern and will not be challenged by the Agencies, absent extraordinary circumstances." To our knowledge, there are no reported antitrust cases finding a health care provider violated the federal antitrust by participating in an exchange of clinical data.

However, competitors engaging in exchanges of competitively sensitive information are viewed differently. Statement 6 of the Healthcare Statements discusses provider participation in exchange of price and cost information. The agencies expressed concerns that exchanging this type of this information will result in reduced competition, increased prices, or reduced quality and availability of health care services. However, the Healthcare Statements provide an antitrust "safety zone" for exchanges. To fall within the safety zone, the following protocols for exchanges need to be followed: (1) the survey or exchange is implemented by a third party; (2) the statistics disseminated are based on data that is at least three months old; (3) the data is from a least five competing providers; (4) no single provider's data accounts for more than 25% of any given statistic; and (5) the information is sufficiently aggregated or masked so the recipients of the information cannot identify the specific prices or costs of particular providers participating in the survey or information exchange.

While information exchanges that do not fit within the safety zone in the Healthcare Statements are not *per se* illegal, they may be subject to challenge to determine whether the exchange "has an anticompetitive effect that outweighs any pro-competitive justification for the exchange." That is, it will be judged under what is called "the Rule of Reason." The agencies likely would treat any exchanges that result in an actual agreement between competitors to fix prices or costs as *per se* illegal.

In 2011, the agencies published a "Statement of Antitrust Policy Regarding Accountable Care Organizations Participating in the Medicare Shared Savings Program" (the SSP Statement).[170] The SSP Statement reaffirmed the agencies' earlier Healthcare Statements regarding information exchanges used to implement Accountable Care Organizations (ACOs) in the SSP.[171]

---

[170] 76 Fed. Reg. 67206 (Oct. 28, 2011).
[171] 76 Fed. Reg. at 67027.

"1. Conduct to Avoid

   a. Improper Sharing of Competitively Sensitive Information

Regardless of an ACO's . . . indicia of market power, significant competitive concerns can arise when an ACO's operations lead to price-fixing or other collusion among ACO participants in their sale of competing services outside the ACO. For example, improper exchanges of prices or other competitively sensitive information among competing participants could facilitate collusion and reduce competition in the provision of services outside the ACO, leading to increased prices or reduced quality or availability of health care services. ACOs should refrain from, and implement appropriate firewalls or other safeguards against, conduct that may facilitate collusion among ACO participants in the sale of competing services outside the ACO."[172]

14.7 Nonprofit Tax Exemption

14.7.1 Unrelated Business Income

For charitable and community organizations exempt from tax under Section 501(c)(3) of the Internal Revenue Code (the Code), revenue directly earned from the organization's mission is exempt from tax. Tax-exempt organizations may set the charges above their costs, with use of those revenues restricted to payment of reasonable compensation and necessary expenses, and otherwise permanently dedicated to the entity's exempt purposes. The direct relationship between the activity and the organization's mission, and not the source of the funds, is what matters, and what keeps the revenue exempt.

However, to prevent tax-exempt organizations from competing unfairly with for-profit businesses, the Code imposes corporate taxes on "unrelated business income." Revenue not directly related to the exempt entity's core purposes is subject to tax, as if the unrelated business income was earned by a regular for-profit entity. If the organization receives income from (1) a trade or business, (2) which is regularly carried on, and (3) which is not substantially related to the organization's exempt purpose, then the nonprofit has received unrelated business income, subject to unrelated business income tax (UBI or UBIT) at regular corporate tax rates. If any of the three UBIT requirements are not met (*i.e.*, the revenue is not from a trade or business, because it is a donation or passive; the activity is irregular or infrequent, and thus not regularly carried on; or the activity is substantially related to the exempt purpose), then the organization does not have UBIT liability. The UBIT determination generally comes down to the third test, whether the activity meets the "substantially related" test, which is a facts-and-circumstances analysis.

Recognized exempt purposes under Section 501(c)(3) include the promotion of health and scientific purposes. An organization furthers scientific purposes if its activities (1) are scientific; (2) constitute research; and (3) are conducted in the public interest.[173] The term "scientific" includes "the process by which knowledge is systematized or classified through the use of observation, experimen-

---

[172] 76 Fed. Reg. at 67029.
[173] Treas. Reg. § 1.501(c)(3)-1(d)(5).

tation, or reasoning."[174] An activity constitutes research "if professional skill is involved in the design and supervision of a project intended to solve a problem through a search for a demonstrable truth" or is "testing done to validate a scientific hypothesis."[175] Scientific research is conducted in the public interest if it is directed toward benefitting the public, such as research carried on for the purpose of discovering a cure for a disease.[176] Organizations should determine whether research activities fit within their exempt mission; the governing documents for academic medical centers likely will list scientific or research activities as part of the organization's charitable purposes.

Moreover, keep in mind that UBIT is a tax on income, which is revenue in excess of expenses. If the exempt organization does not have any income from the activity—if the activity only recovers its costs, properly counted—then the organization has no income to tax. The Internal Revenue Service (IRS) will insist on allocation of income and expenses on a reasonable basis, particularly where an activity serves both exempt and unrelated purposes.[177]

Finally, even if an exempt organization pays UBIT on unrelated business activity income, the IRS will not revoke or deny exempt status if the business generally furthers the organization's exempt purpose and does not become the entity's primary purpose. The IRS may revoke or deny exempt status only where the commercial trade or business is unrelated to the organization's charitable purpose and where the unrelated activity will require "substantial attention" from the organization.[178]

14.7.2 Private Use of Tax-Exempt Bonds

In addition to UBIT liability, exempt providers that have space, equipment, and facilities financed with tax-exempt bonds need to make sure that "private use" of those facilities do not represent more than 5% of direct or indirect use of any bond issue. While there is a "safe harbor" for certain "basic science" research contracts that do not result in private use,[179] the safe harbor is limited to basic research (defined as the original investigation for advancement of scientific knowledge, not having a specific commercial objective).

---

[174] *IIT Research Institute v. United States*, 9 Cl. Ct. 13 (Cl. Ct. 1985).
[175] *Midwest Research Institute v. United States*, 554 F. Supp. 1379 (W.D. MO 1983), aff'd 744 F. 2d 635 (8th Cir. 1984).
[176] Treas. Reg. § 1.501(c)(3)-1(d)(5)(iii)(c).
[177] *See* Internal Revenue Service, *Colleges and Universities Compliance Project Final Report*, available at http://www.irs.gov/pub/irs-tege/CUCP_FinalRpt_042513.pdf (Apr. 25, 2013), at 12–13. On the other hand, if an exempt organization has continuous losses, the IRS may disallow those losses and loss carry-forwards for continually unprofitable activities, but which may not be relevant for exempt organizations anyway. There is not "bright line" guidance on the extent of the "sweet spot" between making too much and too little, but in the UBIT area, the IRS pays more attention to extreme cases, such as where the commercial activity is huge compared to the other parts of the exempt organization, or where the deviation from break-even, in either direction, is in double, or even triple, digit percentages *See* TAM 9636001 (Jan. 4, 1996) (scope of publishing activities went beyond what was needed to educate students); *Iowa State Univ. of Science & Tech. v. U.S.*, 500 F.2d 508 (Ct. Cl. 1974) (television station insufficiently integrated into university's educational operations.
[178] The Tax Cuts and Jobs Act, P.L. 115-97 (Dec. 22, 2017), made two changes to UBIT which may be significant for certain nonprofits. First, the reduction in the corporate tax rate to 21% also reduced the rate at which UBIT taxes are assessed. In addition, the law also requires exempt organizations to calculate UBIT separately for each unrelated business, and net operating loss deductions are allowed only with respect to the particular business from which the law arose. Thus, for exempt organizations (unlike for-profit businesses), losses in one unrelated business no longer can be used to offset income in another.
[179] Rev. Proc. 2007-47.

Providers with tax-exempt bond financing need to keep records and report information on tax-exempt bonds on Schedule K of Form 990 annually. Exceeding the 5% "de minimus" private use limit on any bond issue could result in revocation of the exempt status of the bonds, and major financial liabilities to the facility, the bond issue, and others involved in the financing, unless the provider pays the amount of bond allocable to the private use, either directly or through a defeasance escrow. Particularly extreme cases could result in revocation of exempt status.

Private use may not be an issue if any of the assets used in storing, maintaining, and delivering the information are not bond financed. It may be relatively simple to show that equipment and operations were not financed with tax-exempt bonds, but it is more likely that some providers may have their activities in a building financed with such bonds. In that event, the provider must add up, on an asset-by-asset and bond-issue-by-bond-issue basis, the total amount of private use. The 5% limitation only applies to each bond issue; however, the provider must determine the percentage of private use of each asset, the portion of the asset's original cost paid through the bond, and the percentage of the bond issue represented by that asset, to determine the percentage of private use of the bond issue.

The collection, storage, and delivery of information likely represents a small part of the use of bond-financed building. If equipment used in activities was purchased with tax-exempt financing, then the provider could defease or pay off those bonds, or refinance the debt using taxable debt. Also, some exempt entities purposefully fund at least 8% of capital project cost with equity to provide additional "margin" for private use activities, such as corporate sponsored research. In any case, exempt providers with tax-exempt debt need to make sure that the UBIT does not push any particular bond issue above the 5% limit.

15

Dispute Resolution

Geoffrey A. Drucker
American Health Lawyers Association

15.1 Introduction

Disputes within the health care system are unique in several key respects:

a) *Frequency*: Health care is increasingly delivered by teams of professionals with diverse backgrounds, perspectives, and training who bear enormous responsibility and operate under tremendous pressure with limited resources.[1] Friction between team members is inevitable.

At the organizational level, physician practice groups are merging into hospitals, hospitals are merging into hospital chains, and a variety of health care organizations are banding together into Accountable Care Organizations.[2] Tensions are likely to flare as individuals and groups are severed from their traditional moorings and thrust into new relationships with unfamiliar policies and procedures and a highly uncertain future.

b) *Consequences*: In health care settings, lives are on the line. When personal friction stifles or impedes communication between health care workers, patients may suffer death or serious injury.[3] Other types of health care disputes involve money, not well-being, but because health care spending represents over 16.4% of the Gross Domestic Product,[4] the sums involved can be vast. And profitability determines the quantity and quality of health care that organizations can deliver.

c) *Confidentiality*: Health care disputes, regardless of the subject matter, typically concern sensitive information that patients, providers, and payers wish to keep private.

d) *Ongoing Relationships*: Because collaboration is a cornerstone of modern health care, health care professionals often cannot distance themselves from people with whom they are in conflict. They must find a way to put their differences aside and reengage productively.

---

[1] Pamela Mitchell et al., *Discussion Paper: Core Principles & Values of Effective Team-Based Health Care*, Institute of Medicine (October, 2012) *available at* https://www.nationalahec.org/pdfs/VSRT-Team-Based-Care-Principles-Values.pdf.

[2] Loren Adler et al., *Navigating Health Care Coordination and Industry Consolidation*, Bipartisan Policy Center (June 21, 2013) *available at* https://bipartisanpolicy.org/blog/navigating-health-care-coordination-and-industry-consolidation/.

[3] Gerald B. Hickson et al., *Balancing Systems and Individual Accountability in a Safety Culture*, Chapter 1 in From Front Office to Front Line: Essential Issues for Health Care Leaders (2nd Ed.).

[4] Organization of Economic Cooperation and Development, Health Law Data 2015, *available at* https://www.oecd.org/unitedstates/Country-Note-UNITED%20STATES-OECD-Health-Statistics-2015.pdf.

This chapter explains how attorneys can tailor arbitration, mediation, and conflict management to help health care organizations address these unique challenges.

15.2 Arbitration

In its classic form, arbitration is a contract between two or more parties to adjudicate a dispute privately.[5] A single arbitrator, or a panel of three, hears evidence and renders an award (binding decision) in accordance with a set of rules.[6]

15.2.1 Potential Advantages

Arbitration offers the following *potential* advantages over litigation:

a) *Speed*: In many state and federal courts, cases take years to get to trial because court rules permit attorneys to engage in protracted discovery and bury the other side in motions, and because judicial resources to manage dockets are dwindling.[7] Trials drag on endlessly as creative litigators invoke arcane rules of evidence to conjure up objections to testimony and documentary evidence.

   In arbitration, parties may agree to eliminate or set strict limits on discovery and motions; select an arbitrator or panel who can move a case along expeditiously; minimize the grounds for evidentiary objections; and require that an award be issued within a set period of time.[8]

b) *Finality:* A trial court verdict can be appealed for errors of fact or law. In many court systems two levels of appeal are available. If a verdict is overturned by an appellate court, it may be returned to the trial court for further proceedings.

   Arbitration awards cannot be overturned for errors of fact or law. A court may vacate an arbitration award only upon proof of a serious flaw such as corruption, fraud, evident partiality, misbehavior that prejudices a party's rights, or where the arbitrators exceed their powers or fail to issue a mutual, final and definite award.[9]

---

[5] Some statutes dictate the procedures under which certain disputes must be arbitrated and/or require participation in arbitration. *See* 29 C.F.R. § 4221.5 (ERISSA); Cal. Bus. & Prof. Code § 6200 et seq. (attorney fee disputes).

[6] Some state and federal courts mandate that parties participate in non-binding arbitration. *See* M. Moffitt and A.K. Schneider, *Dispute Resolution: Examples & Explanations* (Wolters Kluwer 2nd Ed. 2011) p. 240). In addition, although it is far less common than binding arbitration, parties may contract for a non-binding award—a recommended decision—to use as a reference point in settlement negotiations. *See* the Non-Binding Consumer Arbitration Rules of the American Arbitration Association *available at* https://www.adr.org/sites/default/files/Non-Binding%20Consumer%20 Arbitration%20Rules.pdf.

[7] *See Task Force on Preservation of the Justice System*, American Bar Association Board of Governors, *available at* https://www.americanbar.org/content/dam/aba/migrated/2011_build/task_force_on_the_preservation_of_the_justice_ system/taskforcenextsteps.authcheckdam.pdf.

[8] *E.g.*, AHLA Rules of Procedure for Commercial Arbitration, *available at* https://www.healthlawyers.org/dr/ Documents/Arbitration%20Rules%202017/Commercial.pdf.

[9] 9 U.S.C. § 10. The Federal Arbitration Act applies to contracts involving "commerce among the several States or with foreign nations." 9 U.S.C. § 1. Since patients, health care employees, drugs, and medical devices routinely cross state lines, the delivery of health care constitutes interstate commerce. *See, e.g., Smith v. Pacificare Behavioral Health Of California, Inc*, 93 Cal.App.4th 139 (2001); *Erikson v. Aetna Health Plans of California*, 71 Cal.App.4th 646 (1999).

Since the Federal Arbitration Act (FAA) reflects a "liberal federal policy favoring arbitration,"[10] courts tend to interpret Section 10 narrowly, overturning an award only when the arbitration process is severely flawed.[11]

Parties cannot confer jurisdiction on a court to vacate an award on any grounds other than those set forth in Section 10.[12] Five federal circuits have held that they, too, lack authority to create additional grounds for vacating award.[13] The other five circuits will vacate an award in the extreme event that an arbitrator purposefully disregarded a well-defined, explicit, and clearly defined law.[14] The Second Circuit explicitly requires that this knowing misapplication of law result in an incorrect outcome.[15] Some of these circuit decisions rest on the theory that, under the FAA, an arbitrator does not have the authority to manifestly disregard the law.[16] Other decisions characterize manifest disregard of the law as a violation of public policy.[17]

c) *Cost:* In litigation, the costs of adjudication (e.g., judge, clerk's office, court room) are publicly funded; whereas parties to arbitration must pay for the arbitrator's time and expenses and the costs of administering the arbitration process. While these charges can mount up, they pale in comparison to potential savings in attorneys' fees. As is indicated above, arbitration may greatly reduce the number of hours spent on discovery, pre-hearing motions, evidentiary objections, and appeals.[18]

d) *Expertise:* Judges and juries often lack sufficient knowledge of health law and health care to render an informed decision. In arbitration, the parties may select an arbitrator who possesses whatever background and experience they deem necessary to weigh the relevant facts and law. They may select a recognized expert on Medicare reimbursement in one case, a board certified cardiologist in another, and a retired hospital executive in a third. By choosing a qualified decision-maker, parties not only increase their chances of receiving a fair reward, they also promote settlement by making the outcome more predictable.

e) *Privacy:* Court proceedings are open to the public and press. Arbitrations are generally private. Only party representatives, witnesses, and the arbitrator attend the hearing. Only the persons

---

[10] *See, e.g., AT&T Mobility LLC v. Concepcion*, 131 S. Ct. 1740 (2011).
[11] *E.g., Stolt-Nielsen v. Animal Feeds*, 130 S. Ct. 1758 (2010); *Bonar v. Dean Witter Reynolds, Inc.* 835 F.2d 1378 (11th Cir. 1988); *Commonwealth Coatings Corp. v. Continental Casualty Co.*, 393 U.S. 145 (1968); *Tempo Shain Corp. v. Bertek, Inc.*, 120 F.3d 16 (2nd Cir. 1997).
[12] *Hall Street Associates v. Mattel*, 552 U.S. 576 (2008).
[13] T.K. Potter III and K.S. Heisterhagen, *Arbitration Vacator: Circuits Split Over Whether Manifest Disregard Survived Hall Street*, Thomson Reuters News & Insight, April 11, 2012.
[14] *See id. See also Westerbeke v. Daihatsu Motor*, 304 F.3d 200, 208 (2nd Cir. 2002).
[15] *American University of Antigua v. Leeward Construction Company*, 826 F.3d 634(2nd Cir. 2016).
[16] *See* 9 U.S.C. § 10(a)(4) and *Arbitration Vacator, supra*. Whether U.S. Supreme Court decisions have deprived courts of the authority to vacate an award for manifest disregard of the law remains in doubt. *See Goldman v. Citigroup Global Markets Inc.*, 834 F.3d 242, n. 13 (3rd Cir. 2016).
[17] *See Arbitration Vacator, supra*. A court may vacate an award only if it violates a public policy "well defined and dominant". General considerations of what may be in the public interest are not sufficient grounds for vacating an award. *D.A. Nolt, Inc. v Local Union No. 30*, 661 Fed. Appx. 200 (3rd Cir 2016).
[18] *Benefits of Arbitration for Commercial Disputes*, American Bar Association Section of Dispute Resolution, p. 3, *available at* http://www.americanbar.org/content/dam/aba/events/dispute_resolution/committees/arbitration/arbitrationguide.authcheckdam.pdf.

directly involved in pursuing or responding to a claim, or administering the claims process, gain access to documents used in arbitration.[19]

15.2.2 Realizing Time and Cost Savings

Is arbitration truly faster and less expensive than litigation? As is the case in many areas of law, the answer is "It depends." If the parties agree to streamlined rules of procedure that limit discovery, motions, and objections, and that empower the arbitrator to narrow the issues to be addressed during the hearing, the savings may be substantial. However, if the parties transform arbitration into scorched earth litigation by consenting to full-blown discovery or unlimited motions, arbitration is likely to cost even more than court proceedings.[20] Similarly, arbitration will be much faster than litigation if attorneys agree to an aggressive timeline, but not if they seek liberal extensions. To move cases off their docket, judges may deny unopposed extensions. Arbitrators, having been hired by the parties, have no incentive to deny extensions agreed to by all parties.

Another key factor is whether the parties opt for a single arbitrator or a panel of three.[21] Since arbitration awards are subject to very limited review, parties often feel more secure vesting decision-making power in a panel rather than in a single individual, especially in high stakes cases. But scheduling becomes more difficult when dates must be cleared with two additional decision-makers. The costs for the hearing, and any pre-hearing conferences attended by the full panel, will triple. Parties may also incur costs for time spent by panel members to confer on procedural and substantive issues and exchange and review draft orders and awards. Parties can control costs somewhat by authorizing the panel chair to rule on procedural and/or evidentiary issues on his or her own.[22]

In short, to save time and money, parties must provide for a streamlined process that, in its most efficient form, vests nearly unfettered authority in a single decision-maker. The more arbitration resembles litigation in form, the more it resembles it in price and delay.

15.2.3 Getting Cases Into Arbitration

Parties can agree to arbitrate a claim at any time, even after litigation has already commenced. But most cases find their way to arbitration through a pre-dispute agreement: a clause inserted into a contact that requires arbitration of any disputes arising out of the relationship created by the contract. Once a dispute arises, it is often too late for parties to agree on a process for resolving them. Communication has deteriorated to the point where an open, objective dialogue about the mutual benefits of arbitration is not going to occur.

---

[19] *See, e.g.*, AHLA Rules of Procedure for Commercial Arbitration, Rules 6.3 and 8.2, *available at* https://www.healthlawyers.org/dr/Documents/Arbitration%20Rules%202017/Commercial.pdf.

[20] Thomas J. Stipanowich, *Arbitration: The New Litigation*, 2010 U. ILL. L. REV. 1; *The College of Commercial Arbitrators Protocols for Expeditious, Cost-Effective Commercial Arbitration: Key Action Steps for Business Users, Counsel, Arbitrators & Arbitration Provider Institutions* (2010), available online *at* www.thecca.net.

[21] Robert F. Copple, *Tapping the Potential of Arbitration: Protocols for Improvement*, 48-NOV ARIZ. ATT'Y 44 (Nov. 2011).

[22] *See* AHLA Rules of Procedure for Commercial Arbitration, Rule 3.5(c).

Arbitration can be either administered or self-administered. Administered means the process is run by an organization with rules of procedure for arbitration and a roster of arbitrators, such as AHLA. Self-administered means the parties select an arbitrator on their own, and the arbitrator and the parties manage the logistics of scheduling teleconferences, exchanging documents, booking a hearing room, etc. In a self-administered arbitration, the parties can require the arbitrator to follow an established set of rules, or they can create their own rules.

Even if parties agree to arbitrate under established rules, such as AHLA's, they have a great deal of leeway to tailor the process as they see fit. Most rules can be amended to meet the needs of a particular situation. AHLA has a free guide that describes the issues to consider in drafting an arbitration clause and provides sample language and drafting tips.[23] The importance of devoting time and attention to drafting an appropriate arbitration clause cannot be overemphasized. A few minutes of thoughtful labor at the front end can save weeks, months, or years of aggravation after a dispute arises.[24]

15.2.4 Employment and Consumer Disputes

Arbitration developed as a means for resolving disputes between two or more companies in the same industry. However, in recent decades, it has become common for businesses in many industries, including health care, to include arbitration clauses in contracts with employees and consumers. In the health care context, "consumer" means an individual who receives health care services, or a person who represents such an individual, such as the son or daughter of a resident in a long-term care facility.[25]

Since business-to-individual contracts are typically drafted by the business and regarded as non-negotiable, individuals frequently argue either that they did not consent to arbitrate, or that, even if they did, the arbitration clause is fundamentally unfair to them and, therefore, should not be enforced.

15.2.4.1 Agreements with Employees

An employer may present an employee with an adhesive (non-negotiable) arbitration clause, so long as it is reasonably fair.[26] If an arbitration clause appears in an employee handbook, a preliminary question is whether the employee assented to it. Many courts have found no agreement to arbitrate where the employee merely received or acknowledged receipt of the handbook,[27] or where the employer retained the unfettered right to alter the existence or scope of the arbitration clause.[28] If the employee handbook is non-binding, the agreement to arbitrate should be in a separate document affirmed by both parties and identified as a condition of employment.[29] The agreement must be binding on both parties.[30]

---

[23] AHLA Guide to Arbitration Clauses, *available at* https://www.healthlawyers.org/dr/SiteAssets/Lists/drsaccordion/EditForm/Guide%20to%20Arbitration%20Clauses.pdf.
[24] *See* John M. Townsend, *Drafting Arbitration Clauses: Avoiding the 7 Deadly Sins*, DISPUTE RESOLUTION JOURNAL, Vol. 58 No. 1 (2003).
[25] For a more precise definition, *see* AHLA Rules of Procedure for Consumer Arbitration, Rule 1.1, *available at* https://www.healthlawyers.org/dr/Documents/Arbitration%20Rules%202017/Consumer.pdf.
[26] *See Johnson v. Circuit City Stores*, 148 F.3d 373, 378–79 (4th Cir. 1998), *aff'd*, 203 F.2d 821 (4th Cir. 2000); *Martindale v. Sandvik, Inc.* 173 N. J. 76, 800 A.2d 872 (2002).
[27] *Arbitrating Employment Disputes: Avoiding 10 Mistakes in Preparing and Implementing a Pre-Dispute Arbitration Program*, SK013 ALI-ABA 829 § II (A) (Paul, Hastings, Janofsky and Walker LLP 2004).
[28] *Dumais v. American Golf Corporation*, 299 F.3d 1216 (10th Cir. 2002.)
[29] *Patterson v. Tenet Healthcare*, 113 F.3d 832 (8th Cir. 1997).
[30] *Mazera v. Varsity Ford Management Services*, 565 F3d 997 (6th Cir. 2009) (applying Tennessee law).

Even signed by an employee, an agreement to arbitrate is contrary to public policy if it curtails his or her substantive rights. For example, an arbitration clause may not impede an employee's ability to enforce statutory rights, raise the burden of proof, or limit damages or attorney's fees.[31]

Arbitration need not offer all the procedural protections available in court, such as full blown discovery or strict rules of evidence.[32] But terms cannot be "so one-sided that their only possible purpose is as to undermine the neutrality of the proceeding."[33] The dividing line between less-than-litigation-but-okay and unacceptable is murky at best. Some courts require that an employee pay no arbitration costs, whereas others require an employee to prove costs are so excessive that they deter the filing of claims.[34]

If a claim does not involve statutory rights, courts will examine whether the process is so unbalanced as to be unconscionable. Standards vary from state to state but typically require proof that: (a) one party had no meaningful opportunity to draft the contract terms, and (b) the terms unreasonably favor the other party.[35] The first prong is often met in employment cases because the arbitration clause is non-negotiable. Case law on the second prong varies widely. There is no judicial consensus on what procedures are unconscionable.[36]

AHLA and other leading arbitration providers have special rules for claims arising out of agreements that employees are required to sign as a condition of employment. They require the employer to pay the forum costs (filing fees, arbitrator's fees and expenses, and possibly other administrative charges) and override any provisions in the arbitration agreement that would limit an employee's statutory rights and remedies or deprive an employee of a fair hearing.[37]

15.2.4.2 Agreements with Consumers

Arbitration of disputes between consumers and health care providers is highly controversial. Opponents have sought to limit the scope and content of consumer arbitration agreements and to restrict who can give their consent. The key legal issues are the validity of:

- Statutes and regulations that purport to ban or limit the arbitration of certain disputes;
- Arbitration agreements that restrict consumer choice or consumer rights and remedies; and
- Arbitration agreements that are signed by someone who arguably did not understand what they were agreeing to or who arguably did not have the authority to sign the agreement.

---

[31] *Green Tree Financial Corp. v Randolph*, 531 U.S. 79, 90 (2000); *Arbitrating Employment Disputes, supra.*
[32] *Gilmer v. Interstate/Johnson Lane Corp.*, 500 U.S. 20, 31–32 (1991).
[33] *Hooters of America, Inc. v. Phillips*, 173 F.3d 933 (4th Cir. 1999).
[34] See *Cole v. Burns International Security Services*, 105 F.3d 1465, 1481 (C.A.D.C. 1997) (arbitrator's compensation and expenses must be paid by employer alone); *Rosenberg v. Merrill Lynch*, 170 F.3d 1, 16 (1st Cir. 1999) (employee can present argument about excessive fees post award to a reviewing court).
[35] See, e.g., *Brown v. MHN Government Services, Inc.*, 306 P.3d 948 (Sct. Wash. 2013).
[36] See *Arbitrating Employment Disputes, supra.*
[37] *Employment Rules Comparison*, available on the AHLA website at https://www.healthlawyers.org/dr/SiteAssets/Lists/drsaccordion/EditForm/Employment%20Rules%20Comparison.pdf.

15.2.4.2.1 Nursing Home Statutes and Regulations

A. State Statutes: The Federal Arbitration Act (FAA) requires that agreements to arbitrate be enforced to the same degree as other types of contracts.[38] So the FAA preempts state laws that single out arbitration contracts for special (negative) treatment, including statutes that bar nursing homes from requiring consumers to arbitrate negligence or wrongful death cases.[39] Courts must determine case by case whether an agreement to arbitrate runs afoul of a statute or precedent applicable to all contracts.[40]

B. Federal Regulations: On October 4, 2016, the U.S. Department of Health and Human Services (HHS) issued regulations forbidding long-term care facilities that participate in Medicare and Medicaid from asking residents to sign pre-dispute arbitration agreements.[41] The regulations permitted a covered facility to ask a resident to sign an arbitration agreement after a dispute arose so long as it took measures to ensure the resident's signature was truly knowing and voluntary.[42]

On November 7, 2016, the U.S. District Court for the Northern District of Mississippi reluctantly enjoined HHS from enforcing the ban on pre-dispute arbitration agreements. In the Court's view, even though the ban was "based on sound public policy," HHS could not institute it on such a thin administrative record without clear authority from Congress.[43] The Obama Administration appealed this ruling to the 5th Circuit, but the Trump Administration subsequently withdrew the appeal.[44]

On June 8, 2017, HHS proposed to remove the ban on pre-dispute arbitration agreements but continue to: (a) require facilities to explain arbitration to residents in language they can understand, (b) preserve the ability of residents to communicate with government officials, and (c) require facilities to make arbitration agreements and final awards available for inspection.[45] Under these revised rules, facilities would have to draft arbitration agreements in "plain language" and post their binding arbitration policy in "plain language" in an area visible to residents and visitors.[46]

15.2.4.2.2 Limitations on Consumer Choice

Long-term care providers often ask incoming residents or their family members to agree to arbitration upon their admission to a facility. Since a delay in care could have serious consequences, the focus is generally on the moving the process along, not on examining and debating the language of a lengthy admission agreement. Thus, a court may deem an agreement to arbitrate unconscionable unless a facility takes steps to make it voluntary. These steps may include presenting the agreement

---

[38] 9 U.S.C. § 2.
[39] *Nitro-Lift Technologies v. Eddie Lee Howard*, 133 S.Ct. 500 (2012) (per curiam).
[40] *Marmet Health Center v. Brown*, 132 S.Ct 1201 (2012).
[41] 81 C.F.R. § 68,867.
[42] 81 C.F.R. § 68,867.
[43] *American Health Care Association v. Burwell*, 217 F. Supp. 3d 921 (N.D. Mississippi 2016).
[44] *American Health Care Assn v. Price*, Case No. 17-60005 (5th Cir). The Court granted a joint motion to dismiss on June 2, 2017.
[45] The proposed regulations do not require facilities to make settlement agreements available for inspection.
[46] 82 Fed. Reg. 26651 (June 8, 2017). Whether Federal Arbitration Act precludes HHS from imposing these less onerous requirements on long-term care facilities is unclear. The issue will be resolved only if HHS finalizes the rules and they are challenged in court. Since the meaning of "plain language" is anything but plain, there appears to be ample opportunity for litigation.

as a separate document, indicating that is not a condition for admission, and affording the resident (or his or her representative) the right to revoke the agreement for a period of time (e.g., 30 days) after signing.[47] In addition, a court may invalidate an agreement if it unfairly limits a consumer's rights or remedies.[48]

15.2.4.2.3 Authority to Agree to Arbitration

In the long term care context, it is not always immediately clear who has the authority to enter into an arbitration agreement on a resident's (or prospective resident's) behalf. Consideration must be given to the following potential parties:

Consumer. When people are admitted to long-term care facilities, their capacity to comprehend and make choices about legal documents may be moderately or severely impaired. Whether a consumer had the requisite capacity to agree to arbitration must be determined on a case by case basis. Advanced age is not, by itself, proof of incapacity.[49]

Power of Attorney. A person can agree to arbitration on a consumer's behalf if he or she has broad power to enter into contracts. A consumer need not specifically grant authority to consent to arbitration.[50]

Relative or Friend. If someone needs medical care, a provider cannot delay admission until the patient regains the capacity to sign legal documents (which may never happen) or a friend or relative arrives with power of attorney (which also may never happen). If the agreement to arbitrate is signed by someone without power of attorney to act on resident's behalf, a court may nevertheless enforce the document based on common law doctrines such as equitable estoppel, implied or apparent authority, and ratification by the principal.[51]

Survivor or Executor. State courts are split on whether an agreement to arbitrate disputes between a health care provider and a consumer applies to an action for wrongful death brought by the consumer's heirs.[52] Some view wrongful death as a cause of action that derives from, and is therefore defined by, the decedent's rights and remedies immediately preceding death. So if the decedent was bound by an agreement to arbitrate, his heirs would be similarly bound.[53] Other courts view wrongful death as

---

[47] See J. Pavlic, *Reverse Pre-Empting the Federal Arbitration Act: Alleviating the Arbitration Crisis in Nursing Homes*, 22 JOURNAL OF LAW AND HEALTH 375, 384–387 (2009); S.M. Scheller, *Arbitrating Wrongful Death Claims for Nursing Home Patients: What is Wrong with this Picture and How to Make it "More" Right*, 113 PENN STATE LAW REVIEW 528, 549–551 (2008). See also Hayes v. Oakridge Home, 908 N.E. 2d 408 (S. Ct. Ohio 2009).
[48] *Ruppelt v. Laurel Healthcare Providers*, 293 P.3d 902 (N.M. Ct. App. 2012).
[49] See, e.g., *Hayes v. Oakridge Home*, 908 N.E. 2d at 413 (resident was 95 years old at the time of admission)
[50] *Kindred Nursing Centers LTD v. Clark*, 137 S. Ct. 1421 (2017). The Supreme Court of Kentucky required specific authority to "waive his principal's fundamental constitutional rights to access the court" and "to trial by jury." The U.S. Supreme Court held that this ruling violates the Federal Arbitration Act because it treats arbitration contracts less favorably than other contracts.
[51] See *Washburn v. Northern Health Facilities*, 121 A.3d 1008 (Pa. Super. 2015). See also *Validity, Construction, and Application of Arbitration Agreement in Contract for Admission to Nursing Home* 50 A.L.R.6th 187.
[52] Compare *Laizure v. Avante at Leesburg*, 109 So.3d 752 (S. Ct. FL 2013) (arbitration agreement binds the signing party's estate and heirs in a subsequent wrongful death case) with *Northern Health Facilities v. Batz*, 993. F. Supp. 2d 485 (M.D. Pa. 2014) (ordering arbitration of survival action but not claim for wrongful death).
[53] *Laizure v. Avante at Leesburg*, 109 So.3d 752 (S. Ct. Fla. 2013).

a separate cause of action granted to family members to recover for their own economic losses, not as beneficiaries of the estate. Under this theory, the decedent does not have the authority to contract away the right of family members to bring a wrongful death action in court.[54] Since each state has its own wrongful death statute or common law right of action, state courts are likely to remain divided on whether a wrongful death action is or is not derivative of a decedent's rights at the time of death.

15.2.4.2.4 Rules of Procedure

Only AHLA has arbitration rules tailored for consumer cases in the health care industry.[55] JAMS accepts consumer cases of all kinds in accordance with minimum standards of fairness.[56] The American Arbitration Association does not accept consumer claims in the health care industry unless the consumer agrees to arbitrate after the dispute arises or a court orders the parties to arbitrate.[57]

15.2.5 Summary

A clause requiring parties to arbitrate disputes arising out of a health care contract helps ensure claims are decided by a neutral with sufficient knowledge of health law and the delivery of health care to render a fair decision. Arbitration also keeps sensitive health-related information out of the public eye. If parties resist the urge to treat arbitration like litigation, they are likely to save a substantial amount of time and money.

15.3 Mediation

In the legal context, mediation refers to settlement negotiations that are assisted by a neutral third party. Neutral means the mediator has no interest in what the terms are and makes no attempt to steer the parties in a particular direction. However, mediators are advocates for settlement and will zealously strive to overcome barriers to agreement.

15.3.1 Advantages for Health Law Cases

The benefits of mediation are comparable to those available through arbitration. Mediations typically last no more than a day, and, except in extremely complex cases such as class actions, rarely extend more than a few days. Thus, mediation is far less expensive and time-consuming than litigation. Since parties select the neutral, they may choose someone with the type of health law or health care background they deem necessary to understand the case. Mediation is informal, so parties can determine where, when, and how they want the process to unfold. If the parties reach an accord, it will be as final and binding as any other settlement agreement. And, as is the case in arbitration, mediation sessions are private so parties can keep sensitive health information out of the public eye.

Mediation obviously compares very favorably to litigation, but parties always have the option to negotiate an agreement on their own, without the additional expense of a neutral. So the real question is what value a mediator adds to the negotiation process.

---

[54] *Pisano v. Extendicare Homes, Inc.*, 77 A.3d 651 (S.Ct. Pa. 2013), cert denied, 134 S.Ct. 2890 (2014).
[55] They are *available at* https://www.healthlawyers.org/dr/Documents/Arbitration%20Rules%202017/Consumer.pdf
[56] They are *available at* https://www.jamsadr.com/consumer-minimum-standards/.
[57] *See* AAA Healthcare Policy Statement issued in 2003.

First, a mediator can secure a deal early on, before both sides have incurred the costs and aggravation associated with discovery, pre-trial proceedings, and trial preparation.[58]

Second, in complex cases, mediation can be highly productive long before the parties are ready to trade settlement proposals. The mediator can help parties structure an efficient and effective discovery process. For example, in lieu of an expensive battle of experts, parties may agree to secure an opinion from one agreed upon expert. A neutral who has worked with the parties on structuring discovery will be well prepared to assist in reaching a deal when the time is ripe to settle.

A third reason for bringing in a mediator is to preserve or restore relationships between health care workers or organizations. Settlement negotiations are typically lawyer-to-lawyer, with no direct contact between clients. Mediation provides a forum in which clients and client representatives can air differences, share information, express emotions, ask questions, apologize, seek or grant forgiveness, and find pathways to move forward.

15.3.2 Mediating Effectively

When parties mediate voluntarily, settlement rates reach as high as 80–85%.[59] A significant percentage of cases settle even when mediation is involuntary (court-ordered).[60] Attorneys can increase their chances of success by learning how to: (a) secure an agreement to mediate; (b) select the right mediator; and (c) prepare to mediate.

15.3.2.1 Agreeing to Mediate

Attorneys are often reluctant to propose mediation for fear of looking weak.[61] They believe suggesting mediation is tantamount to admitting that their client is reluctant to try the case, and, consequently, is willing to make major concessions. Health care attorneys can overcome this barrier to mediation in three ways.

The first is to secure a pre-dispute agreement to mediate. Typically, such a clause requires mediation of any dispute arising out of the relationship created by a contract. Since it is usually hard to predict what type of dispute might arise, or when, it is best not to get too specific about how mediation will work. Here is a sample from the AHLA Guide to Arbitration Clauses:[62]

---

[58] John Lande, *The Movement Toward Early Case Handling in Courts and Private Dispute Resolution*, Ohio St. J. on Disp. Resolution, 24:1 (2008), pp. 103–106.

[59] The McCammon Group has mediated over 16,000 cases with a settlement rate of approximately 85%. *See* https://www.mccammongroup.com/services/civil-dispute-mediation/. The Financial Industry Regulatory Authority (FINRA) has a settlement rate of 80%. *See* http://www.finra.org/ArbitrationAndMediation/Mediation/Overview/. A court connected mediation program achieved an overall settlement rate of 69%, and over 80% of cases settled if, prior to the session, the court had ruled on any pending motions. Naman L.J. Wood, *Can Judges Increase Mediation Settlement Rates? Of "Coase" They Can*, 26 Ohio St. J. on Disp. Resolution 683 (2011).

[60] Bobbi McAdoo et al, *Institutionalization: What Do Empirical Studies Tell Us About Court Mediation?*, Dispute Resolution Magazine (Winter 2003), pp. 8–10.

[61] *See Can Judges Increase Mediation Settlement Rates? Of "Coase" They Can, supra.*

[62] The full guide is *available at* https://www.healthlawyers.org/dr/SiteAssets/Lists/drsaccordion/EditForm/Guide%20to%20Arbitration%20Clauses.pdf.

Prior to filing a claim for arbitration under this clause, a party must request mediation through the AHLA Dispute Resolution Service. No earlier than 60 days after notifying the opposing party that the request for mediation was submitted to AHLA, a party may initiate arbitration through the AHLA Dispute Resolution Service if, for any reason, the matter has not been fully resolved in mediation.

No court will compel the other side to make a reasonable settlement offer or reach agreement,[63] but getting to the table is more than half the battle. Once there, most parties will operate in good faith.

A second way to avoid proposing mediation of a particular case is to propose mediation in every case.[64] A health care organization, or a firm that practices health law, may adopt a policy requiring that mediation be considered for every claim, either before litigation begins or shortly after it is filed. No one is compelled to mediate if, for example, one or both sides see a strong need to establish a legal precedent. With such a policy in place, instead of having to say "Would you consider mediating this case?" and fear sounding weak or desperate, an attorney can say, "Our corporate policy is to considering mediating every claim before surrendering control to a judge, jury, or arbitrator. What is your position regarding mediation?"

A third strategy to avoid directly proposing mediation is to ask a mediation provider such as the AHLA Dispute Resolution Service to broach the subject with the other side. The provider need not mention that it is acting at the behest of the other party.

15.3.2.2 Selecting a Mediator

The key question to ask in selecting a mediator is who both sides will trust and respect. A brief example helps illustrate why these qualities are so critical. Imagine if, at the 11th hour, after a long, hard day of negotiation, the mediator advises Party A that Party B has reached its limit. In the mediator's opinion, if Party A wants a deal it is going to have to bridge the remaining gap between their offers. The first question on Party A's mind should be: Do I trust that the mediator is telling me what he believes is the truth, and is not trying to pull the wool over my eyes to get a deal? The second question should be: Do I respect the mediator's opinion? Do I think the mediator's assessment of Party B's position is accurate, or do I believe Party B has pulled the wool over the mediator's eyes? If Party A trusts and respects the mediator, Party A will reluctantly accept Party B's final offer. If either trust or respect is lacking, Party A may call what it suspects is the mediator's or Party B's bluff, and the deal may fall through.

Since health law is so complex and specialized, parties tend to trust and respect recognized subject matter experts. In disputes involving ongoing relationships, the parties also may require a mediator they can relate to on a personal level, which often means someone with a similar background. Organizations that administer mediations such as AHLA can recommend candidates with the expertise or experience the parties are looking for.

---

[63] A court will compel a party to mediate if it has clearly agreed to do so. *E.g., In re Pisces Foods,* 228 S.W.3d 349 (Ct. App. Tx 2007).
[64] See *The Movement Toward Early Case Handling in Courts and Private Dispute Resolution, supra,* at 107–112.

15.3.2.3 Preparing for Mediation

Preparing for mediation is much different than trial preparation, but no less important.[65] Since most voluntary attempts to reach agreement succeed, mediation is likely to be the most consequential event in the life of a case. In addition to having a thorough knowledge of the relevant facts and law, health care attorneys should create an effective presentation, ensure their client representative is adequately briefed, and have a realistic settlement proposal in hand.[66]

Mediation often begins with a joint session, which means all participants are in the room together. Attorneys often fail to leverage this golden opportunity to tell a compelling story. Audio-visual materials can drive key points home.[67]

If an attorney is representing a health care organization, a key decision is whom to select as the client representative. The representative must have adequate settlement authority, and should also have the personality and skills to help sway the other side. The representative needs to have a firm understanding of his or her role before the session commences.[68]

Attorneys are often extremely reluctant to put a realistic offer on the table. However, social science research has persuasively shown that the party who goes first is able to anchor the conversation on its terms and thereby gain a distinct advantage.[69] So attorneys are well advised to arrive with a proposal they can defend as reasonable. What attorneys should *not* have when mediation begins is a firm bottom line. Instead, they should be willing to let this line shift as they acquire new information.

15.3.3 Combining Mediation and Arbitration

Attorneys need not make an either/or choice between mediation and arbitration. A pre-dispute agreement may provide for mediation first, with arbitration to follow if the parties cannot reach an agreement. Alternatively, parties may agree to mediate after arbitration has commenced.

Parties also may appoint a neutral to both mediate and arbitrate. In Med-Arb, the neutral first attempts to mediate a settlement. If this effort fails, the neutral convenes a hearing and issues an award. As the name suggests, Arb-Med begins in arbitration, but before issuing an award, the neutral attempts to broker a deal. In both processes, the neutral's ability to issue an award provides extra leverage in pushing for an agreement. In a conventional mediation, parties may discount the mediator's assessment of the strengths and weaknesses of their case if they feel it is off the mark. When the mediator *is* the ultimate decision-maker, his or her assessment cannot be ignored.

---

[65] ABA Section On Dispute Resolution, Task Force On Improving Mediation Quality, Final Report 12 (2006–2008), *available at* http://www.abanet.org/dispute/documents/FinalTaskForceMediation.pdf.
[66] Geoff Drucker, *Mediation Advocacy: The View From Across The Table*, The Young Lawyer (2008), *available at* https://www.mccammongroup.com/wp-content/uploads/2013/12/TheYoungLawyer-Jan08-Drucker.pdf.
[67] Alexia Morrison, *Weapons for Peace*, TRIAL (December 2007), p. 36.
[68] *See id.*
[69] Dan Orr and Chris Guthrie, "Anchoring, Information, Expertise, and Negotiation: New Insights from Meta-Analysis," OHIO STATE JOURNAL ON DISPUTE RESOLUTION 21, no. 3 (2006): 623, http://papers.ssrn.com/sol3/papers.cfm?abstract_id=900152.

When agreeing to Arb-Med or Med-Arb, parties need to address whether the neutral may rely on information provided in mediation when issuing an arbitration award. AHLA has developed guidance on how to address this potentially thorny issue.[70]

15.3.4 Summary

Mediation is as private as arbitration and can be even faster and less expensive. Furthermore, in mediation parties retain control over their destiny. They can withdraw from the process at any time, without consequences, unless they agree to settle. Mediation is especially helpful in health care cases where the parties must continue to work together. Unlike litigation and arbitration, which tend to make bad relationships even worse, mediation can bridge differences and restore or improve communication.

If parties arrive at mediation well-prepared, with appropriate settlement authority, they are very likely to reach an agreement. Typically, the biggest challenge is getting to the table. Attorneys can ease the way by agreeing to mediate in advance (in a pre-dispute clause) or by drafting a policy for their health care organization or law firm that requires considering mediation in every case.

15.4 Conflict Management

Conflicts pose problems in all organizations, but in health care institutions the causes and consequences are especially acute. Dysfunctional relationships, often emanating from the stress and fatigue of long hours spent caring for the sick and dying, have been linked to medical errors and preventable adverse outcomes (as well as dissatisfied patients and high staff turnover).[71] In short, workplace conflict can have a direct and immediate impact on patient care. For this reason, The Joint Commission requires hospitals seeking accreditation to manage conflict between leadership groups to protect the quality of care.[72]

Attorneys need not confine their role to helping health care organizations cope with the fallout of mismanaged conflict, such as medical malpractice suits and peer review hearings to withdraw a disruptive physician's credentials. They can also suggest ways of reducing future exposure to liability. Health care lawyers have been at the forefront of efforts to develop new and better ways of managing health care disputes.[73] For example, Carole Houk and Richard Boothman have designed successful programs to resolve disputes arising from adverse medical events through open disclosure and dialogue.[74]

---

[70] *See* AHLA Guide to Arbitration Clauses, 3–4, *available at* https://www.healthlawyers.org/dr/SiteAssets/Lists/drsaccordion/EditForm/Guide%20to%20Arbitration%20Clauses.pdf.
[71] *Behaviors That Undermine a Culture of Safety*, The Joint Commission, Sentinel Alert, Issue 40, July 9, 2008.
[72] *See* Joint Commission Accreditation Standards for Hospitals, Standard LD.02.04.01.
[73] *See id.* for the bibliography.
[74] Carole S. Houk, *Medical Errors: Hospitals with Unexpected Outcomes Explore Alternatives to 'Deny and Defend'*, HEALTH LAW REPORTER, BNA, Vol. 14, No. 5 (February 3, 2005); Biography of Richard C. Boothman, University of Michigan Department of Surgery, *available at* https://medicine.umich.edu/dept/surgery/richard-boothman-jd.

15.5 Conclusion

The suggestions provided in this chapter can be distilled into this sound bite: "Don't wait until it's too late." Friction within the American health care system can quickly heat up into a dispute and boil over into litigation. Lawyers can add value by helping health care organizations manage conflict better right from the start, and by channeling disputes that require third-party intervention into mediation and arbitration. Once parties march down the litigation path, reining them back in is far more difficult. Even if all would benefit from putting their differences to rest quickly, inexpensively, fairly, and privately, severed channels of communication and strong emotions can impede them from changing course.

Index

A

ABANDONMENT OF PATIENT
duty to treat, 2.1
ABBREVIATIONS
table of abbreviations, 1.2
ABORTION
access to abortion facilities, 13.1.1.5
communications between physician and patient, attempts to regulate, 13.1.1.6
conscience laws
  duty to treat patient, 2.1.3
counseling and referral for federally funded clinics, restrictions on, 13.1.1.6
drug-induced abortion, 13.1.1.4
duty to treat patient, 2.1.3
emergency contraception, 13.1.1.4
Freedom of Access to Abortion to Clinic Entrances (FACE) Act, 13.1.1.5
Griswold v. Connecticut, 13.1.1.1
informed consent
  counseling and referral for federally funded clinics, restrictions on, 13.1.1.6
  generally, 13.1.1.3
  special circumstances, statutes requiring, 2.2.1.4
late-term abortions, 13.1.1.3
Partial Birth Abortion Act, 13.1.1.3
Roe v. Wade (See **ROE v. WADE**)
trimester approach, 13.1.1.1; 13.1.1.2
undue burden test, 13.1.1.3
waiting periods, 13.1.1.3
ACCOUNTABLE CARE ORGANIZATIONS (ACO)
generally, 10.8
Medicare
  antitrust issues, 7.2.1.3.1
  Part C coverage, 3.6.4
  shared savings programs, 3.6.3; 5.2.23
stand-alone exemption
  generally, 6.2.3.3
  lessening burdens of government as alternative basis for exemption, 6.2.3.4
waivers of application of statutes, 5.2.23; 5.5.3.17
ACUTE INPATIENT HOSPITALS
Medicare prospective payment system (PPS), 3.8.2
ADOPTION
Employee Retirement and Income Security Act (ERISA) coverage, 8.3.2.6
ADULT DAY SERVICES (ADS) PROGRAMS
home and community-based services (HCBS), 11.6.1
ADVANCE DIRECTIVES
do-not-resuscitate protocols (DNR orders), 2.3.4.3
durable power of attorney for health care, 2.3.4.2
generally, 2.3.4
living wills, 2.3.4.1
AFFILIATES
health care transactions and contracting, 12.1 to 12.9
  affiliation agreements, 12.7.5
  structure of transactions, 12.3.3
tax-exempt issues
  use of taxable affiliates, 6.3.7
AFFORDABLE CARE ACT (ACA)
Medicaid (*See* MEDICAID)
AIDS STATUS
confidentiality of patient medical information, heightened protection of, 2.4.1
ALCOHOL TREATMENT (*See* **DRUG OR ALCOHOL TREATMENT**)
AMBULANCES
Medicare
  Part B coverage, 3.6.2.3
  resource-based relative value scale (RBRVS) fee schedule, 3.9.7

replenishing and restocking
Anti-Kickback safe-harbor regulations, 5.2.18
AMBULATORY SURGICAL CENTERS
Anti-Kickback safe-harbor regulations, 5.2.16
implants in ASCs, 5.5.1.5
ANATOMICAL GIFTS
organ transplantation generally (*See* **ORGAN TRANSPLANTATION**)
Uniform Anatomical Gift Act (UAGA), 13.2.1
ANTI-KICKBACK SAFE-HARBOR REGULATIONS, 5.2
accountable care organization (ACO) waivers, 5.2.23; 5.5.3.17
ambulances
replenishing and restocking, 5.2.18
ASCs, 5.2.16
coinsurance and deductible waivers, 5.2.9
cooperative hospital-services organizations, 5.2.15
discounts, 5.2.6
electronic health records (EHR), donation and receipt of technology, 5.2.22
electronic prescribing, 5.2.21
employees, amounts paid to, 5.2.7
federally qualified health centers (FQHCs), 5.2.19; 5.2.24
group health plans
price reductions, 5.2.11
group practices, investments in, 5.2.14
group purchasing organizations, 5.2.8
investment interests, 5.2.1
60/40 investor rule, 5.2.1.2
60/40 revenue rule, 5.2.1.2
investments in entities in MUAs, 5.2.1.3
large investment interests, 5.2.1.1
small investment interests, 5.2.1.2
managed care organizations
beneficiary incentives, 5.2.10
Medicare coverage gap discount program, 5.2.25
obstetrical malpractice insurance subsidies, 5.2.13
practitioner recruitment, 5.2.12; 5.5.3.18

referral agreements for specialty services, 5.2.17
referral services, 5.2.4
risk-sharing arrangements, 5.2.20
sale of practice, 5.2.3
space and equipment rental, 5.2.2
transportation services, 5.2.26
warranties, 5.2.5
ANTI-KICKBACK STATUTE, 5.1
advisory opinions, 5.1.4
exceptions
Anti-Kickback safe-harbor regulations, 5.2
Hanslester decision, 5.1.2.2
judicial interpretation, 5.1.2
Hanslester decision, 5.1.2.2
pre-*Hanlester*, 5.1.2.1
United States ex rel. Jamison v. McKesson, 5.1.2.3
United States v. Greber, 5.1.2.1
special fraud alerts, 5.1.3
statutory prohibition, 5.1.1
ANTITRUST LAW, 7.1 to 7.7
applicability to health care sector, 7.6
attorneys' fees
private enforcement, 7.5
boycotts, group, 7.2.1.3.4
causation, proof of
private enforcement, 7.5.1
Clayton Act, Section 7
competitors in the relevant market
calculation of each competitor's market share, 7.2.3.4
identification, 7.2.3.3
generally, 7.2.3
Herfindahl-Hirschman Index (HHI)
measure of market concentration level, 7.2.3.5
horizontal merger guidelines, 7.2.3
increase in market concentration resulting from merger
calculation, 7.2.3.5
misleading post-merger market share/concentration statistics, 7.2.3.6
market concentration level
calculation, 7.2.3.5

misleading post-merger market share/
  concentration statistics, 7.2.3.6
mergers and acquisitions, 7.2.3
misleading post-merger market share/
    concentration statistics
  examination of factors, 7.2.3.6
post-merger market share
    calculation, 7.2.3.5
  misleading post-merger market share/
    concentration statistics, 7.2.3.6
relevant geographic market
  defined, 7.2.3.2
relevant product market
  defined, 7.2.3.1
consumer welfare prescription
  purpose of antitrust laws, 7.1.1
coverage, 7.3
damages
  government enforcement, 7.4.1
  private enforcement, 7.5; 7.5.4
  standing, 7.5.3
  treble damages, 7.5
data sharing, 14.6
DOJ antitrust division
  government enforcement, 7.4.1
enforcement
  government, 7.4
  private enforcement, 7.5
exemptions, immunities, and scope of
    coverage
  federal government, immunity of, 7.3.2
  generally, 7.3
  Health Care Quality Improvement Act,
    7.3.8
  insurance business, 7.3.6
  labor unions, 7.3.7
  Local Government Antitrust Act, 7.3.5
  McCarran-Ferguson Act, 7.3.6
  Noerr-Pennington antitrust immunity
    doctrine, 7.3.4
  nonprofit entities, 7.3.1
  solicitation of government action, 7.3.4
  state-action exemption, 7.3.3
Federal Trade Commission
  FTC Act, 7.2.4
  government enforcement, 7.4.2

generally, 7.1
government enforcement
  DOJ antitrust division, 7.4.1
  Federal Trade Commission, 7.4.2
  generally, 7.4
  state Attorneys General, 7.4.3
Health Care Quality Improvement Act, 7.3.8
health care transactions and contracting,
    12.4.1.1
immunities, 7.3
injury
  antitrust injury, private enforcement, 7.5.2
insurance business, 7.3.6
integrated delivery systems (IDSs), 12.4.1.1
labor unions, 7.3.7
local Government Antitrust Act, 7.3.5
market concentration, market share and, 7.1.3
McCarran-Ferguson Act, 7.3.6
mergers and acquisitions
  Clayton Act, Section 7, 7.2.3
Noerr-Pennington antitrust immunity
    doctrine, 7.3.4
nonprofit entities, 7.3.1
Norris-LaGuardia Act, 7.3.7
private enforcement
  antitrust injury, 7.5.2
  causation, proof of, 7.5.1
  damages, 7.5.4
  generally, 7.5
  standing, 7.5.3
  treble damages plus attorneys fees, 7.5
professional regulatory boards, 7.3.3
purpose of antitrust laws, 7.1.1
references, print and website, 7.7
relevant market
  defined, 7.1.2
  market concentration, market share and,
    7.1.3
scope of coverage, 7.3
Sherman Act, Section 1
  agreement, requirement of, 7.2.1.1
  agreements with potential Section 1
    ramifications, 7.2.1.3
  anticompetitive effect, 7.2.1.2
  capacity to conspire, 7.2.1.1

consciously parallel action, 7.2.1.1
conspiracy-in-fact analysis, 7.2.1.1
exclusive-dealing agreements, 7.2.1.3.6; 7.2.2.1
generally, 7.2.1
group boycotts, 7.2.1.3.4
horizontal agreements to exchange pricing information, 7.2.1.3.2
horizontal concerted refusals to deal, 7.2.1.3.4
horizontal market-allocation agreements, 7.2.1.3.3
horizontal price-fixing agreements, 7.2.1.3.1
independent personal stake, 7.2.1.1
meeting of the minds
    unilateral versus concerted action, 7.2.1.1
per se rule
    unreasonable restraint on competition, 7.2.1.2
quick-look or truncated version of rule of reason
    unreasonable restraint on competition, 7.2.1.2
rule of reason analysis
    unreasonable restraint on competition, 7.2.1.2
semi-exclusive dealing agreements, 7.2.1.3.6
single and unified economic interest, 7.2.1.1
tying agreements, 7.2.1.3.5; 7.2.2.1
unilateral versus concerted action, 7.2.1.1
unreasonable restraint on competition, 7.2.1.2
Sherman Act, Section 2
    attempted monopolization, 7.2.2.2
    exclusionary conduct, 7.2.2.1
    generally, 7.2.2
    monopolization, 7.2.2.1
    predatory conduct, 7.2.2.1
    specific intent to monopolize, 7.2.2.2
solicitation of government action, 7.3.4
standing
    private enforcement, 7.5.3
state-action exemption, 7.3.3
state Attorneys General
    government enforcement, 7.4.3
statutes, analysis of
    common elements, 7.2
    Federal Trade Commission Act (FTC Act), 7.2.4
    Sherman Act, Section 1, 7.2.1
    Sherman Act, Section 2, 7.2.2
treble damages
    private enforcement, 7.5
types of issues typically arising, 7.6
unfair methods of competition under Federal Trade Commission Act (FTC Act), 7.2.4

ARBITRATION
administered versus self-administered, 15.2.3
advantages, 15.2.1
agreements to arbitrate
    consumer disputes, 15.2.4.2
    employment disputes, 15.2.4.1
    generally, 15.2.3
combined with mediation, 15.3.3
consumer disputes
    agreements to arbitrate, 15.2.4.2
    generally, 15.2.4
employment disputes, 15.2.4.1
generally, 15.2.5
long term care, 15.2.4.2.2; 15.2.4.2.3
nursing homes, 15.2.4.2.1
rules of procedure, 15.2.4.2.4
savings in time and cost, 15.2.1; 15.2.2
single arbitrator versus panel, 15.2.2

ASCs (*See* **AMBULATORY SURGICAL CENTERS**)

ATTORNEYS' FEES
antitrust law
    private enforcement, 7.5

ATTORNEYS GENERAL
antitrust law
    state Attorneys General
        government enforcement, 7.4.3

AUDIOLOGISTS
Medicare Part B coverage, 3.6.2.2
suppliers, 3.2.7

Index

B

BANKRUPTCY
 health care transactions and contracting, 12.6.3
BEST INTERESTS OF CHILD
 consent to medical treatment, minors, 2.2.4
BEST-INTEREST STANDARD
 end-of-life decision making
  incompetent patients, 2.3.2
BIG DATA (*See* DATA SHARING)
BIOETHICS, 13.1.1.1 to 13.4
BLUE CROSS AND BLUE SHIELD (BC/BS) PLANS
 history of Medicare, 3.1.1
 horizontal market-allocation agreements, 7.2.1.3.3
 insurance regulation
  scope of state regulation, 8.2.7

C

CENTERS FOR MEDICARE AND MEDICAID SERVICES (CMS), 3.1; 3.3.2
 administrative guidelines, 3.3.2.4
 administrative history, 3.3.2.1
 administrator
  rulings, 3.3.2.5
 center clinical standards and quality (CCSQ), 3.3.2.2
 center for Medicaid, CHIP, and survey and certification, 3.3.2.2
 center for Medicare, 3.3.2.2
 center for Medicare and Medicaid innovation (CMMI), 3.3.2.2
 center for program integrity (CPI), 3.3.2.2
 center for strategic planning (CSP), 3.3.2.2
 headquarters, 3.3.2.3
 regional operations, 3.3.2.3
 structural overview, 3.3.2.2
CERTIFIED NURSE MIDWIVES
 Medicare Part B coverage, 3.6.2.2
CERTIFIED REGISTERED NURSE ANESTHETISTS (CRNAs)
 Medicare
  Part B coverage, 3.6.2.2

 resource-based relative value scale (RBRVS) fee schedule, 3.9.4
CHARITIES
 public charities
  tax-exempt issues, 6.1.2; 6.4
   Pension Protection Act (PPA) (*See* PENSION PROTECTION ACT (PPA))
   principal function
    Section 509(a)(1) public charities, 6.4.1
   recurring concepts, 6.1.3
   Section 509(a)(1) public charities, 6.4.1
   Section 509(a)(2) public charities, 6.4.2
   supporting organizations
    control test, 6.4.3.4
    operational test, 6.4.3.2
    organizational test, 6.4.3.1
    relationship test, 6.4.3.3
    Section 509(a)(3) public charities, 6.4.3
   two-part public supported test
    Section 509(a)(2) public charities, 6.4.2
CHILD CUSTODY
 bioethics
  commercial surrogacy
   custody disputes, 13.1.3.2
CHILD NEGLECT
 consent to medical treatment, 2.2.4
CHILDREN OR MINORS
 consent to medical treatment, 2.2.4
CHILD SUPPORT
 qualified medical child support orders, 8.3.2.5
CHOICE OF MEDICAL TREATMENT
 Constitutional protection, 2.2.2
CLAYTON ACT
 labor unions, 7.3.7
 Section 7
  competitors in the relevant market
   calculation of each competitor's market share, 7.2.3.4
   identification, 7.2.3.3
  generally, 7.2.3
  Herfindahl-Hirschman Index (HHI)
   measure of market concentration level, 7.2.3.5

horizontal merger guidelines, 7.2.3
increase in market concentration resulting from merger
calculation, 7.2.3.5
misleading post-merger market share/concentration statistics, 7.2.3.6
market concentration level
calculation, 7.2.3.5
misleading post-merger market share/concentration statistics, 7.2.3.6
mergers and acquisitions, 7.2.3
misleading post-merger market share/concentration statistics, 7.2.3.6
post-merger market share
calculation, 7.2.3.5
misleading post-merger market share/concentration statistics, 7.2.3.6
relevant geographic market, 7.2.3.2
relevant product market, 7.2.3.1

CLINICAL NURSE SPECIALISTS
Medicare
Part B coverage, 3.6.2.2
resource-based relative value scale (RBRVS) fee schedule, 3.9.4

CLONING
bioethics, 13.3.3.2

COBRA (*See* CONSOLIDATED OMNIBUS BUDGET RECONCILIATION ACT (COBRA))

COINSURANCE
Anti-Kickback safe-harbor regulations, 5.2.9

COMMERCIAL SURROGACY
custody disputes, 13.1.3.2
generally, 13.1.3
prohibition and regulation, 13.1.3.1

COMPETENCY
end-of-life decision making
incompetent patients, 2.3.2
refuse life-sustaining medical treatment, right to, 2.3.1
incompetent patients
end-of-life decision making, 2.3.2
treatment decisions, right to make, 2.2.3

CONFIDENTIALITY AGREEMENTS
health care transactions and contracting, 12.8.2
physician/hospital arrangements, 10.3.2.5

CONFIDENTIALITY OF INFORMATION
data sharing (*See* DATA SHARING)
dispute resolution, 15.1
genetic information, 13.3.1
health care transactions and contracting termination of agreements, 12.8.2
patient medical information, 2.4
confidentiality generally, 2.4.1
duty to warn, 2.4.2.2
Health Insurance Portability and Accountability Act (HIPAA) (*See* **HEALTH INSURANCE PORTABILITY AND ACCOUNTABILITY ACT (HIPAA)**, subhead: Confidentiality of patient medical information)
heightened protection, 2.4.1
judicial disclosure, 2.4.2.1
mandatory disclosure, 2.4.2
mandatory reporting of medical conditions, 2.4.2.2
patient release forms, importance of, 2.4.1
reporting of medical conditions, mandatory, 2.4.2.2
use and disclosure of protected health information, 2.4.3.2
violent propensities of patients, duty to warn of, 2.4.2.2

CONSCIENCE LAWS
duty to treat patient, 2.1.3

CONSENT TO MEDICAL TREATMENT
abortion (*See* ABORTION, subhead: Informed consent)
Constitutional protection, 2.2.2
disclosures required, 2.2.1
exceptions to requirement to obtain consent, 2.2.1.3
experimentation, consent for, 2.2.5
forms, 2.2.1.1
HIV testing, 2.2.1.4
human-subject research, 2.2.5
incompetent's right to make treatment decisions, 2.2.3
informed consent (*See* **INFORMED CONSENT**)

mental health procedures, 2.2.1.4
minors, 2.2.4
restraints, 2.2.1.5
right to be free from undesirable personal contact, generally, 2.2.1
special circumstances, statutes requiring, 2.2.1.4
undesired personal contact, right to be free from, 2.2.1
waiver, 2.2.1.3

CONSOLIDATED OMNIBUS BUDGET RECONCILIATION ACT (COBRA)
federal regulation of private health care plans, 8.3.2.1

CONSPIRACY
antitrust law, 7.2.1.1
fraud and abuse, 5.6.6

CONSTITUTIONAL PROTECTION
consent to medical treatment, 2.2.2
end-of-life decision making
 incompetent patients, 2.3.2
right to refuse medical treatment, 2.2.2

CONTRACEPTIVES
access to, 13.1.2

CONTRACTS AND CONTRACTORS
Medicare
 Medicare administrative contractors (MACs), 3.3.3
 private contracts, 3.2.2
 quality improvement organizations (QIOs), 3.3.4
termination of agreements
 confidentiality and ownership of records, 12.8.2
 indemnification provisions, 12.8.1
types of contracts, 12.7 to 12.7.5
 affiliation agreements, 12.7.5
 employment contracts
  compensation, 12.7.1
  independent contractor agreements, 12.7.1
  liability concerns, 12.7.1
  noncompete clauses or restrictive covenants, 12.7.1
 independent contractor agreements, 12.7.1

management and service agreements, 12.7.3
merger and acquisition agreements, 12.7.4
physician recruitment agreements, 12.7.2
purpose of contracts, 12.7

COOPERATIVE HOSPITAL-SERVICES ORGANIZATIONS
Anti-Kickback safe-harbor regulations, 5.2.15

COORDINATED CARE PLANS (CCPs)
Medicare Part C, 3.2.1.3

CO-PAYMENTS
Medicare
 cost-sharing by beneficiaries, 3.2.4.1

COSMETIC SURGERY
Medicare, 3.2.3

COVENANTS NOT TO COMPETE
health care transactions and contracting
 employment contracts, 12.7.1
 termination of agreements, 12.8.3
physicians
 post-termination restrictive covenants, 10.2.2.6
 sale of ownership interest, 10.2.4.4

CREATION OF PROVIDER/PATIENT RELATIONSHIP
generally, 2.1.1

CRIMINAL LAW AND PROCEDURE
fraud and abuse (*See* FRAUD AND ABUSE)
HIPAA privacy rules, violations of, 2.4.3.7
kickbacks
 Anti-Kickback safe-harbor regulations, 5.2
 Anti-Kickback Statute, 5.1
physician self-referral, 5.4
"sunshine law", 5.3

D

DAMAGES
antitrust law (*See* **ANTITRUST LAW**, subhead: Damages)
end-of-life decision making
 unwanted care, 2.3.3

DATA SHARING
antitrust laws, 14.6
Common Rule
 access to data repository, 14.5.5

amendments, 14.5.2.1; 14.5.3.1
applicability, 14.5.1
building a data repository, 14.5.4
generally, 14.5
informed consent, 14.5.3
research exemptions, 14.5.2
waiver, 14.5.3
de-identified data, 14.2.7
drug or alcohol abuse patient records
  access to data repository, 14.3.3; 14.3.4
  building a data repository, 14.3.2
  disclosure restrictions, 14.3.1
  federally assisted program, data obtained by, 14.3.1.2
  generally, 14.3
  identifying information, 14.3.1.1
  re-disclosure protections, 14.3.1.3
  research, access to data repository for, 14.3.4
generally, 14.1
Health Insurance Portability and Accountability Act (HIPAA)
  access to data repository, 14.2.2; 14.2.3
  building a data repository, 14.2.1
  de-identified data, 14.2.7
  minimum necessary standard, 14.2.4
  psychotherapy notes, 14.2.5
  research, access to data repository for, 14.2.3
informed consent, 14.5.3
research exemptions
  Common Rule, 14.5.2; 14.5.2.1
  drug or alcohol abuse patient records, 14.3.4
  Health Insurance Portability and Accountability Act (HIPAA), 14.2.3
  tax exempt organizations, 14.7.1; 14.7.2
state privacy laws, 14.4
tax exempt organizations, 14.7.1; 14.7.2
withholding personal health information as individual right, 14.2.6

DEATH, DETERMINATION OF
organ transplantation, 13.2.1

DEDUCTIBLES
Medicare, 3.2.4.1

DEFINED TERMS
assignment
  Medicare, 3.12.1
disqualified persons
  tax-exempt issues, intermediate sanctions, 6.2.7.3
durable medical equipment, 11.2.2.1.1
entity
  physician self-referral, 5.4.4
fair market value
  physician self-referral, 5.5.4.1
financial relationship
  physician self-referral, 5.4.1
glossary, 1.1
intermittent care, 11.3.2.1
market concentration
  antitrust law, Clayton Act, Section 7, 7.2.3.5
  generally, 7.1.3
program payment
  Medicare, 10.4.3
prosthetic and orthotic devices
  home medical equipment (HME) suppliers Medicare coverage, 11.2.2.1.1
provider
  Medicare, 3.2.7
provider-based
  Medicare, 3.2.8
reassignment
  Medicare, 3.12.2
relevant geographic market
  antitrust law, Clayton Act, Section 7, 7.2.3.2
relevant market, 7.1.2
relevant product market
  antitrust law, Clayton Act, Section 7, 7.2.3.1
supplier
  Medicare, 3.2.7

DENTAL CARE
Medicare, 3.2.3

DHHS OFFICE OF INSPECTOR GENERAL (OIG)
Anti-Kickback Statute
  advisory opinions, 5.1.4

audit and evaluation of Medicare, 3.3.5
fraud and abuse
    corporate compliance programs, 5.8.2

DIAGNOSTIC TESTS
resource-based relative value scale (RBRVS) fee schedule, 3.9.4

DISCLOSURES
confidentiality of patient medical information, 2.4
    HIPAA privacy rules
        use and disclosure of protected health information, 2.4.3.2
    mandatory disclosure, 2.4.2
experience and skill of provider, 2.2.1.2

DISCOUNTS
Anti-Kickback safe-harbor regulations, 5.2.6
tax-exempt issues
    courtesy discounts, 6.3.5

DISCRIMINATION
genetic information
    employment, 13.3.2.2
    generally, 13.3.2
    insurance, 13.3.2.1
Patient Protection and Affordable Care Act
    health status, discrimination based on, 8.3.3.13
    highly compensated individuals, discrimination favoring, 8.3.3.8

DISPUTE RESOLUTION
arbitration (*See* **ARBITRATION**)
confidentiality of information, 15.1
conflict management, 15.4
generally, 15.1; 15.5
mediation (*See* MEDIATION)
physician employment contracts, 10.2.2.7
physician/hospital arrangements, 10.3.2.6
provider reimbursement review board (PRRB), 3.3.6

DNR ORDERS
advance directives, 2.3.4.3

DOJ ANTITRUST DIVISION
government enforcement of antitrust law, 7.4.1

DO-NOT-RESUSCITATE PROTOCOLS (DNR ORDERS)
advance directives, 2.3.4.3

"DONUT HOLE," CLOSING OF
prescription drug costs, 3.6.5

DRUG OR ALCOHOL TREATMENT
confidentiality of patient medical information, 2.4.1
data sharing (*See* **DATA SHARING**)
Mental Health Parity and Addiction Equality Act (MHPAEA), 8.3.2.2

DURABLE MEDICAL EQUIPMENT (DME) SUPPLIERS
home medical equipment (HME) suppliers, 11.2

DURABLE POWER OF ATTORNEY FOR HEALTH CARE
advance directives, 2.3.4; 2.3.4.2

DUTY TO TREAT, 2.1
conscience laws, 2.1.3
creation of provider/patient relationship, 2.1.1
emergency treatment
    "Good Samaritan" laws, 2.1.2
    health care facilities required to accept patients, 2.1.2.1
"Good Samaritan" laws, 2.1.2
health care facilities required to accept patients, 2.1.2
non-emergency treatment, 2.1.2.2

DUTY TO TREAT PATIENT, 2.1
conscience laws, 2.1.3
creation of provider/patient relationship, 2.1.1
"Good Samaritan" laws, 2.1.2
health care facilities required to accept patients, 2.1.2

DUTY TO WARN
mandatory reporting of medical conditions, 2.4.2.2

E

ELECTIONS
tax-exempt issues
    political activity prohibition
        exemption requirements, 6.2.9.1

ELECTRONIC RECORDS
electronic health records (EHR)
    donation and receipt of technology
        accountable care organization waivers, 5.2.23

Anti-Kickback safe-harbor regulations, 5.2.22
tax-exempt issues, 6.3.6
Health Information Technology for Economic and Clinical Health Act (HITECH), 9.3.1; 10.6
stand-alone exemption, 6.2.3.4
physician self-referral, 5.5.3.15
prescriptions, 5.2.21

EMANCIPATED CHILD
consent to medical treatment, 2.2.4

EMBEZZLEMENT
federal health care fraud offenses, 5.6.2.3

EMBRYONIC AND FETAL-CELL RESEARCH
genetic engineering, 13.3.3.1

EMERGENCY MEDICAL TREATMENT AND ACTIVE LABOR ACT (EMTALA)
hospitals, 9.3.2

EMERGENCY TREATMENT
contraception, 13.1.1.4
emergency response systems, 11.6.1
"Good Samaritan" laws, 2.1.2
health care facilities
  accept patients, requirement to, 2.1.2.1
  "Good Samaritan" laws, 2.1.2
health care facilities required to accept patients, 2.1.2.1
health maintenance organizations (HMOs), 8.2.3.3
home and community-based services (HCBS), 11.6.1
hospitals, 9.3.2

EMPLOYEE RETIREMENT AND INCOME SECURITY ACT (ERISA)
any-willing-provider (AWP) laws, 8.1.2
federal regulation of private health care plans
  adopted children, coverage, 8.3.2.6
  cancer, minimum treatment, 8.3.2.9
  Consolidated Omnibus Budget Reconciliation Act (COBRA), 8.3.2.1
  generally, 8.1.2; 8.3.1
  HIPAA's preexisting condition rule, 8.3.2.3
  HIPAA's pre-existing condition rule, 8.3.2.3
  HIPAA's privacy and security rules, 8.3.2.4
  maternity protection, 8.3.2.8
  Mental Health Parity and Addiction Equality Act (MHPAEA), 8.3.2.2
  qualified medical child support orders, 8.3.2.5
  vaccine coverage, pediatric vaccines, 8.3.2.7
historical background, 8.3.1
medical malpractice, 8.1.2
preemption of state provisions
  deemer clause, 8.1.2
  preemption clause, 8.1.2
  saving clause, 8.1.2

EMPLOYEES
Anti-Kickback safe-harbor regulations, 5.2.7
genetic information, nondiscrimination and, 13.3.2.2

EMPLOYER-SPONSORED PRIVATE HEALTH CARE PLANS
regulation (*See* **HEALTH CARE PRIVATE PLANS, REGULATION**)

END-OF-LIFE DECISION MAKING, 2.3
advance directives (*See* **ADVANCE DIRECTIVES**)
"End of Life Choices" Act, 2.3.6
incompetent patients, 2.3.2
medical futility, 2.3.5
physician-assisted suicide, 2.3.6
refuse life-sustaining medical treatment, right to, 2.3.1
right to refuse life-sustaining medical treatment, 2.3.1
unwanted care, damages for rendering, 2.3.3

EQUIPMENT
home medical equipment suppliers (*See* **HOME MEDICAL EQUIPMENT (HME) SUPPLIERS**)
rental of office space and equipment, 5.5.3.1

ERISA (*See* **EMPLOYEE RETIREMENT AND INCOME SECURITY ACT (ERISA)**)

ETHICS
bioethics, 13.1.1.1 to 13.4 (*See* **BIOETHICS**)
nursing facilities, 11.5.3.4; 11.5.4.4

EUTHANASIA
   end-of-life decision making (*See* **END-OF-LIFE DECISION MAKING**)

EXPERIMENTATION
   consent to medical treatment, 2.2.5
   institutional review board (IRB) approval for experimentation, 2.2.5

EXTENDED CARE OR SKILLED NURSING SERVICES (SNF)
   Medicare Part A coverage, 3.6.1.2

EYE CARE
   Medicare, 3.2.3

F

FEDERAL GOVERNMENT
   antitrust law
      immunity, 7.3.2

FEDERALLY QUALIFIED HEALTH CENTERS (FQHCs)
   Anti-Kickback safe-harbor regulations, 5.2.19; 5.2.24

FEDERAL REGULATION OF PRIVATE HEALTH CARE PLANS
   Employee Retirement and Income Security Act (ERISA) (*See* **EMPLOYEE RETIREMENT AND INCOME SECURITY ACT (ERISA)**, subhead: Federal regulation of private health care plans)

FEDERAL TRADE COMMISSION
   antitrust law (*See* **ANTITRUST LAW**, subhead: Federal Trade Commission)

FEE-FOR-SERVICE (FFS) PLANS
   Medicare Part C, 3.2.1.3

FICTITIOUS CLAIMS
   experience and skill of provider, 2.2.1.2
   submitting fictitious or fraudulent claims, 5.6.6

FINES
   Anti-Kickback Statute, 5.1.1
   HIPAA privacy rules, violations, 2.4.3.7
   physician self-referral, 5.4.1

FOOT CARE
   Medicare, 3.2.3

FRAUD AND ABUSE, 5.1 to 5.7.3
   Anti-Kickback safe-harbor regulations
      accountable care organization (ACO) waivers, 5.2.23; 5.5.3.17
      ambulances
         replenishing and restocking, 5.2.18
      ASCs, 5.2.16
      coinsurance and deductible waivers, 5.2.9
      cooperative hospital-services organizations, 5.2.15
      discounts, 5.2.6
      electronic health records (EHR), donation and receipt of technology, 5.2.22
      electronic prescribing, 5.2.21
      employees, amounts paid to, 5.2.7
      exceptions, 5.2
      federally qualified health centers (FQHCs), 5.2.19; 5.2.24
      generally, 5.2
      group health plans
         price reductions, 5.2.11
      group practices, investments in, 5.2.14
      group purchasing organizations, 5.2.8
      investment interests
         60/40 investor rule, 5.2.1.2
         60/40 revenue rule, 5.2.1.2
         generally, 5.2.1
         investments in entities in MUAs, 5.2.1.3
         large investment interests, 5.2.1.1
         small investment interests, 5.2.1.2
      managed care organizations, beneficiary incentives offered by, 5.2.10
      obstetrical malpractice insurance subsidies, 5.2.13
      practitioner recruitment, 5.2.12; 5.5.3.18
      referral agreements for specialty services, 5.2.17
      referral services, 5.2.4
      risk-sharing arrangements, 5.2.20
      sale of practice, 5.2.3
      space and equipment rental, 5.2.2
      warranties, 5.2.5
   Anti-Kickback Statute, 5.1
      advisory opinions, 5.1.4
      Hanslester decision, 5.1.2.2
      judicial interpretation, 5.1.2

Hanslester decision, 5.1.2.2
pre-*Hanlester*, 5.1.2.1
United States ex rel. Jamison v. McKesson, 5.1.2.3
United States v. Greber, 5.1.2.1
special fraud alerts, 5.1.3
statutory prohibition, 5.1.1
corporate compliance programs
federal sentencing guidelines, 5.8.1
generally, 5.8
integrity agreements, 5.8.3
OIG compliance guidelines, 5.8.2
false claims and fraudulent billing, 5.6
civil prohibitions
federal false claims Act, 5.7.1
Fraud Enforcement and Recovery Act (FERA), 5.7.1
Program Fraud Civil Remedies Act, 5.7.3
qui tam actions, 5.7.1
Social Security Act, 5.7.2
conspiracy to defraud, 5.6.6
federal health care fraud offenses, 5.6.2
mail and wire fraud, 5.6.3
money laundering, 5.6.5
racketeering, 5.6.4
Social Security Act, 5.6.1; 5.7.2
submitting fictitious or fraudulent claims, 5.6.6
false statements, making
experience and skill of provider, 2.2.1.2
federal health care fraud offenses, 5.6.2.2
federal health care fraud offenses
false statements, making, 5.6.2.2
generally, 5.6.2.1
theft or embezzlement, 5.6.2.3
home health agencies (HHAs), 11.3.3.4
home medical equipment (HME) suppliers, 11.2.4
hospice services, 11.4.8
integrated delivery systems (IDSs), 12.4.1.2
investment interests
Anti-Kickback safe-harbor regulations, 5.2.1
long term care
compliance program guidelines, 11.5.6.8

false claims actions based on quality of care, 11.5.6.7
mail and wire fraud, 5.6.3
money laundering, 5.6.5
physician self-referral, 5.4
advisory opinions, 5.4.5
prohibited generally, 5.4.1
regulations, 5.4.2
reporting requirements, 5.4.3
Stark exceptions, 5.6
academic medical centers, 5.5.1.4
accountable care organization (ACO) waivers, 5.5.3.17
additional compensation exceptions, 5.5.3.16
additional regulatory exceptions, 5.5.1.6
bona-fide employment arrangements, 5.5.3.2
compensation arrangement exceptions, 5.5.3
compensation conditioned on referrals to a particular provider, 5.5.4.3
compensation methodologies, 5.5.4.2
compliance training, 5.5.3.13
electronic prescribing and electronic health records, 5.5.3.15
fair market value exception, 5.5.3.9; 5.5.4.1
group practice arrangements with a hospital, 5.5.3.7
hospitals, ownership in, 5.5.2.2
implants in ASCs, 5.5.1.5
indirect compensation, 5.5.3.14
in-office ancillary services, 5.5.1.2
isolated financial transactions, 5.5.3.6
manage-care risk-sharing arrangements, 5.5.3.12
medical staff incidental benefits, 5.5.3.11
non-monetary compensation up to $300, 5.5.3.10
ownership and compensation exceptions, 5.5.1
ownership exceptions, 5.5.2
payments for items and services, 5.5.3.8

personal-service arrangements, 5.5.3.3
physical recruitment and retention, 5.5.3.5
physician services, 5.5.1.1
prepaid plans, 5.5.1.3
publicly traded securities and mutual funds, ownership exceptions, 5.5.2.1
rental of office space and equipment, 5.5.3.1
rural providers, 5.5.2.3
special rules for compensation, 5.5.4
"stand in the shoes" analysis, 5.5.3.14
unrelated payments, 5.5.3.4
Stark law, 5.4.1
racketeering
false claims and fraudulent billing, 5.6.4
Social Security Act
false claims and fraudulent billing, 5.6.1; 5.7.2
overpayments, reporting and return of, 5.7.1
Stark law
accountable care organization (ACO) waivers, 5.2.23; 5.5.3.17
physician self-referral, 5.4.1
"sunshine law", 5.3
theft or embezzlement, 5.6.2.3

FREEDOM OF ACCESS TO ABORTION TO CLINIC ENTRANCES (FACE) ACT
bioethics, 13.1.1.5

FUTILITY, MEDICAL
end-of-life decision making, 2.3.5

G

GENETIC ENGINEERING
cloning, 13.3.3.2
embryonic and fetal-cell research, 13.3.3.1
generally, 13.3.3

GENETIC INFORMATION
confidentiality of information, 13.3.1
discrimination based on health status of participants and beneficiaries, 8.3.3.13
generally, 13.3

genetic engineering (See **GENETIC ENGINEERING**)
Genetic Information Nondiscrimination Act (GINA), 13.3.2
human genome project, 13.3
nondiscrimination (See **DISCRIMINATION**, subhead: Genetic information)
Patient Protection and Affordable Care Act, 8.3.3.13

GLOSSARY, 1.1
defined terms generally (See **DEFINED TERMS**)

GRISWOLD V. CONNECTICUT
bioethics of human reproduction, 13.1.1.1

GROUP HEALTH PLANS
Anti-Kickback safe-harbor regulations, 5.2.11

GROUP PURCHASING ORGANIZATIONS
Anti-Kickback safe-harbor regulations, 5.2.8
"sunshine law," reporting requirement sunder, 5.3

H

HANSLESTER **DECISION**
Anti-Kickback Statute, 5.1.2.2

HEALTH CARE FACILITIES
accept patients, requirement to, 2.1.2
emergency treatment
accept patients, requirement to, 2.1.2.1
"Good Samaritan" laws, 2.1.2
health care transactions and contracting, 12.1 to 12.9
non-emergency treatment, 2.1.2.2

HEALTH CARE PRIVATE PLANS, REGULATION, 8.1 to 8.4
annual coverage limits, 8.3.3.1
appeals
Patient Protection and Affordable Care Act
external reviews, 8.3.3.3
internal appeals process, 8.3.3.3
basis of state regulation of private health plans, 8.1
insurable interest, existence of, 8.1.1
McCarran-Ferguson Act of 1945, 8.1.1
Blue Cross and Blue Shield (BC/BS) plans
scope of state regulation, 8.2.7

cafeteria plans, 8.3.3.18
center for Medicaid and state operations, 3.3.2.2
dependent coverage extension, 8.3.3.5
discrimination based on health status, 8.3.3.13
Employee Retirement and Income Security Act (ERISA) (*See* **EMPLOYEE RETIREMENT AND INCOME SECURITY ACT (ERISA)**, subhead: Federal regulation of private health care plans)
essential benefits coverage
   Patient Protection and Affordable Care Act
      generally, 8.3.3.10
      penalty tax for failure to provide health plan with minimum essential coverage, 8.3.3.16
exchanges
   Patient Protection and Affordable Care Act
      employer duty to inform employees of coverage options, 8.3.3.15
      essential benefits coverage, 8.3.3.10
      transparency of information, 8.3.3.7
flexible spending accounts for health, 8.3.3.18
health maintenance organizations
   scope of state regulation, 8.2.3
      description, 8.2.3.1
      regulatory scheme, 8.2.3.2
      typical areas of regulation, 8.2.3.3
highly compensated individuals, discrimination favoring, 8.3.3.8
history of federal efforts to regulate health care, 8.3.3; 8.4
indemnity insurers, 8.2.1
lifetime coverage limits, 8.3.3.1
McCarran-Ferguson Act, 8.1.1
Patient Protection and Affordable Care Act (*See* **PATIENT PROTECTION AND AFFORDABLE CARE ACT**)
penalty tax
   minimum essential coverage, failure to provide health plan with, 8.3.3.16
point-of-service programs, 8.2.4
preexisting condition exclusions, 8.3.3.12
preferred provider organizations, 8.2.2
preventive health services coverage, 8.3.3.4
provider-sponsored networks, 8.2.6
quality reporting, 8.3.3.9
rescission of coverage, 8.3.3.2
small businesses, tax credits for, 8.3.3.14
standardization
   benefit summaries, 8.3.3.6
   coverage explanations, 8.3.3.6
state regulation of insurance business, 8.1.1
   preemption by federal regulation, 8.1.2
   scope of state regulation
      Blue Cross and Blue Shield (BC/BS) plans, 8.2.7
      generally, 8.2
      health maintenance organizations, 8.2.3
         description, 8.2.3.1
         regulatory scheme, 8.2.3.2
      indemnity insurers, 8.2.1
      point-of-service programs, 8.2.4
      preferred provider organizations, 8.2.2
      provider-sponsored networks, 8.2.6
      third party administrators, 8.2.5
third party administrators, 8.2.5
waiting periods, excessive, 8.3.3.11

HEALTH CARE QUALITY IMPROVEMENT ACT (HCQIA)
antitrust law, 7.3.8
hospital disciplinary procedures, 9.3.4

HEALTH CARE TRANSACTIONS AND CONTRACTING
affiliations
   agreements, 12.7.5
   structure of transactions, 12.3.3
bankruptcy, 12.6.3
business development teams and due diligence, 12.2.1
confidentiality
   ownership of records, 12.8.2
consolidation, effect of, 12.1
contracts, types of, 12.7 to 12.7.5
   affiliation agreements, 12.7.5
   employment contracts
      compensation, 12.7.1

independent contractor agreements, 12.7.1
  liability concerns, 12.7.1
  noncompete clauses or restrictive covenants, 12.7.1
independent contractor agreements, 12.7.1
management and service agreements, 12.7.3
merger and acquisition agreements, 12.7.4
physician recruitment agreements, 12.7.2
purpose of contracts, 12.7
corporate structures, 12.4.1 to 12.4.5
  independent practice associations (IPAs), 12.4.3
  integrated delivery systems (*See* **INTEGRATED DELIVERY SYSTEMS (IDSs)**)
  management-services organizations (MSOs), 12.4.5
  physician/hospital organizations (PHOs), 12.4.2
  professional corporations, 12.4.4
current climate of transactions and contracting, 12.9
indemnification provisions
  termination of agreements, 12.8.1
independent practice associations (IPAs) (*See* **INDEPENDENT PRACTICE ASSOCIATIONS (IPAs)**)
integrated delivery systems (*See* **INTEGRATED DELIVERY SYSTEMS (IDSs)**)
integrated or affiliated entities, 12.1
joint ventures, 12.3.2
key issues in structuring transactions, 12.5.1 to 12.5.3
  legal issues, 12.5.3
  operational issues, 12.5.2
  purpose of venture, 12.5.1
legal issues in structuring transactions, 12.5.3
letters of intent, 12.2.3
management and service agreements, 12.7.3
management-services organizations (MSOs), 12.4.5
mergers and acquisitions, 12.1 to 12.9
  agreements, 12.7.4

structure of transactions (see subhead: Structure of transactions)
successor liability, 12.3.1.2
noncompete clauses or restrictive covenants
  employment contracts, 12.7.1
  termination of agreements, 12.8.3
non-disclosure agreements and protected-health information (PHI), 12.2.2
non-interference clauses, 12.8.3
operational issues in structuring transactions, 12.5.2
physician/hospital organizations (PHOs), 12.4.2
physician recruitment agreements, 12.7.2
professional corporations, 12.4.4
protected-health information (PHI), 12.2.2
purpose of venture, 12.5.1
repurchase obligations, 12.6.2
rights to repurchase, 12.6.2
structure of transactions, 12.3.1; 12.3 to 12.3.3
  affiliations, 12.3.3
  asset transactions, 12.3.1.2
  due diligence, 12.2.1
  joint ventures, 12.3.2
  mergers and acquisitions, 12.3.1
    asset transactions, 12.3.1.2
    successor liability, 12.3.1.2
  stock transactions and member substitutions, 12.3.1.1
  successor liability, 12.3.1.2
termination of agreements, 12.8 to 12.8.3
  confidentiality and ownership of records, 12.8.2
  importance of including provisions, 12.8
  indemnification provisions, 12.8.1
  noncompete and non-interference clauses, 12.8.3
termination provisions, 12.6.1
term sheets, 12.2.3
types of contracts, 12.7 to 12.7.5
unwinding transactions, 12.6 to 12.6.3
  bankruptcy, 12.6.3
  importance of planning, 12.6
  repurchase obligations, 12.6.2

rights to repurchase, 12.6.2
termination provisions, 12.6.1
HEALTH INSURANCE PORTABILITY AND ACCOUNTABILITY ACT (HIPAA)
breach of unsecured protected information, 9.3.1
confidentiality of patient medical information
administrative requirements, 2.4.3.1
authorized disclosures, 2.4.3.2
breach notification, 2.4.3.5
business associates, 2.4.3.6; 9.3.1
de-identified information, use and disclosure of, 2.4.3.2
enforcement, 2.4.3.7
generally, 2.4.3
health care transactions and contracting, 12.2.2
notice of privacy, 2.4.3.4
patient access to own information, 2.4.3.3
privacy officers, designation of, 2.4.3.1
sanctions, 2.4.3.7; 9.3.1
training requirements, 2.4.3.1
use and disclosure of protected health information, 2.4.3.2
covered entities defined, 9.3.1
data sharing (*See* **DATA SHARING**)
Employee Retirement and Income Security Act (ERISA)
pre-existing condition rule, 8.3.2.3
privacy and security rules, 8.3.2.4
Health Information Technology For Economic and Clinical Health Act (HITECH), 9.3.1; 10.6
hospitals, 9.3.1
HEALTH MAINTENANCE ORGANIZATIONS (HMOs)
access to specialists, 8.2.3.3
anti-gag clause rules, 8.2.3.3
bonus arrangements, 8.2.3.1
capitation arrangements, 8.2.3.1
continuity of care, 8.2.3.3
direct contract model HMOs, 8.2.3.1
emergency services, prudent layperson standard, 8.2.3.3
enrollee grievances and appeals, 8.2.3.3
financial incentives, 8.2.3.3
group model HMOs, 8.2.3.1
indemnification provisions, 8.2.3.3
independent practice association (IPA) model HMOs, 8.2.3.1
insolvency protection, 8.2.3.3
insurance regulation, scope of state, 8.2.3
mandated benefits/coverage requirements, 8.2.3.3
Medicare Part C, 3.2.1.3
member hold harmless provisions, 8.2.3.3
network adequacy, 8.2.3.3
network model HMOs, 8.2.3.1
percent of premium arrangements, 8.2.3.1
pool/fund arrangements, 8.2.3.1
provider selection and deselection, 8.2.3.3
quality assurance, 8.2.3.3
staff model HMOs, 8.2.3.1
typical areas of regulation, 8.2.3.3
utilization management laws, 8.2.3.3
withhold arrangements, 8.2.3.1
women's health, 8.2.3.3
HEARING CARE
Medicare
excluded services, 3.2.3
HILL-BURTON ACT
history of Medicare, 3.1.1
HIPAA (*See* **HEALTH INSURANCE PORTABILITY AND ACCOUNTABILITY ACT**)
HIV
confidentiality of patient medical information, 2.4.1
testing, 2.2.1.4
HOME AND COMMUNITY-BASED SERVICES (HCBS), 11.6
adult day services (ADS) programs, 11.6.1
case managers and geriatric care managers, 11.6.1
emergency response systems, 11.6.1
friendly visitor and companion services, 11.6.1
homemaker and chore services, 11.6.1
integration mandate
legal developments, 11.6.2

Index

legal developments, 11.6.2
meals programs, 11.6.1
Medicaid quality assurance/quality improvement and oversight, 11.6.3
new freedom initiative (NFI)
   legal developments, 11.6.2
respite care, 11.6.1
senior centers, 11.6.1
transportation services, 11.6.1

HOME CARE PROVIDERS, 11.1 to 11.6.3
certificates of need, 11.3.1
durable medical equipment (DME) suppliers, 11.2.1
fraud and abuse
   home medical equipment (HME) suppliers
      Medicare, 11.2.4
home and community-based services (HCBS), 11.6
   adult day services (ADS) programs, 11.6.1
   case managers and geriatric care managers, 11.6.1
   emergency response systems, 11.6.1
   friendly visitor and companion services, 11.6.1
   homemaker and chore services, 11.6.1
   integration mandate
      legal developments, 11.6.2
   legal developments, 11.6.2
   meals programs, 11.6.1
   Medicaid quality assurance/quality improvement and oversight, 11.6.3
   new freedom initiative (NFI)
      legal developments, 11.6.2
   respite care, 11.6.1
   senior centers, 11.6.1
   transportation services, 11.6.1
home health agencies
   Medicare prospective payment system (PPS), 3.8.7.3
home health care generally, 11.3
home medical equipment (HME) suppliers (*See* **HOME MEDICAL EQUIPMENT (HME) SUPPLIERS**)
hospice care, 11.4.1 to 11.4.9 (*See* **HOSPICE SERVICES**)
long term care generally, 11.5.1 to 11.5.6 (*See* **LONG TERM CARE**)
Medicaid home health agencies (HHAs)
   audits, 11.3.3.5
   coverage, 11.3.3.1
   fraud and abuse, 11.3.3.4
   hospital discharge planning, 11.3.3.6
   moratoria on enrollment, 11.3.3.4
   payment, 11.3.3.3
   qualifications, 11.3.3.2
Medicare, 11.3.2
   "36 month rule", 11.3.2.3
   certification by physician or practitioner, 11.3.2.1
   conditions of participation, 11.3.2.2
   consolidated billing, 11.3.2.4
   coverage, 11.3.2.1
   intermittent care, defined, 11.3.2.1
   low utilization payment adjustment (LUPA), 11.3.2.4
   outlier payments, 11.3.2.4
   partial episode payment adjustment (PEP), 11.3.2.4
   payment, 11.3.2.4
   sanctions for non-compliance, 11.3.2.2
   value-based purchasing program, 11.3.2.4
Medicare Part A coverage, 3.6.1.3
Medicare prospective payment system (PPS), 3.8.7.3
post-acute care providers, 3.8.7.3
scope of chapter, 11.1
state licensure
   durable medical equipment (DME) suppliers, 11.2.1
   generally, 11.3.1

HOME MEDICAL EQUIPMENT (HME) SUPPLIERS
generally, 11.2
Medicare, 11.2.2
   advance beneficiary notices (ABNs), 11.2.2.4; 11.3.2.2
   competitive bidding, 11.2.2.3.3
   consolidated billing
      home health agencies, 11.2.2.5
      skilled nursing facilities, 11.2.2.5

coverage, 11.2.2.1
  categories of coverage, 11.2.2.1.1
    durable medical equipment Medicare administrative contractors (DME MAC) coverage policies, 11.2.2.1.4
  exclusions, statutory, 11.2.2.1.2
  national coverage policies, 11.2.2.1.3
customized items, 11.2.2.3.1
DME rental payment, 11.2.2.3.1
fraud and abuse, 11.2.4
Medicaid, 11.2.3
participation, requirements for, 11.2.2.2
payment, 11.2.2.3
  categories of payment, 11.2.2.3.1
  competitive bidding, 11.2.2.3.3
  inherent reasonableness as basis for payment reductions, 11.2.2.3.4
  updates, 11.2.2.3.2
prosthetic and orthotic devices, 11.2.2.3.1
recompete contracts, 11.2.2.3.3
Recovery Audit Contractors (RACs), 11.2.2.1.4
transitional freeze on DME rates, 11.2.2.3.2
upgrade provisions, 11.2.2.4
state licensure, 11.2.1

HOSPICE SERVICES, 11.4.1 to 11.4.9
certificate of need, 11.4.2
compliance guidance, 11.4.9
continuous home care, 11.4.4.1
defined, 11.4.1
fraud and abuse, 11.4.8
Medicaid
  availability, 11.4.1
  reimbursement, 11.4.7.2
Medicare
  availability, 11.4.1
  conditions of participation, 11.4.3
    generally, 11.4.3
    interdisciplinary group, 11.4.4.2
    provision and supervision of hospice services, 11.4.4.2
    routine home care, 11.4.4.1
    services required, 11.4.4.2
  coverage
    Part A, 3.6.1.4
    election of hospice benefit, 11.4.5
    long term care facilities, agreements with, 11.4.4.1; 11.5.3.2
    physician certification, issues with, 11.4.6
    post-acute care providers, 3.8.7.2
    prospective payment system (PPS), 3.8.7.2
    qualifications for coverage, 11.4.4.3
    reimbursement, 11.4.7.1
    skilled nursing facilities fraud and abuse, 11.4.8
    types of hospice care, 11.4.4.1
    visit data reports, 11.4.7.1
OIG compliance guidance, 11.4.9
physician certification, issues with, 11.4.6
reimbursement
  Medicaid, 11.4.7.2
  Medicare, 11.4.7.1
routine home care, 11.4.4.1
state licensure, 11.4.2
types of hospice care, 11.4.4.1

HOSPITALS, 9.1 to 9.4
accreditation, 9.4
arrangements with physicians (*See* physician/hospital arrangements)
ASCs
  Anti-Kickback safe-harbor regulations, 5.2.16
  implants in ASCs, 5.5.1.5
certificate of need laws
  construction of facilities
    state regulations, 9.2.5
  state regulations
    state licensure, 9.2.1
compliance programs
  federal regulations, 9.3.3
Comprehensive Accreditation Manual for Hospitals, The Official Handbook (CAMH), 9.4
conditions of participation
  federal regulations, 9.3.3
construction of facilities
  state regulations, 9.2.5

Index

cooperative hospital-services organizations
   Anti-Kickback safe-harbor regulations, 5.2.15
discharge planning
  home care providers
    Medicaid HHAs
      hospital discharge planning, 11.3.3.6
disciplinary procedures, regulation of medical staff, 9.3.4
emergencies
  community call plans, 9.3.2
  federal regulations
    treatment of medical emergencies, 9.3.2
employer status of hospitals, 9.3.5
  unionization of nurses and doctors, 9.3.6
excluded provider verification
  federal regulations, 9.3.4
experimentation, institutional review board (IRB) approval for, 2.2.5
federally qualified health centers (FQHCs)
  Anti-Kickback safe-harbor regulations, 5.2.19; 5.2.24
federal regulations, 9.3
  compliance programs, 9.3.3
  conditions of participation, 9.3.3
  Emergency Medical Treatment and Active Labor Act (EMTALA), 9.3.2
  employer status of hospitals, 9.3.5
  Health Care Quality Improvement Act (HCQIA), 9.3.4
  Health Insurance Portability and Accountability Act (HIPAA), 9.3.1
  labor unions
    regulation of unionization of nurses and doctors, 9.3.6
  medical staff
    disciplinary procedures, regulation, 9.3.4
    excluded provider verification, 9.3.4
    treatment of medical emergencies, 9.3.2
health care transactions and contracting, 12.1 to 12.9
horizontal market-allocation agreements, 7.2.1.3.3
hospital outpatient department services (HOPPS) (*See* **MEDICARE**, subhead: Prospective payment system (PPS))
human-subject research, 2.2.5
institutional review board (IRB) approval for experimentation, 2.2.5
joint venture arrangements involving exempt and non-exempt participants
  whole hospital joint ventures, 6.3.4.1
labor unions
  regulation of unionization of nurses and doctors, 9.3.6
licenses
  state licensure, 9.2.1
medical staff
  disciplinary procedures, regulation
    federal regulations, 9.3.4
  excluded provider verification
    federal regulations, 9.3.4
  state regulations affecting medical staff, 9.2.3
  unionization of nurses and doctors
    federal regulations, 9.3.6
Medicare Part A coverage, 3.6.1.1
Medicare prospective payment system (PPS) (*See* **MEDICARE**, subhead: Prospective payment system (PPS))
nurses
  unionization of nurses and doctors
    federal regulations, 9.3.6
Patient Protection and Affordable Care Act
  effect on hospitals, 9.1
patient rights
  state regulations, 9.2.2
patient safety
  state regulations, 9.2.2
physician clinics connected to hospital outpatient departments, 3.2.8
physician/hospital organizations (PHOs), 12.4.2
physicians
  disciplinary procedures, regulation
    federal regulations, 9.3.4
  excluded provider verification
    federal regulations, 9.3.4

state regulations affecting medical staff, 9.2.3
unionization of nurses and doctors
federal regulations, 9.3.6
privacy of patient health information
Health Insurance Portability and Accountability Act (HIPAA), 9.3.1
state regulation to protect patient health information, 9.2.4
relevant product market, 7.2.3.1
scope of chapter, 9.1
solicitation of government action, 7.3.4
standing to sue for antitrust violations, 7.5.3
state regulations
construction of facilities, 9.2.5
medical staff, 9.2.3
patient safety and rights, 9.2.2
privacy of patient health information, 9.2.4
state licensure, 9.2.1
survey of hospital compliance in support of accreditation standards, 9.4
tax-exempt issues
joint venture arrangements involving exempt and non-exempt participants
whole hospital joint ventures, 6.3.4.1
tying agreements, 7.2.1.3.5
types of hospitals, 9.1

HUMAN GENOME PROJECT
bioethics of genetic information, 13.3

HUMAN REPRODUCTION, 13.1.1.1 to 13.1.2.2
abortion (*See* **ABORTION**)
commercial surrogacy, 13.1.3

HUMAN-SUBJECT RESEARCH
consent to medical treatment, 2.2.5

I

INCOMPETENCY
consent to medical treatment
incompetent's right to make treatment decisions, 2.2.3
end-of-life decision making, 2.3.2

INDEMNITY INSURERS
insurance regulation
scope of state regulation, 8.2.1

INDEPENDENT CONTRACTORS
physician/hospital arrangements, 10.3.1
types of contracts
independent contractor agreements, 12.7.1

INDEPENDENT DIAGNOSTIC TESTING FACILITIES (IDTFs)
Medicare Part B coverage, 3.6.2.3

INDEPENDENT PRACTICE ASSOCIATIONS (IPAs)
corporate structures, 12.4.3
model HMOs, 8.2.3.1
physician reimbursement issues, 10.5.2

INFORMED CONSENT
abortion (*See* **ABORTION**, subhead: Informed consent)
data sharing, 14.5.3
disclosures required
generally, 2.2.1
special risk factors by providers, 2.2.1.2
exceptions to requirement to obtain consent, 2.2.1.3
forms, 2.2.1.1
generally, 2.2.1
special risk factors by providers, 2.2.1.2
waiver, 2.2.1.3

INSPECTIONS
hospitals
survey of hospitals in support of accreditation, 9.4
long term care
federal oversight of state inspections, 11.5.6.3

INSURANCE
antitrust law, 7.3.6
creation of physician/patient relationship
when examination for insurer's benefit, 2.1.1
discrimination
bioethics of genetic information
nondiscrimination, 13.3.2.1
funding of buy-outs, 10.2.4.3
health insurance regulation (*See* **HEALTH CARE PRIVATE PLANS, REGULATION**)

INTEGRATED DELIVERY SYSTEMS (IDSs)
corporate structures, 12.4.1
  antitrust considerations, 12.4.1.1
  certificate of need (CON), 12.4.1.5
  fraud and abuse, 12.4.1.2
  generally, 12.4.1
  legal issues, 12.4.1.5
  reimbursement issues, 12.4.1.5
  shareholders employing physicians, potential restrictions, 12.4.1.5
  Stark law, 12.4.1.3
  tax considerations, 12.4.1.4

INVESTMENT INTERESTS
fraud and abuse
  Anti-Kickback safe-harbor regulations, 5.2.1
    60/40 investor rule, 5.2.1.2
    60/40 revenue rule, 5.2.1.2
    investments in entities in MUAs, 5.2.1.3
    large investment interests, 5.2.1.1
    small investment interests, 5.2.1.2

IN VITRO FERTILIZATION
commercial surrogacy, 13.1.3

J

JOINT VENTURES
generally, 12.3.2
health care transactions and contracting, 12.1 to 12.9
horizontal price-fixing agreements, 7.2.1.3.1
tax-exempt issues
  joint venture arrangements involving exempt and non-exempt participants, 6.3.4
    ancillary joint ventures, 6.3.4.2
    whole hospital joint ventures, 6.3.4.1

K

KICKBACKS
Anti-Kickback safe-harbor regulations, 5.2
Anti-Kickback Statute, 5.1

L

LABORATORY TESTING
center for Medicaid and state operations, 3.3.2.2
Medicare
  resource-based relative value scale (RBRVS) fee schedule
    applicability to non-physician practitioners and other suppliers, 3.9.4
  fee schedules for freestanding supplier entities, 3.9.6

LABOR UNIONS
antitrust law, 7.3.7
hospitals
  federal regulations
    regulation of unionization of nurses and doctors, 9.3.6
physicians
  reimbursement issues, 10.5.3

LEASES
Anti-Kickback safe-harbor regulations
  space and equipment rental, 5.2.2
office space and equipment, 5.5.3.1

LICENSED CLINICAL SOCIAL WORKERS
Medicare Part B coverage
  non-physician practitioners, services by, 3.6.2.2

LIFE-SUSTAINING MEDICAL TREATMENT
end-of-life decision making, 2.3

LIVING WILLS
advance directives, 2.3.4
generally, 2.3.4.1

LOBBYING
hospitals, 7.3.4
tax-exempt issues, 6.2.9.2

LOCAL GOVERNMENT ANTITRUST ACT
exemptions, immunities, and scope of coverage, 7.3.5

LONG TERM CARE, 11.5.1 to 11.5.6.9
abuse of residents, combating, 11.5.6.5
arbitration, 15.2.4.2.2; 15.2.4.2.3

dehydration
  enforcement
    prevention of pressure ulcers, dehydration and malnutrition, 11.5.6.4

egregious violations, prosecution, 11.5.6.6

enforcement
  abuse of residents, combating, 11.5.6.5
  egregious violations, prosecution, 11.5.6.6
  false claims actions based on quality of care, 11.5.6.7
  federal oversight of state inspections, 11.5.6.3
  fraud and abuse compliance program guidelines, 11.5.6.8
  OIG and GAO reports, 11.5.6.6
  prevention of pressure ulcers, dehydration and malnutrition, 11.5.6.4
  quality indicator survey (QIS), 11.5.6.1
  stronger enforcement actions, 11.5.6.2
  survey policies and procedures, 11.5.6.1

fraud and abuse
  compliance program guidelines, 11.5.6.8
  false claims actions based on quality of care, 11.5.6.7

grace period
  stronger enforcement actions, 11.5.6.2

hospice agreements with facility, 11.4.4.1; 11.5.3.2

inspections
  federal oversight of state inspections, 11.5.6.3

malnutrition
  enforcement
    prevention of pressure ulcers, dehydration and malnutrition, 11.5.6.4

Medicaid nursing facilities, 11.5.4
  coverage, 11.5.4.1
  qualifications, 11.5.4.2
  reimbursement, 11.5.4.3
  transparency and accountability, 11.5.4.4

Medicare
  prospective payment system (PPS), 3.8.7.3
  skilled nursing facilities (SNFs), 11.5.3
    coverage, 11.5.3.1
    market basket index, 11.5.3.3
    participation, conditions of, 11.5.3.2
    reimbursement, 11.5.3.3
    transparency and accountability, 11.5.3.4

nursing home value-based purchasing demonstration, 11.5.5.4

on-site visits
  stronger enforcement actions, 11.5.6.2

pressure ulcers
  enforcement
    prevention of pressure ulcers, dehydration and malnutrition, 11.5.6.4

quality of care, 11.5.5
  false claims actions based on quality of care, 11.5.6.7
  mandated staffing, 11.5.5.3
  nursing home value-based purchasing demonstration, 11.5.5.4
  quality indicator survey (QIS), 11.5.6.1
  quality information, collection, and publication, 11.5.5.2
  resident assessment instruments (RAIs), 11.5.5.1

resident assessment instruments (RAIs), 11.5.5.1

special focus facilities
  stronger enforcement actions, 11.5.6.2

staffing, mandated, 11.5.5.3
state certificate of need, 11.5.2
state licensure, 11.5.1
survey policies and procedures, 11.5.6.1
value-based purchasing demonstration, 11.5.5.4

LONG TERM CARE HOSPITALS
Medicare prospective payment system (PPS)
  Affordable Care Act updates, 3.8.3.4
  generally, 3.8.3.2

M

MAIL AND WIRE FRAUD
　false claims and fraudulent billing, 5.6.3
MALPRACTICE INSURANCE
　Anti-Kickback safe-harbor regulations
　　obstetrical malpractice insurance subsidies, 5.2.13
MANAGED CARE ORGANIZATIONS
　beneficiary incentives
　　Anti-Kickback safe-harbor regulations, 5.2.10
　Medicaid (*See* **MEDICAID**)
　risk-sharing arrangements
　　Anti-Kickback safe-harbor regulations, 5.2.20
　　physician self-referral, Stark exceptions, 5.5.3.12
MANAGEMENT-SERVICES ORGANIZATIONS (MSOs)
　corporate structures, 12.4.5
MA ORGANIZATIONS
　Medicare
　　certification, 3.7.3
MATERNITY PROTECTION
　Employee Retirement and Income Security Act (ERISA), 8.3.2.8
MATURE-MINOR DOCTRINE
　consent to medical treatment, minors, 2.2.4
MCCARRAN-FERGUSON ACT
　insurance business exemption, 7.3.6
　insurance regulation, 8.1.1
MEDIATION
　advantages, 15.3.1
　agreement to mediate, 15.3.2.1
　combination with arbitration, 15.3.3
　effective mediation, 15.3.2
　generally, 15.3; 15.3.4
　preparation, 15.3.2.3
　selection of mediator, 15.3.2.2
MEDICAID
　Affordable Care Act (ACA)
　　CHIP extension and enhancement, 4.8.8.1
　　DHS payments, 4.8.7
　　effect of, 4.2.2; 4.2.3; 4.8.1
　　eligibility requirements under, 4.4.2
　　improvements to Medicaid services, 4.8.2
　　increased reimbursement for primary care, 4.8.5
　　payment innovations, 4.8.8
　　prescription drug coverage, 4.8.3
　　presumptive eligibility sites, 4.8.4
　　program integrity provisions, 4.8.8.2
　　quality initiatives, funding and support for, 4.8.6
　applying for, 4.4.1
　benefits
　　categorically needy, 4.5.1
　　cost sharing, 4.5.5
　　denial of services for nonpayment, 4.5.5.1
　　drug rebate programs, 4.5.6.1
　　generally, 4.5
　　limitations on covered services, 4.5.4
　　medically needy, mandatory benefits for, 4.5.3
　　optional benefits, 4.5.2
　　prescribed drugs, specific rules for, 4.5.6
　categorically needy
　　benefits, 4.5.1
　　mandatory, 4.4.2.1
　　optional, 4.4.2.2
　center for Medicaid and state operations, 3.3.2.2
　Centers for Medicare and Medicaid Services (CMS)
　　Center for Medicare and Medicaid innovation (CMMI), 3.3.2.2
　　oversight by, 4.3.1
　CHIP extension and enhancement, 4.8.8.1
　corporate compliance program as condition of enrollment, 5.8
　cost sharing, 4.5.5
　delivery systems
　　fee-for-service, 4.7.2
　　state options, 4.7.1
　denial of services for nonpayment, 4.5.5.1
　Disproportionate Share Hospital (DSH) payments, 4.6.1.3; 4.8.7
　drugs
　　rebate programs, 4.5.6.1; 4.8.3
　　specific rules for prescribed drugs, 4.5.6

eligibility
    Affordable Care Act (ACA), 4.4.2
    categorically needy
        mandatory, 4.4.2.1
        optional, 4.4.2.2
    income and resources standards, 4.4.3.1
    medically needy
        financial criteria, 4.4.2.3.1
        optional, 4.4.2.3
    presumptive eligibility sites, 4.8.4
generally, 4.1
home and community-based services (HCBS)
    managed care, 4.7.3.4
    Medicaid quality assurance/quality improvement and oversight, 11.6.3
home health agencies (HHAs)
    audits, 11.3.3.5
    coverage, 11.3.3.1
    fraud and abuse, 11.3.3.4
    hospital discharge planning, 11.3.3.6
    moratoria on enrollment, 11.3.3.4
    payment, 11.3.3.3
    qualifications, 11.3.3.2
home medical equipment (HME) suppliers
    Medicare, 11.2.3
hospice services
    availability, 11.4.1
    reimbursement, 11.4.7.2
List of Excluded Individuals and Entities (LEIE), 10.4.3
managed care
    generally, 4.7.3
    home and community based services (HCBS), 4.7.3.4
    Section 1115 demonstration projects, 4.7.3.3
    Section 1915(b) waiver, 4.7.3.2
    State Plan Amendment (SPA), 4.7.3.1
mandatory participation, 4.9.2
medically needy
    benefits, 4.5.3
    financial criteria, 4.4.2.3.1
    optional, 4.4.2.3
nursing facilities, 11.5.4
    coverage, 11.5.4.1
    qualifications, 11.5.4.2
    reimbursement, 11.5.4.3
    transparency and accountability, 11.5.4.4
optional participation, 4.9.1
original intent of Congress, 4.2.1
physicians
    licensure and credentialing
        exclusion from Medicare/Medicaid, 10.4.3
prescription drugs (see subhead: drugs)
reimbursement and financing
    Disproportionate Share Hospital (DSH) payments, 4.6.1.3; 4.8.7
    innovations, 4.8.8
    non-Federal share of Medicaid expenditures, 4.6.2
    primary care, physician reimbursement for, 4.8.5
    provider payment rates, 4.6.1.1
    upper payment limits, 4.6.1.2
state program
    differences among state programs, 4.3.4
    elements of, 4.3.3
    single state agency, 4.3.2
Supreme Court of the United States rulings, 4.9; 4.9.1; 4.9.2

MEDICAL FUTILITY
end-of-life decision making, 2.3.5

MEDICAL INFORMATION
confidentiality of patient medical information, 2.4

MEDICAL RECORDS
confidentiality of patient medical information, 2.4
    hospitals
        state regulation to protect patient health information, 9.2.4
electronic health records (EHR)
    donation and receipt of technology
        accountable care organization waivers, 5.2.23
        Anti-Kickback safe-harbor regulations, 5.2.22
        tax-exempt issues, 6.3.6
    Health Information Technology for Economic and Clinical Health Act (HITECH), 9.3.1; 10.6

physician self-referral, Stark exceptions, 5.5.3.15
stand-alone exemption, 6.2.3.4
electronic prescribing
  Anti-Kickback safe-harbor regulations, 5.2.21
  physician self-referral, Stark exceptions, 5.5.3.15
health care transactions and contracting
  termination of agreements
    confidentiality and ownership of records, 12.8.2

MEDICAL RESEARCH
  data sharing (*See* **DATA SHARING**, subhead: research exemptions)

MEDICAL SAVINGS ACCOUNTS (MSAs)
  Medicare Part C, 3.2.1.3

MEDICARE, 3.1 to 3.17
  accountable care organizations (ACOs)
    shared savings programs, 3.6.3; 5.2.23
  administration of program, 3.3
    Medicare administrative contractors (MACs), 3.3.3
  Advanced Payment Models (APMs), 3.9.5.1
  American health care industry
    Medicare as substantial financial underpinning, 3.16
  appeals
    Part A, 3.13
      claims appeals, 3.13.1
      cost report appeals, 3.13.2
    Part B, 3.13
      claims appeals, 3.13.1
    Part C, 3.14
      enrollee grievances and appeals, 3.14.1
        determinations during an inpatient stay, 3.14.1.4
        independent review, 3.14.1.2
        judicial review, 3.14.1.3
        reconsiderations, 3.14.1.1
        service terminations, 3.14.1.5
      MA organization contract appeals, 3.14.2
        request for hearing, 3.14.2.1
        request for review, 3.14.2.2
    Part D, 3.15; 3.15.1
  assignment and reassignment, 3.12
    assignment
      defined, 3.12.1
      Part A, 3.12.1.1
      Part B, 3.12.1.2
      Part C, 3.12.1.3
    reassignment
      defined, 3.12.2
      penalties for improper assignment, 3.12.2
    reimbursement, five components, 3.4
  audit and evaluation of programs
    DHHS office of Inspector General (OIG), 3.3.5
  Balanced Budget Act
    Hospital Insurance Trust Fund, 3.16
  Benefits Coordination and Recovery Center (BCRC), 3.2.5
  blended capitation, 3.10
    advance monthly payments, 3.10.1
    determining MA payment rate, 3.10.2
    per-member per-month (PMPM) methodology, 3.10.1
  Blue Cross plans, history of Medicare, 3.1.1
  Blue Shield plans, history of Medicare, 3.1.1
  board of trustees, 3.3.1
  Centers for Medicare and Medicaid Services (CMS), 3.1; 3.3.2
    administrative guidelines, 3.3.2.4
    administrative history, 3.3.2.1
    administrator
      rulings, 3.3.2.5
    center clinical standards and quality (CCSQ), 3.3.2.2
    center for Medicaid, CHIP, and survey and certification, 3.3.2.2
    center for Medicare, 3.3.2.2
    center for Medicare and Medicaid innovation (CMMI), 3.3.2.2
    center for program integrity (CPI), 3.3.2.2
    center for strategic planning (CSP), 3.3.2.2
    headquarters, 3.3.2.3
    regional operations, 3.3.2.3
    structural overview, 3.3.2.2
  certification, 3.7
    MA organizations, 3.7.3

PDP sponsors, 3.7.4
physicians, 3.7.2
providers, 3.7.1
reimbursement, five components, 3.4
suppliers, 3.7.2
CFR
   sources of Medicare regulations
      websites and other resources, 3.17
competitive market-based systems for payment, 3.11
   Part B, 3.11.1
   Part C, 3.11.2
   Part D, 3.11.3
contractors
   Medicare administrative contractors (MACs), 3.3.3
   quality improvement organizations (QIOs), 3.3.4
coordinated care plans (CCPs), 3.2.1.3
co-payments, 3.2.4.1
corporate compliance program as condition of enrollment, 5.8
cosmetic surgery
   excluded services, 3.2.3
cost control
   independent payment advisory board (IPAB), 3.3.7
cost-sharing by beneficiaries, 3.2.4
   co-payments, 3.2.4.1
   deductibles, 3.2.4.1
   low-income beneficiaries, assistance for, 3.2.4.3
   Medigap, 3.2.4.2
   premiums, 3.2.4.1
   supplement policies, 3.2.4.2
coverage, 3.6
   national coverage determination (NCD)
      websites and other resources, 3.17
   national coverage determinations (NCD), 3.6.6
   Part A, 3.6.1
      hospital services, 3.6.1.1
   Part B, 3.6.2
   Part C, 3.6.4
   Part D, 3.6.5

reimbursement, five components, 3.4
deductibles, 3.2.4.1
dental care
   excluded services, 3.2.3
DHHS office of Inspector General (OIG)
   audit and evaluation of programs, 3.3.5
dispute resolution
   payments of more that $10,000
      provider reimbursement review board (PRRB), 3.3.6
eligibility
   determination, 3.3.1
   Part A, 3.5.1
   Part B, 3.5.2
   Part C, 3.5.3
   Part D, 3.5.4
   reimbursement, five components, 3.4
evolution of Medicare policy and law, 3.1.1
excluded services, 3.2.3
eye care
   excluded services, 3.2.3
fee-for-service (FFS) plans
   Part C
      generally, 3.2.1.3
fiscal intermediaries
   Medicare administrative contractors (MACs), transition to, 3.3.3
foot care
   excluded services, 3.2.3
generally, 3.2; 3.2.1
health maintenance organizations (HMOs), 3.2.1.3
hearing care
   excluded services, 3.2.3
Hill-Burton Act, 3.1.1
history of Medicare policy and law, 3.1.1
home care providers and long term care, 11.3.2
   "36 month rule", 11.3.2.3
   certification by physician or practitioner, 11.3.2.1
   conditions of participation, 11.3.2.2
   consolidated billing, 11.3.2.4
   coverage, 11.3.2.1
   intermittent care, 11.3.2.1

Index

low utilization payment adjustment
(LUPA), 11.3.2.4
outlier payments, 11.3.2.4
partial episode payment adjustment (PEP),
11.3.2.4
payment, 11.3.2.4
sanctions for non-compliance, 11.3.2.2
value-based purchasing program, 11.3.2.4
home medical equipment (HME)
suppliers (*See* **HOME MEDICAL
EQUIPMENT (HME) SUPPLIERS**)
hospice services (*See* **HOSPICE SERVICES**)
hospitals
payment
prospective payment system (PPS), 3.8
List of Excluded Individuals and Entities
(LEIE), 10.4.3
long term care
skilled nursing facilities (SNFs), 11.5.3
coverage, 11.5.3.1
market basket index, 11.5.3.3
participation, conditions of, 11.5.3.2
reimbursement, 11.5.3.3
transparency and accountability,
11.5.3.4
low-income beneficiaries, assistance for,
3.2.4.3
manuals and other publications
websites and other resources, 3.17
MA organizations
certification, 3.7.3
market-based systems for payment, 3.11
Part B, 3.11.1
Part C, 3.11.2
Part D, 3.11.3
medical savings accounts (MSAs), 3.2.1.3
Medicare Access and CHIP Authorization Act
(MACRA), 3.9.5
Medicare administrative contractors (MACs),
3.3.3
Medicare Prescription Drug, Improvement,
and Modernization Act (MMA)
hospital outpatient department services
(HOPPS), 3.8.6.2
Part C, 3.2.1.3
national health insurance initiatives, 3.1.1

nursing homes
excluded services, 3.2.3
outlays by Medicare, 3.1
oversight of organization and programs, 3.3.1
Part A
appeals, 3.13
claims appeals, 3.13.1
cost report appeals, 3.13.2
assignment, 3.12.1.1
center for Medicare, 3.3.2.2
coverage, 3.6.1
extended care or skilled nursing services
(SNF), 3.6.1.2
home health services, 3.6.1.3
hospital services, 3.6.1.1
eligibility, 3.5.1
fiscal intermediaries
Medicare administrative contractors
(MACs), transition to, 3.3.3
generally, 3.2.1.1
Part B
appeals, 3.13
claims appeals, 3.13.1
assignment, 3.12.1.2
carriers
Medicare administrative contractors
(MACs), transition to, 3.3.3
center for Medicare, 3.3.2.2
coverage, 3.6.2
ambulance services, 3.6.2.3
community mental health centers,
3.6.2.3
durable medical equipment (DME)
administration of drugs,
11.2.2.3.1
independent diagnostic testing facilities
(IDTFs), 3.6.2.3
non-physician practitioners, services by,
3.6.2.2
outpatient providers and freestanding
supplier entities, 3.6.2.3
physicians' services, 3.6.2.1
prosthetics and orthotics, 3.6.2.3
rural health clinics (RHCs), 3.6.2.3
shared savings programs, 3.6.3

X-ray services, 3.6.2.3
durable medical equipment regional
    carriers (DMERCs)
    Medicare administrative contractors
        (MACs), transition to, 3.3.3
eligibility, 3.5.2
generally, 3.2.1.2
payment
    competitive market-based systems,
        3.11.1
    market-based systems, 3.11.1
    resource-based relative value scale
        (RBRVS) fee schedule, 3.9
sources of revenue, 3.2.1.2
therapy services, caps on, 11.5.3.3
Part C
    appeals, 3.14
        enrollee grievances and appeals, 3.14.1
            determinations during an inpatient
                stay, 3.14.1.4
            independent review, 3.14.1.2
            judicial review, 3.14.1.3
            reconsiderations, 3.14.1.1
            service terminations, 3.14.1.5
        MA organization contract appeals,
            3.14.2
            request for hearing, 3.14.2.1
            request for review, 3.14.2.2
    assignment, 3.12.1.3
    coverage
        basic benefits, 3.6.4.1
        generally, 3.6.4
        supplemental benefits, 3.6.4.2
    eligibility, 3.5.3
    generally, 3.2.1.3
    payment
        competitive market-based systems for
            payment, 3.11.2
        market-based systems for payment,
            3.11.2
Part D
    appeals, 3.15; 3.15.1
    coverage, 3.6.5
    eligibility, 3.5.4
    generally, 3.2.1.4

    payment
        competitive market-based systems for
            payment, 3.11.3
        market-based systems for payment,
            3.11.3
        sponsor payments, 3.12.1.4
payment
    blended capitation, 3.10
    competitive market-based systems, 3.11
    customary charge
        resource-based relative value scale
            (RBRVS) fee schedule, 3.9.1
    hospitals
        prospective payment system (PPS), 3.8
    market-based systems, 3.11
    prospective payment system (PPS), 3.8
    reasonable charge
        resource-based relative value scale
            (RBRVS) fee schedule, 3.9.1
    reimbursement, five components, 3.4
    resource-based relative value scale
        (RBRVS) fee schedule, 3.9
PDP sponsors
    certification, 3.7.4
personal comfort services, 3.2.3
physicians
    certification, 3.7.2
    licensure and credentialing
        exclusion from Medicare/Medicaid,
            10.4.3
    List of Excluded Individuals and Entities
        (LEIE), 10.4.3
preferred provider organizations (PPOs),
    3.2.1.3
premiums, 3.2.4.1
prescription drugs
    Part D, 3.2.1.4
    radiopharmaceuticals, 3.8.6.2
private contracts, 3.2.2
private fee-for-service (PFFS) plans, 3.2.1.3
prospective payment system (PPS)
    acute inpatient hospitals, 3.8.2
        case-mix adjustment, 3.8.2.3
        community-based care transition
            program, 3.8.2.4

Index

determining IPPS rate, 3.8.2.2
diagnosis-related groups (DRGs), 3.8.2.1
disproportionate share hospitals (DSH), 3.8.2.4
ESRD discharges, 3.8.2.4
excluded (pass-through) costs, 3.8.2.4
hospital-acquired conditions, 3.8.2.4
indirect medical education, 3.8.2.4
low-income patients, 3.8.2.4
low-volume hospitals, 3.8.2.4
new technologies and medical services, 3.8.2.4
outlier cases, 3.8.2.4
post-acute transfers, 3.8.2.4
readmissions to hospital, 3.8.2.4
value based purchasing (VBP), 3.8.2.4
creation, 3.8.1
excluded hospitals, 3.8.5
generally, 3.8
hospital outpatient department services (HOPPS), 3.8.6
three-day DRG payment-window rule, 3.8.6.4
unbundling, 3.8.6.5
long term care hospitals, 3.8.3.2
generally, 3.8.3.2
Patient Protection and Affordable Care Act updates, 3.8.3.4
three-day DRG payment-window rule, 3.8.6.4
unbundling, 3.8.6.5
post-acute care providers, 3.8.7
home health agencies, 3.8.7.3
skilled nursing facilities, 3.8.7.1
psychiatric hospitals (*See* PSYCHIATRIC HOSPITALS, subhead: Medicare prospective payment system (PPS))
rehabilitation hospitals
generally, 3.8.3.1
Patient Protection and Affordable Care Act updates, 3.8.3.4
rural-area hospitals, 3.8.4
provider-based
defined, 3.2.8

provider reimbursement review board (PRRB), 3.3.6
providers
certification, 3.7.1
conditions of participation (CoPs) establishing eligibility, 3.7.1
deemed status, 3.7.1
provider agreements, 3.7.1
provider identification numbers (PINs), 3.7.1
reimbursement, 3.4
provider-sponsored organizations (PSOs), 3.2.1.3
provider versus supplier, 3.2.7
qualified Medicare beneficiary (QMB) program
low-income beneficiaries, assistance for, 3.2.4.3
qualifying individual (QI) program
low-income beneficiaries, assistance for, 3.2.4.3
quality improvement organizations (QIOs), 3.3.4
regional PPOs, 3.2.1.3
reimbursement, 3.4
assignment and reassignment, 3.12
certification, 3.7
coverage, 3.6
dispute resolution
payments of more that $10,000
provider reimbursement review board (PRRB), 3.3.6
eligibility, 3.5
payment
blended capitation, 3.10
competitive market-based systems, 3.11
market-based systems, 3.11
prospective payment system (PPS), 3.8
resource-based relative value scale (RBRVS) fee schedule, 3.9
payments of more that $10,000
provider reimbursement review board (PRRB), 3.3.6
provider reimbursement review board (PRRB), 3.3.6

resource-based relative value scale (RBRVS) fee schedule
   ambulance services, 3.9.7
   applicability to non-physician practitioners and other suppliers, 3.9.4
   coding and documentation standards, 3.9.3
   CPT codes, 3.9.3
   fundamentals, 3.9.2
   geographic practice cost indexes (GPCIs), 3.9.2
   historic overview, 3.9.1
   national dollar conversion factor, 3.9.2
   practitioner's current procedural terminology (CPT)
      coding and documentation standards, 3.9.3
   relative value units (RVUs), 3.9.2
   suppliers
      fee schedules for freestanding supplier entities, 3.9.6
review of services
   quality improvement organizations (QIOs), 3.3.4
routine physicals
   excluded services, 3.2.3
secondary payor rule, 3.2.5
shared savings programs, 3.6.3
Social Security Act of 1935, 3.1.1
special needs plans (SNPs), 3.2.1.3
specified low-income Medicare beneficiary (SLMB) program
   low-income beneficiaries, assistance for, 3.2.4.3
statutory sources of Medicare law
   websites and other resources, 3.17
subsidies
   medical residency and allied health-education training programs for teaching hospitals, 3.2.6
   rural hospitals, 3.2.6
supplemental insurance
   Part B, 3.2.1.2
supplement insurance
   cost-sharing by beneficiaries, 3.2.4.2
   Medigap, 3.2.4.2

suppliers
   certification, 3.7.2
   providers distinguished, 3.2.7
   reimbursement, 3.4
   resource-based relative value scale (RBRVS) fee schedule
      fee schedules for freestanding supplier entities, 3.9.6
websites and other resources, 3.17

MEDICARE ACCESS AND CHIP AUTHORIZATION ACT (MACRA), 3.9.5

MEDICARE ADVANTAGE (MA) PROGRAM
Anti-Kickback safe harbor regulations, 5.2.24
Part C, 3.2.1.3
Patient Protection and Affordable Care Act effect on enrollment, 3.16

MEDICARE PRESCRIPTION DRUG, IMPROVEMENT AND MODERNIZATION ACT (MMA)
history of federal efforts to regulate health care, 8.3.3
hospital outpatient department services (HOPPS), 3.8.6.2
Medicare Part C, 3.2.1.3

MEDIGAP
Anti-Kickback safe harbor regulations, 5.2.25
Medicare, 3.2.4.2

MENTAL HEALTH
confidentiality of patient medical information heightened protection, 2.4.1
consent to medical treatment, 2.2.1.4
home and community-based services (HCBS), 11.6.2
Medicare
   community mental health centers, 3.6.2.3
   prospective payment system (PPS) (*See* **PSYCHIATRIC HOSPITALS**, subhead: Medicare prospective payment system (PPS))
Mental Health Parity and Addiction Equality Act (MHPAEA), 8.3.2.2
restraints or seclusion, use of, 2.2.1.5; 9.2.2
violent propensities of patients, duty to warn of, 2.4.2.2

Index

MERGERS AND ACQUISITIONS
  antitrust law, 7.2.3
  health care transactions and contracting (*See* **HEALTH CARE TRANSACTIONS AND CONTRACTING**, subhead: Mergers and acquisitions)
  sale of practice (*See* **SALE OF PRACTICE**, subhead: Mergers and acquisitions)

MIDWIVES
  Medicare
    Part B coverage, 3.6.2.2
    resource-based relative value scale (RBRVS) fee schedule, 3.9.4
  suppliers, 3.2.7

MINORS
  consent to medical treatment, 2.2.4

MONEY LAUNDERING
  false claims and fraudulent billing, 5.6.5

MONOPOLIES
  antitrust law, 7.1 to 7.7 (*See* **ANTITRUST LAW**)

N

NEW FREEDOM INITIATIVE (NFI)
  home and community-based services (HCBS)
    legal developments, 11.6.2

NONCOMPETE CLAUSES
  employment contracts, 12.7.1
  health care transactions and contracting
    termination of agreements, 12.8.3
  physicians
    post-termination restrictive covenants, 10.2.2.6
    sale of ownership interest, 10.2.4.4

NON-DISCLOSURE AGREEMENTS
  protected-health information (PHI), 12.2.2

NON-INTERFERENCE CLAUSES
  health care transactions and contracting
    termination of agreements, 12.8.3

NONPROFIT ENTITIES
  antitrust law, 7.3.1

NORRIS-LAGUARDIA ACT
  labor unions, 7.3.7

NURSE MIDWIVES (*See* **MIDWIVES**)

NURSE PRACTITIONERS
  Medicare
    Part B coverage, 3.6.2.2
    resource-based relative value scale (RBRVS) fee schedule, 3.9.4

NURSES
  extended care or skilled nursing services (SNF)
    Medicare Part A coverage, 3.6.1.2
  hospitals
    unionization of nurses and doctors
      federal regulations, 9.3.6
  labor unions
    hospitals, federal regulations
      regulation of unionization of nurses and doctors, 9.3.6
  Medicare
    resource-based relative value scale (RBRVS) fee schedule
      applicability to non-physician practitioners and other suppliers, 3.9.4
  midwives (*See* **MIDWIVES**)
  Services by non-physician practitioners
    Medicare Part B coverage, 3.6.2.2

NURSING HOMES
  arbitration statutes and regulations, 15.2.4.2.1
  long term care generally, 11.5.1 to 11.5.6.9 (*See* **LONG TERM CARE**)
  Medicare
    excluded services, 3.2.3
  Medicare prospective payment system (PPS)
    skilled nursing facilities
      post-acute care providers, 3.8.7.1
      value-based purchasing program (VBP program), 3.8.7.1

O

OBSTETRICAL PRACTICE
  Anti-Kickback safe-harbor regulations
    obstetrical malpractice insurance subsidies, 5.2.13

OCCUPATIONAL THERAPY
  Medicare
    Part B coverage, 3.6.2.2

resource-based relative value scale
(RBRVS) fee schedule
applicability to non-physician
practitioners and other suppliers,
3.9.4

OIG
Anti-Kickback Statute
advisory opinions, 5.1.4
corporate compliance programs, guidelines
for, 5.8.2
DHHS office of Inspector General (OIG)
Medicare
audit and evaluation of programs, 3.3.5
hospice services
compliance guidance, 11.4.9
List of Excluded Individuals and Entities
(LEIE), 10.4.3
long term care
enforcement
OIG and GAO reports, 11.5.6.6
physician self-referral, 5.4.5

ORGAN TRANSPLANTATION
allocation policies, 13.2.2
brain-death criteria, 13.2.1
determination of death, 13.2.1
generally, 13.2
National Organ Transplant Act (NOTA), 13.2
organ procurement and transplantation
network (OPTN), 13.2
strategies to increase supply of organs, 13.2.1
Uniform Anatomical Gift Act (UAGA),
13.2.1
united network for organ sharing (UNOS),
13.2
Vegetative state, 13.2.1

P

PARENT AND CHILD
consent to medical treatment, 2.2.4
PATIENT CARE, 2.1 to 2.5
abandonment of patient
duty to treat, 2.1
bioethics, 13.1.1.1 to 13.4
confidentiality of patient medical
information, 2.4

breach notification, 2.4.3.5
confidentiality generally, 2.4.1
duty to warn, 2.4.2.2
heightened protection, 2.4.1
HIPAA privacy rules, 2.4.3
judicial disclosure, 2.4.2.1
mandatory disclosure, 2.4.2
notice of privacy practices, 2.4.3.4
patient release forms, importance of, 2.4.1
reporting of medical conditions,
mandatory, 2.4.2.2
consent to medical treatment (*See* **CONSENT TO MEDICAL TREATMENT**)
PATIENT MEDICAL INFORMATION
confidentiality, 2.4
patient access to their own information
HIPAA privacy rules, 2.4.3.3
**PATIENT PROTECTION AND
AFFORDABLE CARE ACT**
appeals
external reviews, 8.3.3.3
internal appeals process, 8.3.3.3
cafeteria plans, 8.3.3.18
Centers for Medicare and Medicaid Services
(CMS)
structural overview, 3.3.2.2
constitutionality, 8.3.3
coverage
annual coverage limits, 8.3.3.1
dependent coverage extension, 8.3.3.5
essential benefits coverage
generally, 8.3.3.10
penalty tax for failure to provide health
plan with minimum essential
coverage, 8.3.3.16
excessive waiting periods, 8.3.3.11
lifetime coverage limits, 8.3.3.1
limits, 8.3.3.1
options, employer's duty to inform
employees of, 8.3.3.15
preventive health services coverage,
8.3.3.4
reporting employer health coverage,
8.3.3.17
rescission of coverage, 8.3.3.2

standardization of coverage explanations, 8.3.3.6
dependent coverage extension, 8.3.3.5
discrimination based on health status of participants and beneficiaries, 8.3.3.13
essential benefits coverage
  generally, 8.3.3.10
  penalty tax for failure to provide health plan with minimum essential coverage, 8.3.3.16
exchanges
  employer duty to inform employees of coverage options, 8.3.3.15
  essential benefits coverage, 8.3.3.10
  transparency of information, 8.3.3.7
flexible spending accounts for health, 8.3.3.18
health care private plans, regulation of, 8.3.3
highly compensated individuals
  discrimination favoring, 8.3.3.8
history of federal efforts to regulate health care, 8.3.3
Medicare
  cost control
    independent payment advisory board (IPAB), 3.3.7
  effect of Act on Medicare, 3.16
  other than acute care hospitals, updates from ACA, 3.8.3.4
  Part C
    competitive market-based systems for payment, 3.11.2
    coverage, 3.6.4
  Part D
    cost sharing obligations, 3.6.5
    "donut hole," closing of, 3.6.5
    shared savings programs, 3.6.3
national practitioner data bank (NPDB), reports to, 10.4.2
penalty tax for failure to provide health plan with minimum essential coverage, 8.3.3.16
preexisting condition exclusions, 8.3.3.12
preventive health services coverage, 8.3.3.4
purposes, 8.3.3
reports
  employer health coverage, 8.3.3.17
  quality reporting, 8.3.3.9
rescission of coverage, 8.3.3.2
small business tax credits, 8.3.3.14
standardization
  benefits summaries, 8.3.3.6
  benefit summaries, 8.3.3.6
  coverage explanations, 8.3.3.6
tax credits for small businesses, 8.3.3.14
tax-exempt issues
  exemption requirements, 6.2.3.2
waiting periods, excessive, 8.3.3.11

PATIENT RELEASE FORMS
confidentiality of patient medical information, 2.4.1

PDP SPONSORS
Medicare
  certification, 3.7.4

PENSION PROTECTION ACT (PPA)
effect of Act, 6.4.4
supporting organizations, 6.4.3.3

PERSONAL COMFORT SERVICES
Medicare, 3.2.3

PHYSICAL THERAPY
Medicare Part B coverage, 3.6.2.2

PHYSICIAN ASSISTANTS
Medicare
  Part B coverage, 3.6.2.2
  resource-based relative value scale (RBRVS) fee schedule, 3.9.4

PHYSICIAN-ASSISTED DEATH, 2.3.6

PHYSICIAN/HOSPITAL ORGANIZATIONS (PHOs)
compensation, 10.3.2.3
confidentiality, 10.3.2.5
corporate structures, 12.4.2
dispute resolution, 10.3.2.6
duties of physician, 10.3.2.2
employee benefits, 10.3.2.4
hospital records, 10.3.2.5
restrictive covenants, 10.3.2.5
status of physician as employee or independent contractor, 10.3.1
term and termination, 10.3.2.1

PHYSICIAN/PATIENT RELATIONSHIPS
  generally, 10.7
PHYSICIANS
  accountable care organizations (ACO), 10.8
  arrangements with hospitals (*See* physician/hospital arrangements)
  certification
    center for Medicaid and state operations, 3.3.2.2
    hospice services
      issues with physician certification, 11.4.6
  compensation
    benefits and perquisites, 10.2.2.3
    employment contracts, 10.2.2.2; 12.7.1
    ownership opportunities, 10.2.2.4
    physician/hospital arrangements, 10.3.2.3
    Stark exceptions, 5.4.1
    tax-exempt issues
      physician incentive compensation, 6.3.2.3
  dissolution of practice
    sale of ownership interest, 10.2.4.5
  employment contracts, 10.2.2
    assignability, 10.2.2.7
    benefits and perquisites, 10.2.2.3
    compensation, 10.2.2.2
    dispute resolution, 10.2.2.7
    duties and responsibilities, 10.2.2.1
    legal compliance, 10.2.2.7
    notice, 10.2.2.7
    ownership opportunities, 10.2.2.4
    post-termination restrictive covenants, 10.2.2.6
    recordkeeping, 10.2.2.7
    term of employment and termination, 10.2.2.5
  equipment, rental of office space and, 5.5.3.1
  group practices, investments in
    Anti-Kickback safe-harbor regulations, 5.2.14
  health care transactions and contracting
    corporate structures
      independent practice associations (IPAs), 12.4.3
    physician/hospital organizations (PHOs) (*See* **PHYSICIAN/HOSPITAL ORGANIZATIONS (PHOs)**)
    employment contracts, 12.7.1
    independent contractor agreements, 12.7.1
    physician recruitment agreements, 12.7.2
  hospice services
    physician certification, issues with, 11.4.6
  hospitals
    disciplinary procedures, regulation
      federal regulations, 9.3.4
    excluded provider verification
      federal regulations, 9.3.4
    physician/hospital organizations (PHOs) (*See* **PHYSICIAN/HOSPITAL ORGANIZATIONS (PHOs)**)
    state regulations affecting medical staff, 9.2.3
    unionization of nurses and doctors
      federal regulations, 9.3.6
  independent practice associations (IPAs) (*See* **INDEPENDENT PRACTICE ASSOCIATIONS (IPAs)**)
  insurance
    sale of ownership interest
      funding buy-outs with insurance, 10.2.4.3
  labor unions
    hospitals, federal regulations
      regulation of unionization of nurses and doctors, 9.3.6
    reimbursement issues, 10.5.3
  licensure and credentialing, 10.4
    exclusion from Medicare/Medicaid, 10.4.3
    medical staff privileges, 10.4.4
    national practitioner data bank (NPDB), reports to, 10.4.2
    state licensure law, 10.4.1
  List of Excluded Individuals and Entities (LEIE), 10.4.3
  malpractice insurance
    obstetrical malpractice insurance subsidies
      Anti-Kickback safe-harbor regulations, 5.2.13

Index

Medicaid
  licensure and credentialing
    exclusion from Medicare/Medicaid, 10.4.3
Medicare
  certification, 3.7.2
  licensure and credentialing
    exclusion from Medicare/Medicaid, 10.4.3
Medicare Part B coverage
  physicians' services, 3.6.2.1
national practitioner data bank (NPDB), 10.4.2
obstetrical malpractice insurance subsidies
  Anti-Kickback safe-harbor regulations, 5.2.13
office space and equipment, rental of, 5.5.3.1
ownership
  Stark exceptions, 5.4.1
ownership of practice
  buy-in, 10.2.3.1
  employment and compensation, 10.2.3.3
  employment contracts
    ownership opportunities, 10.2.2.4
  ownership agreements, 10.2.3.2
  sale of ownership interest, 10.2.4
    dissolution of practice, 10.2.4.5
    funding buy-outs with insurance, 10.2.4.3
    payment terms and collateral, 10.2.4.2
    post-termination restrictive covenants, 10.2.4.4
    valuation of interest, 10.2.4.1
patient relationships, 10.7
physician/hospital organizations (PHOs), 12.4.2
post-termination restrictive covenants, 10.2.2.6
sale of ownership interest, 10.2.4.4
recruitment
  Anti-Kickback safe-harbor regulations, 5.2.12
  health care transactions and contracting
    physician recruitment agreements, 12.7.2

self-referral, Stark exceptions, 5.5.3.5
tax-exempt issues
  physician recruitment incentives, 6.3.3
referral agreements for specialty services
  Anti-Kickback safe-harbor regulations, 5.2.17
reimbursement issues, 10.5
  independent practice associations (IPAs), 10.5.2
  labor unions, unionization issues, 10.5.3
  problems in reimbursement, 10.5.1
representing physicians, 10.1 to 10.8
  accountable care organizations (ACO), 10.8
  characteristics of most physicians, 10.1
  compensation, 10.2.2.2
    benefits and perquisites, 10.2.2.3
    ownership opportunities, 10.2.2.4
  employing a physician, who can employ, 10.2.1.2
  employment contracts, 10.2.2
    assignability, 10.2.2.7
    benefits and perquisites, 10.2.2.3
    compensation, 10.2.2.2
    dispute resolution, 10.2.2.7
    duties and responsibilities, 10.2.2.1
    notice, 10.2.2.7
    ownership opportunities, 10.2.2.4
    post-termination restrictive covenants, 10.2.2.6
    recordkeeping, 10.2.2.7
    term of employment and termination, 10.2.2.5
  licensure and credentialing, 10.4
    exclusion from Medicare/Medicaid, 10.4.3
    medical staff privileges, 10.4.4
    national practitioner data bank (NPDB), reports to, 10.4.2
    state licensure law, 10.4.1
  life cycle of physician-practice association, 10.2
  ownership of practice, 10.2.3
    buy-in, 10.2.3.1
    employment and compensation, 10.2.3.3

employment contracts
    ownership opportunities, 10.2.2.4
    ownership agreements, 10.2.3.2
physician/patient relationships, 10.7
reimbursement issues, 10.5
    independent practice associations (IPAs), 10.5.2
    labor unions, unionization issues, 10.5.3
    problems in reimbursement, 10.5.1
retirement, 10.2.4
sale of ownership interest, 10.2.4
    dissolution of practice, 10.2.4.5
    funding buy-outs with insurance, 10.2.4.3
    payment terms and collateral, 10.2.4.2
    post-termination restrictive covenants, 10.2.4.4
    valuation of interest, 10.2.4.1
telemedicine, 10.6
who is your client, 10.2.1.1
restrictive covenants
    employment contracts, 12.7.1
    post-termination restrictive covenants, 10.2.2.6
    sale of ownership interest, 10.2.4.4
retirement, 10.2.4
sale of ownership interest, 10.2.4
    dissolution of practice, 10.2.4.5
    funding buy-outs with insurance, 10.2.4.3
    payment terms and collateral, 10.2.4.2
    post-termination restrictive covenants, 10.2.4.4
    valuation of interest, 10.2.4.1
self-referral, 5.4
    advisory opinions, 5.4.5
    disclosures
        self-referral disclosure protocols (SRDP), 5.4.6
    entity defined, 5.4.4
    integrated delivery systems (IDSs), 12.4.1.3
    prohibited generally, 5.4.1
    protocols for self-referral, 5.4.6
    regulations, 5.4.2
    reporting requirements, 5.4.3

self-referral disclosure protocols (SRDP), 5.4.6
Stark exceptions
    academic medical centers, 5.5.1.4
    accountable care organization (ACO) waivers, 5.5.3.17
    additional compensation exceptions, 5.5.3.16
    additional regulatory exceptions, 5.5.1.6
    bona-fide employment arrangements, 5.5.3.2
    compensation arrangement exceptions, 5.5.3
    compensation conditioned on referrals to a particular provider, 5.5.4.3
    compensation methodologies, 5.5.4.2
    compliance training, 5.5.3.13
    electronic prescribing and electronic health records, 5.5.3.15
    fair market value exception, 5.5.3.9; 5.5.4.1
    generally, 5.5
    group practice arrangements with a hospital, 5.5.3.7
    hospitals, ownership in, 5.5.2.2
    implants in ASCs, 5.5.1.5
    indirect compensation, 5.5.3.14
    in-office ancillary services, 5.5.1.2
    isolated financial transactions, 5.5.3.6
    manage-care risk-sharing arrangements, 5.5.3.12
    medical staff incidental benefits, 5.5.3.11
    non-monetary compensation up to $300, 5.5.3.10
    ownership and compensation exceptions, 5.5.1
    ownership exceptions, 5.5.2
    payments for items and services, 5.5.3.8
    personal-service arrangements, 5.5.3.3
    physical recruitment and retention, 5.5.3.5
    physician services, 5.5.1.1
    prepaid plans, 5.5.1.3

publicly traded securities and mutual funds, ownership exceptions, 5.5.2.1
rental of office space and equipment, 5.5.3.1
rural providers, 5.5.2.3
special rules for compensation, 5.5.4
"stand in the shoes" analysis, 5.5.3.14
timeshare arrangements, 5.5.3.19
unrelated payments, 5.5.3.4
Stark law, 5.4.1
"sunshine law", 5.3
tax-exempt issues
physician incentive compensation, 6.3.2.3
physician recruitment incentives, 6.3.3
background, 6.3.3.1
community benefit requirement, 6.3.3.2
income guarantees, 6.3.3.3
telemedicine, 10.6

POST-ACUTE PROVIDERS AND SUPPLIERS
home care providers
generally, 11.1 to 11.6.3 (*See* **HOME CARE PROVIDERS**)
hospice care, 11.4.1 to 11.4.9 (*See* **HOSPICE SERVICES**)
introduction to discussion, 11.1
long term care, 11.5.1 to 11.5.6 (*See* **LONG TERM CARE**)

POWER OF ATTORNEY
durable power of attorney for health care, 2.3.4; 2.3.4.2

PRACTITIONERS REPRESENTING EMPLOYERS, PLANS OR PROVIDERS
importance of becoming familiar with regulatory schemes, 8.2

PREEMPTION OF STATE PROVISIONS, 8.1.2
deemer clause, 8.1.2
preemption clause, 8.1.2
saving clause, 8.1.2

PREFERRED PROVIDER ORGANIZATIONS (PPOs)
insurance regulation, 8.2.2
Medicare Part C, 3.2.1.3
regional PPOs, 3.2.1.3

PREMIUMS
Medicare, 3.2.4.1

PRESCRIPTION DRUGS
"donut hole," closing of, 3.6.5
electronic health records (EHR)
donation and receipt of technology
accountable care organization waivers, 5.2.23
Anti-Kickback safe-harbor regulations, 5.2.22
electronic prescribing
Anti-Kickback safe-harbor regulations, 5.2.21
physician self-referral, Stark exceptions, 5.5.3.15
Medicare Prescription Drug, Improvement, and Modernization Act (MMA)
history of federal efforts to regulate health care, 8.3.3
hospital outpatient department services (HOPPS), 3.8.6.2
Medicare Part C, 3.2.1.3
outpatient prescription drugs
Medicare Part D, 3.2.1.4
radiopharmaceuticals, 3.8.6.2
radiopharmaceuticals, 3.8.6.2
"sunshine law," manufacturers' reporting requirements under, 5.3

PRICE-FIXING AGREEMENTS
horizontal agreements, 7.2.1.3.1
manufacturers and wholesalers, 7.5.3

PRIVACY
bioethics of human reproduction
abortion
Roe v. Wade, 13.1.1.1
confidentiality of patient medical information, 2.4
data sharing (*See* **DATA SHARING**)
Health Insurance Portability and Accountability Act (*See* **HEALTH INSURANCE PORTABILITY AND ACCOUNTABILITY ACT (HIPAA)**)
hospitals
Health Insurance Portability and Accountability Act (HIPAA), 9.3.1

state regulation to protect patient health information, 9.2.4
PRIVATE CONTRACTS
Medicare, 3.2.2
PRIVATE FEE-FOR-SERVICE (PFFS) PLANS
Medicare Part C, 3.2.1.3
PRIVATE HEALTH-PLAN COVERAGE
Medicare Part C, 3.2.1.3
regulation of private health insurance plans (*See* **HEALTH CARE PRIVATE PLANS, REGULATION**)
PROFESSIONAL CORPORATIONS
health care transactions and contracting, 12.4.4
PROFESSIONAL STANDARDS REVIEW ORGANIZATIONS (PSROs)
stand-alone exemption, 6.2.3.3; 6.2.3.4
PROSTHETICS AND ORTHOTICS
home medical equipment (HME) suppliers, 11.2; 11.2.2.3.1
Medicare
Part B coverage, 3.6.2.3
resource-based relative value scale (RBRVS) fee schedule, 3.9.6
PROVIDER-BASED
defined
Medicare, 3.2.8
PROVIDERS
certification
center for Medicaid and state operations, 3.3.2.2
defined, 3.2.7
Medicare
certification, 3.7.1
conditions of participation (CoPs)
corporate compliance program, 5.8
establishing eligibility, 3.7.1
deemed status, 3.7.1
provider agreements, 3.7.1
provider identification numbers (PINs), 3.7.1
reimbursement, 3.4
outpatient providers and freestanding supplier entities
Medicare Part B coverage, 3.6.2.3

PROVIDER-SPONSORED ORGANIZATIONS (PSOs)
insurance regulation, 8.2.6
Medicare Part C, 3.2.1.3
PSYCHIATRIC HOSPITALS
Medicare prospective payment system (PPS)
generally, 3.8.3.3
Patient Protection and Affordable Care Act updates, 3.8.3.4
PSYCHOLOGISTS
Medicare Part B coverage, 3.6.2.2
PSYCHOTHERAPY
Health Insurance Portability and Accountability Act (HIPAA) privacy rules, 14.2.5
PUBLIC CHARITIES
tax-exempt issues, 6.1.2; 6.4
Pension Protection Act (PPA) (*See* **PENSION PROTECTION ACT (PPA)**)
principal function
Section 509(a)(1) public charities, 6.4.1
recurring concepts, 6.1.3
Section 509(a)(1) public charities, 6.4.1
Section 509(a)(2) public charities, 6.4.2
supporting organizations
control test, 6.4.3.4
operational test, 6.4.3.2
organizational test, 6.4.3.1
relationship test, 6.4.3.3
Section 509(a)(3) public charities, 6.4.3
two-part public supported test
Section 509(a)(2) public charities, 6.4.2

Q

QUALIFIED MEDICAL CHILD SUPPORT ORDERS (QMCSOs)
Employee Retirement and Income Security Act (ERISA), 8.3.2.5
QUALIFIED MEDICARE BENEFICIARY (QMB) PROGRAM
low-income beneficiaries, assistance for, 3.2.4.3

QUALIFYING INDIVIDUAL (QI) PROGRAM
Medicare
 low-income beneficiaries, assistance for, 3.2.4.3

QUI TAM ACTIONS
false claims and fraudulent billing
 civil prohibitions, 5.7.1
 Fraud Enforcement and Recovery Act (FERA), 5.7.1

R

RACKETEERING
false claims and fraudulent billing, 5.6.4

RADIOLOGY
Medicare
 resource-based relative value scale (RBRVS) fee schedule
  applicability to non-physician practitioners and other suppliers, 3.9.4

REFERRAL SERVICES
Anti-Kickback safe-harbor regulations, 5.2.4

REFUSAL OF MEDICAL TREATMENT
constitutional protection, 2.2.2
end-of-life decision making
 generally, 2.3.1
 incompetent patients, 2.3.2
 unwanted care, damages for rendering, 2.3.3

REGIONAL PPOs
Medicare Part C, 3.2.1.3

REHABILITATION HOSPITALS
Medicare prospective payment system (PPS)
 Affordable Care Act updates, 3.8.3.4
 generally, 3.8.3.1

RELIGION
objections to treatment, 2.2.4

RENTALS
Anti-Kickback safe-harbor regulations
 space and equipment rental, 5.2.2
physician self-referral
 Stark exceptions
  rental of office space and equipment, 5.5.3.1

REPORTS
national practitioner data bank (NPDB), 10.4.2
Patient Protection and Affordable Care Act
 employer health coverage, 8.3.3.17
 quality reporting, 8.3.3.9
physician self-referral, 5.4.3
"sunshine law," manufacturers' reporting requirements under, 5.3

REPRODUCTION
bioethics, 13.1.1.1 to 13.1.2.2
contraceptives, access to, 13.1.2

RESTRAINTS, USE OF
consent to medical treatment, 2.2.1.5

RESTRICTIVE COVENANTS
health care transactions and contracting
 generally, 12.7.1
 termination of agreements, 12.8.3
physicians
 post-termination restrictive covenants
  generally, 10.2.2.6
  sale of ownership interest, 10.2.4.4

RIGHT TO DIE
end-of-life decision making, 2.3

RIGHT TO REFUSE MEDICAL TREATMENT
end-of-life decision making
 incompetent patients, 2.3.2
 right to refuse life-sustaining medical treatment, 2.3.1
 unwanted care, damages for rendering, 2.3.3

RISK-SHARING ARRANGEMENTS
Anti-Kickback safe-harbor regulations, 5.2.20
managed care organizations
 physician self-referral, Stark exceptions, 5.5.3.12

ROE v. WADE
generally, 13.1.1.1
post-Roe developments, 13.1.1.2
transformation of Roe, 13.1.1.3

ROUTINE PHYSICALS
Medicare, 3.2.3

RURAL-AREA HOSPITALS
Medicare prospective payment system (PPS), 3.8.4

RURAL HEALTH CLINICS (RHCs)
Medicare Part B coverage, 3.6.2.3
RURAL HOSPITALS
Medicare subsidies, 3.2.6
RURAL PROVIDERS
physician self-referral
Stark exceptions, 5.5.2.3

S

SAFE HARBOR
Anti-Kickback safe-harbor regulations, 5.2
SALE OF PRACTICE
Anti-Kickback safe-harbor regulations, 5.2.3
mergers and acquisitions
asset transactions, 12.3.1.2
successor liability, 12.3.1.2
SCHIP
center for Medicaid and state operations, 3.3.2.2
SECLUSION OF PATIENT
consent to medical treatment, 2.2.1.5
patient safety and rights, 9.2.2
SECONDARY PAYOR RULE
Benefits Coordination and Recovery Center (BCRC), 3.2.5
Medicare, 3.2.5
SKILLED NURSING FACILITIES (SNFs)
ethics, 11.5.3.4
Medicare
hospice service fraud and abuse, 11.4.8
long term care, 11.5.3
coverage, 11.5.3.1
market basket index, 11.5.3.3
participation, conditions of, 11.5.3.2
reimbursement, 11.5.3.3
transparency and accountability, 11.5.3.4
prospective payment system (PPS)
post-acute care providers, 3.8.7.1
value-based purchasing program (VBP program), 3.8.7.1
SMALL BUSINESS
tax credits under Patient Protection and Affordable Care Act, 8.3.3.14

SOCIAL SECURITY ACT
false claims and fraudulent billing, 5.6.1; 5.7.2
Medicare, history of, 3.1.1
overpayments, reporting and return of, 5.7.1
SPECIAL NEEDS PLANS (SNPs)
Medicare Part C, 3.2.1.3
SPECIFIED LOW-INCOME MEDICARE BENEFICIARY (SLMB) PROGRAM
low-income beneficiaries, assistance for, 3.2.4.3
SPEECH PATHOLOGY
Medicare Part B coverage, 3.6.2.2
STARK LAW
accountable care organization (ACO) waivers, 5.2.23; 5.5.3.17
integrated delivery systems (IDSs), 12.4.1.3
physician self-referral, 5.4; 5.5
STATE LICENSURE
home medical equipment (HME) suppliers, 11.2.1
STEM CELLS
embryonic and fetal-cell research, 13.3.3.1
STERILIZATION
duty to treat patient, 2.1.3
SUICIDE
"End of Life Choices" Act, 2.3.6
physician-assisted death, 2.3.6
SUPPLEMENT INSURANCE
Medicare
cost-sharing by beneficiaries, 3.2.4.2
Medigap, 3.2.4.2
Part B, 3.2.1.2
SUPPLIERS
certification
center for Medicaid and state operations, 3.3.2.2
defined, 3.2.7
Medicare
certification, 3.7.2
reimbursement, 3.4
resource-based relative value scale (RBRVS) fee schedule
fee schedules for freestanding supplier entities, 3.9.6

outpatient providers and freestanding supplier entities
Medicare Part B coverage, 3.6.2.3
SURROGACY
custody disputes, 13.1.3.2
generally, 13.1.3
prohibition and regulation, 13.1.3.1

T
TAX-EXEMPT ISSUES, 6.1 to 6.4.4
affiliates, use of taxable, 6.3.7
application of fundamental exemption requirements, 6.3
affiliates, use of taxable, 6.3.7
compensation arrangements, 6.3.2.1
incentive compensation, 6.3.2.2
courtesy discounts, 6.3.5
electronic health records (EHR)
donation and receipt of technology, 6.3.6
executive compensation, 6.3.2.4
incentive compensation
physician incentive compensation, 6.3.2.3
joint venture arrangements involving exempt and non-exempt participants, 6.3.4
physician incentive compensation, 6.3.2.3
physician recruitment incentives, 6.3.3
purchase and sale of a business or other assets, 6.3.1
benefits of tax-exempt status, 6.1.1
chapter focus, 6.1
community benefit standard
exempt purpose requirement, 6.2.3.1
charity care, 6.2.3.2
non-hospital and non-direct health care providers, 6.2.3.3
recurring concepts, 6.1.3
compensation arrangements
application of fundamental exemption requirements, 6.3.2.1
executive compensation, 6.3.2.4
incentive compensation, 6.3.2.2
physician incentive compensation, 6.3.2.3

physician incentive compensation, 6.3.2.3
"soft contact audits", 6.3.2.4
courtesy discounts, 6.3.5
data sharing, 14.7.1; 14.7.2
derivative theory of exemption, 6.2.4
joint operating companies, 6.2.4.2
parent corporations, 6.2.4.1
discounts
courtesy discounts, 6.3.5
disqualified persons
intermediate sanctions, 6.2.7.3
electronic health records (EHR)
adoption of electronic health information technology, 6.2.3.4
donation and receipt of technology, 6.3.6
executive compensation, 6.3.2.4
exemption requirements, 6.2
derivative or integral part theory of exemption, 6.2.4
joint operating companies, 6.2.4.2
parent corporations, 6.2.4.1
exempt purpose, 6.2.3
information return reporting, 6.2.3.5
stand-alone exemption
charity care, 6.2.3.2
community benefit standard, 6.2.3.1
non-hospital and non-direct health care providers, 6.2.3.3
lessening burdens of government as alternative basis for exemption, 6.2.3.4
intermediate sanctions, 6.2.7
disqualified persons, 6.2.7.3
excise taxes, 6.2.7.1
revocation sanction, relationship of excise tax, 6.2.7.4
lobbying limitation, 6.2.9.2
operational test, 6.2; 6.2.2
organizational test, 6.2.1
political activity prohibition, 6.2.9.1
private inurement prohibition, 6.2.6
public-benefit, 6.2.5
rebuttable presumption of reasonableness, 6.2.7
excess-benefit transactions, 6.2.7.2
unrelated business activities, 6.2.8

exempt purpose
    exemption requirements, 6.2.3
    information return reporting, 6.2.3.5
    recurring concepts, 6.1.3
    stand-alone exemption
        charity care, 6.2.3.2
        community benefit standard, 6.2.3.1
            non-hospital and non-direct health care providers, 6.2.3.3
        lessening burdens of government as alternative basis for exemption, 6.2.3.4
integral-part exempt status
    joint operating companies, 6.2.4.2
    parent corporations, 6.2.4.1
    recurring concepts, 6.1.3
integral part theory of exemption, 6.2.4
integrated delivery systems (IDSs), 12.4.1.4
intermediate sanctions
    disqualified persons, 6.2.7.3
    excise taxes, 6.2.7.1
        revocation sanction, relationship of excise tax, 6.2.7.4
    exemption requirements, 6.2.7
    revocation sanction, relationship of excise tax, 6.2.7.4
joint operating companies
    derivative or integral part theory of exemption, 6.2.4.2
joint venture arrangements involving exempt and non-exempt participants, 6.3.4
    ancillary joint ventures, 6.3.4.2
    whole hospital joint ventures, 6.3.4.1
lobbying limitation
    exemption requirements, 6.2.9.2
more-than-incidental private benefit
    recurring concepts, 6.1.3
operational test
    exemption requirements, 6.2; 6.2.2
organizational test
    exemption requirements, 6.2.1
parent corporations
    derivative or integral part theory of exemption, 6.2.4.1
physician incentive compensation, 6.3.2.3

physician recruitment incentives, 6.3.3
    background, 6.3.3.1
    community benefit requirement, 6.3.3.2
    income guarantees, 6.3.3.3
political activity prohibition, 6.2.9.1
private inurement
    prohibition
        exemption requirements, 6.2.6
    recurring concepts, 6.1.3
public-benefit exemption requirement, 6.2.5
public charity status, 6.1.2; 6.4
    Pension Protection Act (PPA) (See **PENSION PROTECTION ACT (PPA)**)
    principal function
        Section 509(a)(1) public charities, 6.4.1
    recurring concepts, 6.1.3
    Section 509(a)(1) public charities, 6.4.1
    Section 509(a)(2) public charities, 6.4.2
    Section 509(a)(3) public charities, 6.4.3
    supporting organizations
        control test, 6.4.3.4
        operational test, 6.4.3.2
        organizational test, 6.4.3.1
        relationship test, 6.4.3.3
        Section 509(a)(3) public charities, 6.4.3
    two-part public supported test
        Section 509(a)(2) public charities, 6.4.2
purchase and sale of a business or other assets
    application of fundamental exemption requirements, 6.3.1
reasonableness
    rebuttable presumption, 6.2.7
        excess-benefit transactions, 6.2.7.2
rebuttable presumption of reasonableness, 6.2.7
    excess-benefit transactions, 6.2.7.2
sale of a business or other assets
    application of fundamental exemption requirements, 6.3.1
scope of chapter, 6.1
Section 509(a) public charity status, 6.4
stand-alone exemption
    exempt purpose
        charity care, 6.2.3.2

community benefit standard, 6.2.3.1
    non-hospital and non-direct health care providers, 6.2.3.3
    lessening burdens of government as alternative basis for exemption, 6.2.3.4
information return reporting, 6.2.3.5
recurring concepts, 6.1.3
unrelated business activities
    exemption requirements, 6.2.8
unrelated business income tax (UBIT)
    recurring concepts, 6.1.3

TELEMEDICINE, 10.6

THEFT
federal health care fraud offenses, 5.6.2.3

THIRD PARTY ADMINISTRATORS
insurance regulation
    scope of state regulation, 8.2.5

TORT LIABILITY
end-of-life decision making
    unwanted care, damages for rendering, 2.3.3

U

UNFAIR METHODS OF COMPETITION
antitrust law, 7.2.4

UNIFORM ANATOMICAL GIFT ACT (UAGA)
organ transplantation, 13.2.1

V

VACCINES
Employee Retirement and Income Security Act (ERISA), 8.3.2.7

VEGETATIVE STATE
organ transplantation, 13.2.1

VIOLENT PROPENSITIES OF PATIENTS
duty to warn, 2.4.2.2

VITAL STATISTICS
mandatory reporting of medical conditions, 2.4.2.2

W

WARRANTIES
Anti-Kickback safe-harbor regulations, 5.2.5

WOMEN'S HEALTH
Employee Retirement and Income Security Act (ERISA), 8.3.2.9
health maintenance organizations (HMOs), 8.2.3.3
Women's Health and Cancer Rights Act of 1998 (WHCRA), 8.3.2.9

WRONGFUL DEATH
unwanted care, damages for rendering, 2.3.3

X

X-RAY SERVICES
Medicare Part B coverage, 3.6.2.3